D1261847

CURRENT BIOGRAPHY 1954

CURRENT BIOGRAPHY

WHO'S NEWS AND WHY
1954

EDITED BY

Marjorie Dent Candee

THE H. W. WILSON COMPANY
NEW YORK, N. Y.

FIFTEENTH ANNUAL CUMULATION—1954

PRINTED IN THE UNITED STATES OF AMERICA

Library of Congress Catalog Card No. (40-27432)

Preface

In this, the fifteenth volume of CURRENT BIOGRAPHY YEARBOOK, are presented 325 biographies (reprinted from eleven monthly issues and cumulated in one alphabet) of personalities prominent on the international scene, in the arts, sciences, industry, politics, education and entertainment. Also included in this volume are twenty biographies of authors which were originally published in the *Wilson Library Bulletin.* These are indicated in the Index by (WLB) and are listed under the classification **Literature.**

Representing the United States are two new Cabinet members, nine Governors, nine Senators and eight Congressmen. Other countries are represented by presidents, kings, prime ministers, ambassadors, artists, authors, and scientists, a total of eighty. Five winners of Nobel Prizes and four winners of Pulitzer Prizes for 1953-54 and two "Oscars" are also included.

The names are classified into forty-one broad fields ranging from archaeology to technology. (See Classification Section at the end of this volume.) A new classification, **Organizations,** lists the presidents of professional, veterans', fraternal and industrial organizations. Biographees who are not professional authors but who have written books are listed under appropriate headings (such as **Nonfiction** or **Literature**) in addition to their principal vocational field. Fifty-one women in many fields of endeavor are included (and also listed separately at the end of the volume).

Again we publish biographies of individuals first presented in the 1940-1944 volumes (now out of print except for 1943). Among these names (whose sketches have been revised to take account of the intervening years) included in this Yearbook are: Attorney General Herbert Brownell, Jr., Eddie Cantor, Ambassador Henry Cabot Lodge, Jr., Mary Margaret McBride, Foreign Minister Vîacheslav Molotov, Robert Moses, Maestro Arturo Toscanini, Emperor Haile Selassie, and Chief Justice Earl Warren.

Obituary notices of biographees whose sketches were published in past issues, and who died in late 1953 or during the first three-quarters of the year 1954 are included. These are listed under **Necrology** at the rear of this volume as well as in the **Index**.

The assembling of material for these biographies requires painstaking research. When a name is selected a research writer is then assigned who consults *Readers' Guide to Periodical Literature* and many other indexes which lead to a mass of information; "Who's Who's," encyclopedias and other reference works are also culled for biographical and background facts. Information is obtained from Government offices and from commercial and educational organizations. Subjects of the biographies are sometimes interviewed, and asked to confirm or correct facts.

The result of these endeavors is biographical information often unavailable elsewhere. It should be pointed out, however, that these are objective rather than authorized biographies. For the Yearbook these have been revised to include any major changes in an individual's position in the course of the year.

On the pages following are **Explanations** of this Yearbook, **Key To Pronunciation** and **Key to Abbreviations.** At the rear of this volume will be found these indexes:

Biographical References Consulted
Periodicals and Newspapers Consulted
Necrology
Classification by Professional Field
Cumulated Index, 1951-1954
Addenda

NOTE: The index for 1940-1950 is published in the 1950 Yearbook. Separate copies of this index, including the 1951-54 supplement, are available. Inquire of the publisher for price.

M.D.C.

NOTE: Authors whose biographies do not appear in CURRENT BIOGRAPHY may usually be found in TWENTIETH CENTURY AUTHORS, Kunitz & Haycraft, 1942, H. W. Wilson Company, or will be included in the FIRST SUPPLEMENT to that work, scheduled for publication in 1955. Authors of books for young people are included in THE JUNIOR BOOK OF AUTHORS (Second Edition, Revised) edited by Kunitz & Haycraft, 1951, H. W. Wilson Company.

Explanations

Authorities for biographees' full names, with some exceptions, are the bibliographical publications of The Wilson Company. When a biographee prefers a certain name form, that is indicated in the heading of the article: for example, Andrews, T(homas) Coleman means that he is usually referred to as T. Coleman Andrews. When a professional name is used in the heading, as, for example, Cyd Charisse, the real name (in this case Tula Ellice Finklea) appears in the article itself.

The heading of each article includes the pronunciation of the name if it is unusual, date of birth (if obtainable), and occupation. The article is supplemented by a list of references to sources of biographical information, in two alphabets: (1) newspapers and periodicals and (2) books. See the section ***Biographical References Consulted.***

References to newspapers and periodicals are listed in abbreviated form; for example, "Sat Eve Post 217:14-15 S 30 '44 por" means ***Saturday Evening Post,*** volume 217, pages 14-15, September 30, 1944, with portrait. (For full names, see the section ***Periodical and Newspaper Abbreviations,*** in the rear of this volume.) The reference following each obituary notice is to the New York ***Times***; these notices appear for persons whose biographies have been published in ***Current Biography***.

KEY TO PRONUNCIATION

(Based on Webster's Guide to Pronunciation)*

ā	āle	N	Not pronounced, but indicates the nasal tone of the preceding vowel, as in the French *bon* (bôN).	û	ûrn; French eu, as in *jeu* (zhû); German ö, oe, as in *schön* (shûn), *Goethe* (gû'tĕ)
â	câre			ŭ	tŭb
ă	ădd			*ŭ*	circ*ŭ*s
ă	*ă*ccount	ō	ōld	ü	Pronounced approximately as ē, with rounded lips: French u, as in *menu* (mē-nü'); German ü, as in *grün*.
ä	ärm	ô	ôrb	zh	azure
à	àsk	ŏ	ŏdd	'	= main accent
à	sof*à*	oi	oil	"	= secondary accent
ē	ēve	o͞o	o͞oze		
ĕ	ĕnd	o͝o	fo͝ot		
ẽ	makẽr	ou	out		
g	go	*th*	*th*en		
ī	īce	th	thin		
ĭ	ĭll	ū	cūbe		
K	German ch as in *ich* (ĭK).				

(*Exceptions : *th* in then ; main and secondary accents.)

KEY TO ABBREVIATIONS

AAA	Agricultural Adjustment Administration
A.A.A.A.	Amateur Athletic Association of America
A.A.U.	Amateur Athletic Union
ABC	American Broadcasting Company
A.C.L.U.	American Civil Liberties Union
ADA	Americans for Democratic Action
AEC	Atomic Energy Commission
AEF	American Expeditionary Force
AFL	American Federation of Labor
Ag	August
A.L.A.	American Library Association
A.M.A.	American Medical Association
AMG	Allied Military Government
Ap	April
A.P.	Associated Press
ASCAP	American Society of Composers, Authors and Publishers
ASNE	American Society Newspaper Editors
AVC	American Veterans Committee
b.	business address
B.A.	Bachelor of Arts
BBC	British Broadcasting Corporation
B.D.	Bachelor of Divinity
B.L.S.	Bachelor of Library Science
B.S.	Bachelor of Science
CAA	Civil Aeronautics Administration
CAB	Civil Aeronautics Board
C.B.	Companion of the Bath
C.B.E.	Commander of (the Order of) the British Empire
CBS	Columbia Broadcasting System
CCC	Civilian Conservation Corps
C.E.	Civil Engineer
CEA	Council of Economic Advisers
C.E.D.	Committee for Economic Development
CIO	Congress of Industrial Organizations
C.M.G.	Companion of (the Order of) St. Michael and St. George
Com.	Commodore
CWA	Civil Works Administration
CWS	Chemical Warfare Service
D	December
D.A.R.	Daughters of the American Revolution
D.C.L.	Doctor of Civil Law
D.D.	Doctor of Divinity
D.Eng.	Doctor of Engineering
D.F.C.	Distinguished Flying Cross
D.J.	Doctor of Jurisprudence
D.Lit.	Doctor of Literature
D.Mus.	Doctor of Music
DP	Displaced Person
D.Pol.Sc.	Doctor of Political Science
D.Sc.	Doctor of Science
D.S.C.	Distinguished Service Cross
D.S.M.	Distinguished Service Medal
D.S.O.	Distinguished Service Order
ECA	Economic Cooperation Administration
ECOSOC	Economic and Social Council
EDC	European Defense Community
ERP	European Recovery Program
ESA	Economic Stabilization Administration
F	February
FAO	Food and Agriculture Organization
FBI	Federal Bureau of Investigation
FCA	Farm Credit Administration
FCC	Federal Communications Commission
FEPC	Fair Employment Practice Committee
FERA	Federal Emergency Relief Administration
FHA	Federal Housing Administration
FSA	Federal Security Agency
FTC	Federal Trade Commission
G.B.E.	Knight or Dame Grand Cross Order of the British Empire
G.C.B.	Knight Grand Cross of the Bath
GHQ	General Headquarters
h.	home address
H.M.	His Majesty; Her Majesty
HOLC	Home Owners' Loan Corporation
ICC	Interstate Commerce Commission
I.C.F.T.U.	International Confederation of Free Trade Unions
I.L.A.	International Longshoremen's Association
I.L.G.W.U.	International Ladies' Garment Workers' Union
I.L.O.	International Labor Office
I.L.P.	Independent Labour Party
INS	International News Service
IRO	International Refugee Organization
I.T.U.	International Typographical Union
J	Journal
Ja	January
J.C.B.	Juris Canonici Bachelor
J.D.	Doctor of Jurisprudence
Je	June
j.g.	junior grade
Jl	July
K.B.E.	Knight of (the Order of) the British Empire
K.C.	King's Counsel
K.C.B.	Knight Commander of the Bath
L.H.D.	Doctor of Humanities
Litt.D.	Doctor of Letters
LL.B.	Bachelor of Laws
LL.D.	Doctor of Laws
LL.M.	Master of Laws
M.A.	Master of Arts
M.B.A.	Master of Business Administration
MBS	Mutual Broadcasting System
M.C.E.	Master of Civil Engineering
M.D.	Doctor of Medicine
M.E.	Master of Engineering
MGM	Metro-Goldwyn-Mayer
M.Lit.	Master of Literature
M.P.	Member of Parliament
M.P.P.D.A.	Motion Picture Producers and Distributors of America
Mr	March
MRP	Mouvement Républicain Populaire
MSA	Mutual Security Agency
M.Sc.	Master of Science
Msgr.	Monsignor, Monseigneur
MVA	Missouri Valley Authority
My	May
N	November
NAACP	National Association for the Advancement of Colored People
NAB	National Association of Broadcasters
NAM	National Association of Manufacturers
NATO	North Atlantic Treaty Organization
NBC	National Broadcasting Company
N.E.A.	National Education Association
NLRB	National Labor Relations Board
N.M.U.	National Maritime Union
NRA	National Recovery Administration
NRPB	National Resources Planning Board
NWLB	National War Labor Board
NYA	National Youth Administration
O	October
OBE	Officer of (the Order of) the British Empire
OCD	Office of Civilian Defense
OEEC	Organization for European Economic Cooperation
OPA	Office of Price Administration
OPM	Office of Production Management
OPRD	Office of Production Research and Development
OSRD	Office of Scientific Research and Development
OWI	Office of War Information
PAC	Political Action Committee
P.C.	Privy Councilor
PCA	Progressive Citizens of America
P.E.N.	Poets, Playwrights, Editors, Essayists and Novelists (International Association)
Ph.B.	Bachelor of Philosophy
Ph.D.	Doctor of Philosophy
por	portrait, -s
PWA	Public Works Administration
Q.C.	Queen's Counsel
R	Review
RAF	Royal Air Force
RCA	Radio Corporation of America
REA	Rural Electrification Administration
RFC	Reconstruction Finance Corporation
RKO	Radio-Keith-Orpheum
ROTC	Reserve Officers' Training Corps
S	September
SAC	Strategic Air Command
SCAP	Supreme Command for the Allied Powers
SEC	Securities and Exchange Commission
s.g.	senior grade
SHAEF	Supreme Headquarters, Allied Expeditionary Force
SHAPE	Supreme Headquarters, Allied Powers Europe
S.J.D.	Doctor of Juridical Science
SPA	Surplus Property Administration
SSB	Social Security Board
S.T.B.	Bachelor of Sacred Theology
S.T.D.	Doctor of Sacred Theology
S.W.O.C.	Steel Workers' Organizing Committee
T.U.C.	Trades Union Congress
TVA	Tennessee Valley Authority
T.W.U.A.	Textile Workers Union of America
U.A.W.A.	Union Auto Workers of America
UMT	Universal Military Training
U.M.W.A.	United Mine Workers of America
U.N.	United Nations
UNESCO	United Nations Educational, Scientific, and Cultural Organization
UNRRA	United Nations Relief and Rehabilitation Administration
U.P.	United Press
USO	United Service Organizations
U.S.S.R.	Union of Socialist Soviet Republics
U.S.W.A.	United Steel Workers of America
VA	Veterans Administration
V.F.W.	Veterans of Foreign Wars
WAA	War Assets Administration
W.C.T.U.	Woman's Christian Temperance Union
WFA	War Food Administration
W.F.T.U.	World Federation of Trade Unions
WHO	World Health Organization
WLB	War Labor Board
WMC	War Manpower Commission
WPA	Work Projects Administration
WPB	War Production Board

CURRENT BIOGRAPHY
1954

AALTONEN, WÄINÖ (WALDEMAR)
Mar. 8, 1894- Sculptor; painter
Address: Mannerheiminkatu 1, Kulosaari, Helsinki, Finland

The work of the Finnish sculptor Wäinö Aaltonen has been described as a blending of the classical tradition and the folk spirit of his native land to form an original, modern style of his own. His production includes portraits, freestanding figures, and large public monuments in granite, marble and bronze, as well as reliefs, wood carvings, medallions, and paintings. Among his principal works are the statue of Paavo Nurmi, the Aleksis Kivi monuments, *The Goddess of Liberty Crowns Youth with a Laurel Wreath,* and the Delaware Monument in Chester, Pennsylvania. Frequently called "the most important of modern Finnish sculptors," Aaltonen is the only one to have attained an international reputation. Some of his work was exhibited at the Smithsonian Institution in Washington, D.C. in June 1952.

Wäinö Waldemar Aaltonen was born on March 8, 1894, in Karinainen, near the city of Turku in southwest Finland. His father, Matti Aaltonen, was a village tailor; his mother, Ida Katarina (Tähtinen) Aaltonen, was of peasant origin. His grandfathers had been farmers, but there were two sculptors in the family—Aarre Aaltonen and Yrjö Liipola. Although young Wäinö's parents were poor, they encouraged his interest in art, and in 1910 he succeeded in entering the art school of the Turku Art Society, where his training was entirely in drawing and painting.

However, when he was graduated with highest honors in 1915, he decided that his main interest was in sculpture. Consulting his former teachers, the painters Victor Westerholm and Axel Haartman, he was advised to study nature alone and to work on his own, so as not to lose his individuality. In order to help support himself, he served for a time as an assistant to his cousin, Aarre Aaltonen. His works were first exhibited in Turku in 1915 and in Helsinki two years later.

Aaltonen's initial efforts at sculpture include a series of heads of young girls that immediately revealed his mastery of shaping marble and modeling in bronze. It was in the handling of granite, his favorite medium, that he developed his most personal and original style. One of his major contributions to modern sculpture has been the revival of the technique

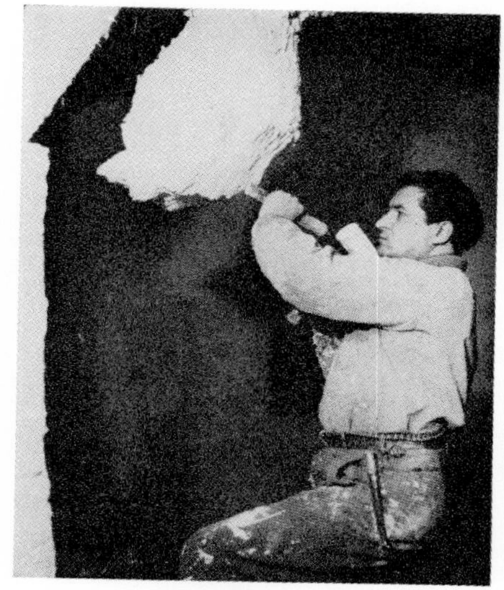

WÄINÖ AALTONEN

of carving directly out of stone—an art that had fallen into decay since the Renaissance. He picked up many technical skills and valuable practical suggestions from the simple stonecutters of his home district of Hirvensalo, and he reportedly found inspiration for his monumental granite style by studying the shapes of rocks worn smooth by the action of the sea.

His first important work in this hard, native material was the blocklike *Granite Boy* (1920), which is said to reflect his early admiration for ancient Egyptian stone sculpture. He also employed red granite for his first large monument, the stylized Soldiers' Memorial at Savonlinna, which dates from 1921 and was commissioned to honor the memory of the Finnish soldiers who died in the War of Liberation of 1918.

From the outset of his career, Aaltonen won a number of fellowships, awards, competitions, and travel grants. He visited Italy for the first time in 1923, and there studied the works of Michelangelo and Donatello, the two Renaissance masters whom he most admired. In the years immediately following, he traveled through France, England, Germany, Russia, and Scandinavia. During this period,

AALTONEN, WÄINÖ—*Continued*

he executed an imposing series of bathing women, in granite and marble, which critics have found related in spirit to the nudes of Aristide Maillol and Auguste Renoir.

In contrast to his static, massive figures in stone, Aaltonen's next major work was in as dynamic and mobile a plastic form as possible. This was the large-sized bronze statue of Paavo Nurmi, the world-champion long-distance runner, which had been commissioned by the government in 1924 to commemorate the victories won by Finland in athletics. Aaltonen depicted Nurmi in the act of running at full speed, with only the right foot touching the ground and bearing the full weight of the body. When the work was placed on exhibition at Aaltonen's first one-man shows in Stockholm (1927) and Paris (1928), the critics hailed it as "a masterpiece" and compared it to the best creations of antiquity and the Renaissance. The statue earned Aaltonen his first international acclaim, and outside Finland it is still his best-known work.

Under the influence of cubism, Aaltonen for a brief period explored the possibilities of semi-abstract, geometric forms in works like *Musica* (1926) and *The Dancer* (1928). It is Oscar Antonsson's opinion that Aaltonen found the cubist style too limited to serve as a vehicle for the expression of emotional values. At about the same time, Aaltonen experimented in such highly stylized compositions as the *Head of a Maiden* and *Figure of a Young Girl* (both 1925) with sculpture carved out of wood and then gilded.

During the late 1920's and early 1930's, Aaltonen executed several important public commissions. These include the four monumental figures in bronze that adorn the Hämeensilta Bridge in Tampere (1930); the memorial *Storm* (1930) at Reposaari, dedicated to the men who lost their lives in the sinking of the Finnish submarine S-2; and the five symbolic nudes, in gilded plaster, for the debating hall of the House of Parliament in Helsinki (1932). Two of Aaltonen's most noted bronze statues have been monuments to the nineteenth century Finnish writer, Aleksis Kivi. One, in Tampere, allegorically represents the poet and his muse (1927); the other, erected in Railway Square in Helsinki, is a monumental seated figure of Kivi (1934).

The Delaware Monument was dedicated to the memory of the first Finnish settlers who landed on the American coast in 1638. Depicting in relief the embarkation and pioneer life in the new world, this granite block was ordered by the Finnish government and presented to the United States as part of the Delaware tercentenary celebrations in 1938. It now stands in Chester, Pennsylvania.

Probably Aaltonen's most famous work in Finland was *The Goddess of Liberty Crowns Youth with a Laurel Wreath* (1940), a marble relief some ten feet high that he carved to celebrate the tercentenary of Helsinki University. Similar in subject to antique Greek metopes and steles, this relief is said to be the most classical in inspiration of all Aaltonen's works. It was destroyed during the aerial bombardment of the Finnish capital early in 1944.

The war years (1939-1945) severely curtailed Aaltonen's creative opportunities, and he spent considerable time during this period working in Sweden, where exhibitions of his sculpture met with both popular and critical success. In the reconstruction period in Finland following the war, he has won many competitions for public monuments. His most recent works include the large granite monument erected in Tampere for the Central Federation of Consumer's Co-operatives (1950); the statue *Binding Friendship* (1952, 1954), which was set up in both Göteborg (Sweden) and Turku; and a number of soldiers' memorials in various Finnish cities and towns.

Throughout his career, Aaltonen has produced a great many portrait busts, in marble, bronze and granite, that have been praised for their psychological penetration and perfection of form. Among the most distinguished are those of Queen Louise of Sweden; the League of Nations' officials, Joseph Paul-Boncour, Albert Thomas, and Joseph Avenol; the Finnish statesmen, Kaarlo Ståhlberg, P. E. Svinhufvud, and J. R. Danielson-Kalmari; the Finnish composers, Jean Sibelius and Toivo Kuula; the Finnish writers, Aaro Hellaakoski, Maria Jotuni, Maila Talvio, Otto Manninen, and J. Lehtonen; and the Finnish artists, Helena Schjerfbeck, Jalmari Ruokokoski, Tyko Sallinen, Westerholm, and Haartman. Aaltonen has also received several commissions for commemorative bronze medallions.

At various times since his graduation from art school, Aaltonen has returned to painting, and worked in oils, tempera, water colors, and pastels. He has treated several themes—notably the figure of *Marjatta and Child,* derived from the national epic *Kalevala*—in both painting and sculpture. Among his paintings are portraits of his mother and father: *The Enraged Kullervo* (1940), and *Silence after Music* (1946).

Although Aaltonen has been variously called a "realist," a "classicist," and an "idealist," the critic Onni Okkonen believes these terms fit only partially an artist of Aaltonen's "rare originality." J. J. Tikkanen has spoken of the freedom with which the sculptor moves among different styles—at times seeking a monumental mass effect, at others a sinewy elasticity, and then again a womanly softness—depending on the nature of his subject and material. According to Bertel Hintze, it is to the union of opposites—"classicism and romanticism, the clarity of the south and the dream of the north, solidity of form and the light shimmering of surfaces"—that the art of Aaltonen owes its particular intensity. "In the wake of Aaltonen there has grown a younger generation of gifted and skillful sculptors," observes Sakari Saarikivi (*Studio*), "and thanks to his example we can state that Finnish sculpture nowadays stands on a far higher level than Finnish painting."

The sculptor has participated in exhibitions of Finnish art in most of the leading cities of Europe. At the Vienna International Art Exhibition in 1936, he received a gold medal award, and the following year he won the grand prize at the Paris International Exposition. His sculpture was on display at the New York and San Francisco world fairs, and he visited the United States for the first time in the summer of 1952 to attend an exhibition of Finnish arts and crafts at the Smithsonian Institution in Washington, D.C. In addition to being represented in many private collections, his work is included in the permanent collections of the Atheneum in Helsinki, and the art museums of Turku, Tampere, and Vaasa in Finland; the National Museum in Stockholm, and the museums of Malmö, Lund, and Göteborg in Sweden; and in the Tate Gallery in London.

The Finnish artist has been awarded the Knight's Cross and the Commander's Cross of the Order of the White Rose of Finland; the Knight's Cross of the French Legion of Honor; the Commander's Cross of the Norwegian Order of St. Olav; the Medal of Prince Eugen of Sweden; and the Stélla della Solidarietà Itáliana. Honorary doctorates have been bestowed upon him by the University of Lund in Sweden (1941) and Helsinki University (1950). In token of Finland's gratitude for his achievements, he received the honorary title of professor in 1940.

In 1948, Aaltonen was elected a charter member of the newly established Finnish Academy. He has been a foreign member of the Swedish Royal Academy of Fine Arts since 1931, and an honorary member of the Italian Accadèmia Culturale Adriatica since 1950. Among the Finnish organizations in which he holds honorary memberships are the Aleksis Kivi Society in both Helsinki and Turku, the Turku Art Society, Turku Artists' Club, Finnish Art Academy, Finnish Society of Artists, Helsinki Rotary Club, and the Educational Association of Lapland. He is also a member of the Kalevala Society, Finnish Federation of Sculptors, Finnish Union of Painters, Finnish-American Society, Finnish-British Society, Finnish-French Society, Dante Alighieri Society, Finnish Association of Anglers, Ursa Astronomy Club, and Finnish Sports Academy.

The sculptor was married in 1919 to Aino Pietiläinen, and they had four children. This marriage was later dissolved, and in 1930 he married Elsa Rantalainen. When Aaltonen visited New York, an interviewer described him as "a stocky man with a fine face and a great head of dark hair." In his youth the artist was fond of wrestling, weight-lifting, and swimming, and his vigorous physique reportedly enables him to work at his sculpture for ten consecutive hours without becoming exhausted. Some critics have attributed his powers of concentration and psychological perception in part to the fact that he has been deaf since childhood.

Aaltonen is "unshakably faithful to the emotional world of the Finnish folk soul, his primary source of inspiration," stated Oscar Antonsson in his monograph. In the opinion of Onni Okkonen, the sculptor has actually opposed "conventional rules of proportion and beautiful form in his effort to create a new classical art, based on typical character traits and physical features of his own people."

References

Renaissance p510+ D '28
Okkonen, O. L'Art Finlandais aux XIXe et XXe Siècles (1932); Wäinö Aaltonen (1945); Finnish Art (1946)
Saarikivi, S. and others. Art in Finland (1952)
International Who's Who, 1953
World Biography (1948)

ABRAMS, BENJAMIN Aug. 18, 1893
Radio corporation executive

Address: b. Emerson Radio and Phonograph Corp., 111 8th Ave., New York 11; h. 993 5th Ave., New York 28

A pocket radio, six inches wide, one and one-quarter inch deep, and weighing less than one pound, was introduced in 1953 by Benjamin Abrams, president of the Emerson Radio and Phonograph Corporation since 1922. Emphasizing radio as a style product instead of a purely technical marvel, Abrams, in 1932, launched the Emerson Model 25-A which is credited with making the nation "small-radio conscious." The portable radio "within two years," Abrams predicted, "is to be the size of a package of cigarettes. A few years more and the wrist radio will emerge from the laboratory" (New York *Times*, June 13, 1954).

Since the end of World War II Abrams has expanded Emerson's activities to include the manufacture of television sets and air conditioning units, and has established a research laboratory in Washington, D.C. Today the manufacture of radio sets accounts for only about 15 per cent of Emerson's business, which in 1953 recorded sales of over $75,000,000. Abrams established a fund in 1952 to support ten educational television stations.

Benjamin Abrams was born August 18, 1893 in Dorohoi, Romania to Solomon and Mollie (Hertan) Abrams. He attended Talmudic and public schools in his native land for about four years. In 1907 the Abrams family immigrated to the United States; it was about this time that Solomon Abrams died. "We had to struggle along all the way," Abrams recalls.

After studying at a New York public school for a year, Benjamin was forced to leave in order to help support his mother, two brothers, and four sisters. After working as a piano tuner for three dollars a week, he became a salesman of subscriptions to *Collier's* and the Hearst magazines for about four years, using "cheap desk clocks as added bait for his customers" (*Forbes*, June 15, 1954). "I always dressed up my propositions for appeal," he remembers. "I always got off the beaten path."

At nineteen, Abrams turned to the "distress merchandising" field, buying and selling the stock of bankrupt dealers. By the time he was twenty-one he had amassed $10,000. He invested in the manufacturing of unbreakable

BENJAMIN ABRAMS

dolls, and lost practically the entire sum within six months. This reverse forced Abrams to abandon a boyhood dream of becoming a lawyer, and he returned to "distress merchandising".

"With only $200 capital, a one-room office, a telephone and six phonographs," states *Forbes,* "he began organizing a crew of phonograph peddlers." Trading as the Grand Talking Machine Company, he began marketing phonographs that he assembled from purchased parts.

Several years later, Abrams obtained the Brooklyn distributorship of the Emerson Phonograph Company. He acquired the assets of the entire concern in 1922, and has controlled it ever since. Radio in this period was an infant industry; the Radio Corporation of America had begun the manufacture of receiving sets about 1922. Abrams, looking to the future, decided to enter this field. (It was at this time that he changed the company's name to the Emerson Radio and Phonograph Corporation.) About a year after assuming control of Emerson he placed on the market a combination radio-phonograph.

In 1932, Abrams was inspired by a visit to a clock factory to begin the manufacture of the Emerson Model 25-A. This compact radio weighed six pounds and retailed at twenty-five dollars, as compared with the fifty dollars charged for the smallest radios, which he described as "bulky tombstones" weighing about twenty-five pounds.

About 200,000 Model 25-A's were sold within two years. "It was more than enough," states *Forbes,* "to convince Abrams, who had begun to think of himself as the Ford of the radio industry, that building small-size, low-priced, mass-produced sets was the way to make Emerson grow. Thanks to this formula, by 1942 Emerson's share in the American radio market had soared from 1½ to 17½%." By the end of 1937 1,000,000 Emerson radios had been sold. Output continued at the rate of 1,000,000 radios a year until World War II, when the corporation's facilities were converted to the war effort.

In June 1946 Abrams exhibited the first two Emerson postwar TV receivers, a table model and a console model. In the summer of 1949 Emerson was producing 1,000 television receivers daily. The Canadian Marconi Company, Ltd. began manufacturing Emerson television and radio receivers on a royalty basis.

At this time Abrams announced that his corporation would soon add a television receiver to its radio line in Italy, thus establishing Emerson as the first American producer to make TV sets available on a mass production basis in Europe. For its fiscal year ending October 31, 1949, the Emerson corporation reported a net income of $3,035,652, as compared with its previous "high" of $2,401,769 in the preceding fiscal year.

Following the announcement by RCA in August 1949 that it was ready to demonstrate a "compatible" color television system using an electronic tube (as contrasted with Columbia's system for broadcasting color images with an outside "adapter"), Abrams expressed the hope that the Federal Communications Commission would "abandon the idea" of adopting any color television standards at that time. He urged that "every possible system be explored" and that standards be set only when receivers can be made economically. "I am still of the opinion that color TV will not become a commercial reality for at least two or three years," Abrams stated (New York *Times,* May 30, 1950).

After the New York state board of regents, contemplating the establishment of a network of eleven educational television stations, applied to the FCC to reserve the necessary channels, the National Association of Radio and Television Broadcasters in May 1951 lodged a protest. Abrams, however, complimented the board of regents on its "forward-looking step."

In June 1952 the Emerson corporation announced the establishment of a $100,000 fund from which grants of $10,000 each would be paid to the first ten educational television stations to go on the air. The first recipient was Station KUHT of the University of Houston in Texas. Other grants have been awarded to the University of California in Berkeley and the University of Pittsburgh, Pittsburgh, Pennsylvania.

Emerson, in 1953, acquired the Quiet Heet Corporation of New Jersey, a producer of private-brand room coolers for Sears Roebuck and Company and Sylvania Electric Products, Inc. In the same year Emerson established a research laboratory at Washington, D.C., where experiments were begun on "the use of transistors in portable television sets" (*Forbes,* June 15, 1954). In September 1953, nearly three months before the FCC approved a new color system that can be received on existing black and white sets, Emerson unveiled "the first commercial compatible color TV set designed for mass production" (New York *Herald Tribune,* September 29, 1953).

On March 1, 1954 Abrams announced that Emerson would rent, not sell, its television color receivers to the public, asserting that his organization did not believe that purchasers of color sets would get their money's worth in the immediate future.

On August 5, 1954 Emerson announced that it has discontinued its color TV leasing plan, and is offering instead a 15-inch color TV set at a retail price of $695. Abrams stated that his company will be among the first to use 21-inch color tubes "when satisfactory performance" is assured (New York *World-Telegram*, August 5, 1954).

The annual report of the Emerson corporation for the fiscal year ending October 31, 1953 listed sales of $75,926,546, an increase of 31 per cent over the $57,664,201 of 1952. Only about 15 per cent of this income was derived from the sale of radio sets. Abrams nevertheless still believes in a limited future for radio, especially in the field of the portable receiver.

Abrams is on the board of the Better Business Bureau of New York City, Radio-Television Manufacturers Association's reorganization committee, Federation of Jewish Philanthropies, Brooklyn Hebrew Orphan Asylum, and United Service for New Americans Joint Distribution Committee. He also serves on the industry advisory committee of the Munitions Board, the committee of the Joint Electronics Industry Commission, and is chairman of the greater New York committee for the State of Israel Bond Issue.

On December 19, 1926 Benjamin Abrams and Elizabeth Sargoy were married; they have three daughters and two grandchildren. *Newsweek* described him as "soft-spoken" and "somewhat melancholy looking". He has said that he is "much too busy" for hobbies or extravagances. Abrams is a light eater of very plain food, "requires eight hours sleep and manages to put some time on the golf course. . . . He likes to read biographies of men who succeeded."

References

Forbes 73:22+ Je 15 '54 por
N Y Herald Tribune p14 Ag 26 '50 por
N Y Post Mag p35 D 27 '48 por
N Y Times III p8 Je 13 '54 por
Newsweek 43:77+ F 15 '54 por

Who's Who in America, 1954-55
Who's Who in American Jewry, 1938-39
Who's Who in Commerce and Industry (1953)

ACHELIS, ELISABETH (a-kā'lĭs) Organization official

Address: b. c/o The World Calendar Association, Inc., 630 5th Ave., New York 20; h. 1 E. 66th St., New York 21

Blackstone Studios

ELISABETH ACHELIS

As president of the World Calendar Association, Inc., Miss Elisabeth Achelis has been urging calendar reform for the past twenty-four years. Nearly 500 different plans have been proposed by various groups to revise the Gregorian calendar, but the one which now has the largest number of proponents throughout the world is the World Calendar. This plan for a perpetual, equal-quarter, twelve-month calendar with holidays being observed on Fridays or Mondays was on the agenda of the United Nations Economic and Social Council (ECOSOC) when that international agency met in the summer of 1954. In addition to making each year the same and each calendar perpetual, ("Do you buy a new watch every year?" Miss Achelis asks), the World Calendar has other attributes that appeal especially to businessmen.

Although many spoke in favor of the World Calendar at the ECOSOC meetings in Geneva, Switzerland, (including the Rev. Daniel O'Connell, head of the Vatican Observatory in Rome), the National Council of Young Israel strongly opposed it on religious grounds. France proposed that the whole project be sent to member Governments for further study.

Elisabeth Achelis and her twin sister, Margaret Julie, were born in Brooklyn, New York to Bertha F. (Konig) and Fritz Achelis, who was president of the American Hard Rubber Company. She is of German descent. Elisabeth attended the Brooklyn Heights Seminary and the Ogontz School in Pennsylvania. The family, which included a brother, Frederic George, moved to New York City when Miss Achelis was in her early twenties.

While at the Lake Placid Club in the summer of 1929, Elisabeth Achelis became interested in calendar revision after hearing a talk on how to simplify life by the late Dr. Melvil Dewey, inventor of the Dewey decimal system for cataloguing books in libraries. In his speech Dr. Dewey discussed the Eastman thirteen-month calendar.

(Continued next page)

ACHELIS, ELISABETH—*Continued*

After painstaking research Miss Achelis discovered a twelve-month, equal-quarter plan conceived in 1834 by an Italian priest, Abbé Marco Mastrofini. She studied the priest's idea and decided that this embodied a realistic solution to the inadequacies of the Gregorian calendar. Miss Achelis christened it the World Calendar and undertook its promotion.

After consultation with her banker, her lawyer, and her minister, the late Dr. Robert Norwood of St. Bartholomew's Church, she incorporated the World Calendar Association on October 21, 1930, assumed its presidency, and engaged Charles Dexter Morris, former Associated Press foreign correspondent, as adviser.

The association's first office was at 485 Madison Avenue in New York City. Its initial promotional activity was the mailing of 30,000 pamphlets to leaders in business, industry, education and politics. Shortly thereafter the *Journal of Calendar Reform,* with Charles Dexter Morris as editor, was founded for international distribution. Steps were taken to integrate the association's support of the World Calendar with that of the Bureau d'Etudes pour la Réforme du Calendrier in Paris and the Parliamentary Committee on Calendar Reform (nongovernmental) in London. Since then Miss Achelis has devoted all her time and energies and a good part of her fortune to the movement. She has spoken to many groups throughout the world and urged calendar reform. She is the author of two books: *The World Calendar* (Putnam's, 1937) and *The Calendar for Everybody* (Putnam's, 1943).

The World Calendar is an attempt to give the year's measuring stick the same stability and permanence enjoyed by other measuring devices such as the clock, the ruler and the scale. It would divide the year into quarters of thirteen weeks each with each quarter beginning on a Sunday. The first month in each quarter would have thirty-one days, the others thirty. Since this accounts for only 364 days an intercalary day would be inserted between December 30th and January 1st. On leap years another extra day would be inserted after June 30th.

Miss Achelis suggests that these intercalary days be observed as world holidays: "Without doubt these days observed throughout the world will foster a greater world unity, cooperation and good will. The world holidays are the friendly handclasps of time."

The World Calendar has other aspects that interest businessmen: each quarter is identical, with thirteen full weeks, seventy-eight business days and thirteen Sundays; days and dates agree from year to year; holidays are stabilized, and can be made to fall on week ends every year.

The principal opponents of change, according to Miss Achelis, are "inertia" and some religious sects that object to the occasional eight-day week (mainly the Seventh-Day Adventists and Orthodox Jews). Calendar reform, she maintains, is a secular and civil and not a religious responsibility. She has been upheld by the Roman Catholic Church and other religious bodies which believe that religious holidays can fit into the World Calendar as readily as into the Gregorian.

Nearly 500 plans to revise the Gregorian calendar (instituted by Pope Gregory XIII in 1582) were presented at two calendar conferences of the League of Nations. Two of these, the Eastman calendar and the World Calendar, were assigned to a committee for further study. Since that time the Eastman calendar has lost popularity. By July 1951 seventeen governments approved the World Calendar. On March 28, 1949 Senator Estes Kefauver introduced a bill in the United States Senate calling for the adoption of the World Calendar at the end of 1950. However, this bill never came to a vote.

Sir Harold Spencer Jones, the Astronomer Royal of the United Kingdom, is an advocate of the World Calendar. Miss Achelis told a *New Yorker* reporter (February 13, 1954): "The outlook for the World Calendar is decidedly promising. Reform is imminent. The fact that India's permanent representative has placed our plan on the agenda of the eighteenth session of the Economic and Social Council, which will commence in Geneva on the twenty-ninth of June, is most encouraging." This time only the World Calendar proposal will be on the agenda. It will offer a "balanced, regular, perpetual and uniform calendar" for universal use. On the other hand, the United States and Great Britain took the position on April 2 at the United Nations that some religious groups seemed to be opposed to the idea and that there did not appear to be any great public demand for such a change (New York *Times,* April 3, 1954).

Miss Achelis has blue eyes and graying hair, weighs 135 pounds and is five feet two and one-half inches tall. She wears earrings to distinguish herself from her identical twin sister, Mrs. Frederick Arendale Sansome. An Episcopalian formerly, Miss Achelis is now interdenominational in religion and independent in politics. She is a member of the Colony Club, Women's City Club, The Town Hall Club, and the National Institute of Social Science. For recreation Miss Achelis enjoys reading and walking.

She was official American observer at the League of Nations Calendar Reform Conference, 1931; a delegate to the Universal Christian Council congresses at Geneva, Novi Sad, Fano, and Oxford, 1932 to 1937; delegate, International Chamber of Commerce, Vienna Congress, 1933; and delegate, International Women's Convention, Budapest, 1937.

The president of the World Calendar Association is a regular contributor to the *Journal of Calendar Reform* and other publications. In an article for *Education* (April 1951), she wrote: "Time measurement went hand in hand with the development of the arts of writing, agriculture, numbering and elementary geometry. . . . Somewhere in every school program there should be a place for basic instruction in regard to the calendar. This ought to cover the history of our system of time measurement and its intricate mathematical problems." She also stated: "In these days of tension and crises, the saving of valuable time, effort, material, and money that this [World Calendar] will make possible, cannot be lightly disregarded."

References

N Y Herald Tribune VIII p8 Mr 9 '47 por
New Yorker 15:21+ D 30 '39; 29:23+ F 13 '54
Achelis, E. The Calendar for Everybody (1943)
International Who's Who, 1953
Who's Who in America, 1954-55

ADAMS, DIANA March 29, 1926- Ballerina
Address: b. c/o New York City Center of Music and Drama, Inc., 130 W. 56 St., New York 19; h. 38 East 52 St., New York 22

"One of the loveliest of artists, and a shining jewel in the City Ballet's crown," such is the tribute paid to ballerina Diana Adams by dance critic John Martin in the New York *Times,* February 22, 1954. In describing her portrayal of the Sugar Plum Fairy in the presentation of *The Nutcracker* ballet he wrote: "There is a glowing quality to her movement like the timbre of a fine voice, and it becomes a pleasure simply to watch her move. . . She brought a fresh and valid beauty to the role."

Miss Adams has been collecting enthusiastic reviews of this kind ever since she danced the title role in *Helen of Troy* in the Ballet Theatre production of 1944. In the decade since that performance she has been actively employed in ballet companies and is now a featured member of George Balanchine's renowned New York City Ballet.

Diana Adams was born on March 29, 1926, in the town of Stanton, Virginia. Her father, Stanley Adams, was an English teacher, and her step-mother, Emily Hadley Adams, taught dancing. While Diana was quite young, the family moved to Memphis, Tennessee, where, at the age of seven, she began taking dancing lessons, and where she attended the Lausanne School.

When Diana was twelve the family came to New York City. Here Diana entered the Gardner School, and continued her study of dancing, first at the Ballet Arts School, where she worked under Edward Caton, and later under the tutelage of Agnes de Mille. Diana's first stage appearance was made in the musical comedy hit, *Oklahoma!* where she appeared in the ballet choreographed by Agnes de Mille. This engagement was followed by a similar one in *One Touch of Venus,* in which the young dancer again appeared in a de Mille ballet.

Diana became a member of Ballet Theatre in 1944. Presented at first in minor roles, she rose rapidly to the rank of soloist. Her portrayal of the Queen of the Wilis in *Giselle* was rewarded with critical praise, and in the presentation of *Helen of Troy,* she created the role of Helen. In the subsequent years of her

Walter E. Owen
DIANA ADAMS

association with the company, Diana was seen in such diverse ballets as *Sylphides* and *Undertow, Swan Lake* and *Jardin aux Lilas.* She thus demonstrated her technical scope in fulfilling both the demands for classical purity of execution required in the older ballets, and the more extensive range of coordination employed in the newer works, in which a somewhat exotic and sensational choreography is dramatically introduced.

At the Jacob's Pillow Annual Dance Festival held in Lee, Massachusetts, in the summer of 1949, Diana appeared in a *pas de deux* with Hugh Laing; entitled *Dear Departed,* it was a humorous work composed by Antony Tudor to music of Ravel. She and Laing were also seen on this occasion in the adagio from the *grand pas de deux* from Act Two of *Swan Lake.* The dance critic of the New York *Herald Tribune* referred to Miss Adams' work in the first number as "particularly winning," and of the second wrote, "Miss Adams discloses, as she did this spring in her appearance with Ballet Theatre, that classic dance is quite within her dancing range."

During this period, in keeping with the demands made upon a modern ballerina, Diana continued her dance training under the instruction of Margaret Krask, an exponent of the Cecchetti method of classical ballet, and under the originator of a number of distinguished modern ballets, the English choreographer, Antony Tudor.

The *Herald Tribune* critic, however, commenting on Diana's appearance in the principal role of *Jardin aux Lilas* in a presentation at the City Center the following spring, wrote, (May 5, 1950), "She is still a soloist—a superior dancer—but not yet a ballerina—poignancy and sadness were present, but they were not enough." Commenting on the same performance, the New York *Times* critic stated that

ADAMS, DIANA—*Continued*

Miss Adams "did a quite entrancing job of it," and of her appearance in *Undertow* on the following night, the *Times* critic commented that Diana "was a fierce and menacing Medusa."

In the fall of 1950 Diana became a member of the New York City Ballet, and on November 9 was featured, in company with Nicolas Magallanes and Melissa Hayden, in a presentation of the Frederick Ashton-Benjamin Britten work, *Illuminations*. John Martin in reviewing the performance for the *Times,* wrote: "Miss Adams as the figure of Sacred Love, for the first time brings to it a mystical, other worldly strength and beauty which it has never had before."

The same critic had further praise for Diana's work later in the month when she made her first appearance in *Symphonie Concertante,* a choreographic arrangement by George Balanchine, artistic director of the New York City Ballet, to music of Mozart. Martin wrote, "Miss Adams captured completely Balanchine's approach to the composition and danced it with enchanting daintiness and supreme elegance" (New York *Times,* November 25, 1950).

Diana's position as one of the company's outstanding ballerinas was well established by the following spring. She had acquitted herself notably in taking up the roles assigned to her from the company's repertoire, appearing as Eurydice in the Stravinsky-Balanchine ballet, *Orpheus,* with Magallanes in the titular role, and having made her first appearance in a presentation of the revised *Baiser de la Fée,* among other assignments. She was now chosen to create the role of Marguerite in *Lady of the Camellias,* which had its premiere on the last day of February, 1951. Based on Dumas *fils'* novel, the ballet was choreographically the work of Antony Tudor; setting and costumes were by Cecil Beaton, and the music employed was Verdi's, although not taken from *La Traviata,* which also makes use of the Dumas story. The two featured dancers were Diana Adams and Hugh Laing.

Unqualified approval came from the critics. The reviewer for *Variety* said, "Diana Adams and Hugh Laing dance the leads superbly, Miss Adams lending a frail delicacy to the heroine." The *New Yorker* critic wrote that Diana was "a lovely and superb embodiment of Dumas' luckless heroine." Walter Terry of the *Herald Tribune* found Miss Adams "utterly irresistible as the fragile, gay, yet loving heroine. Every aspect of a complex character, the physical as well as emotional idiosyncrasies, were superbly realized, tellingly conveyed."

The young dancer has been credited with possessing a distinctive gift for a "basic musicality" in her use of movement. Writing in the Sunday edition of the *Times* on November 25, 1951, John Martin said that Balanchine, the artistic director of the New York City Ballet, had found in Diana Adams "a perfect instrument; under his guidance, she has become the epitome of the lyric dancer . . . .Miss Adams' special gift is simply for movement. It is vividly colored by feeling, but its strength lies in the vital continuity of musical impulse which gives it timbre and substance."

Referring to the Balanchine ballet, *Symphonie Concertante,* John Martin wrote: "Admirably performed though it was superficially, it was not until Miss Adams stepped into one of its solo roles that it took on substance in the musico-choreographic sense."

A year later, the ballerina was again seen in a premiere presentation, this time a much heralded ballet, *Picnic at Tintagel,* based upon the legend of Tristan and Iseult (Isolde) to music of Sir Arnold Bax, with settings by Cecil Beaton. Of this occasion, Louis Biancolli wrote in the *World-Telegram,* (February 29, 1952), "I shall never forget the Isolde of Diana Adams," and the *Herald Tribune* critic expressed his belief that Miss Adams had given "the finest performance in her career."

Other first performances which have engaged the ballerina's talents have been Balanchine's *Bayou,* set to Virgil Thomson's "Acadian Songs and Dances," which had its premiere on February 21, 1952; *Valse Fantaisie,* also choreographed by Balanchine, first seen on January 6, 1953; *The Filly,* choreographically the work of Todd Bolender, presented on May 19 of the same year; and Balanchine's most recent work, *Opus 34,* based on a musical score by Arnold Schoenberg, which made its appearance on January 20, 1954. In repeat performances of standard repertoire numbers, including the twenty-year old Balanchine ballet, *Serenade,* (to Tchaikovsky's music) Diana has continued to win fresh laurels.

When the New York City Ballet decided to present *The Nutcracker* for a number of performances in February, Diana Adams, for example, danced the role of Dewdrop (for which she won an ovation earlier in the week of February 15) and Tanaquil LeClercq danced the role of the Sugar Plum Fairy. When Miss LeClercq became ill, Miss Adams took over this part and in "this essentially bravura role, although she is not a bravura dancer" John Martin commented: "She phrases with extraordinary beauty, not alone in the musical sense but also in her awareness of the choreographer's phrase. . . This provides a real illumination of formal values."

Two motion picture presentations, released in 1954, also feature the ballerina. One is an MGM production made in London with Gene Kelly entitled *Invitation to the Dance;* the other, a Paramount picture made in Hollywood, is *Knock on Wood;* in the latter, Diana Adams is seen in a dance routine with Danny Kaye.

Diana was married to Hugh Laing in 1947. At that time, both dancers were members of Ballet Theatre. Although regarded for some years as an ideal married couple, the marriage terminated in divorce on November 19, 1953. Despite her own early start in dance training, the ballerina advises that "It's better to start later . . . and to develop more facets of your life."

In an interview given to the Washington *Post,* she declared that her idea of a vacation is sleep. On the question of hobbies, she asks, "What time do I have for them?" Nevertheless, she lists sewing and reading mysteries and "thriller" movies as among her favorite occupations. She enjoys cooking, and making some of her own dresses. Diana has brown hair, brown eyes, is five feet seven in height and weighs 120 pounds.

References

N Y Herald Tribune p4 Jl 16 '49
N Y Times II p6 N 25 '51
New Yorker 27:82 Mr 10 '51
Variety 181:56 Mr 7 '51
Washington (D.C.) Post p16 F 14 '53 por
Chujoy, A. (ed.) Dance Encyclopedia (1949)

ADAMS, EDITH Apr. 16, 1927- Singer; actress

Address: b. c/o Columbia Broadcasting System, Inc., 485 Madison Ave., New York 22; h. 91 Sunset Lane, Tenafly, N.J.

EDITH ADAMS

Television demonstrated that it could give to the theatre as well as take from it when it contributed Edith Adams to the cast of *Wonderful Town,* which opened on Broadway in February 1953. In the role of the "lovely and effervescent" Eileen in this musical version of the hit play *My Sister Eileen,* the young singer, whose only previous professional experience had been before the TV cameras, won the critics completely with her beauty, her singing, and her acting.

From a student production at the Juilliard School of Music in 1949 Miss Adams went on a television talent show, won the title of Miss New York Television, became Miss U. S. Television for 1950. She appeared on Ernie Kovacs' TV program for several years. Her latest television job requires her singing and acting on the Jack Paar show.

Edith Enke (Adams, which she took as her stage name, was her mother's maiden name) was born April 16, 1927 in Kingston, Pennsylvania, the second child and first daughter of Sheldon A. and Ada (Adams) Enke. Her Enke ancestors were Pennsylvanians and the singer recalls that after tracing the family to a Hessian soldier who had fought for the British in the Revolutionary War, genealogical research was given up.

Always interested in music, Edith did her first singing in church. The Enke family having moved to Grove City, Pennsylvania, she entered Grove City High School in 1942. She was a joiner, she says, participating in many extracurricular activities in addition to her singing, acting as drum majorette and writing a column for the school paper.

Since her family moved frequently during this period, she later attended Julia Richman High School in New York City for a year, and she spent her junior and senior years at Tenafly (New Jersey) High School. At her last school Edith became a member of the *a capella* choir and the glee club and sang the roles of Buttercup in *H. M. S. Pinafore* and Katherine de Vaucelles in *The Vagabond King* in school productions.

After her graduation in 1945 she commuted daily to New York City to study at the Juilliard School of Music, took some courses in drama at Columbia University, and studied singing with Helen Jepson. She made some summer stock appearances at the Chapel Theater in Ridgewood, New Jersey and the Grove Theater in Nuangola, Pennsylvania.

Television scouts discovered Miss Adams at a student revue entitled *Lose Your Tempo* at Juilliard School in the spring of 1949. Invited to appear on a new talent show, she won the preliminaries but lost in the finals. However, she was given another TV spot and in a contest which followed she became Miss New York Television and later, in the finals at Chicago, Miss U. S. Television for 1950.

At this time the young singer left Juilliard to concentrate on a career in show business and found herself confronted with a problem. Her coloratura soprano, she decided, was unsuitable for popular singing, so she took lessons from Bee Walker, a Broadway coach, and after eight months she had lowered her voice more than two octaves.

Two Canadian night club appearances as Miss U. S. Television in April and May 1951, the first in Toronto at the One Two Club and the second at the Show Bar in Montreal, were her first real professional experience. As a result of an enthusiastic review of these engagements in *Variety,* Richard Rodgers offered her a chorus job in one of the Rodgers and Hammerstein companies with the promise of something more important to follow.

She was also invited to appear on Arthur Godfrey's *Talent Scouts.* She entered the talent contest, singing *Would I Love You,* and lost to a baritone, but she turned down Richard Rodgers' offer when a Philadelphia TV director

ADAMS, EDITH—*Continued*

who had seen her on the Godfrey show asked her to join the Ernie Kovacs program as featured singer, which she did in July, 1951.

The Kovacs show, which originated in Philadelphia at the time Miss Adams joined the cast, was an unrehearsed, uninhibited comedy program variously termed "wacky" and "zany." Commenting on her experience with the group the singer said, "If I seem relaxed and unworried in *Wonderful Town* it's because of the great training I've been getting on Ernie's wild TV show, where it'd be a little ridiculous to feel nervous" (*Cue,* April 4, 1953).

In April 1952 WCBS-TV brought the comedy program to New York City, giving it a morning spot as *Kovacs Unlimited,* and Miss Adams came along in her role of vocalist and "stooge" for the comedian. The *Ernie Kovacs Show,* an hour-long evening program, made its debut at the beginning of 1953. "When she isn't playing patsy to Kovacs, Miss Adams sings and she's pretty special at that, too," said John Crosby in the New York *Herald Tribune* of the singer's contribution to the program, and Harriet Van Horne called her "one of the best assets on the Kovacs show" (New York *World-Telegram and Sun*).

In the fall of 1952 Richard Rodgers, who had failed to gain Miss Adams for his own company, recommended her for the role of Eileen in the scheduled production of *Wonderful Town.* In preparation she spent that fall working with Clytie Mundy, her singing teacher, to regain her previous singing style. A short time after she applied for an audition she developed laryngitis; when she was finally able to appear she sang *Mountain Greenery* and *Why Was I Born?* and read scenes from the script.

The following day she met Rosalind Russell, the show's star, who had the final say on the selection of Eileen from among 300 who had auditioned for the role. With Miss Russell's approval a contract was offered to the young singer; Miss Adams was hesitant about accepting it, worried whether the musical comedy would have a long enough run to warrant her giving up her television work, but she decided to take the chance. It meant not only hard work in rehearsals, but Miss Adams had to diet, and she managed to reduce her weight from 130 to 118 pounds.

Wonderful Town opened in New York at the Winter Garden Theatre on February 25, 1953 and became an immediate hit, winning an award as the best new musical of the season. Based upon the 1940 comedy, *My Sister Eileen,* which in turn was derived from *New Yorker* sketches by Ruth McKenney, it tells the story of two Ohio girls who come to New York in the 1930's and the various excitements and predicaments attendant upon their entry into the life of Greenwich Village.

The critics were enthusiastic about Miss Adams' portrayal of Eileen, the younger of the sisters. "Not only has Miss Adams the vitally necessary good looks and romantic charm . . . and does she sing attractively," said Richard Watts, Jr. in the New York *Post* (March 15, 1953), "but she also reveals a remarkable expert sense of humorous characterization. Her Eileen is always an authentic human being, gentle, innocent but more than a bit guileful, successful but oddly touching, and quietly amusing without ever losing her romantic appeal."

Brooks Atkinson commented in the New York *Times,* "She is a trained singer who can also act. In fact, she can act with a lot of nuance. For Eileen is not a simple character. Although she is genuinely innocent, she also has an instinct for subduing and annexing the predatory male. Miss Adams moves through this elusive character with the greatest of ease, keeping it fresh and sweet and adding just enough worldliness to make it palatable. . . . In her first appearance on Broadway Miss Adams has won a considerable triumph of her own."

For several weeks during the rehearsal of the musical Miss Adams managed to sing two songs daily on the Kovacs show by dashing to the studio in a cab during her lunch hour. This became too distracting, however, and she gave up her television appearances altogether in January 1953. After *Wonderful Town* had settled into its Broadway run, she made a brief return to the Kovacs show from April through July. Her latest venture is the Jack Paar Friday morning program which was premiered on WCBS-TV November 12, 1953. As for the future, Miss Adams says she would like to do one or two more musicals and then act in a straight drama.

The blond singer has been described as "pretty, sweet, naive, candid, shrewd and in the vein of the whim-of-iron girls" (New York *Times Magazine,* April 26, 1953), and, according to cast members of *Wonderful Town,* she "sounds a lot like Eileen offstage." Water skiing, swimming, sewing, and painting are among her many hobbies. Her religion is Presbyterian and she is an independent politically.

References

Cue 22:14 Ap 4 '53 por
N Y Herald Tribune IV p2 Jl 12 '53 por
N Y Times p14 Ap 26 '53 por
N Y World-Telegram p24 O 20 '53
Scholastic 62:6 My 20 '53 por
Blum, D. Theatre World, 1952-53

ADAMS, STANLEY Aug. 14, 1907- Song writer; organization president

Address: b. c/o American Society of Composers, Authors and Publishers, 575 Madison Ave., New York 22

Lyric writer Stanley Adams is the sixth president of the American Society of Composers, Authors and Publishers (ASCAP), comprised of approximately 3,400 members whose songs are played on radio and television, in hotels, restaurants, skating rinks, and wherever music is performed for profit, a total of over 20,000 licensees. Organized by composer Victor Herbert in 1914 to safeguard the rights of composers, ASCAP now collects over $16,000,000 annually.

Adams began his career as a song writer while he was still in college, and although he is a law school graduate he has never practiced as an attorney. He has written the lyrics for more than 100 published songs, some of which have appeared in musical shows on Broadway and in motion pictures. Among his best known songs are *Little Old Lady, There Are Such Things, What a Difference a Day Makes* and *La Cucaracha.*

A native of Manhattan, Stanley Adams was born on August 14, 1907 to Henry Charles and Nan (Josephs) Adams. He attended De Witt Clinton High School, where he was a member of the freshman boxing team, played varsity baseball, and performed in class plays. Graduated in 1924, he entered New York University and later N.Y.U.'s School of Law, receiving the LL.B. degree in 1929. He was elected to the *Law Review,* wrote a column for N.Y.U.'s *Daily News,* and wrote, choreographed and performed in varsity shows.

During his college years he worked on ships, arranging entertainment, and taking parts in amateur theatrical productions. This experience led to his collaboration, in his last year at law school, with the late Fats Waller in the creation of the song *Rolling Down the River.* Written for the Connie's Inn revue, the song became a hit. When Lester Santly, publisher of popular music, heard the song, he offered Adams a contract on his staff, and Adams, after graduating from law school, began his career as a professional song writer.

Adams contributed the song *I'm Not Me, I'm You* to the *Shoestring Revue* in 1929. Three of his songs were presented in Broadway shows in 1933, *Time to Go, Where Can I Find Love* and *You're Everywhere.* The following year he wrote one of his most successful songs, *La Cucaracha,* for the motion picture *Viva Villa,* and collaborated with Xavier Cugat, who wrote the music for *My Shawl;* with Ernesto Lecuona on *Dust on the Moon,* and with Marie Grever on *What a Difference a Day Makes.*

Another of his songs, *Little Old Lady,* was written to music composed by Hoagy Carmichael. According to Adams, he and Carmichael wrote the song for *The Show Is On* (1936), which went into rehearsal in the east while the song writers were working in Hollywood. Because the revue had been hastily assembled, provision had not been made for properly introducing the song, and it was at first discarded. E. Y. ("Yip") Harburg, who was directing the rehearsals, was reluctant to have the song omitted, so he himself wrote the scene in the revue which introduced Mitzi Mayfair as the "little old lady." The song became the hit of the show and a national success.

In 1937, Adams collaborated with Belle Fenstock on *Stranger in the Dark,* which was introduced at Billy Rose's Aquacade. He wrote the lyrics for *Yesterthoughts* in 1940 for the melody composed by Victor Herbert in 1907. Late in 1942, Adams contributed to the composition, *There Are Such Things,* which was for many weeks one of the most frequently performed songs on the major radio networks. Among the songs Adams has written for motion pictures are *I Have So Much More,* for *The Great Lie* (1945), *While You're Away,* for *My Reputation* (1945), and *Duel in the Sun* for the film of the same name (1947).

Jean Raeburn

STANLEY ADAMS

The lyric writer became a member of ASCAP in 1934. The organization was founded in 1914 by Victor Herbert and eight associates in order to protect the copyrights of its members. Membership, which is voluntary, is open only to those who have demonstrated the ability to create or to publish successful music. Together with affiliated societies in other countries, the association, which operates on a nonprofit basis, collects fees for public performances of the works of its composers and 565 publishers who have contributed the 500,000 copyrighted titles in ASCAP's catalogues. (A copyright runs for twenty-eight years, may then be renewed for another twenty-eight years; after which the work is "in the public domain.") Its function is authorized by the United States copyright of 1909 which established the right of composers and publishers of music to be paid whenever their works are performed publicly for profit.

In 1941 ASCAP asked radio broadcasting stations to pay 7½ per cent for the use of its members' music, but the station owners refused. Then ensued a ten month period known as "the great blackout," or the era of *Jeanie with the Light Brown Hair.* No ASCAP music was heard over the ether waves, and the radio stations used chiefly old songs. ASCAP finally won the right to collect 2¾ per cent of the gross intake of the networks.

The networks submit logs to ASCAP which list the number of times a composer's works are played. For Irving Berlin, Cole Porter or Richard Rodgers the revenues may amount from $50,000 to $100,000 a year (*Business Week,* October 10, 1953). Approximately 80 per cent of its income comes from radio and

ADAMS, STANLEY—*Continued*

television. A competitor, Broadcast Music, Inc., was formed by the radio industry in 1940 with its own membership of non-ASCAP composers.

ASCAP is valuable to commercial users of copyright music in that it relieves them of the legal responsibility of obtaining permission for each commercial use. Its membership has grown from 188 at its inception to about 3,400 in 1953. The composers pay dues of ten dollars a year; publishers pay fifty dollars. The dues are used to help needy song writers.

Adams became a member of the board of directors in 1944, and established a reputation as a good administrator and negotiator. He has been among the most active ASCAP board members in committee work during recent years. He was elected to the presidency of ASCAP, at an annual salary of $25,000, on April 23, 1953, succeeding Otto A. Harbach. He was re-elected on April 29, 1954.

ASCAP's president has been a vice-president of the Songwriters Protective Association and a member of the United Nations Educational, Scientific, and Cultural Organization conference for international copyright. He belongs to Delta Beta Phi fraternity and to the Dutch Treat club. Tennis and horseback riding are his favorite sports. He also devotes much time to the staging of nonprofessional plays. Adams is five feet seven inches tall, weighs 152 pounds, and has hazel eyes and black hair.

References

Bsns W p137 O 10 '53 por
Variety 190:10 Ap 22 '53
ASCAP Biographical Dictionary of Composers, Authors, and Publishers (1952)

ADDAMS, CHARLES (SAMUEL) Jan. 7, 1912- Cartoonist

Address: c/o The New Yorker, 25 W. 43d St., New York 36; h. 20 East 35th St., New York 16

Creeping in and out of the pages of the *New Yorker* magazine are some of the most gruesome — yet strangely loveable — characters in the world, the brain children of Charles Addams, one of America's most popular and successful cartoonists. Since he sold his first sketch in 1933, Addams has peopled his drawings with weird creatures such as the witch-woman, the king-size Boris Karloff butler, the children with beetling brows and pointed heads whose sinister appearance and morbid behavior are the delight of countless fans. He is regarded as the funniest spokesman for all the repressed violence that lurks in normal people.

His name has become part of the American idiom. An "Addams house" means a cobwebby, gloomy Victorian structure inhabited by what columnist John McClain calls "a vampire lady and a manservant who has apparently been left over from the Neanderthal age." Addams has capitalized on his peculiar gifts and anthologies of his macabre cartoons have sold over 180,000 copies. "Clearly," says critic John Mason Brown, "Mr. Addams invites us to enter a world which has nothing to do with the one in which we live except that, in the most glorious, undeviating, and giddy fashion, it turns all of its values topsy-turvy" (*Saturday Review,* November 11, 1950).

The creator of these "loveable monsters" whose behavior is outrageously at variance with the normal, is, according to Wolcott Gibbs, drama critic on the *New Yorker,* just a "nice guy, very little different from his other friends."

Charles Samuel Addams was born in Westfield, New Jersey on January 7, 1912, the son of Charles Huey and Grace M. Spear Addams. His father was a manager for a piano company. As a child, Charles read Edgar Allan Poe, Grimms' *Fairy Tales,* and the *Book of Knowledge.* When Selma Robinson, reporter on the New York *Star* (September 19, 1948) asked Addams if there was anything in his childhood which might explain his homicidal cartoons or his gift for the macabre, Addams said helpfully: "In Westfield, once, I broke into a deserted house and drew skeletons all over the walls. The grounds were soggy with rain and there was a fine set of my footprints in the mud around the house for the detectives to see, so each day for a week I wore a different pair of shoes to throw them off the track. It worked out fine. It took the cops a week to find me."

He told Tex McCrary in an interview published in the New York *Herald Tribune* (October 5, 1949) that he did have fun, as a boy, frightening people "but never badly." He related one special trick he played on his grandmother. "We had a dumb-waiter in our house in New Jersey, and I'd get inside on the ground floor, and then very quietly I'd haul myself up to grandmother's floor and then I'd knock on the door, and when she came to open the door, I'd jump out and scare the wits out of her."

As a boy artist, he doodled skulls and bones. "For him," wrote Saul Pett in the San Francisco *Chronicle* (November 1, 1953), "Hallowe'en was a big production. He never dressed as an Indian or pirate, only as a ghost. He was fond, too, of roaming through cemeteries. 'I suppose I was trying to scare myself,' Addams said, 'but all in all, I had a normal healthy childhood.' " His mother worried occasionally about the portent of Charley's doodling, but his father, who had studied to be an architect, encouraged him to draw. He drew cartoons for the Westfield High School paper.

Addams was also interested in medicine, but not enough to study it. He attended Colgate University for one year (1929 to 1930), transferred to the University of Pennsylvania because he had heard they had an art course there. "Only I found out later that it was not art but an architectural course," he recalled. "Anyway, it didn't hurt me at all." The next year he went to the Grand Central School of Art (1931 to 1932), but admits that he spent most of his time in the Terminal, "watching people."

Deciding to become an illustrator, he sent a cartoon to the *New Yorker.* "It was a simple line drawing of a man in his stocking feet standing on the ice and saying: 'I forgot my skates.' It was not very funny," Addams told Selma Robinson, "and I don't know why they ever bought it."

After that he found a job with a Macfadden publication, "sort of a true detective magazine," he recalls. "I did lettering, retouching of photographs and diagrams of the spot where the body was found. It paid me $15 a week, which was almost enough to pay for my sodas and my commutation ticket to Westfield. It was the last and only job I ever had." As a free lance, he sold drawings to *Life,* the old humorous weekly, to *Collier's,* and to other magazines, and averaged fifty dollars a week.

His popularity as a cartoonist began with the publication in the *New Yorker,* January 13, 1940, of his cartoon of a lady skier whose down-hill tracks led to a tree, and mystifyingly on either side of the tree the two tracks of her skis continued in perfectly parallel lines. Addams is pleased that an insane asylum in Nebraska used this drawing to test the mental level of its patients. "Under a fifteen-year level they can't tell what's wrong." He added that he never quite understood the cartoon himself. But from then on his cartoons have appeared regularly in the *New Yorker.* Occasionally, *Collier's* and *Cosmopolitan* also publish them. He served as a private in the United States Army from January 1943 until February 1946, most of the time in a Signal Corps detachment at Astoria, Queens, Long Island, where, with other professional artists, he animated educational film cartoons for the Army, and illustrated manuals.

People like to collect original Addams drawings. Herbert Marshall owns several. Mrs. Ronald Colman bought one showing a psychiatrist asking a woman: "Now, in your dreams of being chased by Ronald Colman and a plumed alligator—which is in the lead?"

"I must admit I have a special fondness," writes John Mason Brown, "for those frightening little brats, those incipient Loebs and Leopolds who most often attract Mr. Addams' attention. I have in mind such of his bantam ogres just about to send a boulder rolling down a hill toward the fancy car in which an inoffensive motorist has his eyes fixed on a sign reading 'CAREFUL! Children at play.' Or the appalling little boy who is reaching in the medicine cabinet in his bathroom to dip an arrow into a bottle marked 'Poison.' Or the same menace again when he is sending a toy school bus straight into the path of an oncoming toy train . . . or the glamour ghoul, the lanky young witch with the chalk-white skin and the hearse-black gown and locks, who is everyone's joy whenever she haunts the pages of the *New Yorker* . . . Monsters young or old, four-legged or two-headed, prehistoric or contemporary, simpering or nonchalant, are very much Mr. Addams' affair. His is a goblin world of bats, spiders, broomsticks, snakes, cobwebs, and bloodletting morons in which every day is Hallowe'en" (*Saturday Review,* November 11, 1950).

His work has been exhibited at the Fogg Art Museum, the Rhode Island School of Design and the Metropolitan Museum of Art (war exhibition). His books are *Drawn and Quartered* (Random House, 1942); *Addams and Evil* (Simon and Schuster, 1947) and *Monster Rally* (Simon and Schuster, 1950). He has contributed to each of the *New Yorker* Albums.

Hugh Blodgett

CHARLES ADDAMS

According to his friend, John O'Hara, the novelist, Addams "is a big man, about six feet one inch, and around 195 pounds, a toxophilist who can handle a sixty-pound pull, but I don't think he'd hurt a fly. I never have seen him lose his temper, although that is not to say he doesn't get mad. He happens to be what is called easygoing, and has a decent contempt for the opinions of mankind. He speaks with a New Jersey twang plus a drawl of his own, and but for the grace of God, which gave him his enormous talent, his sense of humor, and his impatience with banality, he might have become a successful politician."

Addams lives in a cheerful house in Westhampton, Long Island in the summer, does his drawing in the kitchen. His apartment in New York includes a white Angora cat and a black French poodle named Tulip. He once owned two English poodles named Abraham and Strauss in honor of a department store, and a canary named Birdie.

Jinx Falkenberg McCrary once described Addams' apartment as follows: "Half of one wall is covered with murderous and ancient cross-bows. A tired Victorian flyswatter casts batlike shadows on another wall; a huge empty bamboo birdcase makes a chandelier over one light. A human skeleton, under glass, teeters on top of a table in the living room; in the bedroom there is a skull on the dressing table. Liquor bottles on shelves are mixed with other ominous bottles labeled 'ARSENIC' . . ." (New York *Herald Tribune,* October 5, 1949).

Addams likes fast automobiles, owns a Mercedes-Benz and an Aston Martin. He belongs

ADDAMS, CHARLES—*Continued*

to the Sports Car Club of America. He occasionally enters races, but according to his friends frequently "organizes his own races: Addams vs. all the cars on the road from New York City to Quogue, Long Island." He enjoys reading Civil War history, collects medieval armor and uses a piece of an old tombstone as a paper weight. It is marked "Phoebe, 1760" and he found it in an abandoned church yard. In sports, he likes horseback riding, golf, and archery. He was married to Barbara Day, a former model, on May 29, 1943. They were divorced in 1952. Burgess Meredith says that Addams is "really a very gentle and humorous fellow."

References

Look 6:60 D 15 '42; 17:98 My '53
N Y Herald Tribune p23 O 5 '49 por
N Y Star Mag p5 S 19 '48 pors
N Y Sun p14 Ag 31 '48
N Y World-Telegram p1 Ja 30 '43
Reporter 9:37+ Jl 21 '53
San Francisco Chronicle Mag p29 N 1 '53
Sat R 33:25 N 11 '50
Addams, C. Drawn and Quartered (1942)
Addams, C. Addams and Evil (1947)
Addams, C. Monster Rally (1950)
Kobler, J. Afternoon in the Attic
Who's Who in America, 1952-53

ALBERT, EDDIE April 22, 1908- Actor; educational film producer

Address: h: Cahuenga Pass, Hollywood, Calif.

Known for his comic roles in the Broadway plays *Brother Rat, Room Service* and *The Boys From Syracuse,* Eddie Albert is also a successful radio and motion picture actor. Recently, he has become one of the most active personalities in television. He received much acclaim for his performance in the *Studio One* production of George Orwell's *Nineteen Eighty-four,* televised in September 1953. In the role of Winston Smith he demonstrated his talents as a serious actor, and his development from the role of the shy, puzzled, good-natured fellow with the corn-fed grin in which he was "typed" in many films.

During 1954 Albert and his actress-wife, Margo, have made a successful entry into a new field: the night-club circuit. Their 45-minute act has drawn capacity houses at New York's Waldorf-Astoria hotel, and in Miami, Hollywood and Las Vegas.

Since 1945 he has owned a producing company which makes sixteen millimeter educational films for youngsters, and documentary pictures for industrial firms. It was his experience as a Navy lieutenant during the war which made Albert enthusiastic about making such pictures after he had watched the amazing results of the armed forces' training films.

Eddie Albert was born Eddie Albert Heimberger on April 22, 1908 in Rock Island, Illinois, the son of Mr. and Mrs. F. D. Heimberger. When he was a year old, the family moved to Minneapolis, where young Albert attended St. Stephen's parochial school, and subsequently was graduated from Central High School in that city, helping to support himself by working in a soda fountain from six p.m. until one o'clock in the morning.

To help maintain himself while he attended the University of Minnesota, Albert washed dishes, was an usher in a movie house, and later became assistant manager and then manager working nights for Paramount Publix. "They found out I could pull bum theaters out of the red," he recalls. Part of his job in this respect was a weekly master-of-ceremonies stunt in a magic show, his first real stage experience.

Eddie left the university without graduating, and obtained a job as a "song-dance-and-patter man" with a trio on a Minneapolis radio station. Radio announcers kept referring to him as Eddie Hamburger, instead of Heimberger, so he decided to change his name to Eddie Albert. The trio went to Cincinnati, Chicago and to New York, where it broke up, and Albert was on his own.

Hearing that the National Broadcasting Company was looking for a singing team, Albert and Grace Bradt auditioned and got the job. For a year they were on NBC stations every morning at eleven, and were known as *The Honeymooners*—Grace and Eddie. After acting in summer stock, Eddie Albert got his first part on Broadway, in a play called *O Evening Star,* which lasted only a week. But his second try was to prove successful. On his radio show, the young singer-comedian occasionally used guests, and one of these was playwright-producer Garson Kanin. It was Kanin who was responsible for Albert's appearing in the role of Bing Edwards, in *Brother Rat,* in 1936.

This Broadway success established him, and when he appeared in another George Abbott comedy, *Room Service,* with equally good results, he was given a contract with Warner Brothers. He made his movie debut in *Brother Rat,* and in November 1938 returned to Broadway and played in the successful comedy *The Boys From Syracuse.* Called again to Hollywood, he appeared in such films as *Four Wives, Angel From Texas* and *Dispatch From Reuter's,* at a reported salary of one thousand a week.

But the now successful actor was restless. He became fond of taking long trips in a sailboat which he had fitted out for himself, and on one of these he heard rumors of secret submarine fueling stations. He returned with news of Japanese "fishermen" making hydrographic surveys of the coast line. He reported this to Army Intelligence, and after he had finished another picture for Warner Brothers he went to Mexico and turned up facts about German Nazi activities there. He joined the Escalante brothers' circus and toured throughout Mexico. Albert, who worked as the "flyer", or the member who is caught at either end of the act by the "catcher", wandered about between shows, and got information. "I had the perfect disguise," he says. "It was a very profitable trip, despite the Rover Boy overtones. I got solid satisfaction whenever I sent a tip in." He was able to take some motion pictures of use to Army Intelligence.

The comedian joined the Navy in July, 1942 and was sent to the Cornell Officers' Training School, from which he was graduated with the rank of lieutenant (j.g.) in April, 1943. Assigned to the amphibious transport *U.S.S. Sheridan,* he saw action in the South Pacific, including the first landings on Tarawa.

In January 1944 he was recalled to the States for assignment in the Training Films Branch. Before he returned, however, Albert and another lieutenant on Tarawa had vowed that if they returned safely they would dedicate their lives to education on a level that could reach the people. After he became a civilian again, on December 7, 1945, he formed his Eddie Albert Productions, an organization for making sixteen millimeter educational films.

Albert first made five regular pictures in order to get the $200,000 necessary to finance the company.

He appeared in *Rendezvous With Annie,* playing his usual role of a nice young man all wound up in trouble. The film was released in September 1946 by Republic Pictures.

He was a supporting player in *The Perfect Marriage* released January 1947, by Paramount Pictures, as well as in *Time Out of Mind, Smashup: The Story of A Woman,* and *Hit Parade of 1947,* in which he was one of four leading players. The last picture was made by Republic. Albert was seen in 1948 in *You Gotta Stay Happy,* in which he was co-starred with James Stewart. The actor also appeared in *The Dude Goes West* in 1948. By mid-1951, Eddie Albert Productions had completed fourteen twenty-minute sixteen millimeter films, the best known of which was entitled *Human Growth,* a sex-education picture for the eleven-year-old level, made in collaboration with the University of Oregon. This film, widely distributed, received praise and blame, the latter notably from Catholic authorities insisting that such material might better be shown in the home rather than the schoolroom.

In 1949 Albert made the film *Human Beginnings,* aimed at first-graders which shows what a group of six-year-old children believe about the origin of human life as expressed in their own drawings. The second part of the film shows how a young boy and his parents react to the coming of a baby sister into the family. According to Cecile Starr, reviewer of sixteen millimeter films for the *Saturday Review,* "[it] is certainly an eye-opener . . . the drawings and the children's comments about them are something quite new for the public to see and hear . . . it should be remembered that the film is an experimental one, based upon experimental research findings."

Eddie Albert returned to Broadway as the leading man in the musical *Miss Liberty,* wherein he sang, danced, and performed ably, according to Brooks Atkinson on July 24, 1949. The play had a run of 308 performances, after which Albert returned to Hollywood to co-star with Lucille Ball in *The Fuller Brush Girl,* released by Columbia on October 6, 1950.

CBS-TV

EDDIE ALBERT

He then appeared with Betty Grable in *Meet Me After the Show,* and in *You're in the Navy Now,* in *Carrie,* and in *Roman Holiday* in 1953.

After appearing on several television programs, Albert was signed in the fall of 1952 by CBS-TV to do a situation comedy entitled *Leave It to Larry.* The program was not well received, although the critics said Albert was better than his material. On February 25, 1953 the actor began a one-man "personality" show, presented five afternoons a week. The New York *Times* commentator reported that "Mr. Albert tries desperately to be very folksy and warm; but he works so hard at the chore that his manner seems affected after a day or two." However, Albert was well received in *Nothing But the Best* NBC-TV and in Orwell's satire, *Nineteen Eighty-four,* presented on September 21, 1953 on the *Studio One* program.

The *New Yorker* stated: "Eddie Albert, as Winston Smith . . . surprised me by the depth of his performance. I had no idea that Mr. Albert, who turns up all over the television channels . . . in amiable surroundings, could be so moving." The actor also was seen in the initial play of the new *Playhouse on Broadway* series, *Journey to Nowhere,* on October 1, 1953.

His recent television activities include being the narrator on the documentary drama series *Personal Story,* introduced in October 1953 on the American Broadcasting Company's television network, in cooperation with the Federation of Jewish Philanthropies of New York. Albert also appeared on the United States Steel ABC-TV program as the innkeeper in the drama *Outlaw's Reckoning,* on November 3. Albert said, "I prefer acting in TV to any other medium provided the shows are of the caliber of those I have done recently" (New York *World-Telegram and Sun,* October 31, 1953).

(Continued next page)

ALBERT, EDDIE—*Continued*

Eddie Albert was married to Margo, the screen actress, on December 5, 1945 at St. Patrick's Cathedral in New York. They have one son, Eddie, Jr., who was born February 20, 1951. In addition to being an ardent physical culturist, Albert collects first-editions and paints in oils. Besides singing and playing the piano, violin and guitar, he is an avid reader, preferring Bernard Shaw to other authors. He has blue eyes and blonde hair, and "a grin that makes you think of a Penrod grown up."

References

Colliers 108:53 Jl 5 '41
N Y Herald Trib VIII p6+ O 19 '47
N Y Post Mag p3 My 5 '47
N Y Times p20 N 5 '48
New Yorker 29:84 O 3 '53
Variety 188:27 O 22 '52
International Motion Picture Almanac, 1950-51

ALBION, ROBERT GREENHALGH

Aug. 15, 1896- University professor; historian

Address: b. Widener Library, Harvard University, Cambridge 38, Mass.; h. 15 E St., S. Portland 7, Me.

An authority on maritime and naval history, Professor Robert Greenhalgh Albion has taught and written extensively for more than thirty years on these subjects. He had a distinguished teaching career of twenty-seven years at Princeton University, and since 1949 has been Gardiner professor of oceanic history and affairs at Harvard University. Albion has aided in recording the work of the United States Navy and War departments, and the Maritime Commission. He is the author of several books including *The Rise of New York Port, 1815-1860* and *Sea Lanes in Wartime; The American Experience, 1775-1942* (with Jennie Barnes Pope).

Professor Albion has written more than eighty articles in the *Dictionary of American Biography* and others in the *Encyclopædia Britannica, Encyclopedia Americana, Collier's Encyclopedia, Encyclopedia of the Social Sciences, Book of Knowledge,* and quarterly maritime bibliographies in *American Neptune.* His subjects include the overseas expansion of Europe, the history of the British Navy and the British Empire, the development of the American Merchant Marine, the wartime and administrative experience of the American Navy, and general military history.

Robert Greenhalgh Albion was born on August 15, 1896, in Malden, Massachusetts. His father, James Francis Albion, D.D., was a Universalist pastor of the Congress Square Church, Portland, Maine, from 1904 to 1924. His mother, Alice Marion Lamb, was a direct descendant of Thomas Lamb, one of the first settlers of Boston in 1630. He has two sisters: Margaret (Mrs. Albert M. Tripp) and Gertrude (Mrs. Richardson Wright). In 1904 the family moved to Portland, Maine, where Robert was graduated from Portland High School in 1914.

Young Albion majored in economics at Bowdoin College, Brunswick, Maine. In his junior year he attained membership in Phi Beta Kappa. He was editor in chief of the *Bowdoin Orient,* chairman of the Bowdoin Press Club, a member of the Student Council and Theta Delta Chi, and senior captain of the R.O.T.C. He received his A.B. degree, *cum laude,* from Bowdoin in 1918.

During World War I Albion served in the infantry. He entered as a private and attended the Third Officers School at Camp Devens, Massachusetts. Stationed at Camp Zachary Taylor, Kentucky, during the remainder of the war, he was discharged in 1919 with the rank of second lieutenant.

After his wartime service Albion began postgraduate study in history at Harvard University. In this endeavor he was influenced by his father, who had a deep interest in history, by Herbert Bell, then professor of history at Bowdoin (who may have swung Albion's choice away from his alternative interest in a journalism career), and by Portland itself with its docks and its shipping.

After receiving the A.M. degree from Harvard in 1920 he served as Austin teaching fellow from 1920 to 1922. Continuing his graduate studies, Albion received the Ph.D. degree in history from Harvard in 1924. His thesis "Forests and Sea Power; The Timber of the Royal Navy, 1652-1862" was based upon research in the Admiralty records. It was published in 1926 by the Harvard University Press. The book tells the story of the supply of timber to the British Navy from the time when private ships were no longer requisitioned for service (1652) to the age of iron ships (1862). In commenting on the work, Professor Harold D. Lasswell stated: "This monograph is to be welcomed. . . . Such a study gains in timeliness from the prominence of another natural resource in the modern diplomacy of the Powers" (*American Journal of Sociology,* July 1927).

Albion became an instructor at Princeton University in 1922, assistant professor in 1924, associate professor in 1928, and acquired a full professorship in 1939. At Princeton he was director of the summer session and assistant dean of the faculty from 1929 to 1942 and served as faculty member of the council on athletics for ten years. He has been Gardiner professor of oceanic history and affairs at Harvard University since 1949. His present chair was the first of its kind in the United States and was founded by William Howard Gardiner, a former vice-president of the Navy League, and Mrs. Gardiner.

Presently, Professor Albion teaches a two-semester course entitled "Oceanic History and Affairs" (1415 to the present). It stresses the influences that impelled the peoples of Western Europe to expand across the seas in the age of sail; the methods of seafaring, both commercial and naval, and the consequences on early phases of civilization in North America; and technological developments whereby surface seafaring is supplemented by subsurface and aerial means, with special reference to the interests and influences of the United States in oceanic affairs. The course is very popular among the students, and they regard Professor Albion as a "colorful" teacher. He also teaches a course on "Topics in the Expansion of Europe, 1415-1815."

Among his books is *The Rise of New York Port, 1851-1860* (Scribner, 1939), in which he describes the economic and sociological factors which "definitely drew New York ahead of its rivals and established itself as the chief American seaport and metropolis." The initiative of New York merchants, he believes, who took full advantage of nature's bounty, "created a three-cornered trade in the 'cotton triangle'. New York dragged the commerce between the southern ports and Europe out of its normal course some 200 miles to collect a heavy toll upon it . . . to clinch this arrangement New York developed fast ocean packets [as well as coastal packet lines] which operated on regular schedules in the Atlantic shuttle." The first ocean liners were square-rigged, but Professor Albion points out that "whether under sail or steam, most of the crack liners of the world have made New York their western terminus ever since that initial venture . . . they are the true heirs of the Black Ball Line pioneers."

The review of this book in the London *Times Literary Supplement* read in part: "Here one of the greatest themes in modern economic history is treated with a fulness, a depth and width of learning and a lively critical power that call for the highest praise."

In *Sea Lanes in Wartime; The American Experience, 1775-1942* (Norton, 1942), a study of the Merchant Marine and the Navy's experience during the major wars of the United States, written with Jennie Barnes Pope, Albion wrote: "In war after war, from its very earliest days, the United States has had to fight its way by sea. Keeping the sea lanes open has always been one of the main concerns of American foreign policy." Among other books Albion has written are *Introduction to Military History* (Century, 1929), *History of England and the British Empire* with W. P. Hall and J. B. Pope (Ginn, 1937), and *The Navy at Sea and Ashore* with S. H. P. Read (Navy Department, 1947).

The American government has made considerable use of Albion's specialized knowledge. He was lecturer at the United States Naval Finance and Supply School from 1936 to 1941, and expert consultant to the War Department in 1943. From 1943 to 1950 he served on a part-time basis as assistant director of naval history. historian of naval administration, Navy Department, and supervised the preparation of 200 volumes of unpublished analyses of the Navy's administrative history. He was consultant to the Maritime Administration in 1952 and 1953. Professor Albion has lectured at the National War College and the U.S. Naval Academy.

Harvard Univ. News, Walter R. Fleischer

ROBERT GREENHALGH ALBION

Active in professional societies, Albion was president, from 1941 to 1945, and a trustee of the American Military Institute, vice-president of the Economic History Association from 1944 to 1946, vice-president of the Naval Historical Foundation from 1946 to 1950, and a member of the editorial boards of the *Journal of Economic History* and *American Neptune*. He is an honorary life member of the Society for Nautical Research (England), and a member of the American Historical Association and New Jersey Historical Society. His clubs are the Cosmos (Washington, D.C.), Princeton (New York), Faculty (Cambridge, Massachusetts), and Cumberland (Portland, Maine). He also holds honorary membership in the undergraduate clubs, Colonial (Princeton) and Fox (Harvard). The historian is chairman of the library committee of South Portland, which introduced the first library service in that city by arrangement with the Portland Public Library.

The professor was married on August 16, 1923 to Jennie Barnes Pope who has been a collaborator on some of his books. Albion has blue eyes, brown hair, weighs 190 pounds and is nearly six feet tall. His academic honors include the David A. Wells prize from Harvard in 1925 and the honorary Litt.D. degree from Bowdoin in 1948. In that year he also was the recipient of the presidential Certificate of Merit. He belongs to the Universalist Church, and his political affiliation is Republican. His favorite recreations are sailing and the conversion of driftwood into firewood. The Albions spend their week ends and vacations at Mrs. Albion's family home on the sea in South Portland.

References

Directory of American Scholars (1951)
Who's Who in America, 1952-53

ALLEN, ETHAN (NATHAN) Jan. 1, 1904- Baseball coach

Address: b. c/o Yale Athletic Association, New Haven, Conn.; h. 148 Carmalt Rd., Hamden 17, Conn.

Under the leadership of Ethan Allen, who became head coach at Yale University in 1946, Yale's baseball teams have had the most successful seasons in their history, winning two Eastern division titles in the National Collegiate Athletic Association play-offs. Allen spent thirteen years as an outfielder with major league teams after his graduation from the University of Cincinnati in 1926, being one of the few college baseball players to be signed for the major leagues without previous minor league team experience.

After retiring from active participation in baseball in 1938, he became the motion picture director for the public relations department of the National League and made films showing technical aspects of the game. He is the author of three books and a number of magazine articles on baseball, and is the inventor of All Star Baseball, a game based on the sport.

Ethan Nathan Allen was born in Cincinnati, Ohio on January 1, 1904 to David and Laura (Francis) Allen. After attending McKinley Grammar School in Cincinnati, he entered Withrow High School in the same city, and while a student there, participated in football, basketball, baseball, and track. He enrolled at the University of Cincinnati after his high school graduation in 1922, and majored in physical education. He became a member of Beta Theta Pi.

On the university basketball team, Allen averaged 10 points a game, and was placed as center on the 1924 All-Cincinnati basketball team, was selected as All-Ohio guard in 1925, and received a position on the All-State team in 1926. Another sport in which he excelled was track, his record for the 100-yard dash being 9:03.5 seconds and for the 220-yard sprint 22:01.5 seconds. Other marks include 5 feet 10½ inches for the high jump, 22 feet 7½ inches for the broad jump, and 124 feet for the discus throw. Allen served as the captain of the university baseball team in his senior year. He played as an outfielder and his batting record included one stretch of eight hits with four consecutive home runs and a double.

Samuel Kravitt
ETHAN ALLEN

Allen received the B.S. degree from the University of Cincinnati in 1926. While he was still in college three major league baseball clubs, the Cincinnati Reds, the Detroit Tigers and the Cleveland Indians tried to sign Allen for their teams. He went on trips with each club before deciding which offer to accept and eventually picked the Cincinnati Reds. He received a bonus of $8,500 when he signed with the club. An outfielder throughout his baseball career, he bats and throws right-handed and was known as one of the greatest fly-chasers in the game.

Playing against the St. Louis Cardinals, Allen achieved fame by becoming the first player to hit a home run over the center field fence of Redland Field, which was then more than 400 feet from the plate. Allen gives much of the credit for his advancement in baseball to Jack Hendricks, former manager of the Cincinnati ball club. While with the Reds his batting averages were .308 for 1926, .295 for 1927, .305 for 1928. and .292 for 1929. He was judged the best outfielder on the Heydler circuit in 1929

In May 1930 Allen was traded to the New York Giants with Peter Donohue for Clifford Crawford. He hit two home runs with the bases loaded while with the New York team. In 1930 he hit .292, in 1931 .329, and in 1932 .175. After completing a course in postgraduate study he received the M.A. degree in physical education from the Teachers College of Columbia University in 1932. With Bill Walker, Jim Mooney and Bob O'Farrell, he was traded to the St. Louis Cardinals on October 10, 1932 for August Mancuso and Ray Starr. His average for 1933 was .241. He left the Cardinals in 1934 to play with the Philadelphia Phillies, for whom he hit .330 the first year and .307 the second.

Allen was traded to the Chicago Cubs on May 21, 1936 with Curtis Davis for Charles H. (Chuck) Klein and Fabian Kowalik. His average for that year was .295. On December 2, 1936 he was sold to the St. Louis Browns, and he remained with that club during the last two years of his career as a ballplayer. He hit .316 in 1937 and .303 in 1938.

After his retirement, Allen joined the National League public relations department and produced and distributed motion pictures involving personality shots and slow motion sequences to show techniques. These were sent to schools, clubs and service organizations. He also did work as a sports commentator with Vernon (Lefty) Gomez.

During World War II Allen served in Italy with a Special Service Athletic Clinic and produced a sports picture, *Junior Big Leaguers,* for the office of the Coordinator of Inter-American Affairs. He succeeded Robert A. Rolfe as head baseball coach of Yale University at New

Haven, Connecticut in 1946. The teams have since had the greatest success in the ninety-odd year history of baseball at the college, and won the Eastern division title in 1947 and 1948 in the National Collegiate Athletic Association play-offs, thus becoming the intercollegiate champions of the states east of the Mississippi.

"Here are all the answers. A perfect manual of the how's and why's of baseball technique," said Red Barber of Allen's *Major League Baseball; Technique and Tactics.* It was published in 1938 by Macmillan and a 1953 revision appeared entitled *Baseball; Major League Technique and Tactics.* Allen is also the author of *Winning Baseball* (McGraw, 1942) and *Baseball Techniques Illustrated* (Barnes, 1951) which is the first of a series to be presented for beginners or inexperienced coaches. The book describes baseball techniques with a brief text, drawings and diagrams. R. W. Henderson commented, "Exceptionally well written, with dozens of little sketches, clever, illuminative.... Recommended" (*Library Journal*, March 1, 1951). The coach has contributed several articles to *Scholastic Coach* magazine.

In a recent discussion Allen stated that in order for a coach not to become stereotyped he must always be alert to "the conditioning program, the preparation of the players for their respective duties, the evaluation of available personnel, and the intelligent use of strategy in relation to this player ability, the shortcomings of the opposing team, and the stage of the game" (*Scholastic Coach,* February 1952).

All Star Baseball, a game originated by Allen, is according to him "based on lifetime batting records and each player's record is graphed on individual circles. These fit over an At Bat so that each player is potentially the same batter as he is in regular baseball. Participants can select their teams with the knowledge they have about the players; consequently the participant who is the best student of records is usually the winner." The game includes many old-time players such as Babe Ruth, Ty Cobb and Christy Mathewson as well as those of the modern generation. Each year Allen revises the game. Presently he is engaged in preparing a new game, Major Sports.

Allen and Doris Wetzel were married on October 16, 1928 and have two children, Toby and Doris Lee. His hobbies include photography, literature, bridge, movies, and athletics, and he is also an excellent pianist. He is independent politically and a member of the Unitarian Church. He is a Mason and a Shriner, and is a member of the University of Cincinnati "C" Club. Allen has brown eyes, black hair, and is six feet one inch tall, and weighs 180 pounds.

The coach believes that "college baseball in the future should thrive due to the fact that many lower classification professional leagues have had to suspend operations . . . the colleges will have to provide the source of players. It will be just as good a source as many minor leagues and perhaps better since many college coaches have been major league players."

References

Baseball Register (1949)
Official Encyclopedia of Baseball (1951)
Who's Who in American Sports (1928)

ALLEN, HELEN HUNTINGTON HOWE *See* Howe, H. (WLB) Yrbk 54

ALSTON, WALTER (EMMONS) Dec. 1, 1911- Baseball manager

Address: b. c/o Brooklyn National League Baseball Club, 215 Montague St., Brooklyn 2, N.Y.; h. RR No. 2, Oxford, Ohio

Introduced to the press in November 1953 as the man chosen to succeed Charles ("Chuck") Dressen as manager of the Brooklyn National League Baseball Club through the 1954 season, Walter ("Smokey") Alston proved a selection completely surprising to the assembled newsmen. Few New Yorkers were familiar at that time with his name, even though he had a record of over twelve successful years as the manager of minor league clubs in almost every classification from "D" to "Triple A". As manager of the Montreal Royals of the International League, Alston led this Brooklyn "farm" team to victory in the so-called "Little World Series" in 1953.

The Dodgers won their opening game on April 15, 1954 against the Pirates by a score of 7-4, but lost the 1954 National League pennant to the Giants by a score of 7-1 on September 20.

Commenting on Alston's managership three weeks after the season opened, Bill Roeder wrote in the New York *World-Telegram and Sun* (May 7, 1954): "Walt Alston continues to surprise the Dodgers by running the team in anything but the conservative manner expected of him. The players who did not know Alston had been told that he did his job efficiently but rather conventionally. Either that was a false picture, or the man has decided that a big league assignment called for a more daring approach."

Walter Emmons Alston was born on December 1, 1911 at Venice, Ohio, the son of Emmons and Lenora (Neanover) Alston. His father, a farmer, and later a worker at the Ford Motor Company, taught him to play baseball. As a right-handed pitcher on his high school team, Walter earned the nickname of "Smokey" because he pitched such a fast ball. He never had an opportunity, however, to display this skill on professional diamonds. Walter was graduated from the high school in Darrtown, Ohio in 1929.

After entering Miami University at Oxford, Ohio and joining the baseball team, he proved so promising a long-distance hitter that he was moved from the mound to the infield. Alston was also a member of the basketball team at the university, where he majored in industrial arts and physical education and received his bachelor's degree in 1935. "I put myself through college playing pool," the baseball manager told George Trow of the New York *Post.* "I signed to play pro ball the day after I graduated."

Frank Rickey, a brother of Branch Rickey, manager of the St. Louis Cardinals, signed "Smokey" Alston to his first baseball contract as a third base player in 1935 with the Cardinals' Class D "farm" at Greenwood, Missis-

WALTER ALSTON

sippi. During the 1936 season, he was brought up to St. Louis for a trial with the majors. He came to bat only once, and faced Lonnie Warneke of the Chicago Cubs. "I fouled off a couple, then struck out," Alston has recalled.

Returning to the "minors", he became a first baseman. He was a right-handed hitting and throwing first baseman who clouted twenty-five or more "homers" four times in his minor league career. In the summer of 1940, at the prompting of Branch Rickey, he was named by general manager Mel Jones of the Cardinals' Class C "farm" at Portsmouth, Ohio to succeed Charles ("Dutch") Dorman as player-manager.

Alston later served (1941 to 1942) as manager of the Springfield club in the Mid-Atlantic League before his connection with the Cardinals' organization was severed. In the winters between managerial duties then and later, Alston was occupied as a basketball coach and an instructor in physical education and science at high schools near Darrtown, Ohio. "The Board of Education was always nice about it," he told George Trow. "They let me finish the ball seasons even if I was a little late for schoolwork."

In 1944 and 1945 Alston was player-manager in the Trenton, New Jersey team in the Class B Interstate League. For the 1946 season he was appointed player-manager of the Dodgers' "farm" at Nashua, New Hampshire in the Class B New England League. Here he helped to develop the talents of the catcher Roy Campanella and the pitcher Don Newcombe, whose battery work that year brought victory to Nashua in the New England League play-offs.

Less fortunately for himself, the usually mild-mannered Alston became involved at Nashua in an exchange of fisticuffs with Sal Yvars who was then playing for Manchester, New Hampshire. Alston injured his shoulder to such an extent that in 1947 he was forced to end his career as an active player. In that year he managed the Pueblo, Colorado club in the Class A Western League, and won his second triumph in the play-offs.

The victory earned promotion for Alston to the managership of the Dodger-owned St. Paul, Minnesota club in the Triple A American Association. At St. Paul, where the "Saints" finished third in 1948 and first in 1949, Alston helped to develop both the infielder Wayne Belardi and the pitcher Clem Labine.

Already regarded by the Brooklyn organization as "an excellent instructor and strong field leader," Walter Alston was promoted in 1950 to the managership of the Dodgers' top-ranking "farm" club, the Montreal Royals of the Triple A International League. In 1950, when this team finished second, he had under his tutelage the "no hit, no run" game pitcher Carl Erskine.

In 1951 and 1952 the Royals won the International League pennant under Alston's guidance. Among the players who benefited from his instruction during these two years were pitchers Joe Black and John Podres, infielder Bobby Morgan, outfielder George Shuba, and second baseman "Junior" Gilliam who all went on to play for the Dodgers.

On October 8, 1953 the team won by a 7-2 score over the New York Yankees' affiliated Kansas City club of the American Association in the final game of the so-called "Little World Series." Participating in this decisive contest were pitcher Hampton Coleman, catcher Charley Thompson and center fielder "Sandy" Amoros, now with the Dodgers. In all, Walter Alston has had under his tutelage at one time or another some twenty-five members of the Dodgers' 1954 roster.

During the early days of October 1953, while Alston was finishing his fourth year in Montreal, the Brooklyn Dodgers were losing the World Series to the New York Yankees for a second successive time. Not long afterwards, when the Brooklyn "front office" adhered to a policy of limiting agreements to a single year, the Dodgers' manager, Dressen, declined to accept the offered terms.

For several days thereafter, it was generally expected that the Dodgers' field captain, the shortstop Harold ("Pee Wee") Reese would succeed Dressen, but Reese did not wish to undertake managerial duties while still a player. Several former major league managers were then believed under consideration. The astonishment of both sports writers and "fans" was considerable when on November 24, 1953, Walter F. O'Malley, president of the Brooklyn organization, called a meeting of the press and introduced Walter Alston as the man chosen to pilot the Dodgers in 1954.

"O'Malley," wrote George Trow, "made no secret of the fact that Alston has moved to Ebbets Field because he could beat a Yankee team." The sports writers were more surprised to learn that in addition to having no major league managerial experience, the new Brooklyn pilot had witnessed only one game at Ebbets Field, and that he had never seen a World Series game except on television. He had in recent years been fully occupied, at the time of the "baseball classic," with his minor league teams.

Manager Walter Alston made an excellent impression on the sport reporters when they questioned him as to his managerial philosophy and practice. "I'm not one to get into a lot of unnecessary arguments with umpires," he stated quietly, and disclaimed any impatience to apply the new broom by trades with other clubs. "I've got to look at what I've got," he declared. Alston expressed himself as content with a one year contract, which was variously reported as bringing him either $20,000 or $25,000.

On December 1, 1953, the new manager announced that he would be his own third base coach, and would be assisted by Billy Herman and Jake Pitler, two of the three coaches who had served his predecessor; the other coach of the previous season, "Cookie" Lavagetto, had resigned, and was replaced later in December by Ted Lyons, since Alston had requested that "Lavagetto's place be filled with the best pitching coach available" (Rud Rennie in the New York *Herald Tribune*). Asked about Brooklyn's pennant chances in the coming season, Alston replied that "he saw no reason why the Dodgers should not do as well in '54 as they did in '53."

For relaxation "Smokey" Alston goes to the movies, reads sport magazines, or watches basketball and football games. In the winter he likes to do woodworking. His taste in clothes is said to be conservative, and his manner is that of "a quiet, scholarly sort of fellow." The Dodgers' manager has blue eyes and brown hair. He stands six feet two inches tall and weighs 205 pounds.

Walter Alston married Lela Vaughn Alexander in 1930; they have one daughter, Doris LaVerne Alston. Mrs. Alston is also baseball-minded. "She loves the game," her husband has been quoted as saying, "and goes to the ball park with me everyday, but we don't bring it home at night."

References

N Y Herald Tribune p1+ N 25 '53
N Y Post Mag p2 D 13 '53 por
N Y Times p1+ N 25 '53 por
N Y World-Telegram p1 N 24 '53; p31 F 24 '54 por; p29 F 25 '54; p22 F 26 '54
Turkin, H. and Thompson, S. C. The Official Encyclopedia of Baseball (1951)

ANDERSON, ROBERT (WOODRUFF)

Apr. 28, 1917- Playwright

Address: b. c/o The Playwrights' Company, 1545 Broadway, New York 36; h. 14 W. 11th St., New York 11

A "first" play on Broadway, in the opinion of Robert Anderson, is more likely to be the fifteenth or the twentieth or even the fiftieth play written by a dramatist. In his own case, he became a successful Broadway playwright after fifteen years of apprenticeship in the theatre, writing and re-writing plays, trying them out in summer theatres, adapting novels and plays for radio and television, and teaching drama courses. His "first" Broadway play, *Tea and Sympathy*, starring Deborah Kerr, and produced by The Playwrights' Company in the fall of 1953, became one of the outstanding successes of the 1953-1954 season. His play, *All Summer Long*, starring June Walker and her son, John Kerr, was presented on Broadway by The Playwrights' Company in the fall of 1954.

Robert Woodruff Anderson was born in New York City on April 28, 1917, the younger son of James Hewston Anderson and the former Myra Esther Grigg. His father was for twenty-five years an executive of the United Verde Copper Company; he retired in 1929, and later became an agent for Northwestern Life Insurance Company. His brother, Dr. Donald G. Anderson, is now the dean of the Medical School, University of Rochester, Rochester, New York. The family moved to New Rochelle, New York while Robert was in a private grade school. He attended Phillips Exeter Academy, Exeter, New Hampshire where he was on the basketball and track teams, was vice-president of the musical clubs and a member of the senior council.

After he was graduated in 1935 he entered Harvard University and majored in English, joined the dramatic club, wrote musical shows, sang in the glee club and was elected the class poet. He was graduated with the A.B. degree, *magna cum laude*, in 1939. He lists poet Robert Hillyer, drama instructor Hallie Flanagan Davis and Phyllis Stohl, his wife, as those who helped to influence him in his choice of a career.

While at Harvard he seriously considered becoming a singer, but Phyllis Stohl, to whom he showed some of his writing, convinced him that his destiny lay in the theatre. Bob was not convinced about the "destiny" part when his first play turned out to be a rather dour tragedy called *The Sisters*. He refers to this period in his writing as his "transitional low." But he kept on writing. In an all-out effort to learn every angle of the theatre, he wrote twenty-one one-act plays and composed the music, lyrics and books for numerous musicals. He also directed and staged productions, taught drama and writing courses at Harvard (1939-1942), earned his M.A. degree in 1940, and wrote drama criticisms.

It was not, however, until he was commissioned an ensign in the U.S. Navy that he began to concentrate seriously on playwriting. While cruising with the *Alaska* in a temperature of 105 degrees in the South Pacific, he wrote *Come Marching Home*, and submitted it in a $100 contest sponsored by the Army and Navy for the best original drama by a man in uniform. His play won the contest in 1945, and before he could return to mufti, it was produced at the State University of Iowa, The Blackfriars' Guild of New York and the Pasadena (California) Playhouse in 1946.

He then wrote several other scripts, *Boy Grown Tall* and *The Tailored Heart*, which he

ROBERT ANDERSON

now admits were hastily turned out while riveters were working all around him fitting out his ship, and between kamikaze attacks when he was serving on the *Texas*. These plays, and *Come Marching Home*, won for him the National Theatre Conference Fellowship of $2,000. This award made it possible for Bob and Phyllis (whom he had married on June 24, 1940) to live in New York after the war, and for Bob to devote his full time to writing plays. His wife became a play reader for the Theatre Guild. She is now in the play department of the Music Corporation of America.

His first play of the postwar period was *The Eden Rose* (1948). "This play," Anderson recalls, "was optioned several times, but only this year (1954) a star finally decided she would like to do it. But now I have re-read it, and I don't want it done. It was originally done at the Ridgefield, Connecticut, Summer Theatre." His next play, *Love Revisited*, was tried out at the Westport, Connecticut, Country Playhouse. "It didn't go over very well," he admits.

During the young playwright's struggling years in New York, he taught playwriting at the American Theatre Wing (1946-1950). "I believe," he says, "that you can teach the technique of playwriting by exploring successful plays and discovering how they work and why they work. But the artistry, that certain quality which lifts a play—making it particular—this you cannot teach. This you have to leave to the individual. He either has the artistry and taste or doesn't."

He also wrote and adapted plays for radio and television. "I think I must have done about forty radio adaptations for the Theatre Guild," Anderson recalls. Among the plays he adapted which had been written by members of The Playwrights' Company were *Valley Forge* by Maxwell Anderson (no relation to Robert), *The Petrified Forest* by Robert Sherwood, and *Dream Girl* by Elmer Rice.

"*Petrified Forest* was my first radio show," he told a *Current Biography* writer recently. "It presented a number of problems, because radio likes to have many short scenes with a lot of change of locale, and the nature of *Petrified Forest* is that wonderfully trapped in feeling Sherwood gets, as he rounds up all the characters in one room under the gun of Duke Mantee. I finally used an inner monologue device to break up the scenes. *Dream Girl* presented the problem of what to do with the dream scenes. I hit upon the idea of having each dream sequence like a radio serial, a soap opera, with an announcer taking us into each episode."

Other adaptations for Theatre Guild radio programs of which Anderson admits he is proud, were *David Copperfield, The Glass Menagerie, Farewell To Arms, Summer and Smoke, Good-Bye, Mr. Chips;* also for *Robert Montgomery Presents* on television, *Rise Up And Walk* (a story about a man recovering from polio); for Schlitz Playhouse, *Still Life;* for Prudential Playhouse, *Biography* (which starred the late Gertrude Lawrence); and for Studio One, *At Midnight on the Thirty-first of March.*

Refuting the theory that teaching is supposed to be "bad" for playwriting, Anderson says: "All I can tell you is—if you really want to learn to do something, try teaching it. That's how I learned to write plays. As for radio and TV scripts, it was doing them that made a professional writer of me."

The theme for Anderson's play, *Tea and Sympathy,* had been brewing for some time, and after he had finished it early in 1952, he submitted it "with all the temerity of a novice" to Molly Kazan, the wife of Elia Kazan. Mrs. Kazan took Anderson's script to Munich where her husband was directing the film, *Man On a Tightrope.* Meanwhile, Anderson's agent, Audrey Wood, sent the play to Roger L. Stevens, a member of The Playwrights' Company, who said that his firm would sponsor it. When Kazan returned from Europe he agreed to stage the production in the fall of 1953. It was presented by The Playwrights' Company in association with Mary K. Frank and opened at the Ethel Barrymore Theatre on September 30.

The critics acclaimed Anderson as a "brilliant new dramatist" (John McClain, New York *Journal-American*) with "a sensitive feeling for character" (Richard Watts, Jr., New York *Post*). Only Wolcott Gibbs of the *New Yorker* dissented. Anderson sent flowers every Monday to Deborah Kerr's dressing room while she was in the play in token of his appreciation for playing the part as he had conceived it.

The story of the play concerns Laura Reynolds (played by Miss Kerr), the wife of a housemaster in a preparatory school in New England. When Laura arrived to live in this small academic world, the headmaster's wife advised her: "It's best not to get involved in the boys' problems—they'll get over them. Just give them a little tea and sympathy—and always remain just an interested bystander." Laura decides not to heed this advice in the case of young Tom Lee (a shy, retiring boy with artistic and musical interests because of which he is taunted by his classmates). The playwright's premise is that "tea and sympathy" are not enough when a human spirit is crushed. His play was published by Random House and became a Fireside Theatre book club choice for March 1954. In an article "Walk a Ways with Me" in *Theatre Arts* (January, 1954), Anderson paid tribute to Elia Kazan's painstaking direction of the play with a result that it was presented "the way I hoped it would be done."

Anderson adapted a novel by Donald Wetzel, *A Wreath and a Curse,* and entitled it *All Summer Long.* It was tried out in 1953 at the Arena Theatre in Washington, D.C. by Alan Schneider who also directed the Broadway production.

Anderson is six feet one inch tall, weighs 155 pounds, and has brown hair and blue eyes. He is a member of the Harvard Club of New York and the New Dramatists. He was elected a member of The Playwrights' Company in 1953 before his play *Tea and Sympathy* had become a hit.

The Andersons live in a basement apartment in Greenwich Village, and Bob maintains a telephone-less studio nearby. He usually writes plays from 9:30 A.M. to 1:00 P.M., and in the afternoons concentrates on radio and television assignments. The couple has a small weekend home in Rocksbury, Connecticut. His favorite hobbies are gardening and bridge or canasta, and he is still an active tennis player. In both his city apartment and rural retreat there is a piano, for he still likes to write songs and to sing.

The sudden flow of prosperity that accompanies a successful Broadway play is pleasant to the Andersons, of course, but has not changed the already established pattern of their lives combining weekday hard work with weekend relaxation.

References

N Y Herald Tribune IV p2 Ja 10 '54
N Y Times II p3 N 8 '53
N Y Times Mag p17 D 13 '53
N Y World-Telegram p28 O 15 '53
Theatre Arts 38:31 Ja '54
Who's Who in America, 1954-55

ANDERSON, SAMUEL W(AGNER) Feb. 6, 1898- United States Government official; banker

Address: b. c/o United States Department of Commerce, Washington 25, D.C.; h. 5015 Lowell St., N.W., Washington, D.C.

As Assistant Secretary of Commerce, Samuel W. Anderson heads a cabinet *ad hoc* committee whose duties include studying how to encourage the investment of United States capital abroad, how to work out a tariff schedule to advance the "Trade, Not Aid" position of the Eisenhower Administration, and how to liberalize America's foreign economic policy. He attended the Tenth Inter-American Conference held in Caracas, Venezuela during March 1954 and took an active part in trade discussions.

After serving in several posts under two Democratic administrations, Anderson, a Republican, was named Assistant Secretary of Commerce for International Affairs by President Dwight D. Eisenhower and was sworn in on January 28, 1953. For about twenty years he was an investment banker in New York. He was first called to Washington, D.C. in 1941, and directed the aluminum and magnesium expansion program for the War Production Board during the early part of World War II, and later was chairman of the board's requirements committee.

Anderson was associated with Lehman Brothers, New York investment bankers, when he was recalled to Washington in 1948 to work with the Economic Cooperation Administration. The following year, he went to the International Bank for Reconstruction and Development. The Defense Production Administration secured his services in 1951 as "czar" of the aluminum industry.

Samuel Wagner Anderson, son of Samuel Wells and Minne (Wagner) Anderson was born in La Crosse, Wisconsin, on February 6, 1898. His grandfather, Mons Anderson, was a Norwegian emigrant who settled in Wisconsin. Young Anderson decided on a career in finance when he was a student in high school. He entered Williams College in 1916, and in 1918 and 1919 was a student pilot in Naval Aviation. He was elected to Phi Beta Kappa and was graduated from Williams in 1920 with an A.B. degree *cum laude.* He entered Harvard University Graduate School of Business Administration and was a co-founder of the Harvard *Business Review.* He received a Master of Business Administration degree with distinction in 1922.

Immediately after his graduation, Anderson worked as a clerk for Goldman, Sachs & Company, New York investment bankers. He first gained experience in all phases of finance, and later specialized in the issuance of securities and the negotiation of large financial transactions. By January 1931, he was a partner of the company.

He resigned from the firm in January 1932 to become associated with the Interstate Equities Corporation and the Equities Corporation of New York, and other affiliated investment trusts. The firm of Anderson, Allen & Company, investment counselors, was formed in 1935, and later became Anderson & Conrow. Of the several industrial enterprises with which Anderson was associated, the Suchar Process Corporation of New York occupied much of his time from 1939 to 1941.

Under the Roosevelt administration, Anderson was named assistant director of the aluminum and magnesium division of the Office of Production Management (later, the War Production Board). When World War II began he was given full charge of the aluminum and magnesium expansion program. Prior to 1941,

SAMUEL W. ANDERSON

Anderson had had no experience in the aluminum or magnesium industry, but as he explained to Paul P. Kennedy (New York *Times,* December 29, 1952), investigating a new business was an everyday occurrence in investment banking.

In May 1944 he was named program vice-chairman and chairman of the requirements committee of the War Production Board. He held this position until VE Day. He was sent to Mexico City in 1945 as adviser to the American delegation at the Conference on Problems of War and Peace.

Anderson was with Lehman Brothers, New York investment bankers from January 1946 to July 1948. Paul G. Hoffman recalled him to Washington to serve as the industry division director of the Economic Cooperation Administration. Anderson resigned from this post in July 1949 and joined the staff of the International Bank for Reconstruction and Development as chief of the Latin American division of the bank's loan department in October 1949. In connection with proposed loans and other types of assistance considered by the bank, he traveled extensively in South America.

In October 1951 the Office of Defense Mobilization requested the International Bank to grant Anderson a leave of absence to become deputy administrator for aluminum of the Defense Production Administration, in charge of the government's interests. Edwin L. Dale commented in the New York *Herald Tribune* (November 14, 1951) that Anderson's appointment as aluminum "czar" was an effort to end an unhappy chapter in the aluminum expansion program. Three separate government agencies were handling the contracts, while the Justice Department's anti-trust division wanted a fourth producer in competition with the "big three"—Alcoa, Kaiser and Reynolds.

To secure enough metal for an eight billion pound stockpile, after military needs and civilian consumption were taken care of for the forthcoming year (1952), Anderson proposed that the government obtain 1,800,000,000 pounds of Canadian metal. The industry objected to this plan. It was generally believed that Anderson's prediction of a needed increase of ten per cent for the year was overestimated.

According to the New York *Times* (January 5, 1953), figures for the year 1952 showed an increase of twelve per cent. Aluminum had found many new uses—in architecture and in land, sea and air transportation. To fill the demands, the U.S. Government had to borrow much aluminum from Canada and domestic stockpiling was halted in the last four months of 1952. Anderson negotiated agreements with Olin Industries and the Harvey Machine Company to enter the aluminum production business. Alcoa, Kaiser and Reynolds were encouraged to expand their facilities.

As Assistant Secretary of Commerce, Anderson became head of the Bureau of Foreign Commerce and chief consultant to the White House on foreign economic policy. When a study commission, headed by Clarence B. Randall, was established to examine the future U.S. trade policy, Anderson drew up plans and recommendations to present to this commission.

When Milton S. Eisenhower was sent as the special representative of the President on a mission to South America in the summer of 1953, Anderson accompanied him. Anderson returned to South America in March 1954 to attend the Tenth Inter-American Conference in Venezuela. Paul P. Kennedy (New York *Times,* March 18, 1954) reported that Anderson led the fight against preferential trade within the American states and emphasized the need for "multilateral trade in all areas of the world."

In a later session (as reported by the New York *Times,* March 24, 1954), he opposed the Chilean resolution which demanded immediate abandonment of the double tax imposed on foreign investments at home and at the source of gain. His argument that such a resolution would affect the right of a country to tax its citizens was upheld, and a plan to work toward gradual abandonment of the double tax was adopted.

In New York, Anderson is a member of the Downtown Association, and of the Angler's and Harvard clubs. In Washington, he belongs to the Metropolitan Club. His particular hobby is fishing. He likes parties, particularly gatherings where he can take part in discussions.

Samuel W. Anderson and Lorraine Annette Combs were married in 1926. They have a daughter, Mary Lorraine, and a son, Michael Mons. According to Edward J. Michelson (*World,* December 1953), "Anderson's kind of Republicanism is distinguished for its idealism, but critics would find it hard to hang the do-gooder label on him." He has been described as "a tough-minded businessman," and his speed in making important decisions has been called "amazing."

Speaking recently of the battle over U.S. foreign economic policy, Anderson remarked, "I suspect this . . . will be one of the great and significant debates in our whole history."

References

N Y Times p12 D 29 '52 por
Newsweek 41:30 F 16 '53 por
World 1:65 D '53 por
Who's Who in America, 1954-55
Who's Who in Commerce and Industry (1953)
World Biography (1948)

ANDREWS, T(HOMAS) COLEMAN Feb. 19, 1899- United States Government official; accountant

Address: b. c/o Internal Revenue Service, Washington 25, D.C.; American Bldg., Richmond 6, Va.; h. 3811 Chamberlayne Ave., Richmond 22, Va.

Some seventy billion dollars are collected annually from United States taxpayers by the Internal Revenue Service which is now headed by Commissioner T. Coleman Andrews. A former president of the American Institute of Accountants, Andrews came to his present post on February 4, 1953 with experience in state and Federal fiscal matters. He directs the 54,000 employees of this bureau of the U.S. Department of the Treasury.

He is an advocate of simplified income tax procedures which would eliminate "the painful business of filling out income tax forms for 35 million citizens whose entire income is from earnings that are subject to payroll withholding." He also recommends Civil Service examinations for executives in the Revenue Service, and giving field offices greater authority in tax decisions. In July 1953 Andrews inaugurated a door-to-door canvass by agents to collect from tax evaders, a policy which provoked criticism but which brought the government twenty-four dollars for every dollar spent.

Thomas Coleman Andrews was born on February 19, 1899 in Richmond, Virginia, the son of Cheatham William and Dora Lee (Pittman) Andrews. After completing his high school education in Richmond, he obtained a job as an office boy for Armour & Company and within two years became an office manager. From 1918 to 1922, he was employed by F.W. Lafrentz & Company, CPA's, of Richmond, first as junior accountant and then as chief accountant. He served during World War I as a sergeant major in the Students' Army Training Corps.

Having meanwhile studied bookkeeping and auditing in his spare time, Andrews passed the certified public accountant examinations and in 1922 organized his own firm, T. Coleman Andrews & Company. It was this firm, reported *Business Week* (July 21, 1945), which was called in to help clean up fiscal matters "in Kansas City and Jackson County, Missouri after the Pendergast collapse." Subsequently

Wide World

T. COLEMAN ANDREWS

Andrews helped establish the Andrews and Howell management-engineering concern and Bowles, Andrews & Towne, consulting actuaries.

His first public service post was as state auditor of Virginia from 1931 to 1933. While in office he discovered shortages in the accounts of forty-two county treasuries in the state. He also established a system of uniform accounting. In 1933 he accepted appointment as accounting member of the Public Utilities Rate Study Commission of Virginia.

When Andrews became comptroller and director of finance of Richmond in 1938, he displayed an "impartiality [which] perturbed politicians, but brought order to the system and money to the city" (New York *Times*, January 18, 1953). Among his achievements were an investigation of the collection of delinquent taxes, discharge of inefficient employees, reduction in travel allotments for councilmen, and setting up more economical procedures for municipal bond issues. His reforms were responsible in part for bringing to Richmond a council-manager type of government.

Called to Washington in 1941, the accountant was employed on the staff of the director of the fiscal division in the office of the Under Secretary of War before becoming in 1942 a member of the staff of the contract renegotiation division in the office of the Under Secretary of the Navy.

Later, he joined the U.S. Marine Corps, which "loaned" him in 1943 to the Department of State to be chief accountant and transportation director of the North African Economic Board in Algiers. In this post he was attached to the staff of General Dwight D. Eisenhower. For the last year of the war Andrews saw duty in the Central Pacific theater as a staff officer of the Fourth Marine Aircraft Wing.

(Continued next page)

ANDREWS, T. COLEMAN—*Continued*
Discharged in 1945 with the rank of major, he retains this rating in the Marine Corps Reserve.

Returning to Washington in 1945, Andrews organized and was the first director of the corporation audits division of the General Accounting Office. In this new department, where he earned the reputation of being a "bulldog and bloodhound," he was responsible for checking the fiscal activities of government corporations.

One of the agencies to come under his scrutiny was the Reconstruction Finance Corporation, which he criticized sharply in July 1946 before hearings of the House Committee on Expenditures in the Executive Departments. He has stated that government financial procedures "would not be tolerated in any successful business" and has urged "a thorough overhaul of the Federal government's financial and accounting policies" (New York *Times,* January 18, 1953). Andrews was chairman of the accounting and auditing study group of the Commission on Organization of the Executive Branch of the Government (Hoover Commission) in 1948.

A Democrat who supported Eisenhower in the presidential election of November 1952, Andrews was made Commissioner of Internal Revenue in the Republican Administration. He had been recommended by Senator Harry F. Byrd of Virginia. Before being sworn into office on February 4 as the thirty-first Commissioner of Internal Revenue, Andrews was questioned by members of the Senate Finance Committee on the condition of the Internal Revenue Service. The reorganization of the bureau under the previous Administration was regarded as unsatisfactory by many Republicans.

After taking his oath of office Commissioner Andrews made known his objective "to restore the Revenue Service to the great reputation it used to have" (New York *Times,* February 5, 1953). The following months' press reports commented on his indifference to political pressure. He announced in May that vacancies in top positions would be filled through open competitive Civil Service examinations.

The nonpartisan National Civil Service League took notice of the commissioner's apparent determination "to run the tax service along lines of honesty and genuine merit" and expressed its view that if Andrews' reorganization plans were carried out, the Internal Revenue Service "may be on its way to the first real merit system in its history" (Washington *Post,* August 31, 1953).

In a move toward decentralization, Commissioner Andrews gave increased authority to the field offices to make decisions in tax settlements and abolished the bureau's post-audit division in Washington which formerly reviewed tax disputes. While opposition to this change came mainly from Washington's tax lawyers, more widespread criticism was made against the commissioner's program of door-to-door canvassing by agents to seek out tax evaders. The canvass begun in New England in July 1953 brought the government twenty-four dollars for every dollar invested in the drive. To charges of "snooping" and using "Gestapo tactics", Andrews announced that when reports on the canvassing had been evaluated, new campaigns would be undertaken. On November 19, 1953 Secretary of the Treasury George M. Humphrey stated that he had delegated authority to Andrews to make final agreements on tax disputes.

On a National Broadcasting Company television program February 21, 1954, Andrews disclosed that each year twenty-five out of every 100 income tax returns filed contained errors. He listed these errors in this order: (1) mistakes in arithmetic; (2) improper exemptions; (3) incorrect deductions claims; (4) unreported income. He also said that when couples file a joint return both should sign it, and all should attach the withholding statement to their return. Of the 60,000,000 returns filed, he said, 35,000,000 were from people entirely dependent on salaries and wages and he hoped, by 1955, to be able to eliminate the necessity for this group filing a tax form, since their employers can withdraw the correct amount. Such a system would require Congressional approval.

He also urged everyone to keep adequate records of all income "as a regular procedure", and he stated that representatives of the Internal Revenue Service would gladly answer questions on the telephone. "We are just as anxious to correct errors in reporting income in favor of the taxpayer as in favor of the government."

Prominent for many years in the American Institute of Accountants, which in 1947 presented him with an award, Andrews served that association as vice-president (1948-1949) and as president (1950-1951). He is affiliated with the Virginia Society of Public Accountants; Chamber of Commerce of the United States, Virginia and Richmond; Municipal Finance Officers' Association; American Accounting Association; and National Association of Cost Accountants. A delegate of the American Society of CPA's to the International Accounting Congress in Amsterdam, Holland in 1926, he was elected a member of the presiding council of the congress.

Civic and educational interests have made Andrews a member of the sponsoring group of the Graduate School of Business Administration of the University of Virginia, of the advisory board of the University of Richmond School of Business Administration, of the board of the Richmond Memorial Hospital, and chairman of the Virginia Citizens Committee for the Hoover Report. His Greek-letter societies are Beta Alpha Psi, Beta Gamma Sigma, Omicron Delta Kappa (in all of which he is an honorary member) and Pi Kappa Alpha. He is a Mason (Shriner) and in Richmond belongs to the Commonwealth, Rotunda and Country clubs and in Roanoke, to the Shenandoah and Country clubs. His church is the Episcopal.

Andrews married Rae Wilson Reams on October 18, 1919; they have two sons, Thomas

Coleman and Wilson Pittman Andrews. The government official has been pictured as "a jovial, distinguished-looking Virginian with a fine command of Elizabethan English and an enthusiasm for rod and gun."

References

Bsns W p18 Jl 21 '45 por
N Y Herald Tribune p1+ Ja 14 '53 por; p16 F 5 '53
N Y Times p52 Ja 18 '53
Newsweek 41:20 F 2 '53 por
Time 61:21 Ja 26 '53; 62:11 Ag 31 '53 por
U S News 34:84 F 13 '53; 36:62+ O 2 '53 por
Washington (D.C.) Post p2 Ja 15 '53
Who's Who in America, 1952-53

ANOUILH, JEAN (ă"nü'y zhăn) June 23, 1910- Playwright

Address: b. c/o Les Éditions de la Table Ronde, 4 rue Jules-Cousin, Paris 4ᵉ; h. 7 rue St. James, Neuilly-sur-Seine, France

French Embassy Press & Inf. Div.
JEAN ANOUILH

Noted for his contemporary treatment of classical themes, French playwright Jean Anouilh has probably had more "interesting failures" on Broadway during the past decade than any other dramatist. New York producers continue to present his plays, however, for they are both fascinated and mystified by the "sardonic romanticism and ironic humor which shine through the murkiness often obscuring them," as drama critic Richard Watts, Jr. described them.

The New York theatre-going public in early 1954 saw Anouilh's comedy, *Mademoiselle Colombe,* which starred Edna Best and Julie Harris, and ran for sixty performances. Other Anouilh plays, translated into English under the titles *Legend of Lovers, Ring Round the Moon, Cry of the Peacock* and *Antigone,* had met with mixed receptions from American critics, who were frequently unable to understand the warm welcome given to his twenty-five plays by English and European audiences. Besides his work for the theatre, Anouilh has provided synopses for films and for the ballet.

Jean Anouilh was born in Bordeaux on June 23, 1910. His father was a tailor and his mother was reportedly a violinist who played in the orchestra of the casino at Arcachon. As a boy, Anouilh was frequently allowed to stay up at night in order to see operettas presented at the casino—only until the intermission, however. By the time he was ten he was writing short plays and at the age of sixteen he completed his first full-length play. His family moved to Paris where Anouilh attended the Ecole Colbert and later the Collège Chaptal.

After a year and a half at the faculty of law at the Université de Paris à la Sorbonne, Anouilh was obliged to forego further study and to find employment in an advertising concern, the Publicité Damour. In an interview with Michael Horton of the New York *Herald Tribune* (April 2, 1950), he said: "For three years I wrote copy for products ranging from noodles to automobiles. I consider advertising a great school for playwriting. The precision, conciseness and agility of expression necessary in writing advertisements helped me enormously."

His income of 3,000 francs a month was supplemented by the occasional sale of comedy ideas to film producers. With one of his colleagues, Jean Aurenche, Anouilh wrote in 1929 a ten-minute curtain raiser, *Humulus le Muet,* which was published in 1945 and is still used by amateur groups in France.

The author's first long play, *Mandarine,* was written in 1929 but not staged until 1933. The theme of a young girl attempting to rehabilitate a gigolo was considered "a frightful subject" by the *Mercure de France* (February 15, 1933). Anouilh was hired in 1931 as secretary to Louis Jouvet's company. Through the recommendation of actor Pierre Fresnay, Paulette Pax was persuaded to present Anouilh's first serious play, *L'Hermine,* at the Théâtre de l'Œuvre in 1932. The play, which was written about the fear of poverty, ran for thirty-seven performances.

There followed several years of poverty for Anouilh and his wife, during which he wrote *Jézabel,* never produced, but published in 1946, and *Le Bal des Voleurs,* written in 1932, and produced and published in 1938. The latter play, although dealing with the problem of poverty, is described by Edward Owen Marsh in his book, *Jean Anouilh,* as an "enchantingly comic stage entertainment."

In 1934 Anouilh wrote *La Sauvage* which was produced four years later at the Théâtre des Mathurins. His portrait of a poor young girl genuinely in love with her rich fiancé, but doubtful of his ability to comprehend the degradations wrought by poverty, brought this comment from *L'Illustration's* reviewer: "It shows . . . the same neo-romanticism [as his earlier

ANOUILH, JEAN—*Continued*

plays] which betrays itself by a sort of revolt and intellectual anarchism."

The critic Marsh wrote of *Le Petit Bonheur,* Anouilh's 1935 play, that it is evidently one "he appears to want forgotten." In that year the Théâtre des Ambassadeurs presented his *Y'Avait un Prisonnier.* Despite good notices, the play had only a short run, but the sale of its film rights to Metro-Goldwyn-Mayer brought about a change in the fortunes of the Anouilh family, providing them finally with the money to buy a crib for their newborn daughter. "The play was never filmed," said Anouilh to Michael Horton, "but overnight I had a new car and enough money to keep us going for two years."

In 1937 *Le Voyageur sans Bagage* was presented; this drama was concerned with a war veteran who was suffering from amnesia and was forced by a psychiatrist to seek his family. Upon finding out the truth about himself as a boy and about his family, he rejects his past and begins a new life. *L'Illustration,* commenting on the success of the play, discovered it to be a "troubling study of the mystery of personality," presented with "satiric wryness, vigorous observation, and philosophic weight."

A similar problem was considered in his next play, *Le Rendez-vous de Senlis* (1937), in which a husband, disappointed in his marriage, finds the courage to withdraw from the marriage into the satisfactory dream world he has created. In *Léocadia,* written and produced in 1939, Anouilh told the story of a young prince who is freed of his obsession for a dead actress by his new love for a young girl. "Once again," writes Edward Owen Marsh, "it presents the conflict between the dream world and reality, but here reality is finally the more desirable and the more friendly."

The first wartime play by Anouilh was his *Eurydice* in 1941. This restatement of the Orpheus and Eurydice myth was presented to New York audiences in 1952 under the title *Legend of Lovers* with Dorothy McGuire as its star. Joseph Wood Krutch, writing for the *Nation* (January 12, 1952), commented: "It may possibly be that this adaptation. . .is worse than the original, but it is difficult to imagine how the original could have been good."

Anouilh's occupation with modern adaptations of classic Greek themes was also evident in *Oreste* (published in the magazine *La Table Ronde* in 1945). This one-acter was considered part of a study for his *Antigone* (1942), in which Antigone's flouting of the authority of Creon aroused different interpretations in the audience. Katharine Cornell and Sir Cedric Hardwicke played in the American production in 1946.

Roméo et Jeannette, Anouilh's next treatment of a classical theme, reiterated the disastrous love of the chief characters, who were, wrote Marsh "stricken with despair by the contrast between what they feel their love could be and what surrounding reality makes it. . ."

With the one-act tragedy, *Médée* (1946), Anouilh presented, in the character of Jason, a new development in his drama, that of a man content to come to grips with reality rather than to revolt against it. Marsh describes him as a "calmer and more rational hero" than Anouilh had hitherto portrayed, and commented that "for the first time [Anouilh] casts doubt on the virtue of rebellion."

Based on the classical theme of confusion between identical twins, *L'Invitation au Château,* Anouilh's 1947 comedy, was rendered into English by Christopher Fry, and presented in London (1950) and New York (1950) as *Ring Round the Moon.* Of the New York production at the Martin Beck Theater, *Time* (December 4, 1950) wrote that it "seems frequently garrulous and increasingly tenuous and a little too complacently impromptu." On the other hand, actor Alfred Drake (*Theatre Arts,* December 1950) observed that "it dares to be fantastical and serious. . .and succeeds. It is a play of ideas, not poses."

Besides a one-act curtain raiser, *Episode de la Vie d'un Auteur,* Anouilh in 1948 also wrote *Ardèle* (or *La Marguerite*) on the theme of a middle-aged hunchback anxious to marry another hunchback against the wishes of her family. It was produced in Paris in 1949, and in London and New York under the title, *Cry of the Peacock.*

Another one-acter, *L'Ecole des Pères,* came from Anouilh's pen in 1949, and is described by Marsh as "a brilliant exercise in the two main types of Molière comedy." It was followed by *La Répétition* (or *L'Amour Puni*) in 1950, "the story of a pure young girl whose freshness is brutally destroyed by middle-aged decay."

Concerning its production by Jean-Louis Barrault at the Théâtre Marigny, the *Mercure de France* (January 1, 1951) considered the manipulation of the "play within a play" technique to be that of a "master of dramatic art." After the play was presented in French in New York by the Barrault company, Brooks Atkinson called it "a rueful drama that seemed charming and tender and the most intelligible of all the Anouilh plays put on in this country."

Anouilh, in an interview with Isolde Farrell of the New York *Times* (January 3, 1954) described the subject of his play, *Colombe* (1950) as "simple and. . .universal: the plight of a man who loses his wife, when she moves into a world different from his own."

Louis Kronenberger's adaptation of the tragi-comedy of backstage life was presented to New York audiences in January 1954 under the title *Mademoiselle Colombe.* Richard Watts, Jr. of the New York *Post* (January 17, 1954) wrote: "All I can say is that. . .the mood of the narrative, which deals with the ironic triumph of feminine realism over masculine idealism. . .is impressive while the play, itself, is oddly ineffective dramatically."

Described by *Time* as an "amorality play," it provoked this comment about the American reaction from the New York *Herald Tribune's* Walter F. Kerr: "It may be that we can tolerate M. Anouilh's moral ambivalence only at the fringes. . . Or it may be that there is something fundamental in the author's flyspeck philosophy which is ineradicably alien to us."

After *Colombe,* Anouilh wrote *La Valse des Toréadors,* which dealt with a "love that was a failure but that prolonged itself falsely and hypocritically, emptily and pointlessly for a lifetime." Its 1952 production in Paris aroused violent controversy.

For the 1953 Paris season, Anouilh offered *L'Alouette,* a play about Joan of Arc. French critic Jean-Jacques Gautier, of *Le Figaro,* found it an "exceptional work" and commented on the new and joyous Anouilh which the play reveals. On the other hand, Morvan Lebesque in *Carrefour* felt that Anouilh had brought "the sublime to the trivial" (New York *Times,* November 29, 1953).

Because of the varying orientations of his plays, either pessimistic or optimistic, Anouilh divides them into categories, *pièces roses* ("pink plays") or *pièces noires* ("black plays"), to which, with *La Répétition* and with *Colombe* he added the category of *pièces brillantes.* It is the general opinion among French critics that Anouilh has at least overcome his predilection for the *pièce noire* and that in the future audiences can expect more "pink plays" than "black plays."

Jean Anouilh has written the scenarios for such films as *Deux Sous de Violettes, Monsieur Vincent* (which won the Grand Prix du Cinéma Français), *Anna Karénine, Pattes Blanches, Caroline Chérie,* and *Cavalcade d'Amour.* For the ballet, he has written the stories, *Les Demoiselles de la Nuit* (1948), and *Le Loup* (with Georges Neveux, 1953), both used by Roland Petit's troupe, Les Ballets de Paris.

When the Anouilhs occupied an apartment on the Avenue Trudaine in Paris, their rare visitors, reports Françoise Giroud, were surprised to find a shining, spotless upper-middle class interior, and succulent meals prepared by Madame Anouilh herself. The only betrayal of the playwright's preoccupation was one room devoted to his collection of gigantic marionettes and theatrical masks.

Anouilh and his wife, the actress Monelle Valentin, live in a mansion in the Parisian suburb of Neuilly-sur-Seine where they gave a ball for the fifteenth birthday of their daughter, Catherine. Anouilh spends only about three months of the year in Paris, as he prefers to stay at his country house in Brittany or to ski in the French Alps. Slender, blue-eyed, and chestnut-haired, Anouilh usually wears heavy spectacles. Of his ability to write a play in a month, he has said: "It's scandalous to think that I earn my livelihood by amusing myself as much as I do."

References

N Y Herald Tribune V pl Ap 2 '50
N Y Times II p3 Ja 3 '54
Dictionnaire Biographique Français Contemporain (1950)
Giroud, F. Françoise Giroud Vous Présente le Tout-Paris (1952)
International Who's Who, 1953
Marsh, E. O. Jean Anouilh; Poet of Pierrot and Pantaloon (1953)
Who's Who in France, 1953-54
Who's Who in the Theatre (1952)

ANTHEIL, GEORGE (ăn'tīl) June 8, 1900- Composer

Address: 8161 Laurel View Dr., Hollywood 46, Calif.

The American composer George Antheil, who was known as a "coldly mechanistic aesthetic" in the 1920's, has more recently been called a "musical Tom Sawyer," a "parodist," and a "genius." His early works, which portrayed the jazz age and the age of steel, "burst on startled ears" and caused rioting in audiences in Paris and New York; his later works have been praised for their "romanticism," and "robustness," and for their contribution to American music. Antheil's most recent work, *The Capital of the World,* a ballet presented at the Metropolitan Opera House in New York in December 1953, was well received, and Virgil Thomson called it a "master's score."

In addition to his many symphonies, chamber works, ballets, and piano compositions, he has written more than fifteen movie scores. He is the author of numerous magazine articles and four books, among them his autobiography, *Bad Boy of Music* (Doubleday Doran, 1945).

Georg Johann Carl Antheil was born on June 8, 1900 in Trenton, New Jersey, the son of Henry W. and Wilhelmina (Huse) Antheil. His father owned and operated a shoe store in that city. He is of German-Polish ancestry. When he was young, he added an "e" to his first name. He started studying the piano when he was six, and at ten, began composition lessons with Constantin von Sternberg in Philadelphia.

In 1917 he was graduated from the Trenton High School where he had edited the newspaper. At the end of World War I he served in the aviation arm of the United States Signal Corps as a cadet. The war over, Antheil continued his studies with von Sternberg, and in 1919, became a composition student with Ernest Bloch.

After two years with Bloch, Antheil went to the Music Settlement School in Philadelphia where he made the acquaintance of Mrs. Edward Bok and studied under George Boyle. He also gave lessons there in elementary harmony. Hearing that Martin H. Hanson, concert manager, was leaving soon for Europe and might need a concert pianist of the "fiery ultramodern variety," Antheil practiced the piano for sixteen to twenty hours a day for thirty days and then sought an audition with Hanson. The audition was successful, and so in May 1922, Antheil left the United States to concertize in Europe.

In addition to classical works, his programs contained his own compositions and those of other modern musicians. In December 1922 his First Symphony, said to be the first symphonic piece in which jazz was recognized, was given its première by the Berlin Philharmonic Orchestra.

Antheil soon decided to devote himself almost entirely to writing music. He went to Paris, and rented an apartment above Sylvia Beach's bookshop at 12 rue de l'Odéon. On October 4, 1923, he introduced a group of piano pieces, "Mechanisms," "Airplane Sonata," and "Sonata

GEORGE ANTHEIL

Sauvage," at the Théâtre des Champs Elysées. As a result, rioting broke out, and overnight Antheil was famous in Paris as, in his own words, "an anti-expressive, anti-romantic, coldly mechanistic aesthetic."

Among his friends and acquaintances he could now count Gertrude Stein, Pavel Tchelitchew, Ezra Pound, and Ernest Hemingway. Bravig Imbs wrote in his book, *Confessions of Another Young Man,* that Antheil was "assailed by new callers every day . . . a lady from England who thought that it would be sweet to have him roar in her drawing room; . . . a Persian princess with a dachshund which liked modern music; . . . a young American girl who had never seen a composer before and who stared at him speechless as though he were a zoological specimen. . . ."

During this period, Ezra Pound wrote his book, *George Antheil and the Treatise on Harmony,* in which he commented: ". . . Antheil has made a beginning; that is in writing music that couldn't have been written before. 'Interpreting' . . . his age, but doing it without the least trace of rhetoric. He is not local. His musical world is a world of steel bars, not of old stone and ivy."

On the other hand, Henry Prunières (New York *Times,* November 7, 1926) wrote: "George Antheil is a born musician . . . he has the orchestral sense, and undeniable cleverness. His fault seems to lie in his desire to be original at any cost. . . . It is not by wildly pursuing originality that George Antheil will reach it, but in communing with himself and listening to the voice within."

One of Antheil's compositions was the *Ballet Mécanique* which was scored for eight grand pianos, xylophones, percussion instruments, electrical bells, and the sound of a whirling airplane propeller. When the piece was first performed in Paris, it overwhelmed the audience, and when it was introduced in New York on April 10, 1927, the audience "booed, whistled, clapped, and even hissed."

When a shortened "Ballet Mécanique" was played on February 21, 1954 at the fifth Composers' Forum at Columbia University, a reviewer for the New York *Times* wrote: "The work which caused riots in Paris . . . and burst 'on startled ears' in Carnegie Hall, now sounds like an ebullient and lively piece that is actually pretty in places. . . . Instead [of riots] there was a three-minute ovation that necessitated many bows by the composer. . . ."

Shortly after his return to the United States in 1933, Antheil stated: "America must create her tradition in music, and I think she must do it through the theatre. Young composers . . . must give the people something they can see and sing, and then we will have a real American music" (New York *Herald Tribune,* December 29, 1933).

His opera, *Helen Retires,* was written to a libretto by John Erskine. The opera was performed in 1934 at the Juilliard School of Music in New York. A reviewer for the *Literary Digest* (March 17, 1934) wrote: *"Helen Retires* . . . goes to show that native music is coming out of the doldrums." Paul Rosenfeld (*New Republic,* March 14, 1934) commented: "The score has a pleasant, present-day terseness and hardness. . . . But structurally, it is quite unstrung."

Several years after his arrival in the United States, Antheil began doing such film scores for Charles MacArthur and Ben Hecht as *The Scoundrel* and *Once in a Blue Moon.* In 1936 he became a composer for both Paramount and Columbia studios. After writing the scores for *The Plainsman* (1936), *The Buccaneer* (1937), and *Make Way for Tomorrow* (1937), Antheil wrote an article in the *American Scholar* (Summer, 1937) in which he supported the idea that serious music could be written for the films.

In his autobiography, Antheil reiterates the need for good movie scores, because it is through background movie music that "the great larger public taste is being slowly but surely formed." Virgil Thomson has called Antheil's movie scores "soundly effective" and *Time* magazine (July 20, 1953) commented that recently Antheil has written "crackerjack scores for such movies as *Specter of the Rose, The Sniper, The Juggler,* [and] *In a Lonely Place."*

Speaking on the need for new expressions in music, Antheil said: "In the period between the two wars there was a false serenity, and music was intellectualized to the limit. . . . I am very doubtful whether the intellectualized quibbling music that I was a part of will be important again. A return to the romantic and heroic is natural" (*Time,* February 28, 1944).

When Antheil's Fourth Symphony was conducted by Leopold Stokowski with the NBC Symphony Orchestra in 1944, Noel Straus wrote that it had fulfilled Antheil's new intention to write "dramatic, rather than antiheroic" music, but that it leaves one "with the impression that the composer has little of his own to impart that has not been said before" (New York *Times,* February 14, 1944).

Virgil Thomson, however, commented: "He is an American composer, probably the most thorough-going American of us all. He is a musical Tom Sawyer, gay, fanciful, ingenuous, self-confident and comical. . . . He is not in the stuffy sense an imitation of anybody. He is a humorist, a parodist and a great clown. The Fourth Symphony . . . is about the most complete musical picture of an American circus that has ever been made" (New York *Herald Tribune*).

The Fifth Symphony by George Antheil was given its première with Eugene Ormandy conducting the Philadelphia Orchestra. Louis Biancolli wrote: "I found the Antheil symphony a refreshing change from much of the angular, abstract writing we have been getting from many quarters in recent years" (New York *World-Telegram,* January 5, 1949).

Winifred Young played Antheil's Third Piano Sonata on December 29, 1953 in New York. A New York *Times* reviewer wrote: "It is an effective pianistic display piece that also reflects the increasingly conservative style of the one-time Bad Boy of Music. . . . Antheil has in fact come full circle. . . ."

The Capital of the World, a ballet by Antheil based on a short story of Ernest Hemingway, was performed by Ballet Theatre at the Metropolitan Opera House on December 27, 1953. Virgil Thomson was genuinely impressed by Antheil's score and wrote: "Rarely have I heard music for dancing with so much real energy in it . . . it generates physical activity on the stage. . . . It is colorful, too, bright and dark and full of the contrasts that are Spain . . . its orchestration is picturesque, emphatic, powerfully underlined, a master's score" (New York *Herald Tribune,* January 3, 1954).

Among the other works Antheil has written are a Piano Concerto (1926); two operas, *Transatlantic* (1929) and *Volpone* (1953); *Dreams,* a ballet produced by George Balanchine in 1935; three symphonies; two concert overtures, "McKonkey's Ferry" (1948) and "Tom Sawyer" (1950); incidental music to poems by Blake and Shelley and a play by W. B. Yeats; sonatas for violin; chamber works; and numerous piano pieces.

Besides his autobiography, Antheil has written: *Death in the Dark* (Faber, 1930) under the pen name "Stacey Bishop"; *Every Man His Own Detective* (Stackpole, 1937); and *The Shape of the War to Come* (Longmans, 1940). He has also written numerous articles; some on endocrinology appeared in *Esquire;* others on his system of simplified musical notation which he calls "SEE-NOTE" have appeared in magazines in the United States and abroad. He and Hedy Lamarr invented a radio-directed torpedo on which they hold a United States patent.

The honors conferred on the artist are an award from the Société Académique in Paris (1933) and the Bispham Memorial Award (1934). He holds an honorary life membership with the Paris police for his work with them in criminal typing. He received Guggenheim fellowships for the two years, 1931 and 1932. He belongs to the League of Composers (New York City), ASCAP, and the Screen Composers Association.

George Antheil married Boski Markus, a niece of Arthur Schnitzler, the Austrian writer, on November 4, 1925. The couple has one child, Peter. The composer has blond hair and blue eyes; he weighs 140 pounds and is five feet four inches tall. He belongs to the Evangelical church. He is a Democrat. The *New Yorker* has described him as an "intense, bright-eyed man." For recreation he enjoys studying astronomy and endocrinology, and reading—he rereads the novels of Stendhal every year.

References

Etude 64:431 Ag '46 por
Mod Mus 23:78+ Winter '46

Antheil, G. Bad Boy of Music (1945)
Ewen, D. (comp) American Composers Today (1949)
Howard, J. T. Our American Music (1946)
Thompson, O. (ed.) International Cyclopedia of Music and Musicians (1949)
Who is Who in Music, 1951
Who's Who in America, 1954-55

ARCINIEGAS, GERMÁN (är-sēn-yā'gäs hĕr-män') Dec. 6, 1900- University professor; historian

Address: b. c/o Columbia University, New York 27; h. 27 W. 55th St., New York 19

Through his many books which describe much of the history and present-day sociological conditions in Latin America, Professor Germán Arciniegas has introduced North Americans to the countries south of the Equator and to his native country, Colombia. During the past ten years he has been a visiting professor at several universities in the United States including Columbia University, where he has taught Spanish-American literature since 1948.

Professor Arciniegas has a law degree and has been a journalist as well as an educator. He has held diplomatic posts in the service of his country, was twice Minister of Education for Colombia, and was the founder of the Museo de Arte Colonial in Bogotá.

In his most recent book *The State of Latin America* (Knopf, 1952), he discussed the aspirations of the peoples of twenty nations toward the concept of democracy which persists "as a goal to be aimed at, a hope, an ideal yet to be won." Hubert Herring, in the New York *Herald Tribune Book Review* (April 27, 1952), wrote that Arciniegas "is not a neutral in the present fevered contest between dictatorship and freedom, but an eager and able polemicist for the sort of democracy that Colombia represented for years."

Germán Arciniegas was born in Bogotá, Colombia on December 6, 1900, the son of Rafael and Aurora (Angueyra) Arciniegas. The family lived on a farm close to Bogotá, and from an early age Germán helped his father with the farm work. When he went to school in Bogotá, it was necessary to get up at three

Lida Moser

GERMAN ARCINIEGAS

A.M. to do the farm chores and ride horseback into the city in order to reach school by eight o'clock.

After attending the Escuela de Comercio, young Arciniegas entered the Universidad Nacional at Bogotá. In 1920 he became secretary of the Bogotá Students' Association and later was editor of the magazine, *Voz de la Juventud.* He received the LL.D. degree from the Universidad Nacional in 1924. The following year, he was appointed to the faculty of law and political science as professor of sociology.

Arciniegas contributed items to Bogotá's liberal newspaper *El Tiempo* while a student, and continued to write articles after he became a member of the faculty. In 1928 he left the university to become editor of *El Tiempo* and in 1930 he was sent to London as vice-consul. Rather than sever his newspaper connection, he represented *El Tiempo* as London correspondent.

During this period he wrote a book on the historical role of students in Spain and Spanish-American countries called *El Estudiante de la Mesa Redonda* (Pueyo, 1932), and another book entitled *La Universidad Colombiana* (Nacional, 1932).

By 1933 Arciniegas was back in Bogotá as editor in chief of *El Tiempo.* He was elected a member of the House of Representatives of Colombia in that year, re-elected in 1934 and again in 1938. He wrote several books during this period: *Memorias de un Congresista* (Cromos, 1933?), *Diario de un Peatón* (Nacional, 1936), *América, Tierra Firme* (Ercilla, 1937), and *Los Comuneros* (ABC, 1938).

His book about Jiménez de Quesada was translated into English as *The Knight of El Dorado* (Viking, 1942). It recorded the discovery and conquest of New Granada (now Colombia) by Gonzalo Jiménez de Quesada and the founding of Bogotá.

Eduardo Cardenas, (*Saturday Review of Literature,* June 6, 1942) wrote that Germán Arciniegas is an unbiased historian, and that the book "is a serene appraisal of some of the human ingredients that destiny took from the medieval Spain of Doña Juana la Loca and mixed with native stock to form the basic elements of the future man of Hispano America." John Cournos (*Atlantic Monthly,* July 1942) called it "a distinguished piece of work . . . a real thriller for highbrows."

Arciniegas became director of *El Tiempo* in 1939, and later in the same year was appointed chargé d'affaires at the Colombian embassy in Buenos Aires. He spent two years in Argentina and wrote *Los Alemanes en la Conquista de América* (Losada, 1941). It tells about the financial exploits of two sixteenth century German banking families who failed to gain control of Latin America because they were interested solely in treasure.

Alvaro De Silva (New York *Times Book Review,* October 17, 1943) wrote of the English version, *Germans in the Conquest of America* (Macmillan, 1943), that it was as "breathless" as an incredible detective story until one realized that it was "the raw stuff of history" and the villains "all too real."

Upon his return to Colombia from Buenos Aires in 1941, Arciniegas was appointed Minister of Education, a post which he continued to hold in 1942 and to which he was reappointed for the year 1946. There were busy years in between. He traveled extensively, and wrote several books that were published in Mexico, Colombia and Argentina: *Este Pueblo de América* (Cultura Económica, 1945), *En el País del Rascacielos y las Zanahorias* (Suramérica, 1945), and *El Pensamiento Vivo de Andrés Bello* (Losada, 1946).

Columbia University invited him to lecture on Spanish-American literature in 1943. In 1944, he was visiting professor at the University of Chicago, and in 1945 at the University of California, Berkeley, and Mills College in Oakland, California, where he was awarded an honorary doctorate degree.

The Green Continent (Knopf, 1944), an anthology selected and edited by Germán Arciniegas and translated from the Spanish and Portuguese, represented a comprehensive view of Latin America by its leading writers. Angel Flores in *Book Week* (September 3, 1944) said that the anthology reflects Arciniegas' sociological and literary background, and "marks a step forward in providing United States readers with relevant material about Latin America."

His book *Caribbean, Sea of the New World,* translated into English by Harriet De Onís, was published by Knopf in 1946. It gave a detailed history of the Caribbean Sea area from the discovery of San Salvador by Christopher Columbus to the completion of the Panama Canal. J. H. Jackson (San Francisco *Chronicle,* July 11, 1946) recommended the book to North Americans who thought that the new world began with "Raleigh's Virginia Colony or Plymouth Rock", and added that it painted a "gigantic panorama" and at the same time told "a whacking good story."

The New York *Times* reviewer wrote: "Sometimes mocking, sometimes deeply stirred, our poet-historian [Arciniegas] has told a colorful and troubled story, but the last creature to come out of his Caribbean Pandora's box of troubles is a winged hope." "Not the least of the book's virtues," commented the *New Republic*, "are a series of thumbnail biographies of such figures as Amerigo Vespucci, Raleigh, Toussaint, Miranda, Lafitte, William Walker and de Lessep." "It holds the reader with a breezy, informal style," stated the *Saturday Review of Literature*.

While Minister of Education in Colombia, Professor Arciniegas founded the Museo de Arte Colonial in Bogotá. He became a director of the publishing house Ediciones Colombia, an editor of *La Revista de las Indias,* a codirector with Roberto García Peña of the *Revista de América,* and a contributor of articles to such newspapers and magazines as *La Prensa* and *La Nación* (Argentina), and *Cuadernos Americanos* (Mexico).

As early as 1946, political difficulties began in Colombia. There was a split in the Liberal party which had long been in power, and the Conservative party won the election which led to "strong man" Laureano Gómez taking office as president in 1950.

Meanwhile, Arciniegas, who had returned to Columbia University as visiting professor of Spanish-American literature in 1948 (a position he still holds), viewed with alarm the conditions in his homeland and prepared a "documented exposé" of the "struggle between dictatorship and democracy" in the South American countries.

In *The State of Latin America* (translated by Harriet De Onís), it was noted by the book reviewers that Arciniegas had departed from historical interpretation and had supplied an authoritative survey of present-day problems in twenty Latin American nations that hover "between freedom and fear."

Hubert Herring (New York *Herald Tribune Book Review,* April 27, 1952) wrote that the author had written "as a Colombian patriot, in anger against those who have betrayed 'the best of the Latin American democracies'; as a Latin American who comprehends as well as any living man the tormented history of the onetime colonies of Spain and Portugal; and as a friend, often critical, of the United States."

Professor Arciniegas wrote: "Colombia was a nation that had moral authority . . . that owed all its progress to its civilian, representative government. It enjoyed complete freedom of the press and the unrestricted interplay of public opinion. Overnight its liberties were snuffed out, and a new era began, that of the mailed fist." He then quoted reports in the New York *Times, Atlantic Monthly, Life,* etc. alleging that Laureano Gómez assumed office on August 7, 1950 "under the most rigid dictatorship in modern history." (Gómez was overthrown by a "bloodless coup" on June 13, 1953, and later Lieutenant General Gustavo Rojas Pinilla was elected to finish his term of office.)

Arciniegas' book, *En Medio del Camino de la Vida,* was published in 1949 in Buenos Aires by Sudamericana. *Freedom and Culture,* a UNESCO publication (Columbia University Press, 1951) was co-authored by Germán Arciniegas, Julian Huxley, Lyman Bryson, Jean Piaget, Maurice Bedel, Rex Warner and Bart Box. In an article entitled *The Pen is More Powerful,* Herschel Brickell (*United Nations World,* May 1951) called Professor Arciniegas "an ambassador of culture" who had introduced North Americans to their southern neighbors. Arciniegas is now writing a biography of Amerigo Vespucci.

When Professor Arciniegas arrived at Idlewild Airport on September 16, 1953—after a visit to France—he was detained by United States immigration officials and taken to Ellis Island. The New York *Times* (September 18, 1953) reported that he had been held for questioning under the provisions of the McCarran-Walter act, had spent the night in a dormitory, and after an examination of his passport the next morning, had been released with "an apology for the inconvenience."

Columbia University *Alumni News* (December 1953) said that Professor Arciniegas believed that his book *The State of Latin America* was responsible for his trip to Ellis Island, as it had made him "*persona non grata* in half a dozen lands and a political exile from his own." The article further revealed that earlier in 1953, the Colombian government had rewritten the constitution and inserted a clause that branded anyone who wrote or said anything against either Colombia or its government as a traitor.

According to the article, the professor "believes that Gómez compiled an extensive dossier 'proving' him a communist, and had it sent to the F.B.I. with the suggestion that he be extradited as an undesirable." This move failed, and as evidence of the esteem in which Professor Arciniegas is held, the New York newspapers printed editorials and letters of protest.

The academies of Spain and Mexico, and the academies of history in Argentina, Venezuela and Cuba have made Professor Arciniegas a corresponding member. He is also a member of the Academia Colombiana and the Academia Colombiana de Historia. He was named an honorary associate of the National Institute of Arts and Letters in the United States in 1943, and elected vice-president of the American Committee for Cultural Freedom.

Germán Arciniegas was married in 1926 in Medellín, Colombia to Gabriela Vieira. They have two daughters, Aurora and Gabriela. The professor has been described as "mild-mannered, friendly and scholarly." He is a Roman Catholic. He has brown eyes and black hair. As a member of the Liberal party in Colombia, he is an opponent of both fascism and communism and is a strong champion of democracy.

References

N Y Times Book R p26 My 18 '52 por
Córdova, F. Vida y Obras de Germán Arciniegas (1950)
Directory of American Scholars (1951)
Who's Who in Latin America (1951)
World Biography (1948)

ARDALAN, ALI GHOLI (är'dăl"ăn ȧ-lē' gō'lē) Oct. 15, 1901- Iranian delegate to the United Nations

Address: b. c/o Iranian Delegation to the United Nations, 350 5th Ave., New York 1

A delegate from the modern kingdom of Iran (known officially as Persia before 1935), Dr. Ali Gholi Ardalan is Ambassador and Permanent Representative of his country to the United Nations. His appointment in September 1950 preceded by a year the presentation before the U.N. Security Council of the British-Iranian oil dispute, in which Ambassador Ardalan assisted Premier Mohammed Mossadegh in arguing the case for Iran. In 1953 he served on the U.N. *Ad Hoc* Political Committee, and he had earlier headed the Iranian delegation to two sessions of the Economic and Social Council. Ardalan has spent twenty-eight years as a career diplomat in Iranian missions to Germany, the United States, France and Turkey.

Ali Gholi Ardalan was born in Teheran, the capital of Iran, on October 15, 1901, the son of Abdul Hassan and Valieh Ardalan. Soon after his graduation from the University of Teheran with a degree in law and political science, he entered the Persian foreign service and was sent in 1926 to represent his government as attaché to the embassy in Berlin.

While in Germany he studied at the university in Berlin and received his doctorate in law, political science and economics in 1928. The thesis submitted for his degree was published in Germany in the same year under the title, *Persian Economy in World Economy.*

The diplomat first visited the United States in 1932 when he was assigned to the embassy in Washington, D.C. to fill the office of secretary (until 1934). Ardalan's next post was at the Embassy of Iran in Paris, first as secretary in 1936 and then as counselor and

ALI GHOLI ARDALAN

chargé d'affaires in 1941. While serving in the diplomatic mission to Turkey, he was counselor at the embassy in 1943 and minister in 1946. During 1947 he was an Iranian representative on the U.N. Conciliation Commission for Palestine.

When recalled to Iran in 1948 Ardalan was named Under Secretary of the Ministry of Foreign Affairs in Teheran and the following year acting secretary of that ministry. When Nasrollah Entezam, chairman of the Iranian delegation to the United Nations, became Ambassador to the United States and president of the fifth session of the U.N. General Assembly in September 1950, Ardalan became the Ambassador and Permanent Representative of Iran to the United Nations. Since then he has been spokesman for his country on a number of committees and commissions of that world organization.

During the first session of the General Assembly that he attended, Ambassador Ardalan represented Iran on the First (Political and Security) Committee. He later headed the Iranian delegation to the twelfth and fourteenth sessions of the Economic and Social Council. As chief delegate to the U.N. Commission on Narcotic Drugs in 1952 and 1953, he presented Iran's position during May 1952 in relation to a discrepancy in the reported number of tons of raw opium held by that nation.

He also represented Iran on the General Assembly's Second (Economic and Financial) Committee and was present at the second and third conferences on the expanded program of technical assistance (1951 to 1952). In 1953 he spoke for his government on the *Ad Hoc* Political Committee. He was head of the Iranian delegation to the Japanese Peace Conference in San Francisco (1951) and to the International Opium Conference (1953).

Although not a leader in the political activity at home which brought about the expropriation of the properties of the British-owned Anglo-Iranian Oil Company and the nationalization of Iranian oil industry in the spring of 1951, Ambassador Ardalan had a large part in defending Iran's action before the United Nations.

In a speech during 1951 he maintained that certain Asian countries had not succeeded in achieving freedom from economic domination by Western powers. "Asia now aspires to an independent life," he stated. "It wishes to exploit itself its natural riches and resources. All this is nothing else than putting in words the recommendations of the United Nations Charter" (New York *Times,* September 8, 1951).

At the end of September, Ambassador Ardalan said that Iran had rejected the ruling of the International Court of Justice by which the British would be allowed to continue operations in the oil fields until the disagreement was settled because the court could deal only with disputes between nations. He later protested, without success, the decision of the Security Council to consider the oil dispute.

When the Iranian government debated its position before the Security Council in October 1951, it was represented chiefly by Premier Mohammed Mossadegh, who had brought a special delegation to New York from Teheran to argue for the rejection of the British resolutions. Delegates from other nations, reported the New York *Times,* knowing the Premier's reputation for emotional outbursts and fearing that public debate might increase the acrimony between Great Britain and Iran, "noted with interest that the full Iranian case would be stated in the form of a forty-page speech to be read in French by Dr. Ali Gholi Ardalan" (New York *Times,* October 11, 1951).

Discussions in the Security Council left the Anglo-Iranian oil dispute still unresolved. While representing his government in the United Nations in November 1952, Ardalan exchanged points of view over the issue of the nationalization of Iranian oil with the British representative, and disclosed his country's willingness to pay compensation to the British oil company in accordance with the nationalization laws passed by Great Britain.

Earlier, in an article entitled "The Inter-Dependence of the World Economy" which appeared in the *United Nations Bulletin* (July 1, 1952), Ardalan had called attention to Iran's offers of compensation and to her good faith in trying to settle her conflict with Great Britain. The U.N. delegate's main purpose in this article was an explanation of the effect of the economies of underdeveloped countries on world prosperity and the place of oil and nationalization of the oil industry in the economic development program of his government.

Ambassador Ardalan also had a prominent role in April 1952 in the efforts of certain Arab and Asian countries to have the dispute between Tunisia and France added to the agenda of the Security Council. When these efforts were facing defeat, the Iranian representative acted as spokesman for the thirteen Arab and Asian nations in suggesting that the group might call for a special session of the U.N. General Assembly or might reapply to the council in the event of worsening of the Tunisian situation.

On June 20, 1952 these countries asked formally that a special General Assembly session be held to discuss the Tunisian question, but this request failed. The General Assembly's First Committee passed a resolution on December 17, 1953 which expressed the hope that negotiations between France and Tunisia would be continued "on an urgent basis" with a view towards bringing about the self-government of Tunisia.

Ardalan, who was married to Mehri Esfandiary in 1938, has two children, Manoutchehr and Cyrus. Honored by a number of Near East nations, he has received decorations from Iraq, Afghanistan and Transjordan, as well as from his own country.

References

U N Bul 10:214 Mr 1 '51
Who's Who in the United Nations (1951)

ARMSTRONG, EDWIN HOWARD Dec. 18, 1890-Feb. 1, 1954(?) Inventor, electrical engineer; received degree from Columbia University (1913); research associate with Michael I. Pupin at Marcellus Hartley Research Laboratories (1914-1917, 1919-1935); professor of electrical engineering at Columbia University (since 1934); his contributions to modern broadcasting include regenerative circuit (1912), as a signal officer, World War I, he designed superheterodyne circuit (1918), considered basic to radio receivers today; superregenerative circuit (1920); perfected system for static-free radio through frequency modulation (FM) (1939), now widely used in U.S.A., Germany, England, and increasingly in other countries; frequency modulation is also used to provide the sound part of television broadcasting; Armstrong awarded Medal of Honor of Institute of Radio Engineers (1917), Franklin Medal of Franklin Institute (1941), Medal for Merit (1947). See *Current Biography,* (Apr.) 1940.

Obituary

N Y Times p1+ F 2 '54

ARNOW, HARRIETTE SIMPSON (är-nō') July 7, 1908- Author

Address: b. c/o The Macmillan Co., 60 5th Ave., New York 11; h. 3220 Nixon Rd., Ann Arbor R2, Mich.

Reprinted from the *Wilson Library Bulletin,* Sept. 1954

The regional flavor which marks the books of Harriette Arnow is drawn from her heritage of five generations of Kentucky ancestors. Since early youth the author of *The Dollmaker,* acclaimed as one of the outstanding novels of 1954, has wanted to write or tell stories, a tendency she attributes to her background: "My people to begin with lived only a short distance from their childhood homes where generations of forebears had lived; this made, I think, for a great richness of tradition and legend; both grandmothers were good storytellers and were full of hand-me-down stories, some going back to the Revolution. The Civil War had raged through the country of the Cumberland; from this war alone were volumes of stories, for in that section it was less a war between the states than a war between neighbors and even kin. There were stories about the War of 1812, and more about Indians."

Harriette Louisa Simpson was born in Wayne County, Kentucky, July 7, 1908, the daughter of Elias Thomas Simpson and Mollie Jane (Denney) Simpson, both descended from old Kentucky settlers, including Revolutionary soldiers from Virginia and North Carolina. The Simpson children—five girls and a boy—attended grade and high school in Burnside, though the family lived far enough from town for the solitude Mrs. Simpson desired. Young Harriette found story material as she wandered or played in the woods or watched the nearby river.

(Continued next page)

HARRIETTE ARNOW

Soon reading began to interest her more than the countryside. Her parents, both teachers, had been guided by McGuffey in their choice of books, and she became well-read in the standard English and American novelists, and especially in poetry, which she memorized.

At college (Berea and the University of Louisville) she majored in science and earned a B.S. degree; many of her extracurricular hours, however, were spent in such nonscientific activities as writing poetry, grading English papers, and belonging to a literary society. Then, having "fallen in love with mathematics, feeling that it might be a better language than mere words," she went on to graduate study; but by the time she reached integral calculus, her mind turned once more to poetry.

For several years she taught school in Kentucky, until the compulsion to write proved too strong. In 1934 she went to Cincinnati, where she devoted herself to reading and writing, taking jobs—typing, cashiering, waitressing—only "to pay the rent and eat." Her first publications were magazine stories (the earliest ones appeared in "little magazines") and a novel with a Kentucky background, *Mountain Path,* which was highly praised by reviewers when it was published in 1936. In her work, which includes stories and reviews in the *Southern Review,* the *Atlantic Monthly, Esquire,* and the *Saturday Review,* she has been encouraged and influenced by magazine and book editors—Robert Penn Warren, Edward Weeks, Harold Strauss, Granville Hicks—and by the publishers of her novels.

Hunter's Horn, a 1949 best seller and Fiction Book Club selection, was a critical success as well, and was translated into several foreign languages. This tale of a poor farm family and the relentless pursuit of a predatory fox impressed Harold Preece, commenting in *The Churchman,* as "a pastoral of the Kentucky hills and one of the finest 'grass roots' novels . . . in many a year." Realistic, earthy, yet tender and poetic, reviewers found the book a portrait of an isolated, primitive community, but a portrait universal in appeal.

Even greater was the critics' enthusiasm for *The Dollmaker,* the story of Gertie Nevels' struggle to maintain the values she has brought from the Kentucky mountains to a sordid housing project in wartime Detroit. Harnett T. Kane, in the New York *Times Book Review,* pronounced the novel a masterwork of power and comparison, a superb book of unforgettable strength and "glowing richness of character and scene."

In 1939 Harriette Simpson married Harold B. Arnow, now a Detroit *Times* reporter. They lived first on a farm in the Cumberland National Forest, working as writers and farmers, and then, during the war, in Detroit. (Mrs. Arnow has used both locales in her novels and is now writing a nonfictional book about the Cumberland River.) Their present home is near Ann Arbor, Michigan. They have a twelve-year-old daughter and a seven-year-old son. Since her marriage Mrs. Arnow has combined authorship with her main occupation, "housewifery," explaining that she must steal time for writing (often between four and seven in the morning) from marketing, cooking, sewing, gardening, caring for pets, attending PTA meetings, and helping in Girl Scout work.

Mrs. Arnow attends the Disciples of Christ Church (Campbellites). She is a Democrat and a member of the Daughters of the American Revolution and the American Civil Liberties Union.

In her busy life reading still plays an important part. "Authors are like people," she believes. "We turn to them at different times; while living in a crowded section of Detroit, I found myself always picking up Thoreau—the woods, I guess." Other favorites, too, classics of prose and poetry, she reads over and over, and "will go back to again."

References

Sat R Lit 33:12 F 11 '50 por
Warfel, H. R. American Novelists of Today (1951)

ARON, RAYMOND (CLAUDE FERDINAND) Mar. 14, 1905- Author; journalist; university professor

Address: b. c/o Le Figaro, 14 Rond-Point Champs-Elysées, Paris 8ᵉ, France; h. 34, quai de Passy, Paris 16ᵉ, France

One of France's most distinguished journalists and commentators on world events is Raymond Aron, editorial writer for *Le Figaro* since 1947 and author of *The Century of Total War,* published in the United States by Doubleday & Company in 1954. Aron turned to journalism during World War II when he became assistant to General Charles de Gaulle and editor of *La France Libre.* He has had a long career as a professor of social philosophy and is noted for his "dry brilliance" in classroom lectures.

His pro-American views are based on a profound study of the forces of history leading him to conclude that only under American world leadership as opposed to communism can human liberties be preserved.

Born in Paris on March 14, 1905, Raymond Claude Ferdinand Aron was one of three sons of Gustave and Suzanne (Levy) Aron. His father, who came originally from Lorraine, was a professor of law. Raymond's brother Adrien is an international bridge player; his brother Robert is head of the research department of the Bank of Paris and the Netherlands.

Young Raymond entered the Lycée Hoche at Versailles at the age of nine, and received his baccalaureate in 1922. He then studied for two years at the Condorcet in Paris preparatory to entering the Ecole Normale Supérieure for training as a professor. He passed the fellowship examinations in philosophy in 1928, and then studied for a doctorate in letters. His thesis, "Introduction à la philosophie de l'Histoire," presented the idea of relativity in history. It was published by Gallimard in 1938.

In choosing teaching as a lifework, Aron was influenced by the French philosopher Léon Brunschvicg and the German sociologist Max Weber. He began his career in 1930 as lecturer at the University of Cologne, and remained there until 1931 when he transferred to the French Academic House in Berlin.

In 1933 he accepted an appointment as professor of philosophy at the *lycée* in Le Havre. A year later he was made secretary of the center of social studies at the Ecole Normale Supérieure in Paris. He held this post until 1939.

He also served as professor at the normal school in Saint-Cloud (1935-1939) and professor of social philosophy at the University of Toulouse (1939). During this period he wrote *La Sociologie allemande contemporaine* (Alcan, 1935) and *Essai sur la théorie de l'Histoire dans l'Allemagne contemporaine* (Vrin, 1938).

Following the outbreak of World War II, Aron served with the French Air Force until the French defeat in 1940 when he escaped to London to join General de Gaulle and become editor in chief of *La France Libre*.

In 1944 his book *L'Homme contre les tyrans* (Maison Française) was published. Aron then wrote three other political works: *De l'armistice à l'insurrection nationale* (Gallimard, 1945), *L'Age des empires et l'avenir de la France* (Editions Défense, 1946) and *Les Français devant la Constitution* (Editions Défense, 1946). *Le Grand Schisme,* a collection of essays on world problems with particular emphasis on the situation of France during and after the war, was published by Gallimard in 1948.

Raymond Aron was appointed professor at the Institut d'Etudes Politiques of the Sorbonne and at the Ecole Nationale d'Administration after the liberation of France, but continued to bring "a scholar's knowledge and a politician's understanding to the job of newspaper commentary" (as Arthur Schlesinger described it), by writing for *Combat* (1946-1947)

Elliott Erwitt

RAYMOND ARON

and then for *Le Figaro,* one of France's outstanding newspapers.

Since 1947 Aron's articles on international affairs, politics, social and economic problems, and contemporary history have been appearing two or three times a week on the front pages of the newspaper. "Of European writers on current affairs, few have shown more penetration, vigor and courage in the years since the war than Raymond Aron," wrote Arthur Schlesinger in the New York *Post Magazine* (March 14, 1954).

In his articles Aron has consistently opposed French neutrality, and has recommended strong defenses against the encroachments of communism and any other power that he feels will interfere with intellectual and political liberties. He has advocated alliance with the United States, and has emphasized the reconstruction rather than the political aims of the American aid policy.

In an interview published in *U.S. News & World Report,* March 13, 1953, Aron was asked if he had written in favor of the European Defense Army. He replied: "I was in favor of German rearmament even before '50. I was the first Frenchman to come out for that position. In '45 I wrote in favor of German reconstruction, and in '49 and '50 I wrote in favor of rearming the Germans. But I also have many objections to the particular form of the European Defense Community. I personally believe that it is a mistake of the American policy to put together the two ideas of German rearmament and European Defense Community."

In addition to his newspaper editorials, Aron has written articles for such periodicals as *La Table Ronde, France Illustration, Commentary, Foreign Affairs, International Affairs, American Mercury, Saturday Review of Literature* and the New York *Times Magazine.* During his visits to the United States in 1951

ARON, RAYMOND—*Continued*

and 1953, his views were widely quoted. He has stated repeatedly his belief that the majority of Europeans are prepared to accept American leadership since "by itself Europe lacks the power to resist the pressure exercised by Moscow."

"M. Aron has not pretended that everything about the United States is to his liking," wrote Richard Rovere in the *New Yorker,* March 7, 1953, "but he has made strenuous efforts to allay European misgivings about the general drift of American society and to assure European skeptics that the American devotion to freedom is an intense and enduring one." Following the investigations by Senator Joseph R. McCarthy of the Voice of America in February 1953, some of which Aron attended, Aron said that he was unable to see how he could honestly continue to defend the United States against charges that its political life is characterized by fear and hysteria.

The French journalist stated in an interview in *U.S. News & World Report* (March 13, 1953) on the subject "War III—Would France Fight?" that his country hoped to avoid a catastrophic third war but would fight if it had to. "Of course the main idea of the French is to avoid the third war," he said. "There is the fundamental difference between the psychology of the United States and Europe. You think that the third war would be awful, but you hope to win it—and win it decisively. The people of Europe know that in case of a third war there would be no victory for them because the destruction would be such that it would be actually a defeat."

Aron's book, *Les guerres en chaîne,* published by Gallimard in 1951, was brought out in the United States by Doubleday in March 1954 under the title *The Century of Total War.* After outlining the historical background of contemporary world conflicts, Aron explains how modern technology has increased the interdependence of all peoples at the same time that it has devised new weapons of mass destruction. Thus world unity has become not only technologically possible, but capable of being forcibly achieved.

In this situation, Communist fanaticism and American power have both risen to overshadowing heights as competitors for world leadership. Aron's thesis is that World War I set off an ever-widening chain reaction whose end is nowhere in sight. Wars in the twentieth century, in his view, are profound revolutions causing upheavals in economic systems, human behavior, morals, values and basic institutions.

The two problems facing civilized man, as he sees them, are how "to master the dynamism of violence" and how to preserve liberty. Aron believes that the burden of preserving liberty rests with the United States. He recognizes that the American people have taken over their role of world leadership with reluctance and that they need the support of all anti-Stalinists. Wise leadership, he believes, may well prevent the cold or limited war from developing into total war.

Saul K. Padover, reviewing Aron's book in the New York *Times Book Review,* called it "a treatise in the grand style of French political writing . . . erudite, logical, paradoxical, cautiously pessimistic, dryly aphoristic and devastatingly lucid." According to Crane Brinton (New York *Herald Tribune Book Review*): "Raymond Aron is one of the relatively few publicists who can write about current events without losing his head, his temper or his sense of decency."

Arthur Schlesinger (New York *Post Magazine*) comments on Aron's "profound sense of the complexity of history and his detached, unflinching realism about human motives and decisions." "At times," Schlesinger declares, "the analysis becomes exceedingly close and subtle, and the organization is sometimes diffuse and repetitious. But it is a book which repays the closest attention, and it introduces to America one of the distinguished minds of our time."

Raymond Aron was made a chevalier of the French Legion of Honor in 1947. His marriage to Suzanne Gauchon, formerly a teacher of Latin and Greek, took place on September 5, 1933. They have a daughter, Dominique-Françoise, and a son, Laurence. Aron is five feet seven inches tall and weighs 154 pounds. He has blue eyes and blond hair. An independent, he lists no political or formal church affiliations.

For recreation he enjoys playing tennis and watching football matches. Harvey Breit of the New York *Times Book Review* described him in 1951 as a "small, well-knit man with a friendly smile" who likes to walk around cities without guides or conducted tours.

References

N Y Post Mag p12 Mr 14 '54 por
N Y Times Book R p29 Ja 7 '51 por
New Yorker 29:89+ Mr 7 '53
Sat R 37:12 Mr 13 '54 por
Dictionnaire Biographique Français Contemporain (1950)

ARONSON, J(OHN) HUGO Sept. 1, 1891-
Governor of Montana

Address: b. c/o State Capitol, Helena, Mont.; h. 304 N. Ewing St., Helena, Mont.

The governor of Montana, a state whose principal industry is agriculture and whose economy is affected by periods of drought, is J. Hugo Aronson. He is the fourth Republican governor in the history of the state and has had many years of experience as a rancher and farmer. He defeated his Democratic opponent, the incumbent Governor John W. Bonner, in the November 1952 election and took office on January 5, 1953 for a term of four years.

Aronson attained the governorship of the "treasure state," after serving in its Legislative Assembly a^ a representative from 1939 to 1945 and as a senator from 1945 to 1952.

John Hugo Aronson was born on September 1, 1891, in Gallstad, Sweden, the son of Aaron

Johannsen Aronson, a farmer, and Rike (Ryeing) Aronson. He was reared and educated in his native land. When he left for America at the age of twenty, his father told him: "Don't make a promise unless you can keep it. If you can't do that, don't promise anything."

Landing in Boston, he traveled all over the United States and took odd jobs where he found them. He settled in Columbus, Montana and began working there. Friends encouraged him to file a claim on a homestead on the Montana-Wyoming border. He worked in the oil fields with his team of horses, hauling pipe and other equipment. He served in World War I with the 20th Engineers in France.

He returned to his homestead after the war, and his willingness to do all kinds of hard work as a teamster, trucker, oil rig builder, and trucking contractor earned him the name, the "Galloping Swede." Becoming also a rancher and farmer, he learned at first hand the significance of drought in the Rocky Mountain state's economy. The success of his work caused him to be chosen president of the Toole County Bank in Shelby, Montana.

Aronson became city alderman in Cut Bank, Montana in 1935, a post which he retained for four years. He was elected to the House of Representatives of Montana in 1938 and reelected in 1940.

In the election of 1942, Aronson was returned to his seat in Montana's House of Representatives and the Republicans gained control of both houses of the state legislature. He was elected in 1944 to the Senate, the upper house of Montana's Legislative Assembly. Aronson states of this election campaign that "the only reason I am bald today is from getting in and out of Indian tepees trying to get votes from the Blackfeet Indians who live in my county of Glacier."

While Aronson was a member of the Senate in 1949, the Legislative Assembly initiated tax-sharing in Montana by allocating 6 per cent of gross liquor revenues collected in state liquor stores to local governments, raised old-age, unemployment and workmen's compensation benefits, and created a resources development board to encourage new industries to settle in Montana.

A Republican legislature adopted the interstate civil defense and the western regional education compacts in 1951, appointed an interim commission to study reorganization of the state government, created a department of labor and industry, and passed a reapportionment measure which raised membership in the House of Representatives from ninety to ninety-four members. In addition, the Legislative Assembly ratified a proposed amendment to the Federal constitution to limit the president's office to two full terms.

Speaking of his work as alderman and state legislator, Aronson stated: "My every aim was to substitute business for politics. The people's business, it seems to me, should be treated in exactly the same manner as the individual businessman treats his own business. . . . My only thought was, 'What is best for Montana and the nation right now?'"

DeWalt Studio

J. HUGO ARONSON

In a major race for the Republican gubernatorial nomination, in July, 1952, Aronson defeated the state railroad commissioner Leonard C. Young by "52,034 to 20,246 votes" (New York *Times,* July 17, 1952). The following November, when Montana went Republican nationally at the polls for the first time since 1928, Aronson was elected governor by a majority of more than 4,000 votes over his Democratic opponent, Governor John W. Bonner. The "Galloping Swede" stated of his election: "Folks had confidence in me and I had confidence in them."

On January 5, 1953, in his message to the new Legislative Assembly he stated that "Our goal is to do our best for Montana and the nation and to protect the heritage of our children. There is no place for partisan politics, sectionalism or special privilege."

He advocated, among other measures, a balanced budget, the careful consideration of the information given in the "Little Hoover" Reorganization Commission, the "intensive study" of a proposal for the revision of unemployment compensation, the extension of modern facilities to all households, and that all state employees give "full value" to their jobs.

The state was recovering from the effects of record floods in 1952 in the Missouri basin and also from a drought of such intensity as to cause the Defense Electric Power Administration to limit the use and delivery of electricity in Montana and other states when water shortages cut hydroelectric output.

Discussing the promises of the newly elected national Republican leaders for more "grass roots participation in reclamation and river basin developments" in 1953, Aronson stated that "we want nothing of plans which would take away our rights and make us tenants of absentee landlord bureaucrats in Washington."

(Continued next page)

ARONSON, J. HUGO—*Continued*

Meeting with the governors of Oregon, Washington and Idaho, three other members of a Columbia Basin Inter-Agency Committee, in March 1953, in Seattle, Aronson gave his support to an interstate compact which would allow states drained by the Columbia River to handle regional issues blocking interstate development. The question of power shortage was considered; reports of cuts in the Federal dam building program on the lower Columbia River indicated a delay in this source of power. As stated by the New York *Times* (March 26, 1953), final agreement on the governors' interstate compact would be required by all state legislatures and Congress, and was not expected "for four years."

Speaking in Minneapolis, Minnesota on Swedish Day on June 28, 1953, Aronson stated: "Today there is a philosophy that the Government should tell us what to do from the cradle to the grave. I think that we should develop the stamina and the courage to tell the Government what we will do and not waste our energy and our priceless birthright by dependence on Government. But this . . . will require our participation in Government and not leaving it to the politicians."

Aronson is a member of the Chamber of Commerce in Cut Bank, Montana, the Montana Motor Transportation Association, the Montana Bankers' Association, and the Montana Club. He also holds membership in the American Legion, the Veterans of Foreign Wars, and in the Lions, Elks, Masons, Moose, and Shrine organizations. His church affiliation is Protestant.

Aronson's first wife, a French woman whom he married in France during his First World War service, died in 1936. He married Rose McClure, a school teacher and county superintendent, in 1944. They have one daughter, Rika. Aronson stands six feet two inches tall and weighs 200 pounds. He has gray eyes and hair, and his favorite recreation is watching wrestling, boxing, and baseball. Aronson has made four trips back to Sweden (in 1923, 1929, 1936 and 1949) to visit his relatives. Since Aronson knew no English except the words "ham and eggs" when he first came to the United States, he was compelled to order them for his meals for about two months. Even now, he confesses that he advises "When in doubt, order ham and eggs and you will never go wrong."

Reference

N Y Times p3 N 6 '52

ARP, HANS *See* Arp, J.

ARP, JEAN Sept. 16, 1887- Sculptor; painter; poet

Address: h. 21 rue des Châtaigniers, Meudon, Seine-et-Oise, France; b. c/o Valentin Gallery, 32 E. 57th St., New York 22

The smooth, amorphous forms of Jean Arp's abstract sculpture have frequently been compared to clouds which seem to be on the verge of forming into recognizable objects. These forms have not only influenced many contemporary painters and sculptors but have been widely copied in the decorative and commercial arts. Alsatian-born Arp has been closely identified with a number of important movements in modern art including dadaism and surrealism.

Although best known as a plastic artist, Arp has worked in a variety of other media including painted wood reliefs, oil, gouache, collage, engraving and lithography. He is a notable bilingual poet (writing in French and in German) and in the opinion of Georges Hugnet and other French critics his earliest dadaist poems with their imaginative word deformations, puns and grotesque images, were an "historic" contribution to the development of modern poetry. His most recent show of sculpture was at the Curt Valentin Gallery in New York City (March 2-27, 1954).

Art critics have often stated that Arp is one of the few contemporary artists to achieve a harmonious synthesis between "classic" abstraction and "romantic" surrealism. As an innovator of forms, Arp, in the opinion of Robert Coates (*The New Yorker*), has "helped mold the plastic design of a whole generation."

Hans Arp and Jean Arp are identical, Arp using both first names according to whether he writes in German or French. He was born on September 16, 1887, in Strasbourg, Alsace, which at that time was under German rule. His father, Pierre Guillaume Arp, a merchant, was of Danish descent, while his mother, Josephine (Koeberlé) Arp, was French. He has one brother, François. During his childhood, Hans began to draw and to compose poems, and his first verse was published in literary reviews when he was fourteen or fifteen years old.

Educated at the *lycée* in his native city, he left school without graduating in order to devote himself to art. He visited Paris for the first time in 1904 and there he became acquainted with the latest developments in modern painting. Between 1905 and 1907, he studied under Ludwig von Hofmann at the Kunstakademie in Weimar, Germany, and the following year he returned to Paris to continue his studies at the Académie Julian.

In 1909 Arp went to Weggis, in Switzerland, where he worked for several years in solitude and made his first attempts to transcend inherited art forms and achieve an impersonal, non-objective style of painting. While living there, he joined with the Swiss painters Wilhelm Gimmi and Oskar Lüthy and the Russian artist Rossiné to found *Der Moderner Bund*. Arp's works were included in the first exhibition of the *Moderner Bund* at Lucerne, in 1911, and in the group's second show in Zürich the following year.

Meanwhile, Arp had visited the noted Russian painter, Wassily Kandinsky, in Munich, and found Kandinsky's first purely abstract "improvisations" dating from 1911 a confirmation of the direction in which he himself was working. He was associated with Kandinsky, Franz Marc, and Paul Klee in the expressionist group known as *Der Blaue Reiter*, exhibiting with that circle of painters at the Goltz Gallery in Munich in 1912 and contributing to the group's yearbook.

In 1913, Arp was represented at the first German Autumn Salon at "Der Sturm" Gallery, the center of an expressionist group in Berlin. The next year he went to Paris, where he kept in close contact with the leaders of cubism.

Returning to neutral Switzerland in 1915, Arp settled in Zürich, where he lived until the end of the war. One of the most important events in his career was an exhibition held there at the Galerie Tanner in November 1915. Together with the Dutch artists Otto and Adja van Rees, Arp showed wall tapestries and drawings that were completely abstract. It was at this exhibition that he first met Sophie Henriette Gertrude Taeuber, a young Swiss artist who taught at the Kunstgewerbeschule, Zürich (1916-29). They were married in 1921.

Arp has acknowledged that the severely simplified forms of Sophie Taeuber's abstract designs had a decisive influence on his own work. Shortly after their meeting, they both decided to renounce painting in oils on canvas and to work exclusively in new materials. Believing in the concept of anonymous, collective endeavor, they collaborated in 1916 on a number of collages (pasted-paper compositions), woven fabrics, and embroideries that were composed entirely of rectangular planes.

Alfred Barr has stated in *Cubism and Abstract Art* that Arp's geometrical work of 1915-16 was more purely abstract than anything then produced by the Parisian cubists or the Munich expressionists, and anticipated by a year or two the strictly rectangular compositions of Piet Mondriaan and the Dutch *de Stijl* group, with which Arp was associated after the war.

In February 1916, Arp joined with Hugo Ball, Richard Huelsenbeck, Tristan Tzara, and Marcel Janco to found dadaism. (The name "dada,'" a children's word meaning "hobbyhorse," was picked at random from a French dictionary.) Inspired by a bitter contempt for the folly of World War I, the dadaists were in revolt against "the conventional and traditional in both art and life." Dadaism, in Arp's own words, aimed at destroying "the reasonable deceptions of man" and at recovering "the natural and unreasonable order." The center of the dadaists in Zürich was Hugo Ball's Cabaret Voltaire, where Arp hung his pictures, recited his poems, and participated in various dadaist demonstrations.

By 1917, Arp had abandoned the use of rectangular, geometric forms and began to invent the curvilinear, biomorphic forms characteristic of all his later work. He first drew his inspiration for these forms by studying the shapes of roots, broken branches, and stones found along the shores of Lake Maggiore. These free, fluid, irregular forms were employed in an important series of woodcuts he made to illustrate Tzara's *25 Poèmes* (1918) and *Cinéma Calendrier du Coeur Abstrait* (1920). The year 1917 also marks the first of Arp's famous

JEAN ARP

bas-reliefs, a form of expression in which cut-out pieces of painted wood are mounted on a painted panel.

In accordance with the dadaist spirit of irrational spontaneity, Arp at this time began to create whimsical and useless "objects" (*Egg-board*, *Castaway's Bundle*) out of materials either found or manufactured. He also practiced "automatic drawing," in which conscious control is presumably abandoned. And he further experimented with compositions "arranged according to the laws of chance," a process by which torn or cut-out pieces of colored paper were first shaken up and then pasted on a sheet of cardboard just as they had fallen.

At the end of the war, dadaism spread throughout Germany, and later, in 1920, reached Paris. From 1919 to 1920, Arp was a member of the dadaist group in Cologne, which included Max Ernst and Johannes Baargeld. The three artists issued the dadaist periodicals *Die Schammade* and *Dada W/3*, and in April 1920 held a sensational exhibition of their work at Winter's Brauhaus, which was closed by the police. Arp and Ernst signed each other's work indiscriminately and collaborated on a famous series of collages called *Fatagaga* (an abbreviation for *Fabrication de tableaux garantis gazométriques*).

Later, Arp showed work at the International Dada Exhibition in Berlin (1920); took part in the dadaist demonstrations in the Tyrol (1921, 1922); participated in the celebrated Salon Dada at the Galerie Montaigne in Paris (1922); and in 1923 collaborated with the painter, Kurt Schwitters, who lived in Hanover and called his version of dada "Merzism."

Surrealism, a schismatic outgrowth of dadaism, was announced in Paris by the poet André Breton in 1924, and Arp joined the movement shortly thereafter. His work was included in the first collective exhibition of the surrealist painters at the Galerie Pierre in November 1925, and he had his first one-man show in Paris at the Galerie Surréaliste two years later. Arp devoted most of his attention in the 1920's

ARP, JEAN—*Continued*

to constructing painted bas-reliefs. Among the best-known are *Bird in an Aquarium* (c. 1920), *Mountain, Table, Anchors, Navel* (1925), and *Overturned Shoe with Two Heels under a Black Vault* (1928).

In 1926 Arp and his wife settled permanently at Meudon, a suburb of Paris, in a house which Sophie Taeuber-Arp designed. During the next two years, they collaborated with the *de Stijl* artist Théo van Doesburg on the mural decorations for a restaurant in Strasbourg called L'Aubette. The interiors of L'Aubette (since destroyed) have been described by M. Seuphor as the first collective attempt to use abstract art in decorating an important public building. Arp was one of the founding members of the *Abstraction-Création* group, which was organized in Paris in 1931 to promote abstract art.

During the 1930's, Arp began executing three-dimensional sculpture in bronze, stone, or plaster. Most critics agree that in sculpture in the full round Arp has achieved "the fullest realization of his inventive capacities," and Thomas Hess (*Art News*) has called him "one of the great modern sculptors." His ovoid shapes seem to express "the primary forces of growth, movement, and change."

Following the Nazi invasion in the spring of 1940, Arp and his wife fled to southern France and they eventually settled in Grasse, in the Unoccupied Zone. There Arp executed two *Mediterranean Sculptures* and collaborated with his wife and the artists Sonia Delaunay and Alberto Magnelli on a series of abstract lithographs. In November 1942, the Arps succeeded in crossing over to Switzerland. Two months later, Sophie Taeuber-Arp died accidentally, near Zürich.

According to Gabrielle Buffet-Picabia's monograph, Arp was unable to work for a long time thereafter and seriously considered taking religious orders. It was only through the encouragement of friends that he was eventually persuaded to continue his creative work. A series of water colors in 1944 marked his return to artistic activity, but it was not until two years later, after he had moved back to Meudon, that he undertook sculpture once more.

In the opinion of Carola Giedion-Welcker in *Horizon* (October 1946) Arp's art is "one of the purest achievements of our time." This is largely due, she believes, to "a rare sensibility" which enables him "to penetrate and to disclose the mysteries of the natural world in forms so elementary and structurally precise that they seem to belong to the origins of existence."

An exhibition of gouaches by Arp was held at the John Becker Gallery in February 1934. With the revival of interest in abstract art among the younger generation of artists after World War II, Arp gained wider recognition. His first sculpture show was held at the Buchholz (now Curt Valentin) Gallery in 1949. He visited the United States early in 1949, and was commissioned by the architect Walter Gropius to construct a large mural relief (1950) in red wood for the new Graduate Center at Harvard University.

The critics have discerned a new aesthetic orientation in Arp's latest sculptures, which were on view at the Curt Valentin Gallery in New York during March 1954. The forms of such works as *Aquatic* (1953), *Cobra-Centaur* (1952), *Mythical Sculpture* (1949), and *Configuration of Serpent Movements* (1950) are said to be "discreetly and partially figurative," with frequent suggestions of natural and human forms. Howard Devree in the New York *Times,* March 7, 1954 commented: "Arp's marbles and bronzes have a sensuous quality, such that they fairly invite the hand to follow the eye along the curves and rhythms of his beautifully finished pieces. . ."

Arp is well-known for his work in the graphic arts. *Dreams and Projects* is his latest portfolio of text and woodcuts (Curt Valentin, 1952). He has also illustrated many books, most recently Camille Bryen's *Temps Troué* (1951). In addition, he has made abstract designs for rugs, embroideries and Aubusson tapestries. In his monograph *On My Way* (Wittenborn, 1948) he lists a bibliography of his writings including essays, poems, prose poems and a novel *Tres Novelas Ejemplares* (1935) in collaboration with the Chilean poet, Vicente Huidobro.

From 1946 to 1948 Arp was a member of the committee of the Salon des Réalités Nouvelles in Paris, and he has served in the same capacity for the Salon de la Jeune Sculpture (1950-52). His works are represented in museums in Paris, London, Zürich, Basel, Rome, Stockholm, Rio de Janeiro, New York, Philadelphia, San Francisco, and other cities, as well as in numerous private collections.

The artist, who stands five feet seven inches tall and weighs around 150 pounds, has blue eyes and close cropped gray hair. He has been described as "friendly, polite, unchanging, and without any pretensions," and according to Hans Richter, his "wit and good spirits are legendary among those who knew him when he was young." Arp is a Roman Catholic. His favorite reading includes books of pre-Socratic philosophy and philosophical dictionaries, the works of the Church Fathers, and both German romantic and modern poetry.

Maurice Raynal in his *History of Modern Painting from Picasso to Surrealism* wrote: "Arp was always in revolt against the convention of a picture as a framed rectangle. . . . His 'free form' was born of a free interplay of fantasy and the subconscious and was subsequently turned to good account by his infallible instinct for plastic and structural values . . . [and the years have] demonstrated his amazingly rich powers of invention."

References

Art N 47:20+ Ja '49 por
Time 53:37+ Ja 31 '49
Arp, J. On My Way (1948); Wegweiser-Jalons (1951); Dreams and Projects (1952)
Motherwell, R. ed. The Dada Painters and Poets (1951)
Seuphor, M. L'Art Abstrait (1949)

ASCOLI, MAX (ȧ'skō-lē) June 25, 1898-
Publisher; author; educator

Address: b. c/o The Reporter, 136 E. 57th St., New York 22; h. 23 Gramercy Park South, New York 3

The editor and publisher of *The Reporter,* a fortnightly magazine founded in 1949 which interprets national and international news, is Dr. Max Ascoli, scholar and political scientist. He has taught in leading universities in Italy and is a full professor of political science on leave from the New York School for Social Research in New York City.

Author of several books including *The Power of Freedom* (Farrar-Straus, 1949) and *Intelligence in Politics* (W. W. Norton, 1936) Dr. Ascoli believes that there are "responsibilities of . . . intellectuals which they must be aware of if they wish to recognize the share of power that belongs to them." He has said that the purpose of his magazine is "to process the news in order to reach the facts, and to dissect opinions in order to reach a clear idea of an American policy . . . to brief the reader on vital issues." He has stated that his editorial staff is guided by the basic belief "in America, as a nation whose freedom and well-being are inseparably tied to the freedom and well-being of other nations." Moreover, he has confidence in the I.Q. of the American reader "whose capacity to grasp facts and ideas is crudely underrated by most of the existing media of information."

Max Ascoli was born on June 25, 1898 in Ferrara, Italy, the only child of Enrico Ascoli, a wealthy coal and lumber dealer, and Andriana (Finzi) Ascoli. He attended the local schools and *liceo* and earned his LL.D. degree at the Universita Statale di Ferrara in 1920. His first book, published in both Italy and France in 1921, was a critical study of Georges Sorel, the French syndicalist and social philosopher. He wrote *Le Vie dalla Croce* in 1925. The young author was appointed an associate professor of jurisprudence and political philosophy at the Universita Libera di Camerino in the following year. In 1928 he received the Ph.D. degree from the University of Rome.

The increasing power of the Mussolini regime prompted Ascoli to contribute his strongly anti-Fascist opinions to the underground newspapers. Arrested in 1928 in Milan, he feared that his attacks on the government had been identified but he discovered that the police were ignorant of his clandestine literary work and were merely attempting to intimidate him because of his reputation as an anti-Fascist.

After three weeks in jail, he was given two years *ammonizione* (modified house arrest). This was relaxed after six months, nevertheless he was constantly followed by a policeman. The arrest resulted in the termination of his relations with the Camerino university, and suppression of his writings in Italy, and prevented him from accepting a chair in philosophy at the University of Rome which he had won in a competition.

Unable to teach on the mainland, he became an associate professor of jurisprudence and

Halsman

MAX ASCOLI

political philosophy at the university of Cagliari in Sicily in 1929. Here he held the dual distinction of being the only professor who was not a member of the Society of University Professors (a Fascist organization) and the only faculty member who had his own personal policeman. The presence of this functionary at the university was not conducive to academic tranquility and this, together with Ascoli's adamant refusal to join the Fascist party or any of its appendages, led to his dismissal in 1931.

Dr. Ascoli then applied for and received a Rockefeller Foundation fellowship in 1931. Through a personal plea to Mussolini by Senator Gentile, former Fascist Minister of Education who disliked the needless persecution of intellectuals, Ascoli obtained a passport. Nevertheless he was stopped from boarding ship at Naples because the emigration authorities had not been notified of his removal from the "frontier book," which contained the names, pictures, and fingerprints of all persons forbidden to leave the country. Ascoli told the vice-chief of the Naples police the merits of his case and was so persuasive that he was allowed to depart. He boarded the ship by the last gangplank and arrived in the United States a week later, carrying with him a Gauguin painting, a Tintoretto, and a large part of his family's considerable fortune.

A foreign recipient of a Rockefeller Foundation fellowship is expected to return to his native land upon its expiration to write on his findings. When Dr. Ascoli informed the foundation's officials that he did not intend to return to Italy they assisted in securing for him a professorship in political science with the graduate faculty of political and social science at the New School for Social Research in New York City in 1933 and, for the first year paid

ASCOLI, MAX—*Continued*

half his salary. He was dean of the graduate faculty from 1940 to 1941 and is still a member of the faculty and of the board of trustees.

Professor Ascoli became a frequent contributor of articles concerning political subjects to the *Atlantic Monthly, Foreign Affairs, International Journal of Ethics, American Scholar, Yale Review, The Nation, Free World,* and *Social Research.*

In *Intelligence in Politics,* Ascoli asserted that the freedom which a people gain is largely determined by the activities of the intellectuals because their role is one of "reducing hazy collective experiences to terms that the individual being can figure out and assimilate, theirs is the privilege of taking care of expression, which is the most important safety valve . . . of society and makes known as clearly as possible the real condition of society."

The *Saturday Review of Literature* (January 9, 1937) commented on Ascoli's book *Intelligence in Politics*: "He has some important observations to make about how the political and social orders in America are bound in together, observations which are not usually made. . . ." K. N. Llewellyn (*Survey Graphic,* February, 1937) noted that "Ascoli writes as Van Gogh paints, a stroke of scarlet beside a stroke of blue—neither one of them wholly right, in itself—yet both justified."

This volume was followed by *Fascism for Whom?* (W. W. Norton, 1938), written with Arthur Feiler, a colleague at the New School and a pre-Hitler economics editor of the Frankfurter *Zeitung*. "As *fuorusciti* (political exiles)" R. C. Brooks wrote, ". . . one would expect from Messrs. Ascoli and Feiler implacable hostility against the Fascist and Nazi regimes. On the contrary, they give evidence at every point of scholarly detachment and rare critical acumen" (*Saturday Review of Literature,* November 26, 1938).

Dr. Ascoli became an American citizen in 1939 and from 1940 to 1941 served as associate director of cultural relations, Coordinator of Inter-American Affairs. After resigning from this post he founded and was the principal financial supporter of the Committee for the Assistance and Distribution of Materials to Artisans (CADMA), a demonstration of his belief that communism can be eliminated if people have "not only enough to eat but a chance to work." CADMA, a non-profit organization, was established in Italy to revive the handicraft industries which were destroyed by war.

Tools, equipment, capital, and merchandising advice were provided to reactivate the centuries-old skills. Simultaneously, Handicraft Development, Inc., was organized in the United States, with Dr. Ascoli as president, to open markets for the craftsmens' wares and to display them at the House of Italian Handicrafts in New York City. CADMA, a resounding success, was later merged with *Compagnia Nazionale Artigiana,* an Italian government agency, and the American branch was discontinued in 1953 when it had served its purpose. In 1950 Dr. Ascoli gave $200,000 to establish an eye clinic in the Santa Anna Hospital in Ferrara as a memorial to his mother.

After withdrawing from plans to begin a new liberal publication, *United Nations World,* Professor Ascoli and a small nucleus of associates began to implement a dream that has been his since student days—a magazine of his own. Originally conceived as a Washington weekly modelled on the London *Economist* and aimed at influencing government policy, the plans for *The Reporter* were altered; it was to be a liberal fortnightly of facts and ideas dealing with national and international affairs.

The editorial staff moved to New York to escape becoming "virtually a house organ of Congress" and its *Economist* formula was discarded in favor of a magazine "commuting between Sirius and the poolroom" whose "goal will be to strengthen the institutions of freedom in every country of the world."

The first issue (April 19, 1949) had thirty-six pages and a press run of 175,000 (50,000 to newsstands and 125,000 to a selected list of labor leaders, educators, businessmen, and government leaders). It was generally well received but some critics thought that its promise to be "free from obsession with headline news and from the conceit of opinion" was humanly impossible of fulfillment.

The "break even" point of 200,000 circulation and twenty pages of advertisements based on that circulation has not yet been reached (circulation as of August, 1954, over 100,000), but the magazine has succeeded in acquiring some extremely capable reporters who cover the international scene. Among its regular contributors are Bill Mauldin, Mary McCarthy, A. A. Berle, Jr., Marya Mannes and Theodore White. It is owned and financed equally by Dr. Ascoli (general partner) and Mrs. Marion Ascoli (limited—and silent—partner) in a limited corporation with a capital of $1,500,000.

A feature of *The Reporter* is its *Reports from Abroad* in which correspondents carry out the magazine's policy "to present the views of foreign people, what they think of our policies, of the help we are extending to them, how they are affected by anti-American propaganda coming from Moscow or from unconscionable legislators on the Hill."

Commenting on the European situation, Ascoli wrote in an editorial (October 13. 1953): "The unity of Europe cannot remain loose and informal as it has been for centuries. It is exposed to two major dangers: German aggressiveness and the Communist threat. Adenauer himself fears this aggressiveness and believes that a United Europe can check it. The Communist threat from within and without can be met only if Europe organizes itself into a new political entity."

In Ascoli's book *The Power of Freedom,* he asserts that freedom is the "propulsive power of civilization—a power that men have the ability to release and to control . . . this power can drive the men of our time to goals so high and so good that we can only dimly discern them." However, he warns that the "political principles that give character to our society should always be kept one step ahead of the course of economics and technology, in order to exert some control over them. But in an era of supersonic speed our political ideas are trotting along at the restful pace of the horse and buggy."

His marriage to the Italian poetess Anna Maria Maddalene Paolina Giacinta Cochetti (who writes under the name of Anna Maria Armi) was terminated in 1940. Dr. Ascoli, who is six feet tall and weighs 195 pounds, lives in a large house in Gramercy Park, which is packed with periodicals, books, classical records and gadgets. He is married to Marion Rosenwald, a daughter of Julius Rosenwald, the late philanthropist and executive of Sears, Roebuck & Co. They have one son, Peter Max.

References

Atlan 165:168 F '40 por
Christian Sci Mon p6 Mr 6 '40
N Y Herald Tribune My 29 '50
N Y Post Mag p31 Ja 29 '47
Sat R Lit 32:16 Ja 22 '49 por
Who's Who in the East (1951)

The Times, London
COL. JOHN JACOB ASTOR

ASTOR, JOHN JACOB May 20, 1886- Publisher; former Member of British Parliament

Address: b. c/o The Times, Printing House Sq., London E.C. 4, England; h. 18 Carlton House Terrace, London, S.W. 1; Hever Castle, Kent, England

The Times of London, which has been called by Prime Minister Winston Churchill "one of the most powerful and respected institutions in the British Empire", has been directed by Colonel John Jacob Astor since 1922 when he purchased the daily newspaper from Lord Northcliffe's estate. He was a Member of Parliament from the Dover division of Kent from 1922 to 1945. An active director on the boards of numerous British educational and welfare institutions, Astor was elected chairman of the Council of the British Press in 1953. On June 1, 1954 he was re-elected president of the Commonwealth Press Union at the organization's forty-fourth annual meeting.

Although he has lived since childhood in England, John Jacob Astor is American by birth. He is the great-great-grandson of the American merchant and capitalist, John Jacob Astor, who came to the United States from Waldorf, Germany. His father, William Waldorf, who became 1st Baron and 1st Viscount Astor of Hever Castle, Kent, was born in New York City and was at one time a member of the legislature of the state of New York, and between 1882 and 1885 served as U.S. Minister to Italy. His mother was Mary Dahlgren, daughter of James W. Paul of Philadelphia. The family settled in England about 1890 and several years later became British subjects. Viscount Astor had three children, Pauline, Waldorf (2d Viscount Astor) and John Jacob, who was born on May 20, 1886.

John Jacob attended Eton where he played cricket in 1904 and 1905. Later, he studied at New College, Oxford. In 1906, Astor took a commission in the First Life Guards. From 1911 to 1914 he served as aide-de-camp to Lord Hardinge of Penshurst, then Viceroy of India.

As soon as the First World War broke out, in August 1914, Astor was posted to France and in October was wounded at Messines. After his recovery, he served on through the war, and in 1918 became a major. Astor won the French award of chevalier of the Legion of Honor. Just before the Armistice he was severely wounded and the amputation of a foot proved necessary.

In December 1922 he became a Member of Parliament for the Dover division of Kent, as a Conservative. Astor succeeded in holding that seat continuously until 1945. Throughout his career in Parliament he was interested in work for the unemployed, in the British Legion and in hospitals. His continual and absorbing interest has been the freedom and welfare of the British press.

After Lord Northcliffe (Alfred Harmsworth), owner of the *Daily Mail* and *The Times* of London was certified as insane, complicated financial and editorial discussions on the ownership and management of *The Times* ensued (*The History of The Times*, Vol. IV, Part II). By the final arrangements, agreed upon after Northcliffe's death in 1922, Astor owns 9/10 of the shares of the Times Publishing Company, Ltd., and John Walter owns 1/10. Both have equal proprietorial powers during John Walter's lifetime. According to British author Bernard Falk, in *Five Years Dead,* "the earnings of *The Times* did not justify anything like this amount [£1,580,000] being paid for the controlling interest." (The daily newspaper is not connected with the London *Sunday Times,* published by Kemsley Newspapers.)

At the time Astor wrote: "No political party is nowadays content unless some important or-

ASTOR, JOHN JACOB—*Continued*

gan of the press is enslaved to its service . . . surely, a wise object [is] to secure as far as possible the continued independence of one great journal, and through it the perpetuation of the highest standards of British journalism. Such at least were the considerations that actuated the writer to join with Mr. John Walter in . . . purchasing the bulk of the shares in *The Times*" (*Empire Review,* September, 1923). Astor believes that "personal vendettas, mere sensationalism, or calculated demonstration of how much the press can accomplish, are alike foreign to the basic principles of the paper."

The Times of London was first produced in 1785 as the *Daily Universal Register,* changing its name to *The Times* January 1, 1788. Its present circulation is approximately 235,814.

In 1919 a sign was constructed on the front of *The Times* building in Printing House Square with the name of the newspaper in large gilt letters and the Royal Arms in color. Lord Northcliffe's order had read, *"The letters should dominate the building*—not the building the letters. Do not delay. They can easily dominate the street if brains and imagination are used." The gilt letters and Royal Arms were removed after the change in proprietorship in 1922.

It was not long before the aims and ideals of Astor's proprietorship were crystallized by the formation of a trust in August 1924. The trust, which is still in existence, was founded to maintain "the best traditions and political independence of *The Times* newspaper and national rather than personal interests" and "eliminating as far as reasonably possible questions of personal ambition or commercial profit." The trustees are the Lord Chief Justice, the warden of All Souls College, Oxford, the president of the Royal Society, the president of the Institute of Chartered Accountants, and the governor of the Bank of England. Under the provisions of the trust, no ordinary share may be transferred to anyone unless such a person has been approved by this distinguished committee.

"With no pretense either to the experience or journalistic ability of his remarkable predecessor (Northcliffe), Major Astor yet manages to play a decisive, and on the whole successful, part in the conduct of *The Times,*" wrote Bernard Falk in 1937. "He is a shrewd businessman served by admirable advisers, who has the patience to interest himself in all departments of the paper, an interest extending even to matters of detail. Apart from his commercial acumen, he has many gifts invaluable to one charged with the control of a great newspaper. Among these might be mentioned the power of judging with a remarkable degree of accuracy the direction in which the broad stream of public opinion is likely to move. Having a wide circle of friends, and being a member of Parliament besides, he has ample opportunities for acquainting himself with what people of varied interests and occupation are thinking and saying."

It is reported that Astor has a keen interest in the welfare and *esprit de corps* of his staff. Every summer he entertains at his country home, Hever Castle, the newspaper's employees. In addition to his leadership of *The Times,* Astor is a director of Hambros Bank, Ltd., Barclays Bank, and London Guarantee and Accident Corporation, and is chairman of the Phoenix Assurance Company. He was president of the Westminster employment committee from 1924 to 1945, and served on broadcasting committees in 1923 and 1935, Post Office advisory council from 1933 to 1939, BBC general advisory council from 1937 to 1939, and advisory council to Ministry of Information in 1939. During the Second World War he was a lieutenant colonel with the Fifth Battalion of the City of London Home Guard.

As president of the Commonwealth Press Union, Colonel Astor asserted that one of the union's first duties after the war would be to insure freedom in gathering news from every country in the world. He said the union, which is composed of newspapers throughout the British Empire, must aim for "the fastest possible transmission at the lowest possible rates" (New York *Times,* February 14, 1945).

On October 29, 1946 the British House of Commons, on a free vote, decided that there should be a royal commission to investigate the conduct of the press in Britain. The commission held many meetings and heard masses of evidence from 1947 to 1949, and in June of the latter year presented its report to Parliament. One of its recommendations was that the press itself should create a general council to consider recruitment, ethics and a transferable pension scheme in the journalistic profession. Established in 1953, this council is composed of both editorial and managerial representatives of journalism, and its chairman is Colonel John Jacob Astor.

Among Astor's recent activities has been the collection of the names of 28,000 Americans who either died in Britain or on service from British bases during World War II. These names were inscribed in a book of honor, a copy of which Astor presented to President Harry S. Truman on November 25, 1952.

Colonel Astor is the president of Dover College; chairman of Middlesex Hospital; vice-president of the Royal College of Music; president of the Press Club, Newspaper Press Fund, National Association for Employment of Regular Sailors, Soldiers and Airmen, and Kent Council, British Legion; and an honorary freeman of Dover.

Astor married Lady Violet Mary Elliot, younger daughter of the 4th Earl of Minto, and the widow of Major Lord Charles Mercer Nairne in 1916. He and Lady Violet have three sons, Gavin, Hugh Waldorf and John. His clubs are the Turf, Carlton, Royal Yacht Squadron (Cowes), and Hurlingham. In his younger days, Astor was active in several sports, particularly rackets and horseback riding. His more recent recreation is landscape painting, in which he is regarded as highly competent.

Of Astor the Ottawa *Evening Citizen* said, "there are few more modest men in British public life today". According to Bernard Falk, he "has the direct manner of the typical army man. . . . He has a good idea of what he wants to do, and is not easily swayed from a settled objective".

References

Ottawa Evening Citizen Jl 2 '37 por
Burke's Peerage, Baronetage, and Knightage (1953)
Camrose, W. E. B., Viscount British Newspapers and their Controllers (1947)
Falk, B. Five Years Dead (1937)
History of The Times (1952)
Who's Who, 1953

ATWOOD, DONNA 1926- Ice skater
Address: c/o Ice Capades, Inc., 6121 Santa Monica Blvd., Hollywood 38, Calif.

The star of Ice Capades, a $750,000 spectacle of skating virtuosity, is Donna Atwood who has been the head-liner in the show for almost ten years with co-star Bobby Specht and a cast of nearly 200. Miss Atwood came to professional skating from amateur championship competitions—she was at one time holder of the junior women's figure skating title and the national senior pairs' title.

A unique feature about the talented skater is that on her tours of the United States, appearing in the ice show in twenty-five cities for a forty-seven week season, she is accompanied by her twin sons and daughter who, in their infancy, traveled in electrically equipped portable nurseries.

Twentieth Century Fox Films announced on March 15, 1954 that a feature-length CinemaScope production of the Ice Capades extravaganza would be made during the summer and with Donna Atwood featured in the picture.

The birthplace of Donna Atwood was Newton, Kansas, where she lived until she was six years old. At that time, her parents decided to visit Los Angeles, California, for their vacation, remaining through the winter as well. "Then they decided to stay through the next summer," Donna Atwood told Ed Wallace of the New York *World-Telegram and Sun* (September 5, 1953). Besides her ordinary schooling, she had a great deal of training in ballet, tap and acrobatic dancing as a child, which she considers later helped her to achieve balance in figure skating, a sport to which she was first attracted by seeing the Norwegian skating star Sonia Henie in a professional appearance at Los Angeles.

When she was about thirteen years old Donna Atwood began to take a real interest in skating. She told Ed Wallace: "I went to the Polar Palace in Los Angeles and was struggling around on hockey skates, having a perfectly wonderful time, when one of the instructors, John McDonald, offered to help me learn." After six months of instruction she recalls, "I won my first skating contest."

This encouragement spurred her interest in skating so that the following year she took

DONNA ATWOOD

part in the national skating competitions held in Cleveland. In retrospect, she says of that attempt, "I did very badly indeed." There followed a year of intensive work to perfect her skating before she again entered the competitions on a national basis. Then, she states, "I won the junior women's figure skating title and the national senior pairs, skating with Eugene Turner."

Several factors were responsible for Donna Atwood's decision to become a professional skater—because of World War II, both international and Olympic meets were discontinued; and the death of her father also entered into her decision. It was through Belita, who at that time was the star of the Ice Capades, that she was brought to the attention of the ice revue's producers. After seeing a sample of her work at the Polar Palace, she recalls, "They offered me a contract but promised me nothing." She signed at the age of sixteen and joined the show at its Atlantic City headquarters, where she was assigned one of Belita's numbers. When the star resigned from the revue the following year, Donna Atwood succeeded her.

Ice Capades and its cast of 187 toured twenty-five cities during its forty-seven week 1953-54 circuit. The show's opening at New York's Madison Square Garden on September 10, 1953, marked Donna Atwood's first appearance in that city, since she had been on leave the previous year to await the birth of her third child. Walter Terry of the New York *Herald Tribune* was highly impressed by the Ice Capades' version of Walt Disney's *Snow White,* remarking, "Donna Atwood and Bobby Specht, the stars of the show, were delightful as the hero and heroine. Furthermore they skated as well as mimed and their skating was something to remember."

When Miss Atwood and her partner returned to the rink in a later number on the program, "España Mamba," Terry found that

ATWOOD, DONNA—*Continued*

the spectacle "provided them with ample opportunities to display their very special gifts of technical accuracy, grace, professional polish, virtuosity and personal charm."

Of the same "Snow White" number, Ed Wallace of the New York *World-Telegram and Sun* said, "Miss Atwood's solo reveals no skating techniques that couldn't be done by a score of other girls, but it is skated with a beauty and radiance that make it unique." The same reviewer felt that she and Bobby Specht skated "España Mamba," so well "that the ice is merely incidental."

She spoke as well as skated the role of Snow White, to a background of recorded solo voices and the Norman Luboff choir. Miss Atwood, said J. P. Shanley of the New York *Times* "skates beautifully and is something of a dish to see." *Variety's* reviewer reported, "Miss Atwood is delightful as Snow White and projects a romantic quality in her dreamy spins across the ice." Of her all-round capacities, he added, "She demonstrates a blade agility that's hard to beat."

In 1948 Miss Atwood was married to John Harris, producer of Ice Capades. Their children, twin sons, Donald Patrick and Dennis Anthony, and a daughter, Donna Jeannette, accompany their parents on the Ice Capades' tours. "If I couldn't take the children along," Miss Atwood has said, "I would stay home."

In order to travel with the children during their infancy, Mr. Harris designed a special aluminum traveling case, complete with bath, sterilizer, milk warmer, clothes compartments, hot plate, and air conditioner, to accommodate the babies and had it constructed at a cost of $2,100. Planning to retire when her sons reach school age and to live in the Harris' Beverly Hills house, the skating star has said, "I think I'll be all ready to enjoy it after fifteen tours." She considers her small sons objective critics: "My boys determine their mother's standing in the show by the number of comedy acts. They tell me I'm best, except for the clowns."

"She looks," wrote one reviewer, "as if she weren't quite old enough to be elected queen of the sophomore spring dance."

References

Look 14:23 N 7 '50 por
N Y World-Telegram Mag p6 S 5 '53 por

AUCHINCLOSS, LOUIS (ôk'ĭn-klôs") 1917- Author; lawyer

Address: b. c/o Hawkins, Delafield and Wood, 67 Wall St., New York 5; h. 24 E. 84th St., New York 28

Reprinted from the *Wilson Library Bulletin,* Dec. 1954

The narrator of Louis Auchincloss' latest book, *The Romantic Egoists,* is Peter Westmancott, a young New Yorker, who was educated at one of the best Eastern preparatory schools and at Yale University, served as a naval officer during the second World War, practiced law

LOUIS AUCHINCLOSS

for a time with a solidly established New York law firm, became a writer, traveled abroad, and at home and abroad met and mingled with what is still generally though somewhat awkwardly described as "high society." Through all this Peter Westmancott moves quietly, with a shrewdly observing eye and a sharp ear, and an attitude that is both satiric—in that he sees the ludicrousness of his world—and sympathetic—in that he understands and forgives it. With hardly a change in detail Peter Westmancott might be Louis Auchincloss. "No modern American writer obeys the familiar precept, 'Write about what you know' more conscientiously," Orville Prescott said of him. And because Auchincloss' knowledge is soundly based and his technique precise and skillful, he has been hailed as a writer "of unusual brilliance" (by James Stern, in the New York *Times*) and is widely regarded as one of the most promising of younger American novelists.

Louis Auchincloss was born in New York City in 1917 to Joseph Howland Auchincloss and the former Priscilla Stanton. He has two brothers, John W. and J. Howland Auchincloss, Jr., and one sister, Priscilla (Mrs. William F. Pedersen). He spent his childhood there and in Bar Harbor, Maine. His Scottish ancestors had come to America early in the nineteenth century and made their fortune in business. Most of the members of his family, he relates, "are brokers, bankers or investment counselors." Following in that solid tradition, Auchincloss attended Groton, then spent three years at Yale, where he edited the *Yale Lit* magazine, was elected to Phi Beta Kappa, and in his sophomore year, wrote his first novel. The novel was rejected by a publisher and Auchincloss, in what he describes as "a fit of discouragement," transferred to the University of Virginia Law School and prepared to become a lawyer. He continued to write, however, and completed another novel. Once again discouraged, he burned the manuscript and "abandoned writing." In 1941 he took his law degree and entered the New York law firm of Sullivan & Cromwell.

Auchincloss' career as an attorney was abruptly halted by the war. He enlisted in the Navy, saw one year of "torpid shore duty" in the Canal Zone and three years of active sea duty with Atlantic and Pacific amphibious forces. He participated in the Normandy invasion in command of an LST. On war duty, Auchincloss recalls, "I did a great deal of reading, more than I had done in school and college combined, and I started writing again." The product of these war years was his first published novel, *The Indifferent Children* (1947), which appeared under the pseudonym of "Andrew Lee." A sharply-drawn portrait of New York "society" during the war years, *The Indifferent Children* was very well received for a first novel.

On his discharge from the service, Auchincloss went back to his law practice. In his evenings and spare time he continued to write—mainly short stories now. These began appearing in the *Atlantic Monthly,* the *New Yorker, Town and Country,* and other magazines, and in 1950 a collection of eight of his stories was published under the title *The Injustice Collectors.* Another novel, *Sybil,* appeared in 1952. By this time Auchincloss had given up his law practice, but, he reported to Lewis Nichols in the New York *Times* in 1953: "[I] haven't altogether given up the idea of going back." It was from the law in fact—from an article on cross-examination in the *Journal of the Bar Association*—that he got his idea for another novel, *A Law for the Lion* (1953), the story of the impact of a divorce trial on a wealthy New York society family.

Auchincloss' characters have been described by the *New Yorker* as "people who have beautiful manners, plenty of money, and a perfectly ghastly time all around." They live in the narrow, remote world of the very rich and the very well bred. As Auchincloss describes them in one of the stories in *The Romantic Egoists*: "They spoke of their parents and their grandparents, who had been far richer than themselves, with affectionate amusement, laughing at the little snobbishnesses of the past as though such things were as quaint and dead today as Brewster town cars and spun sugar for ice cream, but their laughs, it always struck me, had a note of the reverential, their stories a vibrant chord of nostalgia."

Inevitably Auchincloss has been compared to Edith Wharton and to Henry James. But resemblances, though they may be present, are necessarily superficial. Virgilia Peterson has said of Auchincloss in this connection: "Whereas the well bred, fastidious irony of an Edith Wharton fitted the times of which she wrote, this kind of satire applied to our day seems as anachronistic as the society it depicts. For all its merits, it is out of context today and, as such, curiously lacking in passion and in power to move." If Auchincloss suffers in a comparison with such masters, he nevertheless emerges very well from a critical evaluation of his work in its own terms. At thirty-five he was pronounced (by John Barkham in the New York *Times*) "a mature man of letters," and Orville Prescott, though he considers his work "pale, precise," and limited in its appeal, wrote: "There can be no doubt that Louis Auchincloss is a literary artist."

Auchincloss is still practicing law. Since 1953 he has been with the law firm of Hawkins, Delafield and Wood. He finds writing a solitary business ("I love being tied up and busy all day, with things going on all around") and refuses to follow any conventional discipline in going about it—"Writing can't be pushed. If I start out and say, 'I'm going to do a story,' the whole thing gets thrown away at the end of the day." He is unmarried and lives in New York City.

References

Newsweek 43:107 My 17 '54 por
Martindale-Hubbell Law Directory, 1952

AUSTIN, MARGRETTA (STROUP) Sept. 18, 1907- United States Government official

Address: c/o United States Information Service, American Embassy, 41 Grosvenor Sq., London, W. 1., England

When Mrs. Margretta Austin entered the Department of State's Foreign Service Reserve in September 1952, she was given the title of information and cultural officer for women's affairs in the American Embassy in London, with the task of initiating a program to strengthen understanding between British and American women. Earlier she had been employed by the Department of State in assignments relating to public liaison and information, after having served with the American Council on Education and, in the capacity of civilian consultant, with the Department of the Army.

The only daughter of the Reverend Ner Wallace Stroup and Emma (Cartwright) Stroup, Margretta Stroup was born in Cleveland, Ohio, on September 18, 1907. Her father was pastor of the Windermere Methodist Church in East Cleveland; he traced his ancestry to pre-Revolutionary settlers who had moved to America from Holland and Scotland. Through her mother, who was a public speaker active in religious and women's suffrage work, she is also of English and Alsatian descent. One of her brothers, Cranston Leroy Stroup, a writer, is deceased; her other brother, the Reverend Russell Cartwright Stroup, is pastor of the Georgetown Presbyterian Church in Washington, D.C.

She received her precollege education at Miss Harker's School in Palo Alto, California, where she took part in school dramatics and edited the yearbook. She entered Leland Stanford University in 1923 and after four years was graduated with the B.A. degree, the first student majoring in English to participate in the university's newly inaugurated independent study plan. The following year (1928) she

MARGRETTA AUSTIN

enrolled in education and psychology courses at the University of Southern California and several years later (1943) in Cleveland, she undertook further graduate study in adult education at Western Reserve University.

Margretta Stroup's marriage on July 17, 1929, to Allan Stewart Austin, an engineer and business executive of the Austin Company, did much to stimulate her interest in world affairs. During the third year of Russia's first five-year plan, in the spring of 1930, Mrs. Austin went to the U.S.S.R with her husband, who was engaged to supervise the construction of an automobile plant near Nijni Novgorod.

Remaining there for a year and a half she became acquainted with many phases of Russian society, and on her return home she lectured for two years (1932 to 1934) in Ohio and California on her experiences and observations in the Soviet Union. She also wrote articles for *Christian Advocate* and other publications. In "Home Making Around the Globe," which appeared in *American Home* (May 1934), she discussed such matters of domestic interest as marketing and home decoration in Russia. When her husband's work later took the family to England (in 1938), she contributed feature articles on that country to the Cleveland *Plain Dealer*.

While living in Cleveland during the early years of World War II, Mrs. Austin took part in the work of a number of civic organizations, including the Cleveland Community Fund, the Phyllis Wheatley Home, and the Cleveland Board of Child Health Association. Her main occupation from 1941 to 1943 was as director of the office of information and education of the Cuyahoga County council of civil defense.

For six months during 1944 she conducted a survey of civilian women in war work for the War Department in Washington, D.C. In mid-September of that year she became national executive director of Federal Union, Inc., an organization headed by Clarence K. Streit, which proposed world federation of democratic nations.

As staff associate of the American Council on Education from 1946 to 1950, Mrs. Austin was employed on the Commission for International Educational Reconstruction and the Commission on Occupied Areas, working on reconstruction of schools, exchange of students and books in war-devastated areas. She edited news notes and handbooks for the council and in 1950 was co-editor with Harold E. Snyder of reports on conferences dealing with cultural relations with occupied countries.

One of these reports was on the first national conference on occupied nations, which met in Washington in December 1949 under the auspices of the Commission on Occupied Areas in cooperation with the Department of State. Another, dealing with educational progress in Japan and the Ryukyus, covered the May 1950 conference of major non-government agencies, held under the sponsorship of the council's same commission with the cooperation of the Department of the Army. During 1950 in a temporary post of civilian consultant to the Department of the Army, she also made a special survey on the orientation program for Japanese exchangees.

Mrs. Austin joined the Department of State in September 1950 as chief of the conference section of the division of public liaison. In a speech delivered in early 1952 before the Young Presidents Association in New York, she urged businessmen to help inform the American public on international affairs and to combat communism by extending the knowledge of American democracy abroad. She suggested that Americans make it known in foreign countries that "we now have a modified capitalism that has corrected many of the conditions that Marx first started to fight."

Calling attention to the importance of emphasizing the idealistic concept of democracy, she told the business executives, "We must somehow dispel the idea of America as only a materialistic country. Probably no country has ever been motivated by less material forces than those governing our foreign policy today, and yet to most people all we have to offer is material goods" (New York *Times,* February 16, 1952).

"They think of [women] in the United States as ladies of leisure, a Hollywood version of life where we do our housework by pushing buttons and spend our time either buying clothes, in the beauty parlor or at gay cocktail parties," Mrs. Austin said (Cleveland *Plain Dealer Magazine,* July 19, 1953). It is an impression created, she believes, by American movies and comic books, by the idea that all Americans are rich. However, she has observed that British women are eager to learn the facts about our country. "They welcome an opportunity for intelligent cooperation with our women. They realize that English-speaking countries must become friends and have confidence in each other if we are to save the peace for the free world. The Soviets are doing everything possible, missing no chance to pull us apart."

For a brief period beginning in February 1952 Margretta Austin held the post of acting chief of the State Department's group liaison branch and acting assistant chief of the division of public liaison. The following May she was transferred to the international information administration as information officer for public affairs, a position that she filled until becoming in September 1952 a cultural affairs officer in the Foreign Service Reserve.

In her assignment as women's affairs officer at the American Embassy in London, Mrs. Austin introduced a program to better inform British women about the United States. During her first eight months at the Embassy, headed since February 1953 by Ambassador Winthrop W. Aldrich, she had "contacted seventy-three British women's organizations, talked to some 200 prominent women leaders, made many speeches, appeared on TV, traveled through eight countries, [and] written articles for the house organs of British women's groups" (Washington *Post,* August 23, 1953). She had also received calls from Great Britain's twenty-one women members of Parliament and handled a large correspondence in response to requests for information ranging from questions about manners of American children to problems concerning the United Nations.

One British misconception about America which especially bothers Mrs. Austin, and which she is striving to correct in her articles and in her talks, is the idea that ours is a "godless country," devoted to the material at the expense of the spiritual. "I try to tell them about our church life, the devotion of all denominations, and particularly the American woman's support of the church," she said.

The United States cultural envoy holds a number of awards conferred by the Office of Civilian Defense for her contributions during World War II. She was formerly a member of Cleveland's Women's City Club and College Club and of several organizations from which she withdrew when she took up her present assignment in England. Her church is the Presbyterian and she names the Democratic party as her political affiliation.

By her marriage to Allan Stewart Austin, which was terminated by divorce in 1946, Mrs. Margretta Austin has a son, Richard Cartwright Austin who is studying at Swarthmore College, Pennsylvania. Described as a small, slender woman of marked femininity, she has blue eyes and blond hair and stands five feet four and a half inches tall with a weight of 126 pounds. Golf is her favorite sport, while her other recreations are reading and an appreciation of music and art. She also collects antiques.

References

Cleveland Plain Dealer Mag p7+ Jl 19 '53

Washington (D.C.) Post p16 O 18 '52; p12 Ag 23 '53

Department of State Biographic Register (1951) (Suppl., 1953)

AZUMA IV, TOKUHO Japanese dancer

Address: b. c/o Hurok Artists, Inc., 711 Fifth Ave., New York 22; h. 22 Third Chome (street), Akasaka Tamachi, Tokyo, Japan

The Azuma Kabuki Dancers and Musicians, brought from Japan to America by impresario S. Hurok, and presented under the auspices of H.I.H. Prince Takamatsu, brother of the Emperor, and the Japanese Ministry of Foreign Affairs, were one of the highlights of the 1953-54 New York theatrical season. The leader of the troupe, Tokuho Azuma IV is the third successor to the founder of the Azuma School of Kabuki Dance. Her distinguished reputation throughout Japan stems from her great Kabuki forebears and her exacting training at their hands. By virtue of her many new dance creations in the classical style she has brought "fresh artistic sensibility" to Japanese dancing.

This was the first occasion on which a major Japanese classical dance company had performed in the western world. After six weeks on Broadway, the company set out on a world tour, starting with several U.S. cities. Although steeped in Kabuki lore, Azuma does not appear in the Grand Kabuki Theatre since it bars women. However, her troupe includes several men from the Kabuki Theatre, as well as ten dance dramas which are traditional with the Grand Kabuki group.

Kabuki dances are performed by players costumed in magnificent brocades, accompanied by music produced by drums, flutes, bells, gongs, and samisens. They are a synthesis of music, dancing and drama, a symbolic art form, expressing nuances of light and shade, the joys and sorrows of the human soul. Kabuki remains the oldest classical theatre in the world still maintained by a ticket-buying public.

Tokuho Azuma was born in Tokyo, the daughter of the late Uzaemon XV, one of the most revered actors and dancers of the Grand Kabuki Theatre, and the dynastic head of the Ichimura family which traces back to the early days of the Kabuki traditions, some 350 years ago. Her mother, Masaya Fujima, is today one of the greatest Kabuki-style dancers in Japan. Miss Azuma started her training when she was six, under her parents' tutelage, and except for six years in a regular elementary school, all her training has been in dancing. She also received training from Mitsugoro, head of the Bando School of Dancing, and Kikugoro VI, head of the Onoe School. At fourteen she received a diploma from the Fujima School of Kabuki Dancing.

With the death of her father in 1945 Tokuho Azuma inherited the headship of the Azuma School of Kabuki Dancing, becoming Azuma IV. Such inheritance does not occur simply because one is the son or daughter of the Head. The critics and specialists of the Kabuki Dance decide whether son, daughter, adopted child, or protégé is worthy to inherit the headship of such a dancing school.

Firmly grounded in the tradition, she went on to create her own individual style, which, while maintaining the stature of the Kabuki classics,

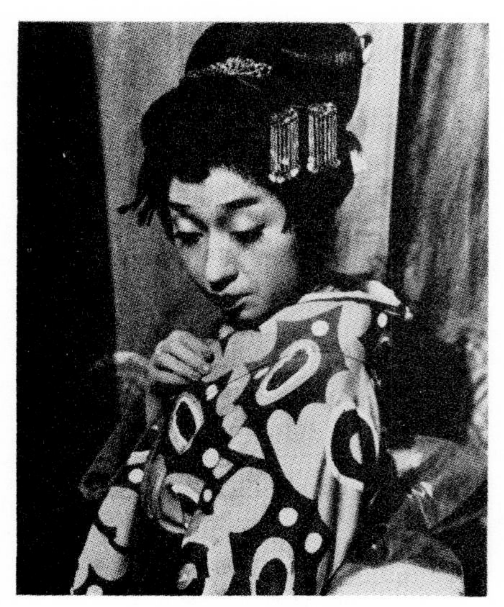

TOKUHO AZUMA IV

added an original element. Encouraged by the plaudits of the critics and experts, she began to form her own groups, the first "Shunto-Kai" (Spring Wisteria Dancing Group), the second with her husband and famous choreographer Masaya Fujima—"Azuma Tokuho Fufu-Kai", (The Tokuho Azuma Husband-Wife Company).

The arrival of Madame Tokuho Azuma and her company of twenty-four at the Century Theatre in New York in February 1954 presented some special problems. They brought four sets weighing twenty-four tons, ten boxes of props, fifteen trunks of costumes, sixty boxes of wigs, four crates of carefully made cypress dancing platforms, (which had to be consecrated) and twelve cases of musical instruments. They also brought a tradition that no shoes should touch their special dancing platforms—which of course included the American stagehands who worked in the theatre, and had to be convinced that they should go about in their stocking feet for four weeks.

The American wardrobe mistress in the theatre also had something to learn, for the Japanese performers refused to use the regular clothes racks provided, and insisted on laying their costumes flat on the floor, which involved a good deal of stooping all evening. Madame Azuma expressed herself as delighted, however, with the cooperation received from their employees and their understanding and appreciation of a different way of doing things. International good will was further aided because on its arrival, the Kabuki troupe presented each member of the backstage crew with a present—while after the opening night impresario Hurok gave each member of the company a crisp, new ten dollar bill. Just a couple of old Oriental customs, on both sides.

New York dance critics while delighted with the Azuma Kabuki dancers, were agreed that here was something very specialized and, to Western eyes and ears, exotic. John Martin wrote in the *Times* of February 19, 1954, "It would be hard to imagine a more completely captivating evening than the one supplied last night. . . . You need know absolutely nothing about Japanese art to enjoy it; all you need is eyes, ears, and a delight in expert theatre performance. It is well also to open your mind and take what you are given on its own terms. In case you have preconceived ideas of what dancing is, be prepared to find no *entrechats* and *tours jetés* here. This dancing is remote from physical virtuosity and is in essence a form of highly stylized acting in terms of movement. It also is inseparable from music, including a fascinating kind of cadenced speech, chanting and actual song, often a loose-jowled falsetto.

"If it is wonderful to listen to it is wonderful to look at. The costumes are both magnificent and subtle. Their colors, the texture of their fabrics, their ornamentation, their extraordinary contours and the way they move are a constant delight. And the stage itself provides a background of great pictorial beauty at all times."

Walter Terry in the N.Y. *Herald-Tribune* of February 19, further warned audiences that they ". . . must not expect to see . . . passages built to smashing climaxes, explicit gesture (except in comedy) or emotional tensions clearly revealed in facial expressions (again, comedy excepted). As a matter of fact it is sometimes difficult to distinguish between fury and bliss. But these differences have compensations, for here is a way of dance, a style of acting in which nuance (of motion and of mood) is exquisitely cherished and in which the element of repose makes possible unhurried savoring of pictorial beauty."

The program includes a charming, formal greeting by the company; a dance by a young lion and an old lion who toss their manes "with delightfully controlled bravura"; a temple scene in which the heroine makes lightning changes of costume before our eyes (symbolizing the life of woman from childhood to old age); a group of folk dances; a dance in which a spider spins a shimmering web; a fragile and "utterly captivating love dance, and a stunning festival scene which, among other things calls upon the services of a drunk, a gracious courtesan, and (with all due respects to Kukla, Fran and Ollie), the greatest dragon I have ever seen."

Faubion Bowers, who was official U.S. Censor of the Japanese theatre during the American occupation, and is the author of *Japanese Theatre*, (Hermitage House, 1952) writing in the *Saturday Review*, February 27, 1954, gave an account of the place of the Kabuki in Japanese life: "The theatrical attitude of the Japanese is different from that of the West. It is an almost compulsory ritual for the family to go together once a year to Kabuki. They may attend either the 'matinee' which lasts from ten in the morning till three in the afternoon, or the 'evening' performance (from four to ten or eleven). If the family is able to afford it, they may spend all day in the theatre—during the intermissions eating in one of the several restaurants . . . shopping for souvenirs . . . or chatting with friends. The several Kabuki theatres of Japan are large and comfortable. The Kabuki-Za, Tokyo, for example, seats around 3,000 people. . . . People casually saunter in and out during performances; lost, wandering children cry for their parents; and nursing babies are fed while their mothers gaze entranced at the onstage spectacle." Audiences feel that applause should be given "at the moment of excellence" instead of at the end. They shout their approval with a variety of phrases, equivalent to "I have waited for this!", or calling the name of their favorite actor.

The Azuma Kabuki Dancers and Musicians which make up the company brought to America were selected from among the masters of this art all over Japan, and they include Kikunojo Onoe, one of the foremost male Kabuki dancers. He has the distinction of having inherited the headship of the Onoe School of Kabuki Dancing from Kikugoro VI, with whom he started training at the age of ten. Kabuki actors are trained to play the parts of young, middle-aged or old men, characters of high or low rank, of heroic or villainous disposition, and women of various stations.

The Grand Kabuki Theatre in Tokyo is traditionally the province of male dancers. However, in the 350 years of its development the Kabuki theatre has at one time or another been entirely performed by women—or by men. The Japanese-American artist and stage designer, Yuji Ito, explained in an article in the New York *Herald Tribune,* February 14, 1954, that "because the Kabuki Theatre is denied to women, the Kabuki dance is open to them, and if a particular woman is excellent enough she may inherit the headship of a Kabuki Dance School from her natural or adopted father" (Thus Azuma IV inherited from her father the headship of the Azuma School of Kabuki Dancing.)

Madame Azuma, who is a Catholic, and her husband Masaya Fujima have a son, Motoyasu Yamada, age twenty-two, who is breaking the tradition, for he wants to be a writer rather than a dancer. Interviewed by a *Current Biography* writer, through an interpreter, Azuma IV, seated with a group of friends on the floor of her dressing room at the Century Theatre, answered all questions readily except one—about her age. The interpreter said: "Azuma says American women don't have to tell age, so she won't either."

References:

Dance 28:14 Mr '53 por
Sat R 37:24+ F 27 '54
Time 63:80 F 22 '54

BACHAUER, GINA May 21, 1913- Pianist
Address: b. c/o National Concert and Artists Corporation, 711 5th Ave., New York 22; h. 41, Highgate West Hill, London, N.6, England

"A truly phenomenal pianist having few peers among pianists of either sex" is the way Madame Gina Bachauer was described by music critic Jerome D. Bohm of the New York *Herald Tribune.* The distinguished Greek pianist by her performance "in the grand tradition of pianists", reported the New York *Times,* "puts herself into the foremost ranks of pianists, male or female." Such critical appreciation was accorded her following her first recital in New York on October 29, 1950. Since then she has toured extensively and has given a concert in New York City each season.

She made her debut in Athens, Greece in 1935 under conductor Dimitri Mitropoulos, her Paris debut in 1937 under Pierre Monteux, and her London debut under Alec Sherman in 1946. During World War II she made her headquarters in Alexandria, Egypt where she gave more than 600 concerts to the Allied forces in the Middle East area.

At her Town Hall recital on February 24, 1954 Madame Bachauer played Bach's *Partita in B Flat* and Liszt's *Sonata in B Minor.* "What a contrast between her Bach and Liszt!" wrote the New York *Times* reviewer. "The Bach was scaled down, seldom rising above a forte. . . . The Liszt was all drama and rhetoric. As an example of bravura playing that never got out of control, and as an example of musical excitement, it represents a school of romantic piano playing that is fast vanishing."

Gina Bachauer was born May 21, 1913 in Athens, Greece. Her parents were Jean Bachauer, a dealer in foreign cars, and Ersilia (Marostica) Bachauer. She has two brothers. She traces her paternal line back 400 years in Austria. Her musical development was fostered, as she herself explains, by the inherent love of music in her entire family.

After her graduation from a secondary school in Athens, she studied with Ariadne Casasis at the Athens Conservatoire where she won the Medaille d'or in 1929. One of her teachers at the Conservatoire was Waldemar Freeman, often a partner in two-piano recitals with Sergei Rachmaninoff. Following her work at the Conservatoire, Gina Bachauer continued her studies in Paris for two years at the École Normale de Musique under its founder, Alfred Cortot. In 1933 she took part in the Vienna Competition for Piano and Song and won the Medaille d'honneur, the highest award.

Gina Bachauer approached Sergei Rachmaninoff in London with a letter of introduction from Waldemar Freeman. Impressed by her playing, the great pianist-composer agreed to give her instruction. Since Rachmaninoff was concertizing widely at that time, Madame Bachauer had to follow him all over Europe for her lessons, studying with him from 1932 to 1935 in London, Paris, Rome, in Switzerland and elsewhere (H. C. Schonberg, New York *Times,* October 10, 1950).

(Continued next page)

GINA BACHAUER

In addition to training her in advanced techniques, Rachmaninoff edited most of her music, not only with the complex fingerings which his insistence on legato, without excessive reliance on the sustaining pedal, demanded, but also with marginal annotation, some of it humorous. As Schonberg notes, "a little round face surrounded by a pair of. . .wings. . .was to remind Miss Bachauer to play like an angel." Another little face wearing glasses, which appeared toward the end of a solo passage, was a reminder for her to glance up at the conductor as a warning not to have the orchestra come in too soon.

The young pianist gave her first major recital in Paris in 1937, and played in concert with the Paris Symphony Orchestra under Pierre Monteux, launching a career which was to take her as recitalist to the principal concert halls and as soloist with the major symphony orchestras in France, Italy, Austria, Yugoslavia, her native Greece, and Egypt.

World War II interrupted her career, and she took refuge in Alexandria where she played to military personnel whose tastes in music often led her far from her accustomed repertoire. She became perforce an adept at "boogie-woogie."

In an effort to resume her concert work, she went to London toward the end of 1945, with little money and few connections. She made her debut in Royal Albert Hall on January 21, 1946, playing the Grieg *Concerto in A Minor* with the New London Symphony conducted by Alec Sherman, and was received most cordially by critics and concert-goers. Since that time Madame Bachauer has played with "all the principal London and provincial orchestras," as the periodical *London Musical Events* puts it, and has given innumerable recitals throughout the British Isles and Eire as well as in Europe and the United States.

After her first recital at Town Hall, in October, 1950 (which, because she was quite unknown to American concert-goers, did not draw a large audience) the artist was immediately booked for a return engagement in 1951. Later in 1951, she appeared as guest soloist with the New York Philharmonic Orchestra under Dimitri Mitropoulos, and during the 1951-1952 season she toured the United States.

Dividing her time, as she does, between Europe and America often makes scheduling a problem. After her second recital in New York (January 1951) for example, she returned at once to England for a six-week tour of Britain in the course of which she played eleven different piano concertos. Then, in April 1951, Madame Bachauer flew back to New York to play in a concert with the New York Philharmonic for the American Greek War Relief Society (May 2, 1951) before returning to Greece and then on tour through Italy, Egypt and France.

The physical stamina which enabled Madame Bachauer to maintain such a pace has reflected itself in her playing. Critics of her New York debut noted that she had chosen an extremely difficult program which she performed with a technique which was "amazing even in these days of extraordinary technical accomplishment." Phrases such as "dizzy velocity," "miracles of virtuosity," "diamond-point sprays of notes," "organ-like sonorities" are typical of her first reviews.

Upon her return recital to a capacity crowd at Town Hall on January 26, 1951, Olin Downes reported as an example of her technical prowess that she "played the *Danse Infernale* [from a transcription of Stravinsky's *Firebird* ballet] as a pianist with twenty hands and contingent fingers—no question about it, a feat of compelling dexterity." Francis D. Perkins of the New York *Herald Tribune* noted Madame Bachauer's "imposing, organ-like mass and sonority . . . technical brilliance and stimulating energy."

This facet of Madame Bachauer's playing has recalled for European critics the memory of the great Teresa Carreño (1853-1917) who was called "The Valkyrie of the Pianoforte." Madame Bachauer has also been praised, however, for "keeping her dynamics down to a minimum, yet getting all the nuance and contrast she desired." Olin Downes observed that in playing Mozart she was capable of "immediately adjusting her scale of sonorities to that of Mozart's style and the tonal capacities of the instrument that Mozart knew," while Francis D. Perkins appreciated "her command of dynamic shadings and the fine gradations of her tone color."

Madame Bachauer has been criticized adversely for speeding up certain passages. But this criticism is generally mingled with expressions of awe at the virtuosity which permits her to play at such a velocity without either loss of clarity by blurring of successive notes, or sacrifice of the basic musical idea to technical display. Her mastery of the piano was expressed in Douglas Watt's review in the *New Yorker* of her January 26, 1951, recital: "It was easy to see from the start that this concert grand was just a kind of complicated toy that she had put in its place long ago."

After her two recitals in Town Hall, Madame Bachauer was heard again in New York with the Philharmonic Symphony Orchestra under Dimitri Mitropoulos in a benefit concert on May 2, 1951, playing the Tchaikovsky *Concerto in B Flat Minor,* her first appearance in this country with an orchestra. The New York *Times* noted that her interpretation of the concerto "was a combination of strength and delicacy." Later in that year Madame Bachauer took part in two more concerts with the Philharmonic.

In her third Town Hall recital, February 6, 1952, Francis D. Perkins of the *Tribune,* who had in January 1951 noted "an occasional sense of premeditation limiting emotional spontaneity," and "that some of the expressive essence of certain works . . . had been incompletely disclosed," now found that "her interpretation suggested a realization of thoroughly thought out expressive intentions." The critic further noted that the artist "again exhibited a remarkable and comprehensive technique, whose display was not the main objective of her performances." Howard Taubman, however, writing in the New York *Times,* observed that this recital which he found to be "the epitome of virtuosity" was "almost feverish in its brilliance . . . her performances were breath-taking but they were also breathless." Taubman reported that in one Scarlatti sonata, the pianist's "hands and fingers moved so rapidly that they almost blurred before the eye, but the notes came out cleanly . . . a performance that caused the blood to tingle."

Madame Bachauer's repertoire, as it has appeared in her American tours, leans toward the brilliantly difficult selections of such as Bach, especially his organ works in concert transcription, Scarlatti, Mozart, Chopin, and Liszt, rather than the "heavier" works of Beethoven or Brahms, although she by no means ignores the more substantial work of the composers in either group. Through her more frequent performance of the brilliant works, reviewers of her recitals have taken note of her technique, her phrasing, and her firm control of dynamics; and critical opinion has been most unanimous in this area. Her less frequent performances of the major works of Brahms and Beethoven have met with mixed criticial judgment and divided opinion.

Her ability to exploit her resources of technique fully was amply demonstrated in her fourth Town Hall recital in as many years on January 23, 1953, when she built her program around the seldom-played, "laborious," as the *Herald Tribune* reviewer phrased it, *Variations and Fugue on a Theme by Bach* by Max Reger. Her performance of this work was called, by the *Times,* "staggering . . . it is hard to imagine it ever played better," while the *Tribune* praised her ability "to embolden (with her dynamo technique) and rejuvenate (with her perfect sense of rhythm and phrase) the intricacies of Reger's work."

Her concert at Town Hall on February 24, 1954 drew varied criticism. The New York *Times* critic commented: "There are many fine pianists before the public, but there are not so many personalities illustrative of the type of artistry where one is always conscious of an original mind, of original ideas, of a keyboard concept idiomatically translated into keyboard practice. Gina Bachauer is one of those personalities. . . . When music requires drama, she has it to spare; when she wants to play the most delicate pianissimo she has it at her command; when a singing line is required, out it sings."

On the other hand, Virgil Thomson wrote of the same concert (at which she played Liszt's *Sonata in B Minor*): "Her piano recital left this listener wondering how so fine a musician could make such ugly sounds . . . the performance could be fairly described, I think, as grand but not beautiful" (New York *Herald Tribune,* February 25, 1954).

The pianist was awarded the Order of the Golden Phoenix (1949) and, in 1950, the Order of the Taxiarchos (Order of St. Michael) which was conferred upon the pianist by H.M. the King of the Hellenes, King Paul of Greece. Madame Bachauer is a member of the Arts Theatre Club of Great Britain. She records for H.M.V. (British branch of RCA Victor) and has recorded on 78 r.p.m. records *Les Funérailles* and the *Hungarian Rhapsody No. 12 in C Sharp Minor* (rev. Saint-Saëns) of Liszt, and the *Toccata, Adagio, and Fugue in C Major* of Bach (arr. Busoni).

In July 1952 Victor released in the United States her performance of the Liszt *Rhapsodie Espagnole* (as arranged for piano and orchestra by Busoni) and Mozart's "Coronation" *Concerto No. 26* on a long-playing record with the New London Symphony conducted by Alec Sherman. This recording was reviewed by Irving Kolodin in the *Saturday Review* who remarked that those who like both works equally would prefer Madame Bachauer's playing of the Liszt to her playing of the Mozart. He found the Mozart "amply spirited but percussive in articulation."

On November 21, 1951, Madame Bachauer married Alec Sherman who had conducted the New London Orchestra when she made her British debut with that organization in 1946. The marriage, Madame Bachauer's second, took place in New York City. The best man was Spyros P. Skouras, president of Twentieth-Century Fox, one of the leading figures in the Greek community in the United States.

The pianist is a brown-eyed brunette, is five feet six inches tall. James Lyons in *Musical America* (February 1, 1954) describes her as "nimble," "redoubtable," with an "irrepressibly sunny spirit." She lists her hobbies as swimming, reading, cooking, and floral decoration. Her taste in music is catholic and she is very interested in contemporary composers, reports *London Musical Events,* but she confesses that for pleasure she prefers to play Bach.

References

Mus Am 71:13 My '51 por; 74:8+ F 1 '54 pors
Newsweek 37:78 F 5 '51 por
Time 57:38 F 5 '51 por

BACKSTRAND, C(LIFFORD) J(ULIUS) July 21, 1897- Business executive

Address: b. c/o Armstrong Cork Company, Lancaster, Pa.; h. 1267 Wheatland Ave., Lancaster, Pa.

Associated with the Armstrong Cork Company for thirty-three years, C. J. Backstrand now serves as president of the firm. He went to work as a student salesman for Armstrong in 1921 and moved steadily up to the presidency of the ninety-four-year-old business whose total assets at the end of 1952 were over $136,000,000. Backstrand is active in civic and educational affairs both locally and nationally, and has served on several committees of the National Association of Manufacturers.

Clifford J. Backstrand was born on July 21, 1897 in Los Angeles, California, to John Ferdinand and Christine (Scott) Backstrand. The family moved to Riverside, California, where young Backstrand attended grammar school and was graduated from the Riverside Polytechnic High School in 1916. His college education at Pomona College, Claremont, California, was interrupted by a year's service in the infantry during World War I; in 1918 he attended Officers' Training School at Plattsburg, New York and Camp Pike, Arkansas. Returning to Pomona College after the war, he was graduated with an A.B. degree in 1920. He spent a year at the University of Pennsylvania and obtained the degree of Bachelor of Science in the field of economics.

Backstrand entered the service of the Armstrong Cork Company on July 6, 1921 as a student salesman in the floor division in Lancaster, Pennsylvania. He became a full-fledged salesman the following year and district manager of the floor division in San Francisco in September 1922. Returning to Lancaster in April 1927, he was appointed assistant sales manager of the floor division. Promoted to assistant general sales manager in 1929 and to general sales manager in 1930, he became general manager of the floor division in 1933 and held that position until 1942.

C. J. BACKSTRAND

In 1935 Backstrand became a director of the Armstrong Cork Company. Three years later he was made a vice-president of the company, and in October 1942 assumed the title of vice-president attached to the president's office. One year later he took on the additional duties of vice-president in charge of manufacture. *Time* magazine has said that he was "largely responsible for boosting the company's war production from $500,000 in 1941 to $39,000,000 in 1944."

Relinquishing his duties as director of manufacturing operations in September 1944, Backstrand worked directly with the president's office in the administration of the company's general affairs. The following year he was named first vice-president, and on April 26, 1950 became president, succeeding Henning Webb Prentis, Jr., who was elected chairman of the board of directors.

The company which Backstrand heads was founded in 1860 in Pittsburgh, Pennsylvania by John D. Glass and Thomas S. Armstrong, who cut bottle corks by hand. This enterprise now produces linoleum, asphalt tile, rubber tile, felt-base floorings, installation sundries and accessories for floorings, wall coverings, corks, corkboard insulation, cork pipe covering, cork composition, textile roll covers, acoustical materials, insulating fire brick, and numerous other specialities. The company is described as "a group of widely diversified businesses" related to each other because either the product is made from cork, serves the same purpose as one made of cork, or helps the marketing of other company products. Its annual research budget is over $1,500,000.

Eighteen plants in the United States employ 13,000 workers, and over 3,000 more are employed in manufacturing and sales activities abroad. Foreign manufacture is carried on at nine plants in Spain, one at Casablanca in French Morocco, and through subsidiaries in England, Canada, France, Portugal, Algeria, and South Africa. A financial report issued by the company in December 1952 showed total net sales for the year amounting to $202,373,467, and total assets of $136,526,755 as of December 31, 1952.

In a "President's Letter" issued in 1953, Backstrand stated that the company planned to pay particular attention to "growth products," defined as "those for which expanding sales opportunities exist in the sharply increasing replacement and modernization market in residential, commercial and institutional building; and products designed to contribute to the advancement of efficient industrial operations and higher living standards generally."

Backstrand's advancement to the presidency of Armstrong is typical of the careers of the firm's executives. A report issued to the stockholders states: "The management of the Company is today, as it has always been, composed of men who have grown up with it." The average record of employment of the principal merchandising and production heads is twenty-four years, and the officers, with few exceptions, have "served for the duration of their business lives." Backstrand is the company's fifth president since its inception ninety-four years ago.

The company supplements the old-age benefits provided by the Federal Social Security Act with a pension plan for its employees, the company contributing about 75 per cent of the money and the employees about 25 per cent. Nearly 1,000 retired employees are receiving pensions.

The Armstrong Company under Backstrand's presidency has utilized television as an advertising medium for its products. On June 6, 1950 the Armstrong Circle Theatre weekly program was inaugurated on the National Broadcasting Company TV network. It presents realistic dramas "of interest to all the family," and has won a faithful nation-wide audience. It has used original scripts by more than fifty new writers.

The executive is also on the board of directors of the Hamilton Watch Company (since 1945) and the Bell Telephone Company of Pennsylvania (since 1953). His educational activities include a directorship of the Wharton School Alumni Association of the University of Pennsylvania, membership on the board of trustees of the Thaddeus Stevens Trade School of Lancaster, on the general committee of the University of Pennsylvania development fund, and of the Pomona College Associates.

He has been a member of the Pennsylvania State Chamber of Commerce committee on basing point price system and of the management advisory committee of the Business Management Services of Community College of Temple University. A member of the National Association of Manufacturers, he served on the committee on distribution in 1949 and the committee on industrial problems in 1951. He was appointed to the board of trustees of the executive committee of the National Security Industrial Association in 1951. Backstrand was the head of the linoleum unit, floor covering and upholstery section of the textile branch of the War Production Board during World War II.

A civic leader in Lancaster, Pennsylvania, Backstrand is president of the board of directors of the Lancaster Free Public Library, a member of the finance committee of the Lancaster county branch of the Pennsylvania Economy League, Inc., and a member of the committee on manufacturing of the Manufacturers' Association of Lancaster. From 1939 to 1942 he was a director of the Lancaster Chamber of Commerce.

He served as director of the Welfare Federation of Lancaster county in 1942, as alternate control officer of the county's defense council, and as a group leader of the Police Reserve. For the past three years he was chairman of the Christian committee of Lancaster's United Jewish Appeal. Organizations in which he holds membership are the Free and Accepted Masons, Phi Beta Kappa, Phi Gamma Delta fraternity, Newcomen Society of England, Pennsylvania Society, Cliosophic Society, the Lancaster County Historical Society, and Historical Society of Pennsylvania.

In 1952, Backstrand received the honorary LL.D. degree from Elizabethtown (Pennsylvania) College and the honorary D.C.S. degree from Franklin and Marshall College.

He was married to Edris Powlison in 1922. They were divorced in 1935. By this marriage he has a daughter, Barbara, now Mrs. H. Alvin Pentoney, Jr. On September 8, 1939 Backstrand married Virginia Parks Biggers. He has served as a vestryman of the St. James' Episcopal Church of Lancaster. His political affiliation is Republican. He holds memberships in the Hamilton, Lancaster Country, Fortnightly, and University clubs.

Backstrand, who has been characterized as a "driver and organizer," finds relaxation in golf, riding and big game hunting.

References

Business Executives of America (1950)
Who's Who in America, 1952-53
Who's Who in Commerce and Industry (1953)

BACON, LEONARD May 26, 1887-Jan. 1, 1954 Poet, author; graduated from Yale University; taught English at University of California (1910-1917, 1919-1923); won 1941 Pulitzer Prize for poetry for *Sunderland Capture* (1940); elected to American Academy of Arts and Letters (1951); other works include *Ulug Beg* (1923), *Ph. D.s* (1925), *Animula Vagula* (1926); *Lost Buffalo* (1930); *The Voyage of Autoleon* (1930); *Rhyme and Punishment* (1930); *Drama and Action* (Life of French poet Rimbaud, 1934); *The Goose on the Capitol* (1936); *Semi-Centennial* (1939); *Bullinger Bound* (1938) and *Day of Fire* (1943); *Atlantic Monthly* published his verse and political essays. See *Current Biography*, (June) 1941.

Obituary

N Y Times p12 Ja 2 '54

BAILEY, CONSUELO NORTHROP Oct. 10, 1899- Speaker of Vermont House of Representatives; government official; lawyer

Address: b. 203 Main St., Burlington, Vt.; h. 1317 Spear St., South Burlington, Vt.

"Mrs. Speaker of the House," as Mrs. Consuelo Northrop Bailey is known in the Vermont legislature, was elected to this post in January 1953, thus becoming the second woman in the history of the United States to preside over a state legislature. "The woman's touch" is evident in the Vermont Assembly now; there are two women in the Senate and fifty-two in the 246-member House. Corsages are given to women legislators on their birthdays. To her five men opponents, whom she defeated for the post of speaker, Mrs. Bailey awarded committee chairmanships in the House, and declared that she was getting "excellent cooperation" from them (New York *Times*, February 1, 1953).

President Dwight D. Eisenhower nominated Mrs. Bailey the only woman member of the

CONSUELO NORTHROP BAILEY

newly created U.S. Post Office Advisory Board, to serve without pay, and her nomination was confirmed by the Senate Post Office and Civil Service Committee on July 7, 1953. In September 1954 Mrs. Bailey received the Republican candidacy for lieutenant governor of Vermont.

A member of the Republican National Committee since 1936, she became vice-chairman of this committee in 1952. Mrs. Bailey was elected to the Vermont General Assembly in 1950 as representative from South Burlington, and re-elected in 1952. This made her the fourth member of her family to occupy the same seat in the state's House of Representatives, which was held by her father in 1902. In 1933 she became the first Vermont woman admitted to practice before the United States Supreme Court, and in 1942 before the United States Customs Court.

Consuelo Northrop was born in Fairfield, Vermont, on October 10, 1899, the daughter of Peter Bent Brigham and Katherine E. (Fletcher) Northrop. Her paternal ancestors were among the earliest settlers of the town and have tilled its soil for four generations. She says: "I became interested in law at an early age because my father had studied law, although he never took the bar examinations" and never practiced "because of ill health."

Reared in Fairfield, Vermont, Consuelo attended grade school in Sheldon and high school in St. Albans. Her extracurricular activities included basketball and debating. After graduating from high school in 1917, with honors, she entered the University of Vermont, majoring in law. In college, she was a member of the Sigma Gamma glee club, the dramatic club and the basketball team. She received her Ph.B. degree from the university in 1921 and was elected to Phi Beta Kappa.

Following her graduation from college, Miss Northrop taught Latin and history at Shelburne High School, Shelburne, Vermont for one year. Her ambition for a law career then took her to Boston University Law School, from which she received an LL.B. degree in 1925. Her first position after passing the bar examinations was a political appointment as the first woman city prosecutor for Burlington, Vermont, which she retained until February 1927.

She was elected state's attorney for Chittenden County in 1926 and was re-elected in 1928, serving until 1931. "I enjoyed being state's attorney more than anything else I have ever done," she says. In this post, during November 1926, she became the first woman lawyer in Vermont to try a murder case, in which a life imprisonment term was assigned to the slayer of a customs officer.

Consuelo Northrop was admitted to legal practice in the Vermont Supreme Court in January 1926, and in the U.S. District Court in March 1927. She was elected state senator for Chittenden County in 1930. While in this post until 1933, she was chairman of the minor courts committee, clerk of the highway traffic committee, and member of the judiciary, state institutions and federal relations committees. Concurrently, she gained additional knowledge of law as secretary from 1931 to 1937 to former U.S. Senator Ernest Willard Gibson. Her admission to practice law before the nation's Supreme Court came in March 1933.

The Vermonter holds fourth seniority rank among her sex in the Republican National Committee. She has been very active in the organization since she joined in 1936, and is the longest serving member from the New England states. The only Vermont woman ever twice elected a delegate to the Republican National Convention, she attended the conventions at Cleveland, Ohio, in 1936 and at Chicago, Illinois, in 1944.

Her other important services included being on the final drafting committee of the National Republican platform in 1944, on the arrangements committee of the Republican National Convention at Philadelphia in 1948, and on the social security legislation committee as chairman from 1948 to 1950. She was the leader of the Thomas E. Dewey-for-president movement in Vermont in 1948.

Elected South Burlington's representative to the Vermont General Assembly in 1950, she was re-elected in 1952. In this post, she served on the House of Representatives rules, aviation and judiciary committees, acting as clerk of the latter. The Vermont House, which is notable for its membership of more than fifty women, gave her strong support.

In her efforts to advance the interests of the Republican National Committee, Mrs. Bailey filled nearly 400 speaking engagements throughout the South, East and West of the United States. Her election as vice-chairman of the committee came in Chicago on July 12, 1952, making her the second New England woman to hold this post.

She reiterated General Eisenhower's statement that "one of the best ways to achieve peace was to keep hope alive in the breasts of those behind the Iron Curtain, convince them that we believe in our own form of government, and maintain trade with free European nations. . . ." (New York *Times*, August 29, 1952). For a brief period in April 1953, she served as chairman of the Republican National Committee, during the election of a new chairman in Washington, D.C.

In her campaign for the speakership of the Vermont House of Representatives in 1952, Mrs. Bailey states that she traveled a little over 4,700 miles, convinced that ringing doorbells in person was the best way to get votes. Her election followed on January 7, 1953, and she became the second woman speaker in a state legislature. (The first was Minnie B. Craig in North Dakota in 1933).

Mrs. Bailey first presided as speaker of the House during the forty-second biennial session of the Vermont General Assembly, when approximately 400 bills were offered. These included a proposal for the largest budget ever suggested by the state.

She announced her candidacy on January 16, 1954 for the Republican nomination of lieutenant governor of Vermont, to oppose former Governor Harold J. Arthur in the September 1954 primary election. In the spring of 1954, she flew to Arizona to address members of the American Association of University Women at Phoenix and at Chandler. She also spoke over the Mutual Broadcasting System coast to coast radio network during a forum conducted by the "Sounding Board" program on March 28, 1954 and on several television programs.

The woman lawyer is the author of *Digest of Primary and Election Laws of Vermont* (1928). From the University of Vermont she received an honorary LL.D. degree in 1952, "the only woman in 161 years, other than Grace Coolidge," awarded this degree by the university (*Independent Woman*, June, 1953). She is director of the Vermont Association of the Blind, and the founder and first president of the Burlington, Vermont, section of Zonta International. Her other organization memberships include the Vermont Bar Association, Champlain Valley Grange, Sigma Gamma, Phi Sigma Pi (honorary debating), and Kappa Beta Pi (international legal). She is on the Vermont State Civil Defense Board and is an ex-officio member of the Republican State Committee. Her church affiliation is Episcopalian.

Consuelo Northrop married Henry Albon Bailey, a Burlington, Vermont attorney, on September 2, 1940. She is five feet five inches tall, weighs 145 pounds, and has blue eyes and brown hair. She often wears blue-colored rimmed glasses and earrings to match. Outside of her political activities, she is the owner and joint operator of the family farm at Fairfield, Vermont. She enjoys gardening, horseback riding and collecting blue and white Bennington china. Vermonters are asking: "Will she one day become governor?" (Rutland *Daily Herald*, January 12, 1953). She herself says: "I am very busy."

References

N Y Herald Tribune p63 Ap 26 '53
Scholastic 62:16 My 6 '53
Who's Who in America, 1954-55

BAIRD, BIL Aug. 15, 1904- Puppeteer
Address: b. and h. c/o Bil Baird Marionettes, 334 W. 70th St., New York 23

BAIRD, CORA Jan. 26, 1912- Puppeteer
Address: b. and h. c/o Bil Baird Marionettes, 334 W. 70th St., New York 23

During the past four years Bil and Cora Baird's puppets have been delighting millions of television viewers all over the United States, not only as features on the Columbia Broadcasting System, but also as guest performers on many other network shows. For more than a decade before, this husband and wife team had been showing their puppets on the stage, in movie houses and night clubs, and in educational and commercial films.

Critic John Crosby of the New York *Herald Tribune* has called their creations "probably the most ingenious puppets to be seen anywhere on television" while the New York *Times'* critic Jack Gould wrote of one show: "To the viewer there was a sense of maturist theatre, not just a toy-like approximation." While the Baird puppets are tremendously popular among children, they also fascinate adults, and today much of the Baird fan mail comes from grown-ups. "People used to seem ashamed to like puppets, but there aren't so many apologies today," Bil Baird has said.

The Bairds have used hundreds of puppets in various shows, but some characters are favorites and appear again and again—such as Snarky Parker, the master of ceremonies; Heathcliff, the talking horse; "J.P.", the young boy with whom children identify themselves; The Spider Lady who casts spells with the words "Elia Kazan!"; Groovy, a rabbit disk jocky; and Bubbles La Rue, a dancing puppet. Of these marionette characterizations, Bil Baird has stated: "We're not trying to imitate people, but to burlesque, satirize, and interpret them" (*Collier's*, August 2, 1952).

William Britton Baird was born in Grand Island, Nebraska on August 15, 1904 and his first puppet was made for him when he was seven by his father, William Hull Baird. The elder Baird was a chemical engineer and general superintendent of the American Beet Sugar Company, and a pioneer in motion picture training films. His mother was the former Louise Hetzel.

Young Baird was fascinated with his puppet, and by the time he was in high school in Mason City, Iowa, he had built a stage in his attic. Using an old auto dashboard for a switchboard, he gave puppet performances of *Treasure Island*. At the State University of Iowa he painted sets for the university players, and was art editor of *Frivol*, the humorous magazine. While playing with a dance band, he also put on puppet shows during intermissions.

After his graduation in 1926, Baird entered the Chicago Academy of Fine Arts where he specialized in stage designing. It was here that he lost the second "l" of his first name and became "Bil" in order to become a member of the Crowned Radish Club which insisted that all members have first names with only three

CBS-TV

BIL AND CORA BAIRD

letters. During this period, he designed sets for Eleanor E. Freer's opera, *Chilkoot Maiden,* which was produced in Chicago, and thereby made enough money to go to France where he often played jazz on his accordion for small-town audiences.

Back in America, Baird went to work for Tony Sarg, the puppeteer, with whom he was associated for five years. At one time he took Sarg's *Ali Baba and the Forty Thieves* on the road for forty weeks of one-night stands, and on returning remarked plaintively, "I never knew there were so many trains in America leaving at five o'clock in the morning." While with Sarg he also worked on many of the gigantic balloons used in the R. H. Macy and Company's Thanksgiving Day parades.

At the Century of Progress Exposition in Chicago (1933 to 1934), Bil Baird put on a show for Swift and Company in which Brooksie, a puppet cow, appeared in seventy shows a day, for a total of 4,500 performances.

By now an experienced puppeteer, Baird branched out on his own in 1935 with a traveling truck puppet outfit. He did commercial shows for such clients as the Shell Oil Company, the Philadelphia *Bulletin* and the Atlantic Refining Company.

When Orson Welles produced Marlowe's *Dr. Faustus* for the WPA Federal Theatre Project in 1936, he commissioned Baird to make puppets to represent the seven deadly sins. Cora Burlar, a young actress who had once been refused a part because she looked too much like Katharine Cornell, was assigned to speak the parts of the puppets Envy, Gluttony and Sloth, and very soon thereafter, she recalls, "I began to notice that the puppets on the *College Humor* magazine covers Bil was doing, were beginning to look like me, slanty eyes, long legs and all." They were married in 1937 and since then, all the characters in their puppet world have been joint creations.

Cora Eisenberg was born on January 26, 1912 in Manhattan, the daughter of Morris and Anne (Burlar) Eisenberg. Her father owned a candy store and some movie houses. After a year at Hunter College in New York, Cora took her mother's maiden name and made her start in the theatre as Cora Burlar. She did small parts in Eva Le Gallienne's Civic Repertory Theatre and in the Neighborhood Playhouse, and she appeared in such productions as *Noah, Valley Forge* and *Winterset.*

Soon after they were married, the Bairds acquired an old carriage house near the Hudson River in New York City which, according to legend, had been an alcohol cutting plant for the Dutch Schultz mob during the Prohibition era. They soon transformed the place into a combination of workshop, warehouse and home, and named it "Fire Horse Manor."

Recently they acquired an adjacent building for part of the puppet population, stage sets and props which they keep on hand. Many of the puppets, stored in numbered boxes, are found via a card index.

While puppets for a television show or commercial film may have to be produced quickly, many Baird puppets grow slowly over the years, and the workshop on the ground floor is filled with heads, arms, legs, and bodies of puppets which are not yet just exactly what the Bairds think they should be. Until a character is fully developed, they do not put it into a show. Bil Baird has said that they use Charles Darwin's *The Expression of the Emotions in Man and Animals* as a textbook for their use of pantomime with the marionettes.

Today the Bairds have a staff of artists, sculptors and technicians, but in the early days they carved, painted and dressed all their puppets, built their scenery, wrote scripts, and composed (and often played) their own music. According to Cora Baird, "Bil fell into this work because it combined all the things he liked—sculpture, dance, music, painting and the theatre."

The Baird puppets are made out of almost everything. Baird once bought four grand pianos for two dollars each, and reported later: "It's amazing how much hard wire you will find in four grand pianos." One drawer in his workshop is labeled "Priceless Junk".

Although their puppets had been seen in Radio City Music Hall and the Roxy Theatre in New York, the Bairds received a new kind of success in 1943 when they played in such night clubs as Le Ruban Bleu, the Persian Room, and the Cotillion Room—and on the stage in the *Ziegfeld Follies.* During the war they made two educational puppet films for the Office of the Coordinator of Inter-American Affairs, *Gardening is Fun* and *A Boy and His Cow.* In *Flahooley,* a musical show which opened in 1951, the Baird puppets replaced the human ballet, and in all, thirty-three of the singing, dancing and talking performers were puppets.

The Bairds have appeared for the last four years as guests on over 150 television shows, including Ed Sullivan's *Toast of the Town,* and *Your Show of Shows.* In 1950 their own television show, *Life with Snarky Parker,* began and ran on the CBS network for forty-eight weeks. Then came the *Whistling Wizard,* a show which ran for forty weeks in 1951 and 1952, and the *Bil Baird Show* which ran for thirteen weeks in 1953.

Bil and Cora Baird have made two educational films with their marionettes for the Bell Telephone Company: *Telezonia* and *Party Lines.* Bil Baird wrote the article on marionettes in the *Britannica Junior; the Boys' and Girls' Encyclopædia* (1947).

The Bairds have a three-year-old adopted son, Peter Britton Baird. Cora Baird has brown eyes, brown hair and weighs 130 pounds. Her husband has blue eyes, brown hair and weighs 150 pounds. In their home, they have paintings by such artists as Fletcher Martin, Julio de Diego and Ethel Magafan, and a collection of rare musical instruments.

References

Am Artist 16:44+ S '52 pors
Christian Sci Mon Mag p10+ D 4 '43
Collier's 130:32+ Ag 2 '52 pors
Cue 22:17 D 19 '53 pors
Dance 27:36+ D '53 pors
N Y Herald Tribune IV p7 My 4 '52
N Y Times II p9 Jl 13 '52
N Y World-Telegram p5 Ja 23 '43
Sat Eve Post 216:24+ S 18 '43 por

BAKER, LOUISE May 18, 1909- Author

Address: b. c/o McGraw-Hill Book Co., Inc., 330 W. 42nd St., New York 36; b. and h. 2733 Sheridan Blvd., Lincoln, Neb.

Reprinted from the *Wilson Library Bulletin,* Mar. 1954

Because Louise Baker learned at the age of eight how to triumph over an above-the-knee amputation, she has won success for herself in several fields. Her wise parents (Adrial and Anna Hersey Maxwell) allowed her to roller skate on her one leg, aided only by an occasional push of her crutches. This admitted her to her neighborhood "gang" and never after—in school, college, home, or business—did she hesitate to attempt anything she wanted to do.

Louise Maxwell was born May 18, 1909, in the southern California town of Upland, and although she has lived in many parts of the country, she still feels the Pacific Coast is her "heart's home." In that small community everyone took her and her handicap for granted, but when her family moved to Los Angeles and she entered Roosevelt High School with its 4,000 students, she suffered the teen-age torture of being "different." However, her friendly fearlessness and executive ability brought her social success. She was made president of the Girls' League, vice-president of the student body, and editor of the school paper and school annual. In her senior year, she was chosen Ephebian—a city-wide Los Angeles high school society. At Pomona College, Claremont, California, she became president of women students, editor of the college daily and of *Manuscript,* a college literary magazine.

LOUISE BAKER

She worked summers as a camp counselor. Besides playing tennis expertly, she made the college swimming, riding, and archery teams, and belonged to Mortar Board and Alpha Delta Mu (journalism honorary). She majored in English and sociology, and received her B.A. degree in 1930. In 1936 she did postgraduate work at Columbia University School of Business, taking secretarial and advertising courses.

"How did I begin to write? . . . Well, I won $3 in an essay contest when I was nine . . . and thought 'What an easy way to make money!' "

Beginning in 1939 with short stories and articles, of which she has sold more than a hundred to top publications, she went on into full-length books, and had the exciting experience of seeing the very first, *Party Line* (1945), zoom into a national best seller and be made into a motion picture. The New York *Times* found it "a heart-warming book full of chuckles and human nature. . . . Several scenes of tragedy and pathos are excellent bits of writing . . . a friendly, candid portrayal of a period in American history."

The following year, Mrs. Baker's publisher—McGraw-Hill—persuaded her to put her own story into a book, and in *Out on a Limb* (1946) she gives an inspiring account of overcoming her handicap and achieving a full, happy, well rounded life. Virginia Kirkus wrote: "This is a humorous . . . approach to a loss which was only physically crippling. The book should have much to hearten amputees." This prophecy was fulfilled, 50 to 100 letters a day pouring in from handicapped persons or their relatives, as condensations appeared in *Cosmopolitan, Omnibook,* and the pocketbook edition of *This is America.* Although called to Hollywood to help write the script for Paramount for the movie made from *Party Line,* and offered a well-paid position there, she felt that her opportunity for real service lay in another opening—with the National Society for Crippled Children (Easter

BAKER, LOUISE—*Continued*

Seals)—and in touring the country to speak on the importance of accepting crippled persons as normal members of society.

Soon after college graduation, Mrs. Baker had taught in two boys' boarding schools, and from this experience and camp counselor days came her third book, *Snips and Snails* (1952), bought by M-G-M. Fanny Butcher of the Chicago *Tribune* commented: "That a book so hilarious . . . can be so touching and also tacitly so vivid an indictment of parents who just don't want to be bothered by their young, is due to Louise Baker's skill and her sense of fun (she certainly knows what little boys are made of)." This was a Family Reading Club choice, and her two earlier books were selections of the Peoples' Book Club.

Sandwiched in with her writing, Mrs. Baker has held other jobs: publicity agent—"Wings of a Century" for the Chicago World's Fair; instructor at Antioch College, concurrently with being assistant to a director and editor of Fels Research Institute, Yellow Springs, Ohio, on a child development study. Her first marriage was to Ramsay L. Harris, a professor at Pomona College, in 1931; her second was to Cecil Sherman Baker, Jr., a writer, in 1939. After this marriage was terminated she married Howard S. Wilson, president of Bankers Insurance Company of Lincoln, Nebraska, in 1952. Mrs. Baker keeps up her service activities as a board member of Child Guidance Center and the Humane Society in Lincoln; as a director of Antioch College; and consultant to the National Society for Crippled Children.

She wears her crutches gaily, with a pair to match each costume. Blue-eyed, with gray-brown hair, a slim figure (5 feet 3 inches tall, and weighing 105 pounds) and sparkling vitality, she makes an attractive appearance. Fond of sports and travel in this and other countries, her favorite recreation is reading, her tastes ranging from Jane Austen to Thurber and Freud. She belongs to the Authors' League, Screen Writers' Guild, and Midland Authors; also to the Lincoln Country Club, University Club, and Fortnightly Club. In politics she is nonpartisan; in religion, Congregational.

References

Time 48:86+ N 4 '46

Baker, L. Out on a Limb (1946)
Lotz, P. H. (ed.) Unused Alibis (1951)
Warfel, H. R. American Novelists of Today (1951)

BALANCHINE, GEORGE (băl'ăn-chīn)
Jan. 9, 1904- Choreographer

Address: b. c/o School of American Ballet, Inc., 637 Madison Ave., New York 22

NOTE: This biography supersedes the article which appeared in *Current Biography* in 1942.

The artistic director of the New York City Ballet Company is George Balanchine, who has been called "the finest choreographer of our time," and is regarded as "the creative genius of the company." He has composed more than eighty ballets which are to be seen in the repertoire of almost every top-ranking ballet company, and particularly in the one with which he is associated, which has "enticed record-breaking numbers of watchers into theatres on two continents."

The choreographer who has been praised for "the lyric grace of his inventions, the cool classicism of his abstract design," has also been noted for his versatility. He has choreographed ballets for operas, musical comedies and motion pictures.

In an interview some years ago, Balanchine stated: "America becomes the new home for ballet." That this is so is largely due to his own artistic contributions, made during the last two decades. With Lincoln Kirstein and others, he founded the School of American Ballet in 1934 from which many of the leading contemporary American dancers were graduated. His book, *Balanchine's Complete Stories of the Great Ballets,* was published in March 1954 by Doubleday & Company.

Georgi Melitonovitch Balanchivadze was born on January 9, 1904, in what was then Saint Petersburg, Russia. His father, Meliton Balanchivadze, was a recognized composer. His mother, Maria (Vassiliev) Balanchivadze, had hoped that her son would enter the military profession, but one day when she happened to be visiting the Imperial Ballet School, a governor of the school suggested that she try to enter her son as a student. She did, and in 1914 he was accepted.

Like other students, young Georgi was fed, housed, dressed, and educated at the expense of the Czar. In addition to school studies, instruction in the Russian Orthodox religion, and music and fencing lessons, the boy received a thorough training in ballet, which included participation in the performances presented at the Mariinsky Theatre. He also appeared at the Alexandrinsky and Mikhailovsky Imperial theatres.

With the overthrow of the czarist regime in 1917, the Imperial Ballet School was closed down. Georgi worked as a bank messenger and a saddler's apprentice, and at nights played the piano for silent films in nearby movie houses. When Anatoli Lunacharski, a writer and ballet enthusiast, was appointed Commissar for Education, the ballet organization was adopted by the new regime and continued to function much as it always had.

Georgi was graduated in 1921 from what had become the Academy of Opera and Ballet, and while still dancing with the state ballet company, he continued his studies at the Conservatory of Music. In 1924 he became a member of a small company which, under the title of Soviet State Dancers, was being sent to Europe on a tour.

The troupe played in Germany and in England during the summer, and then received a telegram from the Soviet government to return at once or be punished. Balanchine later said (*Time,* January 25, 1954), "If we went back, we would be punished anyhow—no food."

He did not go back, but instead went with the troupe to Paris, where Sergei Diaghilev was presenting his Ballet Russe. Diaghilev took Georgi into his company and changed his name to Balanchine. The slight build of the young dancer was not in his favor as a performer, but Diaghilev was quick to recognize his choreographic talent and to use it. Balanchine remained with Diaghilev until the latter's death in 1929, when the company was dissolved.

Among the ballets Balanchine had choreographed up to this time were *Enigma, La Chatte,* and *Apollon Musagète (Apollo).* Of the last-mentioned, Lincoln Kirstein later wrote: "[it] is a work of capital historical importance in the arts of the first half of the twentieth century . . . it demonstrated that tradition is not merely an anchorage to which one returns after eccentric divagations, but the very floor which supports the artist. . . ." (*Theatre Arts,* November 1947).

In 1929 Balanchine went to London where he staged the dances for Cole Porter's production, *Wake Up and Dream.* He became *maître de ballet* of the Royal Danish Ballet at the Royal Theatre in Copenhagen in 1930 where he staged some half dozen ballets. Two years later, he assisted in the organization of the Ballet Russe de Monte Carlo, a derivative of the original Diaghilev company. Among the ballets he composed during this period were *Cotillon* and *La Concurrence,* the latter especially for ballerina Tamara Toumanova. He presented his own company, Les Ballets 1933, in Paris.

Lincoln Kirstein, a wealthy ballet enthusiast, believed that an American ballet company should be founded. He and his associates invited Balanchine to come to the United States in 1933 as the artistic director of the enterprise. The first step taken was the founding of the School of American Ballet in January 1934, and in due time Balanchine-trained dancers were appearing in Balanchine-composed ballets in a variety of companies, both in the United States and abroad.

Balanchine was associated with the Metropolitan Opera from 1935 to 1938. Turning also to Broadway productions, he composed the ballet *Slaughter on Tenth Avenue* for the musical, *On Your Toes* (1936). According to a later statement by Allen Churchill, the show marked "a milestone in American musical comedy—in it for the first time such a show dispensed with a line of girls and offered ballet instead" (*Theatre Arts,* March 1949).

In a South American tour of the American Ballet in 1941, a Brazilian audience saw the première of a Balanchine work entitled *Ballet Imperial,* which made its New York debut in the repertoire of the New Opera Company at the Broadway Theatre the following season. John Martin in the New York *Times* (November 5, 1942) referred to it as "a beautiful job," but Robert Lawrence in the New York *Herald Tribune* called it "a turkey".

In 1940 Balanchine staged the dances for the all-Negro musical, *Cabin in the Sky.* Other musicals to which Balanchine has contributed include: *Babes in Arms, I Married an Angel, Louisiana Purchase, The Lady Comes Across, Dream with Music, Song of Norway, Where's Charley?,* and *Courtin' Time.* Hollywood also engaged the choreographer's talents. Dances by Balanchine were seen in *Goldwyn Follies* (which offered Hollywood's first full-length ballet), *Star Spangled Rhythm,* and *I was an Adventuress.*

GEORGE BALANCHINE

"Since 1940," wrote Allen Churchill (*Theatre Arts,* March 1949), "Balanchine has been occupied with . . . ballets of pure movement, as some symphonies are pure music." This is in accordance with his belief that "a ballet may contain a story, but the visual spectacle, not the story, is the essential element" (quoted by Merle Armitage in *Dance Memoranda*).

Ballets composed by Balanchine between 1940 and 1946 include: *Concerto Barocco, Le Bourgeois Gentilhomme, Danses Concertantes, Symphonie Concertante, Waltz Academy,* and *The Four Temperaments.* In 1946, Ballet Society came into existence and Balanchine became its artistic director. The following year, Balanchine accepted an invitation from the Paris Opera House, for which he composed *Le Palais de Cristal (Symphony in C).*

The Ballet Society had presented his *Divertimento* and *Renard (The Fox)* in early 1947, and when Balanchine returned to the United States, he composed for the society *The Triumph of Bacchus and Ariadne* and *Orpheus.* The latter, set to the music of Igor Stravinsky, was presented by Ballet Society at the New York City Center on April 28, 1948 with Maria Tallchief, Tanaquil LeClercq, and Nicolas Magallanes taking the leading roles.

With Lincoln Kirstein as general director, and with Balanchine as artistic director, the New York City Ballet Company came into existence in 1948. The success of the company has grown with each successive season. Playing to full houses at the City Center, its New York engagements have become ten-week runs, and on tour in the United States, many of its return

BALANCHINE, GEORGE—*Continued*

engagements are for extended periods. It has, to date, made three trips to Europe; the 1953 tour lasted for seven months.

The company has, moreover, fulfilled the purpose for which Lincoln Kirstein invited Balanchine to the United States in 1933, for although European soloists still appear in the cast, the company draws largely on the pupils of the School for American Ballet for its personnel, and the number of American-born, American-trained dancers is constantly increasing.

Over 60 per cent of the ballets presented are choreographed by Balanchine. The repertoire includes works which date from his early period in the United States; *Serenade* was first produced in 1935, and *Le Baiser de la Fée* in 1937. Traditional ballets, such as *Swan Lake* and *The Nutcracker*, have been re-choreographed by Balanchine.

Referring to Balanchine's revision of *Swan Lake*, John Martin (New York *Times*, January 13, 1954) commented: "[It] made strikingly clear . . . how individual is Balanchine's style even in the traditional line." Of the revised *Nutcracker* ballet, set to Tchaikovsky's music, Walter Terry (New York *Herald Tribune*, February 3, 1954) wrote: "Balanchine has worked that miracle of using the traditional movements of the classical ballet and making them seem wholly new. . ."

Original works recently added to the repertoire, many of them showing a modern influence, have also been praised by the critics. Of *Opus 34*, built on a score by Arnold Schönberg and presented in January 1954, Terry wrote: "[It] is harsh in movement and evil in its drama but the unsurpassable craftsmanship, a thing of beauty in itself, of . . . Balanchine is apparent throughout." Robert Sabin, writing in *Musical America*, stated: "The amazingly versatile genius of George Balanchine was brought home to the audience at the première of his new ballet, *Opus 34* . . . a profoundly original composition."

Through the system of Labanotation (invented twenty-five years ago by Hungarian-born Rudolf von Laban) by which all the choreographic movements of a ballet may be recorded, many of Balanchine's ballets have been "transcribed for posterity" (*Time*, January 25, 1954). The growing use of this system "insures that, unlike masterpieces of the past, which went down through the generations by demonstrations and word of mouth, today's ballets can be re-created fairly exactly, and ultimately, that the innovations of a Balanchine need not be distorted by faulty memories."

In addition to his work with the ballet company, Balanchine directed the staging of Igor Stravinsky's opera, *The Rake's Progress*, for the Metropolitan Opera Company in 1953. He won unqualified praise for his work from Virgil Thomson (New York *Herald Tribune*, February 22, 1953) who stated: "The result has been, in my judgment, a most distinguished operatic stage presentation."

The choreographer has had to limit the number of engagements he accepts in the musical comedy and motion picture fields. He rejected an offer to do the dances for the film *Hans Christian Andersen* because of his other commitments.

The choreographer has been married to five distinguished ballerinas. His first wife, Tamara Geva, was a member of the Soviet State Dancers company in which Balanchine left Russia. Alexandra Danilova, well known to balletomanes, was his second wife. Vera Zorina, the third, appeared in motion pictures choreographed by Balanchine, and was seen as Ariel in Margaret Webster's production of *The Tempest*. The daughter of an Osage Indian, Maria Tallchief, who is a leading ballerina with the New York City Ballet, was the fourth Mrs. Balanchine (this marriage was annulled). He is now married to Tanaquil LeClercq, a well-known ballerina of the company.

He enjoys playing two-piano music, baton twirling, and cooking epicurean dishes. He is five feet eight inches tall and weighs 145 pounds. He is a United States citizen.

"Ballet is important and significant—yes," Balanchine said in a recent interview (*Time*, January 25, 1954). "But first of all, it is a pleasure. No one would enjoy watching a group of dancers jump about the stage aimlessly, no matter how well they jumped. After all, a pig can jump—but who wants to see a pig jump?"

Selected References (See also references listed in 1942 biographical sketch)

Theatre Arts 31:37+ N '47 por; 31:37+ D '47; 33:34+ Mr '49 pors
Time 56:42 D 11 '50 por; 63:66+ Ja 25 '54 pors

Amberg, G. Ballet in America (1949)
Armitage, M. Dance Memoranda (1947)
Balanchine, G. Balanchine's Complete Stories of the Great Ballets (1954)
Chujoy, A. The New York City Ballet (1953)
Chujoy, A. (ed.) Dance Encyclopedia (1949)
Martin, J. J. World Book of Modern Ballet (1952)
Who's Who in America, 1954-55
Who's Who in the Theatre (1952)
World Biography (1948)

BALENCIAGA, (CRISTÓBAL) (bă-län-cē'ă"gă) 1896?- Fashion designer

Address: h. 10 av. George-V, Paris 8e, France; h. av. Marceau, Paris 16, France

One of the leading couturiers of France is Spanish-born Cristobal Balenciaga, whose designs are worn by some of the wealthiest and most elegantly dressed women in the world. Although his creations have appeared in many style shows in the United States, he has not been a leader of popular fashion trends as have Christian Dior and Jacques Fath, but rather has dedicated himself to designing for individuals in the grand tradition of the *haute couture*.

American women of moderate incomes have become familiar with Balenciaga's designs through biannual showings of French and

Italian imports which include costumes from his original collections, exhibited alongside American-made copies. These are presented by Gimbel Brothers, Macy's and Ohrbach's, and other department stores in New York and throughout the United States.

His career, begun in Spain, was interrupted by the Spanish Civil War. In 1936 he started a new enterprise in Paris, quickly gaining a prominence in the world of fashion that has been undisputed for almost twenty years. One of Balenciaga's great assets is his profound knowledge of cut and fit—as important to a designer as the knowledge of anatomy is to a painter. "If Dior is the Watteau of dressmaking, then Balenciaga is fashion's Picasso. For like that painter, underneath all his experiments with the modern, Balenciaga has a deep respect for tradition and a pure classic line" (Cecil Beaton in *The Glass of Fashion*). His other great attribute is his color sense "so refined, sharpened to such a remarkable degree, that he can unerringly scan four hundred colors and choose the right one for his purpose."

The name Balenciaga, according to Gilbert Graziani writing in Paris *Match*, has been variously attributed to a Spanish revolutionary and to a Spanish noblewoman. Cristobal Balenciaga was born in Guetaria, a fishing village on the Bay of Biscay. The European editor of the *Woman's Home Companion*, Margaret Thompson Biddle, states that Cristobal's first creation at the age of five was a velvet, "jewel"-studded collar that he designed for his cat.

Cecil Beaton in his book, *The Glass of Fashion* (1954) writes of Balenciaga's youth: "His father was captain of a pleasure boat, catering to the simple outings of simple people. He could not help being amazed by the son who, at a tender age, showed little inclination to swim and fish or lead the life of the peasant children. He preferred, on the contrary, to 'sew like the women' . . . his mother protected the boy and allowed him to continue with his hobby."

His father's death when Cristobal was ten, turned the boy to the serious study of dressmaking, for his mother had to support the family by sewing. Cristobal began by learning how to cut and make his own clothes. He had long been fascinated by the exquisite gowns of the royal ladies who came with the King and Queen of Spain at the turn of the century to visit San Sebastián, a fashionable resort near Guetaria.

Mrs. Biddle relates how Balenciaga particularly admired the elderly Marquesa de Casa Torres, a former great beauty, who always attended mass on Sundays at the village church attired in elegant Paris costumes. One Sunday the fourteen-year-old Cristobal unable to restrain his admiration exclaimed, "How elegant you are!" His interest and enthusiasm was so keen, the Marquesa questioned him and commissioned him to copy her Drecoll suit, giving him a bolt of expensive material with which to work.

When, after several fittings, the suit was finished, Cristobal had the pleasure of seeing the Marquesa wear it to church. The next year

Match, Paris

BALENCIAGA

he made his first visit to Paris and "sat rapt in wonder" at the collections of Worth, Doucet and Drecoll. When his money ran out, he returned home, happy in the conviction that he would become a great couturier.

At the age of twenty, Balenciaga was operating his own dressmaking establishment in San Sebastián. Within a few years he became the leading couturier of Spain. The Spanish Civil War terminated his business, causing him to leave for Paris where he set about the establishment of his present *maison de couture*. After finding an apartment (which he still occupies) and the building on avenue George-V where he still carries on his business, he bought some bolts of material and a dressmaker's dummy, carted them home in a taxi, and began to create the first dresses for his first Paris collection.

His success was steady, his prestige growing every season. Twice a year for nearly twenty years he has presented a "royal spectacle" of two hundred dresses and suits shown in quick succession in the plain white salon of his *maison de couture*. The show, lasting two-and-a-half hours, is open only to carefully screened people. Although cries of "Bravo!" and "Encore!" are frequently heard at opening shows, and the audience often calls upon the designer to appear, Balenciaga never comes out from behind the white satin curtain that separates the mannequins' room from the salon. His determined avoidance of personal publicity has made him an almost legendary character. In the French press he is known as "the most mysterious couturier" in Paris.

Balenciaga creates his collection in an atmosphere of "profound calm". He claims he cannot create in a state of excitement. "I would be like a bull in front of three toreadors, not knowing which one to attack first," he said in an interview for Paris *Match*. Under his

BALENCIAGA—*Continued*

patient and painstaking hands, in almost complete silence (voices are never raised in his establishment), his beautiful collections take form. In addition to his Paris establishment, he now operates dressmaking houses in Barcelona, San Sebastián and Madrid.

Balenciaga's associates in the world of fashion hold the designer in the highest esteem. In the words of "Coco" Chanel, as recounted in Paris *Match*, "The others are draftsmen or copyists, or else they are inspired people or even geniuses, but Balenciaga alone is a couturier. He is the only one who can design, cut, put together and sew a suit or a gown entirely alone."

Known as the *couturier-architecte*, he neither follows nor leads the style, but like a "lone horseman" goes his own way. His style is a combination of French refinement and Spanish intensity. Balance is its keynote. Balenciaga believes that the three elements in a costume are color, cut and ornamentation, each counterbalancing the other. If a suit is bright red, he pares down its cut to the utmost simplicity and does not use trimmings. If a gown is of a soft color, he allows a more elaborate cut and decoration. In his sense of balance lies the secret of the simplicity and almost classic harmony of his creations, while his flawless use of color gives his fashions their dramatic strength.

According to Mrs. Biddle, Balenciaga believes that an elegant woman does not necessarily wear the latest style, but dresses in a manner becoming to herself, choosing clothes of good material and cut which she wears for several years, changing accessories to make them up-to-date. She never wears clothes that are conspicuous or uncomfortable, is never dominated by fashion, but uses it to express her own personality.

The designer does not assist at the fittings of his creations, even those purchased by his most celebrated clients. However, he is always anxious that each dress or suit be worn by the type of woman for whom it was designed. "The sketch is only the beginning of the design," Mrs. Biddle quotes him as saying: "I must think it all through from the fabric to the shoes, until I see the woman all complete as in a colored photograph." Even though his creations are among the most expensive in Paris, they are in such demand that he sometimes has to turn away orders.

Mrs. Biddle wrote: "When I go to look at Balenciaga's collection as a customer, I am sometimes not quite sure that I want to wear some of his extreme models. But I have such faith in his taste that if I am certain a model is becoming I dare to order it. The first year I may be hesitant of wearing it, the second year I wear it and feel the height of fashion and the third year the dress has become part of me."

Since Balenciaga's coats and suits have been described as "a miracle of cut and utter simplicity" (New York *Times*, March 19, 1954) his views on how a woman's suit should fit are respected. "Your belt has nothing to do with the fit of your skirt," he said, "it is only a finishing touch. Your skirt must rest on and hang from the hips, and should fit as well without a belt as with one," he told Mrs. Biddle. "One of the ugliest lines in the world is that of the straight skirt that 'cups under.' This comes from too straight a cut, a lack of proper fitting over the hips, a skimping on the material used. A straight skirt hangs properly when carefully fitted by a series of darts between hipline and waistline."

When asked what constitutes a distinguished woman, Balenciaga quotes Salvador Dali: "A distinguished lady always has a disagreeable air." He regrets that women no longer have the time and the leisure to devote to being elegant and beautiful. His basic assertion is that a woman must have an inner quality that makes her wear her clothes well. As illustration he points out that you may put the same dress on two different women, and one will be vulgar while the other will achieve elegance. He does not believe that women need to vary their clothing often to be well dressed.

The fashion designer, who is of medium height, always dresses in a conservative gray suit, white shirt and black tie. His straight black hair, graying at the temples, is combed back from a high patrician forehead. Balenciaga lives in an apartment on avenue Marceau that has white walls and is furnished in mahogany and an abundance of green sofas. He owns a Renaissance chateau near Orléans. He has broken his leg twice and his ankle once while skiing, but it is still his favorite sport. Balenciaga shuns social gatherings and seldom permits himself to be photographed. "Why should people photograph me? I am not a great scholar, nor a victorious general. . . ." he queried.

Madame Eugenia Errazuriz, the fashionable Chilean beauty who lived in Paris and who inspired such diverse artists as Picasso and Sargent, once paid tribute to Balenciaga when she advised women: "Don't buy five middling-good dresses; much better to have one good one from Balenciaga than a lot for the sake of variety."

References

Paris Match 126:34+ Ag 18 '51 por
Woman's Home C 80:36+ N '53
Beaton, C. The Glass of Fashion (1954)

BALLANTINE, IAN (KEITH) (ē'ăn)

Feb. 15, 1916- Publisher

Address: b. c/o Ballantine Books, Inc., 404 5th Ave., New York 18; h. 440 W. 24th St., New York 11

A plan to publish original fiction and nonfiction in paper-bound and hard-bound editions simultaneously was announced by Ian Ballantine in May 1952. Six months later he put the plan into effect by launching the publishing firm of Ballantine Books, Inc., thereby precipitating considerable controversy and speculation in publishing circles. His method is to finance a low-priced hard-bound edition of a new book through the mass production and distribution of a cheap paper-bound edition. He offered to co-publish under this plan with any publisher of hard-bound books who wished to submit books on a single title basis.

In addition, Ballantine appeared before the Authors' Guild Council of the Authors' League of America to offer a plan for author-publisher relations which would, he claimed, make it possible for the average author to devote full time to his writing instead of writing in the hours left over from a more lucrative job.

Ballantine had gained publishing experience as general manager of Penguin Books, Inc., (1939-1945) and as president and director of Bantam Books, Inc., (1945-1952) one of the first American paper-bound reprint publishers. He has written articles on publishing and taught a sociology course at Columbia University on mass communications media.

Ian Keith Ballantine was born in New York City on February 15, 1916. His father, Edward James Ballantine, a Scottish actor and sculptor, had come to the United States with a Shaw repertory company. His mother, Stella (Commins) Ballantine was born in the United States and was a publicist for the Ben Greet Players, for Jesse L. Lasky and other groups connected with the theatre.

After graduation from Stuyvesant High School in New York City in 1933, Ian Ballantine entered Columbia University. He received an A.B. degree in 1938, and then spent a year at the London School of Economics and Political Science. He had no particular interest in a business career until a thesis he wrote at the London school on low-cost books in the United States attracted the attention of Allen Lane, publisher of Penguin Books, Ltd. Lane was interested because Ballantine had pointed out new possibilities within the copyright law for the importation of British low-cost paper-bound reprints into the American market.

Penguin Books, Ltd., had been established by Allen Lane in 1936, when twenty-five cent American reprints were nonexistent, but before Ballantine returned to the United States, Pocket Books, Inc. had issued in 1939 its first ten titles in similar format. Ballantine organized Penguin Books, Inc., in America in 1939 and remained with the firm until 1945, when he left to establish Bantam Books, Inc., a new publisher of paper-covered reprints.

While president and director of Bantam Books, Ballantine began to study the trends in mass reading tastes. An entirely new market had been successfully tapped. New outlets for books had been secured, and although it seemed that lurid covers were largely responsible for the sales of fiction, there were also some best sellers among the nonfiction titles.

Ballantine used the market research technique of sending men directly to the dealers to determine how many copies of every Bantam title were sold to the public in key cities during a specific period of time. The surveys and resulting sales curves proved accurate, he reported in *Publishers' Weekly* (July 9, 1949), because during the last three years his company "averaged less than one per cent of [its] books returned." He also announced that Bantam would begin a new marketing program for its best sellers and would publish a monthly list of its eight leading reprint titles.

paul george schutzer
IAN BALLANTINE

As a part-time instructor in sociology at Columbia University, Ballantine has dealt extensively with the field of mass communications, and has studied particularly the influences of cheap books, magazines, radio, and television on the American mind.

In building up the paper-bound book business, Ballantine had time for very few extended vacations—none between 1939 and 1948. But an enforced vacation in 1950—after breaking a leg while skiing—gave him the opportunity to envision what David Dempsey (*New York Times Book Review*, May 18, 1952) called, "the most far-reaching development to hit Publisher's Row in a long time." Ballantine formulated his plans to establish a new publishing house (to be known as Ballantine Books) to bring out original fiction and nonfiction in hard-bound editions (starting at $1.50) simultaneously with thirty-five cent paper-bound editions for the newsstand trade. "If successful," Dempsey wrote, "the idea . . . could radically transform the whole conventional publishing set-up."

Outlining his "simulprint" plan to representatives of leading newspapers and trade publications and to literary agents, Ballantine also consulted the Authors' League of America and presented his plan to the Authors' Guild Council. As part of his plan he proposed to pay authors a royalty of ten per cent on the hard-bound edition and eight per cent on the paper-bound edition, with a minimum guarantee of $5,000 three months after publication. This represented a substantial increase over the royalty generally paid on paper-bound reprint editions.

The Saturday Review (June 21, 1952) published an outline of the Ballantine Plan along with the opinions of two publishers of hard-

BALLANTINE, IAN—*Continued*

bound books. Lovell Thompson, trade manager of Houghton Mifflin Company called it a "new daring possibility." On the other hand, Cass Canfield, chairman of the board of Harper & Brothers, wrote that "certain serious problems are involved" and he explained that some publishers were wary because authors might lower the quality of their writing for mass distribution, the review media would vanish, advertising would dwindle, and bookstores would be driven out of business.

During the organization period, Ballantine operated from his home, but on September 6, 1952, *Publishers' Weekly* announced the names of the staff, the move to offices at 404 Fifth Avenue, and the release date of November 7, 1952 for the first four "simulprint" titles: *Executive Suite* by Cameron Hawley, *The Golden Spike* by Hal Ellson, *All My Enemies* by Stanley Wade Baron, and *Saddle by Starlight* by Luke Short (Frederick Dilley Glidden). Houghton Mifflin Company and Farrar, Straus & Young would be the first two copublishers.

The Authors' League of America published an article in its house organ in October 1952 by Ian Ballantine. He reported that arrangements had been made to distribute the hardbound editions to book stores through the sales representatives of Houghton Mifflin Company, while the services of a major magazine distributor would assure wide distribution of the paper-bound editions. He stated that Ballantine books as well as co-published titles would be "backed up with advertising expenditures in traditional book review media on a scale comparable to that of the old-line publishers.

T. J. Wilson, director of the Harvard University Press was quoted in *Publishers' Weekly* (September 6, 1952) as having written: "I still believe there is a good market for serious books in original editions at good prices, and I don't believe that the Ballantine Plan, promising though it may be, or soft-bound publishing in general has yet destroyed that market, or even threatens to within a reasonable period of time."

In a roundup of 1952 news of books and publishing, Joseph Henry Jackson (San Francisco *Chronicle,* January 4, 1953) featured the Ballantine Plan and called it "unquestionably the most significant phenomenon of 1952 in books." He also pointed that "it is a move toward experimentation. And since book publishing is a business as well as an intellectual adventure . . . certain rules of American business have got to apply."

David Dempsey, writing in the *Atlantic Monthly* (January 1953) called the plan ". . . the time bomb that is ticking away beneath the foundations of the publishing industry." He pointed out that Ballantine Books planned an annual anthology of new poetry to be edited by Rolfe Humphries (the collection, *New Poems by American Poets,* was published in the summer of 1953 and received favorable reviews) and other books ordinarily considered too literary for the paper-bound market.

When the book *New Short Novels* (by Jean Stafford, Elizabeth Etnier, Clyde Miller and Shelby Foote) was published by Ballantine Books in 1954, the reviewer for *Time* magazine (February 15, 1954) wrote: ". . . paperback originals worth reading have been extremely rare. . . . The news this week is that writing of a pretty high level has at last shown up between the covers of a thirty-five cent book. No old-line publisher need have been ashamed to sponsor *New Short Novels* between boards. . . ." Also in 1954, Ballantine published *Aircraft Carrier* by J. Bryan, 3d., Lieut. Commander, U.S.N.R., issuing a thirty-five cent paper-book edition simultaneously with a $3.00 cloth edition.

The original plan of thirty titles a year was expanded to sixty, or five a month, in 1953. Mrs. Ballantine, secretary of the company, explained that books contracted for by hardcover publishers must have pretty sure paperbound market possibilities before they are undertaken for co-publishing because of the greater financial risks of mass paper-bound publication and distribution.

While Ballantine was with Bantam Books, he relied to a large extent on market research for his distribution strategy, but now with a relatively smaller list he can depend on fairly close supervision of individual titles. *The Best American Short Stories, 1953,* edited by Martha Foley, for instance, was recently found to be selling best in its paper-bound edition in metropolitan areas, so sales efforts were concentrated there and it was withdrawn from less populated areas.

One of the most successful books in the copublishing series has been the novel, *Executive Suite,* by Cameron Hawley. Although the average newsstand life of the paper-bound book is estimated at three months, this book has been selling well for over a year.

In the New York *World-Telegram and Sun* (March 29, 1954), Sterling North quoted a report by J. K. Lasser & Company which stated that 259,000,000 paper-back books were published in the United States in 1953, as opposed to about 500,000,000 hard-bound books and 900,000,000 crime-comic magazines in the same year.

Ian Ballantine was married on June 22, 1939 to Elizabeth Norah Jones, and as secretary of Ballantine Books, she has shared considerably in his professional life. They have one son, Richard. Their year-round week-end home at Woodstock, New York, is the scene of much excess office work such as manuscript reading.

Politically, Ian Ballantine is independent. He has been active in State Department and other programs distributing American books overseas, and is in the executive reserve of the State Department. Skiing is his only sport or hobby. He is a member of Phi Beta Kappa and of the Players Club in New York. He is five feet, seven inches tall, weighs 160 pounds, has brown hair and green eyes and is softspoken.

References

Pub W 156:131+ Jl 9 '49 por
Who's Who in America, 1952-53

BALMAIN, PIERRE (ALEXANDRE)
May 18, 1914- Fashion designer
Address: b. 44 rue François-Ier, Paris 8e, France; 498 7th Ave., New York 18; h. 32 Quai de l'Ecluse, Croissy-sur-Seine, Seine-et-Oise, France

The French couturier Pierre Balmain has been influential in demonstrating "the vitality and the prestige of the French genius" in the fashion world. While a student of architecture at the Beaux-Arts in 1934, he decided that he would rather work with chiffon and wool than with steel and concrete, and so began his career as a fashion designer with Captain Edward H. Molyneux. He opened his own salon in Paris in 1945 and a New York branch in 1951 which supplies over 200 American stores with Balmain-created fashions.

His designs, based on simplicity and wearability, have been built on a slim silhouette for daytime, a full-skirted one for evening. He has been largely responsible for the popularization of the stole. He designed the costumes for Jean Giraudoux' play *The Madwoman of Chaillot* and other plays and ballets.

Born on May 18, 1914, in Saint-Jean-de-Maurienne in the French Savoie, Pierre Alexandre Balmain was the only child of Maurice Balmain, wholesale merchant, and Françoise (Ballinari) Balmain. The boy studied at the *lycée* in Chambéry where his history professor was Henry Daniel-Rops. On a Sunday in 1932 young Balmain arrived in Paris to study at the Ecole des Beaux-Arts. "When I came out of the metro onto the Place de la Concorde for the first time," he wrote in later years, "the admirable harmony of the architecture of this city I had come to conquer, tore at my heart."

Balmain studied architecture, but even as he designed buildings he surrounded his sketches with designs for dresses. In October 1934 economic necessity brought him with his dress designs to Captain Molyneux, one of the leading couturiers of Paris, who gave young Balmain the chance to work at dress designing in the afternoons while continuing his study of architecture in the mornings. Shortly afterwards, Molyneux advised Balmain to devote full time to dress designing.

The young man remained with Molyneux until 1939 when he was mobilized into the 440th Regiment of Pioneers and assigned to his native Savoie. There he met Gertrude Stein and Alice B. Toklas who encouraged the young soldier's ambition to become an independent couturier. After the capitulation of France, Pierre Balmain returned to Paris to work as an assistant with Lucien Lelong, then considered the "first gentleman of fashion". Christian Dior joined the staff the same year and the two young men were put to work in the same room.

According to Ernest O. Hauser (*Saturday Evening Post,* October 17, 1953), Balmain's "constant yelling, singing and loud laughter so exasperated Dior that the newcomer repaired to a telephone booth de luxe where he created in upholstered silence." The two young men constantly found their best ideas tabooed by

PIERRE BALMAIN

Lelong's "ironclad demureness." However, Lelong's diplomatic resistance to Joseph Goebbels' attempts to close the fashion houses in Paris and transfer the world of fashion to Berlin, saved Balmain from being sent to work in Germany in 1943.

Balmain and Dior "were friendly enough," according to Cecil Beaton in *The Glass of Fashion* (1954), "Balmain was ambitious and dreamed of opening his own establishment. His reveries were catching, and Dior began dimly to entertain similar notions. After the liberation of France, Balmain opened his own successful dressmaking house."

The House of Balmain was established in a four-story apartment building on rue François-Ier. Gertrude Stein and Alice B. Toklas helped to publicize the new enterprise. In the summer of 1946 Miss Toklas wrote: "One day last September Pierre Balmain showed his first collection and suddenly there was the awakening to a new understanding of what mode really was, the embellishment and the intensification of women's form and charm. A dress . . . once more became a thing of beauty, to express elegance, grace and delicacy in silk and wool, in lace, feathers and flowers. . . ."

Balmain takes credit for being the first designer to launch the "New Look," citing the 1945 issues of *Vogue* (to substantiate his claim), which showed his designs with long, bell-shaped skirts, small waists, and accents on femininity. Dior, who has become known as the creator of the "New Look," did not open his own salon until 1946.

However, according to *Collier's Encyclopedia* (1952), four designers are credited with launching the "New Look"—Dior, Balmain, Jacques Fath, and Balenciaga. These men "captured the spirit of youth and revitalized the couture" after World War II. In the designs of all four, "the silhouette was gathered in at the waist, had narrow shoulders, a high bust line,

BALMAIN, PIERRE—*Continued*

a rounded hip line, and a long full skirt. Balmain, disliking fussiness, presented clean-cut gowns, simple yet youthful. . . ."

In November 1946 Balmain visited the United States to promote "closer cooperation between the two fashion capitals of New York and Paris," and to study American styles and American women in order to "adapt his styles to their needs." Speaking before the Fashion Group, Inc., in New York, he said France would never try to "match the American ready-to-wear industry," but would "continue to make her contribution in new ideas."

The designer made a three-months trip around the world by air in 1947, and popularized French styles, especially in the Middle East, India and Australia. His designs for 1949 showed the influence of his travels. "There is great dignity in the Far East," he observed, explaining his use of the Chinese mode to permit free and graceful movement. Although he designed costumes in the styles of the 1920's for a musical show in Paris, he came out against "an artificial revival" of these fashions, saying that although they had "great elegance," they were interpreted in "terrible proportions."

On a visit to the United States in March 1950, Balmain featured a smart airplane travel wardrobe designed for his mother, who accompanied him on his trip. He made fashion news again in 1951 when his collection was described by Eugenia Sheppard as "a thrill a minute, like a roller-coaster ride. Most fun-loving of the Paris designers, Balmain . . . lines mink coats with white Venetian lace . . . and launches umbrellas with flutes built into the handles. Underneath the frivolities, Balmain cannily builds two complete collections. One of them plays up slim skirts and draped hips, and the other goes in for wide skirts lined in color to match romantic petticoats" (New York *Herald Tribune*, August 4, 1951).

Speaking at the New York *Herald Tribune* Forum in October 1952, Balmain explained the postwar trends of the French fashion industry. Before the war, he said, New York stores bought many models from Paris couturiers as well as quantities of material in order to repeat the models in their custom-made departments. American manufacturers also bought in quantity; in addition, there were many rich private customers. During the war, most of the manufacturers in the United States turned to American designers.

The retail stores, unable to get Paris fashions, did the same or else discontinued their custom-made departments. Consequently, following the war, Parisian couturiers found they had lost much of their American market. In 1952 Balmain's Parisian house, which employs over 400 workers, sold 25 per cent of its output to European manufacturers and dressmakers, 40 per cent to private American customers, 34 per cent to private customers from France and other countries, and only 1 per cent to American stores or manufacturers. In order to reach the American market, Balmain in 1951 opened his New York branch for which he has designed special collections planned for American women.

Eugenia Sheppard, describing his 1952 New York collection, wrote: "Balmain keeps his French accent when he designs for Americans. His new ready-to-wear resort collection made right here by Elfreda-Fox and shown by De Pinna at the Plaza . . . is so suave and sophisticated that you can put the plane fare to Paris right back in the piggy bank." In this collection was shown his already-famous giant stole worn over suits, dresses and evening clothes. The basic silhouette was a sheath dress under a cutaway cardigan jacket. Pink and blond shades as well as interesting prints were featured.

Prices of daytime dresses and suits in Balmain's American collection in 1953 started at just over $100, about one-third the price of an original Balmain of similar style in Paris. His collection shown in Washington, D.C., in March 1953 featured the slim silhouette for daytime wear, but showed "full-skirted and fabulous" evening gowns.

After his fall 1954 showing in Paris, Eugenia Sheppard wrote: "Balmain, the perpetual college boy of the couture, still does tricks . . . but they are chic tricks like a high-collared, long-sleeved ermine shirtwaist. . ."

"I believe in simplicity in material as well as in stone and marble," the architect-designer told a reporter, and added that he also believed in "wearability" and in "free and easy movement." Another Balmain conviction is that the French couture offers the world much more than a seasonal change in silhouette: "It offers an ideal of elegance and refinement that follows the moving pattern of life and builds up a perfect testimony of civilization."

Now that Balmain has achieved success in fashion, he frequently draws plans for houses on the borders of his sketches for gowns. His home in the suburbs of Paris was designed entirely by him; it houses his collection of porcelain monkeys. The bachelor designer is five feet ten inches tall and weighs 165 pounds. He is a big, broad-shouldered man with a wide forehead, chestnut eyes, brown hair, and a brown mustache. His religion is Catholic; his political attitude is independent.

Fond of sports, he skis, swims, sails, and rides horseback. He likes music, ballet, art, and the theatre. He also enjoys traveling, and has gone around the world two times. He summarized his travels and his lifework in a treatise entitled *Des Rapports de l'Architecture avec la Couture,* delivered as a speech before an architectural conference and published privately in 1950.

References

N Y Herald Tribune IX p34 O 26 '52 por
Dictionnaire Biographique Français Contemporain (1950)
Who's Who in America, 1954-55
Who's Who in Commerce and Industry (1953)
Who's Who in France (Paris), 1953-54

BARLOW, HOWARD May 1, 1892- Conductor
Address: h. Rte. 1, Bedford, N.Y.

NOTE: This biography supersedes the article which appeared in *Current Biography* in 1940.

The *Voice of Firestone,* a simultaneous television and radio program of concert music featuring a forty-six piece orchestra conducted by Howard Barlow, concluded its last concert over the National Broadcasting Company network on June 7, 1954. The Monday evening series, sponsored for twenty-five years by the Firestone Tire and Rubber Company, has been under the baton of Dr. Barlow since 1943. Practically every major opera singer in the United States has appeared with the Firestone orchestra as guest soloist.

On June 14 the Firestone orchestra moved to the American Broadcasting Company network and will continue on Monday evenings from 8:30 to 9:00 o'clock its TV and radio concert programs, broadcasting from the ABC studios in New York.

An American-born and trained musician, Barlow has fostered American music and has introduced radio and concert listeners to the works of many American composers such as Aaron Copland, Roy Harris, and Howard Hanson.

He was symphonic conductor and general musical director of the Columbia Broadcasting System from 1927 until 1943, during which period he pioneered in the use of symphonic music in radio dramas and on the *March of Time* program. The CBS Sunday afternoon concerts under his direction usually included at least one piece by an American composer. The conductor has made numerous guest appearances with leading orchestras.

Howard Barlow was born on May 1, 1892 in Plain City, Ohio; he is the son of Earl and Nettie (Dunham) Barlow. As the boy grew up, first in Urbana, Ohio and later in Mt. Carmel, Illinois, he showed an unusual aptitude for music. Among his earliest memories are those of his father, a lumber merchant and furniture manufacturer, playing the family upright piano. At Mt. Carmel, Howard was a boy soprano in the church choir and began to study the piano. He proved to have a phenomenal ability to memorize music and today seldom conducts with a score before him.

When Howard was ten years old, his father gave him a mandolin which he quickly mastered. Later, he found an old brass E flat alto horn and learned to play it well enough to become a member of the Mt. Carmel band. On a trip to Chicago with his father, he saw his first musical show—*Madame Sherry.* He was so charmed with the melodies that he sang them all night in the railroad sleeper that took him back to Mt. Carmel.

At the age of eleven, Howard was given the job of conducting the Sunday school orchestra, and for his performances, he bought a large ebony baton from the local store. In the attic of the church, he found an old cello; he

Sarra, Inc.

HOWARD BARLOW

repaired it and in ten days was able to play it in the orchestra.

In 1910 Barlow was sent to Denver, Colorado to recover from a serious bronchial condition. He spent a year on a ranch and then finished his secondary education at the North Denver High School where he was graduated in 1911. The music director of Denver's public schools was Wilberforce J. Whiteman (father of conductor Paul Whiteman). He gave Barlow his only lesson in directing music. Thereafter, Barlow decided to become a conductor. He entered the University of Colorado in 1911, and in addition to the regular studies, took courses in harmony, the history of music, and music appreciation.

When Barlow's father moved his furniture business to Portland, Oregon, he sent his son to Reed College in that city. Howard majored in English since the college had no department of music. He organized the chapel choir, glee club and orchestra. Through the cooperation of the college president, Dr. William T. Foster, he was able to take correspondence courses in music from Columbia University. As a result, when he completed work for the B.A. degree in 1915, he also had won the Richard Butler scholarship for graduate study at Columbia. Louis Koemmenich, conductor of the Mendelssohn Glee Club of New York and the New York Oratorio Society, helped Barlow to get started on his musical career.

While at Columbia Barlow sang in the New York Oratorio Society, the college chapel choir and chorus. He secured his first paying job as a director of a small chorus in Riverdale-on-Hudson. In the summer of 1916 he conducted the Bay View (Michigan) Chautauqua Assembly. During the next school year, he continued his job with the Riverdale choral society and sang in New York churches.

When the United States entered World War I in 1917, Barlow enlisted in the Army,

BARLOW, HOWARD—*Continued*

and served as a sergeant in the infantry. He spent eighteen months in France, during which time he was assigned to the division of criminal investigation. He received a commission as a lieutenant before his discharge in February 1919.

On his return to New York, Barlow resumed his job with the Riverdale choral society and also became director of a small choral group in Staten Island and of the Beethoven association in New York City. In May 1919 he prepared a chorus of school children who accompanied Metropolitan Opera singers at a large music festival in Charlotte, North Carolina. In 1919, he was chosen to conduct at the summer festival of music given at the MacDowell Memorial Colony at Peterboro, New Hampshire, during the biennial meeting of the National Federation of Music Clubs. This helped to establish him as a professional music conductor.

After working with many choral societies the young conductor became musical director in 1922 of the Neighborhood Playhouse in New York City. During the course of his five years with the playhouse, he assisted with both dramatic and musical productions.

Meanwhile, he became interested in fostering American music and in 1923 he organized the American National Orchestra which was dedicated to the performance of at least one composition by an American-born musician at every concert. After two seasons, the orchestra was forced to disband because of inadequate funds.

When the Columbia Broadcasting System radio network was organized in 1927, Barlow was chosen symphonic conductor and music director. He resigned from the Neighborhood Playhouse in order to accept the appointment. On September 18, 1927 at 3:00 P.M., the network was launched with a musical program directed by Barlow. That evening, he conducted the orchestra in music from *The King's Henchman*, the work of the American composer, Deems Taylor. Thus, Barlow showed his future intentions—to raise the level of music on the air and to introduce American composers to radio listeners. With his program and others, Sunday afternoon became the established time for good music on the air.

During the rest of the week Barlow organized other musical series—a cycle of piano and of violin concertos, and special educational programs such as *Understanding Music* and *Understanding Opera*. He was also musical director for such programs as the *Philco Radio Hour* and the *March of Time*. In his programing Barlow sought to include the works of American musicians and conducted many works commissioned by CBS from such composers as Aaron Copland, Roy Harris, Robert Russell Bennett, Howard Hanson, and Randall Thompson. During this period he made over 200 recordings with the CBS symphony orchestra.

Barlow also accepted engagements as guest conductor of the orchestras of Duluth; Rochester; Washington, D.C; Detroit; Chicago; Seattle; Vancouver, and Montreal. From 1940 to 1943 he was the conductor of the Baltimore Symphony Orchestra, and from 1943 to 1945 he was one of the conductors of the New York Philharmonic Orchestra.

In October 1943 Barlow resigned from CBS to accept the post of conductor and musical director for the *Voice of Firestone*, a weekly radio program over the network of the National Broadcasting Company.

November 30, 1953 marked the twenty-fifth anniversary on the air of the *Voice of Firestone*. The initial broadcast was on radio, and the TV program originated on September 5, 1949. When asked why the *Voice of Firestone* adheres to the familiar operatic and musical comedy numbers, Barlow explained that "it wasn't due to any lack of flexibility on his part or on the part of the sponsor. But any time they try to ring anything outside the standard repertoire they are inundated with mail from irate fans" (*TV Guide*, December 4, 1953).

In an interview, the conductor described good music as follows: "To me, good music means simply music that is correctly written and that has the universality of appeal that gives it vitality and endurance." Barlow believes that the conductor has the responsibility of being "absolutely sincere in his dual task of presenting beautiful music to his hearers and performing it as beautifully as he knows how" (*Etude* May 1945). Barlow was honored in 1949 with a LL.D. degree from Reed College. He is a member of the American Federation of Musicians and of Sigma Nu fraternity.

He was married on December 12, 1926 to Jeannette Thomas, of Portland, Oregon. Before her marriage, Mrs. Barlow was known on the New York stage as Ann Winston. Barlow is a Republican. He has blue eyes and gray hair; he is five feet eight inches tall, and weighs 170 pounds. He has been described as "soft-spoken" and "unassuming." For recreation, he enjoys reading. His single favorite piece of music is Wagner's prelude to the opera *Tristan und Isolde*.

In an address on "Practical Music" before the Ohio Music Education Association (reprinted in *Music Educators Journal*, January 1952 and in *Recreation*, February 1953), Barlow recommended "ensemble playing—the forming of groups who make music together because they love music. . . . I wish that there were *more* amateurs in music because it is the amateur who keeps the desire for music growing. . . . With the odds so heavily against your community producing a musician who will win world-wide acclaim, it seems to me far better to try to cultivate a *love* for and understanding of music than to try to find and train great talents."

References (see also references listed in 1940 biographical sketch)

Etude 63:264+ My '45

Ewen, D. Dictators of the Baton (1948)
Thompson, O. (ed.) International Cyclopedia of Music and Musicians (1949)
Who is Who in Music (1951)
Who's Who in America, 1954-55

BARNHART, CLARENCE L(EWIS) Dec. 30, 1900- Lexicographer; editor

Address: b. 141 Parkway Rd., Bronxville 8, N.Y.; h. Baptist Church Rd., Yorktown Heights, N.Y.

Robert Browning Baker

CLARENCE L. BARNHART

The *New Century Cyclopedia of Names,* which is a biographical and geographical dictionary, a literary handbook, and a guide to world history, was edited by Clarence L. Barnhart and published by Appleton-Century-Crofts in March 1954. In this new three-volume reference work, the emphasis has been put on the usefulness of the material and on simplicity of presentation. Barnhart used a system of entry based on the two reference books probably most familiar to the greatest possible number of people—the telephone book and the dictionary.

When the *American College Dictionary* was published in 1947 and the *Thorndike-Barnhart Comprehensive Desk Dictionary* in 1951, their editor, Barnhart, received much praise for departing from certain techniques long used in compiling small-sized dictionaries. One of his practical, scientific methods was relying upon statistical evaluation to determine which words people refer to most frequently and which meanings of a word occur most often. The total sales of the *American College Dictionary* (Random House, 1947) as of May 1954 were 443,044.

Barnhart helped to edit a notable series of school dictionaries between 1929 and 1945 for Scott, Foresman & Company, Chicago publishers.

Maintaining that many lexicographers depend too heavily upon written sources, Barnhart made his dictionaries descriptive of the present-day American-English language both as it is spoken by the people and as it appears in books and the press. He does not seek to judge the correctness of usage, but, as Austin Stevens of the New York *Times Book Review* (December 28, 1947) has expressed it, "he holds with those who believe that the resistance of the language to prescriptive authority is its very glory."

Clarence Lewis Barnhart is of Pennsylvania Dutch ancestry. He was born near Plattsburg, Missouri on December 30, 1900, the son of Franklin Chester and Frances Nora (Eliot) Barnhart. His father was a railroad foreman. Clarence was brought up in Belle Plaine, Kansas and in Hutchinson, Kansas. He was graduated from the high school in Hutchinson in 1919. He went to Transylvania College in Lexington, Kentucky for a year, and then transferred to the University of Chicago in Illinois where he received the Ph.B. degree in 1930. "But long before then he had developed two things no lexicographer gets from any university—a deep love of language and a quick and relentless mind" (*Life,* February 12, 1951).

During three years of graduate work, from 1934 to 1937, Barnhart studied under the late Leonard Bloomfield, a linguist, who at that time was professor of Germanic philology at the University of Chicago. Bloomfield's influence, together with that of the late Edward L. Thorndike, educational psychologist, largely determined Barnhart's scientific approach to language problems.

He worked his way through the University of Chicago as a package wrapper in the shipping room and later as a record clerk at Scott, Foresman & Company, educational publishers. Later (1929) promoted to an editorial assistantship in the company, he met Thorndike and began an association with the famous educator of twenty years during which was produced a notable series of school dictionaries: *Thorndike Century Junior Dictionary* (1935, 1942), *Thorndike Century Senior Dictionary* (1941) and *Thorndike Century Beginning Dictionary* (1945).

One outstanding contribution in the field of dictionary making was the practice introduced in these books of defining a word in terms familiar to the reader. In its review of the earliest volume, *Thorndike Century Junior Dictionary,* the Chicago *Daily Tribune* (February 9, 1935) commented: "The definitions have a refreshing simplicity and directness. They sound like the explanations that a capable teacher would actually give children in the classroom."

Another advance in lexicography that was to affect Barnhart's later work was Thorndike's development of a scientific basis for determining what words should be included in a small dictionary. Over a period of years he employed a staff of readers to ascertain the frequency of words in many types of reading material so that he could define in his dictionary the 30,000 words which most often appear in the language. This investigation, later continued under Professor Irving Lorge at the Institute of Psychological Research at Columbia University's Teachers College, is often called the Lorge-Thorndike semantic count. It now also measures the frequency of use of a meaning of a

BARNHART, CLARENCE—*Continued*

word, thus enabling a small dictionary to limit itself to the most prevalent of the many meanings given to a word.

For a period during World War II, Barnhart took some time away from his work at Scott, Foresman to edit for the War Department the *Dictionary of United States Army Terms* (1943). He was awarded a War Department Certificate of Appreciation in 1946.

Barnhart left Scott, Foresman in 1945 to edit for Random House the *American College Dictionary* (1947), the first entirely new dictionary in twenty years. In deciding upon a basic list of words Barnhart drew from the *New Century Dictionary,* the *Century Dictionary,* the *Dictionary of American English,* and the Lorge-Thorndike semantic count. His office staff of some fifty people worked with 355 specialists to determine the definition of about 140,000 words. The editor reversed the traditional procedure in defining a word when he gave first place to current meaning and secondary place to obsolete and original meanings. He also used a simplified pronunciation system.

Reviews of the *American College Dictionary* commented upon its inclusion of almost all entries (new words, foreign words, geographical and proper names) in one alphabet instead of in separate sections and on its use of spot maps to show geographic locations. The San Francisco *Chronicle* (January 4, 1948) found Barnhart's dictionary "logical, sensible and readable." *Life* considered it "probably the finest 'college' dictionary that has been produced in the United States." It had cost its publishers $544,000.

In order to reach a mass market, Doubleday & Company published in 1951 the *Thorndike-Barnhart Comprehensive Desk Dictionary* to sell for $2.75. This volume, edited by Barnhart, listed about 80,000 of the most frequently used words as determined by the Lorge-Thorndike semantic count. (The title of the dictionary acknowledges dependence upon Thorndike's methods in his school dictionaries; Thorndike had died in 1949). A feature of the dictionary was its attention to "Americanisms"—Barnhart had secured permission to draw from the manuscript of Mitford M. Mathews' *Dictionary of Americanisms on Historical Principles* which was published later in 1951.

A report made by *Publishers' Weekly* (January 1952) on the best-selling books of 1951 showed that the *Thorndike-Barnhart Comprehensive Desk Dictionary* held eighth place on the non-fiction list. Its sales during 1951 had totaled 162,623 copies, not including school or book club sales.

Barnhart was chosen in 1947 by Appleton-Century-Crofts to edit a forthcoming cyclopedia of names. After six years of preparation, the *New Century Cyclopedia of Names* appeared in March 1954 and was welcomed by reviewers as a more than worthy successor to the out-of-print 1894 *Century Cyclopedia of Names.* The new set, prepared at a cost of over $500,000, sells for $39.50.

Since 1947 Barnhart has been president of C. L. Barnhart, Inc., a dictionary editing office which he established in Bronxville, New York. Besides editing dictionaries and reference books, he has been associate editor of the periodical *American Speech* since 1948. During 1945 and 1946 he held an honorary associateship in the Institute of Psychological Research at Columbia University.

He belongs to the American Academy of Political and Social Sciences, American Association for the Advancement of Science, American Dialect Society, American Folklore Society, Linguistic Society, Modern Language Association, and National Council of Teachers of English. He is a member of Phi Beta Kappa, and of the Columbia University Faculty Club, Century Association, and University Club in New York.

Barnhart and Frances I. Knox, were married on February 21, 1931. They have two sons, Robert and David. The lexicographer has blue eyes and light brown hair. He weighs 189 pounds and is five feet ten inches tall. He is a Democrat. He is the originator of a name game to provide mental recreation.

References

Life 30:125+ F 12 '51 por
N Y Herald Tribune p7 N 25 '47; VII p 1 Ja 11 '48
N Y Times Book R p11 D 28 '47 por
This Week p9 Ag 8 '54 por
Directory of American Scholars (1951)
Who's Who in America, 1954-55
Who's Who in New York, 1952

BAX, SIR ARNOLD (EDWARD TREVOR) Nov. 8, 1883—Oct. 3, 1953 British composer; Master of the Queen's Music for Queen Elizabeth II; and of the King's Music for King George VI; studied at Royal Academy of Music (1900-1905); went to Ireland and became a Celt "by conversion"; composed seven symphonies, three concertos, and march played in Westminster Abbey at coronation of Queen Elizabeth II; wrote Irish stories under pen name Dermot O'Byrne; knighted in 1937. See *Current Biography,* (Sept.) 1943.

Obituary

N Y Times p88 O 4 '53

BEALS, RALPH A(LBERT) Mar. 29, 1899- Oct. 14, 1954 Librarian; educator; author; educated at University of California and Harvard University; taught at Harvard and New York University; assisted director of American Association for Adult Education (1933-1939); was assistant librarian at Washington (D.C.) Public Library, professor and director of libraries at University of Chicago, and, since 1946, director of N.Y. Public Library; brought to librarianship broad concepts of public service. See *Current Biography,* (Feb.) 1947.

Obituary

N Y Times p23 O 15 '54

BEAU, LUCAS VICTOR Aug. 3, 1895- United States Government official; Air Force officer

Address: b. c/o Civil Air Patrol National Headquarters, Bolling Air Force Base, Washington 25, D.C.

"Puddle-jumper pilots," "aerial bird dogs," and "Search-and-Rescue patrol"—these are some of the nicknames given to the approximately 35,000 senior members of the Civil Air Patrol (C.A.P.) of which Major General Lucas Victor Beau, USAF, is the national commander. He heads a flight organization of civilian volunteers, "the only trained body in the nation," according to General Beau, "which could be activated in an emergency for civil defense on a minute's notice" (New York *Times*, October 26, 1953).

General Beau began his military career in 1917 as a flying cadet. He was commissioned a second lieutenant in the Air Service and served successively as a recruiting officer, instructor, engineer officer, personnel officer and intelligence officer, rising through the grades to become commanding general of the Mediterranean Air Transport Service in Italy in 1945. In that year he also helped to organize a transportation service for the European theater.

Since his appointment on October 1, 1947 as head of the C.A.P. he has developed the organization into a unified "air force within the Air Force." The C.A.P. has Wing Commands in every state of the Union, Puerto Rico, Alaska, and Hawaii. Its ranks include many former pilots and amateur pilots who contribute their own planes, time and fuel to serve their fellow men. General Beau has been given much credit for developing the fine *esprit de corps* which characterizes the C.A.P. organization.

C.A.P. pilots have helped to save orange crops from freezing by flying low over the groves so as to stir up the air with the blast from their propellers; rescued victims of crashed planes in heavily wooded country; they have ferried sick or injured island residents to mainland hospitals; they have dropped food, fuel and supplies to snowbound ranchers and farmers; they have flown in blood plasma, nurses, doctors, and medicine to disaster areas. Also included in C.A.P. are about 43,000 boy and girl cadets who receive aeronautical education through high schools and local units.

Lucas Victor Beau was born in New York City on August 3, 1895. He was graduated from Mamaroneck High School and entered Syracuse University. He became a member of the New York National Guard and after World War I broke out, he was called to active duty in 1916. He served as a corporal with the National Guard on border patrol duty from June until December of that year. In July 1917 he was sent by the Army to the School of Military Aeronautics at Cornell University. He was graduated with a degree in Military Aeronautics and became an instructor at Eberts Field in Arkansas.

He later went to gunnery school at Wilbur Wright Field, Ohio. By June 1918, he was commissioned a temporary second lieutenant in the Air Service, and shortly thereafter was sent overseas for service at St. Maxient, France, and for training in the Pursuit School at Issoudun. Here, in December 1918, he became a ferry pilot with the Third Army Interceptor Command. Then in quick succession he was assigned to Mitchell Field, New York, February 1919; to Hazelhurst Field, New York, as recruiting officer and instructor from March to November of that year, and then back to Mitchell Field.

U. S. Air Force

MAJ. GEN. LUCAS VICTOR BEAU

"Vic" Beau was commissioned a second lieutenant in the Air Service of the Regular Army on July 1, 1920, and almost immediately was promoted to first lieutenant. There followed other short assignments, at Langley Field, Virginia, back to Mitchell Field for duty with the First Observation Squadron, and finally, in 1922, to Bolling Field, Washington, D.C. Serving first as engineer and supply officer with the headquarters detachment of the Air Service, then in the same capacity for the 18th Headquarters Squadron, he was finally put in command of that squadron.

Most of the next two years were spent in the Philippine Islands at Kindley Field as an engineer officer and with the Second Observation Squadron. By July 1928, Beau was back in the United States, this time as instructor for the Colorado National Guard at Denver, where he remained until August 1933. After graduating from the Air Corps Tactical School at Maxwell Field, Alabama in June 1934, he went on duty with the Fifth Composite Group at Luke Field, Hawaii. A few months later he became commanding officer of the 50th Observation Squadron at that station, and remained in Hawaii until September 1936.

Assigned to March Field, California, he was personnel officer but soon assumed the additional duty of civilian procurement officer, positions he held for two years. Interrupting this assignment for a short period he returned to Alabama to enter the Air Corps Tactical

BEAU, LUCAS VICTOR—*Continued*

School at Maxwell Field again to take the special naval operations course.

After completing the course he once more assumed his duties in California, and in May 1939, became adjutant of the First Wing of the General Headquarters of the Air Force at that station. By July, he had been appointed personnel and intelligence officer for the First Wing and in January 1940 became executive officer. By this time, too, he had had several promotions and now held the rank of major (permanent).

In the Office of the Chief of the Air Corps in Washington, D.C., Major Beau became assistant chief of the personnel division in March 1940. Four months later he took over as chief of the officers' section in the personnel division, and in July of 1941 he was named its head. Back in California, this time at San Bernardino Air Depot, he was commanding officer from February 1942 to November 1943. He had now attained the rank of brigadier general (temporary), and was transferred to Patterson Field, Ohio, as chief of staff of the Air Service Command.

When in 1945 he went to the Mediterranean theater, it was as commanding general of the Mediterranean Air Transport Service in Italy. The following September he was transferred to Wiesbaden, Germany, to organize a transportation service for the European theater. European Air Transport Service, popularly known as E.A.T.S., was set up for the duration of the military occupation of Germany. In building up the airports, establishing the communications networks, and setting the standards of operation, it paved the way for American commercial airlines to operate on an intertheater basis. E.A.T.S. covered the European continent, carried military as well as commercial passengers, and will long be remembered for its uncomfortable bucket-seat, weather-beaten C-47s that had seen combat service during the war.

For these many distinguished services to his country, Major General Beau, assigned this rank on July 21, 1952, has been awarded the Legion of Merit. He is rated a command pilot, combat observer, aircraft observer, and technical observer.

The Civil Air Patrol (C.A.P.) (Office of Civilian Defense) was established by Administrative Order 9 of December 8, 1941 to enlist, organize and operate a volunteer corps of civilian airmen, with their own aircraft and equipment, for wartime tasks. Executive Order 9339 of April 29, 1943, transferred the Civil Air Patrol to the War Department to be operated as an auxiliary of the Army Air Forces. The patrol was transferred to the Department of the Air Force by order of the Secretary of Defense on May 21, 1948 and it was established as a civilian auxiliary of the U.S. Air Force on May 26, 1948.

"During World War II the C.A.P. flew more than 24,000,000 miles in little single-engine put-puts. They patrolled coast lines and flew dangerously out to sea as submarine spotters. They flew along the Mexican border looking for spies and saboteurs; they ferried bombers from factory to airfield, and they flew across the country with secret dispatches. In that duty fifty-one C.A.P. members, including two women, gave their lives. Today C.A.P. is officially designated as the civilian auxiliary of the U.S. Air Force, with authorization to wear Air Force uniforms with C.A.P. insignia" (*Reader's Digest*, June, 1952).

War emergency may act to unify and spur large numbers to effective and unselfish volunteer service, but in peacetime to uphold the interest of such a group to service, with no other incentive than humanitarian need, requires the direction of a man of unique personality. This has been General Beau's task as national commander of the C.A.P. to which he was appointed in October 1947.

Each Wing is staffed with regular USAF officers. The jobs the C.A.P. are expected to perform fall into several categories: 1) To maintain a pool of at least 100,000 selected cadets trained in ground and pre-flight subjects to help furnish pilots for the Air Force. 2) To develop an auxiliary radio communications network within C.A.P. geographic boundaries. 3) To provide anti-submarine patrol along the coasts of continental U.S.A. and Alaska.

In the jargon of C.A.P. members, these are "search-and-rescue" capers. Yet they constitute the most hazardous non-combat flying, over some of America's most formidable terrain where the air is so turbulent that it has been known to bounce the gas out of a plane's carburetor and stall the engine. Let the call go out that "the big flap is on" (emergency call), and a dentist drops his drill, a lawyer rushes from court, and a carpenter puts down his hammer.

Wings in the western states are particularly active. The Rockies hide many lost planes. Probably the biggest mercy mission the C.A.P.'s have participated in was the "haylift" of 1949 when isolated Midwest cattlemen and livestock were rescued. Their small aircraft got into canyons and valleys impossible for larger planes. The "Capers" flew 1,400 "official" hours, used 184 aircraft and dropped more than twenty-five tons of supplies. Several volunteer pilots lost their lives. Feats such as this are routine for C.A.P., and are possible, General Beau declares, since "they join because they want to help do a constructive job."

Although the emphasis in C.A.P. is on air strength, the general and his staff have seen to it that the airmen are backed by a strong ground team—hundreds of member-owned jeeps, horses, swamp buggies, motorboats, and snowmobiles. Tying all these elements together is a radio network of 9,500 stations, the largest non-military radio network in the world. Even with all power gone, C.A.P. would be able to communicate with its stations manned by "ham" operators and taxicab drivers (*Skyways*, May 1952).

"There are other jobs the C.A.P. can do in wartime," wrote General Beau. "Patrol of 600 million acres that hold virtually all our pulpwood and other domestic wood products would be vital" (*Flying*, January, 1951).

Speaking at the northeastern regional conference of C.A.P. in Atlantic City on October 25, 1953, General Beau stressed the importance of the civilian auxiliary of the Air Force in American defense and said that the patrol was assured of having loyal Americans within its ranks since every applicant was investigated by the Federal Bureau of Investigation. He also announced that a C.A.P. junior cadet (from fifteen to twenty years old) who earned a certificate for meeting the patrol's educational and aeronautical requirements would be accepted in the Air Force as an airman third class, a rank which requires the equivalent of two years of college training (New York *Times*, October 26, 1953).

General Beau is married to the former Dulcie Steinhardt.

References

Flying 48:28+ Ja '51 por
Who's Who in America, 1950-51

BEECROFT, JOHN (WILLIAM RICHARD) June 22, 1902- Editor

Address: b. c/o Literary Guild of America, Inc., 575 Madison Ave., New York 22; h. Norfolk Lane, Glen Cove, Long Island, N.Y.

An ability to anticipate the reading preferences of more than 2,000,000 Americans has made John Beecroft, editor in chief of the Literary Guild of America, Inc.—in the words of Bennett Cerf—"one of the most important figures in the book world today." His uncanny accuracy in choosing books which later become popular favorites accounts also for the success of the four other Doubleday and Company book clubs which he edits: the Doubleday Dollar Book Club, Book League of America, Family Reading Club, and Dollar Mystery Guild.

John William Richard Beecroft was born in Superior, Wisconsin, on June 22, 1902, the son of John and Theresa (Batz) Beecroft, his father being English, his mother Austrian. After studying at the normal school in Superior, Beecroft attended Columbia University, receiving his degree in 1924.

Beecroft's first job was with the Crowell Publishing Company, where he wrote a reading guide to Dr. Charles William Eliot's *Five Foot Shelf of Books.* In 1926 he left to roam about Europe and study architecture in Italy. On his return to New York in 1928 he applied for a job with the Literary Guild which had been formed the year before.

Hired by Milo Sutliff, he soon was editing *Wings,* its monthly bulletin. When book sales dropped during the depression he was discharged for a short period, traveled abroad again, and worked briefly for Paramount Newsreel. Soon rehired by the Literary Guild, he succeeded Burton Rascoe as editor in chief in 1937, and in rapid succession became editor of the Doubleday Dollar Book Club and the Book League of America. When the Family Reading Club was started in 1946, and the Dollar Mystery Guild in 1948, he also assumed editorial supervision of these clubs and makes their selections.

Affiliated Photo—Conway

JOHN BEECROFT

While Beecroft has about half a dozen readers who screen for him and submit brief typed reports, he is the final arbiter in the selection of books for the various clubs. Since he personally reads about twelve books a week in manuscript or galley, and skims through twenty-five, Beecroft follows a rigorous schedule which has him in the Literary Guild's Madison Avenue office on Mondays, Wednesdays and Fridays, and in the quiet of his Long Island home in Glen Cove, where he does all his reading, the rest of the time.

"The fact that he is not better known to the general public," wrote Bennett Cerf in the *Saturday Review of Literature* in 1946, "that he has not yet been profiled in the *New Yorker* or glamourized in *Life* is due solely to his own reticence and positive passion for anonymity . . . [he is] inscrutable, efficient, and calm . . . as long as he gets his own way. When he is crossed, the mild and scholarly Beecroft charges his foe with the fury of a hurricane, creating such a furore that all opposition literally dissolves. . . . his eyes are steel blue, and he [has] convinced himself that he [is] something of a cold fish not to be stirred by ordinary emotions. In reality, he is a bowl of mush, a pushover for a cagey moocher or a stray alley-cat." (The Beecrofts have four cats.)

It had been assumed at first, both in the book trade and the Doubleday publishing organization, that since Doubleday owned the Literary Guild, its books would be favored in making selections. "That this is definitely not the case," writes Cerf, "may be attributed directly to John Beecroft. He reacts to high pressure as Hearst does to Russia, and leans backward so far when he considers a product

BEECROFT, JOHN—*Continued*

from the home office that one disgusted Doubleday editor calls him 'The Horizontal Man.' "

Book club selections are made many weeks or even months before the books in question are seen either by the critics or the general public, so that Beecroft relies entirely on his own judgment as to what millions of readers are going to like. Just how he arrives at his decisions, which have so unfailingly found favor with Literary Guild and other club subscribers, has been the subject of a good deal of speculation. He even appears to have an uncanny faculty to foresee changes in public taste.

Merle Miller, writing about book clubs in *Harper's Magazine* (May-June 1948), said of Beecroft, "former employees explain his success not as an intellectual process, but as simple intuition." Beecroft himself says very simply, "I have the same taste as thousands of other book readers." As to any rules or formulae, Beecroft has none except that he very rarely chooses anything but fiction, and that he believes his readers dislike flash backs, and want a forward-moving, fast-paced story with a plot: "Something has to happen to somebody."

Beecroft now reads everything with his eye on five different audiences for as many book clubs, a trick which one publisher compares to the performance of a stock company actor who must keep five different roles in his head at once.

Since the selection of a book for one of the clubs assures its financial success, the pressures brought to bear by publishers would be enormous if Beecroft didn't deliberately side-step them. It is generally admitted that no persuasion works on Beecroft. Publishers send galley proofs of forthcoming books to the Literary Guild office (never to Beecroft); he carries them home to read in big manila envelopes, and in time the lucky publishers are notified. Each year he makes about seventy choices for his various clubs.

Generally shy, retiring and inaccessible, Beecroft nevertheless has firm friends in the literary world, and contacts in all publishers' offices. Once the barriers are down, say these friends, he reveals himself as congenial and humorous. Short and gray-haired, he is rapid in thought and movement. His decisions are quick and his opinions positive.

Beecroft's first choice when he became editor of the Literary Guild was Liam O'Flaherty's *Famine*, which was very well received. Then came *Madame Curie*, for which Beecroft guaranteed an unprecedented 50,000 copies for a book club edition—one of his few non-fiction choices. From then on the Literary Guild and his other book clubs boomed, until by 1948 he was selecting books for 2,500,000 readers all over the United States.

A few of Beecroft's other selections which have become top sellers are *A Tree Grows in Brooklyn* (by Betty Smith, then an unknown), *Rebecca, The Sun is My Undoing, The Black Rose, Anna and the King of Siam*, and *The Last Time I Saw Paris*, as well as W. Somerset Maugham's *The Summing Up*, Edna Ferber's *A Peculiar Treasure*, and Thomas Wolfe's *The Face of a Nation*. On the New York *Times* best seller chart at the end of 1953, four of the top six leaders in fiction were Literary Guild selections; the three most popular books according to the New York *Herald Tribune* (December 27, 1953) were choices of Beecroft.

The editor is a formidable and sometimes dismaying authority on antiques, giving his positive opinion on a piece's authenticity (or lack of it) with complete candor. Both his home in Glen Cove and another he maintains near Deerfield, Massachusetts are furnished with especially fine pieces, and even the furnishings in his office in New York are chosen with great taste.

John Beecroft was married to Melenda Pollen Schmidt in 1940. A descendant of John and Priscilla Alden, and the Treadwells of New York, Mrs. Beecroft graduated from the Comstock School and studied at the American Conservatory of Music at Fontainebleau. Beecroft is a Catholic, his wife an Episcopalian.

He is a member of the University Club in New York. He served on the American Council of Books in Wartime, and he was the American judge of the international committee, All-Nations Prize Novel Competition, 1938-1939. He compiled *The Modern Reader* (Doubleday) in 1939, reprinted in 1941 as *The Modern Reader's Anthology* (Garden City Publishing Co.) Critic Charles Poore of the New York *Times* found this collection "an uncommonly varied potpourri of writing." (August 4, 1939).

References

Sat R Lit 29:28 Jl 27 '46

Who's Who in America, 1952-53

BENAVENTE (Y MARTÍNEZ), JACINTO Aug. 12, 1866-July 14, 1954 Spanish playwright; studied law at University of Madrid; toured Europe with a circus; his first play, *El Nido Ajeno*, produced in 1894; subsequently wrote more than 170 plays; won the Nobel Prize for Literature (1922); best known in the United States for his plays, *Bonds of Interest* (1907) and *Malquerida* (1913); also a noted literary critic for Madrid journals. See *Current Biography*, (June) 1953.

Obituary

N Y Times p27 Jl 15 '54

BENNETT, W(ILLIAM) J(OHN) Nov. 3, 1911- Canadian Government official

Address: b. P.O. Box 379, Ottawa, Ontario, Canada; h. 216 Clemow Ave., Ottawa, Ontario, Canada

Canada's atomic research and development project at Chalk River, Ontario is directed by W. J. Bennett who was appointed president of Atomic Energy of Canada, Ltd., in November 1953. This is a crown company formed by the Canadian government to develop industrial uses of atomic energy and to sell the radioactive isotopes which are its by-product. Bennett is also president of the Eldorado Mining and Refining, Ltd., a crown company which is the sole refiner of radioactive ores in Canada and which operates uranium mines whose productive capacity has been compared with those in the Belgian Congo.

Bennett, who was named president of Eldorado in 1947, and of its subsidiary, Northern Transportation, Ltd., had previous administrative experience in Ottawa as private secretary to Canada's first Minister of Transport, the Right Honorable C. D. Howe, and as his chief executive assistant when Howe was the Minister of Munitions and Supply during World War II.

Of Irish descent, William John Bennett was born on November 3, 1911, to Carl Edward and Mary Agnes (Downey) Bennett. An only child, he was reared in Schreiber, the small Ontario town where he was born, and went to public school there. After attending the collegiate institute at Fort William, Ontario, he entered St. Michael's College at the University of Toronto. In 1934 he was granted the B.A. degree with honors.

After graduation Bennett sought a job in order to finance further studies, with a view to a career in either law or the Department of External Affairs. At this juncture he was offered a position as private secretary to C. D. Howe, a Fort William engineer and businessman who had just been elected to Parliament. Bennett accepted the offer and assumed his duties in Ottawa, Canada's capital, in 1935.

During that year, Howe was named Minister of Railways and Canals, and Minister of Marine; when these two ministries were consolidated, Howe was named the new Minister of Transport. Bennett was called upon to perform numerous administrative tasks in the new ministry, which in that period instituted a reorganization of the administration of the Canadian National Railways (the government-owned nationwide railroad), the establishment of the National Harbor Board, and the founding of the Canadian Broadcasting Corporation and Trans-Canada Airlines.

When, with the advent of World War II, the Right Honorable C. D. Howe was named to head the newly created Ministry of Munitions and Supply, Bennett moved with him to the new department as his chief executive assistant. The department has been given much of the credit for the speedy development of Canada's productive capacity during the war years. The country's uranium production and research in atomic energy were also undertaken by this department.

In 1946 Bennett accepted the post of vice-president and general manager of Eldorado Mining and Refining, Ltd., and the following year became its president, retaining the general management. The organization is a crown company, that is, a government-owned corporate enterprise, formed in 1944 to administer the mining and refining operations of a private enterprise of the same name whose property

Herb Nott & Co., Toronto

W. J. BENNETT

and assets were in that year acquired by the government "as a necessary means for the more effective prosecution of the war" (in the words of the Minister of Munitions and Supply, under whose supervision the new company at first functioned).

The company's product is uranium, which has been called the "raw stuff of atomic power." Eldorado owns and operates Canada's only uranium refinery (located at Port Hope, Ontario), and is by law the sole purchaser of radioactive ore. Until 1948 the company also had a monopoly of prospecting and mining rights for such ore, but in that year these rights were opened to private enterprise under permit of Atomic Energy of Canada, Ltd.

Eldorado directs extensive mining operations at Great Bear Lake in the Northwest Territories, within twenty-six miles of the Arctic Circle, and at Beaverlodge Lake in northern Saskatchewan. These two ore fields put Canada "in the forefront of the coming atomic revolution," in the words of B. T. Richardson (*Maclean's Magazine*, October 15, 1951). An editorial in the New York *Times* (June 12, 1951) pointed out that "the exploitation of the Beaverlodge deposits is of political and military importance."

Since the Eldorado properties are located in undeveloped northern wildernesses, special measures were necessary to make them accessible. Accordingly, the crown company, Northern Transportation, Ltd., was created in 1947 to operate transport facilities to the areas concerned. A subsidiary of Eldorado Mining and Refining, Ltd., it also has as its president W. J. Bennett.

In the fall of 1953 it was announced that W. J. Bennett had been appointed president of Atomic Energy of Canada, Ltd. to succeed Dr. C. J. Mackenzie. On November 1 of that

BENNETT, W. J.—*Continued*

year he assumed the duties of this post in addition to those of his position with the Eldorado and Northern Transportation companies. Atomic Energy of Canada, Ltd. is a crown company formed in 1952 to administer the country's atomic energy program. Bennett is also a member of the Atomic Energy Control Board, responsible for Canada's atomic energy policy.

Soon after being named to his new post Bennett expressed the opinion that with all due regard to security precautions, the Western powers "still stand to gain the most from pooling scientific information as well as material resources." One of Canada's chief sources of atomic energy knowledge is the research and development project at Chalk River, Ontario, put into operation in 1945 by the National Research Council, and now operated by Atomic Energy of Canada, Ltd.

The installations there include chemical separation plants, and laboratories for research in chemistry, nuclear and technical physics, medicine, and biology, as well as a large atomic energy pile, the NRX nuclear reactor. A heavy-water atomic pile, NRX was described as "the world's 'hottest' known reactor from the standpoint of radioactivity produced at any one given time in a given area" (Frank Carey in the Ottawa *Citizen*, December 26, 1951).

Currently in process of construction is a more powerful, thirty-million dollar nuclear reactor, NRU, which is expected to go into operation in 1955. With NRU it will be possible to make tests of use in the projected construction of reactors for the production of power by atomic energy.

An important role played by Atomic Energy of Canada, Ltd. since July 1952 is the marketing of radium and the radioactive isotopes produced at Chalk River. (Formerly, marketing of these products was done by Eldorado Mining and Refining, Ltd.; the sale of uranium is still its responsibility.) In 1953 it was estimated that the Chalk River plant produced more than eighty different kinds of radioactive isotopes for use in industry, medicine, agriculture, and general research, and that an average of fifty shipments a month was made to users in Canada, the United States, Great Britain, Europe and South America. One of the best-known of these isotopes is Cobalt-60, an ingredient which gives its name to the so-called "cobalt bomb," developed by Eldorado researchers for use in the treatment of cancer.

In recognition of his services, Bennett has been awarded the Order of the British Empire (1946) and the Pro Ecclesia et Pontifice (1947). He is a director of the Canadian Metal Mining Association and of the Advisory Mining Committee on Radioactive Minerals. In politics he is a Liberal. His faith is the Roman Catholic.

On November 12, 1936, Bennett married Elizabeth Josephine Palleck, of Fort William, Ontario. The couple has seven children: Paul Jerome, Mary Suzanne, Elizabeth Ann, William John, Barbara Jane and Kristin Mary (twins), and Hilary Joseph. The Canadian executive has brown hair and brown eyes, stands five feet nine inches, and weighs 160 pounds. He belongs to the Rideau Club (Ottawa) and the Edmonton (Alberta) Club. For recreation he turns to gardening or skiing.

References

Financial Post p6 O 17 '53 por
Ottawa Citizen p34 S 18 '53 por
Canadian Who's Who, 1949-51
Directory of Directors, 1953

BERIA, LAVRENTI P(AVLOVITCH)—Mar. 29, 1899- Dec. 23, 1953 Deputy Premier of the Soviet Union under Georgi M. Malenkov until his arrest for "high treason" in July 1953; reportedly executed by a firing squad December 23, 1953; was born in the province of Abkhazia, Georgia, Russia; was graduated from the Polytechnical Institute of Baku (1919); joined the Bolshevik wing of the All-Russian-Social Democratic Labor party (1917); participated in Bolshevik Revolution; and appointed chief of Intelligence Service, Red Army (1922); held numerous posts in O.G.P.U. (Government Political Administration) and later in N.K.V.D. (People's Commissariat of Internal Affairs); leader of the Bolshevik organizations in Georgia and Transcaucasia; appointed (1938) People's Commissar of Internal Affairs and (1941) Commissar under Joseph Stalin of United N.K.V.D.; given control of secret police (1938); rose to power by "purging" Stalin's enemies.

See *Current Biography*, (Dec.) 1942

Obituary

N Y Times p 1 D 24 '53

BEST, EDNA Mar. 3, 1900- Actress

Address: b. c/o Actors' Equity Association, 45 W. 47th St., New York 36; h. Beverly Hills, Calif.

Indicative of Edna Best's versatility as an actress is the record of her 1953-1954 season. Between October 1953 and February 1954 she appeared in two Broadway plays (as an attractive widow in *The Ladies of the Corridor* and as an egocentric harridan in *Mademoiselle Colombe*). In June 1954 she appeared at the Bucks County Playhouse, New Hope, Pennsylvania, in the part of Julia in T. S. Eliot's *The Cocktail Party,* followed by the role of the wistful tourist secretary in *The Time of the Cuckoo.*

Miss Best made her debut on the London stage in 1917 when she played an ingenue role in *Charley's Aunt.* Between 1925 and 1940 she traveled back and forth between London and New York, appearing in many successful plays and films. She is best known to Broadway theatregoers for her role in John Van Druten's *There's Always Juliet* in 1932, for her portrayal of the schoolteacher's wife in *The Browning Version* in 1949, and for her part as the provincial widow in S. N. Behrman's comedy, *Jane,* in 1952.

Edna Best was born on March 3, 1900 in the town of Hove, in Sussex, England to Leonard William and Claire (Romaire) Best. She studied for the stage at the Guildhall School of Music. She made her first professional stage appearance on December 15, 1917 at the St. James's Theatre as Ela Delahay in *Charley's Aunt.* At the New Theatre, in December 1919, she played Nibs in *Peter Pan.* She starred in the 1920 Christmas production at the St. James's Theatre of Sir James Barrie's classic. So triumphant was her portrayal that she returned to the St. James's in 1922 for another Christmas as the mythical Peter.

Subsequent performances were as Blanche Ingram in *Her Temporary Husband* (1923), Catherine in *The Lilies of the Field* (1923), Simone Martin in *The Elopement* (1923), Parks in *Trust Emily* (1923), and Jean Trowbridge in *Morals* (1924). She was also in the comedy *Six-Cylinder Love* and *Fallen Angels,* the latter with Tallulah Bankhead.

Michael Arlen's *These Charming People* opened on October 6, 1925 at the Gaiety Theatre with Edna Best in her first New York appearance. Playing opposite Herbert Marshall, Miss Best as Pamela Crawford "made a pert young thing with a mind of her own, vivacious and attractive, walking a very fine line between boldness and modesty" (New York *Times,* October 8, 1925)

After a short run in *The Way You Look At It* in 1926 the actress achieved her second dramatic success before London audiences in the Margaret Kennedy and Basil Deane dramatization of Miss Kennedy's novel, *The Constant Nymph.* In this play Miss Best played opposite Noel Coward, and later John Gielgud, as Teresa Sanger. She appeared in an "all-star cast" benefit performance for King George's Pension Fund of *The Wandering Jew* in May 1927, and later toured in *The Constant Nymph.*

In April 1928, after performing in London as Cecil Zaidner in *Come with Me,* Edna Best was back on the New York stage. With Herbert Marshall she appeared in Frederick Lonsdale's comedy *The High Road* which opened September 10, 1928 at the Fulton Theatre. Brooks Atkinson wrote that "the central part of all enjoys the rare personal charm that Edna Best brings to it. She plays with simplicity of manner and a gracious skill" (New York *Times,* September 11, 1928).

After two active seasons in London, the actress returned to Broadway, to star with Earle Larimore and Basil Rathbone in Henry Bernstein's *Melo* (1931). "With her clean grace of beauty," Edna Best "catches the impish animation of the wife in the beginning and the limp misery of the conclusion" (New York *Times,* April 17, 1931).

In October 1931 Miss Best returned to London where she created the role of Leonora Perrycoste in John Van Druten's play *There's Always Juliet,* playing opposite Herbert Marshall. The play was brought to the Empire Theatre in New York in February 1932 where,

Alfredo Valente

EDNA BEST

"in the two chief parts, Edna Best and Herbert Marshall added several cubits to their stature as artists" (New York *Times,* February 16, 1932).

After a run of 108 performances in *There's Always Juliet,* Miss Best appeared in several London plays including *Another Language* (1932) and as Cinderella in the Christmas pantomime (1936). In films, the actress was in (Sir) Alexander Korda's *South Riding* (1938) and in *Prison Without Bars* (1939).

At the Henry Miller Theatre in New York, Miss Best portrayed the leading role of Mary Cristof in *Delicate Story* which opened December 4, 1940. With John Cromwell, K. T. Stevens and Ann Dere, she starred in *Yankee Point* at the Longacre Theatre in November 1942.

The actress spent the next few years in her Beverly Hills home, producing the Corliss Archer radio broadcasts. In 1947 she was filmed in Twentieth Century Fox's *The Late George Apley,* based upon John P. Marquand's Pulitzer Prize winning novel, with Ronald Colman, Mildred Natwick, Nydia Westman, and Percy Waram.

Ending her absence from the stage, she joined Maurice Evans in October 1949 in a program of two one-act plays by Terence Rattigan at the Coronet Theatre. As Millie Crocker-Harris in *The Browning Version* and as Edna Selby in *A Harlequinade,* Edna Best scored "something of a return triumph" (Richard Watts, Jr., New York *Post,* October 13, 1949). "The performances of Evans and Miss Best are beautifully matched," wrote Howard Barnes. "Miss Best is utterly convincing. . . . The gifted actress has never been more knowing" (New York *Herald Tribune,* October 13, 1949).

Playing in a revival engagement at the City Center in February 1950, she received glowing

BEST, EDNA—*Continued*

notices when she appeared as the aunt from Poughkeepsie in the Ruth and Augustus Goetz adaptation of Henry James's novel *Washington Square,* known as *The Heiress.* In a cast which included Basil Rathbone and Margaret Phillips, Miss Best was thanked by Brooks Atkinson for "a rich and amusingly breathless performance."

In December 1950, Edna Best appeared at the New York City Center in her first Shavian role as Lady Cicely in *Captain Brassbound's Conversion.* "I have a dreamy part," she told Ward Morehouse. "Lady Cicely is comedy and. . . . She feels that if you're nice to people they'll be nice to you. It's a play written in 1899 but you can still translate modern touches into it" (New York *World-Telegram and Sun,* December 20, 1950). Brooks Atkinson wrote that Miss Best "gives a warm, subtle and infinitely accomplished performance" (New York *Times,* December 28, 1950).

Basil Rathbone and Edna Best starred in S. N. Behrman's comedy, *Jane,* adapted from a story by W. Somerset Maugham, at the Coronet Theatre in New York. Sarah Marshall, Edna Best's daughter, also appeared in this successful vehicle. Of the production Brooks Atkinson noted: "In the field of comic theatre nothing so skillful as this has turned up all season" (New York *Times,* February 2, 1952).

On October 21, 1953 she performed in the Dorothy Parker-Arnaud d'Usseau play, *The Ladies of the Corridor,* at the Longacre Theatre. Although the play lasted only fifty-three performances, Miss Best and the cast, including Betty Field, Frances Starr and June Walker, received the critics' praise. Hers is a "stunning portrait" wrote New York *Herald Tribune* critic Walter F. Kerr (October 22, 1953).

Of her performance in the role of Lulu Ames, "a fiftyish widow transplanted from Akron to New York," critic Henry Hewes in the *Saturday Review* (November 7, 1953) wrote: "Edna Best is most brilliant with acid lines and subtle moments of self-realization in the role." William Hawkins commented: "Miss Best has an uncanny way of acting a role with perfect sincerity while letting you know how contemptuous and comical she feels the character really is" (New York *World-Telegram and Sun,* October 22, 1953).

Co-starred with Julie Harris, Miss Best played in *Mademoiselle Colombe,* adapted by Louis Kronenberger from Jean Anouilh's *Colombe,* which opened at the Longacre Theatre on January 6, 1954. Gowned by Motley in Toulouse-Lautrec-period costumes, disguised with a red wig and a putty nose, she took the role of Mme. Alexandra, a flamboyant actress with a volatile temperament and raucous ways. Walter F. Kerr commented: "Miss Best is wonderfully venomous as she mimics the sort of actress who likes to go to the theatre early in order to dream of the ghosts who have trod the old stage" (New York *Herald Tribune,* January 7, 1954).

The actress was married to Seymour Beard in 1920 and by this marriage has twin sons; this union was dissolved in 1928. In that year she married Herbert Marshall, the actor; they have a daughter, Sarah. This marriage was later terminated and in 1940 Miss Best married Nat Wolff, a radio-TV producer. The couple make their permanent home in Beverly Hills, California. In August 1950 Edna Best became an American citizen. She has blonde hair and blue eyes.

References

N Y World-Telegram p32 O 20 '50 por
Who's Who, 1954
Who's Who in the Theatre (1952)

BIALK, ELISA (bôk) Oct. 4, 1912- Author

Address: b. c/o The World Publishing Co., 119 W. 57th St., New York 19; h. 791 Bryant Ave., Winnetka, Ill.

Reprinted from the *Wilson Library Bulletin* Apr. 1954

At home Elisa Bialk is the wife of L. Martin Krautter, a Chicago advertising executive, and home is Winnetka, Illinois.

At her desk she is realizing a lifelong purpose. She says she cannot remember a time when she did not want to write. It was poetry in the beginning—a poem entered in a contest in her freshman year in high school which won second prize and the interest of Harriet Monroe, editor of *Poetry.* "She was very kind to me," Miss Bialk says, reminiscing. "She introduced me to many well known poets of the time and urged me to write prose because my poetry showed a definite dramatic quality."

Her parents, Martha Holcher and John Nicholas Bialk, were both brought from Ger-

ELISA BIALK

many to the United States by their parents when small children. They met and were married and began to raise their family, four girls and a boy, in Chicago.

Elisa Bialk was born October 4, 1912, and she, too, was married in Chicago, the city which has given rich background to much of her writing. She says, "As a child I lived near and played in Lincoln Park. Now when I begin a book in Chicago, it is as if I see the child that I was, playing in the park of my memory. As long as I can see that child and remember her vividly, I can retain a close bond with all childhood." Before finishing Waller High School in Chicago, Elisa Bialk had begun writing for publication. In addition to fulfilling an aim, it was an economic expedient, for her father had died while she was still in kindergarten. Though she does not hold an academic degree, for the same reason, Miss Bialk says, "I feel as if I had never stopped studying. Most of my academic classes were in the School of Journalism at Northwestern University, taken during my spare time while already writing, and working as a reporter."

For a number of years the short story was Miss Bialk's best medium, pulps giving way when she made her first sale to a "slick" in 1932, at the depth of the depression. *Good Housekeeping* bought five short stories within six weeks. Several of her short stories have appeared in anthologies, notably *The Horse Called Pete*, from which the juvenile book of that name was drawn, and *The Sainted Sisters*. This comedy was made into a play, in which the author participated, was later filmed by Paramount, starring Barry Fitzgerald, Veronica Lake, and Joan Caulfield.

Before her marriage in June 1934, Miss Bialk wrote *On What Strange Stuff*, a novel published by Doubleday in 1935. Reviewers were agreed that her work showed promise. The scene was Chicago and the theme the degree of accomplishment—success or failure—achieved in life by eight characters, told in a series of brief dramatic pictures. After her marriage Miss Bialk gave up the newspaper work she had carried on for years in several guises, reporting a column in the *Lincoln-Belmont Booster*, a Chicago community newspaper, called "On Betty's Beat" and other writing for the Chicago *Daily News*. Her interest in children, as her own grew to story age, influenced her to enter the juvenile field seriously after doing *The Horse Called Pete* (1948). *Taffy's Foal* followed in 1949. This story is for grades three to five. The New York *Times'* reviewer said, "Here is another good horse story by the author of *The Horse Called Pete*. It is not so poignant as that first book, nor so succinctly written, but seven-to-eleven-year-old girls will share Nancy's experiences with pleasure and ready understanding."

In 1950 Houghton Mifflin published *Ride 'em, Peggy*. The Chicago *Sunday Tribune* commented, "There is much fun and information for nine to twelve-year-olds in this entertaining family story. . . ." This was followed by *Wild Horse Island* in 1951 and *Jill's Victory* in 1952. The first, published by Houghton Mifflin, was a Catholic Book Club selection telling how a boy "hunted and hoped and finally found and won his wild filly." The second, brought out by World, is a lively story of modern farm life.

In the fall of 1952 World published Miss Bialk's *Colt of Cripple Creek*, a warm-hearted story of a small boy's growing up. On May 16, 1953 Ruth Harshaw presented Miss Bialk and this book on her radio program, Carnival of Books. With the author was Leslie Wilkinson, the postmaster of Cripple Creek, Colorado, the originator of the campaign to build a new schoolhouse there which led to the writing of the book. The school children sold samples of gold ore for a dollar each and raised more than $20,000 for the project.

Miss Bialk is a member of the Society of Midland Authors and of Theta Sigma Phi honorary organization of women in journalism, and of the Children's Reading Round Table, a Chicago group interested in promoting good reading for children. Her other outside interests are varied, if limited by her profession and the demands of her home life. Her journalistic gifts are used annually to promote a number of worthy causes. Golf and fishing while on family vacations are favorite recreations. In addition, and as a mother there is the travel education of her two daughters—Elena, fifteen and Elizabeth, thirteen—and most summer holidays find them far afield in some corner of the United States.

References

Chicago Sch J 32:sup6 My '51 por

BINGHAM, JONATHAN B(REWSTER)
Apr. 24, 1914- Lawyer; former Government official

Address: b. 10 Rockefeller Plaza, New York 20; h. 5000 Independence Ave., Riverdale, New York 71

The idea of helping the people of underdeveloped areas to improve their standards of living is "practical idealism," Jonathan B. Bingham maintains, and one in the United States' own interests—to help stop the threat of communist expansion and "to preserve the peace in the world." Increased food production and control of diseases are among the major aims of the Point IV Program which is carrying out this principle.

From his service with Point IV (called the Technical Cooperation Administration under the Democratic Administration, and now part of the Foreign Operations Administration) from October 1951 to March 1953, for most of that time as deputy director, Bingham drew the material for his book *Shirt-Sleeve Diplomacy* (John Day, 1954).

Former Ambassador Chester Bowles called the book "an excellent report . . . [it] makes exciting reading for thoughtful Americans willing to understand the new world slowly unfolding in . . . Asia, Africa and South Amer-

JONATHAN B. BINGHAM

ica" (New York *Times*, March 7, 1954). "In this book as nowhere else one can find in readable form the essential factors regarding the "Point IV Program" (*Christian Science Monitor*, March 15, 1954).

"Point IV," Bingham explains, "is an educational program involving teaching, training, demonstrating." It is not a "big give away program," but a joint enterprise in which the people voluntarily cooperate. "In Latin America it is *Punto Cuatro,* in Iran it is *Astle Charom*. . . To millions of people all over the world the words Point IV have come to stand for the idea that the American people are interested in their welfare. . . What was both 'bold' and 'new' about [it] was that a whole nation should commit itself and its resources, as a fundamental part of its foreign policy, to the idea of helping all 'peace-loving peoples' to help themselves."

"Representing the type of younger public servant, not dulled by too much contact with red tape nor carried away by delusions of power," wrote August Heckscher in the New York *Herald Tribune Book Review* (March 14, 1954), "Mr. Bingham seems to have been an ideal man for the post" of Point IV deputy director. He is a New York City lawyer who had held several previous positions in the Democratic Administration.

A descendant of Deacon Thomas Bingham, an American colonist of the seventeenth century, Jonathan Brewster Bingham is the youngest of the seven sons of Hiram and Alfreda (Mitchell) Bingham (now Mrs. Henry Gregor). He was born in New Haven, Connecticut on April 24, 1914—the year during which his father, an historian, author and explorer, began the last of his organized expeditions in South America. Hiram Bingham, a Republican, later served eight years in the U.S. Senate and in 1951 became chairman of the Civil Service Commission's Loyalty Review Board.

Jonathan Bingham entered Groton School in Massachusetts in 1926, where he was editor in chief of *The Grotonian* and also took part in athletic and dramatic activities. After being graduated *summa cum laude* in 1932, he enrolled in Yale University and became chairman of the Yale *Daily News*. A Phi Beta Kappa student, he was granted his B.A. degree with honors in economics in 1936. He later attended Yale Law School, was note editor of the *Yale Law Journal* and took his LL.B. degree in 1939.

Before the outbreak of World War II, he traveled as a free-lance correspondent in Europe and Asia, contributing feature articles to the New York *Herald Tribune*. Bingham was admitted to the New York bar in 1940. He was employed in the law firm of Cravath, de Gersdorff, Swaine & Wood in New York City from 1939 to 1941. In that year he was engaged as counsel for the New York State Labor Relations Board and, then, as counsel for the Office of Price Administration.

During the war, Bingham, who had enlisted as a private in 1943, served in Army Intelligence and was promoted to captain before his discharge in 1945. His work earned him the War Department Staff Citation in 1945. He later served in the Department of State as chief of the Alien Enemy Control Section and as special assistant to Assistant Secretary Spruille Braden (October 1945-April 1946).

Resuming the practice of law in New York City in 1946, Bingham became a partner in Cohen & Bingham, the firm with which he is currently associated. It was in 1946 also that he began his activity in the New York State Democratic party. Early in 1950 he was mentioned (without subsequent nomination) as a possible coalition candidate of the Republican and Democratic parties to oppose Vito Marcantonio, then Representative of New York's Eighteenth Congressional District. A New York *Post* editorial (May 23, 1950) noted that any successful candidate against Marcantonio must be able "to offer more than anti-Communism as his platform." Bingham "understands the nature of the conflict between liberalism and totalitarianism . . . he personifies . . . the integrity and conviction which a candidate must possess to beat Marcantonio."

With his appointment as assistant director of the Office of International Security Affairs, Bingham returned to the State Department in April 1951. He held that post, in which he was responsible for non-European affairs, until October 1951 when he assumed the duties of deputy administrator of the Technical Cooperation Administration.

The fourth point in former President Harry S. Truman's "program for peace and freedom," outlined in his January 20, 1949 inaugural address, was a plan (originated by the late Benjamin H. Hardy in 1948) for aiding countries in need of technical assistance. Truman proposed that the United States "embark on a bold new program for making the benefits of our scientific advances and industrial progress available for the improvement and growth of the underdeveloped areas" of the world. Accordingly, in 1950 the Technical Cooperation Administration was established as part of the State Department, with Dr. Henry G. Bennett as its first director. The enterprise was to be a cooperative one, in which nations would work together through the United Nations and its specialized agencies as far as possible. Capital investment was to be encouraged, and foreign students and technicians were to be brought to the United States for training.

When Dr. Bennett was killed in an airplane crash in Iran in December 1951, Bingham was named acting administrator of the program and served in that capacity until Stanley Andrews took office as administrator four months later. Bingham remained as deputy administrator, resigning in March 1953, subsequent to the establishment of the Republican administration.

By January 1952 Point IV had undertaken 216 projects in thirty-four countries, with the aid of 619 American technicians. Bingham at that time called attention to Point IV achievements in Latin America as the foremost success of the program. Another significant accomplishment was the project in Etawah, India, where wheat production was increased by 50 per cent. It has been estimated that 80 per cent of Point IV work in its early operations related to food, health and education, with food the most urgent consideration.

Point IV technicians teach farmers how to increase production and how to use bulldozers and tractors. Mechanized equipment cannot always be used, however, Bingham explained. "Hoes and scythes may be the best thing in one place and not in another. A fungicide that works here may not work there. The job requires ingenuity and flexibility, as well as determination."

Soon after his return in October 1952 from a trip to survey conditions in countries of the Middle East, Bingham noted that U.S. assistance to Israel had been directed chiefly to the economic problems which had arisen from the influx of refugees and stated that in the two previous years Congress had provided $133,000,000 for Israeli aid under Point IV.

"While others had more intimate contact with the program in one country," Bingham has said, "I had an almost unique opportunity to observe the workings of the whole thing." He discussed Point IV at the New York *Herald Tribune* Forum (March, 1952) and subsequently in several articles, including "Understanding Point Four" (*Department of State Bulletin,* December 29, 1952) and "Can Private Enterprise Do the Job of Economic Development?" (*Foreign Policy Bulletin,* June 15, 1953).

He believes that the American people must, however, be realistic and not expect "the deserts to bloom in a few short years, to expect ignorance, and hunger, and disease to be overcome, to expect, in short, miracles" (*Department of State Bulletin,* December 29, 1952). "Our desire is to help the host government through cooperative methods to achieve progress of which *it* can be proud . . . curious and suspicious at first, the local officials have gradually come to understand that our interest is to see them succeed in *their* efforts. . . ."

Pointing out that great strides have been made in the elimination of malaria, Bingham said that in many areas the villagers themselves cooperated by spraying with DDT. "The incidence of this debilitating disease has dropped in two years from 80 per cent to as little as five per cent," he said, "with a consequent direct effect not only on the welfare of the people but on their ability to work and produce crops. In a number of dry and dusty villages, deep wells have been sunk, bringing to the inhabitants the miracle of clean, fresh water."

In an article for the New York *Times Magazine* (May 10, 1953), he wrote: "The real question is not whether we can afford the relatively small amount that the Point IV Program costs—about one-tenth of New York City's budget—but whether we can afford to let the gaps of poverty and misunderstanding widen between ourselves and more than a billion of our neighbors." Bingham's article in the *Bulletin of Atomic Scientists* (March 1954), "Partisan Politics and Point IV," makes clear that the program cannot succeed without genuine idealism on the part of the people who direct it.

August Heckscher (New York *Herald Tribune Book Review,* March 14, 1954) noted that Bingham writes in his book *Shirt-Sleeve Diplomacy* "with a refreshing sense that to have served the government of the United States, particularly in so novel and challenging a field is one of the privileges of a lifetime." Clarence R. Decker commented in the *Saturday Review* (June 5, 1954): "Although neither sentimental nor polemical, Bingham shares the current anxiety and pleads soberly for rededication to the original point to Point IV. . . The real battle of our time is against the appalling social and economic inequities. . . Bingham sees Point IV as a necessary and noble experiment."

Bingham is counsel to the Far Eastern Association, and on the board of the National Child Labor Committee. He belongs to the American and New York county bar associations and to the Association of the Bar of the City of New York. The lawyer served during 1949-1951 on the Yale Corporation, from 1948 to 1950 as New York state chairman of the Americans for Democratic Action, and on the national board of ADA. His clubs are the Metropolitan in Washington, D.C., and the Coffee House and Yale in New York.

Mrs. Jonathan B. Bingham, the former June Rossbach, is an author. Married on September 20, 1939, the Binghams have four children: Sherrell, June Mitchell, Timothy Woodbridge, and Claudia Rossbach. The brown-haired, brown-eyed lawyer is six feet two inches in height and weighs 175 pounds. He attends the Congregational Church. Music, books and tennis are his chief recreations.

References

N Y Herald Tribune p20 Mr 24 '52 por
Martindale-Hubbell Law Directory, 1952
Who's Who in America, 1954-55

BINNS, JOSEPH PATTERSON June 28, 1905- Hotel executive

Address: b. c/o The Waldorf-Astoria, 301 Park Ave., New York 22; h. 9 North Rd., Darien, Conn.

As general manager and executive vice-president of the forty-seven story Waldorf-Astoria hotel in New York, Joseph Patterson Binns oversees every facet of hotel operation "from plovers' eggs to private police," while keeping a firm hand on the budget. In an average month he welcomes as many as 900 guests from foreign countries and more than 11,000 Americans. When Conrad Hilton bought "the world's best known hostelry" to add to his hotel "empire" in 1949, he chose Binns to head it. Attention to detail is "the amazing thing" in a hotel that serves an average of 6,000 guests daily, 2,000,000 meals annually, has 2,000 rooms, 116 apartments, eight dining rooms, eleven banquet suites, five bars, eight kitchens, and 500 employees.

Binns is also a vice-president of the Hilton Hotels Corporation in charge of the eastern division which includes the Waldorf-Astoria, Roosevelt, Plaza, and New Yorker in New York City and the Mayflower in Washington, D.C. He entered the hotel business about twenty-five years ago as a room clerk at the Chalfonte-Haddon Hall in Atlantic City, New Jersey after studying hotel management at Cornell University and business administration at the Wharton School, University of Pennsylvania.

In World War II Binns was a colonel and served in Europe as chief of supply and service for the Air Transport Command of the Army Air Force. On November 7, 1953 former President Herbert Hoover appointed Binns to head a government task force to study subsistence services provided by Federal departments and agencies.

A. Laviosa

JOSEPH PATTERSON BINNS

He became a director of the Hotels Statler Company on August 6, 1954 when it was acquired by Conrad Hilton, president of Hilton Hotels.

Joseph Patterson Binns, one of six sons, was born in Winona, Ohio on June 28, 1905. He was brought up in Philadelphia. His father, Edward T. Binns, was a Quaker minister, and an elder in the Arch Street Meeting in Philadelphia. His mother was Esther (Brackin) Binns. One of his brothers, Edward T. Binns, is a television actor.

"Joe" received his secondary education at the Westtown School in Westtown, Pennsylvania, and at a Quaker boarding school in Philadelphia, graduating in 1924. He studied business administration for two years at the Wharton School, University of Pennsylvania, and then transferred to Cornell University to major in hotel administration. He was graduated with a Bachelor of Science degree in 1928. While at college he made the All-American Soccer Team, became a member of the honorary theatrical society, "The Ghosts", and belonged to Sigma Chi.

Soon after graduation, Joe Binns began his career as room clerk at the Chalfonte-Haddon Hall Hotel in Atlantic City. Three years later he became the assistant manager of the Claridge Hotel in that city, and a year later, its manager. Then, in 1933, he joined the Cambridge Realty Company as manager, supervising hotels, apartment houses, garages, and office buildings in several cities. Chicago's Stevens Hotel, with its 2,700 rooms, became Joseph Binns's next post. He went there as general manager in 1939. Today, this is the Conrad Hilton Hotel.

By 1942 Binns had enlisted in the Army as a second lieutenant, beginning a protracted Army career under three different commands, from which he emerged a colonel in the Air Transport Command at the end of the war, serving as chief of supply and service. For his service he holds two Bronze Stars for campaigns in northern France, ribbons for the European, Asiatic, Middle East, and Pacific Theaters, the Victory Ribbon, Croix de Guerre, Bronze Star Medal, and Legion of Merit.

Returning to civilian status after the war, Binns became general manager of the Palmer House, a Hilton hotel in Chicago. It was in 1946 that the Hilton Hotels Corporation was formed and Binns was named a vice-president. Conrad Hilton acquired the Stevens Hotel in Chicago, and in New York City the Roosevelt, the New Yorker, and the stately old Plaza, where Binns became manager in 1948. Since prestige is paramount in the Hilton scheme, the atmosphere of the Plaza was kept intact, but cloakrooms and offices were shuffled to make room for lucrative bars and high priced living quarters, and Binns, like all the Hilton managers, saw to it that profits increased.

For ten years after the "new" Waldorf-Astoria opened on Park Avenue in 1931, it lost money—$10,000,000 all told—and its stock never paid a dividend. In 1944 business improved, and in 1949 Hilton bought the Waldorf-Astoria for $3,000,000, a hotel which had cost $26,000,000 to build and furnish. He appointed Binns its general manager and executive vice-president.

Of Hilton's purchase Binns said, "It took courage. The Waldorf is a great civic and social center, but its financial history had always been a dismal failure" (*Reader's Digest*, January, 1952). Currently, however, the Waldorf-Astoria is reputed to be showing a yearly profit of $1,000,000.

The magnitude of Binns's responsibility is indicated in some of the hotel's better known statistics. To serve the 2,000,000 meals consumed during the year, the hotel employs eighty-six chefs, twelve chefs on soup, one plus a staff for sauces, one fry cook plus a staff, a vegetable cook, potato man, a broiler, roaster, and liaison cook, five salad girls, twelve ice cream men, thirty-four pastry cooks, and a corps of pantry helpers who, among other things, clean 3,000 melons and grapefruit daily. There are 155 telephone operators, and the police system is large enough to keep order in a small city—a chief, his assistant, ten house detectives, twenty-five patrolmen, a clerk, and a roundsman.

The problem of dealing with Kings, Queens, Presidents and generals who stay at the Waldorf is handled by an extensive foreign department. Some 400 flags of sixty nations, the emblems of United States officials and of the Holy See are in readiness to be displayed in honor of visiting dignitaries.

Among those who have apartments in The Towers on the twenty-eighth to forty-second floors of the Waldorf are ex-President Herbert Hoover, General Douglas MacArthur, the Duke and Duchess of Windsor, Mr. and Mrs. William Randolph Hearst, Jr., and Mr. and Mrs. Cole Porter. Over the door to Apartment 42A is the official seal of the United States, which establishes that suite as "what is probably the only American Embassy located in a hotel." Its seven rooms were used by U.S. Ambassador Warren R. Austin and are now occupied by his successor, Ambassador Henry Cabot Lodge, Jr., as the U.S. representative at the United Nations.

In his position on the Commission on Organization of the Executive Branch of the Government (Hoover commission), to which he was appointed in November 1953, Binns heads a group of experts on food programs, mass food preparations and service, warehousing, laundry operation and allied fields. It studies installations operated by the military services, the Veterans Administration, the Public Health Service, and other agencies.

Among the clubs to which Binns belongs are the University (New York), University (Chicago), Metropolitan (Washington, D.C.), Wee Burn Country (Darien, Connecticut), Middletown Yacht (Middletown, Connecticut), and Oxford Ridge Hunt (Darien). He is a member of the American Hotel Association.

Binns was described in *Town & Country* (October, 1951) as "a handsome, graying, immaculately groomed Quaker." He has brown eyes and is five feet eleven inches tall. Tennis, one of his hobbies, keeps him lean and fit. His wife, the former Ruth Taplin whom he married on May 1, 1930, shares his love of the sea. Their yacht, "Grey Gull II" is often moored in Nassau. Their daughter is Ruth Anne Binns, a student at Stanford University.

The hotel executive drives a 1912 Rolls Royce he calls "Silver Ghost" which is his particular pride. With it he won a Gold Cup in Springfield, Massachusetts, for the best kept Rolls Royce. "Silver Ghost" is one of the old cars Binns has collected as a favorite hobby, and which he keeps, not at the Waldorf, but at his home in Darien, Connecticut.

A *New Yorker* reporter who accompanied Binns on one of his drives down Park Avenue in the Rolls Royce said that Binns always places carnations in a slender cut-glass vase attached to the doorpost of the elegant blue morocco interior. "I just don't feel right going out in her without flowers," Binns said. In order to pass a motor-vehicle inspection in Connecticut, he had to install a hand windshield wiper and a stop light. He also installed isinglass curtains on either side of the front seat. "In 1912," said Binns, "nobody worried about the chauffeur getting wet, but I'm my own chauffeur and I like a little protection."

"That reminds me," said Binns. "I was driving past Gramercy Park the other night and noticed a lady trying to hail a cab. For a lark, I said 'Taxi, lady?' She started to get in, then noticed I was in evening clothes. We both burst out laughing, and I took her where she wanted to go. A wonderful humanizer, this old girl!" (*New Yorker,* September 6, 1952).

References

New Yorker 28:32 S 6 '52
Who's Who in America, 1954-55

BIRD, WILL(IAM) R(ICHARD) May 11, 1891- Author; Government official

Address: b. Chronicle Bldg., Halifax, Nova Scotia, Canada; h. 35 Marlborough Ave., Halifax, Nova Scotia, Canada

One of the most prolific of contemporary Canadian authors, Will R. Bird has published some 600 short stories and articles and over a dozen books in a writing career covering over thirty years. His historical novels *Here Stays Good Yorkshire* and *Judgment Glen* were co-winners of "All Canada" Fiction awards and both concern the English settlers who came to Nova Scotia just before the American Revolution. Other highly regarded works by Bird include his history *A Century at Chignecto,* his historical novel *The Passionate Pilgrim,* and a travel book entitled *This Is Nova Scotia.*

Bird, a veteran of World War I, has written and lectured on Canadian regiments and battlefields. He was assistant director of the Nova Scotia provincial government's Bureau of Information from 1934 to 1950, when he became chairman of the provincial government's Historic Sites Advisory Council. Bird's novel, *To Love and To Cherish,* was published in Canada in 1953 by the Ryerson Press and in the United States in 1954 by Bouregy & Curl.

William Richard Bird was born on May 11, 1891 at East Mapleton, Nova Scotia. He was

New Liberty, Toronto

WILL R. BIRD

one of the five sons of Stephen and Augusta Caroline Bird; the former was a carpenter, farmer and lieutenant in the Nova Scotia militia; the latter, a schoolteacher. His eldest brother is a minister of the United Church of Canada; the second died of war wounds; the third is the proprietor of an inn at Amherst, Nova Scotia; the fourth was killed in action in World War I.

"Will" Bird was brought up at Amherst, Nova Scotia and was graduated from the academy there in 1906. For some time before the outbreak of World War I he farmed in Alberta, where he took up a homestead. He enlisted in 1916 as a private in the 42nd Royal Highlanders and spent twenty-six months in trenches on the French front. He won the Military Medal for gallantry at Mons and was discharged with the rank of corporal on March 20, 1919.

His literary career stemmed from his war service. "While suffering from blood poisoning, the result of too much poison gas . . . ," he recalls, "I had to sit with my arm in a solution. I read all the material possible. Seeing an offer of $25 for a best fish story, I wrote one, won the money, and was invited to meet the editor of the publication, the Halifax [Sunday] *Atlantic Leader*. I worked for him for two years and have been writing ever since."

He has published 217 articles since 1924 in over sixty publications—Canadian, American, British, and Australian. During the same period, he sold 402 short stories and novelettes "to the same range of publications, with translations in European magazines."

The first work by Bird to appear in book form was *A Century at Chignecto, the Key to Old Acadia* (Ryerson, 1928). It was "the story of the isthmus of Chignecto" and "centered on . . . Fort Beauséjour," the principal bastion between Quebec and Louisburg. It was followed by *And We Go On* (the author's privately printed war reminiscences) and by *Private Timothy Fergus Clancy* (T. Eaton, 1930).

His one-page short story "Paid-up Member" (dealing with a Canadian veteran) appeared in the June 14, 1930 issue of the American magazine, *Collier's*, and was followed in the April 11, 1931 number of the same magazine by "Beyond the Wire," a World War I story.

As many as twenty-three titles by Bird have been included in Edward J. H. O'Brien's anthologies of best short stories and in the O. Henry Award collections. In 1931 the author was commissioned by *Maclean's Magazine* to tour the World War I battle fronts on which the Canadian corps had served. He "covered the ground in four months" and wrote eighteen articles which were later published in book form as *Thirteen Years After* (MacLean, 1932). His visit to the battlefields concluded, Bird toured the five eastern provinces of Canada for two years and lectured in about 111 towns and cities.

Bird was appointed in 1933 to a clerkship in the Nova Scotia provincial government's Bureau of Information, and was made assistant director of the bureau in 1934. He held this post for the next sixteen years, during which he lectured and wrote publicity material. Only two new books by Bird appeared during his first ten years with the bureau, the first being the privately printed *The Communication Trench* (1935), the second the romantic novel, *Maid of the Marshes* (1936).

When the Ryerson Press published his *Here Stays Good Yorkshire* in 1945, Will R. Bird's stature as a man of letters was increased immeasurably. The book was co-winner with Philip Child's *Day of Wrath* of the 1945 Ryerson "All Canada" Fiction Award, and was published in England in 1946 by Hatchards. A reviewer for the London *Times Literary Supplement* observed that the story dealt with the Crabtree family which "in 1772 decided to emigrate from Yorkshire and settle in Nova Scotia," and that the Crabtrees' history was "largely made up of fights with each other and with Indians, neighbors and wild animals, violent love affairs, struggles to possess land and found families, robust religion, and uproarious fun."

Clara Thomas wrote in *Canadian Novelists: 1920-1945* that Tristram Crabtree "emerges as one of the truly great characters of Canadian fiction." She considers *Here Stays Good Yorkshire* "one of the most distinguished and fascinating historical romances written by a Canadian."

The collection *Sunrise for Peter, and Other Stories* was published by the Ryerson Press in 1946. Bird's *Judgment Glen* (Ryerson, 1947) was the co-winner with Edward A. McCourt's *Music at the Close* of the year's "All Canada" Fiction Award. A critic in the *Dalhousie Review* summed up *Judgment Glen* as "another fine novel of the founding of Cumberland county . . . by Yorkshire men." The central character is Helger Fallydown "who through his vanity and egotism brings his family to Nova Scotia that he may leave them there while he returns to expected knightly honors in England."

The Passionate Pilgrim (Ryerson, 1949) impressed one reviewer, Elizabeth A. Wallace, as "a straightforward yarn of adventure" about "an attractive youth, Steve Bonsel, who comes to Boston and later to the neighborhood of Fort Beauséjour after a terrible experience with marauding Indians" (*Queen's Quarterly*).

The Haliburton Society of Nova Scotia made Bird a fellow in 1946 in recognition of his contribution to Canadian literature. He was awarded an honorary Doctor of Literature degree by Mount Allison University at Sackville, New Brunswick in 1949. In 1949-1950 he served as national president of the Canadian Authors' Association. He was appointed chairman of Nova Scotia's Historic Sites Advisory Council in 1950.

Of Bird's *This is Nova Scotia* (Ryerson, 1950; Macrae Smith, 1950), R. C. Gask wrote: "This is by no means merely a tourist book" since "even if the reader never visits Nova Scotia . . . he will feel, after 'journeying' with Mr. Bird, that he knows and likes it well" (New York *Times,* September 10, 1950).

In the following year, Bird added *So Much to Record* (Ryerson) to his list of works. His next book was *To Love and to Cherish,* an historical novel. It provided a picturesque account of a pioneering community as well as a tale of action and romance, and dealt with a young Connecticut farmer who, having been dispossessed by a "patriotic" mob, became one of the Loyalist band which established the town of Shelburne, Nova Scotia. The *Two Jacks* (Ryerson) and *No Retreating Footsteps* (Kentville Publishing Company) appeared in Canada during 1954.

William Richard Bird and Ethel May Sutton, a secretary to the superintendent of a government experimental farm, were married on June 18, 1919 and became the parents of two children. (Their son, Captain Stephen Stanley Bird of the North Nova Scotia Highlanders, died in action at Caen, Normandy on July 8, 1944; their daughter, Betty Caroline, is married to a doctor). The Birds were residents of Amherst from 1919 to 1933, and now live in Halifax, where Will Bird is a member of the Commercial and Men's Canadian clubs and St. George's Society.

He also belongs to the Cornwallis branch of the Canadian Legion, and the Nova Scotia and Canadian Historical societies. He is five feet nine inches in height and 170 pounds in weight, and has brown eyes and hair. For outdoor recreation he enjoys trout fishing. His indoor hobby is book reviewing. He is a member of the United Church of Canada. His political affiliation is with the Liberal party.

References

Canadian Who's Who, 1949-51
Thomas, C. Canadian Novelists: 1920-1945 (1946)

BLACKWELL, BETSY TALBOT Editor

Address: b. c/o Mademoiselle, 575 Madison Ave., New York 22; h. 1170 5th Ave., New York 29

The woman "who raised *Mademoiselle* up from an awkward miss in pigtails" to a poised young lady is Mrs. Betsy Talbot Blackwell. She has been editor in chief of the magazine that is "a fashion bible to the co-ed and white collar girl" since 1937 and under her editorship the magazine has developed a social consciousness as well as a fashion awareness. She has won a number of awards for her efforts toward serving the interests of young business and college women, in guiding them in their choice of careers, in helping the "young marrieds" to become leaders in community life, and in promoting American fashions.

She had more than a decade of experience in fashions and editing before becoming *Mademoiselle's* fashion editor in 1935. From 1923 to 1931 she was on the editorial staff of *Charm* magazine, and later was promoter of children's clothes at Tobe fashion service. From 1947 to 1949, in addition to her work with *Mademoiselle,* she served as editor in chief of the magazine *Living.*

Early in 1954 *Mademoiselle* magazine held its first workshop under the auspices of seven leading women's colleges and the publication's "Jobs and Futures" department. In the words of Mrs. Blackwell the two-day forum "was devoted to discussing with deans and vocational guidance directors of some 120 colleges the job problems of liberal arts women graduates." The results of the forum were published in the February 1954 issue.

Betsy Talbot was born in New York City, the only child of Hayden and Benedict (Bristow) Talbot. Her father, a playwright, newspaper correspondent and author, was the first journalist to obtain an authorized statement from Kaiser Wilhelm II at the end of World War I. Her mother was one of the first stylists in the United States and a former fashion expert with Lord & Taylor in New York City.

Betsy obtained most of her early education at the Academy of St. Elizabeth in Convent Station, New Jersey. She edited the school publication, *The Beth,* and was graduated in 1923. As a part-time student, she later attended the College of St. Elizabeth, also at Convent Station, New Jersey. In choosing her lifework, she states, "probably the most important influences were the professions of my parents."

She began her career at the age of fifteen when she was "a fat, freckle-faced" girl at home on spring vacation from school. With the help of a friend of her mother, she secured a three-week position as a comparison shopper of men's overcoats in a Fifth Avenue department store in New York City.

Miss Talbot's first full-time job came in 1923 as a fashion reporter for the publication *The Breath of the Avenue.* Then followed almost nine years on the staff of *Charm* magazine, where she is quoted as saying she "did everything but set type, and was even sent to

BETSY TALBOT BLACKWELL

Paris for the openings." From 1923 to 1931 she was successively assistant to the fashion editor, beauty editor, and fashion editor.

She became advertising manager of Sisholz Brothers' buying office in New York in 1931. The next year she was with the Tobe fashion service as a promoter of children's clothes. During most of 1933, she remained at home writing, but found she needed "the discipline of an office." That year she was also a volunteer with the Woman's Organization for National Prohibition Repeal. She returned to her former position with Tobe in 1933.

When the magazine *Mademoiselle* was launched in 1935 by Street & Smith, publishers, Betsy Talbot Blackwell joined the staff as fashion editor. She states: "There were two kinds of women's magazines when we started *Mademoiselle* . . . the de luxe luxury magazines with emphasis on Paris fashions [and] . . . the mass women's magazines, not fashion magazines at all. . . . It seemed obvious that there were people in the country with good taste who couldn't afford custom-made clothes. That is the *Mademoiselle* field, good taste at moderate price."

Following the resignation of Desmond Hall as editor in chief of *Mademoiselle* in 1937, Mrs. Blackwell was appointed to the post. Her original ideas and woman's touch began increasing the magazine's circulation. Her plan for making unattractive young women into charming girls by bringing them to Manhattan and outfitting them with smart clothes, hair styles and make-up, increased *Mademoiselle's* circulation to 178,057 in May 1939. By 1953 *Mademoiselle's* circulation was 539,558.)

To further add to the popularity of the magazine. Mrs. Blackwell started a college issue, written and edited by college girls during their summer vacation. These girls come to Manhattan and work under the guidance of *Mademoiselle's* staff. Within the first year of its inauguration, this idea almost doubled the demand for the magazine.

Mrs. Blackwell says that the staff of *Mademoiselle* "is rather young. We try to have it as contemporary with our readers as possible." As guest speaker at a meeting of the Women's Advertising Club in Washington, D.C., she stated that each month *Mademoiselle* "selects an over-all theme and builds an entire issue around it" (Washington *Post,* January 26, 1950).

In January 1950, a low-sale month for most magazines, *Mademoiselle* drew a high circulation with its salute to the Washington, D.C. sesquicentennial celebration. The February 1954 issue of *Mademoiselle* made a significant literary contribution with its publication of Dylan Thomas' verse play and last important work "Under Milk Wood."

In the monthly feature, "Memo from the Editor," which Mrs. Blackwell writes for *Mademoiselle,* she gives news of fashions, and describes parties, visits to meetings and places, entertainment of notables and other items of interest to young women. Although she believes "writing is the hardest way to make a living and the rarest talent," she is trying to encourage young college girls in a writing career. *Mademoiselle* offers annual writing awards to college women and other awards to women writers under thirty years old.

In her frequent trips throughout the United States, Mrs. Blackwell studies clothes, discusses fashions and visits colleges. She told staff writer Carol Taylor of the New York *World-Telegram* (April 2, 1945): "I never have enough sleep. I work too hard and I play too hard, and I'm the healthiest person you know."

Mrs. Blackwell won the Neiman-Marcus Award for Distinguished Service in the Field of Fashion in 1942, and was one of the Key Women of the Year honored in 1947 by the Federation of Jewish Philanthropies for her creative activities. In 1953 she received the Junior Achievement Award for Inspiration to Youth. *Mademoiselle* was awarded in 1954 the Fairbanks Award by the American College Public Relations Association, District II, for its ". . . interest in and accurate presentation of the values of a college education for women." She is a member of the Fashion Group, Inc., Women's National Press Club, Women's National Republican Club, Inc. and Columbia University School of General Studies Council. She is a delegate to the American Assembly. Her church affiliation is Presbyterian.

Betsy Talbot was married to Bowden Washington on December 11, 1925. This marriage was later dissolved, and on April 10, 1930, she married James Madison Blackwell, a lawyer. They have one son, James Madison Blackwell IV. She has "green" eyes and brown hair, and is five feet two and one-half inches tall. She weighs 118 pounds.

Her hobbies include going to football games; collecting miniature antique shoes, dolls and fans; and reading. Pert and modern, with a husky voice, her plea is "please don't call me a career woman. . . ." (New York *World-Telegram,* April 2, 1945). She hopes to make *Mademoiselle* of greater service to young educated women who, she says, "are marrying earlier and having larger families."

References

N Y World-Telegram p13 Ap 2 '45 por
Time 35:55 Ap 15 '40 por
Washington (D.C.) Post p5B Ja 26 '50
Who's Who in America, 1954-55
Who's Who in New York, 1952

BLANCH, ARNOLD (ALDER) June 4, 1896- Painter; teacher

Address: b. c/o Associated American Artists, 711 Fifth Ave., New York 22; h. Woodstock, N.Y.

NOTE: This biography supersedes the article which appeared in *Current Biography* in 1940.

A versatile painter of the American scene, Arnold Blanch held his latest exhibit at the Walker Art Center in Minneapolis during August and September 1953. Blanch, who has been painting for over thirty years, has passed through periods variously termed those of "romanticism," "acid realism," and "abstract expressionism."

The artist has based much of his work on his travels through the United States and Europe. His paintings, as well as his ceramics and book illustrations, show his range of expression and subject matter. His work has brought him many prizes and awards and appears in many public and private collections. He has written books on art and has taught in several well-known American art schools. Blanch is a member of the Woodstock, New York art colony.

Arnold Alder Blanch, born in Mantorville, Minnesota on June 4, 1896, is the son of Louis and Bertha (Alder) Blanch of Swiss and English ancestry. His mother painted china, but as a boy he was more impressed with the reproductions of paintings which his aunt had copied to hang in her home.

He decided to become an artist after his family had moved to Minneapolis and after he had watched students drawing Greek casts in the public library. He entered the Minneapolis School of Art where his aunt paid his first year's tuition. Thereafter, he won scholarships, and one enabled him to go to the Art Students League in New York where he studied under John Sloan and Robert Henri.

After a brief period as a commercial artist, Blanch was sent to France in 1918 with the AEF and whenever he could get a leave, he visited the Paris galleries and museums. After the war, he returned to the Art Students League where he studied until 1921 under such artists and teachers as Kenneth Hayes Miller and Boardman Robinson.

Blanch then took advantage of the AEF university training program and spent a summer painting in the Loire Valley of France. He also worked in England and Italy. He

ARNOLD BLANCH

joined other young art pioneers, in 1923, at Woodstock, New York where he did odd jobs to earn enough money to secure time and materials for painting. Blanch sold some of his pictures during an exhibit in 1926, which enabled him to continue painting and to complete enough pictures for his next show at the Dudensing Galleries in New York City in 1928.

The artist then went to France and painted there for eight months. On his return, he received the Norman Waite Harris silver medal from the Art Institute of Chicago for *Midsummer Landscape,* acclaimed by *Art Digest* (November 1, 1929) as a "modern rendering of a typical American country-side."

Blanch had five one-man shows in the period from 1930 to 1932; two in New York, and one each in Chicago, Minneapolis and San Francisco. While traveling by car to San Francisco to become an instructor at the California School of Fine Arts in 1930, Blanch has written, he came to realize "the expansive and fertile beauty of this country." In San Francisco he discovered that he liked to teach. He was awarded the Anne Bremer First Prize and an Art Association Purchase Prize by the San Francisco Art Association in 1931.

A recipient of a Guggenheim fellowship, the painter went to Europe in 1933 and spent much of his time studying pictures in Spain, France and Belgium. Blanch returned to the United States the following year and according to Harry Salpeter (*Esquire,* March 1938), the artist hoped now to "transpose social feeling to canvas." In explaining Blanch's style during these depression years, Salpeter wrote, "It was as if the artist were saying: 'Look here, I'm angry about this.'"

During the thirties, Blanch worked on various Federal art projects and painted murals in post office buildings in Columbus, Wisconsin, Norwalk, Connecticut and Fredonia, New York. His one-man show at the Rehn Galleries in

BLANCH, ARNOLD—*Continued*

New York in 1935 brought varied reactions from the critics. Edward Alden Jewell, (*Art Digest,* March 1, 1935), called the show "a rather odd mixture, the gamut running from some of the circus performers, gay in color, to drab . . . landscapes. Several of the latter are freighted with macabre symbolism: *The Third Mortgage,* with skeletons hanging from trees; *New England* epitomized . . . by a scarecrow and an ancient scrapped auto." Carlyle Burrows of the New York *Herald Tribune* called the same pictures "spook ridden" and felt that the artist had traveled around the country "looking for old houses fallen into ruin and breathing an air heavy with desolation," but added that the scenes were painted with care and imagination.

For five years, until 1939, Blanch taught at the Art Students League in New York. During this period, he received the Beck Gold Medal Award from the Pennsylvania Academy of Fine Arts, and a third prize at the Carnegie International Exhibition of Paintings in 1938 for a picture entitled *The People.* He visited Mexico, South Carolina and Georgia and taught summer classes at the Colorado Springs Fine Arts Center from 1939 to 1941.

In the spring of 1940, the artist held a one-man show at the Associated American Artists Gallery in New York. *Art News* (April 27, 1940) commented that his work had a delicacy of form and color resembling Japanese prints. *Swamp Folks* and *Swanee River* were cited as examples of his skill in approaching "with the greatest sympathy . . . the human lives which are lived against a background of indescribable poverty and hopelessness. But the emphasis is largely upon the subtle color of brown-gray fields, glimpses of gray water and leaden skies."

Time (April 29, 1940), when featuring Blanch's painting *Negro Preacher,* described Blanch as presenting the American scene "without trimmings" in "bleak, overcast landscapes and figure-paintings."

Grace Pagano wrote, in the *Encyclopædia Britannica Collection of Contemporary American Painting* (1946), that critics continue to disagree about Blanch's work because his paintings fail to fit any pigeonhole, and added, "there will always be those [critics] who will seize upon the acid realism, the irony or the gloomy sentiment, but there will always be others, fortunately, who will see them as art in its finest sense."

Blanch illustrated Dale Lowell Morgan's book, *Humboldt, Highroad of the West* (Farrar and Rinehart, 1943), and in 1945 he received a prize in the Domesday Press Competition for juvenile book illustrations. He illustrated Lee Anderson's book of poems, *Prevailing Winds,* which was privately printed. He wrote two books of instruction, *Methods and Techniques for Gouache Painting* (American Artists, 1946), and *Painting for Enjoyment* (Tudor, 1947), the latter in collaboration with his wife, Doris Lee. Many of Blanch's pictures have been reproduced in other books and in periodicals.

In his monograph, published by the American Artists Group in 1946, Blanch stated that the poet Walt Whitman, and his book, *Leaves of Grass,* in particular, brought him a sense of values. "Whitman," he wrote, "has not only been an impetus to living but has also had an effect on the content of my painting."

Blanch has been a visiting artist at Michigan State College (1944), University of Minnesota (1949), Ohio State University summer school (1952), Florida Gulf Coast Art Center (1951 to 1953), and University of Minnesota's summer school in Duluth (1953).

The artist was awarded first prize for designs by the National Ceramic Exhibition of the Syracuse Museum of Fine Arts in 1949 and again in 1951. The painter's work appears in thirteen public collections including those at the Metropolitan Museum of Art, Whitney Museum of American Art, Carnegie Institute, Denver (Colorado) Art Museum, and Library of Congress.

John K. Sherman, writing in the Minneapolis *Star* of August 11, 1953, stated that the paintings in Blanch's 1953 Minneapolis show revealed "amazing technique . . . buoyant spirit, mastery of . . . pattern and varied textures, and a joy in aligning much amusing detail in flowing all-over designs." The thirty-nine oils, *gouaches,* etchings and ink drawings showed "a wonderful balance . . . between the outer world and the inner vision—the first supplying a colorful abundance of motifs, the second bringing into action a highly personal and versatile treatment."

The artist married Lucille Lundquist, a fellow student at the Art Students League, in 1922. They were divorced in 1939. In 1941 he married Doris Emrich Lee who had been one of his students at the California School of Fine Arts, and who has since become an outstanding American painter. The farmhouse and barn at Woodstock which served as their first home and workshop has been replaced by a studio home which they designed. They have had winter homes in Key West and in Clearwater, Florida.

Since early boyhood, Arnold Blanch has been an enthusiastic fisherman and hunter. He enjoys gardening and reading, but says he finds his thoughts and activities almost completely absorbed by the problems of painting. He is five feet eight inches tall, weighs 175 pounds and has gray hair and eyes. He belongs to the Woodstock Artists' Association and is a Democrat.

References

Esquire p59 Mr '38
Time 35:39 Ap 29 '40
American Artists Group. Arnold Blanch (1946)
Pagano, G. The Encyclopaedia Britannica Collection of Contemporary American Painting (1946)
Who's Who in America, 1952-53
Who's Who in American Art (1953)

BLANCH, MRS. ARNOLD (ALDER) *See* Lee, D.

BLANDY, W(ILLIAM) H(ENRY) P(URNELL) June 28, 1890-Jan. 12, 1954 United States naval officer; graduated from Annapolis (1913); during World War I served on U.S.S. *Florida*; between wars did distinguished work on gunnery; chief of the Bureau of Ordnance (1941-1943); commander, Amphibious Group I, Pacific Fleet (1944-1945); appointed commander of the Joint Army-Navy Task Force One (1946) and directed "Operation Crossroads" at Bikini; commander, Eighth Fleet in Atlantic (1946-1947); commander in chief, Atlantic Fleet (1947-1950); retired in 1950, but returned to active duty in 1953; awarded the Distinguished Service Medal and three Gold Stars. See *Current Biography,* (Nov.) 1942.

Obituary

N Y Times p31 Ja 13 '54

BLOCH, FELIX Oct. 23, 1905- Physicist; university professor

Address: b. c/o Stanford University, Palo Alto, Calif.; h. 1551 Emerson St., Palo Alto, Calif.

Representatives of twelve nations unanimously approved on April 9, 1954, the appointment of Professor Felix Bloch of Stanford University as director of the new European Nuclear Research Center for peacetime uses of atomic energy. The Swiss-American physicist, co-winner (with Dr. Edward Purcell) of the 1952 Nobel Prize for his nuclear induction method of determining the properties of atomic nuclei, has also made many contributions to solid state physics. Among them are two Bloch theorems, the Bloch-Grüneisen relationship, and the Bloch T 3/2 law; his name is applied also to Bloch functions and the Bloch wall. He has been a professor of physics at Stanford University since 1936.

Felix Bloch was born in Zurich, Switzerland, October 23, 1905. His parents were Gustav and Agnes (Mayer) Bloch. Because of the boy's interest in mathematics and astronomy, his father (a wholesale grain dealer) enrolled him in the engineering course at the Federal Institute of Technology. But his first course in elementary physics convinced Felix that physics, not engineering, should be his life work. In 1928 he received his Ph.D. degree from the University of Leipzig, Germany, where Professor Werner Heisenberg, the father of quantum mechanics, was pursuing his researches.

After receiving his doctorate, Bloch returned home and worked as a research assistant there during 1928 and 1929. A Lorentz Fund fellowship took him to The Netherlands in 1930, after which the young Swiss returned to Leipzig as Heisenberg's assistant. In 1931 an Oersted Fund fellowship enabled him to work with Niels Bohr, director of the Institute for Theoretical Physics at the University of Copenhagen. When Hitler came to power in 1933

Wide World

FELIX BLOCH

Bloch was teaching at the University of Leipzig as a *Privatdozent* (lecturer) in theoretical physics. Because of his Jewish faith, his position soon became uncomfortable and he went to Paris, where he lectured at the Institut Henri Poincaré.

In 1933 Bloch also worked in Rome with Enrico Fermi on a Rockefeller Fellowship from the International Education Board. At its conclusion, the Swiss physicist was invited to Stanford University in Palo Alto, California. His title, since 1936, has been professor of physics.

Beginning in 1927, Bloch had made significant contributions to notable scientific publications such as *Zeitschrift für Physik* and *Physikalische Zeitschrift.* (Since 1932, his papers have appeared in *Nature, Physica,* and the *Physical Review.*) Kittel's *Introduction to Solid State Physics* (John Wiley, 1953) gives, in different connections, not less than six theorems, statements, laws and objects to which Bloch's name is commonly applied. From 1928—the outset of the physicist's career—dates the Bloch-Floquet theorem, which specifies the form of wave functions for electrons in a crystal, and the Bloch-Grüneisen relationship, which describes the electrical conductivity of metals as a function of temperature.

What Kittel calls "the Bloch-Floquet theorem" is ordinarily referred to simply as the Bloch theorem; after he had presented it, it was found to be identical with a problem in abstract mathematics that had been solved years earlier by a mathematician named Floquet. Functions satisfying the conditions of the theorem are conventionally referred to by physicists as Bloch functions, and are used in most modern theoretical investigations of the structure of metals.

The Bloch-Grüneisen relationship is so called because Dr. Bloch provided a theoretical ex-

BLOCH, FELIX—*Continued*

planation for Prof. Eduard Grüneisen's empirical findings. Another Bloch theorem, which deals with superconductivity, rules out some of the possible explanations for that phenomenon. The Bloch T 3/2 law describes the dependence on temperature of magnetization in a ferromagnetic material, and the Bloch wall is the name of the transition region between two parts of a ferromagnetic crystal that are magnetized in different directions. This has been shown by experiment to move through the body of the crystal and to have the properties which Bloch predicted for it. The above-mentioned work was done by Felix Bloch in his twenties and is not the contribution for which he was to receive the 1952 Nobel Prize. He was called upon to contribute to *Quantenmechanik der Materie und Strahlung,* of which Max von Laue was senior author. Bloch's books *Elektronentheorie der Metalle* and *Les électrons dans les métaux; Problèmes statiques; Magnétisme* (Hermann, 1934) were published not long after he found it advisable to leave Germany.

Bloch continued his researches on the interaction between matter and radiation. He was intrigued by the neutron, the nuclear particle without electric charge which was discovered by Prof. James Chadwick in 1932. "The idea that a neutral elementary particle should possess an intrinsic magnetic moment had a particular fascination for me," Bloch said in his Nobel Prize speech of acceptance, "since it was in such striking contrast to the then only existing theory of an intrinsic moment which had been given by [Professor Paul Adrien Maurice] Dirac for the electron" (*Science,* October 16, 1953).

An electron acts like a tiny bar magnet, a fact which Dirac had explained as a consequence of its electrical charge. Since the neutron has no charge, it was clear that an entirely different explanation would have to be found for its magnetism, and to that task Bloch addressed himself. New techniques were needed, for the neutron's lack of charge makes it difficult to detect and difficult to control. Also, neutrons can be obtained only from nuclear disintegrations and, according to atomic physicist, Dr. H. D. Smyth, the only means of controlling free neutrons is "to put nuclei in their way so that they will be slowed and deflected or absorbed by collisions."

In 1936 Bloch pointed out that the magnetic moments of the free electron and the neutron could be demonstrated experimentally by observing the scattering of slow neutrons in iron; he stated also that the magnetic scattering would lead to the polarization of neutron beams. These predictions were confirmed the following year by a group of experimenters at Columbia University.

Bloch, the theoretician, turned to experimental work at the University of California cyclotron at Berkeley in 1939, when he and Luis W. Alvarez succeeded in measuring the magnetic moment of the neutron by passing a polarized neutron beam through a region where a weak oscillating field was superimposed on a strong constant field. (It is necessary that the weak field oscillate at the same frequency as that of the neutron's motion around the direction of the constant field.) Their answer was consistent with the magnetic moment of the deuteron minus that of the proton, a fact which tends to confirm that the deuteron is a proton combined with a neutron.

Bloch's peacetime research was interrupted in 1941, when he joined the Manhattan District project which was working to produce an atomic fission bomb. He worked at the new Los Alamos, New Mexico laboratory from 1942 until 1944, when he served as associate group leader in counter-radar research at the Harvard University Radio Research Laboratory. This acquaintance with radio techniques suggested to Professor Bloch a method of "detecting the reorientation of nuclear moments through the normal methods of radio reception. The signals to be detected," he explained in his Nobel Prize address, "would be due to the electromagnetic induction caused by nuclear reorientation and should appear as a voltage difference between the terminals of an external electric circuit" (*Science,* October 16, 1953). For this reason, he chose the name "nuclear induction."

Advantages of the crossed-coil method (which Bloch worked out with the late Dr. William W. Hansen and Martin Packard) are its relative simplicity, its high accuracy and the fact that the direction of the streak on their radar screen shows whether the nuclei are rotating with or against the field. The Bloch method changes the nuclei of water mixtures into tiny radio transmitters, while a Harvard University group headed by Professor Edward M. Purcell independently achieved the same basic results with paraffin, measuring the absorption of energy rather than the production of signals.

So sensitive is the nuclear induction method that Bloch's co-workers have detected in natural water signals arising from deuterium, which constitutes only 0.02 per cent of the water, and from an isotope of oxygen that constitutes only 0.04 per cent. "It was particularly gratifying to me," said the inventor, "to obtain these results from experiments combining the polarization and magnetic resonance depolarization of neutrons with nuclear induction."

In December 1952 Felix Bloch was in Stockholm to receive from King Gustaf VI a Nobel Prize winner's gold medal, diploma, and a check for some $16,500, representing half of the 1952 award in physics, shared by him and Dr. Purcell. The two men have never worked together on research problems but are good friends. Two years later, in April 1954, Bloch was again in the news, when the naturalized American citizen was unanimously named director of the proposed twelve-nation European Nuclear Research Center in Geneva. He has agreed to accept a two-year appointment—beginning in October—and has been granted a leave of absence by Stanford University to permit him to assume his new post.

Felix Bloch became a member of the National Academy of Sciences in 1948; he is a fellow of the American Physical Society, a member of

Sigma XI and of the Schweiz Naturforschende Gesellschaft. Since March 1940 he has been married to a fellow physicist, German-born Lore C. Misch, a professor's daughter whom he met while she was a research associate at Massachusetts Institute of Technology. The Blochs have three sons—George, Daniel, Frank—and a daughter, Ruth.

Professor Block is a dark-haired, heavy-browed, energetic man. He enjoys skiing and mountain climbing. A favorite indoor recreation is playing the piano.

References

N Y Times p21 N 7 '52 por
Nature 170:911 N 29 '52
Science 118:425 O 16 '53 por
American Men of Science (1949)
International Who's Who, 1953
Who's Who, 1954
Who's Who in America, 1954-55

BLOCK, HERBERT L(AWRENCE) Oct. 13, 1909- Editorial cartoonist
Address: c/o The Washington Post and Times-Herald, Washington, D.C.

HERBERT BLOCK

Twice a winner of the Pulitzer Prize for cartooning, in 1954 and in 1942, Herbert Block has been the editorial cartoonist of the Washington *Post* since 1946. He uses the signature "Herblock" on his daily cartoons which are syndicated in 182 newspapers throughout the United States. He is the author of *The Herblock Book* (1952) which contains "text as pungent as the cartoons." "This is the kind of book Will Rogers would have written if he could draw," commented fellow cartoonist Al Capp. Herblock has been called by poet Archibald MacLeish "a masterful satirist of this curious time . . . one of the principal defenders of the Republic." Poet Carl Sandburg has called him "one of the supreme all-time American cartoonists, a great craftsman and, rather distinctly, a pictorial historian of current events."

The 1954 Pulitzer Prize for cartooning was presented to Herbert L. Block for outstanding work during 1953, and cited a cartoon based on Stalin's death published in the Washington *Post* on March 4, 1953, with the caption "You Were Always a Great Friend of Mine, Joseph." It depicts the grim reaper leading Stalin as he clutches the communist's bloody sickle. The New York *Herald Tribune* (May 5, 1954) called it "a remarkable example of Mr. Block's dramatic power."

Block is the winner of the Heywood Broun Award (1950), the American Newspaper Guild Award (1947 and 1948) and many other journalism awards. Some of his best known cartoons are on permanent exhibit in the Rosenwald Collection at the National Gallery of Art in Washington, D.C.

Herbert Lawrence Block was born in Chicago, Illinois on October 13, 1909, the youngest of three sons of David Julian and Tessie (Lupe) Block. "Herb" began to draw at an early age and when only twelve years old won a Chicago Art Institute scholarship and attended evening art classes. He became the only artist in the family. His father was a chemist and one of his brothers became a reporter on a Chicago newspaper.

After he was graduated from high school in 1927 he entered Lake Forest College in suburban Chicago, but remained only two years. He applied for a summer job in 1929 with the Chicago *Daily News*, and the editor, Charles Dennis, a man with a reputation for developing talent, engaged nineteen-year-old Block to fill a staff vacancy. At his father's suggestion he adopted "Herblock" as a pen-name. For four years his two-column-wide humorous cartoons appeared daily on the editorial page. Almost from the first, the *Daily News* syndicated his cartoons.

The Herblock drawings attracted the attention of the Newspaper Enterprise Association and in 1933 Block went to their Cleveland office where he worked for ten years. He gained wide popularity by lampooning issues and personalities and won the National Headliners' Club Award in 1940.

The Pulitzer Prize for cartooning went to Block in 1942 for outstanding work during 1941, and specifically—a cartoon entitled "British Plane" which appeared on March 7, 1941. It showed a German soldier in occupied France searching the sky for an R.A.F. bomber. while Parisians in the background watched.

Block joined the Army in 1943 and after basic training in Arkansas, spent the rest of his Army duty in Florida and New York drawing cartoons for the Information and Education Division. He was a sergeant when discharged in 1946. While on terminal leave, he applied for a job with the Washington *Post.* The publisher, Eugene Meyer, needed a cartoonist. The job gave Block the independence he wanted and the opportunity to visit the

BLOCK, HERBERT—*Continued*

Capitol frequently and follow national events at first hand. He soon became, in the opinion of Eric Sevareid, CBS broadcaster, "the most powerful and effective political commentator in the United States," as well as "a wit and philosopher, one of the brightest figures in the American scene" in the opinion of poet Carl Sandburg.

He won a Heywood Broun Honorable Mention (sponsored by the American Newspaper Guild) for outstanding journalistic achievement in 1947, and the Broun Award in 1948. He shared the 1950 Broun Award with a New York *Post* reporter. The citation mentioned Block's "penetrating and powerful comments" on the political scene. Jane McMaster (*Editor and Publisher*, April 15, 1950) said that a Sigma Delta Chi Award in 1949 pleased Block because the citation called his work "the product of a genuine and integrated philosophy."

Because of the changes of pace from dark, massive "spatterwork figures" to light "billowing" action characters and occasional "Goyaesque" fierceness, Richard H. Rovere (*New Yorker*, February 11, 1950) found the Herblock cartoons "difficult to characterize." One of Block's inventions, known as Mr. Atom, Rovere described as "a torpedo-shaped gray mass with an intricate trigger arrangement . . . and a malignant, leering face, dirty and unshaven."

Among the 194 Herblock cartoons exhibited at the Corcoran Gallery in Washington in January and February 1950, the animated bomb was portrayed peering at a group of politicians. The caption read "How Would You Guys Like a Whole Bunch of Smoke-filled Rooms?"

Many of Block's drawings were exhibited at the Associated American Artists Gallery in New York during May 1950. Several Herblock "classics" were purchased by the Washington National Gallery for the Rosenwald Collection, which made Block the first living American cartoonist to be represented in the Rosenwald group of prints and etchings.

The 1952 Presidential campaign provided wider distribution for Block's drawings. The Post-Hall Syndicate of New York which distributes Herblock cartoons gained new customers in the United States and supplied additional European newspapers. When asked by Erwin Knoll (*Editor and Publisher*, October 4, 1952) how a syndicated cartoonist's work could appear in both pro-Stevenson and pro-Eisenhower newspapers, Block explained that he took "a whack at each side" and sometimes a cartoon was printed beside an editorial that took an "opposite view". He regarded this as a "tribute" to the press in keeping voters informed.

The Herblock Book (Beacon Press, 1952) contained about 400 of Block's "classics". The text—humorous and informative—related the story behind individual cartoons. J. W. Johnson (New York *Herald Tribune Book Review*, October 19, 1952) commented that it was remarkable that a man could "gain distinction merely by talking common-sense boldly and humorously." N. B. Brown (New York *Times*, November 2, 1952) said that the book contained the keenest and best-informed commentaries on "post-war American politics, economics and foreign relations." Commentator Elmer Davis has said that "Herblock makes just as much sense in his prose as he does in his cartoons, and that says much."

Senators Pat McCarran and Joseph McCarthy and the issues they have represented have been favorite targets of the Herblock pen for a long time. In two chapters of his book Block discusses "Fear and Smear" and "The Screaming Whimwhams", illustrated by a group of cartoons expressing Block's dislike of hearsay reports, vigilante tactics, and unsubstantiated evidence in investigation committee hearings.

Block states that the word "McCarthyism" "seems to have originated in the elephant-and-smear buckets cartoon which was first published in March 1950." The drawing shows the G.O.P. leaders trying to get the elephant to stand on a teetering pile of buckets overflowing with red paint labeled McCarthyism and the caption reads: "You Mean I'm Supposed To Stand On That?" One of his most effective cartoons showed the torch of Liberty burning and a man labeled "Hysteria" climbing a ladder carrying a bucket to extinguish freedom's flame. The caption read simply, "Fire!"

Among his powerful anti-Communist cartoons was one depicting the leaders of the Kremlin happily looking at a map of China and the caption reads: "Five Hundred Million of Them—All Expendable." Many of his drawings show the need for better housing, better schools, freedom from censorship in libraries and colleges, and reciprocal trade.

All of Block's—one-a-day—six-days-a-week—cartoons are freshly drawn. He works in a small, cluttered, air-conditioned "ivory tower" in the Washington *Post* annex. He usually makes several rough sketches based on ideas and information that he has compiled, then spends from two to three hours inking in the final selection with a brush and India ink and a graphite stick.

"He uses only a few stock figures such as Uncle Sam, an elephant and a donkey for the two parties, and a little fellow in spectacles and a soft hat to represent the average citizen," wrote William V. Shannon in the New York *Post*. "He has modernized even these stereotypes. Uncle Sam has lost the stripes from his pants and the stars from his vest. Mr. Average Citizen appears a good deal less bewildered than he does in the work of most other cartoonists. Herblock's average man is usually a pretty shrewd fellow who sees through the characters he is watching."

Block is a bachelor and lives in an apartment four blocks away from his office. He is nearly six feet tall, has light brown hair, blue eyes and "a warm smile and a deep mellow voice" according to William V. Shannon of the New York *Post*. He has no hobbies except walking and taking practice shots at golf. He reads constantly, and his office and home are piled high with old newspapers and magazines.

Politically, Block has often been called a "liberal." He complained to Erwin Knoll that "liberal" was an abused word that had been "kicked around" until nobody knew what it meant, that he only tried to present "the right thing, effectively." This philosophy, as applied to cartooning, was brought out by Jane McMaster (*Editor and Publisher*, April 15, 1950) who quoted Block as saying: "First be right, then be effective, then be a good artist."

References

Ed & Pub 83:40+ Ap 15 '50; 85:50 O 4 '52
N Y Post Mag p2 My 23 '54 por
N Y Times p26 My 4 '54 por
Newsweek 31:56+ My 3 '48 por
New Yorker 25:56 F 11 '50
Time 55:38 Ja 23 '50
Who's Who in America, 1954-55

BLUNDELL, MICHAEL Apr. 7, 1907- Member of Kenya Legislative Council; farmer; Minister of Executive Council

Address: b. c/o European Elected Members' Organization, Box 1730, Nairobi, Kenya; h. Box 100, Nakuru, Kenya

MICHAEL BLUNDELL

The leader of the European elected members in the Legislative Council of the British colony of Kenya is Michael Blundell who was chosen for that post in 1948 after experience as a farmer and cattle breeder in the colony dating back to 1925. He had a distinguished military record in World War II for which he received the Order of the British Empire.

Brought into international prominence in 1952 as the spokesman for the white settlers during the outrages perpetrated by the Mau Mau secret society, Blundell has been characterized, in a London magazine, as "Kenya's man of the hour."

In June 1954 Blundell assumed another office in Kenya's government, Minister without portfolio of the Executive Council.

Michael Blundell was born in London on April 7, 1907 to Alfred Herbert Blundell, a London solicitor, and the former Amelia Woodward Richardson. He is of Norman-English extraction on his father's side; an ancestor, Blondel, received from King Richard I a grant of land in Bedfordshire where members of his family still reside.

He was one of five children. His eldest brother, a lieutenant colonel in the British Army, fell in action in 1943; his second brother is a captain in Her Majesty's Navy.

Brought up in London and Yorkshire, he completed his schooling in 1925 at Wellington in Berkshire, where during four years of attendance he played football and edited the school paper. "I was meant to take up the law," he has written, "but I had a passion for gardening and could not face living in a city like London. I think this gardening craze eventually made me think of the open spaces of Africa."

The "open spaces" to which Blundell's attention had turned were the fertile highlands of the former British East Africa Protectorate whose interior had been made accessible less than a quarter of a century earlier by the completion of the Uganda Railway. These highlands, not previously cultivated, had been used for depasturage by the Masai tribe and were also claimed by the Kikuyus who had abandoned the area shortly before the white man came because of sickness, drought and locusts. The Masai, by treaty, were given other lands in exchange. Under the Kikuyu land tenure system, land was held in trust for the entire tribe. Therefore, the loss of land was not merely an economic loss but a failure to maintain the trust of the tribe.

There was an influx of British settlers in the uplands in 1903. "To the British," the Kikuyu scholar Gikonyo Wa Kiano has written, "it seemed only fair that the land . . . should be handed over to the more efficient white farmers" (*Saturday Review,* May 2, 1953).

The protectorate was raised to the position of a Crown Colony in July 1920 under the title of Kenya Colony. The Africans residing there became, according to the Kenya court, "tenants-at-will" of the Crown. Only Europeans were eligible for leaseholds (actual title to land was vested in the Crown) and no native could be engaged as a farm manager without the formal approval of the Governor-in-Council.

Michael Blundell went to the Kenya Colony as a "farm pupil" in 1925. His apprenticeship completed, he was engaged in April 1927 as manager of a farm near Nakuru, and four years later bought an interest in this largely undeveloped property.

Yorke Henderson wrote that Blundell was "one of the first men successfully to take the risk of bringing pedigreed British cattle into Kenya, and one of the pioneers in crossing them with African cattle to produce a breed sturdy

BLUNDELL, MICHAEL—*Continued*

enough to stand the rigours of East Africa" (*Everybody's,* August 10, 1953).

After World War II broke out Blundell entered the African Colonial Force as a second lieutenant of the Royal Engineers. "He used his power of command and ability to speak several native dialects to quell a threatened mass disturbance in the ranks," states Yorke Henderson. "Then he took his troops into Abyssinia a few short weeks after donning a uniform, to fight their way through to Addis Ababa." Subsequently he saw active service in Italian and British Somaliland, Eritrea, and southeast Asia. For gallantry in action in Abyssinia he was made a member of the Order of the British Empire in 1942.

Blundell, also in 1942, became the sole owner of the 1200 acre farm at Subukia, near Nakuru, where he had first been engaged as manager. Shortly after his demobilization as a colonel in 1945, he was appointed a commissioner of Kenya's European Settlement Board.

From the fires of native discontent, emerged, after the war, two secret societies in the Central and Nyanza provinces, the Dini ya Msambwa and the Watu wa Mungu, dedicated to the expulsion of the white settlers, and the Kenya African Union with the African anthropologist and educator, Jomo Kenyatta, (see *Current Biography,* October 1953) as president, for the advancement of the Negro. Another element of restlessness was to be found in the status of the Indian population, which was also prohibited from owning land.

"In 1947," stated Gikonyo Wa Kiano, "the then Colonial Secretary, A. Creech Jones, issued White Paper 191, which proposed that the European, Asian and African races should each have equal representation in a new East African Central Assembly. Considering that Kenya has 30,000 Europeans, 100,000 Indians and 5,500,000 Africans, this was still a long way from democratic equality. But the white settlers in Kenya so frantically harassed the Colonial Office with protests, that White Paper 191 was withdrawn and replaced by another one (210) which accepted the principle of majority representation for the whites."

The colony is administered under the Colonial Office by a governor who is assisted by an Executive Council and a Legislative Council comprised of seven ex-officio members, not more than nine nominated official members, eleven European elected members, five Indian elected members, one Arab elected member, one nominated Arab member, and four African nominated unofficial members.

In the spring of 1948 Blundell ran for the Rift Valley province seat in the Legislative Council. He was victorious in the May election and was chosen leader of the European Elected Members' Organization. Blundell was thus the recognized legislative leader of the "whites" when the "oath takers" of the secret society, Mau Mau (estimated to have a membership of 200,000), circulated extensively among the Kikuyu with the purpose of eliminating the white men from Kenya.

Blundell is believed to have recommended the order by the governor of the Crown Colony, Sir Evelyn Baring, which outlawed the Mau Mau on August 12, 1952. Outrages, however, continued, and during September some forty-three Europeans were killed on Kenya farms and nearly 150 head of cattle slaughtered.

A "state of emergency" was declared on October 21, 1952 and Kenyatta and five associates were arrested and brought to trial on charges of managing the Mau Mau. They were subsequently convicted by the East Africa Appeals Court and their appeal to the Privy Council, which followed, was rejected.

"On Blundell's own farm," states *Time* (March 30, 1953), "the Mau Mau oath administrators arrived one night at the huts, tortured several of his Kikuyus into taking the oath. . . . And the chief oath administrator was a well-dressed, well-educated young Kikuyu whom the Blundells had fully trusted." Blundell advised farmers to "get rid of all Kikuyus, or at least never to let a Kikuyu enter the farmhouse after dark."

Addressing his Rift Valley constituents in December 1952, he declared that he and his colleagues were "dismayed" by the government's "refusal to use the degree of force necessary to deal with Mau Mau." He added that the problem "will not be cured until we make it much more . . . distasteful to be a member of Mau Mau than it is to support the Government."

In an article published in the *Kenya Weekly News* three months later, Blundell asserted "it was negative and unimaginative to regard the future of the Kikuyu as one in which an enormous mallet was to be permanently poised over their heads," since such a policy would "build up a wall of bitterness."

For a considerable time, he continued, "freedom of the press and the independent schools needed to be closely controlled," but as soon as "firm discipline" had been established, he would "make a resolute attempt to provide means by which individual title to land could be established."

Meanwhile he "would like to see location reconstruction committees set up" by Kikuyu chiefs and headmen. "In years to come," he declared, "these might be elected. . . . They should aim at creating forces of government out of and by the Kikuyu people at this level and upward, and not from Nairobi downwards" (London *Times,* December 29, 1952).

In March 1953 Blundell participated in the conferences in London which preceded the announcement by the government of Kenya that it would investigate the problem of underpaid natives. He was again in London for the coronation ceremonies, at which time he conferred with Sir Godfrey Huggins, Prime Minister of Southern Rhodesia, and Roland Welensky, the Northern Rhodesian leader, to "determine whether an arrangement could be made so that the federation move in British Central Africa could be extended to benefit Kenya" (New York *Times,* June 12, 1953).

Speaking in Southern Rhodesia on July 18, 1953, after the Central African Federation (whose purpose will be to end Indian immigration) had been assured by act of the British Parliament, Blundell reminded his listeners of Indian contributions to funds for the defense of Jomo Kenyatta. "He declared that India was organizing African opinion against the European in Africa and that this was the beginning of Indian imperialism. He called for rapid European immigration to stem the Oriental tide" (New York *Times*, July 19, 1953).

Blundell believes that the Europeans must pay the Africans salaries commensurate with their desire for a higher standard of living. The elected members have also suggested that loans be made to African farmers and traders, regulations permitting the African trader to obtain goods at wholesale prices, African reserves be developed to the fullest, educational facilities be improved, and that there be equal opportunity for advancement in public service.

The New York *Herald Tribune* (August 30, 1953) commented that if a program of "reconstruction along political, agricultural and educational lines wins approval there will be good hope of brightening skies in East Africa."

The Christian Science Monitor (December 10, 1953) remarked that the African "wants improved living standards now . . . that will make him socially acceptable to the whites . . . and sufficient opportunity to reach these standards by his own effort. . . That, it seems, is exactly what the whites are unwilling to concede."

Michael Blundell and Geraldine Lötte Robarts, a business secretary, were married on February 25, 1946, and are the parents of one young daughter, Susan Collett Blundell. The leader of the Kenya European Elected Members' Organization, is six feet one inch in height, 220 pounds in weight, and has blue eyes and brown hair. *Time* has described Blundell as "burly, boyish-faced." His favorite recreations are gardening, music, and breeding pedigreed Guernsey cattle.

References

Everybody's (London) p8+ Ag 8 '53 por
Life 34:144+ My 4 '53 pors
Time 61:30+ Mr 30 '53 por

BLUNT, KATHARINE May 28, 1876-July 29, 1954 Educator; was graduated from Vassar College (1898); received Ph.D. degree in organic chemistry, University of Chicago (1907); taught chemistry at Pratt Institute and Vassar; was home economics professor, University of Chicago (1913-1929); elected president, Home Economics Association (1924-26); appointed first woman president of Connecticut College in 1929 where she revised and enlarged the curriculum; became president-emeritus (1943); recalled 1945; again retired 1946; author of *Food and the War* (1918); co-author *Ultra-Violet Light and Vitamin D in Nutrition* (1930); wrote many articles on food chemistry for technical journals. See *Current Biography*, (Dec.) 1946.

Obituary

N Y Times p17 Jl 30 '54

BOK, WILLIAM CURTIS Sept. 7, 1897- Judge

Address: b. 692 City Hall, Philadelphia 7, Pa.; h. 1816 Delancey St., Philadelphia 3, Pa.

Author of a frequently cited opinion about book censorship, Judge William Curtis Bok is president judge of the Court of Common Pleas No. 6 of Philadelphia County, Pennsylvania. His ideas on the freedom to read and on basic human rights were expressed in his speech at the fifth annual National Book Award ceremonies, held on January 26, 1954. He is the

JUDGE WILLIAM CURTIS BOK

author of two books, *Backbone of the Herring* (1941) and *I Too, Nicodemus* (1946), which deal with the life of a trial judge, "combining fact, fiction, disquisitions touched with wit on the behind-the-scenes ways of judges and lawyers" (New York *Times*, September 22, 1946).

In March 1949 Judge Bok wrote his now famous decision (in the case of Commonwealth vs. Gordon) protecting nine American novels against the charge of obscenity. He has also made known his views on censorship and freedom of expression in magazine articles and speeches. A practicing lawyer for fifteen years in Pennsylvania, he has served on the bench since 1936.

The older of the two sons of Edward William and Mary Louise (Curtis) Bok, William Curtis Bok was born in Wyncote, Pennsylvania on September 7, 1897. His father, a native of the Netherlands who had come to the United States in 1870, became editor of the *Ladies' Home Journal* in 1889, thus beginning a service of thirty years that made his name a familiar one throughout the country. His mother, the daughter of the late Cyrus H. K. Curtis, founder of the Curtis Publishing Company, and publisher of the *Ladies' Home Journal*, is a former president of the Settlement Music School and is the founder of the Curtis Insti-

BOK, WILLIAM CURTIS—*Continued*

tute of Music in Philadelphia. His brother is Cary William Bok, the publisher.

In his autobiography, *The Americanization of Edward Bok* (1920), the distinguished editor tells of a memorable incident concerning his son, William. When the boy was ten years old, growing up in the Philadelphia suburb of Merion, he requested as his Christmas present that he be taken to Washington, D.C. and introduced to President Theodore Roosevelt. Because of illness, William had to delay until May 1908 his visit to the White House, where he experienced the great joy of discussing bear hunting with the President. Young Bok heard much about and met other prominent people of the time, especially literary figures, who were among his father's friends.

On graduation from the Hill School in Pottstown, Pennsylvania in 1915, Bok entered Williams College in Williamstown, Massachusetts. During his two years there, English was his major study, while his extrascholastic interests were those he had enjoyed in secondary school: playing baseball and working on the literary magazine. He was a member of Delta Kappa Epsilon fraternity, vice-president of his class in his freshman year and president for part of his sophomore year.

In World War I he served in the United States Navy; he entered with the rank of quartermaster (third class) and was discharged as a lieutenant (s.g.). He then took his legal training from 1919 to 1921 at the law school of the University of Virginia, where he was active in the Raven Society and on the staff of the *Law Review*.

Admitted to the Pennsylvania bar in 1921, Bok at that time established a general law practice in Philadelphia which was to continue until 1936. Meanwhile, beginning in 1925, he held a trusteeship for two years at the Eastern State Penitentiary in Philadelphia and from 1928 to 1932 was assistant district attorney of the county. He acted for a year (1936 to 1937) as judge of Philadelphia's Orphans Court before coming in 1937 to the office he still occupies, president judge of the Court of Common Pleas No. 6 of Philadelphia County.

It was as judge of this court that Bok wrote his well-known opinion involving the definition of obscenity in literature when on March 18, 1949 he ruled that nine novels which certain Philadelphia booksellers had been indicted for selling were not obscene. His decision was later in effect sustained by Pennsylvania's Supreme Court. Some years afterward he referred in a speech to his experience in reading these books: "Holding my nose with one hand, I upheld with the other the right of free speech that they represented. For this I got a certain amount of acclaim."

In protecting the nine novels, some of them the work of William Faulkner, James T. Farrell and Erskine Caldwell, Judge Bok explained that they were "obvious efforts to show life as it is. . . . I cannot be convinced that the deep drives and appetites of life are very much different from what they have always been, or that censorship has ever had any effect on them, except as the law's police power to preserve the peace is censorship. I believe that the concensus of preference today is for disclosure and not stealth, for frankness and not hypocrisy, and for public and not secret distribution. That in itself is a moral code" (quoted in *Publishers' Weekly,* April 2, 1949).

Before winning this "certain amount of acclaim," Judge Bok had acquired an excellent literary reputation as the author of two books—semifictional and, supposedly, semi-autobiographical—dealing with the human and humane side of the law. The first of these, *Backbone of the Herring* (Knopf, 1941), takes its title from the judicial oath used in the Isle of Man: "You swear to do justice between cause and cause as equally as the backbone of the herring doth lie midmost of the fish." Made up largely of histories of cases tried before a certain Judge Ulen, the book also sets forth the reflections and observations of the judge on human behavior and the nature of justice.

According to a reviewer in *Commonweal* (January 23, 1942), "the stories he tells are fascinating, and the incidents strange, but they are such as could happen to any of us. A broad and deep humanity runs through the whole book and we come away hoping that there were more judges like the central figure of the book, Judge Ulen."

Like *Backbone of the Herring,* Judge Bok's *I Too, Nicodemus* (Knopf, 1946), which also has as its main character the patient and kind Judge Ulen, may be described as "an essay on the use of the courtroom as a school for society" (New York *Herald Tribune,* September 12, 1946). "A good judge," the author believes, "must have an enormous concern with life, animate and inanimate, and a sense of its tempestuous and untamed streaming." He must occupy himself as well with the question of Nicodemus, "How can man be born again?" and must strive to help man in his continual rebirth by making the best of the moment.

In narrating the cases brought before him for trial, Judge Bok shows "a sure instinct for the dramatic; his tales, whether they deal with the criminal or the civil side of court, are professional in their artistry. The subtlety of his insights, his characterizations, his observations on human behavior are in the best tradition of our novelists. . . . He can be satirical of pomposity of bench and bar; hilariously funny in his lampoon of rival pettifogger; tender, and caustic; and at all times incisive" (*Saturday Review of Literature,* December 7, 1946).

Praising the book in his review for the New York *Times* (September 22, 1946), Jerome Frank, an appellate judge, promised readers that they would "see life from the angle of a profoundly wise judge who is also a sensitive soul and a gifted artist."

Judge Bok has presented his views on penology, censorship and civil liberties in speeches and magazine articles, among them "Youth Justice" (*Survey Graphic,* June 1940) and "Jury System in America" (*Annals of the American Academy of Political and Social Science,* May 1953). At the opening of the fifth annual Philadelphia Book Show in April 1950, he read a paper entitled "Censorship Through the Open Market Rather than the Police Station." Many of his ideas regarding freedom to write and freedom to read, with censorship stemming from public taste and custom, were reiterated in "The Duty of Freedom," which appeared in the *Saturday Review* (July 11, 1953).

The speaker at the fifth annual National Book Award ceremonies held in New York in January 1954, Judge Bok discussed further the matter of custom in connection with freedom: "I grasp at custom, for custom should be the evolution of the law. Nations with most customs have fewest laws, and their native procedures are instinctive and gracious. . . . Custom is more efficient than law because it is self-executing. . . . With freedom of the press goes the freedom to read or to close the book, and it will linger so long as we retain the power to say no. With the right of free speech goes the right of free silence, particularly when a citizen is challenged without the provision of procedure for a fair fight. And with it the duty, if we do speak, to speak not only freely but fully. . . . The difficulty is not so much with free speech as with free truth," he declared.

He gave special emphasis to the importance of procedure, as quoted by the *Saturday Review* (February 13, 1954): "Unless people have an instinct for procedure their conception of basic human rights is a waste of effort . . . the challenge we face is not the issue between Communism and capitalism but the issue between freedom and slavery, and if we are to act like free men we will win by vitalizing our procedures, not by trying to put handcuffs on a gale of wind."

While serving Pennsylvania since 1949 as a member of the State Planning Board, Judge Bok has also been called upon by the Federal government to fill the positions of panel member of the national and third regional war labor boards in arbitration matters (1942 to 1945), commissioner and deputy chief compliance commissioner of the War Production Board (1942 to 1945), and deputy chief compliance commissioner of the National Production Authority (1950 to 1952). From 1942 to 1945 and from 1950 to 1952 he was special assistant to the United States Attorney General as hearing officer on conscientious objector cases.

The Philadelphia justice has held membership in various committees of the American Bar Association and the American Law Institute, and is a member of the council of the law school of the University of Virginia. He has also given his attention to duties of vice-president of the Curtis Institute of Music and secretary and treasurer of the American Foundation, Inc. In 1937 he attended the coronation in England of George VI as secretary of the American delegation. In politics a Democrat, Judge Bok ran unsuccessfully in 1943 against Judge Claude T. Reno, Republican incumbent, as his party's candidate for Pennsylvania's Superior Court judgeship.

Judge Bok's wife is Nellie Lee (Holt) Bok, a former teacher, whom he married on November 25, 1934; their two children are Rachel and Enid Bok. By a previous marriage, to Margaret Adams Plummer, which began in 1924 and was terminated by divorce in 1933, he is the father of Margaret Welmoet (Bok) Roland Holst and of Benjamin Plummer and Derek Curtis Bok. The judge has gray hair, blue eyes, and weighs 190 pounds with a height of six feet two inches.

His clubs are the Legal Club, Midday Club, Merion Cricket Club and the Franklin Inn of Philadelphia. Active in the sport of sailing, he belongs also to the Cruising Club of America and the Camden (Maine) Yacht Club. He finds recreation, too, in reading and in playing the piano and the bassoon. A member of the Society of Friends, he is said (New York *Times,* September 22, 1946) to have the philosophy "of an Americanized Montaigne with a strong Quaker tincture."

References

N Y World-Telegram p10 S 12 '46
Bok, E. The Americanization of Edward Bok (1920)
Who's Who in America, 1952-53
Who's Who in the East (1953)

BOLT, RICHARD H(ENRY) Apr. 22, 1911- University professor; acoustician

Address: b. Massachusetts Institute of Technology, 77 Massachusetts Ave., Cambridge 39, Mass.; h. 34 Temple St., Arlington 74, Mass.

Exploring the uses of acoustics in a technological age, Richard H. Bolt, one of the leading acoustical scientists in the United States, has studied the effect of aircraft noise on people residing near airports and the use of ultrasound waves in the detection of cancer. He is the director of the acoustics laboratory and associate professor of physics at the Massachusetts Institute of Technology. He de-

RICHARD H. BOLT

BOLT, RICHARD H.—*Continued*

signed the acoustics for the United Nations buildings and was a special consultant on the design of the Royal Festival Hall in London. He has made important theoretical and experimental studies of sound distribution in enclosures.

He is a partner in the firm of acoustical engineers, Bolt, Beranek & Newman, which designed the acoustical features of the Grace Rainey Rogers Auditorium at the Metropolitan Museum of Art which opened on May 10, 1954.

Richard Henry Bolt was born in Peking, China on April 22, 1911 to Richard Arthur and Beatrice Rebecca (French) Bolt, who were both United States citizens. His father, a physician, was a medical director of the American Child Health Association. Three of his grandparents came from Cornwall, England. The boy was reared, for the most part, in California and Maryland. His love of music was one of the determining factors in his career. He began his musical education at an early age at the Peabody Conservatory of Music in Baltimore and appeared in several student recitals. Richard also played the piano and sang in his high school glee club.

After he was graduated from high school in 1928, Bolt entered the University of California where he majored in architecture and received the B.A. degree in 1933. His extracurricular activities as an undergraduate included the presidency of the Wesley Foundation and membership in Chi Alpha Kappa. He then studied for one year at the Heinrich Hertz Institute in Berlin.

It was there that Bolt first saw the opportunities for combining architecture and music in the science of acoustics. Following his return to the University of California he began intensive training in acoustics and physics. He received the M.A. degree in physics in 1937. From 1937 to 1938 he studied as a Hattie Heller scholar and from 1938 to 1939 as a university fellow. His dissertation was entitled "Normal Modes of Vibration and Room Acoustics." Bolt was awarded the Ph.D. degree, the Houghton Memorial Research Award, and a National Research fellowship in 1939.

As a National Research fellow he worked under Dr. Philip M. Morse at the Massachusetts Institute of Technology and contributed to the "wave theory" and the "acoustic impedance" solution of several problems then current in architectural acoustics. Appointed to the physics staff at the University of Illinois in 1940 he continued research and instruction in acoustics, but later he was called back to M.I.T. He did research work there until 1943 when he became a scientific liaison officer in the Office of Scientific Research and Development in London.

Continuing his contribution to the war effort he was made chief technical aide to the National Defense Research Committee (division six, New York) in 1944. He was appointed an assistant professor of physics at M.I.T. in 1945 and in the next year, he became an associate professor of physics as well as director of the acoustics laboratory at M.I.T.

Through theoretical and experimental research Bolt has made many important contributions to the science of acoustics. The Acoustical Society of America honored him in 1942 with the society's biennial award. His researches into the behavior of sound in enclosures led him to investigate such practical problems as the control of noise in apartment buildings. He collaborated with Robert B. Newman on an article dealing with this subject. They noted: "To a considerable extent, trends in contemporary design of dwellings had done much to increase noise control problems. Gone are the old-fashioned bearing masonry party walls and the many halls and dead spaces." The article explained how careful planning in the blueprint stage can avoid the necessity of large expenses after the building is completed (*Architectural Forum,* January 1950).

Professor Bolt helped to design the Royal Festival Hall in London, which has been described as "an acoustic masterpiece," and the acoustics of the United Nations buildings. In planning the Royal Festival Hall, Bolt stated that the basic dilemma was that "science cannot be applied rationally to the engineering of acoustics without a set of standards, and yet the final judges, the audience and the musicians, don't seem to subscribe to any such set. In spite of this the answer must somehow be found in those judges. If they will not all respond alike, one can at least look for an average response" (*Architectural Forum,* August, 1951).

Polls were taken to find which type of acoustics the English audiences and musicians preferred to hear. It was discovered that the average Englishman enjoys the full, singing quality of sound produced in the classical-type concert hall which has a rectangular, box shape and large areas of wood paneling and a deeply coffered ceiling. However, the greater sharpness, definition and loudness of tone achieved by the fan-shaped modern concert hall was also desirable. The acousticians solved the problem by utilizing the characteristics of both the classical and modern types of concert-hall design.

The problem of aircraft noise and its effect on people living near airports has been accentuated by the development of jet airplanes. Since 1952 Bolt has served on a special subcommittee of the National Advisory Committee for Aeronautics which is investigating this question. He has worked on another application of acoustics to an entirely different aspect of modern technology in his research into undersea warfare. With T. F. Burke he wrote a survey report on the basic problems of underwater acoustics research that was published in 1950 by the committee of undersea warfare of the National Research Council. Bolt has been chairman of the Armed Forces-National Research Council Committee on Hearing and Bio-Acoustics since 1953. Another project undertaken by Bolt has been the possibility of detecting tumors and cancers of the brain with ultrasound waves.

The scientist was director of the Ultrasonic Corporation in Cambridge, Massachusetts from

1946 to 1953; and was vice-president and director of the Blen Corporation in Cambridge from 1952 to 1953. Bolt has been a partner in the firm of Bolt, Beranek & Newman, consultants in acoustics, Cambridge, since 1949. His firm designed an efficient air horn for diesel locomotives that would be recognized by automobile drivers.

The organizations in which Bolt holds membership include the American Institute of Physics, American Physical Society, and American Association for the Advancement of Science. He is a fellow of the Acoustical Society of America, American Academy of Arts and Sciences, and Physical Society of London; a senior member of the Institute of Radio Engineers; and president of the International Commission of Acoustics. His club is the M.I.T. Faculty, and he belongs to Phi Beta Kappa and Sigma Xi.

The Acoustical Society of America appointed Bolt to be their delegate to the world congress celebrating the fiftieth anniversary of the discovery of radio by Guglielmo Marconi held at Rome in 1947. At this congress Bolt and L. L. Beranek presented a paper, "Some Recent Developments in Applied Acoustics". In 1949 he delivered a series of lectures on room acoustics at the Royal Institute in London. A steady contributor to the *Journal of the Acoustical Society of America*, Bolt has also written and collaborated on articles that have appeared in *Architectural Forum, Radio News, Architectural Record* and *Science*.

Bolt married Katherine Mary Smith on June 24, 1933. They have three children: Beatrice Herron, Richard Eugene and Deborah Katherine. The acoustician is five feet ten inches tall, weighs 150 pounds and has brown hair and hazel eyes. His favorite form of recreation is music.

References

Acoustical Soc Am J 14:111 Jl '42
American Men of Science (1949)
Who Knows—and What (1949)
Who's Who in America, 1954-55

BOLTE, CHARLES L(AWRENCE) May 8, 1895- United States Army officer

Address: b. c/o Department of the Army, Washington, D.C.

A veteran of both World Wars I and II, General Charles L. Bolte was named Army Vice Chief of Staff on September 14, 1953, to succeed General John E. Hull. Before assuming command of the United States Army in Europe last April, Bolte had headed the Seventh Army in Germany. He previously had held several staff posts in Army headquarters including that of Deputy Chief of Staff for Plans.

Born to Anson Lee and Marion E. Bolte at Chicago, Illinois, on May 8, 1895, Charles Lawrence Bolte completed his secondary education there and entered the Armour Institute of Technology to prepare for a B.S. degree in chemical engineering, which he received in 1917.

U. S. Army

GEN. CHARLES L. BOLTE

An undergraduate at Armour when World War I began, young Bolte promptly joined the student training movement and attended camps at Ludington, Michigan (1914), the Presidio in San Francisco (1915) and Plattsburg, New York (1916). He was commissioned a second lieutenant on November 6, 1916, and subsequently assigned to Fort Benjamin Harrison in Indiana as a training camp instructor.

Called to active duty on his twenty-second birthday, Bolte was ordered to Gettysburg, Pennsylvania, to join the 58th Infantry.

He received his regular Army commission as second lieutenant on October 25, 1917 and was sent to France with the 58th Infantry, 4th Division, as a first lieutenant (permanent) in May 1918. He took part in the Aisne-Marne offensive, was promoted to captain (temporary) in August, and fought in the battle of St. Mihiel. During the Meuse-Argonne offensive in September 1918 he was wounded.

After release from the hospital in January 1919, Captain Bolte was assigned to the 338th Infantry as a company commander at the forwarding camp near Le Mans, France. In March he became adjutant of the 4th Division with the Army of Occupation in Germany. Returned to the United States in the following August, Captain Bolte served as adjutant of a provision regiment of the 4th Division from September 1919 to February 1920, when he was assigned to the Historical Branch of the War Plans Division of the War Department General Staff at Washington, D.C.

He received his permanent status as captain on July 1, and was assigned to the Infantry School at Fort Benning, Georgia, where he remained as an instructor until September, 1921. He was then appointed aide to Major General J. L. Hines at Fort Sam Houston, Texas, and subsequently served under Hines in the office

BOLTE, CHARLES L.—*Continued*

of the Deputy Chief of Staff at Washington, and in the office of the Chief of Staff.

Entering Infantry School at Fort Benning in September 1926, Bolte completed the advanced course there, in June 1930. He proceeded to the Command and General Staff School at Fort Leavenworth, Kansas, graduating in June 1932. He was then ordered to the American Barracks at Tientsin, China, where he served for over three years with the 15th Infantry as an operations officer and company and battalion commander.

Promoted to major (permanent) in 1935, he returned to the United States in April 1936 to take command of a battalion of the 13th Infantry at Fort Devens, Massachusetts.

Four months later he was assigned as a student to the Army War College, graduating in June 1937 and serving as an instructor for three years. In July 1940 Major Bolte became a member of a war planning group at the Army War College, and for several months had temporary duty in the office of the chief of the Air Corps. Three months after promotion to lieutenant colonel (permanent) on August 18, 1940, he was assigned as operations and training officer of the Fourth Army Corps at Jacksonville, Florida.

In May 1941 Lieutenant Colonel Bolte was sent to London, England as officer in charge of war plans for a special Army observer group. He was promoted to colonel (temporary)on December 24, to brigadier general (temporary) on January 17, 1942, and was then assigned as chief of staff of the United States Forces in the United Kingdom. In the following July he was designated the first chief of staff of the new European Theater of Operations. For his service between May 1941 and June 1942, General Bolte later received the Legion of Merit.

In September 1942 he was named assistant commander of the 91st Infantry Division at Camp White, Oregon; then in February 1943 he became commanding general of the newly activated 69th Infantry Division in training at Camp Shelby, Mississippi. Advanced to major general (temporary) on April 26, 1943, Bolte led the 69th Division on the Mediterranean front from the following month until July 1944, when he took over the command of the 34th Infantry Division, then in combat along the Arno River in Italy.

Under their new commander, the "Red Bulls" (as soldiers of this division were nicknamed) broke through the Gothic Line, fought the difficult winter campaign in the Apennines, and on April 21, 1945 with the Second Polish Corps of the British Eighth Army, captured Bologna. At this point, the 34th Infantry Division completed five hundred days of combat, believed to be a record up to that time for American forces in World War II, and had won nearly 22,000 awards.

General Bolte himself won a Silver Star for gallantry in action near Bologna, and the Distinguished Service Medal for his command of the division. In May 1945, after having taken 40,000 German prisoners in a strike up the Po Valley, the 34th Infantry Division rested at Milan and was then assigned to occupation duty in Venezia Giulia.

Soon after the return of the 34th Division to the United States in October 1945, General Bolte was assigned to Army headquarters in Washington as Assistant Chief of Staff, Ground Plans. In August 1946 he became chief of staff of the army ground forces at Fort Monroe, Virginia, and on September 1, 1946, received his (permanent) rank as colonel. He was given (permanent) rank as major general to date from October 5, 1944.

He was appointed director of the special joint planning group in Washington, D.C., in May 1948 and a year later director of the Plans and Operations Division, General Staff, Army. Upon reorganization of Army headquarters March 1, 1950, General Bolte was designated Assistant Chief of Staff for Operations, the position he occupied until February 13, 1951 when he was advanced to lieutenant general (temporary) and became Deputy Chief of Staff for Plans, succeeding Lieutenant General Alfred M. Gruenther, who had been assigned as Chief of Staff, Supreme Headquarters, Allied Powers, Europe.

General Bolte also became chairman of the Inter-American Defense Board, which has its headquarters in Washington, and by August was in a position to assure the Senate Foreign Relations and Armed Services Committees that plans had been prepared under which a number of Latin-American countries would assume "a larger degree of responsibility" for hemisphere defense.

On August 5, 1952 Lieutenant General Bolte took over from Lieutenant General Manton S. Eddy the command of the United States Seventh Army. In the following month he directed the joint Franco-American field maneuver known as "Exercise Rosebush." Drew Middleton asserted the maneuver demonstrated that "the Seventh Army has mastered the techniques of camouflage and dispersion so necessary to an army that would have to fight at the outset without sufficient air cover" (New York *Times,* September 10, 1952).

Lieutenant General Bolte's appointment as commander in chief, United States Army, Europe was announced on February 9, 1953. He succeeded Lieutenant General Manton S. Eddy. When he left this post in September to become Army Vice Chief of Staff in Washington, he said that the 300,000-man Army is being trained intensively. "The combat effectiveness is far and away better than it was two and a half years ago when it was built up to its present strength of five combat divisions. Then it was a garrison army. Today it is a field army." He said that the men exercise in the field more than half their time. "It's very rare that you see a fat soldier," he added (New York *World Telegram and Sun,* September 26, 1953). Foreign honors conferred on General Bolte include a Companionship in the Military Division of the Order of the Bath, the Legion of Honor, the Croix de Guerre with Palm, the Brazilian Medalha de Guerra, and the Italian Military Order of Savoy and Order of SS. Maurizio e Lazarro. An academic distinction received by the general was the honorary degree of Doctor of Engineering conferred on him by the Illinois Institute of Technology in 1944. He was promoted to the rank of general, effective July 30, 1953.

General Bolte married Adelaide Carlton Poore, in 1923. They have two sons, David Endicott and Philip Lawrence, and one daughter, Damara. Both sons are United States Army officers and both were wounded in action in the Korean War.

References

Generals of the Army 1:5+ F '53
N Y Times p13 S 15 '53 por
International World Who's Who (1949)
Who's Who in America, 1952-53
Who's Who in the Regular Army (1925)
World Biography (1948)

BOLTON, FRANCES P(AYNE BINGHAM) Mar. 29, 1885- United States Representative from Ohio

Address: b. 450 House Office Bldg., Washington 25, D.C.; 810 Hanna Bldg., Cleveland, Ohio; h. 2301 Wyoming Ave., Washington, D.C.; Lyndhurst, Ohio

NOTE: This biography supersedes the article which appeared in *Current Biography* in 1940.

The first woman member of Congress to represent the United States in the United Nations General Assembly and the first Congresswoman to be elected from Ohio, Mrs. Frances P. Bolton, Republican, has represented the Twenty-second Congressional District continuously since March, 1940. She was chosen to fill out the unexpired term of her late husband, Chester Castle Bolton, in the House of Representatives of the Seventy-sixth Congress.

During her fourteen years in Congress she has proposed sixty-one bills, twenty-five of which were concerned with social, hygienic, educational and industrial issues oriented towards the betterment of women and minors both at work and in the home.

A woman of great wealth, Mrs. Bolton has devoted a part of her fortune to furthering the profession of nursing. She is the author of the Bolton act of 1943, which established the U.S. Cadet Nurse Corps. Now third ranking majority member of the House Foreign Affairs Committee, she has become an expert on Near Eastern affairs.

Frances Payne Bingham was born in Cleveland, Ohio on March 29, 1885, the fourth of the five children of Charles William and Mary Perry (Payne) Bingham. Among her forebears are some of the first New England settlers in the western reserve area. Her paternal great-grandfather and grandfather were members of the Ohio legislature and her maternal grandfather, Henry B. Payne, was a U.S. Senator.

After the death of her mother young Frances Bingham divided her time between her grandparents' households. She learned to speak French and German fluently prior to her enrollment at the Hathaway-Brown School in

Chase

FRANCES P. BOLTON

Cleveland. Later she studied at the Dieudonne Bornel, Oise, France and at Miss Spence's School for Girls in New York City.

Having a soprano voice of concert calibre she studied at the Mannes Music School in New York. While still very young Miss Bingham volunteered for practical nursing work among tenement families. Thus, she was initiated into the problems of public health which have remained one of her dominant interests.

Miss Bingham was married to Chester Castle Bolton (the son of Mark Hanna's business partner) on September 14, 1907. Her husband built his own fortune in steel which later brought him the title of "richest man in Congress." After her marriage Mrs. Bolton continued her interest in social welfare and nursing.

During World War I she was instrumental in persuading the Secretary of War, Newton D. Baker, to organize the Army School of Nursing. In 1923 she gave $1,500,000 to endow a nursing school at Cleveland's Western Reserve University and reluctantly consented to let it be named after her.

Another of her benefactions financed a log-cabin nursery center in Kentucky. As president of the Payne Fund she encouraged studies of the social value of motion pictures, and radio in education. As vice-president of the American Social Hygiene Association she was active in supporting state and Congressional appropriations for the control of venereal diseases.

Chester Bolton was elected as a Republican to represent the Twenty-second Congressional District of Ohio in March 1929 and was re-elected to the House of Representatives in 1930, 1932, 1934, and 1938. Mrs Bolton accepted in 1937 the vice-chairmanship of the Republican national program committee, and in 1938, membership on the Ohio Republican state central committee. In campaign speeches

BOLTON, FRANCES P.—*Continued*

for her husband, she exhibited "a flair for reducing complex issues to simple terms, for getting across the woman's viewpoint."

Following the death of her husband in 1939 she was asked by Republicans to seek election as his successor, and on February 27, 1940 was chosen to fill out his unexpired term. She defeated her Democratic opponent, Anthony A. Flegler, by 40,882 votes to 24,348, although she made only one campaign speech.

The first of her sex to be elected to Congress by an Ohio district and the seventh woman ever to become a member of the House, Mrs. Bolton was seated in the Seventy-sixth Congress on March 11, 1940. The committees to which she was assigned included those on Indian affairs and the elections of the President, Vice-President and Representatives in Congress.

In September 1941 she became a center of national attention through her speech in opposition to the selective service bill. "I cannot help see in it more danger than defense, more dictatorship than democracy" she said. Re-elected in 1940, Mrs. Bolton was named in January 1941 to the House Foreign Affairs Committee, and dropped all other assignments. In her campaign speeches she had stressed the point that "the United States should fight only to preserve and defend its territorial limits," and in the 1941 session she voted against Lend-Lease. After her country was committed to war, however, Mrs. Bolton gave wholehearted support to the military effort.

She voted for the creation of the Women's Auxiliary Army Corps (March 1942) and authored the Bolton bill to provide Federal aid for the training of nurses and to establish a uniformed nurses reserve. This measure received the Presidential signature on June 15, 1943. Six months later she sponsored another bill to give members of the Army Nurse Corps regular officers' commissions.

Representative Bolton voted in September 1943 for the Fulbright resolution which favored creation of international machinery to establish a lasting peace. She was a member of the Republican Postwar Advisory Council (Mackinac conference). "Mrs. Bolton has been no party hack in Congress," noted *Life,* June 12, 1944. "She voted against the Smith-Connally bill to outlaw strikes and voted for the Administration's soldier-vote bill. . . She voted to sustain the President's tax bill veto."

In 1944 the Congresswoman traveled in England and France to study the care of American wounded in hospitals thus becoming the first woman member of Congress to visit a war theater. She returned to Europe with a Foreign Affairs Committee subcommittee to visit twenty countries in 1945.

Mrs. Bolton was the first woman to head a Congressional mission abroad when in 1947 she toured the Middle East, the Soviet Union and Poland. In 1949 she was appointed by the Speaker of the House to the advisory committee of the Foreign Service Institute. (She is today the third Republican in rank on the House Foreign Affairs Committee).

In June 1949 she wrote an article in the *American Magazine* advocating the inclusion of women in the draft. She sponsored a new "long-range bill for nursing education" in January 1951 calling for about $47,000,000 of Federal aid in the first year of operation. (The measure was opposed by the American Medical Association and was tabled in committee).

Significant votes on domestic issues cast by Mrs. Bolton from 1946 through 1951 were in favor of reasonable profits in OPA ceilings (1946), the Taft-Hartley bill (1947), two-term limit for the presidency (1947), the anti-poll tax bill (1947), displaced persons bill (1948), Mundt-Nixon bill (1948), a cut in Federal spending (1950), and tidelands oil bill (1951).

Prior to the election of 1952 Ohio's Twenty-second District had been the largest in the United States, with a population of more than 900,000. By the reapportionment effective in that year, however, it was reduced to an area with a population of about 305,000, some of the former area becoming a part of the reconstituted Eleventh District. The youngest of Mrs. Bolton's three sons, Oliver Payne Bolton, a lawyer, was elected on the Republican ticket as the Representative of the Eleventh Congressional District to Congress in November 1952. Thus, the Boltons are the first mother and son to sit in the same house of the same Congress.

Believing that Americans must feel responsible for the hardships of others, she "worked valiantly to keep Congress from ignoring the UN International Children's Emergency Fund" (*Christian Science Monitor,* October 26, 1953). President Dwight D. Eisenhower named Mrs. Bolton, on recommendation of the House Foreign Affairs Committee, to be a U.S. delegate to the U.N. General Assembly. As a delegate she successfully led a fight in late 1953 to block a Polish proposal to hear charges by the Nationalist party of Puerto Rico to the effect that this territory was not truly "self-governing."

Her voting record in recent sessions of Congress indicated that she approved of using the Taft-Hartley act to halt a steel strike (1952), of maintaining 90 per cent farm price supports (1952), ending Federal rent controls on September 30, (1952), statehood for Hawaii (1953), private power development at Niagara (1953), and extending the excess profits tax (1953).

At a meeting of the Washington, D.C. chapter of B'nai Brith on February 15, 1954, Representative Bolton said that all religious prejudice must be wiped out if the nation is to preserve any of its freedoms. She said that an attack on any religious group "endangers every one's freedom" (New York *Herald Tribune,* February 16, 1954). In answer to letters from constituents criticizing her for attending "frivolous cocktail parties with United Nations delegates", she replied, "These gatherings have a value in easing diplomatic tensions. . . Our so-called civilized parties," she continued, "where mostly we stand about on weary feet talking first to one and then to another, seem to be the one method we have of making the acquaintance of people who have come together from the four corners of the world to try to lay the foundation stones upon which some day there can be built the structure of peace" (New York *Times,* November 17, 1953).

Speaking at Union Theological Seminary on November 16, 1953 at a tea given in her honor, Mrs. Bolton reminded her audience that she had headed a subcommittee of the Foreign Affairs Committee which had produced the 1948 study and tactics of world communism. She stated therefore that she was very much aware of the Communists' methods and "their never-ending pressures." She asked "Should I be afraid of those whose declared purpose is to destroy all those who differ from them? Would you have me turn away from the opportunity put before us [in the United Nations] of finding cracks in the iron curtain of men's minds, and women's too?"

The Congresswoman is the recipient of honorary degrees from Colgate (1940), Ohio Wesleyan (1942) and Western Reserve (1944) universities, and Baldwin-Wallace (1944), Kenyon (1947), Wooster (1948), and Fenn College (1953). She is the first American woman and second woman to receive the William Freeman Snow award. She also received the Adelaide Nutting award of the National League of Nursing Education.

An honorary life member of the American Social Hygiene Association and the Cleveland Dental Society, she is also a trustee of the Lakeside Hospital, Cleveland, Ohio; Lake Erie College, Painesville, Ohio; Tuskegee Institute; Meharry Medical College, Nashville, Tennessee; and Harmon Association for Advancement of Nursing, Inc; and on the advisory council of the school of nursing of Western Reserve; and the City Hospital of Cleveland. Mrs. Bolton holds membership in the D.A.R., Women's Club of Cleveland, Pen and Brush of New York, League of Women Voters, Society of Women Geographers, and Mt. Vernon Ladies Association.

The mother of three sons, Charles Bingham, Kenyon Castle and Oliver Payne Bolton, she has eight grandchildren. She enjoys music, and her interests include education and medicine. Her church is the Presbyterian. She has been described as "a handsome woman of medium height . . . a trim, erect figure," with white hair and blue eyes who "manages to combine an air of quiet authority with a warmly cordial manner."

References (see also references listed in 1940 biographical sketch).

Christian Sci Mon p2 Mr 11 '40 por; p9 O 26 '53
Ind Woman 32:441 D '53 pcr
J Social Hyg 29:164+ Mr '43 por
N Y Herald Tribune p21 F 26 '43 por; IX p18 O 25 '53 por; p8 O 26 '53
N Y Times II p3 N 8 '42 por; p11 Jl 30 '53
Sat Eve Post 226:25+ Ag 15 '53 por
Betts, A. Women in Congress (1945)
Congressional Directory (1953)
Who's Who in America, 1952-53
World Biography (1948)

BOND, HORACE MANN Nov. 8, 1904-
University president

Address: b. Office of the President, Lincoln University, Lincoln University, Pa.

The fifth president of Lincoln University, an interracial institution in southeastern Pennsylvania, and its first Negro president is Horace Mann Bond. When elected in 1945, he had been president of Fort Valley State College in Georgia for six years; previously he had been chairman of the department of education at Fisk University and dean of Dillard University. As president of Lincoln, Dr. Bond heads

Scurlock

HORACE MANN BOND

the first university to have offered higher academic degrees to Negroes. Under his leadership it has embarked on a program of expansion in 1954, its centennial year.

Horace Mann Bond was born on November 8, 1904 in Nashville, Tennessee, the son of James and Jane Alice (Browne) Bond. His surname was that of the owners of James Bond's mother, who was a slave in Kentucky. His father was a minister who later became engaged in interracial community work, part of the time for the Young Men's Christian Association. His mother taught Latin, and eventually four of the five surviving children in the family chose teaching careers. One brother, James Max Bond, is president of the University of Liberia in Monrovia, Liberia.

Horace was first educated at home, but with such competence that he was graduated from Lincoln Institute near Louisville, Kentucky at the age of fourteen. He has stated that "intellectually, my most important associations and influences arose from the fact that, through the education of my parents in the strongly New England humanitarian-tinged colleges,—Berea College in Kentucky and Oberlin College

BOND, HORACE MANN—*Continued*

in Ohio—I was reared in the moral, political, and social traditions of that stream of American life."

During his undergraduate years at Lincoln University in Pennsylvania, he became president of the athletic association and was sports editor of the college newspaper. He was also a member of Kappa Alpha Psi fraternity, and the scientific society, Beta Kappa Chi, which he helped to establish.

After his graduation in 1923 with a B.A. degree, he received a fellowship to study for the summer at Pennsylvania State College and he continued postgraduate studies during summers and as the occasion offered at the University of Chicago, between 1924 and 1936. He enrolled in that university's social science division of the department of education, and received his M.A. degree in 1926. He wrote his thesis on the personality traits of a group of adult Oklahoma Negroes among whom he had worked for the National Association for the Advancement of Education.

Beginning his teaching activities as an instructor in education at Lincoln University in 1923, he became a professor of education at Langston University in Oklahoma and served as head of the department from 1924 to 1927. He then administered in-service teacher education classes at Alabama State College for Negroes in Montgomery, Alabama from 1927 to 1928.

During the next five years he lectured at Tuskegee Institute, became an instructor, then assistant professor at Fisk University in Nashville, Tennessee, and was simultaneously a research specialist for the Rosenwald Fund. He served as dean of Dillard University in New Orleans, Louisiana from 1933 until 1936.

Of his first book, *The Education of the Negro in the American Social Order* (Prentice-Hall, 1935), E. M. Frazier stated: "Scarcely another book in recent years attacks the problems of Negro life in as fundamental and comprehensive a manner. . . . The objectivity of this study is to be found in its brilliant and fearless analysis of statistical and other types of data in relation to a significant frame of reference. For the first time we see the problem of Negro education in its social and economic setting" (*American Journal of Sociology,* Summer, 1935).

While teaching at Alabama State College for Negroes, Bond had already begun research that was to provide material for his doctoral thesis. In the acknowledgment in his thesis, Bond attributed his first interest in social and economic analysis of educational institutions to two professors at the University of Chicago, Dr. Newton Edwards and Dr. Charles Hubbard Judd.

His thesis, completed in 1936 and entitled "Social and Economic Influences on the Public Education of Negroes in Alabama, 1865-1930" earned him his Ph.D. degree from the University of Chicago and the Susan Colver Rosenberger Prize as the best social science doctoral thesis. It was published as *Negro Education in Alabama; A Study in Cotton and Steel* (Associated Publishers, 1939) and was designated by the American Educational Research Association as one of the six best educational research studies published during the years from 1935 to 1940.

R. N. Davis, in *Social Forces* (October 1939), termed the study "valuable to the historian and the social scientist as well as to persons interested in the field of education." In the *American Sociological Review* (December 1939), C. S. Johnson reported: "The book is characterized by careful research, excellent documentation, and cautious generalizations."

In 1938 Bond became the head of the department of education at Fisk University, and in the following year he was elected president of Fort Valley State College, at Fort Valley, Georgia. Toward the end of his six-year tenure of this post, he was one of a group who made a study of Hampton Institute. In 1945 he served also as a consultant in a survey of higher education in the state of Mississippi.

When Dr. Walter Livingston Wright, who had taught at Lincoln University since 1893 and had been its president for nine years, retired in 1945, Dr. Bond was chosen to become the fifth president. He is the first Negro and the first Lincoln alumnus to hold that post. The university, which celebrates its centenary this year, was founded by members of the Presbyterian faith to give "the advantages of Christian education" to young Negro men. Named originally Ashmun Institute, it became Lincoln University in 1865, adopted a nonsectarian policy, and was the first institution to award higher academic degrees to Negroes.

At present, approximately one out of every eight Negro physicians in the United States received their pre-medical training at Lincoln. With an endowment of $1,000,000 and a distinguished board of trustees, including Dr. Ralph J. Bunche and former Supreme Court Justice Owen J. Roberts, the university plans to increase its faculty and equipment and to triple its enrollment. Simultaneously a policy of encouraging the attendance of white students, so that the interracial character of the college already manifested in its faculty and trustees may extend to the student body, has been announced.

"We are continuing in our primary task of offering higher education to Negro students, but at the same time we are attempting to break through the racial pattern still prevalent in American education," Dr. Bond has stated. "Negro colleges are on the way to becoming colleges for every one."

During World War II, Bond was made a member of the subcommittee on education of the Joint Army and Navy Committee on Welfare and Recreation. He attended the UNESCO seminar on problems of teacher training which was held in England in 1948 and led some of the discussions.

Recently Dr. Bond has made several trips to West Africa, where many Lincoln University graduates are prominent in public and political life. His first visit, in 1949, he describes as having inspired "a great outpouring of nationalistic, pan-African feeling, as the people turned out by the tens of thousands to see their 'African brother' from America."

On his fourth visit, in December 1953, for the Institute of African-American Relations, a philanthropic organization whose purpose is to foster better relations with Africa, he met African leaders and went to Kumasi to attend a conference of West African nationalists.

Nnamdi Azikiwe, a Nigerian leader and a Lincoln graduate of 1930, was the principal speaker. Bond consulted with the president of the Grand Council of French West Africa about beginning a student exchange program and plans to help establish a department of African affairs at Lincoln University.

The educator married Julia Agnes Washington of Nashville, Tennessee on December 27, 1929. They had met at Fisk University and were married in Chicago. They have three children, Jane Marguerite, Horace Julian and James George.

Horace Mann Bond is five feet and nine inches in height with brown eyes and graying black hair. His weight is 180 pounds. He is a Presbyterian and a member of the Republican party. His organizations include the Elks, Masons, and the Lincoln-Civil War Society of Philadelphia. He is a member of the executive committees of the National Child Labor Committee, National Social Welfare Assembly and United Defense Fund. He serves on the editorial staff of the *Journal of Negro Education* and on the advisory staff of *Phylon,* an Atlanta University quarterly. From 1944 to 1945 he was president of the Conference of Presidents of Negro Land Grant Colleges.

President Bond holds the honorary LL.D. degree from Lincoln University (1941) and Temple University (1953). He enjoys watching sports and playing checkers, particularly a variety called "Polish draughts," at which he proved to be a champion in competition in West Africa. He also likes to read science fiction.

References

Opportunity 24:41 Ja '46 por
Leaders in Education (1948)
Who's Who in America, 1952-53
Who's Who in American Education, 1951-52
Who's Who in Colored America, 1950

BORDEN, NEIL H(OPPER) Dec. 7, 1895- Association president; university professor

Address: b. 325 Morgan Hall, Soldiers Field, Boston 63, Mass.; h. 150 Highland Ave., Winchester, Mass.

The recently elected president of the American Marketing Association is Professor Neil H. Borden who believes: "Advertising's outstanding contribution to consumer welfare comes from its part in promoting a dynamic, expanding market. Advertising's chief task from the social standpoint is encouraging the development of new production." Borden has had a teaching and administrative career at Harvard School of Business Administration for over thirty years and is the author of several books.

Fabian Bachrach

NEIL H. BORDEN

His election to the Hall of Fame in Distribution in 1953 is the latest in a series of distinctions earned by his contributions to the study of advertising and marketing.

Neil Hopper Borden was born December 7, 1895 in Boulder, Colorado, one of the seven children of Irene (Gilbert) and Edmund James Borden. His father, an accountant, and his maternal grandparents were pioneers in Colorado. Neil attended Boulder High School where he was active in student government and was graduated in 1914.

Continuing his studies at the University of Colorado, Borden majored in economics. He was elected to Phi Beta Kappa, was a member of Alpha Tau Omega and Acacia, and was on the staff of the college paper. His education was interrupted by service in the Army during World War I. He entered the Army as a private in the medical corps, working as a psychological examiner and was discharged as a student officer in the machine gun corps. Completing the various prerequisites, he received the B.A. degree in 1919 and instructed at the university during the following summer. In the choice of his life's work, Borden has stated that he was influenced by Dean Fred B. Hellems of the University of Colorado.

His first position was as principal of the Lafayette (Colorado) High School from 1919 to 1920. Borden then enrolled at the Harvard Graduate School of Business Administration. At the school he was a research assistant in 1921 and 1922 and received the M.B.A. degree in 1922. Borden remained at the graduate school serving from 1922 to 1930 as assistant dean, from 1925 to 1928 as assistant professor of advertising, from 1928 to 1938 as associate professor, and as a full professor of marketing since 1938.

Among the books he has written are *Suggestions on Report Writing* with Charles A. Glover (Harvard Business School, 1925), *Problems in*

BORDEN, NEIL H.—*Continued*

Advertising (Shaw, 1927), *Determination of Confusion in Trade-mark Conflict Cases* (Harvard Business School, 1937), *The Economic Effects of Advertising* (Irwin, 1942), *Advertising in Our Economy* (Irwin, 1945), *National Advertising in Newspapers* written with M. D. Taylor and H. T. Hovde (Harvard University Press, 1946), and *Advertising, Text and Cases* (Irwin, 1950).

In presenting the findings of a four-and-one-half year study on the effects of advertising, Professor Borden told the American Marketing Association in December 1941 that advertising has been an essential ingredient in expanding the material welfare of the United States. Advertising and aggressive selling have helped to bring a tremendous expansion of new and improved production upon which technological development and increased investment have depended. The New York *Times* December 30, 1941) reported that he warned also that the evidence shows that advertising usually is accompanied by certain dangers, particularly those attending the tendency of business to compete in advertising and thus to bring into the price a large amount of selling costs.

As president of the American Marketing Association, Professor Borden has indicated that one of his present tasks is the restoration of a Congressional appropriation for the business and industrial census. He told the *Christian Science Monitor* (September 30, 1953): "It is my feeling that the changes in our economy, with regard to manufacturing and distribution particularly, have been so rapid during the past decade that to wait until 1958 [when the next business census is scheduled] would fail in keeping up with the speed of the changes with enough accuracy and detail to permit the sort of analyses that would be of most value."

Professor Borden intends to enlist the cooperation of as many of the important national business organizations as possible. "Business must come closer to realizing just what is going on in retail and wholesale circles, . . . to see whether or not it is developing the right sort of outlets for the future," Professor Borden explained. "That's why these censuses are so necessary."

"We know that there have been very marked changes, and we can all note the growing importance, let us say, of our supermarkets. We've also seen the steady trend toward establishing retail business outside the cities in a direct move toward greater decentralization. Any omission of these facts in our present rapidly changing economy would tend to keep us from attaining the high standard of productivity which has stimulated and brought a higher standard of living."

Borden received the research award of the Kappa Tau Alpha Society in 1945, American Marketing Association research award in 1946, American Marketing Association award in 1947 for his contribution to marketing, Distinguished Service Medal in Advertising from Syracuse University in 1949, and the Charles Coolidge Parlin Award. The American Marketing Association gave him its Paul D. Converse Award in 1951 for advancing the science of marketing, and in that year he was elected to the Marketing Hall of Fame.

The professor is a member of the American Economic Association. Active in civic affairs, he served as a director of the Cambridge Y.M.C.A. from 1932 to 1947, on the planning board of Lexington, Massachusetts from 1934 to 1938, on the school committee of Winchester, Massachusetts from 1942 to 1948, and he is now a member of the Winchester Town Meeting and the board of the Winchester Public Library. He belongs to the Harvard clubs of Boston and New York City.

Married to Esther Page on September 11, 1926, Borden is the father of Rosanne, Neil Hopper, John E. P., and Penelope Borden. He is five feet nine inches in height, weighs 163 pounds, has blue eyes and thinning gray hair. For relaxation he enjoys gardening and woodworking. He is an Episcopalian and a Republican. To both his colleagues and his students he is known as "Pete".

References

Directory of American Scholars (1951)
Who's Who in America, 1952-53
Who's Who in Commerce and Industry (1953)

BORNE, MORTIMER Dec. 31, 1902- Artist

Address: 107 S. Broadway, Nyack, N.Y.

The three-color dry point engraving process, by means of which subtle variations of color can be introduced into a print, was first demonstrated by artist Mortimer Borne at a showing of his work in December 1943 at the Grand Central Art Galleries in New York City. Art critic Howard Devree called Borne's "innovations in color dry point very courageous experiments." A meticulous craftsman, Borne brings to his work (which is represented in the permanent collections of leading museums) the talents of the creative artist combined with the skills of the trained mechanic. He is also a teacher of art at the New School for Social Research. His work has been exhibited in graphic art shows since 1926. He began his experiments in color printing in 1936.

Now a naturalized American citizen, Mortimer Borne, the son of Harry and Lena (Warshaw) Borne, was born in Rypin, Poland on December 31, 1902. He attended the *gymnasium* in Gostynin, a town near Warsaw, and it was there that his aptitude for art was first discovered. He accompanied his art teacher on sketching trips and, Borne recalls, "he must have been an impressionist because I vaguely remember that he placed dabs of color on his canvas, which was both incomprehensible and fascinating to me." His teacher helped him to cast in plaster a head of Peter the Great which young Borne modeled from a textbook engraving and which won him a prize in a national school competition.

Schooling and art classes were interrupted for Borne by World War I and were not resumed until 1916 when he and his family came to the United States. Here he continued his art studies in New York at the National Academy of Design, the Art Students League and the Beaux-Arts Institute of Design. He studied under the noted American painter Charles Webster Hawthorne, founder of the Cape Cod School of Art in Provincetown, Massachusetts.

His subjects range widely—farm scenes, landscapes, city scenes, and figures. He has done American scenes—views of Gloucester, Weehawken, Norwich (Connecticut), and New York City. One of his most striking prints in the latter group was *Rainy Night* which won the J. Frederick Talcott Prize of the Society of American Etchers in 1939 and appeared in Albert Reese's collection of *American Prize Prints of the 20th Century*. Another print, *Landscape,* won the Mrs. Henry F. Noyes Memorial Prize of the Society of American Etchers in 1943. He has also done a number of pictures of Palestine—street scenes of Jerusalem and landscapes.

All his prints, the *Art Digest* (April 1, 1942) commented, "are charged with a vigor of both concept and technique." It is in dry point, especially, that Borne has done his most important work. The technique of dry point was developed in the fifteenth century. Although it is often confused with etching, dry point is an independent graphic process. In etching, the artist draws with a needle on the grounded surface of a metal plate which is then bathed in an acid solution. The acid eats away the metal to the proper depth for printing. No acid is used in the execution of dry point. The artist draws with a needle directly upon the metal surface. The burrs thrown up by the needle and the lines of the design hold the ink. The print usually has a richer and deeper tone than an etching.

Borne uses the dry point process with strength and boldness, but, as Leila Mechlin of the Washington *Star* commented, his hand is skilled and capable of subtlety in execution." His works have added richness because of the color process which he has perfected. The earliest color experiments with intaglio (engraving) plates were made in the seventeenth century by Joannes Teyler. Borne's contribution to the process was the development of a color medium "which retains a unified intaglio character without sacrificing subtlety of color-tone variations and rhythm of line" (Manchester *Leader,* April 7, 1945).

This result was accomplished, Borne says," by use of three dry point plates without any supplementary tone media." He cuts and inks the lines on each plate for a different color. The three plates are then printed successively on one sheet of paper to obtain the finished print. In some of his exhibits, Borne demonstrated this color process by showing prints of the various stages through which a flower design passes before its completion as a dry point. The effect is a subtle blend of colors and has been described as "comparable to water color."

Since 1939 when he had his first one-man show at the Delphic Studios in New York City, Borne has exhibited in many shows—at the

MORTIMER BORNE

American International College in Springfield, Massachusetts (1940); Cedar Rapids Art Association (1940); Corcoran Gallery of Art in Washington, D.C. (1941); Museum of Fine Arts in Montreal, Canada (1942); Currier Gallery of Art in Manchester, New Hampshire (1945).

He is represented in the permanent collections of the Library of Congress, Syracuse Museum of Fine Arts, Rochester Memorial Art Gallery, New Jersey State Museum, New York Public Library, National Gallery of Art, and United States National Museum.

Borne has been represented in exhibitions at the Chicago Art Institute (1931), American Institute of Graphic Arts (1937), New York World's Fair (1939), Museum of Modern Art (1940), Metropolitan Museum of Art (1942), Carnegie Institute (1947), Brooklyn Museum (1950), and New York State Fair (1950, 1951).

In 1945 Borne lectured at Sweet Briar College in Virginia. That same year he joined the faculty of the New School for Social Research in New York as a lecturer in art. Here he offers a course in contemporary art aimed at an "understanding of the creative process and the problems which confront the contemporary artist." In his course Borne uses a screen and projector to show students' preliminary sketches in enlarged form for class criticism and instruction.

From time to time he also shows his own pen and ink sketches. Many of these are done in a sketchbook covered to resemble an ordinary printed book so that Borne may draw fellow passengers in the subway without attracting too much attention. "I must have made many hundreds of these sketches," Borne writes, "and I prize some of them above anything else I have ever done."

Borne's ideas on "Art as a Form of Thinking" were presented in 1947 in a "University of

BORNE, MORTIMER—*Continued*

the Air" broadcast which he made for the Office of International Information and Cultural Affairs of the U.S. Department of State. On this program Borne said: "Step by step we are moving to new concepts that bring the terms 'intellect' and 'emotion' together into a single, unified stream of consciousness, the effectiveness of which depends in large measure on the cooperation and integration of these two types of thinking—the one which measures and counts and the other which reflects states of being and qualities."

He contributed an article to the book, *Are You Fed Up With Modern Art?*, edited by Clarence Canning Allen (Rainbow Press, 1952), in which he discussed the idiomatic specialization in modern art. He tried to reconcile the advocates of abstract or object-less painting with those favoring the representation of objects since he believes that the two "schools" should not be mutually exclusive.

In 1938 he was chairman of the Committee for the Interchange of Artists between the Americas and submitted a plan for such an exchange to the Conference on Inter-American Relations in the Field of Art. He concluded with a plea that artists "be given an opportunity to demonstrate that aspirations and interests of the peoples of North and South America are closely and inevitably inter-related. Than the artist, there is no better ambassador of good will."

In 1950 Borne and his wife, the former Rachel Zipes, whom he married in 1929, moved from Brooklyn to an old house in Nyack, New York. Since then he has remodeled the house completely, "with only an occasional help from a plumber and roofer, and improved it with a large skylight studio converted from an old attic." The artist is a member of the Society of American Graphic Artists (formerly the Society of American Etchers) and the National Audubon Society, and is the president of the Rockland Foundation.

Among the artist's related interests are reading—especially the Greek drama (for which he has made a number of illustrations), and books on science, archaeology and mechanical design. During World War II he was employed as a draftsman and worked on designs of mechanical devices. Borne submitted a number of preliminary sketches for new types of war equipment to the National Inventors' Council in Washington, D.C. He designed and marketed several games, among them "Strategy" and "Unconditional Surrender."

His interest in science and mechanics, Borne writes, "derives from a general curiosity as well as an underlying belief that art and the empirical sciences are indissolubly connected and no clear picture of our world surroundings is possible when one or the other facet is neglected."

References

Allen, C. C. ed. Are You Fed Up With Modern Art? (1952)
Who's Who in American Art (1953)
Who's Who in the East (1951)

BORST, LYLE B(ENJAMIN) Nov. 24. 1912- Atomic physicist; astrophysicist

Address: b. c/o New York University, College of Engineering, University Heights, New York 53

When the design of an atomic-powered locomotive that is "technically feasible to construct" was announced by physics professor Lyle B. Borst at the University of Utah, the New York *Times* editorialized on February 11, 1954 that Borst deserves "the credit for having telescoped time."

Although the building of such a locomotive was thought to be a possibility within the next quarter century, Borst's research has made its construction practicable in the near future. He has estimated that construction costs for an atomic locomotive would be $1,200,000, about twice the cost of a four-unit Diesel type. Powered by a reactor, the locomotive would use eleven pounds of uranium annually.

During the course of his career Borst has been closely associated with the developments in the field of nuclear physics. As a graduate student at the University of Chicago, he participated in an experimental research program which was to lead to the atomic bomb. Later affiliated with the Clinton Engineer Works at Oak Ridge, Tennessee, Borst was concerned with nuclear reactor development. When the Atomic Energy Commission established the Brookhaven National Laboratory, Associated Universities, Inc., at Upton, Long Island, New York, for experimental rather than military purposes, Borst was chosen to supervise the design and construction of the $25,000,000 atomic reactor which began operating on August 22, 1950. Since 1951 he has been professor of physics and director of the nuclear research program at the University of Utah, Salt Lake City. In 1952 he offered an explanation of the occurrence of supernovae in the sky.

On August 1, 1954 it was announced that Dr. Borst had been named chairman of the department of physics of the College of Engineering at New York University.

Lyle Benjamin Borst was born on November 24, 1912 in Chicago, Illinois, the son of George William and Jean Carothers (Beveridge) Borst. He received the A.B. degree from the University of Illinois in 1936. He remained on the campus to continue his studies, and in 1937, he was granted his master's degree in physical chemistry.

Young Borst began to work on his doctorate at the University of Chicago, and in 1940 he was appointed an instructor at the university. Borst received the Ph.D. degree in physical chemistry in 1941; his thesis was entitled "The Angular Distribution of Recoil Nuclei, with Notes on the Deuteron Hydrogen-Three Reaction."

Scientists had envisioned the prospect of unleasing atomic energy by splitting the atom, and by 1941, the United States government had recognized this military potential. A research center, the Metallurgical Laboratory, was established at the University of Chicago. The laboratory was engaged in the production of plutonium, under the general supervision of Arthur H. Compton. There, under the guidance of Enrico Fermi, the first self-sustaining nuclear chain reaction was obtained on December 2, 1942.

Borst was a research associate at the Metallurgical Laboratory. The experience gained on this project was invaluable for the young physicist. In 1943 he went to the Clinton laboratories in Oak Ridge, Tennessee, which had been set up by the Manhattan project for research in nuclear physics and the further applications of atomic energy. He remained there as a senior physicist until 1946.

When atomic bombs were dropped on Hiroshima and Nagasaki, the world awakened to the realization that a weapon of such destructive power should be controlled. The national and international regulation of the bomb was considered by some, and an atomic energy control bill was brought before the U.S. Congress. Scientists were called to present their views in November 1945, and Borst represented the Oak Ridge atomic scientists. He joined others in registering disapproval of certain restrictions being imposed on private atomic research, because he feared that such measures would regiment scientists and prohibit the open discussion of ideas.

He became an active member in the newly organized Federation of Atomic Scientists, a group representing about 90 per cent of those working on the bomb. The organization was dedicated to the beneficial use of atomic energy for civilization and to the international control of the bomb to "prevent a competitive armaments race." Borst, spokesman for the association, announced its principles on November 8, 1945 (New York *Times*).

In July 1946 Borst, as a member of the executive committee of the Association of Oak Ridge Engineers and Scientists, refuted charges made by the House Committee on Un-American Activities that Oak Ridge scientific organizations were participating in subversive activities. He also denied that the association had engaged in any plan to disseminate scientific knowledge outside the United States.

Appointed chairman of the department of reactors at Brookhaven National Laboratory in 1946, Borst was placed in charge of the construction of an atomic reactor. The laboratory, supervised by the AEC, but operated by a group of eastern universities, was primarily intended for experimental purposes; namely, the examination of the fundamental nature of the nuclei of atoms, the production of radioactive isotopes to treat certain types of cancer, and the investigation of atomic power in agriculture and industry.

The official dedication of the atomic reactor took place in August 1947, with Borst officiating at the ceremony. The nuclear reactor is an apparatus designed and operated for the purpose of initiating and controlling a chain reaction in a material such as uranium. The reactor was to be housed in a building six to eight stories high, 120 feet long, and 100 feet wide.

LYLE B. BORST

Not until August 1950, however, was this powerful reactor put into operation. At a signal from Borst, the chain reaction was begun by removing the boron control rods. "The full power was to be set at 30,000 kilowatts per hour; at capacity, it would be 50,000 times more powerful than the first atomic pile at the University of Chicago, and fifteen times more powerful than the nuclear reactor for Oak Ridge" (William L. Laurence, New York *Times,* August 23, 1950).

The fissionable atom, in a world at peace, could multiply the wealth of mankind. Borst was determined to show the significance of this premise. In March 1948, he predicted to the American Society of Mechanical Engineers that "industrial applications of atomic energy will be legion but will certainly not be immediate. . . The development of atomic energy since the war has taken a new direction, focusing attention upon beneficial, peacetime application. It has reached a point at which widespread industrial technology is possible and is required, if the nation is to maintain its preeminent position and is to benefit to the fullest extent from the new developments of a new field in a new world" (*Science Digest,* May 1948).

The scientist resigned his position at Brookhaven in 1951, and became professor of physics at the University of Utah. Shortly thereafter, the AEC authorized the university to build a reactor. Borst became chief designer of "hot pot," a reactor similar to the Los Alamos model. It was built to a great extent by his graduate students, and was intended for both a teaching and research laboratory.

The announcement that the first atomic-powered railroad locomotive had been designed was made by Borst on February 9, 1954. "An atomic-powered locomotive," he said, "now

BORST, LYLE—*Continued*

seems around a much closer corner than originally believed" (New York *Times*). Five university staff members and research engineers co-operated with Borst on the design and on the fifty-five page "feasibility study" which he turned over to railroad executives.

Structurally, the locomotive would be designed in two sections. The reactor would be two feet wide, three feet high, and three feet long; it would burn uranyl sulfate, a liquid form of uranium. The steam produced in the reactor would drive the turbine which in turn would drive the electric generators. Adequate protection from radiation is provided by encasing the reactor in a four foot thick steel shield which would weigh 200 tons. The second unit is intended to hold the radiators which would cool the hot air being discharged.

The giant locomotive generates 7,000 horsepower, equal to approximately four Diesel engines. Although the AEC has not released information on the exact cost of uranium, it is believed that it averages about $9,000 a pound. At this price, Borst maintains that his locomotive could compete favorably with other engines. The report stated that "the study is neither complete nor self-sufficient . . . [The] purpose was to find out 'whether an atomic-powered locomotive is in principle technically feasible'" (New York *Times*, February 14, 1954). The project was supported by private funds, and Borst was gratified with the cooperation tendered him by officials of five major railroads and nine manufacturing corporations.

Commenting on the "feasibility" of the locomotive, the editor of *Power* (April 1954) wrote: "In general, both practical railroad men and nuclear engineering experts tend to view various details of the proposal with great scepticism. It would appear that the problems of safety and public relations are more serious than the study suggests."

Using his knowledge of atomic science, Borst attempted to explain the activity of supernovae. His examination suggests that these giant stars which explode in space are "composed of a radioactive form of beryllium that does not exist on earth and can be created only in the atomic reactor" (New York *Times*, February 3, 1952).

According to Robert C. Cowen (*Christian Science Monitor*, March 1, 1952), Borst believes that the "beryllium for the explosion is formed by a reaction, similar to the one that would power a hydrogen bomb. In this reaction the nuclei of two light atoms fuse together to form the nucleus of a heavier atom with a tremendous release of energy . . . [This] collapse . . . may cause the flare-up of the supernova in what appears to earth-bound telescopes as the greatest explosion known in nature."

The scientist has favored the appropriation of large funds from the government to aid atomic research. Speaking as the head of the Federation of American Scientists in 1951, he strongly advised Congress to appropriate adequate sums for the National Science Foundation, lest the entire research and training program be shattered. He was supported by an editorial in the Washington *Post* (September 17, 1951), in which he was quoted as saying: "We run the risk of greatly distorting and weakening our entire research effort if we do not lay special emphasis on the training of new investigators and the development of new fundamental knowledge."

Borst is a fellow of the American Physical Society and the American Association for Advancement of Science. He has been elected to Sigma Xi and Gamma Alpha.

Lyle B. Borst has blue eyes and brown hair; he is five feet ten inches tall, and weighs about 150 pounds. He married Barbara Mayer on August 19, 1939. Their children, John Benjamin, Stephen Lyle, and Frances Elizabeth have already played a small role in the advancement of science, by donating their toy electric train engine to the atomic locomotive project (*Newsweek*, February 22, 1954).

References

Power 98:105+ Ap '54
Ry Age 136:15 F 22 '54
American Men of Science (1949)
Chemical Who's Who, 1951
Who's Who in America, 1954-55

BRANIFF, T(HOMAS) E(LMER) Dec. 6, 1883-Jan. 10, 1954 Airline executive; founder, president and board chairman of Braniff International Airways; president of T. E. Braniff Investment Co.; member of U.S. council of International Chamber of Commerce; Catholic co-chairman of the National Conference of Christians and Jews (since 1946); one of founders of World Brotherhood organizations in Europe; general chairman of "National Brotherhood Week" for 1954; established (with his wife) the Braniff Foundation for religious, educational and scientific projects (1944); made Knight Commander of the Order of St. Gregory and Knight of the Equestrian Order of the Holy Sepulchre. See *Current Biography*, (Apr.) 1952.

Obituary

N Y Times p1+ Ja 11 '54

BRECKINRIDGE, AIDA DE ACOSTA July 28, 1884- Organization official

Address: b. c/o The Eye-Bank for Sight Restoration, Inc., 210 E. 64th St., New York 21; h. 28 E. 63d St., New York 21

The founder and executive director of the Eye-Bank for Sight Restoration, Inc., is Aida de Acosta Breckinridge whose efforts to restore the sight of the blind through corneal graft operations and through the collection of the corneal tissue from the eyes of the dead have been phenomenally successful. Since its founding in 1945 the Eye-Bank has utilized 4,000 eyes for transplanting or research, and seventy-two doctors have been trained to do corneal transplant. There are now eye-banks established in Boston, Chicago, and Winston-

Salem, North Carolina affiliated with the New York office.

Mrs. Breckinridge has long been interested in civic and cultural activities and in promoting child health. She helped to found May Day as National Child Health Day in 1928 and Herbert Hoover appointed her in 1929 assistant director of public relations to the White House conference on child health and protection. She was chairman of the municipal art committee of the City of New York in 1935 and was chairman of the advisory committee on fine arts of the New York World's Fair in 1939.

Aida de Acosta was born in Elberon, New Jersey on July 28, 1884, the daughter of Ricardo and Micaela Hernandez (de Alba) de Acosta. She was educated at the Sacred Heart Convent in Paris. It was on June 29, 1903 that she made a solo flight over Paris in a powered balloon dirigible after being instructed by Alberto Santos-Dumont, a young Brazilian. When she stepped out of the balloon, Santos-Dumont greeted her with these words, "Mademoiselle, you are the world's first woman pilot." When news of the event reached Mrs. de Acosta, she ordered her daughter home, and requested that both Aida and Santos-Dumont keep the exploit secret. Aida de Acosta's flight in the powered craft was not made public until she revealed it at a dinner party in 1932.

The young society girl married Oren Root on November 5, 1908. Her husband, the nephew of the American statesman, Elihu Root, became the president of the Hudson and Manhattan Railroad Company. The couple had a daughter, Alva, and a son, Oren Root, Jr. The marriage was later dissolved.

During World War I, Mrs. Root sold Liberty bonds valued at $2,000,000. She induced Enrico Caruso to sing on the steps of the Subtreasury building on Wall Street in this effort. After the war she served with the American Committee for Devastated France. On her return Mrs. Root became director of the development of publicity and promotion of the American Child Health Association. It was her idea to dedicate May 1st, with its traditional outdoor festivities including the Maypole, to child health. She called on the late Samuel Gompers, president of the American Federation of Labor, asking him to release May 1st for children, and he agreed.

The first National Child Health Day was proclaimed by President Calvin Coolidge in 1928 when he asked that "all agencies and organizations interested in child welfare unite on that day in the observance of such exercises as will acquaint the people of the nation with the fundamental necessity for a year-around program for the protection and development of the health of the nation's children." On April 30, 1953, President Dwight D. Eisenhower proclaimed May 1st as the twenty-fifth Child Health Day.

Mrs. Root first became interested in eye diseases and their alleviation through her own personal experiences. In 1922 glaucoma took the sight of one of her eyes. After a series of medical visits both here and abroad, she consulted Dr. William Holland Wilmer of

Wide World
AIDA DE ACOSTA BRECKINRIDGE

Washington, D.C. Through an operation he managed to save some of the vision in her other eye. He also convinced her that virtual blindness need not end her career. While recovering from this operation Mrs. Root began to think about raising funds among Dr. Wilmer's patients to build a hospital where he could operate and pass on his surgical skill to young doctors, thus helping to restore the sight of many blind or partially blind persons.

Although Dr. Wilmer refused to reveal the names of his patients for this purpose, Mrs. Root managed to contact them and many wealthy people who became interested in her project. The Rockefeller Foundation subscribed $1,500,000 which was matched by other donors, including a gift from Andrew Mellon. In all more than $5,000,000 was obtained and the Wilmer Ophthalmological Institute was founded in 1929 at The Johns Hopkins University with a special chair for Dr. Wilmer.

On August 5, 1927 she married Henry Breckinridge, a lawyer. This marriage was later terminated.

One of Dr. Wilmer's former students, Dr. R. Townley Paton, approached Mrs. Breckinridge in 1944 with the suggestion of founding an eye-bank to supply the much needed corneal tissue. The Eye-Bank for Sight Restoration, Inc. was founded in May 1945 with Mrs. Breckinridge as its executive director. At that time fifteen surgeons were capable of performing the corneal graft, and the acquisition of an eye was a matter of luck, although 15,000 of America's 250,000 blind were in need of the operation. By 1954 the Eye-Bank had trained seventy-two doctors to restore sight through corneal transplant.

In the annual report for 1952 Mrs. Breckinridge stated: "More and more, because of the donation of eyes after death by generous Americans who had signed our forms (which may be obtained at the Eye-Bank), and

BRECKINRIDGE, AIDA DE ACOSTA
—Continued

through the cooperation of their next of kin, and our 169 affiliated hospitals throughout the country, the Eye-Bank is beginning to receive a good supply of eyes—an average of about fifty per month. After the eye surgeons have used the corneas to restore vision, the eyes are returned to us for pathological study, thus opening up new opportunities of investigation in other fields of ophthalmology."

Of particular importance to the Eye-Bank program is the American Red Cross motor corps whose members answer any emergency assignment to deliver eyes from the airport to the hospital. Air lines also give priority to delivering eyes to the designated hospital. It is a real example of teamwork in which the Red Cross and the air lines cooperate all over the country. The great need for speed is apparent since live corneal tissue can be preserved for grafting for only three days after the eyes have been removed.

Doctors in the Eye-Bank's headquarters in the Manhattan Eye, Ear and Throat Hospital, 210 East 64th Street, New York, examine the eyes upon arrival, attend to their preservation, and if the corneas are perfect for grafting, distribute them in turn to qualified surgeons throughout the country who have a waiting list of suitable cases. A surgeon is given the word that it is his turn and his patient is then rushed to the hospital for the operation.

It was announced in the 1953-1954 report that since its inception the Eye-Bank has received approximately 4,000 eyes, and has granted twelve fellowships, several of which were awarded to doctors in China, India, Israel, Switzerland and the Philippines. Mrs. Breckinridge said that "within the last year we have added to the Eye-Bank a national advisory committee—a group of fifteen regional ophthalmologists. Each one stands ready to support us and to give us counsel, and we are proud of meriting their endorsements." The corneal clinic of the Eye-Bank, it was reported, had served 6,000 patients in six years "a haven of diagnosis open to patients regardless of financial station, race or creed."

Dr. Paton, the vice-president of the Eye-Bank, revealed that its laboratory is pursuing research in methods of improving the preservation of corneal tissue, examination of the retinal periphery in eyes, the vitreous humor in relationship to retinal detachment, the corneal basement membrane, glaucoma, and cancer research. He announced: "Twenty years ago, the incidence of success in corneal grafting operations was around 20 per cent. Today, the incidence of success in selected cases is almost 90 per cent."

Mrs. Breckinridge believes that the success of the Eye-Bank program has been due in large part to the cooperation given by America's newspapers and magazines. "If you have an idea to sell and can tell a proper story, you gain your point in this great country of ours," she stated.

She has served on many health and welfare committees and was the director of the medical service division of the Association for Improving the Condition of the Poor, director of the New York committee of the National War Fund in 1943, liaison director of national advertising of the National War Fund in 1944 and 1945. She was director of space advertising of the American Red Cross from 1943 to 1945 and initiated the idea of persuading advertisers to include boosts for the Red Cross in their national advertising. Since 1941 she has been a member of the public relations committee of the New York chapter of the American Red Cross. She is a director of the William Holland Wilmer Foundation. She was national chairman of the women's division of the Willkie Clubs of America in 1940.

The executive director of the Eye-Bank has been described as "warm, enthusiastic, tireless, and inspiring." Her club is the Cosmopolitan. Union College awarded her the degree of Doctor of Humane Letters in 1949. Mrs. Breckinridge believes that "It is wonderful to see . . . it is also wonderful to know that you have helped others to see."

References

N Y Herald Tribune p11 Ag 5 '40 por
N Y Post Mag p3 Mr 2 '52 por
N Y Times p56 N 11 '48
N Y Times Mag p18 Ap 28 '46; p18 N 2 '47 por
N Y World-Telegram Mag p12 Jl 12 '53 por
Read Digest 53:101+ Ag '48
American Women, 1939-40
Who's Who in America, 1954-55

BRINEY, NANCY (WELLS) June 12, 1911- Publisher; editor

Address: b. 575 Madison Ave., New York 22 h. Barrington, Ill.

About 15,000 devotees of drama, 90 per cent of whom live far from Times Square, receive their Broadway theatre once a month by way of the United States Post Office in the form of published versions of current plays. These are selected by Nancy Wells Briney, and distributed by Fireside Theatre, an enterprise originated in 1946 by Mrs. Briney and her husband, Paul, and now sponsored by the Literary Guild of America.

Nancy Wells Briney was born in Louisville, Kentucky, on June 12, 1911, to Edmond Daniel Wells and Elsie Bald Wells. Her father was an eye, ear, nose and throat specialist. She attended Kentucky Home School for Girls and the University of Louisville. While in college she attended Boyd Martin's drama courses and became interested in dramatics. Martin was director of the University Players and Nancy acted in some of the productions. She met another drama student, Paul Briney, and they were married on March 31, 1936.

She began her newspaper career in the advertising department of the Louisville *Herald Post* in 1932, and continued to take an active part, with her husband, in little theatre groups in Louisville. She also wrote articles about the theatre for the New York Junior League Magazine. During World War II she did volunteer work for the Service Men's Center in Indianapolis, where she and Mr. Briney had moved. She also was an active worker in behalf of the Bundles for Britain organization, and for the Army Map Service.

The young couple yearned to see Broadway plays, but they had little opportunity to travel to New York from Indianapolis where Mr. Briney was in the public relations department of a large firm. So they began purchasing published versions of current plays such as Random House occasionally issued. Feeling that there might be other hinterlanders who would like to read these plays, they conceived the idea of distributing plays to those who expressed interest in receiving them. They purchased the bound copies of the plays, beginning with Eugene O'Neill's *The Iceman Cometh* in October 1946, and invested their small savings in the venture. The plan was to distribute four plays a year.

Since the Brineys both held jobs, they worked on their project at night, using the cellar of their apartment as a storage place for the books. They purchased a mailing list of 10,000 names. "This was not a special theatre list, as you might think," Mrs. Briney explained (*Christian Science Monitor* December 14, 1951). "We bought a gift list because we thought the people would be used to buying by direct mail—and that was the way we hoped to sell our idea."

"We made up a letter and sent it out, choosing states as far away from Broadway as California and Texas. We had a fair response—106 subscribers—so we began to order plays from the New York publishers." Mrs. Briney recalled that sometimes the rains flooded the cellar and ruined the plays, but she and her husband kept on, encouraged by the enthusiastic response. They did their own wrapping and addressing.

"We made our selections carefully," said Mrs. Briney. "Sometimes the play would be a comedy, sometimes a musical play, and again something serious. We soon discovered that people who are interested in the theatre are interested in all phases of it. They like to know about plays even if they don't like the plays themselves. They enjoy forming their own opinion, whether the critics approve a play or not."

For two years Mrs. Briney carried on the Indianapolis Fireside Theatre with her husband's help in the evenings and on weekends. They distributed in these two years *The Iceman Cometh, Present Laughter, All My Sons, Years Ago, Born Yesterday, Medea, A Streetcar Named Desire, Mister Roberts,* and *Death of a Salesman.* "Our original subscribers remained loyal, but we made no effort to get new subscribers because we had all we could do to keep up with the business we had. Our basement was getting too crowded. . . Then one day Mr. Briney said he thought we would have to give it up. In a burst of nobility, I offered to give up my job. So we carried on" (*Christian Science Monitor,* December 14, 1951).

However, when her husband accepted another position in 1949 and they moved to New York (he is now assistant vice-president of Allstate Insurance Company) it seemed as if they might have to relinquish the Fireside Theatre project. "I had read of the Literary Guild and A. Milton Runyon, its president, in *Publishers Weekly,* and I went to see him and asked if he would be interested in carrying on the project. He said that he would be willing to give it a try. Tests showed that it could be done successfully on a larger scale. The plan was then expanded to a play a month, at the reduced price of $1.89 each, plus postage."

NANCY BRINEY

With promotion, the subscription list grew to over six thousand members. It now numbers about fifteen thousand, and has had very few resignations. At least 75 per cent of the members order a selection every month. Of the membership, 90 per cent purchased *The King and I,* Oscar Hammerstein's and Richard Rodger's musical version of *Anna and the King of Siam*; 80 per cent chose Shaw's *Caesar and Cleopatra* in combination with Shakespeare's *Anthony and Cleopatra* in the acting version used by Sir Laurence Olivier and Vivien Leigh; and 90 per cent ordered *The Innocents,* William Archibald's dramatization of Henry James' story, *The Turn of the Screw.*

Nancy Briney, continuing as editor, attends Broadway plays and selects twelve a year for her members. A tribute to her astuteness was her choosing *I Am a Camera* by John Van Druten, (dramatized from Christopher Isherwood's short stories) long before it won the New York Drama Critics' Circle award. "I still have editorial supervision of the Fireside Theatre," Mrs. Briney said, "but Mr. Briney is entirely out of it, now, except that he goes with me to see all the shows."

Playwrights like "the immortality of covers," and most producers of plays which are still running on Broadway regard a published script as prestige. Only occasionally does a producer hesitate. Mrs. Briney recalls that she met with

BRINEY, NANCY—*Continued*

resistance from the producers of *Bell, Book and Candle,* since two road companies were going on tour (one starring Joan Bennett, and the other, Rosalind Russell). However, they finally agreed to allow a Fireside Theatre version. It is believed that the published play created additional interest and increased audiences.

Actors who are busy in other productions have told Mrs. Briney that they enjoy reading the plays in book form. Henry Fonda said, "Reading plays is the next best to being there when the curtain goes up." Shirley Booth commented, "I find reading plays the most fascinating form of diversion, to act out roles in one's own living room." Katharine Cornell, Noel Coward, and other theatre people have endorsed the idea.

Mrs. Briney gives credit for the interest in play reading to the growth of community theatres throughout the United States, to Random House, which publishes about half of the plays issued in the Fireside editions, and to the development of drama courses in colleges and universities. Theatre-lovers formerly could not always obtain the published versions of plays still on Broadway. In the early 1900's Mrs. A. Starr Best, head of the Drama League of America, persuaded some publishers to print an occasional new play, and Random House got its start in 1933 with a small edition of Eugene O'Neill's *Ah, Wilderness!*

The Brineys have one son, Timothy Paul, aged six. Mrs. Briney's hobbies include doing over old furniture, painting, and ice skating. She has black hair and green eyes, is five feet five and a half inches tall and weighs 145 pounds. She calls herself a "Southern democrat"; her religion is Episcopalian. She is a member of the New York Junior League and The Woman Pays Club.

References

Christian Sci Mon p4 D 14 '51
Washington (D.C.) Post p6C D 16 '51

BRINEY, MRS. PAUL See Briney, N. (W.)

BROOKE-POPHAM, SIR ROBERT (MOORE) Sept. 18, 1878—Oct. 20, 1953 Commander in chief of British forces in Far East (1940-1942); educated at Royal Military College at Sandhurst; in 1912 formed, with other officers, Air Battalion of Royal Engineers from which Royal Flying Corps was organized; commandant of RAF Staff College at Cranwell (1921-1926); chief of fighting area of Great Britain (1926-1928); air force commander in Iraq (1928-1930); commandant at Imperial Defence College (1931-1933); inspector general of RAF (1935-1936); governor general of Kenya Colony (1937-1939); received Legion of Honor in 1914, and in 1936 was created Knight Grand Cross of Royal Victorian Order. See *Current Biography,* (Oct.) 1941.

Obituary

N Y Times p29 O 21 '53

BROSSARD, EDGAR B(ERNARD) (brŏs'sârd) Apr. 1, 1889- United States Government official; agricultural economist

Address: b. c/o United States Tariff Commission, Washington 25, D.C.; h. 1629 Columbia Rd., N.W., Washington 9, D.C.

The chairman of the United States Tariff Commission, a nonpartisan federal agency which is responsible for investigating foreign trade markets and recommending changes in the duties imposed on imported goods, is Edgar B. Brossard. He was appointed to this post by President Eisenhower in March 1953 for a term ending June 16, 1954, and was reappointed chairman to serve until June 1955. Brossard has been a member of the six-man commission for twenty-nine years.

Recent tariff cases considered by the commission include those pertaining to the importation of Swiss watches, woolen gloves, scissors and shears, fish fillets, and lead and zinc. Domestic producers of these products appeared before the commission which studied each case, reported the findings to President Eisenhower, and recommended in "hardship" cases higher tariffs for foreign goods and lower tariffs when deemed necessary. During the period of Brossard's chairmanship the commission has received over fifty applications for relief under the "escape clause" of reciprocal trade agreements.

Before his U.S. government service, he was a farm management demonstrator in Utah and later, from 1919 to 1923, headed the department of agricultural economics and farm management in the Utah State Agricultural College. He has also served on the Interdepartmental Committee on Scientific and Cultural Cooperation and attended the United Nations Preliminary Conference on Trade and Employment.

Edgar Bernard Brossard, born April 1, 1889 in Oxford, Idaho, is one of the eleven children of Amable Alphonse and Mary Catherine (Hobson) Brossard. His father was a farmer, rancher and prospector, and later became supervisor of highway construction in Utah. Winter sleigh rides to school, summer work on the farm, and the fall roundup are among Brossard's boyhood memories.

Edgar attended Utah State Agricultural College Preparatory School and Utah State Agricultural College, at Logan, Utah, where he majored in economics. At the college he was a four-letter athlete, a member of the student body council, president of the junior and senior classes, athletic editor for the school paper, and president for two years of his fraternity. In addition, he held a variety of part-time jobs—assisting in the college chemistry laboratory, reporting weather conditions for the U.S. Weather Bureau, correcting examination papers, and teaching mathematics at a preparatory school. He received the B.S. degree in 1911.

During the period of 1911 to 1914 Brossard, a member of the Church of Jesus Christ of Latter-Day Saints (Mormon), was a missionary for his church. He traveled extensively through Europe, studied conditions there, and headed the French Mission. Returning to the United States, he became a farm management demonstrator for the state of Utah. In 1916-1917 he did similar work in Minnesota, studying, meanwhile, at the state university.

He earned the M.S. degree from the University of Minnesota in 1917, and during the next year was a student at the graduate school of Cornell University. However, he completed his graduate studies at the University of Minnesota, where he was an instructor in farm management and where he received the Ph.D. degree in 1920. His thesis was "Some Types of Irrigation Farming in Utah." From 1919 to 1923 Brossard was the head of the department of agricultural economics and farm management at Utah State Agricultural College, and he directed research in this field for the Agricultural Experiment Station, at Logan, Utah. Entering the Federal government in 1923, he worked as an economist with the U.S. Tariff Commission. Two years later, he was appointed a member of the commission. (Such appointments are now for six years and are made by the President and confirmed by the Senate. The chairman is designated annually from among the members of the commission by the President.) In his long career with the commission, Brossard has been reappointed at the end of each of his six-year terms and during 1930 he served as its chairman.

When, in 1950, the question of his most recent reappointment came before the Senate, the Washington *Post* commented that Brossard "has gained a vast knowledge of the country's economic problems and an invaluable experience in fact-finding and laying the economic groundwork for government policies . . . That Dr. Brossard . . . has worked primarily as an economist interested in the national welfare is indicated by the widespread bipartisan support accorded him." On March 5, 1953, Brossard was designated chairman of the commission to fill out a term expiring in June, when he was again chosen by the President to fill the chairmanship for the term ending June 16, 1954. He was then reappointed for another one-year term (until June 1955).

The six-member nonpartisan Tariff Commission (there cannot be more than three members from one political party) was created by Congress on September 8, 1916, and its functions and responsibilities have been augmented since by other acts. It is charged with investigating the administration and the fiscal and industrial effects of U.S. customs laws; American tariff policies and their effects; and foreign trade and trade control policies. Reports by the commission are made when required by the President, the House Ways and Means Committee and the Senate Finance Committee, and annually to Congress.

The Agricultural Adjustment Act of 1933 designates the Tariff Commission to determine whether imports are interfering with agricultural programs undertaken by the government. The Philippine Trade Act of 1946 provides for investigations by the commission with regard to the need for quotas on Philippine articles. Under

Washington Press Photo Service
EDGAR B. BROSSARD

the Trade Agreements Extension Act of 1951 the commission investigates concessions which may be granted in proposed trade agreements, and actions which should be taken under the "escape clause" of trade agreements.

Since March 1953 the tariff agency has received over fifty applications from domestic industries. In three relief applications—one dealing with briar pipes, another with screen-printed silk scarves, and a third with hand-blown glass the commission, including Brossard, recommended a higher tariff. On the three items, President Eisenhower either decided against the recommendation or requested further study. These decisions were based, according to most commentators, on the President's desire to maintain and increase trade with friendly countries. Increased duties, he felt, would hinder an important aspect of U.S. foreign policy.

The commission also recommended that an additional tariff fee of ten cents a pound on clean imported wool be granted by the President. The majority report said that since the government's price support program had failed to maintain domestic wool production, the alternative was to aid domestic growers through higher duties on imported wool. President Eisenhower, however, refused to accept the recommendation and instead proposed Congressional action on an incentive payment plan during periods when wool prices are below the desired support level. The President decided in May 1954 in the case of scissors and shears not to increase the present 42% tariff (even though the commission had recommended doubling the duty on German and Italian imports) on the ground that no imminent threat to domestic industry was proved.

In July 1954 the President upheld the recommendations of the Tariff Commission to ir

BROSSARD, EDGAR B.—*Continued*

crease tariffs up to 50 per cent on certain types of watch movements (from Switzerland).

Since the founding of the Interdepartmental Committee on Cooperation with the American Republics (now called Interdepartmental Committee on Scientific and Cultural Cooperation) in 1938, Brossard has been a member of the committee, which coordinates the work of various government agencies in Latin American countries.

The committee laid the groundwork of the Point Four program by encouraging the exchange of students, educators, professionals; establishing cultural centers, maternal and child welfare services, and training grants; and cooperating in research for the improvement of native agriculture and industries.

In order to examine the progress of the committee's program, Brossard visited seven Latin American countries in April and May of 1946 and reported that the projects had made a substantial contribution to mutual good will and friendship. He wrote: "Surely one of the very best ways of establishing peace and cooperation between one nation and another is for their people to work together in daily educational, technical and professional tasks until they know the natural, peaceful, and normal heart's desires . . . of one another" (*Bulletin of the Pan American Union,* November 1946).

As chairman of the Committee for Reciprocity Information, Brossard represents the Tariff Commission on that committee. Created by executive order on October 5, 1949, the committee receives the views of interested persons in any negotiated foreign trade agreements before such agreements are concluded, as provided for by the Trade Agreements Act. The committee is composed of representatives from those government departments and agencies concerned with the operation of the Trade Agreements Act.

Dr. Brossard was an alternate U.S. delegate to the U.N. Preliminary Conference on Trade and Employment (1947-48) which worked on the charter of the International Trade Organization.

The tariff expert is a member of the American Economic Association and American Farm Economic Association; Public School Association of the District of Columbia; alumni associations of Utah State Agricultural College, University of Minnesota and Cornell University; National Grange; and Phi Kappa Phi, Pi Kappa Alpha and Alpha Zeta. He is a Republican and his private club is the Inquirendo. Brossard has blue eyes, brown hair, weighs 230 pounds, and is six feet tall. He enjoys reading and study and likes to watch football, baseball, and tennis. He was married on August 25, 1915 to Laura Parkinson Cowley, a teacher and head of a high school home economics department before her marriage.

References

Who's Who in America, 1954-55
Who's Who in Commerce and Industry (1953)
World Biography (1948)

BROWNELL, HERBERT, JR. Feb. 20, 1904- United States Attorney General

Address: b. c/o Department of Justice, Washington 25, D.C.

NOTE: This biography supersedes the article which appeared in *Current Biography* in 1944.

As administrator of the Department of Justice, Attorney General Herbert Brownell, Jr. is principal legal advisor to President Eisenhower and to all the Federal departments. He is in charge of providing the means for the enforcement of the Federal laws and he also heads the Office of Alien Property, the Immigration and Naturalization Service, the Federal Bureau of Investigation, and the Federal prisons. Responsible to him are more than 30,000 employees, including ninety-four prosecuting attorneys throughout the United States.

Brownell has had more than twenty-five years of experience as a practitioner mainly in hotel and restaurant law in New York City, and a concurrent political career covering two decades. He was one of the top advisors in General Eisenhower's campaign for President in 1952, and was recognized as "the best political strategist of the Republican party" (*Time,* February 16, 1953).

Born in Peru, Nebraska, on February 20, 1904, Herbert Brownell, Jr. is one of the seven children of Herbert and May A. (Miller) Brownell, both descendants of early English settlers in New England, and the great-nephew of William Henry Harrison Miller, U.S. Attorney General from 1889 to 1893. His father joined the faculty of the University of Nebraska when Herbert was about six years of age, and the boy attended primary and secondary school in the state capitol.

After graduating from Lincoln High School in 1920, where he had been president of the debating club and of his class, and managing editor of the newspaper, Herbert Brownell entered the University of Nebraska to pursue a liberal arts course. As president of the college journalism fraternity and editor of the school's *Daily Nebraskan,* he acquired experience in reporting and during his senior year taught a course in journalism at Doane College. He was elected to Phi Beta Kappa society and received the A. B. degree from the University of Nebraska in 1924.

Offered a scholarship to Yale Law School, Brownell accepted in lieu of his original plan for a journalistic career. At Yale he roomed with his older brother, Samuel (now U.S. Commissioner of Education). He edited the *Yale Law Journal,* and graduated *cum laude* in 1927. In the following year he was admitted to the New York bar.

Brownell began his career as a law clerk with Root, Clark, Buckner & Ballantine in New York City in 1927. At the end of two years he accepted a position with the Manhattan law firm of Lord, Day & Lord of which he became a partner in 1932.

Entering politics as a member of the Young Republican Club of New York, he became an election captain in the Tenth Manhattan Assembly District (now the First). The Republican Party selected Brownell as its candidate for the New York State Assembly in 1931 and Thomas E. Dewey to act as campaign manager. Brownell lost in 1931, but won in 1932. Reelected for five terms, he served as assemblyman from 1933 to 1937, and introduced legislation to establish minimum wage standards, liberalize alimony laws and reorganize New York city government. He was named head of the Republican national committee on state affairs in 1934.

Announcing that he would not be a candidate for re-election in 1937, Brownell returned to Lord, Day & Lord and served as general counsel for the American Hotel Association. He was campaign manager for Dewey's unsuccessful bid for the governorship in 1938. In the following year, he accepted the post of chief counsel for the New York World's Fair and contributed to the record of only one case lost among nearly 1,000 lawsuits.

Brownell successfully managed the campaign for Republican Edgar J. Nathan, Jr. for president of New York City's Borough of Manhattan in 1941. He directed Dewey's 1942 gubernatorial campaign, in which the New York Governor received an excess of about 650,000 votes. Going to Albany as one of Dewey's key men in handling patronage, Brownell refused a state cabinet post. "For me," he explained, "politics was winning elections, not getting political jobs" (*Time,* February 16, 1953).

He directed Joe R. Hanley's winning campaign for the lieutenant governorship of New York in 1943. The next year, he was elected chairman of the Republican National Committee, an office he retained for two years. During this period, he reorganized the Republican party, setting up national machinery that would work closer with precinct units. He was manager of Dewey's presidential campaigns in 1944 and 1948.

After retiring from politics for several years, he began working to win the Republican presidential nomination of 1952 for General Eisenhower. Shortly before the 1952 Republican convention, as reported by *Newsweek* (November 23, 1953), with "Taft still in the lead . . . it was Brownell who brought about the coup which won for . . . Eisenhower. [Brownell] flew to Texas, where a governors' conference was being held, and succeeded in inducing nearly all the governors to sign a statement protesting 'the Texas vote steal.' Out of this grew the 'Fair Play Amendment,' under which many of Taft's delegates were unseated."

He advised Eisenhower on the issues to be stressed and other strategy problems. Refusing to go on the campaign train, he said: "The manager should be at the telephone at national headquarters, far enough away to get a bird's eye view" (*Time,* February 16, 1953).

Following the election Brownell became one of President-elect Eisenhower's chief advisors on Cabinet appointments. His nomination as Attorney General was announced in November 1952, and he was the only Cabinet member besides Charles E. Wilson to accompany the President-elect on his Korean tour.

HERBERT BROWNELL, JR.

Sworn in as Attorney General in January 1953, Brownell was admitted to practice law before the U.S. Supreme Court. He has severed his connection with Lord, Day & Lord. Expressing his concept of his new office, he said: "I feel strongly that the Department of Justice is a keystone of the Republic; if it fails, all that our youth has fought to preserve crumbles" (*Time,* February 16, 1953).

Shortly after he took office, Brownell declared that the Department of Justice would no longer withhold prosecution of tax evasion cases on "grounds of ill health" (New York *Times,* February 20, 1953). He became the second administration spokesman to oppose the constitutional amendment proposed by Senator John W. Bricker to limit the treaty-making authority of the President. Expressing his conviction, he affirmed "we can ill afford" to lessen the nation's treaty-making power, "the one great peace-time weapon this country possesses" (New York *Herald Tribune,* April 8, 1953). In May 1953, he made a ruling removing income tax immunity from approximately 400 foreign employees of the United Nations, in accordance with provisions of the Immigration and Nationality Act of 1952.

Concerning the confiscation of German property in this country under the Trading With the Enemy Act of World War II, the Attorney General declared his department "will not issue any orders vesting new or additional German properties" (New York *Times,* April 18, 1953). In commenting on President Eisenhower's government-employee loyalty and security program effective May 27, 1953, Brownell stated: "It eliminates dangerous loopholes and establishes an objective test as to whether a person's conduct is consistent with national security rather than the subjective test as to whether in his mind he was loyal" (New York *Times,* April 28, 1953). On May 8, the Attorney

BROWNELL, HERBERT, JR.—*Continued*
General submitted to Congress the draft of a bill to legalize the use of evidence obtained by wire tapping in Federal cases involving national security or defense (New York *Times,* November 22, 1953).

Summarizing his views on anti-trust policies, the Attorney General declared that "in a dynamic society such as ours every barrier to the entry of new producers must be eliminated in order to maintain our system of free enterprise" (New York *Times,* October 10, 1953). The anti-trust division will endeavor to obtain consent judgment in many cases, that is, settlement without trial or extended court proceedings, as exemplified by the October 1953 court which required the General Electric Company to make public its incandescent lamp patents.

The Attorney General spoke on October 20, 1953, before the New York *Herald Tribune* forum in New York City and recommended that a Federal public defender service be provided with competent counsel in cases of felony and other serious offenses. In an address to the National Education Association's 1953 convention, he said that "law and education must go forward hand in hand" (*Vital Speeches,* August 1, 1953). Brownell presented his brief to the Supreme Court in December, 1953 contending that the court has full power to end segregation in the nation's public schools.

Another important brief was submitted by a group of lawyers, headed by Thurgood Marshall, special counsel of the National Association for the Advancement of Colored People. On May 17, 1954 the Supreme Court held that racial segregation in the public schools violates the Constitution. The decision was unanimous.

Concerning the serious threat of Communist infiltration, Brownell advised the American Veterans of World War II at their convention on September 5, 1953: "I have dedicated myself and the Department of Justice to use every legal weapon to expose and punish the conspirators." The Attorney General proposed a law to compel testimony from witnesses pleading self-incrimination before Congressional committees, by granting them immunity from prosecution. A similar proposal was passed by the Eighty-third Congress and signed by President Eisenhower in August 1954.

On November 6, 1953 Attorney General Brownell in a speech before the Executives Club of Chicago cited as an example of "the failure of our predecessors to defend the government from Communist infiltration" the case of Harry Dexter White. "The records of my department show," he said "that White's spying activities for the Soviet Government were reported in detail by the F.B.I. to the White House . . . in December of 1945. In the face of this information and incredible though it may seem, President Truman subsequently on January 23, 1946, nominated White, who was then Assistant Secretary of the Treasury, for the even more important position of executive director for the United States in the International Monetary Fund" (New York *Times,* November 7, 1953).

On a television and radio broadcast on November 16, Truman answered Brownell by stating that he "first learned of the accusations against White early in February 1946" through an FBI report which "pointed out that it would be practically impossible to prove those charges with the evidence at hand" (*Newsweek,* November 23, 1953). Because of an investigation being carried out it was decided that White's appointment to the International Monetary Fund "should be allowed to take its normal course" since "any unusual action with respect to Mr. White's appointment might well have alerted all the persons involved" (New York *Times,* November 17, 1953).

J. Edgar Hoover, Director of the Federal Bureau of Investigation, stated on November 17 before the Senate Subcommittee on Internal Security: "It is clear that the FBI called to the attention of the appropriate authorities the facts (in the Harry Dexter White case), as alleged by reliable sources, which were substantial in pointing to a security risk, as they occurred. It is equally clear that the FBI did not depart from its traditional position of making no evaluation, and was not a party to any agreement to keep White in public service" (New York *Times,* November 18, 1953).

President Eisenhower declared on December 2 that the government "will have made such progress under the leadership of Attorney General Brownell in weeding out Communists that it will no longer be a serious menace and will not be a political issue in 1954."

Brownell is co-author with C. W. Merritt of *Manual of Laws Affecting Hotels and Restaurants in New York State* (New York State Hotel Association, 1947). The University of Nebraska awarded him a medal for his public service in 1940.

Organizations in which he holds membership include the American and New York state bar associations, Bar Association of the City of New York, New York State Judicial Council, the Order of Mayflower Descendants, and Order of the Coif. Among his clubs are the Century Association, Downtown Association, National Press and Metropolitan (Washington). He is a director of the Gramercy Park Association, and a trustee of the University of Nebraska Foundation and the New York School of Social Work.

The Attorney General announced in a speech at the University of Texas that the Department of Justice is inaugurating a program to bring outstanding law school graduates into the department. "We will make available each year thirty positions to be filled by the best qualified young men and women. Selections will be strictly on the basis of merit. . . The starting salary will be competitive with that offered by the large law firms" (New York *Herald Tribune,* December 6, 1953).

The Attorney General married Doris A. McCarter on June 16, 1934, and their children are Joan, Ann, Thomas McCarter, and James

Barker. Brownell, described by *Time* (February 16, 1953) as "neatly tailored, with an easy smile, low-pitched voice . . . and unassuming air," is five feet ten inches tall and weighs 150 pounds. His hobbies are traveling, puzzles, horseback riding, and walking.

References (See also references listed in the August 1944 biographical sketch)

Life 33:76+ D 22 '52 pors; 34:45 Ap 6 '53
N Y Herald Tribune p9 Jl 1 '44; p50 O 25 '53; II pl N 22 '53
N Y Times IV p6 Je 25 '44
N Y World-Telegram Mag p8 Jl 18 '53
Newsweek 42:27 N 23 '53
Sat Eve Post 225:27+ F 21 '53
Time 60:14 D 1 '52 por; 61:23+ F 16 '53 pors
U S News 35:40 S 4 '53
International Who's Who, 1953
Martindale-Hubbell Law Directory, 1952
Who's Who in America, 1952-53
Who's Who in United States Politics (1952)
World Biography (1948)

Dept. of Health, Education & Welfare

SAMUEL MILLER BROWNELL

BROWNELL, SAMUEL MILLER Apr. 3, 1900- United States Government official; educator

Address: c/o United States Department of Health, Education and Welfare, Washington 25, D.C.

Cited by educators as "an eminent scholar with a warm, humane approach," Dr. Samuel Miller Brownell was appointed thirteenth United States Commissioner of Education by President Eisenhower and took office on November 15, 1953 succeeding the late Dr. Lee M. Thurston. He has had more than twenty-five years of experience in the field of education, including teaching and administration service in secondary schools and in colleges.

Upon assuming his new post, Dr. Brownell received a leave of absence as professor of educational administration in the Graduate School of Yale University, an appointment he has filled since 1938. He also resigned from the presidency of New Haven State Teachers College, an office he had held since 1947.

Samuel Miller Brownell was born in Peru, Nebraska, on April 3, 1900, the elder son of Herbert and May A. (Miller) Brownell. His interest in pedagogy was stimulated by his father who was a professor of science at the University of Nebraska. Samuel attended high school in Lincoln, Nebraska, graduating in 1917. He was president of the student council, active in dramatics and an officer of his class. Referring to his boyhood and to his brother, Herbert, Jr., now U. S. Attorney General, Brownell states: "Herb and I had a paper route and sold milk to help out family finances."

After entering the University of Nebraska in 1917, Brownell left to serve in the Army as a private in 1918. When he returned he earned money toward his tuition by working for a publisher, the student activities office and the bursar's office. His principal scholastic interests were in business and science subjects and he was a member of Phi Beta Kappa, Delta Kappa, the senior honor society, and a participant in the university's dramatic activities.

Having received the A.B. degree from the University of Nebraska in 1921 Brownell served during the next two years as the principal of the demonstration high school at Peru State Teachers College in Nebraska. He recalls that his boyish appearance often caused him difficulty in his position as an administrator and teacher.

Brownell began postgraduate study at Yale University in 1923, and the following year he received the A.M. degree. His work was completed with the aid of a scholarship, which was continued while he studied for a doctorate. During these years, he had the companionship of his brother, Herbert, Jr., who was enrolled in Yale Law School. For his dissertation, Brownell submitted "The Working Hours of Secondary School Teachers in Connecticut." He received the Ph.D. degree in 1926.

After leaving Yale University, Dr. Brownell spent one year as an assistant professor of education at New York State College for Teachers in Albany. He then accepted the post of superintendent of schools at Grosse Pointe, Michigan, where from 1927 to 1938, he is credited with building up one of the best educational systems in the United States. As early as 1931, he suggested that educators recognize the value of radio as a medium of instruction. He stated: "It is not the attempt of each radio broadcast to supply individual help, but if the lesson is well taught by the radio teachers the classroom teachers will have more time to help the backward pupil individually. They are able to watch each pupil in a way that would be impossible if they were

BROWNELL, SAMUEL MILLER—*Cont.*
doing all the teaching for the full class" (*Nation's Schools,* October, 1931).

In another article, Brownell affirmed that ". . . the purpose of public education is to assist parents and other agencies in society to guide the growth of children so that the abilities of each individual are discovered and developed to their fullest extent" (*Education,* June, 1938).

Dr. Brownell accepted an appointment as professor of educational administration in the Graduate School at Yale University in 1938, following service as a visiting professor. He defined progressive education as "the combination of cooperative effort to improve childhood education" by evaluating present techniques and possible innovations with a view to "understanding the individual pupil and helping him to have meaningful experiences . . . for the life that he . . . is to lead." Nevertheless, to the extent that "progressive education . . . becomes a fetish . . . to a particular set of practices, progressive education is in grave danger of dying by its own sword" (*School and Society,* December 10, 1938).

Beginning in 1939, Brownell conducted or cooperated in surveys of school systems in Connecticut, New York, New Jersey, Massachusetts, Rhode Island, Vermont, Nebraska, and California. Such studies indicate, he said, "variations between states in administrative organization . . . conflict between state and local authorities, greater emphasis on responsibilities of state departments of education, and increased pressure for state support of education" (*Review of Educational Research,* October 1943).

In a radio broadcast on August 29, 1943, he urged trained teachers to remain on the job, stating that school children in the U. S. were becoming war casualties due to teacher shortages and lack of parental care at home. "Of what value," he asked, "is winning a military victory and finding that we have a generation of neurotic, disillusioned, incompetent nonthinkers—incapable of meeting the problems of a post-war world?" (New York *Times,* August 30, 1943).

The professor, in 1947, added to his teaching responsibilities at Yale, the administrative functions of the presidency of New Haven State Teachers College. He obtained $3,200,000 from the Connecticut legislature which was used to build a new campus for the college. He recommended "the development of greater . . . mutual understanding between personnel of educational institutions" as "one of the most constructive steps that the profession can take to strengthen education as a force" (*National Education Association Journal,* February, 1951).

Appointed to the position of U.S. Commissioner of Education by President Eisenhower on October 14, 1953, Brownell assumed office on November 15. He has obtained a leave of absence from Yale and has resigned as president of New Haven State Teachers College.

The Office of Education is a branch of the Department of Health, Education, and Welfare which collects and diffuses "statistics and facts as shall show the condition and progress of education in the several States and Territories . . . respecting the organization and management of schools and . . . methods of teaching, as shall aid . . . in the establishment and maintenance of efficient school systems" and it administers funds "appropriated as aids to education."

Commissioner Brownell declared that in his new office he plans "to strengthen and stimulate improvement" in education for "in a democratic society it is a sound position to have education a state function, with the responsibility delegated to the local communities" (New York *Times,* October 25, 1953). He believes that the educational process should be accelerated in order that young people would be able to complete school earlier "so that when students reach college they can go into their major field. . . . In this way students will be able to begin their professional work earlier. . . ." (New York *World-Telegram and Sun,* November 14, 1953).

An increase of 4.8 per cent in college and university enrollment over the last academic year was reported on December 9, 1953 by the Federal Office of Education. Commissioner Brownell said that the increase was due to a record number of high school graduates last spring as well as to educational benefits for war veterans and efforts to interest high school students in continuing their education. Men students, totaling 1,432,474, continued to outnumber women students, who totaled 818,227 (New York *Times,* December 10, 1953). Segregation, Samuel Brownell stated, is "outdated" in American schools and "inconsistent with the Constitution" (*Newsweek,* December 21, 1953).

A plan to recruit teachers by persuading training institutions and boards of education to cooperate on a local level in setting up courses for married women with college degrees was announced by Dr. Brownell and Mrs. Alice K. Leopold, director of the Women's Bureau (New York *Times,* August 12, 1954).

The commissioner is the author of forty-two articles in educational magazines. He has been a summer lecturer at the University of Wisconsin, Cornell University, Harvard University, University of Southern California, and the University of Michigan. A life member of the National Education Association, Brownell also holds membership in the American Educational Research Association, National Society for the Study of Education, National Society of College Teachers, American Association of School Administrators, Connecticut Superintendents' Association, Connecticut Education Association, and National Conference of Professors of Educational Administration.

He is a member of the Kiwanis Club and a member of the board of directors of the Vocational Counseling Service, Inc., New Haven Y.M.C.A., and New Haven Civil Defense, and a member of the advisory committee of the New Haven Armed Services. His clubs are the High Lane (Hamden, Connecticut), Yale Faculty and Mory's (Yale University). The educator is a Republican and a Congregationalist.

He married Esther Delzell, a teacher, on June 23, 1927, and their children are Richard Miller, Dorothy Wilson, Jane Davis, and Ruth Delzell. The commissioner has blue eyes and brown hair, is five feet seven inches tall, and weighs 150 pounds. He likes neat bow ties and considers his "family" his hobby. His goal is a good teacher for every classroom (New York *Times*, October 25, 1953).

References

N Y Herald Tribune p19 O 15 '53
N Y Times p35 O 15 '53; p23 O 19 '53; IV p9 O 25 '53; p16 N 14 '53
N Y World-Telegram Mag p4 N 14 '53
Time 62:50 O 26 '53
Washington (D.C.) Post p1 O 15 '53; p26 O 16 '53
Leaders In Education (1948)
Who's Who in America, 1952-53
Who's Who in American Education, 1951-52
Who's Who in the East (1951)
World Biography (1948)

FRANKLIN R. BRUNS, JR.

BRUNS, FRANKLIN R(ICHARD), JR. May 25, 1912- Philatelic writer and curator

Address: b. c/o Smithsonian Institution, Washington 25, D.C.; h. 7215 13th Ave., Takoma Park, Md.

Through his lectures at hundreds of stamp clubs and his columns as stamp editor of the New York *Sun* and later the New York *World-Telegram and Sun,* Franklin R. Bruns, Jr., has become one of the best-known philatelic journalists in the United States. He was appointed in 1951 as assistant curator, in charge of the Division of Philately, of the Smithsonian Institution in Washington, D.C. He has brought to his care of the national postage stamp collection of over 125,000 stamps his broad, twenty-year experience as author and editor of many books and handbooks on stamps and as a researcher in specialized fields. Some of his notable work was undertaken in his office of philatelic adviser and agent for the Republic of Liberia.

His *Postage Stamps of Elizabeth Regina and the Royal Family* (1953) and *Stamps, A Fascinating Hobby* (1954) are his latest books. Since January 1953 his weekly syndicated column "The World in Stamps" has been published in seventeen leading newspapers through the Hardale Syndicate.

Coming from a family of Germanic origin with forebears who had moved to the United States in the mid-1800's, Franklin Richard Bruns, Jr., was born in New York City on May 25, 1912. He is the only son of Franklin Richard and Anna Sophie (Feuring) Bruns, who also had a daughter, Katharine Elise (recently deceased). In his boyhood in Yonkers, New York, young Bruns combined his regular academic courses at the Roosevelt High School with playing football, and entering into the activities of the dramatic society and writing for school publications.

"Frank" began to collect stamps when he was about eight years old, and received his initial instruction from an aunt, Miss Hattie H. Bruns. "I kept at the hobby steadily through my youth," Bruns recalls, "and always held to two ambitions—to be a newspaperman and to have all the time I wanted to collect stamps."

Enrolling in Columbia University after his high school graduation in 1931, he intended to follow the usual undergraduate curriculum and then to study in the School of Journalism. However, an opportunity of working on the New York *Sun* led him to decide to leave school and learn journalism through employment on a major metropolitan newspaper.

From his first position with the New York *Sun* in 1931 as a classified advertising telephone salesman Bruns advanced to stamp editor in April 1932 and began work on a philatelic column that he was to continue until 1950. When the *Sun* ceased publication in January 1950, he became stamp editor of the newly formed New York *World-Telegram and Sun.* During his years with the New York *Sun* he compiled and edited ten stamp booklets, including *United States Commemorative Notes, Philatelic Agencies of the World, Miniature Sheets of the World, Stamp Collectors Guide and Glossary, British Jubilees and Coronations* and *Postage Centennial-Pan American Jubilees.*

He conducted series of stamp forums for adults and young people, addressed hundreds of stamp clubs on various aspects of the hobby and spoke at a large number of special events and dinners. In his capacity as editor he served as well on executive committees of the 1936 and 1947 International Philatelic Exhibitions held in New York City.

Bruns was also engaged as stamp editor of *Boy's Life* magazine and as editor of the American Stamp Dealers' Association *Bulletin, The Coin Collectors' Journal, Harmer's Stamp Hints, Gimbels' Stamp News* and *The Philatelic Report,* among others. While holding the editorship of *The Collectors Club Philatelist,*

BRUNS, FRANKLIN—*Continued*

a publication of the Collectors Club of New York, of which he is also a past governor and past secretary, he was responsible for the production of such handbooks as *Essays of Egypt* and *Supplement to the History of Free Franking of Mail in the United States.* He also had a share in the publication of *The De La Rue Georgians of South Africa,* parts of a translation into English of the Greece portion of *Kohl Handbuch,* and a special 116-page *Brazil Bull's Eye* centennial issue, 1843-1943. A handbook, *Hawaii,* for which Bruns did the planning and preliminary work, was later made a project of the Philatelic Foundation.

In the position of philatelic adviser and agent for the Republic of Liberia, which Bruns filled from 1947 to 1952, he was responsible for the designing, production and distribution of Liberian stamps. His achievements included the editing of *Liberia* (published by the National Philatelic Museum) and of *Liberian Odyssy* by F. A. Price; the publication of *Liberia's Eighteenth President* by J. Emery Knight and of *Liberia, The West African Republic* (1950) by R. and D. Henries; and the staging of the first all-Liberian philatelic exhibition. Bruns is currently preparing a book to be called *Liberia—Its Postal History and Postage Stamps.*

By his appointment in early 1951 as associate curator, Division of Philately, of the Smithsonian Institution in Washington, D.C., Bruns was charged with custody of the national postage stamp collection. This collection, now containing more than 125,000 stamps, was started many years ago by a contribution of the Post Office Department and has since been increased by donations and by the annual addition of new issues of all countries through the Universal Postal Union. For the previous thirty-seven years the stamp department had grown under the care of Mrs. Catherine Manning, Brun's predecessor, to become "one of the most widely known and frequently consulted philatelic collections in the world" (*Hobbies,* April 1951). Besides discharging such duties as arranging exhibits and supervising cataloguing, Bruns must talk with visitors to the museum and maintain a large correspondence.

After moving to Washington, Bruns continued for a short time as philatelic agent to Liberia and as stamp editor for the New York *World-Telegram and Sun.* In January 1953 he began his syndicated stamp column for the Hardale Syndicate in New York and has since given part of his time to writing "The World in Stamps" for newspapers throughout the country, with a total paid circulation just under 4,000,000 weekly. Some of the papers in which his column appears are Philadelphia *Inquirer,* Fort Worth *Press,* Baltimore *American,* Washington *Post and Times-Herald,* Detroit *News,* Cleveland *Press,* Milwaukee *Journal* and Brooklyn *Eagle.*

Meanwhile, in 1953 his *Postage Stamps of Elizabeth Regina and the Royal Family* and in 1954 his *Stamps, A Fascinating Hobby* were published by the Washington Press of Newark, New Jersey. An earlier volume, *Fell's Profitable Stamp Guide* (Frederick Fell, Inc., New York, 1951), was reviewed in *Wilson Library Bulletin* as "A comprehensive guide for the neophyte in stamp collecting . . . [which] includes chapters not only on starting a collection but also on selling and production of stamps." Among several books Bruns has in preparation are *United States Commemorative Issues, 1893-1943* and *America's History on Postage Stamps.*

On March 31, 1954 the Federal government had its first sale of used stamps, clipped from incoming White House and Administration mail, which netted $339. "Good foreign stamp mixtures may bring about $5 a pound," according to Franklin Bruns, "and domestic mixtures from $3 to $5," he said. From the thousands of stamps offered for sale Bruns culled a handful of valuable ones for the national collections at the Smithsonian Institution. One of these was a surcharge $10 stamp of Nationalist China. This was a "find", because the Nationalist Government on Formosa is not a member of the Universal Postal Union and does not "swap" three specimens of each new issue, as member nations of the union do.

While stamp editor of the New York *Sun,* the philatelist was the recipient of the Colonel Hans Lagerloef Barry Bowl for the outstanding newspaper stamp column for the three years in which the award was offered (1942, 1943 and 1944). His column also won the unique Philatelic Journalists of America Award, and for his paper "Philatelic Exhibition Reform" he was given the American Philatelic Congress plaque at that association's Atlantic City meeting.

Bruns, who is a council member and past president of the American Philatelic Congress and past editor of its annual book (1952), belongs to a number of other philatelic organizations. He has been director since 1935 of the Association for Stamp Exhibitions, Inc.; past president of the Souvenir Issues Association and past editor of its magazine *The Souvenir Issue;* past regional director and member of the publicity committee of the American Philatelic Society and member of its exhibition committees in 1940 and 1947; member of the Society of Philatelic Americans, American Topical Association, American Air Mail Society, Aero Philatelists, Inc., Washington Philatelic Society, Collectors Club of Washington, Essay-Proof Society and American Stamp Dealers' Association. Among the groups in which he maintains honorary membership are Associated Stamp Clubs of the Chesapeake Area, Bureau Issues Association, Bronx County Stamp Club, All Boro Collectors Club, International Stamp Club, Michigan Stamp Club and Franklin Philatelic Society.

The stamp curator and his wife, Priscilla Ann (Garfield) Bruns, who had a career in fashion before her marriage on October 24, 1936, are the parents of Priscilla Lee Bruns, Franklin Richard Bruns 3d and James Harold Bruns. Five feet eleven inches tall, Bruns weighs 175 pounds; his eyes are green and his hair is brown. He is a member of the Lutheran Church and a Mason (Gramatan Lodge, Bronxville, New York). With cub scouting as one of his chief recreational interests, he is a past master of the Boy Scouts (cub pack committee chairman). For relaxation in other forms, he gardens, plays golf and watches baseball games.

In the introduction to *Fell's Profitable Stamp Guide* (1951) Bruns wrote: "Stamps are tiny storybooks—each carrying a message for those who look for it. Nations are born and countries are absorbed, and the little stamp is one of the first heralds. The men and women of history and their deeds find their place in the stamp album. Stamp collecting is truly a visual education . . . geography, history, the arts and sciences, animal and plant life and peoples. . . . Using a single stamp design, a person can spend hours developing the story of its background, its designing, its production and its distribution."

References

Hobbies 56:127 Ap '51
N Y Times II p20 F 18 '51

BRUNSDALE, (CLARENCE) NORMAN

July 9, 1891- Governor of North Dakota

Address: b. State Capitol, Bismarck, N.D.; h. 320 Ave. B, Bismarck, N.D.; Mayville, N.D.

Rudrud Studio

NORMAN BRUNSDALE

In North Dakota, which operates the only state-owned bank, flour mill and grain elevator in the United States, Norman Brunsdale is the Governor. He was elected to this office in 1950 and was re-elected in 1952. Previously he had managed and operated his family's farm lands, held various executive positions with local banks and with a business in Minnesota, and served in the state Senate.

In the June 29, 1954 primary elections for governor, Brunsdale, who is affiliated with the Republican Organizing Committee faction of the North Dakota Republican party, defeated Wallace E. Warner, who was endorsed by the other Republican group, the Nonpartisan League. The New York *Times* (July 1, 1954) noted: "A primary victory in this heavily Republican state [North Dakota] long has been assurance of election."

Clarence Norman Brunsdale was born on July 9, 1891 in Sherbrooke, North Dakota. His mother, the former Anna Margaret Nordgaard, was born in Norway, and his father, Knute H. Brunsdale, in Wisconsin. His paternal grandfather emigrated from Norway to the United States in 1832; his mother's family came in 1861. Brunsdale has four brothers and a sister.

He grew up in Portland, a town in a farming area crossed by the Goose River in North Dakota. There he was graduated in 1908 from Bruflat Academy. He then enrolled in Luther College, Decorah, Iowa, where he managed the gymnastic and basketball teams and majored in languages. In 1913 he received the B.A. degree.

When he left college, he became the manager of the Brunsdale farming interests, "not particularly by choice but by reason of necessity," he has stated, since his father had died in 1899, and he had many family responsibilities. For sixteen years, Brunsdale cared for the acreages owned by his kinsmen in Steele and Traill counties.

Soon he also established himself as a banker and businessman. In 1917 he became associated with the Russell Grader Manufacturing Company of Minneapolis, Minnesota, as a director and third vice-president, positions he held until 1929. He began a thirty-two-year directorship of the Goose River Bank in Mayville, North Dakota in 1918, and served as vice-president of the bank (1924-1940). For a period of thirty years (1920-1950), he was a director of the First National Bank, Portland, North Dakota, and was president of the First and Farmers Bank from 1934 to 1944 and from 1945 to 1950.

He was elected state Senator from the 8th Legislative District for a succession of terms beginning in 1927 and running to 1935, and again from 1941 to 1951. His early years in the legislature covered a period when North Dakota farmers suffered from soil loss, low market prices for their products, depressed land values, bank failures, and crop failures.

The state, home of the Nonpartisan League, dealt with its problems by "its own peculiar blend of Republicanism" and the "middle way" of the Scandinavian countries. A state-owned mill and elevator association was formed to break the control of Minnesota mills over grading and docking North Dakota grain. Buying and selling cooperatives handled a large share of the farmers' business affairs, and advanced social legislation was passed for relief and welfare work.

By the end of World War II, North Dakota was in a cycle of prosperity helped by federal price supports, favorable weather conditions, and higher prices. An active soil conservation program which included planting trees was

BRUNSDALE, NORMAN—*Continued*

begun, and dams were built to overcome the effects of drought.

Brunsdale became increasingly active in politics. In 1943 he acted as president pro tem of the state Senate. He served as majority floor leader in 1945, 1947, and 1949; as chairman of the Republican Organizing Committee during the 1946 campaign, and as national Republican committeeman from 1948 to 1952.

In the North Dakota primaries for the governorship in June 1950, Brunsdale won the Republican nomination. In November 1950, he was elected to succeed Governor Fred G. Aandahl. In 1952 Brunsdale sought re-election, and after defeating Albert Jacobson in the Republican primary in June 1952, he won in the November elections.

One of the problems with which Brunsdale has had to deal since becoming governor has been the rapid growth of the petroleum industry. Oil was discovered near Williston, North Dakota in 1951. C. W. Leifur wrote in *The Americana Annual, 1953:* "Whereas there had been only one producing well in 1951, by November 1952, there were over seventy wells producing oil in commercial quantities." By May 1953, more than 134 oil wells had been completed. At the same time, the state is trying to attract new industries which would use its 600 billion tons of lignite (low-grade brown coal) as a source of power.

Throughout his career, Brunsdale has never lost touch with the farmers. He is still a member of the American Farm Bureau. He has been active in civic and service organizations and in the Rotary Club. He is a baseball fan, a fisherman, and a handy man in his own workshop. He received an honorary LL.D. degree in 1952 from Luther College. His religious affiliation is with the Lutheran Church.

Clarence Norman Brunsdale married Carrie Lajord, a schoolteacher, on August 30, 1924. They have two daughters, Margaret Marie and Helen Lucille (Mrs. Percy Don Williams). The Governor has blue eyes and brown hair. He weighs 176 pounds and is five feet ten inches tall.

References

Who's Who in America, 1954-55
Who's Who in the Midwest (1952)
Who's Who in United States Politics (1952)

BULLARD, SIR EDWARD (CRISP)
Sept. 21, 1907- Geophysicist

Address: b. c/o National Physical Laboratory, Teddington, Middlesex, England; h. Bushy House, Teddington, Middlesex, England

The director of the National Physical Laboratory of England, Sir Edward Bullard, is one of the leading geophysicists of Great Britain. In 1950 he succeeded Sir Charles Darwin (grandson of the naturalist) to the post. The National Physical Laboratory, a research institute which was founded in 1900, issues annual reports and some technical papers which are published by Her Majesty's Stationery Office; other technical papers are printed in the journals of learned societies.

Active as a specialist in geophysics since 1931 when he was appointed demonstrator in geodesy at Cambridge University, Sir Edward has been a reader in experimental geophysics at Cambridge and professor of physics at the University of Toronto. He was made a Fellow of the Royal Society in 1941. During the war, he did special work with the British Admiralty. He was knighted in 1953.

Academic contributions of Sir Edward include papers on the subjects of physics and geophysics with particular reference to gravity, seismology, heat flow, and terrestrial magnetism. Many of these papers have appeared in the British scientific periodical *Nature*. He received his Ph.D. degree in 1939 and his Sc.D. degree in 1948 from Cambridge University.

Edward Crisp Bullard was born on September 21, 1907 in Norwich, England. He is the only son of Edward John and Eleanor Howes (Crisp) Bullard. He has three sisters. His family has been established in Norwich for many years—in that city, his great-grandfather founded a brewery, Bullard and Son, of which Sir Edward is a director. His early childhood was spent in Norwich. He was educated at Repton School and at Clare College, Cambridge University where he majored in physics.

He received the B.A. degree in 1929. While working at Cambridge for the Ph.D. degree in physics, he was a student at Cavendish Laboratory of the late Lord Rutherford who won the Nobel prize for chemistry in 1908. Lord Rutherford was partly responsible for Bullard's specialization in geophysics. He recommended Bullard for the job of demonstrator in geodesy at Cambridge in 1931.

As a student, Bullard had followed the ordinary courses in physics. Sir Edward himself says the choice of geophysics for his main work was "entirely accidental and was due to the difficulty of getting a job during the depression. There happened to be one available in Cambridge at the time when I needed it." Very early in his career the quality of his work won recognition. In 1935 he was appointed Smithson Research Fellow of the Royal Society (he held this title until 1943). In 1936 he won the Sedgwick Prize. He was made a Fellow of the Royal Society in 1941.

During the years as Smithson Research Fellow, Bullard was engaged, among other things, in attempting to find the depth of Paleozoic strata, first in Cambridgeshire, and later, by the use of a submarine, in the sea around the British Isles. For this study, he used a geophonic device of his own design for listening underground.

His contribution in the field of gravity surveys was of far-reaching importance. He helped to combine gravity measures in Great Britain into a coherent scheme which formed a basis for further work on gravity. He was responsible for organizing the results of cooperative research in gravity surveys made all over the world.

The scientist's work during the war as an experimental officer was of a highly specialized nature. At first he was in charge of degaussing in mine sweeping research and development. Later in the war he was made assistant director of operational research at the Admiralty in which capacity he was chiefly concerned with problems connected with the anti-submarine campaign.

In 1944, while Bullard was still employed by the British Admiralty, he was appointed reader in experimental geophysics at Cambridge University. He remained there for the next four years, during which time he was engaged, among other things, in research concerned with the heat flow of the earth. In connection with this, Bullard organized studies in the northern and southern hemispheres.

His investigations in South Africa "showed from measurements of heat conductivity of the rocks at different horizons that the rate of upward flow of heat across any section of a given bore-hole was the same" (*Nature*, December 5, 1953). He also demonstrated that "the outflow is . . . the same in all the continental regions of the globe." This research helps the geophysicists to understand the cause of volcanic eruptions. Also it is hoped that increased understanding of temperature gradients will be of great help to pump designers, mining engineers and oil prospectors in their geophysical problems.

Bullard spent the year 1948-1949 as professor of physics at the University of Toronto. He then became director of the National Physical Laboratory. In 1949 Bullard had determined the question of heat flow through the ocean floor. In order to do this he devised an instrument in the form of "a hollow steel 'spear' which could be driven vertically into the ocean sediments" where it could be "left for about thirty minutes in order to reach thermal equilibrium." With this apparatus, experiments were carried out in the Pacific Ocean—these indicated that the outflow of heat is approximately the same as that through the continents. In 1952, however, when he used the "spear" in the Atlantic Ocean, a lower heat flow was recorded.

His theory about the nature of the earth's core has attracted much attention. According to the New York *Times* (April 5, 1952), he is a "pressure theorist who believes that pressure can transform even rocky surface material into metallic form. He thought that was what might have taken place at the center of the earth. . . . According to this theory, the depth of the outer surface of the core would simply be the depth at which pressure was great enough to bring about the change into a metal. Heat would transform it into a fluid."

At the same time, Bullard also stated, according to the New York *Times,* that "most earthquakes occurred within a few miles of the surface but some started at a depth of 400 miles. Below that the shocks ceased, which suggested that there was insufficient strength in the deeper material to store up the energy necessary for an earthquake."

Gordon Rice, Toronto

SIR EDWARD BULLARD

The scientist rejects the idea "that the earth's field is the result of permanent magnetism" and seeks to explain the observed phenomena in other terms. He propounds the theory that "the core of the earth is capable of making electricity like a dynamo by the movement of a conductor (the core) inside a magnetic field, the whole earth. The electricity in turn acts on the metal core and electromagnetizes both it and the surface of the earth" (New York *Times,* June 1, 1953). According to Bullard, the dynamo theory would explain why there "has been no perceptible diminution in the magnetism of the earth and also why compass variations from true North change irregularly from place to place."

A field of research with which Sir Edward has been concerned is the utilization of solar energy in eucalyptus trees. It is hoped that this source of power can be used by Sir Harry Ricardo's new invention—a light steam engine which uses low-grade fuel, including green wood, and which could be employed in undeveloped but heavily forested regions of the tropics.

According to a report in the New York *Times* (June 27, 1953), "Sir Edward has calculated that quick-growing Indian eucalyptus trees have a yield of nine and one-quarter tons of wood an acre a year. As the wood contains 0.8 per cent of the solar energy reaching the ground in the tropics in the form of heat, Sir Edward has suggested that in theory eucalyptus forests could provide a perpetual source of fuel. He has said that by rotational tree planting and felling, a forest of twenty kilometers square would enable a wood consuming power station to provide 10,000 kilowatts of power."

The scientist was knighted by Her Majesty Queen Elizabeth in Coronation Honors of June 1953. He was awarded the Hughes Medal by

BULLARD, SIR EDWARD—*Continued*

the Royal Society in November 1953. The president, Dr. E. D. Adrian said of Sir Edward at that time: "His clear insight and experimental skill enabled him to tackle difficult problems with a directness and freshness of approach that made them appear deceptively simple." Dr. Adrian concluded with the following comment: ". . . despite the heavy demands of administrative work as director of the National Physical Laboratory during the past four years he has contrived to continue his own geophysical researches and to inspire and facilitate the researches of others."

Sir Edward belongs to the Geological Society of London, Geological Society of America, Royal Astronomical Society, Cambridge Philosophical Society, Royal Society Club, Arctic Circle, Challenger Society, and the Physical Society. He is a member of the Athenæum and president of the National Physical Laboratory's Sports Club.

The year of Bullard's first appointment to the faculty of geodesy in Cambridge (1931) was the year of his marriage to Margaret Ellen Thomas. Miss Thomas was a student when they were married. She is now a novelist. The couple has four daughters: Belinda, Henrietta, Emily, and Polly. Sir Edward is six feet tall and weighs 170 pounds; his eyes are blue and his hair is "greying." He has no political affiliation. He is a member of the Church of England. His favorite recreation is skiing.

References

Nature 164:16 Jl 2 '49; 172:1022+ D 5 '53
International Who's Who, 1953
Who's Who, 1954
World Biography (1948)

BUNKER, ELLSWORTH May 11, 1894-

Red Cross official; business executive

Address: b. c/o American National Red Cross, 17th & D Sts., N.W., Washington, D.C.; h. Putney, Vt.

Through an administrative change which took effect at the beginning of 1954, Ellsworth Bunker became the first salaried president of the American National Red Cross. He succeeded E. Roland Harriman, who now serves as chairman of the board. Associated with the National Sugar Refining Company since 1916, Ellsworth Bunker became president of the company in 1940 and chairman of the board in 1948. In 1951 and 1952 he served as United States Ambassador to Argentina and in 1952 and 1953 as United States Ambassador to Italy.

Born in Yonkers, New York on May 11, 1894, Ellsworth Bunker is the son of George R. and Jean Polhemus (Cobb) Bunker. He was educated at the Mackenzie School in Dobbs Ferry, New York and at Yale University where he majored in economics and history and was a member of the Zeta Psi fraternity. After receiving his A.B. degree in 1916, Bunker worked for the National Sugar Refining Company (of which his father had been one of the founders) and began learning the sugar business by hand-trucking the raw material on a Yonkers dock. He worked his way up through all the refinery operations and spent a total of thirteen years in the operating end of the business.

During this period he was manager of the Warner Sugar Refining Company, a New Jersey concern taken over by National in 1927. Elected a director of the latter, Bunker was, however, because of severe arthritis, compelled to retire for about a year. When he returned to the refining company in 1931 he was appointed secretary. He was advanced to vice-president and treasurer in 1934 and was also elected a director of the American-Hawaiian Steamship Company.

When the U.S. Cane Sugar Refiners Association was organized in 1936 he was chosen to be chairman, a position he still occupies. Promoted to executive vice-president of the National Sugar Refining Company in 1937, Bunker viewed with favor the Jones sugar quota bill.

Bunker became the president of the National Sugar Refining Company in 1940. During World War II he served as chairman of the Cane Sugar Refiners' War Committee, a governmental advisory agency. He was one of the organizers of the Sugar Research Foundation in New York in 1942. Steadily extending his industrial interests, Bunker became a director of the Sugar Association, Inc., Guantanamo Sugar Company of Cuba, Central Aguirre Associates of Puerto Rico, and chairman of the board of the Potrero Sugar Company of Mexico.

In a communication published in the New York *Times* (July 24, 1947), the executive defended the proposed sugar act of 1948.

When W. K. Dick retired as chairman of the board of the National Sugar Refining Company in April 1948, Bunker was elected to succeed him. Within three years, however, the new chairman brought to an end his active business career by accepting the U.S. ambassadorship to Argentina to succeed Stanton Griffis. Bunker's nomination was announced by President Harry S. Truman on February 5, 1951, but his appointment was not acted upon by the full Senate until March 12 and it was May 8 before he could present his credentials to President Juan Perón.

His predecessor, Ambassador Griffis, had left for his new post at Madrid some weeks earlier, and in the interim Argentine-American relations had been seriously strained by the expropriation of the Buenos Aires newspaper *La Prensa* and the attendant reaction in the United States. However, in less than one year in what Anne O'Hare McCormick characterized as a "delicate and difficult post, where we have oscillated from soft policies to hard and back again," Bunker was so successful that "Argentinians constantly compared him to that accomplished and popular diplomat Norman Armour" (New York *Times,* May 7, 1952)

When sixteen members of the U.S. House Interstate and Foreign Commerce Committee were received by Perón on November 22, 1951, the Argentine President referred to Bunker and himself as "good friends." A New York *Times* (April 1, 1953) editorial remarked that the "tact, understanding and firmness" with which Bunker handled his assignment at Buenos Aires "helped to set Argentine-American relations in correct focus for the first time in years."

Through a shuffling of diplomatic posts in early 1952, Truman, on February 20, nominated James C. Dunn, U. S. Ambassador to Rome, to succeed David K. E. Bruce, the new Under Secretary of State, in Paris. On the following day President Truman named Bunker as Ambassador to Italy. This appointment was confirmed by the Senate on March 12, 1952. "Mr. Bunker never saw Italy, even as a tourist, until he arrived to take over the embassy," observed Anne O'Hare McCormick, adding that this was "not a total disadvantage . . . for a man of diplomatic temperament and warm interest in human problems."

Bunker displayed both qualities in the course of the next eleven months, during which he participated in negotiations after the closing down in Italy of several churches of the Protestant Church of Christ. He was succeeded by Clare Boothe Luce in April 1953, after having accomplished what a New York *Times* editorial pronounced "a remarkably fine job" in a diplomatic post which "has been a difficult one in recent years because of the problems of Italian politics and economy."

On November 16, 1953 the American National Red Cross announced that the former diplomat would become its first salaried president on January 1, 1954 and that the president of the organization E. Roland Harriman would move into the newly created office of chairman of the board, with Bunker taking over the chief executive duties at an annual stipend of $30,000.

The American National Red Cross, which was founded by Clara Barton in 1881, has been chartered as a quasi-official agency of the U.S. government since 1905. Its principal purposes are (according to the *U. S. Government Organization Manual*) "to furnish volunteer aid to the sick and wounded of armies in time of war, to perform all duties with which the national society of each nation acceding to the treaties of Geneva is charged, to act in matters of voluntary relief. . . . and as a medium of communication between the people of the United States and the Armed Forces. It is further charged with providing a system of national and international relief to mitigate the sufferings caused by pestilence, famine, fire, floods and other great calamities."

The organization, which is administered through a national headquarters at Washington, D.C. and four area offices, consists of 3,700 local chapters and 4,200 branches. It is supported by popular subscription to annual fund raising campaigns. The goal of the 1954 campaign was announced as $85,000,000.

In his new Red Cross post he sees a great challenge and opportunity for public service. In other countries he has witnessed a lack of individual social responsibility resulting in tragic intervention by the state. In the Red Cross with its millions of volunteers he sees a strong bulwark against the dangers of the over-paternalistic state.

ELLSWORTH BUNKER

Although Bunker resigned the board chairmanship of the National Sugar Refining Company on February 16, 1951, he remains a director of this concern and of the American Hawaiian Steamship Company. He is also a director of the General Baking Company, and a trustee of the Atlantic Mutual Insurance and Centennial Insurance companies.

Actively interested in civic affairs and education, he is a trustee of the New School for Social Research, Marlboro College at Marlboro, Vermont, which he had helped to found, Union Settlement of New York, (an interracial, nonsectarian neighborhood house in Harlem), Nutrition Foundation, Arthritis and Rheumatism Foundation, and a member of the Council of Foreign Relations.

Ellsworth Bunker and Harriet Allen Butler of Yonkers were married on April 24, 1920 and are the parents of Ellen (Mrs. Fernando Gentil), John and Samuel Bunker. The Red Cross official is six feet one inch in height, weighs 175 pounds, and has gray hair and blue eyes. He enjoys farming. Bunker believes that "Voluntary effort is the essence of American democracy and no finer expression of it exists than the work of the Red Cross."

References

Christian Sci Mon p3 My 17 '51 por
N Y Herald Tribune II p1 F 11 '51 por; p7 F 22 '52; p15 N 17 '53 por
N Y Times p6 F 6 '51 por; p3 F 22 '52 por; p26 My 7 '52; p8 N 17 '53 por
Business Executives of America (1950)
International Who's Who, 1953
Poor's Register of Directors and Executives, 1952
Who's Who in America, 1952-53
Who's Who in the East (1953)
World Biography (1954)

BURKE, THOMAS A(LOYSIUS) Oct. 30, 1898- United States Senator from Ohio; lawyer

Address: b. Senate Office Bldg., Washington 25, D.C.; h. Lee House, Washington 5, D.C.; 13509 Drexmore Ave., Cleveland, Ohio

The interim Senator from Ohio, Thomas A. Burke, Democrat, is occupying the seat in the United States Senate left vacant by the death of Senator Robert A. Taft. At the time of his appointment in October 1953 by Ohio's Governor Frank J. Lausche, Burke was completing his fourth full term as mayor of Cleveland. He will serve in the Eighty-third Congress until December 1954 at which time the successful candidate in the November 1954 election will fill the two remaining years of Senator Taft's term. Burke is a candidate for this seat, and was nominated at the Democratic primaries on May 4, 1954 without opposition. He opposes Representative George H. Bender, a Republican.

Burke, a lawyer by training and one-time Cleveland law director, is regarded as politically a middle-of-the-road Democrat who has had the support of organized labor. He has had nine years of experience in city administration —holding the office of mayor longer than anyone else in Cleveland's history.

Thomas A. Burke, a native of Cleveland, was born on October 30, 1898 to Thomas A. and Lillian (McNeil) Burke. His father was a surgeon and his grandfather an Irish immigrant who became a captain on Lake Erie steamers. During his boyhood he heard much from his father of Cleveland's reform mayor, Tom Loftin Johnson, and so became interested in politics at an early age. He attended parochial schools, Loyola High School, and the College of the Holy Cross, a Jesuit institution in Worcester, Massachusetts. In his junior year he transferred for one term to Georgetown University in Washington, D.C.

After receiving his B.A. degree *cum laude* from Holy Cross in 1920, Burke studied at Western Reserve University School of Law in Cleveland. He was graduated in 1923 with the LL.B. degree and in the same year was admitted to the Ohio bar. Appointed assistant prosecuting attorney of Cuyahoga county, he entered public service in 1930 and after six years in that post was named in 1937 special counsel to the attorney general of Ohio to prosecute vote frauds. Burke's early career was devoted largely to private law practice in Cleveland, for part of the time (1937-1941) as a member of the firm of McConnell, Blackmore, Cory & Burke.

Frank J. Lausche, mayor of Cleveland in 1941, chose Burke to be city law director, a vice-mayor post which made him the city's chief executive when Lausche became Governor of Ohio in 1945. This appointive term and his subsequent election to four two-year terms gave Burke a record tenure as mayor. He was one of Cleveland's largest vote-getters, defeating his Republican opponent in 1947 by 82,000 votes which established him as Cleveland's "Mr. Democrat".

In his 1951 campaign he received the support of the three Cleveland newspapers: the *Plain Dealer*, Scripps-Howard *Press* and the *News*. "Burke was a notably effective and popular mayor," wrote William V. Shannon (New York *Post*, February 28, 1954). "His proudest accomplishments were the reorganization of the city's tangled transit system and his plan for the beautification of Cleveland's lake front." The city and the railroads had been arguing for nearly a hundred years about control of the lake front. Burke negotiated a settlement whereby the railroads got possession of two miles of lake front that they needed and the city took control of the other six miles.

While Burke consistently had the backing of labor, he showed firmness in dealing with labor in times of crises. During the December 1949 strike of employees of the city's transit system, he planned to call the National Guard and sought a back-to-work injunction. Liberal representation was granted to labor on the Community Relations Board, a committee building interracial understanding which Burke considered "as important to the city as the physical improvements outlined by the City Planning Commission" (*Christian Science Monitor*, October 22, 1953). While Burke was mayor, Cleveland became one of the few cities to attain enactment of a fair employment practices law.

Under his administration nearly $400,000,000 in tax money was spent on city government operations, "with never a breath of scandal" (New York *Times*, October 18, 1953). In a municipal program costing more than $200,-000,000, Cleveland bought land for recreational purposes, laid out new parks, opened "the country's first downtown airport," and began improving the streets and the rapid transit system.

Another innovation was a charter amendment giving the mayor the power to appoint and dismiss the city's police chief at will. In support of the amendment, which was carried to victory in the November 1951 election, Burke said: "As long as I am responsible for preserving the peace, I should have a free hand in naming the police chief" (*Christian Science Monitor*, December 5, 1951). Senator Estes Kefauver praised Burke as one of the officials who had "applied the brakes on organized crime in Cleveland" (*Saturday Evening Post*, April 21, 1951).

Mayor Burke was urged by his political supporters to campaign for the U.S. Senate against Senator Robert A. Taft in 1950 and against Senator John W. Bricker in 1952, but each time he declined to seek the Democratic nomination. In September 1953 he also refused renomination as Cleveland's mayor, intending to return to private law practice, "with a view," according to the New York *Herald Tribune* (October 18, 1953), "to earning more than the city's $15,000-a-year salary."

He was thus free on October 12, 1953 to accept appointment by Governor Lausche to succeed Senator Taft, who had died in July 1953, as Senator from Ohio. While often differing with Taft on political issues, Burke had much admiration for the Republican Senator.

His appointment gave the Democrats a majority in the Senate, with the roster reading Democrats, forty-eight; Republicans, forty-seven; and independents (Senator Wayne L. Morse), one. He early indicated that he did not intend to upset the Republican control of committees and that he believed that his party should not oppose President Eisenhower's program for purely political purposes.

Before taking his seat in the second session of the Eighty-third Congress, Burke indicated that he would probably side with Senators who opposed cuts in defense expenditures, stating that if he had been in the Senate earlier in the year he would have voted against the Air Force appropriation reductions.

In January 1954 Burke was assigned to the Senate Committee on the District of Columbia. This appointment was welcomed in a Washington *Post* editorial (January 15, 1954) as a "real boon" to the community in view of the Senator's nine-years experience as mayor of Cleveland. Among the changes that Burke has advocated (informally) for Washington are national representation, more public housing and attraction to the city of industry other than government. He also favors granting the district bond-issuing authority to finance in part the proposed municipal public works program and thinks that consideration should be given to public ownership of the transit system and to problems of stream polution.

When Senator Burke retired from the Senate Committee on the District of Columbia to become a member of the Government Operations Committee in May 1954, he stated, "I don't think you'll have first-class government until Washington gets home rule."

On legislative measures brought before the Senate in early 1954, Burke voted against adoption of a conference report to discharge indebtedness of the Commodity Credit Corporation to the amount of $681,769,703 (February) and opposed the proposed Senator Bricker constitutional amendment to curb presidential treaty-making powers (February).

He was a leading opponent of the bill (passed by the Senate on March 15 and later signed by President Eisenhower) which gave to the states rate control over all natural gas received and used within their borders. Burke contended during the debate that it would cost consumers millions of dollars by placing some distributors under state regulation instead of under the Federal Power Commission (New York *Herald Tribune*, March 28, 1954).

Senator Burke voted in favor of a bill providing for United States participation in the building of the St. Lawrence Seaway, and for the ratification of a mutual security treaty with South Korea. When a bill to grant statehood to Hawaii and Alaska came before the Senate in April 1954, Burke voted with the majority of senators for the passage of the proposed legislation. He favored the adoption of a Constitutional amendment giving eighteen-year-olds the franchise, and in a roll-call vote

Wide World

THOMAS A. BURKE

taken in early June 1954, he supported President Eisenhower's public housing program.

"Clearly, Burke does not believe in the Congressional maxim that freshman members should be seen and not heard," noted the Washington *Post* (February 28, 1954). "He lit into the Republican claim that the Administration had fired 2,200 'security risks' and he lashed out at Senator Joseph R. McCarthy." In his column of February 13, 1954 Drew Pearson commented on Burke's speech on Lincoln's birthday in which he discussed the subversives-in-government issue and quoted a number of statements of Lincoln illustrating opposition "to sacrificing principle for political gain."

In early December 1953 Burke stated that he intended to seek the Democratic Senatorial nomination in 1954. Burke's name was unopposed at the primary election in May 1954.

For a short period in the fall of 1953 Burke was president of the U.S. Conference of Mayors. He is a member of the Shaker Heights (Ohio) Country Club, Cleveland Athletic Club and Phi Alpha Delta fraternity. He is a Roman Catholic and belongs to the Knights of Columbus. He received an honorary degree from John Carroll University in 1943 and the College of the Holy Cross in 1954.

Burke married Josephine Lyon (whom he met while he was a student at Georgetown University and she was a student at Trinity College) on June 25, 1924. They have two married daughters, Jo Ann and Barbara, and five grandchildren. He has been described as "a solidly-built man of average height with black hair going gray, brown eyes . . . and a ready smile" (New York *Post*, February 28, 1954).

The *U.S. News & World Report* (October 23, 1953) described Burke as "a quiet kind of man with a flashing wit and a tendency to be

BURKE, THOMAS A.—*Continued*

conservative." The genial, round-faced statesman has also been described as a person of "captivating manner."

When Burke opened the Cleveland Indians' baseball season eight years in a row, he threw left-handed, and invariably wide of the plate. But he is "pitching his Congressional actions right down the middle" (*Christian Science Monitor*, October 22, 1953).

His chief recreations are playing gin rummy and reading biography. His favorite book of recent years is Robert Sherwood's *Roosevelt and Hopkins*. "He is a vigorous worker who often puts in twelve hours at his desk." He told a New York *Post* reporter that he preferred to run for Senator instead of for Governor. "I wanted to take a crack at Washington," he said.

He gave up golf two years ago because of lack of time. He shot "a fair game—in the nineties, maybe you'd better say the high nineties."

References

N Y Herald Tribune p1+ O 13 '53 por
N Y Post Mag p2 F 28 '54 por
N Y Times p1+ O 13 '53; p13 O 17 '53
N Y World-Telegram p7 O 17 '53 por
New Repub 129:4 O 26 '53
Time 62:29 O 19 '53
Washington (D.C.) Post p1+ O 13 '53 por
American Catholic Who's Who, 1954-55
Who's Who in America, 1954-55

BURNET, SIR (FRANK) MACFARLANE Sept. 3, 1899- Virologist; physician

Address: b. c/o Walter and Eliza Hall Institute of Medical Research, Sydney Rd., Parkville, Melbourne, N.2, Australia; h. 10 Belmont Ave., Kew, Victoria, Australia

One of Sir Macfarlane Burnet's most important contributions to the control of infectious diseases (such as influenza) is the technique he developed for cultivating bacterial viruses in chicken embryos. Dr. Burnet, director of the Walter and Eliza Hall Institute of Medical Research at the Royal Melbourne Hospital, Melbourne, Australia since 1944, is an internationally renowned microbiologist and virologist who has made important discoveries regarding poliomyelitis and herpes.

Dr. Burnet was knighted in 1951, and in 1952 he was given one of the Albert and Mary Lasker Awards of the American Public Health Association "for fundamentally modifying our knowledge of virus disease and the inheritance of characteristics by viruses." His book, *Natural History of Infectious Disease* (Cambridge University Press, 1953), is a revision of an earlier one, and contains a new chapter on antibiotic drugs. His article, "The Influenza Virus" (*Scientific American*, April 1953), explored the idea that the organism which causes influenza is curiously changeable, thereby making it difficult to anticipate epidemics with vaccines.

Frank Macfarlane Burnet was born in Traralgon, Victoria in Australia on September 3, 1899, the son of Frank Burnet and the former Hadassah McKay. Early in his youth he showed a keen enthusiasm for birds, butterflies and beetles. These interests endured, and led him to study biology and medicine at Geelong College, Geelong, Victoria. After his graduation, he entered the University of Melbourne and received the M.D. degree in 1923. His first professional assignment was as resident pathologist at the Royal Melbourne Hospital.

While a Beit fellow at the Lister Institute of Preventive Medicine in London, England in 1926, he began researches into bacteriophages and viruses. For his work he won a Ph.D. degree at the University of London in 1927. He returned to Australia in 1928 and became assistant director of the Walter and Eliza Hall Institute of Medical Research at the Royal Melbourne Hospital.

Dr. Burnet specialized in bacteriophages—microorganisms which are smaller than bacteria and which are agents for destroying bacteria. He described the "phenomenon of lysogenesis or 'carrying' of a bacteriophage, active against other bacteria, by an organism which is itself apparently unaffected" (*Nature*, December 13, 1947). By this and similar studies, he showed how bacteria as well as bacteriophages could be classified.

Having been a Rockefeller fellow at the National Institute for Medical Research in London from 1932 to 1933, Burnet returned to his duties as assistant director of the Walter and Eliza Hall Institute in 1934. He continued his research and concentrated more and more on viruses pathogenic to vertebrate animals. He showed that psittacosis is endemic in wild Australian parrots. He also threw new light upon the epidemiology of herpes and poliomyelitis.

He developed several techniques for cultivating viruses in living chicken embryos. The present procedure is to inoculate certain parts of the chick embryos with throat washings taken from persons stricken with a virus disease. After the incubation period, the chicken embryo contains enough virus to cause red blood cells to clump together, i.e., to agglutinate (a test which determines the presence of the virus).

The techniques of Dr. Burnet aided medical researchers to isolate the virus of specific diseases ranging from influenza to poliomyelitis. He is well-known also for his use of these techniques in immunological and other studies of viruses, particularly influenza. In 1944 Dr. Burnet became director of the Walter and Eliza Hall Institute of Medical Research and a professor of experimental medicine at the University of Melbourne, positions which he still holds.

Studying the manner in which red blood cells agglutinate in the presence of different virus germs, Dr. Burnet "found that an enzyme produced by cholera vibrios has an action on blood cells which is quite similar to that of influenza viruses, and is capable of blocking the union between virus and susceptible cell" (*Nature,* December 13, 1947). This discovery points to one possible approach to the study of the chemotherapy of virus infections.

Having observed the periodic waves of influenza which encircle the world about every other year, and utilizing his method of cultivating virus in chicken embryos, he discovered how each successive wave of influenza was due to a mutant of the previous virus which had all but disappeared since man had developed immunity to it. People who earned immunity to the original virus strain find their body defenses useless against the new strain and have to be either infected or inoculated to develop an immunity against the current influenza virus strain.

Chosen to receive a 1952 Lasker Award by the awards committee of the American Public Health Association, headed by Dr. Frank G. Boudreau, Dr. Burnet received his citation from Dr. Hugh R. Leavell, chairman of the executive board of the A.P.H.A.

The citation read in part: "The observation [by Dr. Burnet that viruses were not present as such in the bacterial cells from which they arose] now stands as a landmark in biology as a whole, the initiation of a new concept of the phenomenon of life." His discovery that influenza viruses "are able to merge with virus particles of other types and give rise to new offspring which combine the characteristics of both parents but differ from each . . . may clarify basically the entire matter of virus behavior. . . ." (*American Journal of Public Health,* December 1952).

Dr. Burnet takes a sober view of using "miracle" sulfa drugs and antibiotics such as penicillin, streptomycin, and aureomycin indiscriminately but admitted their efficacy: "It is not too much to say that at the present time no acute infection occurring in a previously healthy individual will result in his death if he reaches a well-equipped hospital before irreparable damage has been done to his tissues." He warned, however, that germs are capable of mutating into new strains, and that the new species might be resistant to sulfa drugs and antibiotics (*Time,* August 3, 1953).

On the other hand, according to Dr. Burnet, "the mumps virus . . . apparently caused much the same symptoms in Hippocrates' time, 2,500 years ago, as it does today, and we can find only trivial immunological differences among present strains of the virus" (*Scientific American,* April 1953). He also found that the virus is mostly active against children and newborn babies who have never been exposed to it.

Besides bacteriophages and viruses, Dr. Burnet studied staphylococcal toxins, poisons produced by staphylococci. He was the first to make formolized staphylococcal toxoid, and he also proved that a rickettsia virus is the cause of Australian Q fever.

His books, *Biological Aspects of Infectious Disease* (Cambridge University Press, 1940),

Australian Information Bureau

SIR MACFARLANE BURNET

Production of Antibodies (Macmillan, 1941), and *Virus as Organism* (Harvard University Press, 1945), are considered classics in their fields. The 1953 revision of Dr. Burnet's first book is called *Natural History of Infectious Disease.* He has written other books and numerous articles for technical journals.

Awarded honorary Sc.D. degrees by both Cambridge University and the University of Western Australia, Dr. Burnet also holds the titles of F.R.S. (1942), F.R.C.P. (1953), F.R.E.C.P. (1953), and F.R.A.C.P. He won the Royal Medal of the Royal Society in 1947. He was the Dunham lecturer at Harvard Medical School (1944), Croonian lecturer of the Royal Society (1950), and Herter lecturer at The Johns Hopkins University (1950).

Dr. Burnet received Germany's highest scientific award, the Emil von Behring Prize, in 1954 for his research in virus diseases. The prize consisted of a medal, a scroll, and 5,000 German marks ($1,190).

He was married on July 10, 1928 to Linda Druce, a schoolteacher. They have two daughters, Elizabeth and Deborah, and a son, Ian. Sir Macfarlane is five feet ten inches tall, brown-haired and blue-eyed, and weighs 180 pounds. His one hobby is painting, but his professional work keeps him too busy to pursue it as much as he would like to. He has been described as "somewhat shy", but a fascinating speaker on the lecture platform.

References

Am J Pub Health 42:1615 D '52 por
Nature 160:839+ D 13 '47
Sci Am 188:14 Ap '53
Time 60:79+ D 8 '52; 62:42 Ag 3 '53 por
Who's Who, 1953
Who's Who in Australia, 1950
Who's Who in British Science, 1953
World Biography (1948)

BURNETT, HALLIE SOUTHGATE—Dec. 3, 1908- Author; editor

Address: b. c/o Henry Holt & Co., Inc., 383 Madison Ave., New York 17; h. Setauket, Long Island, N.Y.

Reprinted from the *Wilson Library Bulletin* Jan. 1954

Hallie Southgate Burnett, who has described herself as "an addict of the unpublished word—not my own but others, strangers all," had to wait until her late thirties before settling down to writing novels (her basic interest in the world of letters). With two novels to her credit so far and a couple of anthologies of her own in the libraries, she is in her second decade as an editor of *Story* (the magazine of the short story in book form), as vice president of the Story Press (now with A. A. Wyn, Inc.), and as discoverer of other people and their literary talents (among them Norman Mailer and Truman Capote).

HALLIE SOUTHGATE BURNETT

By heritage Hallie Southgate Burnett is American, of Dutch, Scotch, and French-Huguenot ancestry on one side, and Dutch and English on the other. She was born December 3, 1908 in St. Louis, Missouri, daughter of John McKnight Southgate, one of the state's leading engineers and a one-time famous athlete of the Missouri School of Mines. Her mother, the former Elizabeth Baker, was until recently in charge of book binding for the library of that college. "Like most other writers of longer fiction," the author says, "my first writing was short stories. The first one turned up a few years ago in some old papers of my grandmother, for whom it was lovingly written. It was a highly moral tale, written at the age of seven, about a little boy who was very, very good. At ten I won my first literary prize. It was a hat. The story was about a boarding school where I'd never been, a Chinaman I'd never seen, and an emerald bracelet the like of which I have never yet owned."

Hallie Southgate had little formal schooling, but she spent her life around colleges as the daughter and niece of trustees. During the 1930's, then married to Robert Abbott, from whom she was later divorced, she was a faculty wife at Yale University and later at Union College. Meanwhile, she was writing and winning prizes for her writing—among them a national contest sponsored by *Story*. Although that story was not published, her next one some years later went to *Story*, and it was recommended and accepted by the two women editors, Bernardine Kielty and Martha Foley, and then approved for publication by Whit Burnett, the other editor.

In 1942 Hallie Southgate married Whit Burnett. She spent the next ten years reading other people's manuscripts instead of writing her own. Mrs. Burnett belongs, as the poet Margaret Widdemer says, to the "interruptible sex." She lives in busy domesticity with their two children, John, ten, and Whitney Ann Beekman, seven, a collie dog, one Blue Persian male and one White Persian female, and several Persian kittens, in a 1695 house in Setauket, a little town on the North Shore of Long Island. After the Burnetts settled there in 1948 the incoming manuscripts elevated the rural post office from third class officially to second. Life in the country gave Mrs. Burnett more time for writing, "partly because (my own theory) I found I also had to be cook and part-time nurse (my mother takes the other part) and these pastimes so increased my pleasure in life that anything seemed possible; and so I wrote my first novel, *A Woman in Possession* (Dutton, 1951) experimentally (just as I tried my first *coq au vin*) and when it was rather well received, I felt fine. My second book, *This Heart, This Hunter* (Holt, 1953), developed out of a short story. It also grew from a long time interest in how men satisfied their desire for power."

Both of Mrs. Burnett's novels have had college town backgrounds and have dealt sensitively with the emotional problems of intelligent people. Ray Pierre wrote in the *Saturday Review of Literature* of *A Woman in Possession*: "Mrs. Burnett understands the anatomy of love. She painstakingly dissects an ailing marriage in a deft and polished prose. . . ." Joseph Henry Jackson, of the San Francisco *Chronicle*, found the promise of this first novel fulfilled in *This Heart, This Hunter* which he described as "a truer novel than most, written with a simple warmth and knowledge that are rare these days."

In October 1953 appeared *Story No. 4*, which Mrs. Burnett coedited with Whit Burnett, the fourth of a series of semi-annual volumes of new short stories issued in book form under the Story Press imprint with A. A. Wyn. An earlier compilation in 1950 was for Dutton—*Story: The Fiction of the Forties*. With Eleanor Gilchrist she edited *Welcome to Life*, stories of parenthood; and she worked with Whit Burnett on such anthologies as *Time To Be Young, The Seas of God,* and *The World's Best.* Currently she is working into book form for children the travel and history notes on France (with photographs by herself, her husband, and their son John) chronicling a 5,000 kilometer journey through France, in which she tried to explain to her two children (and her husband) the historical past of France from the time of Caesar and the Gauls. (She denies this, though, and says all she was doing was trying to teach it to herself.) Her next novel, Mrs. Burnett says, is going to be about the publishing business. There will be no hero.

BURNETT, MRS. WHIT *See* Burnett, H. S. (WLB) Yrbk 54

BURNS, EDWARD MCN(ALL) Feb. 18, 1897- University professor; author

Address: b. c/o Department of Political Science, Rutgers University, New Brunswick, N.J.; h. Logan Lane, River Rd., New Brunswick, N.J.

Rutgers News Service

EDWARD MCN. BURNS

An historian and political scientist who has managed to extricate himself from the rigors of his own disciplines and examine both subjects from a broad philosophical viewpoint, Edward McN. Burns, author of the widely-used college textbook, *Western Civilization: Their History and Their Culture,* has asserted that "most progress worth mentioning in the past resulted from the growth of intelligence and tolerance and herein lies the chief hope for a better world in the future."

A teacher of history and political science at Rutgers University for twenty-three years, Dr. Burns became chairman of the department of political science in 1951. He has written a number of books including *James Madison: Philosopher of the Constitution,* and *David Starr Jordan: Prophet of Freedom.*

Edward McNall Burns was born in Burgettstown, Washington County, Pennsylvania on February 18, 1897, one of the four children of James McNall and Lucy Idelta (Gilliland) Burns. His ancestors who were of Scotch-Irish stock have resided in the vicinity of Burgettstown since colonial days and were predominantly preachers and, like his father, farmers. As a farm boy, young Burns often avoided his chores in order to read history books. He was graduated from Burgettstown High School in 1915; here his extracurricular activities included debating, public speaking and football.

Determined to continue his studies in college, he taught for two years at a rural school to earn his tuition before entering Washington and Jefferson College for a year. He served as a sergeant in the Army corps of engineers during 1918 and later enrolled in the University of Pittsburgh. The student was elected to Phi Alpha Theta (national honorary historical fraternity) and after receiving the A.B. degree in 1925 he remained at the university as an assistant in political science. He received the M.A. degree at Pittsburgh in 1927. Two of his professors, Dr. Alfred P. James and Dr. Elmer D. Groper, Burns believes influenced him to become a college teacher.

Continuing his formal education, Burns pursued postgraduate courses at the University of Chicago from 1926 to 1929, Columbia University from 1929 to 1930, Princeton University from 1933 to 1934, and received the Ph.D. degree from his alma mater in 1935. The title of his dissertation was "The Political Philosophy of James Madison," a subject long neglected because of the enormous mass of material which had to be integrated and studied. He spent many weeks in the Library of Congress reading approximately ninety volumes of Madison's manuscripts.

The scholar became associated with Rutgers University in 1928 as an instructor in history and political science and was promoted to assistant professor of history in 1931, associate professor of history in 1941; professor of history in 1947; chairman of the department of history and political science in 1950; professor of political science and chairman of the department of political science when the latter became an independent department in 1951.

In 1938 Rutgers University Press published Burns' *James Madison: Philosopher of the Constitution,* a revision of his dissertation. In the book the author asserts that "Madison was a true aristocrat in many ways, who regarded governing as the most honorable of professions, a profession requiring the most thorough knowledge of political science and the deepest instinct of political morality." Recognizing despotism as the greatest evil, Madison envisaged a popular democratic government predicated on the separation of powers and a system of checks and balances. It was Madison's ideals, Dr.

BURNS, EDWARD MCN.—*Continued*

Burns believes, "more than those of any other man" that "determined the original character of the Federal Constitution."

In reviewing the book, Benjamin F. Wright, now president of Smith College wrote, "In spite of the difficulties of his subject, Mr. Burns has written one of the most satisfactory studies of an American political thinker that we have. It is . . . a very careful and comprehensive survey of Madison's political and constitutional thought" (*American Political Science Review,* December, 1938). David Page stated ". . . the book sets a high standard for subsequent volumes" (*Boston Evening Transcript,* August 27, 1938).

A standard freshman text in many American colleges and universities, *Western Civilization: Their History and Their Culture,* was published by W. W. Norton in 1941 and its fourth edition appeared in February of 1954; it has also been translated into Spanish. In it Professor Burns defines civilization as culture which has reached "a stage of advancement in which writing has come to be used to a considerable extent, some progress has been made in the arts and sciences, and the political, social, and economic institutions have developed sufficiently to conquer at least some of the problems of order, security, and efficiency in a complex society."

In one of his articles, Dr. Burns characterized the liberal as one who cannot be an "opponent of change except in relation to certain values essential to freedom or to social progress. Even those he must be willing to reinterpret from time to time in the light of new conditions. Likewise, liberalism is basically opposed to the methods of the radical. The liberal refuses to subscribe to the dictum that the end justifies the means. He believes, rather, that the two are interdependent, that the choice of means may condition the end, even to the extent of perverting or destroying it" (*Antioch Review,* September, 1948).

In Dr. Burns' view scholarship affords civilization the opportunity of evaluating the flow of events thereby endowing each generation with courage and insight so desperately needed by man in his endeavor to deal with the problems of his society. In his most recent book, *David Starr Jordan: Prophet of Freedom,* Dr. Burns sets forth as its purpose "to present the social and political ideas of Dr. Jordan, in the belief that they constitute a body of wisdom that Americans can ill afford to ignore." Although Jordan, who was the first president of Leland Stanford University, received little recognition, "in the range and originality of his achievements, Jordan surpassed nearly all of his contemporaries among college presidents."

Among the variety of the ideas of Dr. Jordan, perhaps the most basic was the belief that "government should be *of* and *by* the people" in the first instance. The evils of the modern political state, "ignorance, corruption, self-seeking" are deplorable indeed, but a remedy cannot be found in benevolent despotism. While the people may err, it must always be that they determine their own destiny. This book was completed after three and a half years of research and study and was published in 1953 by the Stanford University Press in the United States and by the Oxford University Press in Great Britain, India and Pakistan.

Presently preparing a new book, Dr. Burns will analyze the ideas of what has made America great as expressed in the writings of its leaders from Benjamin Franklin to Dwight D. Eisenhower. The leaders whose writings have been studied will include statesmen, philosophers, educators, historians, literary men and scientists. Some have emphasized our Puritan heritage as the source of the nation's greatness, others have insisted that Anglo-Saxon institutions, factors of race, or equality of economic opportunity have been the principal causes. The study will include also an examination of the ideal of the future America and conceptions of the factors that could contribute to its decline.

Active in the faculty affairs of Rutgers, Dr. Burns has been secretary of the faculty of the College of Arts and Sciences since 1943. In 1950 he was chairman of the faculty committee which cooperated with a committee of the board of trustees in selecting a new president for the university. (The final choice of the university was Dr. Lewis Webster Jones). After serving for two terms on the university council, Burns was elected in 1953 to the university senate. The professor has asserted, "I believe with H. G. Wells that civilization is a race between education and disaster. No influence can surpass that of education in endowing man with the capacity to solve his numerous and distressing problems, but education to be effective must be grounded upon a careful and rigorous use of the scientific method. Indoctrination is not education, neither is the spinning of plausible theories which do not have a firm foundation in factual knowledge."

The professor was a lecturer in the South Orange and Maplewood (New Jersey) Adult School from 1935 to 1940. He is a member of the board of directors of the New Brunswick Urban League. He also holds membership in the American Historical Association, American Political Science Association, American Association of University Professors, Phi Beta Kappa, Tau Kappa Alpha, and Pi Sigma Alpha. Popular with the student body for his lectures and graduate seminars, Burns was named by a student poll in 1942 as the "best teacher" on campus and has several times been chosen as the "most scholarly" faculty member.

Dr. Burns married Marie Katherine Bentz on June 29, 1936. Mrs. Burns was formerly a school teacher in Flemington, New Jersey and met her husband as a student in a summer session course which he instructed. The couple have one daughter, Eleanor Witherspoon Burns. Dr. Burns has blue eyes and brown hair, is five feet ten inches in height and weighs 165 pounds. His favorite hobbies are reading and traveling.

References

Directory of American Scholars (1951)
Who's Who in America, 1952-53

BURNS, H(ENDRY) S(TUART) M(ACKENZIE) Apr. 28, 1900- Business executive

Address: b. c/o Shell Oil Company, 50 W. 50th St., New York 20; h. 1060 Fifth Ave., New York 28

Because of his ease before public gatherings and his way with a story, the president of Shell Oil Company, H. S. M. Burns, has become a popular speaker for business and oil industry groups. His "Myth of Monopoly" speech, delivered at the November 1953 meeting of the American Petroleum Institute, was enthusiastically received and has since been widely quoted.

"Max" Burns joined Shell in 1926 and learned all phases of the oil business in England, South America and the United States. After ten years of full responsibility in Colombia he was transferred to New York in 1946 and became a senior vice-president. On July 1, 1947 he was elected president and director. In 1951 Shell entered the ranks of corporations whose annual sales total over one billion dollars. Shell's 1953 annual report showed a consolidated net profit of $115,406,585, or $8.40 a share, compared with a net of $90,872,834, or $6.61 a share in 1952. During 1953 the company sold more and made more than ever before in its history; it sold $1,269,551,000 worth of petroleum products.

Hendry Stuart Mackenzie Burns was born in Aberdeen, Scotland on April 28, 1900, the son of John Stuart and Anne (Mackenzie) Burns. He attended Robert Gordon's College from 1914 to 1917. After serving with the Royal Artillery during World War I, he entered Aberdeen University where he received the B.Sc. degree with honors in 1922. He won the Ferguson scholarship to Cambridge University and was made a scholar of Clare College and in 1925 received his master's degree in mathematics and physics.

During the following year Burns came to the United States and joined the Shell Oil Company in California as a geophysicist, and in 1927 transferred to the manufacturing and supplies department. He trained in a refinery, got the "feel" of being a service station attendant and even rode a tank truck. In 1928 the young man was made assistant to the division manager in Seattle. He was promoted to assistant general manager in 1932 and served as general sales manager from 1934 to 1936.

After ten years of this thorough experience, he went to London and then moved to Venezuela to be second in command of Shell's interests there. Shortly thereafter Shell began operations in Colombia, South America, and Burns was sent there in 1936 to organize the local company. As Burns says, he was sent to Colombia to find oil, and he was lucky and found it. "His overseas bosses also found that he got on famously with the Colombia people—he taught himself Spanish and avoided all local political involvements" (*Fortune,* September, 1951). Burns remained in his Colombian post until 1946 when he came to New York and was made senior vice-president.

Hal Phyfe

H. S. M. BURNS

The Shell Oil Company is the American member of the Royal Dutch Shell group. The group originated as two separate organizations, the Shell Transport & Trading Company, Ltd., of London and the Royal Dutch Petroleum Company of the Hague. Both of these had begun, in the 1880's, to produce and refine petroleum products in the East Indies. To oppose the Standard Oil Company of New Jersey, a competitor, they joined forces in 1907 by establishing two new companies, De Bataafsche Petroleum Maatschappij, The Hague for exploring and preparing petroleum, and The Anglo Saxon Petroleum Company, London for transportation purposes. The two old companies maintained separate existences, but the possessions of both were combined under the two new companies, Royal Dutch owning 60 per cent and Shell 40 per cent.

The Supreme Court of the United States, in 1911, ordered the dissolution of the Standard Oil Company of New Jersey under the Sherman anti-trust act. Taking advantage of this development, the Royal Dutch Shell group began operations with a small marketing company in the United States. The Shell organization on the West coast was one of the largest producers of crude oil in California by 1920, owned a flourishing refinery in the San Francisco Bay area, and another at Wood River, Illinois, a 500 mile pipe line near St. Louis, Missouri, and producing oil properties in numerious mid-continent fields.

In 1929 Shell took over the New England Oil Refining Company and the New England market has so expanded that in 1954 the company employs nearly 600 in its marketing division.

On July 1, 1947 Max Burns became president of Shell. Two years later when Shell Oil, Inc. was absorbed by a holding company, Burns was elected president of the newly named Shell Oil Company. During his presidency, Shell

BURNS, H. S. M.—*Continued*
has been the recipient of much attention, with its shares climbing from $24 in 1947 to over $90 in 1954. Its growth has been "sound and steady" and it is today "the fifth largest producer of crude oil in the United States, and one of the five biggest petroleum marketers" (*Christian Science Monitor,* February 6, 1954). Today, although the Royal Dutch Shell group owns 65 per cent of its stock, the Shell Oil Company operates as an American business with an almost totally American staff. Except for exploration and production in Western Canada, Shell Oil Company confines its operations to the United States.

In his speech, "The Myth of Monopoly," at the annual meeting of the American Petroleum Institute in Chicago on November 9, 1953, Burns pointed out that the term monopoly applied to the oil business was inaccurate. "The fact that so many brands of petroleum products are available in every community of the United States," he said, "and that there are so many rival claims for superiority . . . must in itself make any talk of monopoly in the oil business stand out as the fairy tale which it is."

He also pointed out that "many people, for one reason or another, usually political, who, in order to perpetuate the myth of monopoly [say] that bigness is a sin and amounts to the same thing as monopoly. They play upon the emotional phenomenon that has been noted by psychologists, that people are inherently distrustful and fearful of big things. The emotional reaction is the basis of the old fairy tales about Jack, the giant killer, but the people of America have surely got over such childish superstitions. Of course, the oil industry is a big business. But its bigness arises from the fact that it is made up of many businesses and it has to be big in order to furnish some 600 gallons of petroleum products per year for every man, woman and child in the United States.

"America," Burns continued, "has reached its high level of productivity and its high standard of living because of the bigness of its industries. If there were not a big automobile industry, or a big railroad industry, or a big aviation industry, we should all have had to come to Chicago for these meetings in a horse and buggy. . . . Big business encourages, stimulates and relies on small business. In 1938 there were less than 10,000 oil jobbers. Today there are over 14,000. In my own company, 40 per cent of our business is done through independent jobbers and they all seem to flourish . . . refuting the charge that smaller groups are squeezed out."

Shell's president has his own ideas regarding public relations. "Once, on a tour of the Northwest, a reporter asked him: "How do you set the price of gas?' Burns stared at the veteran newsman as if to ask whether he'd never heard of supply-and-demand, answered bluntly: 'We charge all that traffic will bear.' " His public relations aides were discomfited, explaining that Burns was simply expressing the basic theory of the free enterprise system. "Their explanations were unnecessary. Not a journalist at the press conference quoted Burns out of context" (*Forbes,* April 1, 1952).

Max Burns has been described as "a big chap, over six feet, well conditioned, husky and ruddy of countenance . . . witty and gregarious . . . has a reputation for tremendous drive and singleness of purpose" (New York *Herald Tribune,* December 19, 1950). "There is usually a twinkle in Burns's eye, for he enjoys life tremendously. He says he never worries once a step is taken. 'That kind of worrying kills people', he adds with a soft burr he has never lost. 'It's worrying post facto' " (*Fortune,* September, 1951).

After an expensive "wildcat" in Beckham County, Oklahoma had failed to promise oil after the drilling crew had used the $50,000 budget. Burns promptly ordered them to "blow" another $10,000 because one man had seen an "oil wiggle". A few feet farther down Shell struck a 100,000,000 barrel pool of oil.

Burns is a director of the American Petroleum Institute, International Lubricants Corporation, Shell Oil Company of Canada, Ltd., Shell Exploration (New Brunswick) Ltd., Shell Exploration Alberts, Ltd., Shell Canadian Tankers, Ltd., Shell Oil Company of British Columbia, Ltd., and Shell American Petroleum Company. He belongs to the St. Andrews Society (New York), Burns Society, and American Society of Magicians. His clubs are the Racquet and Tennis (New York), Pacific Union (San Francisco), Sewanhanka Corinthian Yacht, and Piping Rock (Long Island).

On January 24, 1929 Burns married Dorcas Jackson of San Francisco. Their sons are Peter Mackenzie and Michael Jackson Burns. The president of Shell enjoys fishing and boating. Deeply interested in art, Burns has said that, if he doesn't actually retire to Florence, Italy, at least, he plans to spend a lot of time there.

References

Forbes 69:18+ Ap 1 '52 por
Fortune 64:124 S '51 por
N Y Herald Tribune p40 D 19 '50 por
Business Executives of America (1950)
Who's Who in America, 1953
Who's Who in Commerce and Industry (1953)

BUSH, PRESCOTT S(HELDON) May 15, 1895- United States Senator from Connecticut

Address: b. Senate Office Bldg., Washington 25, D.C.; h. Grove Lane, Greenwich, Conn.

NOTE: This biography supersedes the article which appeared in *Current Biography* in 1942.

Elected in November 1952 to fill the remainder of the term of the late Senator Brien McMahon, Prescott S. Bush, Republican, of Connecticut, was one of five Senators appointed at the close of the first session of the Eighty-third Congress to President Eisenhower's Foreign Economic Policy Commission. Since 1930 Bush has been a partner in a leading private banking firm in New York City. For seventeen years he was the moderator of the Representative Town Meeting in his home community of Greenwich, Connecticut.

He was a candidate for the Senate in 1950, and in his campaigning used television, zany orchestras and a quartet composed of former Yale Whiffenpoofs to acquaint the electorate with his personality.

One of the four children of Samuel Prescott and Flora (Sheldon) Bush, Prescott Sheldon Bush was born in Columbus, Ohio, on May 15, 1895. He is descended on the paternal side from an English settler who came to Cape Cod, Massachusetts in the middle of the seventeenth century. Reared in Columbus (where his father, a steel manufacturer who later helped to launch the Community Chest movement in this country, was in business), Prescott attended local public grade schools for eight years. He then enrolled at St. George's School in Newport, Rhode Island, where he was graduated in 1913. On entering Yale University, New Haven, Connecticut, he established himself as an all-round athlete, playing for three seasons on the varsity baseball team, as well as on the football team and (in 1914) the golf team. He was a member of Skull and Bones and president of the Yale Glee Club. (Subsequently he became president of the Yale Glee Club Associates and as second bass in the All-Time Whiffenpoofs Quartet, has been acclaimed by contemporaries as "the hottest close-harmony man" at Yale in a span of twenty-five years.)

In his junior year Bush joined the Connecticut National Guard and for a number of weeks during 1916 saw action as a private on the Mexican border. He returned to Yale and received the B.A. degree in 1917.

Called to World War I service in the latter year, Prescott S. Bush received a captain's commission in the American Expeditionary Force and served with the 158th Field Artillery Brigade through the Meuse-Argonne offensive; following the armistice he was assigned to the Army of Occupation in Germany and was stationed at Seventh Army Corps headquarters until April, 1919 when he was returned to the United States for demobilization.

Back in civilian clothes, Bush found a job with the Simmons Hardware Company in St. Louis, Missouri. He later worked for the Stedman Products Company (from 1922 to 1924) and for the United States Rubber Company (from 1924 to 1926), before becoming vice-president of W. A. Harriman and Company, a private banking firm in New York City.

When the present New York banking house of Brown Brothers, Harriman and Company was established through a merger in 1930, Bush became a partner in the new firm. He also served as a director of the Columbia Broadcasting System, the Prudential Insurance Company of America, the Vanadium Corporation of America, the Simmons Company, the Rockbestos Products Company, the Dresser Industries, Inc., the Pennsylvania Water and Power Company (chairman of the board of directors), the Pan American Airways Corporation, Hydrocarbon Research, Inc., and the United States Guarantee Company.

PRESCOTT S. BUSH

As an amateur sportsman, Bush competed in a number of golfing tournaments and served for eight years as a member of the executive committee of the United States Golf Association (he served successively as secretary, vice-president and president from 1928 through 1935).

A resident of Greenwich, Connecticut since 1924, Bush was active on behalf of the Greenwich Defense Council, the Greenwich Hospital Association, the Boys' Club of Greenwich, and the Connecticut Society for Mental Hygiene. He held the moderator's chair of the Greenwich Representative Town Meeting for seventeen years, until his election to the United States Senate in 1952.

In February 1942 Prescott Bush was named national campaign chairman to conduct the second annual U.S.O. drive for funds to provide recreational services for the armed forces. Some five thousand cities and towns raised more than $33,000,000 during the year. In April 1943 Bush was appointed by Winthrop W. Aldrich to head the 1943 to 1944 campaign of the National War Fund, Inc., an amalgamation of some 600 war relief agencies other than the Red Cross but which included the U.S.O.

Bush's consistent success in the solicitation of funds brought him the chairmanship of the Connecticut Republican State Finance Committee in 1947.

In July 1948 Bush was a delegate-at-large to the Republican national convention in Philadelphia. Two years later (1950), he was nominated by Republicans of the Nutmeg State to oppose the election to the United States Senate of the Democratic incumbent, William Benton, an interim appointee.

The candidate conducted a brisk, aggressive and at times, a highly unconventional campaign. He enlivened political rallies by singing bass in a quartet made up of former Yale

BUSH, PRESCOTT S.—*Continued*

Whiffenpoof singers or by "strumming the guitar" with the so-called Brooklyn Sym-phoney Orchestra, the musical outfit which plays at Brooklyn Dodgers' games and which he had hired for the campaign. In his speeches he discussed the issues of "Korea, communism, confusion and corruption." He lost his contest with Benton on November 8 by approximately 1,000 votes out of the 862,000 cast.

After the death of Brien McMahon, Senator from Connecticut, in the summer of 1952, a special election was held to determine his successor. Bush, nominated as the Republican candidate in September 1952, ran against Representative Abraham A. Ribicoff, Democrat, of Hartford, Connecticut.

In an automobile "stumping" trip up the industrialized Naugatuck Valley, Bush linked his campaign with that of the presidential candidacy of General Eisenhower. He defeated Representative Ribicoff in November by a reported 559,586 votes to 529,213.

Upon entering the Senate, he was given a leave of absence from Brown Brothers, Harriman and Company. He also resigned his directorates of several corporations.

Assigned to the Public Works, and to the Banking and Currency committees in the Eighty-third Congress, the Senator led a successful movement in the banking committee to set the life of the pending Defense Production Act at two years instead of the one year originally contemplated. In a debate on the Senate floor, Bush defended the inclusion in the pending bill of stand-by authority for the President to "freeze" prices, wages and rent for ninety days in case of "grave national emergency."

The Senator voted (July 1953) against cutting the total amounts in the Mutual Security Program authorization bill and against an amendment to the foreign aid authorization bill to send surplus farm crops abroad. He favored a bill which would make special quota immigration visas available to Italian nationals as well as to Italian refugees.

In national affairs, Bush supported the offshore oil bill, voted against increasing Federal grants to states for building hospitals, and favored the sale of government rubber plants to private interests. He stood with the Administration on limiting the appropriations to the Air Force.

Outside the Senate, the legislator has defended the Eisenhower Administration policies relative to "sound dollars and debt management" and criticized "the financial community all over the United States" for "trading against the government in the Treasury bond market" (New York *Herald Tribune,* July 3, 1953).

In September, when an important New England manufacturing concern announced the transfer of part of its operations to Mississippi, Senator Bush promised that in the next session of Congress he would seek legislation to prevent Southern states from using Federal aid as a basis for giving tax abatements to influence new industries to settle in the South.

An Episcopalian in faith, Prescott S. Bush is a trustee of the Episcopal Church Foundation of the United States and a director of Seabury House. He was Connecticut chairman of the United Negro College Fund in 1951. The Senator belongs to the American Legion and the "40 and 8;" his clubs include the Field, Links, Lunch, Yale and Round Hill, and he is a member of the National Institute of Social Sciences. He served as a trustee of Yale University from 1944 to 1950, and in June 1952 was elected to a second six-year term. He received an honorary M.A. degree from Yale University in 1944.

He married Dorothy Walker of St. Louis in 1921. They have five children, Prescott Sheldon, Jr., George Herbert Walker, Nancy (Mrs. Alexander Ellis, Jr.), Jonathan James, and William Henry Trotter, and eight grandchildren. The Senator, described as a "towering, handsome man," is six feet four inches tall. He is a low handicap golfer—he shot a 66 in the U.S. Seniors Championship at Apawamis in 1951 to set an all-time course and tournament record for eighteen holes.

References (See also references listed in the May 1942 biographical sketch)

N Y Herald Tribune p7 F 13 '42 por; p8 Ap 12 '43; p17 S 29 '50; p9 N 5 '52
N Y Sun p23 F 13 '42 por
N Y Times p10 F 13 '42; p8 Ap 12 '43 por

Business Executives of America (1950)
Congressional Directory (1953)
Poor's Register of Directors and Executives, United States and Canada, 1952
Who's Who in America, 1952-53
Who's Who in Commerce and Industry (1953)
Who's Who in New England (1949)
Who's Who in New York, 1952

BUTLER, HUGH (ALFRED) Feb. 28, 1878-July 1, 1954 United States Senator from Nebraska; was born in Iowa and his family took up a homestead near Cambridge, Nebraska; was graduated from Doane College (1900); bought a grain elevator and flour mill (1908); organized the Butler-Welsh Company in Omaha (1918) which developed into one of the leading firms of grain dealers in the Middle West; became a member of the Republican National Committee (1936); elected to the U.S. Senate (1940) and became a leading isolationist who upheld the tradition of the Republican "Old Guard" through three terms in the Senate; was a spokesman for the farm and cattle blocs, and a protectionist; opposed Social Security system, administration "secrecy", particularly on the Yalta treaty, lend-lease aid to Britain, the Marshall Plan, aid to Turkey and Greece, and, later, intervention in Korea; but he voted for United States membership in the United Nations. See *Current Biography,* (Feb.) 1950.

Obituary

N Y Times p19 Jl 2 '54

BUTLER, JOHN MARSHALL July 21, 1897- United States Senator from Maryland; lawyer

Address: b. Senate Office Bldg., Washington 25, D.C.; Mercantile Trust Bldg., Baltimore 2, Md.; h. 221 Upnor Rd., Baltimore 12, Md.

A "political unknown" when he began his campaign for his first elective office in 1950, Republican John Marshall Butler on November 7 of that year won over veteran Senator Millard E. Tydings for a six-year term in the United States Senate. Maryland's new legislator, whose career for some twenty-three years previously had centered almost exclusively on his private law practice in Baltimore, is a strong exponent of reduced Federal spending. As a member of the Senate Judiciary Committee in the Eighty-third Congress, Butler in 1953 headed an investigation of communist influence in labor unions in connection with hearings on labor legislation which he had proposed.

John Marshall Butler is of Scotch, Irish, English and French descent, with Huguenot forebears who settled in America in the seventeenth century. He was born to John Harvey and Eunice West (Riddle) Butler on July 21, 1897 in Baltimore, Maryland. In childhood he sold newspapers, was employed in a mattress factory, and later worked as an office boy in a law firm.

After twenty-six months of military service during World War I, Butler attended night school and then enrolled in The Johns Hopkins University. He became a star right tackle on the football team. At the end of his second year, in 1921, he left the university to work in his father's real estate business. During the next few years he studied at night to complete courses for his LL.B. degree which was granted in 1926 by the University of Maryland School of Law.

Having been admitted to the Maryland bar that same year, Butler in 1927 joined the Baltimore firm of Venable, Baetjer & Howard, of which he has been a partner since 1939. Interested in civic affairs, he was a member from April 1947 to June 1949 of the City Service Commission of Baltimore. While advancing in his law practice he took little active part in politics until in the late 1940's he attended a number of conferences of prominent members of Maryland's Republican party.

With the encouragement of national and state GOP leaders, Butler entered the Republican primary in 1950 and, although he lost in popular votes to John Markey, gained the Senatorial nomination by a larger unit vote count. The Democratic candidate in the Congressional election was Senator Millard E. Tydings, who had represented his state in the Senate for twenty-four years and who had recently headed a subcommittee to investigate charges made by Senator Joseph R. McCarthy that communists were employed by the State Department. In his many speeches in all parts of Maryland and in frequent radio and television appearances Butler used as a major issue of his campaign the allegation that Tydings had "whitewashed" these charges.

Fabian Bachran

JOHN MARSHALL BUTLER

Butler's campaign held the attention of the press for several months after his victory over Tydings on November 7 by about 43,000 votes. The former Senator accused Butler of using a pamphlet entitled "From the Record", issued under the name of Young Democrats for Butler, with an alleged "composite" picture "showing Tydings in deep conversation with Earl Browder, former Communist leader" (New York *Times*, February 28, 1951). Tydings later sent a letter on April 5, 1951 to the Senate charging that Butler had "violated Federal and Maryland election laws" relating to excessive and unreported campaign expenditures (Washington *Post*, April 6, 1951).

Butler stated that he "did not personally disburse any campaign funds, but was involved involuntarily in the matter of a bill owed William Fedder [a Baltimore printer] for printing". He added that although he had not authorized such a bill, "it was up to me to see that he did not suffer even if it took my last cent" (Washington *Post*, September 13, 1951).

A Senate subcommittee was formed to investigate Tydings' complaint. The report issued by the subcommittee after four months of inquiry denounced the campaign tactics which had been used in behalf of Butler by his campaign manager and other supporters. A subsequent Justice Department inquiry did not advise action in the matter. The general sentiment in the Senate was that election campaign laws should be revised.

Shortly after the opening of the first session of the Eighty-second Congress the freshman Senator from Maryland was assigned to the Senate District of Columbia, Post Office and Civil Service committees. Having opposed in the spring of 1951 the Kefauver-Taft bill for home rule in the district, he co-sponsored in July a substitute bill which he believed would

BUTLER, JOHN M.—*Continued*
accomplish the objective of self-government in a constitutional manner.

In his first foreign policy speech, made in Washington in January 1951, Senator Butler expressed his view that the President does not have the constitutional right to send troops to the Atlantic Pact nations. "Let us call a halt," he urged, "to this move to place a standing Army of the United States troops in Europe as part of an international army until all constitutional provisions have been met" (Washington *Post,* January 21, 1951).

The following April he voted in favor of a measure not to have additional troops assigned to Europe without consent of Congress. Butler's viewpoint on international cooperation had earlier been expressed: "I'm not an isolationist and never will be. I was on the radio in 1939 trying to get the United States to take action to help Finland when Russia attacked her. We must protect ourselves abroad, we can't sit in our own back yard and let the world go by. We've got to help" (Washington *Post,* November 17, 1950).

An advocate of economy in government, the Maryland legislator supported in 1951 a number of bills to reduce Federal spending: a cut in Government civil payrolls; $10,000,000 cut in reclamation funds; reduction in soil conservation funds; and a decrease in European economic aid. His voting record in 1952 shows him approving an offshore oil bill giving title to the states; a measure to abolish the Reconstruction Finance Corporation; a proposal to use the Taft-Hartley act in the steel strike; and a move to shelve the St. Lawrence seaway power project.

On May 15, 1953 Senator Butler called on the Administration to rid its ranks of what he called "crypto-Socialists" who have dug into jobs where they could influence policies of the Federal government. He stated that they are to be found for the most part in agencies in the economic and social fields and are usually lawyers and economists. Their assumptions, he said, are that "Business is evil and to be regimented; labor unions are good . . . employers are wicked; the Federal government is progressive and should increasingly supplant the states . . . wages are good, profits are sinful. . ." (New York *Times,* May 16, 1953).

Concern for economy is also evident in the Senator's opposition in 1953 to an allocation of an additional $400,000,000 for jet bombers. One of a large number of Senators who sponsored an equal-rights-for-women amendment, Butler in July introduced an unqualified plan (without special privileges) and voted "nay" to a rider keeping protections for women. On other measures before the first session of the Eighty-third Congress, he approved bills to sell government-owned rubber plants and to admit into the United States refugees from communist countries, and opposed a bill to penalize nations trading with the Soviet bloc.

Senator Butler's committee assignments in the Eighty-third Congress were to Government operations, Interstate and Foreign Commerce, and the Judiciary. He was also made a member of the board of visitors to the Coast Guard Academy. On the Judiciary Committee, the Baltimore Republican was a leader in defending a proposed constitutional amendment to curtail the treaty-making powers of the President.

The Senator introduced a bill in April 1953 to prevent the National Labor Relations Board from certifying communist-dominated labor unions as collective bargaining agents for workers and to give to the Subversive Activities Control Board the responsibility of determining whether a union is so controlled. "We can't save this country," he maintained, "if we can't keep communists out of unions, especially out of positions of authority" (New York *Times,* August 7, 1953).

In connection with hearings on his bill Butler was named by the Senate internal security subcommittee of the Judiciary Committee to head investigations which began in November on communist infiltration of labor unions. He noted on a television program *Youth Wants to Know* on November 22, 1953 that while labor unions have made progress in eliminating communist influence, they should be given greater help by Congress.

Addressing the Maryland Junior Chamber of Commerce in May 1953, the Senator suggested that more young people were needed in local, state and Federal governments because of the "idealism" of youth, "its ability to take a fresh look at our problems and a willingness to initiate changes and assume risks." He thought that young businessmen in particular should assume greater responsibility: "During the past twenty years there has been a suspicion and distrust of businessmen in government circles. But that is rapidly changing with the new Administration's policy of turning to men from industry and trade to administer the complex machinery of government" (Washington *Post,* May 24, 1953).

Butler, on April 5, 1926, married Marie Louise Abell, whose family had founded the Baltimore *Sun.* Their children are John Marshall, Jr., Edwin Franklin Abell and Maria Louise Butler. The blue-eyed, graying blond-haired Senator is described as having a "breezy, man-of-distinction manner. It includes both quick friendliness and quiet dignity." He stands about six feet tall, with a weight of 180 pounds and has a "pleasant baritone" voice. The Senator is a member of the American, Maryland and Baltimore bar associations. He belongs to the Country Club and Maryland Club and he is an American Legionnaire. His church is the Methodist.

References

N Y World-Telegram p17 N 11 '50 por
Nation 177:387+ N 14 '53
Time 65:21 N 20 '50
U S News 27:45 N 17 '50
Washington (D.C.) Post p3B O 29 '50 por; p14 N 17 '50 por

Congressional Directory (1953)
Who's Who in America, 1952-53
Who's Who in United States Politics (1952)

BUTTS, ALFRED M(OSHER) Apr. 13, 1899- Architect; inventor

Address: b. c/o Holden, Egan & Associates, 215 E. 37th St., New York 16; h. 3421 80th St., Jackson Heights, Queens, New York 72

The man responsible for the word game "Scrabble," which has attained widespread popularity in the United States during the last two years, is architect Alfred M. Butts, who invented it in 1933. "No game in the history of the trade has ever sold so rapidly and few have shown such promise of consistent, long-term popularity," commented *Life* (December 14, 1953). An important co-worker in effecting the success of the game, James Brunot, began marketing it in 1948; over 1,100,000 games have been sold to date. According to *Look,* "Everyone's playing it . . . from India's Premier Nehru to Dagmar."

Alfred Mosher Butts was born in Poughkeepsie, New York, on April 13, 1899, one of the five sons of Allison and Arrie Elizabeth (Mosher) Butts. Both his parents' ancestors were farming families in Dutchess county, New York. His father was a Poughkeepsie lawyer and his mother a teacher in that city. His brother, Norman, is a landscape architect in Atlanta, Georgia, and two brothers, Allison and Wilbur, are professors at Lehigh and Chattanooga universities, respectively. A brother Ralph, who was a lawyer, died in 1933.

The family was game-loving and frequently played chess, checkers and their variations. With his brothers, Alfred introduced into the game of anagrams an innovation in the form of a black square as a joker which he later made an integral part of "Scrabble".

Alfred attended Poughkeepsie High School, where he was editor of the yearbook and from which he was graduated in 1917. He then entered Pratt Institute in Brooklyn, New York and majored in architecture. During World War I he served as a private in the Students' Army Training Corps. He later attended the University of Pennsylvania and received the Bachelor of Architecture degree in 1924. As an undergraduate he was a member of the chess team.

Beginning his career as a draftsman, Butts entered the New York architectural firm of Arthur C. Holden and Associates in 1924. During the depression, he recalls, "I was out of a job . . . and I just decided I would invent an adult game" (New York *Post,* January 17, 1954). After classifying board games into three groups—chance, skill and a combination of both—he decided that the last was the most promising. As quoted by Fern Marja in the New York *Post,* he declared ". . . the third category hadn't been developed at all. There was no way of scoring. So I said, 'All right, I'll see if I can develop something in anagrams.' "

His initial version of "Scrabble" was completed in 1933 for use in his own home. It was played without a board and the letters were assigned various values related to their frequency of use in the English language. Vowels received a low one-point value each, and the consonant "Z" the count of ten.

Calvacca, 1954
New York Post Corp.

ALFRED M. BUTTS

During the 1930's, Butts continued to experiment with his invention and to improve it. "When we played at home," he stated, "we used old anagram letters, mahjong racks and kept score on a cribbage board." His wife was his most frequent partner and shared his enthusiasm for games.

In his opinion the important factor that advanced his invention was the use of a playing board of 225 squares, some of which double or triple the value of letters or words. To replace the earlier anagram letters, he developed a set of 100 small wooden blocks bearing letters of the alphabet. His attempts to interest leading manufacturers in his product failed, and for a brief period before returning to his former position with the New York architectural firm in 1935, he thought of manufacturing his own product. He completed the modifications of the game in 1938, and made about 500 sets for his friends.

A decade after the inventor had produced his final version of the game, his friend James Brunot, former executive director of the President's War Relief Control Board, opened an assembly plant in the living room of his home in Newtown, Connecticut. With the aid of his wife, he began production of the game, christening it "Scrabble". Although this proved to be a money-losing project for four years, in 1952 sales of the sets increased from sixteen games daily early that year to around 411 each day during the last quarter. Advertising was largely by "word of mouth . . ." and by "leaflets" enclosed with the sets (*Life,* December 14, 1953).

Regarding mounting "Scrabble" sales, Butts states: "Jim Brunot has all the headaches and I just collect royalties." Sets are produced to sell at three different prices. Brunot has assigned the production of the least expensive

BUTTS, ALFRED M.—*Continued*

set, now called "Skip-a-Cross" to the Cadaco-Ellis Company of Chicago, and the medium-priced three dollar set to Selchow & Righter Company of New York. The wooden blocks of this set are made of mountain maple by a factory near Adolf Hitler's Berchtesgaden hide-out in Bavaria. Brunot, who became associated with the manufacture of "Scrabble" because he wanted a small business in the country, continues the manufacture of the de luxe set which is made of plastic tiles.

Of the many letters Butts and Brunot receive from fans of the game some are written in "Scrabble" form. Most letters are in regard to commercial suggestions which for the most part have been rejected, and requests for replacing missing blocks, lost on beaches or eaten by dogs who like the chemical coating.

Although Butts outlaws slang and foreign words in playing "Scrabble", as well as obsolete terms, he accepts musical scale notes and letters of the Greek alphabet. He considers an "unabridged" dictionary the "final authority" in the game. Convinced that his game should not be taken "too seriously," he said, "I play 'Scrabble' for fun."

In the field of architecture, Butts, who is still with the Holden firm, is the designer of the $6,500,000 Charles W. Berry housing project on Staten Island, New York City. His article "Pre-planning Low Cost Housing Projects to Meet Economic Requirements" (*American Architect,* March 1933) is a mathematical study of housing costs and rent. In this he states that "the dominant factor determining the rent of low cost housing is the rate of interest to be paid on the investment. . . ." He includes a rent estimating chart based on capital charges plus taxes and total cost per room.

Butts is described by Fern Marja as "professorial-looking . . . friendly, diffident, bespectacled, with bright blue eyes and an unexpectedly boyish laugh." His hair is brown, and he stands five feet seven inches tall and weighs 155 pounds. He is a Republican and his church affiliation is Protestant.

The architect married Nina Ostrander on October 3, 1925, a biological technician and teacher. The couple still enjoys playing "Scrabble" and Butts explains, "Nina knows more words and spells better than I, but my architectural training helps me to plan better." Once, while playing the game with his brother, Alfred produced the word "zinc" which Allison Butts made into "dezinc". Upon challenging the word, Alfred discovered it in the Merriam-Webster dictionary: it had been put there on the authority of Professor Allison Butts.

Aside from playing "Scrabble", Alfred Butts enjoys collecting stamps and old cigarette cards, cutting and making jigsaw puzzles, and drawing. Six prints of his drawings of New York scenes are in the Metropolitan Museum of Art.

References

Life 35:101+ D 14 '53
Look 17:50+ D 29 '53 pors
N Y Post Mag p2 Ja 17 '54 por
Time 62:17 Jl 20 '53
Who's Who in American Art, 1940-41

CAMERON, CHARLES S(HERWOOD)
June 22, 1908 Organization executive; physician

Address: b. c/o American Cancer Society, Inc., 47 Beaver St., New York 4; h. 44 Addison Ave., Rutherford, N.J.

Following the announcement of the American Cancer Society on June 21, 1954 that cigarette smokers from fifty to seventy years of age have a higher death rate than non-smokers, Dr. Charles S. Cameron, medical and scientific director of the society, said: "I do believe we'll see a change in smoking habits among doctors and some change in the smoking habits of the American people within a year." The report, made by the American Cancer Society (ACS), on a study in nine states during the past two and a half years, was presented to the American Medical Association at its annual convention, held in San Francisco.

The study was conducted by 22,000 trained volunteers who interviewed 187,766 men between fifty and seventy years of age (both smokers and non-smokers), and was directed by Dr. E. Cuyler Hammond with his associate, Dr. Daniel Horn. The researchers agreed that the study was "so conclusive" that the big problem now is to find out the agent in cigarettes that accounts for the higher death rate (cigar and pipe smoking did not have a significant effect on the death rate). However, Dr. Cameron differed with his colleagues who were convinced that heavy smoking "causes" cancer. It is possible, he said, that glandular disturbances may cause or predispose to cancer (New York *Times,* June 23, 1954).

Since he was appointed medical and scientific director of the ACS in 1948, Dr. Cameron has been one of the leaders in the fight against the disease which fills one out of every fourteen general hospital beds in the United States. He has said that "while it is possible today to cure half of all cases of cancer, we are actually curing only one-half of that half" and attributed this to failure to detect the disease in time (New York *Times,* October 3, 1953).

Dr. Cameron has been clinical assistant surgeon at the Memorial Hospital in New York City since 1947, and clinical assistant visiting surgeon at the James Ewing Hospital, since 1950. He became special consultant to the cancer control grants section of the National Cancer Institute of the United States Public Health Service in 1948.

Charles Sherwood Cameron was born in Philadelphia, Pennsylvania, on June 22, 1908, the son of Charles Sherwood and Ella (Baker) Cameron. After receiving the A.B. degree from the University of Pennsylvania in 1931, he entered Hahnemann Medical College, Philadelphia, which awarded him the M.D. degree in 1935. He interned for the next two years at the Philadelphia General Hospital and then served there as surgical resident in 1937 and 1938.

Awarded a Rockefeller fellowship in cancer surgery, Dr. Cameron undertook postgraduate studies at the Memorial Hospital in New York City from 1938 to 1942. He came under the influence of several of the nation's outstanding scientists, including the late Dr. James Ewing. Dr. Cameron recalls Dr. Ewing's statement that "in terms of their behavior and their structure, there were more kinds of cancer than there were of other diseases combined" (*U.S. News & World Report,* November 6, 1953).

During service with the U.S. Navy Medical Corps from 1942 to 1946, Dr. Cameron continued his cancer research. He was chief of the tumor service during 1945 and 1946 at Brooklyn Naval Hospital in New York. He contributed an article to the *Journal of the American Medical Association* (April 28, 1945) on the "Anastomosis of Vas Deferens," and reported that "the male sterilization process can be reversed by a second operation." In the *United States Naval Medical Bulletin* (July 1946), he described cancer in the naval service.

Following his discharge from the Navy with the rank of commander in 1946, Dr. Cameron became assistant medical and scientific director of the American Cancer Society. Later in 1946 he was made professional service director of the society. He served as acting director from November 1947 to March 1948, when he was advanced to the offices of medical and scientific director, and of vice-president.

The physician established the ACS clinical fellowship program in 1948, which annually provides more than one hundred fellowships for one-year training in cancer diagnosis and treatment. He later instigated a grant-in-aid program to promote projects in cancer control, and supported a three-year study by the statistical department in tumor classification, which is reported in the *Manual of Tumor Nomenclature and Coding.*

In his work with the ACS, Dr. Cameron is expanding the program of assistance to doctors in the fight against cancer. Clinical monographs written by cancer authorities are being provided to many practicing physicians, hospital resident doctors, and medical students. From the society's medical library, which has one of the most complete files of technical information on cancer in the world, monthly bibliographies are available to professional workers. A medical journal, *Cancer,* is issued every two months to over 5,000 physicians on the subscription list. Dr. Cameron is the editor of *CA- A Bulletin of Cancer Progress* which reaches about 50,000 doctors and is directed toward the interests of general practitioners.

The doctor has declared that "today the family physician plays the leading role in cancer control since it is he who has the opportunity to guide the patient to early diagnosis and prompt, aggressive treatment." He has also said: "If 100,000 family physicians would spend three and one-half hours a week, giving one-half hour examinations" each year to individuals over forty-five years of age, they "would cover 85 per cent of the people who do get cancer, and most of these cancers could be caught fairly early" (Washington *Post,* September 25, 1949).

In cooperation with the National Cancer Institute of the U.S. Public Health Service, Dr. Cameron has developed a program for doctors

DR. CHARLES S. CAMERON

which includes a series of training films on cancer diagnosis. He aided in promoting several conferences to make cancer prominent in the thinking of medical leaders. The first National Cancer Conference was held in Memphis, Tennessee, in 1949.

In answer to criticism by a number of doctors that the ACS public education campaign is creating a nation of "cancerophobes," Dr. Cameron stated that replies on questionnaires sent to 100 representative psychiatrists indicate "that the harmful effects of cancer publicity are not as serious as the more extreme critics would have us believe" (New York *Herald Tribune,* October 29, 1949).

In his article entitled "Progress in Cancer Research" (*American Journal of Nursing,* April 1950), Dr. Cameron wrote: "Not long ago cancer was a concern of only the surgeon, the radiologist, the pathologist and, of course, the patient. Now it calls forth the efforts of the internist, the botanist, the cytologist, the biologist, the nuclear physicist, the chemist, the virologist, geneticist, and endocrinologist."

As reported by *Newsweek* (April 24, 1950), Dr. Cameron has said that "95 per cent of all cases of skin cancer are curable if taken early enough. Eight or nine out of every ten breast cancers can be cured by prompt surgery. Three-fourths of the uterine cancer (greatest killer of women) can be cured while the disease is still confined to the cervix. . . ."

Concerning cigarette smoking and its possible relationship to lung cancer, Dr. Cameron advised that "if you are young and do not smoke, or if you are a beginning smoker without the ingrained habit, do not smoke." He himself smokes about six to eight cigarettes a day. However, after the results of the two-and-a-half-year survey were announced in June 1954, he has "tapered off," and is trying to smoke cigars or a pipe instead.

(Continued next page)

CAMERON, DR. CHARLES S.—*Continued*

Reporting in 1951 that only two states in the nation, New Hampshire and Connecticut, had enough cancer detection and treatment clinics to meet ACS recommendations, Dr. Cameron said that an additional 891 clinics were needed in the United States and that the society planned to spend $1,000,000 a year during the next five years in order to stimulate the opening of new cancer clinics (New York *Times,* March 28, 1951).

As one of the medical authorities answering the questions of U.S. Congressmen during a House Appropriations Committee hearing in 1953 on funds for the National Cancer Institute, Dr. Cameron advised that statistics of the Metropolitan Life Insurance Company showed "there has been an 11 per cent decline in the death rate from cancer . . . in a ten-year period" among women policyholders (*U.S. News & World Report,* May 29, 1953).

In answer to a question about whether the medical profession felt cancer was a communicable or a hereditary disease, Dr. Cameron told the U.S. House Interstate and Foreign Commerce Committee: "I think the widely held view is that human cancer is not communicable. There are evidences of certain heritage relationships for certain kinds of cancer."

Late in 1953, the ACS sponsored what Dr. Cameron calls "an unprecedented effort in post-graduate education" for doctors in a series of weekly "live" closed-circuit color telecasts reaching seven cities from the east coast to the Midwest. In 1954 the society launched a tour for science writers to major cancer research centers on the east and west coasts of the United States as a part of its public education program. "Everywhere scientists were working on chemotherapy," wrote Earl Ubell (New York *Herald Tribune,* March 28, 1954). "There are now in use half a dozen chemicals which temporarily kill cancers. . . ." Over station NBC-TV on April 25, 1954, Dr. Cameron conducted a half-hour television program which brought attention to cancer's seven danger signals and presented seven case histories of cured patients.

Dr. Cameron became president of the Commission on Cancer Control of the International Union Against Cancer in May 1953. He has written many articles in professional medical journals. He is a fellow of the American College of Surgeons, and is chairman of the program committee of the New York Cancer Society. His organization memberships include the New York Academy of Sciences, World Medical Association, American Medical Association, Inter-Society Cytology Council, Public Health Cancer Association of America, and James Ewing Society. His religious affiliation is Episcopalian.

Dr. Cameron is slim and of medium height, and has blue eyes and brown hair. His hobbies include playing the organ and gardening.

References

N Y Times p37 My 10 '53 por
Who's Who in America, 1954-55
Who's Who in New York, 1952

CAMROSE, WILLIAM EWERT BERRY, 1ST VISCOUNT June 23, 1879-June 15, 1954 British publisher; first worked on newspapers (Wales) and *Investor's Guardian* in London; started *Advertising World* in 1901; with brother (later Lord Kemsley) bought a publishing business (1905), the *Sunday Times* (1915), *Financial Times* (1915), numerous other publishing concerns and paper mills, the Amalgamated Press (1926), and *Daily Telegraph* (1928); acquired *Morning Post* in 1937; was made a baronet (1921), member of peerage (1929) and Viscount of Hackwood Park (1941). See *Current Biography,* (Oct.) 1941.

Obituary

N Y Times p31 Je 16 '54

CANDAU, MARCOLINO G(OMES) May 30, 1911- International health organization official; physician

Address: b. c/o World Health Organization, Palais des Nations, Geneva, Switzerland; h. Mies, Switzerland

Internationally known as an expert in public health education, Dr. Marcolino G. Candau of Brazil succeeded Dr. Brock Chisholm of Canada as director-general of the World Health Organization (WHO) in July 1953. Dr. Candau was elected to the post on May 11, 1953 for a five-year term by the World Health Assembly which was meeting in Geneva, Switzerland. His job is to supervise the work of thousands of doctors, nurses and sanitary engineers to help control diseases in many areas of the world. Any nation may receive help from WHO whether or not it is one of the eighty-four member countries represented in this largest specialized agency of the United Nations.

During 1953, although handicapped by a reduction in funds received under the U.N. technical assistance program, WHO helped seventy-four countries in over 330 health projects, and started active programs against twenty-seven major infections, including malaria, yaws, and tuberculosis (New York *Times,* April 4, 1954).

Dr. Candau began his work with WHO in April 1950 at Geneva, as director of the division of organization of public health services. He came to the United States in 1952 to serve as deputy director of the Pan-American Sanitary Bureau, the regional office of WHO for the Americas. Between 1934 and 1950, he occupied various city, state and national health posts in Brazil.

Marcolino Gomes Candau was born in Rio de Janeiro on May 30, 1911; he is of French-Portuguese ancestry. He earned his way through the School of Medicine of the State of Rio de Janeiro by tutoring his fellow students in anatomy, and received the M.D. degree in 1933. Although he engaged in private practice as a physician, his interest centered in public health. In 1936 he received a state scholarship which enabled him to take a special course in public health at the University of Brazil. From 1934 to 1938, he served in various city health departments, including São João Marcos, Sant' Ana de Japuiba, and Nova Iguassú.

At the age of twenty-seven, in 1938, the young doctor became assistant director-general of the Rio de Janeiro State Department of Health. Concurrently, he was appointed assistant professor of hygiene at the School of Medicine, Rio de Janeiro. He also did medical field work as a medical officer in the Northeast Malaria Service. When he received a Rockefeller Foundation fellowship in 1940, he came to the United States for a year's study at the School of Hygiene and Public Health, The Johns Hopkins University, Baltimore, Maryland. Returning to Brazil the following year, he became chief of the Niterói Health Center.

During World War II, Candau was assistant director of the medical service set up to care for mobilized workers who were producing rubber in the valley of the Amazon River. In the late 1940's, he was made director of a cooperative public health program of the Brazilian government and the Institute of Inter-American Affairs, known as the Serviço Especial de Saúde Pública (SESP). In addition, he was assistant professor of epidemiology in the Oswaldo Cruz Institute, a research center of the Brazilian government.

Dr. Candau was appointed director of the division of organization of public health services of WHO, at Geneva, Switzerland, in April 1950. His responsibility was to advance technical planning for the organization's member nations through its regional offices. A little more than a year later, in June 1951, he succeeded Dr. Martha Eliot of the United States, to the post of assistant director-general of WHO in charge of advisory services.

The physician became deputy director in 1952 of the Pan-American Sanitary Bureau in Washington, D.C. Before Dr. Candau left Geneva for his new post, Dr. Brock Chisholm, then director-general of WHO, declared: "Dr. Candau has been one of the main architects of the World Health Organization's policy and program in relation to advisory services to governments. . . . His wide practical experience in the improvement of economically underdeveloped areas has been of invaluable assistance to WHO and has been an essential factor in the development of WHO's program of technical assistance" (*United Nations Bulletin,* February 1, 1953).

While with the Pan-American Sanitary Bureau in 1952 and 1953, Dr. Candau coordinated and supervised WHO's public health programs throughout the Americas. As described by *Américas* (June 1954), he was "well liked by his colleagues and by his staff." His work brought him increased international recognition, particularly as an expert in public health education.

At the sixth World Health Assembly, held in May 1953, Dr. Candau was elected director-general of WHO by a vote of 47 to 16. He assumed the duties of office in July 1953. During his inaugural address, the doctor referred to the "almost staggering responsibility" connected with his new post, and advised that he

Wide World

DR. MARCOLINO G. CANDAU

was assuming it "with humility, but also with strength based on the certitude" that he was "free from commitments to any national, racial, or political group . . ." (*Américas,* June 1954). In becoming WHO's chief administrator, Dr. Candau also became *ex-officio* secretary of the annual World Health Assembly, of the executive board, which meets twice a year, and of all commissions, committees and conferences of the organization.

WHO works on the principle that the highest attainable standard of health is physical well-being; that this standard must be reached by all in order to achieve world peace; that unequal health standards in different countries is a common world danger; and that all people are entitled to the benefits of all medical, psychological, and related knowledge. In April 1948 WHO gained sufficient governmental ratifications to become a permanent international group.

Speaking before the General Assembly of the United Nations in October 1953, Dr. Candau called for closer cooperation between the U.N. and WHO. He said, according to the *United Nations Bulletin* (October 15, 1953), that "investment in health is the best way to develop the world's human and material resources" and that WHO's regional committee meetings in Asia and Africa had led to the "adoption of a series of imaginative yet sound blueprints to raise the low health conditions" in those areas.

In his message presented on U.N. Day in 1953, he emphasized that "modern methods of sanitation still have to be extended to vast areas where insect-borne and intestinal diseases continue to afflict large numbers of the people." He expressed his belief that nutritional science and new agricultural techniques need to be combined to improve diet standards throughout the world (*United Nations Bulletin,* November 1, 1953).

Describing the plans of WHO at the World Health Assembly held in Geneva in May 1954,

CANDAU, DR. MARCOLINO G.—*Cont.*

Dr. Candau declared: "Member countries can now depend more and more on WHO for assistance in improving their epidemiological services for the protection of their peoples against outbreaks of epidemics . . ." and "in improving their population and health statistics" (*United Nations Bulletin,* May 15, 1954). He added: "I hope that man will have the wisdom to decide, once and for all, that the only enemies worth fighting are ill-health, poverty and ignorance."

In an eighty-page study which was released on June 5, 1954, WHO reported that in campaigns against infections carried on in the post-war era with penicillin, nearly 16,000,000 persons have been examined and 4,000,000 people treated. An example of one of the results was given: in Haiti, 100,000 workers who were afflicted with yaws have returned to productive labor "with a consequent increase in national production of $5,000,000 a year" (New York *Times*).

Dr. Candau is the author of numerous studies in the field of public health. In his article "The World Needs Nurses!" (*Rotarian,* May 1954), the doctor wrote: "It will take decades even to approach a solution" of the shortage of nurses in the world, and "we can reach it only by international action." He added that "in Burma, India, Malaya, Mexico, Thailand, Turkey, and Israel short courses of from three to twelve months have been organized for local nurses with the assistance of WHO nursing instructors."

Organizations in which Dr. Candau holds membership include the American Public Health Association (vice-president 1949-1950), Inter-American Association of Sanitary Engineering, and Royal Society of Tropical Medicine and Hygiene. Armando S. Pires, writing of Dr. Candau in *Américas* (June 1954), states: "People who know him describe him as 'charming,' 'fired with an infectious enthusiasm,' 'decisive'."

Marcolino Gomes and Ena Candau, who were married in 1936, have two sons, Marcos and Nelson. Dr. Candau is about five feet eight inches tall and weighs around 200 pounds. The doctor is a capable canasta player, is a connoisseur of tasty dishes and wines, and likes to add to his knowledge of languages. He is said to be "an emotional, intensely human person" who "never forgets a name" (*Américas,* June 1954).

He and his wife have sometimes rented a summer home (summer in Brazil is in December and January) in Petrópolis, a mountain resort near Rio de Janeiro. At their home near Geneva, Dr. and Mrs. Candau frequently entertain large numbers of visiting dignitaries and journalists.

References

Américas 6:13+ Je '54 pors
N Y Times p6 My 12 '53 por
U N Bul 14:119 F 1 '53 por; 14:401 Je 1 '53 por
International Who's Who, 1953
World Biography (1954)

CANFIELD, CASS Apr. 26, 1897- Publisher

Address: b. c/o Harper & Brothers, 49 E. 33d St., New York 16; h. 152 E. 38th St., New York 16

"I am a publisher," Cass Canfield once told a meeting of the New York Library Association, "a hybrid creature, one part stargazer, one part gambler, one part businessman, one part midwife, and three parts optimist."

Most of Cass Canfield's life has been spent in an atmosphere of books. Having served as president of Harper & Brothers from 1931 to 1945, he has been chairman of the board of the publishing house since 1945. He is also a director of Bantam Books, Grosset & Dunlap (reprint firms) and the American Book Publishers Council. The publisher has held several government posts, on the Board of Economic Warfare, in the Foreign Economic Administration and in the Office of War Information.

Canfield stated that in this particular period of human development, librarians, educators, authors and publishers have had thrust upon them "a major role in keeping alive a thoughtful, intellectual approach to the world around us. The intellectual approach is an individual one; it is nurtured by creative thinking which depends in large degree on the reading of serious books" (*Library Journal,* June 1, 1951).

Cass Canfield was born in New York City on April 26, 1897 to Josephine (Houghteling) Canfield and Augustus Cass Canfield, an engineer. He has two sisters, Laura and Mary. His preparatory school was Groton, from which he was graduated in 1915, and his college Harvard, from which, after he had served in the First World War as a second lieutenant, he received his A.B. degree in 1919. At Harvard he was on the freshman football team and was third marshal of his class.

He spent a year in England at Oxford University, followed by a journey around the world, in the course of which young Canfield traversed southern China on foot. Later he pursued studies at the Sorbonne in Paris.

Beginning his career as a securities analyst for Harris, Forbes and Company, Canfield later worked for the New York *Evening Post,* first as a reporter and then in the business department. In 1923 and 1924 he aided in establishing the magazine *Foreign Affairs.*

Having attracted the attention of one of the New York *Evening Post's* advertising clients, Harper & Brothers, he went to work for the publishing firm in 1924 and was made manager of their London office. In that capacity he did much to enhance the Harper list of British authors, being responsible for the publication in the United States of such writers as E. M. Delafield, Philip Guedalla and J. B. Priestley.

Upon his return to the United States in 1927 Canfield became assistant book editor in the New York office of Harper's. His rise in the publishing world was rapid; in 1929 he was made executive vice-president, and in 1931 president.

Harper & Brothers was founded in 1817 by J. & J. Harper and has been intimately associated with the development of American and

English letters. The company has published the work of William Thackeray, Charles Dickens, George Eliot, Mark Twain, Herman Melville, and many other noted authors. *Harper's Magazine* has been an integral part of the firm since 1850. (From 1857 to 1916 it also published *Harper's Weekly*.)

During Canfield's years with the firm, Harper & Brothers has steadily added to its distinguished list of authors. He is credited with persuading John Gunther to write *Inside Europe*, and has himself edited numerous manuscripts despite the pressure of executive responsibilities.

Canfield's publishing career was interrupted in 1942 by service on the Board of Economic Warfare; he was made chief of its blockade and supply branch, dealing with the blockade of the Axis powers and with the sending of supplies overseas. He participated in the negotiations of a war trade agreement with Sweden, and was a special adviser to the American Ambassador in London.

After his fifteen months' leave of absence to permit the carrying out of these duties, Canfield returned to Harper & Brothers in August 1943. For a time he acted as special consultant to the Foreign Economic Administration in Washington. In 1945, the year of his election as chairman of the board of Harper's, he was granted another leave so that he might act as director of informational activities in France for the Office of War Information. He returned to his publishing post in June of that year.

In the publishing field, Canfield has been active in fostering constructive programs. He was instrumental, as president of the National Association of Book Publishers (a precursor of the American Book Publishers Council) from 1932 to 1934, in instituting the Cheney report, a highly significant survey of the American publishing industry. Upon his retirement from the presidency of the association, he announced the final draft of the industry's NRA code.

Canfield was chairman of the publishers' committee of the New York Book Fair in 1937. He has spoken and written frequently on problems of publishing. His professional credo is "to present to the public the work of new authors of talent; to publish books of cultural and historical value; to keep in print worthwhile books; to present in book form every point of view that has validity and is worthy of expression" (*Saturday Review of Literature*, April 17, 1948). However, he also stated: "The book publisher who takes himself too seriously as a custodian of culture is always a joke and sometimes a menace" (*Saturday Review*, June 21, 1952).

Believing that books should be published at low prices, Canfield is a director of two reprint firms, Grosset & Dunlap and Bantam Books. He wrote "in our time the two most important changes in publishing have been the development of book clubs and of reprints in the form of paper-covered books."

Pursuing the subject of paper-bound originals in the *Saturday Review*, June 21, 1952,

CASS CANFIELD

Canfield wrote: "Even though the sales of a first novel in cloth are sometimes less than 3,000 copies, the loss to the publisher is not disastrous. But in the paper publishing set-up, where a sale of at least 100,000 is necessary to cover costs, experimentation becomes a far more hazardous procedure."

The publisher was married to Jane Sage White, a sculptor, on May 27, 1938. He has two sons, Michael Temple and Cass Canfield, Jr., by a previous marriage to Katharine Emmet which ended in divorce in 1937. He has been described as "essentially modest in expression, both written and spoken." He is an Episcopalian and a Democrat. He is five feet eleven inches tall, weighs 175 pounds, has brown hair and blue eyes.

Canfield is a member of the executive committee and council of New York University and a director of Freedom House. His clubs are the Century Association and the Harvard Club of New York. For special publication he edited the letters of his great-grandfather, General Lewis Cass, American statesman and officer of the War of 1812. Canfield is proud of the fact that Harper & Brothers is largely owned by employees. Recently, he commented that with television "we must take into account the danger that fewer and fewer children will grow up in the atmosphere of books."

The New York *Herald Tribune* commented that Cass Canfield "combines a sharp interest in current affairs with a canny diagnostic sense and resourceful talent for dealing with problems of book publishing."

References

N Y Herald Tribune p11 Ja 23 '45; p37 N 16 '50 por
Sat R Lit 31:24 Ap 17 '48
Who's Who, 1953
Who's Who in America, 1952-53
Who's Who in New York, 1952

CANTOR, EDDIE Jan. 31, 1892- Comedian
Address: b. c/o National Broadcasting Co., Sunset and Vine, Hollywood 28, Calif. h. Beverly Hills, Calif.

NOTE: This biography supersedes the article which appeared in *Current Biography* in 1941.

When Eddie Cantor was stricken with a heart ailment in September 1952, thousands of persons took time out to send him letters, telegrams and cards saying "Get well, Eddie." This is one example of how the banjo-eyed entertainer has held the affection of the public over a period of forty years.

First winning fame on the stage, the comedian has successively won new listening and viewing audiences in motion pictures, radio, and television. He launched his television career in 1950 as the star of the *Colgate Comedy Hour*, a Sunday night program on the National Broadcasting Company network. Cantor's spectacular stage successes included *The Ziegfeld Follies*, (1917-1919), *Kid Boots* and *Whoopee*. He first achieved radio popularity in 1931.

He has also starred in numerous motion pictures. In 1953 Warner Brothers made a film, *The Eddie Cantor Story*, which portrayed his colorful career. The comedian has won numerous awards for his humanitarian services and his "never-ending charity to those in need." He has made hundreds of appearances at benefits, has aided the U.S. Treasury bond drives, the Red Cross Blood Donor campaign, and has given countless performances before soldiers at the battlefronts and in hospitals. He raised $60,000,000 for the Bonds-for-Israel drive.

On June 22, 1954 Cantor signed contracts with Ziv Television Programs Company to make thirty-nine half-hour television programs on film, and a like number of recorded radio programs, for seven years. He is one of the first major comedians active in television to decide to by-pass a network in favor of distributing his filmed programs directly to sponsors on individual stations (New York *Times*, June 23, 1954).

Cantor was born Edward Israel Iskowitz on Eldridge Street on the lower East Side of New York City on January 31, 1892. By the age of two he was an orphan, his mother, Minnie, and father Michael Iskowitz, a poor violinist, having died within a year of each other, and the boy's grandmother, Esther, took charge of him.

Although the domestic employment agency his grandmother managed brought her very little remuneration it became for young Eddie excellent source material. He sang and clowned his way on street corners for pennies, including in his repertoire imitations of the girls who applied for jobs at his grandmother's agency. At twelve, Eddie was sent to a Y.M.H.A. summer camp for orphaned boys and at the entertainments was applauded for his mimicry and impersonations. He never finished grade school, tried job after job but was fired for being too comical, and then in 1908, persuaded by his childhood sweetheart, Ida Tobias, he tried his talents at Miner's Bowery Theater Amateur Night. He won the $5 prize, and, beginning his career as Edward Cantor, he was hired a week after his $5 triumph for $15 a week in a downtown burlesque house. Cantor went on tour with its show *The Indian Maidens*, which closed abruptly, leaving him stranded.

In quick succession he obtained these jobs—as a singing waiter at a Coney Island saloon (where the pianist was Jimmy Durante), as an actor playing the Zukor-Loew vaudeville circuit, after which he was hired by the vaudeville team, Bedini and Arthur. For their juggling routine Arthur appeared in blackface, and it was at his insistence that Cantor first "blacked up" with burnt cork. Cantor was engaged by Gus Edwards in 1912 to play a blackface butler in the *Kid Kabaret* revue. Following that, he fulfilled a London engagement in Charlot's Revue, again in the blackface that had captured the fancy of audiences.

With money in his pockets, Cantor proposed to Ida Tobias, "the belle of Henry Street," and they were married on June 9, 1914. She has continued to be the inspiration of his life. When given a small part in a musical play, *Canary Cottage*, Cantor built up the bit with consent of producer Oliver Morosco into a big role and scored a success.

The famous producer Florenz Ziegfeld sought Cantor's services as a comedian. In 1916, under Ziegfeld's exclusive management, Cantor appeared in the *Midnight Frolic* on Gotham's New Amsterdam Roof and won immediate acclaim. Cantor's triumphs under the Ziegfeld aegis continued for three successive years in the *Follies* (1917-1918-1919). Billed as the "Apostle of Pep" in the 1919 edition (considered the greatest of them all) Cantor lived up to the description. One reviewer observed, "Eddie Cantor still gallops all over the stage, sings some comedy numbers in the well-known Cantoresque manner and scores a smashing hit."

At the time Cantor worked almost entirely in blackface and wrote his own humorous lyrics, often on timely topics. With America's entrance into World War I, Cantor devoted much time, too, to selling Liberty bonds and entertaining soldiers.

The comedian appeared in George Lemaire's *Broadway Brevities* and then under the Schubert banner in *The Midnight Rounders* (1921). One of Cantor's greatest musical comedy successes was in *Kid Boots*, which opened at the Earl Carroll Theater in 1923. Three years later he was called to Hollywood to star in the cinema version of the hit show. The second of his great personal triumphs was in the Ziegfeld production, *Whoopee* (1928) (a musical comedy version of Owen Davis' farce, *The Nervous Wreck*) which ran for 223 performances.

The stock market crash of 1929 deprived Eddie Cantor of all his amassed earnings of $2,000,000 invested in stocks. Cantor wrote of this experience in a humorous book entitled *Caught Short!* (Simon & Schuster, 1929), the popularity of which helped him recoup his losses. *Gotham Life* called it "A book you will enjoy, a book you will chuckle over, a book that you simply must have."

Cantor's autobiography *My Life Is In Your Hands* (written with David Freedman) was serialized in the *Saturday Evening Post* and published in book form by Harper (1928). With Freedman, Cantor wrote *Yoo-hoo, Prosperity! The Eddie Cantor Five-Year Plan* (Simon & Schuster, 1931); *Your Next President!* (Smith, 1932); *Ziegfeld, the Great Glorifier* (King, 1934). Cantor wrote a paper-back book, *Since Ma Is Playing Mah Jong* (Witmark, 1928) and *Between the Acts* (Simon & Schuster, 1930).

Cantor's first radio appearances in 1931 were as guest on the Rudy Vallee Show and star for one performance on the Chase and Sanborn Show. His own weekly series on Sunday nights over Station WEAF followed and won acclaim for Cantor's successful transition from the stage to radio. Cantor brought from the footlights an innovation at that time for radio—a live audience. For an hour before each broadcast he held a dress rehearsal for the studio audience. The jokes that the preview audience liked were left in the script, and the rest deleted. Cantor believed that a few hundred people in the audience could make the show better for the vast invisible audience. He also discovered such new talent as Deanna Durbin, Bobby Breen, and Dinah Shore. Harry Einstein, who was Parky Karkas on Cantor's weekly series, became one of radio's foremost stooge characters.

By 1936 Cantor was the highest paid star on radio, but in 1939 he was out of a job. A speech which he made at the New York World's Fair attacking certain public figures as fascists caused him to be labeled a controversial figure. "Nobody in radio would touch me," said Cantor, "until my good friend, Jack Benny, used his influence to get me back on the air." With America's entrance into World War II, Cantor's radio career resumed as star of NBC's *Time To Smile.*

Cantor also made a succession of motion pictures that included *Palmy Days* (1931), *The Kid From Spain* (1932), *Roman Scandals* (1933), *Strike Me Pink* (1936), *Ali Baba Goes To Town* (1937), and *Forty Little Mothers* (1940).

After an absence of twelve years from the Broadway stage, Cantor returned in 1941 to star in *Banjo Eyes,* a musical comedy version of the popular stage play *Three Men On A Horse.* The role Cantor played as Erwin, a modest greeting card writer who could pick racetrack winners, was judged a particularly happy one for him.

Critic David Burnham in *The Commonweal,* January 9, 1942 said of Cantor's acting in *Banjo Eyes.* "Here is a nimble, versatile, expert comedian who depends not at all upon his audience's sentimental memories. The radio has tended to preserve the 'Margie' Eddie, but the movies have developed an Eddie who can delight the eye with significant pantomime. Definitely, this is a comic with a frantic, impish style entirely his own."

Songs that Cantor helped to popularize—traditional with him when he does his numbers—include "If You Knew Susie," "Dinah," "Making Whoopee," "Ma, He's Making Eyes at Me." "Toot-Toot-Tootsie," and "Ain't She Sweet?"

EDDIE CANTOR

Cantor's television debut occurred in September, 1950 on the *Colgate Comedy Hour,* NBC-TV, Sunday nights. "I didn't jump into TV," remarked Cantor. "I waited until 1950, the year 5,000,000 more television sets were sold . . . after all, Cantor likes to play to full houses." Of Cantor's initial video appearance, *Cue* reported, "No musical comedy seen on television has a more violent pace. . . . He (Cantor) did everything that was expected of him—rolling his eyes, clapping his hands, power-housing the skits and winding up with a black-face reprise of a few of the songs he's been identified with through the years. . . . No surprises, but no disappointments."

Jack Gould of the New York *Times* praising the program called it "a sort of Cavalcade of Cantor . . . a lesson in pure songs salesmanship and personality. . . ." A dissenting vote was cast by critic John Crosby, who thought Cantor dwelt too extensively on "the glories of his own past." In a later week the reviewer wrote, "I'm happy to report that Mr. Cantor on subsequent shows has thrown away his memories for the time being and proved what a redoubtable entertainer he can be. . . ."

New in the Cantor program was his vignette characterization of Maxie the Taxi, which he has continued as a regular feature on the *Comedy Hour.* Cantor appears on one show a month. He has rotated with such entertainers as Dean Martin and Jerry Lewis, Fred Allen, Bobby Clark, Donald O'Connor, Jimmy Durante, and others. He thus avoids the grueling test of a weekly series, has two weeks rehearsal instead of one, and "fewer pressure headaches" (*Time,* September 25, 1950).

Discussing his views on an industry-wide code of censorship for TV, Cantor said that the network and the sponsor should supervise performers instead of calling in someone to set up rules. "Censorship will not stop with just deleting a blue joke," he said, "it will also

CANTOR, EDDIE—*Continued*

become political" (New York *World-Telegram and Sun,* January 12, 1952).

Cantor also does a one-man stage show, *Forty Years in Show Business,* touching on many aspects of his career in the theatre, and in 1949 and 1950 gave single performances of it before capacity audiences in Carnegie Hall, New York City. Songs, anecdotes and tales about the parade of celebrities in his life feature the show, about which it has been said, "His (Cantor's) self-assurance, stage presence and timing, combined with humility are virtues that should be studied profitably by neophytes of show business."

The sixty-year old star suffered a heart attack in 1952 which curtailed his activities for some weeks. Upon recovery, Cantor resumed his work on the *Comedy Hour,* his recordings of a disc jockey type of radio program for NBC, and his other activities. *The Eddie Cantor Story,* Cantor's film biography, produced by Warner Bros., was released in 1953 to theatres and was well received. Seventeen of the Cantor song hits were pre-recorded and his records "dubbed in," while Keefe Brasselle, twenty-seven-year old star of the picture, mouthed the words as Larry Parks had done when playing Al Jolson in *The Jolson Story.*

Outside of his career commitments, Cantor always finds time for philanthropies. He was credited by President Franklin D. Roosevelt with having coined the phrase *March of Dimes,* and each year he has participated in the appeal to raise funds to combat infantile paralysis. The United Jewish Appeal and the boys' camp where he had spent his early summers are charities to which Eddie Cantor is deeply devoted. In the innumerable benefits in which he has performed, he has also raised money for a Negro Catholic church, a medical clinic, and a host of other philanthropies.

Cantor is the recipient of the New York University Award, Temple University Award, War Veterans Award, Williamsburg Settlement Gold Medal Award, Michael Award, and on January 29, 1952 was cited by the Mayor of the City of New York for his service to humanitarian causes.

On Cantor's sixtieth birthday, January 31, 1952, 1800 persons filled the Hotel Commodore ballroom in tribute to the comedian and in recognition of his activities in behalf of the State of Israel. Vice-President Alben W. Barkley, in behalf of the Israel bond drive, presented to Cantor a gold relief plaque of a map of Israel and said that Cantor's life "has been a noble testament of devotion and self-sacrifice for the Jewish people and all mankind."

Cantor is five feet seven inches tall and weighs about 140 pounds. He has black hair and staring brown eyes, his most prominent feature, which accounted for his being nicknamed "Banjo-Eyes." He has been described at sixty as looking like forty and acting like twenty. "The only thing that dates Eddie is his remarkable fund of personal anecdotes which cover forty-two years in show business," observed Howard McClay of the Los Angeles *Daily News.*

Eddie and Ida Cantor are the parents of five daughters—Marjorie, Natalie, Edna, Marilyn, and Janet. Like their mother, the bevy of daughters is widely known to radio and video audiences because of Cantor's frequent humorous references on his programs to his family life. The comedian, whose hobbies are collecting old records and reading, has said of his career of dispelling gloom, "Laughter is the world's oxygen tank."

Eddie Cantor occasionally writes articles for national magazines. In December 1951 he wrote one entitled "God Help Me" in the *Ladies' Home Journal*: "In these days of suffering and confusion, the whole universe is praying, and it must keep God pretty busy. Wouldn't it be fine if we helped Him? . . . There is a tendency today to feel that our efforts are inconsequential in shaping the destiny of the world . . . [but] think of the potentialities of a world praying, in humility and sincerity, 'God, let me help You, instead of 'God help me'."

The secret of real security, Cantor believes, is the power of prayer. In an article entitled "Greater Than The H-Bomb" (*Reader's Digest,* September, 1953) he wrote: "I'm convinced my early battle for life was won by Grandma Esther and her only weapon against poverty: prayer. . . . The overwhelming force of a nation united in prayer would result in a security that no man-made weapon could destroy."

In an article in the *Saturday Evening Post,* October 27, 1951 "How I Beg For Money" Cantor told how "one small man with a rather small voice could wheedle, cajole, serenade and joke the American people out of $250,000,000 in cash." "Raising money for other people has taught me how to live," Cantor said.

"I have learned," Cantor wrote, "that service is the rent we pay for our room on earth, and I try to be a good tenant. I have learned that he who believes that charity begins at home is right, but he's wrong if it ends there . . . in all my years of association with philanthropy I never knew anyone who had a breakdown from overwork for charity and never knew a man who went bankrupt because of what he gave . . . I love a dollar. But nowadays I spend one week out of four in hard travel from one end of the country to the other working for free for other people".

The Veterans of Foreign Wars on August 4, 1954 named Eddie Cantor as the winner of its Al Jolson Award, given annually to the entertainer contributing most to the morale of service men at home and abroad.

References (see also references listed in 1941 biographical sketch)

Coronet 30:72 O '51
N Y Journal Amer 4-P My 25 '52
Read Digest 59:13 O '51; 63:7 S '53
Sat Eve Post 224:32 O 27 '51
This Week p4 Ja 31 '54
Motion Picture and Television Almanac, 1952-53
Who's Who, 1952
Who's Who in America, 1952-53
Who's Who in Jewry 1938-1939
Who's Who in the Theatre (1952)

CARDON, P(HILIP) V(INCENT) Apr. 25, 1889- United Nations official; agronomist

Address: b. c/o Food and Agriculture Organization of the United Nations, Viale delle Terme di Caracalla, Rome, Italy; h. 1730 Crestwood Drive, N.W., Washington 11, D.C.

At the seventh session of the United Nations Food and Agriculture Organization held in Rome in December 1953, P.V. Cardon was elected director-general for a two-year term. The American agriculturist had been suggested by United States Secretary of Agriculture Ezra Taft Benson as a possible successor to Norris E. Dodd. For many years associated with the U.S. Department of Agriculture, Cardon has frequently been a delegate to international agricultural meetings, and has, wrote the Washington *Post*, "the requisite research and technical qualifications in good measure."

The birthplace of Philip Vincent Cardon was Logan, Utah, and the date of his birth, April 25, 1889. He was one of seven sons born to Thomas Barthelmy and Lucy (Smith) Cardon, who also had four daughters. His father, of French descent, was born in the Italian Piedmont and in 1854 came to the United States where he served with the Union army during the Civil War, and later distinguished himself in business and agriculture. Also in 1854 his mother emigrated from England to the United States, where, aged slightly more than a hundred years, she died in 1952.

Reared in Utah—at Logan and Cache Valley ("a mountain valley in which early fur trappers 'cached' their furs"), Philip attended secondary school in Logan and was graduated in 1903 with highest honors. He attended Brigham Young College for a year. He entered Utah State Agricultural College, and received the Bachelor of Science degree in 1909.

Besides being on the honor roll, Cardon played baseball and football, edited the college paper for two years, participated in dramatic activities, and did farm and ranch work. His graduate studies were done at the University of California (Berkeley), which awarded him a Master of Science degree in 1933.

In 1909 Cardon joined the staff of the Utah Agricultural Experiment Station in Nephi. Shortly thereafter he was named a special agent of the bureau of plant industry, and was attached to the Nephi station of the U.S. Department of Agriculture. Subsequently he became scientific assistant in agronomy, and later, assistant agronomist to the Nephi station, of which he was also superintendent from 1910 to 1914.

At Nephi, wrote the *Journal of the American Society of Agronomy* (December 1948), Cardon's "early studies . . . on the relationship of summer fallow tillage to moisture penetration and retention by the soil broke a pioneer trail." From 1914 to 1918, Cardon studied cotton in the south for the USDA, and from 1918 to 1920, wheat in Montana.

For the next two years Cardon devoted himself to academic pursuits, first as professor of agronomy at the Montana State College and its experiment station in Bozeman (1920 to 1921), and then as director of the southern branch of the Utah State Agricultural College in Cedar City (1921 to 1922). From 1922 to 1925 he was the editor of the *Utah Farmer*. Establishing himself in Logan again in 1925, Cardon served as farm economist with the Utah State Agricultural Experiment Station until he was named its director in 1928, a post he held for five years.

P. V. CARDON

Appointed regional director for subsistence homesteads by the U.S. Department of the Interior, Cardon supervised this work in 1933. He returned to the Department of Agriculture the following year as regional director for the southwestern states of the land policy section of the Agricultural Adjustment Administration. Cardon was sent to Washington in 1935 to act as principal agronomist in charge of the forage crops and diseases division of the USDA's bureau of plant industry and in 1939 he became assistant chief of this bureau.

The forage crops work was reported in the *Journal of the American Society of Agronomy* (December 1948). Cardon "organized the cooperative forage improvement program throughout the United States, including the Regional Pasture Laboratory at State College, Pennsylvania, and the Regional Soybean Laboratory at Urbana, Illinois." He also helped to organize the Regional Salinity Laboratory at Riverside, California.

Cardon was next associated with the Agricultural Research Administration of the USDA as assistant administrator (1942 to 1945) and as research administrator (1945 to 1946). He went back to the bureau of plant industry as special assistant to its chief in 1946, but returned to his work with the Agricultural Research Administration in 1948.

In 1952 he became director of the graduate school of the USDA. This graduate faculty,

Cardon wrote in the March 13, 1953 issue of *Science*, had been founded by the department in 1921 to provide advanced study opportunities for its young scientists under the tutelage of the department's officials. He pointed out that the school now has an undergraduate program as well, and although the school offers credits for its courses, it does not grant any degrees.

Put forward by Secretary of Agriculture Benson as a candidate for the director-generalship of the U.N. Food and Agriculture Organization in September 1953, P. V. Cardon was elected to that office in December 1953. Despite what Edmund Stevens of the *Christian Science Monitor* (December 8, 1953) characterized as "an undercurrent of chafing irritation, especially among small nation delegations, at what they consider the highhanded American domination of the conference and organization," Cardon was elected by sixty-seven of the seventy-one member nations at the seventh world conference of the FAO in Rome. He succeeded Norris E. Dodd for a two-year term in the $18,000-a-year post.

Established at Quebec on October 16, 1945, the FAO is dedicated to improving nutrition and living standards, to implementing the efficiency of production and distribution of all food and agricultural products, and to aiding the expansion of the world's economy. To do so, reports the *Pocket Almanac*, "it promotes the global exchange of new types of plants; spreads advanced techniques; . . . combats epidemics of animal diseases; . . . and provides technical assistance" in nutrition, erosion, reforestation, irrigation, and fertilization.

At the seventh FAO session, three new nations—Libya, Iran and Yemen—were admitted to membership, the FAO's council was increased from eighteen to twenty-four member countries, and the budget was raised from $5,250,000 to $6,000,000. A major conclusion of discussions at the session was that member nations should plan their agricultural production so that too great surpluses or shortages in one area would be avoided.

Prior to the establishment of the FAO, Cardon had been a member of the technical secretariat of the International Conference on Food and Agriculture held in 1943 at Hot Springs, Virginia, at which he was also secretary of the committee on agricultural production. At the 1945 Quebec meeting of the United Nations Food and Agriculture Conference, where the FAO was founded, he was on the American delegation, and served as vice-chairman of the commission on agriculture. In 1946 he was consultant to a special meeting of officials of the FAO held in London.

Sent in 1947 as a delegate to the third conference of the FAO in Geneva, Cardon was elected chairman of the standing advisory committee on agriculture, of which he subsequently became permanent chairman.

At the fourth and fifth conferences of the FAO, held at Washington, D.C. in 1948 and 1949, Cardon was a member of the American delegation. At the sixth, convoked in Rome in 1951, he was again an American delegate and was elected a member of the co-ordinating committee and chairman of the working party on the program of work and associated long-term problems.

Other international meetings to which Cardon has been a delegate are the Fourth International Grassland Congress (1937) in Great Britain (he was chairman of the American delegation, and had spent the five previous months studying grassland practices in fifteen European countries), and the Sixth International Grassland Congress (1952) at Pennsylvania State College (he was president of the congress). He was an American delegate to the Third Inter-American Conference on Agriculture, held in Caracas, Venezuela, in 1945, and an alternate delegate to the fourth, held in Montevideo in 1950.

In 1945 and 1946 he was a member of the Mexico-United States Agricultural Commission. Chairman of the Ninth Congress of the International Seed Testing Association in 1950 at Washington, D.C., Cardon was also that year chairman of the section on agriculture and forestry of the Alaskan Scientific Conference (also held in Washington).

For the Department of Agriculture, Cardon has served on a committee which surveyed the United States to determine the possibilities of the industrial use of farm products. For several years he was also a member of the department's committee on training in land-grant colleges. In a liaison capacity, Cardon represented the USDA on the Atomic Energy Commission. In 1948 he was given the USDA's Distinguished Service Award "for outstanding service and exceptional leadership in the advancement of agricultural science."

Utah State Agricultural College awarded Cardon an honorary LL.D. degree in 1948, and Montana State College awarded him an honorary Sc.D. degree in 1953. He is a fellow of the American Association for the Advancement of Science and of the American Society of Agronomy. His alumni fraternities are Phi Kappa Phi, Alpha Zeta, and Pi Kappa Alpha. He is a member of the American Farm Economics Association and the Washington Botanical Society. He also holds membership in the Rotary Club. Cardon's religious affiliation is with the Church of Jesus Christ of Latter-day Saints (Mormon).

Articles by Cardon have appeared in the Utah State bulletins, U.S. Department of Agriculture bulletins, Montana State bulletins, *American Miller, National Wool Grower, Market Growers' Journal, Breeder's Gazette, Farm and Fireside, Agricultural Leaders Digest, Better Crops,* the *Journal of Farm Economics,* and the *Journal of the American Society of Agronomy.* He has also contributed to *Successful Farming, Agronomy Journal,* and the *Chemurgic Digest.* Cardon's speeches have been reprinted in the proceedings of a number of congresses and conferences.

By his marriage on September 17, 1913 to Leah Ivins, a former home economist, P. V.

CARDON, P. V.—*Continued*

Cardon is the father of two daughters, Lucy Elizabeth (Mrs. Calvin L. Rampton) and Margaret Ivins (Mrs. Gerald Wessler), and a son, Philippe Vincent Cardon, Jr. The FAO director is five feet nine inches tall, weighs 185 pounds, and has brown eyes and brown hair. For reading he prefers either histories of the western United States or biographies. For recreation he enjoys painting and gardening (with special attention to growing azaleas).

References

Am Soc Agron J 40:1110+ D '48 por
Farm & Home Sci 9:4 S '48
N Y Herald Tribune p5 D 10 '53
N Y Times p15 S 29 '53
U N Bul 16:53 Ja 1 '54 por
American Men of Science (1949)
Who's Who in America, 1952-53
Who's Who in the South and Southwest (1952)

LESLIE CARON

CARON, LESLIE July 1, 1931- Ballet dancer; actress

Address: b. c/o Metro-Goldwyn-Mayer Studios, 10202 W. Washington Blvd., Culver City, Calif.

The French-American ballet dancer, Leslie Caron, whose elfin charm, straight bangs, turned-up nose and blue eyes have become familiar to American movie and theatre audiences, began her American career in 1951 when she appeared in *An American in Paris*, produced by Metro-Goldwyn-Mayer. The picture won seven Academy awards, and the young dancer's name was made. Prior to her Hollywood role she had made a sensational success in Paris with the *Ballet des Champs-Elysées*. She made her American stage debut in 1954 with Roland Petit's *Les Ballets de Paris*.

American movie goers have seen her in the motion picture *Lili*, a Metro-Goldwyn-Mayer production which has been playing at the 52nd Street Trans-Lux Theatre in New York City for a record run of over eighteen months. For her role of a ragamuffin orphan Miss Caron won an Academy award nomination in 1953. Her latest motion picture role is as Cinderella in MGM's *The Glass Slipper*. She received the English "Oscar" (British Film Academy) in March 1954 for her role in *Lili*.

Leslie Caron, born in Paris, July 1, 1931, is the daughter of a French chemist, Claude Caron, and an American-born mother, Margaret (Petit) Caron. Mrs. Caron, who was born in Topeka, Kansas, and trained in ballet at the Cornish School in Seattle, achieved success as a dancer in the 1920's, appearing in *What's in a Name, The Greenwich Village Follies, Pin Wheel Revue*, and *Sweet Little Devil*. After her marriage she made France her home, and Leslie's childhood was spent in the Paris suburb of Neuilly.

When she was eleven, Leslie began the study of ballet but during the Nazi occupation of Paris she and her brother Aimery were sent to live with their grandparents in Cannes, returning after the liberation. The girl was educated at the Convent of the Assumption and continued her study of ballet at the National Conservatory of France.

Leslie began her professional career at sixteen when she became a member of the Ballet des Champs-Elysées, an organization headed by Roland Petit, which had come into existence in 1945. Doing bit parts, Leslie attracted attention of the dancer-choreographer David Lichine, who selected her for the principal role in his ballet *La Rencontre*. Based upon the story of Oedipus and the Sphinx, the action of the ballet depicted the Sphinx, infuriated by Oedipus' ability to answer her riddle correctly, tumbling from the top of a trapeze and hanging head down for more than five minutes. The ballet was presented in April, 1948, with Leslie as the Sphinx, and the sixteen-year-old dancer, previously an unknown, made an immediate hit.

The actor-dancer, Gene Kelly, and his wife, Betsy Blair were in the audience one night. Impressed by the young dancer's ability, they went backstage after the performance to congratulate her, but Leslie had gone home. Nothing further came of the incident at that time; Leslie continued to work with the company, in Paris and on tour, her career interrupted for a period by the anemia from which she suffered. But when Gene Kelly returned to France in 1950 in search of a French leading lady for the film, *An American in Paris*, for which he had been engaged, he remembered Leslie. When he reached her he gave her a scene to study, and arranged for a screen test in which he played opposite her. The film was flown to Metro-Goldwyn-Mayer in Hollywood, where producer Arthur Freed and director Vincente Minnelli approved Gene's selection, and a cable, engaging Leslie, was dispatched. At three days notice,

CARON, LESLIE—*Continued*

the young dancer, accompanied by her mother, emplaned for the United States.

While waiting for the filming of *An American in Paris,* the studio executives, impressed as much by Leslie's personal charm and acting ability, as by her dancing, cast her in a straight role in a dramatic film, *The Man with a Cloak,* with Joseph Cotten and Barbara Stanwyck; the film was not released, however, until after *An American in Paris.*

Inspired by Gershwin's music of that name, *An American in Paris* included several other of Gershwin's compositions. It starred Gene Kelly, with Leslie Caron, Oscar Levant, Georges Guetary, and Nina Foch in the supporting cast. The film had its debut in 1951 and became the winner of seven Academy awards. Of Leslie's part in contributing to the success of the film, Thomas Wood in the New York *Herald Tribune* wrote: "Not the least spectacular aspect of *An American in Paris,* the lush, technicolor extravaganza that has been hailed in conservative circles as just about the most colossal musical ever produced, is the introduction of a little, twenty-year-old, fawn-faced French ballerina named Leslie Caron." The film concluded with a brilliant seventeen-minute ballet, danced by Gene and Leslie and a company of 120 which, according to the same critic, was "easily the most musical sequence ever staged for a motion picture." Other motion picture critics likewise hailed the discovery of Leslie, the reviews tending to emphasize the "piquant," "puckish," "elfin" quality of her personality.

On the strength of the success of her first film appearance, Leslie was signed to a long-term contract by MGM. In her next film, *Glory Alley,* Leslie, portraying an entertainer in a New Orleans night club, both acted and danced. *The Story of Three Loves* cast her in the part of a French governess, which Bosley Crowther of the New York *Times* referred to as a "talkative, priggish, thankless role," in making the point that her fifth film assignment, *Lili* was better suited to her because, "Miss Caron is a girl who flowers in all her delicate enchantment when she is given a role in which to dance."

In *Lili* Leslie played opposite Mel Ferrer, taking the part of a teen-age waif who gets a job with a French provincial carnival show. Otto L. Guernsey, Jr., in the New York *Herald Tribune,* referred to the film as "a piece of candy-colored sentiment," but said, "Whatever it is that Leslie Caron has got—whether it is limpid charm, sweetness or something else—it permeates *Lili.*"

In an interview given to the New York *Times* in March, 1953, Leslie, who was in New York to publicize the openings of both *The Story of Three Loves* (at the Music Hall) and *Lili* (at the Trans-Lux Fifty-second Street Theatre), picked *Lili* as her favorite role to date. The story, she said, "came straight to my heart. It has no glamour or beauty in the conventional sense but I never had a chance before to do a picture that causes both pity and laughter."

An American stage debut was made by Leslie at the Broadway Theatre in New York on January 19, 1954, when, through the courtesy of MGM, she appeared in *Les Ballets de Paris* with Roland Petit, with whom she first danced in Paris. Her vehicle on this occasion was a ballet called *Deuil en 24 Heures,* or *The Beautiful Widow,* arranged by Petit.

In the New York engagement, while finding little to commend in the offering as a whole, John Martin of the *Times* said of Leslie that, "even in an unbecoming hair-style she is as cute as a button and could easily steal a far better show than this one." Walter Terry in the *Herald Tribune* wrote, "Miss Caron does not have much to work with but she manages to be winsome." Of her dancing, the same critic said that she was "a pleasantly accomplished dancer," but "not yet a great one, either technically or stylistically."

Shortly after Leslie's arrival in America, her mother returned to France and Leslie was joined by her brother Aimery for whom she kept house while he studied chemistry at Palos Verdes College. During Leslie's second year in Hollywood, she met George Hormel II, heir to the meat-packing fortune, and they were married in Las Vegas, on September 23, 1951. On January 20, 1954 it was announced that George had entered suit for divorce. He was granted the divorce on March 31 in Los Angeles on testimony that Leslie preferred "the intense artistic life to life with him" (New York *Times,* April 1, 1954).

Leslie is five feet three-and-one-half inches in height and weighs 110 pounds; her eyes are blue and her hair is brown. She designs and makes many of her own dresses. Self-supporting since she was sixteen, she is quoted in an interview with Sidney Skolsky of the New York *Post* in 1952 as saying, "Everything I have, I have paid for myself." Anemia has continued to be something of a problem for her. In an interview with Marie Torre of the New York *World-Telegram* in 1953, Leslie stated, ". . . it is too strenuous for me to work in a ballet company, but I can dance in the movies. And I can act." One of her ambitions is to play the role of Bernard Shaw's St. Joan.

The petite dancer admits that she wears out more than two pairs of ballet slippers a week during rehearsals. For hobbies, she enjoys painting: "Pictures of people," she said, "not real people. People I invent." She also likes to cook. Her favorite color is black and her favorite Parisian designer is Christian Dior.

References

Mus Am 74:14 F 1 '54
N Y Herald Tribune p16 Ja 20 '54 por
N Y Post Mag p5 F 24 '52 por
N Y Times II p5 Mr 8 '53
N Y World-Telegram Mag p19 Mr 14 '53 por
Silver Screen 22:38 Ap '52 por
Washington (D.C.) Post p37 Mr 23 '54 por
Motion Picture and Television Almanac, 1953-54

CARPENTER, J(ULIUS) HENRY, REV. DR. Jan. 7, 1893-June 16, 1954 Clergyman; organization official; executive secretary Brooklyn division of the Protestant Council of the City of New York since its formation in 1944; was graduated from Colgate University (1917) and received a master's degree in religious education, Boston University (1924); was an instructor at New York University (1930-1936); was active in the Inter-Church World Movement in the 1920's; headed Tour Committee of the Cooperative League of the U.S. and led groups of Americans in the study of cooperatives in many foreign countries; toured the U.S. and China in the interest of United China Relief; was a member of the board of directors of the World Parliament of Religions; author of articles in religious journals; active in the cooperative movement and religious pacifism. See *Current Biography,* (Feb.) 1943.

Obituary

N Y Times p23 Je 18 '54

Hessler

GERTRUDE S. CARRAWAY

CARRAWAY, GERTRUDE S(PRAGUE) Aug. 6, 1896- Woman's organization official; editor; writer

Address: b. c/o 1776 D St., N.W., Washington 6, D.C.; h. 207 Broad St., New Bern, N.C.

When Gertrude S. Carraway was elected on April 23, 1953 to the office of president general of the Daughters of the American Revolution (D.A.R.), she became the first such officer from North Carolina, the first newspaper woman ever chosen, and the first in many years to be elected without an opposing ticket (New York *World-Telegram and Sun,* June 8, 1953). She succeeded Mrs. James B. Patton to this post.

As guest of honor at a reception of the D.A.R. Round Table of Greater New York on June 8, 1953, Miss Carraway said that "patriotic awareness and appreciation of American history can come through education" (New York *World-Telegram and Sun*). She declared that the program of the D.A.R. to spread interest in American history among young people would offer "thousands of prizes and good citizenship medals" in schools and colleges all over the United States.

The D.A.R., with a membership of 170,000, is composed of women descendants of those who "with unfailing loyalty rendered material aid to the cause of independence as a recognized patriot, as a soldier or sailor, or as a civil officer in one of the several colonies or states" (*Encyclopedia Americana*). Its objects are to perpetuate the memory of the spirit of the men and women who achieved American independence, to foster knowledge, freedom and patriotism, and to aid in securing for mankind the blessings of liberty. It has more than 2,500 chapters whose members aid in educational work among immigrants, and who establish scholarships for students of American history.

For more than two decades Miss Carraway has served the D.A.R. in other offices. Editor of its magazine since 1950, she was vice-president general of the national society from 1949 to 1950 and state regent of North Carolina from 1946 to 1949. She served as a member of the national resolutions committee for seven years, from 1945 to 1952. Previously, she was for two years vice-chairman of the building promotion committee, and for nine years vice-chairman of the press relations committee.

Gertrude Sprague Carraway was born in New Bern, North Carolina, on August 6, 1896, the daughter of John Robert Bennett and Louise (Elgie) Carraway. She traces her ancestry to the Stuart kings of Scotland and says her first American ancestors, Patrick and William Stuart, came from that country to Bladen County, North Carolina, in 1739. Her paternal grandfather was Major Daniel T. Carraway of the Confederate Army. Her brother is Brigadier General William E. Carraway of the United States Army.

Miss Carraway attended the public schools in New Bern. Her extracurricular activities in high school were basketball, debating, and editing the student publication. After graduating in 1912, she entered the Woman's College at the University of North Carolina, at Greensboro where she was active in the debating, literary and dramatic societies. She received her B.A. degree in 1915.

After college, she took home correspondence courses in journalism and attended two summer sessions at Columbia University. She had an opportunity during her summer postgraduate study at Columbia to substitute in the editorial offices of the New York *Times* for assistants who were on vacation. For four years, from 1915 to 1920, Miss Carraway taught English, French and history in Jacksonville, Reidsville, and Smithfield, North Carolina, and during World War I worked as a volunteer on the Exemption Board.

Her first full-time newspaper job was editing the Smithfield (North Carolina) *Observer* from

CARRAWAY, GERTRUDE S.—*Continued*
1920 to 1922. She also contributed to the Fairchild Publications, New York, the David C. Cook papers, Elgin, Illinois, and to newspapers in North Carolina and Virginia.

The New Bern *Sun-Journal* offered Miss Carraway a post as city editor in 1924, and she continued to serve also as correspondent for several North Carolina and Virginia dailies, and as a feature writer for New York and North Carolina papers and periodicals. For a pseudonym she used the name S. Carr. As Margaret Kernodle states in the Washington *Post*(February 1, 1953), Gertrude Carraway was "so good in finding news, and getting it printed . . . that she was asked by the North Carolina D.A.R. to be State publicity chairman before she was a member of the organization."

Gertrude Carraway surrendered her editorial post with the New Bern *Sun-Journal* in 1937 and became a free lance journalist. She contributed to the New York *Times,* the New York *Herald Tribune,* and the *Christian Science Monitor,* and wrote for trade journals and farm papers. In addition, she sold a number of her juvenile stories. During the late 1930's she served as manager of public relations, advertising and publicity for Caplon-Smith Company, Inc., in New Bern.

In World War II Miss Carraway was publicity director for the American Red Cross in Craven County, North Carolina. She was also state vice-chairman, women's section, of the war finance committee, organized under the United States Treasury Department to promote the sale of war savings bonds and stamps. She christened a Liberty ship and launched other vessels. Her publicity work for the North Carolina D.A.R. had earned her the post of national vice-chairman of the press relations committee.

Miss Carraway's interest in historical sites led her to become secretary of Tryon's palace commission in 1945, which supervised the restoration of the edifice built by colonial Governor William Tryon in New Bern in 1767, and called "the most beautiful building in all colonial America" (New York *Times,* April 21, 1951). The next year she became D.A.R. state regent of North Carolina, retaining this office until 1949. She was editor and publisher in 1948 of *Coastal Topics,* a summer publication of New Bern.

While serving as vice-president general, and as editor of the D.A.R. magazine, Miss Carraway succeeded in getting the publication on a profitable basis. "I put to use the same idea I used in state publications," she said; "we made our money from advertisements from individual states" (Washington *Post,* February 1, 1953).

Upon election to president general, Miss Carraway accepted the broad blue ribbon of office with the statement that the D.A.R. will endeavor "to make our citizenry and membership so strongly pro-America that our country will be able to withstand attacks from without . . . and subtle attacks from within" (Washington *Post,* April 25, 1953).

Among other national D.A.R. officials, Miss Carraway was received on April 24, 1953, at the White House by Mrs. Dwight D. Eisenhower, who had just become a member-at-large of the organization.

At its Sixty-second Congress which elected Miss Carraway to its highest office the D.A.R. adopted resolutions against Federal aid to education and health, reciprocal trade treaties, United Nations genocide and human rights pacts, or attempts through the United Nations or other media to bring about a world government. They declared the United States should have air power unsurpassed by any country in the world, approved the Bricker "treaty-limiting" amendment, and favored Congressional investigation of subversives.

Miss Carraway is the author of several historical booklets including *The Flying Marines, U.S. Marine Corps Air Station, Cherry Point, North Carolina* (1946), and *New Bern, Cradle of North Carolina* (1941) (with A. T. Dill, Jr.). Her three books are *Carolina Crusaders,* a story of the North Carolina Federation of Women's Clubs; *Crown of Life,* a history of the Episcopal Church in eastern North Carolina; and *Years of Light,* a chronicle of the St. John's Masonic Lodge, No. 2, A.F. & A.M., New Bern, North Carolina.

For her outstanding World War II service, Miss Carraway received twelve awards of merit, including those from the United States Treasury Department, the American Red Cross, the Elks, and the D.A.R. She is on the executive board of the North Carolina State Department of Archives and History and is a trustee of the University of North Carolina. Her organization memberships include the Order of the Crown, the National League of American Pen Women (Washington, D.C. branch), and Colonial Dames of America. Her church is Episcopalian.

Described as a "woman who likes clothes and knows how to wear them" by Margaret Kernodle (Washington *Post,* February 1953), Miss Carraway is five feet two inches tall and weighs 138 pounds. She has blonde hair and sparkling hazel eyes. The D.A.R. official enjoys travel and people, and says her recreations are "reading, radio, television, and drama." She affirms that "we could perform miracles if we could harness our nation's womanpower" (Washington *Post,* March 27, 1953).

References:

Washington (D.C.) Post p48 F 1 '53
Who's Who Among North American Authors (1939)
Who's Who in Journalism, 1928

CASTAGNETTA, GRACE (căs-tan' yĕ-ta)
June 10, 1912- Pianist; composer

Address: b. c/o Columbia Lecture Bureau, 113 W. 57th St., New York 19; h. 383 Union Ave., Wood-Ridge, N.J.

Since Grace Castagnetta played her first public concert at the age of seven she has given recitals throughout the United States, Canada, Europe and Scandinavia, and has appeared as piano soloist with the world's major symphony orchestras. She is also a composer, teacher and improviser, and she has arranged music for seven songbooks, six of them in collaboration with the late Dr. Hendrik Willem van Loon. The pianist frequently appears as a guest artist on radio and television concert programs, and she has recorded several albums.

Recognized as an accomplished exponent of the little understood art of improvisation, Miss Castagnetta has brought to concertgoers the exciting experience of witnessing musical creations based on themes suggested by her audiences. Describing her gifts for spontaneous musical utterance, the late Leonard Liebling, editor of the *Musical Courier,* wrote: "Here are no tricks—here are poetry and dramatic expressiveness musically revealed in the moment of their birth."

Grace Sharp Castagnetta was born in New York City on June 10, 1912. Her father, Francis Aloyius Castagnetta, is of Italian extraction, and her mother, Grace Lee Sharp, is of Scotch parentage. She began to play the piano by the time she was able to walk, making up tunes and repeating whatever music she heard. At the age of seven she received a scholarship from Dr. Nicholas Elsenheimer, and within the year gave her first full-length recital at Carnegie Chamber Music Hall.

Grace's family moved to Wood-Ridge, New Jersey, where she attended Rutherford High School and was a member of the debating society. In 1926 she was sent to Germany on a four-year scholarship for study at the Hochschule für Musik and was graduated *cum laude.* With the help of the widow of Hans von Bülow she was presented to the Berlin music public and made her debut at the historic Singakademie. The New York *Times* (September 28, 1928) told of the "sensational debut of the diminutive American pianist." A tour of leading German cities followed.

Returning to the United States, she won a scholarship for further study at the Curtis Institute of Music in Philadelphia in 1934. She found no easy path to success, however, for the economic depression prevailed, and instead of concertizing she toured the country as an accompanist in a vaudeville act. She feels that she learned more from this experience than from the Hochschule—more about music, and more about people. She recalls playing Bach and Brahms on tinny pianos, and keeping up her practicing in between four shows a day.

Joining the staff of the Columbia Broadcasting System in 1935, she "filled in" with piano music whenever a radio program was too short, or when mechanical difficulties prevented programs coming in from other cities. Her ability to improvise was of help as she played themes for such varied personalities as Alexander Woollcott, H. V. Kaltenborn, Raymond Gram Swing, Tony Wons, "The Mystery Chef" and the "Voice of Experience."

After playing a Bach-Brahms program over the Columbia network, Miss Castagnetta received a complimentary letter from the author, Dr. Hendrik Willem van Loon. Subsequently, she and van Loon collaborated on a series of songbooks published by Simon and Schuster: *The Songs We Sing* (1936); *Christmas Carols* (1937); *Folk Songs of Many Lands* (1938); *Songs America Sings* (1939); *Last of the Troubadours* (1939); *Life and Times of Johann Sebastian Bach* (1940); and also *Good Tidings* (American Artists, 1941).

GRACE CASTAGNETTA

Miss Castagnetta arranged a collection of Robin Hood ballads, with Anne Malcolmson (Houghton Mifflin, 1947). She has also recorded several albums of piano music for Timely, Musicraft and RCA Victor.

She made her debut in Town Hall in 1937 and soon earned a national reputation as a concert pianist. She introduced the custom of improvising on themes suggested by the audience (almost universal in Beethoven's time, but extinct in ours) at her Town Hall recital on April 28, 1942. Before deciding to do this, (according to Henry Simon, music critic on *PM*) she discussed the advisability of the procedure with musical friends. "There wasn't any question about her being able to do it," wrote Simon. "Most of us had heard her do it either at private homes or in out-of-town recitals and knew her extraordinary mastery of the ticklish art. The question was almost solely: Is it dignified enough for a Town Hall recital?"

"So Miss Castagnetta made herself familiar with the long and honorable history of improvisation. Bach did it; Mozart did it; Beethoven did it; Liszt did it; Why not, then, Castagnetta?"

Since her 1942 concert she has made improvisations on themes suggested by the audience a feature of her annual recital at Town Hall. Enthusiastic audiences attest to her skillful "pianism," her "fine musicianship," "imagination and deft technique."

Comments like the following are typical of those received from music critics: "Gifted with temperamental charm and a fabulous facility in improvising, Miss Castagnetta is an artist who does not have to rely on these qualities,

CASTAGNETTA, GRACE—*Continued*

for her approach to the standard repertoire is as vivid and alive as her own creative work. . . ." (*Musical America,* April 25, 1946).

The pianist admits that she has "improvised all her life." "My mother tells me I improvised before I was two, and I improvised publicly before I was four. The embarrassing thing about this is—I have no idea *how* to improvise! Thousands of letters come to me asking for how-counsels. I can't give them because I don't know. I know that the mechanics of improvising root in rhythm and a sure knowledge of harmony, but that does not explain how you get the top-line."

In an article, "Relax and Improvise," Miss Castagnetta wrote, "I have discussed this with psychologists and they seem to feel that what happens in improvisation is a complete taking-over of the sub-conscious, freed from all the plannings of the where-do-I-go-from here school of thought. . . . I know that I cannot plan an improvisation. The pattern takes over by itself, and I don't know what's going to come out before the listener knows it" (*Etude,* December, 1949).

"In this day of music at the turn of a dial," she believes, "enormous advantages will result from individual and active participation. In music as in other matters, one should stand captain of one's soul!" However, she thinks that children should not be started off at the keyboard too young. For the average child, seven is a good age to begin. "By all means," she advises, "let Johnny and Mary sit down and pick out tunes and fill in chords. All they like! But let them also understand that this is not improvising. Improvising must make sense, it must come out of form and discipline. Study and practice should supplement the improvising. The child should have the excitement of finding things out for himself."

Miss Castagnetta was a guest of President and Mrs. Franklin D. Roosevelt at the White House on the occasion when she was soloist with Hans Kindler's National Symphony Orchestra in Constitution Hall. She recalls that she occupied "an enormous room—the famous Lincoln Room—and dressing in such a setting filled one with a sense of overpowering awe and solemnity. On the way to the concert, riding in a big black limousine with a motorcycle escort, I was feeling like a princess, when all of a sudden I heard a yell and looked out of the window. I saw a dilapidated car and in it were two students I had known in Stockholm. They waved and gesticulated and howled 'Hey, Gracie!' And I waved back, etiquette or no etiquette. They trailed us all the way to Constitution Hall."

Shortly before World War II she toured the Scandinavian countries and gave recitals in Oslo, Copenhagen, Stockholm and Helsinki. She was further honored by a visit to the composer Jan Sibelius, at his home in Finland. During the war she gave hundreds of concerts at Army camps and she continues to give programs at veterans' hospitals. She also holds classes among the patients, encouraging them to improvise on various musical instruments.

Her own compositions include four piano sonatas, several preludes, études and songs. She has arranged for the piano George Gershwin's *Concerto in F,* some of Bach's Chorales, and Vivaldi's *Concerto in D.* At her most recent concert in Town Hall, on November 28, 1953, she introduced her composition *Sonata Essay, The Quest.*

The pianist has black curly hair and brown eyes, is five feet tall and weighs 99 pounds. Her hobby is watching baseball and she admits to being "an ardent, long-suffering Giant fan." She says that the only time she begrudges the time for piano practice is during the baseball season, particularly when the Giant and Dodger teams are battling it out. She devised a silent practice keyboard so that she could listen on the radio to her favorite team and appease her conscience by exercising on the keyboard during the games. So devoted a fan is she that she never arranges her Carnegie or Town Hall recitals until she checks on the dates of the World Series.

"I have one advantage over a baseball pitcher," says Miss Castagnetta. "If the pitcher's legs go bad, he might still be a young man but his career is finished. At least, I can sit down, and still play the piano when I'm quite an old lady."

She owns two cats, one named John Gunther after the famous correspondent, and one named Johnnie Mize, after her baseball hero.

Miss Castagnetta is a member of the American Musicological Society and the Academy of Political Science. Her political affiliation is Republican and her church is the Presbyterian.

References

Etude 67:18 D '49 por
Newsweek 19:77 My 11 '42
Who's Who in the East (1951)
Who's Who in Music (1951)

CATTON, (CHARLES) BRUCE (căt'tŭn)
Oct. 9, 1899- Author

Address: b. c/o Doubleday & Company, 575 Madison Ave., New York 22; h. 6301 Bradley Blvd., Bethesda 14, Md.

Reprinted from the *Wilson Library Bulletin* June 1954

Winning the 1954 Pulitzer Prize for history with his *A Stillness at Appomattox* was a high point in the career of Bruce Catton, who has turned a favorite recreation—the study of the Civil War—into a vocation. The third of a trilogy on the Union Army of the Potomac (*Mr. Lincoln's Army* appeared in 1951 and *Glory Road* in 1952), *A Stillness at Appomattox,* published in 1953, is a rich expression of a lifelong interest—an interest shown in boyhood encounters with old Civil War soldiers at Fourth of July celebrations and in a young reporter's Memorial Day series in the Cleveland *Plain Dealer* on the dwindling number of veterans in "The Fading Line of Blue." Catton's latest book is *U. S. Grant and the American Military Tradition* (1954); still in progress are a history of the Northern side of the war for Doubleday's "Mainstream of America" series, a boy's life of General Sheridan, a study of the origins of the war, and an extended life of General Grant.

Charles Bruce Catton was born in Petoskey, Michigan, October 9, 1899, the son of George Robert Catton and Adella Maude (Patten) Catton. His family moved to nearby Benzonia when his father, a Congregational minister, became principal of Benzonia Academy, a small preparatory school. Benzonia, he recalls with nostalgia, was "about as small a small town as there ever was, and I think about as pleasant a place, in the last of the preautomobile age, for a child to grow up."

Catton attended Benzonia Academy and entered Oberlin College in 1916. He left college during World War I to enlist in the Navy. After two years' service he returned to Oberlin, where his extracurricular activities included waiting on table in the village hotel for his board and helping to edit the college paper. But at the end of his junior year he left to become a professional newspaper man, choosing his career "more or less automatically."

From 1920 to 1926 he reported for the Cleveland *News*, the Boston *American*, and the Cleveland *Plain Dealer*; from 1926 to 1941 he was with the Newspaper Enterprise Association service—writing editorials and book reviews, running a Sunday section, or acting as a Washington correspondent. His more creative attempts of the 1930's, a couple of novels, he now dismisses as "quite worthless."

In 1942 Catton became a government man, serving as director of information for the War Production Board and holding similar posts after the war with the Department of Commerce and the Department of the Interior. It was his W.P.B. experience which provided background for his 1948 book, *The War Lords of Washington.* Thought by some reviewers to be too journalistic in style, this "documented report of the civil war waged in Washington by the dollar-a-year appointees" was praised by others as warm, idealistic, and thought-provoking and was selected by the Book Find Club.

Since 1952 he has devoted all his time to literary work, and although his Washington columns and book reviews have appeared in *The Nation* for several years, his chief occupation has been Civil War history. Gathering material from diaries, letters, and soldiers' reports, he wrote *Mr. Lincoln's Army*, the story of the early years. A New York *Times* review by A. F. Harlow lauded Catton's "rare gift of doing enormous research and then presenting it in what is almost a motion picture in color of march, camp and field, with brief, vivid close-ups of generals." When Catton continued with the chronicle of the bloody 1862-1863 campaigns in *Glory Road*, Avery Craven, in the Chicago *Sunday Tribune*, called the work "military history . . . at its best. . . . [He] has come remarkably close to catching the feelings and reactions of citizen soldiers. . . . He imparts an air of reality to camp and battle."

BRUCE CATTON

The final volume was *A Stillness at Appomattox,* which also won the 1954 National Book Award with this citation: "Mr. Catton has combined historical accuracy with poetic insight to present the story of the Army of the Potomac in the final years of the Civil War. Writing from the point of view of the citizens who found themselves soldiers, he has reaffirmed the great American tradition of a peace-loving people who, faced with necessity, can also produce greatness in war." *A Stillness at Appomattox* (a Book-of-the-Month Club selection) was acclaimed by critics, military men, historians.

T. Harry Williams, in the *Sunday Review,* noted the impact of the main theme: the change by which "war was becoming hard, relentless, even cruel—in short, modern and total." Most critics stressed Catton's special qualities as historian-journalist: as he explained in his National Book Award acceptance speech: "What both the reporter and the historian are really looking at is people on the march. . . . What we see, if we look closely, is that the sum of many small victories won by individual human beings . . . is . . . a victory for all of us. . . . Out of sight, somewhere, something great is moving. When the reporter or historian does his job faithfully, now and then we get a glimpse of it."

Bruce Catton and his wife, the former Hazel Cherry, live in Bethesda, Maryland, near Washington, D.C. Their only child, William Bruce Catton, is now at work on his Ph.D. degree in history at Northwestern University. Catton is a Presbyterian in religion, a Democrat in politics, and is a member of the National Press Club and is current president of the Civil War Round Table of Washington.

References

Who's Who in America, 1954-55

CAULFIELD, (BEATRICE) JOAN June 1, 1922- Actress

Address: b. c/o Columbia Broadcasting System, Television City, Hollywood, Calif.

An estimated audience of fifteen million watches actress Joan Caulfield every Saturday night over a CBS-TV channel, the "live" show being telecast from the CBS West Coast studio in Hollywood, California. Miss Caulfield, who is Mrs. Frank Ross in real life, plays a modern young housewife in a popular domestic series called *My Favorite Husband,* which co-stars her with actor Barry Nelson.

The program opened in September 1953 as a TV continuance of a radio show which had starred Lucille Ball. It is well on the way to becoming one of the best of the married-couple shows and has earned for Joan Caulfield the TV fans' title "favorite wife." Before the camera, she is Liz Cooper, lovely and slightly scatter-brained helpmate of a young bank executive, George Cooper (Barry Nelson). They are characters created by Isabel Scott Rorick in her best-selling books, *Mr. and Mrs. Cugat* and *Outside Eden.*

Before achieving her present TV success, Miss Caulfield acted in the Broadway show *Kiss and Tell,* toured in stock plays, and made a series of movies and personal appearances, becoming well known to film goers during the past eight years. As a Harry Conover model, her ash-blonde beauty put her in the front ranks of the cover girls as far back as 1942. Her face and figure have graced dozens of magazines and newspapers, but not to her inner satisfaction. She wanted, from early girlhood, to be lauded for her acting ability, not just for her looks.

Joan Beatrice Caulfield was born in Orange, New Jersey on June 1, 1922 to Mr. and Mrs. Henry R. Caulfield, the second of three daughters. Her father, an airlines executive, and her mother favored Joan's ambition.

Stage-struck at a tender age, Joan took part in class plays while receiving her early education in both parochial and public schools. She continued her interest in dramatics at Theodore Roosevelt Junior High School and at Miss Beard's, a private school in Orange, New Jersey. She was graduated from the Lincoln School of Teacher's College in 1939, then attended Columbia University for two and one-half years.

At Columbia, she was associated with the Morningside (Heights) Players and learned the first steps in professional acting as well as some of the mechanics of play production, including how to paint scenery. She earned her tuition by working for the Harry Conover Agency as a model, posed for fashion pictures ranging from *Mademoiselle* covers to mail order catalogues for housedresses.

On May 11, 1942, her photograph was used as a cover for *Life* magazine. She wore a becoming hat for the "head-shot" which was titled "Fluffy Ruffles."

Having heard that George Abbott, Broadway producer, was casting for the musical, *Best Foot Forward,* Miss Caulfield who was not quite twenty years old, walked into his office.

George Abbott's astute secretary ushered her in to see the producer. He offered her a bit part in another musical, *Beat The Band,* in which she played a gold-digger named Veronica. The musical was short-lived, but Miss Caulfield's career was not.

Producer Abbott cast Joan in the role of Corliss Archer in F. Hugh Herbert's comedy, *Kiss and Tell,* which opened March 17, 1943 at the Biltmore Theatre. She was an instant hit. In an interview with Douglas Gilbert (New York World Telegram, March 19, 1943) Joan said: "Remember, I had virtually no theatrical training. Mr. Abbott has taught me everything. . . . I have had numerous offers from studios and I have turned them down. It's only a matter of decency. Imagine Mr. Abbott's trust—giving me, an untried and untrained actress the leading role. He said I had one thing—sincerity. I hope I have. But I have something else, too. I have gratitude."

Eventually she succumbed to the lure of the screen and stardom. In 1944 after one year and two months with *Kiss and Tell,* she accepted an offer from Paramount after being besieged by ten movie studios. Her sister Betty, then seventeen, continued in the understudy role of the play which ran for 480 performances. Producer George Abbott warned Joan that she would regret leaving Broadway, but at the time, she was eager to appear in motion pictures and was given a leading part in *Miss Susie Slagle's* opposite Sonny Tufts. When the film was released in 1945, the girl from New Jersey received the critics' praise, along with a contract to do *Blue Skies* with Bing Crosby.

During the filming of *Blue Skies* Miss Caulfield had her first bitter experience with "Hollywooditis," which sometimes afflicts the over-confident novice. After she told a studio executive that she could dance she was assigned to dance with Paul Draper, a professional. When she learned that he was secretly trying out other girls for the dance part, and she was about to lose her role in the picture, she stormed into the producer's office, according to a story in *Cosmopolitan* by Martin Scott (January 1954), and asked that she either be given the job or that her contract be destroyed. Two days later the producers put Joan back in the picture but replaced Draper with Fred Astaire. She found him easy to work with, learned the "fancy footwork" by diligently rehearsing.

She was signed the same year to the costume-comedy, *Monsieur Beaucaire* with Bob Hope. She hoped for a part in *An American Tragedy,* but instead was given another light role in *Welcome Stranger* with Bing Crosby. She had a clause in her contract which allowed her to return to Broadway for six months of a year for stage work. Although she made a visit to New York in 1946 she found no role for her on Broadway.

Continuing to make films for Paramount, she appeared in *Dear Ruth* with William Holden (it was released in 1947), was a guest artist in

Variety Girl, and was loaned to Warner Brothers studio for *The Unsuspected,* with Claude Rains in the lead. Miss Caulfield, in an interview with Erskine Johnson,N.E.A. correspondent, (N.Y. *Herald Tribune,* June 3, 1953) confessed that she "went Hollywood," forgot to be her natural self and began playing at being a movie star, lowering her voice, striking poses and imitating other screen figures. "I blame Hollywood and myself and Hollywood's star system," she added.

She appeared in *Petty Girl,* which relied strictly on her looks. Her beauty had been touted from the moment she went to Hollywood to make her screen debut. Luella Parsons wrote on September 2, 1945 (*Journal American, Pictorial Review*), "Certainly she is the prettiest natural beauty since Marion Davies."

Writers vied with descriptive phrases: "A Dresden shepherdess," "lovely as a pink porcelain statuette," "frank as a flower, and looks it," "blonde good looks, refreshing as the first breath of air in a country resort," "hair the color of straw, honey and sparkling lemonade," and even the artist George Petty, who draws the calendar girls said Joan was what he "had meant all the time" (*Life,* February 1950).

But Joan Caulfield still wanted to act, not to be "just a decoration." She also missed the reaction of theatre-goers. On January 26, 1946, she told William Hawkins, drama reporter for the New York *World Telegram,* "I don't think you can ever get over the stimulation of live audiences."

Miss Caulfield played a melodramatic cinema role with John Payne in a picture called *Larceny,* released in 1948, then made another movie, *The Lady Said No* with David Niven. Neither offering was sensational according to the reviews although Miss Caulfield built up box-office receipts by going on tour with the latter picture. It was produced by her husband Frank Ross who has since made a name for himself as producer of *The Robe.*

She barnstormed in summer theatres in 1948, playing Sally Middleton in *The Voice of The Turtle,* with John Payne, and in *Claudia,* and *Dream Girl* in Arizona stock with ex-football star Bronco Magurski in the cast. She continued taking drama lessons with coach Michael Chekov between shows.

Previous to her current TV show, Joan Caulfield made a guest appearance on a Ford Theatre program (NBC-TV) with Herbert Marshall in *The Girl in the Park.* In October 1950 she played a leading role in Maxwell Anderson's *Saturday's Children* for Lux Video Theatre over CBS. She was selected for the subject of a *This Is Your Life* telecast and was spotted on the program by Harry Ackerman of the CBS West Coast division and given a bid to play Liz Cooper in *My Favorite Husband.*

The series, which began Sept. 12, 1953 was complimented by Jack Gould in the New York *Times* Magazine (December 27, 1953), "As

CBS-TV

JOAN CAULFIELD

restful a vision as there is on the screen, she [Joan] makes the Liz in 'My Favorite Husband' seem both appropriately kittenish and skittenish yet always becomingly female. . . . She imparts the credibility and charm to the young housewife coping eagerly with the rigors of married existence." The show is directed by Norman Tokar and the script by Sol Sachs and Nate Monister of *Duffy's Tavern* success. Its rating is steadily increasing. The Simmons Company and International Silver Company sponsor *My Favorite Husband* on alternate weeks.

Ben Gross, TV columnist for the New York *Daily News,* interviewed the actress during a recent visit to California and reported March 7, 1954 her opinion that "the movies still think in terms of pretty faces and beautiful legs. They pick the prettiest girls, not the best actresses." She claimed that she was "much happier" in television because she had a chance to act with "group effort, group feeling." She prefers a "live" audience in the TV studio.

She was married on April 29, 1950 to Frank Ross (former husband of actress Jean Arthur). He has been referred to by one writer as the "Pygmalion" who began the re-carving of Joan Caulfield's career. They live in Beverly Hills at "Liberty Hall," a U-shaped house built around a swimming pool, which had served as a retreat for John Barrymore. It was built in Spanish hacienda style by King Vidor of the silent screen era. There is a 12th century sundial in the middle of the swimming pool to add to the interest of the Provincial French furnishing selected by Mrs. Ross who says she has "tinkered with antiques for years."

The actress plays a fair game of golf, likes tennis, swimming and skiing, dislikes housework, enjoys rumba dancing and listening to

CAULFIELD, JOAN—*Continued*

jazz records (Chicago style). She likes to read best sellers, prefers to wear sport clothes and uses Lanvin's "Arpege" perfume. She rises at six A.M. and studies her TV script until eight o'clock. Her husband predicts that "TV will give her confidence. She'll really blossom."

References

Cosmop 136:26 Ja '54 pors
Life 28:75 F 6 '50 por
Look 10:45 Ja 8 '46 pors
N Y Herald Tribune IV p 1 D 23 '45
N Y Journal American p15 S 2 '45; p3 Mr 12 '50 pors
N Y Post Mag p2 Je 14 '47 pors
N Y Sunday News II p12 Mr 14 '54 por
N Y Times Mag p17 D 27 '53
N Y World-Telegram p8 Ag 5 '49
N Y World-Telegram Mag p16 Ag 22 '53
T V Guide 2:15 Ja 8 '54
This Week Mag p16 Ja 17 '54
Motion Picture and Television Almanac, 1953-54

CAVANAH, FRANCES (ELIZABETH)

Sept. 26, 1899- Author

Address: b. c/o Macrae Smith, 225 S. 15th St., Philadelphia 2, Pa.; c/o Row, Peterson & Co., 1911 Ridge Ave.,Evanston, Ill.; h. 1411 Chicago Ave., Evanston, Ill.

Reprinted from the *Wilson Library Bulletin* Feb. 1954

"Just think," wrote a fourth-grade girl to Frances Cavanah, "if it hadn't been for you I never would have known that Balboa discovered the Pacific!" This refreshing reaction, typical of young readers, explains why Frances Cavanah enjoys writing and editing for children. Author of a dozen books, and coauthor and editor of more than a dozen others, Miss Cavanah is well known as both an editor and a writer.

FRANCES CAVANAH

Born September 26, 1899, in Princeton, Indiana, of Irish, English, Scottish, and French Huguenot descent, Frances Elizabeth Cavanah grew up in Mount Vernon and Evansville. Her father, a teacher and school principal, died when she was young. Her family background undoubtedly gave Miss Cavanah the first impetus towards the subjects she chose later to write about. The first Cavanahs came to North Carolina from Ireland in the early 1700's, while the first American ancestor of her maternal grandfather, Thornton Neale, arrived in Virginia in 1649. His nephew was later known as General "Stonewall" Jackson.

Thornton Neale did not approve of slavery, so as a young man he left the South for southern Indiana, where he became a pioneer farmer and an ardent supporter of the new Republican party.

From the time Frances Cavanah was nine she yearned to write. The first person to encourage her was a grade teacher in Evansville, Bettye McCutcheon, now retired. In junior high school, Frances won a writing contest on "My Favorite Character in *Little Women*" (Jo, of course). That was the deciding factor in her early resolution to be a writer.

Her first job after graduating from De Pauw University was in Chicago, as book review editor of *The Continent,* a Presbyterian magazine no longer published. From there, Miss Cavanah went to *Child Life,* where she remained fifteen years, the last eight as associate editor. She contributed frequently to the magazine, and read letters from literally thousands of youthful subscribers. One comment was about her own stories, which later became her first book, *The Treasure of Belden Place*: "Those children are always doing the things I want to do." Another: "I'd like to correspond with someone my own age. How old is Frances Cavanah?"

Perhaps her most rewarding experience as an editor was as director of biography for Row, Peterson and Company, where Miss Cavanah was editor of the *Real People* series, a group of forty-eight biographies of leaders in American and world history. A number have been translated into other languages. Just preceding this assignment, she was biography editor of the 1947 revision of *World Book Encyclopedia,* and anthology editor of the 1949 revision of *Childcraft.* Of *Real People,* prepared for use in the schools, Miss Cavanah says: "We tried to show history in human terms. I feel it is very important for children to realize that history is made by people, and that it is a continuing process to which they, in time, will have a chance to contribute."

This idea motivated her as coauthor of two basic elementary histories, *Our New Land,* and *Our New Nation.* The same motif runs through all of Miss Cavanah's work—her four "city" books, *Benjy of Boston,* etc., which show the influence of various nationalities in American communities; her historical books, *A Patriot in*

Hoops, Boyhood Adventures of Our Presidents, and her highly successful *Our Country's Story,* also translated into Korean, which has sold over 100,000 copies in its different editions.

Miss Cavanah's own favorite is *They Knew Abe Lincoln.* As a child, she was thrilled by the knowledge that Lincoln had grown up almost in the next county. She wondered what it must have been like to have known him, what friends he had made during those fourteen years in Indiana, what his family thought of him. She based her book largely on Lincoln's own statements, and those of people who had been closely associated with him as a boy. The *New Yorker* commented, "Adds up to an illuminating portrait," while the *Horn Book* remarked, "Presented with flavor and humor."

Miss Cavanah's publishers, Macrae Smith, are enthusiastic about her new book, tentatively entitled *Through the Golden Door* to be published later this year. Intended primarily for young adults, the book will show how this country looked to the succession of newcomers who have been arriving on these shores since our beginnings.

Miss Cavanah is tall and slender, her brown hair touched with gray. She is gay, full of fun, and humor frequently glints from her blue eyes. Her little chuckle bubbles up at the slightest provocation. She is very fond of the theatre, and would rather read plays than anything else, although biography ranks a close second. In 1953, she spent several months in Europe, gathering material for future books. For many years her home has been in Evanston, Illinois, where she lives part of each year. Much of her research is done in the Library of Congress.

In October 1952 Miss Cavanah's alma mater called her back to bestow on her a citation for meritorious achievement and service. At the DePauw Inaugural Convocation, with Mary Beard, William Oatis, and other famous sons and daughters of the university, she was cited for attaining "distinction as writer and editor of books for young people."

References

Chicago Sch J 32:sup10 My '51 por
American Women, 1939-40
Who's Who in Chicago and Illinois (1950)

CHAMBERLAIN, SAMUEL Oct. 28, 1895-
Photographer; etcher

Address: b. c/o Hastings House Publishers, Inc., 41 E. 50th St., New York 22; h. 5 Tucker St., Marblehead, Mass.

Portraying with his camera the native charm of the American countryside, Samuel Chamberlain has photographed many beautiful and famous scenes which have been collected into about forty books including *Beyond New England Thresholds* (1937), *Fair is Our Land* (1942) and *Behold Williamsburg* (1947), all published by Hastings House.

SAMUEL CHAMBERLAIN

He is also known as the official etcher of colonial Williamsburg in Virginia and for the annual photographic Engagement Calendars published by Hastings House.

An epicurean, Chamberlain has contributed articles for more than a decade to *Gourmet* magazine and is the author of *Clémentine in the Kitchen* and with Narcissa Chamberlain of *Bouquet de France.* His most recent book is *Soft Skies of France* (Hastings House, 1953).

Samuel Chamberlain was born on October 28, 1895, the son of George Ellsworth and Cora Lee (Summers) Chamberlain in Cresco, Iowa. His mother had been a teacher in the State Normal School at River Falls, Wisconsin and his father was a graduate physician. The family gradually migrated westward. Samuel's early years were spent in Bismark, North Dakota. By the time he was ready for high school, the family lived in Aberdeen, Washington, where Dr. Chamberlain became the first surgeon in this frontier area. Samuel entered the University of Washington in 1913, but transferred to the Massachusetts Institute of Technology in 1915. His mother had influenced him to study architecture.

Two years later, young Chamberlain enlisted in the American Field Service of the French Army and later served with the United States Army Ambulance Service. He received the Croix de Guerre. Although he returned to M.I.T. after the war, Chamberlain, stimulated by the architecture and rural life of France, desired to record the picturesque rather than design it.

After discovering that commercial art was not satisfying, he saved money to return to France where he became an architectural travel writer and illustrator. His articles of France accompanied by sketches began to appear in *Century, American Architect, Pencil Points,*

CHAMBERLAIN, SAMUEL—*Continued*

Arts and Decoration, Architectural Record, and other periodicals.

An American Field Service traveling fellowship was awarded to Chamberlain in 1923, and he studied etching in Paris under Edouard Léon. In 1925 and 1926 he was an assistant professor of architecture at the University of Michigan, but later in 1926, a Guggenheim fellowship provided the opportunity to study etching with Malcolm Osborne, R.A., at the Royal College of Art in London.

The Architectural Book Publishing Company published several books by Chamberlain: *Sketches of Northern Spanish Architecture* (1926), *Domestic Architecture in Rural France* (1928) and *Tudor Homes of England* (1929). In the early 1930's Chamberlain settled in Marblehead, Massachusetts. He began to concentrate on the New England scene with etchings on post cards and won a commission from Yale University for a series of etchings commemorating the Connecticut Tercentenary in 1935. While in the midst of this work, he submitted a collection of enlarged prints of New England houses to his publisher, P. Wenzel. The collection was rejected but attracted the attention of Wenzel's grandson, Walter Frese, who decided to publish the book himself.

A Small House in the Sun (1936) by Samuel Chamberlain was the first book published by Hastings House, a new firm headed by Frese. The book heralded Chamberlain's career as a photographer. *Cape Cod in the Sun* (1937) *Gloucester and Cape Ann* (1938) and *Historic Boston in Four Seasons* (1938) soon followed. The annual Engagement Calendars created by Chamberlain and published by Hastings House, began with photographs of New England scenes. They grew in popularity and other American areas became the subjects of the calendars.

The artist's interest in early Americana led him to Virginia when the late Rev. Dr. W. A. R. Goodwin and John D. Rockefeller, Jr. recreated Williamsburg as the eighteenth century colonial capital. Chamberlain's work on the project was selected for exhibition at the Grand Central Galleries in New York. The New York *Times* (March 3, 1940) commented that his etchings captured the charm of the eighteenth century frame of living. He was named official etcher for colonial Williamsburg. His book *Behold Williamsburg* (Hastings House, 1947) contains several reproductions of exhibited etchings.

An enthusiasm for French cooking, a rare collection of "gastronomic literature" and a French cook whom the Chamberlains brought to the United States, inspired the artist to assume the name Phineas Beck for a series of articles published in *Gourmet* magazine and as a book *Clémentine in the Kitchen* (Hastings House, 1943). The Boston *Post* (December 14, 1943) called the latter "the gift of gifts for the gourmet, the epicurean, or anyone nostalgic for rural France." The book, which contains dry points by Chamberlain and line drawings by Henry Stahlhut, sold over 100,000 copies by 1953. *Bouquet de France, an Epicurean Tour of the French Provinces* (Gourmet, 1952) was written with his wife.

As a specialist in photo intelligence, Chamberlain served in World War II with the U.S. Army Air Force and held the rank of major when discharged in 1946. The Legion of Merit and Bronze Star were conferred upon him in 1944 and he was made a chevalier of the Legion of Honor in 1949.

Among his approximately forty books, *France Will Live Again* (1940) *This Realm, This England* (1941) and *Fair is our Land* (1942) "in particular, embrace Mr. Chamberlain's success as an artist, photographer and editor" (Roland Sawyer, *Christian Science Monitor,* June 19, 1948). R. S. Brooks, *Springfield Republican* (May 11, 1952) described *Frontier of Freedom* (1952) as "outstanding both as a historical record and as an exhibition of artistic photography." Neil Martin (*Christian Science Monitor,* December 3, 1953) pointed out that the photographs in *Soft Skies of France* (1953) gave "subtle color" to the luster of French architecture through shaded grays and blacks.

Walter Frese related in his article "Samuel Chamberlain and the American Scene" (*Publisher's Weekly,* August 2, 1947) that the artist, because of his talent as an etcher and his architectural training, was particularly suited to record "the infinite variety of his native land in photographic accuracy and a beauty of composition which few photographers achieve."

Frese revealed that Chamberlain's books are compiled from photographs collected over a period of time, often after several trips to an area to get the best shots at the right moments.

The etcher received from the Paris Salon honorable mention for his work in 1925 and the Bronze Medal in 1928; the Kate W. Arms Prize (1933) and the John Taylor Arms Prize (1936) from the Society of American Etchers; and the Fine Arts Medal of the American Institute of Architects in 1947. He has been a lecturer at M.I.T. His prints are in the collections of the Metropolitan Museum of Art, Library of Congress, New York Public Library, Boston Museum of Fine Arts, Art Institute of Chicago, British Museum (London), Victoria and Albert Museum (London), and Bibliothèque Nationale (Paris).

During a trip from France to the United States, Chamberlain met Narcissa Gellatly on shipboard. They were married on April 27, 1923 and returned to France to live in the little town of Senlis, north of Paris. Their two daughters, Narcisse and Stephanie, were born there. The family now live in a seventeenth-century house in Marblehead, Massachusetts, which they took great pleasure in restoring. This has been described in *Old Rooms For New Living,* by Narcissa Chamberlain, with photographs by Samuel Chamberlain (Hastings House, 1953). Chamberlain is a tennis fan, but no longer plays the game. He has brown hair, blue eyes, is five feet ten inches tall and weighs 170 pounds. Politically, he is a Democrat. His church affiliation is Episcopalian. Because his photographs have been so widely published, it has been said that he did not take them all. Mr. Chamberlain has stated that he has taken all of them, unaided. There are about 20,000 negatives in his files.

The artist is a fellow of the American Academy of Arts and Sciences, and a member of the National Society of Arts and Sciences, National Academy, Society of American Graphic Artists, Société de la Gravure Originale, and in Boston of the Club of Odd Volumes, Colonial Society and Tavern Club.

References

Am Artist 10:17+ Ap '46
Christian Sci Mon p6 Je 19 '48 por
Pub W 152:412+ Ag 2 '47

Who's Who in America, 1954-55
Who's Who in American Art (1953)

GABRIELLE CHANEL

CHANEL, GABRIELLE (BONHEUR)

1883?- Fashion designer

Address: b. and h. 31 rue Cambon, Paris 1er, France

After fifteen years of retirement, Gabrielle "Coco" Chanel presented a fashion collection in Paris in February 1954 that has "permeated" contemporary Parisian couture with the elegant simplicity which characterized Chanel's styles in the "flaming 20's." Inventor of the famous perfume Chanel No. 5, the designer in 1919 "took women out of the prison of tight corsets," lowered waistlines, shortened skirts, and introduced a "poor girl look" which combined pearls with jersey, and which offered a youthful appearance and comfort. At the height of her career, she was the richest couturier in Paris. Although she retired in 1938 when women shifted their preference to Schiaparelli, Chanel continued to operate her perfume business. Aroused because Paris fashion has been taken over by men designers, she decided to make a comeback in 1954.

"The spirit of Chanel has made itself widely felt in the creation of the fall styles," commented Virginia Pope, fashion editor of the New York *Times* (July 11, 1954). "The magic of her name evoked the simplicity of style for which she was famous during the Thirties. The easy lines, the use of wool jersey, the red that bore her name, and her extravagant use of jewels all will be important features of the coming season."

Gabrielle Chanel was born probably in 1883 near Issoire in the province of Auvergne, France in a convent-hospital where a nun gave her the middle name, Bonheur. Chanel often amused her friends by telling them conflicting stories of her childhood, saying once that she was raised in a stable, and another time that she had a sheltered life with a governess. There is a story that she cut up the curtains in the living room as a child to make dresses for her dolls. Her other youthful enthusiasm was riding horses.

Orphaned at an early age, the country-bred girl at seventeen went to Deauville with her sister to work in a hat shop. In 1914 they arrived in Paris where Chanel opened a tiny millinery shop, having "no capital beyond her native Auvergnate shrewdness." Since she often went horseback riding in the Bois de Boulogne early in the morning, when the cocks were crowing, she was nicknamed "Miss Cocorico," contracting it later to "Coco" Chanel.

According to Kathleen Cannell in the *Christian Science Monitor* (February 8, 1954), Chanel became a girl-groom at a de luxe stable. Wearing chic riding togs, she brought around the horses for the glamorous debutantes of the World War I period. Feeling cold one day, she pulled on a polo player's jumper and suddenly conceived the idea of making jersey pullovers for women. Charles Ritz, an American fashion importer who had met Chanel at the stables, started her on the road to fame by giving her some bolts of a wool-jersey fabric that he had bought but could not sell to his rich clients because "it looked too much like winter underwear." "Coco" fashioned the beige jersey into draped turbans with tubular pullovers to match, sold them to the equestriennes in the Bois, and thus launched the sweater line and jersey of the "beige decade."

Described by *Vogue* as "a revolutionist, a non-conformist, a lone rebel who let women out of the prison of tight corsets," Chanel introduced a "new look" to the 20's. Tearing down the "monstrous constructions of net and feathers that crowned women's heads," she designed simple hats to conform naturally to the shape of the head. Then, wrote Miss Cannell, "she lowered the waistline, shortened the skirt, flattened the hourglass figure into the paper doll, stripped off trimmings to make way for great hunks of ostentatiously fake costume

CHANEL, GABRIELLE—*Continued*

jewelry." The "Chanel Look," which came in directly after World War I when women were prepared by wartime uniforms to accept "untrammeled standardization," was a paradoxical combination of elegance and casualness, and above all offered comfort to women.

During the 20's, Chanel became "unchallenged queen regnant of Paris fashion," building her "flair for simple elegance" into a million-dollar business with headquarters at 31 rue Cambon, Paris. At her career's height, she was running four businesses—couture (twenty-six sewing ateliers employing some 2,400 workers); a textile house; perfume laboratories; and costume jewelry. In addition she was said to own most of the rue Cambon.

Among the directors of her many enterprises were Paul Iribe, famous French interior and stage designer, and poets Pierre Reverdy and Jean Cocteau. Count Etienne de Beaumont once headed her costume jewelry shop. Her perfume No. 5 (Chanel's lucky number) was brought out in 1922 in simple containers, contrasting with heavy expensive bottles containing other perfumes. It became and still is the most famous perfume in the world.

Chanel had induced women to cut their hair during the 20's; and she was the first to make skirts shorter. She herself—small, black-haired, with brilliant dark eyes and beige skin—personified the Chanel Look. Her habitual costume was a loose jersey cardigan jacket worn over a white shirt, the jacket sleeves turned back to reveal white cuffs. With it she wore a short pleated skirt. Around her neck she hung a "mess of real pearl ropes, jumbled with red or green stones, obviously fake." For a short period in the early '30's she worked with real stones. Chanel introduced semi-precious stones in barbaric settings. Her own fabulous collection of real jewels includes twenty-four strings of pearls.

She personally supervised every detail of her workrooms. At final rehearsals before openings, Chanel would lie on her stomach to see that the hems hung right as the mannequins paraded before her. Once after going away for a rest before a fashion opening, she returned to find none of the final details to her liking, and furiously ripped everything apart. Since there was not time to sew them all together again, dozens of gowns of lace and chiffon were modeled with raw, irregularly-cut hemlines. The press called these "airy, floaty" effects a "stroke of genius" and the unfinished hem inadvertently became a Chanel trademark.

Chanel always showed her new collections on the fifth day of the month. She would sit on the top step of the curved mirrored staircase in her gold and white salon, with twenty-five or so of her close friends on the steps below her. Among them were often celebrated artists of the time—Stravinsky, Diaghilev, Bérard, Dali. Instead of coming out six steps apart as in other fashion shows, her tall mannequins would walk out slowly, her shorter mannequins quickly, as she had instructed them.

For many years Chanel rose at seven, went to bed early each night. For a short time during the early 30's she relaxed her regime and became one of the personalities of the international set. At a waltz ball in 1934, where most of the women were plumed and décolleté, Chanel created a sensation by appearing in extremely covered-up black taffeta, wearing a small black pillbox adorned with a headlight jewel, and carrying a demure bunch of white flowers. For one of her own fantastic parties she draped a cloth-of-gold tent over the terrace of her eighteenth-century house in the Faubourg St.-Honoré.

When Chanel's dressmakers went on strike in June 1936, the "strong-nerved" fashion designer told them that since the shop could not earn enough to pay what they demanded under her management, they could run it themselves and she would stay on as an unpaid stylist. Convinced that she needed more capital, the strikers tried to get her some from the Socialist treasury. Failing in this they marched back and formally refused to take over the shop. Mlle. Chanel in turn refused to keep it open. Three weeks later, the strikers called off their strike and Chanel, "svelte, smart and lively in her middle age," reopened her establishment.

The designer's place as top headliner in fashion was threatened during the 30's by Schiaparelli, Alix and Balenciaga. The struggle between Italian Schiaparelli and Chanel lasted ten years, ending in 1938 when "almost overnight the women of Paris, followed sheeplike by the women of the world, turned from 'Coco' to the invader from Italy, with her exaggerated feminine conceits, her tassels, her flaming colors, and 'parachute' silhouettes" (*Time,* February 15, 1954). "Chanel wanted the tricot sailor frock with the long sweater, the short skirt,' said Schiaparelli. 'I took the frock, I altered the line . . . Voilà! Chanel ees feeneesh!' "

Time in August 1938 had reported that Chanel "aimed to clothe rather than astonish" and that her new collection showed her celebrated simplicity. But by the end of 1938, with her workrooms and output reduced by more than half, Chanel, "solvent but disillusioned," quit fashion designing. Although she closed her couture houses, she continued her perfume business at 31 rue Cambon, where after the expulsion of the Germans in World War II, G.I.'s queued up to buy the famous No. 5. In 1953 Chanel personally supervised the redecoration of her New York perfume showrooms.

Fashion reporters announced in February 1954 that the "biggest headline of current Paris fashion openings is the comeback of Chanel after 15 years' retirement. . ." Claiming her competitive spirit had been aroused because Paris couture had been taken over by men (Fath, Dior, Balenciaga, Balmain, Dessès), she designed a new collection and presented it on February 5th. The first model stepped out in a plain Navy cardigan suit carrying a card with No. 5 for luck. Other models showed an easy supple silhouette with hemlines fourteen inches from the ground for day, ankle length for cocktail wear. For evening, skirts were bouffant and cleared the floor. Included in the collection were several little jersey dresses as well as Chanel's famous blazer suit.

"There was more than a show of feline claws as the fat cats of the fashion world crowded in. . ." reported *Time*. A London critic called the showing a collection for mothers, adding, "Though personally we like to see Mums with a bit more dash." *Le Figaro's* writer observed: "It was touching; one might have thought oneself back in 1925." *Vogue* reported that the fashion world had expected Chanel to surprise it in 1954 as she had in 1919. "The surprise was that none appeared. . . Chanel followed her [past] ideas so closely that the public, whipped to a frenzy of expectation by the extraordinary advance publicity gasped in surprise at the unchanged simplicity and many of them gasped in disappointment."

Most critics agreed, however, that although Chanel's simplicity was not new, its influence on 1954 fashion was unmistakeable. "All the Paris couture (except Fath) is permeated with the easy underdone sort of clothes that were the basis of Chanelism at its height." "In the midst of all the scratching and meowing," *Time* reported, ". . . the buyers are buying." On May 2, 1954, the New York *Journal-American* stated that after the opening shock had subsided, "Chanel had prevailed again, and Paris was busy turning out simpler, Chanel-type clothes."

The designer's ideas have changed but slightly during her retirement. She believes that unless a fashion becomes popular it is not a fashion but an eccentricity. She wants women to look pretty and young in dresses that are comfortable and allow freedom of movement. Of skirt lengths, she says they should vary with the individual woman, according to what looks best on her. Jewels, real or false, are still part of her theory of elegance. She no longer wants to dress a few hundred private clients, but is interested in dressing thousands of women, especially older ones whose waistlines have spread.

"There are too many men in this business," she told the New York *Journal-American* (May 2, 1954), "and they don't know how to make clothes for women. All this fantastic pinching and puffing. How can a woman wear a dress that's cut so she can't lift up her arm to pick up a telephone?" However, in *Vogue* (February 15, 1954) she was reported as saying that when she wants an opinion about what she has done, she asks her men friends. "Not professionals in the couture, just friends. I value their reactions much more than women's."

Described in *Vogue* as "a spare, taut, compressed figure hung with jewels," Chanel wears enormous eye-glasses. Her face is broad, shrewd, with widely-spaced eyes, a wide mouth and pencilled eyebrows. She has powerful sculptor's hands. When she speaks in her low muted voice, she leans forward, "her angular jaw thrust out like a Toulouse-Lautrec lithograph of Yvette Guilbert." Miss Cannell described her as "a miniature sphinx, a petite, sunburned woman."

The fashion designer lives in a cluttered four-room apartment, two floors above her salon on rue Cambon, filled with art treasures, rare books, Coromandel screens, bronzes, rock crystal, rose quartz, jade animals and mirrors. There she has her meals and entertains her friends, but she sleeps in a plain, white-walled room at the Ritz Hotel across the street. She likes travelling, especially in America.

Missia Sert once said, "Coco doesn't know the difference between relaxation and boredom." It was to escape boredom that she made her fashion comeback. To her critics, she says: "I prefer vitriol to honey." According to *Vogue*, "Chanel is a tradition so strong that today she can hardly compete with the strength of her own aura."

References

Christian Sci Mon p4 F 8 '54
Life 36:49+ Mr 1 '54 pors
Time 63:28 F 15 '54 por
Vogue 123:82+ F 15 '54 pors

CHARISSE, CYD Mar. 8, 1923- Dancer; motion picture actress

Address: b. c/o Metro-Goldwyn-Mayer Studios, 10202 West Washington Blvd., Culver City, Calif.; h. Beverly Glen, Los Angeles, Calif.

One of the most striking dancers in motion pictures today, Cyd Charisse began her professional career with the Ballet Russe with which she toured the United States and Europe. Since then, her work has developed as a result of continuous experience in numerous films. An upswing in her popularity with moviegoers which began with her sensational dancing in *Singin' in the Rain* and continued with her fiery performance in *Sombrero*, resulted in her being co-starred with Fred Astaire in *The Band Wagon* in 1953.

Cyd Charisse, whose real name was Tula Ellice Finklea, was born in Amarillo, Texas on March 8, 1923 to Ernest E. Finklea, a jeweler, and his wife, Lela (Norwood) Finklea. Miss Charisse is of Scotch, Irish, French, English, and American Indian ancestry. Her father encouraged her to study ballet and equipped her room with a practice bar and a full-length mirror. At the age of eight she began dancing lessons.

She received her academic education at Amarillo Grammar School, and, after her family had moved to Hollywood, at the Hollywood Professional School. After a year of studying ballet under Nico Charisse, she had an audition with Colonel de Basil of the Ballet Russe. Immediately signed for work with the company, the young dancer toured the United States for a season.

When the Ballet Russe was about to leave for Europe, the dancer received word of her father's grave illness. She returned to his bedside and the company sailed without her. After the death of her father, she rejoined the Ballet Russe which was still touring Europe. "We saw the great capitals of the world," she has said, "only through hotel windows."

With the outbreak of World War II Miss Charisse returned to Hollywood. The dancer and choreographer David Lichine, who had known her as a fellow member of the Ballet

CYD CHARISSE

Russe, introduced her to director Gregory Ratoff, who gave her a role as a dancer in the film *Something to Shout About,* produced by Columbia in 1942.

In the following year, she was given another small dancing part in *Mission to Moscow.* Robert Alton cast her for the role of the ballerina in the film *Ziegfeld Follies* in 1945, and in the same year, she also appeared in *The Harvey Girls.*

The dancer worked in four pictures in 1946: *Three Wise Fools, Fiesta, The Unfinished Dance,* and *Till the Clouds Roll By.* The last of these was a musical based on the life and works of Jerome Kern, and Cyd Charisse's name was included in the billing. The next year she appeared in *On an Island with You.* Another dancing part was assigned to her in *Words and Music* in 1948 and in *The Kissing Bandit* which featured Frank Sinatra. In a review of the latter film in the New York *Times,* Bosley Crowther commented that her "thundering *Dance of Fury* . . . marks the best spectacle in the film." Cyd Charisse was elected a Star of Tomorrow in 1948.

In *East Side, West Side* which featured Barbara Stanwyck and James Mason and was produced in 1949, Miss Charisse had her first speaking part. Although Gotham Gargoyle in the New York *Herald Tribune* of December 23, 1949 commented that she was "attractive enough in the role of a model," Irene Thirer in the New York *Post* reported: "Cyd . . . just about steals the works. She's so lovely that you forget she is actually a dancer doing her first straight acting job."

Cyd Charisse appeared in *Tension* and in *The Adventures of Don Renegade* before she appeared in *Singin' in the Rain* in 1952. This film, a technicolor musical based on show business, played an important part in the progress of the young dancer. The story and screen play were written by Adolph Green and Betty Comden, Gene Kelly directed the film and Miss Charisse appeared in the character of the "Guest Artist." Bosley Crowther in the New York *Times* of March 28, 1952 praised the "lovely dream dance" which Cyd Charisse did with Gene Kelly. She was scheduled to play the leading feminine role opposite Gene Kelly in *An American in Paris,* but marriage and motherhood kept her out of pictures for a year.

Miss Charisse appeared in 1952 in *The Wild North* which featured Stewart Granger and in which she played the part of a half-breed Indian girl. Commenting on this film, Marie Torre in the New York *World-Telegram and Sun* of May 12, 1952, wrote "Cyd Charisse is both warm and pleasing to the eye."

The success which Miss Charisse had made in *Singin' in the Rain* was continued by another hit at the end of 1952, *Sombrero,* in which she danced around an Aztec idol in a tempestuous scene on a mountain side. Then came *The Band Wagon* in 1953, a technicolor screen musical based on "show business" which was directed by Vincente Minnelli and for which Adolph Green and Betty Comden wrote the story and the screen play. Cyd Charisse was now co-starred with Fred Astaire. William Hawkins, in a review in the New York *World-Telegram and Sun* on July 10, 1953, wrote that her work was at times "amateurish," but Bosley Crowther stated in the New York *Times* that she danced "beautifully." Miss Charisse made her latest appearance in the film *Brigadoon,* followed by *Kismet,* and the *Songs of Solomon.*

The dancer married her ballet teacher, Nico Charisse, in France on August 12, 1939. By this marriage she has a son, Nicky, who was born in Hollywood on May 7, 1942. The Charisses were divorced in 1947. She was married to the singer, Tony Martin, on May 9, 1948. On their honeymoon, they traveled through Europe and she had the chance to see the cities which she had missed seeing on her first trip abroad. The Martins have a son, Tony, who was born on August 28, 1950. They live in a suburb of Los Angeles in a white colonial house whose walls are hung with French originals, Degas prints and the sheet music of Tony Martin.

Miss Charisse is five feet, six inches tall, and weighs 115 pounds. Her eyes are brown, and her hair is dark brown. She came to use the name Cyd because a young brother called her "Sid" when trying to say "sister."

She likes French poodles, swimming, black coffee and steaks done medium rare. In commenting on her work in motion pictures, Miss Charisse has stated, "If by some chance I had to give up either acting or dancing, I'd choose to keep on dancing" (*Saturday Evening Post,* December 6, 1952).

References

N Y Post Mag p5 Ag 10 '52 por
N Y World-Telegram Mag p24 Jl 12 '53
Newsweek 42:48+ Jl 6 '53
Motion Picture and Television Almanac, 1952-53

CHARLESWORTH, JAMES C(LYDE)

May 21, 1900- Political scientist; university professor

Address: b. Institute of Local and State Government, University of Pennsylvania, Philadelphia 4, Pa.; h. 7125 Penarth Ave., Upper Darby, Pa.

The American Academy of Political and Social Science, which has an international membership of more than 17,000, announced on June 8, 1953 that Dr. James C. Charlesworth had been elected as its new president, succeeding Dr. Ernest Minor Patterson. The academy was organized at Philadelphia in 1889 "to provide a forum for the discussion of political, social and industrial problems confronting the United States and other countries."

Dr. Charlesworth has been a member of the faculty of the University of Pennsylvania since 1939 and a full professor of political science since 1945. In addition to the presidency of the academy, he is continuing as supervisor of the educational program of the Institute of Local and State Government at the University of Pennsylvania. During World War II he was chief of the management planning branch in the office of the Adjutant General.

One of the five children of James and Priscilla (Hawkins) Charlesworth, who were both natives of England, James Clyde Charlesworth was born on May 21, 1900 near Greensburg, Pennsylvania. He was taken at an early age to Donora, Pennsylvania and attended public schools there. While he was a student in high school his father was invalided by an accident and James had to help support his younger brothers. Starting as a water carrier for a labor crew, he worked sixty hours a week at a steel mill, continuing his high school course in the evenings.

After graduation he moved to Pittsburgh where he was enrolled in the night school of Carnegie Institute of Technology from 1921 to 1923. During 1922 to 1924 he worked by day as assistant to the chief engineer of the Miller Machinery Company. Subsequently, Charlesworth transferred to the University of Pittsburgh, where he attended day sessions for about a year and a half, qualifying for his B.A. degree in political science in 1926. In his quest of a higher education and in his choice of a field of interest, Charlesworth was influenced (he told *Current Biography*) by the clergy at the Oakland Methodist Episcopal Church in Pittsburgh.

An instructorship in political science at the University of Pittsburgh enabled him to study for the M.A. degree which he received in 1927. "The Legislature of Pennsylvania" is the title of his master's thesis. He attended Harvard University during 1928, then returned to the University of Pittsburgh to teach, study and work on his doctoral thesis, "Implementation of the Pact of Paris." Five years later he acquired the Ph.D. degree and was promoted to assistant professor. Charlesworth was advanced in 1935 to associate professor and appointed supervisor of his department's course in government service.

JAMES C. CHARLESWORTH

The Chancellor of the University of Pittsburgh, John Gabbert Bowman, attempted in 1939 to enforce a new "code" of amateur standards in football, which appeared to threaten the university's football fame. The late John Bain (Jock) Sutherland, the university's coach, resigned and a group of students staged a "walkout" in protest. The strikers invaded Charlesworth's classroom while he was reading Plato's *Republic*, and the professor went into action and several blows were struck. Charlesworth was quoted: "Philosophers should take action once in awhile. I don't believe the schools should be run by self-appointed and noisy groups" (*Saturday Evening Post*, November 4, 1939).

Professor Charles Rohlfing, chairman of the department of political science at the University of Pennsylvania, offered Dr. Charlesworth in 1939 an associate professorship in political science at the Wharton School of Finance and Commerce. He accepted this position and also undertook the supervision of the educational program of the affiliated Institute of Local and State Government which had been established as a training and service unit. The institute prepares selected college graduates for government service, offers in-service training programs for employees already engaged in public work, and encourages more effective citizenship among other selected groups including undergraduates.

The political scientist became director of the graduate division of the Wharton School in 1942. After serving as director of personnel and training for the Philadelphia Regional Civilian Defense Council, Charlesworth entered the Army as a major in 1943. During the following year he became chief of the management planning branch in the office of the Adjutant General. For his service he was awarded the Legion of Merit in 1945.

(Continued next page)

Dr. Charlesworth was advanced to a full professorship at the University of Pennsylvania in 1945, while he was still in the Army. Promoted to lieutenant colonel, he was discharged in 1946 and resumed his several duties at the university. The professor now offers courses in the theory of public administration, and objectives and administrative problems in local and state government.

In this period he wrote *Government Administration* (Harper, 1951) in which he stated: "Efficiency is not the prime desideratum in a republican form of government; efficiency-within-liberty should be the heart of the administrator's credo. The administrative instrument of education is conspicuously appropriate to this end. The more we develop the uses of education, the closer we bring the state and the citizen together and the longer we postpone the collapse of democratic society."

Active for many years in the functions of the American Academy of Political and Social Science, Dr. Charlesworth contributed to the May 1942 issue of the *Annals of the American Academy of Social and Political Science* a paper entitled "The Regulatory Agency: Detached Tribunal or Positive Administrator?" which argues on behalf of the latter and cites "the power of public opinion" which forced supplanting of three early World War II boards by "the hierarchical, unified, nondeliberative and powerful organization under Donald M. Nelson." (This paper is included in the 1950 revision of *People, Politics and the Politician,* edited by A. N. Christensen and E. M. Kirkpatrick).

Professors Rohlfing and Charlesworth were the co-editors of the September, 1948 number of the *Annals,* which was devoted to the subject "Parties and Politics: 1948" and opened with a paper by Charlesworth entitled "Is Our Two Party System Natural?" (He believes it is.)

Since 1949 the professor has been associate editor of the *Annals* and in March 1952 was co-editor with Clarence N. Callender of the issue devoted to "Ethical Standards in American Public Life." The September 1952 number, under the personal editorship of Charlesworth, concerned the "Meaning of the 1952 Presidential Election."

Dr. Charlesworth was elected president of the American Academy of Political and Social Science, effective in June 1953. He succeeded Dr. Ernest Minor Patterson who was unanimously chosen president emeritus after a tenure of twenty-three years. The new president is continuing his administrative and professorial assignments at the University of Pennsylvania.

"From its organization in 1899," states the University of Pennsylvania catalogue, "the American Academy of Political and Social Science . . . has been associated with the University of Pennsylvania, and particularly with the Wharton School."

Each winter the Academy of Political and Social Science holds public meetings, and an annual meeting in the spring extending over two full days and including six sessions. The papers of permanent importance presented at these meetings are included in the *Annals of the American Academy of Political and Social Science.* The present international membership of the academy of over 17,000 individuals and institutions is largely attributed to the prestige of its meetings and the scholarly value of the *Annals.* (Academy membership includes about 3,500 libraries in the United States and abroad.)

The political scientist has served as a consultant to the Pennsylvania Labor Department and Pennsylvania Civil Service Commission. He is a member of the American, Pennsylvania, Western, and Southern political science associations, and American Society for Public Administration of which he served as the first president of the Philadelphia regional chapter from 1947 to 1949. His Greek letter societies are the Pi Sigma Alpha and Pi Gamma Mu. He is an Episcopalian and an Independent.

Professor Charlesworth was married on August 14, 1928 to Dorothy Louise Coy (who died in 1945). He married Berenice Lucille Steward on July 6, 1946. He has two daughters, Audrey Elaine and Sylvia Jean, by the earlier marriage, and one daughter, Pamela Steward, by the second marriage. He has gray eyes and brown hair, is five feet seven inches in height and weighs 170 pounds. His favorite outdoor exercises are golf and hiking. He is the trails chairman of the Philadelphia Trail Club, director of the Horseshoe Trail Club, and a member of the Appalachian and Potomac Appalachian mountain clubs.

References

Ann Am Acad 288:1 Jl '53
N Y Times p17 Je 9 '53 por

America's Young Men, 1938-39
Directory of American Scholars (1951)
Who's Who in America, 1954-55

CHERRY, FRANCIS A(DAMS) Sept. 5, 1908- Governor of Arkansas; lawyer

Address: b. State Capitol, Little Rock, Ark.; h. 18th & Center, Little Rock, Ark.

In his campaign for election to the governorship of Arkansas, Judge Francis A. Cherry attracted much attention through his use of a new radio technique known as "Talkathon" by means of which he reached more voters than any other candidate in the state's history. Regarded as a novice in politics, he nevertheless carried sixty-seven of the seventy-five counties of Arkansas to score an impressive victory over former Governor Sidney S. McMath for the Democratic nomination on August 14, 1952. He was elected Governor on November 4 for a two-year term.

In 1954 he was defeated by Orval Faubus for a second two-year term in the primary held in August.

"An entire state is pulling itself out of the mire by its own bootstraps," Governor Cherry told Godfrey Sperling, Jr., in an interview in the *Christian Science Monitor* (August 10, 1953). "This is revolution—revolution, that is, Arkansas style. Towns that were once sleepy are now bustling with new buildings, new community activities, new morale. . . . We believe that we have discovered a formula of self-help which not only will provide progress and development for this state but which might well be applied anywhere in the world where people are anxious to improve their economic and social life." In ten years great progress has been made.

Governor Cherry has favored President Dwight D. Eisenhower's proposal that eighteen-year-olds should be allowed to vote. "They should have a voice in Government," he declared. After the Supreme Court ruling prohibiting racial segregation in the schools, the Governor said that Arkansas would not approach the ruling with the idea of being an "outlaw." He stated, "Obviously it will take a good deal of time to work it out. I only hope what has happened does not set back the advances Negroes have made in Arkansas in the past several years" (New York *Times*, May 19, 1954). He added that the first step toward conforming with the decision will be the appointment of a Governor's committee on segregation.

Before his gubernatorial victory, Cherry's only political office had been that of chancellor of the Northeast Arkansas Chancery District, a post he won in 1942, after five years of private practice as a lawyer, in Jonesboro, Arkansas.

Francis Adams Cherry was born in Fort Worth, Texas on September 5, 1908, youngest of the five children of Haskille Scott Cherry and Clara Belle (Taylor) Cherry. His father a railroad conductor, moved the family to El Reno, Oklahoma, and later to nearby Enid, Oklahoma, where Cherry attended Enid High School.

Upon his graduation in 1926 he entered Oklahoma A. and M. College at Stillwater, Oklahoma and majored in pre-law. When he had completed his courses there in 1930 he obtained whatever jobs were available during that depression period. He worked as a dishwasher and later drove an ice truck through the Ozark mountains. "If you don't think that's hard work you ought to try it," Cherry said recently. He managed to save thirty-seven dollars and went to Fayetteville, Arkansas in 1933 and enrolled at the University of Arkansas Law School. After paying his tuition of eighteen dollars he had only nineteen dollars left to live on for the year. He was sorely tempted to buy a railroad ticket back to Oklahoma but classmates helped out by lending him their books. "We were all impoverished in those depression days," recalled Bayard Taylor, "but Francis was more impoverished than the rest of us." Despite outside jobs, he made good grades and was elected president of the senior class.

After receiving his Bachelor of Law degree in 1936, Cherry went to Little Rock, Arkansas, and was befriended by a young attorney, Leffel Gentry, who gave him a desk in his office. Gentry later became chairman of the State Democratic Committee and manager of Cherry's successful campaign in 1952. Cherry moved to Jonesboro, Arkansas in 1937 and entered law practice as a junior partner with Marcus Feitz.

Arkansas Pub. & Inf. Comm.

FRANCIS A. CHERRY

The young lawyer served as a U.S. Commissioner and as a referee for the Workmen's Compensation Commission before running for the offices of chancellor and probate judge of the Twelfth Chancery District in Northeast Arkansas. After a mere five years as a resident of that district, he became the youngest chancellor in recent Arkansas political history being nominated over a long-time incumbent in 1942, for a six-year term.

He waived his judicial deferment and sought to enter the Armed Services through the Selective Service but without success. He then secured a commission in the U.S. Navy in 1944 and served for two years, returning to the bench of the Chancery in January, 1946. He was re-elected for another six-year term in 1948, there being no opposition to his candidacy.

When the stumping began for the Democratic nomination for Governor in 1952, Chancellor Cherry was given little or no chance for the nomination, among the five who were in the running. The campaign took on national significance because of the support given to Governor Sidney S. McMath by President Harry S. Truman. Speaking six weeks before the August run-offs, Truman personally endorsed McMath in his dedication speech at Bull Shoals Dam in the Ozarks.

"Talkathon", used only once before as a political device, is a marathon radio broadcast, whereby Cherry talked for twenty-four and a half consecutive hours to both a visible and a radio audience, using microphones and answering over 5,000 questions that came to him from all parts of the state over a battery of telephones. Before the balloting on July 29 Cherry made twenty more "Talkathons", none shorter than three hours (*Newsweek*, August 25, 1952). He called Governor McMath "Harry's boy" and declared that Arkansas

CHERRY, FRANCIS A.—*Continued*

voters resented outside interference in their state elections (New York *Herald Tribune,* August 14, 1952).

Throughout his energetic "Talkathons" the Judge parried those who pointed out that he was not born in Arkansas by stating, "I'm here because I wanted to be; the others are here just because they happened to be born here." He was further quoted, in the Arkansas *Democrat* on August 13, 1953 as saying: "I fell in love with the state, and decided it would be my home."

In the final election on August 12, he won a victory of more than 100,000 votes over McMath in by far the largest total vote in any Arkansas election. With 2,277 of the 2,301 precincts reported, Cherry amassed 235,173 votes, while McMath received 137,900 votes. Judge Cherry credited his victory to his having answered all questions fully and openly, and admitting frankly when he did not know the answers.

After his inauguration on January 13, 1953, Governor Cherry put into operation his major legislative program, which included legislation for the adoption of a new State Fiscal Code, the revising of the Revenue Stabilization Act covering major expenditures, and a proposed Constitutional amendment for revision of the property tax system. He also encouraged the development of new industries for the state.

Arkansas' chief industries are agriculture, lumbering, and mining (coal, manganese and bauxite). Its population is about 2,000,000. To bring in new industries the University of Arkansas sent professors to help communities decide what types of industry would best fit into their economy. The project works under the title of Arkansas Economic Council, State Chamber of Commerce, and the Associated Industries of Arkansas, as an official state operation. Experts were sent to New York, Chicago, Detroit, and other cities, and many of Arkansas' raw materials are now used in manufacturing which were not utilized before. Farming, too, has been diversified and has often replaced cotton. Truck farming, soy beans, hay, grains and timber were developed in communities where the people were at first slow to respond. The 270 communities which have adopted new methods have made many civic improvements in municipal buildings, pavement of streets, fire departments, mosquito and fly control.

"If only representatives from the underprivileged areas of the world could see what has been done in Arkansas during the past ten years they would go home talking about the 750 new industries in Arkansas . . . and the $1,000,000,000 of new investments," said Governor Cherry. "And, most of all, they would talk about the community enthusiasm which did the job. Capital is still necessary. And education—lots of it. Arkansas found its capital and education right here—one from people digging deep into their jeans, the other from the University of Arkansas" (*Christian Science Monitor,* August 10, 1953).

Francis Adams Cherry was married to Margaret Frierson on November 10, 1937. The couple met while students at the University of Arkansas, where Mrs. Cherry was campus queen in 1933. They have three children, Haskille Scott III, Charlotte Frierson and Francis A. Cherry, Jr. The Governor is a Presbyterian, a member of the Kappa Alpha and the Delta Theta Phi (Legal) fraternities.

He has blue-green eyes, silvery gray hair, and is five feet eight inches tall, with a weight of one hundred seventy pounds. He is a member of the Little Rock Consistory, Shrine, United Commercial Travelers, American Legion, Fraternal Order of Eagles, Order of Amaranth, and is a past president of the Lions Club of Jonesboro.

References

Arkansas Democrat p8 Ag 13 '52
N Y Herald Tribune p5 Ag 14 '52
N Y Times p16 Ag 14 '52
Newsweek 40:76 Ag 25 '52 pors
Who's Who in America, 1954-55

CHIANG CHING-KUO (jĭ-äng'jēng gwô)
1906- Chinese military leader
Address: Taipei, Formosa

One of the most controversial figures in the Far East is Lieutenant General Chiang Ching-kuo, the forty-eight-year-old son of Generalissimo Chiang Kai-shek, President of the Chinese Nationalist Government on Formosa. His supporters believe that he is doing an admirable job in ferreting out Communist agents. His critics object to his dictatorial methods, resulting, they claim, in loss of civil liberties for Chinese citizens.

Described by Joseph W. Alsop, Jr. in October 1953 as "the rising man and perhaps the strongest man after his father" on the island of Formosa, Chiang Ching-kuo has been head of the political department of the Ministry of Defense. On June 25, 1954 a United Press dispatch stated that in a government reshuffling he had been succeeded by Lieutenant General Chang Yi-ting, but that reliable sources expected Chiang Ching-kuo to be promoted to a higher position in the Nationalist government.

He spent the years 1925 to 1937 in the Soviet Union, and in exercising his present authority he has been accused by several journalists and by Dr. K. C. Wu (former Governor of Formosa) of "employing police state techniques he learned from the Communists" (*Look,* June 29, 1954).

On the other hand, William C. Bullitt, former Ambassador to Russia, insists that Chiang Ching-kuo has "performed a vital service for his country" in ferreting out Communists. "There is no more intense enemy of the Communists than Chiang Ching-kuo "(*Look,* August 24, 1954).

Chiang Ching-kuo was born in Chekiang province, China in 1906 to Chiang Kai-shek and his first wife. This union with a girl of the Mao family had been arranged by relatives when Chiang Kai-shek was fifteen and it ended in divorce. In an article (translated for *Scholastic*, March 15, 1943) Chiang Ching-kuo recalls his father's insistence on self-reliance. ("Don't ask money from me," the boy was admonished. "Be strong and create your own future.") He learned such English as he knows while attending a school at Shanghai. He was arrested at the age of fifteen for leading a student "strike." Later he continued his education in Peking.

After the death of Dr. Sun Yat-sen, who was instrumental in founding the Chinese Republic, Chiang Kai-shek in 1925 became a member of the Kuomintang triumvirate which ruled China. The elder Chiang was officially chairman of the Military Affairs Commission. In 1925 (the year prior to the *coup d'état* which made him the virtual dictator of China) Chiang Kai-shek entered his son in the Soviet military academy at Leningrad. The younger Chiang remained in the Soviet Union for the next twelve years, but whether he did so willingly or not is a matter of speculation.

Early in 1936, when Chiang Kai-shek was fighting the Chinese Communists, the Leningrad newspaper *Pravda* published an "open letter" in which Chiang Ching-kuo denounced his father as "the enemy of the whole people, and therefore the implacable enemy of his son," and in describing his life in the Soviet Union stated that "after studying in various schools until 1930, he went to work in a plant as an ordinary laborer, rising steadily until he became head of his department, with 4,000 workers under him at a salary of 700 rubles a month and an apartment to himself" (as quoted in the New York *Times*, February 12, 1936).

On the other hand, it has been asserted that he was expelled from the Leningrad military academy after only two years because of "anti-Stalinist activity," and spent the next seven "in forced labor camps" (*Time*, February 1, 1954).

The outbreak of Sino-Japanese hostilities in July 1937 was followed by the conclusion of a Russian-Chinese nonaggression pact on August 29, 1937. Chiang Ching-kuo then returned to China. Reconciled with his father, he asked the generalissimo "for an administrative job 'under the worst possible conditions'" (*Newsweek*, October 7, 1946). He was assigned in 1940 as commissioner for the Fourth Administrative District of Kiangsi province, and was charged with reindoctrinating its 3,000,000 inhabitants.

The younger Chiang, who became a member of the new provisional government of Kiangsi in December 1943, remained as such until the Japanese overran the province in 1945. During World War II he also directed a training school for political officers at Chungking.

From 1945 to 1947 Chiang Ching-kuo served as Foreign Affairs Commissioner for the Northeast, participated in conferences relating to the future of Manchuria, and in December 1945, revisited Moscow to discuss with Joseph Stalin "Manchurian and other topics of mutual Sino-Russian interest."

Wide World

CHIANG CHING-KUO

In August 1948 the Chinese Nationalist government promulgated stringent price-control regulations to combat inflation and the black market, and Chiang Ching-kuo was sent to Shanghai as deputy economic control supervisor. After his arrival he told a "cheering throng" that the "new economic policy" was a "socialistic, revolutionary movement" aimed at "unpatriotic business men" (New York *Times*, October 13, 1948). More than one hundred "Tigers" (black marketeers) were arrested, and merchants were forced "to sell goods below cost for the public benefit."

However, the "new policy" failed, and on October 31 the government announced a new regulation based on accepting inflation. Chiang resigned as Shanghai's "economic czar," and in the following month, with the rank of major general, took command of a tank force on the Suchow front.

When the Chinese Nationalist government moved to Formosa in early December 1949, Chiang Ching-kuo became chairman of the Taiwan (Formosa) Provincial Kuomintang Headquarters. Thus, he was to exercise what has been characterized as "virtual control" over the ruling Kuomintang party. In March 1950 when Chiang Kai-shek resumed the Presidency (which he had resigned the previous year) he named his son as the head of the political department of the Ministry of National Defense. (His army rank was that of lieutenant general.)

On October 2, 1950 it was announced that Chiang Ching-kuo would institute a military "self-reliance program." The 500,000 soldiers of the Nationalist Army were required to raise crops and livestock and to do "other service jobs usually awarded to contractors." He also established "political officers" in every echelon, and these officers "responsible to him only . . .

CHIANG, CHING-KUO—*Continued*

also functioned as a secret police" (*Time*, February 1, 1954). Some critics believe this program is similar to one promulgated by Mao Tse-tung, Chinese Communist leader.

Dr. K. C. Wu, who was Governor of Formosa from 1949 to 1953, has said that Chiang Ching-kuo "organized a Youth Corps modeled after the Hitler Youth and the Communist Youth" (*Look*, June 29, 1954). The former Governor who "split" with the Chiang regime and went into exile in the United States, stated that Chiang Kai-shek "would not agree" to legalizing an opposition party, and that "when the Seventh Kuomintang Conference convened in the summer of 1952, he himself hand-picked all the delegates, three-quarters of them his son's stooges."

Chiang Ching-kuo served on the central reform committee of the Kuomintang from 1950 to 1952, and in 1952 he became a member of the Central Committee of the Kuomintang.

By the spring of 1953 speculation began as to the identity of the new president, in the event of the death or retirement of Chiang Kai-shek. "According to the constitution," stated Robert Franklin (New York *Herald Tribune*, March 15, 1953), "the Prime Minister should succeed . . . but there are many here who feel that the generalissimo's son will eventually emerge as the next leader of the Chinese Nationalists. Such is certainly Chiang Ching-kuo's own aim."

Joseph W. Alsop, Jr., who visited Formosa later in 1953, commented in the New York *Herald Tribune* (October 30) on "the emergence of the generalissimo's son as a major power," stating that he "appears to be a man of the highest capacity, brilliantly intelligent, absolutely honest, hard as nails," although "not . . . a 'democratic leader.'" Alsop felt that the "present tendency" was for Chiang Ching-kuo "to ally himself with the old bad lots."

Ambassador William C. Bullitt, on the other hand, maintains that Chiang Ching-kuo "is a man of first-rate character and ability, who works extremely hard" as head of a Formosan "FBI" to catch traitors in both the army and civilian life." To call Free China 'totalitarian' or 'a police state' is grossly unfair" (*Look*, August 24, 1954).

In defense of his use of communist techniques, Chiang Ching-kuo has declared that "the basic objective is to eliminate communism and any tactic that helps toward that end should be used."

Chiang Ching-kuo married a blonde Russian woman in 1934 whom he is said to have met while working as an engineer in the Ural Mountains. They have two sons and a daughter. The Chinese leader is "of medium height, weighing perhaps 130 pounds, athletically built."

Dr. Hu Shih, one of China's most respected scholars, and a member of the editorial board of the fortnightly *Free China*, entered an emphatic rebuttal of Dr. Wu's denunciation of Chiang Kai-shek's regime and of his son Chiang Ching-kuo. Writing in the *New Leader* Hu Shih stated: "Freedom of speech and the press [in Formosa] is now shared by all who have the moral courage to speak out. . . . Elections have been and still are quite free" (*Time*, August 16, 1954).

References

Collier's 112:11+ Jl 31 '43 por
Look 18:39+ Je 29 '54 por
N Y Herald Tribune II p3 S 19 '48 por
N Y Sun p16 F 3 '44
N Y Times p12 F 12 '36; IV p2 S 19 '48; p2 Ja 20 '51; N 17 '51 por
New Yorker 29:143+ N 7 '53
Newsweek 13:23 F 6 '39; 28:51+ O 7 '46; 32:34 S 27 '48
Reporter 10:18+ Ap 27 '54
Scholastic 42:17 Mr 15 '43
Time 52:39 S 20 '48 por; 63:17 F 1 '54 por
China Handbook, 1953-54

CHRISTOPHER, GEORGE T. Oct. 2, 1887-June 7, 1954 Former automobile company executive; son of a coal miner; born in a log cabin in Indiana; obtained electrical engineering degree (1911); worked on 155-mm. cannons, Army Ordnance Department, World War I; joined General Motors (1918) as vice-president, Delco-Remy Electric Company; later held same position at Oldsmobile, Pontiac, and Buick; president, Packard Motor Car (1942-1949); developed mass-production of Rolls-Royce engines and greatly improved aircraft engines during World War II, especially the P-51 Mustang Fighter. See *Current Biography*, (Nov.) 1947.

Obituary

N Y Herald Tribune p28 Je 9 '54

CHUTE, CHARLES LIONEL Aug. 4, 1882—Sept. 25, 1953 Social worker; executive director of National Probation and Parole Association (1921-1928), and vice-president since 1948; received A.B. degree from Oberlin College (1904); M.A. from Columbia University (1910); graduate of New York School of Social Work; investigator for National Child Labor Committee (1910); secretary Pennsylvania Child Labor Association (1912); secretary New York State Probation Commission (1913-1920); leader in ten-year effort which secured passage of Federal Probation Act (1925); wrote and lectured on juvenile delinquency and crime prevention. See *Current Biography*, (Sept.) 1949.

Obituary

N Y Times p85 S 27 '53

CLAIRE, INA Oct. 15, 1895- Actress

Address: h. 1000 Mason St., San Francisco 8, Calif.

After an absence of seven years, Ina Claire, generally regarded as the outstanding "high comedienne" of the American theatre, has returned to Broadway to play in *The Confidential Clerk* by T. S. Eliot. When the play opened at the Morosco Theatre on February 11, 1954, the critics were unanimous in their praise of Miss Claire's acting in the role of Lady Elizabeth Mulhammer. "She gives a mettlesome, radiant, comic performance in which every detail is carefully mitered," wrote Brooks Atkinson in the New York *Times*. "It's wonderful having her back again, lightening the world with her ironic humors." *The Confidential Clerk* closed on May 22nd after a run of 116 performances.

Miss Claire began her career as a child entertainer and achieved eminence in vaudeville, later in musical comedy, and then in such successes as *The Last of Mrs. Cheyney, End of Summer, Biography, The Fatal Weakness* and others of the "drawing room comedy" *genre*. She has appeared in motion pictures including *The Awful Truth* and *The Royal Family of Broadway*.

Ina Claire was born Ina Fagan, in Washington, D.C., on October 15, 1895 of Irish ancestry. She was one of two children born to Joseph Fagan and the former Cora B. Lieurance Claire. When she was very young her father was killed in an accident in the Ford Theatre in Washington, D.C. Even as a child Ina did imitations of the boarders in the boardinghouse where she and her mother lived.

Ina Fagan attended Holy Cross Academy, until the eighth grade, when she and her mother embarked on a tour of the vaudeville circuits. "I was all of thirteen," Miss Claire recalls. "Somebody once told me I was as good as Elsie Janis." Included in her act was the imitation of Sir Harry Lauder which won her wide acclaim.

The young actress learned how to get "the necessary four bows" and thus stay on the vaudeville bill. She traveled on the Orpheum and on the Keith and Proctor circuits, and believes that those were the places to really learn the business, doing three shows a day.

In 1911 Ina Claire entered the musical comedy field, appearing in *Jumping Jupiter*. Her outstanding success of that period was in the musical *Quaker Girl*, in the role of Prudence, a part she played for 240 performances, beginning in October 1911. She made her first appearance on the London stage in October 1913, playing Una Trance in *The Girl from Utah*. After playing in *The Belle of Bond Street* she returned to New York and appeared in *Lady Luxury*. She was in Ziegfeld's *Follies of 1915* in which she did imitations of Jane Cowl and other stars.

It was in the part of a maid-adventuress in *Polly with a Past* in 1917 that the actress made her debut in the straight comedy roles. David Belasco produced this play; it ran for 315 performances and it made Ina Claire famous. She was next seen in the Belasco production of *The Gold Diggers*, in 1919. She played this role for nearly two years. Miss Claire made her first film in 1915. She repeated her successful stage role in *Polly With A Past* in a motion picture version of the play.

There followed a long series of starring vehicles, most of them drawing room comedies in which Ina Claire usually played a lighthearted, charming sophisticate. Noel Busch (*Life*, February 10, 1947) said that her career

INA CLAIRE

does credit to the taste of audiences. "Certainly it is not to the detriment of the American stage that it has produced at least one comedienne who inspires, rather than . . . pretentious tributes, merely smiles, and reasoned compliments, and the feeling of delight." Miss Claire was seen in *Bluebeard's Eighth Wife*, 1921; *The Awful Truth*, staged by Henry Miller, in 1922; *Grounds For Divorce*, in which she was co-starred with Philip Merivale at the Empire Theatre in the 1924 season (commemorated by the inclusion of Miss Claire's portrait in the Empire Theatre gallery). Audiences recall with fondness her role in *The Last of Mrs. Cheyney*, by Frederick Lonsdale, in which she played 252 performances in New York. These last two plays remain among her favorites as types of "manor house comedy" she now feels is too infrequently seen on the stage.

After these plays, most of which were outstanding successes, Miss Claire went to Hollywood, where she made the film version of *The Awful Truth* in 1929. This was followed by *The Royal Family of Broadway* in 1930; *Rebound* in 1931; and *The Greeks Had a Word For Them* in 1932. Miss Claire has said: "I have been ashamed of my movies. I never believed what I was saying. The plots are really for children" (*Cue*, January 30, 1954). Ina Claire returned to the legitimate stage during 1932 and was cast in S. N. Behrman's *Biography*, playing the role of Marion Froude, a portrait painter. The play, a success, was taken to London for the 1934 season, with Miss Claire again in the leading role.

She told Helen Ormsbee: "I'm the sort of actress they call difficult at rehearsals. That's because for quite a while I keep looking at the play as a whole, instead of at my part. I feel detached," she explained. ". . . But all of a sudden the day comes when I begin to see my part, to know the women. Then things are better.

CLAIRE, INA—*Continued*

Still, I'm rather shy at rehearsals, especially comedy, for in comedy the audience works with you and what can you do without it? Hearing an audience laugh is the only thing I miss when I'm away from the theatre," Miss Claire said (New York *Herald Tribune,* November 17, 1946).

The actress appeared in *Ode to Liberty* in 1934. This was followed by the S. N. Behrman comedy *End of Summer* in 1936; *Once Is Enough* and *Ninotchka* in 1938; *The Talley Method,* another S. N. Behrman comedy in which she played Enid Fuller in 1941.

It was not until five years had passed that Ina Claire returned to Broadway in *The Fatal Weakness* in 1946. Richard Watts, Jr. wrote (New York *Post,* November 20, 1946) of her portrayal of the role of Mrs. Espenshade: "It brings back that unfailingly brilliant actress, Ina Claire, after far too long an absence. Miss Claire has always been a resourceful comedienne and a quietly effective emotional player, but I have never seen her in finer form than in George Kelly's comedy, as she exhibits all her gifts for humor and character."

John Mason Brown (*Saturday Review of Literature,* December 21, 1946), although criticizing the play, paid tribute to Miss Claire. "In its darkest moments she shines like a candle made of diamonds. Where there is no comedy she creates some. She creates it by the machine gun rapidity of her speech, by the contagious smile which keeps dancing in her eyes, by the mere twinkle of her personality."

During Miss Claire's last seven-year absence from the Broadway stage she has lived on Nob Hill, San Francisco. With her husband, William R. Wallace, Jr., a lawyer, she has made many visits to Europe, seeing plays in London and Paris. She has also visited the southwest to observe the Indian tribal customs and dances near Taos and Santa Fe, New Mexico. Although many plays were submitted to her, she told Ward Morehouse (*Theatre Arts,* August, 1951), that "she hasn't quit Broadway, but she is in no hurry to get back.... Find me a play," she said. "A good play. A good part. Not just one of those that I've played a thousand times." Morehouse predicted that the right kind of play would bring her back.

When Ina Claire received the script of T. S. Eliot's London hit *The Confidential Clerk,* she said, "It's exactly the kind of play I've wanted. It's delicious, really. And it would take that kind of play to get me away from San Francisco, which we love." The play opened on February 11, 1954, and again the artistry of the leading American "high comedienne" was acclaimed.

Walter Kerr (New York *Herald Tribune,* February 12, 1954) wrote that Miss Claire who still looks "like a dazzling line-drawing from the most fashionable magazine of the '20's, is delectable beyond belief."

"To read the text after seeing the play," wrote Brooks Atkinson (New York *Times,* February 21, 1954), "is to appreciate the brilliance [Ina Claire] imparts to it in her acting. She is an exhilarating person on the stage—trim, sparkling, alert, and ironic. Very much the mistress of the part, she has found the key words that define it in the dialogue and given them space, style and emphasis in the playing. Out of Mr. Eliot's meticulous words she has created a magnetic character."

The hazel-eyed, blonde-haired Miss Claire has often been voted one of the ten best dressed women in America. She was married to James Whittaker, a newspaperman, in 1919, from whom she was divorced in 1925. On May 9, 1929 she married John Gilbert, the silent screen star; they were divorced in 1931. Ina Claire married William R. Wallace, Jr. on March 16, 1939. For recreation she enjoys reading and traveling, and often accompanies her husband on hunting or fishing trips. They have a 500-acre ranch and "a sort of adobe house that runs along a hill" in the Valley of the Moon in Sonoma county. "She retains," wrote Ward Morehouse, "that bright-as-a-candy box look, she dresses tastefully . . . [and] has wit and buoyance and great intelligence."

Despite her success as a comedienne, Miss Claire has always had the "conviction that she is a better actress than the producers ever thought she was, her protest against being typecast . . . in artificial and delightful plays that have never given her the opportunity to display histrionic depth" (*Theatre Arts,* August, 1951). She told William Hawkins once that her ambition was to play Peter Pan in Barrie's play, and Joan in Shaw's *Saint Joan* (New York *World-Telegram,* January 24, 1947). "I wish now I'd played up my real name of Fagan and done more varied parts."

References

Cue 23:10 Ja 30 '54 por
Life 22:51+ F 10 '47 pors
Theatre Arts 35:26+ Ag '51
Who's Who in the Theatre (1952)

CLARK, BENNETT CHAMP Jan. 8, 1890-July 13, 1954 Circuit Judge of U.S. Court of Appeals; former Democratic Senator from Missouri (1933-1945); was graduated from University of Missouri (1914); served as lieutenant colonel, World War I; practiced law in St. Louis; past national commander of American Legion; son of Champ Clark, Speaker of the House of Representatives (1911-1919).

See *Current Biography,* (Nov.) 1941.

Obituary

N Y Times p27 Jl 14 '54

CLARK, J(OSEPH) J(AMES) Nov. 12, 1893- United States Naval officer

Address: b. c/o Fleet Post Office, San Francisco, Calif.; h. 324 E. 8th St., Chelsea, Okla.

The Commander of the United States Seventh Fleet from May 1952 until his retirement at the end of 1953 was Vice Admiral J. J. ("Jocko") Clark. He is a veteran of action in both World Wars and a naval aviator since 1925.

An expert in carrier warfare, Clark participated in or directed important raids on Marcus and Wake Islands, Iwo Jima, and Okinawa during World War II, when he was frequently referred to as "the fightingest admiral in the Pacific." Vice Admiral Clark assumed command of the Seventh Fleet on May 20, 1952.

Joseph James Clark, one of the eight children of William Andrew and Lillie Belle (Berry) Clark, was born November 12, 1893 at Pryor, in what is now Oklahoma. His father, a rancher and farmer, was a native of nearby Tahlequah; his mother came from the neighborhood of Memphis, Tennessee. The elder Clark was listed on the Cherokee tribal rolls as of one-quarter Cherokee descent; in Navy records his celebrated son is described as one-eighth Indian.

When he was seven, Clark's parents moved from the ranch where he was born to another ranch north of the town of Chelsea. There the elder Clark raised wheat, oats, corn and Hereford cattle, and his son rode a pony, ran coyotes with hounds, trapped skunks and hunted ducks with a rifle.

The youth, who had just passed his fourteenth birthday when the former Indian and Oklahoma Territories were admitted to the Union as the state of Oklahoma, attended Willie Halsell College at Vinita, Oklahoma, and Oklahoma Agricultural and Mechanical College at Stillwater, Oklahoma, before becoming a plebe (freshman) at the United States Naval Academy, Annapolis, Maryland, in 1913. He is said to have been the first appointee with Indian blood ever to be enrolled at Annapolis.

Towards the end of their second year as midshipmen, "Jocko" Clark (as he was nicknamed) and twenty of his classmates took revenge for previous treatment at the hands of upper classmen by "hazing" the plebe baseball team; the offenders were identified and were "turned back a year" as penalty. Jock "studied diligently after that, and finished in the top fourth of his class. But the Navy's records will always show, for purposes of promotion, that the Admiral's class was 1918 instead of [1917] when he actually graduated" (*Life,* January 22, 1945).

About two months after the United States entered World War I, and on receiving his ensign's commission, Clark was assigned to the armored cruiser *North Carolina* engaged in escorting troop convoys across the Atlantic. Following the war he remained at sea, serving on the destroyers, *Aaron Ward, Aulick* and *Brooks* in the Near East and as executive officer of the *Bulmer,* employed by the American Relief administration and the Near East Relief.

"Jocko" Clark, who subsequently commanded the *Brooks* for a short period, returned to the United States with the keen desire to enter naval aviation, but realization of this ambition was delayed by an ankle injury which left him with a slight limp. However, after one year from 1923 to 1924 as an instructor at Annapolis, he was accepted for flight training, and was finally designated naval aviator at Pensacola, Florida, on March 16, 1925. In the ten years that followed, Clark saw sea duty with Aircraft Squadrons, Battle Fleet, successively as flight officer with Utility Squadron One, aviation officer of the battleship *Mississippi,* and aviation

U. S. Navy

VICE-ADM. J. J. CLARK

technical adviser to the commander of the Battleship Division Three. He commanded Fighting Squadron 2-B of the *Lexington* in 1931 and 1932 and was air officer of that carrier in 1936 and 1937.

His shore duty on regular rotation during the period between the wars included tours as executive officer of the Naval Air Station, Anacostia, D.C., and as aeronautical member of the Navy Department's Board of Inspection and Survey. In 1938 Clark was assigned to Pearl Harbor, Hawaii, as both executive officer of the Fleet Air Base and commanding officer of Patrol Wing Two, and was so engaged until September 1939. He was inspector of naval aircraft at the Curtiss-Wright Corporation in Buffalo, New York in 1940, and executive officer of the Naval Air Station at Jacksonville, Florida, during 1940 and 1941.

Returning to sea in 1941, he served as the executive officer aboard the carrier *Yorktown.* Clark participated in the first Navy task force raid on the Marcus and Gilbert Islands on January 31, 1942. In the ensuing spring he was given responsibility for "commissioning" the U.S.S. *Suwannee,* a former tanker converted to aircraft carrier. "He refused to permit 'abandon ship' drill on the *Suwannee* . . . announcing, 'You boys are going to bring her home'" (*Life,* January 22, 1945). He commanded that carrier through the invasion and occupation of French Morocco.

For this "outstanding service," Clark received a Letter of Commendation with Ribbon; in addition, he was promoted from commander to captain and was given command of the new carrier *Yorktown* even before she was commissioned at Norfolk, Virginia, April 4, 1943.

The *Yorktown* and its aircraft raided Marcus Island, August 31, destroying three quarters of the Japanese installations there (a feat for which Captain Clark received another Navy

CLARK, J. J.—*Continued*

commendation). Subsequently, the carrier also attacked Wake, Jaluit, Makin, Kwajalein and Wotje Islands; and for his part in the various raids Clark was awarded the Silver Star Medal for conspicuous gallantry.

President Roosevelt nominated Clark for advancement to rear admiral on January 24, 1944. Two days later Clark was personally commended by Admiral Chester W. Nimitz "for the performance of his ship," and early in the following month the newly elevated rear admiral was re-designated as a task group commander of carriers and screening vessels operating alternately with the First and Second Carrier Task Groups of the Pacific Fleet.

In operations under the general command of Vice Admiral Marc A. Mitscher, Clark and his carrier aircraft struck three times at Iwo Jima and Chichi Jima before the Fourth of July, and blasted 206 Japanese planes out of the air, destroyed fifty-four more on the ground, sank seven ships, probably sank six more, and damaged thirty-three after which new attacks on the Bonin Islands early in August resulted in the destruction of twenty-eight enemy naval vessels. (His insistence on teamwork at this period and later was such that he required all pilots in his command to read Frank Graham's book *The New York Yankees.*)

Rear Admiral Clark's striking power was a major factor in the naval battle of the Philippines, October 1944, and his carrier fleet subsequently played a prominent part in the capture of Okinawa and made strafing attacks on the Japanese home islands themselves. For his 1944 and 1945 war service, Clark received the Navy Distinguished Service Medal twice, as well as the Legion of Merit with Combat "V" and the Navy Cross.

Returned to the United States in June 1945 for new duty as chief of the Naval Air Intermediate Training Command at Corpus Christi, Texas, the naval commander so often referred to as "The Chief" by his men was actually made an honorary chief of the Sioux tribe in ceremonies at Yankton, South Dakota, on the following September 3. (His tribal name is Thunderbird). A year later in September 1946 Clark was appointed Assistant Chief of Naval Operations for Air.

In an address to the Wings Club in New York several weeks later (October 18) Admiral Clark not only denied that surface carriers were obsolescent, but referred to "the possibility that the Navy could develop a submersible aircraft carrier capable of launching planes carrying atomic bombs" (New York *Times,* October 19, 1946).

In November 1948 Clark succeeded Rear Admiral Ralph E. Jennings as commander of Carrier Division Four, a designation he retained through the outbreak of the Korean War and until August 1950, when he became commander of the Naval Air Bases, Eleventh and Twelfth Naval Division.

His first tour of duty in Korean waters began on October 3 of the year following, when he succeeded Rear Admiral John Perry in command of the fast Carrier Task Force 77. Clark was in command of Carrier Division Three when, late in February of 1952, he was recalled to the continental United States to become Commander, First Fleet, with the rank of vice admiral on March 24.

Admiral Clark was back in the Orient, by May 20, 1952, having taken over command of the Seventh Fleet from Vice Admiral Robert P. Briscoe, who had succeeded Vice Admiral C. Turner Joy as commander of all naval forces in the Far East. The bulk of the Seventh Fleet was, and is, concentrated in Korean waters, but certain units were assigned to patrol the Taiwan Strait in accordance with President Truman's directive of June 28, 1950 "to defend Formosa against attack by the Chinese Communists and at the same time prevent re-entry on the mainland by the Nationalist forces (New York *Times,* February 9, 1953).

In this connection, Clark visited Taipei with Major General Ernest M. Moore of the Air Force about two weeks later. After conferring with Chinese Nationalist officers, Clark expressed the belief that "carrier-based fighters of the United States 13th Air Force would be able to beat back any Communist attempt to bomb Formosa." He thought the chances of a Communist invasion of Formosa "remote," but likely to be "bigger" if "an armistice is reached in Korea" (New York *Times,* June 9, 1952).

In his first address to Congress late in January 1953, President Eisenhower informed the legislators that the Navy would no longer be required to protect Communist China from Nationalist attack. The Far Eastern Command announced on February 8 that the Seventh Fleet was "manned and ready" for any result of "policy changes affecting the Orient."

After the signing of the Korean truce on July 26, 1953, Admiral Clark said at a press conference in Hong Kong that the United States was not encouraging Generalissimo Chiang Kai-shek's Nationalist government in Formosa to attempt an invasion campaign against Communist China.

"Our government is at peace, and we do not encourage an invasion of the mainland," he declared (New York *Times,* August 23, 1953).

Composition of the Seventh Fleet was described by the Navy as including Carrier Task Force Seventy-seven, comprising the *Kearsage, Philippine Sea, Oriskany* and *Valley Forge,* which were stationed off both the east and west coasts of Korea, a cruiser force including the *Rochester, Los Angeles* and *Toledo,* numerous destroyers, a "substantial force" of minesweepers, amphibious units under Rear Admiral W. E. Moore, and approximately one hundred supply and repair vessels.

Rear Admiral Alfred M. Pride has succeeded to Clark's command of the Seventh Fleet.

Admiral Clark was selected for the Oklahoma Hall of Fame in 1952 and on November 21 was decorated with the Korean Medal of Military Merit, Taiguk, with Silver Star, by President Syngman Rhee. He has also received the Merito Naval Medal from Mexico and the Peruvian Flying Cross. He is the recipient of many United States campaign medals as well as the Navy Occupation Service Medal, the

United Nations Medal, Presidential Unit Citations, with three Stars, the World War I Victory Medal, with one Bronze Star, American Defense Medal, with Combat "A", and the Navy Expert Pistol Shop Medal.

The Admiral is an Episcopalian and a Freemason. His clubs are the New York Yacht, New York Athletic and the Chevy Chase. He was married to the former Shannon Kelly Jensen, an investor and the owner of a bank at Pharr, Texas, on May 12, 1946. Clark's two daughters, Mary Louise and Catherine Carol, are the children of an earlier marriage. Five feet eleven inches in height and 185 pounds in weight, the brown-haired, brown-eyed naval officer is very proud of his Cherokee heritage.

References

Life 18:41+ Ja 22 '45 pors
N Y Sun p18 Jl 30 '46
N Y Times p26 Ja 30 '44; p3 My 20 '52
International World Who's Who (1949)
Jensen, O. Carrier War (1945)
Who's Who in America, 1952-53
World Biography (1948)

Columbia Pictures

MONTGOMERY CLIFT

CLIFT, MONTGOMERY Oct. 17, 1920-
Actor

Address: b. c/o Columbia Pictures Corporation, 729 7th Ave., New York 19; c/o Music Corporation of America, 598 Madison Ave., New York 22

In his first role on the New York stage in eight years Montgomery Clift appeared in the revival of Anton Chekhov's *The Sea Gull* which opened at the Phoenix Theatre on May 11, 1954. His recent motion pictures have included *I Confess* (Warner, 1953), *Indiscretion of an American Wife* (Columbia, 1954), made in Rome with Jennifer Jones as co-star, and *From Here To Eternity* (Columbia, 1953). Clift was one of the five nominees for the best actor award ("Oscar) of the Academy of Motion Picture Arts and Sciences for 1953 for his portrayal of Private Prewitt in *From Here to Eternity*, a runner-up honor he had also received in 1948 for his performance in *The Search* and in 1951 for his role in *A Place in the Sun.* Before his movie career, Clift had appeared in thirteen Broadway plays including *There Shall Be No Night, Our Town* and *The Skin of Our Teeth.*

Montgomery Clift was born in Omaha, Nebraska on October 17, 1920 to Mr. and Mrs. William Brooks Clift. He has a twin sister, Ethel, and an older brother, William Brooks, Jr. The family moved to Chicago when the twins were eight months old, and soon afterwards to New York where their father became a stockbroker.

At the age of thirteen, while visiting in Sarasota, Florida with his parents, "Monty" got a part in a little theatre production of *As Husbands Go.* The following summer he was given a small part, without salary, in *Fly Away Home* at Stockbridge, Massachusetts.

On January 15, 1935 young Clift made his debut on Broadway in *Fly Away Home*, starring Thomas Mitchell, which played for about six months. As Prince Peter he appeared for 169 performances in Moss Hart's musical comedy, *Jubilee* which opened on October 12, 1935. This was followed by two unsuccessful plays in early 1938, *Yr. Obedient Husband* and *Eye on the Sparrow.* In *Dame Nature* he had a leading role and attracted good press notices. Afterwards, he made a trip to Mexico where he contracted amoebic dysentery, thus becoming ineligible for military service.

He played a role in *Life With Father* but was dismissed from the cast after five performances because he was not suited to the role. For two seasons he appeared in Robert Sherwood's Pulitzer Prize play *There Shall Be No Night* starring Alfred Lunt and Lynn Fontanne at the Alvin Theatre, New York, and on the road. This experience, Clift says, gave him the opportunity to study the acting techniques of the famous couple.

His next appearance was in Thornton Wilder's *The Skin of Our Teeth,* which won the Pulitzer Prize, opened on November 18, 1942 at the Plymouth Theatre and played for 239 performances. Of Clift's portrayal of Henry in the play, Douglas Hubbard (*Theatre Arts,* March 1944) commented that it was outstanding, and called the actor "a young man of quiet gallantry and great seriousness of purpose."

In a revival of Wilder's *Our Town,* a Pulitzer Prize play, at the City Center, Clift's part as George Gibbs was rated as excellent by Howard Barnes (New York *Herald Tribune,* January 11, 1944). He was next seen in Lillian Hellman's hit *The Searching Wind* at the Fulton Theatre. Offers came from Hollywood studios, but Clift, wary of the usual

CLIFT, MONTGOMERY—*Continued*

seven-year contract, and feeling he still had a great deal to learn about acting, declined.

His next part was in *Foxhole in the Parlor* in 1945. Howard Hawks saw him in *You Touched Me* by Tennessee Williams and Donald Windham, and offered him $60,000 to play a part in *Red River,* a western picture. When Clift accepted the part, in 1946, he was $1,300 in debt and had been collecting unemployment insurance (*Saturday Evening Post,* August 27, 1949).

After playing a cowboy in *Red River* (1948), Clift was filmed in Germany as a young American soldier in *The Search* (1948), MGM's picture about Europe's lost children. His next picture was *The Heiress* (1949) with Olivia de Havilland. Augustus Goetz, who wrote, with his wife, both the stage and screen versions of *The Heiress,* stated that the fortune hunter, Clift's part, "is warmer and more sympathetic on the screen than it was on the stage" (*Saturday Evening Post,* August 27, 1949).

The actor received $100,000 for his work in *The Heiress.* After its completion he left for a trip to Europe and Israel. He very often stayed at third-rate hotels. When he returned he explained, "It's inconceivable to me that any young actor who had the fare didn't go to Palestine. There was one of the few really new countries carved out since the American Revolution. Everything was dramatic and challenging—perfect source material for acting."

For his work in *The Search* and *Red River, Look* magazine (March 1, 1949) presented Clift with an Achievement Award as "the most promising star on the Hollywood horizon." The *Motion Picture Herald* poll (1949) gave him top rating as the exhibitors' choice of "stars of tomorrow." *Good Housekeeping* (October 1949) called him a most convincing GI in *The Search,* said he rode as though born in the saddle in *Red River* and played the cad role in *The Heiress* to perfection.

In Germany Clift made *The Big Lift* (1950) for Twentieth Century Fox. He appeared in *A Place in the Sun* (1951), based upon Theodore Dreiser's novel *An American Tragedy* with Shelley Winters and Elizabeth Taylor. For his role as the struggling youth who goes to the electric chair for a murder he intended but did not commit, Clift was nominated for the Academy of Motion Picture Arts and Sciences award.

Under Alfred Hitchcock's direction, Clift played the young priest in the murder-melodrama *I Confess,* a Warner Brothers picture. In *From Here to Eternity* he appeared as Private Robert E. Lee Prewitt, for which he was nominated for an "Oscar". The picture was honored as the best film of 1953 by the Academy of Motion Picture Arts and Sciences, and received seven other academy awards.

While in Rome, *Look* (July 19, 1949) reported, Clift recognized Vittorio De Sica on the street and asked him for a part in a movie because of his admiration for De Sica's direction of *Shoe Shine.* Columbia gave Clift the opportunity of working with the director, in his first English-language film, as the distrait young Italian-American professor in *Indiscretion of an American Wife* (1954).

In May and June of 1954 Clift appeared in a revival of Chekhov's *The Sea Gull* at the off-Broadway Phoenix Theatre and, with others in the cast including Judith Evelyn and Maureen Stapleton, received $100 a week. The adaptation was by Clift and co-actors, Kevin McCarthy and Mira Rostova. Brooks Atkinson (New York *Times,* May 12, 1954) commented that Clift's "lonely, brooding Constantin is beautifully expressed without any foolish pathology." John Beaufort of the *Christian Science Monitor* (May 15, 1954) remarked that "Clift plays Constantin in a kind of choked-in fashion. . . . As for his manner of speech, it may be suitable for Private Prewitt but it is not good enough for Chekhov's struggling young author."

It has been explained that Clift's disinterest in clothes and de luxe apartments is a result of his precarious years on the stage. The success he achieved in his first two pictures came as a surprise to him, but he wanted to continue leading his own life without conforming to the Hollywood social pattern. The brown-haired, blue-eyed movie star is six feet tall and weighs 155 pounds. He loves children and enjoys swimming, sailing, photography, reading, and popular music. He seldom goes to night clubs or parties and the only professional club to which he belongs is The Players. Clift is a bachelor.

"Acting is make-believe, but you can carry it too far," Clift has said. "To be convincing, an actor must share, or at least be aware of, experiences familiar to the audience. Otherwise you're making faces in an emotional vacuum and nobody knows what . . . you're trying to express."

References

Am Mag 147:42+ Je '49 por
Look 13:57+ Jl 19 '49 pors
N Y Herald Tribune IV p1+ My 9 '54 por
N Y World-Telegram p9 My 1 '54
Theatre Arts 28:174+ Mr '44 por
Who's Who in the Theatre (1952)

COBLENTZ, STANTON A(RTHUR) (cŏb'lĕnts) Aug. 24, 1896- Author; editor

Address: b. and h. P.O. Box 332, Mill Valley, Calif.

The editor of *Wings,* a quarterly magazine of verse, is Stanton A. Coblentz who for over twenty years has been a leading exponent of traditional poetry in the United States. In 1952 the Lyric Foundation annual award of $1,000 was given to him in recognition of his efforts "to encourage simplicity, clarity and discipline in the writing of poetry." He is the author of thirty volumes including poetry, science fiction and novels.

His latest book is *From Arrow to Atom Bomb* (Beechhurst, 1953), a psychological history of warfare "from its stone-ax infancy and its bow-and-arrow youth down to the instruments of wholesale annihilation provided with mechanized transport at supersonic speed, characteristic of our more enlightened age" (*Christian Century,* October 28, 1953). Coblentz concludes that according to all the evidence war is not an "instinctive" human activity, and therefore is not "natural" and "not inevitable."

Stanton Arthur Coblentz was born on August 24, 1896 in San Francisco, California, the son of Mayer and Mattie (Arndt) Coblentz. His father had come to the United States from Alsace-Lorraine at the age of sixteen. The family lived at first in San Francisco, but later moved to Stockton, California where Mayer Coblentz managed the local office of an insurance company. Stanton was graduated from high school in 1913; he entered the University of California at Berkeley, California where he was active in the debating society and was on the college chess team. After graduating in 1917 he did post-graduate work and received the M.A. degree in 1919. His thesis was "The Poetic Revival in America."

While still a student, Coblentz won a prize for peace poems offered by the San Francisco *Chronicle,* and marketed book reviews to the *Argonaut.* For a year he wrote daily feature articles for the San Francisco *Examiner,* and in 1920 went to New York City where he reviewed books for the New York *Times,* New York *Sun, Bookman,* and *International Book Review.* He began to compose verse, which appeared in a collection, *The Thinker and Other Poems* (White, 1923). The next year he edited an anthology, *Modern American Lyrics* (Minton), which was followed by *Modern British Lyrics* (Minton, 1925) and his first sustained prose effort, *The Decline of Man* (Minton, 1925).

Three books by Coblentz were published in 1927. *The Literary Revolution* (Frank-Maurice) continued the trend of his master's thesis. In *Marching Men* (Unicorn) he wrote a full-length study of the story of war. *The Lone Adventurer* (Unicorn) was a sustained romance in rhyme royal. Meanwhile, he contributed regularly to the *American Mercury,* university quarterlies, New York *Times Magazine, Literary Digest, Canadian Bookman Survey,* and *Christian Century.*

His prolific output included interviews with Albert Einstein and G. K. Chesterton for *Success* magazine, and science fiction.

He relates, "I was, in fact, one of the earliest writers of modern science fiction, having contributed extensively to the earliest magazines in the field, at a time when neither I nor anyone else suspected that this form of fiction would ever be widely popular."

Wonder Stick (Cosmopolitan Book, 1929), a prose tale of adventures among the "beast-men" was followed by *Shadows on a Wall* (Poetic publication, 1930); a history of various beliefs concerning death and immortality, *Answer of the Ages* (Cosmopolitan Book, 1931); and a sonnet sequence *Enduring Flame* (Paebar, 1932).

Wings, a magazine which was to become a major organ for "traditional" poets, was founded by Coblentz in 1933. That same year *Songs of the Redwoods, and Other Poems* (Overland), was published and then *Merry Hunt, and Other Poems* (Humphries, 1934) and *Pageant of Man* (Wings, 1936). Of the latter work the British poet, Lord Dunsany, remarked: "With a vast vision, sometimes stepping aside to look at our planet from 'the midstream of the Milky Way,' and sometimes peering close at the lives of men and women in streets and offices of American cities, he examines the way of life; and one feels as he lays down this book that one has read one of the prophets." In the *Saturday Review of Literature,* William Rose Benét wrote, "His reach exceeds his grasp by a good deal," and A. M. Sullivan commented, "A prodigious and often ponderous effort in rhymed pentameter. The philosopher dominated the poet in much of the work. . . ."

STANTON A. COBLENTZ

A far cry from poetry was *Villains and Vigilantes* (Wilson-Erickson, 1937) which was called a "strange and thrilling history" of pioneer justice in California (New York *Times,* January 18, 1937). The author returned to California in 1938 and settled in Mill Valley, just north of the Muir Woods across the Golden Gate from San Francisco, and continued to publish *Wings.*

Songs by the Wayside (Wings) appeared in 1938 and another volume of poetry, *Senator Goose and Other Rhymes* (Wings) in 1940. A collection of editorials from *Wings, Triumph of the Teapot Poet* (Wings, 1941), was a "declaration of hostility" against what he considered the radical wing of versemakers. He then wrote: *Winds of Chaos* (Wings, 1942); *Green Vistas* (Wings, 1943); *Armageddon* (Wings, 1943); his third anthology *Music Makers* (Ackerman, 1945); a novel, *When the Birds Fly South* (Wings, 1945); and *The Mountain of Sleeping Maiden, and other Poems* (Wings, 1946). In *An Editor*

COBLENTZ, STANTON A.—*Continued*

Looks at Poetry (Wings, 1947) he advises hopeful rhymesters.

After an excursion in full-length science fiction, *The Sunken World* (Fantasy, 1948), reprinted in England as a pocketbook, he published *Unseen Wings* (Beechhurst, 1949), his fourth anthology. Of *Garnered Sheaves* (Wings, 1949) the reviewer in the *Saturday Review of Literature* (October 22, 1949) wrote that Coblentz "attacks big subjects, treats them in clear, adequate and rhythmic language. He is always discursive, technically accurate, but not always inspired in his treatment of enigmas of mankind."

In *New Poetic Lamps and Old* (Wings, 1950), Coblentz assailed the poets of the school of T. S. Eliot and Dylan Thomas. Favoring traditional prosody and a positive philosophy, he attacked those he considered defeatist and obscurantist as practitioners of a verse by no means free: "They have walled themselves about with more tabus than a tribe of aborigines; they have written *thou shalt not* in a code of a thousand commandments."

He affirmed: "I am sustained by the belief that poetry offers an answer to the inchoate gropings and questionings within millions of breasts. And I am upheld by knowing that poetry has long shed and may still shed a radiance not quite of this earth, the illumination of law rather than the confusion of license, the splendor of truth rather than the murkiness of chaos. . . ."

The year 1952 was one in which Coblentz received the Silver Medal of the Commonwealth Club of California for the best book of poetry that year by a Californian, and the $1,000 award of the Lyric Foundation for Traditional Poetry. This foundation was established by the late Virginia Kent Cummins in 1949, and the first award was granted to Robert Hillyer.

In the preface to Coblentz' *Time's Travelers* (Wings, 1952), Lord Dunsany wrote: "It is not for me from three thousand miles away to say who is the greatest living poet on the continent of America; I can only say who is the greatest one that I know . . . and the greatest poet I can see to the west is Stanton Coblentz."

The poet's latest work is a study of the psychological history of war, *From Arrow to Atom Bomb,* in which he traces from primitive times the basic causes he believes produced resorts to arms, and observes that "war has been largely if not entirely the product of psychological urges." He concludes that the cure must correspond: "Our political leaders . . . must be trained for their responsibilities. . . . As men seek diplomas today in medicine or engineering, so they must work for degrees in statecraft, and only the graduates of acknowledged institutions should be qualified to compete for high government positions."

The Houston (Texas) *Chronicle* called the book "a searching piece of work . . . a disturbing piece of writing." The Rochester (New York) *Democrat and Chronicle* believed that "in assembling in one volume the thoughts of many writers and philosophers on the subject of warfare, Mr. Coblentz has done a major service." From the Raleigh (North Carolina) *News and Observer* came the opinion that "his main premise is sound: if a habit of thinking makes wars, another habit of thinking can stop them." James Thompson observed that "the Coblentz viewpoint . . . is conveniently lacking in some of the practical details of attaining this state of mind, the masters of the Kremlin being who they are" (Chicago *Tribune*).

Don Fabun (San Francisco *Chronicle,* February 7, 1954) wrote: "Coblentz has endeavored to trace this bloody history and at the same time to account psychologically for the war madness that underlies the development of ever-more destructive weapons. . . . The psychological reconstruction appears the result of thinking more wishful than objective."

The poet was married on June 23, 1922 to Flora Bachrach, a schoolteacher.

He is a member of the Authors League of America, and is a Democrat. Coblentz is five feet ten inches tall and weighs 169 pounds; he has blue eyes and brown hair with tinges of gray. He enjoys hiking, listening to music, and a wide variety of reading ranging from belles-lettres to anthropology.

"War is not a convulsion of nature," concludes Coblentz. "It is not caused, like the earthquake... nor is it like the hurricane.... It is produced primarily by one thing: the mind of man—the ideas, the will, and the emotions of man. This means that it can be checked or controlled only by one thing: the mind of man—the ideas, the will, and the emotions of man."

References

Who's Who in America, 1954-55

COBLENTZ, W(ILLIAM) W(EBER)
Nov. 20, 1873- Physicist

Address: 2737 Macomb St., N.W., Washington 8, D.C.

About fifty years after W. W. Coblentz made his first investigations of the infrared spectra, his work is still finding continually wider application in science, while the importance of his discoveries for technology and industry is becoming every day more fully recognized. The distinguished pioneering physicist conducted most of his research at the United States National Bureau of Standards, where he headed the section on radiometry until his retirement in 1945. Since then he has acted as a consultant to the Bureau of Standards, the American Medical Association and the Pittsburgh Plate Glass Company.

Among some 500 scientific papers produced by Dr. Coblentz are his reports in the 1920's on planetary temperature measurements, findings which are credited with having stimulated the imagination of popular writers as to the possibilities of some form of life on other planets. He has been many times honored for his development of instruments and methods in radiometry as used in astronomy, medicine and other scientific fields, most recently (1953) by the Society for Applied Spectroscopy.

On a farm in Ohio's rural Beaver Township, William Weber Coblentz was born on November 20, 1873 to David and Catherine M. (Good) Coblentz. The scientist has told in his autobiography, *From the Life of a Researcher* (Philosophical Library, 1951) that according to all traditions the paternal side of his family came from Coblenz, Germany. His great-grandfather, John Coblentz, moved from Frederick, Maryland to Ohio in 1804. When William was about three years old, his mother died, leaving him and his younger brother to grow up under the care of their father's second wife, their aunts and their grandmother.

Spending much of his childhood on farms in Ohio, the boy had early contact with the wonders of nature. He collected tree roots which had grown into the shape of all the letters of the alphabet and some of the numerals. His formal education began in 1880 when he entered the district school, Webster Hall. At the age of eleven he showed his mechanical ability by constructing a threshing machine on which he made improvements from time to time and for which he obtained a patent. "The half-dozen and more patents, granted me in recent years," he later wrote in his autobiography, "have never produced any thrill in comparison with the dreams that came to me as a care-free youth. . . ."

Coblentz received most of his secondary school education at Poland (Ohio) Union Seminary, where he earned his tuition by working as a janitor. After graduating in 1894, he enrolled in Rayen High School in Youngstown in order to complete its high school course and then took an additional year for postgraduate study. He entered Case School of Applied Science (later called Case Institute of Technology), and was granted a B.S. degree in 1900.

His intention had been to become an electrical engineer, but as a graduate student at Cornell University he met Professor Edward L. Nichols, head of the department of physics, who suggested that he work on infrared absorption spectra. His M.S. degree was conferred by Cornell in 1901 and two years later he completed requirements for his Ph.D. degree, after submitting the thesis "Some Optical Properties of Iodine."

At the recommendation of Nichols, Coblentz was given a research associateship by the Carnegie Institution of Washington, D.C., thus he remained at the university for two years as an honorary fellow. The results of his investigations, on infrared absorption, reflection, and emission spectra were published in three volumes by the Carnegie Institution (1905 to 1908) under the title *Investigations of Infra-red Spectra.*

Since very little work had been previously done in this field, Coblentz has come to be regarded as a pioneer in the research on this subject and in its practical application. His early papers "have served as a guide to a vast army of technical workers who have extended the exploratory work which he conducted" (*Journal of the Optical Society of America,* November 1953).

Harris & Ewing

W. W. COBLENTZ

In May 1905 Coblentz became a laboratory assistant at the National Bureau of Standards in Washington, D.C. Established in 1901, the bureau "is the principal laboratory of the Federal Government for fundamental research and related technical activities in physics, mathematics, chemistry and engineering." In addition to maintaining national standards of physical measurements, it "carries on research leading to improvement of standards and related measurement methods and instruments in keeping with demands for greater precision and the opening of new fields of science and industry" (*U.S. Government Organization Manual, 1953-54*).

Dr. Coblentz remained with the Bureau of Standards until 1945, much of this time under the supervision of Dr. Samuel W. Stratton, the first director of the bureau, who influenced the younger man's career. During these forty years, while he advanced to associate physicist and then to physicist, Coblentz was in charge of the section on radiometry, which he helped to establish.

In his autobiography, he quoted the primary function of his section, as described in the proposed budget of the bureau for 1937: "To investigate the absorptive, emissive and reflective properties of matter for thermal radiation of various wave lengths, commonly designated ultraviolet, visible and infrared rays; and the practical application of this information for commercial and medical purposes."

An article in the *Journal of the Optical Society of America* (November 1953) has praised the physicist's "exceptional skill in construction and operation of delicate apparatus" and the unparalleled scope of "his surveys of optical and photoelectric properties of materials." Practical application of his laboratory findings has been extensive, including such objects as ultraviolet ray lamps and protective eye goggles for use with intense flames. Infrared

COBLENTZ, W. W.—*Continued*

absorption techniques growing out of his researches are widely used in industries such as petroleum, rubber, plastics, and textiles. Among the applications for which Coblentz has received patents are those on photoelectric signaling devices and thermopiles. These patents are either dedicated to the public or held in trust for it.

In investigations apart from his work at the Bureau of Standards, Dr. Coblentz undertook research in stellar radiation at Lick Observatory in California in 1914 and in stellar and planetary temperature measurements at Lowell Observatory, Flagstaff, Arizona during 1921, 1922, 1924, 1926, 1929, 1934, and 1938. As a member of the Harvard eclipse expeditions, he had the opportunity to study at Middletown, Connecticut the radiation of the corona during the solar eclipse in January 1925 and at Benkoelen, Sumatra, in January 1926. He took ultraviolet solar measurements at various research stations in Europe, including the one on the Jungfrau in 1932, and at San Juan, Puerto Rico in 1935.

A bibliography of Coblentz's scientific writings (published in the *Journal of the Optical Society of America,* February 1946) listed 412 titles. There have been additions since then. Most of his important work has appeared in the scientific publications of the Bureau of Standards and in reports to professional journals. He has contributed also to more popular periodicals.

Along with publications of the Bureau of Standards like *Temperature Estimates of the Planet Mars* (1925), he wrote a number of magazine articles including "Temperature of Mars" (*Science,* November 7, 1924) and "Can Life Exist on Mars?" (*Scientific Monthly,* April, 1925). It was such information set forth "nearly thirty years ago that sent fiction writers and comic-strip artists off into the flights of fantasy that have gained momentum year after year" (Washington *Evening Star,* November 21, 1953).

At the time of Coblentz's retirement from the bureau, he was engaged in research on radiation energy in the ultraviolet wave lengths which prevent such diseases as rickets. He continued, without pay, to complete this study and has since served in an advisory capacity at the bureau. He has also remained as a member of the A.M.A. council on physical medicine and rehabilitation.

On his eightieth birthday in November 1953 Dr. Coblentz was honored by special tributes from his fellow scientists of the National Bureau of Standards and the world. In that month the *Journal of the Optical Society of America* published thirty-eight papers on infrared research in honor of the pioneer in that field. Earlier in 1953 he received the medal of the Society for Applied Spectroscopy. Other awards conferred on the scientist are the Howard N. Potts Medal of Franklin Institute (1910), Janssen Medal of the Institute of France (1920), John Scott Medal (1924), Gold Key of the American Congress of Physical Therapy (1934), Rumford Medal of the American Academy of Arts and Sciences (1937), and Frederic Ives Medal of the Optical Society of America (1945).

Professional associations with which Coblentz is affiliated include the American Association for the Advancement of Science, National Academy of Sciences, American Astronomical Society, Washington Academy of Sciences, Philosophical Society of Washington, American Physical Society, Optical Society of America, American Society of Psychical Research, Washington Academy of Medicine, and Society of the Sigma Xi.

He is a member also of the committee on solar radiation of the International Union of Geodesy and Geophysics and a member of the International Committee on Measurement and Standardization of Ultraviolet for Use in Medicine, and a corresponding member of the Illuminating Engineering Society and the Société Française de Physique.

At the Bureau of Standards Coblentz met Catherine Emma Cate, also a government employee, whom he married on June 10, 1924. Before her death in 1951 she had become well known as a writer of juvenile stories and of verse. Their children, Catherine Joan and David William, are deceased.

At eighty Coblentz was described as a gray-haired "sharp-eyed, sharp-witted" scientist (Washington *Post,* November 23, 1953). Concerned with the subject of psychic phenomena, he has summarized his investigations in this field in a chapter of his autobiography. He is interested in nature and has made studies of the firefly, cicada and the formation of ice on plants. He also enjoys music and gardening.

References

Nature Mag 46:543 D '53
Opt Soc Am J 36:61+ F '46; 43:939 N '53 por
Washington (D.C.) Evening Star p2A N 21 '53
Washington (D.C.) Post p21 N 23 '53 por
American Men of Science (1949)
Coblentz, W. W. From the Life of a Researcher (1951)
National Cyclopædia of American Biography Current Volume E, 1937-38
Who's Who in America, 1950-51

COLE, ALBERT M(CDONALD Oct. 13, 1901- United States Government official; lawyer.

Address: b. Office of the Administrator, Housing and Home Finance Agency, Washington 25, D.C.; h. Holton, Kans.

As administrator of the Federal Housing and Home Finance Agency, Albert M. Cole has been studying low rental units, slum clearance, and urban redevelopment for possible solutions to the nation's housing problems. He has "constantly maintained that politics are 'out' in the development and operation of public housing" (*Christian Science Monitor,* July 3, 1953).

The United States Senate on March 9, confirmed, 64 to 18, President Dwight D. Eisenhower's nomination of Cole, who succeeded Raymond M. Foley in the $17,500-a-year post on March 11.

Elected to Congress four times, he represented the First Congressional District of Kansas from 1945 to 1952. For twenty years prior to 1945 he practiced law in Kansas. He had also been a county attorney, and, from 1941 until 1944, state senator. Cole is a Republican.

Albert McDonald Cole was born in Moberly, Missouri, on October 13, 1901, the son of Walter I. and Mary B. Cole. When he was eight years old, the Cole family moved to Topeka, Kansas, where he received his elementary education. He attended Sabetha High School and Washburn College in Topeka, and received his LL.B. degree from the University of Chicago in 1925. The next year he was admitted to the bar and started to practice law in Holton, Kansas.

Later, he also maintained law offices in Topeka. From 1927 until 1931 he was attorney of Jackson County, Kansas. For the next twelve years he was a member and president of the Holton School board. In 1941 he was elected to represent Jackson and Atchison counties in the state senate, where he served until 1944. During the same period he was a member of the Kansas Legislative Council. Then in 1944 the voters of the traditionally Republican First Congressional District elected him to the House of Representatives.

During the first session of the Seventy-ninth Congress, Cole voted in support of a bill to establish a permanent Committee on Un-American Activities and also voted affirmatively to extend the Trade Agreements Act to 1948, on an anti-poll tax bill, and on the Employment-Production Act, 1945. Towards the close of the session he joined a group of House Republicans who declared their determination to express their own opinions regardless of the views of their party leaders.

In the second session, Cole voted affirmatively to extend until 1947 the Selective Service Act of 1942, on an amendment to permit reasonable profits under OPA ceilings, and to grant a loan of $3,750,000 to England. An "announced foe of one Federal housing phase, subsidies for low-rental living quarters" he opposed the appropriation of $477,500,000 for housing subsidies (*U. S. News & World Report,* April 17, 1953).

Re-elected to the House in 1946, Cole cast his vote in the first session of the Eightieth Congress in support of limiting the presidency to two terms, extending rent control from June 30, 1947 to February 29, 1948, the Greek-Turkish Aid Bill, statutory authority for the Voice of America, and abolishing the poll tax.

In the second session he supported a Republican-sponsored tax reduction bill, a bill extending rent control until March 31, 1949, and another repealing Federal taxes on oleomargarine. He also voted in favor of a tidelands oil bill, legislation continuing the Trade Agreements Act for one year, and the Wolcott housing bill, which provided for the construction by public housing authorities of 500,000 low-rent housing units over a period of five years. In November 1948, he was elected to Congress a third time.

As a member of the House Banking and Currency Committee in 1949, Cole played a part

Wide World

ALBERT M. COLE

in the investigation of the Lustron Corporation which, he charged, had wasted funds borrowed from the Reconstruction Finance Corporation. When the House Banking and Currency Committee voted to study possible government operation of the Lustron Corporation if the RFC should foreclose, Cole commented, "This looks like an effort to put the Government into the prefabricated housing business. I don't think the Government has any business getting into it at all" (New York *Times,* February 16, 1950). In August 1950, he again charged the RFC with lax supervision over its loans to Lustron.

In the first session of the Eighty-first Congress, Cole voted against extending the Rent Control Act to June 30, 1950, in favor of continuing the Economic Cooperation Act of 1948 (the Marshall Plan) until June 30, 1950, to eliminate the public housing section of the long-range housing bill, against the bill itself (the Housing Act of 1949), for an anti-poll tax bill, and for a 50 per cent reduction of military aid to Europe.

During the second session he voted against a bill to grant economic aid to Korea and Formosa, and supported a voluntary-compliance FEPC bill. In March he joined five other Republican Representatives in sponsoring an amendment to the charter of the Commodity Credit Corporation providing for an increase of $2,000,000,000 in the agency's borrowing authority to permit it to use more private facilities in its operations. Cole's proposal "that agricultural surpluses be disposed of at terminal stages through regular channels of trade rather than by the Commodity Credit Corporation was voted down on the ground that, as the New York *Times* reported, "the cost of handling such trade through middlemen in the wheat field alone would be as great as the entire adminis-

COLE, ALBERT M.—*Continued*

tration of the price support program at present" (March 24, 1950).

In March he voted to strike loans for housing cooperatives out of a housing bill; in June he voted to grant an additional $2,000,000,000 for farm price supports. Arguing against any further extension of rent control, he declared that fears of chaos and skyrocketing rents were baseless, since investigation by the Bureau of Labor Statistics of decontrolled areas showed only a median 10 per cent increase in rents. Cole was re-elected to Congress for his fourth term in November 1950 by a majority of 30,000. Early in the first session of the Eighty-second Congress Cole voted to extend the draft and in support of the principle of universal military training; to reduce the government's civil payrolls; and in favor of limiting public housing in 1952 to 5,000 units. Again opposing continuance of rent control, he asserted that in requesting it the Truman Administration was trying to "pressure" Congress into passing a "socialistic defense housing bill."

An opponent of the Administration's price control program, he proposed an amendment to protect the profits of meat processors on every item under control, and voted favorably on legislation allowing a "reasonable profit" under all price ceilings. On March 4, 1952, during the second session, he voted to shelve the universal military training bill, to limit public housing to 5,000 units, and to reduce the TVA appropriation by $14,000,000.

In the following months he voted to cut Federal jobs by 10 per cent, to reduce economic aid to Europe by $615,000,000, and to end consumer price controls on June 30, 1952 and Federal rent controls on September 30, 1952.

His bid for a fifth term in Congress failed when his constituents elected a Democrat, Herman Miller, by a majority of 38,000. Cole's defeat has been attributed to his refusal to oppose the plan by Army Engineers to build Tuttle Creek Dam, a highly unpopular project among the farmers of the area.

The nomination of Cole for his present post was denounced by many Democrats on the ground that while in Congress Cole had opposed the Housing and Home Finance Agency's public housing and slum clearance bills, yet now he would be asked to administer that agency's program. Cole stated that his past record on housing legislation did not mean that he would "attempt to scuttle any program Congress has decided on." Questioned by the Senate Committee on Banking and Currency on March 2, 1953, he stated: "I believe the government should gradually get out of the housing business. I think government should support the housing industry and not supplant it" (New York *Times,* March 9, 1953). Cole was confirmed by the Senate 64 to 18.

As the director of the Housing and Home Finance Agency, which was established by the President's Reorganization Plan of 1947, Cole must guide the government's activities in housing toward the objectives set forth in the Housing Act of 1949.

Cole also supervises the housing research program, the Alaskan housing program, Federal loans and grants to local public agencies so that they can clear slums and make land available for private or public redevelopment, the administration and liquidation of war and veterans' emergency housing, the lending to educational institutions for the construction of housing for students and faculties, and the lending for prefabricated houses.

Stating that the "Eisenhower budget" provided for thirty-five thousand new low-rent public housing units for fiscal 1954, as against 75,000 proposed by former President Truman, Cole stated in March 1953 that the figure was "set by the executive office of the President with my concurrence."

Cole urged the Senate appropriations subcommittee to reject an order approved by the House to halt all new public housing, and on May 6 the subcommittee voted to restore funds for the 35,000 housing units requested by the President.

On September 13, 1953 President Eisenhower appointed Cole chairman of a new advisory committee on government housing policies and programs which includes twenty-one members representing the fields of banking, real estate, architecture, insurance, labor, housing, and city planning.

Returning from a nationwide tour of "shirt-sleeve" conferences with builders, Cole predicted that new houses in 1954 may exceed 900,000 (*Business Week,* September 19, 1953). Speaking at the American Bankers Association convention, Cole warned that unless banks and other lending institutions make home building loans available at reasonable rates, the government may have to step in with direct aid to home builders.

At the insistence of Cole, several of the FHA staff were dismissed on charges of accepting "kickbacks" or gratituties from those profiting from Federally guaranteed housing projects (New York *Times,* April 24, 1954). Cole asked Congress for funds so that the FBI could investigate "criminal violations among contractors all over the country" (New York *Post,* August 1, 1954).

The FHA lowered down payments and extended loan repayment periods on government-insured houses, starting on August 10, 1954, to carry out the 1954 Housing Act. Cole set up a national voluntary mortgage credit extension committee to facilitate the flow of loans.

Albert Cole is married to the former Emily Corbin of Kansas City. They have two children, Mrs. Kitty Kaul, and Will, who is at present in the armed forces. Cole is a Scottish Rite Mason and a member of Phi Alpha and Kappa Sigma fraternities.

References

N Y Times p18 Mr 9 '53 por
U S News 34:67 Ap 17 '53
Washington (D.C.) Post p12 F 26 '53
Congressional Directory (1951)
Who's Who in United States Politics (1950)

COLE, W(ILLIAM) STERLING Apr. 18, 1904- United States Representative from New York

Address: b. c/o House Office Bldg., Washington 25, D.C.; h. 109 E. Steuben St., Bath, N.Y.

Since becoming chairman of the congressional Joint Committee on Atomic Energy in April 1953, W. Sterling Cole has been largely responsible for all atomic energy legislation introduced in Congress.

On September 6, 1954 President Eisenhower, using nuclear fission, broke ground at Shippingport, Pennsylvania for the first commercial atomic power plant. Cole, speaking at the ceremonies, said that a new world agency for peacetime development of atomic energy would include a reactor school to train representatives of friendly nations.

The Republican legislator, who is also a senior member of the House Armed Services Committee, represents New York's Thirty-seventh District. First elected to the Seventy-fourth Congress in 1934, the lawyer has been returned to every subsequent Congress, most recently in the November 1952 election. Cole is at present a member of the Republican Policy Committee and the House Patronage Committee.

William Sterling Cole, one of the sons of Ernest Ethelbert and Minnie (Pierce) Cole, was born in Painted Post, New York on April 18, 1904. Educated in upstate New York, he attended Colgate University for his B.A. degree and was graduated as a Phi Beta Kappa student in 1925. His LL.B. degree was conferred in 1929 by the Albany Law School of Schenectady's Union University.

Before studying law, Cole had taught during 1925 and 1926 in the public schools in Corning, New York, not far from the town of Bath, where he began his law practice in 1930. With his brother, Robert Cole, he established the firm of Cole & Cole and still shares a law practice in Steuben county.

The candidate on the Republican ticket for a seat in the Seventy-fourth Congress, Cole was elected in 1934 at the age of thirty to the House of Representatives from New York's Thirty-ninth District. When that district was merged with the Thirty-seventh in 1952, Cole ran against Congressman Edwin A. Hall in August of that year to win a primary contest for the Republican nomination. In the Eighty-third Congress he represents the newly formed Thirty-seventh District, comprising the upstate counties of Steuben, Chemung, Tioga, and Broome.

During his freshman year (1935) in Congress, Representative Cole was appointed to House committees on education and the District of Columbia and to a special committee to investigate the American Retail Federation. In the course of his nineteen years in Washington, his committee assignments have included insular affairs, conservation of wildlife resources, postwar military policy, Naval affairs, armed services and atomic energy, with special prominence in the last three named.

During the early years of the New York Republican's political career, he voted in favor of the social security bill (1935) and against the

U.S. Navy

W. STERLING COLE

work relief bill (1935), the Eccles banking bill (1935), the Wagner housing bill (1937), and farm parity payments (1939). He also opposed an appropriation of $1,500,000,000 for relief in 1938 (1937) and an additional $100,000,000 for work relief in 1939 (1939).

The Congressman voted to create a permanent committee on un-American activities (1945), to submit to the states a constitutional amendment for House participation in the ratification of treaties (1945), to allow reasonable profits in OPA ceilings (1946), for the Case strike control bill (1946), and against draft exemption for teen-agers (1946).

Generally favoring expenditures on postwar foreign assistance, Cole supported the Greek-Turkish aid bill (1947), six billion dollars foreign aid authorization (1948), extension of the Economic Cooperation Act of 1948 to June 30, 1950 (1949), Korea-Formosa economic aid (1950) and the $2,700,000,000 Economic Cooperation Administration extension bill (1950). On domestic issues he voted for the two-term limit for the presidency (1947), the anti-poll tax bill (1947) and against the long-range housing bill (1949). His record on government economy measures indicates that he approved a $600,000,000 cut in Federal spending (1950) and a reduction in government payrolls (1951).

In the first session of the Eighty-third Congress, meeting in 1953, the Representative opposed statehood for Hawaii and a proposal to continue the public housing program, but favored private power development at Niagara, extension of the excess profits tax to December 31, 1953, and a $4,400,000,000 foreign aid appropriation.

The ranking Republican on the Naval Affairs Committee, he opposed, unsuccessfully, in 1946 a provision of the reorganization act to merge that committee with the House Military Affairs Committee to form the Armed Services Committee. In 1947 he led in organizing opposition

COLE, W. STERLING—*Continued*

against the Army-Navy unification bill, which was, however, given favorable action in Congress. Cole, who is a lieutenant commander in the U.S. Naval Reserve, testified in June 1947 during hearings before the House executive expenditures committee that he had sent queries to more than 200 officers in the Navy and other branches of the armed forces and had found general disfavor toward some features of the proposed unification legislation.

A bill to give to the United Nations International Children's Emergency Fund the $1,229,240 earned during the war by conscientious objectors in the United States was submitted by Cole in June 1947. The idea was supported by the Society of Friends.

Several months later he headed an armed services subcommittee which made a two months' tour of part of the Orient and Europe. On its return to Washington in November the group recommended conclusion of an early peace treaty with Japan, retention of three naval bases in Japan and establishment of other U.S. bases in the far Pacific.

Representative Cole filed in January 1951 a bill to give a place to the commandant of the Marine Corps on the Joint Chiefs of Staff. The previous year he had sponsored a resolution for world disarmament under U.N. direction, but in April 1951 in the face of much opposition in the House of Representatives he argued in favor of a bill for universal military training, pointing out that "the foreseeable future offers no reasonable expectation that times will remove the need for a strong military establishment" (New York *World-Telegram and Sun,* April 6, 1951). Cole's amendment to this controversial bill, allowing the trainees to choose their own season for training, was offered in March 1952.

Soon after Congress met in early 1953, members of the Joint Committee on Atomic Energy encountered a deadlock of several months over whether to select a member of the Senate or of the House as chairman of their committee, a post held in the previous Congress by the late Senator Brien McMahon. Eventually deciding on a rotation plan, the committee on April 1, 1953 chose Representative Cole as its leader for the two-year duration of the current Congress.

This committee was formed in 1946, with Cole as one of its members, and has the function of initiating legislation regarding atomic and hydrogen power. Since the Atomic Energy Commission is required by law to inform the committee on all atomic energy matters, Cole "undoubtedly knows as many facts about atom and hydrogen power as any man in America" (*Christian Science Monitor,* October 12, 1953).

Upon assuming the chairmanship Cole announced that among the first undertakings of the committee would be the consideration of changes in the Atomic Energy Act of 1946 to allow for private atomic power development for peacetime industrial uses. As a result of a two-month hearing completed by the committee in mid-1953, the chairman made it known that he would introduce a bill toward that end in the second session of the Eighty-third Congress.

He urged the adoption of a large-scale hydrogen bomb program to meet the challenge of the Soviet Union, which he believed would soon be capable of devastating the United States. In a speech in Indianapolis he also spoke of the need for prayer in the atomic-hydrogen age: "If we are to prevail . . . our ultimate reliance must lie . . . not in the realm of material things, but in the realm of the spiritual" (*Christian Science Monitor,* October 16, 1953).

The responsibility of informing the American people of the March 1, 1954 thermonuclear bomb test at Eniwetok was given to Sterling Cole. He said: "We have passed another milestone. We now have a deliverable hydrogen weapon that can be dropped anywhere in the world" (it exploded with the force of 15 megatons (15,000,000 tons of TNT).

On April 7, 1954 Cole issued a statement following Senator Joseph R. McCarthy's charge that the development of the hydrogen bomb had been deliberately held up for eighteen months. Cole told of vigorous debate among the members of the Joint Atomic Energy Committee as to the technical feasibility of a thermonuclear weapon, and as to the transfer of money and experts from fission [atomic] bomb preparation. To many of the committee "the prospect of such potentially devastating weapons was morally repugnant." He concluded by saying that the delay was "not sinister", nor "does it imply that those who opposed President Truman's final decision [to proceed with the development of the hydrogen bomb] were motivated by a desire to lessen our military strength."

On the question of exchanging atomic information with other nations, Cole expressed his opinion in December 1953 that greater cooperation with Great Britain, Canada and other free countries would be desirable. He does not approve of revision in the law that would permit disclosure of information on the "construction or fabrication" of nuclear weapons.

Appearing on CBS's television program, *Man of the Week,* Cole urged the administration to earmark more money for "basic research" on defensive atomic weapons. He also stated that the United Nations should give Russia three or four months to accept President Eisenhower's plan for the peaceful use of atomic power. If Russia does not accept, he added, interested nations should get together and try to work out the plan themselves.

Several weeks later the Congressman revealed that he was encouraging the government to release motion pictures of the 1952 hydrogen explosion at Eniwetok which he described "as visual evidence of the devastating effect of the hydrogen weapons" (New York *World-Telegram and Sun,* January 25, 1954).

A long-time advocate of government economy, Cole regularly supported reduction in Federal expenditures and in 1952 sponsored a bill to decrease spending by abolishing free mailing privileges for Congress and government agencies. In October 1953 the Representative from New York disclosed that he had changed his views on balancing the budget in favor of appropriating an increase of ten billion dollars annually for defense.

His 1954 voting record indicates that he opposed raising the personal income tax exemptions from $600 to $700, movie ticket tax relief, and U.S. participation in the St. Lawrence seaway. He voted for a bill making evidence obtained by wire tapping admissible in court cases involving sabotage, against an amendment requiring the approval of a Federal judge to intercept telephone messages, and for the atomic energy bill. The latter became a law on August 30.

Cole, who is interested in problems of education and who introduced a bill in 1947 to establish a Federal board of character education, is a trustee of Elmira College, a past trustee of Colgate University (1944 to 1950) and a past member of the board of education in Bath (1933 to 1935). He is a trustee of Woodlawn Foundation, Inc. His fraternities are Sigma Nu, Pi Delta Epsilon and Delta Sigma Rho and he is a Mason, a Shriner and a member of the Knights Templar.

The "short, gray and handsome" Congressman, as *Time* described him, has been married since July 3, 1929 to Mary Elizabeth (Thomas) Cole and is the father of three sons: William Sterling, Thomas Ernest and David Aaron. He is a member of the Presbyterian Church.

References

Empire State Mason 2:11 O '53 por
N Y World-Telegram p31 N 15 '46
Time 61:24 Ap 13 '53 por
Biographical Directory of the American Congress, 1774-1949 (1950)
Congressional Directory (1953)
Martindale-Hubbell Law Directory, 1952
Who's Who in America, 1952-53
Who's Who in United States Politics (1950)
World Biography (1948)

COLLIER, CONSTANCE Jan. 22, 1880-
Actress

Address: h. 157 W. 57th St., New York 19

The English actress Constance Collier was the recipient in April 1954 of an American Shakespeare Festival Theatre Award for distinguished service in training and guiding actors in Shakespearean roles. To older generations of theatre-goers she is known as one of London's greatest stars where she created memorable interpretations of Juliet, Portia, Lady Macbeth, Cleopatra and other roles under the aegis of Sir Herbert Beerbohm Tree. American audiences recall her portrayal of Mary, Duchess of Towers in *Peter Ibbetson* (1917) with John and Lionel Barrymore, and her role as Carlotta Vance in *Dinner At Eight* (1932).

She played in W. Somerset Maugham's drama, *Our Betters,* for a run of 548 performances at the Queen's Theatre, London. "One of the most beloved figures in her profession," wrote Daniel Blum in *Great Stars of the American Stage,* "she probably knows more famous people intimately than any living person." She has appeared in many Hollywood films. Today

Marcus Blechman

CONSTANCE COLLIER

she devotes most of her time to coaching actresses. Among her celebrated pupils are Katharine Hepburn, Jennifer Jones, Anita Colby, Gene Tierney, and Margaret Truman.

Constance Collier was the professional name assumed by Laura Constance Hardie, daughter of Cheetham Auguste Hardie, a Shakespearean actor, and his actress wife, Elezia Collier. She was born on January 22, 1880 on Windsor Hill, Berkshire, England, in the shadow of Windsor Castle. (She has had "the deep honor and privilege" of the friendship of the late H.R.H. Queen Mary most of her life.)

When Constance was only four years old she appeared as Peasblossom in a touring revival of *A Midsummer Night's Dream.*

Constance was only six years old when engaged by the actor-manager Wilson Barrett to appear in his company at the Theatre Royal, Hull, Yorkshire, as Cissy in Henry Arthur Jones's and Henry Herman's melodrama, *The Silver King.* The young girl proved naturally gifted as both a singer and dancer, and made her London stage debut at the Criterion Theatre on July 22, 1893 in the chorus of Lecocq's light opera *La Fille de Madame Angot.*

Her acting ability and striking beauty attracted producer George Edwardes who chose her for one of his famous Gaiety Girls at the Gaiety Theatre. Later, in 1896, Miss Collier rejoined Wilson Barrett at the Lyric Theatre, appearing first as Ancaria and later as Mercia in Barrett's celebrated play, *The Sign of the Cross.* She went to Paris and studied for a time under the great French actor, Coquelin, who acted with Sarah Bernhardt where she met "the divine Sarah".

Slender, graceful, and with dark hair, eyes and complexion (inherited, she says, from distant Portuguese forebears) Miss Collier scored her first real personal triumph at the Comedy Theatre in London in the year

COLLIER, CONSTANCE—*Continued*

1898 as the gypsy Chiara in H. V. Esmond's play *One Summer's Day*. An even more important event in her career was her engagement late in 1901 by H. Beerbohm (later Sir Herbert) Tree for his company at His Majesty's (now Her Majesty's) Theatre in London. In Stephen Phillips' *Ulysses* the "strikingly handsome" and "regal" young actress presented a memorable stage picture on her entrance (through a trap) as the goddess Minerva, and the following year appeared as Roma in Hall Caine's *The Eternal City*.

She played the leading feminine role of Poppoea in 1906 in Phillips' *Nero*. Miss Collier remained with Beerbohm Tree for seven years, gaining wide Shakespearean experience as well as renown in such roles as Mistress Ford in *The Merry Wives of Windsor,* Portia in *Julius Caesar,* Viola in *Twelfth Night,* and Cleopatra in *Antony and Cleopatra* in which play she appeared in a command performance before the Emperor of Germany and was decorated by him. She also appeared in many Royal Command performances in London.

She made her Broadway debut (in support of William Gillette) as Anne-Marie in Henry Bernstein's drama *Samson* at the Criterion Theatre, October 1908. Miss Collier returned to Stratford-on-Avon in 1909 to play Portia in *The Merchant of Venice* to Henry Ainley's Shylock. Back in New York in October, she was seen as Agnes de Croucy in Bernstein's *Israel*. She appeared as Imogen Parrott in a revival of Pinero's *Trelawny of the "Wells"* (Empire Theatre, January 1, 1911) and in the title role of Paul Wilstach's dramatization of *Thais* (Criterion, March 14, 1911). She portrayed Nancy Sykes in an all-star production of *Oliver Twist* at the New Amsterdam on February 26, 1912. (She was seen in this role at His Majesty's, London, in the previous year). At the Lyric, New York on November 25, 1912 Miss Collier followed Julie Opp Faversham in the role of Portia in William Faversham's revival of *Julius Caesar,* and beginning February 9, 1914 played Emilia in *Othello*.

While visiting the William Favershams at their country home in England in July 1914 Miss Collier met Eva Le Gallienne and coached her in the role of Ariel. "It was one of many fascinating lessons," Miss Le Gallienne wrote in her autobiography *At 33*. "She tried to make me see the values in the beautiful speeches, to bring out the music without losing sight of the meaning. She explained to me the two chief dangers in reading Shakespeare's verse: the one, to intone in a stilted fashion losing all feeling of reality; the other, precisely the opposite, in the effort to be natural, the complete disregard of poetic metre. She was a ruthlessly honest teacher." She also gave Miss Le Gallienne the opportunity to make her professional debut in Maeterlinck's *Monna Vanna* in which Miss Collier was starred at the Lyric Theatre.

During the first year of World War I Miss Collier was very ill, lost most of her savings, and, according to Lionel Barrymore's recollections in *We Barrymores,* "took a small apartment in a hotel in Jermyn Street and made a habit of going to bed at nine o'clock. She had reasons to suspect that her brilliant career was ended. But on an air raid night she received a telephone call from Sir Herbert Tree." Through him she met John N. Raphael, the Paris correspondent of the London theatrical weekly, *The Stage*. He submitted his dramatization of George Du Maurier's novel *Peter Ibbetson* to Miss Collier who did extensive rewriting and induced the Countess of Huntingdon to put up £500 for a "special matinee" production, the receipts to go to a World War I charity. Leading players were persuaded by Miss Collier to donate their services, with the result that *Peter Ibbetson* received its first performance at His Majesty's Theatre on the afternoon of July 23, 1915, with Owen Nares as Peter, Henry Ainley as the villainous Colonel Ibbetson, and Miss Collier herself as Mary, Duchess of Towers.

In late 1915 she went to Hollywood to make her motion picture debut in the D. W. Griffith film *Intolerance*. Beginning March 20, 1916 she played Mistress Ford in *The Merry Wives of Windsor* to the Mistress Page of Henrietta Crosman and the Falstaff of Thomas A. Wise at the Criterion Theatre in New York. Both actresses later supported Sir Herbert Tree in the same play at the New Amsterdam (May 21, 1916).

Hoping to secure a New York production for *Peter Ibbetson,* Miss Collier (as related by Lionel Barrymore in *We Barrymores*) brought the script to America and, with the expert assistance of playwright Edward Sheldon, revised it. She persuaded John Barrymore to play the title role of the romantic lover. Subsequently, (as related by Gene Fowler in *Good-night, Sweet Prince*), Miss Collier and "Ned" Sheldon, Alexander Woollcott (the drama critic), Robert Edmond Jones (the scenic designer) and Margaret Carrington (the elocution teacher), formed what they termed a "Barrymore Board of Regents" to further the career of the actor (whom Miss Collier still considers the greatest actor in her experience).

Peter Ibbetson had a triumphant première at the Republic Theatre in New York on April 18, 1917 with John Barrymore as Peter, his brother Lionel as Colonel Ibbetson, and Miss Collier as Mary, Duchess of Towers. It ran for 71 performances and subsequently on a long tour during which Miss Collier and John Barrymore played to crowded theatres in the United States and Canada.

After appearing as Mrs. Cheveley in a revival of Oscar Wilde's *An Ideal Husband* (Comedy, New York, September 16, 1918) during which her husband, Julian L'Estrange, who was acting in the play with her, died. Miss Collier left the cast and returned to London where she did not appear until February, 1920 at the Savoy Theatre.

She began a run in *Peter Ibbetson,* with Basil Rathbone as Peter and Gilbert Hare as the Colonel. A decade later Miss Collier and Deems Taylor adapted the piece as the libretto for Taylor's opera *Peter Ibbetson,* first sung by Edward Johnson (Peter), Lawrence Tibbett

(Colonel Ibbetson) and Lucrezia Bori (Mary) at the Metropolitan Opera House, New York City, on February 7, 1931. Later in that year (April 8) the play itself was revived under Miss Collier's direction at the Shubert Theatre, New York, with Dennis King, Charles Coburn and Jessie Royce Landis in the leading roles.

From September 12, 1923 to January 3, 1925 Miss Collier enjoyed, at the Queen's Theatre in London, the longest continuous run of her career; the play, which had 548 performances, was W. Somerset Maugham's cynical comedy-drama *Our Betters,* with Miss Collier enacting the Duchess de Surennes. During the run of this piece Miss Collier collaborated with Ivor Novello (the young composer of the famous war song *Keep the Home Fires Burning*) under the collective pseudonym of "David L'Estrange" on the *apache* melodrama *The Rat* in which Novello had a long run at the Prince of Wales's Theatre beginning June 9, 1924.

Miss Collier enlisted the interest of the manager of the Haymarket Theatre, London, in a production of *Hamlet* in 1925 with John Barrymore which she staged and in which she played the Queen. (Gene Fowler in *Good Night, Sweet Prince* tells of her infinite tact and patience in dealing with Barrymore during his tempestuous moods and alternate periods of despair.). *Hamlet* opened on February 19, 1925 and ran for twelve weeks, with standing room only for every performance. (Bernard Shaw sent Barrymore a long letter attacking him, not as an actor, but as a person who dared to alter and cut Shakespeare's play.)

All the young and aspiring actors in London, Miss Collier recalls, tried to get into the *Hamlet* company. "Boys used to come in," she said, "proud and happy to have been chosen for the role of Laertes. Little did they know what was in store for them. When it came time for the graveyard scene, Jack would fight violently . . . the young actor would come from the encounter dripping with blood!"

She staged a London production of *Down Hill,* another "David L'Estrange" play which starred Ivor Novello at the Queen's Theatre in June, 1926. Returning to New York, Miss Collier appeared at the Klaw Theatre beginning November 4, 1927 as Herodias in Philip Barry's *John.* At Henry Miller's Theatre on February 20, 1928 she repeated, in a revival of *Our Betters,* her brilliant London success. When S. N. Behrman's dramatization of Enid Bagnold's then anonymous novel *Serena Blandish* was presented by Jed Harris at the Morosco Theatre, New York on January 23, 1929, Miss Collier scored a triumph as the Countess Flor di Folio. At the Longacre Theatre on March 18, 1930 Miss Collier endowed Anastasia in G. B. Stern's *The Matriarch* with an "Oriental opulence of character" which was "very striking." At the Music Box Theatre on October 22, 1932 she made a strong impression as Carlotta Vance. (an impersonation of the actress Maxine Elliott), in Edna Ferber's and George S. Kaufman's *Dinner at Eight.* Her last appearance on the New York stage was as Madame Bernardi in *Aries Is Rising* at the John Golden Theatre in November, 1939.

In 1929 Miss Collier moved to Hollywood under contract to Metro-Goldwyn-Mayer studios and was seen in support of Greta Garbo, Katharine Hepburn, Fred Astaire and other stars. Her performances as a "martinet professor" with Simone Simon in *Girls' Dormitory* (1936) and as the "endearingly British" Duchess of Glenalvon with Edward G. Robinson in *Thunder in the City* (1937) led to a seven-year contract with Twentieth Century-Fox. Subsequently freelancing, Miss Collier was (wrote Bosley Crowther in the New York *Times*) "excellent . . . as a blowsy aunt" in support of Paulette Goddard in the film *Kitty* (1946). She "clowned" effectively with Bob Hope in the travesty version of *Monsieur Beaucaire* (1946); gave a hilarious performance as the "broken-down grande dame" in *The Perils of Pauline* (1947), based on the career of Pearl White; played Lady Markby to the Mrs. Cheveley of Paulette Goddard in *An Ideal Husband* (1948); and was seen as Tina Cosgrove in the José Ferrer-Gene Tierney horror film *Whirlpool* (1950).

At a Shakespeare's birthday celebration held in New York City by the American Shakespeare Festival Theatre and Academy on April 29, 1954, Miss Collier received a "distinguished service to Shakespeare" award for "the training and guidance she has given to young actors as well as stars in the interpretation of Shakespeare's plays."

Constance Collier was married in 1912 to the English actor Julian L'Estrange, who was leading man to Maxine Elliott, Florence Reed, Billie Burke and other American actresses. He died in 1918. Her book of reminiscences *Harlequinade: The Story of My Life,* published by John Lane in London in 1930, carried a grateful foreword by Noel Coward, whom she had early encouraged and who had been an *habitué* of the Fifty-Fifty club operated in London in 1925 by Miss Collier and Ivor Novello.

Noel Coward once wrote, "Constance Collier as a person possesses all the range and variety appropriate to an actress of her reputation. I have seen her radiantly charming, tremendously funny and very tragic, but always, no matter through what crises she may be passing, there emanates from her a vitality and zest for life which makes her the most stimulating and entrancing of companions."

Miss Collier once said that she always kept three books at her bedside, the Bible, Trelawny's *Recollections of Shelley and Byron,* and *Peter Ibbetson.* In her preface to her autobiography, *Harlequinade,* she wrote: "I cannot bear talking of the past. All that matters to me is the present and the future. I am a good listener. My interest in other people's joys and sorrows is quite genuine, and makes me very popular."

Eva Le Gallienne in her autobiography *With A Quiet Heart* quotes Constance Collier after they had lunched together one day in 1937: "Whatever my work may be at the moment I do it to the fullest extent of my powers and with great enjoyment. Should anyone comment on the anachronism of my supporting Shirley Temple in *Wee Willie Winkie* and start talking of my great parts at His Majesty's with

COLLIER, CONSTANCE—*Continued*

Beerbohm Tree, I merely remark that I was myself at that time, and at this time I am still myself—but in another period. Life is never static . . . we must not go on clinging to the old and the past."

The noted actress has always been very fond of pets. At present she has a parrot, Mimsie, and a thirteen-year old dachshund given to her by Katharine Cornell. For many years she had a pet monkey. "My father," she recalls, " loved birds, and could talk their language. Mimsie was born in an incubator and, having never heard bird voices, understands humans. She thinks she's a woman!" Miss Collier, with Mimsie, recently appeared on a television program with Lilli Palmer. Miss Collier is spending the summer in Venice with her friend, Katharine Hepburn, who will be making the film, *The Time of the Cuckoo,* on location.

Miss Collier's friends cherish two famous descriptions of her: Sir Herbert Tree said "She is a passion flower with a sense of humour" and Sir Gerald DuMaurier said "She was born in a prompt corner and swallowed a powder puff."

References

Atlan 175:105+ Mr '44
N Y Herald Tribune VI p3 Jl 24 '38; V p3 Je 22 '47
N Y Times X p4 Ja 24 '37
Photoplay 47:289 My '35 por
Barrymore, L. and Shipp, C. We Barrymores (1951)
Blum, D. C. Great Stars of the American Stage (1952)
Collier, C. Harlequinade (1930)
Fowler, G. Good Night, Sweet Prince (1944)
Hartnoll, P. (ed.) Oxford Companion to the Theatre (1950)
Le Gallienne, E. At 33 (1934)
Motion Picture and Television Almanac, 1954
Who's Who, 1954
Who's Who in the Theatre (1952)

COMPTON, KARL T(AYLOR) Sept. 14, 1887-June 22, 1954 Physicist; atomic scientist; chairman of the corporation of Massachusetts Institute of Technology since 1949 and president (1930-1949); was graduated from Wooster College, Ohio (1908); Ph.D. degree, Princeton University (1912); taught physics at Reed College (1912-1914); served in World War I as aeronautical engineer in Signal Corps; was professor of physics at Princeton (1919-1930) where he assembled a group of research workers in atomic physics; he made important contributions to the knowledge of photo-electric effect, structure of crystals by X rays, fluorescence and dissociation of gases and thermionic emission; as president of M.I.T. broadened the curriculum; introduced a five-year plan of study combined with industrial cooperation; was closely associated with the development of the atom bomb and defended its use against Japan, stating that the bomb had saved at least 50,000 American soldiers' lives (the Army's estimate of casualties for initial landings on the main islands of Japan); appointed in 1948 by President Truman the head of the seven-man Research and Development Board of the National Military Establishment, reporting directly to the Secretary of Defense on military weapons and counter-measures against the atom bomb; was a prolific writer on scientific subjects (over 300 papers on thermionics, electric emission from hot filaments and spectroscopy, etc.); received the civilian Medal of Merit (1946) for outstanding services to his country and crediting him with being "personally responsible for hastening the end of World War II;" was named (1951) to the five-member National Security Training Commission by President Truman to detail a plan for universal military training of eighteen-year-old boys; received many awards for his research including the Rumford Medal; was president of the American Association for the Advancement of Science (1935-36), American Society for Engineering Education (1938-39), American Physical Society (1927-29); served in 1946 as a member of the President's personal committee on atom bomb tests; held that science and religion are in accord. See *Current Biography,* (Mar.) 1941.

Obituary

N Y Times p 1+ Je 23 '54

CONAN DOYLE, ADRIAN *See* Doyle, A. (M.) C.

CONLEY, EUGENE (THOMAS) Mar. 12, 1908- Singer

Address: b. c/o Columbia Artists Management, Inc., 113 W. 57th St., New York 19; h. 60 W. 58th St., New York 19

After nearly a decade of success as a radio singer, and as a leading tenor with the Salmaggi, San Carlo and New York City Opera companies, Eugene Conley made his debut at the Metropolitan Opera House in 1950 in the title role of Gounod's *Faust.* Critics acclaimed him as "a true lyric tenor" who sang "with a degree of stylistic finish not often encountered here nowadays in French opera." He is the only major singer, American-born and completely trained in the United States, to sing a leading role in an opening performance at La Scala Opera House in Milan, Italy, where in December 1951 he was warmly praised for his performance of Arrigo in Verdi's *I Vespri Siciliani.*

He sang the role of the Rake in Igor Stravinsky's *The Rake's Progress* which had its premiere at the Metropolitan Opera on February 15, 1953. He also sang the tenor lead in a broadcast performance in 1953 of Beethoven's *Missa Solemnis* with the NBC Symphony conducted by Arturo Toscanini (recorded by R.C.A. Victor and released in March 1954).

Eugene Thomas Conley was born in Lynn, Massachusetts on March 12, 1908 to Reuben A. and Josephine (Farnsworth) Conley. His father was a surveyor who, in his spare time, played the violin at local dances. Both of his grandfathers had fine tenor voices. Eugene was at first given piano lessons, but, as he grew up, he began to cultivate his voice with the help of local teachers. As both singer and tap-dancer he enjoyed the Saturday night musical get-togethers organized by his father. Later he was soloist with his high school glee club and in several local churches. His youth, however, was by no means wholly devoted to musical studies. He was a member of the Boy Scouts of America, played baseball with his high school team, and competed in track meets.

After graduating from high school he obtained work with the General Electric Corporation to pay for his vocal lessons. Young Conley later joined the Boston Male Choir and toured the country with that group. As his professional career developed he sang with the Handel-Haydn society in *The Messiah,* with the Boston Apollo Club, and as soloist with the Commonwealth Symphony.

During the early thirties Conley began singing regularly on a small radio station in Boston where his repertoire included everything from operatic arias to popular ballads. Thus he became known throughout New England, and he soon attracted the attention of radio station WWJ, owned and operated by the Detroit *Daily News.* He was engaged to sing for this station under contract for about three years. His steadily growing reputation interested the National Broadcasting Company who brought him to New York. Now for the first time he was heard on nation-wide broadcasts. From 1939 on he was heard either on his own programs such as *NBC Presents Eugene Conley,* or as a regular participant in the *Magic Key* program (NBC) and, later, on Columbia's *Golden Treasury of Song* (1941) and Mutual's *Operatic Review.* One of his notable early performances was singing the Brahms *Liebeslieder* Waltzes with Arturo Toscanini's NBC Symphony Orchestra.

The young tenor's success in radio never obscured his ambition to sing grand opera. Continuing to study voice with Harriot E. Barrows and Ettore Verna, in September 1940 he made his operatic debut at the Brooklyn Academy of Music as the Duke in Verdi's *Rigoletto* with the New York La Scala Opera Company. It was not known by the audience that Conley sang the role without rehearsal, with Verna prompting and directing him from the wings.

After several more appearances with that group during the 1940-1941 season, he was engaged by the San Carlo Opera Company (also of New York) for the following season. He sang with the Cincinnati Summer Opera in *Faust* in July 1942 and in the fall appeared in leading roles with the Chicago Opera Company.

Military service interrupted Conley's professional activity. Between 1942 and 1945 he served with the United States Air Force and performed for the benefit of the Army Air

Bruno of Hollywood

EUGENE CONLEY

Force Aid Society and in the show *Winged Victory,* the cast of which was drawn entirely from Air Force personnel. While *Winged Victory* was playing in New York during the spring of 1944, Fortune Gallo, the impresario of the San Carlo Opera Company, (pleading the severe wartime shortage of tenors) obtained permission from the Air Force for Corporal Conley to sing with his company. He appeared in five operas between April 26 and May 7, 1944, donating his earnings to a war relief agency.

Resuming his operatic career after the war, Conley diversified his activity with concert tours and radio work. He sang with the New York City Opera Company and during the 1945-1946 season he toured with the National Grand Opera Company. The tenor gave his first Town Hall recital in New York on December 30, 1946, singing art songs, folk songs and only one well-known operatic aria. His audience, however, demanded more opera, and the artist obliged them with several tenor arias. He was praised generally for his vocal technique, diction and voice quality.

Early in 1947 he helped to organize a group known as the American Lyric Theatre along with Winifred Heidt, the mezzo-soprano, and others drawn chiefly from the staff of the New York City Opera for the purpose of presenting opera in English. They presented Rossini's *The Barber of Seville,* Offenbach's *The Tales of Hoffmann* and Bizet's *Carmen.*

Making his first trip to Europe in 1947, he sang the role of Rodolfo in Puccini's *La Bohème* at the Paris Opera Comique for his European debut and received an ovation for his performance. Later that year, he joined Winifred Heidt in New York in a revival of Massenet's seldom heard opera, *Werther*—it was the first performance in thirty-seven years—and it was favorably reviewed.

(Continued next page)

CONLEY, EUGENE—*Continued*

By the end of 1947 Conley's repertoire included virtually all of the major lyric tenor roles in English, Italian, French, and German opera. He was one of five outstanding figures in the entertainment field to receive the 1948 award of the Linguaphone Institute for his "excellent diction in singing." His popularity in Europe increased greatly during his 1948 tour which took him to the major opera houses in Stockholm, Paris, London, Milan, Naples, Florence, Turin, and Genoa for a total of twenty-two performances in eight weeks.

Conley's voice was "dubbed" onto the sound track of an Italian film of the opera *Faust* under the musical direction of one of the conductors of La Scala. He was invited to La Scala for a special revival of Bellini's *I Puritani* (The Puritans) in 1949. The very first tenor aria in the opera includes a D Flat above high C, a formidable challenge to the soloist and one of the reasons why the opera is so rarely performed. Conley met this challenge and became an immediate favorite with operagoers in Milan. When he returned to La Scala to sing in Verdi's *I Vespri Siciliani, L'Italia* found his high notes "bell-like and sure" but his movements "uncertain and indefinite." *L'Unita* stated that his high notes were "impeccable" (*Time,* December 17, 1951).

Conley made his debut at the "Met" on January 25, 1950 in the title role of *Faust.* In the course of his four seasons with the opera company he has sung ten other lyric roles and the critics have used their finest superlatives to describe his interpretation of such parts as Pinkerton in Puccini's *Madam Butterfly,* the Duke in Verdi's *Rigoletto* and Alfredo in Verdi's *La Traviata* and Cavaradossi in Puccini's *Tosca.* On occasion he has been criticized for a lack of warmth in his voice and by Olin Downes in the New York *Times* for seeming to force his voice in apparent effort to produce a larger tone. His high notes have been generally praised for their clarity.

He has sung at New York's Lewisohn Stadium, the Hollywood Bowl and other outdoor summer theatres here and abroad. Twentieth Century Fox's short film *Of Men and Music* was released in 1951 with Conley as one of the featured singers. Between seasons of the Metropolitan Conley has toured South America and the Caribbean area, stopping to concertize in Puerto Rico at the University of Puerto Rico where he also participated in the ten-day Caribbean festival of opera in June, 1954.

In an article (*Etude,* March, 1950) giving advice on the training of the voice, Conley stressed the necessity of seeking the guidance of a competent teacher. The tenor referred to the often difficult problem of locating the voice on the basis of its color and timbre, noting that many young singers "type" themselves by range instead of by voice color. He noted that often only an experienced teacher can determine where the voice actually lies. Discouraging the attempt to imitate a particular singer, he suggested that the tyro develop his own style of singing consistent with the nature of his own voice.

He belongs to the Air Force Association, The Bohemians and to the S.P.E.B.S.Q.S.A., the Society for the Preservation and Encouragement of Barber Shop Quartet Singing in America which each year sponsors a nationwide contest of male quartets. His recorded operatic arias were among the first long playing releases of London FFRR, and he sings the role he created of the Rake in Columbia's recording of *The Rake's Progress.*

The singer was married on March 9, 1948 to Winifred Heidt, the mezzo-soprano. He has a son, Eugene, by a former marriage. Blue-eyed and with brown hair, Conley is five feet seven inches tall and weighs 170 pounds. A lover of the outdoors, he is a camera enthusiast and enjoys landscape painting. His New York apartment contains hundreds of framed color photographs of his tours, bright paintings, figurines and trophies from his travels. Before crossing the ocean, however, he acquired extensive musical experience in his own country. "I firmly believe," he said "that many of the best teachers in the operatic field may be found right here in the United States" (*Opera News,* February 27, 1950).

He is proud of his manual dexterity and his ability to take a motor apart and put it together again which helps him to concentrate on his music, especially when he has to learn a new operatic role.

References

Mus Courier 133:13 My 1 '46
Opera N 15:9 F 27 '50
Time 58:68 D 17 '51
Who is Who in Music (1951)

CONNELL, ARTHUR J(OSEPH) July 17, 1898- Veterans organization official; businessman

Address: b. c/o American Legion National Headquarters, 700 N. Pennsylvania St., Indianapolis 6, Ind.; h. Huntly Rd., Portland, Conn.

The national commander of the world's largest veterans' association, the American Legion, is Arthur J. Connell who was elected at the Legion's thirty-fifth annual convention in St. Louis, Missouri in September 1953. The New England business executive, who had served in the Navy from 1918 to 1921, has long been prominent in the veterans' organization, rising from post commander to national executive committeeman before assuming the Legion's top executive position for the 1953-1954 term. He was succeeded by Seaborn P. Collins, Jr., in September 1954.

Arthur Joseph Connell, one of the seven children of John Joseph and Mary (Dever) Connell, was born in Boston, Massachusetts on July 17, 1898. He attended Phillips Exeter Academy in New Hampshire where he participated in football and baseball activities and was the assignment editor of the *Exonian,* a semi-weekly, and the managing editor of the yearbook. Following graduation in 1916, he pursued an economics and English curriculum at Harvard University.

In his freshman year at Harvard, Connell volunteered for service in World War I and in June 1918 became a seaman second class in the U.S. Naval Reserve in Boston. During the next three years, until September 30, 1921, he was stationed at a number of bases in the New England area: Hingham Naval Station and Bumpkin Island, Wakefield Range (Massachusetts) and Bay Harbor (Maine). Returning to Harvard after the war, he received the A.B. degree in February 1921. He later attended Harvard Graduate School of Business Administration and began his career as an advertising salesman.

The Navy veteran settled in Middletown, Connecticut and joined the American Legion, advancing through the ranks from commander of the Milardo-Wilcox Post No. 75 of Middletown, to commander of the seventh district of Connecticut. In this post he established an aircraft warning service in 1941.

He was elected national vice-commander for the 1942-1943 term and from 1947 to 1953 Connell held the office of the Legion's national executive committeeman. As the official representative of the organization, he was present during September 1952 at the memorial dedication in Suresnes, France and at the pilgrimage to American military cemeteries in Europe.

The American Legion, which received its charter from Congress in 1919, has a membership of approximately 3,000,000, with about sixty departments and 17,000 posts. Its members are veterans of World Wars I and II who served in the armed forces of the United States or who "as American citizens entered the armed forces of a government associated with the United States in war." Besides obtaining benefits for veterans and directing its efforts toward strengthening national defense and combating forces subversive to the established democratic form of government, the Legion is engaged in a variety of community projects, including recreational youth activities and an extensive child welfare program.

When the American Legionnaires met in St. Louis in early September 1953 for their thirty-fifth annual convention, Arthur J. Connell was one of five candidates for the office of national commander. In the polling on September 3 at the closing session of the four-day meeting, he received 2,751 votes, with his closest contender polling only 274. Commander Connell succeeds Lewis K. Gough, of California, who had been the fourth consecutive World War II veteran to hold the Legion's commandership. Connell is the first World War I veteran to be elected commander since 1949.

Upon receiving the national commander's red cap from his predecessor, Connell declared: "We see no early prospect for reducing the defensive strength of our armed forces. Moreover, with hostilities suspended in Korea, we must take an additional responsibility for public understanding and support of an adequate preparedness program" (New York *Times,* September 4, 1953).

Several resolutions relating to national defense were adopted at the convention, including recommendations for maintaining the Air Force

ARTHUR J. CONNELL

at "a level far above the minimum necessary for national safety," building up a Merchant Marine of modern ships and operating a program of universal military training together with selective service. In a report on civil defense the Legion warned that the present defense setup was inadequate to meet a real emergency.

The day after he had been made the Legion's new commander, Connell sent a message to the annual convention of the Jewish War Veterans, meeting in Chicago. He affirmed that the American Legion and the Jewish veterans' organization "have always stood together in those things which patriotic Americans have always fought for—promotion of genuine Americanism, adequate national security, the welfare of our disabled comrades and their dependents" (New York *Times,* September 5, 1953).

During an address in late September in New York, Commander Connell remarked that American Legion officers in the past had been "too ready to give their opinions and I am opposed to this policy." He suggested that matters concerning the Department of State and the Department of Defense are better left to those agencies to handle. Promising that the fight against communism and other forms of subversion would be given full attention by his administration, he observed that while the fixing of guilt was not the responsibility of the Legion, the dissemination of information bearing on anti-Americanism was of deep concern to the veterans' organization.

In his annual report made public August 27, 1954, Connell reaffirmed the Legion's support of a universal military training program. He led the Legion's convention parade of over 75,000 in Washington, D.C. on August 31.

The American Legion sponsors the discussion program "Youth Wants to Know" over NBC-TV each Sunday in which high school students interview Senators, Congressmen, Cabinet mem-

CONNELL, ARTHUR J.—*Continued*

bers and others on their views in regard to domestic and foreign policies.

Connell is president and treasurer of Connell's, a clothing firm in Middletown, Connecticut and vice-president of the George H. Ellis Company, a printing house in Boston. He also serves as vice-president of the New England Clothiers and Furnishers Association.

Known for his leadership in civic activities, he is vice-president of the Greater Middletown Community Chest, Inc., secretary of the Connecticut Veterans' Home and Hospital Commission, incorporator of the Middlesex Memorial Hospital, director of the Borough of Stannard Beach Association, and president and treasurer of the Joan Connell Foundation. For seven years he was chairman of the Middletown Selective Service Board 33. He is a member of the Rockfall Corporation, Chamber of Commerce and the Elks.

Connell's wife is the former Patrice Finlay, whom he married on January 16, 1924. Their daughter, Joan, is deceased. The commander has brown eyes, gray-brown hair and is six feet one inch in height and weighs 195 pounds. He is a Roman Catholic and is politically independent. His recreations include baseball, golf and swimming. On his return to Middletown from the Legion convention, Commander Connell was greeted by leading city and state officials who joined with 25,000 spectators in a celebration to honor him.

Reference

N Y Times p1+ S 4 '53 por

CONROY, PAT(RICK DOMINIC) 1900-
Canadian Government official

Address: b. c/o Embassy of Canada, 1746 Massachusetts Ave., N.W., Washington, D.C.; h. 3331 Quesada St., Washington, D.C.

Supplementing the traditional "silk-hat diplomacy" by the use of labor attachés, the Canadian government created a new post for this purpose and appointed Pat Conroy as labor attaché in its Embassy in Washington, D.C. Canada is thus following a procedure established by Great Britain and the United States in appointing labor attachés to diplomatic missions.

Conroy was chosen for the post in January 1952, some months after his resignation from the chief administrative office of the Canadian Congress of Labour. He had served on the executive committee of the CCL, one of Canada's two central labor organizations, from the time of its formation in 1940, and as its secretary-treasurer and organization director since 1941.

In the course of World War II he served on a number of government committees; his services were recognized with the award of Member of the Order of the British Empire. A miner by trade, Conroy rose through a succession of local and district posts in the United Mine Workers of America to "a post of outstanding leadership in the Canadian labour movement" (*Labour Gazette,* February 1952). He has represented Canadian labor at several international meetings. He has a long record of opposition to communism in trade unions.

Patrick Dominic Conroy was born in 1900 into an Irish family living in the town of Baillieston, near Glasgow, Scotland, where his father was a miner. Good at his studies, Patrick won a scholarship on reaching the top grade, the sixth, at the local school, but could not afford to accept it. His father having died when he was eight years old, it was necessary for him to help support the family of seven children.

Accordingly, at the age of thirteen, he went to work in the coal mines, where his first job was shoveling coal from the miners at the coal face. For this his apprentice's pay was the equivalent of $.50 a day; after four years, he became a miner, and his pay was equivalent to $1.75 a day. Encouraged by his mother, he spent his evenings studying.

When nineteen years old, Conroy immigrated to Canada to find work in the coal mines of Drumheller, Alberta. After a few months in that city, Conroy went to the United States. He worked as a lumberman in Washington, Oregon and California, as a laborer and timekeeper with construction gangs in Oklahoma and Kansas, and as a miner in Kentucky, Colorado and New Mexico. He returned to Canada in 1922 and settled in Drumheller.

A member of the British Mineworkers' Federation in Scotland, Conroy in Canada joined the United Mine Workers of America, and became a member of Local 3857, Drumheller. Shortly after his return from the United States, the union fought a successful seven-month strike against a 50 per cent cut in wages, and Conroy was elected to the committee of his local.

Well-versed in union procedure from his Scottish background, he applied his spare time to a study of labor economics to such good effect that, in the words of the *Labour Gazette* (February 1952), "he became a specialist in this field and acquired a mastery of the written and spoken word that was later to make him a national figure in company-union negotiations and in convention arenas, where his voice was the voice of labour." He became secretary of the committee of his local, then advanced through a succession of local and district union offices to become vice-president of District 18 (Western Canada) of the United Mine Workers in 1935. At that time he ceased underground work in the mines.

As vice-president of District 18 U.M.W., Conroy was a delegate to the convention at which the Canadian Congress of Labour was formed in 1940. The congress is a central labor organization comprising both national and international unions, developed when the All-Canadian Congress of Labour decided to amalgamate with the Canadian branches of CIO unions which had been expelled from the Trades and Labour Congress (the other national labor organization in Canada) in 1939.

The way was opened for this amalgamation when the CIO granted complete autonomy to its Canadian branches. Conroy was elected a vice-president of the new body, and in 1941 became its secretary-treasurer. As such he was chief administrative officer, and has been called "chief architect" of the success of the CCL. The congress undertook a program of organizing new unions, mostly on an industrial basis, with Conroy as national director of organization, and within a decade tripled its membership to an estimated 350,000.

As secretary-treasurer of the CCL, Conroy had a strategist's role in respect to strikes staged by member unions. A tribute to him in the *Canadian Unionist* (a CCL publication) credited him with an important part in the settlement of several of Canada's biggest strikes, notably the Kirkland Lake gold miners' strike of 1942, the steel strike of 1943, and the strike at the Ford Motor Company of Canada in 1945.

He was frequently spokesman for the Congress or its members before Parliamentary committees on labor legislation, old age pensions and similar questions, and before labor relations boards. During World War II he served on the Minister of Labour's consultative committee, on the National War Finance Advisory Committee, and later was a member of the Postwar Reconstruction Committee.

The labor leader has represented Canadian labor on committees of the International Labor Organization, at the Commonwealth Labor Conference in London in 1943, and at the World Trade Union Conference in London in 1945. He attended the constitutional convention of the World Federation of Trade Unions held in Paris in 1945, and being elected a member of its executive board, took part in the drafting of its constitution.

However, when this organization appeared to be dominated by the communist faction, Conroy withdrew and assisted in the organization of a new body, the International Confederation of Free Trade Unions. At the founding conference in London in December 1949, he was elected to its executive board. His activities in the confederation included participation in the setting up of the Inter-American Regional Organization at a convention held in Mexico City in 1951, attendance at the congress of the ICFTU in Milan (July 1951) and service on several of its committees.

Conroy's opposition to communism began early in his career. At Drumheller he withdrew from the newly organized Canadian Workers' Party when he observed that it was controlled from abroad. His opposition continued throughout his career with the CCL, and he is credited with a leading part in its campaign to free its ranks from communists and communist-dominated unions.

He was the congress spokesman at conventions where such unions protested their suspension or expulsion. Conroy has expressed disapproval of any tendency to identify anti-communism with the interests of particular segments of the population, and has stated: "We have to fight communism . . . because it's a threat to everybody's liberty and to the values we all live by."

Pat Conroy announced his resignation from office at the 1951 annual convention of the

Capital Press Service, Ottawa

PAT CONROY

CCL, held in Vancouver. The CCL executive committee finally accepted his resignation with expressions of regret. The grounds given by Conroy for his resignation included an implied lack of confidence in his judgment shown in the congress' failure to re-elect a former executive committee member. News commentators saw in this an expression of belief on the part of the labor leader that Canadian labor should insist on a greater degree of autonomy in its relations with the international brotherhoods.

In an appreciation of Conroy's work on behalf of labor, the *Canadian Unionist* (December 1951) wrote: "His calmness, his judgment, his sincerity, impressed the executives of great corporations and won him many friends even among those whose interests are traditionally opposed to those of labor. The same qualities won for him the respect and loyalty of the rank and file."

The magazine went on to quote from a memorandum to the National War Labour Board in which Conroy incidentally stated his philosophy of organized labor, saying, ". . . unions are living organisms, representing the everyday aspirations of a large number of our peoples and . . . their aim is to establish a standard of life consistent with the rights and dignity of every human being."

On January 16, 1952, it was announced that Pat Conroy had been appointed labor attaché to the Canadian Embassy in Washington, D.C. A newly created post, it carried the same status and salary as that of commercial attaché. A concept that emerged during World War II when Great Britain appointed a labor attaché in Washington, D.C., it was taken up by the United States and then by Canada.

Creation of such posts had long been recommended by Conroy, who had urged on the Canadian government the merits of such representatives. He claimed that the value of "silk-hat diplomacy" was limited, and that the use of

CONROY, PAT—*Continued*

labor men to contact labor circles abroad was a necessity. The idea of offering the former CCL executive the post had Cabinet approval.

Acclaiming the government's action and its choice of a representative, the *Ottawa Journal* wrote: "Pat Conroy, often referred to as 'the Philip Murray of Canada,' is by common consent the most literate, able and experienced labor leader [in] this country in a generation."

The duties of the Canadian labor attaché have been defined as twofold: to keep the Canadian Department of Labour in touch with labor developments abroad and to explain the Canadian labor situation abroad. Writing on the meaning of the Conroy appointment, Michael Barkway (*Saturday Night*, March 29, 1952) noted Conroy's personal relations with top labor leaders in the United States, and the peculiar relation of Canadian labor to American in that many unions in both Canadian congresses are affiliates of the CIO or the AFL.

Barkway also wrote: "If we should get back into times of serious labor unrest, it is very likely that more and more Canadians would get more and more indignant about unions which look across the border for their leadership. It is also likely that the Canadian government would be very glad to have a trusted Canadian voice with direct access to the highest leaders of the 'international' unions."

In 1948 Saint Francis Xavier University (Nova Scotia) presented him with an honorary LL.D. degree. He is a member of the Roman Catholic Church. In 1940 he married Esther Green of Cleveland, Ohio. Mrs. Conroy was a schoolteacher and sales executive before her marriage. The couple has one daughter, Anne.

Rather short in stature, Conroy has broad shoulders, weighs some 150 pounds, and is built, in the words of Blair Fraser writing in *Maclean's Magazine*, "like a good welterweight." He has blue eyes; his wavy hair is predominantly gray, but with traces of red; he gives a general impression of ruddiness. His hobbies are reading and gardening; he smokes a pipe. Barkway wrote that Conroy "talks quietly and decisively . . . he comes straight to the point, and generally stays there."

References

Canadian Unionist 25:379 D '51
Labour Gazette 52:153 F '52
Maclean's Mag 60:8 Ag 1 '47
Sat Night 65:37 F 7 '50; 67:8+ Mr 29 '52 por

Canadian Who's Who, 1949-51

COOK, DONALD Sept. 26, 1901- Actor

Address: b. c/o Actors Equity Assn., 45 W. 47th St., New York 36

Adding to his long list of expert characterizations, Donald Cook is playing a glib cartoonist in the hit comedy, *King of Hearts*, which opened on April 1, 1954 at the Lyceum Theatre in New York City. The role marks his fifteenth on the Broadway stage since 1926. He has also played parts in forty-five motion pictures and has made numerous radio appearances. His first starring role was in 1946 in John Golden's production of *Made In Heaven!* Brooks Atkinson, drama critic of the New York *Times*, applauds Cook's current role and his "crisp, dapper, almost farcial style that he has perfected through many amusing seasons."

Drama lovers remember Cook most vividly for his suave interpretations as Tony Kenyon, advertising executive, with the late Gertrude Lawrence in *Skylark* (1939); as David Naughton, the young husband in *Claudia* (1941); as the volatile husband in *Private Lives* (1948) opposite Tallulah Bankhead, and as David Slater, the middle-aged playboy with the "built-in Southern accent" in *The Moon is Blue* (1951) in which he played for 924 performances.

Donald Cook was born in Portland, Oregon on September 26, 1901 to Frank R. and Edith (Parker) Cook. His father and uncles were in the banking business and it was presumed that young Donald would follow in this tradition. He was educated in Portland public schools, and was graduated from the University of Oregon (Portland) with a degree in agriculture. For a time he sold bonds and was a bank clerk, but the lure of the footlights began one night when he teamed with a partner for an amateur song and patter act at The Wigwam in San Francisco.

The team of Cook and Wadhams obtained a four months booking in vaudeville and toured through little western towns and down to Amarillo, Texas. The booking agent who was to meet them there to send the act to Chicago failed to appear. Donald, undaunted, made his way to Emporia, Kansas, where he sang in movie theatres. He moved on to Kansas City, Missouri, and worked there at odd jobs as a bellhop, elevator boy, grocery clerk, and cattle counter in the stockyards. Finally he secured a job as a lumber salesman, and in the evenings, organized a little theatre group and studied drama.

His efforts were rewarded when he attracted the attention of actress Margaret Anglin who was then on tour. His two years with the Kansas City Community Players were not wasted. In the summer of 1925, encouraged by letters of introduction from Miss Anglin to three producers, Donald arrived in New York. Two of the producers turned him down. The third, George C. Tyler, was in Europe.

During the waiting period, Cook studied voice and dancing. When Tyler returned he interviewed Cook and sent him to Minneapolis to join a star-studded company playing on the road in *The Rivals*. The cast included Chauncey Olcott, James T. Powers, and Mrs. Minnie Maddern Fiske. Cook listened to all the advice from these experienced thespians, but was especially grateful to Mrs. Fiske who coached him in his role as Captain Absolute. He still attributes his "fundamental knowledge of comedy technique" to her patient teaching.

His next step was into stock as Donn Cook with the Hartman Stock Company. In the New York *Times* (April 15, 1952), he stressed "the importance of stock companies as training schools for aspiring performers," deplored the use of the "star system in summer theatres," and urged the members of the Stock Managers Association to "utilize the apprentice as well as the professional performer."

As John Roberts in *Seed of the Brute,* Cook appeared at the Little Theatre in his first Broadway show which opened on November 1, 1926 and played for eighty performances. This was followed by a part as Rowlie Bateson with Pauline Lord in *Spellbound,* a mystery melodrama presented at the Earl Carroll Theatre in November 1927.

His first real acclaim was received for his role of Jim Hutton in *Paris Bound* with Madge Kennedy at the Music Box Theatre in December 1927. In this play he used the telephone conversation technique for which he has become famous. He enacted Stephen Ferrier in *Half Gods* at the Plymouth Theatre in 1929, and Bill Truesdale in *Rebound* (Plymouth, February 1930) opposite Hope Williams. In this play he developed the style of playing husband roles in "acid fashion." Since then, Cook has often been lauded for his ability to portray the character of the slightly world-weary "man of distinction" who is inclined toward cynicism in his observance of the opposite sex.

Hollywood beckoned in 1930 and during the next seven years, Cook appeared in thirty-seven screen offerings. His most praised role was in Warner Brothers' picture *Man Who Played God* (1932) with George Arliss and a newcomer, Bette Davis. Among the other pictures in which Cook appeared were *Public Enemy, Showboat, Viva Villa, Frisco Jenny* (with Ruth Chatterton), *Jennie Gerhardt,* and *Private Jones.* For the most part he acted in film versions of murder and mystery stories.

Joining a summer stock group he appeared, according to *Variety* (July 7, 1937), in the comedies *Let Us Be Gay, The High Road, Pride and Prejudice, Remote Control,* and *Dearly Beloved.* In subsequent summer tours, he acted in *Romance* with Cornelia Otis Skinner, *Our Town* with Thornton Wilder, and *It Can't Happen Here* with Sinclair Lewis. In February 1938 he was cast as Laddy Sears in *Wine of Choice* at the Guild Theatre with the late drama critic Alexander Woollcott. He also played Gerald Spinner in *American Landscape* at the Cort Theatre in December 1938.

He turned out an excellent portrait of Tony Kenyon in *Skylark* which opened at the Morosco Theatre in October 1939 with the late Gertrude Lawrence. Brooks Atkinson commented in the New York *Times* (October 13, 1939) that Cook gave "an attractive, mettlesome performance." The actor's next long run hit was in 1941 as David Naughton in *Claudia* at the Booth Theatre with Dorothy McGuire. At the same time, he played in radio dramas.

After fifty-six weeks in *Claudia,* Cook returned to Hollywood to appear in several screen productions including *Patrick the Great, Bowery to Broadway, Murder in the Blue Room, Blonde Ransom, Our Very Own,* and others, bringing his total motion picture output to forty-five.

DONALD COOK

Returning to Broadway on March 13, 1945 in the Philip Barry satire *Foolish Notion* at the Martin Beck Theatre, Cook played the role of Gordon Roark opposite Tallulah Bankhead for 104 performances before going on tour.

Between 1946 and 1948 he played opposite Tallulah Bankhead in a revival of Noel Coward's comedy *Private Lives* on a fifty-three week cross-country tour and then opened at the Plymouth Theatre on October 4, 1948 for a Broadway run. He was first starred by producer John Golden in *Made in Heaven!* (October 24, 1946) as Zachary Meredith, a commuter in a marital farce by Hagar Wilde, which ran for ninety-two performances. He next appeared as Dr. Philip Graham in a murder play *Portrait in Black* which opened at the Booth Theatre May 14, 1947, and closed after sixty-two performances.

The Moon is Blue by F. Hugh Herbert opened on March 8, 1951 at the Henry Miller Theatre and received enthusiastic reviews. Cook got a "run-of-the-play contract," outlasted four leading ladies (Barbara Bel Geddes, Maggie McNamara, Janet Riley, and Betty Oakes), and played the role of the martini-drinking neighbor of the hero for 924 performances. "At no time," he said, "did I find this long and uninterrupted employment onerous. . . . After three seasons in *Private Lives,* my long stay in *The Moon is Blue* seems like a tropical vacation" (New York *World-Telegram and Sun,* March 8, 1953).

The summer of 1953 marked Donald Cook's entry in a National Broadcasting Company domestic comedy called *My Son Jeep* in which he played a small town physician. In the winter of 1954 he appeared in Columbia Broadcasting System television dramatizations. As

COOK, DONALD—*Continued*

the megalomaniac cartoonist in *King of Hearts,* a comedy by Jean Kerr and Eleanor Brooke, Cook is proving to be "a knave of diamond quality." He plays with a "steady, glib absurdity."

In 1952 Cook served as chairman of a personnel committee of the Actors Equity Association. He received a gold medal in 1941 from the New York Academy at The Lambs Club for giving "the best light comedy performance of the year" in *Claudia.*

Donald Cook is married to the former Princess Gioia Tasca di Cuto of Palermo, Sicily. He owns a New Jersey farm and plans to build a house at Fire Island. He told Ward Morehouse that his hobby is weaving. "I took a course in weaving," he said, "when I was with Tallulah in San Francisco in *Private Lives,* and I've found it fascinating. I have two looms now. . . . During the run of *The Moon Is Blue* I took a course in real estate" (New York *World-Telegram and Sun,* May 5, 1954). Among his hobbies are photography and raising Hungarian sheep dogs.

References

N Y Herald Tribune IV p2 My 20 '45 por
N Y World-Telegram p28 Je 25 '52
Pictorial R p12P F 3 '52 pors
Motion Picture and Television Almanac, 1953-54
Who's Who in the Theatre (1952)

COOLIDGE, ELIZABETH SPRAGUE
Oct. 30, 1864—Nov. 4, 1953 Music patron; founder of the Berkshire Festivals on South Mountain, Pittsfield, Mass.; established scholarships for gifted musicians; gave $600,000 in 1926 to Library of Congress to endow chamber music programs and collections; donated Sprague Hall to Yale University; began a pension fund for musicians of Chicago Symphony Orchestra; commissioned many chamber-music compositions; and was a member of the Legion of Honor of France. See *Current Biography,* (Aug.) 1941.

Obituary

N Y Times p31 N 5 '53

COOPER, ALFRED DUFF *See* Norwich, A. D. C., 1st Viscount

COTTERELL, (ALAN) GEOFFREY
Nov. 24, 1919- Author

Address: b. c/o J. B. Lippincott Co., E. Washington Sq., Philadelphia 5, Pa.; h. Ham Frith, Grove Park, Wanstead, E.11, England

Reprinted from the *Wilson Library Bulletin,* Nov. 1954

In October 1951, shortly before his fourth novel, the first to be published in the United States, was released here, Geoffrey Cotterell landed in New York and started on an informal tour of the country. In Buffalo he bought a

GEOFFREY COTTERELL

1940 Chevrolet for $125. About four months and 10,000 miles later he sold the car in Atlanta, Georgia, for $180.

A detailed description of his findings during his cross-country tour came in 1953 when his novel *Westward the Sun* was published here. For the novel, told in the first person, of an English girl who marries an American soldier, reaches its climax when its protagonist arrives in the United States as a "war bride" and describes her reactions to our country. In a subsequent interview with William Du Bois of the New York *Times,* Cotterell revealed that, in addition to his general observation of the United States, he had talked to a great many real English war brides in the course of his tour, so that the Linda Ferrers of his novel emerges as a composite of the lives and experiences of many like her.

The youthful author of this novel was born in Southsea, Hampshire, England, November 24, 1919, to Millicent Louise (Crews) Cotterell and Graham Cotterell, a dental surgeon. He was christened Alan Geoffrey Cotterell. (Anthony Cotterell, his older brother, was a journalist—an important factor in Geoffrey's choice of writing as a profession.)

Geoffrey Cotterell received his education from Bishops Stortford College, a secondary school in Hertfordshire. He left this school at the age of seventeen, spent about a term at Berlin University and then returned to begin studying toward a degree in economics at University College, London. He soon decided, however, that what he really wanted to do was write. Early in 1937, therefore, he left University College and began to submit stories to the pulps. He recalls that he sold one almost at once. It was called "She Was a Bad One, He Thought," and brought him £5. After that sale, he writes, he "lived in a gale of rejection slips," which continued almost unabated until just before the war when there was "a detectable improvement." Not in the least abashed about his long apprenticeship in the pulps, he has said: "What the pulp writer learns is that a writer must write with total sincerity, that it is fatal to be patronizing. And he learns that there has to be a story. . . . If I'm readable now it's because of what I learned then."

After the outbreak of war he became a gunner (1940) in the Royal Artillery attached to anti-aircraft units at various stations in the United Kingdom, reaching the rank of major in 1943. During the postwar occupation he worked in Hamburg with the Control Commission attached to the German News Service for whom he went on the air in German as "The Voice of the Military Government" on a question-and-answer program.

While he was still serving in the war, Cotterell wrote his first full-length novel, *Then a Soldier.* It was published in England in 1944, and was very well received.

After the war his second and third novels, *This Is the Way* (1947) and *Randle in Springtime* (1950) were published in England. Cotterell was introduced to the American reading public with *Strait and Narrow* in the spring of 1951. It is the story of an Englishman driven by political ambition and the desire to rise above his social background into an unhappy marriage, and of his downfall brought about as the result of a tragic liaison with the wife of a Dutch underground worker during his army service in World War II. British reviewers had praised the book as the work of "a devastatingly competent writer with a flair for authenticity that is little short of ventriloquism" *(New Statesman and Nation),* and at the same time had felt that while the "novel is accomplished and credible and sound . . . it leaves no deep impression" *(Times Literary Supplement).* Reviewers in the United States, however, found the book "a novel of substance and strength . . . convincing as well as highly entertaining" (Chicago *Sunday Tribune*). The New York *Times* commented that "Mr. Cotterell largely shares Mr. Marquand's gifts of observation, wit, irony and narrative skill."

Geoffrey Cotterell, as are most young writers, has been beset by comparisons. In addition to J. P. Marquand, he has reminded a London *Daily Telegraph* reviewer of Thackeray while the *New Statesman and Nation,* in its review of *Westward the Sun,* found that "he comes nearer to Mr. Somerset Maugham than any English novelist." It is perhaps significant that he lists both Marquand and Maugham among his favorite authors. Readers of *Westward the Sun* may also catch a little of the flavor of another favorite, J. D. Salinger *(The Catcher in the Rye)* in the reactions of Linda Ferrers to New York City and its inhabitants.

Westward the Sun, a Book-of-the-Month Club selection, was praised by James Hilton in the *Herald Tribune* as "featherweight in its approach, and perhaps for that reason worth more than volumes of set pieces about Anglo-American relations." Other reviewers noted that the ending of the novel seemed contrived and expressed the wish that Cotterell had expanded Linda's experiences in the United States and had dealt more fully with her adjustment to our society. Both C. V. Terry in the New York *Times* and Harrison Smith of the *Saturday Review* note that the major problem of the novel is Linda Ferrers' practical imprisonment in her social stratum, a class status she is unable to break out of in England. Cotterell addresses himself frequently to this social question and makes it the focal point of his study of contemporary British society as it appears in his novels.

In 1953 he visited the United States again and an article on his previous travels appeared in the magazine *Holiday* for January of that year. Cotterell is a bachelor and, by published accounts, highly eligible. He is a six-footer with wavy brown hair, grey-blue eyes, and weighs a trim 180 pounds. His principal hobby is golf. He lives in a suburb of London, belongs to the Church of England, and is a Conservative in politics.

References

N Y Herald Tribune Book R p10 O 7 '51 por; p3 Mr 18 '51 por
N Y Times Book R p8 Ap 1 '51
Author's and Writer's Who's Who (1948-49)
Who's Who, 1954

COTY, RENÉ (JULES GUSTAVE) (kō"tē' rē-nā') Mar. 20, 1882- President of the French Republic; lawyer

Address: b. and h. Palais de l'Elysée, Paris; h. Rue Offenbach, Étretat, Seine-Inférieure, France

After a number of candidates had failed to be chosen at the 1953 joint session of Parliament to succeed Vincent Auriol as President of the Fourth French Republic, René Coty was elected on the thirteenth ballot as the new chief of state of France. An Independent Republican, Coty who was inducted into the Presidency on January 16, 1954, has had more than thirty years of legislative experience.

Both a Deputy and Senator before World War II as well as an Under Secretary of State, Coty served after the war as a representative of the Seine-Inférieure to the two constituent assemblies of 1945 and 1946 and to the National Assembly of the Fourth Republic, and entered the Council of the Republic in 1948. In parliament he was known for his efforts for constitutional reform and for European union.

René Jules Gustave Coty was born on March 20, 1882, in the port city of Le Havre, where his father was director of a private school. Reared in a scholarly atmosphere, he obtained two *baccalauréat* degrees—in science and in letters. Subsequently he received the degrees of Licentiate of Letters and Licentiate of Law, the second of which enabled him to become a member of the bar of his native city in 1902. Practicing law in Le Havre from 1902 to 1932, Coty acted as president of the local bar association for two years (1928 and 1929).

(Continued next page)

French Embassy Press & Inf. Div.
RENÉ COTY

When World War I was declared, he volunteered for service in the infantry and showed such distinction on the field of battle that he received not only the Croix de Guerre but also the Croix du Combattant Volontaire.

Entering civic politics in 1907, Coty represented his district in Le Havre for a year before being elected a municipal councilor. After his World War I service was ended, he was chosen in 1919 to be a general councilor of his department, the Seine-Inférieure, and became president of the general council in 1931. He first entered the field of national politics in 1923 with his election to the Chamber of Deputies, to which he was returned in 1924, 1928, and 1932. As a member of the "Left" Republican group, he was appointed to its directing committee.

Coty was prominent in two committees of the Chamber of Deputies, on both of which he served as vice-president: that on the merchant marine, and the one on the reform of the state. It was about this time that one of his major interests became apparent, since he advocated proposals to modify the proportional representation system and to strengthen the authority of the French presidency, which was quite limited under the constitution of 1875.

Awarded his first Cabinet post in 1931, when he was named Under Secretary of State for the Interior, Coty moved from Le Havre to Paris, where he opened a law office. He handled so many bankruptcy cases, remarks *Time,* that he "became known as the 'amiable liquidator.'" Elected in 1935 to the Senate, Coty remained in that office until 1940. At the joint session of the two French houses in Vichy on July 10, 1940, Coty was one of 569 parliamentarians who voted for Marshal Pétain's single act proposal which Pétain used to establish his own government the next day.

Following the war he was among the two hundred or so of those (who had thus voted) to be restored to their political rights by a jury of honor appointed to review the cases of the men responsible for France's transition to a dictatorship (New York *Times,* December 24, 1953). During the years that France was occupied, Coty remained aloof from politics, for, although he was elected to the council of his department, he refused to enter upon the office.

Under the Provisional Government formed by General de Gaulle in 1944, Coty was elected in both that year and the succeeding to the constituent assemblies which paved the way for the Fourth French Republic. Chosen on the Independent Republican ticket from the Seine-Inférieure, he was frequently heard in opposition to the constitutional projects sponsored by the Provisional Government, according to *Figaro* (December 24, 1953). Particularly, wrote Lansing Warren of the New York *Times,* the Norman representative "opposed the system of the all-powerful National Assembly that was adopted in 1946."

When the Fourth Republic came into being, Coty was returned by his department to the National Assembly, in which he served for two years (1946 to 1948). Coty was appointed to the Foreign Affairs Committee. On November 24, 1947, he was named Minister of Reconstruction and Urbanism in the Cabinet formed by Robert Schuman. He retained that post in the ministry of André Marie and in the next Schuman Cabinet, but was replaced on September 11, 1948 when Henri Queuille became Premier.

Due to Coty, more than 34,000,000 francs were allotted in 1947 for reconstruction, a sum far beyond the previous year's budget, observed *Figaro.* On November 7, 1948, Coty was elected to the Council of the Republic, to which he was returned in the elections of May 18, 1952. Continuing his early interest in constitutional reform, Coty in May 1950 was author of a proposal to effect a compromise between proportional and majority representation.

The 1951 report on constitutional revision drawn up by the committee on universal suffrage, of which he was a member, was presented to the council by Coty. Similar work was encharged to him in 1953 by the council when he was named to coordinate the preliminary suggestions on the projected revision of the constitution. Coty served as vice-president of the Council of the Republic and as president of the European Parliamentary Group.

In mid-December 1953 the National Assembly and the Council of the Republic were convoked in joint session at Versailles to elect a second President of the Fourth Republic (Vincent Auriol, the first, had refused to offer his candidacy for re-election). After a week of voting on possible candidates, the deliberations almost broke down over political, religious, and personal differences of opinion.

In the eleventh round of balloting, the relatively obscure name of Coty first appeared; the compromise candidate received the largest number of votes in the twelfth round, but it was only in the thirteenth, that Coty received the absolute majority of 477 which marked his victory over remaining candidates Marcel-Edmond Naegelen (329) and Louis Jacquinot (21).

Thus, on December 23, 1953, France acquired a new President, after a series of deliberations that had brought the Parliament strong criticism both from the domestic and foreign press for its week-long incapacity to choose a successor to Auriol.

The President of the French Republic serves for seven years, with the possibility of being re-elected once. As France's chief of state, he has many duties, but perhaps the most important is his nomination of premiers who must then be approved by the National Assembly. In an article in *Commonweal* (January 15, 1954) it was noted that "while the President of the Republic has very limited power directly to influence government policy, his position above the parties gives him a considerable amount of indirect influence on the course of French affairs."

Described by Joan Thiriet in the *Christian Science Monitor* as conforming "to the pattern of not-too-young, middle-class, not-too-wealthy, family men that France traditionally has chosen for Presidents," Coty, as an Independent Republican, is considered a moderate conservative.

As President-elect, Coty spent several weeks of tutelage under Auriol; by mutual agreement they decided to retain Joseph Laniel as Premier (traditionally the French Premier resigns when a new President is inducted), and at their suggestion the incumbent Premier sought a vote of confidence in the National Assembly on January 6, which was granted by a decisive majority and which enabled his Cabinet to remain in power during the four-power conference in Berlin in early 1954. (On June 13 President Coty accepted Laniel's resignation and Pierre Mendès-France was appointed Premier.)

The French people were anxious to know the attitude of the incoming President on the European Defense Community since he had been a delegate to the Consultative Assembly of the Council of Europe in Strasbourg. Coty, according to an editorial in the *Christian Science Monitor* (December 26, 1953), presumably feels "that the European political community should be established first, or at least be assured, before a joint defense force—in other words, that there must be a policy-making body to determine how the European Army is used."

On January 16, 1954, René Coty was sworn in as the second President of the Fourth Republic, in a simple inauguration held at the Palais de l'Elysée. At the same time Auriol passed to him the gold chain of the leader of the Legion of Honor, a post also held by the President of the Republic. (Coty had not previously been a member of the organization.) The President's salary is about $11,400 a year, but the perquisites of the office include $45,000 for automobile purchase and maintenance, $125,000 for miscellaneous expenses, and the use of the Presidential hunting lodge at Rambouillet.

When he took up residence in the palace, Coty was accompanied by his wife, the former Germaine Corblet, whom he had married on May 21, 1907, having won the young daughter of a Norman shipbuilder by quoting from the poetry of Alfred de Musset. By their daughters, the Cotys have ten grandchildren; Geneviève has six daughters, and Anne-Marie one son and three daughters.

Music and book collecting are two interests of President Coty, both well in evidence at his house in Étretat. Other characteristics of the President that have been noted by observers are his tendency to chain-smoke, his ability always to secure a hearing from his colleagues although he is quiet and conciliatory, and his stamina in night legislative sessions. He is president of the French Port Association.

Most observers have commented on the increased prestige of the French Presidency, created by Auriol's personal capacities and contributions. The New York *Times* added, "A man who survived untarnished through thirty years of. . .parliamentary life in France and who has won such respect from his colleagues must have qualities that will fit him for the post of President. . . .Coty may prove great in his own right, but at the very least he will owe much to his illustrious predecessor."

References

N Y Times p3 D 24 '53
Time 63:22 Ja 4 '54 por
Dictionnaire Biographique Français Contemporain (1950)
International Who's Who, 1953

COULTER, JOHN B(REITLING) Apr. 27, 1891- United Nations official; United States Army officer

Address: b. c/o United Nations Bldg., New York 17; h. 2022 Columbia Rd., N.W., Washington 9, D.C.

A long-range project for the rehabilitation of Korea is the United Nations Korean Reconstruction Agency which is directed by Lieutenant General John B. Coulter, U.S.A. (Ret.). He has been authorized to spend $130,000,000 for reconstruction projects during the fiscal year from July 1953 to July 1954. The program includes spending $20,000,000 for repairing Korea's industrial facilities, $36,000,000 for machinery and building equipment, $9,000,000 for health and sanitation, $8,000,000 for mining reconstruction, $5,000,000 for housing, and $3,300,000 for education.

Soon after his retirement in January 1952 from the U.S. Army after forty years of service, General Coulter was named chief of the Washington office of the UNKRA. In May 1953 Secretary General Dag Hammarskjöld announced that Coulter had been appointed to succeed J. Donald Kingsley as agent-general of the UNKRA for a two-year term. In this position Coulter is responsible to the U.N. General Assembly which created the agency in December 1950. He holds the rank of assistant secretary general of the United Nations.

(Continued next page)

U. S. Army

LT. GEN. JOHN B. COULTER

General Coulter served in both world wars and in the Korean conflict, where he was commander of the Eighth Army in Korea. In September of 1951, he returned to the United States for assignment to the Office of the Chief of Staff of the Army at Washington, D.C.

John Breitling Coulter was born in San Antonio, Texas, on April 27, 1891, the son of Mr. and Mrs. Thomas H. Coulter. He was graduated from the West Texas Military Academy in 1911, and was commissioned as a second lieutenant in the Regular Army on November 30, 1912.

The young lieutenant was first assigned to the 14th Cavalry at Brownsville, Texas. During the border trouble with Mexico in 1916, he saw his first action in the Battle of San Ygnacio. He was promoted to first lieutenant on July 1, 1916, and was assigned in August as aide to the district commander, Brigadier General William A. Mann.

He went to Washington, D.C. in February 1917 for mustering duty and in March became instructor of the District of Columbia National Guard. On May 15, 1917 he was advanced to captain, and was later assigned again as aide to General Mann, at that time commanding general of the 42nd (Rainbow) Division. Coulter served with him in France between October 1917 and January 1918.

After returning to this country, Coulter spent five months on duty at Governors Island in New York, and then was sent to Camp Meade, Maryland. There he joined the 808th Infantry as commander of the 2nd Battalion with which he again sailed for France in August 1918. He had been promoted to the rank of major on June 7, 1918. In France he took part in the action at Saint-Mihiel and in October he began studying at the General Staff College at Langres, France. He was graduated in January 1919 and was then assigned as adjutant of the 159th Infantry Brigade.

When he came back to the United States, Coulter served in the personnel branch of the War Department general staff. He later moved to Fort Des Moines, Iowa, as commander of the 2nd Squadron of the 14th Cavalry. He completed a course at the Cavalry School, Fort Riley, Kansas, in June 1922, and after a short period at Camp Meade, Maryland, he was made chief of the matériel section, Office of the Chief of Cavalry, and subsequently executive officer.

Coulter was a graduate of the Command and General Staff School at Fort Leavenworth, Kansas in June 1927. He was then assigned to Fort Bliss, Texas, where he served both as a squadron commander with the 8th Cavalry and as assistant plans and training officer of the 1st Cavalry Division.

Following his graduation from the Army War College, which he attended from August 1932 to June 1933, Coulter continued his studies at the Naval War College, and was graduated in June 1934. He was sent to the Military Intelligence Division at Army Headquarters, Washington, D.C., where his duties included those of chief of the Latin American section and chief of the military attaché and foreign liaison section.

Upon being promoted to lieutenant colonel on August 1, 1935, Coulter was named executive officer of the 4th Cavalry Regiment at Fort Meade, South Dakota. He took command of that regiment in December 1940. He became a colonel in June 1941, and on October 31, 1941 was advanced to the rank of brigadier general.

After commanding the 3rd Cavalry Brigade at Phoenix, Arizona and the 2nd Cavalry Division at Fort Riley, Kansas, Coulter was assigned in July 1942 to the 85th Infantry Division at Camp Shelby, Mississippi, as assistant commander. In February 1943 he assumed command of the division, and was made a major general a month later. In December 1943 he moved with his division to the North African theater of operations from which he led it into Italy in March 1944.

The 85th Division, which formed part of the U.S. Fifth Army, was the first all-selective service unit to see action in Italy, and took part in the drive on Rome in the spring of 1944. Coulter won a reputation as an expert on mountain warfare during this offensive.

Milton Bracker (New York *Times,* October 30, 1944) wrote this about the 85th and the 88th divisions: "They have had plenty of losses. . . . But the important thing is that the men of these divisions, whether they live or die, will have shared in one of the most important accomplishments in American military history: the establishment of proof that the people's army called into being by the Selective Service Act of 1940 had what it took."

Coulter was sent back to the United States at the end of World War II, and commanded the Infantry Replacement Training Center at Fort McClellan, Alabama. In May 1946 he was named deputy commander of the Fourth Army at Fort Sam Houston, Texas.

The major general took command of the 7th Infantry Division (part of the U.S. Pacific forces) in January 1948, and later became deputy commander of the U.S. Army forces in Korea. Upon assuming this post, General Coulter issued this statement: "I am aware of the great responsibilities . . . which have been entrusted to my care. It is my earnest desire that I fulfill my mission successfully and further cement the long-standing friendship between Korea and the United States" (New York *Times,* August 27, 1948). In January 1949 he was appointed commanding general of the I Corps in Japan.

Sent to the United States in March 1950, Coulter was made deputy commanding general of the Fifth Army in Chicago, and later took charge of the I Corps at Fort Bragg, North Carolina. The North Korean forces invaded South Korea on June 25, 1950, and Coulter left for Korea with the I Corps on August 18, 1950. He commanded it there until September 11, 1950, when he took over the command of the IX Corps.

At ceremonies near the Korean battle front on February 15, 1951, Coulter received his third star, that of lieutenant general. He was named deputy commander of the Eighth Army in Korea. On May 29, 1951, Lieutenant General Coulter was also assigned as General Matthew B. Ridgway's liaison representative to the United Nations Commission for the Unification and Rehabilitation of Korea. He held these two positions until September 1951 when he was assigned to the Office of the Chief of Staff of the Army in Washington, D.C. He retired on January 31, 1952.

Because of his wide experience in Korea General Coulter was selected to head the Washington office of UNKRA and on May 1953 his appointment as agent-general of the United Nations agency was confirmed. He went to Korea in August to set up headquarters in Seoul and to supervise the reconstruction projects. Reporting to the United Nations on October 23, 1953 on the progress of the rehabilitation work in Korea, General Coulter said that the UNKRA and United States programs in Korea were geared to operate without duplication of effort.

The U.N. agency, he explained, is emphasizing long-range efforts to restore educational and medical facilities and to develop the agriculture, forestry, and fishing industries. The United States' own $1,000,000,000 rehabilitation program is of shorter range, and has military considerations in mind (New York *Times*). One of the most successful new projects in Korea reported by General Coulter has been the introduction of a new type of housing construction using earthen blocks. The UNKRA plans to erect 5,500 of these shelters along designs prepared by Koreans.

In addition to the Distinguished Service Medal with one Oak Leaf Cluster, the Silver Star and the Bronze Star Medal, Coulter was awarded an Oak Leaf Cluster to the Silver Star for rallying U.N. troops during an enemy attack on the eastern portion of the defense perimeter in Korea on August 28, 1950. While in Korea he also received the Air Medal with five Oak Leaf clusters and the Distinguished Flying Cross. His foreign decorations include the Mexican Military Merit, Italian Order of Sts. Maurice and Lazarus (Grade of Commander), British Order of the Bath, and French Legion of Honor. Coulter is married to the former Marion Ainsa and they have one son, John Breitling Coulter, Jr.

On October 24, 1953, the eighth birthday of the United Nations, General Coulter expressed confidence that steady progress toward economic stability can be achieved in Korea. "United Nations experts are working shoulder to shoulder with the Koreans and with United States aid authorities in the multi-nation task of carrying out a well-planned and thoroughly coordinated program aimed at healing the wounds of war," he said.

References

Gen Army 1:5+ O '53 por
N Y Herald Tribune p6 My 31 '51; p7 My 13 '53 por
N Y Times p4 F 16 '51 por
Time 57:30 Mr 5 '51 por
U N Bul 14:366 My 15 '53
Washington (D.C.) Post p5M S 17 '50 por; p1 F 16 '51 por
Who's Who in America, 1954-55

COUSINS, (SUE) MARGARET Jan. 26, 1905- Editor; writer

Address: b. c/o Good Housekeeping, 57th St. & 8th Ave., New York 19; h. 255 Clinton Ave., Dobbs Ferry, N.Y.; 130 E. 61st St., New York 21

Successfully pursuing two careers as both editor and writer, Margaret Cousins is managing editor of *Good Housekeeping* and is also well known to readers of popular magazines as the author of more than a hundred short stories. Before becoming associated with Hearst Magazines, Inc. in 1939, and assuming the editorship of *Good Housekeeping* in 1945, she had acquired years of journalistic training through her work on *Southern Pharmaceutical Journal* and on *Pictorial Review.* She is the author of three books of which *Ben Franklin of Old Philadelphia* (Random, 1952) is the most recent.

Miss Cousins believes that the large-circulation magazines have discovered and fostered much new writing talent, and she regards "The Slicks" as an opprobrious term which does not accurately describe her own and contemporary publications which frequently publish "quality" stories that find their way into the anthologies. "It also happens," she wrote in *Saturday Review* (February 17, 1951) "that the editors of mass magazines unearth talents in their unsolicited mails, nurture them for months, and then stand on the sidelines while the author makes a reputation somewhere else."

Of French-Irish ancestry on her father's side and with Scottish and Welsh forebears on her mother's, Margaret Sue Cousins was born in Munday, Texas on January 26, 1905. She is descended from early settlers in America whose families later moved from the Southeast to Texas. Her maternal grandfather, then a fourteen-year-old boy, and her paternal great-grandfather both fought in the Confederate Army during the War between the States. Texas is

MARGARET COUSINS

the native State of her parents, Walter Henry Cousins, Sr., and Sue Margaret (Reeves) Cousins.

Her father worked as a cow-puncher and camp cook in the Panhandle. "He wanted to be a doctor, but settled for pharmacy," Miss Cousins recalls. "He said he always carried his pharmacy books and a Roget's *Thesaurus* in the chuck wagon. He was an omnivorous reader, and he had a brilliant vocabulary. He wrote charming humorous stories and folk ballads." After becoming a registered pharmacist he operated drug stores in Knox County and Wichita Falls, Texas. He later owned and published the *Southern Pharmaceutical Journal,* a drug trade magazine in Dallas which is still published by Miss Cousins' brother, Walter.

Largely through the influence of her father, who read to her from the writings of Dickens, Poe, Artemus Ward, O. Henry, and other authors, Margaret Cousins became interested in a literary career while still a young girl. At Bryan Street High School in Dallas, from which she was graduated with honors in 1922, she was class poet and devoted much of her free time to school publications.

Entering the University of Texas, at Austin, she chose English literature for her major subject and won the D.A. Frank Poetry Prize. She joined the Theta Sigma Phi (journalistic society), the Scribblers, and the Reagan Literary Society; was staff member of the *Texas Ranger,* staff member of the *Longhorn Magazine* and issue editor of the *Daily Texan.* She also belonged to the fencing team, the student council, and Alpha Chi Omega (social sorority).

When Miss Cousins left the university with a B.A. degree in 1926, she worked first as an apprentice on her father's *Southern Pharmaceutical Journal,* where she was advanced to associate editor in 1930 and to editor in 1935. While writing for this trade magazine and taking responsibility for its make-up and content, she began to look "further afield." As related by Fredrika D. Borchard in an article about Margaret Cousins in the Houston *Chronicle Rotogravure Magazine* (June 21, 1953), "She sent a couple of pharmaceutical articles to the *Southern Druggist* and soon found herself covering the Southwest for its editor."

The editor of *Pictorial Review* offered Miss Cousins a position on the staff of that magazine in New York. Becoming assistant editor of *Pictorial Review* in 1937, Miss Cousins read manuscripts, wrote blurbs, contributed short stories and verse, and was author of its "Baghdad on the Subway" column.

After *Pictorial Review* ceased publication Miss Cousins managed to find employment in 1939 as a copy writer in the promotional department of Hearst Magazines, Inc., in New York. During the next few years she read manuscripts on a free-lance basis and wrote fashion captions for Hearst's *Good Housekeeping,* to which she had been a contributor at least as early as 1930, when her poem "Indian Summer" appeared in the November issue. In 1940 five of her short stories and a poem "Spring Again" were accepted by *Good Housekeeping,* and in 1942 she became its associate editor. Three years later she was made managing editor.

Good Housekeeping, a monthly magazine which was established in 1885, has a current circulation of over 3,000,000 and offers verse and stories chiefly of interest to women, and sections on home building and decoration, child care, entertainment, food, shopping, health, fashions, sewing, and other domestic subjects. Since 1938 the editor of *Good Housekeeping* has been Herbert Mayes, whom Miss Cousins credits with having had the strongest influence on her career.

In addition to her editorial work, Margaret Cousins has continued to write stories for *Good Housekeeping,* among them, "Inconstant Star" (December 1946), "Letter to Mr. Priest" (November 1947), "The Man Who Won the Waldorf" (August 1952), "Life of Lucy Gallant" (May 1953), "The Believer" (December 1953) and "Quarrel" (February 1954). She has also written for other leading large-circulation magazines, including the stories "Papa and the Petunia Chintz" (*House Beautiful,* July 1943), *"Consuelo"* (*American Magazine,* May 1946), and "Virginia's Madness" (*Woman's Home Companion,* December 1952). *Ladies Home Journal, Cosmopolitan, Redbook, Mademoiselle,* and *Glamour* are some of the other magazines that have published her fiction.

About 100,000 stories are submitted each year to *Good Housekeeping.* Miss Cousins once said, "Every editor has nightmares in which she dreams of sending back a manuscript that might turn out to be a classic." She admits that, on occasion, one of her own stories is rejected by some editor. "Sometimes I'm a frustrated writer, sometimes I'm a frustrated editor. But either way, I know one thing: A good story, give it time, will always sell itself" (Houston *Chronicle Rotogravure Magazine,* June 21, 1953).

In the non-fiction field, Miss Cousins contributed seven articles in 1942 to *House Beautiful,* dealing with a variety of subjects: "Can You Spend an Evening at Home Alone?" (March), "Giving Requires Good Sense" (June), "Do You Entertain Because You Have To?" (October), "The Art of Writing a Good Letter" (November), among others. Her article "Opportunities for Free-Lance Writers in the Post-War World" in *The Writer,* (October 1945) describes *Good Housekeeping*'s editorial policies, and in "What the Editors Want" (October, 1949) she defined again the requirements for her magazine.

A talk entitled "Books and the Modern Magazine" made at the Woman's National Book Association on May 24, 1949, concerned in part the efforts of the mass magazines to combine high quality with popular appeal. "No writer need write down to a popular audience today," Miss Cousins said. "He has to write up, since it is more difficult to write simple, lucid prose about subjects which have universal appeal than it is to write the oblique, incidental, fragmentary sort of thing young writers think of as literature" (*Wilson Library Bulletin,* October 1950).

An article by Miss Cousins on a related subject, "Combing the Haystack" (*Saturday Review* February 17, 1951) deals with "the role of the large-circulation magazine in the discovery and fostering of new writing talent." Among the charges and criticisms she answers are the assertions that such publications "are wedded to formulas from which there can be no departure" and that "mass magazines subsist by the star system."

In her opinion, magazines persuade people "to acquire reading habits, and the book market is automatically increased." She points out that *Good Housekeeping* has in the past few years published material by Thomas Mann, Maeterlinck, Jules Romains, Somerset Maugham, Sinclair Lewis, John Van Druten and "many others we think of as prestige writers. Certainly Mann and Romains were presented to many readers who had never before read them." She regards serialization of books in magazines as a boon to book sales.

The earliest of Margaret Cousins' three books is *Uncle Edgar and the Reluctant Saint,* (Farrar, Straus, 1948). Related in the first person, it concerns a six-year-old girl who spends Christmas on a snowbound Texas train. "The story will amuse older boys and girls and their elders, especially their elders," commented H. A. Masten in his review for the New York *Herald Tribune* (December 19, 1948). "The author writes humorously and presents amazingly well the feelings of a child."

Her book *Ben Franklin of Old Philadelphia* (1952), a publication of Random House's Landmark Series for young readers, was praised by the *Commonweal* critic: "A felicitous writer makes the grand old man of American diplomacy, invention, and common sense, and orderer of the nation's business into a living friend" (November 21, 1952).

Virginia Kirkus commented: "As a sympathetic, conversational account of Benjamin Franklin's life, this is a lively catalogue of his remarkable inventions as well as an appraisal of his stature as an editor and statesman."

A collection of Miss Cousins' Christmas stories that had appeared in magazines from 1941 to 1951, *Christmas Gift,* was published by Doubleday Company in late 1952. In each of the eight stories, observed E. J. Fitzgerald, "the miracle of Christmas works the expected transformations in the hearts or circumstances of the characters" (*Saturday Review,* November 27, 1952). To Rose Feld (New York *Herald Tribune,* December 14, 1952) the story "White Kid Gloves" had "a sort of O. Henry flavor" and "The Homemade Miracle" seemed "rewarding not only as a holiday story but as a piece of short fiction which encompasses within its narrow framework the life of a town."

"Maggie", as she is known to her friends, is five feet five inches tall and weighs 170 pounds. Her eyes are hazel and her hair is light brown. She is interested in some private charities and with her brother she supports an endowment fund for the Pharmaceutical Library of the University of Texas in memory of her father, and gives to the Nurses Loan Fund at Baylor Hospital in memory of her mother. She is a Baptist and a Democrat.

"My free-lance writing," Margaret Cousins has said, "can hardly be considered a hobby, but I love to write better than anything. After that I like to keep house and entertain friends. I have never felt the need for or had time for a hobby and have never collected anything but people." Away from work she also enjoys the theatre, travel, cooking, horseback riding, and swimming. In her pursuit of two successful careers, she admits that she is "a happy, fortunate creature."

"When I'm working," she confesses, "I look the way nobody ought to see me, with either a cigarette or my tongue sticking out of the corner of my mouth."

References

Houston Chronicle Rotogravure Mag p8 Je 21 '53

American Women, 1939-40

COWEN, JOSHUA LIONEL Aug. 25, 1880- Business executive; inventor

Address: b. c/o Lionel Corporation, 15 E. 26th St., New York 10; h. 945 5th Ave., New York 21

In the past fifty-four years Joshua Lionel Cowen, the inventor of the first toy electric train, has seen his miniature rail empire extend over 25,000 miles of track. As a result of his lifetime devotion to trains and of his inventive ability, his Lionel Corporation has been selling millions of dollars worth of locomotives, cars, track, and accessories to American boys, their fathers, and railroad hobbyists every year.

The corporation produces two-thirds of all the model electric trains made in the United States. Cowen is probably the first toymaker to have his products used in the "Cold War." In 1951 he presented a dazzling display of trains

Globe Photos

JOSHUA LIONEL COWEN

for an exhibition in West Berlin which lured some 500,000 young Communists over for a wide-eyed look at the products of capitalism (*Pathfinder Town Journal,* December 1953).

Since 1945 Cowen has been chairman of the board of the Lionel Corporation whose sales volume reached a new high of $32,975,506 for the fiscal year ending in February 1954. This figure includes the sales of the corporation's two subsidiaries: the Airex companies, the largest manufacturers of spinning type fishing tackle in the United States, and the Linex Corporation, manufacturer of stereo color cameras and accessories (New York *Times,* May 18, 1954).

Joshua Lionel Cowen was born in New York City on August 25, 1880, one of the nine children of Mr. and Mrs. Haymen Cowen. His father was a real estate man. When Joshua was about seven years old, he made a steam engine which exploded in the family kitchen. After a few years at Public School 96, he was sent by his father to the Cooper Union school to study handicrafts.

About this time he outlined plans for an electric doorbell, but abandoned this project when his instructor told him nothing would ever replace knuckles as a means of announcing oneself. He went to City College for a time, and then, at the age of sixteen, to Columbia University where he studied engineering. One semester of this was enough for him, and he left to take a job assembling battery lamps for the Acme Electric Lamp Company. He spent his evenings working in the plant on his own ideas, and developed what he thinks was one of the first dry-cell batteries in America.

He also invented (and patented) a fuse to set off the magnesium flash powder used by photographers. When news of this device reached U.S. Navy officials, he was invited to Washington, D.C. Eighteen-year-old Cowen appeared before a board of admirals in a rumpled suit (in which he had slept on the train coming down), and carried an old shoe box containing samples of his device. He was taken for a messenger boy until he inquired: "You the gentlemen interested in photography fuses?" The admirals awarded the boy a contract to equip 24,000 mines with detonators. After renting a loft in downtown New York, Cowen went to work. When completed, the job netted him a profit of $12,000.

Then he began to build galvanic and faradic batteries and cytoscopic lamps. His next invention was a tube equipped with a small dry cell and a tiny electric bulb—which today we recognize as a flashlight, but which Cowen placed in a flowerpot to illuminate the flowers. He had a salesman named Conrad Hubert who went on the road to sell the lighted flowerpots. Cowen had not perfected the tubes, however, and occasionally they failed to work. This irritated him, so he gave the device to Hubert who developed it into the Eveready flashlight, from which Hubert made a fortune, and when he died left an estate of $15,000,000.

In 1900 Cowen built a small, battery-run electric fan to cool his shop. Then the weather changed, and, looking at the idle fan, he got to tinkering again. Soon the fan's motor was mounted with a dry cell on a small flatcar and was running around a circle of track made of strips of brass mounted on wooden ties—and model railroading was on the way.

Cowen sold his first model railroad for four dollars to a novelty shop which immediately ordered six more. At first the trains were used chiefly as eye-catchers in store windows. Soon Cowen raised the price for a car and thirty feet of track to six dollars, and orders began to pour in from all over the country. He gave his middle name (Lionel) to the enterprise.

In 1907 the flatcar was replaced with a locomotive modeled after a real electric engine—one which the Baltimore & Ohio Railroad was using to pull trains through a Baltimore tunnel. Sales soared to $25,000 a year, and by 1908 the Lionel rolling stock included coal cars, cabooses, cattle cars, boxcars, and day coaches. Pullmans with lighted interiors came later. The Lionel trains were first run on batteries, but as the country became electrified, Cowen adapted the equipment to run on house current. At first this was unsuccessful as too many children received jolting shocks, but after a short while, he devised a means of overcoming this difficulty.

Never satisfied and forever working on new and more accurate models, Cowen has produced some novel additions to his railroad system almost every year since he started. The sequence switch which appeared in 1926 was one of the most important of these. Now, from a distance, and merely by pushing various buttons, a model railroader can turn switches, pull trains into stations, back them onto sidings, and couple and uncouple cars.

Later came milk cars which could discharge tiny milk cans, and other cars which could unload coal or logs. One of the Lionel Corporation's most elaborate side-attractions is an operation switch tower with a switchman posted outside. When a train comes, he hurries upstairs to the tower room to throw the switches and to notify the watchman who runs down a flight of stairs carrying a tiny pouch.

Down the years it has become apparent that freight trains are more popular than passenger cars; you can do more with them. Cowen provides his railroaders with a wrecking car, and writer Ben Hecht, an ardent model railroader who specializes in fancy wrecks, likes to stage a miniature disaster and then restore order simply by manipulating switches. Other famous Lionel train devotees are Dr. James B. Conant, who set up his tracks in the president's house when he was at Harvard University, and actor Robert Montgomery, who once had so big a layout that he had to cut holes in his walls so that trains could run from room to room.

During World War II, the U.S. Navy asked Cowen to turn out binnacles and compasses, and from 1941 to 1945 the plant at Irvington, New Jersey was given over to war work. Lionel's most recent development is called Magne-Traction which uses a magnetic attraction between the wheels and rails to allow greater speeds on curves. With this a locomotive pulling a string of cars can negotiate a curve at the equivalent of 180 miles per hour, and crawl up a 20 per cent grade. "It's positively wonderful," Cowen admits.

Some years ago a customer pointed out that a New York Central tender Lionel had just produced had three less rivets than its full-sized prototype, and inventor Cowen was deeply disturbed. "It was true. We don't yet know how it happened," he mourned. He created the special job of rivet-counter and since then, there has been no trouble along these lines.

According to Don Wharton in the *Pathfinder Town Journal* (December 1953), Cohen's trains have been put to many different uses. For example, an Indian rajah laid out tracks so that food could be hauled around the dinner table to guests. The U.S. armed services have used the trains for occupational therapy in hospitals, and in the Cleveland Clinic radiation laboratory, a Lionel locomotive, freight car and track are used to carry radioactive materials in and out of shielded vaults.

Cowen married Cecilia Liberman on February 2, 1904. She died in 1946. Their two children are Lawrence, now president of the Lionel Corporation, and Isabel (Mrs. Harold Brandaleone). Cowen's second wife is the former Lillian Herman, whom he married in November 1949. He has been described as a "blunt", and "restless" person, and a man who works "in the same purposeful way that the drivers on a steam engine function." He is often called "Josh" or "J.L." He is five feet five inches tall. Robert Lewis Taylor (*New Yorker,* December 18, 1947) reported that to some Cowen looks like Senator Herbert Lehman of New York or "an anxious cherub."

The manufacturer recently purchased a home in West Palm Beach where he enjoys fishing and photography—and playing bridge and gin rummy. Joshua Lionel Cowen, however, is a man whose chief interest and fun in life has been the production of more and more perfect model trains. It's a happy combination that now runs the Lionel company with Larry, the son, handling the over-all direction and the father, Josh, supplying the manufacturing experience.

References

Collier's 126:31+ D 16 '50 por
N Y Times III p3 O 19 '52 por
N Y World-Telegram II p11 N 29 '52 pors
N Y World-Telegram Mag p10 D 19 '53 por
New Yorker 23:38+ D 13 '47
Newsweek 40:54 D 29 '52 por
Read Digest 64:133+ Ja '54
Who's Who in Commerce and Industry (1953)

COWLES, JOHN (cōls) Dec. 14, 1898-
Newspaper publisher

Address: b. c/o Star and Tribune Bldg., Minneapolis, Minn.; h. 2318 Park Ave., Minneapolis, Minn.

"Our goal at the *Star* and *Tribune*," wrote John Cowles, publisher and president of the two Minneapolis newspapers, "is to try to publish the best newspapers of general circulation, edited for all educational and economic and occupational groups in our area, that is humanly possible to produce, and to give leadership on our editorial pages to the shaping of sound public opinion."

Cowles began his career with the Des Moines, Iowa newspapers owned by his father, the late Gardner Cowles, Sr. He moved to Minneapolis in 1935 when his family acquired the *Star,* and became the publisher of the Minneapolis *Tribune* in 1941. He is chairman of the board of the Des Moines Register and Tribune Company, Cowles Magazines, Inc., (publisher of *Look* magazine), and Cowles Broadcasting Company (which owns radio and television stations in Iowa, South Dakota, Minnesota, and elsewhere). He was appointed a member of the Business Advisory Council for the Department of Commerce in 1952 and was a consultant to the National Security Council in 1953.

"The Minneapolis newspapers are among the trail blazers in the country, in exploring such neglected areas of news as education, science, religion, and government as contrasted with news of politics," wrote Cowles in the article which appeared in *Newsmen Speak* (University of California Press, 1954). "We also try to go deeper than the superficial aspects in reporting news of crime." "Our primary function," he commented, "is to serve as community and regional newspapers of record for all the people in the upper midwest. In doing that, we are trying to serve the highest common denominator of our readers' interest, not the lowest, and we are constantly trying to raise that common denominator."

(Continued next page)

JOHN COWLES

John Cowles was born at Algona, Iowa on December 14, 1898, the second boy in a family of three boys and three girls. His father, the late Gardner Cowles, Sr., was at that time a small-city banker and investor in Kossuth county real estate. His mother, whose maiden name was Florence Call, had been an art student and schoolteacher before her marriage. The artist Russell Cowles is the eldest son; Gardner ("Mike") Cowles, Jr., editor of *Look,* is the youngest.

Gardner Cowles, Sr., had purchased the Des Moines *Register and Leader* in 1903 for $300,000, built up its circulation, and made it profitable within eight months. He bought the Des Moines *Tribune* in 1911, the *Star* in 1924, and the *Leader* in 1927, and merged the latter two with the *Register* and *Tribune,* thus eliminating the last newspaper competition in Iowa's capital city.

John Cowles was graduated from Phillips Exeter Academy in New Hampshire in 1917, and entered Harvard University at Cambridge, Massachusetts. He served as a private in the United States Army in 1918, and then returned to Harvard and took his A.B. degree "as of" 1921.

Joining the staff of the Des Moines *Register,* he worked in the advertising department. After a "jack-of-all-jobs" apprenticeship, John was made general manager. "Mike" Cowles also joined the organization. In the 1920's, the two brothers called upon George Gallup to make a public opinion survey of reader interests in newspapers.

Gallup reported that people preferred pictures to type and particularly "related" pictures. Accordingly, sequence pictures were substituted for isolated shots in their rotogravure section, and "this, along with exceptional sports coverage, increased the Sunday circulation 50 per cent."

John Cowles, who has been described as sharing his father's "absorption in circulation and advertising," began in 1929 a four-year term as director of the Audit Bureau of Circulations; also in 1929 he was elected a second vice-president of the Associated Press. He became a first vice-president of the A.P. in 1930, and was a member of the board of directors from 1934 to 1943.

The two sons induced their father in 1935 to permit them to buy for $1,000,000 the then struggling Minneapolis *Star.* "Mike" Cowles remained at Des Moines and in 1937 launched the picture magazine *Look,* while John Cowles moved to Minneapolis to take charge of the *Star.* "Into it," wrote *Newsweek,* "John poured the Des Moines formula: pictures, features, bright writing, honest and thorough reporting, and small shots of well-deplored sin." The *Star* circulation rose from 78,000 to 155,000 between 1935 and 1939.

The process of eliminating competition began when the Cowles family bought the Minneapolis *Journal* for $2,500,000. It was merged with the *Star.* In 1941 the morning *Tribune* was taken over, and also the evening *Times,* which for a while was continued as a nominally "independent" journal.

Today, Minneapolis has only two daily papers, both Cowles-owned: the morning *Tribune* with a circulation of 195,412 (Sunday edition: 616,060) and the evening *Star* which reported 289,695 readers in 1953. Politically the Cowles papers have been characterized by John Cowles himself as "intelligently conservative" and by others as "liberal Republican."

John Cowles was the author of the article on American newspapers in the anthology *America Now* (Scribner, 1938), as well as of the essay "The Future America Faces" which appeared in the *Proceedings of the Academy of Political Science* of May 1941.

The brothers were introduced to the late Wendell L. Willkie in 1940, and became leading supporters of his presidential candidacy. After the election, John Cowles accompanied Willkie on his trip to England. On his return, Cowles wrote a series of articles entitled "Britain Under Fire" which appeared in the Minneapolis *Star* and other papers in 1941.

A strong advocate of Lend-Lease, the Minneapolis publisher was appointed as special assistant to Lend-Lease Administrator Edward R. Stettinius, Jr. beginning January 1943, and in April and May of that year undertook for Stettinius a "survey mission" which carried him first to North Africa and then to England. After his resignation in the following July, he was awarded the Presidential Certificate of Merit.

In an article published in *Look* (December 25, 1945), John Cowles wrote in favor of the unification of the U.S. armed forces. He became a member of the Hoover Commission's Committee on the National Defense Establishment in 1948. Cowles was a strong champion of the "Voice of America" and in December 1947 urged Congress to increase the appropriation for the U.S. Information Service abroad by $5,000,000.

In the summer of 1951, John Cowles visited western Europe, the Near East, Pakistan, India,

Hong Kong and Japan. On his return he wrote in *Look* (October 9, 1951) that "we will be making a blunder almost as calamitous as the one we made in China if we don't support Nehru's government in India." In the article he cited the Point Four program of technical assistance as "probably the most effective way to help the economically backward nations of Asia."

The publisher's business interests are reflected by his directorships in General Mills, Inc.; Equitable Life Insurance Company of Iowa; and First National Bank of Minneapolis. John Cowles was a member of the Board of Overseers of Harvard University from 1944 to 1950 and president of the Harvard Alumni Association in 1953.

He is a trustee of the Ford Foundation, Gardner Cowles Foundation and Eisenhower Exchange Fellowships, Inc., as well as of Carleton College, Phillips Exeter Academy, Minneapolis Foundation, and Minneapolis Art Institute. He is a member of the national policy committee of the American Assembly, Columbia University, and a member-at-large of the American Council of Learned Societies.

Honorary degrees conferred on John Cowles have included an LL.D. from Boston University in 1941 and a Litt.D. from Jamestown College in North Dakota in 1946. He was the recipient of a centennial award from Northwestern University in 1951, a year in which the distinguished service award of the University of Missouri School of Journalism went to the Minneapolis *Star* and *Tribune*.

Cowles married Elizabeth Morley Bates July 18, 1923: they have two daughters, Elizabeth Morley (Mrs. Arthur A. Ballantine, Jr.) and Sarah Richardson (Mrs. John M. Bullitt), and two sons, John and Russell.

The publisher belongs to Sigma Delta Chi, of which he became honorary national president in 1953. He is an honorary member of Alpha Kappa Psi, as well as a member of the Sons of the American Revolution. His clubs are the Minneapolis, Woodhill, Minneapolis Athletic, and Minikahda in Minneapolis; the Metropolitan in Washington; the Chicago Club; and the Harvard clubs of Boston and New York.

Newsweek has characterized John Cowles as "husky, amiable, open-faced." Dale Kramer wrote that ". . . behind the squarish face, the big-rimmed spectacles and the air of quiet self-confidence are the drive and ability which demolished Minneapolis publishing opposition. . ." (*New Republic*, December 1, 1947).

Despite criticism for having no newspaper competition in Des Moines and Minneapolis, John Cowles has stated that the trend toward monopoly in newspaper publishing is going to continue because of rising costs. He defended his noncompetitive papers by pointing out that they "are better able to resist the constant pressure of immediacy . . . they don't have to scramble hard for circulation . . . and they have a deeper feeling of responsibility because they are alone in their field. Nobody has a monopoly on responsibility. Competitive or not, all newspapers must be more responsible than they are, must demonstrate by their daily performance that they deserve their freedom. . ." (*Time*, May 14, 1951).

In the article which appeared in *Newsmen Speak*, John Cowles pointed out that a newspaper is "an educational institution. The great majority of Americans drop out of school by the time they are seventeen or eighteen. Most of them get the bulk of their information and ideas and enlightenment on current affairs, during the ensuing fifty years, from newspapers." He wrote that "a good newspaper reporter . . . ought to know as much in his field as a good college instructor knows in his" and should be able to "inform the layman without insulting the intelligence of the specialist."

In the article, Cowles also gives his credo for newspaper publishing: "The primary obligation of a newspaper is to give its readers the news, all the news, without bias or slant or distortion or suppression, in the news columns. . . On our editorial pages we express our opinions and viewpoints as vigorously and persuasively as we know how, but there is a complete separation between our editorial pages and our news columns."

References

New Repub 117:19+ D 1 '47
Newsweek 34:52+ Jl 4 '49 por
PM Mag pm10+ My 14 '44 por; pm13+ My 21 '44 por; pm13+ My 28 '44
Time 26:26+ Jl 1 '35 por; 37:61+ My 12 '41 por

Business Executives of America (1950)
Stearns, H. E. ed. America Now (1938)
Stewart, K. N. and Tebbel, J. Makers of Modern Journalism (1952)
Who's Who in America, 1954-55
Who's Who in Commerce and Industry (1953)
World Biography (1948)

COX, ALLYN June 5, 1896- Mural painter
Address: h. 135 E. 40th St., New York 16

The frieze in the rotunda of the Capitol in Washington, D.C. which Allyn Cox, New York mural painter, completed with a thirty-two foot fresco, was dedicated by President Eisenhower on May 11, 1954. The 300-foot painting depicts 400 years of American history, and Cox's final panel shows scenes from the Civil War, the Spanish-American War, and the Wright brothers' first flight.

For his fresco, the artist was awarded the gold medal in painting by the Architectural League of New York. He is known for his murals and decorations in homes, banks, universities, and libraries, and during World War II did a number of altarpieces for the armed services. Early in 1954 he started work on two large murals, eighteen by forty-seven feet, for the George Washington Masonic National Memorial at Alexandria, Virginia.

Allyn Cox was born in New York City on June 5, 1896, the son of Kenyon and Louise Howland (King) Cox. Both his parents were artists. He received his schooling in New York, and was graduated in 1910

Pan-American Photo Service, Inc.

ALLYN COX

from the Allen-Stevenson School for Boys. He then studied at the National Academy of Design in New York. In 1915-1916 he was a student at the Art Students League where he returned as a teacher in 1940-1941.

He received a fellowship in painting from the American Academy in Rome in 1916, and spent the following four years studying there, with time out in 1917-1918 for service as a first lieutenant with the American Red Cross in Italy. Upon his return to New York, he began to accept commissions to do murals and decorative paintings for private residences, clubs, churches, and college buildings.

From 1925 to 1927, Cox was at work on the ceilings for the W. A. Clark Library in Los Angeles, California. The following year he was commissioned to do the murals for Dumbarton Oaks near Washington, D.C., and the decorations for the National City Bank in New York City. His murals for the Continental Bank in New York were completed in 1932. In the meanwhile, beginning in 1931, he was painting the panels of the building of the law school at the University of Virginia in Charlottesville, which he finished in 1934.

The decorations for the ballroom of the Cosmopolitan Club in New York City came from Cox's brush in 1940, the same year in which he was commissioned by the United States Lines to do the decorations for the *S.S. America.* The muralist, working under the auspices of the Citizens' Committee for the Army and Navy, completed a number of altarpieces and other decorative work for the armed forces during World War II. Shortly after the war was over, he received a commission from the Guaranty Trust Company to furnish the murals for its branch bank in Radio City in New York.

Subsequently he contributed a number of decorative panels to the George Washington Masonic National Memorial in Alexandria, Virginia during 1947 and 1948. In 1954 he began work there on two large murals. The subjects are: "George Washington and Brethren Celebrating St. John's Day, Philadelphia 1778," and "George Washington Laying the Cornerstone of the Capitol." The project is expected to be completed in 1956.

When the United States Congress voted appropriations to complete the fresco-frieze surrounding the rotunda of the Capitol, Allyn Cox was chosen to execute the work. The 300-foot historical frieze was begun in 1859 by Constantino Brumidi, the Italian artist political refugee who spent the last twenty-five years of his life decorating the Capitol with murals, medallions and frescoes. The plan of Congress was to have fifteen panels, beginning with the landing of Columbus and ending with the discovery of gold in California. Brumidi, who slipped from his scaffolding sixty feet above the rotunda floor in 1879, died several months later. Other panels depicting events in American history were executed by Filippo Costaggini and Charles A. Whipple.

According to a decision made by a joint Congressional committee in 1952, Cox was required to depict three events in completing the frieze: a handshake between Union and Confederate soldiers following the peace in the Civil War, a naval gun crew in action during the Spanish-American War, and the first flight of Orville Wright in his biplane, with his brother, Wilbur, steadying the wing on the take-off.

Cox recalled to a *New Yorker* interviewer (March 7, 1953) that, as a child, he had been taken by his mother to see the frieze in the Capitol: "I decided then and there that I would like to round out those thirty-two feet. Last June, to my astonishment, I was offered the commission." Of the topics chosen for execution, he observed: "I spent most of the summer developing a composition that would contrive to show all these events without seeming hopelessly overpopulated. Another problem was to keep my figures from looking too unlike old Brumidi's."

Like his predecessors on the project, Cox has employed the grisaille technique—painting in tones of gray and white—on a ground of wet plaster. "Once hard, the fresco becomes lighter and more sparkling as the white lime and sand in the plaster shine through," wrote Raymond J. Blair in the New York *Herald Tribune* (November 22, 1953). "The finished painting resembles marble, and, although flat, gives the appearance of bas-relief sculpture." Cox began his three panels in August 1952 and finished them in June 1953, when he started the last part of the work—cleaning the older portions of the frieze. He touched up cracks with a tempera paint made of cottage cheese, lime and pigment.

When President Eisenhower dedicated the completed Capitol dome frieze in May 1954, he spoke to more than 800 persons including the combined membership of both houses. Just before the President spoke, Mrs. Cox, the wife of the artist, pulled the switch that illumined the thirty-two foot panel he had painted. Cox was introduced by Representative Thomas A. Jenkins (Republican of Ohio), author of the resolution for the completion of the frieze depicting 400 years of American history (Washington *Post*, May 12, 1954).

Other work by Cox may be seen in the Princeton University Museum, Parrish Art Museum at Southampton, New York, and at the Norfolk Naval Hospital. He lectures and writes frequently on the fine arts. One of his studies appeared in the September 1950 issue of *Antiques* in which he described his research for the decoration of niches and panels in the early nineteenth century Alsop house being preserved by Wesleyan University in Middletown, Connecticut.

Allyn Cox has received a medal from the Los Angeles Museum of Art (1926), and two awards from the American Artists Professional League, in 1945 and 1952, the latter being for the best in the show of the New York chapter. He is an associate of the National Academy of Design, president of the American Artists Professional League, and a past president of the National Society of Mural Painters. In 1952 he was appointed a painter member of the New York City Art Commission, to serve for three years. He is a member of the Municipal Art Society, Architectural League of New York, and Fine Arts Federation of New York. Cox is a trustee of the Abbey Fund and a director of the Ernest Peixotto Memorial Fund. His club is the Century Association of New York.

On April 30, 1927, Allyn Cox was married to Ethel Howard Potter. He is five feet eleven inches tall, and weighs 160 pounds; he has brown hair and gray eyes. He has been described by the *New Yorker* as a "lithe and witty" painter who "like most muralists, paints big." His New York home and studio are installed in a former church, built in the nineteenth century, and still decorated by the original glass windows. During the summer, Cox lives at Essex, Massachusetts, where he is able to indulge in his favorite recreation of gardening.

References

New Yorker 29:21+ Mr 7 '53
Who's Who in America, 1954-55
Who's Who in American Art (1953)
Who's Who in New York, 1952

COX, WALLY Dec. 6, 1924- Actor

Address: b. c/o National Broadcasting Company, 30 Rockefeller Plaza, New York 20

The character of Robinson Peepers, a high school science teacher, as portrayed by Wally Cox, has become familiar to television audiences since he was first introduced in July 1952. In April 1953 *Mr. Peepers* was named as one of the eleven outstanding programs of television and radio to win the annual Peabody award. Prior to his success in this role, Cox was heralded by critics for his humorous performance in the musical comedy, *Dance Me A Song*. A popular night club entertainer, he also appeared on some thirty-five radio and television programs.

Wallace Maynard Cox was born on December 6, 1924 in Detroit, Michigan. His father, George Wallace Cox, is an advertising copywriter and his mother, the late Eleanor Frances Atkinson, was the author of mystery stories written under the pen name Eleanor Blake. When Wally Cox was still young, his parents were divorced and Cox moved with his mother and sister Eleanor to New York. After receiving his high school education, Cox, who had become interested in the study of botany, enrolled in City College in New York in 1942.

His studies were interrupted, however, when his mother was stricken with partial paralysis, and Cox had to become the family breadwinner. He found work as a shoe-weaver, and later as a silversmith and puppeteer apprentice.

Drafted by the Army, Cox was sent for training to Camp Walters, Texas. Long marches and Texas heat resulted in heatstrokes which hospitalized him. After four months in the Army in which he was successively a message man in infantry, barracks guard, and a volunteer hospital worker, Cox received an honorable discharge.

Undecided about his future career, Cox took an aptitude test and was advised that his talent lay in manual activities, particularly in arts and crafts. Enrolling in the school of industrial arts at New York University, Cox concentrated on the study of handicrafts. In 1946 he went into business for himself as a silversmith, making tie clasps, cuff links, and shirt studs for New York haberdashers which netted him about forty dollars a week.

While at a social gathering, Cox gave a comic monologue—his impression of a soldier he had once met. Encouraged by the laughter and urged by his sister to repeat the monologue at another party, Cox continued as an informal entertainer at parties and added new monologues to his repertoire.

His friend, actor Marlon Brando, was a further influence on Cox's decision to become an actor. Invited to parties attended by theatre people, Cox took up their suggestion that he join a dramatic group. He became affiliated with the American Creative Theater Group whose director advised Cox to develop several of his monologues into a night club act.

In December 1948 at a theatrical party Cox so impressed one of the guests, Judy Freed, that she arranged an audition for him with Max Gordon, owner of a café, the Village Vanguard. Put to work that same night after the audition, Cox gave a monologue which gibed at sociological lectures. He was so well received by the Village Vanguard audience that his one-night engagement was extended into months.

Variety's critic commented, "He (Cox) is still among the ranks of parlor entertainers, but he has a comedic approach that's somewhat out of the ordinary . . . shows promise.

NBC-TV

WALLY COX

His material is authentic and his characterizations amusing."

From the Village Vanguard Cox moved on to the Blue Angel, a café in mid-town Manhattan, where his monologues delivered in quiet, droll style soon won recognition from critics and audiences. In his New York *Herald Tribune* column, John Crosby observed: "His night club monologues were . . . full of elaborate, stuffy detail which was terribly important in the lives of small, unimportant people . . . and he invested these small facts with such great earnestness that he was hilarious and curiously poignant." Cox's numerous monologues, all written by himself, included such characterizations as a bank president turning down a young man who wished to finance a night club, a camp counsellor lecturing his thirteen-year-old "men" against cutting initials on trees, and a drugstore cowboy.

After two years of successful night club engagements, Cox gained the attention of theatrical producer Dwight Deere Wiman who hired him to appear in his new musical revue, *Dance Me a Song.* Although the revue, which opened at the Royale Theatre in New York in January 1950, did not for the most part win critical approbation, Cox scored a personal triumph. William Hawkins of the *World-Telegram and Sun* reported, "Wally Cox has a warm and winning manner of understanding mad narratives as if they were humdrum. It is unusual delivery, unpretentious, and lazily effective." In his New York *Post* column Richard Watts, Jr. commented, "Just put him down as the humorous find of the year." Before *Dance Me a Song* closed, Cox already had more than twenty offers from major movie studios, night clubs, Broadway producers, and for radio and television appearances. Cox's reaction was, "I was pleasantly surprised."

During the next two years, Cox entertained at the Persian Room of New York's Plaza Hotel and on numerous television and radio programs which included the shows of Perry Como, Ed Sullivan, Garry Moore and Arthur Godfrey. In October 1951, Cox had his own radio show over station WNEW, in which he acted as a "discless disc jockey."

A *Philco Television Playhouse* production of *The Copper,* written by David Swift, in which Cox played the role of a humorous man "who could not seem to make a move without causing some monumental commotion" pointed up to Philco's producer Fred Coe the possibilities that could be realized by harnessing Cox's unique personality to a television series. The result was *Mr. Peepers,* a situation comedy starring Wally Cox as Robinson Peepers, high school science teacher.

The program, a summer replacement, made its debut in July 1952 over NBC-TV network under the sponsorship of the Ford Dealers of America. Once again Cox won personal acclaim for his work. In his *Herald Tribune* column John Crosby was not too favorably impressed by the handling of the plot entanglements of *Mr. Peepers,* but predicted, "Whether *Mr. Peepers* goes or not, I'm sure Cox will be around for a long time."

When *Mr. Peepers* ended its series run on September 25, 1952 for lack of a sponsor, over 8,000 letters deluged the network from fans demanding the return of the program. The following month *Mr. Peepers* was returned to television audiences over NBC-TV and sponsored by the Reynolds Metal Company.

Steadily rising in popularity and Nielsen rating (a system of evaluating audience response), in April 1953 *Mr. Peepers* was accorded the Peabody award, with the board that determined the award describing Cox as a "genuinely funny man," and the program as one which has brought "genuine pleasure to millions of viewers." In June 1953 Cox was one of the stars on the Ford Motor Company's mammoth fiftieth anniversary program and again was singled out for critical approval. Cox began acting in summer theatre productions in 1953, playing the part of Irwin in *Three Men on a Horse* at the Plymouth, Westport, Ogunquit and other playhouses.

More and more the development of *Mr. Peepers* has turned from emphasis on situation to emphasis on character. Cox tries to avoid jokes and unbelievable gags.

Off screen, too, Cox seems to be the embodiment of Robinson Peepers. "We both have trouble with mechanical things," commented Cox. "We understand the theory behind them, but they don't seem to work for us." Cox prefers performing on television to night club monologues which he calls "tid-bits" as characterizations. "Mr. Peepers gives me a third dimension," Cox observed. He stands five feet six inches tall with a weight of 130 pounds. It is said that Cox retains the "same gentle imperturbability and rare naturalness" that characterized him in his earlier days and his income of forty dollars a week. As Robinson Peepers, Cox earns $1500 a week.

Cox's interest in the bucolic life and in botany still persists. Speaking of himself as always having been a "flower-watcher," he recalls that on week-end leaves during his Army days in Texas, he took out books on wild flowers at the camp library and spent the time tracking down specimens. Robinson Peepers also displays a considerable interest in botany. Two days a week Cox, who resides in a Manhattan Riverside apartment, spends his time building a house with his own hands on a wooded two-acre knoll in Rockland county. He enjoys carrying rocks and chopping wood. On June 7, 1954 he married Marilyn Gennaro.

Cox has written several plays and short stories, which are said to be of a whimsical vein. For the past four years he has been undergoing psychoanalysis, and when at first he had difficulty memorizing his lines for television, his psychiatrist explained that he was impatient with acting because his real desire was to write. He maintains his interest in wood carving, chess, and working silver and gold jewelry. He travels to his country home by motorcycle.

References

Am Mag 156:26+ O '53
Collier's 131:67+ Ja 3 '53
Cosmopolitan 135:122+ O '53
Good H 137:14+ N '53
N Y Herald Tribune IV p7 N 30 '52
N Y Times Mag p14 Ja 11 '53
N Y World-Telegram Mag p15 F 21 '53
Newsweek 40:66+ N 10 '52
Time 60:42 Jl 28 '52

CREEL, GEORGE (EDWARD) Dec. 1, 1876—Oct. 2, 1953 Journalist, author; newspaperman for Kansas City *World* and New York *Journal*; editor and publisher of Kansas City *Independent* (1903-1908); writer for Denver *Post* (1908); editor of *Rocky Mountain News* in Denver (1911-1913); organized and directed President Wilson's Committee of Public Information (1917-1918); chairman of San Francisco's labor board (1933); chairman of the National Advisory Committee of Works Progress Administration (1935); appointed adviser of United Mine Workers' office of bituminous welfare and retirement fund (1949); contributed many articles to national magazines; wrote a book of verse, *Quatrains of Christ* (1908); and several books concerning political subjects. See *Current Biography,* (June) 1944.

Obituary

N Y Times p17 O 3 '53

CROSBY, ROBERT (BERKEY) Mar. 26, 1911 Governor of Nebraska; lawyer

Address: b. State House, Lincoln, Neb.; h. 621 W. 5th St., North Platte, Neb.

The Governor of Nebraska, "the cornhusker State", is Robert Crosby, who believes industrialization of an agricultural state is possible. The lessons of the droughts are well learned, he has stated, and "expanding soil conservation practices coupled with wider use of irrigation are among the highlights of progress."

Flying in a little airplane labeled "Operation Honesty", Governor Crosby has traveled around his state, urging citizens to file honest personal property tax reports. If all did so, he declared, real estate taxes could be cut 25%. He has been reluctant to introduce sales or income taxes into Nebraska, and has endeavored to attract industries on the basis that Nebraska is "the white spot of the nation," taxwise.

Elected on the Republican ticket in November 1952, Governor Crosby has had fourteen years of political experience beginning with a term in the Nebraska Legislature in 1940. In the interim he served three terms in the Legislature, during two of which he was chosen speaker. He was elected in 1947 as lieutenant governor.

On April 17, 1954 Governor Crosby named Mrs. Eva Bowring, vice-chairman of the Nebraska Republican party, to serve out the late Senator Dwight Griswold's term in the United States Senate. He then announced that he would not file for re-election to the governorship but would instead file as a candidate for the Senate seat. In the August primary election for the Republican Senatorial nomination, Crosby was defeated by U.S. Congressman Carl T. Curtis.

Robert Berkey Crosby was born in the prairie town of North Platte, Nebraska, on March 26, 1911. His parents, Mainard E. Crosby and Cora May (Berkey) Crosby, taught in country schools and attended the University of Nebraska. Bob's great-grandfather ran for governor of the state on the Populist ticket in 1890; both of his grandfathers were homesteaders. Their Norwegian, Danish, English and Pennsylvania Dutch ancestry was typical of the Midwestern pioneers.

In high school, Bob played tennis, debated on the school team, served on the student council, and managed the yearbook. He was graduated at the age of sixteen, second in his class. Entering Hastings College, he was elected president of the freshman class, although he looked "more like a 14-year-old than a college man." This "pleasant, serious young chap" continued his extracurricular tennis and debating, and became a member of a gospel team and officiated as a student-minister at church services in nearby towns. His junior and senior years were spent at the University of Minnesota from which he received the A.B. degree *cum laude* in 1931 after earning his way by waiting on tables and preparing breakfasts for the Faculty Club.

Following his mid-term graduation, Crosby worked for the State Highway Department for nine months until he entered Harvard Law School in September, 1931. There his first year's record earned him a partial scholarship but he was unable to accept it because already the depression had struck deep into the economic life of Nebraska. He was forced to give up his studies and spend a year at manual labor before he could return to Harvard. In 1935 Crosby received his LL.B. degree.

The first few years were difficult for the struggling young lawyer. Nebraska was so hard hit by drought during the worst of the

Ralf

ROBERT CROSBY

depression that most of its citizens could not afford legal services. After several months in North Platte, Crosby went to Omaha to apply for a job in the office of District Judge Henry Beal. The Judge did not need assistance, but Crosby insisted, "My father told me that if I went to work for you, I'd learn a lot. You can pay me whatever you want, my father will help out."

Judge Beal offered Crosby seventy-five dollars a month which he promptly accepted. With his first brief, Crosby demonstrated his ability by invoking a relatively unknown legal principle. This won Beal's client $4,000 more than the sum for which he had originally asked. It was through Judge Beal that Crosby got his first experience in politics, in the presidential campaign of 1936.

Upon entering state politics, he told Dean James Landis of the Harvard Law School, "I took my sheepskin out the door and turned to the right instead of the left," as many of his classmates were then doing. His direction is the one usually taken by his agricultural constituents. Knowing that Nebraskan voters traditionally shun an Omaha claimant to the governor's chair, Crosby left Omaha thirteen months after moving there, and returned to North Platte in 1937. Three years later he had won a seat in the Nebraska Legislature.

Since then he has never been out of politics, except while he served in the Navy as a lieutenant from 1944 to 1946. He spent his indoctrination training at Harvard Business School and his term of administrative work in San Francisco. He was still in the service when he filed for the lieutenant governorship in 1946.

A month after his election in 1947 he made the startling proposal to abolish the office to which he had just been elected on the ground that since Nebraska's adoption of a one-chamber Legislature in 1934 there has been no need for this "part-time official."

Later he repeated his argument in "Why I Want to Get Rid of My Job," an article he wrote for *State Government* in 1947. At present the speaker, usually the presiding officer of the legislative house, is secondary in Nebraska to the lieutenant governor who is chairman of the chamber.

"The lieutenant governor who wants to get along in Lincoln," said Crosby, "is just a parliamentarian, nothing else. The speaker could do that job just as well. And some other full-time elected state official could be named to act in case of the death or incapacity of the governor."

So earnest was his conviction that he refused to run for re-election in 1948. Instead, he served as assistant state chairman of the Republican party until 1950 when he acted as campaign manager for Val Peterson who was then governor, and who remained in office until Crosby won in 1952.

Crosby's campaign against Walter Raecke (Democratic candidate), a fellow-legislator and his former roommate, was both polite and informative. He outlined in his speeches the changes he considered necessary, among them a plan for a cabinet of department heads to coordinate state affairs. He stated his conviction that Nebraska needed to develop more industries to balance its agriculture, but he recommended that small plants be built in small towns, and not giant plants which would bring an influx of employees from outside the state.

After his election Governor Crosby, who had made an intensive study of the duties of his office, set to work to introduce new industries. Recently he cited some of the results of his state's efforts: the establishment of a $4,000,000 plant in Omaha to convert corncobs into furfural (a chemical solvent used in plastics and nylon) which provides jobs for 100 workers; a $25,000,000 chemical plant south of Omaha which will give work to 450; research on the safflower plant (with seeds like sunflower) gives promise of producing an oil better for paint than linseed oil; wheat straw is being made into cardboard boxes (*Christian Science Monitor,* August 28, 1953).

Robert Crosby married Elizabeth Daisy Ehlers, daughter of a Nova Scotian sea captain, on September 29, 1934; they are the parents of a son, Robert Mainard and a daughter, Susan Mary. The one objection to political office that Crosby has voiced is that it takes him too much away from home. He says, "I enjoy my family and owe a duty to them. . . I would not want the governorship to unreasonably interfere with as normal a home life as the duties of that office will permit."

The Governor belongs to the Presbyterian Church, the Kiwanis Club, Elks Club, American Legion, and Pioneer Ad Club. He is a member of the Lincoln county and Nebraska bar associations, United Commercial Travelers and North Platte Chamber of Commerce and has served as the Lincoln county chairman of Civilian Defense and campaign chairman of the Community Chest.

In December 1953 Governor Crosby initiated a well-planned move he calls "Operation Honesty" by which he hopes to arouse Nebraska taxpayers against a sense of complacency that treats falsified personal property tax returns lightly. "The personal tax dodger," he said "cheats his neighbor." The governor's office has been probing tax figures in preparation for the "showdown." He declared that he had given up the idea of prosecution of tax evaders "partly because I could not find an evasion so flagrant but that it was probably duplicated a hundred times in our state and it seemed unfair to single out one evader." In 1953, he pointed out, real estate accounted for 67 per cent and personal property only 33 per cent of the state's evaluation. If the balance can be restored, most home owners would get the benefit of a cut on their home taxes (*Christian Science Monitor,* December 3, 1953).

Recently he has shown that Nebraska's unique unicameral Legislature has produced great savings in salaries and operation. His only criticism of it is that it is nonpartisan.

Governor Crosby said that he would never have filed as a candidate for the United States Senate against Senator Griswold, who was a close friend. After Griswold's death, however, he announced that he would run for the six-year term, opposing State Senator Tarry Carpenter in the November election. However, he was defeated in the primary held in August.

References

Christian Sci Mon p3 Ag 26 '53; p4 Ag 28 '53; p33 D 3 '53
N Y Times p68 N 9 '52
Omaha Sunday World-Herald Mag p4G+ Ja 4 '53 por
Time 63:23 Mr 15 '54 por
Who's Who in America, 1954-55
Who's Who in United States Politics (1952)

CROSS, BURTON M(ELVIN) Nov. 15, 1902- Governor of Maine; business executive

Address: b. State House, Augusta, Me.; h. Blaine Mansion, Augusta, Me.

Sworn in as the Governor of Maine in late December 1952, Burton M. Cross succeeded Frederick G. Payne. An advocate of states' rights and local government, Cross had previously served his state in its House of Representatives and as a state senator from 1945 to 1952. He also was president of the Senate and believes that "the strictest test of a legislator is whether he interprets the will of the majority or gives in to the din of the minority."

In the Maine election held on September 14, 1954, Governor Cross was defeated for second term by Democratic candidate Edmund Muskie.

Burton Melvin Cross was born on November 15, 1902 in a Gardiner, Maine farmhouse (built by his great-great-grandfather in 1840), the son of Burton Melvin Cross and Harriet (Thompson) Cross. His father was a member of the Augusta school board and a deputy sheriff in Kennebec county. Burton was eight years old when his father died. At the age of twelve he was able to drive a team of horses and work with his two brothers to help keep the family farm operating smoothly. An enthusiast for track work, Burton became a familiar sight as he ran through the countryside or practiced field games in a homemade sand pit.

Graduating from Cony High School in Augusta in 1920, the farm boy became a professional florist in 1926. Unable to fulfill his ambition to be a lawyer, Cross resolved to "help make the laws." When he reached the age of thirty-one he was persuaded by his friends to become a member of the City Common Council in Augusta. He served for four years, and was president of the council and also of the Board of Aldermen.

Elected to the House of Representatives in 1941 and 1943, he later was a member of the Senate, serving from 1945 to 1952. He was majority floor leader in 1947 and in 1949 became the president of the Senate. Observers report that while presiding over the Senate, Cross "ruled with impressive firmness."

As senator his achievements included the building of the Augusta toll bridge and the establishment of a town road improvement fund, which to a great extent eliminated a so-called pork barrel allocation. In 1941, as a representative in the state Legislature, he had introduced a bill to provide roads of military importance by authorizing a $2,000,000 bond issue. Five years later, in 1946, he was chairman of the important ways and bridges committee. The following year he became chairman of the motor vehicle committee. For six years he served as chairman of the Maine Commission on Interstate Cooperation. In 1948 he was elected first vice-president of the Council of State Governments.

The legislator devoted his energies during World War II to extensive fund raising for the Red Cross and helping other humanitarian agencies. He was also active in civilian defense.

Speaking at a Republican rally in June 1950, Cross declared that individual states are in danger of being submerged by centralized government. "Our towns are the last bulwark of governmental freedom," he said. "We in Maine are fortunate to have so many small towns." He pointed out that citizens "don't get Federal aid without Federal control, nor state aid without state control." His defense of the Highway Commission, under attack in 1950 was, "It is handling Federal and state funds ably, and it is laboring under a handicap imposed by heavy spring frosts and constantly overloaded trucks" (Portland *Press Herald*, June 8, 1950).

Strong winds in February 1952 destroyed the largest of the six greenhouses that comprise Cross Flowers, Inc., of which Cross has been president since 1945, ruining 6,000 carnations, a six-months' growth. His firm has a high reputation and represents the work of skilled growers. Cross's activity in the business is an outgrowth of his early farm training and his interest in the land and what it produces.

During his campaign for the governorship Burton Cross traveled more than 40,000 miles

Mansur

BURTON M. CROSS

in a hired station wagon in nine months of tough campaigning, doing most of the driving himself, and visiting 225 communities. He restated his beliefs concerning state and local government. "The county system and town meeting are the very heart of our system in Maine," he insisted, adding that the problems of government "can best be solved on the state level."

With the state of Maine doing an annual business amounting to $60,000,000, the candidate thought it "advisable that citizens take deep interest in their government and find out what is done with their money . . . . every agency in government should be put on a businesslike basis."

Insisting (at considerable risk to his position) on a full probe of Maine's liquor scandal, Cross argued that if the people know what is going on corruption and favoritism cannot flourish. He cited the gain in dictatorships where there is "privacy in public affairs."

Elected to the highest governmental post of Maine on September 8, 1952, Governor Cross took office for a two-year term in December, one week ahead of the usual schedule because his predecessor, Frederick G. Payne, had resigned as governor to take his seat as a United States Senator.

Speaking in 1954 at a Lincoln's birthday meeting of the Young Republican Club in Belfast, Maine, Governor Cross said: "Our Maine Development Commission's industrial division has been responsible for new pay rolls in excess of $6,000,000 coming into Maine in the past year. We have lost almost no old line industries, and a new emphasis on electronics and machine tools is extremely encouraging. Even in the face of a difficult textile market we are seeing a new $1,000,000 plant erected in Ellsworth, another substantial firm in Eastport, and many others in the process of negotiation. A magnificent job has been done in reactivating facilities at the South Portland shipbuilding yards where a new atomic pipe plant has been installed. Our mineral research division is continually making surveys and exploring the possibilities of furthering the development of Maine's mineral resources. . . We will know within a year or even less the results of the 'Nossen' process on manganese deposits in Aroostook."

In answer to charges that economic hard times existed in Eastport, Washington county, because the sardine industry was affected by the scarce catch in 1953, Governor Cross said at his weekly press conference on February 1, 1954 that the picture was not so black as painted by Gerald White, publisher of the now defunct *Weekly Sentinel*. He cited figures from the state bank commissioner showing a $1,000,000 increase in Washington county bank deposits during the past three years (New York *Times*, February 8, 1954).

"We are also finding new and better ways of utilizing our fisheries potential with greatly expanded canning and freezing plants," he said. He pointed to the fact that Maine did a $200,000,000 vacation travel business in 1953, an increase of over $86,000,000 in five years.

Since attaining the governorship Cross has tried to improve state transportation facilities. He commented on February 15, 1954: "The Maine Turnpike will spend over $50,000,000. The highway program involves at least $20,000,000 besides maintenance costs. Paper companies are spending millions in expansion programs. The $1,000,000 ferry terminal at Bar Harbor is a new venture that may be of far-reaching importance to the traveling public. Millions of dollars have been allocated and contracts in the process of being let at the various government airfield installations from Brunswick to Limestone."

Recently Governor Cross hailed seaweed as a possible bargain tidbit for cows and chickens: "Alone seaweed contains more than 15 per cent protein and will sustain cows. Mixed with Aroostook oats it might solve the grain cost problem of the cattle and poultry industry and make this state independent of Western grains." On June 16, 1953 he fought to a draw in a milking contest in competition with New Hampshire Governor Hugh Gregg, marking National Dairy Month.

He was married on November 1, 1927 to Olena R. Moulton of Augusta. They have three daughters, Mrs. Barbara Butler, Nancy (attending the University of Maine), and Burtina, at school in Augusta. Cross's eighty-five-year-old mother now makes her home with her son in the Blaine Mansion, across the street from the State House in Augusta.

The governor is a trustee of the Augusta Savings Bank and the national, state and local chambers of commerce, a past master of the Cushnoc Grange, a member of the State and National Grange, a director of the Society of American Florists and a founder of the Augusta General Hospital. He is a past president of the Augusta Rotary Club, a 32d degree Mason, and a member of Scottish Rite and Kora Temple Shrine. His faith is the Episcopal. An enthusiastic fresh-water fisherman, he is proud of a seven and three-quarter pound salmon he took from Sebago Lake.

On January 6, 1954 Cross announced that he would seek re-election and added that he would "throw his hat in the ring" at the state's Republican primary scheduled for June 21, 1954. He was unopposed on the Republican ballot.

References

Portland (Maine) Evening Press S 9 '52
Portland (Maine) Press Herald F 19 '52
Who's Who in New England (1949)

CURTIS, CARL T(HOMAS) Mar. 15, 1905- United States Representative from Nebraska

Address: b. House Office Bldg., Washington 25, D.C.; h. Minden, Nebraska

Known in Congress as a "watchdog" of social security legislation, Carl T. Curtis, Republican Congressman from Nebraska, has done much to inform his coworkers and the public about the system and the improvements he feels it needs. He advocates extending social security coverage to persons in almost every occupation and recently stated: "Most people who have given any attention to social security are agreed that a national social security system cannot work with the greatest degree of success without universal coverage or nearly so."

Active in the proposal and consideration of numerous other bills, he has served for sixteen years in the House of Representatives, is a member of the House Ways and Means Committee, and in 1953 was chairman of the social security subcommittee.

He is a candidate for the U.S. Senate on the Republican ticket in the November 1954 elections.

Carl Thomas Curtis was born in Kearney County, Nebraska on March 15, 1905, the son of Frank O. Curtis and Alberta Mae (Smith) Curtis. His ancestors were early settlers and farmers in Nebraska. Brought up in Kearney County, Carl attended the high school in Minden, Nebraska and played football and took part in debates. After his graduation in 1923, he attended the University of Nebraska and Nebraska Wesleyan University.

Although he began his career as a teacher, Curtis soon turned to the law, and after being admitted to the bar in 1930, established a private practice in Minden. He also became the attorney for Kearney County and served for four years. Elected in 1938 as a member of the United States House of Representatives, Curtis has been returned to the House every two years since then by his constituency, the First Congressional District of Nebraska.

Besides voting on questions of national and international importance, Curtis has often proposed his own bills or presented his own arguments on labor, foreign aid, agricultural, trade, tax, and social security problems. He voted against allowing $100,000,000 in additional funds for work relief in 1939, and for the Smith anti-strike bill (1941), Case strike control bill (1946), and the banning of portal-to-portal pay suits (1947). He favored the Taft-Hartley labor bill (1947), raising the minimum wage from $.40 to $.75 an hour (1949), and invoking the Taft-Hartley law to halt the steel strike (1952).

The Congressman wrote in 1947 that a reduction of the individual income tax was needed to stimulate consumer spending and thus to prevent a downward trend in business for the year (New York *Times*, February 21, 1947). He voted twice in 1947 to override the President's veto of the bill by which income taxes would be greatly reduced; this reduction was effected by law. The next year he voted for the Republican tax reduction bill of $5.6 billion.

When the House Ways and Means Committee was investigating the Administration's tax proposals in 1951, it became evident that President Harry S. Truman wanted to collect a 20 per cent excise on all shampoos that contained 5 per cent or more soap. Curtis, a member of the committee, spoke against the tax to the commissioner who was being questioned and said: ". . . You tax practically everything a woman must buy. . . . You know as well as I do that women's clothes are not designed for pockets. So she has to use a purse and you tax that. You tax her household equipment. Now this shampoo thing is another tax on women" (New York *World-Telegram and Sun*, February 7, 1951). In that year he voted against a $5.7 billion tax increase.

Since agriculture is one of the chief sources of income of Nebraska, Curtis has been particularly interested in Federal legislation which concerned the farmer. He supported bills to continue farm parity payments (1939) and to provide $212,000,000 for parity payments (1940). He disapproved of allowing the government to sell its wheat below the parity price (1942). In 1949 he voted in favor of continuing the parity price support system instead of changing to the Brannan plan of direct subsidies to farmers. Curtis favored increasing the price support program by $2 billion in 1950.

In foreign trade legislation, Curtis voted against extending the Reciprocal Trade Agreements Act in 1940, 1943, 1945, and 1949, but in 1948 he favored extending the act for one year. That year, however, he charged that the negotiators of the new agreement had disregarded the interests of agriculture and referred to a claim of the Nebraska Farm Bureau Federation that a recent 50 per cent reduction in the butter tariff "constitutes an excessive contribution to world trade by the industry." Curtis also said that "tariff reductions by the State Department are forcing nations to resort to most vicious kinds of trade barriers, inviting the enmity of other nations and working against the peace of the world" (New York *Times*, January 10, 1948).

In the consideration of certain foreign aid bills, Curtis voted in 1941 against the lend lease

CARL T. CURTIS

bill and four years later in favor of giving a second $1,350,000,000 to UNRRA. When approval of a $3,750,000,000 loan to Great Britain was asked of Congress in 1945, Curtis voted against it. He did not support the Turkish-Greek foreign aid bill of $400,000,000 (1947), authorization of $6 billion for foreign aid (1948), extension of the Economic Cooperation Act of 1948 (1949, 1950), or foreign assistance appropriations (1951, 1953).

Curtis has, however, favored allowing foreign refugees to enter the United States. Earlier hostility to this program on the part of some Congressmen was believed to have been moderated by the information that few refugees, if any, were Communists, and by the need for farm hands and other workers in this country. In 1948 and again in 1953, the Congressman voted in favor of two bills, by which over 400,000 refugees would be allowed to enter the United States.

During his years of service in the House of Representatives, Curtis has become increasingly interested in solving the problems of social security. He announced on February 12, 1947 that he would propose an amendment to the Social Security Act of 1935 by which self-employed professional persons, business owners and employees of state and local governments would be covered. The consideration of changes in the social security system was, however, postponed until 1948.

Curtis voted in 1948 to override the presidential veto of the social security bill by which newspaper and magazine vendors were excluded from coverage under present laws. In 1949 he voted in favor of the first comprehensive revision of the Social Security Act. The bill would extend the coverage of the old age and survivors' insurance system to about 10,000,000 more persons, including self-employed persons, domestic workers, and some public employees.

Retirement annuities would be increased and permissable earnings after retirement would be raised from $14.99 to $50 a month. The tax base would be raised from the first $3,000 to the first $3,600 of earnings a year, and the rate of pay roll taxation would increase gradually from 1½ per cent each for employers and employees in 1950 to 3¼ per cent in 1970.

Curtis later called the social security program a "grossly unsound and ineffective tool" and sought for the overhauling of the system "even though it proves necessary to abandon completely those concepts upon which the current program rests" (New York *Herald Tribune*, March 2, 1950).

After pointing out certain flaws in the system, Curtis suggested that benefits be extended without a "needs test" to all elderly people who do not qualify under a wage-records program, because they have worked as faithfully as those who do qualify. These payments would be financed by employer-employee contributions, by taxes added to the income tax (the amount of tax would depend on the yearly need of funds), and by doing away with the wage-records system.

Curtis voted in 1952 against a bill which would have raised the monthly benefits of most of the 4,500,000 persons receiving social security aid. The earnings limit for retired persons over sixty-five was raised from $50 to $75 a month.

When President Dwight D. Eisenhower asked that the old age insurance coverage be extended, Chairman Daniel A. Reed of the House Ways and Means Committee appointed a subcommittee with Curtis as chairman "to develop facts that will lead to the improvement of the social security laws."

Speaking in Cleveland on May 31, 1953, Curtis said that the system was "a tangle of legalistic snarls and contradictions" and stated that of the 13,400,000 persons over sixty-five now in the United States, 8,400,000 were not covered by social security legislation (New York *Times*, June 1, 1953).

Curtis' subcommittee began its hearings in July. Later Curtis stated that Congress should be guided by two fundamental principles in its social security legislation: "1) That an aged person should not be regarded as cast off and useless; that we should encourage him in his desire to do and to serve and to feel that he is wanted and needed in our society; and 2) that our program must have fiscal soundness. It must not be a detriment to our private enterprise economy. An irresponsible government can promise large benefits extending far into the future. This can be a major factor contributing to national insolvency" (*Christian Science Monitor*, October 29, 1953).

During the subcommittee's investigations, Curtis stated that although he used to believe that the government "had a contractual obligation to fulfill [social security] benefits," citizens partaking in the program were not protected by written contracts as they would be by private firms. If Congress wished to, it could change the provisions of the law whenever it voted to do so. Arthur J. Altmeyer, former social security commissioner, replied that although no actual policies or contracts existed, "the full faith and credit" of the United States lay behind the social security rights created by the law.

As authorized by previous legislation, the rate of 1½ per cent pay roll tax for social security on both the employer and employee rose to 2 per cent each on January 1, 1954. President Eisenhower favored keeping the 1½ per cent tax, but Curtis supported the higher rate on the ground that "the increase in the rate is necessary for the financial soundness of the insurance program" (New York *Times*, December 18, 1953).

Using the information gathered by his subcommittee, Curtis presented a bill to Congress on January 6, 1954. He proposed that everybody over sixty-five be made eligible for Federal aid to the extent of at least $45 a month, regardless of need, and be allowed to earn $1,000 a year while still receiving benefits. The Federal relief program would be ended. Taxes would be extended to almost all employed persons under sixty-five and to dividends, rents, etc. as well as to wages. The Curtis plan was described as abandoning the "insurance" principle of the present system (by which each worker builds up a retirement fund for his old age) to a pay-as-you go policy (by which today's workers would support today's aged) with the present social security trust fund of $9 billion held in reserve for emergencies (New York *Herald Tribune*, December 30, 1953).

On January 14, 1954, President Eisenhower proposed that greater benefits be provided for more workers without disturbing the system in principle. The President's plan advocated much that had been suggested by Curtis, including greater coverage, a pay-as-you-go provision, increased monthly benefits, maintenance of the present trust fund for reserve purposes, and liberalization of the "retirement (needs) test" to yearly earnings of $1,000. He did not suggest, however, as Curtis did, to "blanket in" all present aged persons who don't get benefits (New York *Herald Tribune*, January 15, 1954).

Congress passed and sent to the White House a social security bill on August 20. The bill embodied many of the President's recommendations. It was made a law on September 1.

Curtis is a Mason (Scottish Rite) and a Shriner. He is a member of the Odd Fellows and Elks associations, Theta Chi fraternity, the Rotary club, and the Nebraska Bar Association.

The Congressman married Lois Wylie-Atwater, a teacher, on June 6, 1930. They have two children: Claramae and Carl Thomas, Jr. Curtis is blue-eyed and brown-haired, and is five feet seven inches tall, and weighs 160 pounds. He is a Presbyterian and a former trustee of the Hastings Presbytery in the Nebraska Synod.

References

Congressional Directory (1954)
Who's Who in America, 1954-55

DAVENPORT, RUSSELL W(HEELER)

July 12, 1899-Apr. 19, 1954 Editor; author; served with U.S. Army (1917-1919) and received Croix de Guerre; was graduated from Yale University (1923) where he was managing editor of Yale *Literary Magazine;* member research staff of *Time* (1923), reporter of Spokane (Washington) *Review* (1924-1925); published novel *Through-Traffic* (1930); joined editorial staff of *Fortune* (1930), became managing editor (1937); promoted Wendell Willkie's campaign for presidency (1940); became chairman of *Fortune* board of editors (1941), chief editorial writer *Life* (1942-1944); served in World War II with 11th Armored Division as correspondent for *Collier's* and New York *Post;* received Purple Heart; after the war was on the editorial staffs of *Life* and *Time* until 1952; collaborated with editors of *Fortune* on *U.S.A., The Permanent Revolution* (1951); author of *My Country* (1944), a long poem expressing his devotion to America and his internationalist viewpoint; since 1952 at work on a book dealing with human liberties as executive director of the Institute of Creative Research. See *Current Biography,* (Jan.) 1944.

Obituary

N Y Times p29 Ap 20 '54

DAY, DORIS Apr. 3, 1924- Singer

Address: b. c/o Warner Brothers Studios, Burbank, Calif.

Motion picture exhibitors who regard singer Doris Day as one of the film industry's top box-office attractions attribute her popularity to her steadfast refusal to make pictures about serious subjects. She contends that "happy pictures about happy people" are what the public wants. A leading personality in the entertainment world since 1948, Miss Day has established herself in radio, as well, and her recordings for Columbia Records sell nearly five million annually. Her latest pictures are *Calamity Jane* and *Lucky Me.*

She made her theatrical debut at the age of four when, in a wavering voice that has since developed into one of Hollywood's most valuable vocal properties, she rendered *I's Gwine Down to the Cushville Hop* before an indulgent audience in a Masonic hall in Cincinnati, Ohio. Since then she has become variously known as "The Golden Tonsil", "The Tomboy with the Voice", "The Girl We would Like to Take a Slow Boat Back to the States With" (by soldiers in Korea), and "The Prettiest Three-Million-Dollar Corporation With Freckles in America."

Doris von Kappelhoff was born in Cincinnati on April 3, 1924, the second child and first daughter of Alma Sophia and Frederick Wilhelm von Kappelhoff. She inherited a theatrical bent from her mother (who named her after a favorite actress, Doris Kenyon) and her musical talent from her father, who was a church organist and choir master and a pro-

DORIS DAY

fessional teacher of violin, piano, and the theory of classical music.

Her parents were amicably separated in 1936; Mrs. Kappelhoff took their son Paul (age fifteen) and Doris (age twelve) to suburban Evanston, where she worked in a bakery to support the family and pay for dancing lessons for Doris.

Simultaneously attending public school and studying dancing, Doris appeared as an amateur performer wherever invited and it was one of these appearances, plus a touch of adolescent *l'amour,* that put her into show business. Watching from the wings at a service club show while a fellow amateur tapped his heart out on the stage, Doris remarked to a woman nearby that the boy was "cute". The lady elaborated on this teen-age accolade in flowery fashion and, after the show, introduced him as her son, Jerry Doherty.

Before the evening was over Jerry and Doris were partners and, as Doherty & Kappelhoff, they won a $500 prize as the best dance team in Cincinnati in a contest run by the Alms & Doepke department store. This recognition almost automatically suggested Hollywood and at an interfamily conference in the Kappelhoff kitchen it was decided that the two mothers should take the team to California for study under Louis DaPron, a leading teacher of tap dancing.

Despite a few professional appearances by Doherty & Kappelhoff and part-time work by both mothers, the cost of lessons, food, and an apartment in Glendale strained their pooled finances and it was decided to recruit a real money-maker by returning to Ohio and persuading Mr. Doherty, a dairyman, that his future lay in California.

To their surprise Mr. Doherty agreed and, while he was winding up his affairs, the young dancers were further heartened by a short engagement with a touring Fanchon and Marco stage show. This was Miss Day's last good fortune for several years for, on the night before their return to the west coast, her right leg was badly crushed in an automobile accident at Hamilton, Ohio.

Miss Day was confined to hospitals for fourteen months before the leg finally mended. Unable to dance (a premature attempt re-broke a bone) she took to singing popular songs for amusement and her mother, hearing her, quickly revived the dream of a stage career for her daughter and arranged singing lessons with Grace Raine at a discount, taking in sewing to pay for them.

Hard work by mother and daughter paid off when Doris got a job singing on "Karlin's (department store) Karnival" over WCPO. There was no salary but she was "on the air" and Barney Rapp, a band leader planning his own night club, heard her singing *Day After Day* and offered her a club date at twenty-five dollars a week and advised her to change her name from Kappelhoff to something more suitable for billing purposes.

Doris toyed longingly with such classy substitutes as Marmaduke or LaPonselle but Rapp arbitrarily christened her Day after her rendition of *Day After Day.* It seemed prosaic to her but there was one consolation: "I'm glad you didn't catch me singing the *Gotterdammerung,"* she told Rapp.

This engagement led to tours singing in the bands of Bob Crosby, Fred Waring, and Les Brown. In New York City, in March 1941, she married Al Jorden, a trombone player in Gene Krupa's band whom she had met in Cincinnati. The marriage, most of it spent on the road, was not successful and in February 1943, exactly a year after the birth of their son Terry, they were divorced.

Returning to Cincinnati, Miss Day appeared briefly on a local station and then, leaving Terry with her mother, she rejoined Les Brown's band for a three-year tour. Early in 1946 she married George Weidler, trumpet-playing brother of the child movie actress Virginia Weidler, and became a trailer-housewife in the San Fernando Valley while Weidler worked in Hollywood for CBS. The marriage lasted only a year and they separated.

Al Levy of Century Artists (talent) Agency secured for Doris an interview with Michael Curtiz, the director who was seeking a "name" singer for *Romance On The High Seas.* Upset by her break with Weidler (they were divorced in 1949) Miss Day cried during most of the interview, but so impressed Curtiz that, after a screen test, he decided to risk a $1,000,000 production on a lachrymose and unknown girl. He had no reason to regret it, for while Bosley Crowther in the New York *Times* expressed the critical concensus on the picture with "woeful banality", Miss Day received general praise.

Since *Romance On The High Seas* (1948) she has starred in fourteen Warner Brothers pictures, with *Lucky Me* and *Yankee Doodle Girl* being produced by Marty Melcher's new independent producing company and released by Warner Brothers in 1954.

Miss Day's other pictures are: *My Dream is Yours, It's A Great Feeling* (1949); *Young*

Man With a Horn, Tea For Two, The West Point Story (1950); *Lullaby Of Broadway, On Moonlight Bay, Starlift, Storm Warning, I'll See You In My Dreams* (1951); *The Winning Team, April In Paris* (1952) and *By The Light Of The Silvery Moon* (1953).

Surprisingly versatile in all of them, she has been praised for her singing and called a "sincere and moving" actress by *Variety* and "a pert performer" and "effective dancer" by the New York *Times.* In 1950 she received the Laurel Award as "the leading new female personality in the motion picture industry", and in 1952 was named one of the top ten money-making film stars in a poll conducted by *Motion Picture Herald.*

As a singer and leading lady on the Bob Hope NBC radio show for two seasons (1948-1950) and on her Doris Day CBS show (1952-53) she was welcomed everywhere by her film and "platter" fans and her success in radio and films has been equalled with her recordings of songs from her film musicals. As leading money-maker for Columbia Records for over four years, and a top popular vocalist of either sex according to three separate disc jockey polls, she makes about twelve records yearly (twenty-four sides) with annual sales of nearly five million.

The critics generally felt that she was miscast in her role in *Calamity Jane*, released in October 1953. *Variety* commented: "Doris Day works very, very hard at being 'Calamity', and is hardly realistic at all. She'd register fine as a country girl in calico or a cutie from the chorus line, but strain shows through in her essaying of the hard and dynamic 'Calamity' character." Otis L. Guernsey, Jr. in the New York *Herald Tribune* wrote (November 5, 1953): "Miss Day stomps and hollers her way around the town of Deadwood like Betty Hutton in a holiday mood. . .it is all romance, with as much humor as the lithe and determined Miss Day can squeeze out of her role."

On her twenty-seventh birthday in 1951 Miss Day married Marty Melcher, her agent. Her fabulous and diverse income (reputed to be $500,000 yearly) and over $3,000,000 in contracts led him to suggest that she incorporate herself. Very blonde, very blue-eyed, very freckled, five feet five and three-quarter inches tall, 120 pounds, Miss Day lives with her husband, mother and son, in an unpretentious house (by Hollywood standards) in the San Fernando Valley where she swims, plays volley ball and gardens. She has an aversion to nightclubbing. She is a Christian Scientist and she neither smokes nor drinks.

"She lives," writes Louella O. Parsons in *Cosmopolitan*, January, 1954, "in the belief that happiness has to be made—and can be made—by the individual. In her sunny exuberance, she seems to be a living proof of it."

References

Am Mag 147:113 My '49
Collier's 125:16+ Ja 7 '50 pors
N Y Herald Tribune p3 IV D 13 '53
This Week p16+ My 17 '53
Motion Picture and Television Almanac, 1953-54

DEAN, ARTHUR H(OBSON) Oct. 16, 1898- Lawyer; former United States Government official

Address: b. 48 Wall St., New York 5; h. Mill River Rd., Oyster Bay, Long Island, N.Y.

A specialist in international and corporate law, Arthur H. Dean was appointed on September 15, 1953 a Special Deputy Secretary of State with the rank of Ambassador. He was given the difficult assignment of conducting on behalf of the United States and the United Nations the negotiations preliminary to the political peace conference intended to bring an end to the Korean war. A partner since 1929 in the law firm of Sullivan & Cromwell, New York City, Dean has had extensive legal experience in Far Eastern matters.

In negotiations with Red Chinese and North Korean emissaries which began on October 26, 1953, Dean repeatedly stated the United Nations' position that Russia should not be permitted to participate in the conference as a neutral. On December 9, 1953 the Communists rejected an offer submitted by Dean for a political Korean conference to be held within twenty-four to forty-eight days after the preliminary conference ended. The proposal would seat, besides the belligerents, a number of nonbelligerent countries without voting power, and Russia, who would vote in order that she be bound by the decisions. South Korea did not support Dean's proposal. Dean returned to the United States after talks were broken off on December 12.

On January 14, 1954 Arthur H. Dean called a press conference after he had heard charges of "appeasement" against him by Senator Herman Welker, Republican, of Idaho. Dean defended his membership in the Institute of Pacific Relations (which had been called a Communist front) and said that he had remained a trustee of the institute in order to get evidence on Frederick Vanderbilt Field's [alleged] Communist activities, "and then a number of trustees and myself forced his resignation."

Dean stated further: "I am and always have been consistently anti-Communist. Communism is repugnant to every idea for which I stand. In my judgment it should be fought tooth and nail. I am against the appeasement of the U.S.S.R., Red China, North Korea or any other Communist government. I am not in favor of the recognition of Red China or its admission to the United Nations" (New York *Times*, January 15, 1954).

Arthur Hobson Dean was born to William Cameron and Maud Campbell (Egan) Dean in Ithaca, New York on October 16, 1898. He studied at the Ithaca High School and after graduation enrolled at Cornell University in 1915. He helped to earn his college expenses by working as a night clerk at the Ithaca Hotel and as a bookkeeper in the First National Bank of Ithaca.

His studies were interrupted by America's entrance into World War I. He served with the Navy in 1918 and after the armistice he returned to Cornell and was awarded the A.B. degree in 1921. He then entered Cornell Law

Blackstone Studios

ARTHUR H. DEAN

School where he became managing editor of the *Cornell Law Quarterly* and was elected to Phi Delta Phi (legal fraternity). He received the LL.B. degree in 1923.

Admitted to the New York bar in the same year, Dean secured a position with Sullivan & Cromwell, a New York City firm which specializes in international law, and of which Secretary of State John Foster Dulles was a partner.

Dean, in collaboration with Tokyo lawyers, worked out a bond issue of the Nippon Power Company which was based on the first true open and indenture structure ever created in Japan and which was offered to the American public. Advanced to a full partnership in Sullivan & Cromwell in 1929, Dean frequently acted as counsel for English and American banking firms in corporate reorganizations, recapitalizations and financing of industrial firms, public utilities and railroads in America, Germany, Japan, France, and Italy.

Arthur H. Dean was named to the Dickinson committee formed by the Department of Commerce at the request of President Franklin D. Roosevelt. He participated in preparing materials which were later used in drafting the Securities Exchange Act of 1934. The act created the Securities and Exchange Commission, a quasi-judicial agency, whose objective is to protect the public and investors against malpractices in the securities and financial market.

Dean assisted in drafting the Trust Indenture Act of 1939 by which the interests of purchasers of debt securities issued under mortgage indentures and sold publicly are safeguarded through eliminating exculpatory clauses and including protective provisions in indentures. He also took part in drawing up the Investment Company Act of 1940 which provides for the registration with the Securities and Exchange Commission of investment trusts and companies and subjects them to regulation by prescribed standards. The lawyer has served on several advisory committees to the commission.

An officer in the Coast Guard Reserve during World War II, he instructed and supervised classes in navigation and piloting during 1941 and 1942. At this time he was publicly critical, as counsel for the Investment Bankers Association in December, 1943, of Rule U-50 of the Securities and Exchange Commission regulations. He was counsel for the Baltimore & Ohio railroad in adjustment proceedings involving $500,000,000 in debt securities.

Governor Thomas E. Dewey appointed Dean a trustee of Cornell University in 1945. Three years later he became chairman of the Cornell board of trustees' executive committee. He has served as chairman of the subcommittee on finances of the Cornell board of trustees, vice-chairman of the board of trustees of New York state's university system, a member of the joint administrative board of the New York Hospital-Cornell Medical Center.

When Dulles became a U.S. Senator in 1949, Arthur H. Dean succeeded him as the senior partner of Sullivan & Cromwell. In the following year he was the annual Dickinson lecturer at Harvard Graduate School of Business Administration. When the government brought an anti-trust action against seventeen investment banking concerns in 1950, Dean successfully defended five of these firms, namely, Lehman Brothers of New York, First Boston Corporation, Glore Forgan & Company of Chicago and New York, Goldman, Sachs & Company of New York, and Blyth and Company of San Francisco.

Dean's knowledge of the Far East was first drawn upon by the Eisenhower Administration when he accompanied Secretary of State Dulles, Assistant Secretary of State for Far Eastern Affairs Walter S. Robertson, and the U.S. Ambassador to the United Nations, Henry Cabot Lodge, Jr. to Korea in the summer of 1953. In August he acted as an adviser to Lodge in regard to the special session of the U.N. Assembly which dealt with Korea.

Dean is the author of *Business Income Under Present Price Levels* (1949) and has served as *rapporteur* for the International Chamber of Commerce Association. He has contributed articles to *Fortune*, the New York *Herald Tribune* and to several law journals. In a recent article the lawyer stated: "The power to formulate and execute . . . foreign policy was intentionally concentrated by the founding fathers in the Federal Government, particularly in the President and Senate . . . the Bricker Amendment [would] shift this constitutional ordering . . . by augmenting Congressional powers and by requiring participation of the States. . . . The powers of the sovereign state would thus be emasculated" (*Foreign Affairs*, October, 1953).

On October 21, 1953 Dean left for the Far East as a Special Deputy Secretary of State to assume what was characterized as possibly "one of the most important diplomatic roles ever assigned to an American" (New York *Herald Tribune*, October 4, 1953). Although he was authorized to agree on a time and place for a peace conference, Dean was not to negotiate any change in the U.N. position.

The U.N. specification was that the conference delegates should be representatives of the nations that sent fighting forces to Korea, namely, the United States, fifteen other U.N. members and South Korea on one side, and North Korea and Communist China on the other, as well as the U.S.S.R., if the Communists invited the Russians to sit with them.

After seven weeks of unproductive discussions, Dean broke off the negotiations because "the Red Chinese delegate . . . accused the United States of America of perfidy or deliberate treachery in connection with the release of prisoners by President Rhee on June 17 and 18 after General Harrison had signed the terms of reference on June 8" by which prisoners who did not wish to return to their native countries would be in the custody of a Neutral Nations Repatriation Commission. However Dean said that negotiations would be resumed if the Communists apologized and indicated that they did want a conference.

The diplomat began his trip back to the United States on December 16, 1953. In a report to the American people on December 21 he stated that the "Chinese Communists are determined to keep North Korea politically and economically integrated into their own economy. They believe that at a long drawnout conference the American negotiators will be forced by American public opinion to give in in order to have a successful conference" (New York *Times*, December 22, 1953).

Dean is a trustee of the Bank of New York, a director of the Solvay American Corporation, Crowley-Republic Steel Corporation, Henry L. Crowley and Company, Inc., American Agricultural Chemical Company, Cornell Aeronautical Laboratory, and Mexican Light and Power Company, and general counsel of the American Metal Company, Ltd.

Active in legal associations, Dean has served on the committee of state legislation, as chairman on the committee of federal legislation and on the executive committee of the Association of the Bar of the City of New York, and on the committee of corporate law of the New York State Bar Association. He also holds membership in the American Judicature Society, American Society of International Law, International Law Association, Cornell Law Association, New York Law Institute, New York County Law, and the American Bar Associations.

He is a director of the Visiting Nurse Association and the Association for the Aid of Crippled Children, a trustee of the North Country Hospital (Long Island) and the Hochschild Foundation, chairman of the board of the Breen Vale School (Long Island), a member of the finance committee of the Carnegie Foundation for the Advancement of Teaching, and a member of the Foreign Policy Association, Japan Society, Inc., Academy of Political Science, and American Academy of Political and Social Science. Dean served as chairman of the Institute of Pacific Relations from 1950 to 1952. His clubs are the Cold Spring Harbor Beach, Lloyd Neck Bath, Inc., Piping Rock, Century Association, Lunch, Recess, University, and the Metropolitan (Washington D.C.).

Mrs. Dean is the former Mary Talbott Clark Marden. The couple, who were married on June 25, 1932, have two children, Nicholas B. Marden and Patricia Campbell. Dean's church is the Episcopalian.

References

N Y Herald Tribune p7 S 16 '53 por; II p2 O 4 '53 por
N Y Times p14 Ja 17 '50 por
N Y World-Telegram p11 D 19 '53 por
Who's Who in America, 1952-53
World Biography (1948)

DEAN, WILLIAM F(RISHE) Aug. 1, 1899- United States Army officer

Address: b. c/o Sixth Army Headquarters, San Francisco, Calif.; h. 2518 Etna St., Berkeley 4, Calif.

After spending three years in Communist prisoner of war camps in North Korea, Major General William F. Dean was liberated in September 1953. His own account of his capture, his valiant efforts to escape, and the ordeal of Communist "brainwashings" is given in *General Dean's Story* (as told to William L. Worden), published by the Viking Press in 1954. The story first appeared in condensed form in the *Saturday Evening Post*.

As the first recipient in the Korean hostilities of the Congressional Medal of Honor, awarded him *in absentia* in September 1950, General Dean was hailed for his heroism at Taejon, where he had directed the Twenty-fourth Infantry Division in its self-sacrificing stand against the Communist invaders. He had been reported missing in action after the battle. When he came home to the United States in September 1953, he was again honored as a hero who symbolized the courage and endurance of the American soldier in long captivity.

"I've spent most of my adult life trying to learn to be a decent infantry officer," the commander said in *General Dean's Story*. In the last months of World War II he led the Forty-fourth Infantry Division in a victorious drive through Germany and Austria. Before being stationed in Japan prior to the outbreak of the Korean War, he served as military governor of South Korea from October 1947 to August 1948.

William Frishe Dean, the eldest of four children of Dr. Charles Watts and Elizabeth (Frishe) Dean, was born on August 1, 1899 in Carlyle, Illinois, where his father practiced dentistry. In his boyhood, William was fond of outdoor activity, and enjoyed reading books. He was graduated from Carlyle High School in 1918 as valedictorian of his class.

Having failed to get an appointment to West Point, Dean attended the University of California in Berkeley, where his family had moved

U. S. Army

MAJ. GEN. WILLIAM F. DEAN

from Illinois. During part of 1918 he served with the Students' Army Training Corps and in the time he could spare from his studies was employed as a patrolman on the Berkeley police force. He is said to have also paid his university expenses by taking jobs as a streetcar motorman, a stevedore and as a short-order cook.

"I should have received an A.B. degree in 1921, but flunked a course in legal contracts, and so didn't get it until a year later," Dean has explained. "I never did get the Doctor of Laws degree toward which I was aiming, but never cared too much. I'm always disturbed by victories of technicalities over equity, and would have made a bad lawyer" (*General Dean's Story*).

By examination, Dean, who had been commissioned a second lieutenant in the Infantry Reserve in 1921, received his commission as a second lieutenant of infantry in the Regular Army in 1923. His first post was with the Thirty-eighth Infantry at Fort Douglas, Utah, where he spent three years. After another three years (1926-1929) in the Canal Zone, first at Camp Gaillard and then Fort Clayton, he returned for further duty at Fort Douglas. He remained in the United States until 1936, serving at two posts in California and taking courses at the Command and General Staff School in Fort Leavenworth, Kansas.

From Hawaii's Schofield Barracks, where he had been stationed for two years, Captain Dean was sent in September 1938 to the Army Industrial College in Washington, D.C. He completed other courses in the Chemical Warfare School at Edgewood Arsenal in Maryland in 1939 and was graduated from the Army War College in Washington in June 1940. In the early years of World War II Dean (who was promoted to major in July 1940) held a series of staff positions in the nation's capital, including assistant to the secretary of the General Staff and chief of the requirements section of the Army Ground Forces.

During these years, which brought Dean a number of promotions—lieutenant colonel in December 1941, colonel in August 1942 and brigadier general in December 1942—his chief desire was to secure an assignment with combat troops. This goal was realized in 1944 when he was named assistant commander of the Forty-fourth Infantry Division, then on maneuvers in the United States. In August of that year he moved with the division to France and in December became its commander.

The Forty-fourth Division is credited with having captured about 30,000 prisoners in its drive through Germany and Austria and in having helped to force the surrender of the Nineteenth German Army. For his "extraordinary heroism" in a mission near Enchenberg, France in December 1944, Dean was awarded the Distinguished Service Cross. "He personally led an infantry platoon through one concentration of enemy fire after another," the citation stated, "and succeeded in destroying the opposing enemy batteries" (quoted in *Life,* July 31, 1950). Dean also received the Distinguished Service Medal and the Bronze Star Medal. His earlier work with the Army Ground Forces in Washington brought him the Legion of Merit. He was advanced to major general in March 1945.

General Dean brought his victorious division back to the United States in July 1945. He later became class director of the command class of the Fort Leavenworth Command and General Staff School and in June 1946 was made assistant commandant of the Army college there.

Appointed U.S. military governor for South Korea in October 1947, the general held that office during the 1948 elections and until the inauguration of the Korean Republic in August 1948. He took command of the Seventh Infantry Division in Japan in January 1949 and from June to October of that year was chief of staff of the Eighth Army in Japan. Desiring to return to duty with troops, he succeeded in being assigned commanding general of the Twenty-fourth Infantry Division, with headquarters in Kokura, Japan. Later, on July 3, 1950 he was named commander of all U.S. forces in Korea.

When the forces of the North Korean communists crossed the thirty-eighth parallel in Korea on June 25, 1950, the Twenty-fourth Division was ordered to South Korea to halt the Red advance. A front-line general, as he had shown himself to be in World War II, Dean led his division in a series of delaying actions until he was separated from his troops in an attempt on July 20 and 21 to hold the town of Taejon.

His heroism during this battle was described in the citation accompanying the Congressional Medal of Honor, which was presented to him *in absentia* on September 30, 1950. "He personally and alone attacked an enemy tank while armed only with a hand grenade. He also directed the fire of his own tanks from an exposed position with neither cover nor concealment while under observed artillery and small arms fire. When the town of Taejon was finally overrun he refused to insure his own safety by leaving with the leading elements but remained behind organizing his retreating forces, directing stragglers, and was last seen assisting the wounded to a place of safety."

According to S. L. A. Marshall (New York *Times Book Review*, May 9, 1954) several military officials have criticized Dean's behavior at Taejon, believing that he should have been leading and commanding his men, and not playing the role of a rifleman.

For a year and a half after the Taejon action the Western world knew nothing of the fate of General Dean. Then on December 19, 1951 his name appeared on a prisoner of war list issued by the communists. Shortly afterward a news report by communist correspondent Wilfred Burchett, who interviewed Dean, told of the general's capture by the North Koreans on August 25, 1950. During the previous month Dean, weak and injured, had wandered behind enemy lines in a vain effort to find his way back to American forces, had gone for twenty days without food, and although determined to kill himself rather than become a prisoner, had been betrayed into communist hands by two South Koreans pretending to befriend him. (These betrayers, who had turned Dean over to the Reds for the equivalent of five dollars, were later captured by the government of South Korea. Dean in the fall of 1953 made unsuccessful pleas to President Syngman Rhee that they be pardoned.)

He told the story of his life in a series of articles in the *Saturday Evening Post* beginning on January 23, 1954. One dramatic incident concerned Dean's fear that he might be tortured into revealing military secrets and his unsuccessful attempt to commit suicide rather than disclose information that would aid the enemy.

Reviewers of *General Dean's Story* commented on the tone of self-depreciation and lack of stuffiness which distinguishes the account from the usual memoir writing of military leaders. "This is one of the warmest of books, though it treats of a bitterly cold ordeal," observed S. L. A. Marshall. "Its delightful humor, recurrent amid the recounting of excruciating personal experiences, is worthy of an exalted spirit capable of seeing all things in proportion in any circumstances."

On his arrival in the United States in September 1953 amid much public acclaim, General Dean was astonished to find that he had come to be regarded as a hero in captivity as well as in battle. He described himself as "not a hero—just a dog-faced soldier" (New York *Times*, September 27, 1953). In other public statements he urged clemency in handling cases of American war prisoners who had "confessed" to germ warfare charges and later (March 1954) testified at a court of inquiry investigating Marine Colonel Frank H. Schwable. During a television interview in October he said that his experience in Korean prison camps had convinced him that in his capacity as an Army officer he had never sufficiently stressed to his soldiers the information and education program on American institutions.

On December 17, 1953 Dean was named deputy commander of the Sixth Army, Presidio of San Francisco, California, to assume his post on January 1. Among the honors that have been conferred on the general since his repatriation have been South Korea's Order of Taeguk, Korean Presidential Unit Citation, U.S. Presidential Unit Citation, and Alumnus of the Year Award of the University of California. In June 1954 he was adopted into the Crow Indian Tribe of Montana.

General Dean's wife is the former Mildred Dern, whom he married on August 25, 1926. They have a son, William Jr., a daughter, Marjorie June (Mrs. Robert B. C. Williams), and two grandchildren. The white-haired general is six feet tall and weighs 190 pounds. He has been described as an affable man, fond of family life and outdoor sports. He is an Episcopalian.

"Now that I'm home," the Taejon hero said in *General Dean's Story,* "the only special taste I retain from North Korea is for garlic. I can sit and eat garlic like popcorn." He retains also from his captivity the lesson he learned about the conflict between communist and free nations: ". . . we must present a factual world better than the communist dream; . . . we must have political answers simple enough for the dullest to understand; . . . we must, each of us, know and understand the things for which we fight. An army can be a show window for democracy only if every man in it is convinced that it does fight for a free world, for the kind of government he wants himself. . . ."

References

Life 29:26 Jl 31 '50 pors; 35:42 S 14 '53 pors
N Y Herald Tribune II p1 Jl 9 '50 por; II p1 D 23 '51 por; p1+ D 24 '51 por; p3 S 4 '53; p1+ S 5 '53
N Y Sunday News p80+ F 3 '52 pors
N Y Times p2 Jl 3 '50 pors; p1+ D 19 '51 por; p1+ D 24 '51; p3 S 4 '53; p3 S 5 '53
Newsweek 36:17+ Jl 31 '50 por; 43:104 My 10 '54 pors
Pathfinder 59:5 Ja 9 '52 por
Sat Eve Post 226:17+ Ja 23; 22+ Ja 30; 28+ F 6; 25+ F 13; 30+ F 20; 30+ F 27 '54 pors
Sat R 37:20+ My 15 '54 por
Scholastic 59:17 Ja 16 '52 por
Time 58:18 D 31 '51 por; 62:33 S 14 '53 por; 27+ D 7 '53 pors
Washington (D.C.) Post p1+ D 24 '51 por

Dean, W. F. and Worden, W. L. General Dean's Story (1954)
Who's Who in America, 1954-55
World Biography (1954)

DECOURSEY, ELBERT (dè-côr' sē) Apr. 12, 1902- United States Army officer; pathologist

Address: b. c/o Armed Forces Institute of Pathology, 7th St. and Independence Ave., S.W., Washington 25, D.C.; h. 3247 Chestnut St., N.W. Washington 15, D.C.

"Your most potent defense against the atom bomb is to know the truth about it. . . ," stated Brigadier General Elbert DeCoursey, director of the Armed Forces Institute of Pathology. Since August 1945, when Dr. DeCoursey arrived in Nagasaki, Japan, as director of the Army group of the Joint Commission for the

Department of the Army

BRIG. GEN. ELBERT DECOURSEY

Study of the Effects of the Atomic Bomb in Japan (succeeded by the Atomic Bomb Casualty Commission), he has studied 15,000 case histories of survivors of A-bombings in Japan.

DeCoursey, who is now also serving as chief of pathology of the Army Medical Service Graduate School and chief consultant in pathology for the armed forces, believes that "the A-bomb hysteria that many Americans have" is the result of false rumors and distorted facts about the results of atomic explosion. In two articles by General DeCoursey (as told to Bruce Jacobs) in the *American Weekly* (January 24 and January 31, 1954), it is explained what these effects actually are.

Elbert DeCoursey was born April 12, 1902 in Ludlow, Kentucky to Elizabeth (Carter) and William B. DeCoursey, a railroad supervisor. He was brought up in Covington, Kentucky and attended Holmes High School where he played football and was a member of the school band and glee club.

After he was graduated in 1920, he entered the University of Kentucky for his pre-medical studies. His extracurricular interests included the band, theatrical activities, glee club, Delta Tau Delta, Phi Mu Alpha (music), Alpha Chi Sigma (chemistry), and Phi Beta Pi (medicine). After receiving the A.B. degree from the University of Kentucky in 1924, he entered the Johns Hopkins University School of Medicine. He took his M.D. degree in 1928. DeCoursey believes that his high school English and physics teachers, Dean C. R. Melcher of the University of Kentucky, and Major P. E. McNabb of the Army Medical Corps influenced him in the choice of his career.

The young doctor was commissioned a first lieutenant in the Army Medical Corps Reserve on June 12, 1928, and served a year's internship at the Fort Sam Houston station hospital in Texas. He was given his first lieutenant's commission in the Regular Army Medical Corps on August 1, 1929.

Further training in the Army Medical School and the Medical Field Service School prepared Lieutenant DeCoursey for the post of pathologist at the Panama Canal Zone Board of Health Laboratory, a position he held from 1932 to 1934. He had been promoted to the rank of captain August 1, 1931. His work at the Canal Zone merited a letter from Dr. Lewis B. Bates stating that DeCoursey was destined to become a leader in American pathology.

Transferred to Washington, Captain DeCoursey held several posts in this period. From 1935 to 1939 he was assistant director of the Army Institute of Pathology and assistant curator of the Army Medical Museum. He also instructed at the Army Medical School and at George Washington University in ophthalmic pathology.

DeCoursey, promoted to the rank of major in 1938, returned in the following year to the Medical Field Service School. Upon completion of the advanced course, he became a pathologist at the Brooke General Hospital, Fort Sam Houston, Texas and on June 8, 1942 became a lieutenant colonel (temporary). After two years as commanding officer of the Ninth Service Laboratory, Fort Lewis, Washington, he was given command, in November 1943, of the Eighteenth Medical General Laboratory. The following July DeCoursey was made a colonel (temporary) and became laboratory consultant to the Pacific Theater of Operations.

It was on this assignment that the work which has been DeCoursey's chief interest began. The pathologist recalls: ". . .while the bodies of the victims were still stacked in their macabre setting, I arrived in Nagasaki to study the effects of A-bombing on the human body. . . . I examined a constant stream of A-bomb survivors and performed countless autopsies on the bodies of those who had died."

From this study, the Joint Commission for the Study of the Effects of the Atom Bomb in Japan (of which DeCoursey was a member) determined that only 10 per cent of the deaths had been due to radiation, the most generally feared of the bomb's effects. The life of the rays emitted is too short (about two minutes) to allow them to do any more damage.

Heat and air blast were the greatest killers; but, stated DeCoursey, "if the people of

Hiroshima and Nagasaki had used American methods of medical treatment, [prompt hospitalization], fire fighting and rescue work, they could have cut their death toll in half."

Cancer, sterility, blindness, deafness, and loss of hair, all feared as after-effects of radiation, were discovered by the commission to have little or no relation to the rays. Cancer did not develop, and sterility and loss of hair which occurred were found to be only temporary.

Much work remains to be done before definite statements can be made about the hereditary effects of radiation upon children born to parents who were exposed, but DeCoursey's belief is that there will be no danger of adverse effects upon them.

Over and over he has stressed the importance of resisting panic in the event of atomic attack. He feels that the best way to come through such an attack with as few casualties as possible is for every survivor to lose no time in going to the assistance of others. ". . .Nuclear warfare is a terrible thing," he said, "but the A-bomb is not the death rattle in the throat of civilization." DeCoursey served in 1946 as pathologist for the Bikini atomic bomb tests and observed the effects of the explosion on the target area and target animals.

"Today's A-bomb and the more powerful H-bomb . . . are more destructive than the bombs exploded over Japan," General DeCoursey declared. "But so far as radiation is concerned, they are little, if any, more dangerous than the earlier atomic weapons."

In October 1946 DeCoursey became chief of the laboratory service at Brooke General Hospital, Fort Sam Houston, Texas. He was named commandant of the Research and Graduate School of the Army Medical Center in Washington, D.C. in 1948. He became deputy director of the Armed Forces Institute of Pathology, Washington, D.C. in June 1949 and in August 1950 was appointed director of the institute which is charged with the preservation and study of survivors of A-bombings in Japan. In 1950 DeCoursey received the rank of brigadier general, and was made chief consultant in pathology for the armed forces and chief of pathology of the Army Medical Service Graduate School.

General DeCoursey has been awarded the Legion of Merit. He is a member of the National Board of Medical Examiners, Joint Panel on Atomic Warfare, Academy of Medicine (Washington, D.C.), Pathology Study Section of the U.S. Public Health Service, Radiation Research Society, and Advisory Editorial Board of the *American Journal of Clinical Pathology.*

He is Army member of the National Advisory Cancer Council and consultant to the division of biology and medicine of the Atomic Energy Commission.

The general is also a diplomate of the American Board of Pathology; a fellow of the American College of Physicians, College of American Pathologists, American Society of Clinical Pathology, and American Medical Association; and a member of the American Society of Tropical Medicine, Washington Society of Pathologists, International Society of Hematologists, American Association for the Advancement of Science, and American Association of Pathologists; and a director of the Gorgas Memorial Institute.

He is co-author with J. E. Ash of the *Atlas of Opthalmic Pathology* (American Academy of Opthalmology & Otolaryngology, 1942), and the author of several chapters in the Armed Forces Special Weapons Project's *Radiological Defense* (1950).

Articles by General DeCoursey have appeared in the *American Journal of Tropical Medicine, American Journal of Pathology, South Dakota Journal of Medicine and Pharmacy, Journal of the Tennessee State Medical Association, Bulletin of the United States Army Medical Department, Radiology,* and *Cincinnati Journal of Medicine.*

Elbert DeCoursey married Esther Fertig on June 16, 1928. He is five feet ten inches tall, weighs 160 pounds, and has brown eyes and gray-black hair. He is a Baptist. For relaxation he enjoys listening to symphonic music and watching football, baseball and basketball games. He has also become interested in the problems of classical and scientific education.

References

Gen Army F '53 por

American Men of Science (1949)
Who Knows—and What (1949)
World Biography (1948)

DE GALARD-TERRAUBE, GENEVIÈVE *See* Galard Terraube, G. de

DE GASPERI, ALCIDE *See* Gasperi, A. de

DENHAM, R(OBERT) N(EWTON) Oct. 23, 1885-June 18, 1954 Former United States government official; attorney; educated at universities of Missouri and Michigan; practiced law in state of Washington (1910-1917); was a second lieutenant in World War I; served in New York with Irving National Bank (1920-1929) and Eldridge & Company (1930-1933); worked as special counsel to U.S. comptroller of currency (1933-1934); joined the National Labor Relations Board as trial examiner (1938) and was its general counsel from 1947 to 1950. See *Current Biography,* (Oct.) 1947.

Obituary

N Y Times p86 Je 20 '54

DICKSON, MARGUERITE (STOCKMAN) Nov. 14, 1873—Oct. 11, 1953 Author; began career as a teacher in Brooklyn, New York; wrote a series of American history textbooks; a decade ago started writing "junior" novels of which the best known are *Lightning Strikes Twice, Roof Over Our Heads,* and *Turn in the Road.* See *Current Biography,* (Yrbk) 1952.

Obituary

N Y Times p27 O 12 '53

DISNEY, DORIS MILES Dec. 22, 1907-
Author

Address: b. c/o Doubleday & Company, Inc., 575 Madison Ave., New York 22; h. Maiden Lane, Plainville, Conn.

Reprinted from the *Wilson Library Bulletin* June 1954

In her pleasant, modern home on Maiden Lane in Plainville, Connecticut, Doris Miles Disney recently completed *Trick or Treat,* her seventeenth mystery story; mailed it to Doubleday, who have always published her books, and started a new one. (Mrs. Disney, who should not be confused with Dorothy Cameron Disney,

DORIS MILES DISNEY

another writer of mysteries—but often has been—is not related by marriage to Walt Disney, either.) Anthony Boucher has praised her books not only for workmanlike plotting, but for their "acid etching of the everyday." Such novels as *That Which is Crooked* (1948) and *Do Unto Others* (1953) have been called curious and absorbing combinations of case-history and novel.

One of the four daughters of Edward L. Miles, a farmer, and the late Elizabeth Anne (Malone) Miles, and herself the mother of a ten-year-old also named Elizabeth, Mrs. Disney finds some of her keenest critics inside her own family circle. Her niece, nephews, and daughter "are particularly concerned that in my next book I kill a man. I hadn't realized until they called it to my attention that I have been slaughtering an undue percentage of women."

Born December 22, 1907, in the small town of Glastonbury, Connecticut (where the *t* is silent), Doris Miles attended the local high school, where she "inevitably" edited the school paper. She spent some years in Springfield, Massachusetts, and worked in an insurance office in Hartford—hence her sure knowledge of the intricacies of life insurance as shown in *Family Skeleton.* On June 19, 1936, Doris Miles was married to the late George J. Disney; during the war, when Mr. Disney was in the Navy, she stayed with his family in Philadelphia. Asked to account for her daily life since, Mrs. Disney has quoted from a tale told her by her daughter, "full of witches and giants and magic" and a heroine who had a tough time. "Fifteen years went by," said Elizabeth.

"Something must have happened to the girl all that time," objected her mother.

"No," said Elizabeth. "Of course she got up every morning and took in the milk and supported herself but nothing much happened to her."

When not housekeeping, gardening, or working with the local Woman's Club and P.T.A., Mrs. Disney puts in three hours a day writing. She finds it easiest to concentrate on plots when washing dishes, a job she dislikes.

Mrs. Disney sold her first book in 1943, "the sale coinciding with the arrival of Elizabeth." *Compound for Death* was praised by the *Saturday Review of Literature* for its "pleasant, relaxing style." *Murder on a Tangent* (1945) was followed by *Dark Road* (1946), which the *New Republic* thought "grim and highly interesting"; Isaac Anderson in the *Times* called it "an unusually fine example of the detective story in reverse." Virginia Kirkus called *Who Rides a Tiger* (1946) "a romantic mystery with art and substance", and James Sandoe thought *Appointment at Nine* (1947) "a very satisfactory tale," although he and other critics objected that a key piece of evidence had been withheld from the reader. *Enduring Old Charms* (1947) considered the familiar case of a young fortune-hunter married to an aging woman, and the *Saturday Review of Literature* called it "grim—but good." *Testimony by Silence* (1948) was a treatment in an American setting of a famous British *cause célèbre,* the Bravo Case (also the basis of Joseph Shearing's *So Evil My Love*). *That Which is Crooked,* "a penetrating study of a warped mind from childhood through adolescence" (New York *Times*) was followed by *Count the Ways* (1949). This murder novel, with its title from Elizabeth Barrett Browning's sonnet, seemed "routine" to the *New Yorker,* whose critic, however, praised its "quiet, well-behaved prose."

Family Skeleton (1949), received critical acclaim, was published in a pocket edition, and was sold to Hollywood. In the film version it was retitled "Stella" and starred Ann Sheridan. It concerned an obstreperous uncle in a Ring Lardnerish family who was accidentally killed at a picnic. The family buries him, and hopefully tries to collect insurance. O'Neill, Mrs. Disney's pleasant young detective, is the sleuth in *Fire at Will* (1950). Drexel Drake called this a "well-set-up and deeply snarled puzzle," and *Straw Man* (1951), a Mystery Guild selection, "a shrewdly woven fabric of circumstantial evidence." Some reviewers objected to the murderer's being identified half-way in the latter book. *Look Back on Murder* (1951) was also a book club selection (Unicorn). The *New Yorker* thought *Heavy, Heavy Hangs* (1952) "a somewhat conventional item, but pleasantly and lucidly written." *Prescription for Murder* (1953), with its young woman doctor, was a study in infatuation.

Doris Disney is blue-eyed and brown-haired, and of medium height and weight. She manages a full, busy life with easy competence. Her young daughter and a large, complacent tomcat, Mickey, insure that she has few dull moments. She gardens, swims, and plays bridge in season, and reads a little of everything—especially mystery stories.

References

Who's Who in America, 1954-55

DITCHY, CLAIR W(ILLIAM) Apr. 12, 1891- Organization official; architect

Address: b. c/o American Institute of Architects, 1735 New York Ave., N.W., Washington 6, D.C.; 5 W. Larned St., Detroit 26, Mich.; h. 1630 Houstonia, Royal Oak, Mich.

CLAIR W. DITCHY

Quoting Friedrich von Schelling's statement that architecture is "music in space, as it were frozen music", Clair W. Ditchy has written that he finds a "felicitous" analogy between music and the structural art (*Journal of the American Institute of Architects,* April 1948). A well-known architect, Ditchy was elected as president of the American Institute of Architects in June 1953. Representing 9,500 members, he is concerned with the problems of how to acquaint the public with services the architect has to offer, how to educate young architects without too closely adhering to either traditional or modern forms, and how to keep architecture as an expression of the national culture.

He was re-elected president on June 19, 1954 at the organization's eighty-sixth annual convention.

Made a fellow of the American Institute of Architects in 1944 for distinguished service to his profession, Ditchy was national secretary of the institute from 1947 to 1953. Having successfully practiced privately for more than thirty years, he has specialized in the design of schools, hospitals and housing projects.

Clair William Ditchy was born at Kelleys Island, Ohio on April 12, 1891, the son of Peter and Julia (Monaghan) Ditchy. He attended the University of Michigan and received an A.B. degree there in 1911 and a B.Arch. degree in 1915. The young architect began his professional career in the office of Albert Kahn in Detroit, where he was employed from 1915 to 1917, and from 1919 to 1921. He served from 1917 to 1919 as a lieutenant with the American Expeditionary Forces.

Ditchy entered private practice as an architect in Detroit, Michigan in 1921. For the academic year 1927 to 1928, he taught design at the College of Architecture and Design of the University of Michigan. He became a special writer in his field for the Detroit *Free Press* from 1928 to 1929. After joining the American Institute of Architects in 1924, he served within the next several years as director, secretary, vice-president and president of the Detroit chapter, and as director, vice-president and president of the Michigan Society of Architects.

He showed an early interest in improving relations between architects and the public in an article, "How to Interview an Architect" (*Architect and Engineer,* July 1933), in which he wrote in a light vein: ". . . the average architect . . . would feel much more kindly disposed toward the rest of the world if it paid some attention . . . to him now and then. As matters now stand, the average person (based on 1932 statistics) knows there is such a thing as an architect, but the idea of ever engaging one to do anything for him seldom enters his head."

Together with three colleagues in his field, the architect on May 15, 1935 formed the Small House Associates of Detroit which would act as a paid architectural service promoting the building of better small homes, a field generally regarded by architects as unremunerative. In an article "Practical Small House Practice" (*American Architect,* June 1936), Ditchy wrote: "We entered the field with open minds, realizing that our first efforts must be largely experimental . . . that we must try everything and anything that was honest and direct."

A year after the founding of the associates, Ditchy affirmed among other points, that building "the small house is an extremely difficult problem which requires extensive study" and that "there is no room economically for both the builder (or general contractor) and the architect in the building of a single house [of small size]."

Becoming regional director of the Great Lakes division of the American Institute of Architects in 1938, Ditchy held this office until 1941. Discussing the extent to which the National Defense program influenced building in

DITCHY, CLAIR W.—*Continued*

1940, he declared: "The architectural profession is being profoundly affected by the activity of the national program . . . this work has served as a stimulus to private initiative, and firms and individuals who had set aside their building programs for the time being are now scanning the increased activity in business . . . and are preparing to proceed with their building expansion" (*Architect and Engineer,* December 1940).

He acted as president pro tempore of the American Institute of Architects at the annual convention in 1941. Three years later his design of a municipal garage for Royal Oak, Michigan, (pictured in the *Architectural Record,* July 1944), provided housing for offices, repair shops and storage, in addition to space for a garage and allowed for independent expansion of each of the four categories.

Elevated to the rank of fellow of the American Institute of Architects in 1944, Ditchy was cited for "his outstanding practice, his adherence to the ideals of the Institute, and his contribution and service in various capacities. . ." (*Journal of the American Institute of Architects,* September 1944). Addressing the annual convention in April 1945, as president of the Detroit chapter, he said: "We do not want wildcat financing, shoddy buildings and misplaced subdivisions after this war as we had after World War I. We have an unparalleled opportunity for long-range planning. . ." He also declared that glass and solar heating would be used more extensively in building projects during the postwar period (New York *Times,* April 24, 1945).

Among notable buildings the architect has designed are the Highland Park General Hospital and the Climax Molybdenum Laboratory. His Alice Crocker Lloyd Hall at the University of Michigan in Ann Arbor was designed in 1945; costs of labor and material made necessary a "simple and direct" plan. Ditchy made extensive use of glass "with natural vistas increasing the rooms' attractiveness" (*Architectural Record,* April 1951). In collaboration with others, he worked on the Brewster Homes and Parkside Homes housing projects in Detroit.

Ditchy served from 1945 to 1948 on the American Institute of Architects' jury which elects new fellows. Of the trend in architecture toward specialization, he said that the public should know who the specialists are, and who the able ones are in the field. Churches, schools, large houses and factories he listed among the "types of work which have occupied the architect to the virtual exclusion of all other work" (*Journal of the American Institute of Architects,* August 1945).

Appointed national secretary of the American Institute of Architects in 1947, Ditchy filled this post until June 1953. In an address at the testimonial dinner on February 19, 1948 which honored Professor Jean Hébrard of the University of Michigan College of Architecture and Design, he related architecture to music. "In the architectural product of a period," he said, "the extent to which its buildings sing, or merely speak, or are silent, or . . . shout raucously . . . is the mark of its culture" (*Journal of the American Institute of Architects,* April 1948).

The architect attended the eighth Pan-American Congress in Mexico City. Later he wrote: "Ciudad Universitaria, probably the most comprehensive and stimulating current architectural achievement of our hemisphere, attains a harmony of site planning, architecture and landscaping which in many instances reaches a high superlative. . . . Both in material and form, it is inherently a part of the land from which it springs" (*Journal of the American Institute of Architects,* January 1953).

Ditchy was elected as president of the American Institute of Architects on June 18, 1953 at the annual convention in Seattle, Washington. In a message to the convention, he spoke of the need for the increased effectiveness of the program of public relations and affirmed: "Our strength lies in the 9,500 loyal members who . . . are dedicated to the task of improving our communities and imbuing them with an ennobling spiritual and cultural quality" (*Journal of the American Institute of Architects,* August 1953). The members of the institute passed a resolution calling for a "free and natural development of the fine arts" in the United States, and opposed the creation of any laws which might result in government supervision or control in the field (New York *Times,* June 20, 1953).

"Long-laboring, devoted, genial and progressive Clair Ditchy was elected at the head of a slate generally known as progressive" (*House & Home,* July 1953). At the 1954 convention of AIA, held in Boston, Ditchy was re-elected president.

Articles by Ditchy in the field of architecture have appeared in national and foreign magazines. He is a past director of the Michigan Engineering Society, and was formerly on the board of founders of the Engineering Society of Detroit, of which he served as first secretary, director and assistant treasurer. He has been active in the Citizens' Housing and Planning Council of Detroit as director and secretary, in the Associated Technical Societies of Detroit as chairman, and in the Detroit Interprofessional Council as secretary and vice-president. He is an honorary member of Tau Sigma Delta and Sigma Rho Tau fraternities and a member of Alpha Chi Rho, of which he has served as national president.

Ditchy married Berenice Bookmyer on June 22, 1920, and their children are Diane, Elaine and Julie. The architect recommends that one must look for leadership to those who are "courageously developing a purity of architectural expression which is consonant with our times and techniques and which will accommodate the potentialities of our present civilization" (*Journal of the American Institute of Architects,* April 1948).

References

Am Inst Arch J p135 S '44

Who's Who in America, 1952-53

DIXON, SIR PIERSON (JOHN) Nov. 13, 1904- British government official

Address: b. c/o United Kingdom Delegation to the United Nations, 350 5th Ave., New York 1, N.Y.; h. 17 S. Eaton Pl., London, S.W. 1, England; Faun's Green, Egham Hill, Surrey, England

Great Britain's permanent delegate to the United Nations is Sir Pierson Dixon who succeeded Sir Gladwyn Jebb in March 1954. A foreign service career man since 1929, Sir Pierson holds the rank of Ambassador in his new post. He became principal private secretary to Foreign Secretary Anthony Eden in 1943, attended the Allied conferences at Casablanca, Yalta, Cairo, Quebec, Moscow, and Potsdam, and was private secretary to the late Foreign Secretary Ernest Bevin from 1945 to 1947. From 1948 to 1950 he was Ambassador to Czechoslovakia which gave him firsthand experience behind the "iron curtain."

In mid-1950 Sir Pierson was called back to London to become Deputy Under Secretary of State for political affairs, and later for economic affairs in the Foreign Office. Long interested in classical scholarship and archaeology, he is the author of *Farewell, Catullus* (1953), a novel of imperial Rome, and *The Iberians of Spain and Their Relations with the Aegean World.*

On taking office as United Kingdom representative, Sir Pierson voiced the hope that the United Nations could live up to the ideals of its founders. "We have a unique opportunity to win the struggle for peace and security," he declared. On April 8, 1954 he joined with representatives of the United States and France in urging a general discussion of Jewish-Arab differences rather than continued debate in the Security Council on individual incidents of "acts of hostility."

One of four children, Pierson John Dixon was born on November 13, 1904 at Englefield Green, Surrey, England, and is named after his father, a landowner. (His mother was Helen Barbara Beales before her marriage. Dr. A. D. Dixon, formerly of the Indian Civil Service, is his brother.) The Dixons later resided in Bedfordshire, where Pierson attended Bedford School from 1916 to 1923.

Entering Pembroke College, Cambridge University, he received first class honors in both parts of the classical tripos and was awarded the Montague Butler prize for an original poem. His epic *Corcyra,* written in the manner of Virgil and attacking dictatorship, was published in 1925. Dixon received the Stewart of Rannock scholarship, the Craven scholarship and the Porson prize. He held the title of Beatson scholar when elected to a fellowship at Pembroke shortly after receiving his B.A. in 1927. While an undergraduate he played Rugby football and rowed in the college "eights."

After working during the summer of 1927 in the United States as a manual laborer in a national park in Wyoming, Dixon entered the British School of Archaeology in Athens under a Craven studentship. The scholar taught classical studies at Pembroke in 1928-1929. During this period he studied at the Sorbonne and the

SIR PIERSON DIXON

Ecole des Sciences Politiques. Dixon received the M.A. degree from Cambridge in 1932. For about three years, beginning in 1929, he reviewed books for *The Times* of London and the *Times Literary Supplement.*

The Civil Service certificate as a third secretary in the Foreign Office was granted to him on October 11, 1929. Dixon served in London until Novemebr 10, 1932, when he was transferred to the British embassy at Madrid. Stationed at Ankara, Turkey, Dixon remained there approximately two years as a second secretary. He was assigned on February 24, 1938 to Rome, and later became an acting first secretary.

His first book, *The Iberians of Spain and Their Relations with the Aegean World* (Oxford University Press, 1940), considered the influence of Greek art on that of the so-called "Golden Age" of Iberian civilization. In 1941 he accompanied Foreign Secretary Eden on the mission to the Middle East, Greece and Turkey that led to the dispatch of the British expeditionary force to Greece. Dixon acted as chargé d'affaires to the Greek government in London in the latter part of 1941; and for several months served on the staff of Harold Macmillan, the British minister resident at Allied Forces Mediterranean Headquarters at Algiers.

Returning to the Foreign Office, Dixon handled problems of the anticipated surrender of Italy. His promotion to acting counsellor and principal private secretary to Foreign Secretary Eden became effective on November 26, 1943. He accomapnied Eden to the Yalta, Cairo, Quebec, Moscow, and Potsdam conferences. He was with (Sir) Winston Churchill in Italy in August 1944 when Tito came to Naples for his first meeting with a western statesman; in Athens in 1944 on a mission which helped to save Greece from the Communists; and on D-Day when the Allied leaders revealed their

DIXON, SIR PIERSON—*Continued*

plans to General Charles de Gaulle. Dixon attended the United Nations organizational conference at San Francisco in 1945.

When Bevin replaced Eden as Foreign Secretary in 1945 Dixon was retained as private secretary. He accompanied his chief to the foreign ministers' meeting held at Paris in the summer of 1946, and in the following year participated in discussions on United States aid to Europe.

The designation of Pierson Dixon as Ambassador to Czechoslovakia prompted a tribute in *The Times* of London. "For four years Mr. Dixon has had the job that is probably the most strenuous in the Foreign Office. . . . He has been at the inner heart of affairs without a break, attending the war conferences and all the international conferences since then. There was never an end to the work; after the routine sessions of the conferences came private talks among the foreign ministers, often until the early hours, and then reports to be sent off home. Both Mr. Eden and Mr. Bevin relied on his powers of judgment and his unflagging efficiency."

The diplomat received his formal appointment as Ambassador Extraordinary and Minister Plenipotentiary at Prague on January 20, 1948. His experience in Czechoslovakia included the Communist coup of February 1948 and the closing by the Klement Gottwald Government of the British Information Services. Like the American Ambassador, he "was accused of plotting against the Red regime" (New York *Herald Tribune*, November 29, 1953).

The Ambassador was created a Knight Commander of St. Michael and St. George on January 1, 1950. He succeeded Sir Gladwyn Jebb as Deputy Under Secretary of State for political affairs and head of the international organization department of the Foreign Office on June 5, 1950. At this time he was also named United Kingdom representative on the Brussels Treaty Permanent Commission with the rank of Ambassador.

Sir Pierson was the British delegate at the Atlantic Treaty Council meetings in 1950, 1951, 1952, and 1953, and visited the United States for conferences in September 1951 and March 1953. He signed the three-power memorandum on Trieste in May 1952, and in July of the year following (having meanwhile become Deputy Under Secretary of State for economic affairs) he headed his country's delegation to the Anglo-Italian economic committee.

He has written articles on shooting and stalking for such periodicals as *Country Life* and *The Field.* His novel *Farewell, Catullus* (Hollis & Carter) was published in 1953 and concerned the Roman poet and the corrupt society of which he was a part. "Sir Pierson Dixon appears to have drawn upon a great many sources . . . but chiefly upon the evidence of the poems" (London *Times*).

On November 23, 1953 the Foreign Office announced that in March 1954 Sir Pierson would succeed Sir Gladwyn as Permanent United Kingdom Delegate to the United Nations. (Sir Gladwyn was appointed British Ambassador to France to succeed Sir Oliver Harvey.) The New York *Times* (November 24, 1953) noted that Sir Pierson's "debating style . . . will differ from Sir Gladwyn's," but should be "no less effective." An editorial in the same newspaper commented: "It is a tribute to the importance with which the United Nations . . . is regarded that men of this caliber are sent to this post."

On April 9, 1954 Sir Pierson proposed that the U.N. Disarmament Commission set up a subcommittee which would hold closed-door discussions of the atomic disarmament problem, and would report back to the commission by July 15. Referring to the seriousness of the situation because of the development of the hydrogen bomb, he stated, "My government believes that no effort should be spared in this task of trying to devise a disarmament program under effective controls. We can contribute to these goals if we can talk together in private about practical problems, try to see each other's viewpoints and to narrow the difference between us."

He married Alexandra Ismene Atchley, daughter of Shirley C. Atchley, in 1928. They have a son, Piers, and two daughters, Jennifer (Mrs. Peter Blaker) and Corinna. The diplomat attends Church of England services. He is a member of the Marlborough-Windham Club, and enjoys tennis, swimming and shooting. Sir Pierson is five feet ten inches in height, weighs 140 pounds and has blue eyes and auburn-colored hair.

The diplomat was made a Companion of St. Michael and St. George in 1945, a Companion of the Order of the Bath in 1948, and an honorary fellow of Pembroke College in 1951. The foreign service officer has been characterized in the New York *Times* as "a scholar, quiet and reflective in manner, and with an incisive mind."

Sir Pierson believes that there is no hesitation in Britain or the United States to "fight for our way of life" but that the "essence" of the West's current problem is "how to safeguard our way of life and see that it is maintained without matters coming to the issue of arms" (New York *Herald Tribune*, April 30, 1954).

References

Christian Sci Mon p2 N 24 '53
London Times p14 Je 25 '27
N Y Herald Tribune p1 N 24 '53 por; II p1 N 29 '53 por
N Y Times p1 N 24 '53 por
Author's and Writer's Who's Who (1948-49)
Burke's Peerage, Baronetage, and Knightage (1953)
Debrett's Peerage, Baronetage, Knightage and Companionage (1953)
International Who's Who, 1953
International Year Book & Statesmen's Who's Who, 1953
Kelly's Handbook to the Titled, Landed and Official Classes, 1951
Who's Who, 1953
World Biography (1948)

DODGE, CLEVELAND E(ARL) Feb. 5, 1888- Business and foundation executive

Address: b. 40 Wall St., New York 5; h. "Greyston," Riverdale-on-Hudson, New York 71

Vice-president and director of Phelps Dodge Corporation, Cleveland E. Dodge represents the fifth generation of his family in this copper dealing firm. He also follows ancestral tradition in philanthropic services promoting public welfare. One of the founders in 1930, of the Near East Foundation, and president until July 1953, Dodge is currently executive committee chairman. He is also chairman of the executive committee of the YMCA of New York City, which he served as president from 1925 to 1935, and of the Protestant Council of the City of New York, in which he held the presidency from 1943 to 1950. The industrialist was head of the Woodrow Wilson Foundation in 1940.

On January 29, 1954 the National Council of Churches of Christ in the U.S.A. announced that Cleveland E. Dodge, had been named 1954 Protestant "Layman of the Year." He received the national Russell Colgate Distinguished Service Citation, given annually for outstanding achievement in Christian education, in Cincinnati at the annual meeting of the Council's Division of Christian Education on February 8.

Cleveland Earl Dodge was born in New York City on February 5, 1888, the son of Cleveland Hoadley and Grace (Parish) Dodge. His father was graduated from Princeton University in the class of 1879 with Woodrow Wilson, and was an intimate friend of the late president of the United States. An aunt, Grace Hoadley Dodge, played an important part in the founding of Teachers College, Columbia University. His twin brother, Bayard Dodge, is president-emeritus of the American University of Beirut in Lebanon.

Dodge received his elementary and secondary school education at the private Browning School in New York City, which he entered when he was about eight years of age and continued there until he went to college. He believes he benefited from the school's efforts to offer students some knowledge of the "manual arts" through visits to factories and industrial plants. He was a member of the school's debating team.

Entering Princeton University in 1905, he majored in what was then called "the department of politics, history, and economics." Explaining that Woodrow Wilson was president of Princeton "during all my four years there," Dodge recalls that Wilson "used to give the lectures in politics." Dodge received his A.B. degree from Princeton University in 1909.

Beginning a business career in 1910 with the Phelps Dodge Corporation, where four generations of his family had preceded him, Dodge rose to the office of vice-president in 1924. During World War I, from 1917-1919, he served as an officer in the 304th Field Artillery, 77th Division, United States Army. In the next year, he began a second career—that of philanthropist—and accepted the post of trustee, and shortly after of treasurer, of the Near East Relief. This organization, largely established and supported by the elder Dodge, helped to build good will and understanding by its aid to the Near East; it was succeeded by the Near East Foundation in 1930.

Fabian Bachrach

CLEVELAND E. DODGE

Dodge was named president of the YMCA of New York City in 1925, and held this office ten years. "The Association," he states, "does a great deal to give the kind of help to young men in character-building and in educational courses they require to get ahead in a job." During his presidency, he promoted a survey that revealed the need for more recreational centers for young men, resulting in a campaign which raised over $5,000,000 to expand the work of the metropolitan YMCA.

When the Near East Foundation was incorporated in 1930, Dodge, an original founder, was elected president. His task was to help plan the kind of aid the foundation gives to Near Eastern countries, upon invitation of their governments, to help the people help themselves. He encouraged the foundation's activities in Greece, Syria and Iran, where use is made of native resources to improve agriculture, home and child welfare, health, literacy and the training of leaders in such fields. The basic policies of this program were followed by the United States Technical Cooperation Administration under the "Point Four" plan.

As vice-president of Phelps Dodge Corporation, in 1932 Dodge led a protective tariff fight on copper imports coming into the United States, declaring that "foreign output had not been reduced as radically" as this country's, during a period of surplus stocks and world overproduction. He expressed the belief that ultimate improvement in the situation could come only from "increased consumption" (New York *Times*, April 20, 1932).

(Continued next page)

DODGE, CLEVELAND E.—*Continued*

At the ceremony on January 16, 1933, marking fifty years of service of the YMCA of New York City, Dodge affirmed that "changed conditions" were in part "responsible for increased delinquency" among youth, and partly defended parents against charges that they were not training their children properly. "Today," he said, "parents must try to create artificially the surroundings natural in rural or semi-rural committees where wholesome work and play opportunities abound" (New York *Times,* January 17, 1933).

Dodge was one of the leading businessmen in April 1935 who concurred with the proposal of the New York State Chamber of Commerce that Congress provide a nonpolitical national banking and currency commission to study the reorganizing and modernizing of the country's banking system. Speaking at the annual meeting of the Phelps Dodge Corporation, he favored the National Recovery Administration Copper Code, and urged its continuance "at least until surplus copper stocks in the United States could be liquified" (New York *Times,* April 17, 1935).

The philanthropist was made chairman of the executive committee of the YMCA of New York City in 1935, after serving ten years as the association's president. He was the recipient of the annual award in 1940 of the Hundred Year Association of New York, Inc. for his "outstanding service to the City of New York." Upon accepting the medal, he declared that hard work, individual effort and saving money were virtues that "must become accepted again if the country is to continue to prosper" (New York *Herald Tribune,* March 15, 1940).

Dodge became president of the Woodrow Wilson Foundation in 1940, and has been a trustee many years. Under his leadership, in 1950 the foundation began a study to relate the domestic and foreign policies of the United States in order to promote the "full and effective functioning" of the government in world affairs (New York *Times,* September 11, 1950). That same year the foundation presented an award to President Harry S. Truman for his efforts in strengthening the United Nations, and gave to the archives of the United Nations the Woodrow Wilson Memorial Library of the records of the League of Nations.

Upon the formation in New York City in 1941 of the Interdenominational Committee for Religious Education on Released Time, Dodge was elected chairman. He reported in February 1943 that 100,000 public school children in New York City were being released by the state legislature for one hour, one day each week, for instruction in their religious faiths in nearby churches. "A democracy cannot prosper without religion," he said (New York *Times,* February 5, 1943).

Cleveland E. Dodge became president in 1943 of the newly organized Protestant Council of the City of New York, including more than 1,000 Protestant churches in the city's five boroughs. He declared that "every Protestant church, educational and welfare activity in the city will be given new life through the coordinating efforts of the Council" (New York *Times,* June 30, 1944). In 1950, he was chosen executive committee chairman of the organization.

In March 1947 Dodge accepted the chairmanship of the executive committee of the New York City division of the YMCA World Youth Fund, a section of an extensive campaign in the U.S. and Canada to finance the restoration of YMCA installations in twenty-two war-devastated countries. That same year he served as vice-chairman of the Protestant Fund of Greater New York, established in September 1946 by the Protestant Council of the City of New York and the Federation of Protestant Welfare Agencies to coordinate the financing of religious, educational, and welfare efforts of the city, particularly those benefiting children. Dodge declared that an outstanding need of the city was "a more adequate program for religious education" (New York *Times,* April 10, 1947).

Dodge terminated his presidency of the Near East Foundation on July 1, 1953 to become chairman of the board of directors. "My duties are essentially unchanged," he stated, "in spite of the technical variation in title." He assists in planning the policies, budget, and projects of the foundation. The philanthropist is the author of "Mediterranean Demonstration" (*Survey,* August 1944), and "Activities for Men" (*Recreation,* January 1934).

As a business leader, Dodge believes "it is a healthy trend that corporations are feeling more obligations for public welfare." He affirms that "most business men feel there ought to be a direct connection between corporation gifts and the direct benefits to present or future employes, in the form of education, hospitals, better housing, or other aids."

New York University awarded him an honorary Doctor of Laws degree in June 1952, citing that Dodge ". . . humbly regarding private means as a public trust ever since his undergraduate days at Princeton, has adorned the family tradition with his liberal patronage of numerous agencies of human welfare." At the ceremony marking the 100th anniversary of the YMCA of New York City on June 3, 1953, he received the gold key of the Order of the Red Triangle.

He is a director of the City Bank Farmers Trust Company of New York City, the National City Bank of New York, the Southern Pacific Company, the Merchants Refrigerating Company, the B. F. Goodrich Company, the Brooklyn Bridge Freezing and Cold Storage Company and a trustee of the Atlantic Mutual Insurance Company. He is chairman of the board of trustees of Teachers College, Columbia University, a trustee of the Grant Foundation and the American Museum of Natural History and a director of the Greater New York Fund. From 1941 to 1945 he served as alumni trustee of Princeton University. His memberships include the American Institute of Mining and Metallurgical Engineers and the Mining and Metallurgical Society of America of which he was president in 1937. He is a Democrat and a Presbyterian. His clubs are the Union, Downtown, University and Sleepy Hollow.

Dodge married Pauline Morgan in 1919, and their children are Elizabeth, Cleveland E. Jr., and Joan. The philanthropist, who has blue eyes and wavy graying hair, is of slender build, stands six feet one-half inches tall, and weighs 194 pounds. He says the best way to meet the stress of modern living is with "a good education, hard work, and good character."

References

Who's Who, 1953
Who's Who in America, 1952-53
Who's Who in Commerce and Industry (1953)
Who's Who in New York, 1952
World Biography (1948)

DONEGAN, HORACE W(ILLIAM) B(ADEN), RT. REV. May 17, 1900- Clergyman

Address: b. Synod House, Cathedral Heights, New York 25; h. The Bishop's House, Cathedral Heights, New York 25

When Horace W. B. Donegan was formally installed as twelfth Bishop of the Protestant Episcopal Diocese of New York on November 18, 1950, succeeding Bishop Charles K. Gilbert, he said: "The church . . . must support the measures being taken by the United Nations to resist aggression, that all who love liberty may be secure in a free world" (New York *Times,* November 19, 1950). As head of the largest and wealthiest Protestant Episcopal diocese in the United States, he administers the activities of more than 450 clergymen in over 200 parishes and missions. His diocese extends approximately 4,700 square miles from New York City to Albany, and its annual income is around $10,000,000. It includes famous churches such as Trinity, in New York's financial district, and the Cathedral of St. John the Divine in New York City (which, when completed, will seat 10,000 and will be second in size only to St. Peter's Basilica in Rome, Italy.)

Speaking to Episcopal clergymen and laymen attending a conference in April 1954 on work with Puerto Ricans in New York, Bishop Donegan chided those members of his diocese who tend to regard their church as "exclusively Anglo-Saxon." He added: "Any church which has its wagon hitched to a one-cultural racial group is doomed to diminishing influence and numbers. Some don't seem to understand that all men are equal under God" (New York *Herald Tribune,* April 24, 1954). He protested on March 23, 1954, the refusal of an organization of Episcopal laymen (the Church Club) in New York to admit a Negro judge as a member, affirming that "in the Episcopal Church there was no room for prejudice based on race or creed" (New York *Times,* April 16, 1954).

Called "a broad, middle-of-the-road churchman" (*Newsweek,* November 7, 1949), Donegan has had a rapid rise in the Protestant

Dorothy Wilding Photo
BISHOP HORACE W. B. DONEGAN

Episcopal Church since his ordination as deacon in 1927, and priest in 1928. After serving as rector of St. James's Protestant Episcopal Church in New York City from 1933 to 1947, he was consecrated suffragan bishop of New York in 1947, and was unanimously elected coadjutor bishop of New York, with right of succession, in 1949.

Horace William Baden Donegan was born in Derbyshire, England, on May 17, 1900, the son of Horace George and Pembroke (Hand) Donegan. His father, a physician, died while Horace was a young boy. With his mother, he immigrated in 1910 to the United States. From an early age he attended church regularly and says he "enjoyed every minute of it" (New York *Post,* February 22, 1953). His high school education was received in Toledo, Ohio, and he attended St. Stephen's College (now Bard College), Annandale-on-Hudson, New York. He later spent approximately two years at Oxford University, England, and then entered the Episcopal Theological Seminary at Cambridge, Massachusetts, from which he received a B.D. degree in 1927. For a brief period, he studied at the Harvard University Divinity School.

Ordained a deacon in the Protestant Episcopal Church in 1927, and a priest in 1928, he fulfilled the boyhood ambition he had held with his younger brother, Harold, to enter the ministry. He served as assistant rector of All Saints Church, Worcester, Massachusetts (1927-1929), and as rector of Christ's Church, Baltimore, Maryland (1929-1933). He became rector of St. James's Protestant Episcopal Church, New York City in 1933. During the summers of 1935 and 1936, he visited Great Britain where he preached in various cathedrals and churches.

He was chosen an alternate delegate to the General Convention of the Protestant Epis-

DONEGAN, HORACE—*Continued*

copal Church in 1940. Addressing the parents in his parish on December 22, 1940, he offered ten commandments for bringing up children, including religious example and respect for each child's individuality. He warned that the parents' "own faith (or lack of it) communicated" to the children (New York *Times,* December 23, 1940). He said in his sermon on March 16, 1941, that "modern man is amazingly clever but not compassionately wise . . . we are too dependent upon our cleverness" (New York *Times,* March 17, 1941).

Dr. Donegan accepted an invitation extended by the Most Reverend William Temple, Archbishop of Canterbury and Primate of England, to visit Great Britain in the summer of 1944 as a representative of the Protestant Episcopal Church in the United States. He was appointed president of the standing committee of the Diocese of New York of the Protestant Episcopal Church in July 1946. His name was placed among the candidates for Protestant Episcopal Bishop of Rhode Island in November 1946, to succeed the Right Reverend James De Wolf Perry, but he was not elected.

He issued a statement on May 3, 1947, withdrawing his name as a candidate for the office of suffragan bishop of New York "in the interests of harmony and unity in the diocese" (New York *Herald Tribune,* May 10, 1947). However, yielding to the endorsement of both "high" and "low" church groups, he rescinded his withdrawal two days later, and on May 13, 1947, was elected to the post at the Diocesan Convention.

Following his consecration as suffragan bishop in October 27, 1947, Donegan remained in this office two years. He was then unanimously elected bishop coadjutor of the diocese, with right of succession to the bishopric upon the retirement of Right Reverend Charles K. Gilbert. When congratulating Donegan on his election, Bishop Gilbert declared that "never before in the history of the diocese has such unanimity occurred" (New York *Times,* October 26, 1949). In accepting the "sacred trust" of his new post, Donegan said it involved "far more than mere honor or privilege."

He was installed as Bishop of the Protestant Episcopal Diocese of New York on November 18, 1950 at a ceremony attended by nearly 5,000 people in the Cathedral of St. John the Divine. He assumed the outstanding problem of the diocese, which concerns shifting populations from city to suburb, leaving urban parishes with small congregations and little financial support, and overcrowding suburban churches. Some of his time is spent visiting various parishes throughout his changing diocese, helping with perplexing questions. "But he is seldom long away from the great unfinished cathedral at its hub. . . . More than 50,000 persons come to see St. John's every year on tours" (*Newsweek,* April 19, 1954).

Also interested in civic reform, Bishop Donegan appointed a committee with clergy and lay members to study the problem of young drug addicts in 1951. He called attention to "the appalling lack of adequate police protection" in New York City and to the "substandard housing." His requests for reforms brought support from civic groups such as the Citizens Union and the City Affairs Committee (New York *Post,* February 22, 1952).

Commenting upon the newspaper publicity given to the conversion to Roman Catholicism of an Episcopal Church rector in 1952 without equivalent notice of withdrawal from Romanism of a Catholic priest to enter the Episcopal Church the same year, Donegan said a "widespread erroneous notion" of conversions moving in one direction had resulted (New York *Herald Tribune,* May 25, 1953). He declared that out of 3,474 adults received into his diocese within one year, 193 had been Roman Catholics. Answering a criticism that genuine authority was lacking in the Protestant Episcopal Church, he affirmed "there is authority in the Episcopal Church, but not authoritarianism" (New York *Herald Tribune,* May 25, 1953).

The Bishop helped to draft in 1953 a list of questions contained in a statement, *A Profile of the Mayor of New York,* for use by the three leading political parties in New York City in examining and selecting Mayoralty candidates. He was one of seventeen churchmen signing a letter in February 1954 requesting the U.S. Senate to investigate "professional witnesses" and "public accusers" who "traduced" citizens (New York *Times,* February 16, 1954).

As quoted by the New York *Herald Tribune* on January 5, 1954, he expressed confidence that "a religious reawakening is in progress in the United States;" and on Palm Sunday, 1954, he declared the most "alarming feature" of modern life is "not wickedness but rather moral irresponsibility and apathy" (New York *Times,* April 12, 1954).

On April 27, 1954 the Bishop announced that a non-sectarian Community Club for the Aged would be opened at the Cathedral of St. John the Divine, where three rooms would be set aside for crafts, hobbies and recreational activities.

An advocate of "free speech in the pulpit," Bishop Donegan declared that the clergy should take a stand "on the religious and moral issues of our day." He said, however, that he did not advocate the church's indorsing political candidates or proposed legislation, but he advised clergymen: "Let there be no doubt as to where you stand with regard to right or wrong" (New York *World-Telegram and Sun,* May 11, 1954).

Bishop Donegan is the author of several articles in religious publications. He received an honorary D.D. degree from New York University in 1940, and from the University of the South in 1949. Hobart College awarded him a Doctor of Sacred Theology degree in 1948, and General Theological Seminary gave him this degree in 1949. He is a trustee of the Cathedral of St. John the Divine, the New York City Mission Society, and the New York

Chapter of the American Red Cross. He is a Mason and a member of Kappa Gamma Chi fraternity. He was named honorary vice president of Forest Neighborhood House, in New York City, in April 1954.

The Bishop is honorary president of the board of managers of the Seamen's Church Institute of New York and is vice president of the Episcopal Actors' Guild. He holds membership in the National Council of the Protestant Episcopal Church in the U.S.A., St. George's Society, The Pilgrims, and Holland Lodge. His clubs include the Union League (New York) and the National (London).

In "The Bishop's Message", published in the *Bulletin of the Diocese of New York* (May, 1954) Bishop Donegan launched an appeal for $600,000. "Funds are required," he wrote, "for new dormitories, libraries, classrooms and faculty residences at our eleven seminaries; for churches, chapels and parish houses in Japan; for new buildings, dormitories, and recreational facilities at our five Negro educational institutions in the South; for the completion of the reconstruction of buildings destroyed in Manila in World War II; for adequate accommodations at St. Just's School, Puerto Rico. . . ."

The clergyman reportedly weighs "135 pounds" and is "five feet seven" inches tall... with a bold face and steel blue eyes" and hair "close-cropped and black" (New York *Post,* February 22, 1953). He enjoys reading biography, playing and singing Gilbert and Sullivan operettas, painting landscapes in oil, and occasional golf and swimming.

On May 11, 1954 the delegates to the 173rd annual convention of the Protestant Episcopal Diocese of New York voted unanimously to reject the city of Houston, Texas, as a site for the church's next triennial general convention in 1955 unless an immediate guarantee of a completely non-segregated meeting can be given (New York *Times,* May 12, 1954). Bishop Donegan in his address to the convention said that there had never been "such a wholesome ferment within the church seeking to end segregation or exclusion on the grounds of race or color." He praised Presiding Bishop Henry Knox Sherrill's decision to hold the general convention in some other city because of racial segregation in Houston (New York *Herald Tribune,* June 10, 1954).

The decision to hold the Protestant Episcopal Convention in 1955 in the racially heterogeneous city of Honolulu, Hawaii was announced on June 18, 1954.

References

N Y Herald Tribune p28 N 19 '46; p 1 N 19 '50
N Y Post Mag p2 F 22 '53
N Y Times p16 My 14 '47; p 1 O 26 '49
Newsweek 34:75 N 7 '49; 43:71 Ap 19 '54
Time 61:60 Je 1 '53
Religious Leaders of America, 1941-42
Who's Who in America, 1954-55
Who's Who in New York, 1952
World Biography (1948)

DONOVAN, WILLIAM J(OSEPH) Jan. 1, 1883- Former United States Ambassador to Thailand; lawyer

Address: b. c/o Donovan, Leisure, Newton, & Irvine, 2 Wall Street, New York 5; h. 1 Sutton Pl. S., New York 22; Chapel Hill Farm, Berryville, Va.

NOTE: This biography supersedes the article which appeared in *Current Biography* in 1941.

The United States Ambassador to Thailand between July 1953 and September 1954 was Major General William J. Donovan, who was appointed to the post by President Eisenhower. He has a distinguished record in World War II as the organizer and director of the Office of Strategic Services (known to the public as the "cloak-and-dagger boys" who worked for United States intelligence behind enemy lines) which was the precursor of the Central Intelligence Agency. He was awarded the Congressional Medal of Honor for valor in World War I as colonel of the "Fighting 69th." During the peacetime years he practiced law in New York City and was active in New York state and national politics.

The OSS operated in five theaters of war and during the conflict Donovan became "one of the greatest spymasters of all time. His fabulous intelligence and sabotage network," wrote Frederic Sondern, Jr. (*Reader's Digest,* October 1947), "was unquestionably a vital factor in our beating the Axis as quickly as we did." Donovan sent agents into Germany, occupied France and northern Italy equipped with radios who sent out information on troop movements, bomb hits, and morale, and whose propaganda, sabotage and underground resistance won the acclaim of the late President Franklin D. Roosevelt.

"Whether we like it or not," said General Donovan, when recommending that OSS be continued after World War II as an independent intelligence agency with a civilian at the head, "we have many enemies in the world today, and we must know exactly what they are doing. . . We must counter Soviet subversive attacks and help to build resistance in countries Russia attempts to subjugate. We must take the offensive on the psychological front" (*Atlantic,* May 1948).

William Joseph Donovan was born January 1, 1883 in Buffalo, New York to Timothy P. and Anna (Lennon) Donovan. His father was a railroad yardmaster who was also active in Republican county politics. His brother, Vincent, who became a Dominican friar, attained recognition as an authority on religious art and history.

Bill Donovan attended St. Joseph's Collegiate Institute in Buffalo, Niagara University and Columbia University where he was prominent on the football team. Graduated from Columbia University with an A.B. degree in 1905, Donovan entered the university's law school. After receiving the LL.B. degree in 1907, he practiced law with the Buffalo firm of Love & Keating.

Department of State

WILLIAM J. DONOVAN

In 1912 he formed a partnership with Bradley Goodyear which later became O'Brian, Hamlin, Donovan & Goodyear.

Beginning his military career in 1912, Donovan organized Troop One of the First Cavalry, New York National Guard. With this unit he later served on the Mexican border as a captain. In 1916 he was sent by the Rockefeller Foundation to Europe to assist in relief work for Poland.

After the United States entered World War I, Donovan served with the 27th (Rainbow) Division of the American Expeditionary Force, the 51st Brigade, and, finally, with the 165th (the former 69th New York Infantry Regiment) Infantry Division. A full colonel by the time of the Meuse-Argonne operation, Donovan was awarded the nation's highest military decoration, the Congressional Medal of Honor, for his conduct in action on October 14 and 15, 1918.

Three times wounded, Donovan was one of two soldiers to receive the Congressional Medal of Honor, the Distinguished Service Cross, and the Distinguished Service Medal in World War I. He subsequently donated his Congressional Medal of Honor to his regiment. In addition, he was decorated by France and England.

Believing that the Orient would be the scene of the next major war, Donovan traveled in China, and in Siberia, as an unofficial observer of the anti-Bolshevik movement led by Admiral Aleksandr Kolchak in 1919. In the following year he resumed his law practice, and in 1922 was the Republican candidate for lieutenant governor of New York; he was defeated with Governor Nathan L. Miller by the Democratic ticket headed by Alfred E. Smith.

Appointed U.S. District Attorney for western New York in 1922, Donovan broke up a narcotics ring in seventeen counties and obtained several convictions for prohibition violations. During 1923 he served on the U.S. delegation to a customs regulations conference with Canada which drafted a treaty providing for the prosecution of international crimes. The treaty was approved by the U.S. Senate in 1925. In this period he served as a counsel to the New York Fuel Administration.

Harlan Fiske Stone, then Attorney General, appointed Donovan Assistant Attorney General in charge of criminal matters in 1924. In 1925 when Stone became an Associate Justice of the U.S. Supreme Court, Donovan was named assistant to Attorney General John G. Sargent and served in that post until 1929.

After Herbert Hoover was elected to the Presidency, he offered Donovan the governor-generalship of the Philippine Islands. However, Donovan declined the appointment and returned to the practice of law as senior partner of Donovan, Leisure, Newton & Lumbard (now Donovan, Leisure, Newton & Irvine).

Named U.S. commissioner and chairman of the Rio Grande Compact Commission in 1928, Donovan undertook similar posts on the Colorado River Commission in 1929. He was retained by the Association of the Bar of the City of New York and the New York and Bronx county bar associations as counsel in bankruptcy investigations and served as counsel to the commission for revision of the New York state public service laws.

Donovan was the Republican candidate for Governor of New York in 1932, and was decisively defeated by Herbert H. Lehman. Subsequently he became an opponent of the "New Deal." When in October 1937 the Federal government prosecuted fifty-seven oil men for alleged violations of the Sherman anti-trust act, Donovan headed the attorneys for the defense.

When the Italians invaded Ethiopia in October 1935, Donovan went to Rome and was permitted by Benito Mussolini to observe the campaign. He was again in Europe in the summer of 1938. "The Spanish Civil War was raging," Donovan wrote in *Life* (September 30, 1946). "I believed Spain to be, ideology aside, a laboratory for weapons of the next war, and I went there to observe their performance."

When Colonel Frank Knox joined the Roosevelt Cabinet as Secretary of the Navy in 1940, he sent Donovan to England as his "unofficial observer" to study British military strength and intelligence. After Donovan's return in August Secretary Knox released the series of five articles by Donovan and Edgar Ansel Mowrer which were published in various newspapers (as well as in pamphlet form by the American Council on Public Affairs) under the title *Fifth Column Lessons for America.*

From December 1940 to March 1941 Donovan was on a secret government mission in Yugoslavia, Greece and the Middle East. He observed "resistance" movements and was later accused by the Germans of having masterminded the *coup d'etat* which overthrew the regent of Yugoslavia, Prince Paul, whose government had adhered to the Axis pact in 1941.

"Upon my return," wrote Donovan, "Roosevelt called me to Washington and asked me to draft a plan for a new intelligence service cut to fit a global war. 'You will have to begin with nothing,' he said in effect. 'We have no intelligence service.'" Subsequently Colonel Donovan was appointed coordinator of information, a civilian post in which he reported to the President, and analyzed and correlated intelligence.

On June 13, 1942 the Office of Strategic Services was created by executive order and Donovan was appointed its director. Unlike its successor, the OSS was a military agency responsible to the Joint Chiefs of Staff. It was charged with providing "a secret intelligence service working behind enemy lines, sabotage, morale subversion, guerrilla organization, and aid to partisan resistance" (John Chamberlain in *Life,* November 19, 1945). Under the direction of Donovan undercover operations were set in motion. In its three years of existence the OSS employed 12,000 people and spent $135,000,000 (*Reader's Digest,* October 1947).

The OSS together with British agents and Captain Max Manus, a Norwegian resistance hero, sunk the 17,000-ton German troopship *Donau* which aided in preventing Nazi reinforcements from reaching the Battle of the Bulge. From Gorgona, Capraia and Elba, advanced spy units informed the Allied air forces concerning German ship movements and directed the bombing of oil installations on the Italian mainland. About six months before Rome fell, OSS officers had infiltrated that city. Surrender in northern Italy came after the head of the Storm Troopers in Italy leaked a rumor to Allen W. Dulles in Switzerland that Albert Kesselring was ready to accept defeat.

From French North Africa, the OSS sent secret agents into France. They established twenty-eight active radio chains that were operating prior to D-Day. One agent mapped three-fourths of the French Mediterranean coast. Another learned the range, trajectory and location of twenty batteries on each side of Marseilles and the location of German observation posts and electric controls. Such information reaching North Africa by radio, carrier pigeon, pickup plane or couriers, helped inestimably in the preparations for the invasion of southern France.

In the autumn of 1942 twenty OSS men jumped from a plane into the northern Burmese jungle and organized the naked, monkey-eating tribe of the Kachins. The OSS-led Kachins accounted for 5,447 Japanese in the guerrilla warfare that took pressure away from the Assam-Chungking supply route. Another exploit was the rescue of the late General Jonathan M. Wainwright from a Japanese prison camp by a parachute team. The topographical maps turned out by the OSS were said to have been "preferred . . . to all others" by Prime Minister (Sir) Winston Churchill.

Donovan was promoted to the rank of brigadier general in April 1943 and to major general in November 1944. For his services during World War II he received an Oak Leaf Cluster to his Distinguished Service Medal, rank of honorary Knight Commander of the Order of the British Empire, commander of the French Legion of Honor, Italian Order of the Crown, Santi Mala Medal and first class rank in the Most Exalted Order of the White Elephant from Siam, and the Papal Lateran Medal and Order of St. Sylvester. He was the recipient of the Alexander Hamilton Medal by the Alumni Association of Columbia College, and the Buffalo University Chancellor's Medal.

On October 1, 1945 the Office of Strategic Services was terminated by executive order and its functions were distributed to the Department of State and the War Department. Because of its activities the OSS was able to assemble a large part of the evidence against Nazi war criminals. General Donovan was appointed to aid Supreme Court Justice Robert H. Jackson in the Nürnberg war crimes trials.

He resigned shortly afterwards to resume his law practice. In August 1946 Donovan was retained as legal counsel by Siam in a border dispute with French Indochina. In February 1947, when the Army Officers Reserve was activated, Donovan was one of the first group of general officers to be assigned to it.

Strongly in favor of the Marshall plan even before it "became concrete on December 19, 1947," General Donovan contributed to the *Atlantic* (May, 1948) an article entitled "Stop Russia's Subversive War" in which he characterized the European Recovery Program as "vital" to the combatting of "an enemy who is in this for keeps." As chairman of the American Committee on United Europe, he made a number of speeches advocating a Western European Union. Later he described the Schuman plan as "the linchpin of the United Europe" (*Atlantic,* February 1952).

Speaking on August 25, 1952 to 1,200 former and present commanders of the American Legion, Donovan called the Truman Administration's policy of "containment" "a futile strategy which betrays an ignorance of the nature of the enemy." He set forth proposals for undercover work and urged that technical aid to other nations be increased so that the United States could win allies against Russia (New York *Herald Tribune,* August 26, 1952).

General Donovan returned to government service through nomination by President Dwight D. Eisenhower on July 29, 1953 as the Ambassador to Thailand and his appointment was confirmed by the Senate. He was sworn into office on August 12. Donovan recalls that during World War II, forty Americans and forty Siamese were dropped by parachute into Siam, which the Japanese occupied. They sent intelligence to Allied forces (New York *Herald Tribune,* August 26, 1952).

It was announced on February 13, 1954 that the United States would increase the size of its Military Assistance Advisory Group in Thailand by one-third. Thailand attributed this increase to the efforts of Ambassador Donovan. Later that year Joseph and Stewart Alsop (New York *Herald Tribune,* June 21, 1954) reported that the Ambassador was urging the formation of a federation of Thailand, Laos

DONOVAN, WILLIAM J.—*Continued*

and Cambodia to form a common defense against communist attack or infiltration.

General Donovan resigned as Ambassador to Thailand on September 15, 1954 and was succeeded by John E. Peurifoy.

The Ambassador is a member of the American, New York state, and District of Columbia bar associations, the American Law Institute and the Association of the Bar of the City of New York. He belongs to Phi Delta Phi and Phi Kappa Psi. His clubs are the Buffalo, in Buffalo, New York; University, Metropolitan and Chevy Chase in Washington, D.C.; and River, University and Cedar Creek in New York. Donovan is also a director of the American Cancer Society.

To the honorary LL.D. degrees conferred on Donovan by Niagara University (1919), University of Notre Dame (1929) and Syracuse University (1931) was added in June 1947, an LL.D. from Columbia University for "directing with imagination and deadly efficiency the men who fought in the shadows" in World War II, as well as in recognition of his legal and other activities.

Donovan married Ruth Rumsey of Buffalo on July 14, 1914. They have a son, David Rumsey. Their daughter, Patricia, is deceased. The Ambassador is a Latin scholar and reads an average of three books a week on war, politics or economics. He has a good baritone voice, enjoys watching baseball and prize fights, and likes walking. Donovan is a little under six feet in height and has been described as stocky and muscular. His eyes are blue; his hair gray. During the war he usually worked eighteen hours a day and his enthusiasm was quickly communicated to his associates. "His men would have cheerfully gone to hell with him," Father Duffy, chaplain of the 69th once said. "And as a priest, I mean what I say."

There are conflicting stories as to why Donovan was nicknamed "Wild Bill"; one refers to his prowess on the football field; another to his daring in battle.

References (see also references listed in 1941 biographical sketch)

Atlan 181:27 My '48; 189:58 F '52
Christian Sci Mon Mag p6 Mr 29 '41 pors
Collier's 116:12+ O 6 '45 por
Life 19:118+ N 19 '45 pors; 21:108+ S 30 '46
N Y Herald Tribune X p2 F 2 '41 por; II p3 Je 10 '45 por; p27 Ap 15 '46
N Y Times p4 My 17 '45 por; VI p12 O 7 '45 por; p7 F 8 '47; p22 Je 4 '47
Read Digest 51:67+ O '47 por
Time 46:23 O 1 '45 por; 47:24 F 4 '46; 62:18 Ag 10 '53

American Catholic Who's Who, 1948-49
Martindale-Hubbell Law Directory, 1952
National Cyclopedia of American Biography Current Volume G, 1943-46
Who's Who, 1954
Who's Who in America, 1954-55
Who's Who in Law, 1937
World Biography (1954)

DOYLE, ADRIAN (MALCOLM) CONAN

Nov. 19, 1910- Explorer; author

Address: 60 Quai Gustave Ador, Geneva, Switzerland; Box 180, British P.O., Tangier, Morocco

The youngest of the surviving sons of Sir Arthur Conan Doyle, author of the Sherlock Holmes detective stories and novels, is Adrian Conan Doyle, who is the principal administrator of his late father's literary properties. He is also known as a big-game hunter and fisherman, zoologist and explorer. He is the coauthor, with John Dickson Carr, of *The Exploits of Sherlock Holmes*, twelve reconstructions of Sherlock Holmes tales, each of which takes its beginning from a reference to the case in the original Holmes stories. They were published in *Life* and in *Collier's* in 1952 and 1953 prior to publication in book form in March 1954 by Random House.

"By sticking strictly to the original ingredients and prose style of Sir Arthur Conan Doyle," commented *Time* (April 5, 1954) "authors Carr and Doyle [in *Exploits*] have handled the job very well. But only Sir Arthur's ghost is likely to be really critical of this loving attempt to relight the master's dottles." They have attempted, said *Life*, "one of the most difficult literary feats in the world." Doyle is also the author of *Heaven Has Claws* (1953), an account of an expedition he made in 1950 to the Indian Ocean in quest of rare marine specimens.

Born near Crowborough in Sussex, England on November 19, 1910, Adrian Malcolm Conan Doyle was the second of the three children of Sir Arthur Conan Doyle and his second wife, Lady Doyle, the former Jean Elizabeth Leckie. (Sir Arthur had one son, the late Captain Kingsley Conan Doyle, and one daughter, Mary Conan Doyle, by an earlier marriage).

Adrian's brother, Denis Percy Stewart, is his senior by about eighteen months; their sister is Lena Jean Annette. They are descended on the paternal side from Irish Catholic landed gentry.

Adrian passed nearly all his earlier years at Windlesham, the family's five-gabled manor house near Crowborough. For a short time he attended a "preparatory" (private grade) school away from home, but was prepared for matriculation at Cambridge University by a tutor. He passed the entrance examinations, but instead of going into residence at Cambridge in 1928, accompanied his parents on a visit to South Africa, Rhodesia and Kenya.

"I have been influenced only by my father's encouragements," Adrian Conan Doyle has written in response to a *Current Biography* query regarding his choice of work and avocations; and indeed the bond appears to have been very close between Sir Arthur and the offspring of his very happy second marriage. John Dickson Carr has noted in his 1949 biography that Sir Arthur changed perceptibly from the heavy Victorian to the mere companionable Georgian type of parent. Carr recorded that when Adrian was not yet six years old and near death from pneumonia, the father fired the little boy's will to live by showing him pictures of mediaeval knights in armor and recounting the story of the battle of Agincourt.

Another incident is recounted by the biographer; during the 1928 trip to Africa, young Adrian happened to use the word "ugly" in connection with a certain lady, and was reprimanded with a sharp blow followed by the paternal injunction to remember henceforward that "no woman is ugly." The youngest of the Doyle sons also shared his father's mediaevalist hobbies and his enthusiasm for sport, including fishing and hunting; in late youth, furthermore, he developed a passion for automobile racing. In the months following the South African trip, Adrian would frequently "take his 70-year-old father on 120-mile an hour jaunts around the racetrack" (*Life*, March 22, 1948). "From 1928 to 1938," Adrian Conan Doyle writes, "I drove in more than one hundred International Motor Races and speed events."

He was married to Anna Anderson on May 23, 1938, and made with his wife in that year "an expedition into the German Cameroons to try and capture live specimens of the hairy frog which had never been brought into captivity." "We succeeded," he adds, "and the specimens were presented to the London Zoological Gardens." The following year (1939) Adrian and Anna Doyle planned a five-year expedition to the Pacific to secure specimens of marine life, but this project was abandoned after the outbreak of World War II, during which he served in the Royal Navy.

Sir Arthur died on July 7, 1930 and left his estate to Lady Doyle. With her subsequent death and the probating in April 1941 of her will, the administration of the Sherlock Holmes and other literary properties passed to a family trust known as The Sir Arthur Conan Doyle Estates, and Adrian Conan Doyle became their principal executor.

Adrian Doyle described his father's personal powers of deduction in a letter to the London *Times* (October 28, 1943) in which he wrote: "My father had a mind with all the characteristics of a microscope," he wrote, adding that while Dr. Joseph Bell (the Edinburgh medical professor upon whom Sherlock Holmes was admittedly largely modelled) "did indeed help to develop" his father's "immense powers of observation . . . it must be placed on record that those powers were indubitably innate." ("For the mental prototype of Sherlock Holmes," he asserted, "we need search no farther than his creator").

This letter was followed up some time later by Adrian Conan Doyle's brief monograph *The True Conan Doyle*, which was published by Murray in London in 1945 and by Coward-McCann in New York in 1946, and to which General Sir Hubert Gough contributed a preface.

In the spring of 1948, Adrian Conan Doyle and his wife were living in the New Forest

Madame Yevonde

ADRIAN CONAN DOYLE

area of Hampshire, and it was here that a photographer for *Life* found him expressing "disgust with modern civilization, politics, the Labor government and contemporary British sports" by tilting in mediaeval armor with his friend Douglas Ash. This revolt against the conditions of post-war life in England prompted Doyle and his wife to make a year-long trip through France, Switzerland, Italy and Sicily before they acted on the advice of Denis Conan Doyle to take up residence in Tangier, Morocco.

At Tangier the younger Doyle was frequently visited by the American-born mystery novelist John Dickson Carr, who was then preparing the new *Life of Sir Arthur Conan Doyle* which was published in the United States by Harper and Brothers later in 1949. It was at Tangier, too, that Doyle was inspired, through news of huge shark and manta ray observed off the Seychelles Islands, to organize with his wife, and his secretary Corneille Benoist, and some friends, an expedition to the Indian Ocean in search of rare big-game fish which began in 1950. (For various reasons the expedition was diverted to the waters off Mafia Island). In the Kinasi Pass, Doyle caught a *Carcharodon Carcharias*, or as the Australians term it, the White Death shark, one of the most ferocious killers of the deep. It was about twelve feet long, was nearly six feet in girth and weighed 1,360 pounds. He and his wife caught and photographed many types of rare fish, broke the eighty-pound test line record, and filmed the ruins of an ancient palace on the island of Songa Manara.

Their next safari will be for larger sharks and giant manta ray in the Arabian Sea where they plan to photograph them at a depth of twenty-five feet.

(Continued next page)

DOYLE, ADRIAN CONAN—*Continued*

Doyle's book *Heaven Has Claws* (Random House, 1953) describes this expedition. John Barkham of the New York *Times* wrote that it was "one of the most exciting chronicles of adventure to be published in many a month," while Bernard Kalb of the *Saturday Review* found it "crammed with fascinating fish talk." E. F. Walbridge, reviewing it for the *Library Journal,* noted that the book "literally deals with some very queer fish" and was "rife with *noblesse oblige.*"

A popular attraction at the 1951 Festival of Britain was the "reproduction" of a room (with carefully selected furnishings) which Adrian Doyle and the librarian C. T. Thorne achieved for the Borough Council of St. Marylebone of Sherlock Holmes's celebrated quarters at 221B Baker Street. (The street is actually located in London but the number 221B is, of course, wholly imaginary although many visitors to London inquire about it.)

The exhibition was later transferred to the Plaza Art Galleries in New York City, where it was on view for several weeks beginning July 2, 1952.

Adrian Doyle accompanied the exhibition to America, where John Dickson Carr was then residing, and the two resumed the discussion of a project they had conceived some time previously of collaborating on a new series of Holmes stories to be entitled *The Exploits of Sherlock Holmes,* and which, in addition to reproducing as closely as possible Sir Arthur Conan Doyle's style, would be scrupulously true to the late nineteenth century in every detail.

They worked together at odd moments through the late summer of 1952 and subsequently also at Tangier, with the result that the first story in the new series, "The Adventure of the Seven Clocks," was published in *Life,* December 29, 1952. A full account of the method of collaboration, was described in the article by Herbert Brean entitled "How Holmes Was Reborn" in the same issue of *Life.*

Subsequent stories in the "first series" of *Exploits* were given pre-book form publication in successive weekly numbers of *Collier's* beginning May 23, 1953. The first of the *Collier's* stories, "The Adventure of the Black Baronet," was also seen in dramatic form on the *Suspense* television program on May 26, with Basil Rathbone in the role of Sherlock Holmes.

Joseph Henry Jackson in the San Francisco *Chronicle,* March 17, 1954 commented on the "new" Sherlock Holmes stories: "Both reconstructors have taken pains. . . . Yet it is not quite enough. Try as you like, you can't quite 'be' someone else; and neither the able Mr. Carr nor the original author's own son quite makes it. . . . But general readers, as well as the dyed-in-the-wool fans, will make up their own minds."

Jackson made the point that in comparing the *Exploits* with the original Holmes stories "something depends upon whether you compare . . . with the early or with the 'middle' Holmes. As was said at the time, when Sir Arthur yielded to public clamor after killing off Holmes, and brought him back to life again, Holmes was never quite the same afterward." Of the twelve tales, the two that seemed to Jackson best are "The Adventure of the Highgate Miracle" and "The Adventure of the Sealed Room."

Vincent Starrett in the *Chicago Sunday Tribune* (April 4, 1954) commented: "Pastiches have their own interest, however. They keep 'the game afoot' and best of all, they lead the reader back to the great works themselves. All the great heros have their apocrypha. Not all the king's horses could persuade me to say that these uncanonical tales compete successfully with the authentic adventures of Sherlock Holmes; but no Sherlockian should dismiss them without a reading. . . . There is a certain satisfaction in seeing the old master stride across the page again, even if he is not in his best form."

Doyle is a Fellow of the London Zoological Society, is a member of the Authors' Club and the Brooklands Automobile Racing Club in England, and the Tangier Diplomatic Club and the Automobile Club du Maroc in northern Africa. He is just over six feet in height and weighs about 190 pounds; he has grey eyes and brown hair. He collects keys from mediaeval castles and cathedrals and also enjoys oil painting.

References

Life 24:42+ Mr 22 '48 pors; 33:62+ D 29 '52 por

Carr, J. D. Life of Sir Arthur Conan Doyle (1949)

Doyle, A. C. Heaven Has Claws (1953)

DU PONT, PIERRE SAMUEL Jan. 15, 1870-Apr. 5, 1954 Industrialist; philanthropist; helped organize E. I. du Pont de Nemours & Co., Inc.; became its treasurer, vice-president, president (1915-1919), chairman of board (1919-1940), and honorary chairman (1940-1954); served as board chairman of General Motors; active in Delaware government as member of State Board of Education (1919-1921), tax commissioner (1925-1937, 1944-1949), and liquor commissioner (1933-1938); built schools for Negro and white children; improved public highways; supported Association Against the Prohibition Amendment; aided war veterans and universities. See *Current Biography,* (Sept.) 1940.

Obituary

N Y Times p29 Ap 6 '54

DURGIN, C(ALVIN) T(HORNTON) Jan. 7, 1893- Maritime college president; former United States Navy officer

Address: b. New York State Maritime College, Fort Schuyler, New York 61

The oldest maritime school in the country, the New York State Maritime College, is headed by Vice Admiral C. T. Durgin, U.S. Navy (retired), who has had thirty-five years of active naval service. He succeeded Vice Admiral Herbert Fairfax Leary in September 1951 to the presidency of the school which trains young men to become officers in the American Merchant Marine and the U.S. Naval Reserve. More familiarly known as "Fort Schuyler", it is one of four State maritime academies (with college status), the other three being in Massachusetts, Maine, and California.

During the course of his naval career Durgin advanced in the air divisions to Deputy Chief of Naval Operations for Air in 1949-50, the top aviation post in the Navy. The following year he assumed command of the First Task Fleet, the main naval force in the Pacific, then served as president of the Board of Inspection and Survey in the Office of the Chief of Naval Operations from March to September, 1951.

The veteran aircraft commander was one of the few senior naval officers who engaged in carrier warfare in the Atlantic, Mediterranean and Asiatic waters during World War II. For his covering defense of troop landings at Iwo Jima and Okinawa in the Pacific area in 1945 he won the Distinguished Service Medal.

Born in Palmyra, New Jersey, on January 7, 1893, Calvin Thornton Durgin is the son of Frank L. and Sara (Bowl) Durgin. He attended public schools in his native town, then was appointed in 1912 to the U.S. Naval Academy, Annapolis, Maryland, from the Second Congressional District of New Jersey. At the Academy, he played football and was a member of the varsity lacrosse team. Graduating in 1916, he received a B.S. degree and was commissioned an ensign in the U.S. Navy.

From 1916 to 1918 Durgin was assigned consecutively to the battleships USS *Minnesota* and *Connecticut.* The following year, in addition to serving on the USS *Dixie* and USS *Kimberly* of the Destroyer Force training station at Queenstown, Ireland, he was engineer officer on the USS *Craven* at this base. He began his training for an aviation career at the Naval Air Station in Pensacola, Florida, in September 1919. Upon completing this instruction, he was designated Naval Aviator on May 27, 1920, then continued his studies at Pensacola until the following July, in order to get added knowledge of NC (Navy-Curtiss) seaplanes.

After initial flight duty at the Naval Operating Base in Hampton Roads, Virginia, Durgin began service in October 1921 with the USS *Aroostook,* flagship of Air Squadrons in the Pacific, where he remained until May 1922. He then studied aeronautical engineering at the Naval Postgraduate School at Annapolis for one year, and continued these studies at the Massachusetts Institute of Technology, where he received his M.S. degree in June 1924.

At the U.S. Naval Aircraft Factory in Philadelphia, Durgin acquired practical experience in the aeronautical engine laboratory between 1924 and 1926. He then served for the next three years with battle fleet aircraft squadrons on the carriers USS *Langley,* USS *New Mexico,* and USS *West Virginia,* acting successively as observation wing commander, observation squadron commanding officer, and staff aide to the battleship divisions commander. An important

U. S. Navy

VICE-ADM. C. T. DURGIN

assignment came to him in 1929 as fleet aviation officer on the staff of the Commander-in-Chief of the United States Fleet on the flagship USS *Texas.* One year later he went to the office of the Chief of Naval Operations, where he served in the ship movements section until 1932.

The naval officer received positions of increasing responsibility during the 1930's. After returning to sea service on the USS *Saratoga* from 1932 to 1934, he was stationed at the Naval Air Station in Norfolk, Virginia, where he became executive officer in July 1935. He served aboard the carrier *Yorktown* from her commissioning in September 1937 to May 1938. He joined the flagship USS *Wright* of the Aircraft Scouting Force as executive officer in 1938 and in 1939 became commanding officer. That same year he commanded the Utility Wing of the Pacific Fleet, attached to the USS *Rigel,* tender, until ordered in June 1940 to the Bureau of Aeronautics, where he soon became director of the flight division.

Shortly after the United States entered World War II, Durgin received command of the aircraft carrier USS *Ranger,* operating with the Atlantic Fleet. For his skillful employment of the carrier in the assault on French Morocco in November 1942 he received a Letter of Commendation with Ribbon and combat distinguishing device, *V,* from the Commander-in-Chief of the Fleet. His promotion from the rank of Captain to Rear Admiral in the United States Navy followed in February 1943.

Assigned to shore duty in March 1943, Durgin took command of Fleet Air, Quonset Point, Rhode Island. He retained this post until 1944, and was cited for his outstanding services and awarded the Legion of Merit. His citation stated "he was directly responsible for the highly successful organization, administration and training of aircraft carriers . . . in cooperation

DURGIN, VICE-ADM.—*Continued*
with Commander Fleet Operational Training Command. Atlantic Fleet."

Presenting the third Army-Navy E production award to Carl L. Norden, Inc. on April 13, 1943, before an audience of 15,000 of the company employes and their families at Madison Square Garden in New York City, Durgin stated: "Let us add star upon star to our E pennant until it becomes a star-spangled banner of awards" (New York *Times,* April 14, 1943). A few days later on April 25, 1943, he spoke at the commissioning exercises of the Navy's $8,000,000 air station at Atlantic City, New Jersey, saying that, in servicing fleet battle units, the station would "bring this war to a successful end more quickly" (New York *Times,* April 25, 1943).

Durgin provided air support for the invasion of southern France in August 1944 as the commander of a task group of United States and British carriers and lighter units from both navies operating with the Atlantic Fleet. A citation (and Gold Star) commending his services described him as "determined and aggressive in the fulfillment of a vital assignment . . . contributing materially to the early establishment of the beachhead and the rapid advance of the occupying forces." A few months later, he assumed command of the escort carrier group of the Pacific Fleet, skillfully covering the landings in Lingayen Gulf of United States forces at Mindoro and Luzon in the Philippines, and the operations against Japanese-held Iwo Jima, Okinawa, and other islands.

Durgin's ships were exposed to severe aerial attacks by the enemy, but he coordinated combat air and anti-submarine patrols and "met with his entire combat strength any threat to the amphibious operations."

At the end of the Okinawa campaign, the Navy revealed that escort carrier planes commanded by Durgin had flown 35,000 sorties, more than previously flown during World War II by this type of aircraft. Pilots flew four-hour missions daily, sometimes two totalling nine hours in the air. "That's too much," Durgin said, as quoted by the New York *Times* (June 28, 1945). He added that the durability and performance of the pilots, ships' companies, and ships were "far beyond" his expectation. "It was the kind of job we didn't know we could do," he declared. Cited as "a brilliant and courageous leader," Durgin was awarded the Distinguished Service Medal for his "meritorious services."

Immediately following the Japanese surrender, Durgin aided in the evacuation of ex-prisoners of war, and headed a mission which investigated the effects of the war on the islands of Truk. Returning to the United States in December 1945, he served briefly on the board to survey the continental naval shore establishment in the Office of the Chief of Naval Operations. In July 1946, he took command for two years of the Navy Air Bases in San Diego and San Francisco, California. His next assignment placed him as Commander of Fleet Air, Jacksonville, Florida, from November 1948 until May 1949, when he was appointed Deputy Chief of Naval Operations, the top aviation post in the Navy. With the approval of President Harry S. Truman in December 1949, Durgin was promoted to the rank of Vice Admiral, and in March 1950 the President nominated him commander of the First Fleet in the Pacific.

As head of the Pacific First Fleet task force in March 1950, Durgin left Pearl Harbor with twenty warships, 6,600 men, and a submarine and jet plane force for southeast Asia. He said: "You know what the show of our flag did to jack up democratic hopes in the Mediterranean; that's what we plan to do in the Western Pacific" (New York *Times,* May 12, 1950). A year later he returned to the Office of Chief of Naval Operations as president of the board of inspection and survey. The Maritime College was established in 1874 when the entire training was conducted aboard the former ship *St. Mary's.* The school achieved college status in 1948, when it became a part of the New York State University. It has a student body of 500 cadets.

The president of the State University of New York, Dr. Alvin C. Eurich, announced the appointment of Admiral Durgin as head of the New York State Maritime College on March 7, 1951. He assumed the presidency on September 1, 1951 after his retirement from the Navy.

The Maritime College operates a 6,000 ton twin screw vessel, *Empire State,* which takes 400 cadets on ten-week training cruises, making stops at many foreign ports.

Admiral Durgin was asked by the House Merchant Marine subcommittee on March 3, 1954 whether the federally-supported United States Merchant Marine Academy at Kings Point, New York should be continued. Admiral Durgin replied that he was not advocating the closing of "Kings Point" and if asked "yes or no" whether he thought it should close, he would say "no." He said, however, that he considered such education to be in the province of state or private schools, as in other technical education (New York *Herald Tribune,* March 4, 1954). As an economy measure, it was proposed that the State Maritime Colleges absorb the Federal academy training program, but no decision has been made.

Durgin is the author of a chapter in the book *Battle Stations!* (William H. Wise & Co., 1946), largely a photographic account with brief stories by participating admirals of naval operations in World War II. Included among honors awarded to Durgin are the Legion of Merit and two Gold Stars with Combat V, the Navy Expeditionary Medal (USS *Connecticut*), World Wars I and II Victory Medals, and the Philippine Liberation Ribbon with one bronze star. He has received the rank of honorary commander, military division, in the Order of the British Empire, and rank of Chevalier in the French Legion of Honor as well as the Croix de Guerre with Palm. On October 7, 1916, he married Myrtle Fest of Philadelphia, and their children are Calvin Thornton, Phyllis, and Jean.

Admiral Durgin is five feet eleven inches tall, weighs 180 pounds, has hazel eyes and graying black hair. On July 1, 1954 he received from the New York County Post of the American Legion a scroll for "outstanding achievement in youth education."

References

N Y Times p59 Mr 8 '51

Who's Who in America, 1954-55

EARLY, WILLIAM ASHBY Dec. 8, 1905-
Educational association president

Address: b. 1201 16th St., N.W., Washington 6, D.C.; h. 1426 N. Quincy St., Arlington, Va.

Elected president of the National Education Association in July 1953, William Ashby Early has earned a reputation since his entry into the teaching profession in 1931 not only for his devotion to the ideals of education and his efforts at defining the goals of the nation's schools, but also for his emphasis on the role of the school, the teacher and the citizen in community life. He has been superintendent of schools of the counties of Norfolk and Arlington in Virginia.

Twenty thousand delegates to the ninety-second convention of the National Education Association, meeting in New York City, adopted a resolution on July 2, 1954 asking that segregation end in the nation's public schools; delegates from only two states opposed the resolution.

Miss Waurine Walker was elected to succeed William Early as president of the NEA for 1954-55.

William Ashby Early was born in Nelson county in Virginia on December 8, 1905, the son of Louis Hunter and Louise (Wheeler) Early. His father, a Methodist minister, was descended from a distinguished Southern family including Bishop John Early of Bedford county in Virginia who was a pioneer advocate of free public education, General Jubal Anderson Early of the Confederate Army, and Governor Peter Early of Georgia. In addition to William, the Earlys had two daughters, Alice Wheeler and Louise.

Young Early attended Randolph-Macon Academy, a high school administered by the college of the same name founded in the late 1700's through the efforts of Bishop John Early. For extracurricular activities he served as assistant manager of the baseball team and as business manager of the YMCA handbook. After being graduated from Randolph-Macon in 1923, he entered Emory and Henry College, in Emory, Virginia where he was awarded the A.B. degree in 1927.

Embarking on his career in education in the fall of 1931, Early became an instructor of science and social studies at Clarksville High School in Clarksville, Virginia. It was while teaching at Clarksville High that he met and married Glenna Hamlin Jones, a secretary, on June 16, 1933. It was then, too, when the

Will Bond

WILLIAM ASHBY EARLY

depression was causing economic difficulties for local teachers, that the young instructor raised his voice in behalf of better conditions. With his meager family budget as a basis for his request, he presented the local school board with a plea for an increase in teachers' salaries.

Five years after he had taken his first teaching job, William Early became principal of LaCrosse High and Elementary School in LaCrosse, Virginia. Later, he was the principal of Madison Heights High and Elementary School at Madison, Virginia from 1939 to 1943. After pursuing postgraduate courses in education at Duke University, Early received the M.A. degree in 1941.

During World War II he accepted the challenging position as principal of Alexander Park School in Norfolk, Virginia. Alexander Park was a Federal housing project with enough families to send 4,000 pupils to the school. Although his task of supervising 110 teachers occupied much of his time, he organized a community civilian defense program, established Boy and Girl Scout troops, and a Civic League, and participated in Sunday school and church activities.

Just after his service as principal of Alexander Park High, Early was named in 1947 to a seat on the American Council of Education. As a representative of the American Association of School Administrators, of which he is still a member, he was spokesman for superintendents, supervisors and principals of all the schools in the nation.

Following his success with the Alexander Park program, he was appointed in 1946 superintendent of the Norfolk county school system which has 16,300 pupils, forty-three schools and 610 teachers under its jurisdiction. Recognition of his long service to education in Virginia came in 1949 when the young superintendent was elected to a two-year term as president of

EARLY, WILLIAM A.—*Continued*

the Virginia Education Association. Early was named superintendent of schools in Arlington county, Virginia in July 1949.

Writing in an article for the *School Executive* (January 1951) he recommended that "because the lives of so many citizens are interlaced with the schools, the superintendent should have a deep sense of duty. This is his first responsibility. None of his 'extracurricular activities' are so important to the community as that he . . . run a good school system."

In administering his school system, Early has emphasized that the superintendent must consider the major objective of providing proper facilities for the education of the students. Thus he has decried "false economies" in school building programs, asking, "are we going to pursue the ruinous course of false economy . . . or are we going to face the fact that schools are educational living spaces for children?" (*School Executive,* December 1950). The educator believes that "schoolpeople have failed to play their part as partners in the design and construction of school buildings."

In June 1952, Early was appointed superintendent of schools in Chatham county and Savannah, Georgia. In this post he was among the 7000 educators attending the ninety-first annual conference of the National Education Association at Miami Beach, Florida, in July 1953. During the sessions addressed by Attorney General Herbert Brownell, Jr. and Lewis K. Gough, national commander of the American Legion, Early was elected NEA's president for the term of 1953-1954. He had served as the president of NEA's division of county and rural area superintendents in 1948 and 1949 and later as president of the rural department of NEA.

The NEA was founded in 1857 and was originally known as the National Teachers Association. Its purpose is to "elevate the character and advance the interests of the profession of teaching and to promote the cause of popular education in the United States." At present the organization has a membership of more than 500,000 and an affiliated membership of 950,000.

The delegates at the July 1953 convention condemned the "efforts of those who advocate book burning, purges, or other devices which restrict freedom of thought, and which are, in effect, an expression of lack of confidence in the integrity, loyalty, and good judgement of the American people" (*Christian Science Monitor,* July 10, 1953). The convention denounced teachers who utilize the constitutional protection against self-incrimination or refuse to talk about their past or present Communist affiliations.

As long as U.S. citizens continue to place their faith in the common man and not in "self-appointed totalitarian guardians," our country will remain free, President Early told the eighth National Conference on Citizenship in September 1953. For this reason, he said, American schools should teach students about communism "as a measure of defense against our most potent threat."

Repeating the platform adopted by the NEA concerning communism, Early said: "Teaching about communism does not mean advocacy of communism. Members of the Communist Party should not be employed in our schools." He asserted that the extent to which education was available to the rural populations of the world might measure the extent of freedom in the world tomorrow. "We are in a struggle to win the friendship" of all the uncommitted peoples of the world, he told the conference.

Writing in the September 1953 issue of the *Journal of the National Education Association* Early appealed to every citizen to "reaffirm his loyalty and dedication to our country and its institutions" on Loyalty Day, November 9. "During these crucial days," he wrote, "when the course of democracy is being determined in the court of world opinion, it is singularly important for all of us to restate our faith in the American way—to pledge, frequently and publicly, our sincere allegiance to the flag of the United States and to our republic."

A member of Phi Delta Kappa, the educational fraternity, Early is also a life member of NEA and is a member of the editorial board of the *School Executive.* He served as vice-president of the Amherst Rotary in 1945, the Portsmouth Rotary in 1948, on the board of the Norfolk county recreational department, the Norfolk County Tuberculosis Association, and as chairman of the Portsmouth district of the Tidewater Area Council of Boy Scouts.

The educator is five feet nine inches in height and weighs 165 pounds; he lists his eyes as blue and his hair as black, "turning gray." Reading and fishing are his favorite hobbies. The Earlys have one son, William, Jr.

References

Va J Ed 42:12+ Ja '49 por
Leaders in Education (1948)

EBBOTT, PERCY J(OHN) Oct. 23, 1887- Banker

Address: b. c/o The Chase National Bank of the City of New York, 18 Pine St., New York 5; h. 825 5th Ave., New York 21; Crow Hill Rd., Mt. Kisco, N.Y.

The Chase National Bank of the City of New York of which Percy J. Ebbott is the president, has become widely known since World War II for its campaign to "humanize" banking. Its advertisements aim to persuade people of average income that "it pays to do business with Chase." Ebbott's forty years in the commercial banking field have given him a breadth of experience and outlook to aid him in heading one of the world's largest banks whose deposits in 1954 totaled $5,174,415,072 and whose assets amounted to $5,678,726,511. He has been associated with the bank since 1930 as a vice-president, becoming president in 1949. In 1953 he introduced a liberal benefit program for the bank's nearly 10,000 employees.

The son of Harry M. and Lucretia Caroline (Edwards) Ebbott, Percy John Ebbott was born in Fort Atkinson, Wisconsin on October

23, 1887. He was graduated from the high school in Fort Atkinson in 1906, and then attended Oberlin College in Ohio. He received the B.A. degree from the college in 1910, and spent the next year in Ohio as a special agent for the Hudson Underwriters, Inc., of New York. Returning to Wisconsin in 1911, he was one of the organizers of the R. L. Kenyon Company of Waukesha, which manufactured portable cottages and camping equipment.

Ebbott entered the banking field in 1913 when he was employed by the National Park Bank as an assistant cashier. The following year he received his first district assignment and was given the Southwest territory of the United States to cover.

On his first trip there, the story has been told, Ebbott "went naïvely equipped with dinner clothes, mouse-colored spats and a derby." He traveled with a group of "road-hardened district bankers" who always stopped at Fort Worth, Texas, for a banquet. Ebbott, who had been told of the "formality" of the dinner, appeared there "resplendent in a forest-green tuxedo—everyone else, of course, in business suits. . . . So well did he parry the joking that by the end of the evening he was the party favorite and the entire company signed his stiff shirt front" (New York *Times*, March 11, 1951).

During World War I, Ebbott served as a captain in the United States Army Air Force. After he received his discharge in 1919, he returned to the National Park Bank and became an assistant vice-president. The Seaboard National Bank secured his services as vice-president in 1923 and he retained that position when the Seaboard merged with the Equitable Trust Company in 1929.

A subsequent merger of the Equitable Trust Company and the Chase National Bank in 1930 brought Ebbott to the Chase where he began his duties as a vice-president. In 1935 the bank apportioned its wide commercial and banking activities by districts, and he was put in charge of a territory covering thirteen Midwestern and Southwestern states. Ebbott was considered one of the best judges of credits at Chase, and was "prominently identified" with the development of the "term" loan, a type of credit which covers a period of years. In September 1947 he became a senior vice-president of the bank.

In January 1949 Ebbott was made president of the Chase National Bank and a member of the board of directors. In a statement issued when he became president, he said: "I am pleased, humble and hopeful—pleased with the opportunity, humble because I realize my own limitations, and hopeful because I am aware of the power of the men and women who comprise the Chase staff. . . . If we are of good intent, competent, imaginative, and gracious in our daily contacts with the public . . . people will say: 'I like to do business with the Chase.' The benefits which can accrue from this magnitude of daily opportunities to advance the prestige and usefulness of the bank are almost without limit. Everyone likes to play on a

PERCY J. EBBOTT

winning team, and like all good team players, we must remember that the effort of every individual in the group is important" (*Finance*, March 15, 1953).

Since World War II, the Chase National Bank's advertisements in subways and buses, on radio and television, and in newspapers have been used to persuade the person of average income that he would receive friendly service at the Chase bank and at any of its twenty-eight New York City branches. One successful advertisement, which showed a picture of a Siamese rufous-necked hornbill bird who had escaped from a Manhattan pet shop and landed on a window sill in the bank's Pine Street offices, had the caption: "Somebody told me to talk to the people at Chase."

Referring to the series of advertisements, *Finance* magazine (March 15, 1953) wrote: "The vigorous and imaginative efforts in that campaign, stemming largely from Percy Ebbott's forty years of diversified experience in the banking business, can be traced back, in the last analysis, to his basic concept that banking service is a team function."

Ebbott's conviction that industry and banking are interdependent has recently been expressed in a newspaper advertising program describing the contributions of various American industries to the economic growth of the United States, and the way in which banks have helped make these contributions possible. The series, unusual in that a business other than the advertiser's received the more prominent display, prompted an enthusiastic response from both industrialists and bankers, the latter feeling that the good will created by the campaign would extend to banking as a whole as well as to the Chase National Bank.

Winthrop W. Aldrich, chairman of the board of the Chase bank for nineteen years, resigned his post early in 1953 to become U.S. Ambas-

EBBOTT, PERCY J.—*Continued*

sador to the Court of St. James, and was succeeded by John J. McCloy. In an address to stockholders, Aldrich said of the bank's president: "In leaving, I have entire confidence that our bank is in good hands. Percy J. Ebbott . . . is a widely-experienced and exceedingly able commercial banker with a great number of friends throughout the nation. He has done much for the Chase and will continue to do more. . . . Together, Mr. McCloy and Mr. Ebbott will guide the bank in the days to come with wisdom, energy and foresight" (*Finance*, March 15, 1953).

In January 1953 Ebbott was elected a director of the International Paper Company and in February 1953, a director of the New York Central Railroad Company (a position he held until June 1954), both vacancies having been created by the resignation of Winthrop W. Aldrich. On assuming these directorships, Ebbott said: "I don't take on two more jobs just to advertise the Chase bank or the name of Ebbott. It's just that I believe a banker can't know too much about the various industries which banks serve" (*Finance*, March 15, 1953).

He elaborated his viewpoint, as quoted in the same article: "I've always regarded banking as a business that's secondary to other industries. I think the success or failure of a commercial bank is directly related to how well its management understands the way other industries function." Other corporations of which Ebbott is a director have afforded him the opportunity to acquire knowledge of varied fields of commerce: Allied Stores Corporation, Nash-Kelvinator Corporation, Moore-McCormack Lines, Inc., Refrigeration Discount Corporation, Belding Heminway Company, Inc., Discount Corporation of New York, and 825 Fifth Avenue Corporation.

An employees' benefit program instituted by the Chase in 1953 was termed "one of the most important accomplishments in the bank's history" by Ebbott, and he stated that the plan would allow the bank's 9,600 employees "to participate more directly in the rewards and risks of our economic system" (New York *Times*, June 2, 1953). Principal points in the program were a more liberal retirement plan, for which the bank would underwrite the entire cost, a new family benefits plan, and a new thrift-incentive plan, to which both the bank and the employees would contribute.

Ebbott is also vice-chairman and a director of The Chase Bank, an overseas affiliate of the Chase National Bank. He is a member of the executive council of the American Bankers Association, the state policy committee of the New York State Bankers Association, and in 1942 served as president of the Association of Reserve City Bankers, an organization in which he has been active for many years. He serves on the trustees' committee of the New York Community Trust and on the board of the New York Clearing House. He is a member of the New York Chamber of Commerce.

The banker belongs to the Bedford Golf and Tennis Club of Mount Kisco, New York, and to the Bond, Economic, Links, Union, and University clubs of New York City. He is a governor of the Bankers Club of America and a life trustee of Oberlin College. Ebbott received an honorary LL.D. degree from Lawrence College in Appleton, Wisconsin in 1950.

Percy J. Ebbott and Elizabeth Camp of San Antonio, Texas were married on January 1, 1923. They have two sons, John Percy and Peter Camp Ebbott. The banker is often called 'Perce" by his friends, and has been described as a "ruddy-faced, friendly Midwesterner."

References

Finance p43+ Mr 15 '53 por
N Y Times p37 Ja 28 '53 por
Who's Who in America, 1954-55
Who's Who in Commerce and Industry (1953)
Who's Who in the East (1953)
World Biography (1954)

ECHOLS, OLIVER P(ATTON) Mar. 4, 1892-May 15, 1954 Aircraft official; former U.S. Army Air Force officer; rose from second lieutenant (1916) to major general (1942); during World War II was chief of Matériel Division of Air Force; chief of civil affairs division of War Department (1946-1947); after retirement from Air Force was president of Aircraft Industries Association (1947-1949) and chairman of board and chief executive of Northrop Aircraft Corporation (1949-1954). See *Current Biography,* (Dec.) 1947.

Obituary

N Y Times p86 My 16 '54

EDELMAN, MAURICE Mar. 2, 1911- Member of British Parliament; author

Address: b. c/o House of Commons, London, S.W. 1, England; h. Lindisfarne, Chesham Bois, Buckinghamshire, England

Describing himself as an "orthodox" member of the Labour Party, Maurice Edelman has represented Coventry North in Britain's Parliament since 1950, and was a representative for Coventry West from 1945 to 1950. An expert on European affairs and a founding member of the Council of Europe, he is vice-chairman of the British Council which, he says "interprets the British way of life," and acting chairman of the Anglo-French Parliamentary Relations Committee.

He combines a writing career with his political life, having written two novels and several political books. His novel *Who Goes Home* (J. B. Lippincott Company, 1953), about the House of Commons, was a recent selection of the Book Society in England and a Book of the Month choice in France. The Parliamentarian was the recipient of the Coronation Medal in 1953.

Maurice Edelman was born in Cardiff, Wales, on March 2, 1911, the son of Joshua and Ester (Solomon) Edelman. His father, of yeoman stock, is an artist, and his mother is descended from a long line of scholars. He has two sisters and one brother. He attended elementary school in his native town, and was graduated from Cardiff High School in 1929. His competence won him a scholarship, giving him standing as an exhibitioner during his college career at Trinity College, Cambridge University, where he majored in modern languages.

Upon receiving his B.A. degree from that university in 1932, Maurice worked for a London industrial firm as supervisor of research development of timber and plastics until 1941. In that year the University of Cambridge awarded him an M.A. degree.

Edelman began his writing career in 1933, when he published *Duet* in collaboration with H.A.N. Cole (E. Goldstein, 1933), a collection of poems which the London *Times* Literary Supplement critic called "carnivorous." Later, he published a number of articles in leading political magazines in Britain and the United States. In "Folk Song in March Time," *New Statesman & Nation* (September 10, 1938), he wrote that "the chief theme of Soviet song, as indeed of Soviet life, is work and defense." Discussing peacetime conscripts in a letter to this magazine on May 20, 1939, he stated: "The only true *quid pro quo* for conscription of men is conscription of wealth or the means of production."

His first political book, *G. P. U. Justice,* was published by Allen & Unwin, London, in 1938. It was based on the notes of Peter Kleist, and it described the German engineer's experiences in a Moscow prison. The reviewer for the *New Statesman & Nation* (June 4, 1938) called the story "an objective account of Soviet methods."

Three years later Edelman's book, *Production for Victory, not Profit* was published by Gollancz. This included many quotations from newspapers, and Parliamentary speeches and conversations on the nationalizing of industry. He proposed the conscription and nationalization of war industry and its public administration at cost in order to abolish private profit. He is also the author of *How Russia Prepared* (Penguin, 1942).

Upon his return to England in 1945, Maurice Edelman got into politics "fairly fortuitously." As a newspaper reporter sent to cover a Labour party conference, he found himself selected to stand for election. He was elected a Labour Member of Parliament for Coventry West, near London. He likes his work, including "the rough and tumble of election campaigns." "The House and my constituency take all my time," he said. "An M.P. is always being badgered by his constituency. He can try to strike a balance between being a welfare worker and a statesman, but statesmen have a way of being voted out at the next election" (New York *Herald Tribune,* October 11, 1953).

As a war correspondent for the London publication *Picture Post* from 1943 to 1945, Edelman was accredited to the British and United States forces in France and North Africa. In

Bassano Studios, London

MAURICE EDELMAN

1944 he published an account of his war experiences, *France, The Birth of the Fourth Republic* (Penguin, 1944), which became a best seller.

The writer made his first visit to the United States in 1946, and for the British Information Services talked about Britain in a radio interview with Alma Dettinger over the New York *Times* station WQXR. He published an article in the *New Statesman & Nation* (July 6, 1946) in which he discussed "Peace with Russia," and declared that "through the creation of joint trading corporations at points of Anglo-Soviet rivalry, it may be possible to unite Anglo-Soviet interests."

The Labour party member expressed his opinion on the future of Trieste in a letter to the London *Times* on May 17, 1946. He declared: "It is clear that a national award of Trieste to either Italy or Yugoslavia would not only create a permanent *casus belli* between the two countries but also make Trieste a focus of potential conflict between Britain and Russia." He urged that Trieste be made a free port and city with sovereignty vested in the United Nations.

Writing in the London *Times* on January 11, 1947, Edelman advocated a potential organization for Palestine "midway between absolute partition and federation." He wrote that "if the partition is to achieve its object of pacifying the country . . . it must be carried out so that the Arabs have political freedom without fear of Jewish domination, the Jews have independence to control immigration to succour Jewish survivors of Eastern Europe, and Britain has freedom of communications and security of cantonment for troops."

As a delegate in 1948 of the Anglo-French Parliamentary Relations Committee, Maurice Edelman participated in many informal conferences between the two countries' parliamentary representatives. As quoted by the Lon-

EDELMAN, MAURICE—*Continued*

don *Times* (December 11, 1948), he affirmed that "good relations with France were the cornerstone of western union."

The Parliamentarian published a pictorial biography of *Herbert Morrison* (Lincoln-Prager, London, 1948), whom he ranks "second to Atlee" in the Labour party. The *New Statesman & Nation* book critic on December 18, 1948, stated that "Mr. Edelman avoids both the platitudinous and the sycophantic, and has an easy, happy style; the story he tells is genuine." In an article for the *New Statesman & Nation* (June 12, 1948) entitled "Labour and the Middle Classes," Edelman declares "it is the technician, the scientist, the engineer, the manager who will promote the nation's prosperity . . . and Labour Government and trade unions should, by providing facilities for study and necessary experience, promote the passage of manual workers into technical and administrative ranks."

Maurice Edelman was nominated in Parliament on June 3, 1949, a House of Commons delegate to the first session of the Consultative Assembly of the Council of Europe, which met in August 1949 at Strasbourg, France. At the assembly on August 22, 1949, he was appointed a member of the economic committee. Reporting in *New Statesman & Nation* (August 20, 1949), Edelman stated: "The first Assembly has made Europe think in terms of a European Parliament . . .; we can, therefore, hope that in the course of time, the Consultative Assembly of the Council of Europe will become a European institution, respected as a legislature drawing its sap . . . from the people of Europe as a whole."

At the annual meeting of the Franco-British Parliamentary Relations Committee in May 1950, Edelman was elected vice-chairman, a position he retained until he became acting chairman in 1953. Chosen a British parliamentary delegate to the Consultative Assembly of the Council of Europe at Strasbourg in August 1950, the Labour Party adherent proposed the establishment within the council of an Atlantic "joint purchasing board, a European man-power board and a food board" (New York *Herald-Tribune,* August 9, 1950). In the line of thinking of this proposal, he states, the International Materials Conference was established in 1950. At the 1950 assembly in connection with the Korean War, he was the chief author, with two Belgian Socialist leaders, of the Declaration of Strasbourg, which called for support against aggression wherever it exists, and which was described by Edelman as "a check on the atmosphere of war tension . . . in the Council of Europe" (London *Times,* August 25, 1950).

Expressing his opinion on the (Robert) Schuman plan at the 1950 Consultative Assembly of the Council of Europe, Edelman declared he considered the need was urgent for a European coal and steel organization, "subordinate to the Council's Committee of Ministers and advised by the Assembly" (London *Times,* August 15, 1950). He believes the present iron and steel authority is derived from the Schuman plan, and "is the first working functional supranational authority."

Serving as a United Kingdom delegate to the third session of the Consultative Assembly of the Council of Europe in 1951, Maurice Edelman said there was need for "a raw materials council to coordinate the needs of all nations of the free world" (New York *Times,* May 9, 1951). He holds the conviction that the European Defense Community (E.D.C.) is an outgrowth of the European army concept proposed to the Council of Europe by Winston Churchill, but he says that "defense is not a concern of the Council of Europe." It is his opinion that "trade unions are not adequately represented in the Council."

The Member of Parliament published his first novel, *A Trial of Love* (Wingate, London) in 1951. It is set in Algiers during World War II and deals with a successful journalist who seeks self-integration through observing and experiencing the conflict. The critic for *New Statesman & Nation* (November 3, 1951) writes: "Fleet Street's fairy godmother has waved her hand over this book, endowing it with wit, pace and incident."

In his second novel, *Who Goes Home* (J. B. Lippincott Company, Philadelphia, 1953), Edelman is concerned with the conflicts in the private and public lives of members of the House of Commons and with Anglo-American relations. Of this book, the reviewer for the London *Times* (January 21, 1953) writes: "The situation which Mr. Edelman develops with skill and authority contains many of the elements of classic tragedy." The novel was the Book Society's Choice in England and the Book of the Month selection by the Franco-British Book Selection Committee in Paris.

Maurice Edelman married Matilda Yager in 1932, and their two children are Sonia and Natasha. The Labour Party member has black wavy hair, thick eyebrows, and dark eyes. He was described by Mary Margaret McBride in a radio interview in September 1953 on station WABC of American Broadcasting Company as "one of the best-dressed men I have ever interviewed." Edelman is five feet ten and one-half inches tall and weighs 168 pounds. His faith is Jewish. His favorite sport is tennis.

References

N Y Herald Tribune Book R p2 O 11 '53

Who's Who, 1953

EDMAN, IRWIN Nov. 28, 1896- Sept. 4, 1954 University professor; philosopher; born in New York; was graduated from Columbia University (1917) and began lecturing in philosophy department (1918), becoming head of the department in 1945; combined with pragmatism a special interest in esthetics; popular speaker on radio forums; contributed articles and light verse to academic periodicals and popular magazines; wrote many books, best known is *Philosopher's Holiday* (1938); was elected (1953) a vice-president of the National Institute of Arts and Letters; was foremost American writer on philosophy of George Santayana; expressed his political faith in *Fountainheads of Freedom* (1941), which set forth the history of democracy and his belief that "resources of the common man have only begun to be tapped." See *Current Biography*, (July) 1953.

Obituary

N Y Times p51 S 5 '54

EL-GLAOUI, THAMI el-MEZOUARI, *See* el-**GLAOUI, T. el-M., Pasha of Marrakech**

EL MALLAKH, KAMAL (ĕl măl-äk') 1920- Egyptologist; architect; art critic

Address: b. c/o Egyptian Government's Department of Antiquities, Cairo, Egypt; h. 173 Fouad St., Zamalek, Cairo, Egypt

Wide World
KAMAL EL MALLAKH

A perfumed ship built for an Egyptian Pharaoh more than 4,700 years ago to carry his soul across the heavens was discovered on May 26, 1954 in a subterranean corridor beside the Great Pyramid of Giza, south of Cairo, Egypt by the thirty-four-year-old Egyptologist and architect, Kamal El Mallakh. He penetrated into the corridor where the solar ship of Cheops (or Khufu), king of the Fourth Dynasty, had been hidden from view since about 2,750 B.C. The announcement of his discovery excited scholars and archaeologists throughout the world because Egyptian tombs and pyramids were usually plundered repeatedly.

El Mallakh has had an active career as an architect and archaeologist, with journalism as a side line. He writes frequently for the London (England) publication, *Studio*, and for Egyptian State broadcasting publications and newspapers. He has restored stonework at Giza, at Canopus, and on the tail of the Great Sphinx. He is also one of the Middle East's notable art critics, and an artist with several oil paintings on exhibit in Cairo's Museum of Modern Art. He is a reserve Army engineer, a magazine illustrator, and was formerly a teacher.

Kamal El Mallakh was born in 1920 in Assuite in Upper Egypt, the son of William El Mallakh and the former Alice El Mankabadi. He has five brothers and two sisters. His father, now retired, was an official in the National Bank of Egypt. His family claims to be one of pure ancient Egyptian stock. One brother is an architect in Cairo and another brother is a postgraduate student at Rutgers University, New Brunswick, New Jersey. Kamal studied at the Faculty of Arts at Cairo University (known also since 1942 as Fouad I University) where he received his degree in architecture in 1943, and won a First in Merit honor. He joined the Military Engineering Reserve in 1943. He is now working on a thesis for his doctorate in archaeology and Egyptology at the university in Cairo.

During 1943 El Mallakh taught at the Faculty of Arts and later in that year was appointed assistant director of archaeological works of Giza and Lower Egypt. He was advanced to director in 1951. Among his assignments have been the restoration of the crumbling stonework on the Great Pyramid of Cheops at Giza and on the pyramid of Khephren where he reopened the entrance. He also restored the Temple of Philae, which is submerged during the Nile flood season in the reservoir behind the Aswân dam. Early in May 1954 he made major Greco-Roman discoveries at Canopus on the Mediterranean shore of the Nile Delta (New York *Times*, May 27, 1954).

In May, 1954 El Mallakh was in charge of workmen building a road for the convenience of tourists visiting the pyramids, and when they demolished an ancient wall and uncovered a 150-yard row of massive limestone blocks, each slab three feet by three feet by six feet and sealed with pink gypsum, he suspected that the blocks might be the roof of a long underground chamber. He ordered his masons to chisel a hole into one of the blocks, and after he had peered in and seen a fifty-foot wooden boat and smelled a fragrant perfume, he realized that he had found Cheops' funeral ship.

"Peering into darkness," El Mallakh recalled, "through the small opening we saw to our great surprise the upper part of a solar boat, embedded in the corridor with long pieces of wood which looked like oars on both sides. . . . The way the boat was tightly covered we assumed it was a 'night boat.' Ancient Egyptian kings always surrounded their tombs with two kinds of solar boats—day boats, in which they believed their souls would follow the sun on its journey to eternity by daylight, and night boats for journeying from sundown to sunrise" (New York *Herald Tribune*, May 27, 1954). The fragrance of sycamore and cedar wafted through the aperture.

Archaeologists and Egyptologists, at first skeptical, soon hailed El Mallakh's find as im-

EL MALLAKH, KAMAL—*Continued*

portant as the discovery in 1922 of King Tutankhamen's jewel-filled tomb (the only other unlooted Egyptian relic which has been found—the alabaster sarcophagus opened by Dr. Zakaria Ghoneim in June 1954 was empty). On May 30, 1954, Egyptian government officials, scholars and archaeologists were permitted to inspect the solar ship, and peered through a ten-inch opening in the limestone rock.

When interviewed by NBC commentator Wilson Hall in Cairo on June 13, 1954, El Mallakh said: "I am proud that this dreamlike thing happened to me—it is more vivid than an Arabian Nights tale—when I saw the solar ship of King Cheops. I am also proud to be the youngest and first Egyptian ever to make an important find, since the other important discoveries were made by foreigners."

When asked if he thought King Cheops—if he were alive today—would be surprised to discover how famous he had become, El Mallakh replied, "I believe that in their primitive way, our ancestors with their imagery visualized television and radio—sending the *thoughts* of solar ships through the air—just as we send *words* today."

After inspecting El Mallakh's find, Egypt's Premier Gamal Abdel Nasser on June 12 lauded the young discoverer and said that he had "inscribed his name in history for all time." Colonel Nasser's visit to see the solar ship of Pharaoh Cheops was regarded as a public demonstration of support for El Mallakh, who had accused senior Egyptologists of "jealousy" in seeking to oust him from participation in further investigation of his discovery of the funerary craft. The Department of Antiquities decided that El Mallakh would be one of a five-man commission to pursue the investigation.

On June 16 it was announced by Major Salah Salem, Minister of National Guidance of Egypt, that El Mallakh would be sent to New York for the opening of the Egyptian Tourist Bureau there and for a lecture tour. Until his departure for the United States, El Mallakh, according to Dr. Mustafa Amer, head of the Department of Antiquities, planned the shifting of the limestone blocks and preserving and removing the solar boat. Arriving in New York on October 5, as one of a seven-man mission, El Mallakh said he looked forward to exploring "in the shadow of the pyramids of the living."

El Mallakh believes that the pharoahs' love of symmetry makes it "practically certain" that Cheops placed two more ships north of the Great Pyramid. He is supported in his theory by Dr. William C. Hayes, curator of Egyptian art at the Metropolitan Museum of Art in New York. Since his discovery of the first ship, El Mallakh has been busily prospecting in the north or entrance side of the area where countless thousands of visitors have walked. He noticed worn traces of an enclosure wall of precisely the same type as the one on the south side. He believes these walls were built in the sixth and seventh centuries B.C. by Saitic kings, who held the ancient Pharaohs and their works in great reverence. The later monarchs, El Mallakh told Kennett Love, New York *Times* correspondent, possibly learned of the concealed solar ships and built the walls to camouflage them (New York *Times,* July 7, 1954).

The archaeologist, a bachelor, is six feet tall, weighs 165 pounds, has dark hair and brown eyes, and is soft-spoken and shy. He lives with his older brother in the island suburb, Zamalek, near Cairo. For recreation, he enjoys swimming, painting, and reading. His church affiliation is Christian (Coptic). He is also art critic of the Akhbar-el-Yom chain of newspapers for which he writes weekly articles.

References

N Y Times p4 My 27 '54
Newsweek 43:54+ Je 7 '54 por

ELY, PAUL (HENRI) (ā-lē') Dec. 17, 1897- French Commander-in-Chief and High Commissioner in Indochina

Address: b. Ministère de la Guerre, 231, blvd. St.-Germain, Paris 7e, France; Saigon, Viet-Nam, Indochina

"It is not for a soldier to make believe that a compromise peace is better than a victory," said General Paul Ely, French Commander-in-Chief and High Commissioner in Indochina, when he announced on July 22, 1954 the Geneva agreement temporarily partitioning Viet-Nam between French-Allied nationalists and the Communist-led Vietminh. "This is an anguished peace," he declared, "but the solution chosen at Geneva is the one which safeguards best the major interests and the future of the state, the army and the Viet-Namese nation." The agreement calls for the evacuation of French troops and personnel from Hanoi and its environs within 300 days and for elections to create a unified government in Viet-Nam within two years from July 21, 1954.

Appointed to the "most thankless job in the world" on June 3, 1954, General Ely succeeded General Henri Navarre as military head and Maurice Dejean as civilian director in French Indochina. The general, who entered the French Army in 1915, was chief of staff of France's armed forces in 1953 and early 1954, and previously had represented his country on the Standing Group of the North Atlantic Treaty Organization (NATO).

Paul Henri Ely was born in Salonika, Greece on December 17, 1897, the son of a French civil servant and his wife. He spent his early childhood in Crete, where he developed a liking for the ancient Greek philosophers. He received most of his education in Brest, France, and completed his high school training there.

When the German armies marched toward Paris, he enlisted as a foot soldier with the French 46th Infantry Regiment on March 2, 1915. He learned trench warfare fighting along the Marne River, and was wounded twice. His outstanding conduct brought him the Croix de Guerre with two citations.

Ely entered the St. Cyr military academy, France's West Point, in 1917, and was graduated in 1919 as a second lieutenant. He was assigned to the army general staff, and was admitted to the Ecole de Guerre in 1928. "With a lack of haste characteristic of him," he attained the rank of captain in 1930 (*Match,* June 1954). In 1939 he was promoted to the rank of major.

In World War II, experience with the "Maginot-line thinking in the French Army" made Ely "a hardened foe of defensive, positional warfare" (*U. S. News & World Report,* June 18, 1954). In June 1940 he was severely wounded, and his right hand was crippled so that he now writes and shakes hands with his left hand. For his bravery, he was awarded the Croix de Guerre with two citations.

Following the surrender of France to Germany in 1940, Ely left the hospital where he was recovering from his wounds, to serve as delegate of the provisional government in Algiers to the resistance forces in France. In 1942 he joined the Free French Forces of the Interior (F.F.I.)—the military organization of the French underground movement—as a lieutenant colonel and as assistant head. He was given the rank of colonel in 1944 and was named as liaison officer between the Allied headquarters in London and the French National Resistance Council.

He made a number of hazardous English Channel crossings to furnish the Allies in London with information on German military strength and movements. He was given a mandate to replace Jacques Chaban-Delmas as the military delegate of General Charles de Gaulle, but refused this promotion, claiming it was not justified because the post was well filled. His characteristic modesty, wrote Jean Farran in *Match* (June 1954), in this instance meant that "he . . . remained a colonel, and it was Chaban-Delmas who became a general."

A few weeks before D-Day, Ely landed on the Normandy Beach and later joined the Allied army as a Maquis colonel. He stayed in France after its liberation from the Germans. He was awarded the Medal of the Resistance with rosette and received the rank of brigadier general in charge of infantry training in 1945. The next year he became a major general, and during 1947 was commanding officer of the 7th Military Region.

Ely became chief of staff to the inspector general of the French armed forces—General Jean de Lattre de Tassigny—in January 1948. He went to London as head of the French delegation to the military committee on Western union in 1948 and 1949, and won recognition "as a compromiser able to work well with allies" (Washington *Post,* June 11, 1954).

He was advanced to the rank of lieutenant general in 1949, and in October of that year, was sent to Washington, D.C. as French representative on the three-man Standing Group of NATO. In Washington, *Newsweek* (June 14, 1954) claims, "few [men] were happy at the idea of sharing military secrets with a 'foreigner' " but in 1951, when Ely succeeded General Omar N. Bradley as chairman of the group, he won the respect of the members.

French Embassy Press & Inf. Div.

GEN. PAUL ELY

Military planners admired Ely's capacity for work and concentration, and his adherence to personal principles. When his belief that Germany should contribute to Western defense conflicted with that of Jules Moch, then France's Defense Minister, Ely offered to resign his Washington post, but was refused. After his appointment on August 5, 1953 as chief of staff of the French armed forces, Ely returned to Paris. In December 1953 he also became president of the military committee of NATO.

In February 1954 he undertook a mission with René Pleven, at that time the Defense Minister of France, to investigate the French military position in Indochina. Upon his return to Paris in March, Ely was sent by France's Committee of National Defense to Washington, D.C. for "an exchange of views on the Indochina situation" with U.S. military advisers. Ely declared that "American aid for Indochina is constant and almost of a daily character," and described the struggle for Dienbienphu as "a very tough battle" with the Vietminh forces holding out for "some kind of success in view of the Geneva conference" (New York *Herald Tribune,* March 23, 1954).

Following the return of General Ely to Paris, the U.S. Department of Defense announced on March 26, 1954 that it would send twenty-five additional B-26 planes to Indochina on a "temporary loan basis" with supplies of ammunition and parachutes (New York *Times*). American financial assistance to Indochina was then totaling about $1,000,000,000 a year.

After the fall of Dienbienphu on May 7, 1954, Ely was sent to Indochina with General Raoul Salan and General Pierre Pélissier, to prepare a report on which the French Cabinet might base requests to its allies for aid, and to the French parliament for appropriations. He returned to Paris within three weeks, and recommended the reinforcement of troops and

ELY, GENERAL PAUL—*Continued*

equipment in the Red River delta, and the replacement of General Navarre, then Commander-in-Chief of the French forces there. The French Cabinet moved to send additional fighting divisions to Indochina.

General Ely was named Commander-in-Chief and High Commissioner in Indochina by the French Cabinet on June 3, 1954, thus receiving control over both civil and military operations. He declared upon his arrival at Saigon on June 8, 1954, that the joint authority delegated to him reaffirmed France's "solidarity with the Associated States of Indochina" (New York *Herald Tribune,* June 9, 1954).

Jean Farran wrote that "French opinion was astonished at the nomination of an 'unknown general.'" He added: "Ely is not one of those men who in coming to the hour of combat make as much noise as the artillery. It is less for his reputation than for his qualities of good sense, work potential, and intelligence that he was chosen."

After an inspection of the defenses of the Coi (Red) River delta, Ely left for France on June 17, 1954, to present several alternative military plans to the government of Pierre Mendès-France. He declared before returning to Indochina on July 2, 1954 that the withdrawal of French Union forces from the southern delta area was not indicative of abandoning to Vietminh troops the entire region which includes Hanoi, the capital of North Viet-Nam.

"I have regrouped my forces in order to assure, under the best conditions, this defense [of the delta]," Ely said. On July 9, 1954, from French Indochina he affirmed that Hanoi "will be defended" and French Union forces would fight to retain Haiphong, the port from which they received American supplies. The arrangements for an armistice in Indochina were signed in Geneva on July 21, 1954, and brought the fighting in the Associated States to a close.

The truce is being supervised by commissions composed of representatives of India, Poland and Canada. A majority vote of a commission would settle any issue except one which might "lead to a resumption of hostilities." Unanimous vote would be required on such issues, and such cases would be referred to meetings of the ambassadors of the Geneva conference.

When France transferred the Palace of Norodom to the Viet-Namese government in September 1954, General Ely said that France had decided to grant Viet-Nam its independence before the end of 1954. He declared that the present policy of France toward the Associated State of Viet-Nam could be summed-up as one of "full independence, full support" (New York *Times,* September 8, 1954).

General Ely is a grand officer of the French Legion of Honor. He has been awarded the Legion of Merit and the King's Medal for Courage. "When the cravat of the Legion of Honor was put around his neck," wrote Jean Farran "his first gesture was to take it off and put it in his pocket. This quality [modesty] is the key to his character." He does not like to wear the military uniform, but prefers the navy blue suit and Homburg hat of the high-ranking civil servant.

The General is married, and during his work with the resistance forces in France his wife was taken in reprisal from France for a two-year internment in the German Ravensbrück prison camp, an experience which severely injured her health. The general reads the Greek philosophers in the original language for recreation, and also enjoys fishing. He keeps a large collection of cats and pigeons. He rises at five in the morning, drinks "only mineral water," and is always on time (*Match,* June 1954).

He does not look like a general but "more like a professor of mathematics" (*Match,* June 1954), and has said: "By birth and inclination I am of a contemplative nature—but life forced me to be a man of action" (Washington *Post,* June 11, 1954). He is called the "rarest of French generals: a quiet, shy man who seldom raises his voice—and never in public" (*Newsweek,* June 14, 1954).

References

Le Monde Je 5 '54
Match 272:11+ Je '54
N Y Herald Tribune p4 Je 4 '54
N Y World-Telegram p7 Je 12 '54 por
Newsweek 43:41 Je 14 '54 por
Washington (D.C.) Post p13 Je 11 '54 por
Dictionnaire Biographique Français Contemporain (1954)

EMMONS, GLENN L(EONIDAS) Aug. 15, 1895- United States Government official; banker

Address: b. c/o Department of the Interior, 18th and C. Sts., N.W., Washington 25, D.C.; h. Crestwood Apts., 3900 16th St., Washington, D.C.

Emphasizing the differences among Indian groups in their ability to assume self-management, Glenn L. Emmons, United States Commissioner of Indian Affairs, said: "Some people speak of the Indian problem as though it were just one group of people with one set of troubles . . . it is far more complex than that" (Washington *Post,* November 2, 1953). Emmons, who was sworn in on August 10, 1953, as Commissioner, is attempting to introduce a plan which will improve the educational, health and economic conditions of about 350,000 Indians. He has stressed education as the "important key to ultimate relinquishment of all control over Indians."

The Commissioner has been the president of the First State Bank of Gallup, New Mexico since 1935. He has served as the national treasurer of the American Bankers Association, and has taken an active part in community affairs.

Glenn Leonidas Emmons was born in Atmore, Alabama on August 15, 1895, one of the seven children of Martha Jane (Huggins) and

John Davidson Emmons, a businessman. His ancestors came from England to the United States in 1666. His brother, the late Reverend Doctor Grover C. Emmons, was the founder and editor of the church periodical, *The Upper Room*.

When Glenn was nine years old, his family moved to Albuquerque, New Mexico, where he attended public schools. After school hours he worked as a ranch hand, a news "butch" on the Santa Fe Railway, a forest service fireguard, and a locomotive fireman.

Emmons was captain of his high school football team and president of the athletic association. After being graduated in 1914 from Albuquerque High School, he entered the University of New Mexico in Albuquerque, where he majored in Latin and Greek, played football, was business manager of the university annual, *The Mirage*, and was a member of Pi Kappa Alpha. During two of his three years in college, he served as class president.

Leaving college in 1917 Emmons entered the U.S. Air Service and was commissioned a first lieutenant. He commanded the 84th Aero Squadron at Kelly Field, Texas until July 1918, and then went to England in command of Air Force detachments.

Upon return to civilian life, Emmons decided that he wanted a career in banking. He explains: "The principal person who influenced me in this choice was Guy Rogers, who was in the First National Bank of Albuquerque when I was a boy." In Gallup, New Mexico, known as "the Indian capital of the Southwest," he worked as transit clerk in the State Bank in 1919, advancing to the position of teller the next year. After his brother, John, organized the First National Bank of Gallup in 1921, Emmons became the assistant cashier. His promotion to cashier came in 1924, followed by the office of vice-president in 1928. From 1930 to 1933, he served on the Board of Regents of the University of New Mexico.

During the national banking holiday in 1933, the First National Bank of Gallup was discontinued, paying every depositor 100 cents on the dollar. The closing of the bank led to a rumor that there was a shortage in accounts. This rumor temporarily blocked, in July 1953, the Senate's confirmation of Emmons' nomination by President Dwight D. Eisenhower as Indian Commissioner, until Senator William Langer of North Dakota was "entirely satisfied" it was false (New York *Times*, July 29, 1953).

When the closed bank was reorganized as the First State Bank of Gallup in 1934, Emmons became vice-president, advancing in 1935 to the office of president and chairman of the board of directors, from which his brother retired. Glenn L. Emmons served as vice-president for New Mexico of the American Bankers Association (A.B.A.) during 1940 and 1941, and was president of the New Mexico Bankers Association. On the national level, he was on the A.B.A.'s commission on country bank operations in 1945 and 1946, a member of the public relations council in 1946 and 1947,

GLENN L. EMMONS

of its executive council in 1948, and national treasurer from 1949 to 1951.

In the course of his banking career, Emmons won the confidence and admiration of the Navaho Indians, who often came to him for business advice. The banker recognized their problems and needs, and was in sympathy with their desire for "increasing assumption of initiative and responsibility . . . in management of their own personal and tribal affairs" (New York *Times*, October 28, 1953).

During World War II, Emmons served as chairman of the McKinley county selective service board in New Mexico, and as chairman of the war bond committee for San Juan, Valencia and McKinley counties. He was the Republican nominee for Governor of New Mexico in 1944, but was defeated by Governor John J. Dempsey, the incumbent. In 1948, the state's Republican party endeavored to draft Emmons as its gubernatorial candidate, but he declined.

Emmons was sworn in as Commissioner of Indian Affairs on August 10, 1953, succeeding Dillon S. Myer, who resigned. His appointment was called by Oliver La Farge, head of the Association on American Indian Affairs, a victory over "phony spokesmen" for Indians (New York *Times*, July 16, 1953).

The Bureau of Indian Affairs was created in the War Department in 1824, and was transferred to the Department of the Interior in 1849. It acts as trustee with respect to Indian lands and funds, assists in making the most effective use of these lands, provides public services such as education, and public health and welfare aid, where these services are not available to Indians from other agencies. The ultimate goal of the bureau is to abolish the need for its own existence by guiding those Indians who wish to enter normal channels of American economic and social life, and collaborating with other Indian people in develop-

EMMONS, GLENN L.—*Continued*

ing Indian responsibility for the management of their property and affairs. According to the *U.S. Government Organization Manual,* the bureau "has the same purpose and responsibilities toward the natives of Alaska."

In his own words, Emmons' administration policy is to "liquidate the trusteeship of Indians as quickly as possible" (New York *Times,* July 16, 1953). His "Emmons plan" advocates reclamation of tribal lands and water resources, and the development of tribal industries.

President Eisenhower signed a bill on August 15, 1953 which transferred, from Federal to state courts, jurisdiction over criminal and civil cases involving Indians who live on reservations in California, Minnesota, Nebraska, Oregon, and Wisconsin. Referring to this law at the sixth annual convention of the Governors' Interstate Indian Council, in October 1953, Emmons said that the idea that only the Federal government can handle the welfare of the Indians is disappearing and the trend is now toward the states accepting more responsibility.

A series of recommendations to provide the Bureau of Indian Affairs with greater services was approved by Douglas McKay, Secretary of the Interior, on January 19, 1954. The recommendations included postponement of further construction of "relatively high cost boarding schools" on the Navaho Indian reservation, concentration on "inexpensive facilities of a semipermanent nature that could increase the number of children in day schools," and transferring the responsibilities of the bureau's branch of health to the U.S. Public Health Service in the Department of Health, Education and Welfare (New York *Times,* January 20, 1954).

"My belief," Emmons has stated, "is that the major forces now holding many of the Indian people back from full realization of their own potentialities are . . . ill health, lack of educational opportunities and poverty. By creating conditions favorable to the development of initiative and self-reliance, I believe we can hasten the day when the Indian can take his proper place in our local communities on an equal footing with his non-Indian neighbor" (*Rotarian,* August 1954).

Outside his professional interests, the Commissioner serves as director of the New Mexico Chapter of the Arthritic Foundation and vice-chairman for New Mexico of the Newcomen Society of England (a scientific society). He is also a past commander of the Gallup American Legion Post, and a former president of this community's Country and Kiwanis clubs.

Emmons was married to Dorothy Frances Hockaday, a teacher, on June 11, 1924. He stands five feet eleven inches tall, weighs 170 pounds, and has blue eyes and brown hair. He is a Mason, Shriner, Elk, and an Episcopalian. His hobbies are golf, spectator football and reading. The New York *Herald Tribune* wrote: "It is reassuring . . . to the general public to know that a sympathetic and understanding friend of Indians sits in the Commissioner's chair" (May 7, 1954).

References:

N Y Herald Tribune p15 Jl 16 '53; p15 Ag 2 '53
N Y Times p22 Jl 16 '53 por
Who's Who in Commerce and Industry (1953)
Who's Who in America, 1954-55

EYÜBOGLU, BEDRI RAHMI (ā'ū-bōgl") 1911- Painter; poet

Address: Istanbul, Turkey

The Turkish painter, Bedri Rahmi Eyüboglu, has been described by *Time* as having "one foot firmly planted on either side of the Bosporus," and painting pictures "that could never have been done farther east of Paris or west of Bagdad." He has attempted to achieve a synthesis of Turko-Oriental artistic traditions and modern Western techniques, and his ornamental, decorative, and stylized paintings depicting peasant life have earned him the reputation of being one of the most talented younger Turkish artists. His first American exhibition was held in Philadelphia, Pennsylvania in the fall of 1953, and his second, in September 1954 at the Wildenstein Gallery in New York City.

Eyüboglu received his early training at the Academy of Fine Arts in Istanbul, later studied in Paris, and then returned to Turkey to become a member of the avant-guard "Group D. More recently, he has made important contributions in the field of the decorative and applied arts. He is equally well-known in Turkey as a poet.

Bedri Rahmi Eyüboglu was born in 1911 in Trabzon, a city on the Black Sea in northern Turkey. His father, who was in the government service for many years, taught himself French, so that he could aid in the cultural training of his children. Bedri Rahmi first showed an interest in literature, and during his youth wrote the draft of a long novel. In his diary, he describes how he used to get his eldest brother to do his homework for him in painting class, since he himself was not interested in art at that time. It was only after he entered senior high school that he began to reveal a talent for painting.

In 1928, when he was seventeen years old, Eyüboglu enrolled in the Academy of Fine Arts in Constantinople (later Istanbul), the foremost art school in the country. There he worked under Ibrahim Calli, the leader of the impressionist painters in Turkey, who later turned to a modified expressionist style, and Nazmi Ziya, an important impressionist landscape painter. After two years at the Academy, Eyüboglu went to Paris and entered the atelier of the French cubist painter, André Lhote, with whom a number of other young Turkish artists have studied.

During his three-year stay in Paris, Eyüboglu began "to understand painting in a deeper sense." At first, he came under the influence of the post-impressionist masters, Cézanne, Gauguin, and van Gogh. Later, he studied the works of Picasso and other modern painters of the School of Paris, and was particularly impressed by the decorative style of Matisse and Raoul Dufy. In Eyüboglu's earlier paintings, according to Nurullah Berk *(Modern Painting and Sculpture in Turkey),* he was markedly influenced by Dufy's picturesque idiom, with its use of flat planes of contrasting colors and rapid calligraphic manner of drawing.

On his return to Turkey, Eyüboglu became associated with the advanced group of modern artists known as "Group D." Founded in Istanbul in 1933 by five painters and a sculptor, "Group D" was comprised of artists of diverse tendencies who were reacting against the realism and impressionism of the Turkish painters of the 1914 generation. Since it was the fourth important association of artists in the development of contemporary Turkish painting, the group had chosen to adopt as its name the fourth letter of the alphabet.

Among its members were Cemal Tollu, Nurullah Berk, Zeki Faik Izer, Elif Naci, Abidin Dino, Eşref Üren, Sabri Berkel, Arif Kaptan, and Eyüboglu's wife, Eren Eyüboglu, (whom he met in Paris and married in 1936) who is considered "the best Turkish woman painter of today." Like Eyüboglu, most of them had studied in Paris, and they were eager to introduce the cubist and fauve styles of modern French painting to their native country. They promoted this cause with numerous exhibitions and articles.

By 1937, "Group D" had sponsored eight exhibitions in Turkey, and its members had shown individually or together in Vienna, Moscow, Leningrad, Venice, Athens, and Bucharest (where Eyüboglu had a one-man show in 1935). The year 1937 marked the reorganization of the painting section of the Academy of Fine Arts in Istanbul by the French painter, Léopold Lévy, who invited several members of "Group D," including Eyüboglu, to join that institution's teaching staff.

Nurullah Berk has written that it was "Group D" which "had the privilege of establishing in Turkey a pictorial feeling rich in its spiritual nature, that was profoundly thought out and intellectually elaborated."

During the 1940's, Eyüboglu progressively broke away from the influence of the School of Paris that had dominated the painters of "Group D," and sought a more national form of expression based on his own country's artistic traditions and on the depiction of the Turkish scene and characteristic Turkish types. Spending much of his time in the villages of Anatolia, he chose his subjects from rural life, and found inspiration in Turkish folk art and folklore. In technique, he abandoned the delicate brushwork and preference for pastel colors that had marked his European apprenticeship and gradually evolved a more original style characterized by strongly accentuated designs, vivid color harmonies, and the use of ornamental arabesques and decorative motives. To John Steegman (*London Studio,* May 1946), it seems that Eyüboglu's fondness for organized pattern and glowing color is "the logical and reasoned expression of a purely Turkish feeling." As Berk has stated it, Eyüboglu "brought a new flavor to modern Turkish painting."

Sabah
BEDRI RAHMI EYÜBOGLU

Eyüboglu is especially well-known for his series of café scenes *(Coffee Inn in Corumda, Old Café, Café Scene in Anatolia),* which are said to reveal an almost Hogarthian robustness in the depiction of down-to-earth subjects. Examples of his more recent highly stylized manner, in which the figures are boldly outlined in black, are *A Country Woman and Her Child, Farmer Family,* and *Peasant Woman.* In his latest works, such as *Ox Shoeing, Kariye, Karacaoglon,* and *Istanbul,* he has experimented with a mosaic-like technique using tiny dots of pure color.

As a firm believer in a return to the national tradition and to popular art in particular, Eyüboglu has lately tried to reach a wider audience through his work in the applied arts. During the last few years, he has devoted considerable time to making designs for hand-printed fabrics, as well as for ceramics, carpets and kilims, and interior decoration schemes. "The possibilities are limitless," he has said about the decorative arts. Business people have become interested in his work in this field, and the new Hilton Hotel under construction in Istanbul will reportedly be decorated with curtains he designed.

In 1953 the Turkish government invited Eyüboglu and his wife to design *basma*—painted cloth often worn as a headdress by Moslem women—for mass production by the state-controlled textile factory at Nazilli. In Eyüboglu's words, the project "will make art available to thousands of the people; it is multiple art."

(Continued next page)

EYÜBOGLU, BEDRI RAHMI—*Cont.*

Eyüboglu's paintings were represented in "Fifty Years of Turkish Painting and Sculpture," the first large retrospective exhibition of modern art in Turkey, which was held at the pavilion of the Academy of Fine Arts in Istanbul in 1937. Exhibitions of his work in Turkey have taken place almost every year since his first one-man show there in 1941. His paintings attracted favorable critical attention when they were included in the exhibition, "Peinture turque d'aujourd'hui, Turquie d'autrefois," at the Musée Cernuschi in Paris in 1946.

The first American exhibition of Eyüboglu's work took place at the Print Club in Philadelphia in November 1953. It included over thirty of his gouaches, serigraphs, lithographs, woodcuts, and fabrics. The show was arranged for by Mrs. John Wintersteen, the club's president, who had seen some of Eyüboglu's work during a recent visit to Turkey. Reviewing the exhibition for the Philadelphia *Inquirer,* Gertrude Benson wrote: "His work is a strange marriage of the East and West: stylizations, inspired by Byzantine mosaics, Persian miniatures, Anatolian folk art, and a technical sophistication reminiscent, at times, of the work of Matisse and Dufy. But the final result is his own, strongest and most original in some of his gouaches of peasants and their children, in a lithograph like *Istanbul,* and in some of his woodcuts."

In an article on the arts in modern Turkey (*London Studio,* June 1945), Derek Patmore has written: "Bedri Rahmi's work is especially interesting because although extremely modern in technique it emphasizes the Turkish spirit. His paintings and drawings have recaptured the color and dramatic quality of the Anatolian scene, and his work reveals that his technique is sure and firm. Bedri Rahmi is the most Turkish of the young painters. He emphasizes the contrasts in Turkish life, and his painting is full of the passion, color, and depression which is characteristic of the Turkish scene. For these reasons, he may one day be hailed as a great painter."

In addition to being a painter, Eyüboglu is, according to Patmore, "one of the most brilliant" of the younger Turkish poets. He is said to be an exponent of "pure" poetry, which relies solely on words and symbols for its effect. Among Eyüboglu's published books of poetry are *Tuz (Salt,* 1952), which he illustrated with drawings; *Yaradana mektuplar (Letters to God); Kara Dut (Black Mulberries); and Ressam Nazmi Ziya (To Nazmi Ziya, the Painter).* His forthcoming books include *Yukule—leye mektuplar (Letters to Ukulele); Hikâyeler (Short Stories);* and *Resim Sanati (The Art of Painting).* He frequently contributes essays and poems, as well as illustrated travel sketches about his visits to various parts of the country, to Turkish newspapers.

The Turkish artist has a ground-floor studio situated on an alley just off one of the main streets of Istanbul. He works best between midnight and three in the morning—"almost painting in my sleep," as he describes it. *Time* reported that he sells most of his pictures for under fifty dollars, and according to a friend, "if you express a special interest in something he has done, he'll insist on giving it to you." Regarding his work, Eyüboglu has said: "My goal is to evolve an art as unique as Persian miniatures and Matisse, and as Turkish as our coffee and tobacco and figs."

Berk wrote: "Ornamental, decorative and stylized with its often unsubtle contrast of black and strong values, Bedri's art has brought a new flavor to Turkish art."

References

Studio 129:181+ Je '45; 131:129+ My '46

Time 62:70+ S 14 '53

Berk, N. Modern Painting and Sculpture in Turkey (1953)

FABIAN, ROBERT (HONEY) Jan. 31, 1901- Journalist; former police official

Address: b. c/o Kemsley Newspapers Ltd., Kemsley House, Gray's Inn Rd., London, W.C. 1, England; h. 13 Bramlet Way, Ashstead, Surrey, England

With a record of twenty-five years with the Criminal Investigation Department at New Scotland Yard, and twenty-eight years in the service of the London police, Detective-Superintendent Robert Fabian has earned some forty commendations, and the highest award for bravery obtainable by a member of the metropolitan force. Since his retirement in June 1949 he has become a journalist, and a writer of crime feature stories for a chain of British newspapers.

He is the author of the book *Fabian of the Yard,* published in London in 1950 and New York in 1953, which describes some thirty of his leading "cases." A series of "television shorts" based on this book is scheduled for showing on American networks in 1954. His latest book *London After Dark* was published in February 1954 by the Naldrett Press, London.

Grandson of a Manx sailmaker and the son of Andrew Pinwill Fabian, a seagoing engineer, Robert Honey Fabian was born January 31, 1901 at Ladywell near London. He has two brothers, Rupert, now a gold miner, and Abram, an engineer, and a sister, Ellen. His mother was the former Ada Eliza Taggart, a schoolteacher. It was originally intended that Robert should follow in his father's footsteps and attend Trinity College, Dublin. After graduating in 1912 from elementary school at Catford he entered Borough Polytechnic, a London trade school. He was trained as an engineering draftsman and after passing his examinations held a number of drawing jobs, including one with a concern which specialized in ships' telephones and other electrical equipment; but his heart was never in this kind of work. One evening in the spring of 1921 he returned home from work to find an old friend of his parents, Inspector Frederick Rolfe of the Metropolitan police, taking tea. "Listening to Rolfe jovially talking about life in the force," Fabian states, "made me realize. . . there was a good chance it would suit my ego better than any drawing office."

With the inspector's help, he filled out an application and delivered it at the Lewisham police station. Having met the physical and other requirements, he reported for duty on May 17, 1921.

After eight hard weeks of basic police training, twenty-year old Fabian was "posted" as a police constable attached to the Vine Street police station (near London's Piccadilly Circus). The area included some fashionable residential streets, much of the West End theatrical district, the Soho "Latin quarter," and various hotbeds of organized vice. Fabian pounded a nightbeat for a number of months; then in 1922 he was suddenly able to turn his draftsman's training to advantage by making a ground plan of a Soho night club on which a raid was contemplated.

As a result he became "temporarily attached" to the Vine Street vice squad and in the course of duty gained invaluable knowledge and understanding of the local underworld and its personalities. In 1922 he was "confirmed" in his constable's appointment, and in 1923 he "applied for consideration" for the Criminal Investigation Department. Having been accepted as a candidate, he began the probationary period as a plain-clothes detective.

Fabian was still a probationer when in 1924 he assisted in the apprehension of Robert Augustus Delaney, the first of the "cat burglars". He attended the Detective Training School at Hendon and passed the examination for detective-sergeant in 1925, although he did not receive his actual promotion until some five years later.

The young detective kept in good physical condition by playing cricket and Rugby (with the London Welsh team) and by boxing, which he learned from the actor and former pugilist, Victor McLaglen. He touched neither alcohol nor tobacco until he was thirty. "It was his youthfully innocent good looks that brought him his first success as a detective," observed Stanley Jackson *Illustrated London News* (October 24, 1953). "In a notorious Soho club, the rendezvous of some of London's toughest gangsters, he mixed with the ruffians and their women, who called him 'The Little Water Drinker' and had no suspicion he was looking for a murderer. His sharp eyes and ability to stick on the job helped him to trap Emile Berthier on a cross-Channel steamer."

As a detective-constable, he was at the Vine Street station until 1929. He then began eighteen months of duty as a clerk in the criminal record office at headquarters. (By that time he had solved two murders as well as forgery and larceny cases, and had earned fifteen commissioner's commendations).

Fabian received his long-delayed promotion to detective-sergeant in April 1930, and in the same year was transferred to the Marylebone divisional C.I.D. He was working out of the

Kemsley Picture Service, London
ROBERT FABIAN

station in Marylebone Lane when in September 1932 he arrested "the first armed robber to hold up a West End jeweller's shop in broad daylight."

Later promoted to detective-inspector, Fabian was reassigned to Marlborough Street station, and in 1937 stopped a "bogus count bent on marrying a U.S. heiress by noting that his shoes had not been polished under the instep" (*Time,* August 17, 1953).

By the following year (1938) Detective-Inspector Fabian was back at the Vine Street station and was working in his office when on the night of June 24, 1939, a homemade bomb, presumably planted by an Irish Republican, exploded in nearby Piccadilly Circus. Rushing out to investigate, Fabian noticed a brown paper parcel on the edge of the sidewalk which he suspected contained another bomb. No fire bucket was at hand, so he carried the parcel at top speed to Vine Street, where he dropped it in water; it was later found to have contained forty ounces of high explosive.

For this display of courage Fabian was rewarded on August 3 with "a cheque for fifteen pounds drawn on the Police Reward Fund" (London *Times*) and on February 6, 1940 with the so-called "Victoria Cross" of the police, the King's Medal for Gallantry. He received the medal at Buckingham Palace from the hands of His Majesty King George VI, and today keeps it in the same drawer with another medal of a very different character, presented by "the men of London's underworld" and inscribed: "For bravery, 24-6-39. From the Boys."

Between 1943 and 1945 Fabian was the chief of Scotland Yard's "Flying Squad" which uses many different kinds of vehicles, all of which are equipped with radio and can be rushed to any part of London. Ordinarily, the authority of the Yard, which is technically a division of the Metropolitan police, covers only the county

FABIAN, ROBERT—*Continued*

of London, but in cases of special difficulty its aid may be requested by the chief constables of other shires.

Thus when in October 1946, the body of a girl (subsequently proven to be that of Dagmar Peters) was found on Wrotham Hill, Kent, the aid of Scotland Yard was sought. To Fabian was delegated the task of identifying both the corpse and the murderer with "only a hair-net tangled among the dead twigs" as an initial clue. The Wrotham Hill crime, with the scope it afforded for detective work of the Sherlock Holmes variety, is regarded as Fabian's most brilliantly concluded murder investigation.

Another spectacular case was the shoot-and-run killing of Alec de Antiquis near Tottenham Court Road in London in April 1947. The principal clue to the murderer was a label under the lining of a coat and Fabian, now promoted to chief-inspector, solved the murder with this bit of evidence.

After his advancement to detective-superintendent, Fabian decided to retire from the Metropolitan police in June 1949, following twenty-eight years of service. He is now a crime feature writer for Kemsley Newspapers, Ltd., which publishes the London *Daily Graphic* and *Sunday Times,* and several provincial newspapers.

A number of Fabian's articles were assembled in his book *Fabian of the Yard* (published by Naldrett, London, 1950). A series of television "shorts" based on the thirty-odd cases recounted in this book was subsequently produced by Anthony Beauchamp for the British Broadcasting Company.

An American edition of *Fabian of the Yard* was published in New York by the British Book Centre in the summer of 1953 and was favorably reviewed. "There is human warmth in it and no hysteria, no bitterness, no sensationalism," noted Meyer Berger in the New York *Times,* while Joseph Henry Jackson of the San Francisco *Chronicle* was impressed by the "economy" and "nice sense of drama" with which each story was told.

In an introductory chapter Fabian stressed the importance of teamwork in criminal investigation and the "special qualities of character" necessary to the successful detective. "He must be tactful, courageous, painstaking and vigilant. . .and should be a wizard at jigsaws." A concluding chapter giving a practical illustration of the structure and operating procedure of Scotland Yard is followed by a unique glossary of British thieves' jargon.

Married to Letitia Stockwell on May 9, 1925, Fabian is the father of Peter Robert Fabian. The journalist has hazel eyes and dark brown hair, is five feet ten inches in height and weighs 180 pounds. "His well-muscled frame is packed into the suitings of Saville Row." He enjoys shooting, golf, gardening, swimming, and chess. He belongs to the Church of England and the Conservative party.

References

Illus Lond N p50 O 24 '53 pors
Fabian, R. Fabian of the Yard (1953)

FAIRCHILD, DAVID (GRANDISON)
April 7, 1869- Aug. 6, 1954 Botanist; author; educated at the Kansas State College of Agriculture; was director of U.S. Department of Agriculture's section of foreign seed and plant introduction (1906-1928), and agricultural explorer for government; brought to United States more than 200,000 species of plants (including Mexican cotton, Russian wheat, and Japanese rice) gathered in his world travels; established Fairchild Tropical Garden in Florida; wrote *The World Was My Garden* (1938), and numerous other books. See *Current Biography,* (July) 1953.

Obituary

N Y Times p13 Ag 7 '54

FARNSWORTH, JERRY Dec. 31, 1895-
Artist; teacher

Address: b. 4823 Harry Higel Ave., Sarasota, Fla.; h. 3482 Flamingo, Sarasota, Fla.; "Five Elms," North Truro, Cape Cod, Mass.

One of the notable portrait and figure painters in contemporary America is Jerry Farnsworth who has been a consistent favorite in national juried art shows. He is rated "among those rare few who can combine figure and portrait to create a work of art in the finest sense" (*Art Digest,* November 1, 1942). In the *American Artist* (December 1949), Ernest W. Watson states that Farnsworth produces "the kind of painting that inherits the ideals and technical competence of the old masters . . . his canvases are quiet and competent, invariably conceived and executed with good taste. His color is rich and subtle. . . . There is scarcely a museum of importance that does not own a Farnsworth portrait or figure painting."

His works are in such representative museums as the Metropolitan Museum of Art, Whitney Museum of American Art, Pennsylvania Academy of the Fine Arts, Isaac Delgado Museum of Art (New Orleans, Louisiana), and Houston Museum of Fine Arts (Texas). They are also in many private collections. The artist established the Farnsworth School of Art at Cape Cod in 1933 and later a winter branch at Sarasota, Florida, and has taught in both schools with his wife, Helen Sawyer, also a well-known painter.

Jerry Farnsworth was born in Dalton, Georgia on December 31, 1895, the son of Samuel and Lavinia (Pou) Farnsworth. His father, a local storekeeper, died when Jerry was three years old, and his mother, a trained nurse, supported the family. Jerry attended public schools in New Orleans, Louisiana and in other southern areas until his mother moved with the family in 1911 to New York City where the boy entered Stuyvesant High School. There had never been an artist in his family and his interest in art did not develop until he was twenty.

Farnsworth has stated that he began as a "Sunday painter" after a chance visit to a Sunday art class conducted by Clinton Peters in New York City. He then realized that art had a significant meaning for him and that he wanted to pursue it as a career. While serving during World War I as a yeoman with the United States Naval Reserve Force in Washington, D.C., he attended night classes at the Corcoran School of Art. After the war, he worked on the staff of the *Nation's Business* magazine in Washington, D.C. Deciding to give all his time to art, he went to Provincetown, Massachusetts in 1921 to study painting with Charles W. Hawthorne.

His marriage to Helen Alton Sawyer took place on August 26, 1925. He received the third Hallgarten prize of the National Academy of Design in 1925 and again in 1927. He gave courses in New York City at the Art Students League and at the Grand Central School of Art, and in his own school at North Truro in Cape Cod each summer, beginning in 1933. He was made an associate member of the National Academy of Design in 1933 and an academician in 1935.

Farnsworth, who believes that art in America moved toward new goals after its break with the French School, has said: "I don't believe in labels. I myself don't know where I belong, with what group of painters. . . . I believe every artist should be an individualist, appreciative of the giants of the past and interested the while in every new manifestation which presents itself" (*Modern American Painting,* Dodd, 1948). Grace Pagano, in the *Encyclopædia Britannica Collection of Contemporary American Painting* (1946) states that Farnsworth "has developed in the oldest American tradition of all—conscientious realism."

The artist received the first award of $300 for his painting *The Yellow Bird* at the "American Art—Without Isms" exhibition, held in 1939 at the Grand Central Art Galleries in New York City. Farnsworth's painting of a young girl called *Memories,* exhibited in 1939 at the "Recent Paintings by a Group of American Artists" show in the Milch Art Gallery, New York City, won immediate praise and was reproduced in three of the city's newspapers. Emily Genauer wrote in the New York *World-Telegram* that the painting was "an object lesson in what American contemporary portraiture can be and too rarely is" (*Art Digest,* October 15, 1939).

The artist's oil, *Annabella,* a semi-nude, was purchased by the Metropolitan Museum of Art, New York City, in 1940. The following year his *Truro Child* was bought by the New Britain (Connecticut) Institute. The Whitney Museum of American Art added Farnsworth's *My Neighbor Miss Williams* to its permanent collection in 1942.

During 1942 and 1943, Farnsworth was Carnegie visiting professor of art, and artist in residence at the University of Illinois in Urbana. He served on a jury which judged 285 entries in the First Annual Exhibit of Central Illinois artists. In the fall of 1942, the University of Illinois presented a retrospective show covering ten years of Farnsworth's work, including fifty-four oils and twelve drawings. Previous prize winners, *The Guide, The Yellow Bird,* and *Jan de Groot,* were shown, as well as

Steinmetz

JERRY FARNSWORTH

the semi-nude portrait, *Sally,* which had earned high recognition in 1940 at The Pennsylvania Academy of the Fine Arts.

Also included among the paintings were the "strongly modeled figure" of a girl reading, *Emily;* and the "richly-colored likeness" of an elderly Negro preacher (*Art Digest,* November 1, 1942). James Grote Van Derpool, then head of the university's art department, stated in a foreword to the exhibit catalogue that Farnsworth "in achieving enduring expression has premised his procedure on values that are permanent."

Jerry Farnsworth was commissioned in 1945 by the Order of DeMolay to paint an oil portrait of President Harry S. Truman's mother, Martha Ellen Truman, as a Christmas gift for the Chief Executive. The portrait was presented in December 1945, and hung in Truman's study in the Oval Room of the White House.

The artist's *The Spring Hat,* an oil painting, was included in the *Encyclopædia Britannica Collection of Contemporary American Painting.* In the book, Grace Pagano wrote that "Farnsworth's paintings might not force a first, quick glance, but the glance when it happens will be a lingering and delighted one. . . . Never wrathful, never violent, he manages his quiet chords with a sublimated Puritan kind of sensuousness."

A colored reproduction of his painting *The Dancer* is included in *Modern American Painting.* A photographer's record of the development of *My Friend Stephen,* an oil portrait of a young boy, is reproduced in the *American Artist* (December 1949). It demonstrates the artist's belief in keeping "the highlights in a portrait subdued."

Among Farnsworth's still-life pieces is *The Pink Sugar Bowl,* which "stands out for its expert play of light" (*Art Digest,* November 1, 1942). In his article "On Painting Still Life"

FARNSWORTH, JERRY—*Continued*

(*American Artist,* February 1949), the artist calls this "the purest form of painting." He also states that still-life painting is "the chamber music of painting . . . the artist's playtime, his time to study, to relax, to enjoy and to observe."

He has frequently been commissioned to do art work for advertising projects. In 1945 he prepared an advertisement for the DeBeers Consolidated Mines. His drawings have been reproduced by such popular magazines as *McCall's* and his cover designs have appeared on periodicals like *Arts and Decoration* (May 1934). He has exhibited both nationally and internationally.

The artist is the author of the book *Painting with Jerry Farnsworth* (Watson-Guptill, 1949), called ". . . a primer for the novice or painter" (*Art News,* September 1949). It tells about how to get a free art education and how to make a living as an artist, and gives the author's ideas on technique. The volume is illustrated with color plates and half tones and includes examples of Farnsworth's work.

Jerry Farnsworth won the second prize of the Society of Washington Artists (1924), the Golden State Prize of the Grand Central Art Galleries (1928), and the Thomas B. Clarke Prize of the National Academy of Design (1933). He received the academy's Thomas Proctor Prize in 1935, its Isador Medal in 1936, its Altman Prize in 1938, and its Maynard Portrait Prize in 1952.

Other of his awards include the first prize (president's) of the Grand Central Art Galleries (1939), honorable mention of the Art Institute of Chicago (1940), portrait prize of the National Arts Club (1941), purchase prize of the Los Angeles, California, museum (1945), and first purchase prize of the High Museum of Art (Atlanta, Georgia) for his *Loraine of Truro* (1946). He is a member of the Society of Washington Artists and the Provincetown (Massachusetts) Art Association. His clubs include the Salmagundi and the National Arts in New York City.

The artist has gray eyes and hair, is five feet eight inches tall, and weighs 168 pounds. His political affiliation is Republican. Farnsworth likes "sailing, gardening and woodworking." In the words of Ernest W. Watson, "Jerry Farnsworth ranks high in favor with those who know and love good painting" (*American Artist,* December 1949).

References

Am Artist 13:30+ D '49 por

Boswell, P. Modern American Painting (1948)

Who's Who in America, 1954-55

Who's Who in American Art (1953)

Who's Who in New England (1949)

Who's Who in the South and Southwest (1952)

FARNSWORTH, MRS. JERRY See Sawyer, H. (A.)

FARRAR, JOHN (CHIPMAN) (făr'ẽr) Feb. 25, 1896- Publisher; author

Address: b. c/o Farrar, Straus and Young, Inc., 101 5th Ave., New York 3; h. 16 E. 96th St., New York 28

"Publishing is the most exciting business in the world," John Farrar once told the students in his class at Columbia. "There is only one thing more exciting to me than the birth of a best seller: the reading of a great unpublished manuscript, whether it becomes a best seller or not—but so many of them do. To have read *Three Soldiers, John Brown's Body, The Seven Pillars of Wisdom* and *Anthony Adverse* before the fact was more exciting than when the first 1000 copy order came in."

Well known in publishing circles for over thirty years, John Farrar is editor and chairman of the board of Farrar, Straus and Young, a New York publishing company organized since the end of World War II. His co-partners are Roger W. Straus, Jr., and Stanley Young. Farrar has had a distinguished literary career as a poet, playwright, short story writer, teacher, critic, and editor.

He was the editor of the New York literary monthly *The Bookman* from 1921 to 1927, and a partner in the publishing firm of Farrar and Rinehart from 1929 to 1944. He is a veteran of the United States Air Service in World War I, and served with the psychological warfare branch of the Office of War Information in World War II.

Born in Burlington, Vermont, on February 25, 1896, John Chipman Farrar is the son of Edward Donaldson Farrar and Sally (Wright) Farrar. His father was an advertising man "of the Pear's soap era"; his mother was a teacher and librarian who worked for many years at the central branch of the New York Public Library. An early influence on his career was that exerted by Byron Clark, the head of the Burlington Young Men's Christian Association.

Farrar's first printed work, *A Pageant,* was published in Burlington in 1910, when he was only fourteen; it was followed two years later by *Fire Water,* a play subtitled "An Abnaki Indian Allegory", and in 1914 by *Dreams of Boyhood.*

Graduated from high school in 1914, John entered Yale University in New Haven, Connecticut. He formed a close friendship with a fellow Yale student, Stephen Vincent Benét, whose elder brother, William Rose Benét, then a publisher's reader, introduced the two young men to the Poetry Society of America. Both Benéts were major influences on Farrar's career, he has said.

Farrar was only a sophomore when his book of verse, *Portraits,* was published by the Yale University Press. With a second group of "Portraits", a number of "Songs for Children," and other poems, it was included in 1919 in *Forgotten Shrines,* a volume in the "Yale Series of Younger Poets".

From July 1917 to February 1919, Farrar was a first lieutenant in the U.S. Army Air Service, and acquired the war experience on which he drew to write the one-act play *Nerves*, produced by the Yale Dramatic Association in the spring of 1919. Farrar, who received his A.B. degree from Yale in the summer of that year ("as of" 1918), had been the chairman of the Yale *Literary Magazine*. He was also the co-editor with John Andrews, Stephen Vincent Benét and Pierson Underwood of *The Yale Book of Student Verse, 1910-1919* (Yale University Press, 1919).

Farrar received much encouragement and guidance from the late Sidney Howard, a literary critic for the humorous weekly *Life* and well-known playwright. In 1919 Farrar began his journalistic career under John O'Hara Cosgrave as a reporter and feature writer for the Sunday magazine section of the New York *World*. He did so well that in 1921 he was offered, and accepted, the editorship of the New York literary monthly, *The Bookman*, published by George H. Doran Company. In the same year the Yale University Press published Farrar's *Songs for Parents*, which was praised by Amy Lowell in the *Literary Review* as "a most joyous and delightful volume" and by the New York *Times* as "forty-two frisky and friendly memories of childhood."

Timothy Tubby's Journal, a "take-off of the visiting British novelist" published anonymously by Doran in 1922, was the work of John Farrar, who in the same year completed collaboration with Prosper Buranelli on *Gold-Killer; A Mystery of the New Underworld* (Doran) which appeared under the pseudonym of "John Prosper." Also in 1922 Farrar edited *The Bookman Anthology of Verse* (First Series) for Doran. In March of the following year, in addition to his editorial duties on *The Bookman*, he wrote in alternation with Stephen Benét, a signed book column which appeared in *Time* magazine. This he continued until 1924.

Doran published *The Bookman Anthology of Essays* in 1923 (edited by Farrar) as well as seven one-act plays by Farrar which were collected under the title *The Magic Sea Shell and Other Plays for Children*. His one-act war drama *Nerves* was included in the *Atlantic Book of Junior Plays* (Little, 1924). A performing text was published in 1930 by Samuel French. A three-act version (in collaboration with Stephen Vincent Benét) was produced on Broadway in September 1924. *Nerves* was withdrawn after only two weeks, as was *That Awful Mrs. Eaton*, an historical piece about Andrew Jackson, presented at the Morosco Theatre on September 29.

A delightful playlet by Farrar alone, *The Garden at the Zoo* was included in M. A. Jagendorf's *One-Act Plays for Young Folks* (Brentano's, 1924), while in the same year Doran published Farrar's collection of thirty-two poems under the title *The Middle Twenties*, and *The Literary Spotlight*, which Farrar edited. He was the dramatic critic for the magazine *Charm* in 1924 and 1925, and the motion picture critic for the *Ladies' Home Journal* in 1925 and 1926.

He began teaching at New York University in the early twenties, and directed the Bread Loaf Writers' Conference at Middlebury College, Vermont, in its first three years (1926-1928).

Blackstone Studios

JOHN FARRAR

Farrar, who had become an editor in George H. Doran's Company in 1925, edited a second series of *The Bookman Anthology of Verse* in 1927, while two of his short stories, "The Captain's Shower Bath" and "Miss Miranda's Romeo", which appeared in *Collier's* in the same year, were included in anthologies. The first is to be found in James G. Dunton's collection *C'est la Guerre! The Best Stories of the World War* (Stratford, 1927), and the second in Paul M. Fulcher's *Short Narratives* (Century, 1928).

The Bookman having been sold to Burton Rascoe and Seward Collins in April 1927, its former editor remained with the George H. Doran Company until the latter was merged with Doubleday, Page and Company to form Doubleday, Doran and Company, whereupon he became a director of the combined firm for two years. With Stanley Rinehart, another Doran editor, John Farrar had been largely responsible for contracting with Stephen Benét for the writing of his celebrated narrative poem *John Brown's Body*.

In 1929 Stanley Rinehart and his mother, the mystery novelist Mary Roberts Rinehart, and Farrar formed the new publishing firm of Farrar and Rinehart, Inc. John Farrar was editor, vice-president and chairman of the board. "Steve" Benét became the firm's principal reader, and urged publication of its biggest best seller, Hervey Allen's *Anthony Adverse* (1933).

Among Farrar's writings in the 1930's were *Songs for Johnny-Jump-Up* (Smith, 1930); *Indoor and Outdoor Plays for Children* (Noble, 1933); and *Jack* (French, 1935). He also became interested in radio, and edited and assisted in the direction of the National Broadcasting Company's production of Archibald MacLeish's *The Fall of the City* (1937) as well as three

FARRAR, JOHN—*Continued*

later programs by Stephen Vincent Benét: *Letters to Hitler, They Burned the Books,* and *Listen to the People.* Farrar also conducted a sixteen weeks author-interview series on WEVD.

Shortly after the death of Stephen Vincent Benét on March 13, 1943, Farrar contributed to the *Saturday Review of Literature* the memoir "For the Record" which was reprinted later in the year by Farrar and Rinehart along with a bibliography and William Rose Benét's companion memoir "My Brother Steve." In June 1943, John Farrar took a leave of absence from his firm to join the psychological warfare branch of the Office of War Information, and from September of that year until the following July was stationed at Algiers in North Africa.

At New York between September 1944 and December 1945, he was in charge of the O.W.I.'s Overseas Publications; he edited *U.S.A.,* which was distributed abroad in a dozen different languages, and also the first three issues of *Die Amerikanische Rundschau,* the first American magazine to go into Germany after the end of the war in Europe.

While still with the O.W.I., Farrar gave (1945) a lecture course on "Modern Writing" at the Town Hall in New York. In 1945 and 1946 he conducted writing classes at the U.S. Naval Hospital, St. Albans, Long Island. Subsequently (1946-1948) he gave a publishing course in the Columbia University extension program, and from 1949 to 1951 directed the Marlboro Fiction Writers' Conference at Marlboro College in Vermont.

It was announced in September 1944 that John Farrar would not return to Farrar and Rinehart (now Rinehart and Company). "The brief notice assigns no reason for the change, but it is understood that disagreement over matters of policy are responsible," commented Harry Hansen in the New York *World-Telegram,* and added that it was "inconceivable" that John Farrar "should stay out of book publishing for long." Early in 1946 Farrar and Roger W. Straus, Jr. launched a new publishing house with Farrar as editor and chairman of the board, and Straus as president. The new firm (the name of which was changed from Farrar, Straus and Company to Farrar, Straus and Young when Stanley Young became a partner in 1951) scored its first outstanding success in 1947 with Carlo Levi's *Christ Stopped at Eboli.* It has since published many other works of Italian authorship, including the novels of Alberto Moravia.

The firm, which recently took over the lists of the Creative Age Press and Pellegrini and Cudahy, publishes also the fictional works of Robert Graves, Charles Jackson, Shirley Jackson, Edmund Wilson, Charles Williams, and François Mauriac. Notable among the nonfiction issued under its imprint have been *Miracle at Kitty Hawk; The Letters of Wilbur and Orville Wright* (1951) and *Secret Conversations, 1941-1944* (1953) of Adolf Hitler. Farrar, Straus and Young is one of the firms associated with Ballantine Books in issuing paper-back editions of certain of their works simultaneously with regular cloth-bound "trade" editions.

A special interest has been taken by both John Farrar and Roger Straus in their series "City and Country Readers," which includes *State of Mind* (1948), edited by Robert N. Linscott; *World From Jackson Square* (1948), edited by Etolia Basso; *White Pine and Blue Water* (1950), edited by Henry Beston; and *Western Gate* (1952), edited by Joseph Henry Jackson, dealing with Boston, New Orleans, Maine, and San Francisco respectively.

John Farrar has been president of the New York Center of the P.E.N. Club, 1951-1954; he is also a member of the Federal Grand Jury Association (executive committee 1949-), the Writers' Board for World Government, and the National Conference of Christians and Jews. He was made an honorary member of the Phi Beta Kappa fraternity at New York University in 1946; his Yale fraternity is the Alpha Delta Phi (national secretary 1954-). His clubs are the Century Association and Yale in New York and the Elizabethan in New Haven.

He was married to the former Margaret Petherbridge on May 28, 1926. She is now the crossword puzzle editor of the New York *Times;* she has edited a series of crossword puzzle books for Simon and Schuster, and is now an advisory editor with her husband's firm. John and Margaret Farrar are the parents of one son, Curtis Farrar, and two daughters, Alison (Mrs. George W. Wilson) and Janice (Mrs. Peter Weeks) and they have four grandchildren.

Politically, the publisher describes himself as a "Vermont Republican," while his faith is the Episcopalian. Farrar, who is five feet nine inches in height and weighs about 160 pounds, has blue eyes and red hair. Baseball is his favorite spectator sport (he is a Yankee fan), and teaching and "translating from the Italian" are his avocations.

References

N Y Times p13 My 29 '26
N Y World-Telegram p22 S 14 '44; p12 O 6 '45
Benét, W. R. and Farrar, J. Stephen Vincent Benét (1943)
Farrar, J. ed. The Literary Spotlight (1924)
Who's Who in America, 1954-55
Who's Who in the East (1953)
World Biography (1948)

FARRINGTON, JOSEPH R(IDER) Oct. 15, 1897-June 19, 1954 United States Delegate from Hawaii; newspaper publisher; born in Washington, D.C., reared in Hawaii; attended Punahou Academy, Honolulu and then University of Wisconsin (roomed with former Governor Philip La Follette) and was graduated (1919); enlisted in U.S. Army and commissioned a second lieutenant in 1918; was a reporter for the Philadelphia *Public Ledger* (1919) and Washington correspondent; represented his father's paper, the Honolulu *Star-Bulletin* (1924-1933) and became general manager in 1934; was president of the Hilo (Hawaii) *Tribune Herald* and the Honolulu Lithograph Company, Ltd.; began his drive for statehood for Hawaii in 1930 and was elected to the Territorial Senate; promoted a plebiscite in which Hawaiians voted two to one in favor of statehood; was a delegate to Congress since 1942; won "an immediate statehood" plank in the Republican platform in 1952. See *Current Biography,* (May) 1948.

Obituary

N Y Times p84 Je 20 '54

FELTIN, MAURICE, CARDINAL May 15, 1883- Archbishop of Paris

Address: Archevêché de Paris, 32 rue Barbet-de-Jouy, Paris 7e, France

French Embassy Press & Inf. Div.

MAURICE CARDINAL FELTIN

The Archbishop of Paris, Maurice Cardinal Feltin, has long been admired in France for his "vigorous development" of various social projects in the areas under his jurisdiction. He had served as Bishop of Troyes, and Archbishop of Sens and of Bordeaux, before he became the Archbishop of Paris in 1949. In 1953 he was elevated to the Sacred College of Cardinals. He received citations for his courage as an ambulance driver in World War I and distinguished himself in World War II by his opposition to the invaders of France.

Cardinal Feltin is one of three French Cardinals who journeyed to Rome in November 1953 to defend the French worker-priest movement to the Vatican. For ten years these priests have been wearing overalls instead of cassocks, have worked in factories, and have shared the life of the workers. Cardinal Feltin stressed the importance of these priests as missionaries in ending the "long estrangement between French workers and the Roman Catholic Church."

Pope Pius XII protested against the "waywardness" of some of the worker-priests (who had reportedly become "tinged with Marxism") and accordingly, the delegation of Cardinals laid down "five imperatives for future conduct" of these worker-priests. The movement will continue in France, although greatly modified.

Maurice Feltin was born May 15, 1883, at Delle, in the territory of Belfort. He was graduated from the Collège de Saint-Ignace. After completing his studies at the Séminaire Saint-Sulpice near Paris, he was ordained in the Roman Catholic priesthood in 1909, and became curate of the church of Sainte-Madeleine at Besançon. When World War I broke out, he volunteered for ambulance duty and served with the rank of sergeant in the Fourteenth Regiment of the French Army. His courageous conduct brought him the French military medal and several citations, and his war record, too, was one of the elements responsible for his being named a Chevalier of the Legion of Honor on November 5, 1931.

Appointed senior priest of the church at Giromagny in 1920, he served there until 1925 when he returned to his original parish of Sainte-Madeleine in Besançon to become its rector. On January 1, 1927, he was also named its honorary canon. He was raised to the Bishopric of Troyes on December 19, 1927, and his consecration as a Bishop took place in Besançon on March 11, 1928 at the hands of Cardinal Binet.

Bishop Feltin devoted himself to the work of his new diocese and soon his pastoral letters received wide attention, chiefly because of their attacks on religious ignorance. He was named Archbishop of Sens on August 16, 1932, and during his three years in this position, he did notable work, especially "for the economically disinherited" (according to the *Dictionnaire Biographique Français Contemporain*).

When Cardinal Andrieu of Bordeaux died, Archbishop Feltin was named to succeed him and was inducted into his new post on December 16, 1935. Since Monsignor Maglione, then the Papal Nuncio at Paris, had besought him to create an archdiocese worthy of Bordeaux, he started by building a large seminary and by opening a seminary for those who had entered the priesthood late in life.

In addition, Archbishop Feltin founded a vacation retreat for young seminarians in the Pyrenees. He accelerated the construction of such new churches in his See as Saint-Victor, Sainte-Bernadette, Sainte-Monique, and Sainte-Jeanne d'Arc at Arcachon and Saints-Anges at Quatre-Pavillons, and of a chapel at L'Alouette.

Keeping almost all his parochial schools in operation, the Archbishop also established new ones. To the priests in his See, he accorded an annual allowance. He aided the Catholic Action group in its activities, and gave it a local chapter house. The Archbishop organized weeks for study and retreat, and devoted particular attention to the charitable groups of the archiocese.

The record of Archbishop Feltin during World War II and the occupation of France

FELTIN, MAURICE, CARDINAL—*Cont.*
was marked by his denunciations of the brutal methods used by the Nazis and by his efforts to save those whom they persecuted. He was able to rescue Rabbi Cohen and others from the Gestapo. Archbishop Feltin also preserved the Torah of the Bordeaux synagogue. According to the *Dictionnaire Biographique Français Contemporain,* the Archbishop showed "notable intransigence" toward the German invaders.

Upon the death of Emmanuel Cardinal Suhard, Archbishop of Paris, Archbishop Feltin was named his successor in August 1949, and was enthroned as Archbishop of that city on October 8, 1949 in the Cathedral of Notre Dame. Among his other activities in this position, he became president of the international movement, *Pax Christi.* He received the Red Hat of the Cardinal from Pope Pius XII on January 12, 1953.

In Paris, Cardinal Feltin, like his predecessor, encouraged the worker-priest movement, which had been organized in July 1943 as the *Mission de Paris,* inspired by a book by Abbé Henri Godin and Yvan Daniel entitled *La France, Pays de Mission?* The idea spread to all of France during the post-war period. The worker-priests numbered about twenty-five in Paris in 1953.

When the worker-priest movement was condemned by the Vatican in 1953, Cardinal Feltin found himself one of the foremost spokesmen of the Gallican church. The higher French clergy was summoned by the Papal Nuncio, Monsignor Paul Marella, in the name of the Papal Consistory to hear its order to recall from the factories and shipyards the French priests who had carried their ministry to the worker. The Consistory deplored the action of two French priests who participated in Communist-led strikes against SHAPE's General Matthew B. Ridgway in 1952, and the attitude of the seminary at Limoges toward the nationwide strikes of 1953 (*Match,* October 3-10, 1953).

On hearing that the experiment must be put to an end, reported *Match,* Cardinal Feltin "claimed once again for the French episcopate the privilege of regulating this painful problem by itself." Soon after, in his official bulletin, the Cardinal stressed the necessity for the existence of the worker-priests since "the great painful fact that marks our era is the separation that exists between the workers' world and the church."

In the same communication he brought attention to four dangers which might beset the worker-priest; confusion between the temporal and spiritual aspects of his mission, erroneous notions about the church's hierarchy, misconception of the law of charity, and excessive independence foreign to the church's rule of obedience. Later, at Lisieux, he called for reforms in the worker-priest movement, but said that it must not be abolished.

With Pierre Cardinal Gerlier of Lyon, and Achille Cardinal Lienart of Lille, Cardinal Feltin was received by the Pope at Castel Gandolfo on November 5, 1953. Pointing out that it would be dangerous to suppress the mission of the worker-priests entirely, the French Cardinals asked for the establishment of a statute on the mission to avoid possible future deviations. Upon the successful completion of their conversations, the Cardinals and the Pope in mid-November expressed "the formal will of the church not to abandon at any price the effort it is pursuing for the evangelization of the working masses. . . ."

Rules for the future regulation of the worker-priests agreed upon were that they must be chosen individually by their bishops, be attached to a religious community rather than stay independent, refrain from temporal commitments (particularly association with trade-union movements), spend only limited time each day in manual work, and receive specialized and "pertinent" training in Catholic doctrine and in spiritual leadership.

The members of the high French clergy in January 1954 issued orders which in effect required all priests to conform to the new regulations as of March 1, 1954. The French newspapers were critical of the part-time work requirement, because it would separate the priests too sharply from the workers and prohibit them from joining the unions to which most other French workers belong.

According to Louis Rougier in *Saturday Night,* March 27, 1954, "The Holy See and the French Episcopate seem to have come to a compromise. . . . The very expression 'Worker-Priests' is to be changed to 'priests of the Workers' Mission.'"

The principal speaker of the 1953 Week of Catholic Intellectuals, which was devoted to the topic of the Living God, Cardinal Feltin stated: "The disinherited strata of society must be the object of increased solicitude. The presence of God must be manifested without a doubt by laymen, but also by priests. . . ." (*Le Figaro,* November 16, 1953).

References

Commonweal 50:584 S 23 '49
France Illus 374:640 D 13 '52 por
Britannica Book of the Year, 1954
Dictionnaire Biographique Français Contemporain (1950)
International Who's Who, 1953
Who's Who in France (Paris), 1953-54

FINGESTEN, PETER (fĭn-gĕs'tĕn) Mar. 20, 1916- Sculptor; teacher

Address: h. 36 W. 86th St., New York 24: b. c/o Pace College, 41 Park Row, New York 38

"I think one cannot help but grow spiritually on the immense latent strength of this country," wrote German-born sculptor Peter Fingesten on the occasion of his one-man show at the Dubin Galleries, Philadelphia, Pennsylvania in April 1953. "Here one learns directness, forcefulness and simplicity, for everything is measured on a larger scale. This applies to art as well."

Fingesten, who has won recognition as an accomplished sculptor in the expressionist style, came to the United States in 1939 on a fellowship to the Pennsylvania Academy of Fine Arts. His first American exhibition took place in Philadelphia the following year. He has had a total of thirty-two one-man shows in Europe and the United States, his latest being at the Sculptors Gallery in New York City in April, 1954. He is a member of the faculty of Pace College as an assistant professor of art.

His work ranges from straight portraiture to "fantastic flights in symbolism," and he is especially fond of creating multiple masks or of breaking up fragments of the body "to make a fresh corporeal arrangement." His favorite medium is concrete, to which he adds pigments and other elements in order to obtain a variety of colors and textures.

The son of Michel and Bianca (Schiek) Fingesten, Peter Fingesten was born in Berlin on March 20, 1916. His father, who was in an internment camp in Italy in 1943, was a painter, etcher, and illustrator; he was most noted for his *ex-libris* bookplates, of which he designed over 2,000.

Peter received his first training in art from his father and at the age of sixteen he had his first one-man show in Berlin. After graduating from the Real-Reform Gymnasium in 1930, he entered the Hochschule für Bildende Künste in Berlin and won a scholarship in sculpture. He obtained his bachelor's degree in 1934, and a master's degree a year later.

By the time he was eighteen, Fingesten had already begun to teach sculpture. At this period he specialized in wood carving, and he found expressionism the most satisfying idiom. He was influenced by the famous German expressionist sculptors, Wilhelm Lehmbruck and Ernst Barlach, as well as by ancient Cambodian sculpture.

The years of Fingesten's European apprenticeship, from 1935 to 1939, took him from Berlin to Vienna and Paris. Eventually he settled in Milan, Italy where he absorbed elements of baroque sculpture into his expressionist style. He won the first prize in sculpture at the Bianco-Nero International Exhibition in Milan in 1937. Dr. Fede Paronelli published a monograph entitled *Catalogo delle Opere di Peter Fingesten* describing his sculptures: *Christus, Eternity, Greek Souvenir, Portrait of the Composer Pietro Albergoni, In the River of Time, Woman in the Wind,* and *Flying Torso.*

Early in 1939, Fingesten's works were shown jointly with those of Picasso at a Milan gallery. The exhibition was visited by King Zog of Albania, who commissioned Fingesten to do a monumental stone head. Before the completed work could be delivered, however, Italian troops invaded Albania and the King was forced to flee the country. But Fingesten had been paid, and with this money he bought passage to the United States, arriving with five dollars and fifteen sculptures.

Awarded a Quaker fellowship to continue his studies at the Pennsylvania Academy of Fine Arts, he settled in Philadelphia and remained there until 1943. According to *Time* (March 4, 1940), he was assisted financially by a patroness, Mrs. Joseph Wasserman, the widow of a wealthy rugman. For a studio, Fingesten used a shed in suburban Oak Lane, lent him by Temple University.

PETER FINGESTEN

The first one-man exhibition of Fingesten's work in the United States was held at Philadelphia's Warwick Galleries in February 1940. "One of the most individual and imaginative art shows of the season" was the verdict of the *Christian Science Monitor*'s critic. *Time*'s reviewer declared that Fingesten's work was neither abstract nor academic but employed "a selective symbolism that packs more into a fragment than many sculptors get in a whole figure."

A New York debut followed in April 1941 with an exhibition of thirty sculptures at the Marie Sterner Gallery. Melville Upton (New York *Sun*), believed that Fingesten's portrait busts and symbolical masks presented his talent most effectively. Summing up the show for *Art News,* Doris Brian wrote: ". . . in an energetic effort to defeat ennui his style breaks out in all directions, and there are some interesting results. He can get away with sculpting a painter's subject, as in *Sad Cupid,* or he can take a traditional theme like the *Annunciation* and give it a novel and tragic turn. What Fingesten likes best is to defy the rules of gravity by making a charming torso float in the air or by suspending a head on an arm which emerges from nowhere."

In 1942 he was awarded a sculpture prize at the Woodmere Gallery in Philadelphia and exhibited twenty-four pieces at the Newman Galleries in April of that year. Comparing this with his previous show, Dorothy Grafly (Philadelphia *Record*) felt that the sculptor was more mature and less mannered. "He treats the human form with greater interest in flow of relative masses, and less in hills and hollows," she

FINGESTEN, PETER—*Continued*

observed. "With this development has come an increase in suavity (as in *Young Woman* and *Dancer*), yet the sculptor has relinquished none of his purposefulness. His art is still alert, active, idealized rather than personalized in its handling of figures." He exhibited again in Philadelphia at the Coleman Art Gallery in 1944.

Fingesten became an American citizen in 1943. In August of that year he entered the U.S. Army as a private. Assigned to the Technical Intelligence Staff of the Corps of Engineers, he served in the European Theater of Operations. At the beginning of 1945 *American Artist* reported that he was convalescing at a U.S. Army station in England. He was then working on a large-scale relief depicting the early stages of the Normandy invasion. "I have attempted to interpret the real spirit that imbues the liberating force and power of the army to which I belong," he explained. Since Fingesten had no regular tools to work with, he substituted a tongue depressor for a modelling tool and used iodine and foot powder as coloring media.

In June 1946 he joined the faculty of the Department of Arts and Sciences at Manhattan College, in New York City, as a lecturer in the history of art and architecture. In August 1946 he had a one-man show at the Woodstock (New York) Playhouse and in February 1947 at the Contemporary Arts Gallery in New York.

According to Royal Cortissoz (New York *Herald Tribune*), the twenty-four pieces shown were "consistently good," some notable for graceful lines of modelling, others for strong composition; there was "a definite streak of originality in the sculptor," as exemplified in such works as *Stratospheric Sensation* and *Totem*.

Among the works Judith Kaye Reed (*Art Digest,* March 1, 1947) singled out for special praise were *Elegy, Lament,* and *Astarte*. On the other hand, Edward Alden Jewell stated in the *Times*: "The accent is on forms fantastic, bizarre and, frequently it may be felt, rather mannered in their straining for effect. Sometimes the symbolism will seem spontaneous and plausible, again forced and obscure."

The sculptor's *Totem of the Races* was awarded the $1,000 fellowship of the Louis Comfort Tiffany Foundation for the year 1948. This same work received a $100 prize in a contest held in January 1951 by the Committee on the Art of Democratic Living. It was then exhibited throughout the country under the sponsorship of the American Federation of Arts.

Since 1950 Fingesten has been an assistant professor at Pace College, in New York City, where he teaches painting and sketching as well as history of art and architecture. His third New York show, which was made up of sixteen medium and small-sized pieces, opened at the John Heller Gallery in September 1951. Reviewing it for *Art Digest,* Dore Ashton wrote: "The artist carries the impetus of expression in his slightly asymmetrical portrait of a seer, *The Contemplative.* Other works probe the occult traditions of culture, for example *Totem of a New Age,* a Janus-headed, horny piece, and *Totem of Innocence,* a triple image well set in an imaginary quadrature." Larry Campbell remarked in *Art News* that Fingesten pursued "a mood of desperation," projecting fragments of clay—"usually in the form of a morsel of anatomy—from nowhere, without the use of armatures."

At his one-man show held at the Dubin Galleries in Philadelphia in April 1953, seventeen of his works were displayed. In April 1954 his sculpture was shown jointly with the work of Otto Georg Hitzberger at the Sculptors Gallery in New York. In his review of this dual exhibition for the New York *Times,* Stuart Preston wrote that Fingesten was represented by "some strong heads and by equally unequivocal semi-abstract forms." Among the new works on view at these two shows were *Meditation, At Rest,* and *Corea,* all dating from 1953.

Fingesten works chiefly in cement, which offers him "a degree of 'liberation' from traditional practices that makes it an extremely pliable medium." After completing the clay model, he prepares the composition for the plaster cast which becomes a "negative" to receive the Portland cement mixed with marble dust. (At this point, he often adds ground coloring pigment to the dry cement; steel wool, metal filings, or crushed carborundum are also sometimes added.) The mixture, while wet and with the consistency of a stiff paste, is then pushed into the "negative" with the hands. It sets quickly, and after only twenty-four hours the mould can be chipped off. The raw cast is then washed, dried, and sandpapered.

The real interest of cement as a medium, according to Peter Fingesten, is in the coating, or finishing, of the raw cast. Cement, with its great porosity and absorbent quality, takes almost any color. The pigments are mixed with casein, acids, ammonia, subspirits, various oils, waxes, turpentine, petroleum, alcohol, or shellac, to obtain a variety of colors and textures. By these methods, the "living patina," or surface of the cast, is made to resemble bronze, wood, or stone.

Works by Fingesten are represented in several European museums, and in private collections in Paris, Milan, Philadelphia, and New York. The sculptor has lectured on art at New York University, Pennsylvania State College, and the University of Pennsylvania. During the summer of 1950, he served as a lecturer on Buddhism and Hinduism at the Asia Institute in New York. He is the author of *Maxims for Young Artists* (Hyacinth Press, 1947) and *Ex Libris by Michel Fingesten* (1954), and has published several articles on adult education and art history in the *College Art Journal.* Organizations in which he holds membership are the College Art Association, American Association of University Professors, American Society of Aesthetics, and the American Society of Ex Libris Collectors and Designers.

The sculptor was married on May 7, 1943, to Faye Simons, a ceramist. He stands five feet five inches tall, weighs 160 pounds, and has brown eyes and black hair. In personality he has been described as "friendly," "spontaneous," and "colorful," and his students at Pace reportedly call his class "The Hour of Charm."

Peter Fingesten attends Riverside Church in New York City. While working, he usually makes no preliminary sketches, preferring to think "directly in form"; he models in wet clay without the support of any armature, since he finds lead pipes and aluminum wires very restricting to the imagination. One of his maxims is: "Creation is like a race between the conception and the medium in which the artist is invariably the loser."

References

Am Artist 7:23 Ja '43 por
Time 35:55+ Mr 4 '40 por
Who's Who in America, 1954-55
Who's Who in American Education, 1951-52

EDDIE FISHER

FISHER, EDDIE Aug. 10, 1928- Singer
Address: b. c/o Milton Blackstone, 221 W. 57th St., New York 19

At twenty-six, Eddie Fisher, baritone singer, "the curly haired darling of the juke box set," currently heading his own TV and radio show, *Coke Time*, on the National Broadcasting Company network, is heard over 700 stations. His recordings, issued by RCA Victor, have had phenomenal sales topping the ten million mark during the past year.

His rise to popularity has been swift; five years ago he was earning thirty dollars a week as a member of the entertainment staff of a summer hotel in the Catskills. "Fisher's boyish charm, his artfully tousled hair, the appeal of the success saga which catapulted him from the Borsht Belt to Broadway without marring his unsophistication, are among the keys to this current show biz phenom," *Variety* states.

Edwin Jack Fisher, the son of Joe and Kate Fisher, was born in Philadelphia, Pennsylvania, August 10, 1928, one of a family of seven children who grew up in the poorer section of South Philadelphia. Eddie aspired to be a singer and at an early age entered local amateur contests. Singing in a synagogue as a boy gave him some musical training, and he has said that he got his unsophisticated delivery "from helping Dad hawk fruits and vegetables from a truck when I was a kid."

When he was thirteen, Eddie won a Horn and Hardart *Children's Hour* radio contest, and during his high school years with his pal Joey Forman, now a comic, he appeared on local radio stations among them WFIL, earning from fifteen cents up to eighteen dollars a week. At seventeen, he tried out as a singer for Buddy Morrow's band and got the job which brought him to New York. His next engagement was with Charlie Ventura's band, playing in the suburbs of New York.

The young singer auditioned for Monte Proser, then directing the Copacabana, but as Fisher lacked a few months of being eighteen, the legal age required for a night-club performer, Proser put him in touch with the agent, Milton Blackstone, who booked Fisher at Grossinger's hotel in the Catskills as a staff singer for the summer. There Fisher met Bob Weitman, manager of the Broadway Paramount Theatre, and this led to an engagement at the Paramount as an "intermission singer" at a salary of seventy-five dollars a week. Shortly after, now being eighteen, he was engaged to sing in one of the Copacabana productions of the season of 1946. But the young singer went through the usual ups and downs at the start of his career, with frequent periods of unemployment.

In 1948 he won an Arthur Godfrey Talent Scout contest. Eddie Cantor heard Fisher sing on Labor Day, 1949 at Grossinger's and at once engaged him for the Cantor show on a cross-country tour that proved highly successful. As a result, RCA Victor signed Fisher to a contract. "In one year, this boy will be America's most important new singer of popular songs," Cantor predicted, and within a year, Fisher had won the title "America's Most Promising New Male Vocalist" in the annual nationwide poll of disk jockeys, conducted by *Billboard* magazine.

In the following year Fisher was called upon at short notice to substitute for a singer at Bill Miller's Riviera. The young baritone rendered such ballads as *I Wanna be Loved, Wanderin'* and *There's No Tomorrow*. "When the reviews appeared next morning," *Time* Magazine reported, "Fisher was described as 'merely wonderful', 'a sensational singing voice and style.'"

RCA Victor, which had previously issued Fisher's songs on its second-string Bluebird label, now began putting them out on its larger selling black label. Fisher moved into the Paramount Theatre as a headliner at a $1,000

FISHER, EDDIE—*Continued*

a week fee, and the bobby-soxers had a new idol.

Inducted into the Army in April 1951, Fisher, after four months' basic training, was assigned to the U.S. Army Band and Air Force Recruiting. Of his appearances on TV for the Army, *Variety* commented, "His fresh, clean-cut handling of ballads is solid lure to the younger crowd, both male and female, and his wearing of the army khaki adds a glamor touch."

Heading an Armed Forces Review, Fisher was sent on overseas tours touching at Hawaii, Wake Island, Japan, Korea, Alaska, and the Aleutians, and also toured in Europe with stop-offs at Iceland and Greenland, giving more than 150 shows. Sidney Fields in the New York *Mirror* quotes Fisher as saying, "The Army gave me a lot more than I gave it. Why, I did shows I never would have done. In the rain, the mud, off the backs of trucks, without a mike, and sometimes even without music" (New York *Daily Mirror,* April 16, 1953).

During his two years in uniform, Fisher continued to make records while on furloughs, scoring ten hits in two years which totaled over 7,000,000 sales. *Variety* estimated that on his return to civilian life his royalties from RCA Victor would amount to $330,000. Discharged from the Army April 10, 1953, Fisher stepped immediately into a three-week's engagement at the Paramount Theatre, heading the bill, and began, in the words of a *Collier's* writer, "bringing sweet pressure to bear on the heart of the American adolescent." "Not since Sinatra had it happened," Chris Kane in *Radio TV Mirror* wrote of a second appearance by Fisher at the Paramount a few months later. "The kids were bringing their lunches . . . and sitting through five shows. . . . They were swooning for Eddie, not Frankie . . . a brand-new generation of high-school students . . . had it bad."

Fisher's own television and radio show, *Coke Time,* sponsored by Coca Cola and presented over the National Broadcasting Company's TV network and the Mutual Broadcasting System, made its debut April 29, 1953. In addition to his regular TV and radio work, he fills many engagements, and also appears at numerous charity affairs. In May 1953, he made a two-week headline appearance at the Palladium in London.

"The fans were there in force on opening night," *Variety* reported, "greeting each new song with an unrestrained enthusiasm and constantly clamoring for more." While in England, Fisher sang at a charity ball attended by Princess Margaret Rose. He did not ask the Princess for a dance because, he said, "They told me it was customary for her to do the asking. I kept hoping she would."

In the TV presentation in November 1953 entitled *Dinner for the President,* Fisher appeared before President Eisenhower at the White House, and at a Christmas party for the New York Foundling Home, before Cardinal Spellman. Between Christmas 1953 and New Year's, Fisher, at the request of the Army, made several appearances before the Armed Forces stationed in Germany and France.

Through his multiple activities, TV and radio, night club engagements, and recordings, Fisher grosses about $700,000 a year according to an estimate made by *Variety* (March 31, 1954). Millions of Victor disks have been sold, including three 1,000,000 best sellers, *I'm Walking Behind You, O, My Papa* and *Anytime.* From appearances on TV and radio shows other than his own, Fisher receives an approximate $250,000, and an estimated equal amount from his night club appearances, for which he receives as much as $7,500 for a week-end engagement alone.

Coke Time in the 1953-54 season, reached 707 TV and radio stations which, according to a *Collier's* article, represents "more outlets than have ever been given to any other performer."

Fisher's family continues to live in Philadelphia, but not in the neighborhood in which he grew up. He bought them a luxurious home and set one of his brothers up in the candy business. The singer is unmarried. His manager is still Milton Blackstone, who first booked him into Grossinger's. Fisher is five feet eight inches in height, weighs 135 pounds, and has black hair and brown eyes. Harriet Van Horne of the New York *World-Telegram,* has described him as having "tousled locks, a fine, big voice, and the air of a wanton choir boy."

References

Am W p20 N 1 '53
Collier's 131:65 Je 27 '53 pors
Look 18:27 Mr 23 '54 pors
N Y Daily Mirror p26 Ap 16 '53 por
N Y World-Telegram p6 My 29 '53
Time 56:64 S 4 '50 por
Variety 190:53 My 20 '53; 194:1 Mr 31 '54

FISHER, HARRY L(INN) Jan. 19, 1885- University professor; organization official; chemist

Address: b. c/o University of Southern California, Los Angeles 7, Calif.; h. 4116 Santo Tomas Dr., Los Angeles 8, Calif.

The field of rubber chemistry and technology has been the concern of Dr. Harry L. Fisher for over thirty years. In 1954 he became the president of the American Chemical Society, representing nearly 70,000 scientists, for a one-year term. He is also an internationally known authority on the chemistry of vulcanization and is the holder of over forty patents in the field of organic chemical synthesis, rubber and synthetic rubber. Since January 1953 he has directed the research at the Rubber Technology Foundation of the University of Southern California, Los Angeles.

In 1952 he forecast that odor may be completely eliminated from rubber goods, that there is the possibility, if no carbon black is used, that tires can be made in any color to complement the color of automobiles. Dr. Fisher said, "Synthetic rubber tires are likely to be manufactured with very little or no fabric. Tires may last the lifetime of a car."

Working on the theory that the reaction of sulfur is but an example of a general principle, Dr. Fisher demonstrated that many nonsulfur compounds could produce practical rubber vulcanizates. He also discovered adhesives for attaching rubber to rubber and rubber to metal. His research led to a series of thermoplastic resinous materials which could be used as substitutes for such products as shellac, balata, and gutta-percha. Dr. Fisher received the Charles Goodyear Gold Medal in 1949 "for outstanding achievement in rubber chemistry."

Harry Linn Fisher, one of five boys, was born in Kingston, New York, January 19, 1885, the son of George Edwin and Emma Adelia (Bray) Fisher. His father was a locomotive engineer on the New York, West Shore and Buffalo Railroad. The family moved later to Weehawken, New Jersey, where young Harry was reared. After being graduated from high school in Union, New Jersey in 1901, he took courses in stenographic skills.

These studies were financed on a four-dollar-a-week job as messenger boy for Swann and Finch and the Gorham Manufacturing Company. After he had completed his courses, Fisher was employed in 1903 as a stenographer by the New York, New Haven and Hartford Railroad, and later that year by the West Shore Railroad.

Realizing that he had not found his true career, he attended a one-year refresher course at the Dwight School, New York City, in 1904, and then entered Williams College, Williamstown, Massachusetts. During his first two years at Williams, Fisher majored in classical languages, but in his junior year he changed to chemistry.

His extracurricular activities were track and debating. He was appointed the Dean's private secretary in his sophomore year. When he received his A.B. degree in 1909 he was awarded a scholarship for further study at Columbia University where, in 1910, he acquired the M.A. degree in organic chemistry.

For the next two years Fisher served as an assistant in organic chemistry. Then he became an instructor at the Cornell University Medical College in New York City. His doctorate dissertation, "The preparation and properties of 5-amino-6-quino-linecarboxylic acid, and some compounds derived therefrom," was prepared during this period, prior to his receiving the Ph.D. degree in 1912 from Columbia University, which then retained Dr. Fisher as an instructor in organic chemistry. His thesis was published in 1912 by Eschenbach.

While teaching at Columbia from 1912 to 1919, Fisher began investigating the chemistry of rubber and resins. At the conclusion of World War I, Dr. Fisher left teaching to become a research chemist with the Goodrich Rubber Company, Akron, Ohio. For the next seven years (1919-1926), he served in this capacity.

The United States Rubber Company hired Fisher in 1926, as a research chemist in the development department in New York City and

Harris & Ewing

HARRY L. FISHER

in Passaic, New Jersey. During his ten-year service with this organization the special emphasis of his researches was the study of the methods of vulcanizing rubber without the use of sulfur. He experimented with quinone oximes, certain secondary amines, chlorinated quinones, and others. These experiments and discoveries helped to clear up the mysteries of rubber vulcanizing, the process of which was long thought to be limited to the application of sulfur and heat.

Nevertheless, the exact chemistry vulcanization at this time was still uncertain, for as Fisher wrote in his paper, "The Chemistry of Rubber" (*Chemical Reviews,* March 1930), "The practice generally precedes the theory, and, in this case [vulcanization], with the practice well developed, science apparently has a long way to go before it will provide complete explanations."

The chemist was director of organic chemical research of the Air Reduction Company, Stamford, Connecticut from 1936 to 1941, when he joined the United States Industrial Chemicals, Inc., of Stamford, serving in the same capacity until his retirement in 1950. In World War II he worked in the Office of Synthetic Rubber, polymer research branch, Washington, D.C.

After his retirement Dr. Fisher became administrative assistant in the division of chemistry and chemical technology of the National Research Council, and organizing secretary of the Twelfth International Congress of Pure and Applied Chemistry, held as part of the World Chemical Conclave in New York, September 1951. He also supervised the arrangements for the Sixteenth Conference of the International Union of Pure and Applied Chemistry, a part of the World Conclave. Following these services, he was appointed special

FISHER, HARRY L.—*Continued*

assistant to the director of the Office of Synthetic Rubber, Reconstruction Finance Corporation, a post which he held until January 1953.

Dr. Fisher noted in an article in *Chemical Engineering* (July 1952) that synthetic rubbers which have a high resistance to abrasion have already been developed without the use of carbon black. He maintained that "if these can be developed and made on a large scale, tires and other goods would be better than today." Not only may synthetic rubbers be manufactured in less time, he predicted, but they will need much less equipment to produce the same amount of the product.

In January 1953, he was appointed as the first director of education and research for the $100,000 Rubber Technology Foundation of the University of Southern California, Los Angeles. Since taking office he has been teaching a course called "New Developments in Rubber Chemistry and Technology," for engineering students, and directing laboratory work in which the developments are made available to the rubber industry.

Dr. Fisher is the author of *Laboratory Manual of Organic Chemistry* (Wiley, 1920) which is now in its fourth edition, and *Rubber and Its Use* (Chemical Publishing Company, 1941). Two of his more recent articles are "Rubber plus Chemistry" (*Journal of Chemical Education,* June 1951), and his contribution to the fifth annual review of "Chemical Engineering Materials of Construction" of a survey of "elastomers" (the generic term proposed by Fisher for substances having the properties of rubber compounded from the words elastic and polymer) which appeared in *Industrial and Engineering Chemistry,* October 1951. He has also had articles published in such magazines as the *Journal of the American Chemical Society* and *Chemical and Engineering News.*

The National Association of Manufacturers, in 1940, presented Fisher with the Modern Pioneer Award for developments in attaching rubber to metal. He was president of the American Institute of Chemists from 1940 until 1942. The chemist was chosen the Edgar Marburg lecturer in 1941 by the Society for Testing Materials.

The division of rubber chemistry of the American Chemical Society honored Fisher with the Charles Goodyear Gold Medal Award in 1949. It was said of him in the presentation speech by John T. Blake, of the Simplex Wire and Cable Company, that he might take a well-earned place beside his distinguished predecessors, and that he had manifested the commendable qualities of persistence and endurance in following a path to a goal. On December 8, 1952, the American Chemical Society announced that its nearly 70,000 members had named Dr. Fisher president-elect, to serve in 1954. He has been an active member of the society since 1910. Dr. Joel H. Hildebrand succeeded him as president in 1955.

Williams College conferred an honorary D.Sc. degree on Fisher in 1953. He is a fellow of the Institution of the Rubber Industry (Great Britain). He belongs to the Chemists' Club, New York City and the Cosmos Club, Washington, D.C. His Greek letter fraternities are Phi Beta Kappa, Sigma Xi, Phi Lambda Upsilon (honorary chemical society, of which he was national president, 1916-18), and Alpha Chi Sigma.

On June 7, 1910, the scientist married Nellia Edna Andrews, a piano teacher. They have three children, Helen, Ruth (Mrs. Francis B. Rosevear), and Robert Andrews Fisher. Dr. Fisher is five feet eight and one half inches tall, weighs 154 pounds and has brown eyes and gray hair. His favorite pastimes are color photography, singing and mountain climbing. He is a Republican and a Congregationalist.

References

Am Mag 157:21+ Ap '54 por
Chem & Eng N 25:3058 O 20 '47 por; 27:1721 Je 13 '49 por
N Y Times p23 D 9 '46
Rubber Age 72:511 Ja '53 por
American Men of Science (1949)
Who Knows—and What (1954)
Who's Who in America, 1954-55

FITZ GERALD, LESLIE M(AURICE)

Aug. 18, 1898- Organization official; oral surgeon

Address: b. c/o American Dental Association, 222 E. Superior St., Chicago 11, Ill.; 718 Roshek Bldg., Dubuque, Ia.; h. Rolling Ridge Farm, Dubuque, Ia.

The president of the American Dental Association (1953-1954) is Leslie M. Fitz Gerald, who has had a long record of service in the organization. He has held the posts of chairman of the committee on economics, member of the House of Delegates, chairman of the section on oral surgery, and member of the editorial board of the *Journal of Oral Surgery,* the association's house organ. Fitz Gerald has been an opponent of socialized medicine, believing that it would lead to a socialized national economy.

The United States, according to the American Dental Association (A.D.A.), has 93,726 dentists, or one for every 1,677 persons. The association's *American Dental Directory, 1954* lists 85,970 civilian dentists and 7,756 serving in the armed forces. There are also 599 dentists in U.S. territories and possessions. The A.D.A. reports that in general, the east and west coasts are served by more dentists in proportion to the population than any other section of the country.

An A.D.A. survey revealed that public demand for dental care has nearly doubled in one generation. Less than one-fourth (30,000,000) of the nation's population in 1929 had their teeth fixed; in 1952 more than 42 per cent—some 65,000,000 persons—received professional dental care. From its membership, the association collected in May 1954 contributions of dental instruments and equipment which were placed aboard the "Help Korea Trains," to be sent to the National Seoul University College of Dentistry whose equipment was destroyed or stolen by the Communists during the fighting in Seoul.

Dr. Fitz Gerald has practiced dentistry in Dubuque, Iowa, since 1920 and has taken an active part in the civic affairs of his community. He was a lieutenant commander in the Dental Corps of the U.S. Navy in World War II, and has acted as consultant in oral surgery to the central office of the Veterans' Administration and to Admiral Lamont Pugh, surgeon general of the U.S. Navy.

The fourth of five children of Edward A. and Emma (Daly) Fitz Gerald, Leslie Maurice Fitz Gerald was born in Cresco, Iowa, on August 18, 1898. His father, an implement dealer, died while the boy was very young, and Mrs. Fitz Gerald was left with the care of her four sons and one daughter. The boys contributed to the support of the family by working at various jobs. All five children managed to attend college. Leslie entered the State University of Iowa in 1916 after his graduation from high school in West Union, Iowa. He selected dentistry as his major and became a member of Omicron Kappa Upsilon, honorary dental fraternity. He also belonged to the Xi Psi Phi society. In 1919 he was graduated from the university with the D.D.S. degree.

Fitz Gerald spent one year following his graduation as resident in oral surgery at the State University of Iowa Hospital and then set up his own practice in Dubuque in 1920. In that year he began his active participation in the work of dental organizations and became the president of the Dubuque Dental Society. (He also filled this post from 1932 to 1933.) He was a member of the House of Delegates of the A.D.A. and he held the presidency of the State University of Iowa College of Dentistry Alumni Association from 1931 to 1932.

The committee on economics was another group within the A.D.A. to which Fitz Gerald belonged; he was a member of it for fourteen years and acted as chairman for five years. He was elected president of the American Society of Oral Surgeons for two terms (1941-1942 and 1942-1943), and served as the president of the Iowa State Dental Society from 1942 to 1943. He was also a member of the board of trustees of the latter organization for nine years.

He was made a fellow of the American College of Dentists and has served since 1945 as chairman of its committee on oral surgery. In 1948 he became the chairman of the section on oral surgery of the A.D.A. and held the chairmanship of its advisory committee to the Bureau of Economic Research and Statistics from 1948 to 1951.

The dentist has been a member of the editorial board of the *Journal of Oral Surgery* since 1950 and a member of the committee on internships and residencies of the A.D.A.'s Council on Dental Education since 1951. He became a candidate for the presidency of the A.D.A. in 1952 and was made president-elect in 1952 to fill the 1953-1954 term.

LESLIE M. FITZ GERALD

The dental association's position on the fluoridation of drinking water to reduce tooth decay was outlined in a statement prepared for a House Commerce Committee hearing on a bill to outlaw fluoridation. The association's chairman on legislation said: "Every responsible national health agency in the country" favors fluoridation. The A.D.A. told Congress it is safe "beyond any reasonable doubt" (New York *Herald Tribune*, May 27, 1954). Backers of the bill called it "mass medication."

Believing that socialized medicine would lead to a socialized national economy, Fitz Gerald opposed the program at a time when many dentists held that the change was inevitable. He not only presented his case to dentists but lectured before many medical groups in an effort to gain adherents for his position (*Dental Items of Interest,* August, 1952).

Among other positions which Fitz Gerald has held are those of chief of the oral surgery staffs of St. Joseph's, Finley, and Xavier hospitals. He was a co-founder of the American Board of Oral Surgery, is a diplomate of the group, and has served as its secretary. Other dental and medical organizations of which he is a member include the Fédération Dentaire Internationale, International College of Dentists, Chicago Dental Society, Dubuque County Medical Society, and International College of Anesthetists. The North Carolina State Dental Society has made him an honorary member.

As a speaker, Fitz Gerald has appeared before meetings of the A.D.A., American Society of Oral Surgeons, and Chicago Dental Society; at state and district meetings in Pennsylvania, Iowa, Illinois, Minnesota, Wisconsin, Texas, Tennessee, North Carolina, and Georgia; at the State University of Iowa, Temple University,

FITZ GERALD, LESLIE M.—*Continued*

St. Louis University, and Emory University; and at the Thomas P. Hinman Midwinter Dental Meeting at Atlanta, Georgia. He has published many articles on dentistry, among them "Oral Surgery for the General Practitioner" in *Dental Items of Interest* (May, 1932) and "Fundamental Principles of Oral Surgery" in the *Iowa State Dental Bulletin* (February, 1950). He has contributed to the *Iowa State Dental Bulletin* biographies of Dr. John Van Der Bie Conzett and Dr. Ralph A. Fenton, both of whom Fitz Gerald credits with influencing his career.

Civic affairs have claimed an important portion of Fitz Gerald's time. He has served as president of the Dubuque Junior Chamber of Commerce (1923-1924), Dubuque Rotary Club (1930-1931), Dubuque Boy's Club (1931-1932), and Dubuque Community Chest (1931-1932); he was a director of the Dubuque Chamber of Commerce (1924-1930); and he has been vice-president of the Centralia Community Fire Department since 1947. He has served as vice-president of the Dubuque Thrift Plan Industrial Bank since 1931, and as director of the Dubuque Building and Loan Association. He is a member of the Elks Club, American Legion, Forty and Eight, and the Dubuque Golf Club. He belongs to the Farm Bureau and the Guernsey Breeders Association.

On October 8, 1921 Fitz Gerald and Marcelle Dorothy Meis were married. They have three daughters: Shirley Ann (Mrs. F. D. Gilloon, Jr.), Patricia (Mrs. J. A. O'Brien III), and Jacqueline (Mrs. F. Benjamin Merritt II). The dentist has blue eyes and brown hair; he is five feet ten inches tall, and weighs 175 pounds. His political affiliation is Republican. He is a Catholic and a member of the finance committee of the Church of Nativity. He is called "Fitz" by his friends. Raising Guernsey cattle on his Rolling Ridge Farm is one of the oral surgeon's principal interests; he also enjoys golf.

References

Dental Items of Interest Ag '52
Who's Who in America, 1954-55
Who's Who in the Midwest (1952)

FORBES, B(ERTIE) C(HARLES) May 14, 1880-May 6, 1954 Publisher; born in Scotland; worked for Dundee (Scotland) *Courier;* helped to found *Rand Daily Mail* in South Africa (1901); came to New York (1904); worked for *Journal of Commerce;* business and financial editor, New York *American* (1911-1916); became U.S. citizen and founded *Forbes* magazine (1917); until 1942 wrote for Hearst and other newspapers; helped to found Investors League, Inc. (1942); author; received Freedom Foundations award (1949). See *Current Biography,* (Mar.) 1950.

Obituary

N Y Times p24 My 7 '54

FOWLER, R(OBERT) M(ACLAREN) Dec. 7, 1906- Canadian association executive; government official; lawyer

Address: b. c/o Canadian Pulp & Paper Association, Sun Life Bldg., Montreal, Quebec, Canada; c/o Newsprint Association of Canada, Sun Life Bldg., Montreal, Quebec, Canada; h. 36 Summit Circle, Westmount, Quebec, Canada

As president of the Canadian Pulp & Paper Association and the Newsprint Association of Canada, R. M. Fowler is the spokesman for the eighty Canadian companies which in 1953 were the leading exporters of pulp and paper and the largest producers of newsprint in the world. He also serves as director of the pulp and paper division of the Dominion's Department of Defense Production. He is a lawyer by profession.

Robert MacLaren Fowler was born to Edward Bruce and Genevieve W. (Amey) Fowler at Peterborough, Ontario, on December 7, 1906. He majored in mathematics as an undergraduate at the University of Toronto, and received the B.A. degree there with honors. By this time, his thoughts had turned toward the law ("The same mental processes," he argued "are needed to solve a mathematical problem as to solve a legal problem").

Accordingly, he began preparation for admission to the Ontario provincial bar by "reading" law in the chambers of McMaster, Montgomery, Fleury & Company at Toronto, and attending classes and lectures at Osgoode Hall Law School. He took his law degree with honors in 1931, and in the same year, was "called" to the Ontario bar.

He then returned to McMaster, Montgomery, Fleury & Company and built up a successful practice as a barrister. In 1937 he accepted an appointment as a member of the staff of the newly created Royal Commission on Dominion-Provincial Relations—known popularly as the Rowell-Sirois commission. It held hearings in every province of the Dominion and its report (largely the work of Fowler), was published under the title "Design for a New Dominion" in four issues of *Maclean's Magazine* during the summer of 1940.

The report, which was "approved in general terms" by the Dominion Parliament in 1940, recommended "a redistribution of tax power, confining to Dominion authority all income taxes, inheritance taxes, and taxes on corporations," in return for which the Dominion would "assume all provincial outstanding debts," and take over unemployment relief and old-age pensions.

Fowler, who had transferred his personal law practice to the firm of McCarthy & McCarthy in Toronto in 1939, remained associated with this firm until the end of World War II. He then became connected with the Ottawa law firm of Gowling, MacTavish, Watt, Henderson, & Osborne.

"Fowler got into the pulp and newsprint business by accident," Frank Lowe has written in *Saturday Night* (February 2, 1952). "In 1942 he went to Ottawa as secretary and general counsel of the Wartime Prices and Trade Board. There he was called in as legal adviser for the board on newsprint and pulp questions." At the end of the war, the pulp and paper manufacturers asked him "to get them unwound from controls." In 1945, accordingly, Fowler moved to Montreal to take over the presidency of both the Canadian Pulp & Paper Association and the Newsprint Association of Canada.

As president of the Newsprint Association, Fowler predicted in July 1946 that a price increase of $6.70 a ton would be necessary to "compensate Canadian producers" of newsprint for the recent upward revaluation of the Canadian dollar. In a statement in October to a subcommittee of the United States House of Representatives interstate commerce committee, Fowler defended Canadian price increases for newsprint and emphasized that in Canada the "immediate task" was to "find a means of maintaining current rates of production" in a field in which an acute international shortage continued to exist.

When Fowler went to Montreal in 1945 it was in the belief that the Canadian paper industry could be freed from controls within four or five years. Instead, the continuation of a newsprint shortage, and the exigencies of the "cold war," made more governmental supervision of industry necessary, and on April 1, 1951, the Department of Defense Production was established.

On April 18, 1951, the department (of which the Right Honorable C. D. Howe became the head) classified newsprint as an "essential material" in order "to insure that the government could more carefully scrutinize and, if necessary, regulate the international trade" in this predominantly Canadian commodity, about 90 per cent of which was then going to the United States.

A factor in this decision was a demand by foreign countries for larger shares in Canadian newsprint. These shares could not be increased without government controls. A special pulp and paper division of the department was therefore instituted with Robert Fowler as director.

On April 25, 1951, in an address to the American Newspaper Publishers Association, Fowler warned that "if a price ceiling should be imposed by the [U.S.] government, limiting what a publisher in the United States can pay for his newsprint, I think that would legally operate to suspend all [U.S.] contracts with Canadian mills" and cause the "diversion of some newsprint to the 'essential' needs of overseas countries." The reaction in the United States to Fowler's speech was unfavorable.

It was then announced that the Abitibi Power & Paper Company, Canada's third largest newsprint manufacturing concern, would raise the price of newsprint in the New York area to $116 a ton on July 1, 1951. The U.S. Director of Price Stabilization, Michael V. DiSalle, promptly denounced the $10 a ton increase as "unilateral action," and claimed that since he had been given only twenty-four hours notice of the price jump, he had had no opportunity to make "representations" (*Newsweek*, June 25, 1951).

Karsh

R. M. FOWLER

Rumors were heard that the United States might retaliate by cutting down on armaments contracts with Canadian firms, but Fowler stood his ground, and stated that the company had been authorized to increase its price. Defense Production Minister Howe also gave official approval to the price raise as "justified by recent wage boosts and freight-rate increases" (*Newsweek*). "I don't think people of another country have any right to level charges at a business in Canada," Fowler has said in connection with American criticisms of the Canadian industry (*Saturday Night*, February 2, 1952).

Tension over the foreign demands for newsprint began to ease. In 1952 Canadian production reached a new high, and was responsible for a total of 5,690,000 tons out of the total world output of 10,656,000 tons of newsprint. At a forum on Canadian resources at Town Hall, New York in March 1953, Fowler asserted that the international newsprint shortage had already "disappeared," this point being further stressed in an end-of-the-year report released by the Newsprint Association of Canada in January 1954.

Later in January, in his capacity as president of the Canadian Pulp & Paper Association, Fowler stated that the Dominion's paper industry had spent more than $1,000,000,000 on plants since the war and that in 1953 alone $110,000,000 was spent on new construction, machinery, and equipment (New York *Times*, January 30, 1954).

His report set the total of paper and pulp export products in 1953 at $876,000,000 and newsprint production at 5,721,296 tons. Exports of newsprint were recorded as 5,334,287 tons as compared with 5,297,881 tons in 1952.

Fowler is a director of the Canadian Welfare Council, a member of the executive committee of the Canadian Chamber of Commerce and of

FOWLER, R. M.—*Continued*

the board of governors of the Montreal General Hospital, and a member and past president of the Canadian Institute of International Affairs. His clubs are the St. James's and the University in Toronto. He belongs to the Anglican (Episcopal) Church.

He married Sheila Gordon Ramsay, daughter of A. Gordon Ramsay, on June 23, 1934. They have four children. He has been described as a "tall (over six feet), slim man with the gray just starting to appear in his hair," and as "easy to talk to, relaxed in manner, and an excellent listener." His associates speak of him as "a wit of some renown" who has "been known to reply to an office memo with a fast bit of doggerel." For recreation he enjoys sketching and painting.

References

Sat Night 67:22 F 2 '52 por
Canadian Who's Who, 1949-51

FOYLE, GILBERT (SAMUEL) Mar. 9, 1886- British bookseller

Address: b. c/o W. & G. Foyle, Ltd., 119-125 Charing Cross Rd., London W.C. 2, England; h. Durley Court, Eastbourne, Sussex, England

FOYLE, WILLIAM ALFRED Mar. 4, 1885- British bookseller

Address: b. c/o W. & G. Foyle, Ltd., 119-125 Charing Cross Rd., London W.C. 2, England; h. Beeleigh Abbey, Maldon, Essex, England

Foyle's of Charing Cross Road, London, known as the largest bookshop in the world, observed its fiftieth anniversary in January 1954. Its founders, William Alfred Foyle and Gilbert Foyle, are still in charge of the business which carries a stock of over 4,000,000 books, both new and secondhand, on thirty miles of shelving. It is known to thousands of United States tourists as a fascinating place to browse. The Foyle brothers also do a big mail order business, receiving as many as 35,000 letters a day from distant places, and their book club has a membership of more than 250,000.

The bookshop had its origin in a few small dealings in secondhand books by Gilbert and William Foyle from the kitchen of their home in Shoreditch, London. In 1904 they leased a shop on Charing Cross Road. They took larger premises in 1912, and in 1929 expanded laterally and backward into neighboring Manette Street. In the distant days of their youth the Foyles made £10 turnover on their first year's trading. They now average more than £2,000,000 a year and the number of books sold annually totals over 5,000,000.

W. & G. Foyle, Ltd. also includes an art gallery, a literary agency, a record shop, a publishing house and a lecture bureau. The organization employs nearly 600 persons. But despite the vastness of the business it has not become pretentious. "Perhaps its most endearing characteristic," according to the New York *Times* (January 4, 1954), "is that, for all its size, it manages to preserve the informal atmosphere of a small bookshop. . . . As in all good bookshops, there is no rule against browsing. You can read a book through at Foyle's if you can do it on your feet."

William Alfred Foyle was born March 4, 1885 and Gilbert Samuel on March 9, 1886. The lives of the Foyle brothers have run along parallel lines. They are the sons of William Henry Foyle, a Shoreditch wholesale grocer, and his wife, born Deborah Barnet. The name dates back to the Normans, having been spelt successively De Froyle, Froyle, and Foyle. W. H. Foyle's family comprised five boys and two girls. William and Gilbert were both educated at Owen's School, Islington, London (both winning junior and senior St. Leonard's scholarships).

They studied at King's College, University of London, for a year. Both were intended for the Civil Service, and sat for their entrance examination in 1900, but both failed. William became a clerk to (Sir) Edward Marshall-Hall, K.C., a noted advocate in the criminal courts, while Gilbert entered the offices of the Shoreditch borough council.

Out of apparent failure was to spring success. "Having no further use for their Civil Service examination text books," says the booklet *Foyles Fifty Years*, "they decided to sell them through a small advertisement in an educational periodical. The advertisement brought in so many replies that the brothers were quick to see that the book trade offered good opportunities for success." A legend that the business started from a barrow in Holywell Street was denied by Gilbert Foyle in a letter to the London *Bookseller*.

What actually happened is described in *Foyles Fifty Years*: "Their first 'shop' was their parents' kitchen. But gradually room after room began to bulge with secondhand books until, with an excitement brought about by what they regarded as a tremendous speculation, they took a disused shop in Islington at a rent of five shillings weekly." Their first catalogues were written out by hand, and prospective customers were requested to return them after perusal.

In 1903, when William was eighteen and Gilbert seventeen, they took a larger shop at Station Parade, Peckham, south of the Thames, for which they paid a weekly rent of 10s. (roughly $2.30). They gave up their office jobs, worked late into the evenings and even on Sundays, and (wrote The *Bookseller*), "took no half days. They cooked their meals (sausages and mash was their staple diet, they say) at the back of the shop. And steadily they built up a reputation for being able to supply books on even the most out-of-the-way subject."

"To prevent their landlord from learning how young they were," commented the New York *Times*, they negotiated their lease, too, by mail. When they hired their first shop assistant, they thought they had made real headway, but the man absconded with their takings and forced the young partners to economize by walking to and from work for weeks." This was at 131 Charing Cross Road, in the heart of London's bookselling quarter, to which a move was made in 1904.

Eight years later they were able to take larger premises farther down the road, at Nos. 119 and 121. In 1929, says *Foyles Fifty Years,* "William and Gilbert Foyle saw their dreams realized when the then Lord Mayor of London, Sir Kynaston Studd, officially opened their impressive new five-floor building in Manette Street" (which is a small cul-de-sac, off the main road, between Nos. 119 and 121).

This "big, sprawling bookshop" is visited by many of London's celebrities as well as students, schoolteachers, librarians, actors, artists, lawyers and "just ordinary browsers." Walt Disney has browsed among its fine collection of art books. The late George Bernard Shaw and H. G. Wells were frequent visitors as are Noel Coward, J. B. Priestley and Sir Compton Mackenzie. Of the more than 35,000 daily inquiries for books are included subjects as varied as trained seals, high blood pressure, flying saucers, fingerprints, poultry farming, linoleum manufacture, rainfall statistics, and peasant dances, as well as many orders for technical books in a wide range.

Already, in 1920, the enterprising brothers had started a side line, Foyles Educational, Ltd., which supplies books and stationery to schools and educational authorities. In 1929 three new departments were opened. One was concerned with the sale of gramophone records; the second, Foyles Lending Libraries, Ltd., established book-lending agencies which have spread to hundreds of little stationers' shops all over England. The third, on the top floor at Manette Street, was the Foyle Art Gallery, which gives group and one-man shows.

Foyle's "literary luncheons" were inaugurated in 1930 and have become an outstanding feature of London's social life. Despite the "blitz" and wartime austerities, these luncheons continued without interruption under the management of William Foyle's daughter, Christina. When she was seventeen, she had suggested the idea to her father who approved and added two words of counsel: "Aim high." The monthly luncheons were originally held at Holborn Restaurant, with 350 to 400 guests. In the late 1930's they were held at Grosvenor House, attended by 1,400 to 1,800 persons. They are now held at the Dorchester Hotel, Park Lane.

Through the years they have included among the guests of honor distinguished personalities in many walks of life—among them, celebrities as diverse as John Drinkwater, Sophie Tucker, Lord Louis Mountbatten, Jimmy Durante, Anthony Eden, the Archbishop of Canterbury, T. S. Eliot, Hedda Hopper, Randolph Churchill, the Emperor of Ethiopia, Dr. Eduard Beneš and Chico Marx. William Foyle, as chairman, introduces the guests. Since 1949 one "literary luncheon" each year has been devoted to poets and poetry, on which occasion William Foyle presents the Foyle Poetry Prize, a check for £250. The recipients thus far have been Edwin Muir, Christopher Fry, the late Dylan Thomas, Roy Campbell and Walter de la Mare.

The Foyle brothers started three more successful ventures in 1937—Foyle's Book Club (which has over 250,000 members), a publishing house (John Gifford, Ltd.), and a literary agency. In 1944 Foyle's took over the

GILBERT FOYLE

Lecture Agency, originally founded in 1879. It now supplies speakers for 300 discussion groups and literary or luncheon clubs. Among its many lecturers are Neville Cardus, the Manchester *Guardian's* cricket reporter and music critic; the novelist L. A. G. Strong; the conductor Sir Adrian Boult; and the historian Arthur Bryant.

Gilbert Foyle served in World War I as a private in the Royal Army Service Corps and was a member of the Home Guard in World War II. He lives at Eastbourne, the Sussex watering place, where he serves on the borough council, and is a member of the Rotary Club. He has the honor of being a Freeman of the

Keystone Press Agency, Ltd., London

WILLIAM ALFRED FOYLE

FOYLE, GILBERT and WILLIAM—*Continued*

City of London. He is a fellow of the Zoological Society and of the Royal Society of Arts. In 1951 he lodged securities of some £20,000 value with the London County Council to form the Gilbert Foyle Educational Trust, to help young people through the universities. His hobbies are country walking and motoring. He is Conservative in politics and belongs to the Church of England.

William Foyle, who lives at the historic Beeleigh Abbey in Essex, is not only a bookseller by trade but a bibliophile in private life. His private library comprises more than 10,000 volumes, and says *Foyles Fifty Years*, "has been visited by book collectors and museum curators from all parts of the world. It includes rare editions of the greatest works in literature." For many years he has given an annual Foyle Prize to the most promising student at public schools and universities. He is the author of *First Editions and their Values*, and with G. H. Fabes, *Modern First Editions: Points and Values* (Foyle, 1929-32). He is a commander in the Order of the Red Cross of Estonia. He belongs to the Savage and Devonshire clubs. Apart from reading, his hobby is fishing. Like his brother, he is Conservative in politics and belongs to the Church of England.

William Foyle married Christina Tulloch on August 14, 1908 and has a son, Richard, and two daughters, Christina and Winifred. Gilbert Foyle married Ethel Ellen Cook on September 21, 1911, and has two sons, Eric and John. The second generation of the Foyle family is active in the firm, "playing no small part in promoting its continued progress."

References

Bookseller Je 13 '53 pors; Ja 9 '54 pors
N Y Times p17 Ja 4 '54
Sat R Lit 33:14+ O 7 '50
Time 58:82+ Ag 6 '51 por
Fabes, G. H. Romance of a Bookshop, 1904-1929 (1929)
Foyles Fifty Years, 1904-1954 (1954)
Who's Who, 1954
World Biography (1948)

FRANCE, PIERRE MENDÈS- *See* Mendès-France, P.

FRANCO (Y BAHAMONDE), FRANCISCO (fräng'kō ē bä"ä-môn'dā frän-thēs'-kō) Dec. 4, 1892- Prime Minister; Chief of State; Generalissimo of the armed forces of Spain

Address: Madrid, Spain; El Pardo Palace, El Pardo, Spain

NOTE: This biography supersedes the article which appeared in *Current Biography* in 1942.

With the signing of a defense agreement between the governments of the United States and Spain on September 26, 1953, Generalissimo Francisco Franco scored his greatest postwar diplomatic triumph. U.S. officials affirmed, according to a New York *Times* report, that "the Spanish dictatorship would be strengthened through United States economic and military assistance," and some Spanish observers thought that "Franco's personal power and prestige will be greater than ever." Franco himself described the accord as "the most important achievement of our contemporary foreign policy."

The conclusion of the agreement, which climaxed some three years of study and about a year and a half of negotiations, is an indication of the survival powers of one of the most controversial figures on the international political scene of the past fifteen years, a dictator whose downfall has been frequently predicted during that period. Since his emergence in 1939 as the leader of Spain, Franco has often been denounced on the one hand as a onetime associate of Hitler and Mussolini and the head of a totalitarian state, and saluted on the other as the man who saved Spain from chaos and communism.

Francisco Paulino Hermenegildo Teódulo Franco y Bahamonde was born in El Ferrol, Spain on December 4, 1892, the son of Nicolás Franco, a naval officer, and Pilar (Bahamonde) Franco. Francisco Franco received his early schooling at El Ferrol's School of the Sacred Heart and at the naval school there. Because examinations for the Academia de Marina were temporarily suspended, he entered the Academia de Infantería in Toledo in August 1907. He was commissioned a second lieutenant in the Army in July 1910.

Between 1912 and 1926 Franco participated in many engagements in North Africa. Sent to Melilla in February 1912, he soon became a captain. In 1916 he was wounded and was sent back to Spain, decorated with the Cross of María Cristina and promoted to the rank of major. For the next three years he performed garrison duty at Oviedo.

At the end of that period he requested further service in Morocco, and was assigned to the Spanish Foreign Legion there. He was deputy commander of the Legion from 1920 until 1923, and commander in chief from 1923 until 1927. He had become a lieutenant colonel in 1923, and a brigadier general in 1926. He is credited with playing a prominent role in the final defeat of the Rif chieftain, Abd-el-Krim. During 1926 he studied at the French École Militaire in Saint-Cyr-l'École under Marshal Henri Philippe Pétain, who became a personal friend.

Franco served as director of the Academia General Militar at Saragossa from 1927 until 1931. In that year King Alfonso XIII fled from Spain and a Republic was established. The Saragossa academy was dissolved on suspicion of being promonarchist and Franco was sent into semi-banishment as captain general of the Balearic Islands. He returned to the mainland in 1933 when a right-wing government was elected, and the following year, he suppressed an uprising in Asturias so brutally that he gained the nickname, "the Butcher." Gil Robles, Minister of War, appointed him chief of the Army general staff in 1935.

When the Popular Front was voted into power in February 1936, Franco was again sent into semi-exile, this time to the Canary Islands as commander in chief. On July 17, 1936, following the assassination of a prominent right-wing politician, a carefully organized revolt against the government broke out, a revolt that was to develop into the Civil War. After the death of General José Sanjurjo in July 1936, Franco became the leader of the rebel forces and in October 1936 was proclaimed head of the Nationalist government and Generalissimo of the Army. His regime was recognized by Germany and by Italy in the following month.

The Civil War raged for more than two and a half years, and by the time it was over, about a million persons had been killed and the country's economy badly damaged. The Republican side received weapons and personnel from Soviet Russia, but Italian and German aid helped Franco to build even stronger forces.

Early in 1937 Franco appointed a national council to rule the country, formed the single party, the Falange (the Spanish Phalanx of Traditionalist and Offensive National Syndicalist Juntas) and proclaimed himself the leader (*El Caudillo*).

Franco's troops launched their final offensive in December 1938, captured Barcelona in January 1939 and in March ended the war by taking Madrid. The Spanish and German governments had signed a cultural agreement in January 1939, and by April 1939 Spain had signed the anti-Comintern pact.

England and France on February 27, 1939, and the United States on April 1, 1939 recognized Franco's regime, and the Pope commended Franco for having brought "mercy and justice" to Spain. According to a correspondent for the London *News Chronicle,* there were a million political prisoners in Spain in 1940, while every week the Spanish press itself reported hundreds of executions. Franco became Prime Minister of Spain in August 1939.

During the Second World War Franco vacillated between conducting a foreign policy favorable to the Axis powers and one favorable to the Allied governments. Thus it was expressed in *10 Eventful Years*: "During the first years of World War II, when the Axis was victorious, Franco affirmed Spain's solidarity with Germany and Italy in the struggle against 'Bolshevism.' When Allied arms began to triumph he hastened to profess his neutrality and denied that Spain had been fascist or secretly allied with the Axis powers."

Certain details of Franco's relations with Rome and Berlin have come to light only in recent years, with the release of captured enemy documents. One group of these documents, published in 1946 by the U.S. Department of State under the title *The Spanish Government and the Axis,* shows Franco's close ties with the Axis, his plans to enter the war against the Allies at a favorable moment and his schemes to obtain Gibraltar and French Morocco.

Franco declared Spain's neutrality in 1939, but on June 12, 1940 altered her status to one of nonbelligerency. According to Sir Samuel Hoare (Viscount Templewood), then Ambassador to Spain, Franco said to him on June 22, 1940: "Why do you not end the war now? You can never win it."

Wide World

GEN. FRANCISCO FRANCO

When Hitler conquered France, Franco sent the German dictator a message: "In the moment when the German armies under your leadership are bringing the greatest battle of history victoriously to an end, I should like to deliver to you the expression of my enthusiasm and admiration as well as that of my people. . . ."

Shortly afterwards Franco wrote to Mussolini: "Since the beginning of the present conflict it has been our intention to make the greatest efforts in our preparations in order to enter the foreign war at a favorable opportunity. . ." Franco's specific conditions for entering the war on the side of the Axis were noted by the German Ambassador to Spain on August 8, 1940: "1. Fulfillment of a set of national territorial demands, Gibraltar, French Morocco, that part of Algeria colonized and predominantly inhabited by Spaniards (Oran), and further the enlargement of Rio de Oro, and of the colonies in the Gulf of Guinea; 2. Making available military and other assistance required for carrying on the war. . . ." (See Sir Samuel Hoare: *Complacent Dictator*).

Although Spain never actively participated in the war, relations between Franco and the Axis dictators continued for a time to be marked by expressions of esteem. In September 1940 Hitler awarded him the gold cross of the Order of Merit of the German Eagle.

At a meeting with Mussolini in Italy in February 1941, Franco affirmed the "identity of views" between Spain and Italy on all common problems. On February 26, 1941, he wrote to Hitler: "I consider as you do yourself that the destiny of history has united you with myself and with the Duce in an indissoluble way." However, rather than take any step "inconsistent with the honor of Spain," he rejected a German demand for territorial facilities to fly military aircraft through Spain to Africa in

FRANCO, FRANCISCO—*Continued*

March 1941 (New York *Herald Tribune,* March 12, 1941).

In the meantime, Spain had made commercial agreements with Great Britain and other non-Axis powers. In March 1940 an Anglo-Spanish trade agreement was signed and in July a payments and trade agreement between England, Portugal and Spain was concluded. Later, further agreements were reached with Great Britain, Argentina and other nations.

Spain's nonbelligerency was of considerable assistance to the Axis. Franco allowed German tankers to use bays along the Cantabrian coast for refueling submarines, permitted the recruiting of soldiers for the Spanish Blue Division which fought with German troops on the eastern front, and relayed news to the Axis of Allied convoys passing through the Strait of Gibraltar.

On Franco's fiftieth birthday, Hitler sent him greetings and a German automobile. Franco told the National Council of the Falange on December 8, 1942: "The liberal world falls a victim to the cancer of its own errors, and with it falls the commercial imperialism of the financial capitalists and their millions of unemployed" (New York *Herald Tribune,* December 9, 1942).

A month earlier, immediately after the American troops landed in North Africa, President Roosevelt had given Franco assurances that the United Nations harbored no aggressive intentions against Spain, and Franco had replied with a message emphasizing the "relations of friendship which unite our people and which should be preserved."

German diplomatic documents published in Moscow at the end of 1946 disclosed that in February 1943 Franco tried to negotiate peace between Great Britain and Germany because of the "Bolshevik danger." In October 1943 Franco announced that Spain had assumed a position of "vigilant neutrality." A United States Department of State publication in June 1944 referred to the dictatorship of Franco as one indebted to Hitler, and in October of that year Prime Minister Churchill rejected Franco's offer of "common action" against Russia, and repudiated Spain's claims to share in "peace settlements or future world organization."

On October 22, 1945, Franco issued a decree constituting the Charter of Rights; it granted freedom of worship, the right of petition and freedom of expression—provided that these did not conflict with the "fundamentals of the state." A law was also passed which created the institution of popular referendum for the ratification of important legislation. Early the following year he promised that his country would become a democracy when the people were "fully prepared."

The U.N. General Assembly called on its members to bar Spain from membership in February 1946. The next month England, France and the United States issued a declaration stating that "so long as General Franco continues in control of Spain, the Spanish people cannot anticipate full and cordial association with those nations of the world which have . . . brought defeat to German Nazism and Italian Fascism. . . ." It also expressed the hope that "patriotic and liberal-minded Spaniards" would persuade Franco to retire.

On December 12, 1946 the U.N. General Assembly passed a resolution asserting that "in origin, nature, structure and general conduct, the Franco regime is a fascist regime patterned on, and established largely as a result of aid received from, Hitler's Nazi Germany and Mussolini's Fascist Italy." In addition, the Assembly urged U.N. members to recall their senior diplomats from Spain and prohibited international agencies connected with the United Nations from allowing Spanish participation in their sessions. The United States and many other nations withdrew their ambassadors or ministers from Madrid and maintained only a chargé d'affaires there.

Ever since Franco's assumption of leadership, reports emanating from Spain have spoken of the country's disastrous economic conditions and of widespread dissatisfaction. A *Time* story of December 1946, stated: "Spain's economy is sliding inevitably down the chute to bankruptcy."

Less than two years later L. Bus Fekete wrote in *Life* that there was "not much love lost between Franco and his Spaniards. At least 20 million thoroughly disapprove of him." Nevertheless, the U.N. action against him was failing to achieve its purpose partly because, the article continued, Spaniards "resent it furiously if the outside world attempts to advise them on how to conduct their national affairs." The U.N. diplomatic boycott of Spain was ended in November 1950 when the General Assembly voted to revoke its resolution of December 12, 1946.

The resumption of full diplomatic relations between the United States and Spain was foreshadowed by new contacts between the two nations and by Congressional approval of a $62,500,000 loan to the Spanish government in August 1950. On February 5, 1951 Stanton Griffis was sworn in as the new American Ambassador to Spain. The late Admiral Forrest P. Sherman began consultations in July 1951 with Franco about the possibility of a defense agreement.

Britain and France had expressed opposition to such an agreement on the grounds that it would imply a withdrawal of American forces to Spain in the event of war with Russia, and would necessitate a reduction of military assistance to the Atlantic pact countries.

On January 6, 1952, Franco told the Spanish Council of the Kingdom: "Thanks both to God and the tenacity of Spaniards, the sun of our hopes begins to shine in the world." On December 31, 1952, he declared: Spain is now "sought after by those who in years past scorned our offer to cooperate against communism." On September 26, 1953, the American Ambassador to Spain, James Clement Dunn, and the Spanish Minister for Foreign Affairs, Alberto Martín Artajo, signed the agreement which gives the United States the right to use "a number of Spanish air and naval bases for the defense of Western Europe and the Mediterranean" (New York *Times,* September 27, 1953). The U.S. government having undertaken to provide military and economic aid, it agreed to furnish a total of $226,000,000 to implement the accord.

Of the negotiations, the New York *Times* (August 30, 1951) commented: "One of the clear facts that Americans must face is that if we go ahead with this agreement, we will be helping to perpetuate Franco in power as long as he lives and cares to remain the dictator of Spain. This will be our responsibility in the face of history." After the signing of the accord, an editorial in the New York *Herald Tribune* (September 27, 1953) stated: ". . . it is to the common interest of both nations—to say nothing of the interest of the non-Communist world as a whole—to make the agreements signed yesterday into a reality, into a strong weapon against aggression."

The New York *Times* on October 31, 1953 reported that the Falange had just held its first National Congress since the end of the Civil War, "and it looks as if there was a deliberate intention to show that the recent military agreement with the United States does not mean any advance toward democracy."

Under the Law of Succession of 1947, Spain was declared a kingdom, Franco was named Chief of State for life and was given the right to choose his successor. A concordat which, according to Franco, establishes Roman Catholicism as the state religion of Spain was signed in the Vatican on August 27, 1953.

Among other awards, the Spanish dictator holds the Medalla Militar and the French Croix de Mérite Militaire et Naval. He was presented with the American Legion's Medal of Merit on April 11, 1951 and is also a commander of the Legion of Honor.

His residence, El Pardo, was built by the Emperor Charles V in 1543 as a hunting lodge. Franco was married to the former Carmen Polo y Martínez Valdés in 1923; their only child, a daughter called "Carmencita" (María del Carmen Franco y Polo) is married to Dr. Cristóbal Martínez Bordiu Ortega y Bascarán, Marqués de Villaverde. Franco is somewhat less than five feet four inches tall and is said to live simply and to enjoy hunting and fishing.

References (See also references listed in 1942 biographical sketch)

N Y World-Telegram p18 N 22 '50
Newsweek 38:32+ Ag 27 '51 pors
Collier's 120:42+ Jl 5 '47
Sat Eve Post 218:18+ Ag 4 '45 por
Time 42:29+ O 18 '43; 47:26+ Mr 18 '46 pors
U S News 31:36+ Ag 3 '51 pors; 35:69+ O 9 '53 pors
Diccionario Biográfico (1950)
International Who's Who, 1953
International Yearbook and Statesmen's Who's Who, 1953
10 Eventful Years (1947)
World Biography (1948)

FRASER, IAN FORBES Mar. 13, 1907-

Educator; director of American Library in Paris

Address: b. 129 av. des Champs-Elysées, Paris 8, France; h. 149 W. 12th St., New York 11

Regarded as "one of the strongest weapons against communism", the American Library in Paris with its six new branches in the French provinces is headed by Ian Forbes Fraser. "While not organized to fight communism," he states, "our libraries constitute show windows of the American way of life that every Fren[illegible]man can sample. We do not resort to [illegible] of propaganda. But when you give the [illegible] the light they will find the right path. [illegible] that is what the Communists fear."

The American Library in Paris is the o[illegible] American library abroad entirely created a[illegible] maintained by private initiative, and is now in its thirty-fifth year of service. Since Fraser's appointment as director in February 1947, he has dispensed information about America to the French and about the French to Americans. He has delivered lectures in the United States on Franco-American relations. In France, under his leadership, the library has extended its services to all parts of the country. Before becoming library director, Fraser was an instructor in French and assistant to the dean of Columbia College.

Ian Forbes Fraser was born on March 13, 1907, in Aberdeen, Scotland, the only child of John Fraser, a journalist and lecturer, and the former May Webster. His family immigrated to Halifax, Nova Scotia, when Ian was five years old. A year later the Frasers moved to Montreal, Canada, where they remained until their son was thirteen. In 1920 they became residents of New York City where Ian attended George Washington High School, from which he was graduated in 1925. He was active in the student government association of the school and served as president of ARISTA.

At Columbia College, where Fraser majored in French, he won a Pulitzer scholarship and membership in Phi Beta Kappa. He was business manager of the Columbia *Spectator* and a member of Phi Sigma Kappa fraternity. During the summers he worked as counselor and later director of the New York *Herald Tribune* fresh air camps. After receiving his A.B. degree in 1929, Fraser continued his study of French at the University of Paris, and earned his *diplôme* in 1930.

He then studied at Columbia University, where he prepared a thesis entitled "Bibliography of French-Canadian Poetry" (later published by the Institute of French Studies). He was awarded the M.A. degree in 1933. He received the Ph.D. degree in 1939; his thesis, "The Spirit of French Canada," was published that year by the Columbia University Press. Fraser was influenced in the choice of his lifework as an educator by Alexander Guy Holborn Spiers, professor of French, and Horace Taylor, economics professor, at Columbia University.

Fraser began his career in 1930 as an instructor in French at Columbia College, and held this post until 1947. From 1932 to 1937 he was

IAN FORBES FRASER

social director of the men's residence halls at Columbia University; during 1937-1947 he served as assistant to the Columbia College dean. In addition, from 1940 to 1942, Fraser directed the Maison Française at Columbia University.

His teaching career was interrupted in 1942 by the war. He began his service as a first lieutenant with the Air Corps Intelligence, Eighth Air Force and Air Ministry in London. In June 1944 he participated in the Normandy landing with the Provisional Engineers Special Brigade Group. He then worked with the history section of ETOUSA and the U.S. Ninth Army until the crossing of the Rhine. Fraser holds six campaign stars on an ETO medal and a Bronze Star Medal.

After the end of hostilities he organized and commanded the American Military University in Paris for the U.S. Army. Known as the Paris Study Center, it provided educational opportunities for some 3,000 officers and enlisted men between June 1945 and March 1946. For his service as an educator Fraser was made Officer of Public Instruction and chevalier of the Legion of Honor by the French government in 1946. After the center closed, Fraser returned to the United States. He was retired from active duty with the rank of lieutenant colonel in July 1946 and then resumed his teaching and advisory work at Columbia College.

Six months later Fraser returned to France to serve as director of the American Library in Paris. Incorporated on May 20, 1920 as a private nonprofit institution, it was the outgrowth of a library formed to serve the armed forces of World War I. After the war, American residents of Paris took over the book collection and the American Library Association established an initial endowment fund of $25,000.

The library, first located at 10 rue de l'Elysée, was moved in 1936 to 9 rue de Téhéran. In November 1953 it was moved to new and larger quarters at 129 avenue des Champs-Elysées. The building contains a large reference section; special collections in literature, history, biography, and the social sciences; reading rooms for newspapers and magazines, and current books; and a children's room.

Under Fraser's directorship the American Library in Paris has extended its facilities. In January 1948 its first branch was opened on the Left Bank at 173 boulevard Saint-Germain in rooms made available by the Carnegie Endowment for International Peace. In connection with the opening, Fraser was a guest on several radio programs, and a television program. Jefferson Caffery, then U.S. Ambassador, speaking at the ceremonies, stressed "the importance of making available to the people of France not only coal and wheat but also the creative efforts of our writers and philosophers and the achievements of our economists and men of science." *L'Humanité,* French Communist newspaper, in reporting the event, called the library "a menace to France . . . spreading its ideological propaganda into the very heart of the cultural center of Paris."

In 1948 Fraser arranged for the creation of deposit collections in the municipal libraries of Rouen, Le Havre and Reims. Duplicate books and magazines were turned over as gifts to high school, college and other French libraries. In 1948 the library also began its mail service through which books are sent by post each month to all parts of France to serve subscribers who have no other access to books in English.

The American Library in Paris celebrated its thirtieth anniversary at special ceremonies at the Bibliothèque Nationale on May 13, 1950. At that time, André Siegfried spoke on the subject, "French-American Intellectual Exchange," and analyzed the benefits which France and the United States derive from each other. According to *Library Journal,* he also paid "tribute to the efforts of the American Library in Paris, where, as he pointed out, much of the documentation for his famous book, *America Comes of Age,* was obtained" (September 15, 1950).

At the end of that year, funds were made available for the creation of library branches in key provincial cities. During 1951 these were established at Roubaix, Toulouse and Rennes; Grenoble and Montpellier were added in 1952, while in May 1953 a branch was opened at Nantes.

"At a time when it is of paramount importance to tell our story abroad and to replace suspicion and misconceptions with mutual trust based on knowledge, the success of enterprises such as the American Library in Paris and its branches is doubly gratifying," commented the New York *Times* (December 2, 1951). "American books can be ambassadors of good will, and we should commend and support our librarians in their effort to make them available to all those who wish to read them."

At the end of 1953 the American Library in Paris had 3,448 subscribing members who borrowed during that year 108,208 books and magazines for home reading. The Left Bank branch had 670 members and circulated 21,218 books and magazines. At the six branch libraries, a total of 3,879 borrowing members were enrolled and 159,754 books and magazines were circulated for home reading. Thousands of readers who were not subscribing members used the free reading room facilities of all the libraries. Approximately 80 per cent of the books and magazines went into French homes.

The main library's collection in 1953 numbered about 80,000 books and 220 magazines regularly received. Of the 4,106 volumes added in 1953, 1,142 were purchased by the library, while the remaining 2,964 were received as gifts from friends in France and the United States. A private board of trustees administers the American Library in Paris, which cooperates with the U.S. Information Service Documentation Center in order to avoid duplication.

Under the direction of Mrs. William B. Olmsted, Jr., a New York headquarters of the American Library in Paris, Inc., has been established at 159 East 63d Street, New York 21.

Fraser has made annual lecture tours in the United States since 1951. He has called attention in his lectures to the growing anti-American attitude of the French and the success of communist propaganda abroad. He has urged greater understanding and support by Americans of France's anti-communist policies.

In an article describing the functions of the American Library published in the *Wilson Library Bulletin* (December, 1952) Fraser wrote: "The influence of the library extends far beyond the limits of Paris, or even of France, and readers from many lands have found within its walls their first contact with the American principle of the free dissemination of knowledge which must be the basis of all democratic education."

The educator is the author of a textbook, *French Reviewed* (Farrar & Rinehart, 1941). Since 1948 he has been a professor at the Ecole Supérieure de Guerre in Paris. He has been chairman of the selection committee of the University of Free Europe in Exile in Strasbourg since 1951. His clubs are the American Club of Paris, University Club of Paris, American Association of Teachers of French, American Library Association, and Modern Language Association.

The Portland *Oregonian* (February 20, 1954) describes Fraser as the "intellectual ambassador to France" with a "library-quiet" manner. He is five feet ten inches tall and weighs 170 pounds. He has blue eyes and brown hair that is turning gray. He is a bachelor. He gives his political affiliation as independent, his church affiliation as Presbyterian. Reading and music are his favorite recreations.

References

Library J 72:238 F 1 '47 por
Directory of American Scholars (1951)
Who Knows—and What (1949)

FRASER, JAMES EARLE Nov. 4, 1876—Oct. 11, 1953 Sculptor; best known works include *End of the Trail* and the buffalo nickel; studied art in Chicago and Paris; became associated with Augustus St. Gaudens; statues for which he was famous include those of Benjamin Franklin, Theodore Roosevelt, Alexander Hamilton, Albert Gallatin, John Ericsson, and General George S. Patton, Jr.; received gold medal of National Institute of Arts and Letters and American Academy of Arts and Letters, Medal of Honor of National Sculpture Society and Century Association, and Saltus medal; created a Knight of the Order of Vasa by King of Sweden. See *Current Biography,* (July) 1951.

Obituary

N Y Times p27 O 12 '53

FREAR, J(OSEPH) ALLEN, JR. Mar. 7, 1903- United States Senator from Delaware; agriculturalist

Address: b. c/o Senate Office Bldg., Washington 25, D.C.; h. 622 S. State St., Dover, Del.

Delaware's Democratic Senator, J. Allen Frear, Jr., is a Dover agriculturalist and bank director who was elected to a six-year term in November 1948. Named to the Senate Banking and Currency Committee in 1949, he proposed a bill to amend the Securities Exchange Act of 1934. His other committee assignments have been to the District of Columbia, Post Office and Civil Service, and Finance.

Frear is seeking re-election to the Senate in November 1954. Opposing him is Republican Representative Herbert B. Warburton.

Born on a farm near Rising Sun, Delaware on March 7, 1903, Joseph Allen Frear, Jr., is the son of Joseph Allen and Clara (Lowber) Frear. He has one sister, now Mrs. J. W. Wilson. During his boyhood in Rising Sun he attended rural schools, later preparing at Caesar Rodney High School to enter the University of Delaware in Newark, where he received his B.S. degree in 1924.

Before his graduation from the university young Frear had, in 1922, established agricultural interests in Dover, Delaware. In time he became operator of three farms in the state and was also concerned with retail distribution of milk, fuel, farm machinery, and fertilizer. Interested in banking, he was a director of the Federal Land Bank, Baltimore, Maryland from 1938 to 1946, and chairman of the board from 1946 to 1948. He holds directorships in the Farmer's Bank in Dover and the Baltimore Trust Company in Camden (Delaware).

He served as state commissioner for Delaware State College in Dover from 1936 to 1941. He was a member as well of the state commissions for Old Age Welfare (1937-1948) and for Delaware State Hospital (1946-1948). His work for the state government was interrupted in 1943 when he joined the Army to serve in World War II until 1946, with two years' overseas duty. He is now a major in the Reserve.

(Continued next page)

Wide World

J. ALLEN FREAR, JR.

Frear campaigned in 1948 for a seat in the U.S. Senate, and was elected with strong labor backing on November 2. During his first session in the upper chamber, Frear supported the Barkley antifilibuster ruling (March), voted against eliminating segregation in public housing (April), and supported Federal aid to education (May), the North Atlantic Security Pact (July), and the extension of the Trade Agreements Act to June 12, 1951 (September).

In April 1949, the Senator answered criticism of the Administration's national housing program, which included provisions for improving homes and other buildings on submarginal farms. Such aid, he explained, was intended "to remove hazards to health and safety of the farm family and community." Pointing out that loans would be made only for "adequate or potentially adequate farms," he urged approval of the measure on the ground that on the farm "the ideas and ideals of more than a quarter of America's future citizens are being developed" (New York *Times,* April 19, 1949).

As a member of the Senate's Banking and Currency Committee and chairman of its subcommittee on the Securities and Exchange Commission, Frear, on August 8, 1949, introduced a bill to amend the Securities Exchange Act of 1934. This proposal was designed to make the major provisions of the act applicable to all unregistered corporations with assets of at least $3,000,000 and with no less than 300 stockholders. Investors in such companies would thus be given the protection afforded to companies listed on the national exchanges, which are under the supervision of the Securities and Exchange Commission.

Full hearings on Frear's bill, which had the support of the President, Harry S. Truman, were held in February 1950 before the Senate subcommittee headed by the Delaware legislator. While the measure was, in general, endorsed by the New York Curb Exchange, the New York Stock Exchange and the Investment Bankers Association of America, it was opposed by the National Association of Manufacturers and several other organizations.

Frear discussed his bill before the New York Security Dealers Association in December 1950, stating that it would contribute to the solution of the nation's financial problem of increasing "the interest of the public in direct investment, as distinguished from indirect interest through their banks and insurance policies" (New York *Times,* December 9, 1950). "The investment industry is and must be a vital part of our great tradition of free enterprise," the Senator stated. "Perhaps its greatest compliment lies in the fact that Soviet Russia has no such organization."

During the second session of the Eighty-first Congress Senator Frear, then chairman of a subcommittee of the Post Office and Civil Service Committee, sponsored a bill in March 1950 to have postmasters appointed under civil service rules. He was serving also at this time on the Senate's District of Columbia Committee. His voting record on some of the key issues of 1950 showed him in support of an appropriation of $45,000,000 for the Point IV Program (May) and in opposition to an additional $2.7 billion for the Marshall Plan (July) and to the $100,000,000 loan to Spain (August). He favored overriding the President's veto of the Communist-subversive control bill (September).

The Senate banking subcommittee, of which Frear was a member, issued in early 1951 a critical report on the lending activities of the Reconstruction Finance Corporation. On February 6 Frear demanded that two RFC officials be discharged for allowing the agency's policies to be influenced by "favoritism." (Later, in April 1952, he voted to abolish the RFC.) While occupied with the work of the Banking and Currency Committee, including a trip to South America in November 1953, Frear was also concerned with his duties on the Democratic Steering Committee and the Finance Committee, to which he had been assigned at the opening of the Eighty-second Congress in January 1951.

On economy measures in 1951, the Delaware Democrat favored reductions of 10 per cent in government civil pay rolls; $10,000,000 in reclamation funds; and $130,000,000 in soil conservation. The following year he voted "yea" to cuts in foreign aid and to override the President's veto of the McCarran-Walter immigration bill, and against giving power to the President to seize the steel plants. Frear, who approved the use of the Taft-Hartley act in the steel strike in a June 1952 vote, had earlier (April) proposed that the Banking and Currency Committee urge settlement of the dispute by allowing an hourly fifteen cent wage increase to the workers and a price increase of three dollars to five dollars a ton to the steel industry.

The Congressional roll call of 1953 indicates that Frear voted for the offshore oil bill; the use of foreign aid to cut farm surpluses; profits tax relief for small businesses; and to sell government-owned rubber plants. A bill that he introduced in the Eighty-third Congress in April proposed the abolition of the Federal Social Security System and transfer of funds to the states to establish and operate their own programs of old age and survivors insurance.

In early 1953, with Senator Homer Ferguson (Republican) of Michigan, Senator Frear reintroduced their bill of 1950 to revive the War Damage Corporation Act of March 1942 under which householders paid a small sum in annual premiums for insurance against damage by foreign bombs in the United States.

In the 1954 session Frear voted against U.S. participation in the St. Lawrence seaway (January); for the (John W.) Bricker amendment which would limit the President's treaty-making powers (February); for granting statehood to Hawaii and Alaska (April); against continuing 90 per cent supports for basic crops through 1955 (April); for a constitutional amendment fixing the membership of the Supreme Court at nine justices and requiring retirement at the age of seventy-five (May); and against the eighteen-year-old vote amendment (May).

Frear joined with Senator Walter F. George, Democrat of Georgia in June 1954, in an effort to increase income tax exemptions, now $600, by $200 a year this year and $400 a year thereafter. When this failed to win support, Senator George on June 28 proposed a $100 increase in personal income tax exemptions, effective next year, and Senator Frear was one of the co-sponsors of the George amendment (which was defeated).

The Senator is president of the Kent General Hospital board in Dover, a member of the American Hospital Association, Delaware State Farm Bureau, Chamber of Commerce, Kent Horse Show Association, American Legion, and Veterans of Foreign Wars. He is a Mason (Knight Templar, Consistory and Shriner) who in 1949 was elected Grand Master of the Grand Lodge of Delaware. His fraternity is the Sigma Nu and his clubs are the Dover, Rotary (past president in Dover), Delaware Motor, and Maple Dale Country. He holds an honorary LL.D. degree from Bethany College.

Senator Frear married Esther Viola Schauer on February 11, 1933; they have a son, Fred and a daughter, Clara Louise. His religious affiliation is Congregational. He has been quoted in the New York *Times* as expressing himself in opposition "again and again toward any thought of showing a bended knee before the brutality of the Russian puppets in Korea or elsewhere."

References

Congressional Directory (1954)
Who's Who in America, 1954-55
Who's Who in United States Politics (1950)

FREDERICK, PAULINE News commentator

Address: b. c/o National Broadcasting Company, 30 Rockefeller Plaza, New York 20

The first woman to win the DuPont radio news commentator award is Pauline Frederick, who has succeeded in establishing herself in a field hitherto reserved for men. In June 1953 she joined the National Broadcasting Company staff as a news analyst after a distinguished career as a correspondent for the North American Newspaper Alliance and as commentator for the American Broadcasting Company. She made notable coverage of the 1952 political conventions, the United Nations during the Korean crisis, and various trials of spies and Communists. (She is no relation of the late motion picture actress of the same name.)

When she received the eleventh Alfred I. DuPont Award for "meritorious service to the American people" in 1953, the citation paid tribute to Miss Frederick for "exemplifying the best traditions of news commentary" and "avoiding the slickness, automatic orthodoxy and superficial sensationalism characteristic of much news commentary today . . . without making concessions to a vulgarization of either thought or style" (*Variety,* March 31, 1954).

Pauline Frederick was born in Gallitzin, Pennsylvania, the second of three children of Matthew P. Frederick, an official of the Pennsylvania State Department of Labor, and Susan (Stanley) Frederick. While still in high school, Pauline began to report school and social events for three newspapers in Harrisburg. Upon her graduation from high school, she had the choice of continuing her newspaper career or going to college. She chose the latter, and attended the American University in Washington, D.C. She received the B.A. degree in political science and the M.A. degree in international law.

She had originally intended to become a lawyer, but a history professor persuaded her to try journalism since he felt there were already too many lawyers, particularly in Washington, D.C. Miss Frederick then set out to interview diplomats' wives. She called up the Czechoslovakian Legation to ask for an appointment with the Minister's wife. The secretary asked where the article would appear. "Why, that depends on the story I get," Miss Frederick replied. She got the interview. The same technique worked with the Chinese Ambassador's wife. Now she had to sell the stories. She started with the editor of the Washington *Star,* who not only accepted them, but hired her to write a weekly feature.

In the mid-1930's Miss Frederick covered the Department of State for the *United States News* (now *U.S. News & World Report*). Her next job was with the North American Newspaper Alliance. In 1938, after six years of newspaper experience, she started to work in radio with a part-time job helping the commentator, H. R. Baukhage, to prepare his scripts. "Stay away from radio," he advised her. "It doesn't like women." Miss Frederick, however, did not follow his advice. She accepted an offer from the National Broadcasting

PAULINE FREDERICK

Company for occasional radio interviews. She stayed in Washington for the next seven years, and did both newspaper and radio work.

Pauline Frederick's real opportunity came in 1945 when she became a war correspondent for the North American Newspaper Alliance and went on a world tour of nineteen countries. She later covered the trials of the German war criminals in Nuremberg.

She was sent as the only American correspondent on the American military train that returned to Cracow, Poland, the Wit Stowosz altar, a famous art treasure that had been taken by the Germans during the occupation of Poland. She used this opportunity to observe how Soviet Russia, through the Polish Communist party, was rapidly taking control in that country and suppressing freedom. She reported in the New York *Times* (May 22, 1946) after her return to Nuremberg, how members of the Red Army stationed in Cracow and the Polish Communists had fired upon a spontaneous parade of people who had just attended a Mass at the church where the altarpiece had been replaced.

Miss Frederick joined the American Broadcasting Company's news staff in June 1946, the first woman to cover political events for them. Beginning in September 1947, she shared the United Nations "beat" with commentator Gordon Fraser. In that year she was the only woman among 135 men on a B-29 mission sent to the inauguration of the President of Uruguay.

Among her next assignments were the 1948 Democratic and Republican conventions, the presidential campaign and inauguration, the trial of the eleven Communist leaders, the perjury trial of Alger Hiss, and the espionage trial of Judith Coplon and Valentin Gubitchev.

In May 1949 Miss Frederick spent several weeks in the best tradition of Richard Harding Davis. She had been covering the negotiations (between Philip Jessup and Jacob Malik) which led to the lifting of the Berlin blockade. On the day that these were completed (May 4), she emplaned for Germany and flew both directions on the airlift and then rode on the first train into Berlin. From Berlin she flew to Warsaw where she broadcast the Polish reaction on the day (May 14) that the German Communist Gerhart Eisler, who had jumped bail in New York to sail on the Polish liner *Batory,* was removed from the ship in England. She then went to Paris for the opening of the meeting of the Council of Foreign Ministers.

During this period, Miss Frederick appeared on at least five morning newscasts and three telecasts weekly. Her only non-news program was *Pauline Frederick's Guest Books,* a telecast presented every Saturday evening on ABC-TV. She organized and wrote this show.

She had the first radio interview with former King Michael of Romania, and his mother, Princess Helen, one hour after they had arrived in the United States; and the first long-distance telephone interview with Selden Chapin, American Minister to Hungary, concerning the trial of Joseph Cardinal Mindszenty. She was the only American woman commentator to cover the Korean crisis in the United Nations. From her observations of world politics, she has stated her belief that international relations are basically human relations and that policies which are aimed at achieving world peace should consider the backgrounds of the people "on the other side of the street."

In June 1953 Miss Frederick rejoined NBC's staff. Her discussions of national and world events are now heard for fifteen minutes Mondays through Fridays in the early afternoon on her program, *Pauline Frederick Reporting.* In addition, she has a program of interviews, *Listen to the Witness* which is on the air early Sunday afternoon. She also is heard on many NBC special news broadcasts such as the United Nations special session on the Korean truce in August 1953, and she reports the news on NBC's *Weekend,* a Sunday afternoon two-hour program.

Miss Frederick is occasionally a panel member of NBC's television program, *Citizen's Union Searchlight.*

In recognition of her accomplishments, Pauline Frederick has received many awards, including the Theta Sigma Phi National Headliner Award for being the outstanding woman in radio; the American University alumni achievement award; honorary membership in the Harrisburg (Pennsylvania) Club of the Soroptimist International Association; honorary membership in the Columbus (Ohio) Chapter of Theta Sigma Phi; and a citation from the International House at Alabama State Teachers College in Jacksonville.

Miss Frederick lives in an apartment from which she can see the United Nations' permanent home along New York's East River. Her usual workday is from 4:30 in the morning to 8 at night. She has a French poodle named Patrick. She has been described in the New York *Times* (December 5, 1948) as a "tall, lissome brunette of mellifluous voice and photogenic figure."

Television columnist and former movie actress Faye Emerson wrote in the New York *World-Telegram and Sun* (March 12, 1954): "Pauline Frederick . . . This good-looking brainy gal has been doing a crack job on NBC-radio and has just won a highly coveted award, so why not her own TV show? . . . There is room for a few ladies on television to talk about something besides cooking and fashions. . . . Women have minds, too."

References

Ed & Pub 82:42 Jl 23 '49 por
N Y Times II p15 D 5 '48
Newsweek 30:66 O 27 '47 por
Radio-TV Mirror 37:5 F '52 por

FREITAG, WALTER August 14, 1889- Labor union official

Address: Wetterstr. 59, Herdecke a.d. Ruhr, Germany

One of the important leaders in Western Germany is Walter Freitag who was elected on October 17, 1952 the president of the 6,000,000 member German Federation of Trade Unions (DGB). He is also the head of the German Metal Workers Association, the most powerful union in the federation with a membership of 1,600,000. A Social Democrat for forty-five years, he is a deputy of the Bundestag at Bonn.

Walter Freitag was born on August 14, 1889 in Remscheid, the son of a laborer. After receiving an elementary school education, he became an apprentice to a toolmaker. At the age of eighteen he turned to trade unionism and socialism, joining the German Metal Workers Association and the Social Democratic party the next year. He was in charge of the German Metal Workers Association in Remscheid in 1919, and in 1920 headed the Hagen district of the association. Becoming president of the Social Democratic party for the district of Hagen-Schwelm in 1931, he was elected in the following year to the Prussian Landtag from which he was dismissed by the Nazis in 1933. He was imprisoned for two years at the Neusytrum concentration camp and later at the Lichtenburg camp.

During World War II Freitag worked in a steel plant and was constantly watched by the Gestapo. At the end of the war he became one of the founders of the new metal workers union and the Social Democratic party in southern Westphalia. He served as a member of the Landtag of North Rhine-Westphalia from 1946 to 1949, when he was elected to the Bundestag on the Social Democratic ticket.

The labor leader became the president of the metal workers union for the British zone and Bremen in February of 1947, and for the three Western zones in 1950. Kurt Schumacher, then president of the Social Democratic party, led the unsuccessful move in 1950 to elect Walter Freitag president of the DBG. At the 1952 convention a last-minute attempt to prevent Freitag's election by a compromise plan whereby the federation would be headed by a triumvirate proved ineffectual and Freitag was elected by

Bildstelle des Deutschen Gewerkschaftsbundes, Düsseldorf

WALTER FREITAG

a plurality of 184 to 154 with eighteen abstentions. This convention resolved to work for economic reforms which would guarantee full employment, co-determination, nationalization of basic industries, provision for adequate living standards for the overaged and incapacitated, and insure the workers a fair share of the economic profits. In these demands the union has been supported by the Social Democratic party, the labor element in the Christian Democratic party, and by influential church groups, namely, the German Catholic Convention and the Congress of the German Protestant Church.

His affiliation with the Social Democratic party commits Freitag to oppose the European Steel and Coal Community (Schuman plan) as a usurpation of Germany's economic potential. This party also believes that the European Defense Community and the Convention of Relations Between the Three Powers and the Federal Republic (Bonn peace pact) will operate to prevent national unity and would dislocate current economic prosperity, upset the labor market and lower the standard of living. While strongly anti-communist, Freitag desires unification of West and East Germany, a view which differs somewhat from the foreign policy of Chancellor Konrad Adenauer and Secretary of State Walter Hallstein.

It was feared that the election of a socialist to the presidency of the federation would encourage a split in the ranks of labor. Prior to the Nazi dictatorship, the trade union movement was continually torn by political strife between the Social Democrats, the communists and the Catholic center. When the federation regained its freedom in 1945, it united on the basis of forsaking, at least outwardly, old political affiliations.

Since Freitag took office, there appears to be very little dissension. The convention re-

FREITAG, WALTER—*Continued*

jected the resolutions on rearmament, the delegates asserting the subject was a political one and, therefore, should be avoided. The new president endorsed this view, although he has stated that the cost of rearmament must not fall primarily on the working class. Nevertheless Hedwig Wachenheim wrote "Herr Freitag must show wisdom, courage and flexibility—in short, statesmanship, if he wants to avoid a split in the unions. . . ." (*Foreign Affairs*, January 1953).

The drive for co-determination to which Freitag is expected to give new impetus, goes deeply into the history of German trade unions. In form it is a partnership between labor and management in each industry, but in principle co-determination is the assertion by labor of the right of the organized working class to share in shaping the entire economic development of the country through participation in management. The aim is not merely participation of the workers in a given factory or mine, but a share in the direction of the German economy by the federation as the representative of the working class. (A management class is to grow out of the working class.)

The election of Freitag promises no let-up in the struggle to get government enactment of co-determination throughout all of Germany's industries. In the Ruhr where it was adopted in May 1951 for the coal and steel industry, the workers have a right to sit as directors, on the same basis as owners, with veto over naming of plant managers. The Adenauer government is willing to extend co-determination to the basic industries and such state enterprises as Federal railroads and post office, depending upon the experience gained in the coal and steel industry.

These demands of German labor are not new. They appeared in the broad scheme of "economic democracy" embodied thirty years ago in the Weimar constitution which provided that labor should cooperate on equal terms in "the entire economic development of the productive forces" of the country. Freitag has strong convictions about enforcing this program.

Walter Freitag is a member of the advisory council of the Schuman Plan Administration and a member of the executive committee of the International Metal Workers Association.

References

Commonweal 58:49 Ap 17 '53
N Y Times p3 O 18 '53
Wer ist Wer? (1951)

GALARD TERRAUBE, GENEVIÈVE DE

Apr. 13, 1925- Nurse

Address: b. c/o Ministère de l'Air, Paris, France

The attention of the world was focused on the heroic defense of the Indochinese fortress of Dienbienphu early in 1954. During the fifty-six days of siege preceding the fall of the garrison, only one woman remained to tend the wounded—French flying nurse Geneviève de Galard Terraube. Her heroism and devotion during those harrowing days caused her to be known as the "Angel of Dienbienphu."

Daughter of an aristocratic French family, Mademoiselle de Galard Terraube had volunteered for service in Indochina, and when the garrison defended by Brigadier General Christian de Castries and his 12,000 troops fell, she refused to leave the wounded. Recognition of her courage and conscientiousness was expressed by the United States Congress which in July 1954 invited her to be its guest in the United States.

From feudal times the Galard family has been notable for its service to France. Of Gascon origin, the family contributed three of its sons to the Crusades—including Guillaume II, who helped to organize the fleet for Palestine in 1218; three to bishoprics of the Church; and two to royal councils, for Géraud was Chamberlain to Charles VII and Hector both Councillor and Chamberlain to Louis XI. In provincial councils the Galard family was represented by Pierre, Seneschal of Quercy (1340), Jean, Seneschal of Armagnac, and his nephew who became Governor of that Province.

Through the centuries a career at arms has attracted a number of the men of the family, one of whom, Hector de Galard, served under Jeanne d'Arc at the siege of Orléans in 1429. The historic siege of La Rochelle in 1628 occasioned the death of Philippe, Baron de Terraube, one of the foremost captains of the period. In the eighteenth century Louis-Antoine, Marquis de Terraube and officer of the French Navy, was responsible for much of the navigation and cartography of the region of French Guiana, to which he voyaged three times, and on which he wrote a guide for colonial development, *Tableau de Cayenne ou de la Guiane Française*. Among contemporary members of the family, the head of its eldest branch died in 1940 in a German prison camp, another, the Comte d'Ussel, in a concentration camp, and a third, Henri, is at present serving as a lieutenant with the French Foreign Legion in Indochina. A cousin, Hector de Galard, a French newspaperman, "seems to have been mainly responsible for obtaining Geneviève de Galard Terraube's release from Communist captivity," according to Edmond Taylor in the *Reporter*, July 20, 1954.

Born in Paris April 13, 1925, Geneviève de Galard Terraube is one of the two daughters of Vicomte Oger de Galard Terraube and his wife, the former Germaine de Préville. Her sister, Marie-Suzanne, is now Madam Tristan de Villepin, wife of a cavalry officer. Geneviève's father who had been an army officer, died when she was nine years old. The major part of her childhood was spent in Paris, where she attended the Louise de Bettignies School, but during the Occupation of France the family passed four years in Toulouse, where she was a student at a Dominican convent. With her sister and cousins, she spent the summer vacations at the family's Château de Labatu in Terraube (Haute-Garonne).

After successfully completing the examinations for the two parts of the *baccalauréat,*

Geneviève de Galard Terraube entered the Ecole du Louvre for a course in fine arts, at the same time pursuing a course in home economics at another school. During the same period she was also studying at the Sorbonne, from which she received her certificates for proficiency in English in 1948 and 1949.

At the age of twenty-five, Mademoiselle de Galard Terraube decided to undertake the study of nursing, with the result that she received her diploma as a social and medical assistant from the Red Cross in 1950, and the State nursing diploma two years later, when she qualified for it by ranking first in her class. Subsequently she fulfilled the requirements for the diploma from the Paris School of Social Work.

Her decision to enter the air-borne nurses' unit—*Infirmières Pilotes et Secouristes de l'Air*—was a difficult one. "Like Florence Nightingale," observed Malvina Lindsay of the Washington *Post,* "she found her conservative family opposed to her undertaking. It was considered shockingly unconventional for her to assume such an arduous, hazardous life as [that of] an air force nurse, even though the unit she joined was an elite one, largely staffed with girls from aristocratic families. Yet she went firmly ahead. She is said to have been motivated by religion [she is a devout Catholic], by the military tradition of her family and by her own desires to serve where she was most needed." By the end of 1952, Geneviève de Galard Terraube had successfully completed the examinations for the air-borne unit and had signed a contract to serve in its re-grouping centers as well as in Africa and Indochina.

Since 1935 a select group of French nurses had been members of the IPSA, a small and elite women's association which had been formed to provide nurses and first-aid workers for troops evacuated by ambulance planes, and to encourage pilot training among its members. It was to this group that the Minister of War Prisoners and Deportees appealed in 1945 to supply qualified Red Cross nurses for French deportees returned by plane from Germany, and later, to whom another appeal was addressed by the Minister of France Overseas, to accompany back to France civil servants affected by long service in Africa and Madagascar.

When it became evident in 1946, that there was a need for similar nurses to serve in Indochina, the French Military Air Transport Service (*Groupement des Moyens Militaires de Transport Aérien*) secured the legal establishment of the association and organized competitive examinations for the recruitment of thirty-five nurses for service in the Far East. The accepted candidates must fulfill the usual requirements for nurses in the armed forces, as well as "be physically fit to serve in the Air Force . . . and have the aptitudes required of all flying personnel," and "pass written and oral examinations in medicine, aviation, and colonial medicine, geography and English, as well as a psychological and physical examination."

By volunteering for this group, Mademoiselle de Galard Terraube undertook to perform the usual nursing required by the sick and wounded either in war or peace, as well as the duties of

French Embassy Press & Inf. Div.
GENEVIEVE DE GALARD TERRAUBE

stewardess to whatever women and children might be passengers on board airplanes, and of assistant to the captain in administrative work or in case of distress or emergency. Like her colleagues, she is familiar with rescue practice, emergency and distress signals, and theoretical instruction in aviation.

Beginning her first tour of duty on April 29, 1953, she was assigned to Hanoi for a three-month period to care for the wounded in transit from the battle areas to Saigon. Following her assignment to Paris on August 1, she spent the summer of 1953 on service between there and North Africa, before entering upon six weeks of service in the Sahara during September and October. When she had completed her leave in November, she returned to serve in North and West Africa until she was returned to Indochina in January 1954 for her second tour of duty in evacuating the wounded.

Mademoiselle de Galard Terraube's heroic service at Dienbienphu began on March 28, 1954, when the helicopter in which she had made a routine flight to pick up wounded from the fortress (a vital point for the control of a rich rice-producing valley), was knocked out of commission on the airstrip by enemy artillery fire. All other women had already been evacuated from the garrison, which was being held against invading Vietminh forces by Brigadier General Christian de Castries and 12,000 men under his command, drawn from French, North African, Viet Namese, and Foreign Legion forces. Of these almost 1,200 lay wounded under the care of nineteen doctors in underground shelters at the time the flying nurse was stranded at the fortress.

She went to work immediately in aid of the doctors, remaining on duty at times for twenty-four hour stretches and assisting surgeons in as many as twenty-five operations a day. Although soldiers had rigged up a tent for her lined with

GALARD TERRAUBE, GENEVIÈVE DE
—Continued

the red and white silk from parachute drops, observers of her heroic duty during the many days of siege doubted that she often used it —most of the time she slept briefly on a spare stretcher in the hospital, wearing her oversize camouflaged fatigues and sneakers. Her conscientiousness and devotion far beyond the exigencies of duty came to be a symbol of mercy and pity to the wounded, and inspired their characterization of her as their "angel."

Despite volunteer reinforcements parachuted in, and valiant hand to hand fighting in the last twenty hours of its defense, Dienbienphu fell on May 7 before overwhelming Vietminh, and Chinese Communist forces. In those last days, Mademoiselle de Galard received the Legion of Honor and the Military Cross with palms from General de Castries "for courage under fire." When the fortress fell, she maintained her gallant stand by refusing the enemy's offer to evacuate her by air: she preferred to stay with the wounded.

Upon her early release from captivity, Mademoiselle de Galard was sent back to France, where her grateful Government bestowed upon her the Air Medal and the Silver Medal of Honor of the Air Medical Service. Subsequently, pursuant to the presentation of a resolution in her honor to the United States Congress by Representative Frances P. Bolton of Ohio, that body invited the French heroine to visit this country—the first time such an invitation had been extended to a woman, and the third time, since the Congressionally-sponsored visits of the Marquis de Lafayette in 1824 and of Louis Kossuth in 1851, that a foreign national had received one.

Arriving in New York on July 26, 1954, for a three-week tour of the United States, Mademoiselle de Galard Terraube was accorded an official parade of welcome witnessed by more than 250,000 spectators. Her first press conference brought a number of requests for explanation of her two letters to Ho Chi Minh, leader of the Vietminh, the first of which she said had been written to felicitate him on his birthday (when he had promised to release over 700 wounded French prisoners), and the second to thank him for her own release and to beg for the liberation of the doctors and male nurses who had been with her at Dienbienphu.

In reply to the congratulations extended to her, Mademoiselle de Galard asserted: "I do not deserve this honor, for I have only done my duty. This honor is intended, through me, for those whose life I was proud to share in Dienbienphu, and for the nurses, for all the nurses, who devote themselves to the best of their ability to alleviating the sufferings of the wounded."

"You can understand," she continued, "that at this very moment my thoughts go to all those who were killed in that far distant land, to those who are still over there, all deserving much more than I the honor which you do me."

After receiving a scroll of honor from New York's Mayor Wagner, and awards from the American Nurses Association, the National League for Nursing, and Columbia University, the French nurse left the following day for Washington. For the following three days she stayed in the capital, where she witnessed a session of Congress and received the Medal of Freedom from President Eisenhower. The citation accompanying the medal read, in part: "Her service to her comrades, marked by the courage of a woman in battle and by the devotion of a nurse to her sworn duty, has been unsurpassed in this century."

Other awards received by Mademoiselle de Galard Terraube are the silver fellowship pin of the American Red Cross, and the gold medal of the city of Lima, Peru.

The blue-eyed, chestnut-haired nurse on her arrival in New York wore the white dress uniform of her corps, bearing on one sleeve the patch of an honorary private in the French Legion. Frequently referred to as a lieutenant, Mademoiselle de Galard explained that this is an assimilated rank and that actually French military nurses have no rank. During her sojourns in Paris, she shares the modest apartment of her widowed mother, filled with mementoes which recall the illustrious past of the family, in the "unfashionably aristocratic Parc Monceau quarter." When she has time to devote to sports, Mademoiselle de Galard prefers to ski, swim, or play tennis. "Always smiling and cheerful," said one French wounded soldier, "she was wonderful."

References

N Y World-Telegram Jl 26 '54 por
Newsweek 43:38 My 31 '54 por
Reporter 11:26 Jl 20 '54 por
Time 63:23 My 31 '54 por

GASPERI, ALCIDE DE Apr. 3, 1881-Aug. 19, 1954 Former Premier of Italy; at age of seventeen joined Irredentist movement; editor of Irredentist newspaper *Il Nuovo Trentino* (1905-1910); in 1911 elected by Irredentist population of Trento to Austrian parliament; elected to Italian Chamber of Deputies on Popular party ticket (1921-1924); took refuge during Benito Mussolini's regime in Vatican (1929-1943); Minister without portfolio (1944); Foreign Minister (1944-1945); Premier (1945-1953); presented case of defeated Italy at peace conference in Paris (1946); visited United States (1947) and obtained increased U.S. aid; his skill in compromise was regarded as a significant factor in preventing chaos in postwar Italy; a consistent friend of West. See *Current Biography* (Dec.), 1946.

Obituary

N Y Times p 1+ Ag 19 '54

GHULAM MOHAMMED. See Mohammed, G.

GIPSON, LAWRENCE HENRY (gĭp'sŭn)
Dec. 7, 1880- Historian; educator
Address: b. c/o The Library, Lehigh University, Bethlehem, Pa.; h. "Rotha," Panther Rd., Rydal, Pa.

The compilation and writing of eight volumes of a proposed eleven-volume work entitled *The British Empire Before the American Revolution* has occupied Professor Lawrence Henry Gipson of Lehigh University since 1927. The latest volume, *The Great War for the Empire: The Culmination, 1760-1763* was published in January 1954. Gipson received Columbia University's Loubat Prize in 1948 for the first six volumes, and the university's Bancroft Prize in 1950 for the seventh volume.

"Now that volume eight is available . . . the monumental character of Gipson's achievement is beyond dispute," observed Geoffrey Bruun (New York *Herald Tribune Book Review,* January 17, 1954).

After heading the department of history and government at Lehigh University for twenty-two years, Dr. Gipson became a research professor of history at the Lehigh Institute of Research in 1946. He is now a research professor of history emeritus. *Jared Ingersoll; A study of American loyalism in relation to British colonial government* and *Lewis Evans* (Historical Society of Pennsylvania, 1939) are among his other books.

Lawrence Henry Gipson was born in Greeley, Colorado on December 7, 1880, to Albert Eugene and Lina Maria (West) Gipson. He is descended from early settlers of New England. His sister Alice was academic dean and professor of English at Lindenwood College for Women, St. Charles, Missouri. James Herrick Gipson, president of Caxton Printers, is his younger brother. Most of Lawrence's boyhood was spent at Caldwell, Idaho where his father edited the *Idaho Odd Fellow* and the *Gem State Rural and Live Stock Farmer.* Lawrence attended Caldwell High School, and, later, the Academy of the College of Idaho in Caldwell, where he did long distance running.

"While a youth in Idaho," he recalls, "I drove a stagecoach; I also learned the printing trade before entering the University of Idaho and to a great extent met my expenses by acting as a newspaper reporter." He won an oratorical prize, and a prize in English literature.

Gipson received the A.B. degree in 1903 from the University of Idaho in Moscow. In the following year he successfully competed for the first Rhodes scholarship to be granted in Idaho. In 1907 he was awarded the B.A. degree from Oxford University in England.

Upon returning to the United States, Gipson served as a professor of history for three years at the College of Idaho. He continued his studies at Yale University in New Haven, Connecticut as a Farnham fellow in history in 1910 and 1911. President James A. MacLean of the University of Idaho and President William Judson Boone of the College of Idaho, Gipson believes, were important influences in his choice of history as a field of endeavor.

LAWRENCE HENRY GIPSON

At Wabash College in Crawfordsville, Indiana, Gipson was a professor and head of the department of history and political science from 1911 to 1924. In 1917 he had studied at Yale as a Bulkley fellow. After submitting his thesis, "Jared Ingersoll; A study of American loyalism in relation to British colonial government," Gipson received the Ph.D. degree from Yale in 1918. For his thesis he won the MacFarland Prize and the Porter Prize. *Jared Ingersoll* was published by the Yale University Press in 1920. The book was chosen for the Justin Winsor Prize of the American Historical Society.

Dr. Gipson became the head of the department of history and government at Lehigh University in Bethlehem, Pennsylvania in 1924. In 1927 he was awarded a grant by the American Council of Learned Societies "to assist in the . . . study of the last twenty-five years of the Colonial Period preceding the outbreak of the American Revolution." Two years later Gipson received from the Social Science Research Council an additional grant "to visit Ireland, Scotland, England, and France" in connection with this study.

The first three volumes of Gipson's *The British Empire Before the American Revolution* were issued by Caxton Printers in 1936. They were entitled *Great Britain and Ireland, The Southern Plantations* and *The Northern Plantations.* When the eighth volume appeared in 1954, Geoffrey Bruun recalled: "It was clear that Professor Gipson . . . intended to reduce the part played by the thirteen American colonies to scale and judge it against the background of British imperial affairs" (New York *Herald Tribune Book Review,* January 17, 1954).

The fourth volume of *The British Empire* was entitled, *Zones of International Friction:*

GIPSON, LAWRENCE HENRY—*Cont.*

North America, South of the Great Lakes Region, 1748-1754 (Knopf, 1939).

Zones of International Friction: The Great Lakes Frontier, Canada, the West Indies, India, 1748-1754 (Knopf, 1942) was fifth in the series. Knopf published the sixth volume in 1946, *The Great War for the Empire: The Years of Defeat, 1754-1757.* It concerned the perilous situation of the English-speaking people in North America during the first three years of the French and Indian war. This book was received by the reviewers with respect, even by those who were troubled by Gipson's theme which (as Stanley Pargellis wrote in the *Yale Review,* Autumn, 1946) is "nothing less than the reinterpretation of the American Revolution from a Tory point of view."

Transferred in 1946 to the Lehigh Institute of Research, Gipson became a research professor in history. After the seventh of the series, *The Great War for the Empire: The victorious years, 1758-1760* (Knopf, 1949) appeared, A. L. Burt wrote that its publication "makes Parkman's classic *Montcalm and Wolfe* quite obsolete except as a piece of literature . . . it [Gipson's work] utilizes the enormous mass of raw material that has become available since Parkman laid down his pen" (*Canadian Historical Review,* December 1949).

The historian occupied the Harold Vyvyan Harmsworth Chair in American History at Oxford University in 1951 and 1952. He became research professor of history emeritus in 1952 at Lehigh University. Recently, his researches have been supported by grants from Lehigh, the Rockefeller Foundation and the United States Educational Commission for the United Kingdom.

After the eighth volume of *The British Empire* was published by Knopf in 1954, Geoffrey Bruun noted that Gipson "continues to challenge conventional verdicts . . . a number of characters consistently belittled by 'Whig' historians are partly rehabilitated. George II and George III emerge as more conscientious and intelligent rulers than standard American texts imply."

Among his other books are *Studies in Colonial Connecticut Taxation* (Lehigh University, 1931); *Charles McLean Andrews and the Reorientation of the Study of American Colonial History* (Lehigh University, 1935); and *The Moravian Indian Mission on White River* (Indiana Historical Bureau, 1938). He has contributed many articles to historical journals.

Gipson is a fellow of the Royal Historical Society, and a member of the American and Pennsylvania historical associations, American Academy of Political and Social Science, Historical Society of Pennsylvania, American Rhodes Scholar Association, Conference on British Studies, American Association of University Professors, and Phi Alpha Theta. He has been on the board of editors of the *American Historical Review* since 1946. He has been a trustee of Ogontz junior college since 1947. His club is the Franklin Inn in Philadelphia.

The scholar married Jeannette Reed, a teacher, on October 8, 1909. He is five feet seven inches tall and weighs about 135 pounds. His eyes are gray-blue and his hair, brownish-gray. For recreation he enjoys hiking and gardening. He is a Republican and a Congregationalist. Lehigh University awarded him the Hillman Award in 1947. Gipson holds the honorary D.Litt. degree from Temple University (1947), the L.H.D. from Lehigh University (1951) and LL.D. degree from the University of Idaho (1953).

References

N Y Times p26 My 27 '48 por; p7 Ja 12 '51 por
Directory of American Scholars (1951)
Who's Who in America, 1954-55
World Biography (1954)

el-GLAOUI, THAMI el-MEZOUARI, PASHA OF MARRAKECH (l-glou'ē) 1874?-

Address: Marrakech, French Morocco

Considered the "single most powerful man in French Morocco," Hadj Thami el-Mezouari el-Glaoui, the Pasha of Marrakech and Lord of the Atlas, is one of the world's richest men. He rules as a feudal lord over 3,000,000 Berber tribesmen with an army of about 300,000 men.

Opposing the growing strength of the Istiqlal, a nationalist party seeking independence, el-Glaoui in August 1953 succeeded in deposing the pro-Istiqlal Sultan, Sidi Mohammed ben Mulai Youssef, and replacing him with pro-French Sidi Mohammed ben Moulay Arafa. After this *coup d'état,* the eighty-year-old Berber chief narrowly escaped assassination in February and again in March 1954 by terrorists.

The Pasha was a militant supporter of France in her establishment of the Protectorate of Morocco in 1912. In recent years he has favored the installation in Morocco of United States strategic air bases, several of which have been completed.

Thami el-Mezouari was born about 1874 at Telouet in the Grand Atlas Mountains, the fifth son of Sidi Mohammed el-Mezouari, a powerful chief of South Morocco. The family is of Berber stock and is descended from the Prophet Mohammed and Idrīs, founder of the first recorded Moroccan dynasty.

Trained as a warrior and leader, the young Berber learned to ride horseback and to bear arms. Morocco, at the turn of the century, was torn by internal conflict and threatened by foreign invasion. When his oldest brother, Si Madani, Lord of Tafilelt, led a movement to overthrow the Sultan, Abd-ul-Aziz, Thami el-Mezouari commanded an important company of warriors. After bitter fighting, the Sultan was succeeded by his brother, Mulai Hafid in 1908, and Si Madani became Grand Vizier (Premier) and Thami el-Mezouari was named Pasha of Marrakech, a position he has held since that time.

Sultan Mulai Hafid was unable to establish order and relied more and more heavily upon foreign aid, largely from France and Spain.

In 1911 a revolt broke out and France sent an expedition to occupy Fès. The German gunboat *Panther* appeared at Agadir on July 1, 1911 for the purpose of protecting the interests of Germany. An international crisis was precipitated but a settlement was reached between Germany and France in November 1911 by which French protection was, in essence, recognized, and France guaranteed Germany economic opportunities in Morocco.

The Sultan of Morocco signed a treaty with the French on March 30, 1912 establishing the Protectorate. Fighting alongside of the French troops of Louis Hubert Lyautey, first Resident General of Morocco, el-Glaoui and his Berber horsemen were largely instrumental in bringing the tribal chiefs under the rule of the central power.

The Pasha then interested himself in the agricultural development of his country under French direction. The building of roads, railroads, docks, schools, and hospitals was also started by the French. Legislative power, until then arbitrarily exercised by pashas and kaids, was submitted to the control of French authorities. The French position in Morocco was still insecure when World War I broke out and French troops were needed at home, but el-Glaoui and Si Madani gave their solemn oath to maintain order and respect the French *status quo* for the duration of hostilities. After the war the French government showered el-Glaoui with gifts, granted him loans and decorated him with medals and ribbons.

At the outbreak of World War II, el-Glaoui put Morocco's strength solidly behind France. He had no sympathy for the Vichy government under Marshal Henri Philippe Pétain. German commissioners with credentials from the Vichy government sought an audience with el-Glaoui to draw up an armistice agreement, but he refused to receive them.

He was the only Moroccan chief to help rally the forces of the Resistance, hiding arms from the German inspectors and giving the Allies formal assurance of his aid. He was presented with the Medal of the Resistance. His son, Si Mehdi, died "gloriously" as a cavalry lieutenant in 1944 during the Italian campaign.

Under the French Protectorate, Morocco has undergone vast industrial development. French colonists numbering about 400,000 have directed the building of factories and hydroelectric works, the irrigation of the soil and the mining of rich mineral deposits. Progress has been slower, however, in the development of institutions of self-government and social welfare for the Arabs and Berbers.

In 1953 only 7 per cent of the Moslem children were in schools. Although the need for technical workers is great, few training schools for Moroccans exist, and the French fill most of these posts.

A strong nationalist party, Istiqlal, was formed about 1944. Sidi Mohammed who became Sultan in 1927 gave it his support. On a state visit to Tangier in April 1947 the Sultan proclaimed his country's solidarity with the Arab League countries, a statement contrary to the spirit of the Moroccan-French Protectorate.

French Embassy Press & Inf. Div.

THAMI EL-MEZOUARI EL-GLAOUI
PASHA OF MARRAKECH

The pashas and kaids of Morocco were generally hostile to the Istiqlal, seeing in it a threat to their authority and to public order. In answer to frequent attacks in the nationalist press that he was "fighting against his country's independence," el-Glaoui said: "Morocco is not yet ready to live in a state of complete independence. It still has need of French assistance in many fields. . . If France abandons us we shall be the prey of other nations. . ." (*France Illustration*, August 1953).

At a religious feast at the Sultan's palace in Rabat, el-Glaoui warned the monarch: "You are not the Sultan of Morocco but the Sultan of the Istiqlal and you are leading the Empire to ruin." The Pasha was told to leave the palace and never set foot in it again.

The Sultan in 1951 defied a demand by Marshal Alphonse Juin, then Resident General of Morocco, that he disown the Istiqlal or abdicate. Riots broke out in Casablanca in December 1952. The Istiqlal was quickly broken up, its leaders banished to the Sahara Desert under strong guard. Writing in *Scholastic* (September 23, 1953), Kenneth M. Gould stated that the Istiqlal is "strongly anti-Communist and few native Communists have gained a foothold in Morocco."

According to Michael Clark (New York *Times*, August 23, 1953) the Istiqlal "was careful to avoid joint action with the Communist party so as not to compromise its position with the United States and at the United Nations. But the action of the two parties has almost always been parallel and simultaneous. . ."

In May 1953 el-Glaoui rounded up many of the 353 Berber pashas and kaids to sign a petition to the French government asking for the deposition of the Sultan. This petition was

el-GLAOUI, THAMI—*Continued*

never answered, for although the French sympathized with el-Glaoui's movement, they were bound by the 1912 treaty to protect the Sultan's sovereignty.

The Pasha, on August 4th, began a triumphal tour of Morocco with leaders of the Moslem confraternities, associations that had been attacked by the Sultan as "strongholds of superstition." On August 11 they gathered near Meknes to swear solemn oaths to remain united and to work until success had been achieved. Against the advice of the French government and the Arab League, the deposition of the Sultan went forward.

Sidi Mohammed ben Moulay Arafa, an uncle of the Sultan, was proclaimed head of the Moroccan Empire by a vote of 300 tribal chiefs on August 15, 1953. Resident General Augustin Guillaume provided Sidi Mohammed ben Mulai Youssef and his two sons with transportation to Corsica. Satisfied, el-Glaoui declared: "Morocco is saved. Now I can die."

Claire Sterling in the *Reporter* (April 13, 1954) explained the fall of Sidi Mohammed ben Youssef by a dispute over three reforms proposed by the French which violated the treaty of 1912. The three reforms provided for better courts of appeal, but took away the Sultan's personal jurisdiction over these courts; granted rights to Moslem industrial workers in trade unions where Europeans would be guaranteed 50 per cent control; and in municipal elections all Moslem candidates would be selected by the Residency and 50 per cent of the seats would be reserved for the French. The former Sultan refused to sign these proposals.

On February 19 and on March 5, 1954, el-Glaoui narrowly escaped assassination in Marrakech. He claimed that Arab League fanatics were behind the attempts on his life. "The aim of these national extremists, like that of the Communists, is to stir up continual disorder in North Africa," he said.

American military air bases in French Morocco costing about $420,000,000 have great strategic importance since they permit bombers to take off and reach any part of Europe within four hours. The Pasha told John G. Norris of the Washington *Post* that although the recurrent disorders do not endanger the American bases, he thinks the French authorities "are not tough enough on the extremists for fear of repercussions abroad" (Washington *Post*, March 21, 1954).

Opinions differ as to el-Glaoui's popularity in Morocco. According to Claire Sterling, "he is the most hated figure in the country. . . . His income is enlarged by a cut of 50 per cent on all fortunes bequeathed by rich Moslems who die in his domain, and special taxes imposed on the local populace. . . ." (*Reporter,* April 13, 1954). The Pasha is the owner of "uranium, gold, lead, manganese and cobalt mines as well as huge herds and farms worked by thousands of tenant farmers" (Washington *Post*, March 21, 1954).

The Pasha still actively administers his domain and has "several strong sons who think as he does to take over when he goes." Described as "a realist accustomed to command," "cunning and ruthless," the Pasha is grudgingly respected even by his enemies. Tall, thin, straight, with a "stony" face and "cold black" eyes, he speaks quickly, decisively, and with many gestures. "A devout old-fashioned Moslem, his concubines are numbered by the hundreds, his cooks by the dozen," wrote *Newsweek* (August 24, 1953). The Pasha has four wives, the limit permitted under Moslem law.

In addition to his Moroccan palaces, el-Glaoui maintains living quarters in London, Paris and Vichy where he takes the waters annually. He is a friend of Sir Winston Churchill and on his travels is everywhere greeted by officialdom. Once considered the best horseman in Morocco, he is a devotee of horse racing. He also enjoys playing cards and shoots golf in the 60's on his private course. The Pasha often wears Moorish dress: jelab, turban, golden slippers, and pistol and curved sword strapped to his waist. He is equally at home in western surroundings.

References

France Illus 401:71+ Ag '53 por
N Y Herald Tribune p3 Mr 15 '54
N Y Times p 1+ Ag 15 '53 por
Newsweek 20:51 N 2 '42 por; 62:43 Ag 24 '53 por
Time 62:20 Ag 31 '53 por
U S News 35:55+ S 4 '53 por
Washington (D.C.) Post p3B Mr 21 '54
Rogers, J. A. World's Great Men of Color (1946-47)

GLICK, MRS. FRANK See Kirkus, V.

GONZÁLEZ, CÉSAR (gŏn-ză'lĕz sĕ'sĕr) Dec. 14, 1904- Ambassador from Venezuela to the United States

Address: b. c/o Embassy of Venezuela, 2445 Massachusetts Ave., Washington 8, D.C.

An exponent of mutual friendship among the Americas, César González, Venezuelan Ambassador to the United States since October 28, 1952, has been in the diplomatic corps of his country for twelve years, including service as Ambassador to Mexico and Ecuador, and representative to the United Nations. Dr. González was elected to both houses of the Congreso Nacional, and was Minister of Interior in 1942.

Taking issue with those who protest against the weaknesses of the United Nations, González pointed out, in the *United Nations Bulletin* (October 15, 1950), how long it takes for great ideas to grow and take root. How long, for example, did it take to establish juridical norms that today give stability to individual relations. "Slowly but surely," he said, "the United Nations is advancing toward the realization of its purposes. If it did not exist today the world would be at the mercy of chaotic situations."

César González was born on December 14, 1904 at San Cristóbal, state of Táchira, Venezuela, to Dr. Rubén González and Dolores Martínez de González. His father was a prominent Venezuelan jurist. César attended the Universidad Central de Venezuela in Caracas, and was graduated with the degree of Doctor of Political Sciences in 1929. He later took postgraduate law courses at the Sorbonne in Paris and the Université de Lausanne in Switzerland. In 1929 he wrote *El Concepto Latinoamericano de la Nacionalidad* which recounted the origin and history of the peoples of South and Central America, and traced the growth of their need for mutual friendship.

Entering politics in 1930, González was elected to the lower house of the Congreso Nacional for a two-year term. He was secretary to the Venezuelan delegation to the League of Nations in 1932. From 1936 to 1941 González practiced law. Elected to the upper house in 1941, he served as vice-president of that chamber, was president of the finance committee, and a member of the committee on foreign affairs. He also served as legal consultant to the Ministry of the Treasury.

At the conference of foreign ministers of the American Republics, held in Rio de Janeiro in 1942, Dr. González acted as an adviser to the Venezuelan delegation. Later that year, he was appointed Minister of Interior in the government of Isaías Medina Angarita, and from May 1943 to November 1945 he served as his country's Ambassador to Mexico.

When the Inter-American Conference on the Problems of War and Peace was held in Mexico in 1945, Ambassador González represented Venezuela, and participated in the formation of the Act of Chapultepec which was signed by twenty American nations. It called for mutual aid in preserving American boundaries; this was to be operative in cases of aggression by an American as well as a non-American state for the duration of World War II.

This conference was followed by another conference, in 1947, at Petrópolis, Brazil, at which nineteen nations signed the Inter-American Treaty of Reciprocal Assistance. By its terms, the signatories pledged to attempt to settle all inter-American disputes peacefully, before they are referred to the United Nations. It also provides for united defense against aggression under an agreement that "an armed attack . . . against an American state shall be considered as an attack against all American states. . . ." The treaty became effective December 3, 1948.

The career diplomat's next assignment was the Venezuelan ambassadorship to Ecuador where he served from September to October 20, 1945. From 1946 to March 1950 he served as chief of the western hemisphere affairs section of the Department of Security Council Affairs of the United Nations, a position within the world organization. In April 1950 he was appointed Permanent Representative of Venezuela to the United Nations, and chairman of his delegation to the fifth session of the General Assembly. At this session the United Nations endorsed U.S. intervention in Korea on June 27, 1950. Afterwards, González

CESAR GONZALEZ

urged "all members to strengthen the U.N.'s peace-loving authority 'both legally and morally' " (New York *Times,* September 28, 1950).

While González was serving in the United Nations Secretariat, a coup ousting the Acción Democrática government in Venezuela, occurred on November 24, 1948. A three-man military junta composed of Lieutenant Colonel Carlos Delgado Chalbaud, Lieutenant Colonel Marcos Pérez Jiménez, and Lieutenant Colonel Luis Felipe Llovera Páez was established, and the Acción Democrática party was outlawed on December 9, 1948. The junta resigned on December 2, 1952, and the armed forces appointed Pérez Jiménez as provisional President. A new constitution was ratified on April 15, 1953 which provides for the direct election of the President and members of the lower house of the Congreso Nacional, and contains a Bill of Rights. On April 19, 1953 the Constituent Assembly elected Pérez Jiménez as the constitutional president for a five-year term.

The Venezuelan government selected Dr. González as its Ambassador to the United States on October 28, 1952, to succeed Dr. Antonio Martín Araujo who resigned. The new Ambassador declared in an address before the Pan-American Society of the United States that unity in the western hemisphere was "more operative than that of the United Nations," despite differences in Latin-American and Anglo-Saxon cultures. He explained that the American peoples came "to these new lands impelled by the same desire of freedom" (New York *Times,* January 8, 1953).

Dr. González emphasized that the modern U.S. investor in Latin America does not go there to exhaust the sources of raw materials, but to develop the industrial potential of the country in which he is investing, because he is convinced of the indivisibility of prosperity. "Nothing is gained by accumulating riches that

GONZÁLEZ, CÉSAR—*Continued*

impoverish [others]. . . . The creation of real wealth consists in diminishing the number of the poor, in strengthening the weak and in making productive and happy all those to whom he can subsequently sell the products of our ingenuity or industry." (*U.S. News & World Report* [June 26, 1953] noted that North American investments represented 56.25 per cent of total foreign investments in Venezuela, which in 1952 amounted to 2.3 billion dollars.)

The closeness of economic ties between the United States and Venezuela is also shown by the fact that González' country is South America's biggest buyer of U.S. goods (*Life*, September 13, 1954). It is estimated that 10 per cent of all the iron ore smelted in America in 1955 will come from Venezuela.

In three articles by Sydney Gruson on Venezuela in the New York *Times* (December 13, 14, and 18, 1953), after 300 political prisoners were released (leaving reportedly 500 prisoners accused of antigovernment activities), it was stated: "So far as a first-time visitor to Caracas could discover, no torture or beatings are involved in police work at this time. There may have been before, but despite repeated charges by exiled Venezuelan leaders [such as Valmore Rodriguez, former president of the Senate], competent observers have not found any supporting evidence." Ambassador González stated: "The present constitutional government respects human rights."

The Ambassador is the author of *Discursos en el Monumento a Bolívar,* published in 1944 by the department of foreign information of Mexico, and, with Salvador Pineda, *Dos Evocaciónes de Bolívar* (1945). The latter commemorated the 160th birthday of Simón Bolívar, and was published by the Mexican government's directory of social action. González received the Order of the Liberator from Venezuela, Order of Boyacá from Columbia, Order of Merit from Ecuador, Aztec Eagle from Mexico, and Legion of Honor from France.

Georgina Cortez Guzmán and González were married in 1944; the couple has a daughter, María Dolores, and a son, Rubén. The Ambassador has been described as a "tall, alert, quiet man," who has always spent much of his time studying inter-American affairs. He is a member and former president of the Colegio de Abogados de Caracas, Venezuela, a member of the American Society of International Law, honorary member of the Ordem dos Advogados do Brasil, and corresponding member of the Institute of Social Sciences of Mexico. Dr. González is a Roman Catholic.

References

U N Bul 9:394 O 15 '50 por
Venezuela Up-to-date 3:1 N '52 por
International Yearbook and Statesmen's Who's Who, 1954
Who's Who in Latin America (1951)
Who's Who in the United Nations (1951)
World Biography (1954)

GOODMAN, BERTRAM Sept. 21, 1904-
Painter; lithographer

Address: b. c/o Artisans Gallery, 32 W. 58th St., New York 19; 74 Grove St., New York 14; h. 299 W. 12th St., New York 14

A New Yorker, born and bred, Bertram Goodman has been painting the metropolitan scene in lyric mood for over thirty years. He still finds no need to seek inspiration in distant places but continually discovers themes "derived from the experience of living in a great metropolis."

Since Goodman's first picture was exhibited at the American Water Color Society in 1922 he has been represented in many national juried group shows. He has had one-man shows in New York; Youngstown, Ohio; New Orleans, Louisiana; Maitland, Florida; and Dallas, Texas. His lithographs are in the permanent collection of the Library of Congress and in the New York Public Library Print Collection and the Museum of the City of New York.

His most recent one-man show was in December, 1953 at The Artisans Gallery in New York City which received critical approval. Goodman describes his work as expressionism (the subjective approach by an artist to a thing seen, at once symbolic and actual). A thorough craftsman, he prepares his own canvas, grinds his own colors, using the technique of the old masters, to obtain the results he wishes. He has executed work in water color, tempera and allied media, oil, and lithography.

The son of Rose (Kantrowitz) and Saul Goodman, Bertram Goodman was born on September 21, 1904 in New York City. He has a twin sister, Hilda. His father is a clothing salesman. Bertram always drew, even at the age of three. He attended Stuyvesant High School from 1920 to 1922 and won a medal for drawing in his sophomore year. He left to enter the School of American Sculpture, headed by the late Solon Borglum. Here he drew and modeled horses, studied human anatomy and might have become a sculptor, he says, if drawing had not appealed to him so strongly.

Enrolling at the Art Students League of New York, he studied with Kenneth Hayes Miller and later with Thomas Hart Benton. While attending art classes five nights a week he worked during the day at various jobs. For a time he was a quotation board boy in a stockbroker's office. This was the era before the mechanical electrical board, he recalls, and he grew very expert at inserting the new quotations, but he confesses that he often drew sketches on the ticker tape.

At the age of eighteen Bertram first submitted his work in a professional show—the American Water Color Society—at the Vanderbilt Gallery. His water color *Manila Islands* received favorable comment. Several of his water colors were accepted for the 1923 show of the Pennsylvania Academy of the Fine Arts and the American Water Color Society, and in 1925 at the Brooklyn Museum, and in 1926 at the Chicago Art Institute.

His oil paintings *Pneumatic Drilling* and *The Tunnel Diggers* were exhibited in a group show in 1932 at the Museum of Modern Art (at that time located in the home of Colonel William Barbour). The New York *Sun* critic commented on Goodman's first one-man show at the Midtown Galleries in 1932: "Bertram Goodman catches the roll of a ship at sea and sends one's thoughts to voyaging gayly with the *Ventilators,* content alike with the prospect and the dashing way in which his water colors are handled." In the same show, his oil painting *Grandmother* of his own grandmother received especial praise.

Commissioned in 1934 to paint a twenty-foot portable mural *The Evolution of Tools* for Madway's, hardware merchants, in Philadelphia, Goodman executed it in tempera on gesso. The mural was exhibited at the Midtown Galleries in New York. It depicted the tools used by cave men, by craftsmen of the Renaissance, and by twentieth-century workmen. In 1936 the artist painted a mural at the Theodore Roosevelt High School in New York which portrayed the development of the printed word, from the monks in the scriptorium to Johann Gutenberg and William Caxton; the mural also depicted papermaking, engraving, lithography, linotype, photogravure and offset methods. Goodman also executed a mural in the United States Post Office at Quakertown, Pennsylvania.

During World War II the artist was production manager for Sherman & Associates, a firm that published repair and maintenance manuals for combat machines for the armed forces. He directed the work of 300 architects and engineers. This experience developed his draftsmanship, and in his recent one-man show of oil paintings at The Artisans Gallery, the New York *Herald Tribune* art critic commented (December 13, 1953). "Goodman likes to draw, and paints much like a draftsman making a vigorous sketch. His figures are attenuated, somewhat monumental in form, suggesting a composite of the style of El Greco and Reginald Marsh. This artist puts much of his emphasis on life, painting bowlers, people in the subway, performers of the circus and vaudeville stage, but escapes from the limitations of banality and factualness . . . a spirited and handsome show."

His water color *Scenic Railway* won first prize in the Screen Publicists Guild show, held in 1946 at the Barbizon Plaza Galleries, and in 1947 his gouache *New York* received the Purchase Prize at the Abraham Lincoln High School Gallery. *Harlem Bridge* won the 1947 water-color award given by the Village Art Center. The late John Taylor Arms wrote Goodman a letter stating: "Congratulations to the jury who recognized your accomplishment and deep spiritual power."

In the late 1940's Goodman became increasingly interested in color lithography which requires a sharp understanding of paint "film". The artist was asked to exhibit his lithograph prints at the Butler Art Institute, Youngstown, Ohio; Research Studio, Maitland, Florida; Hudson Park Library, New York City; Buffalo (New York) Print Club; Print Club of Albany; and Kansas City (Missouri) Art Institute and School of Design. His lithographs, *Broadway Auction* and *Greenwich Village,* are in the permanent collection of the Library of Congress.

BERTRAM GOODMAN

As the artist developed he became preoccupied with the inner manifestations of things seen rather than with their exact external appearance, and the figures in his paintings became more elongated and distorted. The critics have referred particularly to his brilliant colors. These he achieves by grinding his colors and preparing his canvases with greater or lesser quantities of oil and experimenting with media of different drying speeds. Of his colors the *Art Digest* (December 15, 1953) commented: "Brilliant vermilion, purples and greens are drawn from the backgrounds into the figures to give them an unearthly glow and a plastic reality. There is something of the prophet here, something of the visionary who understands guilt and human corruption."

Art News (December 1953) commented on Goodman's recent show. "The Artisans Gallery exhibits paintings and drawings which give a retrospective glance over his past work and bring it up to the present. His former painting is almost overtly professional, with a skillful grouping of figures caught in theatrical movement. . . . Later, however, he tends to elongate his figures and the draftsmanship, which is quite good, is content to lose itself in a distortion which changes the scene and gives the pictures, now only dimly colored, a strangeness and a poetic quality which formerly did not appear."

"The figure is the core of Goodman's art," wrote Frederick Stevens Licht in *Art Digest* (December 15, 1953). "His precise sense of proportion justifies the violent contortions and eliminates the haphazard element from his work. He has, too, the gift of integrating anatomic elements so that they clarify a single animating or significant gesture."

(Continued next page)

GOODMAN, BERTRAM—*Continued*

The artist is a member of the governing council of the Society of American Graphic Artists, a director of the Village Art Center, and a member of Artists Equity Association, Philadelphia Print Club and Brooklyn Society of Artists. He was chairman of the jury of admissions for the Abraham & Straus show in 1953, sponsored by the Brooklyn Society of Artists. Goodman served as technical director of the yearbook of the Artists Equity Ball in 1952 and 1953. In 1952 he was on the graphic arts jury of the Louis Comfort Tiffany Foundation, and in 1953 on the graphic arts jury of the National Association of Women Artists.

The artist married Marie Caputa (who is a teacher in New York public schools) on August 18, 1928. His hobbies are watching football and reading philosophy, anthropology and art history. Goodman is five feet eleven inches tall, weighs 160 pounds, has brown eyes and black hair. He is an enrolled Democrat. He holds art classes in his studio on the top floor of a bank building at 74 Grove Street. He is regarded as one of the most gifted art teachers in "The Village". He names the artists, Mahonri Young, Harry Wickey and Alfred Jones, lithographer, as those who most influenced his career.

For the past three years he has been art instructor at the Seamen's Church Institute of New York, where he has directed the execution of a "composite" marine mural in which more than thirty-five merchant seamen-artists have contributed their talents. He also enjoys teaching teen-age artists.

Goodman is an artist who believes that "man is the sum of all things in nature," and so he depicts him on canvas in lyric and expressive activities. "Although humanity has been reproduced endlessly through the ages in all media," he feels that "it is possible to find in the mores of our contemporary life the essence of image-making with a new vitality."

References

Pictures on Exhibit 17:26 D '53
Who's Who in American Art (1953)

GOUDSMIT, SAMUEL A(BRAHAM) (goud'smĭt) July 11, 1902- Physicist

Address: b. c/o Physics Department, Brookhaven National Laboratory, Upton, New York

One of the leading physicists in the United States is Dr. Samuel A. Goudsmit, discoverer of the electron-spin theory at the age of twenty-three, and currently senior scientist and chairman of the physics department at the Brookhaven National Laboratory, Upton, Long Island, New York. He readily agrees with the popular view that recent developments in the field of atomic energy may affect future generations profoundly, but he is also concerned with the immediate effect of many aspects of atomic work, such as restrictions and screenings on the scientists themselves.

As quoted by Daniel Lang in the *New Yorker*, November 14, 1953, Dr. Goudsmit deplores "so many travel restrictions now [which] keep scientists of different countries from getting together to talk science—the science of nature's secrets. We need each other's ideas or our research will run dry."

In 1944 Goudsmit was appointed civilian chairman of Alsos, a top secret mission to Europe whose purpose was to uncover information on the progress made by the Nazis in the development of an atomic bomb. His book, *Alsos,* was published in 1947 by H. Schuman. Dr. Goudsmit is the editor of the *Physical Review,* the semi-monthly publication of the American Physical Society.

Samuel Abraham Goudsmit was born in The Hague, The Netherlands, on July 11, 1902. His father, Isaac Goudsmit, was a prosperous businessman, and his mother, Marianne (Gompers) Goudsmit, owned a fashionable hat shop in The Hague. While he was growing up, Samuel enjoyed helping his mother plan hat styles for each new season. His first contact with physics came at the age of eleven when he read the chapter on spectroscopic phenomena in a textbook on elementary physics belonging to his older sister. Although his imagination was greatly aroused by what he read, Goudsmit did not at the time imagine that he was to have a career in this branch of science.

After graduating from high school, he enrolled at Leyden University as a physics student primarily because his best grades had been in mathematics and science. His mild interest in physics was soon transformed into a passion under the influence of one of his teachers, the renowned physicist Paul Ehrenfest.

Professor Ehrenfest recognized that the unique talents of his young student were intuitive rather than logical or analytic. Goudsmit made rapid progress under his teacher's guidance. When he was only eighteen he produced a paper, based on his own research, dealing with the double lines in the spectroscopic image of the alkali metals (e.g., sodium).

While he was still an undergraduate, he took a course in detective techniques at the University of Amsterdam; but he had to wait about twenty years for his first official "case."

His academic career was brought to a climax by what may have been the greatest single achievement of Goudsmit's life. At the age of twenty-three he and a fellow student, George Uhlenbeck, announced their theory of electron spin. Up until that time the electron was thought to be static in its orbit (as the moon is in its orbit around the earth). Goudsmit and his colleague worked out the theory that the electron spins as it moves in its path around the nucleus (as the earth does in its orbit around the sun). Their theory provided an explanation for the fine lines manifested in the spectroscopic images of the elements, and helped to advance the general theory of the electron and its behavior.

"Physics must forever be in debt to those two men for discovering the spin," declared Professor I. I. Rabi, a Nobel Prize winner and professor of physics at Columbia University. "It was a tremendous feat," Rabi said on another occasion. "Why those two men never received a Nobel Prize for it will always be a mystery to me."

Four years later, Goudsmit ironically referred to himself as a "has-been." He later explained this remark by saying, "as a physicist's career goes, it was to be expected. A scientist can do useful work all his life, but if he is to carry learning one big step forward, he usually does so before he is thirty. Youth has the quality of being radical, in the literal sense of the word—of going to the root. . . After a scientist passes his creative peak, it seems to be the most useful thing he can do is teach the status quo to the youngsters, who may then attack it with all their irreverent curiosity and so perhaps arrive at fresh knowledge."

The publication of the electron spin theory established both its authors as important physicists. Goudsmit was awarded a Rockefeller Fellowship which enabled him to study in Germany, where he and Dr. Edmund Back succeeded in measuring the spin of the atomic nucleus by means of high resolution spectroscopy of bismuth, one of the few elements in which the separation of the hyperfine lines of the spectrum is great enough to permit such an analysis. This was the first time this had been done, and it marked the practical limit of spectroscopic measurement.

Goudsmit came to the United States in 1927 to join the physics department at the University of Michigan. Prior to his departure he married Jaantje (Jeanne) Logher, a former designer in his mother's millinery shop.

Dr. Goudsmit left for America with many regrets. He was leaving his parents, his friends, his homeland, his revered teacher, Ehrenfest, and something more vague which Goudsmit calls "the string-and-sealing-wax era" of physics. By this last reference he meant the period when European physics was an obscure science, and when a small, poorly paid band of physicists, hampered by insufficient budgets but filled with the excitement of discovery, fashioned their own primitive equipment and made notable discoveries.

Goudsmit was an instructor in the physics department at the University of Michigan, 1927-1928; an associate professor from 1928 to 1932; and a professor, 1932-1946. In addition to doing research he assumed the unfamiliar task of teaching, and found that he enjoyed the classroom, his students, and academic life. He held open house for his students every Friday night with his wife acting as hostess.

He continued his study of atomic structure, writing numerous papers and collaborating in the writing of two books on the subject. *The Structure of Line Spectra* (with L. Pauling) appeared in 1930; and *Atomic Energy States* (with R. F. Bacher) was published in 1932. Although these works have been important contributions to physics, Goudsmit, the self-styled "has-been," feels they are completely overshadowed by the momentous discovery of the electron spin.

Honors accrued by Goudsmit before the outbreak of World War II included a Guggenheim Foundation Fellowship in 1938 which he

Brookhaven Nat. Lab.
SAMUEL A. GOUDSMIT

used to visit Paris and Rome; and a visiting lectureship at Harvard in 1941.

With the coming of war, Goudsmit became a staff member of the Radiation Laboratory at the Massachusetts Institute of Technology where he worked on the secret radar-research project. His work at M.I.T. as head of a group of scientists investigating the theory of radar was interrupted in 1943 when he was sent to England to help unravel a riddle for the Anglo-American Air Forces. The problem that faced him was why Royal Air Force crews were satisfied with their radar and American fliers, using the same equipment, were not. Goudsmit found that the Americans had the wrong type of radar for the kind of planes they were using.

The success of this sleuthing assignment led to Goudsmit's appointment as the head of the secret mission sent to Europe in 1944 to find out what progress German scientists had made in developing atomic weapons. The mission was christened "Alsos," a Greek word meaning grove, in honor of the military chief of the mission, General Leslie R. Groves. The story of the mission is told in Dr. Goudsmit's *Alsos,* a popularly-written book that has aroused much controversy since its publication by Henry Schuman in 1947.

According to Goudsmit's Holmesian-like logic, the key to the case was Dr. Werner Heisenberg, Germany's outstanding physicist and one of Goudsmit's oldest friends. As the Allied forces advanced into Germany towards the end of the war in Europe, Heisenberg's laboratory containing much data dealing with atomic research was taken. Shortly after, Heisenberg himself was captured.

After questioning Heisenberg and examining the scientific evidence on hand, Goudsmit concluded that the Germans had only a vague notion of the working of an atomic bomb and

GOUDSMIT, SAMUEL A.—*Continued*

that their ideas about a uranium pile were in a very elementary stage. Goudsmit found no mention in any of the captured material on atomic pile control and he even discovered an uncertainty as to whether element 93 or 94 is explosive.

Heisenberg later contradicted all of Goudsmit's conclusions. He maintained that the lack of laboratories equipped for nuclear research coupled with the lack of interest in atomic energy on the part of the Nazi military administration and the effects of the protracted bombings were responsible for the failure of the German scientists to produce an atomic bomb. In an article in the British periodical *Nature* (August 16, 1947), he stated further that when he and his co-workers realized that they could not succeed for these reasons, they turned to the more feasible project of an atomic engine. This explanation was supported by Waldemar Kaempffert in the New York *Times* (October 26, 1947) in his discussion of the conflicting reports.

With the war over, Goudsmit found himself unable to return to the campus at Michigan. As he said in his interview for the *New Yorker*, "I felt caught up in the violent upsurge of everything associated with physics that had followed Hiroshima, and I wanted to be more closely associated with it than seemed possible on a university campus. . . I had the feeling that it was my duty to take an active part in scientific developments in order to—yes, at the time I perhaps even meant it literally—to help save the world."

He joined the faculty of Northwestern University in 1946, partly in hopes of reawakening his interest in the academic world and also to give him time to think out the meaning of his contemplated role in the future of physics. His feelings were transformed into actions when he became senior scientist at Brookhaven in 1948. Two years yater, he was appointed Chairman of Brookhaven's Physics Department, adding the heavy burden of administering one of the world's largest centers for atomic research to his tasks as senior scientist.

Dr. Goudsmit recalled that physicists before the war gave themselves up to a single-minded study of the laws of the universe, but "now we help the Defense Secretary figure out his budget, we brief the President on the nation's nuclear stockpile. We teach physics to Navy officers who will run nuclear-powered submarines . . . we talk with Air Force generals about atomic-driven planes and plan offensive and defensive tactics. . . . From timid pedagogue to eloquent Jeremiah—all in the space of a few short years" (*New Yorker,* November 7, 1953).

During the disagreement between Senator Joseph R. McCarthy and the United States Army over the question of the Army's assiduity in eliminating presumed security risks from its scientific ranks, Dr. Goudsmit associated himself with a committee of the Federation of American Scientists whose members believe that repeated investigations of the Signal Corps Engineering Laboratories at Fort Monmouth, New Jersey are not only wasteful of money, but are harmful to the morale of the scientific personnel (New York *Herald Tribune,* April 26, 1954).

Dr. Goudsmit is a fellow of the American Physics Society, the Netherlands Physics Society and the National Academy of Sciences. He is also a member of the National Research Council. For his work on the Alsos mission, Dr. Goudsmit was awarded the Medal of Freedom and the Order of the British Empire. The scientist and his wife have one daughter, Esther Marianne.

His friendliness for people and his concern for human problems are regarded by some as unique qualities for a physicist. Mariette Kuper, who is executive assistant to the director of Brookhaven, put it this way: "They (the other physicists) go around talking their special language, like monks in India. Sam talks the language the rest of us talk."

References:

New Yorker 29:47+ N 7; 46+ N 14 '53 pors
American Men of Science (1949)
Who's Who in America, 1954-55

GRANTHAM, SIR ALEXANDER (WILLIAM GEORGE HERDER) Mar. 15, 1899- Governor and Commander in Chief of Hong Kong

Address: Government House, Hong Kong

Responsible to the British government for the "peephole in the Bamboo Curtain," Sir Alexander Grantham is the Governor and Commander in Chief of the Crown Colony of Hong Kong. Known also as Hiang-Kiang, the place of "sweet lagoons", Hong Kong has recently become important to the Western world as a means of obtaining information about the Chinese Communist regime, but it has also presented many political and economic problems to Great Britain.

Sir Alexander's six-year term as Governor would normally have expired in 1953, but it has been extended for another two years. As early as 1922 Grantham held a Colonial administrative post in Hong Kong. He later served as Colonial Secretary in Bermuda and Jamaica, as chief secretary of Nigeria, and as Governor of the Fiji Islands and High Commissioner for the Western Pacific before returning to Hong Kong in 1947.

Born on March 15, 1899, Alexander William George Herder Grantham is the son of Frederick William Grantham and Alexandra von Herder. He was educated at Wellington College, and then at Royal Military College (Sandhurst). In 1917 he received his commission in the 18th Hussars. Grantham's training was not, however, exclusively military. He received the Master of Arts degree at Pembroke College, Cambridge, and in 1922 was appointed to the colonial service in Hong Kong.

Called to the Bar at Inner Temple in London in 1934, Grantham in that same year attended the Imperial Defense College, and in 1935 was appointed Colonial Secretary for Bermuda. After three years in Bermuda, he went to Jamaica, the largest island in the British West Indies, to serve as its Colonial Secretary.

His experience in the field of colonial administration was widened through his work as chief secretary of Nigeria from 1941 through 1944, and enlarged yet further by his two years, from 1945 to 1947, as Governor of the Fiji Islands and High Commissioner for the Western Pacific. He was made a Knight Commander of St. Michael and St. George in 1945.

When Sir Mark Aitchison Young retired from the Governorship of Hong Kong in 1947, Sir Alexander was chosen by the Colonial Office to succeed him. The history of Hong Kong and the events which have followed Sir Alexander's appointment as Governor illustrate the strategic economic and geographical situation of this colony.

Before the British occupation of Hong Kong it was a desolate area inhabited by a small fishing population. During the Opium War which began in 1839, Hong Kong Island was used as a naval base by the British and in 1841 it was ceded to Great Britain. In 1860 China ceded Kowloon Peninsula to Great Britain, and in 1898 the New Territories (an area north of Kowloon Peninsula on the mainland) was leased to England for ninety-nine years. These three areas comprise the British Crown Colony.

Since the inauguration of the Chinese Republic in 1911 Hong Kong has been a home for refugees fleeing either from their own people or from the foreign enemy. During the years from 1925 to 1927, a boycott excluded British trade from all the ports of southern China. Relations improved considerably, however, during the Sino-Japanese War, as Chiang Kai-shek was aided by the munitions which reached their destination through Hong Kong. Again the area was inundated with refugees and many camps were opened by the government. In 1941 Hong Kong itself was attacked and fell to the Japanese, but in 1945 the British returned, and re-established their government.

Although certain reforms in the government of Hong Kong were proposed during the term of office of Sir Mark Young, and were to come into effect soon after his retirement, the reforms for the most part have not yet been put into effect. Sir Alexander did not abandon the question of constitutional development, but considered the time inopportune for changes of a major character.

With the difficulties arising from the war between the Nationalists and Communists in China, the dislocation of normal trade, the strikes and labor disputes, the overcrowding and congestion owing to the influx of thousands of refugees, Sir Alexander was given certain emergency powers in December 1949.

The British government recognized the Chinese Communist government in January 1950. In 1951 Sir Alexander said that the U.S. embargo of December 8, 1950 on exports to Communist China, Hong Kong and Macao was already showing its effects in reduced trade, and that conditions in China created

British Inf. Services
SIR ALEXANDER GRANTHAM

serious problems for Hong Kong, particularly in the overcrowding due to the squatters who menaced public health, security, law and order (London *Times*, March 9, 1951). The United Nations embargo on sending arms or strategic materials to Red China (voted on May 18, 1951), further prevented Hong Kong from trading freely with her neighbor.

More than two years later, trade was still a crucial problem. In an interview between Sir Alexander Grantham and Leonard Slater (published in *Newsweek*, November 2, 1953), Sir Alexander stated that the U.N. blockade against Communist China had had a drastic effect on the economy of Hong Kong whose "major trading partner" is China, and that trading with the other Asian countries could "never take the place entirely of China."

When asked how the Hong Kong traders felt about the U.N. embargo, Sir Alexander replied: "Hong Kong traders feel about the embargo much as a man feels when you give him a knife and tell him that it is in the interest of the community at large that he should cut his throat; for that, in effect, is what Hong Kong has done by implementing the United Nations embargo. Hong Kong traders consider the embargo realistic so far as truly strategic materials are concerned, but not as regards semi-strategic materials which can be used for civil as well as warlike purposes."

In Sir Alexander's opinion, if large scale trading with Communist China were not resumed, Hong Kong could survive, but the burden of sheltering over a million refugees from the mainland would become increasingly onerous.

In December 1953 Hong Kong's Governor opened the colony's eleventh annual exhibition of local manufacturers. According to *Time* (December 28, 1953) "the profusion of low-priced local goods displayed was the most hopeful answer yet to Hong Kong's evil spirit—

GRANTHAM, SIR ALEXANDER—*Cont.*

Red China, which is only a few miles away. The United Nations embargo on trade with China has piled up goods . . . for want of customers. The biggest hope for Hong Kong's survival has been to develop its own exports."

"Without Hong Kong's cheap labor and the ingenuity of Chinese businessmen," concluded *Time,* "the U.N. embargo on trade with Red China would have led to mass unemployment in the colony, and in turn to strong pro-Communist sentiment. With the new prosperity of home-grown industry, Communist agitators are conspicuously out of favor with Hong Kong Chinese."

A report in *Travel* magazine (February 1953) stated that since Hong Kong is a free port, goods from all over the world are sold there cheaper than in their country of origin. "Hong Kong is the only place left in China where Chinese goods are available to the free world. Hundreds of factories from Shanghai and Canton have moved down into the 391-square-mile Crown Colony and are busy turning out brocade, summer shantung suits, camphorwood chests, carved ivory, jade, porcelain and silk."

In an article for the New York *Times* (January 24, 1954), Preston Schoyer reported that Indonesia was Hong Kong's best customer in 1953, and that "65 per cent of Hong Kong's total trade (about $1,120,000,000) has nothing to do with China. . . ." However, this means "sickness, not health" for Hong Kong as the drop in the China market "has brought on an over-all decline in business of more than 30 per cent since 1950."

George W. Long, writing in the *National Geographic Magazine* February, 1954 quoted a Hong Kong merchant after the United Nations embargo had affected his business: "Fortunately, the slump is less than we feared. For one thing, our new industries employ thousands. Also, Hong Kong merchants for years have been opening up new markets, especially in Southeast Asia—countries like Malaya and Indonesia. . . . Not keeping all our eggs in one basket has paid off. . . . Somehow Hong Kong hangs on, in spite of wars, embargoes and Bamboo Curtains."

As reported by Jim G. Lucas in the New York *World-Telegram and Sun* (March 11, 1954), Sir Alexander suggested that the West offer to relax its embargo to a certain extent in exchange for peace in Indochina. If Communist China would withdraw its support of Ho Chi Minh (pro-Communist leader of the Indochinese rebels), the West might then, he suggested, permit the export of such semi-strategic goods as tires, petroleum, machinery, and rolling stock to the Chinese mainland.

The Governor also said (as reported by Lucas) that many people felt that the embargo hurts Hong Kong more than Red China because Western goods still reach the mainland through the Communist-held islands surrounding the Crown Colony. Communist China now gets 75 per cent of her imports from the Soviet Union and its satellites, and 25 per cent from the West, but Sir Alexander believes the People's Government would like to increase its trade with the West, so that it would be less dependent on the Soviet Union.

The New York *World-Telegram and Sun* (March 11, 1954) commented editorially: "So desperate are the British for trade, they cannot be relied upon to count the costs in terms of appeasement, or in weakening the structure of Allied unity on doing business with the enemy."

In a recent speech Sir Alexander poked goodnatured fun at the American embargo on the importing of Chinese-made goods into the United States. "Among these articles," he said, "are pressed ducks, bred in Hong Kong, but in many cases the eggs from which the ducks are hatched come from China. A problem that worried Washington for months was this: Were the ducks . . . Chinese ducks or Hong Kong ducks? It wasn't as though the duck from the Chinese egg had red feathers. . . . It was decided that common sense should prevail, and the position was taken that the ducks, regardless of where the eggs came from, should be given the benefit of Hong Kong nationality" (*New Yorker,* March 27, 1954).

When Adlai Stevenson visited Hong Kong he sent back a report to *Look* magazine (May 19, 1953) in which he said: "Hong Kong is a two-way listening post and I heard much that was sobering about Red China from American, British and other allied sources. The consensus was that it's dangerous to assume that most Chinese are praying for Nationalist liberation. . . . We must somehow match the patience and persistence of communism in an area where time is measured not in months or even years but in decades and generations."

Governor Thomas E. Dewey in his book *Journey to the Far Pacific* told of his reunion with Sir Alexander Grantham, whom he had met when Grantham was Colonial Secretary of Bermuda. "We sat down for a briefing on conditions in [Hong Kong] and in Red China," Dewey wrote. "He quite naturally reflected the views of his government, on which we had disagreed vigorously in our correspondence; we now found we still disagreed on many topics, but that made our long and thorough discussion of the Far East sharper and more interesting."

When Sir Alexander acceded to the request of the British Colonial Office to remain as Governor until July 1955, the announcement caused "widespread gratification among Chinese and British alike. The great part he has played in Hong Kong's recovery and development is generally and gratefully acknowledged. Sir Alexander and Lady Grantham have added to their popularity by the direct personal interest they take in all constructive and social welfare activities in the colony. The Governor is also widely regarded as a symbol of the colony's stability and confidence in the future, especially among the Chinese populace" (London *Times,* August 4, 1953).

The foreign officer was made a Companion of the Order of St. Michael and St. George in in 1941, and Knight Grand Cross of the Order of St. Michael and St. George in 1951. He received the honorary LL.D. degree from the University of Hong Kong in 1952.

He married Maurine Samson of San Francisco on October 25, 1925. Sir Alexander is a member of the Church of England. He belongs to the Travellers Club in London.

References

Burke's Peerage, Baronetage, and Knightage (1953)
International Who's Who, 1953
International Yearbook and Statesmen's Who's Who, 1953
Kelly's Handbook to the Titled, Landed and Official Classes, 1951
Who's Who, 1953
World Biography (1948)

GREENSTREET, SYDNEY (HUGHES) Dec. 27, 1879-Jan. 18, 1954 Actor; was a tea planter in Ceylon (1899-1901); made theatre debut at Ramsgate, England in *Sherlock Holmes* (1902); came to U.S. with Ben Greet company (1904); played in Shakespearean repertory, knew by memory over 12,000 lines of Shakespeare's plays; appeared in *Lady Windermere's Fan, R.U.R., The Admirable Crichton,* and *There Shall Be No Night;* made screen debut in *The Maltese Falcon* (1941); played in such films as *Casablanca, Passage to Marseilles, The Hucksters,* and *Flamingo Road.* See *Current Biography,* (May) 1943.

Obituary

N Y Times p27 Ja 20 '54

GREENWOOD, ARTHUR Feb. 8, 1880-June 9, 1954 British Labour party leader; began career teaching at the University of Leeds and Huddersfield Technical College; member of House of Commons since 1922; Minister of Health (1929-1931); member of War Cabinet, and Minister Without Portfolio (1940-1942); Lord Privy Seal (1945-1947) and Paymaster General (1946-1947); active in Labour party for forty years and became its chairman in 1952; author and co-author of books on social welfare, politics, and international relations. See *Current Biography,* (Oct.) 1940.

Obituary

N Y Times p31 Je 10 '54

GREENWOOD, JOAN Mar. 4, 1921- Actress

Address: b. c/o Henry Sherek, Ltd., 40 Pall Mall, S.W. 1, London, England; h. 4 Wentworth Studios, Chelsea, S.W, 3

Making an auspicious Broadway debut on February 11, 1954 at the Morosco Theatre in T. S. Eliot's play, *The Confidential Clerk,* British actress Joan Greenwood played the role of Lucasta (a slightly raffish ingenue) and won both critics and audience by her "provocative, poignant and betwitching" performance. Dancing lessons in childhood started her on a career which has included important roles on the British stage since 1938. During the past six years audiences in the United States have become acquainted with her acting in several very popular British films including *Tight Little Island,* and with Alec Guinness in *Kind Hearts and Coronets* and *Man in the White Suit.*

JOAN GREENWOOD

The borough of Chelsea, London, counterpart of New York's Greenwich Village, was the birthplace of Joan Greenwood on March 4, 1921. Her father was the late Sydney Earnshaw Greenwood, an artist of considerable note. Her mother was the former Miss Ida Waller. Her parents encouraged her interest in dancing and permitted her to take lessons when she was eight years old.

She received her academic education at St. Catherine's School, Bramley, Surrey, while she continued to study ballet dancing. After reaching her fourteenth birthday she entered the Royal Academy of Dramatic Art in London. She had already discovered that she had a knack for mimicry.

Her initial professional stage appearance was at the Apollo Theatre, London on November 15, 1938. She played Louisa in Moliere's *Le Malade Imaginaire.* The following year she portrayed Timpson in *Little Ladyship.* In 1939, she played the part of Little Mary in Clare Boothe Luce's *The Women,* a play which was revived at the Strand in the spring of 1940. It was seen by the late actor, Leslie Howard, who was so impressed by the animated teen-aged actress that he made her his leading lady in a film, *The Gentle Sex,* which was presented to the public in 1942. Meantime, she pursued her career with an appearance in a revue called *Rise Above It,* and in the role of Wendy in J. M. Barrie's *Peter Pan* in which she achieved great personal triumph. Miss Greenwood went on a two-year tour with the *Peter Pan* production. It was during this tour that she decided to relinquish stardom in juvenile roles and to try for adult parts.

(Continued next page)

GREENWOOD, JOAN—*Continued*

She devoted herself wholeheartedly to studying for more mature roles. In 1943 she played Netta in *Striplings,* Henriette in *Damaged Goods* and in Shaw's *Heartbreak House,* undertook the portrayal of Ellie Dunn which had been enacted by Deborah Kerr. After a successful London run Miss Greenwood toured in *Heartbreak House* and in 1944 played a season with the Worthing Repertory Company.

From the light-hearted roles and character-in-comedy parts, she stepped into her first serious role when in 1944 she played Ophelia in *Hamlet* during a season with the Donald Wolfit Company. Next, she was cast as Celia in *Volpone,* then increased her dramatic range in 1945 with the Oxford Playhouse, playing such varied roles as Lady Teazle, Cleopatra, and eventually Nora in Ibsen's *A Doll House.* After spending the next three years in films she played the role of Bertha in *Frenzy* at the St. Martin's Theatre in 1948 and Sabina Pennant in *Young Wives' Tale* in 1949 at the Savoy Theatre, London.

According to Ward Morehouse of the *World-Telegram and Sun,* who interviewed Miss Greenwood (the story appeared March 9, 1954 in his column "Broadway After Dark"), the role in the Ibsen drama was a real challenge. "I played in Helsinki, Finland and Copenhagen with *A Doll's House,*" she said. "I suppose it was a mad thing to do, but I love the part." On her recent Scandinavian tour she was acclaimed for her sensitive portrayal of Nora.

Miss Greenwood's charm, mobile face and acting talent received consistently favorable comment even though some critics "panned" the screen offerings, as in *Saraband,* a historical costume piece in which she appeared with Stewart Granger. She was cast as the tragic Sophie-Dorothea, who fell in love with a swashbuckling adventurer.

Luke-warm criticism, at least in the United States, of the movies, *The White Unicorn* and *The Smugglers,* in which Miss Greenwood co-starred, did not reflect on her acting ability. As Sibella in *Kind Hearts and Coronets* which starred Alec Guinness, she had a screenplay more suited to her talents and as a villainess with a "provocative exterior" was lauded by the New York *Times,* (June 15, 1950).

Again, in the summer of 1951, when the *Man In the White Suit* was shown in American movie houses, Miss Greenwood was termed "delectable" in her support of Alec Guinness, witty and brilliant British film comedian. Her experience in pictures includes *They Knew Mr. Knight, Latin Quarter, Girl In A Million, The Man Within, Bad Sister, The October Man, The Tight Little Island, Bad Lord Byron, Train of Events, Flesh and Blood, Young Wives' Tales, Mr. Peek-a-Boo* and *The Importance of Being Earnest,* adapted from Oscar Wilde's play. A New York *Times* reviewer reported Miss Greenwood's performance as Gwendolen Fairfax as "a lady to the fingertips" (December 23, 1952).

In 1951 Miss Greenwood was selected by producer Irene Selznick as replacement for Lilli Palmer in John van Druten's play, *Bell, Book and Candle.* Unfortunately, no male lead could be found to substitute for star Rex Harrison and the play was therefore not resumed although Miss Greenwood made a quick trip from London to New York in the spring of 1951 for a conference.

Under Henry Sherek's management she returned to this country in December 1953 to begin rehearsals for the T. S. Eliot play in which she is currently appearing with Ina Claire and Claude Rains at the Morosco Theatre in New York. "The part I'm doing," said Miss Greenwood, "is that of Lucasta, who is all unsettled. She's a girl who rushes about with a nice mask on and who finally settles for just being safe" (New York *World-Telegram and Sun,* March 9, 1954).

John Beaufort of the *Christian Science Monitor* wrote, "The same Joan Greenwood who has looked out bewitchingly from many a British film makes a dazzling United States stage debut. Her presence is electric and her movements are marvelously graceful." Beaufort's observation (February 20, 1954) is directly related to the fact that Joan Greenwood has retained as an adult hobby, her childhood love of ballet dancing.

The actress told the *Daily Mirror* writer, Sidney Fields, (March 1, 1954) that she had overcome her first dread of Gotham's noise and confusion. "New York is amazing," she commented. "People leap at you, but it's sweet. I like bearhugs." She also revealed that she had found the ultimate security in acting because she loses herself "in being other people." She also confided that she is in reality "a rebel," and that once during the filming of *Saraband,* she yielded to her "childish passion" for a circus and ran off for a week to take part in an acrobatic stint with a circus troupe.

Summarization of Miss Greenwood's personality by various reviewers and interviewers has included such descriptions of her as "volatile," "an instinctive actress," "a charmer," "a pretty elf," and "a strawberry blond bombshell." This last comment was by columnist George Freedley, in "On Stage and Off" in the New York *Morning Telegraph,* who added, after seeing Miss Greenwood in *The Confidential Clerk,* "She is an out-of-this world comedienne. I hope she stays with us for a long, long time in one play or another."

Miss Greenwood has reddish-blond hair and green-blue eyes. She is five feet and one inch in height. Her most attention-getting characteristic is her voice. William Hawkins of the *World-Telegram and Sun* described her speech delivery (February 12, 1954): "Miss Greenwood plays in a voice that sounds like Lynn Fontanne imitating Carol Channing, and with a brittle style that is artifical but always purposeful."

Her next film will be *Father Brown,* playing opposite Alec Guinness.

References

N Y Daily Mirror Mr 1 '54
N Y World-Telegram p36 Mr 9 '54
Motion Picture and Television Almanac, 1953-54
Who's Who in the Theatre (1952)
Winchester's Screen Encyclopedia (1948)

GREGG, HUGH Nov. 22, 1917- Governor of New Hampshire

Address: b. State House, Concord, N.H.; h. R.F.D. 2, Nashua, N.H.

When Hugh Gregg was elected Governor of New Hampshire in November 1952, a few days before his thirty-fifth birthday, he had already been a practicing lawyer, an industrialist, Army intelligence officer, and mayor of Nashua, New Hampshire. He had helped to avert an economic depression in his home city by inducing new firms to take over closed textile plants and to employ Nashua's workers.

Hugh Gregg was born November 22, 1917 in Nashua, New Hampshire, the son of Harry A. and Margaret R. (Richardson) Gregg. He attended Nashua public schools, and was graduated from Phillips Exeter Academy at Exeter, New Hampshire in 1935. He received the A.B. degree from Yale University in 1939, after majoring in psychology. He entered Harvard Law School and completed his course in June 1942, receiving his LL.B. degree and becoming a member of the New Hampshire bar in that year. (Later, in 1948, he was admitted to the Massachusetts bar.)

Inducted into the Army in April 1942, Gregg served as a special agent in Army counter-intelligence in North Africa, Burma, India, and China. After the war, he became treasurer of Gregg and Son, Inc., one of the largest mill-works manufacturers in the East and, in 1946, a partner in the law firm of Sullivan and Gregg, and a director of the Indian Head National Bank. He was also made president of the Nashua Fresh Air Camp, Inc., director of the New England Council, treasurer of Alan Gregg, Jr., and a member of the Family Foundation, Inc.

A Republican in a normally Democratic town, and a member of a well-to-do family in a highly industrial community, Hugh Gregg aroused scepticism over the possibility of his being elected when he announced in 1947 that he was going to run for Alderman-at-Large in Nashua. But he was elected, after what was locally called a "whirlwind campaign," and was sworn into office January 1, 1948.

Gregg had been in office about six months when a major crisis occurred in Nashua. Textron, Inc., employing 3,500, or one-third of the town's workers, closed its textile plants. The alderman helped to establish the Nashua-New Hampshire Foundation, a community corporation which raised $100,000 for a down payment on the idle plants and gave a $400,000 morgage for the rest. Then he led the drive to induce new industries to come into the plants. The result of his efforts was 2,500 new jobs for the unemployed.

Widely acclaimed for his part in averting an economic disaster, Gregg decided to run for mayor in the 1949 elections, although he had served only one-half of his four-year term as alderman. Many citizens were again doubtful of the possibility of his success.

In this contest, Gregg himself did the door-bell ringing. His campaign was based on a record of his accomplishments in the City Coun-

Fotomart

HUGH GREGG

cil. He had helped to establish a central purchasing agent to save the city money; he had instituted an itemized city budget instead of one with lump figures; he had stopped the floating of bond issues for small non-capital expenditures, such as the purchase of fire equipment. Gregg defeated his opponent, incumbent Mayor Oswald S. Maynard, by 661 votes. (Dr. Maynard later supported Gregg's candidacy for governor.)

At his inauguration on January 1, 1950 as mayor, Gregg stated that the tax burden at that time was as much as the citizens of Nashua could bear. His success in reducing taxes, initiating budgetary controls, and reorganizing municipal departments attracted the attention of Governor Sherman Adams, who asked him to serve on the New Hampshire Reorganization Commission as chairman of the Fiscal and Tax Committee.

It was reported that the thirty-three-year-old Mayor never missed a meeting of the City Council or the Public Works Commission. He arrived at his desk each morning at six-thirty, lunched on a stool at the five and ten cent store and usually ended the day with a speech or meeting. He made occasional trips to Boston and New York to meet industrialists in order to promote the economic interests of Nashua.

Mayor Gregg also assisted the neighboring Canadian community of Rimouski when it was ravaged by fire. He headed a relief committee which sent tons of foodstuff and clothing to Rimouski. He remembered, although only a boy at the time, how sympathetic citizens across the nation and in Canada as well had helped Nashua when it had suffered a similar disastrous fire.

Of his accomplishments as mayor the *Boston Traveler* commented, "Politicians failed . . . to figure on the organizing ability and the unlimited energy of the young World War II

GREGG, HUGH—*Continued*

veteran. . . . His sincerity, straightforwardness and his record won him many friends and supporters. Under the leadership of Gregg, Nashua has again taken its rightful place as one of the outstanding cities in New England. . . . With the experience as chief executive of the city, his legal training and education, this thirty-three year old leader is slated to go places in state and national life."

While still serving as mayor, Gregg was again inducted into the Army, in November 1950, and served as a counter-intelligence officer in the Korean crisis, until April 1952.

Gregg has dealt with labor problems, both as a businessman and city official. He negotiated a pay raise for the employees of his own company, members of the CIO, and worked with four AFL unions in the city government while mayor. He has also been a member of the New Hampshire Industrial Advisory Committee.

As a candidate for the gubernatorial nomination in the fall of 1952, Gregg defeated his three opponents, with 46,670 votes to less than 30,000 for the other three combined. Succeeding Sherman Adams, now administrative assistant to President Eisenhower, Gregg was inaugurated on January 7, 1953. He stated, "Remember this: no government, Federal or state, can give you anything which it has not first taken from you" (New York *Times*, January 25, 1953).

Governor Gregg attracted immediate attention by submitting the biennial state budget on February 3, nearly a month earlier than has been the practice in recent years. Proposing a revision of the entire state tax structure, he included in his present budget voluntary pay rises for state employees, increased state aid for education and expansion of the state Planning and Development Commission.

A town meeting was held April 12, 1953 at Bristol, New Hampshire, with Governor Gregg as moderator, to discuss the United Nations. Delegates to the U.N. from Indonesia, Panama and Greece, Dr. L. N. Palar, Eusebio A. Morales and Alexix Kyrou, respectively, were present. The meeting voted to adopt a town in each of these foreign countries with the hope of promoting international understanding by providing Yankee scientific knowledge.

Cognizant of the economic significance of the port of Boston to all of New England, Governor Gregg designated May as "Port of Boston Month." In a proclamation he urged businessmen of New Hampshire to "ship via Boston."

He decided not to be a gubernatorial candidate in the 1954 primary.

A bill providing for an investigation by the state Attorney General's office into subversive activities in New Hampshire was signed by Governor Gregg on June 12, 1953. It approves the expenditure of at least $10,000 and directs the Attorney General to conduct investigations as privately as possible.

Hugh Gregg married the former Catherine Marshall July 24, 1940. They have two sons, Cyrus W. and Judd Alan. Gregg is over six feet tall, weighs 190 pounds, and has blue eyes and black hair. He received the honorary LL.D. degree from the University of New Hampshire in 1953. He belongs to the Congregational Church; is a member of the American Bar Association, the New Hampshire Bar Association, the Massachusetts Bar Association, the American Legion, and the Veterans of Foreign Wars. His clubs are the Rotary, Appalachian Mountain, Nashua Fish and Game, Lone Pine Hunters and New England Sled-Dog.

References

N Y Times p25 S 11 '52; p47 Ja 25 '53; p3 Ap 17 '53
Worcester (Mass.) Sunday Telegram N 26 '50
Who's Who in New England (1949)

GRISWOLD, DWIGHT P(ALMER) Nov. 27, 1893-Apr. 12, 1954 United States Senator from Nebraska; former Governor of Nebraska; served as assistant cashier, and then cashier and a director of First National Bank of Gordon, Nebraska (1919-1922); editor and publisher of Gordon *Journal* (1922-1940); elected to Nebraska house as a Republican (1920); state senate (1925-1929); elected Governor (1940); re-elected (1942, 1944); was director of internal affairs of U.S. Zone in Germany (1946-1947); director of American Mission for Aid to Greece (1947-1948); elected to Senate in November 1952 to fill unexpired term of the late Senator Kenneth S. Wherry. See *Current Biography,* (Dec.) 1947.

Obituary

N Y Times p31 Ap 13 '54

GUTHRIE, (WILLIAM) TYRONE July 2, 1900- Theatrical director; playwright

Address: b. c/o Shakespearean Festival, Stratford, Ontario, Canada; h. Annagh-ma-Kerrig, Doohat Newbliss, County Monaghan, Eire

The British theatrical director, Tyrone Guthrie, is best known on this side of the Atlantic for his direction of Bizet's *Carmen,* presented at the Metropolitan Opera House in New York in January 1952, and for his staging of *Richard III* and *All's Well That Ends Well* at the Shakespearean Festival held at Stratford, Ontario in 1953. He also directed a second festival at Stratford during the summer of 1954, with *Measure for Measure,* starring James Mason, as one of the productions. The total attendance during the 1954 season was 125,155 people.

Guthrie was in charge of productions at London's celebrated "Old Vic" Theatre between 1933 and 1945, and as administrator of the Old Vic Sadler's Wells organization from 1939 to 1945, and 1951 to 1952. He has also written plays for the radio and the stage and has directed modern and grand operas.

The son of Dr. Thomas Clement Guthrie, physician and surgeon, and the great-grandson of Dr. Thomas Guthrie, a famous preacher and philanthropist, William Tyrone Guthrie is of

Scots ancestry on the paternal side. His mother, the former Norah Power, was a granddaughter of the celebrated early nineteenth-century Irish comedian Tyrone Power (the great-grandfather of the motion picture actor of the same name). William Tyrone Guthrie was born at Tunbridge Wells, Kent, England on July 2, 1900. He attended Wellington College in Berkshire, and later enrolled at St. John's College, Oxford, where he received his Bachelor of Arts degree in ancient history and philosophy in 1923.

Guthrie made his professional debut in the summer of 1923 as an actor and assistant stage manager at the Oxford Playhouse under James Bernard Fagan. Some months later he joined the British Broadcasting Company station at Belfast, Ireland, where he worked as announcer, script writer and director. He was director of the Scottish National Theatre troupe in 1926-27. Rejoining the BBC in 1928, Guthrie became one of the first writers of plays designed expressly for radio performance. Two of his scripts, *Squirrel's Cage* and *The Flowers Are Not for You to Pick,* enjoyed much popularity, and (together with *Matrimonial News*) were later published in London by Cobden-Sanderson, 1931.

British Inf. Service
TYRONE GUTHRIE

An important point in Tyrone Guthrie's career was reached in 1929, when he was engaged by the late Anmer Hall to direct productions at the Festival Theatre in Cambridge. In the next two seasons Hall and Guthrie brought to the stage a series of experimental productions accenting "expressionist" playwriting and stagecraft, which are now acknowledged to have been of pioneering significance.

In 1930 Guthrie crossed the Atlantic to do a series of radio plays for the Canadian Broadcasting Corporation. He rejoined Anmer Hall as stage director at his new little Westminster Theatre in London, which opened with James Bridie's *The Anatomist.* A subsequent presentation at the Westminster was Pirandello's *Six Characters in Search of an Author,* for which Guthrie obtained stunning yet simple scenic effects through shadows cast by a ladder and furniture on an otherwise bare stage.

Subsequent productions at the Westminster reflected the principles enunciated in his long essay *Theatre Prospect* (published in book form in London by Wishart in 1932), which "predicted a break with materialism and a revival of romance as a reaction from rationalism and *bourgeoisie"* (Sewell Stokes in *Theatre Arts,* April, 1943).

So impressed was the critic and novelist J. B. Priestley by the Pirandello production that he engaged Guthrie to stage his play, *Dangerous Corner,* at a London "West End" theatre, the Lyric on Shaftesbury Avenue, in May, 1932. Shakespeare's rarely revived *Love's Labour's Lost,* staged by Guthrie at the Westminster "as an Elizabethan masque" likewise impressed the late Lilian Baylis, who engaged Guthrie to direct in the season 1933-34 the popular-priced Shakespearean repertory company which then shuttled between the "Old Vic" Theatre on the south side of the Thames in London and Sadler's Wells Theatre on the north.

This was the season in which Charles Laughton was a member of the Vic-Wells troupe, appearing under Guthrie's direction in Shakespeare's *Henry VIII, Measure for Measure, The Tempest* and *Macbeth,* and also in Chekhov's *The Cherry Orchard,* Congreve's *Love for Love* (for which Guthrie prepared the acting version), and Wilde's *The Importance of Being Earnest.* Guthrie also directed George Hayes in *Richard II* for the Stratford-on-Avon Festival of 1933, and in 1934 the London productions of Jay Mallory's *Sweet Aloes* at Wyndam's and James Bridie's *Mary Read* at His Majesty's Theatre.

In "Some Notes on Direction" (published in *Theatre Arts,* November, 1944) Guthrie expressed his belief that "the function of a theatrical director has often, and rightly, been likened to that of an orchestral conductor."

New York had its first glimpse of a Guthrie-directed play when the Theatre Guild presented Dodie Smith's *Call It a Day* (starring Gladys Cooper and Philip Merivale) at the Morosco Theatre in January, 1936. Guthrie also re-staged *Sweet Aloes* at the Booth Theatre, New York, in March before rejoining the Vic-Wells organization in September, 1936, for a renewed association which was to last for the next nine years. Laurence Olivier made his first appearance in *Hamlet* in an Old Vic-Tyrone Guthrie production in January, 1937 and in November Guthrie directed Sheridan's *The School for Scandal* for John Gielgud.

Guthrie's production of *A Midsummer Night's Dream* at the "Old Vic" in 1938, with Vivien Leigh as Titania, is recorded in *The Oxford Companion to the Theatre* as a "delight," although Herbert Farjeon deplored the director's tendency "to produce Shakespeare's

GUTHRIE, TYRONE—*Continued*

comedies 'just like ballets.'" Also in 1938, Guthrie returned briefly to acting, giving a memorable performance as the missionary in the Charles Laughton film *The Beachcomber*.

Appointed in 1939 the administrator of the "Old Vic" and Sadler's Wells as well as director of plays, Guthrie staged a notable "modern dress" *Hamlet*, with Alec Guinness in the title role. Following the partial destruction of the "Vic" by German air action in 1940, the company made numerous tours of the battlefronts. The company resettled in London at the New Theatre in 1944. Ralph Richardson appeared in September, 1944 in a much-praised Tyrone Guthrie production of Ibsen's *Peer Gynt*, and subsequently in several Shakespeare plays.

About a year later Guthrie resigned his post with the Vic-Wells organization and became a director of the "Company of Four" at the suburban Lyric Theatre in Hammersmith. He revisited the United States in March 1946 to stage for the Theatre Guild an adaptation of Leonid Andreyev's *He Who Gets Slapped* written by his wife, Judith Guthrie. "Tyrone Guthrie has directed as though he were staging a circus, which indeed he is," was a comment of Lewis Nichols in the New York *Times* on this production of a piece which had previously been treated as murky Russian symbolism.

He made a quick reputation as a director of grand opera when he staged Benjamin Britten's opera *Peter Grimes* at the Royal Opera House, Covent Garden, London in 1946 and also a revival of Rostand's *Cyrano de Bergerac* for the "Old Vic" company at the New Theatre. In 1947 he staged Verdi's *La Traviata* at Covent Garden and *He Who Gets Slapped* at the Duchess, and went to Tel Aviv in Israel to stage Saul Chernikhovsky's Hebrew translation of *Oedipus Rex* for the Habimah players (later produced in New York at the Broadway Theatre on May 22, 1948). He staged the Sophocles tragedy for the Finnish National Theatre at Helsinki in 1948 and Shakespeare's *The Taming of the Shrew* in 1949.

He revived Sir David Lindsay's old Scottish morality play *The Three Estates* at the 1948 Edinburgh Festival and in 1949 with a "delightful" revival of Allan Ramsay's 18th Century Scottish pastoral comedy *The Gentle Shepherd*. In addition, he directed Shakespeare's *Henry VIII* for the Stratford-on-Avon Festival of the same year.

At the medium-sized Sadler's Wells Theatre on February 22, 1949, Guthrie directed an English-language production of Bizet's *Carmen* with such striking effect that Rudolf Bing later engaged him to direct the Metropolitan Opera production in New York. On December 13, 1949 he staged Verdi's *Falstaff* at Sadler's Wells and at the Lyric, Hammersmith on July 17, 1950 directed (with Basil Coleman) the first London performance of the adaptation by Benjamin Britten of John Gay's *The Beggar's Opera* to which Guthrie contributed some of the dialogue.

For the Edinburgh Festival of 1950, Guthrie directed Eric Linklater's *The Atom Doctor* and James Bridie's *The Queen's Comedy*. Also in 1950 he staged *Hamlet* for the Gate Theatre in Dublin and Miles Malleson's free adaptation of Molière's *The Miser* for the "Old Vic" company during their final months at the New Theatre. Guthrie directed the Sadler's Wells production of Rossini's *The Barber of Seville* on November 28, 1950.

The London première of Guthrie's own play, *Top of the Ladder*, was given at the St. James's Theatre on October 11, 1950 starring John Mills. The London *Times* described it as a play concerning "a man whose life is dominated by an unconscious jealousy of his father." The playwright "hammered with varying degrees of strength" the point that "all parents desire that the lives of their children shall be mere extensions of their own." Guthrie used "under a symbolic ladder" the "few bits and pieces of scenery once familiar in the expressionist heyday." *Top of the Ladder* failed to attract the general public; but it had its admirers and was included by J. C. Trewin in the 1949-50 volume of *Plays of the Year*. The acting text was published by Samuel French in 1952.

The "Old Vic" Theatre on the Waterloo Road was repaired and in November, 1950 was reopened. In June, 1951 Guthrie was recalled to the managership of the Vic-Wells organization. Donald Wolfit appeared in Christopher Marlowe's *Tamburlaine the Great* in September 1951, using the adaptation prepared by Guthrie and himself (later published in London by Heinemann). Guthrie directed Shakespeare's rarely performed *Timon of Athens* (May 28, 1952). He resigned from the "Old Vic" that summer.

While his production of *Carmen* was in preparation for a première at the Metropolitan Opera House in New York on January 31, 1952, Guthrie wrote an article for the program noting the influence of the ballet on theatrical design and expressing his view that the dominant theme of the opera was that "physical love and physical cruelty, creation and destruction, are poles of the same axis."

Virgil Thomson, reviewing *Carmen* in the New York *Herald Tribune*, found Guthrie's direction "fresh and mostly quite vivid." Douglas Watt wrote that "Mr. Guthrie's unrelenting attempt to keep *Carmen* a forceful and realistic dramatic work—the music aside—is continuously evident," (*New Yorker*, February 9, 1952). "What we are most aware of is how much more vigorous this is than former productions. . . . The familiar story was treated with such urgency that it was like seeing a fresh and vigorous stage work for the first time. It was a striking occasion."

At the Edinburgh Festival on August 18, 1952 Guthrie directed Joseph Mitchell's ballad opera *The Highland Fair*, as adapted by Robert Kemp. At the "Old Vic" on May 6, 1953 Guthrie staged *Henry VIII* (with Alexander Knox as Wolsey and Gwen Frangçon-Davies as Katherine) of which Harold Hobson remarked in the *Christian Science Monitor* that "he discovers in it climaxes which Shakespeare never suspected."

Richard III and *All's Well That Ends Well* were staged by Guthrie for the first Shakespeare Festival at Stratford, Ontario for performances on alternating evenings in July and August 1953, with Alec Guinness and Irene Worth heading the company. Although Brooks Atkinson of the New York *Times* thought the *Richard III* "overproduced," he observed that "Guthrie's production of *All's Well That Ends Well* and the acting of Guinness and the rest of the company" had "resulted in the composition of a little gem of imaginative theatre." Walter Kerr in the New York *Herald Tribune* reported that the "traditionally intractable" *All's Well* was performed in Edwardian costume on a platform under a canvas awning, resulting in "an evening of irresistible humor," while "stirring up an astonishing amount of emotion along the way."

A record of the festival by Guthrie and others was published at Toronto later in the year under the title *Renown at Stratford.* The initial Shakespeare festival in Ontario was also the subject of a documentary film in color, *Stratford Adventure* (released in the spring of 1954). During the winter 1953-54 Guthrie completed a new comedy *Haste to the Wedding;* first presented at the Crest Theatre in Toronto on May 5, 1954, it followed "the Restoration play pattern in modern clothes, plus Shakespearean undertones in staging" (*Variety*).

Re-engaged to direct a second festival in the summer of 1954, Guthrie discussed plans and prospects in an article "Problems of the Next Stratford Festival" which appeared in the December 12, 1953 number of the Toronto weekly, *Saturday Night.* He pointed out that other cities named Stratford may start Shakespearean festivals "with more spectacular programs and with more ballyhoo." He emphasized that a serious Shakespearean Festival is "not big stuff in terms of tourist attraction, but it is big stuff in terms of the development of Canadian Theatre. The thing not to be afraid of is being thought Arty, Highbrow, Long-haired. The people who buy tickets had better be prepared to have these labels hung about their necks, and not feel too bowed down in consequence. . . . Stratford's customers will be those who want to see a Shakespeare play competently and seriously acted in appropriate surroundings, which implies leisure without dullness." He discussed the growing influence of the ballet on acting and direction "in terms of rhythm and plasticity" in an article in the New York *Times Magazine,* April 20, 1952.

Attendance at the 1954 productions at Stratford, Ontario topped the 1953 total attendance. The 1954 program included *Measure for Measure, Taming of the Shrew,* and *Oedipus Rex.*

An honorary LL.D. was conferred on Guthrie by the Scottish University of St. Andrew's. He is six feet four inches in height, has brown hair, and blue eyes. Mrs. Guthrie, who is author of the play *Queen Bess,* presented by the "Old Vic" at Bristol, England in 1943, is the former Judith Bretherton. The Guthries were married in 1930.

"What is so refreshing about Guthrie," wrote Sewell Stokes, "is that for all his taste and quality, he is not noticeably a highbrow. One has the feeling that he wants his audiences to *enjoy* what he has given them. . . . To be a dictator in the theatre, while retaining the affection of his players, is an accomplishment of which any director may justly feel proud."

References

N Y Times Mag p2 Ja 26 '53
Theatre Arts 27:237+ Ap '43
Hartnoll, P. (ed.) Oxford Companion to the Theatre (1950)
Sobol, B. (ed.) Theatre Handbook (1940)
Who's Who, 1953
Who's Who in the Theatre (1952)

HAILE SELASSIE I, EMPEROR OF ETHIOPIA (hī'lĕ sĭl-lä' syĕ) July 17, 1891-

Address: Imperial Palace, Addis Ababa, Ethiopia

NOTE: This biography supersedes the article which appeared in *Current Biography* in 1941.

Among the royal visitors to the United States in recent years, few have so stirred the imagination of the American people as His Imperial Majesty Haile Selassie I of Ethiopia, who began his first tour of North America in May 1954. The Emperor is remembered for his eloquent although fruitless appeal to the League of Nations in 1936, calling for collective security against the Italian invaders of his kingdom.

Haile Selassie is the temporal and spiritual ruler of one of the oldest Christian domains, Ethiopia (generally known as Abyssinia prior to World War I) in eastern Africa. Ethiopia is a charter member of the United Nations Organization, and several battalions of the Swedish-trained Ethiopian Imperial Guard fought with U.N. forces in Korea. In September 1953 Ethiopia ratified a new treaty of "friendship and commerce" with the United States. Later, in May, 1954 it was announced that he had signed an agreement granting the United States ninety-nine-year military base rights in Ethiopia (New York *Times,* May 15, 1954).

Tafari Makonnen assumed the name of Haile Selassie in 1928 when he was crowned Negus (King). He was born at Harar on July 17, 1891, the son of Ras Makonnen, governor of Harar and trusted adviser of Emperor Menelik II. Tafari is believed to be descended from Menelik I, the son of King Solomon and the Queen of Sheba.

Reared in the Coptic Christian faith, the boy commenced his secular education at the age of seven under private European tutors. Tafari

Wide World

HAILE SELASSIE I, EMPEROR OF ETHIOPIA

was appointed governor of Gara Muleta in Harar province when he was fourteen years old. He was governor of Salale when his father died in 1906.

Tafari studied for a year at a French mission school in Addis Ababa. At this time he was considered in line for the throne. However, in 1909, Emperor Menelik, redesignated the succession, naming Lij Yasu, his grandson, as heir presumptive.

Menelik II died in 1913 and Lij Yasu assumed the reins of government although he was never crowned. Handsome and athletic, Yasu was at first popular, but soon alienated the Christians among his subjects by encouraging Mohammedanism and polygamy. In 1916 he was excommunicated by the Ethiopian church, and the Rases proclaimed Zauditu, the daughter of Menelik, as Empress, and Tafari as heir presumptive and regent. (He had meanwhile become governor of Sidamo and later governor of Harar.) Tafari was given the title of Ras (prince), and was invested with the insignia of the Cordon of the Order of the Crown of Solomon.

Almost all visitors to Ethiopia during Ras Tafari's regency paid tribute to his ability, patriotism and progressive views. He obtained a seat for Ethiopia in the League of Nations in 1923. (Admission was at first opposed because of the institution of slavery in the country, whereupon Tafari promised to abolish the slave trade, which he did in the following year, and provided for the gradual emancipation of the slave population.)

In 1924 Ras Tafari paid his first visit to Europe, and after returning to his own country he introduced many reforms. Four years later he was crowned Negus, decreasing considerably the authority of Empress Zauditu. He sought to counterbalance Anglo-French influence by concluding with Italy a treaty of "perpetual amity." In March 1930, Tafari defeated an armed revolt against him organized by Empress Zauditu's consort. The latter was killed, and the Empress herself died shortly afterwards.

On November 2, 1930 Tafari became His Imperial Majesty Haile Selassie I, King of Kings of Ethiopia, Lion of Judah, and Elect of God. The monarch proclaimed a new constitution in July 1931.

Four years later an armed clash occurred on the border of Haile Selassie's empire and the Italian colony of Eritrea. The Italians used the incident as an excuse to invade Ethiopia in October 1935. Pressing inland, they captured Addis Ababa on May 5, 1936. Haile Selassie escaped to Palestine, and then proceeded to England.

Having failed to enlist British support for his cause, he addressed the League of Nations in a speech on June 30, 1936. He pleaded for military sanctions against Italy, declared that international morality was "at stake," and predicted that if the League failed to enforce the conditions of its Covenant it would be "digging its grave." However, only mild economic sanctions were voted and were never seriously enforced. On November 18, 1938 Great Britain formally recognized King Victor Emmanuel III of Italy as the Emperor of Ethiopia, and the union of Ethiopia, Eritrea and Italian Somaliland under the name of Italian East Africa. Selassie retired to a temporary home at Bath in England.

After Italy entered World War II on the side of Germany, Haile Selassie was recognized by Britain as an ally. Later an Allied-supported invasion of Ethiopia was launched. The Italian troops, cut off from help from home, were routed, and on May 5, 1941, Haile Selassie was able to re-enter Addis Ababa, although the final Italian surrender did not occur until November.

By the terms of an Anglo-Ethiopian agreement concluded on January 31, 1942, the autonomy of Ethiopia and the authority of Haile Selassie as Emperor were formally recognized by Great Britain. Nevertheless, the status of Ethiopia until after the end of World War II was that of a virtual dependency of Britain. On May 17, 1943 *Time* noted that "the actual chores of government are handled (through agreement) by British civilian and military commissioners."

The Anglo-Ethiopian agreement was renewed, in December 1944, for an additional two years. However, the aid and advice of other powers have gradually supplanted that of the British. An agreement ratified in December 1944 permitting U.S. aircraft to use American-built airfields in Ethiopia, and a meeting between Haile Selassie and President Franklin D. Roosevelt after the Yalta conference aboard the U.S.S. *Quincy* paved the way for an extension of American interests in Ethiopia.

By 1947 the Sinclair Oil Company had been granted a fifty-year oil-prospecting concession, and the American Trans-World Airlines had reorganized the air services. Swedish officers undertook the training of the Ethiopian air force, and operation of the railway was returned to the French.

In the summer of 1946 Ethiopia began to press claims for the former Italian colony of Eritrea. The monarch appointed in August 1947 a New York University law professor, Albert H. Garretson, as adviser on "all legal questions to come before the Ethiopian foreign office" including "the problem of the peace settlements and . . . certain territorial questions."

On April 1, 1950, in a speech broadcast from Addis Ababa while a U.N. Commission of Inquiry for Eritrea was making its survey, the Emperor stressed the "identity of dress and manners" and "virtual identity of language" in Ethiopia and Eritrea as well as "Ethiopia's vital need for access to the sea and return to her control of her ancient port of Massaua." (Eritrea had been part of the Ethiopian empire prior to the 1890's.)

The U.N. General Assembly voted on December 2, 1950 to federate an "autonomous Eritrea" with Ethiopia "under the sovereignty of the Ethiopian crown." Under the terms of federation, which became effective September 15, 1952, Eritrea (with a population of about 1,000,000) has its own constitution, an elected legislature and chief executive, and controls most of its internal matters. Ethiopia is responsible for defense, foreign relations, trade, and finance.

Despite the Emperor's efforts Ethiopia remains a backward nation. It is true that slaveholding was made illegal in 1942, and a strong central administration now functions. Nevertheless, because of the continued illiteracy of the vast majority of its estimated 10,000,000 inhabitants, Ethiopia has not instituted universal suffrage.

"I have three priorities in my country," Haile Selassie told Francis Ofner (*Christian Science Monitor,* August 19, 1950). "I first want to expand education. My second ambition is to develop communications. And the third—I want to secure employment for all Ethiopians." In the field of education, progress has been made; Ethiopia in 1954 has nearly 600 schools with about 60,000 pupils. Haile Selassie I University, now under construction, will include a College of Liberal Arts, College of Law, College of Medicine, and a College of Science.

Nevertheless (as *Time* noted October 13, 1952), "the country does not have a single native graduate engineer, architect, chemist, or agricultural expert," and Haile Selassie "must rely on foreign help to bolster his ministries," such help being at the present time mainly American.

"The claim that Ethiopia is now a democratic government," according to *Christian Century* (June 9, 1954), "under a constitutional monarch, is farcical. Actual power continues to be held firmly by feudal lords and landlords . . . who see to it that very little reliable information as to what is actually going on in the country ever reaches the well-meaning Emperor."

Haile Selassie paid a visit to the United States, Canada and Mexico from May to July of 1954. This was his first trip to the United States. In Washington, D.C., he was an overnight guest of President Dwight D. Eisenhower at the White House. Addressing a joint session of Congress on May 28, the monarch referred to the principle of his 1936 plea which he said had been "vindicated" in Korea. "We felt that nowhere can the call for aid against aggression be refused," he declared. "It is either a universal principle or it is no principle at all" (Washington *Post,* May 29, 1954).

From Washington, he visited New York, Boston, Ottawa, and other cities, and received cordial welcomes. He inspected an American agricultural college and the Grand Coulee Dam, and received honorary degrees from Howard, Columbia and Montreal universities. The Emperor was accompanied by his third and youngest son, a granddaughter, and consultants, including three Cabinet ministers.

Americans regretted that the Empress Waizero Menin, a great-granddaughter of Menelik II, was unable to accompany her husband to the United States. The imperial couple were married in 1912 and had six children, Crown Prince Asfa Wusen Haile Selassie; Prince Makonnen Haile Selassie, Duke of Harar; Prince Sahle Haile Selassie; Princesses Lilt Kaluma Work and Tsahai (both are deceased); and Princess Tenegn Work.

The Emperor is deeply religious, strictly adhering to the fasts of the Coptic Christian faith. He is five feet four inches in height and weighs about 100 pounds. He has "an olive complexion, a thin hooked nose, tiny fluttering hands . . . and thin, sensitive lips." His black hair and beard show little sign of graying.

His Majesty is insistent on the deference due to royalty. However, he quickly puts his visitor at ease, and his smile is infectious and expansive, even though his "characteristic expression" is said to be "a singular mixture of melancholic sadness and cold determination" (Curtis Lubinski, Washington *Post,* May 23, 1954). One of his favorite relaxations is viewing American motion pictures. Another is listening to the music of Beethoven.

References (see also references listed in 1941 biographical sketch)

Christian Sci Mon Mag p5 Ag 19 '50 por
Life 23:57 N 10 '47 por; 34:103+ My 4 '53 pors
N Y World-Telegram p4 My 22 '54 pors
Scholastic 64:9+ Ap 21 '54 por
Time 41:35+ My 17 '43 por; 54:32 N 21 '49 por
U N Bul 8:397 My 1 '50
U S News 36:16 My 28 '54 por
Washington (D.C.) Post p1B+ My 23 '54 por

International Who's Who, 1953
Powell, E. A. Beyond the Utmost Purple Rim (1925)
Rogers, J. A. World's Great Men of Color (1946-1947)
Sandford, C. Ethiopia Under Haile Selassie (1946)
Ten Eventful Years (1947)
Who's Who in America, 1954-55
World Biography (1954)

HALL, WILLIAM EDWIN Mar. 25, 1878-
Lawyer; boys' organization official
Address: b. 41 East 42d St., New York 17; h. Old Church Rd., Greenwich, Conn.

For thirty-eight years William Edwin Hall, a lawyer and corporation official, has served as president of the Boys' Clubs of America, a post commanding no salary. The organization is one which Mayor LaGuardia once defined as "typically American because it preserved the boy's individuality, provided an outlet for his emotions and energy and taught him to be a good loser."

Hall, whose activity in the Boys' Club began nearly forty years ago, has stated that there

Underwood & Underwood
WILLIAM EDWIN HALL

are "millions of boys who need the help of clubs, and they have not yet been reached." He believes that Americans must fight to wipe out the "disgraceful record of juvenile delinquency" by offering positive programs to help boys "become sound citizens so that we may have a strong, God-fearing America."

William Edwin Hall was born March 25, 1878 in St. Marys, Pennsylvania. His father, an ex-Congressman from Pennsylvania, was James Knox Polk Hall and his mother, Kate M. Hyde. He attended the Haverford School from which he was graduated in 1896.

Following studies for one year at the Lawrenceville School, he entered Yale University. Young Hall was awarded a Ph.B. degree in 1900. He then studied law at Harvard University, receiving the LL.B. degree in 1903. Admitted to the bar in New York in 1904, he started his practice with the law firm of Sherman and Sterling.

"The way I got the Boys' Clubs in my veins," Hall has stated, "was when I first became a volunteer leader in the Boys' Club of New York on Tenth Street and Avenue A in 1914." After a year as a group leader, he was asked to become treasurer of the Boys' Clubs of America and in 1916 was elected president at the annual meeting in Scranton, Pennsylvania. David W. Armstrong, executive director of the organization, remembered that day in a tribute thirty-five years later to Hall. ". . . a gentleman who was to be the inspiration and guiding light" of the Boys' Clubs of America.

In the decades since, Hall has influenced many outstanding men to become members of the national board of directors. An important milestone was reached in 1936, when he interested Herbert Hoover in the movement and Hoover became chairman of the national board. Hall also was instrumental in securing the appointment in 1941 of David W. Armstrong as national executive director. This choice of Armstrong created what came to be known in Boys' Club circles as "The Big Three"—Herbert Hoover, William Edwin Hall and David W. Armstrong.

During World War II some 150,000 Boys' Club members served in the armed forces; younger boys who were organized as "Victory Volunteers," sold war bonds, planted victory gardens, collected metal and paper for defense plants, worked on farms and made splints and stretchers.

"Since I was elected president in 1916," Hall claims, "I have probably spent one-third of my waking hours in the promotion of more Boys' Clubs in the United States." He has often said that the two things of most interest to him are the Boys' Clubs and his family.

In recent years the growth of the organization has been very rapid. When Hall first became president, there were forty-three Boys' Clubs in the membership and the national budget was less than $3,500. Today, there are 375 clubs with 350,000 members from small towns and large cities throughout the country, and a budget of almost eight million dollars.

The lawyer has also participated in governmental affairs. He was appointed in 1917 by Secretary of Labor William B. Wilson as national director of the United States Public Service Reserve, which operated during the war period under the Department of Labor. Its purpose was to recruit labor for plants and to move it to essential centers. Hall was also the national director of the Boys' Working Reserve and the acting assistant director general of the United States Employment Service.

From 1914 to 1915, he served as secretary and member of the executive committee of the Commission for Relief in Belgium. For his efforts on behalf of that nation, King Albert of Belgium awarded him a medal.

Hall also was vice-chairman of the New York City commission on crime prevention from 1928 to 1933. He has been a trustee of the Children's Aid Society of New York for twenty-five years and a president of the National Institute of Social Sciences (1937 to 1942). He is now its vice-president.

He was also a member of the committee on welfare and housing for the New York World's Fair, is a member of the Association of the Bar of the City of New York, of the Berzelius

Society, of the Pilgrims of the United States, and of the St. Georges Society of New York.

Hall is a member of the law firm of Hall, Cunningham and Haywood, a member of the advisory committee of the Grand Central Branch of the Chase National Bank and president of the Trojan Powder Company. He is chairman of the board of St. Mary's National Bank, St. Mary's Trust Company, the Duriron Company, the Speer Carbon Company, and the International Graphite and Electrode Corporation.

He is a director of the Russell Snow Plow Company, the General Reinsurance Corporation, the North Star Reinsurance Company, the American Surety Company, the Greenwich Trust Company, and the Surety Fire Insurance Company. His clubs are the Downtown Association, Union, Yale, Union League, Greenwich Field, Round Hill Country, Beach, and Tuxedo.

Recognition for his devotion to the boys of America has been accorded Hall by a gold medal from the Catholic Youth Organization, a silver buffalo from the Boy Scouts of America, and a Boys' Exposition Medal from the Metropolitan Boys' Club Workers Association.

In 1936 Harvard University conferred on him an honorary Master of Arts degree and in the same year he received a gold medal from the National Institute of Social Sciences. In 1950, he was named a Pennsylvania ambassador for the year and presented with a plaque by Governor James H. Duff.

William Edwin Hall is an Episcopalian and a senior warden of Christ Church, Greenwich.

While an undergraduate at Yale, Hall met Marguerite Wood. They were married on April 5, 1904. The Halls have three daughters, Marguerite Brinckerhoff, Susan Archdeacon and Constance Clark.

References

N Y Times p25 Ap 10 '41 por
Who's Who in America, 1952-53
Who's Who in Commerce and Industry (1953)
Who's Who in New York, 1952

HAMLIN, TALBOT (FAULKNER)

(tôl'bŭt) June 16, 1889- Former university professor; architect; author

Address: c/o School of Architecture, Columbia University, New York 27.

Frequently in a long career, first as a practicing architect, and then for the past thirty-eight years as a teacher in Columbia University's School of Architecture and the author of many books and articles, Professor Talbot Hamlin has made clear his philosophy. He believes that buildings exist primarily for people and not as expressions of any particular style or dogma, and that "today's buildings should be modern because people are modern."

Hamlin is a man, wrote *Columbia Alumni News* (July 1953), "who can rise above the feuds of his often bitterly divided profession [traditionalism vs. functionalism] and earn the accolade of 'this country's foremost architectural historian and critic.'" His most recent major achievement was the editing of a monumental four-volume work, *Forms and Functions of Twentieth-Century Architecture* (Columbia, 1952), generally regarded as "the definitive work for this half-century." He is co-author of *We Took To Cruising* (Sheridan, 1951), and is now completing a critical biography of Benjamin Henry Latrobe, one of the architects of the Capitol in Washington, D.C.

His retirement was announced in June 1954 and he is devoting his time to writing, painting water colors and cruising in his boat, three activities in which he has demonstrated his professional ability.

Talbot Faulkner Hamlin was born in New York City on June 16, 1889. Much of his childhood was spent in the neighborhood of Columbia University where his father, Alfred Dwight Foster Hamlin, was a member of the faculty of the School of Architecture. His grandfather was Cyrus Hamlin, a missionary who established Robert College in Turkey. His mother was Minnie Florence (Marston) Hamlin.

After his graduation from the Horace Mann School in New York in 1906, Hamlin attended Amherst College, Massachusetts, where he received the A.B. degree in 1910. He went to Columbia University the following year and received the Bachelor of Architecture degree in 1914. The same year he went to work as a draftsman for the firm of Murphy & Dana in New York. In 1920, he was made a partner, and the firm became Murphy, McGill & Hamlin. Among its clients was Ginling College in Nanking, China, which took him overseas in a supervisory capacity in 1922. Other construction with which Hamlin was concerned were buildings of the College of New Rochelle in New Rochelle, New York. In 1925 the name of his firm became McGill & Hamlin.

In 1930 he went into business for himself, but the depression was a bad time for architects. Many years before this, however, in 1916, Hamlin had started his career at the Columbia School of Architecture as a lecturer in extension courses. From 1934 to 1945 he was also librarian of the Avery Library in the School of Architecture, and from 1935 to 1945, of the Fine Arts Library. He was made a full professor in 1947. His early interest in social conditions and his background of social responsibility acquired in his home, Hamlin has written, led to his deep interest in housing and city planning.

In 1916 Hamlin published the first of the many critical books on architecture for which he is known. This work was *The Enjoyment of Architecture* (Duffield) of which Claude Bragdon wrote in *Dial* (January 11, 1917): "His book is full of the fine enthusiasm of youth without the rawness of youth . . . but the great defect of Hamlin's attitude toward American architecture is his incorrigible optimism."

This optimism was not so great, however, that it prevented Hamlin from writing books

Volpe Studios

TALBOT HAMLIN

and magazine articles in which he was sometimes very critical of American architectural fads. While he has written enthusiastically of Frank Lloyd Wright, he has steadfastly been against modern or any other school of architecture simply as a fad or style. He has often pointed out that today's architecturally important buildings nearly always serve some socially useful purpose, whereas fifty years ago such buildings were chiefly homes for wealthy individuals.

He has commented on the "underlying romanticism of Americans . . ." and their "almost wistful search for beauty." In the *New Republic* (August 4, 1941), Hamlin wrote that structures built in the past five years were "better, simpler than the buildings of twenty years ago . . . less ornamental . . . no Ionic columns, Romanesque arches, etc. . . ." He found that "American architecture is emerging."

In a critical appraisal of an exhibit of the work of Frank Lloyd Wright at New York's Museum of Modern Art, Hamlin wrote: "Of the importance of Wright's accomplishment, of the brilliant inventive unconventionality that has always marked his work, there can be no question. . . ." He concluded that Wright was "a liberating creative genius who has made over the world's vision of what buildings may be" (*Nation,* November 30, 1940). Eleven years later in the *Nation* (February 10, 1951), Hamlin again praised Wright as "America's greatest architect."

As to the use of the phrase "modern architecture," Hamlin once commented that as early as 1631 a Dutch architect, Hendrik de Keyser, published a volume entitled *Architecture Moderna.* Speaking before the Architectural League of New York in March 1950, Hamlin said: "No thinking architect today disagrees with the fundamental principles of so-called modern architecture . . . we are not any longer concerned with a great many of the dogmas of early modern architecture . . . all these things have gone into the stream of tradition and we accept them and use them, or do not use them, as we see fit . . . we have come to realize that the real purpose of architecture is to contribute to an environment that will make people happy. . . . For the first time in almost a century we are designing for the whole man."

In 1926 Hamlin published *The American Spirit in Architecture* (Yale); in 1939, *Some European Architectural Libraries* (Columbia); and in 1940, *Architecture Through the Ages* (Putnam). *Books* (June 9, 1940) acclaimed the last-mentioned work as "the most comprehensive, authoritative and interesting one-volume history of architecture in English," and also stated: "Hamlin writes from a wide knowledge of recent archeological and technical discoveries, as well as traditional history, and the material he has selected covers an amazingly wide range."

Hamlin's next work was *Greek Revival Architecture in America* (Oxford, 1944). In 1947 he rewrote *The Enjoyment of Architecture;* the new book was published by the Columbia University Press under the title *Architecture, An Art for All Men.* (This work was done on sabbatical leave, while on his boat.)

In his introduction to the book, Hamlin wrote: "These three decades [since the publication of *The Enjoyment of Architecture*] have seen a revolutionary change in the architecture of the whole world. . . . Architectural movements which thirty years ago were merely little pinpricks in an almost universal complacency, have grown into well-nigh universal acceptance; no longer revolutionary, the basic principles which lie behind what is generally termed 'modern architecture' have established their validity."

With his wife, Jessica, he published in 1951 *We Took to Cruising,* with his own sketches and photographs. This was an account of a cruise from Maine to Florida in the *Aquarelle II,* a thirty-three foot cabin cruiser built according to Hamlin's specifications.

The New York *Times* (July 4, 1954), reporting Hamlin's retirement from Columbia University quoted him as saying: "New York architecture is dead, killed by high land cost and a striving for the last tenth of 1 per cent of rent. Manhattan is getting to be one vast slum with oases of luxury apartments for the wealthy." He proposed that a new development plan for New York and surrounding areas be studied, with more attention given to providing parks in outlying boroughs and more action on limited-dividend slum-clearance housing projects in Manhattan by savings banks and insurance companies.

The architect contributed to the *Encyclopædia Britannica* (fourteenth edition) and the *Dictionary of American Biography.* He is a fellow of the American Institute of Architects, an honorary associate of the New York Historical Society, and for many years was on the architectural committee of the Museum of Modern Art in New York City. He also served on the architects' advisory committee of the Federal

Public Housing Authority. He is a member of Phi Beta Kappa, and in 1952 was awarded a D.Sc. degree by Dickinson College, Carlisle, Pennsylvania.

Hamlin has blue eyes, light brown hair, is five feet eight inches tall, and weighs 150 pounds. Glasses, a white moustache, and a Vandyck beard give him a conventional professorial appearance. A man of independent thought, firm convictions, and cheerful manner, Hamlin never hesitates to speak when he feels it necessary. For many years he was on the Columbia University Council, a high faculty body; members recall that at a meeting, he would listen quietly for awhile, and then would deliver a trenchant observation which would demolish all opposition.

He was married to Hilda B. Edwards on September 11, 1916. They had three children, Wilfrid Gardner, Talbot Fancher, and Norman Anderson Hamlin. This marriage ended in divorce, and on November 17, 1926, he married Sarah H. J. Simpson, who died in 1930. His third wife is the former Jessica V. Walters, to whom he was married on June 10, 1931. He belongs to the Halloween Yacht Club in Stamford, Connecticut. He is a Socialist. An excellent water-colorist, his work has been exhibited on many occasions. He has an "almost childlike wonder and delight in everything in life—from folk songs to bridges" (*Columbia Alumni News,* July 1953).

References

Columbia (University) Alumni N p22 Jl '53 por
Who's Who in America, 1954-55
Who's Who in New York, 1952

HAMMOND-INNES, RALPH *See* Innes, (R.) H.

HARRER, HEINRICH (här′rẽr hīn′rĭk) July 6, 1912- Geographer; author; mountain climber

Address: b. c/o Liechtenstein Verlag, Vaduz, Liechtenstein; c/o E. P. Dutton & Co., Inc., 300 4th Ave., New York 10; h. Kitzbühel, Austria

The author of the popular travel book, *Seven Years in Tibet,* Heinrich Harrer, has spent most of his life thousands of feet above sea level. He was in the Alps during much of his childhood and has climbed peaks in three continents. Disdaining expensive equipment and fanfare, "he prefers the mid-highest unclimbed to the highest unclimbed" mountain, according to Lewis Nichols in the New York *Times* (April 11, 1954).

The accident of his internment in India just before the outbreak of World War II and the daring of his escape led Harrer to a unique adventure in Tibet that he fortunately recorded in his diaries. Before the material was organized into a book, Lowell Thomas and his son, who met Harrer in Lhasa in 1949, predicted in "Escape to Shangri-La" (*Collier's,* March 11, 1950): "The story . . . may rate as one of the top adventure yarns of our time." Harrer's book became a best seller in 1954 in the United States.

Born at Hüttenberg, Austria, a town in the province of Carinthia, on July 6, 1912, Heinrich Harrer was one of the four children of Josef and Johanna (Penker) Harrer. Most of his childhood was spent in the nearby Alps, where he climbed the mountains during the summers and skied in the winter. His family moved to Graz, capital of the neighboring province of Styria, and there Heinrich attended the *gymnasium,* from which he was graduated in 1933.

During his years at Graz University, where he majored in geography and physical training, he continued his mountaineering. He won a place on the Austrian Olympic ski team in 1936, and the next year, he led in the downhill race of the world students' championships.

After his graduation in 1938, his plans for the future were clear: "I began to feel," he wrote, "that the only worthwhile ambition was to measure my strength against the mountains." Incessant practice, despite such mishaps as a nearly fatal 170-foot fall, fitted him for his first hazardous project, the conquest of the north wall of the Eiger, a 13,040-foot peak of the Bernese Alps in Switzerland. Although many had died vainly trying to scale the last 6,700 feet of this precipice, and further attempts had been forbidden by the Swiss government, Harrer and three companions accomplished the feat in the summer of 1938.

During the autumn of that year Harrer kept in shape as a physical training teacher, hoping to win an invitation to participate in a reconnaissance expedition to the Himalayas planned for 1939. When his chances appeared dim, he signed a contract to take part in a ski film. After rehearsals had begun, he received a telephone call to leave for India in four days. "I broke my contract without an instant's hesitation," he writes, "traveled home to Graz, spent a day in packing my things, and on the following day was en route for Antwerp. . ."

His goal was Nanga Parbat, 26,660 feet high, in Kashmir, another unclimbed mountain that had claimed many victims. The German expedition spent almost a year preparing and reconnoitering. In August 1939 they had finished their preparations and were in Karachi, waiting for a ship to take them back to Europe, when the imminence of war ended their hopes. Fearing internment by the British, they made a break for the Iranian border, but were caught and arrested a few hundred miles outside of Karachi two days before the outbreak of hostilities.

Harrer was one of a group interned at Ahmadnagar. He made his first attempt to escape while being transferred by truck to Deolali, but his companion was caught and Harrer returned to the convoy before he was missed. Later that year he was moved to the huge P.O.W. camp near Dehra Dun, in sight of the Himalayas, and he planned persistently to reach the peaks he had come to India to climb.

Joining forces with an Italian prisoner, General Marchese, he learned Hindustani, Japanese

HEINRICH HARRER

and Tibetan, studied travel books, and copied maps. In May 1943 the two cut the camp wires and set out for the Ganges headwaters, but after eighteen days they were caught. Again Harrer spent months in preparation, and left the camp on April 29, 1944, disguised as an Indian laborer. Another fugitive, who became Harrer's companion for the next seven years, was Peter Aufschnaiter, leader of the German Himalaya expedition. The two met at Nelang, ten days out of Dehra Dun. On May 17, 1944, they crossed the Tsangchokla Pass into Tibet.

For the next twenty months Harrer and Aufschnaiter made their way from the western corner of that untraveled land, across inhospitable plateaus and mountain passes towards the capital city of Lhasa in the southeast. Several times they were ordered to leave the country, and they pretended to set out for India and later for Nepal, but each time they backtracked, and by a combination of tact, subterfuge, and audacity they were able to reach the "forbidden city" of Lhasa on January 15, 1946. Hungry and ragged, they squatted in the courtyard of a wealthy citizen, who made them welcome. Soon all Lhasa, more curious and amused than hostile, flocked to see them.

They evaded another order to leave in February 1946, and by making themselves useful, Aufschnaiter as an engineer and Harrer as a gardener, the two Europeans were gradually accepted. Their invitation to visit the parents of the Dalai Lama, secular and religious ruler of Tibet, was followed, two years later (in 1948), by inclusion on the reception list for the royal New Year festivities.

Later in 1948 Harrer was made a salaried official of the government. His duties included translating foreign news and articles into Tibetan, directing a flood control project, and photographing special events. He rented his own home with a stable and garden, and in addition to his salary, received the services of a personal attendant, a messenger, and a groom from the government.

Having made friends and a place for himself in the community, Harrer decided to settle permanently in Lhasa. His status seemed assured when he was invited to meet the Dalai Lama. Soon he became the ruler's tutor and friend. "No other non-Tibetan has ever had such an experience," observed Roy Chapman Andrews in the New York *Herald Tribune Book Review* (February 28, 1954).

Again events frustrated Harrer's plans. Communist Chinese forces crossed the border into Tibet in October 1950, and the Dalai Lama prepared to leave Lhasa. Harrer preceded him, departing for southern Tibet in November. "It was with a heavy heart that I left the house which had been my home for so long, my beloved garden, and my servants who stood around me weeping," he has written. The Dalai Lama found it expedient to return to his capital, but Harrer regretfully left the country in March 1951. His photographs of the plight of Tibet illustrated an article, "The Flight of the Dalai Lama," in *Life* magazine (April 23, 1951).

Reluctant to leave the Himalayas, Harrer joined forces with a New Zealand mountaineer named Thomas. With minimum equipment, at an expense of less than $200 from Delhi and back, the pair climbed the previously unconquered peak of Panch Chuli. Then Harrer started back to Europe, and arrived there in January 1952.

Within a month he began to work the material of his diaries into a book, which was published by the Viennese house of Ullstein as *Sieben Jahre in Tibet* in October 1952. It sold widely in Germany and, in translation, in France, the Netherlands, Italy, Spain, Norway, Sweden, and Finland (*Publishers' Weekly,* December 12, 1953). Meanwhile Harrer was off to further adventures, this time in South America. He made the first ascent of a 21,000-foot Andean peak in Peru; then he explored the upper reaches of the Amazon River by canoe.

In November 1953 the German publishers Heering released *Meine Tibet Bilder,* a volume of Harrer's photographs with brief commentary. An English translation by Richard Graves of the earlier work, called *Seven Years in Tibet,* was published in London by Hart-Davis in 1953, and was chosen as a Book Society selection. The work was printed in New York by E. P. Dutton & Company, and was the March 1954 selection of the Book-of-the-Month Club. The author was the recipient of a Christopher literary award in 1954 for using his talents in a "constructive way" in writing the book.

In the spring of 1954, following the American publication of his book, Harrer began a lecture tour of the United States. Temporary confinement to cities was an experience, according to Lewis Nichols, which afflicted Harrer with "a sense of claustrophobia." The tour, interrupted by a summer of mountain climbing in Alaska and a winter visit to Austria, will be resumed in 1955. When in America, Harrer makes his headquarters in Indianapolis, Indiana, where his wife's brother-in-law is an officer stationed at Fort Benjamin Harrison.

In 1938 Harrer married Charlotte Wegener, daughter of the geophysicist Alfred Lothar Wegener, whose writings deeply influenced Harrer in his university years. Their son, Peter, is now a student at the *Werkschulheim* in Salzburg. While Harrer was interned in India he was divorced. In December 1953 he married Margarethe Truxa, a fashion designer. She shares his enthusiasm for skiing and hiking, but, according to Lewis Nichols, "has a curious lack of interest in ascending high, unclimbed mountains."

Harrer has blond hair, blue eyes, and a "wiry" build. He is just under six feet in height, and weighs about 170 pounds. He is a Protestant. His clubs are the Himalayan of Calcutta, India, and the Himalayan Stiftung of Munich, Germany. He enjoys studying ethnography, and on his recent trip to Peru, according to Peter Fleming, he "sought for and found close ethnic similarities between the Indians and the Tibetans" (*Book-of-the-Month Club News,* February 1954).

References

Book-of-the-Month Club N p4 F '54 por
N Y Times Book R p21 Ap 11 '54 por
Harrer, H. Seven Years in Tibet (1954)

HARRIS, MRS. IRVING DROUGHT

See McCardell, C.

HAYCRAFT, HOWARD July 24, 1905-

Publisher; author; editor

Address: b. The H. W. Wilson Co., 950-972 University Ave., New York 52

NOTE: This biography supersedes the article which appeared in *Current Biography* in 1941.

On January 1, 1953 Howard Haycraft became president of The H. W. Wilson Company, New York, world's largest publishers of library indexes and reference books, succeeding Halsey W. Wilson, founder and first president of the firm, who became chairman of its board of directors. (Wilson subsequently died March 1, 1954; see obituary sketch in this volume.) A member of the Wilson Company staff since 1929 and vice-president of the company since 1940, Haycraft is well known in publishing and library circles. He is known to an even wider public for his studies in the art and the history of the detective story. His *Murder for Pleasure: The Life and Times of the Detective Story* (Appleton, 1941) is generally considered to be the standard and definitive history of the *genre.*

Howard Haycraft was born in Madelia, Minnesota, July 24, 1905. His father, Julius Everette Haycraft, who died in 1951, was a lawyer and state legislator and later a judge of the district court. Judge Haycraft was a descendant of English, Welsh, Dutch, and Huguenot French settlers, and his father, in turn, had homesteaded in Minnesota after serving in the Union Army. Haycraft's mother, Marie (Stelzer) Haycraft, was a school teacher before her marriage; her parents had come to Minnesota from Germany in the 1850's and lived through the Indian uprisings of the Civil War period. Today she resides in the tree-shaded home in Fairmont, Minnesota, where the family moved in 1914. Haycraft has one sister, Mrs. George C. Hellickson, of Minneapolis, Minnesota.

After finishing high school in Fairmont, Howard Haycraft entered the University of Minnesota, Minneapolis, in 1923, with the intention of studying law. An early and lively interest in journalism, however, soon dictated a change in plans. Before college Haycraft had worked on the daily paper in his home town after school hours and during vacations. At the university he began writing for the student daily newspaper and for the Minneapolis papers. In 1926 he became chief editor of the student paper, the *Minnesota Daily,* serving for two terms, 1926-1927 and 1927-1928.

Following graduation from the university, where he received his B.A. degree in 1928, Haycraft spent a few months at the University of Minnesota Press, then only a year old, in charge of advertising and promotion. But the call of the metropolis was too strong, and he left for New York, joining the staff of The H. W. Wilson Company in January 1929.

In his twenty-five years of association with the Wilson Company, Haycraft has handled a wide variety of administrative and editorial assignments. Among his first jobs were the promotion of such then-new Wilson publications as the *Education Index* and the *Art Index,* and handling correspondence for the original "Bookmobile." For one year, 1930, he edited the *Wilson Library Bulletin.* With Stanley J. Kunitz he edited the Wilson Authors Series of biographical literary dictionaries, including *Authors Today and Yesterday* (1933), *The Junior Book of Authors* (1934 and 1951), *British Authors of the Nineteenth Century* (1936), *American Authors: 1600-1900* (1938), *Twentieth Century Authors* (1942), and *British Authors Before 1800* (1952).

Haycraft became an officer of The H. W. Wilson Company in 1934 when he was elected to the board of directors. From 1934 to 1939 he also served as assistant secretary of the company. In 1940 he became vice president. During these pre-war years his time and duties were divided among the editorial, promotion and business correspondence departments, giving him an extensive background of the company's organization and activities.

Early in 1942, after being rejected for active military service because of poor eyesight, Haycraft went on leave of absence to Washington as a civilian consultant to the Secretary of War. In this capacity he was associated for several months in the writing and production of the War Department's pocket "G.I. Guides" to foreign countries, including the widely publicized *Guide to Great Britain,* and also of educational manuals sponsored by the American Council on Education.

In December 1942 he received a limited service commission as a captain in the Army Special Services Division (then charged with the

HOWARD HAYCRAFT

education, recreation and information of United States troops), and for the next three years he served as the division's purchasing and contracting officer. Early in 1946 he was discharged with the rank of major and a citation for the Army commendation ribbon.

Returning from the Army to The H. W. Wilson Company, Haycraft assumed certain of the administrative duties which had been supervised chiefly by Halsey W. Wilson since the firm's founding in 1898, or by the company's first secretary, Edith M. Phelps, prior to her retirement in 1947 after forty years' service. These included notably administration of the company's unique "service basis" method of pricing, and the related system of consulting its library subscribers through frequent and detailed questionnaires, as well as coordination of the editorial and press schedules of the company's more-than-a-score of recurrent publications. Among these are *Readers' Guide to Periodical Literature, Cumulative Book Index, Book Review Digest, Industrial Arts Index, Standard Catalog Series,* etc.

At the same time, other administrative functions were being assumed by two other directors of the company, Arthur Rigg, head of the business department, and Charles J. Shaw, head of personnel. As John L. Lawler wrote in his *The H. W. Wilson Company: Half a Century of Bibliographical Publishing* (University of Minnesota Press, 1950): "Wilson was doubtless interested only in promoting efficiency when he appointed capable men like Howard Haycraft, Charles Shaw, Arthur Rigg, and others to important executive posts. . . . Yet at the same time he was providing for the future by building a competent force that could manage the firm at a later period when he would be unable to supervise directly its operations. . . .Thus the company today is much more than the shadow of one man. Without Wilson the firm undoubtedly could not have survived its infancy or the early and middle periods of its growth. If it is now so well organized that it could carry on without him—as some day it must—that detracts nothing from Wilson. On the contrary, that fact is a measure of his success: he has built for far more than a lifetime."

Therefore, when Halsey W. Wilson was elected chairman of the board of directors in December 1952 (in response to his request to be relieved of active duties after fifty-four years of service, to devote more time to plans and policies), Howard Haycraft was elected president, Arthur Rigg vice-president and treasurer, and Charles Shaw secretary and director of personnel. Today these three direct the day-to-day operations of the company in close and frequent consultation. In matters of larger policy, they have the advice of the company's full board of directors which includes Edith M. Phelps, former secretary; Florence A. Arnold, editor of the *Agricultural Index;* John Jamieson, editor of general publications; and Louis J. Bailey, formerly librarian of the Queens Borough Public Library, Jamaica, New York.

Addressing meetings of the American Library Association in 1953, Haycraft pledged to the library profession continuance of the policies of consultation and cooperation which had guided the company for so many years under the presidency of H. W. Wilson. Haycraft also likes to stress his belief in "team work of the Eisenhower variety" in the company's internal as well as external relations, citing the company's growth as one evidence of this need.

At its founding in 1898, the company had only two employees—H. W. Wilson and his wife Justina—until a few months later they were joined by Miss Marion E. Potter (who continued active with the company until a month before her death in June 1953 at the age of eighty-three).

Today the company employs more than 400 persons; it is one of the few firms which performs all publishing operations under one roof; and its annual volume of business exceeds $2,000,000.

Evidence of Haycraft's belief in cooperation with the library profession is found currently in his personal participation in work with several committees of the American Library Association which are engaged—at the company's invitation—in surveying and studying the Wilson periodical indexes. Other library groups will probably be asked to participate as these studies reach the more specialized fields. Haycraft is additionally familiar with library problems as a director of the Forest Press, Inc., publishers of the *Dewey Decimal Classification,* a position he has held since 1951. He is also a member of a joint committee of the American Book Publishers Council and the American Library Association to study mutual problems of publishing and librarianship. Politically, he considers himself a middle-of-the-road independent.

Like many busy executives, Haycraft has long found relaxation in reading detective stories. Unlike most fans, however, his interest has been more active than passive. He began collecting and studying detective fiction many years ago. In 1938 he edited the first of several anthologies in the field—*The Boys' Book of Great Detective Stories* (Harper). This was followed by a *Boys' Second Book* (Harper, 1940), *Crime Club Encore* (Doubleday, 1942), a non-fiction collection *The Art of the Mystery Story* (Simon & Schuster, 1946), and *Fourteen Great Detective Stories* (Modern Library, 1949).

In the course of his early researches on the detective story, Haycraft discovered that there was no book available which supplied a factual history and analysis of detective story writing. Lacking such a book, he decided to write one himself, and—after three years of work, nights, weekends and holidays—he completed *Murder for Pleasure: The Life and Times of the Detective Story.* The book was published by Appleton in 1941, the centennial year of the detective story. In 1942 it was published in England by Peter Davies.

The late William Lyon Phelps called *Murder for Pleasure* "a real contribution to the history of the detective story . . . extremely well written and salted with wit and humor." Vincent Starrett wrote: "Seldom are scholarship and entertainment so happily blended as in this remarkable and necessary book."

The success of *Murder for Pleasure* led to what Haycraft calls his "second career" as critic and consultant in the field of detective and mystery fiction. In 1941 and 1942 he was mystery critic for *Harper's Magazine,* and he served *Ellery Queen's Mystery Magazine* in a similar capacity from 1946 to 1948; he has also contributed articles and criticism to most of the leading literary and reviewing journals. In 1947 he received the Mystery Writers of America "Edgar" award for criticism. Since 1948 he has served as editorial consultant to the Doubleday Mystery Guild, a book club under the aegis of the Literary Guild, reading and reporting on between 250 and 300 mystery manuscripts a year. He finds, he says, that the book club job affords an ideal foil and relaxation from his Wilson Company duties.

In June 1954 Haycraft received the Outstanding Achievement Award of the University of Minnesota. The award was presented at the twenty-fifth anniversary dinner of the university library school, held during the annual conference of the American Library Association in Minneapolis.

In October 1942 Haycraft married Molly Randolph Costain, daughter of the novelist and historian Thomas B. Costain (see *Current Biography* May, 1953), who, before her marriage, was employed by the literary agency of Curtis Brown, Ltd. The Haycrafts have an apartment just off Washington Square in New York City and a summer cottage on the South Shore of Long Island. His hobbies—besides reading and collecting detective fiction—are sailing, watching baseball, listening to music, and travel.

References

Publisher's W 163:205 Ja 17 '53
Sat R Lit 34:32 F 3 '51

Who's Who in America, 1954-55
Who's Who in the East (1951)

HAYES, SAMUEL P(ERKINS) Dec. 17, 1874- Psychologist; educator

Address: b. and h. c/o Perkins Institution and Massachusetts School for the Blind, 175 N. Beacon St., Watertown 72, Mass.

An authority on color blindness and on the psychology of the blind, Dr. Samuel Perkins Hayes has earned a national reputation as head of the teacher-training department of the Perkins Institution and Massachusetts School for the Blind for the past thirteen years. He was a teacher of psychology at Mount Holyoke College in Massachusetts between 1906 and 1940, and was in charge of its psychological laboratory from 1906 until its destruction by fire in 1917.

He has specialized in the administration and interpretation of achievement and intelligence tests of blind children. He wrote the book, *Contributions to a Psychology of Blindness* (American Foundation for the Blind, 1941) and has contributed articles on blindness to encyclopedias and to professional journals. He is chairman of the National Committee on Psychological Research for the Blind, formed by ten prominent psychologists in May 1949 under the auspices of the Federal Security Agency (now the Department of Health, Welfare and Education).

Born in Baldwinsville, New York, on December 17, 1874, Samuel Perkins Hayes was the second of the three sons of the late M.D.L. and Mary Ellen (Perkins) Hayes. His father was a regional agent for an insurance agency. Samuel was brought up in Rochester, New York, and went to Amherst College in Massachusetts after being graduated in 1892 from the Rochester Free Academy, where he was a member of the Pi Phi debating fraternity.

Musically talented like his parents, both of whom were singers, Samuel played the piano for the gymnastics classes at Amherst, and for occasional visiting opera troupes. He was the organist at the college chapel in his junior and senior years, and played the guitar with the Amherst Mandolin Club on a tour of English resorts in the 1894 summer vacation.

Hayes was a member of Chi Phi fraternity, was elected to Phi Beta Kappa, and was graduated from Amherst with the A.B. degree in 1896. He then worked as an insurance salesman. In 1899 he entered Union Theological Seminary in New York City to satisfy "the interest aroused by Professor Charles E. Garman, the inspiring teacher of philosophy at Amherst."

He also took courses in sociology at Columbia University, and received both the B.D. degree from the seminary and the M.A. degree from the university in 1902. His divinity thesis was entitled "An Historical Study of the Edwardian Revivals." The young student decided not to make the ministry his career, and in the fall of 1902, he went to Clark University in Worcester, Massachusetts, where he studied psychology under President G. Stanley Hall and Professor Edmund Clark Sanford.

After his marriage in 1903, Hayes attended lectures at the University of Berlin in Germany

SAMUEL P. HAYES

(1903-1904), and returned briefly to the United States to study psychology at Cornell University, Ithaca, New York in the summer of 1904. With his wife he went to Paris, where they both attended lectures in psychology at the Université de Paris and the Collège de France.

Early in 1905 Hayes resumed postgraduate work at Cornell where he majored in psychology under Edward Bradford Titchener and Madison Bentley. He was elected to Sigma Xi, and received the Ph.D. degree in June 1906. His doctoral thesis, "A Study of the Affective Qualities," was published in the *American Journal of Psychology* that year.

In the fall of 1906 Hayes joined the faculty of Mount Holyoke College at South Hadley, Massachusetts, as an associate professor of psychology and head of the psychological laboratory. He was advanced to a full professorship in 1909. He became interested in the case of a student in his experimental group who had, he has said, "red-green blindness in one eye, the other eye being normal—a condition reported in only a half a dozen cases up to that time." He discussed this case in a paper, "The Color Sensations of the Partially Color-Blind," which criticized current teaching methods and was published in the *American Journal of Psychology* (July, 1911). "After that article," he has written, "I specialized in color blindness."

Professor Hayes was "particularly interested in adapting for the blind tests of achievement in school subjects and the Binet intelligence tests" and in 1916 became visiting consultant on testing to the Pennsylvania Institute for the Instruction of the Blind at Overbrook, Pennsylvania. He is the author of several of the institute's pamphlets including one entitled *Self-Surveys in Schools for the Blind* (1921).

The fire which destroyed the Mount Holyoke psychological laboratory in December 1917 consumed all but a few pages of Hayes's lecture notes and data, including a collection of family histories of the heredity of color blindness gathered partly in America and partly in England in 1912. "The effect," he has said, "was to make definite my change of interest from color blindness to the blind."

In 1919 he was made visiting consultant on testing at the Perkins Institution at Watertown, Massachusetts, and subsequently contributed to the publications of the Perkins Institute Research Department some eight pamphlets, the earliest of which (1922) was entitled *Preliminary Study of the Influence Upon School Success of the Age at Which Vision Is Lost.*

By 1920 he had begun making regular contributions to the publication *Outlook for the Blind,* and in 1925 became visiting consultant on testing to the American Foundation for the Blind in New York City. He is the author of the pages on the psychology of blindness in *What of the Blind?*, a book edited by Helga Lende and published by the foundation in 1938. He has contributed articles to the *Mount Holyoke Alumnae Quarterly.*

The psychologist was honored with the title of professor emeritus when he left Mount Holyoke College in 1940. He then joined the staff of the Perkins Institution and Massachusetts School for the Blind as resident head of the department of personnel and research. The school, which has an enrollment of about 250 persons and a faculty of 85, was established in 1829 to teach "educable children with less than 20/200 vision." It offers the equivalent of a elementary and secondary public school education as well as a three-year course in tuning and a two-year normal course in music. Under the auspices of Harvard University it also provides a training course of one year for college graduates on the history of the education of the blind and on "special methods" of instruction.

Addressing a section of the National Education Association at Boston in 1941 on "Mental Measurements for the Blind," Hayes reported that " 'tests' indicate that the 'wonderful memory' of the blind is an illusion," and that the "handicap of blindness and the slowness of braille reading produce a two year retardation all through the educational process."

Since 1941 he has directed the department of teacher-training at the Perkins Institution and Massachusetts School for the Blind. He is the author of the section on blindness in the *Encyclopedia of Child Guidance* (1943), on mental measurement for the blind in the *Encyclopedia of Vocational Guidance* (1948), and on measuring the intelligence of the blind in *Psychological Diagnosis and Counseling of the Adult Blind* (1950), edited by Wilma Donahue and Donald Dabelstein, and in *Blindness* (1950), edited by P. A. Zahl.

Speaking at the National Conference on Pre-School Blind Children in New York in March 1947, Hayes declared that "experts are not yet certain that measuring tests for children under three years old and younger are dependable," and that "response to training" is the "acid test."

He is a life member of the American Psychological Association and a member of the American Association of the Instructors of the Blind. A phase of his work in which Dr. Hayes takes particular pride is the series of "Chapel Talks" he has been delivering at various schools for the blind on such subjects as "The Duty of Success", "Workers, Jerkers, and Shirkers", "Habit" (after William James), "Why be Polite?", and "Busybodies".

Samuel Perkins Hayes and Agnes Hayes Stone were married on July 23, 1903; since the death of Mrs. Hayes in October 1948, Dr. Hayes has lived at the Perkins Institution. He has five children and eleven grandchildren, about whom he writes a regular "round robin" letter to his friends. His sons are Lyman Stone Hayes and Samuel Perkins Hayes, Jr., director of the Foundation for Research on Human Behavior.

His daughters are Mrs. Mary Ellen Woodcock, Mrs. Janet Card Renshaw, and Mrs. Betsy Wanton Fredell. All the sons and daughters are, like their parents, musical, and in the words of their father (who added the cello to his instruments when he was forty-five and is a member of the Association of Amateur Chamber Music Players) "used to have many combinations of voice and instruments." He has been a photography enthusiast since his late teens.

Hayes enjoys playing bridge and is an expert amateur tennis player. He is a member of the Longwood Cricket Club in Brookline, Massachusetts, and in the winters, plays at the Longwood Indoor Tennis Club with "a mature group called the 'gray beards.'" His religious affiliation is with the Unitarian Church; an "independent" in politics since college days, he votes according to his "best judgment" of the candidates. He is five feet four inches tall, and weighs 140 pounds. He has blue eyes and his hair, once brown, is now "practically white."

References

American Men of Science (1949)
Leaders in Education (1948)
Who's Who in America, 1952-53
Who's Who in New England (1949)

HAYES, SAMUEL P(ERKINS), JR. Jan. 28, 1910- Social psychologist; economist

Address: b. c/o Foundation for Research on Human Behavior, 1141 E. Catherine St., Ann Arbor, Mich.; h. 1701 Morton St., Ann Arbor, Mich.

The Foundation for Research on Human Behavior, at Ann Arbor, Michigan, has as its first director Dr. Samuel P. Hayes, Jr. who was appointed to this post in October 1953 after several years of government service. In 1952-1953 he was assistant director of the Mutual Security Agency in charge of Far Eastern operations. Keenly interested in the Point IV Program, he headed an Economic Cooperation Administration mission to Indonesia in 1951-1952. Previously he had taught at Mount Holyoke and Sarah Lawrence colleges, and had been associated with Young & Rubicam, Inc., and Dun & Bradstreet, Inc. in New York City.

The third of the five children of Samuel Perkins and Agnes Hayes (Stone) Hayes, Samuel Perkins Hayes, Jr. was born on January 28, 1910 at South Hadley, Massachusetts, where his father was professor of psychology at Mount Holyoke College. He was brought up in South Hadley and received his secondary education at The Loomis School, Windsor, Connecticut, where his extracurricular activities included photography, nature study. and playing tennis and the violin.

After being graduated from Loomis in 1926 he followed a family tradition by entering Amherst College in Massachusetts. He majored in economics, and was greatly influenced in the choice of his lifework by Willard L. Thorp, at that time professor of economics at Amherst.

He was a member of the college glee club, choir, string quartet, and band, and served as photographic editor of the *Amherst Student*. In tennis he won the National Junior Indoor Doubles championship in 1928, was runner-up in the New England Intercollegiates in 1930 and 1931, and in his senior year, captained the Amherst team. He was elected to Phi Beta Kappa and received the A.B. degree from Amherst in 1931 with highest honors.

The winner of a Moore fellowship for graduate work in philosophy, Hayes went from Amherst to Yale University in New Haven, Connecticut, where he studied and did three years of laboratory and administrative work as an assistant in psychology at the Institute of Human Relations. His thesis was called "Voters' Attitudes Toward Men and Issues"; he received the Ph.D. degree in 1934 and was elected to Sigma Xi.

He joined his father on the faculty of Mount Holyoke College in 1934. and taught introductory, social and applied psychology there for the next three years. During 1935 he lectured on social psychology at the American International College in Springfield, Massachusetts. Awarded a Social Science Research Council postdoctoral fellowship, Hayes went to the University of Chicago in 1937 and made a special study of the psychological aspects of politico-economic movements. The results of this study were published in a series of four articles in the *Journal of Social Psychology* in 1937 and 1939. His article, "Note on Personality and Family Position" in the *Journal of Applied Psychology* (August, 1938) was based on studies of seventy-six women students at Mount Holyoke.

For two years (1938-1940) Hayes was on the faculty of Sarah Lawrence College in Bronxville, New York, where he taught economics and statistics. Interested also in labor in relation to political attitudes, he wrote the chapter on the psychology of conciliation and arbitration in *Industrial Conflict: A Psychological Interpretation* (Dryden, 1939), edited by G. W. Hartmann and T. Newcomb. While at Sarah Lawrence, he collaborated with a faculty colleague, Willis Fisher, on the paper entitled "Maladjustment in College predicted by Bern-

Department of State

SAMUEL P. HAYES, JR.

reuter Inventory Scores and Family Position" (*Journal of Applied Psychology*, February, 1941).

Dr. Donald A. Laird, in an article published in the Stamford, Connecticut, *Advocate* (February 5, 1941) on the subject of college women, reported Dr. Hayes as having noted that "women are not as consistent as men in their attitudes towards governmental questions" and are "more on the side of international cohesion and socialistic changes than their husbands."

In 1940 Hayes became senior staff member in charge of market and economic research at Young & Rubicam, Inc., in New York City. While he was with this advertising agency, he prepared the article "Potash Prices and Competition" (*Quarterly Journal of Economics*, November, 1942).

He joined the Office of Price Administration in Washington, D.C. in 1942 as associate chief of the service trades branch. The Lend-Lease Administration (later absorbed into the Foreign Economic Administration) sent him to Algiers in 1943 as chief of requirements and distribution on the North African Economic Board. In 1944 he was transferred to London as head requirements officer with the mission for economic affairs, and in 1945 was assigned as a special representative to Norway and Denmark.

Hayes became associate director of marketing and research at Dun & Bradstreet, Inc., in New York City in 1945. While with this firm he became (1946) a member of the editorial committee of the *American Statistician*, contributed the chapter on France to Mordecai Ezekiel's *Towards World Prosperity* (Harper, 1947), and wrote articles for the *Journal of Marketing* and the *Political Science Quarterly*.

Returning to government service in 1948, Hayes was for two years a special assistant to the assistant secretary of state for economic affairs in the U.S. Department of State in Washington, D.C. After President Harry S. Truman had introduced the Point IV plan in January 1949 for technical and other aid to underdeveloped areas abroad, Hayes wrote papers on the subject for several publications, including the *American Statistician*, *Department of State Bulletin*, and *Annals of the American Academy of Political and Social Science*.

He was appointed deputy chief of the U.S. economic survey mission to southeast Asia in 1950, and director of the program planning and advisory staff of the Technical Cooperation Administration in the Department of State in 1950-1951. Then he went to Indonesia in 1951 as chief of the Economic Cooperation Administration's special economic and technical mission. In September 1952 Hayes succeeded Clarence R. Decker as assistant director of the Mutual Security Agency (which absorbed ECA) in charge of the Far East Program.

In a chapter on "Personality and Culture Problems of Point IV" which he wrote in a book edited by Berthold Hoselitz, *The Progress of Underdeveloped Areas* (University of Chicago Press, 1952), Hayes stated that "the administrator of an economic development program must be continually alert to note cultural or psychological resistances and to seek ways around them or, better, to find positive support in existing psychological and cultural traits."

He gave an example of this in reporting a study told by a Point IV agricultural expert who was working in a part of India where wild antelopes were becoming serious pests. As the Indian name (*neilgai*) for these antelopes, means "blue cows," and "as cows are sacred to Hindus, orthodox Hindus would not kill them. . . They were not really cows, however, and a government decree was promulgated changing their name from *neilgai* to *neilghora* (literally, 'blue horses'). Hindus then felt free to shoot them. . . ." Two articles by Hayes appeared in the *New Republic* in May 1954 and were entitled "Anti-Communist . . . but!" in which he stated that U.S. security requires a much more positive foreign economic development program.

"Quite apart from any humanitarian or economic interest in what is happening in [underdeveloped] areas," he wrote, "the political and military interests of the United States require that we understand this unrest and do something about it. If we don't, the Communists *will*. In fact, while we don't, the Communists *are*. . . . If this is a contest we want to win, we can't leave our opponent alone on the field while we wait to be asked to play!" (*New Republic*, May 17, 1954).

He wrote: "Discontent, unrest and change are rife in the undeveloped countries. . . . They are partly a protest against racial inferiority, a rejection of economic, 'exploitation.' They reflect an impatience with low levels of living, and the impact of better communications. In some areas, it has infected only the city-dwellers. In others, it pervades a large part of the population."

The appointment of Hayes as the first director of the Foundation for Research on

Human Behavior was announced on October 17, 1953. The foundation, "a nonprofit corporation which pools contributions from business and other organizations," aims "to increase the scientific knowledge of human behavior, and to promote the use of this knowledge by industry, government and social welfare agencies." A three-year nationwide program includes seminars for organization officials and research personnel, publication of research reports, and experiments in applying new research findings to operations.

Under the direction of Hayes, the research focuses on the "effectiveness of organizations and methods of supervision and administration; the economic motivation and behavior of consumers, employees, investors and businessmen; attitudes and behavior regarding national and international issues; processes of communication, influence and change. . . ."

Samuel Perkins Hayes, Jr. and Alice Mary Cable of Lima, Ohio were married on March 25, 1937 and have a daughter, Susan, and a son, Jonathan. Mrs. Hayes, a violinist, and her husband (whose instrument of choice is now the viola) are members of the organizing committee of the Association of Amateur Chamber Music Players. With his father, Hayes was a runner-up in one of the National Father and Son Tennis Doubles Tournaments.

His clubs are the Cosmos in Washington, D.C., the Yale in New York City, and the Edgemoor Tennis at Bethesda, Maryland. He is a fellow of the American Psychological Association, and a member of the American Economic, American Statistical, and National Planning associations. His political affiliation is with the Democratic party. He is five feet ten inches tall and weighs 175 pounds. He has blue eyes and brown hair.

References

Ann Am Acad 268:35 Mr '50
N Y Times p37 O 18 '53 por
Directory of American Scholars (1951)
Who's Who in America, 1954-55

HAYS, WILL H(ARRISON) Nov. 5, 1879-Mar. 7, 1954 Motion picture executive; first "czar" of the film industry; admitted to Indiana bar (1900); attorney for Sullivan, Indiana (1910-1913); chairman of the Republican National Committee (1918-1921); postmaster general under President Harding (1921-1922); president (1922-1945) and advisor (1945-1950) for the Motion Picture Producers and Distributors of America, Inc.; active in the American Red Cross, Boy Scouts of America and other organizations. See *Current Biography,* (July) 1943.

Obituary

N Y Times p 1+ Mr 8 '54

HEAD, WALTER W(ILLIAM) Dec. 18, 1877-May 3, 1954 Former business executive; former president of Boy Scouts of America; worked his way through a Missouri normal school; teacher and principal in Missouri; began business career as cashier of De Kalb State Bank; appointed state and national bank examiner (1906-1908); vice-president and then president of Omaha National Bank (1917-1929); president of national bank division of American Bankers Association (1923-1924); president of Morris Plan Corporation of America (1931-1933); a founder and president of General American Life Insurance Company of St Louis (1933-1951); president of Boy Scouts (1926-1946); chairman of Missouri War Finance Commission during World War II. See *Current Biography,* (Apr.) 1945.

Obituary

N Y Times p29 My 4 '54

HENNINGS, THOMAS C(AREY), JR. June 25, 1903- United States Senator from Missouri; lawyer

Address: b. c/o Senate Office Bldg., Washington 25, D.C.; Boatman's Bank Bldg., St. Louis, Mo.; h. 2429 Kalorama Rd., N.W., Washington, D.C.; 34 Washington Terr., St. Louis, Mo.

Prominent in the Eighty-third Congress as one of the "liberal" Democrats, Thomas C. Hennings, Jr., senior Senator from Missouri, was an articulate opponent of "McCarthyism." With seventeen other Senators he proposed a "code of fair procedures" for investigating committees in May 1954, which stipulated that witnesses at Congressional hearings should be entitled to counsel, and should be given an opportunity to cross-examine accusers. He was also instrumental in defeating Senator John W. Bricker's amendment which sought to limit the President's treaty-making powers. In January 1954 Hennings was named secretary of the Senate Democratic Conference.

Prior to his election to the Senate in November 1950, Hennings had served in the House of Representatives from 1935 to 1940, and was a circuit attorney in St. Louis. The Senator is presently senior partner of Green, Hennings, Henry, and Evans, a St. Louis law firm.

Thomas Carey Hennings, Jr. was born on June 25, 1903 in St. Louis, Missouri to Sarah P. (Wilson) and Thomas Carey Hennings, an attorney. His mother is a descendant of Dr. Antoine Poullaine, a physician to the Marquis de Lafayette, who settled in Georgia. Tom attended public grade school and Soldan High School. He was a page at the 1916 Democratic national convention.

After being graduated from high school in 1920, Tom attended Cornell University, Ithaca, New York, where he was a member of the track team and Delta Kappa Epsilon. He received the A.B. degree in 1924, and entered the School of Law, Washington University in St. Louis. Young Hennings was graduated with the LL.B. degree in 1926. Admitted to the Missouri bar in that year, he joined a St. Louis law firm.

His first government position was that of assistant circuit attorney for St. Louis from 1929 to 1934. Outgrowing "a reputation as a

THOMAS C. HENNINGS, JR.

playboy" (*U.S. News & World Report,* November 17, 1950), Hennings made an impressive record as a prosecutor. During this period he lectured on criminal jurisprudence at Benton College of Law in St. Louis. He was appointed a colonel on the staff of the Governor of Missouri in 1932.

The Democratic party of the Eleventh Congressional District of Missouri nominated Hennings as their candidate for the U.S. House of Representatives in 1934; he was elected in November. During his three consecutive terms in the House, Hennings supported the Administration's policies on the floor and as a member of the Foreign Affairs Committee. In July 1940 he submitted a bill to permit children from Great Britain to be brought to this country in American vessels.

The Congressman resigned from the House in December 1940 to become a candidate for circuit attorney in St. Louis and was unopposed for both the nomination and election. In the summer of 1941, he was called from the U.S. Naval Reserve to active duty as a lieutenant commander. He was assigned to Puerto Rico as the naval aide to then Governor Rexford Guy Tugwell. Later he served in Washington and the Pacific Theater. Because of "physical disability incurred in the line of duty," he reverted to inactive status in 1944, and returned to his position of circuit attorney.

After Senator Harry S. Truman was nominated as the Democratic vice-presidential candidate in 1944, "the late FDR recommended that Tom Hennings take Truman's place," wrote Drew Pearson (Washington *Post,* January 14, 1951). "But Truman wanted his senatorial shoes filled by . . . Frank Parks Briggs." Hennings, in 1945, was named by the Truman administration, at the request of Paul V. McNutt, then High Commissioner of the Philippines, as a special assistant to then Attorney General Tom Clark to investigate "collaborationist" activities in the Philippines.

In 1950 Hennings decided to oppose Senator Forrest C. Donnell, a Republican, for re-election. At a news conference on January 5, 1950, President Truman told reporters that he would like the Democrats to nominate Emery Allison, president pro tem of the Missouri State Senate. Subsequently, the state CIO, the Governor, and the mayor of St. Louis supported Allison.

The decisive factor in the primary campaign was opposition to a new city charter proposed for St. Louis. City voters turned out in record numbers for the primary, and carried Hennings to victory over Allison by only 3,301 votes.

In the ensuing campaign Hennings endorsed most of Truman's record and program, although he opposed the (Charles F.) Brannan farm plan and compulsory-health insurance. On November 7, 1950, he defeated Donnell by approximately 93,000 votes, being the only Democratic candidate for the Senate to unseat a Republican.

When the Eighty-second Congress convened in January 1951, Hennings was assigned to the Committee on Public Works and on Rules and Administration. He also served on a subcommittee which upheld in August 1951 the seating of John Marshall Butler as Senator from Maryland but denounced the methods used to defeat Butler's opponent, former Senator Millard E. Tydings. The subcommittee's report was approved by the Rules and Administration Committee on August 8, 1951.

In the fall of 1951 Hennings was assigned to a subcommittee to consider the resolution of William Benton, then Senator from Connecticut, calling for the expulsion of Senator Joseph R. McCarthy of Wisconsin from the Senate. After McCarthy had asked Hennings to "disqualify himself" from the subcommittee, on the grounds that one of his law partners had consented to serve as counsel for a Communist, and that his firm represented the St. Louis *Post Dispatch* (which was editorially critical of McCarthy's methods), Hennings accused McCarthy of "distortion and deceit" in an effort to divert attention from the move to oust him (Washington *Post,* September 22, 1951).

During 1951 the Senator cast his vote to increase taxes by 5.5 billion dollars; against cutting government civil pay rolls by 10 per cent; for cutting the annual leave of federal employees; against an amendment limiting public housing to 5,000 units; against the authorization of rent increases up to 37 per cent of 1943; for UMT and the extension of the draft; against reduction of appropriations for the armed forces from sixty-one billion dollars to fifty-five billion dollars; and against an absolute ban on Allied trade with the Soviet bloc.

In the 1952 session he favored giving power to the President to seize the steel plants; using the Taft-Hartley act in steel strikes; and the extension of the Defense Production Act, and against reinstating the cheese embargo amendment of the Defense Production Act.

He opposed the tidelands oil bill; the abolition of RFC; and cutting T.V.A. appropriations by $46,000,000.

In the Eighty-third Congress, Hennings was assigned to the Judiciary, and Rules and Administration Committees, and also served on the Minority Policy Committee. Serving on a subcommittee of the Judiciary Committee in 1953, charged with studying juvenile delinquency, Hennings participated in hearings to determine the influence of the "horror" comic books.

On August 17, 1954 Hennings cautioned the courts against adopting a "get tough" policy against teenage delinquents, and suggested the "treatment" approach which he believes has never really been attempted because of insufficient funds.

With Carl T. Hayden of Arizona and Robert C. Hendrickson of New Jersey, he sponsored in June 1953 a bill to amend the Federal Corrupt Practices Act in order to bring political primaries and party conventions under Federal regulation, and to increase the ceiling on spending of the national committees for one calendar year from $3,000,000 to $10,000,000.

His 1953 voting record indicates that he supported an amendment designating Federal revenues from outer shelf offshore areas to the support of education; selling twenty-eight synthetic rubber plants owned by the Federal government; increasing soil conservation appropriations from $195,000,000 to $225,000,000; he favored retaining benefits granted to women by law in a constitutional amendment giving equality under the law to both sexes; an amendment to use foreign aid to cut farm surpluses; and opposed an amendment calling for pressuring France to grant full self-government to Indochina. On June 16 he criticized "book-burning" (removing books from overseas libraries).

Votes cast by Hennings in 1954 were for the St. Lawrence seaway (January); against the Bricker amendment (February); for the one billion dollars excise tax cut (March); for Hawaii and Alaska statehood (April); against a constitutional amendment to limit the Supreme Court permanently to nine members (May); against a constitutional amendment which would lower the voting age to eighteen (May); against the atomic energy bill (July); for an amendment by Senator Hubert H. Humphrey, Democrat of Minnesota, to make membership in the Communist party a crime (August).

The Senator is a member of the American, Missouri and St. Louis bar associations, American Judicature Society, Cornell Law Association, and Phi Delta Phi (law) fraternity. He is a director of the Navy League, Urban League, Big Brothers of America, Inc., Missouri Association for Social Hygiene; and a member of the Missouri Social Welfare League, University Investment Syndicate, St. Louis Chamber of Commerce, American Legion, Veterans of Foreign Wars; and a trustee of the Missouri Historical Society.

His clubs are the Missouri Athletic, Cornell, Jefferson, University and Noonday in St. Louis; National Press and Burning Tree in Washington; and Cornell and Mexico Pilgrims in New York.

Senator Hennings' first marriage was to Josephine Silva Halpin, a St. Louis radio announcer. In 1949 he married Elizabeth Stallcup; the couple has two daughters, Sue and Karla. The Senator is over six feet tall, weighs 175 pounds, and has broad shoulders and blue eyes. He is a Presbyterian. The Central College of Fayette, Missouri conferred the LL.D. degree on him in 1954.

In a speech in Valley Forge, Pennsylvania, Hennings said that "when a public official not only boasts of his own violations of law but encourages employees of the U.S. government to violate their oaths of office as well . . . the Democrats . . . cannot shift the responsibility to the Republicans on the ground that it is solely their problem. And the Republicans can no longer indulge in the luxury of appeasement at any price" (New York *Times,* June 14, 1954).

References

Christian Sci Mon p6 Ag 3 '50
Time 39:12 Je 15 '42
U S News 29:46+ N 17 '50
Washington (D.C.) Post p3B N 26 '50 por

Biographical Directory of the American Congress, 1774-1949 (1950)
Congressional Directory (1954)
International World Who's Who, 1948-49
Who's Who in America, 1954-55
World Biography (1954)

HEPBURN, AUDREY May 4, 1929- Actress

Address: b. c/o Paramount Pictures Corp., Paramount Bldg., 1501 Broadway, New York 36

At the age of twenty-two, Audrey Hepburn reached stardom after her first performance in her first role on the dramatic stage. The time was November 24, 1951, the place Broadway, and the occasion was her portrayal of the title role in *Gigi,* a play adapted by Anita Loos from a short novel by the late French writer, Colette.

Twenty-one months after this dramatic triumph, Miss Hepburn was starred in her first American-made motion picture, *Roman Holiday,* which opened on August 27, 1953 at Radio City Music Hall. For her role in this film she received the 1953 Academy of Motion Picture Arts and Sciences award ("Oscar"). She made her next Broadway appearance with Mel Ferrer in *Ondine,* a play by Jean Giraudoux, adapted by Maurice Valency, which opened on February 18, 1954. The play won an Antoinette Perry ("Tony") award.

Named the best movie actress of 1953 by the New York Film Critics and *Film Daily,* Miss Hepburn received these awards within six years

AUDREY HEPBURN

of the time she began her professional career as a member of the chorus in a London musical show.

Audrey Hepburn was born in Brussels, Belgium on May 4, 1929. Her father, J. A. Hepburn-Ruston, was a businessman, of English and Irish ancestry. Her mother, Ella van Heemstra, is a Dutch Baroness. Their marriage was terminated by divorce when Audrey was ten. She has two older half-brothers. Her grandfather, Baron Arnoud van Heemstra, was at one time the Governor of Surinam (Dutch Guiana).

Audrey Hepburn was attending a boarding school in England when World War II broke out in 1939. Her mother, thinking that England was unsafe, took her to Arnhem, Holland, but the German armies swarmed into Holland in May 1940.

As a consequence, mother and daughter endured the hunger, deprivation and terror resulting from the occupation. Audrey saw one of her brothers dragged away to a Nazi labor camp. Her uncle and cousin were executed. She herself escaped from Nazi officers who were forcing youngsters to work in their kitchens. During this period, however, she attended school, and took her first ballet lessons in Arnhem. She took part in furtive amateur shows given to raise money for the Dutch underground.

After the war, she studied ballet in Amsterdam and then, in 1948, she returned to England where she enrolled in Marie Rambert's ballet school. She "tried out" for a part in the English production of the musical show, *High Button Shoes,* and receiving an assignment in the chorus, was started on her professional career. She next secured a small part in the revue *Sauce Tartare,* and subsequently in *Sauce Piquante,* a show in which she did a solo dance. She was seen by Mario Zampi who selected her for a part in *Laughter in Paradise;* this was her first appearance in motion pictures. Then came another small role in *One Wild Oat,* followed by a bit in the *Lavender Hill Mob.*

Her next film engagements were in the *Young Wives' Tale,* which was again only a small part, and in the *Secret People.* During this period, Audrey Hepburn studied dramatics under Felix Aylmer, a British actor who had at one time coached Charles Laughton.

Cast for another motion picture role in *Nous Irons à Monte Carlo,* Audrey Hepburn was with the film company in Monte Carlo where the picture was being shot in both French and English. The French novelist, Colette, told the story in the *American Weekly* (March 23, 1952): "She [Miss Hepburn] was there with a group of cinema people, led by Ray Ventura, the European orchestra leader and producer . . . the moment I saw her I could not take my eyes away. 'There,' I said to myself incredulously, 'is Gigi!' . . . That afternoon I offered her the part in the Broadway play."

In an article in *Theatre Arts* (July 1952), Gilbert Miller, the Broadway producer, told how he had been searching for a young actress who would meet the requirements of the title role in *Gigi.* Anita Loos, the adapter of *Gigi* received a letter from Maurice Goudeket, Colette's husband, which told of Colette having seen Miss Hepburn and being immediately convinced that this was the girl for the part. Miller related that later ". . . we named her for our Gigi—a young actress whom we had never seen on a stage, indeed, a young actress whose two years' stage experience had been confined to dancing bits in topical revues."

Gigi, directed by Raymond Rouleau with scenery by Raymond Sovey, was presented at the Fulton Theatre in November 1951 by Gilbert Miller. It deals with a young Parisian girl of 1900. In the New York *Times* (November 26, 1951), Brooks Atkinson commented: "Audrey Hepburn [is] a young actress of charm, honesty and talent . . . as Gigi she develops a full-length character from artless gaucheries in the first act to a stirring climax in the last scene. It is a fine piece of sustained acting that is spontaneous, lucid, and captivating."

Walter F. Kerr wrote in the New York *Herald Tribune,* that Audrey Hepburn "brings a candid innocence and a tomboy intelligence to a part that might have gone sticky, and her performance comes as a breath of fresh air in a stifling season." William Hawkins in the New York *World-Telegram and Sun* observed "Audrey Hepburn in the title role has unquestionable beauty and talent . . . and acts with grace and authority, if in this case without much relaxation." A reviewer for the *New Yorker* said that Audrey Hepburn "is nearly perfect as Gigi." The play enjoyed a long run on Broadway, and later went on tour for eight months.

Previous to Miss Hepburn's arrival in New York to appear in *Gigi,* she had been given a screen test by film director William Wyler, with the result that when the play closed she worked in Rome under his direction and under contract to Paramount Pictures Corporation. In August 1953 the film, *Roman Holiday,* opened in New York with Miss Hepburn playing the role of a princess of a mythical kingdom who goes on an escapade with an American newspaper man (played by Gregory Peck) through the highways and byways of Rome.

Of her acting in her first American-made motion picture, a reviewer in the New York *Times* wrote that "she is a slender, elfin and wistful beauty, alternately regal and childlike in her profound appreciation of newly-found, simple pleasures and love." Paul V. Beckley in the New York *Herald Tribune* reported: "A remarkable young actress . . . carries off the finale with a nicety that leaves one a little haunted."

Audrey Hepburn is five feet seven inches tall and weighs about 120 pounds. She has brown hair, brown eyes, and a slim figure. As pets, she prefers birds and poodles. In referring to her own work, Miss Hepburn has said, "I'm halfway between a dancer and an actress. I've got a lot to learn."

Miss Hepburn was married on September 25, 1954 to actor Mel Ferrer in Burgenstock, Switzerland.

References

Am W p10+ Mr 23 '52 por
Life 35:127+ D 7 '53 pors
N Y Herald Tribune IV p2 D 9 '51 por
N Y Post Mag p5 O 18 '53 por
N Y World-Telegram p3 O 27 '51 pors
New Yorker 27:32 D 8 '51
Time 62:60+ S 7 '53 pors
Washington (D.C.) Post p9+ Mr 9 '52 por
Motion Picture and Television Almanac, 1953-54

HERBERT, ELIZABETH SWEENEY

Aug. 22, 1899- Organization official; editor; home economist

Address: b. c/o McCall's Magazine, 230 Park Ave., New York 17; h. 1918 James St., Syracuse, N.Y.

American homemakers are the professional concern of Mrs. Elizabeth Sweeney Herbert, who was installed as president of the American Home Economics Association in June 1952 and who has been household equipment editor of *McCall's* magazine since 1944. As a woman who manages both a business career and a home, Mrs. Herbert sets a clear example of the dual role possible for women today.

Elizabeth Sweeney was born on August 22, 1899 at Clifton Springs, New York, the eldest of three children of John Edward and Elizabeth (Kelley) Sweeney. She attended primary and secondary public schools at Clifton Springs. Enrolling in the College of Home Economics, Syracuse University, she received a B.S. degree, *magna cum laude,* in 1942, and received her M.S. degree in 1947. She joined the staff of *McCall's* magazine as editor of household equipment in 1944.

She was an assistant professor of foods and nutrition for two years, and of household technology for four years at Syracuse University, while she was doing graduate work. Additional experience as home service director of the New York State Properties Associated Gas and Electric System further widened her experience in the home economics field.

The problems of women as exclusively homemakers and the more complicated situations when they are both home maker and outside worker, require expert advice on the one hand and efficient scheduling and equipment on the other. Mrs. Herbert, in speeches and articles, clarifies these problems to a notable degree. Speaking before the Twelfth Annual Congress on Industrial Health in Pittsburgh on January 19, 1952 she outlined the motivations for combining two careers, suggesting the need for economic gain as well as outside stimulation.

She pointed out, however, that such gains and stimulation intensify the housewife's problems, for with the division of her time and energy, she must plan to have adequate time for her husband and children and proper equipment to effect good management on a tight schedule. A clarification of the elements that comprise good management and proper equipment requires the counsel of home economics experts.

Mrs. Herbert said of the home economist employed by business or industry that "she must be . . . able to adjust to constantly changing situations and people. Alertness, resourcefulness, and imagination are essential, for she must be able to originate and develop for successful use ideas that are practical yet new and unusual" (*Journal of Home Economics,* June, 1952). The home economist in a business organization must explain the needs of the consumer of the company's products to management, and must also advise the consumer. That this responsibility has been fulfilled is evidenced by the growing employment of home economists in industry.

In her position as household equipment editor of *McCall's* magazine, Mrs. Herbert writes a series called "This is How I Keep House." She gathers material for these articles by flying to many part of the country to interview typical couples who are keeping house under varying circumstances. She lists laundry and grocery shopping as the biggest problems, but believes they can be solved with ownership of automatic washers and deep freezers. Her approach is always practical in nature. In discussing recipes she points out how much easier it would be to include a suggestion of the equipment needed.

During the immediate postwar years, she had the narration and production responsibility for five moving picture "shorts" made for *McCall's* magazine. These demonstrated the proficiency gained by the proper use of household equipment and elucidated the problems in home management.

When proposed budget cuts by the administration threatened the program for vocational home economics education, Mrs. Herbert appeared before the House of Representatives' subcommittee on appropriations for the Department of Health, Education and Welfare in April 1953 to plead for a restoration of funds.

(Continued next page)

ELIZABETH SWEENEY HERBERT

She told the committee that Federal support of vocational home economics has meant establishment of such departments in thousands of high schools, has created strong teacher education programs, has brought closer relationships between home and school and has furthered programs of adult education. Rather than retrenchment, she argued that "the current need is plainly for a stronger program of vocational home economics for girls, boys and adults."

When the United States National Commission for the United Nations Educational, Scientific and Cultural Organization met in January 1952, Mrs. Herbert represented the American Home Economics Association in a consideration of problems relating to the international organization. Among the subjects discussed at the conference were the needs of coordination of the domestic program with international programs and beginning instructive techniques at the "grass roots" level.

When Mrs. Herbert was voted the most outstanding woman in the field of home economics for the year 1952 by a poll taken by the women's department of the Syracuse (New York) *Herald American,* the honor simply crystallized her continuing progressive activities. These have included such affiliations as equipment committee chairman of the American Home Economics Association and chairman of the program-of-work committee.

She is past president of the New York State Home Economics Association and represented her association on the council and consumer goods committee of the American Standards Association. When she was named vice-chairman for home economics on the 4-H Clubs' Builders' Council in 1951, Mrs. Herbert took still another step in the widening arc of related fields. She was elected by the board of trustees of Cornell University in June 1953, as a member of the council for the New York State College of Home Economics for a three-year term. The most recent recognition of her talents was her appointment as a member of the advisory committee of Pratt Institute in Brooklyn, New York. The home economist is a member of Omicron Nu, Pi Lambda Theta and Phi Kappa Phi.

The American Home Economics Association which Mrs. Herbert heads has headquarters in Washington, D.C. and represents about 20,000 home economists. Mrs. Herbert sent a letter to Secretary of Agriculture Ezra Taft Benson because her members had been "unable to find out what was happening to [the Bureau of Human Nutrition and Home Economics] the one unit in the Government set up to do research in behalf of 33,000,000 homemakers." She particularly asked Secretary Benson in view of "the prestige that the Bureau has earned over the years" that its name should not be changed. She noted that more than 146,000,000 copies of its publications had been distributed in the past thirty years (New York *Times,* October 26, 1953).

On January 29, 1949 she married Dr. Leo J. Herbert and it is to their home in Syracuse, New York she commutes on alternate weeks in order to fulfill her twin roles of professional woman and homemaker. The *Christian Science Monitor* described Mrs. Herbert as "a smiling, gray-eyed blonde, who feels deeply that child care and family relations should be a must in the education of all young people." To this can be added her own observation that "Women themselves do not place a high enough value on training for their jobs as homemakers." She states that her particular hobby is gardening.

Reference

Christian Sci Mon p6 Jl 3 '53

HERBERT, MRS. LEO J. *See* Herbert, E. S.

HERBLOCK, *See* Block, H. L.

HIGGINS, DANIEL PAUL Sept. 12, 1886-Dec. 26, 1953 Architect; youth leader; entered architectural firm of John Russell Pope (1905), became a partner (1922); formed Eggers & Higgins (1937); worked on designs for Constitution Hall, National Gallery of Art, numerous prisons, hospitals, homes, embassies, college buildings, housing projects; chairman of board of Catholic Youth Organization; member of Board of Education of New York City; and member of boards of Boys' Club of America, Police Athletic League, Madison Square Boys' Club, and Boy Scouts of America. See *Current Biography,* (Dec.) 1950.

Obituary

N Y Times p60 D 27 '53

HILLARY, SIR EDMUND (PERCIVAL) *See* Hunt, Sir (H. C.) J.; Hillary, Sir E. (P.); and Tenzing Norkey

HITCHCOCK, CHARLES B(AKER) Mar. 16, 1906- Organization executive; geographer; explorer

Address: b. c/o American Geographical Society, 156th St. & Broadway, New York 32; h. R.F.D. 5, Ridgefield, Conn.

"The process of map making is a never-ending job" in the opinion of Charles B. Hitchcock, director of the American Geographical Society which maintains over 250,000 maps—the world's largest collection. The Boston-born geographer, trained as a geomorphologist at Harvard and Columbia universities, has spent much time in the field as an explorer and a cartographer, particularly in Venezuela. He became director of the society in September 1953 after serving for twenty-three years in various posts of the society.

The American Geographical Society co-ordinated the observations of the solar eclipse on June 30, 1954 made by United States and foreign scientists, the U.S. Air Force and the U.S. Naval Observatory. For almost a year before the eclipse, the society sent reconnaissance teams to determine the best observation sites and planned for the provision of necessary equipment. The observations were taken at ten "stations" strung out from Canada to Iran; as the moon's shadow swept past, each observatory determined the instant of totality, i.e., the time when the moon was centered in front of the sun. "If such calculations were not made, the error of fitting the North Atlantic to missile warfare would increase about ten times" (*Time*, May 17, 1954).

Among recent achievements announced by the American Geographical Society (whose 4,000 members are aided by the society's technical maps and data) were the finding of the elusive and mysterious headwaters of the Orinoco River in December 1951 by Dr. José M. Cruxent; of two 8,000-foot sandstone mountains in Venezuela by William H. Phelps, Jr., in February 1954; and the ruined Inca city of Cahuamarca, Peru by Victor Von Hagen in May 1954.

Born on March 16, 1906 in Boston, Massachusetts, Charles Baker Hitchcock is the son of John and Esther Mary (Baker) Hitchcock. With the example of several relatives before him, he specialized in geology at Harvard University where he received the A.B. degree in 1928. He received the M.A. degree from Columbia University in 1933.

Hitchcock's training in geomorphology was supplemented with practical experience in the field in 1929 when he joined a reconnaissance expedition to the mountains of southwest Venezuela under the auspices of the American Museum of Natural History. While the other members of the group collected natural history specimens, Hitchcock made maps of the area and acquired experience that was to serve him well in his later expeditions to the back country of Venezuela.

Upon his return to the United States in 1930, Hitchcock was brought into the staff of the American Geographical Society by its director, the late Isaiah Bowman, who in-

CHARLES B. HITCHCOCK

fluenced him to make geography his lifework. Thus began a long association with the society.

This famous society (not to be confused with the National Geographic Society of Washington, D.C.) was founded in 1852. Among its purposes, according to its amended charter of April 8, 1871, are "the collection and diffusion of geographical, statistical, and scientific knowledge, by lectures, printed publications, or other means"; and the permanent establishment in the City of New York of an institution for supplying such information for public uses.

Since its founding, the society has helped Peary, Mikkelsen, Stefansson, Byrd, Wilkins, Ellsworth, Mawson, and Ronne, all polar explorers, as well as explorers of South and Central America. During World War I, it lent maps of Europe to the United States government, because the War Department then had little cartographic material. The society supplied the maps which aided in the invasion of North Africa during World War II.

The geographer was assigned to assist in the preparation of the 107-sheet "Millionth Map" of Hispanic America which had been started in 1920. Appointed head of the department of Hispanic American research in 1938, he assumed direction of this map project which was completed in 1945. Considered to be "the best integrated and most accurate map of that continent" (*Britannica Book of the Year*, 1952), it marks a milestone in Hispanic-American cartography, and shows the entire continent on a scale of one inch to sixteen miles. It has been used in the settlement of a number of international boundary disputes. This map was later reduced to the scale of 1:5,000,000 and presented as a bipolar oblique conic conformal projection.

Hitchcock has served the American Geographical Society as assistant director, 1943-1948; acting director, 1949; chairman of the

HITCHCOCK, CHARLES B.—*Continued*

advisory committee on American cartography, 1948 to the present; and member of its Research and Development Board, 1949. As executive secretary, 1950-1953, he forcefully presented to the public and the society's members the valuable character of the work of the society and the need for financial assistance to continue and expand its services.

He warned that lack of funds would reduce the society to "intellectual bankruptcy" which he identified with the purely custodial functions of maintaining its maps, 3,000 atlases, and its 130,000-volume library. Unless financing were secured, he said, the society's medical geography program, ice field research, Latin American surveys, map making, and publication of a monthly geographical bibliography and the *Geographical Review,* its scholarly quarterly, would have to be discontinued (New York *Herald Tribune,* March 2, 1952).

Hitchcock's work for the society was recognized in August 1953 when he was appointed its director to succeed George H. T. Kimble who had resigned. At this time, it was said that Hitchcock's "broad concept of geography" had been a "driving force in the society's researches in disease, climate, natural resources, population potential, and land use."

The society's "World Atlas of Disease," now in preparation, will contain about twenty-five maps showing the world distribution of all major diseases. Its Juneau ice field research project on glacial fluctuations and their relation to climactic conditions in Alaska is directed by the society under contract with the U.S. Office of Naval Research and in cooperation with the U.S. Army, Air Force, and Forest Service.

Continuing his interest in the Venezuela back country after his first trip there, Hitchcock returned to the uncharted Orinoco River country on the expeditions of William H. Phelps, Jr., in 1947, 1948, 1949, and 1951. The society furnished Dr. José M. Cruxent, director of the Natural Sciences Museum in Caracas, Venezuela, who was looking for the source of the Orinoco River, with a composite map based on the data given by the earlier Rice, Dickey, and De Oliviera expeditions. Dr. Cruxent was able to send in late 1951 the following cablegram to Hitchcock: "Greetings from the headwaters of the Orinoco" (*Scholastic,* February 13, 1953).

On January 30, 1953, Hitchcock and Phelps left Caracas, Venezuela, to explore a remote area in the Sierra de Perijá Mountains on the border of Colombia and Venezuela. They were seeking for the undiscovered headwaters of the Macoita and Aponcito rivers. Unfortunately, the desertion of their porters (because of the cold weather) forced them to return without completing their mission, although they could report to the Venezuelan government that some of the riparian land was unfit for farming.

Hitchcock was the United States delegate to the International Geographical Congress at Amsterdam, Holland (1938), and to meetings of the Pan American Institute of Geography and History at Lima (1941), Caracas (1946), Buenos Aires (1948), Santiago (1950), and the Dominican Republic (1952). He is an honorary member of the Sociedad Venezolana de Ciencias Naturales, and a corresponding member of the Sociedad Geográfica de Lima.

He belongs to the Association of American Geographers (he was treasurer in 1948-1949), the Arctic Institute of North America, New York Academy of Sciences, and the American Association for the Advancement of Science. He is a member of the Explorers Club of New York City. He contributed a chapter to Louise A. Boyd's *The Fiord Region of East Greenland* (American Geographical Society, 1935), and has written articles for technical publications.

On December 3, 1931 Hitchcock married Agnes Murchie; they have three daughters: Gail, Suzanne, and Esther Lee. Hitchcock has blue eyes and gray-brown hair. He is five feet eleven inches tall and weighs 190 pounds. In June 1954 he was awarded an honorary Doctor of Science degree from Temple University, Philadelphia, Pennsylvania.

References

N Y Times p27 F 26 '53; p43 Ag 30 '53 por
Scholastic 60:6 F 13 '52 por
American Men of Science (1949)
Who's Who in America, 1954-55

HOBBS, LEONARD S(INCLAIR) Dec. 20, 1896- Business executive; engineer

Address: b. United Aircraft Corp., 400 Main St., E. Hartford 8, Conn., h. 36 Norwood Rd., W. Hartford, Conn.

One of aviation's highest awards—the Collier Trophy—was awarded in 1953 to Leonard S. Hobbs whose "daring gamble" produced the J-57 split-compressor turbojet engine, main power source of America's new giant bombers and supersonic fighters. Known in aviation circles as "Luke" Hobbs, he has been associated with Pratt & Whitney Aircraft since 1927, and is vice-president for engineering of the United Aircraft Corporation. Shortly after World War II Hobbs headed a team of hundreds of specialists who developed the J-57 which is now "the most powerful aircraft power plant in the world" (*Collier's,* December 25, 1953).

It has been estimated that some 1,400,000 hours of design effort were spent developing this J-57 gas turbine, the world's first engine to be put into production in the 10,000-pound thrust class. It was laid down in 1948, and in April 1952 it powered the Boeing B-52 on its first test flight. In its first application as a fighter power-plant, the J-57 drove North American Aviation Corporation's F-100 Super Sabre through the air at supersonic speeds in level flight—the first conventional aircraft in history to achieve that performance. Hobbs is also known for his work on the development of the modern aircraft carburetor dating back to 1923, and the lead-silver-indium bearing known in the trade as the "Hobbs bearing".

Leonard Sinclair Hobbs was born on December 20, 1896 in Carbon, Wyoming, a boisterous mining town, now not only completely abandoned, but so obliterated by wind and sagebrush that it no longer appears on any map or in any postal guide. His father, Charles Sinclair Hobbs, was a civil engineer and contractor, and his mother was the former Lillie Mae Amos. Construction was booming all through the West, and the Hobbs family was constantly on the move as the elder Hobbs worked on railroads, surveyed the Montana-Canadian border, and laid out innumerable towns, some of which have disappeared and others of which are now thriving communities. Hobbs remembers his father pointing to a flat sweep of Texas plain and saying "Here's where we are going to build the town of Harlingen"—which by 1950 had over 23,000 inhabitants. Hobbs recalls that he grew up knowing there were only two classes of men: those who resolved their differences by court action, and those who resorted to guns and knives. The family settled down in Brownsville, Texas, where he attended high school, graduating before he was fifteen. He then attended the Agricultural and Mechanical College of Texas, and received his B.S. degree in 1916.

LEONARD S. HOBBS

Awarded a Fellowship at the Kansas State College, he studied there the following year and became an instructor. In World War I, Hobbs served as a lieutenant of engineers in the 42nd (Rainbow) Division. Returning in 1919, he resumed his studies at Kansas State and was awarded his Master of Science degree in 1920.

His first job was as a civilian experimental engineer for the Army Air Corps at McCook Field. At the end of World War I the United States found itself third in air power, and a vigorous effort was being made to develop new planes and engines. During his three years there (1920-23), Hobbs received a fundamental grounding in engine design, working with, among others, the late George Jackson Mead, who designed the Wasp Engine.

It was also during his stay at McCook Field that Hobbs acquired the name "Luke" by which he is known chiefly today among his friends. There was a comic strip character popular during that period known as Luke McGlook, who wasn't given to much serious effort, and since Hobbs was always absorbed in his work, dubbing him "Luke" amused people, and the name stuck. In 1923 Hobbs joined the Stromberg Motor Devices Company, where he did important work on the aircraft carburetor.

In 1927 he joined Pratt & Whitney as a research engineer, and has been with this company in one capacity or another ever since. Today he is vice-president for engineering of the Pratt & Whitney Aircraft Division of United Aircraft Corporation. Among the projects, on which he again worked with George Mead, was Pratt & Whitney's radial air-cooled engine, which was advanced to a point at which its horsepower was doubled. Hobbs also developed the R-2000 engine for the Douglas DC-4 transport which did an important job in World War II. During 1936 Hobbs conducted a year of almost round-the-clock investigation, developing the lead-silver-indium bearing, frequently known in the trade as the "Hobbs bearing".

Describing the development of the J-57 for Pratt & Whitney, Hobbs said (*Collier's*, December 25, 1953), "[It was] a big gamble. We faced a mighty tough situation. Not only were we five years behind the other companies, but some of them could draw on years of experience in the steam-turbine field. We were running a poor race. We decided that it would not be enough to match their designs, that to get back in the race we would have to 'leapfrog' them—come up with something far in advance of what they were thinking about."

At that time jet engines in service had power ratings of about a 4,000-pound thrust; but Hobbs decided to design an engine of 10,000-pound thrust, which could be used in supersonic fighters. After three years of intensive work the first workable engine was built, and in 1952 it passed its Air Force qualification test on schedule—one of the few experimental engines in history to do so.

As for his part in the development of the J-57, Hobbs says, "No man can claim credit for a project such as this. It took the combined efforts of a great many people: Andy Willgoos, who headed up the early research work; Wright Parkins, Pratt and Whitney's engineering manager, who took over after Andy's death, and 1,500 Pratt and Whitney engineers."

In *Aviation Week* (May 17, 1954), Hobbs traced briefly the history of aircraft jet engine development. He stated that in 1921 the Frenchman M. Guillaume was granted a patent on a jet turbine-propelled airplane, and that it was not until May 15, 1941 that Sir Frank Whittle's jet engine was first used. The actual first flight was "the German Heinkel jet turbine-propelled airplane on August 27, 1939." He does not think that the Russians who claim credit for "firsts" in connection with jet airplanes have

HOBBS, LEONARD S.—*Continued*

offered any valid evidence to prove their claim. As explained by James J. Haggerty, Jr. in *Collier's* (December 25, 1953), "All engines prior to the J-57 had single-compressor units. At normal speeds they operated satisfactorily. But a jet engine cannot operate at a constant speed, and when the single compressor turned slower or faster than its optimum, its power dropped and its rate of fuel consumption increased. The duel-compressor system in the J-57 consists of two units . . . each has a different design optimum, and each can work at its own most efficient speed, independently of the other. The engine therefore can operate efficiently over a wide choice of speeds. . . ."

The Collier Trophy, donated in 1911 by the late Robert J. Collier, editor and son of the founder of *Collier's* magazine, is awarded annually. The massive trophy which is the work of sculptor Ernest Wise Keyser, remains in the custody of the National Aeronautic Association. Hobbs received a miniature replica which was presented by President Eisenhower on December 17, 1953, at a dinner given in celebration of the fiftieth anniversary of man's first powered flight by the Wright brothers at Kitty Hawk.

Installed in a North American YF-100 Super Sabre, Leonard Hobbs's J-57 indeed justified all the excitement on October 29, 1953. In a trial over the flat sand bed of California's Salton Sea, it attained a speed of 754.98 miles an hour. While research aircraft have gone faster, this engine set a new world's record for this course. The J-57 is a turbojet which on that flight produced the equivalent of 40,000 horsepower.

Leonard Hobbs has studied the engine and its history from Heron of Alexandria, the Greek physicist who built the first "jet" engine in the third century A.D., through Watt and Lenoir, down to the present. This has taken him into the study of military campaigns in Europe, and our own Civil War. When he can find the time, Hobbs plays golf (shooting between 85 and 90) with Frank Caldwell, United Aircraft's research director, who won his Collier Trophy in 1933 for the development of the controllable-pitch propeller. "I'm sure Luke Hobbs has figured out all the mathematical angles of the golf swing," Caldwell said.

"Luke" Hobbs is of medium height, weighs 165 pounds, has grey eyes and light brown hair. He was married to Idamae (Achue) Hobbs on November 8, 1926. He is a Fellow of the Institute of Aeronautical Sciences, received the Certificate of Merit in 1948, and was elected an honorary member of Tau Beta Pi in 1953. He is a member of the Farmington (Connecticut) Country Club, and the Hartford (Connecticut) Golf Club.

References

Aviation W 60:34 My 17 '54 por
Collier's 132:28 D 25 '53 por
Time 62:47+ D 21 '53 por

Who's Who in America, 1954-55
Who's Who in Commerce and Industry (1953)
World Biography (1954)

HOEY, CLYDE R(OARK) Dec. 11, 1877-May 12, 1954 United States Senator from North Carolina; was publisher of Shelby *Star* (1894-1908); in state House of Representatives (1899-1902); elected state senator (1902); appointed assistant U.S. attorney (1913-1919); elected to Congress (1919); Governor (1937-1941); served in U.S. Senate since 1945; as chairman of permanent subcommittee on investigations studied "5-per centers" and RFC. See *Current Biography,* (Oct.) 1949.

Obituary

N Y Times p29 My 13 '54

HOLDEN, WILLIAM Apr. 17, 1918- Motion picture actor

Address: b. c/o Paramount Studios, Hollywood, Calif.; h. Hidden Village, San Fernando, Calif.

Cast repeatedly as "the nice-looking young man next door," William Holden has recently played more varied roles in pictures. On March 25, 1954 he was presented with the Academy of Motion Picture Arts and Sciences award as the best male screen actor of 1953. The award is one of the "Oscars" conferred annually for distinguished achievement, and is a result of a poll of 13,000 workers in the film industry.

The academy selected Holden for his acting in *Stalag 17* (Paramount) in which he portrayed an American airman in a German prisoner of war camp. Holden's first starring role was in Columbia's *Golden Boy* in 1939 and he has since appeared in about thirty pictures. He is under a fourteen-year contract which ends in 1965 with Paramount, but he is free to act in several pictures for other studios.

Holden was born William Franklin Beedle, Jr. on April 17, 1918 at O'Fallon, Illinois. His father, William Franklin Beedle, is a chemist who became the head of the George W. Gooch Laboratories, and his mother is a former schoolteacher. His brother Robert was killed in action as a Navy fighter pilot in World War II.

When Bill Beedle was very young the family moved to California. He attended grade school at Monrovia and South Pasadena, and South Pasadena Junior College. His father, who hoped that Bill would follow a career in the natural sciences, put him to work during summer vacations in a chemical laboratory. For hobbies Bill played the clarinet, rode motorcycles and sang in the Oneonta Congregational Church choir. He took a course at junior college in radio drama and acted in several radio plays on station KECA.

During this period he appeared in a play, *Manya,* at the Playhouse Theatre in the role of Madame Curie's grandfather. A talent scout, Milt Lewis, was impressed by young Beedle's performance and Paramount gave him a small part in *Million Dollar Legs* (1939). For acting purposes he assumed the name William Holden.

His first starring role was in 1939 as the young violinist-prizefighter in *Golden Boy,* playing opposite Barbara Stanwyck. He still sends Miss Stanwyck roses each year on the anniversary of the day when the picture got under way and she coached the young novice in movie technique. For the part, Holden took boxing and violin lessons. The reviewers acclaimed his acting in the film and he soon had plenty of work. He appeared in *Invisible Stripes* (1940), *Our Town* (1940), *Those Were the Days* (1940), *Arizona* (1940), *I Wanted Wings* (1941), *Texas* (1941), *Remarkable Andrew* (1942), and *Fleet's In* (1942).

Enlisting in the Army, Holden served more than three years and was graduated as a lieutenant from the Army Air Force Officers Candidate School at Miami Beach, Florida. In 1943 he took the necessary steps to use William Holden as his legal name.

There was a tiny notice in the New York *Herald Tribune* (September 11, 1945) stating that Holden had returned to the Columbia lot after service with the Air Force. Richard Dyer MacCann (*Christian Science Monitor,* May 25, 1951) pointed out that this period was the most difficult of the actor's career. For seven months he had no work. Then he was in thirteen pictures in three years.

In 1947 he appeared in *Blaze of Noon,* and in *Dear Ruth* with Joan Caulfield. Of his part as the aviator on furlough in the latter, a New York *Times* reviewer commented: "There is an easy naturalness about William Holden's performance . . . that was not apparent in his previous acting" (June 11, 1947). Holden portrayed a widower-pioneer who marries a bond slave in *Rachel and the Stranger* (1948) and an ex-GI student in *Apartment for Peggy* (1948).

His role as a psychopathic gangster in *The Dark Past* (1948) lifted him out of the typecasting which he disliked and to which he referred as his "Smiling Jim" portrayals. The New York *Times* critic (December 23, 1948) noted: "William Holden is excellent as the dream-shackled gunman, who is . . . ruthless, nervous and explosively dangerous. . . ." His next films were *The Man from Colorado* (1949), *Streets of Laredo* (1949), *Dear Wife* (1950), and *Union Station* (1950).

In *Sunset Boulevard* (1950) Holden appeared opposite Gloria Swanson. The picture won an Academy award for its story and screenplay. Its director, Billy Wilder, credited Holden with much of the picture's success. The movie reviewers warmly praised Holden's acting in the role of Joe Gillis, a down-at-the-heels writer. On August 11, 1950 a New York *Times* critic wrote: "Holden is doing the finest acting of his career. His range and control of emotions never falters and he engenders a full measure of compassion for a character who is somewhat less than admirable." As a result of his acting he was nominated for an "Oscar" in 1950.

The cinema actor's subsequent film was *Born Yesterday* (1950) in which he portrayed an intellectual reporter who awakened a social conscience in an ex-chorus girl, acted by Judy Holliday who won an Academy award for her part. Holden's next assignment was in *Force of Arms* (1951). In *Submarine Command* (1952) he played a grim naval officer. He appeared as a jockey's agent in *Boots Malone* (1952) and a reporter in a Kefauver-type of crime investigation in *The Turning Point* (1952).

WILLIAM HOLDEN

In 1953 Holden starred in *The Moon is Blue* and *Escape from Fort Bravo. Look* magazine's award for 1953 was presented to Holden for "the year's best performance as a scrounging cynical prisoner of war who turns hero" in *Stalag 17,* based on the play by Donald Bevan and Edmund Trzcinski. Otis L. Guernsey, Jr. in the New York *Herald Tribune* (July 2, 1953) remarked: "Holden acts in quick, hard punches of character playing a realist who likes his own comforts and is willing to be an outcast or a hero in order to get them. He forms a kind of bridge between the humor and the drama in a solid performance." The *Christian Science Monitor* (June 30, 1953) stated: "Mr. Holden is excellently hard-eyed and taciturn as the shrewdly opportunistic Sefton." The actor was the recipient of the Academy of Motion Picture Arts and Sciences award for his role in this picture as the best male actor of 1953.

In 1954 Holden is playing in *Forever Female, Executive Suite, Sabrina Fair* with Humphrey Bogart and Audrey Hepburn (who received the 1953 Academy award as the leading female actress), *The Country Girl,* and *The Bridges at Toki-Ri.*

The Woman's Press Club of Hollywood gave Holden in 1951 the "Golden Apple" award for being one of the "most cooperative" stars. He is rarely at odds with the studios for which he works, although he has received suspensions for refusing to make any motion pictures whose scripts he considered below standard. He believes that "It's necessary to capture the fancy of the public—but also to stimulate their thinking."

(Continued next page)

HOLDEN, WILLIAM—*Continued*

The movie star is first vice-president of the Screen Actor's Guild, guild delegate to the Hollywood Coordinating Committee which arranges entertainment for troops overseas, a member of the Motion Picture Industry Council, Permanent Charities Committee, Community Chest, Motion Picture Relief Fund, and Parent-Teachers' Association. He has maintained a regular schedule of veterans' hospital appearances since World War II.

William Holden married Ardis Ankerson (known to movie audiences as Brenda Marshall) on July 13, 1941. They have three children: Virginia (Mrs. Holden's daughter by a former marriage), Peter Westfield and Scott Porter. The actor dislikes intrusion on his private life and is respected as a "solid citizen" of the Hollywood community. He has light brown hair, hazel eyes, is six feet tall and weighs about 170 pounds. He enjoys working around his home, painting fences, and gardening.

An actor should be fully prepared for his role, Holden believes, and should know all the other parts in a picture so that there exists complete understanding. After working with director Billy Wilder, Holden said he might try directing a picture. He was described by director John Farrow as one of the "most competent, sensitive and skillful men in the business."

References

Christian Sci Mon II p9 My 25 '51
Collier's 127:30+ Je 2 '51 pors
Look 18:123 Mr 22 '54 pors
N Y Post Mag p10 Jl 24 '49 por; p5 Jl 5 '53 por
Washington (D.C.) Post p16+ Jl 23 '50 pors; p4 N 23 '52 por
Motion Picture and Television Almanac, 1953-54

HOLLENBECK, DON Mar. 30, 1905-June 22, 1954 Radio and television commentator; studied at the University of Nebraska, left before graduating to become a Nebraska *State Journal* reporter (1926) and later was on the Omaha *Bee News;* became picture editor in New York for the Associated Press (1937) and in San Francisco (1939); national affairs editor, *PM* (1941); served with U.S. Office of War Information during World War II, and broadcast reports of the Fifth Army's amphibious assault at Salerno; joined the Columbia Broadcasting System's news staff (1946); on his *CBS Views the Press* programs (1947-1950) he criticized news handling from a liberal viewpoint and won the George Polk Award for distinguished reporting (1949); did a nightly news comment on television and participated in the CBS network's *You Are There* series; death by suicide. See *Current Biography,* (Feb.) 1951.

Obituary

N Y Times p16 Je 23 '54

HOLM, HANYA Modern dancer; teacher; choreographer

Address: b. c/o Hanya Holm School of Dance, 743 8th Ave., New York 36

Hanya Holm, who composed and staged the dances for the prize-winning musical comedy, *The Golden Apple,* is one of the foremost women exponents of modern dance. She has been active in the concert field of dancing, has received several awards for her choreography, is the first choreographer to have registered her work with the Copyright Office in Washington, D.C., and at present serves on the staff of two colleges. The dances she created for the Broadway musicals *Kiss Me, Kate* (1948), *Out of this World* (1950), and *My Darlin' Aida* (1952) won audience approval and critical acclaim.

The daughter of Valentin and Marie (Moerschel) Eckert, Hanya Holm was born in Worms, Germany. She received her early education in a German convent, studied at Hoch Conservatory and at the Dalcroze Institute in Frankfurt am Main, and was graduated from the Dalcroze Institute at Hellerau. Hanya saw one of the recitals of Mary Wigman, a principal exponent and creator of the modern dance, and her future career was immediately determined. She became a student at the Mary Wigman Central Institute in Dresden, from which she was graduated, and a member of the original Wigman group which began to tour Europe in 1919. She also appeared in one of the first productions of Max Reinhardt's *The Miracle.*

She became the chief instructor and co-director of the Mary Wigman Central Institute. She was also a dance director in Ommen, Holland for two summers and in 1930 she functioned as assistant director and co-dancer with Mary Wigman in the antiwar memorial pageant, *Totenmal,* presented at Munich. In 1931 the Mary Wigman New York school was founded and at Miss Wigman's request, Hanya Holm came to New York to operate it. In 1936 the school became the Hanya Holm Studio, and later, the Hanya Holm School of Dance.

Having assembled and trained a company of her own, she presented them in an American debut in 1936 in Colorado. A short tour of Midwestern colleges followed, and then an appearance at the Bennington Dance Festival of 1937. There Miss Holm presented a major work, *Trend,* which was hailed by John Martin of the New York *Times* as "one of the most substantial pieces of artistry yet to be contributed to these festivals." The work was presented by Hanya Holm and her company in their New York concert debut at Mecca Temple (now the New York City Center) in December 1937.

Two other compositions, *Dance Sonata* and *Dance of Work and Play,* were offered at Bennington in 1938, and during the 1938-1939 season, Miss Holm made her first transcontinental tour. She included in her repertoire two works, *Metropolitan Daily* and *Tragic Exodus.* The former, a newspaper satire, was the first modern dance composition to be televised by the National Broadcasting Company. The latter work won *Dance Magazine's* annual award for the best group choreography in dance for the year.

They Too Are Exiles was added to the repertoire in a second transcontinental tour made the following season. Of the appearance of the company at the Goodman Theatre in Chicago, Claudia Cassidy wrote in the Chicago *Journal of Commerce* that it was "in every way one of the finest we have had in the modern school," while Eugene Stinson of the Chicago *News* considered "Miss Holm the one choreographer in modernist style who has completely realized a system of pure dance."

A New York concert at the Mansfield Theatre in March 1941 featured *The Golden Fleece, an Alchemistic Fantasy,* the joint work of Alex North, Kurt Seligmann and Hanya Holm. The surrealist ballet proved, in the opinion of the New York *Times* critic, "of considerable less importance than the character of the company itself," of which he wrote: "It is a sheer joy to see an ensemble move so beautifully and with such a sense of being an ensemble."

Miss Holm initiated the summer dance sessions at Colorado College, Colorado Springs, in June 1941, thus establishing a dance center in the West. This association has been continued without interruption to date and has included an annual presentation at the Colorado Springs Fine Arts Center. Frequently, the presentation of a new work in Colorado was followed by its presentation in New York. Outstanding among numerous works were *Namesake,* with music by Roy Harris, and *Orestes and the Furies,* set to music by John Colman. On May 26, 1947 a *PM* reviewer wrote: "Combining, as she does, the thoroughness of the Mary Wigman method with the creativeness of the American modern dance, Miss Holm is undoubtedly one of the finest dance teachers in America."

The offering, *Ballet Ballads,* by the Experimental Theatre in 1948 included choreography by Hanya Holm for *The Eccentricities of Davy Crockett.* Opening at the Maxine Elliott Theatre as a showing to its own membership, the Experimental Theatre production met with such success that it was transferred for a Broadway run to the Music Box Theatre. Miss Holm next staged the movement for *The Insect Comedy,* by Josef and Karel Čapek; it was performed by the New York City Theatre Company at the City Center in the early summer of 1948.

The choreographer composed the dances for the Cole Porter production, *Kiss Me, Kate,* which opened at the New Century Theatre on December 30, 1948. This was her first work for a Broadway musical show, and John Martin wrote in the New York *Times*: "Nobody could have stepped more gracefully into a new field than Hanya Holm has done in her transition from the concert dance to show business. The dances she has created . . . have about them the ease and finish of a veteran." Her next assignment was for the incidental choreography in García Lorca's *Blood Wedding,* presented by New Stages.

HANYA HOLM

Miss Holm, one of the founder-directors of the New York City Dance Company, presented her *Ozark Suite* at the City Center in December 1949. Her next choreographic assignment was to do the dances for another Cole Porter show, *Out of This World* (New Century, December 1950). Walter Terry wrote in the New York *Herald Tribune* that "Hanya Holm . . . has created some fine dance passages for a gifted ensemble and for the dance star. . . ." She then went to London to direct dance rehearsals for the English production of *Kiss Me, Kate* (Coliseum, March 1951). Returning to New York, her work was next seen on Broadway in *My Darlin' Aida,* a musical play presented at the Winter Garden Theatre in October 1952.

An off-Broadway presentation claimed Miss Holm's talents in the production of *The Golden Apple* which opened at the Phoenix Theatre on March 11, 1954 (it was later transferred to the Alvin Theatre). The show is a musical with book and lyrics by John Latouche and music by Jerome Moross. In it the stories of the *Iliad* and the *Odyssey* were adapted to a turn-of-the-century American locale. It received both the New York Newspaper Guild's Page One Award for Theatre and the New York Drama Critics' Circle Award. Virgil Thomson wrote in the New York *Herald Tribune*: "Miss Holm's dance design is nothing short of brilliant, especially when it is comic."

John Martin, dance critic of the New York *Times* commented (May 2, 1954): "There is almost nothing in *The Golden Apple* that looks like a dance 'routine', yet Miss Holm's mark is strong upon the whole production. . . . There is a charming little dance, formal and full of style, celebrating the return of the soldiers . . . a wonderfully funny one called

HOLM, HANYA—*Continued*

By Gonna-Goona Lagoon, and the *Circe* scene, [all] unified theatre pieces."

An adviser of the Dance Notation Bureau, Miss Holm has included the system for recording choreography devised by Rudolf von Laban in her curriculum for dance students. In March 1952 the complete choreographic score of the dances originated for *Kiss Me, Kate* was registered for copyright in Washington, D.C., a history-making event in the dance field. The entire script, photographed on microfilm, is now on file at the Library of Congress.

In addition to her affiliation with Colorado College, Miss Holm is a consultant professor of the dance department at Adelphi College, Garden City, New York. She has given frequent lecture demonstrations and has spoken at over sixty colleges. In 1939 she was chosen to represent women in art at the centennial celebration at Duke University. She has written several articles on the dance, including one for *The World Book Encyclopedia* (Field, 1954) and one entitled "The Mary Wigman I Know," published in *The Dance Has Many Faces,* edited by Walter Sorell (World, 1951).

She has been variously described as "a blond and blue-eyed cricket," and a "little German powerhouse." She is five feet two inches tall and weighs 110 pounds. She became a United States citizen in 1939. Her hobbies are numerous, including chess and handicrafts. She enjoys playing the piano, painting, wood carving and "making things out of nothing;" lack of time made her give up embroidery and fine sewing. She was married and divorced before coming to the United States, and has one son, Klaus Holm, who is a stage designer and lighting expert. The lighting for *The Golden Apple* was one of his latest assignments.

References

N Y World-Telegram p36 D 14 '49 por
Chujoy, A. (ed.) Dance Encyclopedia (1949)
Martin, J. Dance: The Story of the Dance told in Pictures and Text (1947)
Who's Who in America, 1954-55

HOOTON, EARNEST ALBERT Nov. 20, 1887-May 3, 1954 Anthropologist; university professor; educated at University of Wisconsin and Oxford University (Rhodes Scholar); began teaching anthropology at Harvard as instructor (1913) and from 1930 was professor; studied ancient inhabitants of Canary Islands: Indians of Pecos, New Mexico; criminals in Massachusetts; adult Irish males; and generations of Harvard graduates; wrote numerous books including *Up from the Ape* (1931), *Apes, Men and Morons* (1937), and *Why Men Behave like Apes and Vice Versa* (1940); known also as a wit, and composer of light verse. See *Current Biography,* (Yrbk.) 1940.

Obituary

N Y Times p29 My 4 '54

HOOVER, HERBERT (CLARK), JR. Aug. 4, 1903- United States government official; engineer

Address: b. c/o Department of State, Washington 25, D.C.; h. 915 Orlando Rd., San Marino 9, Calif.

On August 18, 1954 the United States Senate confirmed unanimously President Dwight D. Eisenhower's nomination of Herbert Hoover, Jr. as Under Secretary of State. Hoover succeeds General Walter Bedell Smith who resigned after a long career in public service. The appointment of Hoover followed his success as special consultant to Secretary of State John Foster Dulles in helping to settle the three-year-old Anglo-Iranian oil dispute.

Following announcement of Hoover's appointment many newspapers made favorable editorial comments on the choice. "He has a notable capacity for adjusting himself to difficult situations," commented the Washington *Post* (August 22, 1954). The *Christian Science Monitor* (August 19, 1954) observed: "Although his diplomatic experience is limited, those who have dealt with him in the last few months have often been impressed by the combination of soundness, candor, and circumspectness he has shown."

A mining engineer like his father, Hoover advised Iran on its oil policies as a private citizen ten years ago. He has served other countries in a similar capacity, and has been decorated for his services by a number of South American governments. Hoover holds several patents for his inventions of oil detecting instruments. His recent work in Iran, which demanded both technical knowledge and diplomatic ability, exhibited, in the words of the New York *Herald Tribune,* "diplomatic leadership and ingenuity," and "remarkable skill" in handling a "delicate task."

Herbert Clark Hoover, Jr. was born in London, England, on August 4, 1903 to Lou (Henry) and Herbert Clark Hoover, then a successful mining engineer and later the thirty-first President of the United States. (He has a younger brother, Allan Henry Hoover.) His father traveled widely in connection with his work, and one of the younger Hoover's earliest memories is of "riding into a town in Australia while sitting on a wagon load of gold."

Joseph Jerry Perling, author of *Presidents' Sons* (Odyssey, 1947), describes Hoover's early years in these terms: "Up to the time of his father's nomination and elevation to the Presidency, the life of Herbert, Jr., paralleled the unpublicized careers of other American youths whose parents possessed education, wealth and wide friendship." He earned his B.A. degree at Stanford University in 1925. Three years later he received a M.B.A. degree from Harvard Business School, where he was an instructor and a member of the research staff in 1928 and 1929. In 1928 he was awarded a grant by the Guggenheim foundation to survey air routes on the west coast of the United States.

Interested in radio, Hoover became an amateur, or "ham," at the age of twelve; at one time he held a Federal license for a radio research short wave station. In 1929 he became communications engineer of Western Air Express. "When, in August, 1929, the airship *Graf Zeppelin* made its round-the-world cruise," Perling related, Hoover "spoke over a coast-to-coast network on the 'Roads of the Sky.' He predicted that commercial planes would be equipped with two-way telephones by which pilots could be in constant communication with landing fields. . . . A week later, young Hoover was engaged to describe the *Graf Zeppelin's* visit to Los Angeles." Unexpectedly, his "hard-driving career," as *Newsweek* (March 22, 1954) phrased it, suffered a check. "Reporting for duty as a reserve lieutenant with the then Army Air Corps, he was found to have tuberculosis. A year in a sanitarium followed."

Following his recovery, Hoover was employed as communications engineer by Transcontinental and Western Air, Inc. (TWA), from 1931 until 1934. The next year he was a teaching fellow at the California Institute of Technology. Having developed radio and electronic devices for the discovery of oil, he founded the United Geophysical Company at Pasadena in 1935. The firm employed 1,000 persons and did $7,000,000 worth of business annually, prospecting for oil for governments and companies all over the world. Between 1940 and 1947 he took out patents on several oil locating devices.

In February 1940 he described to the American Institute of Mining and Metallurgical Engineers a new oil divining rod which he called a "mass-spectrograph," a mechanism of extreme sensitivity used to separate and identify "the minute amounts of gases that have seeped up to the surface over a period of hundreds of millions of years from hidden oil wells 10,000 feet below." In March 1942, together with an associate, Hoover obtained a patent covering a new method of mapping the subterranean structure of the earth's crust. In March 1947 he patented a portable seismometer.

Meanwhile, in 1936, Hoover had become president of another company, Consolidated Engineering Corporation of California. Upon the outbreak of World War II "he devoted his inventive mind," in Perling's words, "to the construction of testing mechanisms which later made American war planes supreme in combat." In August 1941 *Time* reported: "Last week Herbert Clark Hoover, Jr. was an able young geophysicist. This week he is becoming an important defense manufacturer. To his Consolidated Engineering Corp., big Sperry Gyroscope Co. turned over one whole branch of its business: instruments to measure vibration and strain (in airplanes, ships, etc.)."

By the time he was forty, Hoover was not only head of two large companies, and a director of several others, but also a technical consultant to the governments of Venezuela, Brazil, Chile, Peru, and other countries.

On September 12, 1953 the Department of State announced that Hoover, a Republican, had been appointed special adviser to Secretary of State Dulles on international petroleum problems. The New York *Herald Tribune* commented that the assignment was "in excellent

Wide World

HERBERT HOOVER, JR.

hands. The son of the former President is no stranger to Iran and her problems, having been invited by the Iranian government in 1944 to give his advice as an oil engineer on the establishment of concessions to British and American oil corporations." *U.S. News & World Report* hailed the appointment in these words: "Herbert Hoover, Jr. . . . may be the man who will finally make sense out of the British-and-Iranian oil dispute."

The dispute arose in May 1951 when Mohammed Mossadegh, then Premier of Iran, nationalized the oil fields owned by the British-controlled Anglo-Iranian Oil Company. Seizure of the fields was followed by the sharp curtailment of Iranian oil exports, a British commercial blockade, and the rupture of diplomatic relations between Great Britain and Iran on October 22, 1952.

After Mossadegh's deposition, it appeared that Premier Fazlollah Zahedi, his successor, was willing to enter into negotiations with the British. By October 11, 1953 the Zahedi government announced its willingness to reach a settlement with the British over the nationalization of the oil fields and refineries, and to resume diplomatic relations.

Meanwhile, however, oil production in other Middle East countries had expanded considerably, and as Robert C. Doty pointed out in the New York *Times,* it was expected that "by 1955 European oil-refining capacity" would be "47 per cent greater than in 1951," so that resumption of full-scale oil production and refinement in Iran would entail vexing economic and political problems.

For the period that Hoover served as the Secretary of State's special adviser he crossed the Atlantic fourteen times, virtually commuting between Washington, London and Teheran. He was not authorized to negotiate or propose solutions; he was assigned only to

HOOVER, HERBERT, JR.—*Continued*

gather information. However, it was understood that because of his international standing as an oil consultant his opinion would be highly valued by all interested parties.

Early in his mission Hoover reported that he had been "deeply impressed" by the sincere desire of everyone he talked with to find a "dignified and constructive approach to the problem of Iranian oil." At the Bermuda conference of December 1953 Secretary Dulles and British Foreign Secretary Anthony Eden agreed that Iran's refineries be rehabilitated and its oil marketed by a consortium consisting of five American companies (Standard Oil Company of New Jersey, Standard Oil Company of California, Socony-Vacuum Oil Company, Inc., The Texas Company, and Gulf Oil Corporation) in conjunction with British (Anglo-Iranian Oil Company, Ltd.), French (Compagnie Française des Pétroles), and Dutch (Royal Dutch Shell Company) interests. On advice of the National Security Council, the American companies were granted immunity from anti-trust action on this operation.

"The entire strategy," according to the New York *Herald Tribune,* "was engineered by Herbert Hoover, Jr." The New York *Times* reported that this strategy had made so favorable an impression that he had been offered "several top jobs in the Eisenhower Administration," but that, averse to desk work, he had declined. The Anglo-Iranian oil dispute was at length settled on August 5, 1954, when the four-nation consortium and the Iranian government reached a twenty-five year agreement on the operation of Iran's oil industry.

Hoover described the agreement, according to Walter Kerr, as "by far the biggest business deal that has ever been concluded—a fair bargain and a victory for no one" (New York *Herald Tribune,* August 9, 1954). Under the agreement the ownership of the British-built oil industry is to be transferred to the Iranian government for $70,000,000, and the American, Dutch and French firms will pay $600,000,000 to the Anglo-Iranian Oil Company, Ltd. for 60 per cent of the new consortium.

President Eisenhower wrote Hoover that the settlement was due "in significant measure to your expert knowledge of the international oil business, to your persistence and to your skillful diplomacy." On August 10, 1954 a resolution was introduced in Congress to award the Medal of Freedom to Hoover in recognition of his services. A week later the President nominated him as Under Secretary of State to succeed General Walter Bedell Smith, who was retiring from government service to become executive vice-president of the American Machine & Foundry Company. The Foreign Relations Committee, "in an extraordinary one-hour night session" unanimously approved the nomination, and less than twenty-four hours after it had been submitted, the full Senate confirmed it.

Before accepting his present post, Hoover was chairman of the board and a director of the United Geophysical Company, Inc., and a director of the Southern California Edison Company, the Union Oil Company of California, and the Brea Chemical Company, Inc. He is a trustee of the California Institute of Technology and of Claremont Men's College in California. The governments of Venezuela, Chile and Peru have conferred decorations on him. He is a member of the American Institute of Mining and Metallurgical Engineers, American Association of Petroleum Geologists, and Society of Exploration Geophysicists. His clubs are the University (New York), Bohemian (San Francisco) and California (Los Angeles).

He married Margaret Watson, a classmate through grammar school, high school and college, on June 25, 1925. The Hoovers have three children, Margaret Ann (Mrs. Richard Tatem Brigham), Herbert, III, and Joan Ledlie (Mrs. William Leland Vowles). The new Under Secretary of State has been described as "ruggedly handsome, with gray hair and blue eyes."

References

N Y Herald Tribune p12 S 13 '53 por; II p 1 N 1 '53 por; p10 Ag 18 '54; II p3 Ag 22 '54 por
N Y Times p1+ Ag 18 '54 por
Newsweek 43:48 Mr 22 '54 por; 44:25 Ag 30 '54
Washington (D.C.) Post p15 Ag 24 '54
Perling, J. J. Presidents' Sons (1947)
Who's Who in America, 1954-55
Who's Who in Engineering, 1948

HOPKINS, JOHN JAY Oct. 15, 1893-
Business executive; lawyer

Address: b. c/o General Dynamics Corp., 445 Park Ave., New York 22; 1200 18th St., Washington, D.C.; h. 2800 Woodley Rd., Washington, D.C.

Variously described as "a financial wizard," an "empire builder" and the "Mr. Atom" of American industry, John Jay Hopkins is chairman of the board and president of General Dynamics Corporation. The organization he heads consists of three divisions: the Electric Boat of Groton, Connecticut; the Canadair Limited of Montreal, Canada; and the Electro Dynamic of Bayonne, New Jersey. A fourth, the General Atomic Corporation, is an inactive unit formed to develop nuclear power for industrial uses whenever such development becomes feasible.

Through a vote of stock-holders on April 29, 1954, General Dynamics Corporation was merged with Consolidated Vultee Aircraft Corporation. Hopkins said that the merged company would represent "one of the strongest arms of the free world's defense effort," and was "moving swiftly" in the fields of hydrodynamics, aerodynamics and nucleodynamics.

Hopkins, who joined the Electric Boat Company as a director in 1937 with an extensive background as a corporation lawyer, business administrator and financier, became vice-president in 1942 and president in 1947. As indicated by his winning of an Horatio Alger award in April 1953, his career is a success story that began in humble circumstances.

Born in Santa Ana, California, on October 15, 1893, of English, Irish and Scottish forebears, John Jay Hopkins was the third of the five children of the late Reverend John Thomas Hopkins, a Presbyterian minister, and the late May Irene (Hymer) Hopkins. His two brothers became engineers; one of his sisters became a school principal, and the other a physician who has done pioneer research work on epilepsy.

Hopkins has related that his father, who never earned more than $100 a month, "attracted everyone who was in trouble. So we knew what it was to give more than we had." While in grammar school, young Hopkins began to deliver newspapers; by the time he finished high school in Fullerton, California, he was managing several paper delivery routes. During high school and college years he also worked summers in sugar plants.

From 1911 until 1914 he attended Occidental College in Los Angeles, where he was president of his freshman class and participated in football, basketball, track, and tennis. He then transferred to the University of California at Berkeley and earned his A.B. degree in 1915. Following graduation, he worked for a year in the offices and refineries of the Standard Oil Company of California.

Deciding to be a lawyer, he entered Harvard Law School in 1916, but the next year he enrolled as a seaman, second class, in the United States Naval Reserve, at the San Pedro, California Officers' Training School. On completion of the course he was commissioned an ensign in the U.S. Naval Reserve Force and after World War I was over, he remained on inactive duty as a reserve officer until 1923. Meanwhile, in 1919, he returned to Harvard Law School, which awarded him the LL.B. degree in 1921.

Hopkins then joined the New York law firm of Cravath, Henderson, Leffingwell & de Gersdorff (now Cravath, Swaine & Moore) as a $3,000-a-year associate specializing in business and corporation law. Through oil investments, he multiplied his salary many times. He opened his own offices in 1925 and practiced in New York City and Los Angeles until 1932.

Serving as special assistant to Secretaries of the Treasury Ogden L. Mills and William H. Woodin in 1932 and 1933, he worked particularly on problems of international war debts, railroad administration, customs, taxes, and banking administration. For the next three years he was general counsel and a director of Mayflower Associates, Inc., a trust that specialized in oil and mining investments. From 1936 until 1941 he maintained a law and business office in New York City.

Hopkins had become a director in 1937 and vice-president in charge of finances and contracts in 1942 of Electric Boat Company, a submarine building firm with achievements in marine and electrical engineering and manufacturing dating back to 1880. During World War II, the company built eighty-two submarines, more than all other private American builders combined, and more PT boats than any other shipbuilding firm.

JOHN JAY HOPKINS

At the end of the war Hopkins determined, in the words of Henry R. Sutphen, chairman of the executive committee of the Electric Boat Company, to build "an industrial structure more broadly based to withstand the shifting tides of defense expenditure . . . [and] the business cycle, and better equipped to develop suitable manufacturing opportunities in the field of heavy industry. . ."

Convinced of the need for diversification, Hopkins sought to ensure, as *Business Week* (May 2, 1953) expressed it, "a civilian potential to balance munitions work . . . [and] one kind of military product to offset another." In pursuance of this policy, he initiated in 1946 his company's acquisition of Canadair Limited, Canada's largest airplane producer, for $8,000,000. Canadair, which recently expanded its facilities to a total of four plants occupying more than 3,000,000 square feet, is currently building F-86E Sabre jets and the T-33 Shooting Star trainer, and is participating in Canada's guided missile program. Hopkins is chairman of the board and managing director of Canadair Limited.

In 1947 Hopkins became president of Electric Boat Company, which in April 1952 changed its name to General Dynamics Corporation. Electric Boat Company, now a division of General Dynamics, finished at the end of October 1953 the first of two attack-type submarines ordered by the Peruvian government. The division produced the first atomic submarine, the *Nautilus,* which was launched on January 21, 1954. It was commissioned by the Navy, September 1954.

General Dynamics Corporation obtained control in April 1953 of Consolidated Vultee Aircraft Corporation (Convair) for $8,700,000 in cash and $910,000 in stocks. Hopkins succeeded Floyd B. Odlum as board chairman of Convair. The company, which has a backlog of more

HOPKINS, JOHN JAY—*Continued*

than one billion dollars in orders, had a net income of $10,400,000 in 1952.

As *Time* reported when the transaction took place: "Convair has the Government contract to develop an aircraft driven by atomic propulsion. Since Hopkins' own company already has the Navy's contract to build its two atomic submarines, the merger, in effect, made Hopkins the 'Mr. Atom' of U.S. industry." Irvine W. Reynolds commented in the San Diego *Union*: "The empire that Hopkins is putting together is looking toward a new frontier—an unexplored region in which land, sea and air transportation would look to nuclear energy as a principal source of power. Convair may provide Hopkins with the missing link in this grandiose triangle."

At the seventh annual meeting of the American Schools and Colleges Association in April 1953, Milton S. Eisenhower presented Hopkins with an Horatio Alger award. The object of this award is "to guide and direct the attitudes and ideals of American youth toward the benefits of our free enterprise system" (New York *Times,* April 9, 1953).

He told the Canadian Chamber of Commerce on November 1, 1951: "If anything will call a halt to the Communist plan for world domination and the complete wrecking of what we consider to be our 'way of life,' . . . it is the picture confronting history's most powerful Czar of a forbidding industrial strength standing behind the armed forces of the United Nations."

On January 28, 1953 at the sixty-third annual meeting of the Edmonton (Alberta) Chamber of Commerce he declared: "We in Canada and the United States have a common language and literature, common institutions, common ideals and common purposes which have been handed down to us . . . by our common ancestors. . . We need each other. We both recognize it, hence we should work together harmoniously."

Hopkins is chairman of the board of the National Security Industrial Organization, a vice-chairman and member of the executive committee of the American Enterprise Association, a member of the U.S. Chamber of Commerce, on the board of directors of the Canadian Council of the International Chamber of Commerce, a trustee of the Committee for Economic Development, and a director and chairman of the legislative committee of the Shipbuilders' Council of America.

In 1928 and again in 1932 he was a delegate to the Republican National Convention. He served under Herbert Hoover in 1939 as national vice-chairman and director of organization of the Finnish Relief Fund. His clubs include the Metropolitan, Garden City Golf, National Republican, Yacht, Wings and the Harvard Law (all of New York); the Metropolitan and National Press (Washington, D.C.); Burning Tree and Columbia Country (Maryland); Royal Nassau Sailing (Bahamas); St. Andrews' Royal and Ancient Golf (Scotland); and the St. James' and Kanawaki Golf (Canada). Hopkins is the sponsor of the International P.G.A. Team Matches for the Hopkins International Golf Trophy and of the Canada Cup International Invitation Twosomes Matches.

The industrialist was married to Ruth Smith on June 26, 1917; they have one daughter, Lianne (Mrs. Clement Conger). Hopkins is a Presbyterian. "His main interest outside of business," the New York *Times* stated, "now that he is entering his 'late youth' is golf."

References

N Y Mirror Mr 8 '53 por
N Y Times III p3 Mr 8 '53 por
Time 61:93+ Ap 6 '53 por
Business Executives of America (1950)
Who's Who in America, 1952-53
Who's Who in Commerce and Industry (1953)

HORMEL, JAY C(ATHERWOOD) Sept. 11, 1892-Aug. 30, 1954 Meat packer; chairman of the board of George A. Hormel and Company; president from 1928 to 1946; was graduated from Shattuck Military Academy, Faribault, Minnesota (1911); studied three years at Princeton University, leaving before graduation to become a director (1914) in his father's meat-processing firm; served in World War I as a lieutenant in the Quartermaster Corps; developed new methods for canning spiced ham (trade name, "Spam") in 1937; established a guaranteed annual wage for Hormel's 9,000 employes; for many years was chairman of the American Legion employment committee. See *Current Biography,* (July) 1946.

Obituary

N Y Times p21 Ag 31 '54

HOVDE, BRYN(JOLF) J(ACOB) May 17, 1896-Aug. 10, 1954 Educator; housing executive; educated at Luther College, Decorah, Iowa (A.B. 1916); University of Iowa (M.A. 1919, Ph.D. 1924); second lieutenant in Coast Artillery Corps, U.S. Army; taught at Luther College (1919); assistant professor of history and social science at Allegheny College (1924-1926) and University of Pittsburgh (1927-1937); director of public welfare in Pittsburgh (1936-1938); administrator of Pittsburgh Housing Authority (1938-1944); chief of Division of Cultural Cooperation in State Department's Office of Public Affairs (1944) accompanied U.S. delegation to United Nations conference in San Francisco (1945) as a technical expert; delegate (1949) to UNESCO conference in Paris; elected president of the New School for Social Research (1945), resigned in 1950; was executive director, Pittsburgh Housing Association since 1952; was an outspoken critic of the Soviets, and also called for a balance between patriotism and personal freedom; former president, New York Chapter, Americans for Democratic Action, and National Public Housing Conference. See *Current Biography,* (Jan.) 1946.

Obituary

N Y Times p25 Ag 11 '54

HOWE, HELEN Jan. 11, 1905- Author; monologist

Address: b. c/o Simon & Schuster, Inc., 630 5th Ave., New York 20; h. 1158 5th Ave., New York 29

Reprinted from the *Wilson Library Bulletin,* Mar. 1954

When Helen Howe's first novel, *The Whole Heart,* was published she says she was the only member of her family up to then *not* to have written a book. Her father, M. A. DeWolfe Howe, is the author or editor of more than forty volumes, most of them biographical. Her two brothers, Quincy Howe, a radio commentator, and Mark DeWolfe Howe, a professor at Harvard Law School, are both writers. The latter was editor of the *Holmes-Pollock Letters* and the *Holmes-Laski Letters.* In addition, Miss Howe's mother, Fanny Huntington Quincy Howe, contributed frequently, although always anonymously, to the *Atlantic Monthly,* and was the author of several volumes of light essays.

Helen Huntington Howe was born in Boston, January 11, 1905, and was brought up there. She was so attached to her family and home that when she was sent to boarding school, only twelve miles away, she was so homesick she went to bed for three days. She survived this, and after being graduated from Milton Academy in 1922, attended Radcliffe College for a year. There she acted in college plays, and decided upon a career in the theatre. For ten years before she made her début as a dramatic monologist in 1933, Miss Howe worked and studied, preparing herself for the field in which Ruth Draper and Cornelia Otis Skinner have pioneered. Like them, too, she wrote her own monologues. She has given programs in London, New York, in forty-five states, and also at the White House. For two seasons after *The Whole Heart* appeared, she delighted enthusiastic audiences at the Blue Angel night club in New York.

This first novel caused considerable stir in 1943 although critical opinion on it was divided. "The outstanding woman's novel of this season," the Boston *Globe* stated flatly, while *Time* called it "a remarkable first novel . . . by turns howlingly funny, shrewd, sinister, ferocious, painful . . . an impressive, realistic piece of work." Dissenting voices were raised, however. Among them was the *Atlantic Monthly*: "Miss Howe did not quite trust herself as a novelist, and in her timidity she fell back upon her technique as a monologist."

Three years later, her second book, *We Happy Few,* was published. Shakespeare furnished an ironic title for a picture of the life of a tightly knit circle of Harvard professors and their families before and during World War II. The New York *Times* said: "Miss Howe satirizes the intellectual snobbery, the hot-house preciousness, the elaborate personalities. . . . The sarcasm would not be so telling did she not convey, expertly, the snob appeal of being exclusive." Unquestionably *We Happy Few* lacked the compelling tug on the emotions *The Whole Heart* possessed. Bernard De Voto, writing in the New York *Herald Tribune Book Review,* said: "Miss Howe is a better novelist here than she was in *The Whole Heart.* Though there is less feeling in this book, its content is harder and firmer and her skill has greatly increased. . . . The first half of her novel . . . is as good as anything that has come out of New England in two generations."

HELEN HOWE

Miss Howe's most recent book, *The Circle of the Day* (1950), appeared first in a woman's magazine and then was a selection of the Literary Guild. This story of a day in the life of a woman—her tenth wedding anniversary—when she learns that her husband has been unfaithful and that she has to make a decision affecting her entire future, is one many readers found satisfying. The tight time limit Miss Howe imposed on herself, that of less than twenty-four hours, is in itself a revelation of her skill as a writer. The *Christian Science Monitor* commented: "There is a tidiness about *The Circle of the Day* which preserves all three of the classical unities, in pleasing contrast to the formlessness of many similar contemporary novels. . . . Within its neat compass, it is a satisfying novel." The New York *Herald Tribune Book Review* had even higher praise: *"The Circle of the Day* is a thoughtful, purposeful book whose deeper merits . . . do not fully emerge until the whole pattern of this excellent novel is revealed."

Miss Howe was married in 1946 to Reginald Allen, at present assistant manager of the Metropolitan Opera Company. For three years they lived in Hollywood, where Mr. Allen was West Coast representative for the J. Arthur Rank Organization. They now make their home in New York, and spend vacations in their house in Somesville, a village on Mt. Desert Island, Maine, where they sail, walk, climb, and romp with their two dogs.

(Continued next page)

HOWE, HELEN—*Continued*

She is petite—five feet tall, and weighs 115 pounds—with blue eyes and brown hair. Her favorite authors are Jane Austen, Henry James, Proust, and Dickens. At present, she is working on another novel, and although she will not discuss it, her comment on her own writing may give a clue. "It is inevitable, I suppose," she says, "that much of what I have written and, I fear, will write must be colored by my early years. I'd *like* to write about Iowa farmers or Welsh miners, but I am doomed, like any other writer, to write about what I know, and I only wish it were more." Miss Howe occasionally appears professionally in her monologue programs, and she tells fairy stories to underprivileged children at a New York recreation center. She is turning more and more to writing, chiefly because, as she says, "the long tours of one-night stands just don't fit in with the serenity of a happy marriage!"

References

N Y Herald Tribune Book R p3 Je 4 '50 por
N Y Times Book R p12 Je 4 '50 por
American Women, 1939-40
Who's Who in America, 1954-55

HOWELL, CHARLES R(OBERT) Apr. 23, 1904- United States Representative from New Jersey; insurance broker

Address: b. House Office Bldg., Washington 25, D.C.; 1 W. State St., Trenton 8, N.J.; h. E. Curlis Ave., Pennington, N.J.

First elected to the House of Representatives in November, 1948 and re-elected in 1950 and 1952, Congressman Charles R. Howell represents the Fourth Congressional District of New Jersey. A successful insurance broker when elected to the New Jersey House of Assembly in 1944, he authored his State's first fair employment practices legislation during the following year.

Harris & Ewing

CHARLES R. HOWELL

Representative Howell agreed on March 9, 1954 to accept the Democratic designation for United States Senator at the polls in November, opposing Republican candidate Clifford P. Case.

In 1949 Congressman Howell devised a questionnaire for his electorate in order to ascertain their opinions on domestic and foreign issues. It proved so successful that he used it again in succeeding years. The Representative introduced bills in the Eighty-second and Eighty-third Congresses, whose purpose is to encourage the fine arts in our national culture.

Youngest of the four children of Robert Wilson Howell, a bank officer, and Harriet Newton (Bumsted) Howell, Charles Robert Howell was born in Trenton, New Jersey on April 23, 1904. He prepared for college at The Hoosac School in Hoosick, New York, where his extracurricular activities included football and dramatics. Graduated in 1923, Howell entered Princeton University. After studying there for a year and half, he left to become associated with a Philadelphia bank and a Trenton insurance agency.

He established himself as an independent broker and agent in 1928 and began to specialize in life insurance. Howell pursued evening courses at the University of Pennsylvania in 1936 and 1937 and received the Chartered Life Underwriter designation from the American College of Life Underwriters in 1940. Although he still maintains his insurance business in Trenton, he spends very little time on this enterprise.

Of his entrance into politics Howell has stated: "I started as a Republican, which was my family background, but was influenced by Roosevelt and the depression and by my father-in-law, William P. Howe, Sr. I got interested in government, switched to the Democrats, and became active in the Party."

Elected as a Democrat to the New Jersey House of Assembly in 1944, Howell in the following year introduced the original fair employment practices bill, a measure which placed compliance on a voluntary basis and which was the model for proposed legislation elsewhere. He was re-elected in 1945.

In the summer of 1946 Howell began his first campaign for election to Congress as Representative of the Fourth Congressional District which embraces Mercer and Burlington counties. In an address at Trenton on October 16, 1946 he assailed both "reactionary Republicans" and Southern Democrats, asserting that their re-election could "bring about a condition under which Communism, Fascism and other radical ideologies could seriously threaten our American system of free enterprise." He lost the election to the incumbent, Frank A. Mathews, Jr., a Republican.

During his next bid for a Congressional seat in 1948, he mobilized the labor sentiment of industrialized Trenton against his new Republican opponent, Albert C. Jones. Howell polled, in November, a larger vote than had ever been recorded in his district by any candidate, Republican or Democratic.

Seated in the Eighty-first Congress in January, 1949, Representative Howell was assigned to the House Committee on Education and Labor. During this session he voted for extending Federal rent controls to June 30, 1950 (March), the Housing Act of 1949 (June), the anti-poll tax bill (July), extending the Trade Agreements Act to June 12, 1951 (February) and the Economic Cooperation Act of 1948 (Marshall plan) to June 30, 1950 (April).

In the second session of the same Congress he favored loans to housing cooperatives (March) and President Truman's plan to establish a Federal department of health (July), and the "voluntary compliance" F.E.P.C. bill; he voted against the Lodge-Gassett constitutional amendment in July. Representative Howell, who helped to restore captured Mexican battle flags, was decorated by the Mexican Government in 1950.

Shortly after his election to Congress, Howell began to inform his constituents of his views by a weekly radio broadcast over three local stations, and a weekly column which he prepared for approximately thirty newspapers published in his district.

Later he created a questionnaire for his electorate based on important national and international issues. His first questionnaire was mailed in 1949, to about 6,000 persons and returned by 2,150; in 1950 the questionnaire reached 20,000 and he received responses from about 3,000. Congressman Howell continued to use the questionnaire during the next three years.

His voting record in the first session of the Eighty-second Congress (1951) was negative on such issues as restoring the old powers of the rules committee (January), assurance of "reasonable profits" under all price ceilings, and passage of the tidelands oil bill. The Congressman favors extension of the Selective Service Act and institution of universal military training (April) and the full appropriations asked by the Truman Administration for foreign military and economic aid.

Representative Howell sponsored a bill in the Eighty-second Congress to encourage fine arts programs in colleges and universities which passed the House but in the Senate was "lost in the rush for adjournment." After the Eighty-third Congress convened in January 1953 he presented two bills which would provide for a Federal department of fine arts and education, a national war memorial commission, a theatre and opera house in the nation's capitol "dedicated to the fuller growth and development of the fine arts," and appropriation of funds for establishing a Smithsonian Gallery of Art. This legislation would also authorize scholarships and graduate fellowships; and it has been endorsed by the Federation of Women's Clubs, American Council on Education and American Publishers Council.

Congressman Howell served on the New Jersey legislative committee to investigate the causes of juvenile delinquency in 1946 and 1947. He has been president of the Trenton Association of Life Underwriters, vice-president of the New Jersey Association of Life Underwriters, a member of the Mercer County Regional Council of the State Division against Discrimination, Trenton Council on Human Relations, National Conference of Christians and Jews, and a member of the advisory council of the department of politics at Princeton University; he is also a member of the Lions, Elks, and Eagles. A former president of the Trenton Kennel Club, he raises Airedales and other terriers. He enjoys bowling, badminton and bridge.

Mrs. Howell is the former Inez Wood Howe, whom he married on October 3, 1928. The Congressman is six feet two and a half inches in height, and weighs around 202 pounds; his eyes and hair are brown. Representative Howell belongs to the Protestant Episcopal Church.

References

Congressional Directory (1953)
Who's Who in America, 1952-53
Who's Who in the East (1951)
Who's Who in United States Politics (1952)

HULL, JOHN E(DWIN) May 26, 1895-
United States Army officer

Address: b. c/o Headquarters, Far East Command and United Nations Command, APO 500, c/o Postmaster, San Francisco, Calif.; h. Tokyo, Japan

In Tokyo on October 7, 1953 General John E. Hull succeeded to the dual post relinquished by General Mark W. Clark and became Commander in Chief of the United Nations Forces in the Far East and of the Far East Command. As Commanding General of the United States Army Forces in one of the most critical areas of the world, he must carry out American policies which combine "hard-headed realism with probably the highest idealism ever applied in world affairs." The new Far East commander, who had become Vice-Chief of Staff and a four-star general in 1951, has done work with atomic weapons and has had broad experience in military planning and administration.

Since most of Hull's assignments during his more than thirty-five years in the Army have been of "behind-the-scenes" importance, he was little known to the public before President Dwight D. Eisenhower appointed him to the Far East post. One of the crucial problems that confronted General Hull following the "uneasy" Korean truce was the disposition of the unrepatriated prisoners of war.

The youngest of nine children of Joseph Milton and Mary Ann (Mealey) Hull, John Edwin Hull was born in Greenfield, Ohio on May 26, 1895. He was brought up on the family farm where he helped with the chores and presumably developed the rugged build which helped him later when he played football at Miami University (Oxford, Ohio). One of his coaches has been quoted as saying that "Ed

U. S. Army

GEN. JOHN E. HULL

Hull was one of the steadiest players I ever saw in football. He was the player the coaches wanted—but most reporters didn't see him because he was always at the bottom of the pile" (*Newsweek*, September 21, 1953).

As a student, Hull intended to become a physician, but after his graduation with an A.B. degree in 1917 he accepted a commission as a second lieutenant in the infantry reserve and was assigned to active duty on August 15 of that year. The following October he received his regular Army commission and was stationed with the 58th Infantry Regiment at Camp Green in North Carolina.

Sent overseas in May 1918, the young officer fought with the 4th Infantry Division in the Vesle sector, the Toulon sector, and the Aisne-Marne, Saint-Mihiel and the Meuse-Argonne offensives.

After the Armistice on November 11, 1918, Captain Hull served with the American forces in Coblenz, Germany and returned to the United States in August 1919 for duty at Camp Dodge, Iowa. The years between the two world wars were spent at various posts in the United States and at Schofield Barracks in Hawaii where Hull played football on several Army teams.

Hull also attended a number of Army schools during this period and taught military subjects there and in universities. After a course in 1923 and 1924 at the Fort Benning (Georgia) Infantry School, he became assistant professor of military science and tactics at the University of Wisconsin. He later (1932) completed the advanced course at Fort Benning and was graduated in 1936 from the Command and General Staff School at Fort Leavenworth, Kansas, to which he returned as an instructor in 1938. Meanwhile he served as assistant professor of military science and tactics at Louisiana State University and was graduated from the Army War College in Washington, D.C. in June 1938.

Hull, who had been promoted to lieutenant colonel, was assigned in November 1941 to the war plans division of the War Department general staff in Washington, D.C. He remained with this division (redesignated the operations division in March 1942) during most of the war and, having been advanced to the rank of brigadier general, he became chief of the division's European section in charge of handling operational matters in the European theater. He was made chief of the theater group in January 1943 and supervised operational matters in all overseas theaters of war.

In his next wartime post, to which he was assigned in October 1944, Major General Hull was assistant chief of staff for operations on the War Department's general staff, and was responsible to the chief of staff on strategy, plans and operations of the Army. He was named in February 1945 as a member of the executive committee of the Research Board for National Security which was established by the National Academy of Science.

Newsweek (September 21, 1953) quotes an official Army history as crediting Hull with having "more intimate experience in integrating strategy with overseas operational requirements and the resources of the zone of interior than any other Army officer in World War II."

It has been said that Hull was greatly disappointed that he did not receive a combat command in Europe or the Pacific during World War II. Not long after the defeat of Japan he was sent, in July 1946, to Fort Shafter, Hawaii as commanding general of the U.S. Army Forces, Middle Pacific, and commander of the Hawaiian Department.

While in this capacity, John E. Hull was named in October 1947 commander of Operation "Sandstone" to assume charge of the testing of atomic weapons undertaken in the spring of 1948 at Eniwetok by Joint Task Force Seven. Lieutenant General Hull revealed in May, after the nuclear explosions had taken place, that the strength of the task force had been about 9,800 men and that the tests were "literally and truly field laboratory tests designed to determine how bombs now under development by the United States would work and to determine their efficiency" (New York *Times*, May 19, 1948). During 1948 and 1949 he served as the commanding general of the U.S. Army in the Pacific.

Hull's achievement in directing the Eniwetok test made him a logical choice in January 1949 for the directorship of the Weapons Systems Evaluation Group, newly created by Secretary of Defense James V. Forrestal to decide upon the effectiveness and need of the present and future weapons for the armed forces. One project of this highly secret group of military and scientific personnel was the testing of the Air Force's controversial B-36 bomber and a study of its place in the whole strategic bombing system. As reported by Carl Levin of the New York *Herald Tribune* (February 12, 1950), Hull emphasized the importance of the group's establishing "such a reputation for infallibility that its recommendations will be accepted unanimously by the Joint Chiefs of Staff, and that the Joint Chiefs' decision, in turn, will be accepted by the Congress and the public as best for the national security."

Remaining at the Pentagon in his next assignment, Hull became in January 1951 deputy chief of staff for operations and administration at the Department of the Army headquarters. On August 1 of that year he took up new duties as Vice-Chief of Staff of the Army and at the same time received promotion to four-star general. The Army's highest-ranking observer at the atomic blast in Nevada on April 22, 1952, General Hull described the troops' exercise held in conjunction with the test as successful, but pointed out the necessity for developing nuclear artillery to supplement air-borne atomic weapons. For part of the following month the Vice-Chief of Staff lectured in England as a participant in the annual exchange of military lectures between the United States and Great Britain.

When announcement was made on September 11, 1953 that General Hull had been chosen to succeed General Clark as supreme commander in the Far East, many press reports commented that Hull's name was unfamiliar to the public. He has described himself as "just the general that nobody knows." A New York *Herald Tribune* editorial (September 13, 1953) observed that Hull seemed "admirably fitted for the exacting and many-sided duties of his new post. Despite the Korean truce, the Far East is an extremely critical point in the American defense pattern. It demands constant vigilance . . . and diplomatic skill." Hull also holds the office of Governor of the Ryukyu Islands.

On his arrival in Tokyo in October 1953 the new Commander in Chief of the U.N. Forces and the U.S. Far East Command spoke of his ambition to contribute to peace in the Far East and urged Japan to build up her strength against Communist aggression.

In a message marking the eighth anniversary of the founding of the United Nations, Hull told the U.N. Troops in Korea, "Your action in Korea has proved in terms of sacrifice and blood our determination to make the United Nations Charter a living document" (New York *Times*, October 25, 1953).

During his first months in the Far East General Hull was mainly concerned with the "explosive" issue of the unrepatriated prisoners of war who under the terms of the Korean armistice agreement were being held in custody by Indian troops for a period of 120 days. Hull insisted that 22,000 anti-Communist North Korean and Chinese captives refusing repatriation should be released as civilians when that period expired on January 22, 1954.

He rejected a ruling of India's General K.S. Thimayya, chairman of the Neutral Nations Repatriation Commission, that the prisoners be held until an international political conference could convene to determine their fate. "For the United Nations Command now to agree to further and indefinitely prolonged captivity of these prisoners of war," Hull wrote, "would negate the very principle of human rights for which so many men of this command have fought and died" (New York *Times*, January 17, 1954).

After a compromise was reached and the prisoners had been returned to their original captors as POWs between January 20 and January 22, Hull proclaimed the 22,000 anti-Communist prisoners to be free civilians.

After conferring with U.S. officials in Washington, D.C. in February 1954, General Hull announced that "for the present we will have to maintain our combat strength" in Korea and that the two American divisions now being withdrawn from Korea are being replaced by two South Korean divisions.

On August 20 it was announced that the U.S. Second Infantry Division would be withdrawn from Korea and other units subsequently. The regrouping is regarded as technical and strategic.

Among General Hull's military decorations are the Silver Star, the Distinguished Service Medal with two Oak Leaf Clusters, and the Legion of Merit. He received the awards of the Army Occupation of Germany (World War I), Victory Medal (World War I) with four battle clasps, American Defense Medal, the American Theater Medal, the European-North African-Middle East Medal, the Victory Medal (World War II), and the National Defense Service Medal. He has recently been awarded the Korean Service Medal and the United Nations Service Medal.

Other honors conferred on General Hull are Honorary Commander, Order of the British Empire; Knight Commander, Liberian Order of African Redemption; Grand Cordon of Yun-Hui, China; Order of Military Merit, Degree of Grand Officer, Brazil; Philippine Legion of Honor (Commander); and Military Order of Ayacucho, Grade of Commander, Peru. Hull received the honorary degree of Doctor of Military Science from the Pennsylvania Military College in Chester on June 2, 1953.

Miami University (Oxford, Ohio) conferred on General Hull an honorary Doctor of Laws degree on June 3, 1954.

Hull is a Mason and a member of the Elks, Phi Delta Theta, the American Legion, and Veterans of Foreign Wars. His clubs include the Army and Navy (Washington, D.C.), Army and Navy Country (Arlington, Virginia), and Chevy Chase Country (Maryland).

His wife is the former Sara Lucile Davis, whom he met in college and married on August 21, 1919. His religion is Methodist. The general is six feet tall and is said to have an easy manner of self-confidence and to handle his military assignments with modesty, loyalty, and concern for detail. For recreation, he enjoys golf and fishing.

References

Gen Army 1:34 F '53 por; 1:28 S '53
N Y Herald Tribune p1+ S 12 '53 por; p3 S 12 '53; II p1 O 18 '53 por
N Y Times p1+ S 12 '53 por
Time 62:33 S 21 '53 por
Who's Who in America, 1952-53

HUNT, SIR (HENRY CECIL) JOHN
June 22, 1910- British Army officer; mountain climber
Address: b. c/o The Staff College, Camberley, Surrey, England; c/o Lloyds Bank Ltd., 6 Pall Mall, S.W. 1, London, England; h. Weir Cottage, Knighton, Radnorshire, Wales, England

HILLARY, SIR EDMUND (PERCIVAL)
July 20, 1919- New Zealand apiarist; mountain climber
Address: 730 Remuera Rd., Auckland, S.E. 2, New Zealand

TENZING NORKEY 1914- Nepalese mountaineer
Address: Darjeeling, India

Several hours before she was to be crowned Queen of England in June 1953, Elizabeth II learned that she had been presented with an extraordinary coronation "gift." On May 29 a British expedition sponsored by the Joint Himalayan Committee of the Royal Geographical Society and the Alpine Club had ascended Mount Everest in the Himalayas, the world's highest peak. The success of the undertaking was widely and hopefully acclaimed as an omen of the high British achievements to be realized under her reign. The two-man team that actually stood on the "roof of the world" consisted of Edmund Hillary, a New Zealand beekeeper, and Tenzing Norkey, a Sherpa mountain guide. Organizer and leader of the expedition was Colonel John Hunt, a British Army officer with extensive mountain climbing experience.

Knighted by Queen Elizabeth in July 1953, Sir John Hunt and Sir Edmund Hillary received this honor because of their "conquest of Mount Everest." In Sir John's book describing their experiences *The Conquest of Everest,* tribute is paid to Tenzing Norkey who was given the George Medal, Britain's highest civilian award, for his part in the cooperative enterprise.

Henry Cecil John Hunt was born in India on June 22, 1910 to Captain C. E. and Ethel Helen (Crookshank) Hunt. Both his father and his maternal grandfather served in the Indian Army. His mother's great-uncle was Sir Richard Burton, the nineteenth century explorer, orientalist and translator of the *Arabian Nights.* Hunt's brother Hugh is a theatrical producer and director in London. Captain Hunt was killed in France in 1914, and his widow was forced to raise their children on an Army pension.

Partly because such holidays were relatively inexpensive, she took the boys to Alpine resorts during their summer vacations, and it was there that John Hunt first became interested in mountain climbing. Before he went to Marlborough College, according to a biographical sketch in the London *Observer* (January 14, 1953, John had traversed Piz Palu

British Inf. Services
SIR JOHN HUNT

and during his first year at Sandhurst [the English military academy], "traversed the Meije, a long exacting climb for an eighteen-year-old." By the time he led the Mount Everest expedition in 1953, he had ascended some sixty peaks in the Alps.

After Hunt was graduated from Sandhurst with high distinction, winning the King's Gold Medal and the Anson Memorial Sword, he was commissioned a second lieutenant in the King's Royal Rifle Corps in 1930. He was assigned to service at Lucknow, India where, during the civil disobedience campaign of the following year, he volunteered for service in the Indian Police.

According to the London *Observer,* "he had a strong sense of Britain's moral responsibility to Indians, and a conviction that Christian values should be applied to the solution of social problems. . . . He taught himself to live like an Indian, not to play the romantic spy, but because he thought that by mixing with the Indians and winning their confidence he was doing all that an individual could to remove the distrust which, he felt, had produced the disobedience campaign." He was promoted to the rank of lieutenant on January 30, 1933.

During these years, Hunt spent his leaves climbing mountains. In 1935 he took part in his first major mountaineering expedition, and journeyed with James Waller's party to Peak K36 in the Karakoram Range. The group lived for a month above 18,000 feet, ascended as high as 24,500 feet, and, to ensure fresh food, transported live sheep and goats over snow passes and across glaciers.

Two years later he joined another Himalayan expedition, this time to the Kanchenjunga massif. Here he obtained "his first unforgettable view of Everest," and acquired "more experience of working with the Sherpas who have played such an essential part in all Everest expeditions culminating in Tenzing's triumph." In 1940 he took part in a third Himalayan expedition. He was promoted to captain on August 1, 1938, served as acting major from September 23, 1940 until December 22, 1940, as temporary major from December 23, 1940 until January 5, 1941, and held that rank again from October 24, 1941 until May 14, 1944.

During World War II Hunt saw a great deal of active service. In recognition of his combined military and mountaineering experience, he was appointed chief instructor of the Commando Mountain and Snow Warfare School in 1942. The next year he rejoined the King's Royal Rifle Corps, and fought with it through Italy. His battalion was decimated at the battle of the Sangro River; he saved many of his men under fire, and for his heroism was awarded the Military Cross.

The battalion was ordered home, but rather than return to England, Hunt "wangled a job as second-in-command of another battalion. . . . There he smote the Hun with such fierce persistency that he soon became battalion commander, and rose within a few months to the rank of [acting] brigadier."

On August 3, 1944, in recognition of his achievements in the Italian mountains as commanding officer of the 11th Indian Infantry Brigade, Hunt was made a Companion of the Distinguished Service Order. He was made a Commander of the Order of the British Empire in 1945. At the end of the war he was sent to Greece, where he organized mountain training courses on Mount Olympus for his troops. From 1946 to 1948 he was a general staff officer with the Middle East Land Forces, and in 1950 and 1951 served on the Western Europe committee of the commanders-in-chief.

Later in 1951 he became a staff officer at SHAPE (Supreme Headquarters, Allied Powers Europe), and was associated with the Allied Land Forces Headquarters in Central Europe. He was promoted to the permanent rank of colonel on June 25, 1951. At the time the successful Everest expedition was planned, he was attached to the 1st British Army Corps. At present he is assistant commandant of The Staff College in Camberley, England, and holds the rank of temporary brigadier.

The Joint Himalayan Committee of the Royal Geographical Society and the Alpine Club began in 1951 to plan for a full-scale attempt to climb Mount Everest in 1953. The mountain, which was named after Sir George Everest, Surveyor General of India more than a century ago, is situated on the border between Tibet and Nepal; it soars to a height of 29,002 feet. Tibetans call the mountain Chomolungma, "Goddess Mother of the World."

It was not until 1920 that the Dalai Lama of Tibet granted permission to the Royal Geographical Society to ascend the mountain. Between 1921 and 1952 eleven assaults were made, nine of them British, and two Swiss. In the course of these attempts at least fifteen lives were lost. The most famous Everest disaster occurred in 1924, when George Mallory, an English schoolmaster, and Andrew Irvine, of Oxford University, were observed very close to the peak and then were lost sight of forever.

After the Chinese Communists invaded Tibet in 1950, it became necessary to investigate the feasibility of taking a southern route up Mount Everest, through Nepal. This reconnaissance was accomplished in 1951, with satisfactory results, by a British party under the leadership of Eric Shipton. Shipton was also designated to head the 1953 expedition, but he withdrew in October 1952 because of "a friendly difference of opinion" with the sponsors over questions of size and organization.

Hunt thereupon assumed leadership of a group of British climbers: Major Charles G. Wylie, the expedition's organizing secretary; Dr. Michael Ward, its medical officer; Dr. L. Griffith Pugh, its physiologist; Dr. Charles Evans, a surgeon; Wilfrid Noyce, a schoolmaster and writer; George Lowe, another schoolmaster; Thomas R. Stobart, a photographer; George C. Band, a student of geology at Cambridge University; Michael Westmacott, an ex-president of the Oxford University Mountaineering Club; James Morris, a correspondent of the London *Times*; Thomas D. Bourdillon, a rocket expert who took part in Shipton's 1951 reconnaissance expedition; and Alfred Gregory, a travel agency executive. Edmund Hillary joined the group in India; Tenzing Norkey joined it in Nepal.

Colonel Hunt organized his expedition with the comprehensiveness and care for detail of a commander plotting the strategy of a major military operation. For several months, according to an account in *Life* (June 29, 1953), he "sent his mountaineers out to train on the steep tors of Scotland, then in the Alps of Europe. Finally, after reaching Nepal in March 1953 they continued their training and acclimatization on the frozen approaches to Everest itself." By the time the party was ready to make the assault, it had enlarged by the addition of 362 Nepalese porters and thirty-six Sherpa guides, and was accompanied by some 10,000 pounds of baggage which included new lightweight oxygen equipment.

The expedition reached its base camp about April 12, 1953. Within less than a month the entire party was at Camp IV, at a level of 21,200 feet. In all, nine camps were established; the last one was 1,100 feet from the peak. Hunt sent ahead two teams of two men each to attempt the summit. The first team, consisting of Bourdillon and Evans, failed of ultimate success, but prepared the way and brought back valuable advice for the second team, Hillary and Norkey.

These two men set out from Camp IX on the South Col at 6:30 A.M. on May 29 and reached the South Peak about 9:00 A.M. "The final ridge," Hillary stated, "was of high Alpine standard and we finally got to the top at 11:30 A.M. . . . I felt . . . good at the top. It was a beautiful day with a moderate wind. As we got there, my companion threw his arms

HUNT, J. AND HILLARY, E.—*Continued*

around me and embraced me." His companion, Tenzing, said that he was "very happy and not particularly tired." The beekeeper and the guide remained on the peak about twenty minutes before they descended. "Hillary, the New Zealander, along with Tenzing, the Sherpa, 'Tiger of the Snows,'" the New York *Times* asserted editorially, "will take his place with Sir Walter Raleigh and Sir Francis Drake."

Edmund Percival Hillary, "a quiet-spoken, shy perfectionist," was born in New Zealand on July 20, 1919, the son of Percival Augustus and Gertrude (Clark) Hillary. He became interested in mountain climbing while still a schoolboy; at the age of fourteen, he spent a weekend on Mount Ruapehu, and, according to his mother, "has been tremendously keen on climbing ever since." Before long he began to spend two seasons a year in his country's Southern Alps "to perfect his rock-climbing technique and learn ice work." During World War II he served in the Royal New Zealand Air Force as a navigator with a Catalina patrol squadron in the South Pacific. After the end of the war, although he had been seriously wounded, he determined to resume mountain climbing.

He went on the New Zealand Garhwal expedition in 1951. Because of his skillful ice technique, the New Zealand Alpine Club named him to accompany Eric Shipton in 1951. The next year he was a member of a British expedition to Cho Oyu in the Himalayas. Hillary began to keep bees in 1936, and since then, with the exception of the war years, he has spent seven or eight months each year as a beekeeper, and the remaining months climbing mountains. In 1946 he became a partner in an apiary with his brother, W. F. Hillary. He married Louise Rose, whose father is president of the New Zealand Alpine Club, on September 3, 1953. Hillary is six feet three inches tall, and has been described in *Senior Scholastic* (February 17, 1954) as "lean" and "rawboned."

British Inf. Services
SIR EDMUND HILLARY

British Inf. Services
TENZING NORKEY

Tenzing Norkey was born in the village of Tami, Nepal in 1914, but has lived in Darjeeling, India for more than twenty years. Although he is unschooled, owing to financial circumstances, he is able to speak five languages—Hindi, Gurkhali, Tibetan, Bengali, "and an English," in Gordon Graham's words, "which makes up with its richness in mountaineering lore what it may lack in grammar or syntax." Reputed to be "the toughest of a tough race," he was early captivated by "inspiring stories of mountain climbing from his parents and grandparents and ran away from home to become a porter in a British expedition in 1935."

The following year he participated in another British expedition, and in 1938 climbed to 23,000 feet. In 1952 he was a member of a Swiss expedition and reached a record 28,215 feet up Mount Everest, only to be driven back by blasts of stone and ice and by lack of oxygen.

Before the 1953 expedition he had lived with his family in one room; after the announcement of his triumph, two public subscriptions, one in India and one in Nepal, raised money with which he has built a new home. Plans were made to appoint him director of a mountaineering school to be established by the Indian government. After studying at the Swiss Mountaineering School in the Bernese Alps during the summer of 1954, Tenzing returned to India and became director of the new mountaineering institute there.

He is president of the Sherpa Association. His wife, Anglahmu, was born in India, but is of Sherpa descent. They are the parents of two teen-age daughters, Pem Pem and Nima, who attend a school at a Catholic convent near Darjeeling. Tenzing is five feet three inches tall, and has been described as "a handsome, brown-skinned man with a ready smile."

"The courage and fortitude of the victors," *Time* wrote, "were in no way diminished by the evident fact that they could never have stood so high except for the work of the team, and the planning of Colonel . . . Hunt." Hunt wrote an exhaustive account of the expedition, which was published in England under the title *The Ascent of Everest* (Hodder, 1953), and in America as *The Conquest of Everest,* (Dutton, 1954) with a final chapter contributed by Hillary.

Harry C. James, reviewing it for the *Christian Science Monitor,* wrote in part: "*The Conquest of Everest* is an eloquent, swift-moving, factual account. . . . In a world torn by personal ambition and nationalism, it is good to turn . . . to the final sentence in this account of one of the most imaginative undertakings in our time: 'There is no height, no depth, that the spirit of man, guided by a higher Spirit, cannot attain.' "

A motion picture of the expedition made by Stobart and Lowe, entitled *The Conquest of Everest,* was received with equal enthusiasm as "a thrilling account of a thrilling exploit, perfectly edited and strikingly photographed"; the movie won a Robert J. Flaherty Award, given by City College in New York.

Numerous honors and awards were showered upon the members of the expedition, individually and collectively. Hunt and Hillary were knighted; Hillary was created a Knight Commander of the Order of the British Empire. Since he is not a Briton, Tenzing was not eligible for knighthood; he was, however, invested with the George Medal. King Tribhuvana Bir Bikram of Nepal conferred on him the Star of Nepal, the highest honor he can bestow on a subject, and invested Hunt and Hillary with the Order of the Strong Right Arms of the Gurkhas.

On December 8, 1953, Hunt and Hillary were unanimously elected honorary members of the Royal Institution of Chartered Surveyors. Chamonix, France, an Alpine mountain climbing center, made Tenzing an honorary citizen in January 1954. On January 29, 1954, the American Geographical Society awarded its Cullum Medal to the expedition; on February 11, President Eisenhower presented Hunt and Hillary with the Hubbard Medal, the highest honor which the National Geographic Society confers, and in March 1954, George V. Allen, U.S. Ambassador to India, presented the medal to Tenzing in Darjeeling. Hunt was awarded the badge of a Soviet Mountaineer, First Class, during a lecture trip to Moscow in June 1954.

Of the many written tributes to Hunt's leadership may be cited these words from the London *Observer*: "Hunt knows that a climbing party is held together not by military discipline but by friendship and common enthusiasm; and mountains to him have always been far more than a technical or a physical challenge . . . his accounts of running downhill on skis with Athens spread out below . . . reveal a man with a feeling for the poetry as well as the problems of mountains."

He married Joy Mowbray-Green in 1936. His wife is "almost as tough as her husband, able to cope with an obstinate primus [stove] when bivouacking high on an exposed mountain ledge." The Hunts have four daughters. The soldier-mountaineer is tall and fair-haired, and has blue eyes.

References

Christian Sci Mon p9 Jl 2 '53 pors
N Y Herald Tribune p17 Je 8 '53
N Y Times p14 Je 2 '53 por
Washington (D.C.) Post p1+ Je 3 '53
Hunt, Sir J. The Conquest of Everest (1954)
Malartic, Y. Tenzing of Everest (1954)
Who's Who, 1954

HUNT, LESTER C(ALLAWAY) July 8, 1892-June 19, 1954 United States Senator (Democrat) from Wyoming; was graduated from St. Louis University College of Dentistry (1917); practiced as dentist in Wyoming (1917-1934); Army officer in World War I; Hunt took postgraduate courses in dentistry at Northwestern University; resumed his practice in Wyoming (1920); active in community affairs; served one term as president of Fremont county Medical and Dental Society; served in state government of Wyoming as president of Board of Dental Examiners (1924-1928), member of legislature (1932-1934), secretary of state (1935-1943), and governor (1943-1949); elected to U.S. Senate (1948) on Democratic ticket; was member of Senate Armed Services and Crime Investigating committees; death by suicide. See *Current Biography,* (Mar.) 1951.

Obituary

N Y Times p 1+ Je 20 '54

HUTCHESON, WILLIAM L(EVI) Feb. 7, 1874—Oct. 20, 1953 Former labor union president; began work as a carpenter; elected second vice-president of Brotherhood of Carpenters in 1912; first vice-president in 1913; president (1915-1952); since 1952, president emeritus of United Brotherhood of Carpenters and Joiners; member of War Labor Board during World War I; directed labor division of Republican party (1932, 1936); became first vice-president of AFL in 1940; appointed to national council of America First Committee in 1941; and was director of Home for Aged Carpenters. See *Current Biography,* (Sept.) 1943.

Obituary

N Y Times p29 O 21 '53

HUTCHINS, ROBERT MAYNARD Jan. 17, 1899- Foundation executive; former university president

Address: b. c/o The Fund for the Republic, 1 E. 54th St., New York 22

NOTE: This biography supersedes the article which appeared in *Current Biography* in 1940.

The Fund for the Republic, established in 1953 by the Ford Foundation with an outright grant of $15,000,000, is headed by Dr. Robert Maynard Hutchins. He had been an associate director of the Ford Foundation from 1951 until his appointment to the presidency of the Fund for the Republic in May 1954.

When Robert Maynard Hutchins announced in 1951 that he would resign from his post as chancellor of the University of Chicago to become associate director of the Ford Foundation, a bewildered student asked, "How can a myth resign?" With his resignation on June 30, 1951, a colorful and contentious era at the University of Chicago ended.

During his twenty-two years as president and chancellor, Hutchins introduced such controversial changes at the university as the "Chicago Plan," the "Great Books" program and the minimizing of athletics. His own writings have presented his educational theories to the public; his latest books are *The Conflict in Education in a Democratic Society* (Harper, 1953) and *The University of Utopia* (University of Chicago Press, 1953). Although he was branded by some as a fanatical liberal, ominously medieval by others, even his severest critics admit that Hutchins' ideas had one good effect—they made educators recognize the need for re-examining teaching methods in American colleges.

Robert Maynard Hutchins was born in Brooklyn, New York on January 17, 1899, the son of William James and Anna Laura (Murch) Hutchins. His father was a Presbyterian minister who became a professor of theology at Oberlin College and later the president of Berea College in Kentucky.

When Robert was sixteen he entered Oberlin College. His education was interrupted by World War I, when he enlisted in 1917 in the ambulance service of the United States. He then served with his unit in Italy and was awarded the Italian *Croce di Guerra* in 1918.

After the war, Hutchins continued his studies at Yale University. He received his bachelor's degree with honors in 1921 and was elected to Phi Beta Kappa. He entered the Yale Law School and combined studying with teaching, at the Lake Placid School in New York (from 1921 to 1923) and while acting as secretary of Yale (from 1923 to 1927). Having received the LL.B. degree in 1925, he began teaching at the Yale Law School and became a full professor in 1927. In the same year, he was appointed acting dean of the law school and in the following year was appointed dean.

While in this post he hoped to insure a "quality product" in the graduates of the school by making higher entrance requirements and by setting higher standards of scholastic work. He established an honors program of study for the final year of certain qualified students and broadened the basic law curriculum to include studies in other social sciences. He also helped to organize the Yale Institute of Human Relations.

When Hutchins became dean of the Yale Law School at twenty-nine, he was regarded as refreshingly precocious. After he became president of the University of Chicago in 1929 at the age of thirty, he became one of the most controversial figures in American education.

Stating that "we have confused science with information, ideas with facts, and knowledge with miscellaneous data" and that students must primarily come to college "to think," Hutchins began to plan for a new program of education at the university.

In accordance with his objection to "uneducated specialists," Hutchins sought a system by which students would have to study in the four fields of the biological, physical, and social sciences and the humanities, and would be able to obtain a degree as soon as they passed the board of examiners' final "achievement" examination.

Convinced that the last two years of high school duplicated the first two years of college, Hutchins advocated a plan which offered a four year liberal arts program starting in the usual junior year of high school. The plan went into effect in 1937. The university decided in 1942 to award the bachelor's degree for this program and to use placement tests as the basis of admission to the university instead of the high school credit system.

Hutchins introduced a "Great Books" course at the University of Chicago in the early nineteen-thirties, and his plan was adopted by Dr. Stringfellow Barr, president of St. John's College, Annapolis, Maryland, at that time.

Determined to carry this program to the general public as well as to colleges, Hutchins began giving adult courses in the great books in 1946 and was editor in chief of *Great Books of The Western World* (Encyclopaedia Britannica, 1952), a 32,000 compendium of Western culture containing in fifty-four volumes 443 works by seventy-four authors from Homer to Freud.

In 1937 Hutchins was responsible for the reorganization of Chicago Law School in founding a "fundamental, rather than a vocational, curriculum" to include courses in psychology, philosophy, and economics.

Some of the faculty, including social scientist Harry D. Gideonse and George Mead, head of the philosophy department, resigned in protest against Hutchin's ideas. He provoked further opposition by abolishing intercollegiate football at the university in 1939.

Before Pearl Harbor, Hutchins argued against American participation in the war since America was "morally unprepared." "I am not a member of the America First Committee," he stated, "I should like to join a committee for Humanity First."

During World War II the University of Chicago had a large part in the development of the atomic bomb. The $2,000,000,000 government research program there led to the first "controlled" chain reaction experiment at Stagg Field on December 2, 1942.

After the war, Hutchins no longer maintained an isolationist position, which he called an "anachronism" in the atomic age. He campaigned for the establishment of a world organization and for the international civilian control of atomic energy.

When told at the August 12, 1945 University of Chicago Round Table Discussion that world organization was a thousand years off, Hutchins said that the atomic bomb "may frighten us into . . . those positive political steps necessary to the creation of a world society, not a thousand or 500 years from now, but now."

Active in the formation of the Committee to Frame a World Constitution, Hutchins has served as its president since 1945. Hutchins wrote in an article entitled the "Bomb Secret is Out!" that "our only salvation lies in establishment of international morality, a mutual acceptance of the futility of further warfare and a mutual avowal to keep the peace" (*American Magazine*, December 1947).

Hutchins did a great deal to build up the scientific departments at the University of Chicago. Under his administration, the university adopted a $12,000,000 peacetime nuclear and metals research program to be conducted at three new institutes. Two Nobel prize-winning scientists were made a permanent part of the faculty in 1945: Harold C. Urey and Enrico Fermi.

Resigning as president of the University of Chicago in 1945 Hutchins became its chancellor. He took a year's leave of absence from the university in 1946 in order to devote more time to his work as chairman of the board of editors of Encyclopaedia Britannica, Inc.

Hutchins was chosen in 1947 to head the thirteen-man Commission on the Freedom of the Press. He has been a consistent advocate of cooperation between universities. For example, the universities of Texas and Chicago combined their astronomy departments; four denominational schools have organized the federated theological faculty at the university. A cooperative mid-west inter-library center was established on the University of Chicago campus with fourteen other universities and institutions included among its members.

In 1948, under his direction, the University of Chicago organized a two-year project to help re-establish cooperation between higher education in Germany and the United States, and to exchange professors between the universities of Chicago and Frankfurt.

Hutchins has been an equally vigilant and eloquent defender of academic freedom. To him, a university is a community of scholars and must stand for something other than what the vocal minorities or majorities demand at the moment. His test for membership in a university faculty is the competence and integrity of the individual. For this reason, he opposed the loyalty oath for any university faculty members. In 1950 as the controversy over the oath raged, Hutchins announced that the University of Chicago senate had approved in principle the voluntary contribution by professors of two per cent of their salaries for a year to assist any University of California teacher discharged over failure to take the non-communist oath.

Stephen Lewellyn
ROBERT MAYNARD HUTCHINS

When questioned in 1949 by the Illinois seditious activities legislative committee about subversive activities at the University of Chicago, Hutchins declared emphatically that "the legislature and the university are both opposed to Communism." It is his firm belief that the most effective way to combat communism is "to maintain and develop . . . the western traditions of freedom," for the danger facing democracy comes mostly from those who mistakenly repress the free spirit upon which it is built (New York *Times*, April 22, 1949).

Hutchins' main doctrines have been expanded in his books, *No Friendly Voice* (University of Chicago Press, 1936), *The Higher Learning in America* (Yale University Press, 1936), *Education For Freedom* (Louisiana State University Press, 1943), *The Conflict in Education in a Democratic Society* (Harper, 1953), and *The University of Utopia* (University of Chicago Press, 1953). He has written numerous articles for both popular and learned periodicals.

Hutchins became an associate director on June 30, 1951 of the Ford Foundation whose purpose is to "further the cause of peace, advance education, strengthen democratic institutions, promote economic stability, and increase knowledge about individual behavior and human relations." As one of six associate directors, Dr. Hutchins has responsibilities which cover the whole range of the foundation's activities, but his particular work is in education.

His appointment as president of the Fund for the Republic was announced on May 24, 1954. The fund is an independent organization that aims to support "activities directed toward the

HUTCHINS, ROBERT MAYNARD—*Continued*

elimination of restrictions on freedom of thought, inquiry, and expression in the United States and the development of policies and procedures best adapted to protect these rights." The Fund has made grants of $240,000 to the Southern Regional Council for its work in interracial relations and $50,000 to the American Bar Association for an analysis of the operations of Congressional investigating committees.

In *The Conflict of Education in a Democratic Society,* Dr. Hutchins discusses the prevailing theories on education and then advances his own choice of "an intellectual discipline" that fits a man to solve new problems, grasp new facts, meet new needs, and remold the environment "to make it conform to the aspirations of the human spirit."

Hutchins was awarded an honorary M.A. degree from Yale University in 1922, and an honorary LL.B. in 1925. He received honorary LL.D. degrees from the University of West Virginia, Lafayette College and Oberlin College in 1929, Williams College (1930), Berea College (1931), Harvard University (1936), Tulane University (1938), University of Copenhagen (1946), University of Frankfurt (1948), University of Stockholm (1949) and Rollins College (1950). The University of Illinois conferred on him an honorary Litt.D. in 1947.

He served as chairman of the Commission on International Economic Relations (from 1933 to 1936) and of the Goethe Bicentennial Foundation (1949). He is an honorary member of the Chicago Bar Association and is an officer of the French Legion of Honor. The city of Frankfurt, Germany awarded him the Goethe plaque in 1949.

He holds membership in the Yale, Metropolitan and the Century clubs in New York; the Authors in London; and the Chicago, Commercial, University, Union League, Tavern (honorary) and Law (honorary) clubs, Chicago.

He married Maude Phelps McVeigh, a young sculptress, in 1921. He has three daughters, Mary Frances Ratcliffe, Joanna Blessing, and Clarissa Phelps by this marriage which ended in divorce in 1948. On May 10, 1949, he married Vesta Sutton Orlick.

Hutchins ascribes his excellent health to the fact that whenever the impulse to exercise comes over him, he lies down until it passes over. Hutchins enjoys reading German novels, fishing and cooking. He has been described by John Gunther as a man who "boils with vision, likes idiosyncrasy and is completely fearless and independent."

References (see also references listed in 1940 biographical sketch)

Coronet 25:163 Mr '49
Time 54:58 N 21 '49

Leaders in Education (1948)
Who's Who, 1953
Who's Who in America, 1952-53
Who's Who in American Education, 1945-46
World Biography (1948)

IBN SAUD, KING OF SAUDI ARABIA

1880—Nov. 9, 1953 Won his kingdom by the sword; established himself in 1912 as head of state of Nejd; in 1915 signed treaty of friendship with British government; proclaimed King of Arabia of the Sauds in 1926; constantly added new territories to his kingdom and named it Saudi Arabia in 1932; remained neutral during World War II; introduced modern improvements in his desert domain; acquired large revenues through leasing oil concessions to American companies; member of Wahhabi sect of the Mohammedan faith; father of about 140 children. See *Current Biography,* (Feb.) 1943.

Obituary

N Y Times p1+ Nov 10 '53

INGALLS, (MILDRED DODGE) JEREMY

Apr. 2, 1911 Poet; teacher

Address: b. c/o Longmans, Green & Co., Inc., 55 Fifth Ave., New York 3; Rockford College, Rockford, Ill.; h. 501 College Ave., Rockford, Ill.

Reprinted from the *Wilson Library Bulletin,* May 1954

In the foreword to Jeremy Ingalls' first volume of poetry, published in the Yale Series of Younger Poets in 1941, the late Stephen Vincent Benét wrote: "It is not the easiest task in the world to introduce Miss Ingalls' work; not because the work is difficult but because it is different." Now, more than a decade later, Jeremy Ingalls is an established and highly regarded poet, scholar, teacher, and—more recently, with the publication of *The Galilean Way*—she has made her mark as a religious philosopher. But Benét's words retain their validity. She is a poet, he commented, "at once mature and sensitive . . . whose work is entirely and originally her own, and in whom intellectual force is combined with a consistent spiritual philosophy."

Although she has lived for many years in the Middle West, Mildred Dodge Jeremy Ingalls (she does not use her first two names) was born April 2, 1911 in the Atlantic coast town of Gloucester, Massachusetts, and lived there until she entered college. Her father, Charles Augustine Ingalls (now president of the Cape Ann National Bank in Gloucester), and her mother, the former May Estelle Dodge, can trace their New England ancestry back to the early 1600's.

Jeremy Ingalls was an only but not a lonely child. She was raised with a spate of cousins and friends her own age and had a hearty and happy childhood. She had an ardent and unquenchable thirst for knowledge. The fortunate location of Gloucester only a short distance from the museums and concert halls of Boston helped in some measure to satisfy that longing. More important was her reading. At twelve she was deep into Dante and one day stumbled upon an English account of the Buddhist theory of Nirvana ("I recall it as a rather dizzying afternoon"). At fourteen she was working her way

JEREMY INGALLS

through Balzac, Goethe, Confucius, Sun Yat-sen, and Nietzsche. She majored in English literature and classical Greek at Tufts College in Medford, Massachusetts (B.A. 1932), and her college career glittered with honors such as Phi Beta Kappa, editorship of the college literary journal, the Goddard Prize in English, and a scholarship for her studies toward the M.A. (1933) at Tufts.

From 1934 to 1941 Miss Ingalls taught mathematics, general science, English, and American literature at the Gloucester High School. In the latter year two books by her were published—one, the result of an interest she had pursued eagerly since childhood, a group of short stories on legendary themes called *A Book of Legends.* The other was the collection of poems which won her the Yale Younger Poets prize—*The Metaphysical Sword.* In these poems was illustrated the depth and variety of the poet's background—classical, mythological, Biblical, oriental. Ruth Lechlitner commented in *Books* on Miss Ingalls' "excellent command of ideas to frame the essential human factor," and Elizabeth Drew, in the *Atlantic Monthly,* singled out for praise the precision and economy of her language—"she has direct, edged irony which goes straight to its mark."

In 1943, after two years as assistant professor of English at Western College in Oxford, Ohio, she received a Guggenheim Fellowship and in 1944 an American Academy of Arts and Letters grant. These awards enabled her to complete her most ambitious work to date, the long narrative poem *Tahl* (1945).

Tahl is the story of a young musician living in contemporary times but somehow transcending time. As Miss Ingalls explains it, the Tahls of this world are "the kinds of people who, during the surface breakdowns of tribes and nations, have always been the transmitters of the essentials of human dignity." It is a difficult poem, carefully and elaborately worked out. "It is a world in itself," John Holmes wrote in the Boston *Globe,* "created by a rich, vigorous, modern mind. . . ."

The inquiring human spirit, which is essentially the subject of *Tahl,* is also the subject of Miss Ingalls' recently published prose work, *The Galilean Way,* subtitled "A Book for Modern Skeptics." Miss Ingalls is not a skeptic. Her own religion is Episcopalian, but in this volume she speaks simply as a Christian. Drawing upon her extensive knowledge of Buddhism, Hinduism, Islam, Judaism, and Confucianism, as well as her close reading and interpretation of the teachings of Jesus, she has written a book which, Dr. W. Russell Bowie of the Virginia Theological Seminary finds, "has a message both for the mind and for the spirit." Another admirer of the book is Dr. Reinhold Niebuhr of the Union Theological Seminary who read and approved of the manuscript before it was published.

Since 1948 Miss Ingalls has been on the faculty of Rockford College in Illinois. There she has been resident poet and has taught Chinese history, English literature, creative writing, and from 1950-1952 she was chairman of the division of arts. She also lectures from time to time in comparative religions. She teaches the first semester of each academic year and goes on leave the second semester, generally to the Southwest, where she writes. For relaxation Miss Ingalls enjoys playing various musical instruments "poorly but happily" and translating Chinese classical texts. In addition to the Guggenheim and American Academy grants, she held a scholarship from the National Republic of China in 1945 and 1946, received the Shelley Memorial Award for poetry in 1950, the Lola Ridge Memorial Award in 1951, and in 1952 a Ford Foundation fellowship for Asiatic studies.

References

Directory of American Scholars (1951)
Who's Who in Chicago and Illinois (1950)
Who's Who in the Midwest (1952)

INNES, (RALPH) HAMMOND July 15, 1913- Author

Address: b. c/o Alfred A. Knopf, Inc., 501 Madison Ave., New York 22; h. Ayres End, Kersey, Suffolk, England

Reprinted from the *Wilson Library Bulletin,* Sept. 1954

Three years ago, May Lamberton Becker, in her New York *Herald Tribune* department, The Reader's Guide, printed several columns of suggestions from readers for a list of books of "high adventure," recent publications worthy to be considered with those of John Buchan. "Everything that Hammond Innes ever wrote," was one such suggestion. Innes has also been called "the best contemporary writer of the adventure story."

(Continued next page)

Erich Hartmann
HAMMOND INNES

He was born Ralph Hammond Innes at Horsham, England—the Shelley neighborhood—July 15, 1913. His father, William Hammond Innes, a bank manager, was a descendant of the Scots clan of Innes, the smallest clan in Scotland. His mother was Dora Beatrice (Crisford) Hammond Innes. Innes' early years were spent in small Hampshire towns, and he was graduated from Cranbrook School into a depression in 1931. He became a schoolmaster for exactly one term. In 1932 Innes was an industrial correspondent for the *Financial News,* learning to write compressed and forceful sentences under the direction of Maurice Green, now city editor of the London *Times.*

His first novel, *The Doppelganger,* was published by Herbert Jenkins in 1934. This, and three other novels, earned him about £120. In 1936 Innes married Dorothy Mary Lang, a repertory actress, now a playwright, who is a descendant of Andrew Lang. He published *Wreckers Must Breathe* and *The Trojan Horse* before he joined up with the Royal Artillery in 1940 and became Gunner Innes, helping to defend the badly blitzed fighter aerodrome of Kenley during the Battle of Britain. During an early watch of 2 to 4 A.M., he wrote the novel *Attack Alarm* (1942), which, serialized in the *Saturday Evening Post,* enthralled Americans and gratified the New York office of the British Ministry of Information. It was "a genuine thriller of action and suspense, of plot and intrigue, of spies and fifth columnists," said David Tilden in the New York *Herald Tribune.*

For the next four years Major Innes—as he then became—was busy with the Eighth Army, taking part in the Sicily landings, being hospitalized, and then working with the Mediterranean group of army newspapers directed by Hugh Cudlipp, of the *Sunday Pictorial.* He edited the Florence edition, covered the invasion of Southern France, and wrote *Dead and Alive,* a novel about his experiences helping break up networks of black markets and gangs of counterfeiters in Rome and Naples. At Cortina, Innes took a brief, hard course in skiing; when he returned to England to a thatched cottage in Aldbourne, Wiltshire, he put this to good use in another successful thriller, *The Lonely Skier* (1947), titled *Fire in the Snow* in the United States. The New York *Times* thought it a fine example of "the top-drawer British psycho-thriller," and the late Will Cuppy called the book "fast, exciting and likeable." For *Gale Warning* (1948)—serialized in England by the B.B.C. and in America in the *Post*—Innes drew on his memories of freighters and convoys in the Mediterranean. William Weber in the *Saturday Review of Literature* called this tale of piracy and adventure "first-class."

Before writing *The Killer Mine* (1949) Innes went down a Cornish tin mine to the 1,400 fathom level. The *New Yorker* thought this tale of liquor-running "aimed—and rather successfully, too—at admirers of the grim and atmospheric." In *Cocos Bay* (1950), a story for boys, fifteen-year-old Johnny Keverne goes exploring on an island off the coast of Costa Rica. *The Survivors* (1950) was a novel of a whaling expedition undergoing shipwreck and hardship in the Antarctic. Critics had many reservations about *Angry Mountain* (1951); the late Lisle Bell thought it almost a caricature of the Innes-style thriller. Its quick successor, *Air Bridge,* showed two ill-assorted men working on a fuel-saving engine for the Berlin airlift. "Mr. Innes is a whale of a writer," said Rex Lardner in the New York *Times.* Canada is the setting of *Campbell's Kingdom* (1952), which, James Sandoe wrote, was managed "with very considerable skill, silkily but with vigor."

To write *The Naked Land* (1954), a novel of adventure, Innes and his wife spent the winter of 1951-1952 in Morocco, "chiefly south of the Atlas Mountains in the 'Zone of Insecurity,' living in the French *beau geste* forts and traveling down into the Sahara." They traveled recently all along the Russian frontier of Norway, commissioned by the American magazine *Holiday,* which also sent them on a tour of the Trucial Coast, often referred to as "The Pirate Coast." Innes also has covered "the Oman coast, all the islands off, the more inaccessible oil survey expeditions, and the whole of the Hadhramant—the valley with the skyscraper cities, previously chiefly covered by Freya Stark."

His chief recreation is yachting and ocean racing, sailing his own 10-ton ocean racer, *Triune of Troy.* Innes is brown-eyed, with thinning brown hair, and he stands 5 feet 8 inches and weighs about 170 pounds. He has a house, Ayres End, in the old weaving village of Kersey, Suffolk.

References

Collins' Magazine for Boys and Girls p36+ Summer '48 pors
Who's Who, 1954

IVES, CHARLES E(DWARD) Oct. 20, 1874-May 19, 1954 Composer; part-time organist and choirmaster (1898-1902); entered insurance business (1898); partner, Ives and Myrick insurance firm (1909-1930); credited with first use of atonality, polyharmony and polyrhythms; awarded Pulitzer Prize (1947) for *Third Symphony;* wrote *Second Pianoforte Sonata; Concord, Massachusetts, 1840-60;* many other compositions including 114 songs and four symphonies. See *Current Biography,* (Jun.) 1947.

Obituary

N Y Times p31 My 20 '54

JACKSON, ROBERT H(OUGHWOUT) Feb. 13, 1892- Oct. 9, 1954 Associate Justice of the U.S. Supreme Court; author; educated at Albany Law School and Chautauqua Institute; admitted to New York bar (1913); was general counsel for U.S. Bureau of Internal Revenue (1934-1935) and assistant attorney general (1936-1938); as Solicitor General (1938-1940), fought for New Deal legislation; appointed Attorney General (1940) and to Supreme Court (1941); known for liberal convictions, for vigor and clarity of his opinions, for his frequent dissents; was chief prosecutor for U.S. in Nuremberg trials of Nazi war criminals (1945-1946). See *Current Biography,* (Oct.) 1950.

Obituary

N Y Times p 1+ O 10 '54

JAMALI, MOH(AMME)D. FADHEL 1903- Former Premier of Iraq

Address: h. Taha St., Baghdad, Iraq

Serving in six cabinets of the Kingdom of Iraq between the years 1946 and 1953, Dr. Mohd Fadhel Jamali occupied the post of Minister of Foreign Affairs, and during this period also headed his country's delegation to the United Nations at most of the sessions of the General Assembly. He resigned from his government office early in 1953 but was recalled by King Faisal and on September 16 was appointed Premier and Minister of Interior with authority to select a new cabinet.

On August 4, 1954 a Reuters dispatch from Baghdad, Iraq announced that Nuri al-Said, pro-British leader of the Constitutional Union Party, had formed a new Cabinet to succeed the caretaker Government of Arshad al-Umari, who had taken office after the resignation of the Government of Dr. Fadhel Jamali on March 8.

Mohammed Fadhel Jamali was born in 1903 at Kadhimain in what was then a part of the Ottoman Empire. He is the son of Sheikh Abbas al Jamali and Alwiyah Bahiya. His father was a local leader of the Shi'ites, one of the two principal religious sects of Islam. At the age of seven young Jamali entered the mosque school in Kadhimain, where he was taught to read the Koran.

Later he studied at a new school in Kadhimain which adopted western methodology and which was conducted by the "Young Turks" of the Society of Union and Progress, a Persian school in Kadhimain directed by Hajji Ali Akbar Arabi, an exponent of the Pan-Islamic movement, a state-controlled school in Baghdad, and the Khalesi Institute. Having decided to become a teacher, Jamali entered the Elementary Teachers' Training College, where he was graduated first in his class in 1920.

The new government of Iraq, which was recognized by the British who held the Iraqi mandate after World War I, established six scholarships to the American University of Beirut in Lebanon. One of the first six recipients of the scholarship, Jamali received the B.A. degree in education in 1927. The student was president of Urwat ul Wuthqu (nationalist college society), a member of the Students' Union (English-language society), the Brotherhood Society, an interfaith organization promoting mutual understanding.

Jamali secured, in 1927, an appointment at the Higher Teachers' Training College in Baghdad where he became an advocate of education for girls as well as boys. In 1929, he received a Macy grant from the International Institute of Columbia University's Teachers' College to study at the college. He received the M.A. degree in 1930.

The British mandate in Iraq was terminated in October 4, 1932 and Iraq was admitted to the League of Nations. Jamali returned to his native country to be Iraq's attaché on the Commission of Educational Inquiry which was sent to Baghdad. Afterwards he became supervisor general in the Department of Education. By June 1934 he had fulfilled all the requirements for the Ph.D. degree granted him by Columbia. His thesis was entitled *New Iraq; Its Problems of Bedouin Education.*

Dr. Jamali served for ten years in Iraq's Department of Education and Public Instruction under a succession of Ministers, and also lectured on education, philosophy and school management at the Higher Teachers' Training College. He wrote several papers at this time including "Whither Education in the Arab World" (1935), "Education in Modern Turkey" (1937), and "Educational Trends in Germany, England, and France" (1938).

He joined the Ministry of Foreign Affairs in 1942, and was promoted to director general (with the rank of Minister) in 1944. A member of the Iraq delegation to the United Nations Conference on International Organization in San Francisco in 1945, he signed the United Nations Charter for Iraq.

One of the founders of the Arab League, Jamali was Iraq's spokesman against Zionism before the Anglo-American Inquiry Commission on Palestine. On June 1, 1946 he was named Minister for Foreign Affairs in the new government headed by Arshad el Umary.

In an interview, Foreign Minister Jamali suggested as an alternative to the Anglo-American Inquiry Commission's recommendation that 100,000 Jews be permitted to enter Palestine, that America "open her doors" to displaced persons "and not merely shed tears while seeking a solution of the problem at the

United Nations
MOHD. FADHEL JAMALI

expense of small nations" (New York *Times*, June 28, 1946). Dr. Jamali was a delegate to the first General Assembly of the United Nations in 1946 and to the London conference on Palestine of that year.

As president of the Arab League, he warned President Truman's special representative George A. Brownell that "revolution throughout the Arab world" could be expected if Arab rights in Palestine were violated. (New York *Times*, November 21, 1946.)

Again speaking for the Arab League, Dr. Jamali in London in February 1947, argued for an immediate termination of the British mandate of Palestine, in accordance with provisions of the League of Nations Covenant. (If Palestine were promptly given independence, the Arabs would have a majority in the population. Zionists, on the other hand, wanted termination of the British mandate to be postponed until substantial Jewish immigration had been achieved, or, alternatively, partition of the Holy Land into separate Arab and Jewish states).

Co-chairman of the Iraq delegation to the U.N. General Assembly at New York in the autumn of 1947, Foreign Minister Jamali made notable speeches against the partition of Palestine. The General Assembly voted 33 to 13 to partition Palestine into two states, Arab and Jewish. All of the Asiatic countries, including India, either voted "no" or abstained, and after the vote was announced the six Arab delegations "arose and strode out of the Assembly chamber" (*Time*, December 8, 1947).

After yielding his portfolio as Minister of Foreign Affairs at the end of 1948, Dr. Jamali served briefly as Envoy Extraordinary and Minister Plenipotentiary to Egypt. From April to September 1949, he was again Iraq's Foreign Minister and was his country's permanent U.N. delegate through the sessions of 1949 and 1950. At that session he introduced a resolution calling for the immediate independence of Libya, and on November 3, 1949 made "an unusual attack on both the Western powers and the Soviet bloc for dividing the organization" of fourteen small countries seeking admission (New York *Times*, November 4, 1949).

A year later, in October 1950, in a United Nations speech on "Seven Pillars of Peace," Dr. Jamali urged that "members should reaffirm their adherence to the Charter and its basic principles," and that "underdeveloped countries" in the Middle East "should be given both technological and financial assistance" through "an arrangement like that of the Marshall Plan."

Made president of Iraq's Chamber of Deputies in December, 1950, Dr. Jamali served until August 1, 1952, when he again became Foreign Minister in the cabinet then formed by Mustapha el Umary.

As chief delegate to the U.N., Jamali charged in a general debate in October, 1952, that "the United Nations handled the Palestine situation in such a way as to turn out of their homes one million innocent Arabs, Moslems and Christians alike," and further warned that "serious thought should be given to revising the Charter" to do away with the Security Council veto. (Later in the month, the General Assembly's special political committee approved a $23,000,000 program to assist Arab refugees in the Middle East). Jamali remained Foreign Minister and chief U.N. delegate after the overthrow of the Umary government by General Nur Aldin Mahmoud in November, 1952. In the following month he helped to prevent a proposal to force the Arab States and Israel to meet in "face to face negotiations" over Palestine from obtaining a necessary two-thirds majority vote.

He was one of the authors in December, 1952 of a proposal by thirteen Arab nations calling on the French government and the Sultan of Morocco "to enter into negotiations to reach an early peaceful settlement." He resigned his post as Foreign Minister in January 1953 and was succeeded by Jamil el Madfai who in turn resigned in September to give way for a new cabinet headed by Dr. Jamali.

The recipient in 1945 of an honorary Doctor in Foreign Service degree from the University of Southern California, Dr. Jamali is an officer (Grade One) of the Orders of Natha and Hamayuni of the Hashemite Kingdom of Jordan and Iran, and has also been decorated by Spain, China, and his native country. He is a Mason, a member of the board of the Red Crescent Society, president of the Iraqi New Educational Fellowship Society, and vice-president of the Iraqi P.E.N. Club.

He married Sarah Hayden Powell, a young Canadian-born teacher of American parentage, in 1933, whom he had met while attending summer school at the University of Chicago in 1930. After their marriage his wife became a Moslem but retained her American citizenship. They have three children, Laith, Usameh and Abbas.

Dr. Jamali lists swimming and ballroom dancing as favorite recreations, and he enjoys listening to classical music and collecting mementos. Brown-haired and brown-eyed, he stands at five feet six inches, and weighs around 165 pounds.

He still believes that the "conscientious observation of the [U.N.] Charter constitutes the best way for a harassed world towards peace."

References

Asia 35:556+ S '35
Christian Sci Mon p2 N 14 '47
N Y Herald Tribune p33 Ap 27 '47; II p5 S 14 '47; p4 S 18 '53
N Y Times p6 O 30 '52
U N Bul 2:508 My 13 '47 por
Author's and Writer's Who's Who (1948-49)
International Who's Who, 1952
Who's Who in Egypt and the Near East, 1953
Who's Who in the United Nations (1951)
World Biography (1948)
World Diplomatic Directory (1951)

Shelburne Studios, Inc.
WILLIAM J. JAMESON

JAMESON, WILLIAM J(AMES) Aug. 8, 1898- Attorney

Address: b. c/o American Bar Association, 1140 N. Dearborn St., Chicago 10, Ill.; c/o Coleman, Jameson & Lamey, 516 Electric Bldg, Billings, Mont.; h. 67 Park Hill Rd., Billings, Mont.

The president of the American Bar Association for 1953-1954, William J. Jameson, succeeded Robert G. Storey to this office on August 28, 1953, after practicing law in Billings, Montana for thirty-one years and participating actively in the association since 1936. Past occupants of the unsalaried office have included Joseph H. Choate, Alton B. Parker, President William Howard Taft, Charles Evans Hughes and John W. Davis. At the time of Jameson's election as president, the ABA had a membership of 48,000 and through affiliated organizations represents about 135,000 attorneys.

On March 22, 1954 Jameson declined the invitation by the U.S. Senate permanent subcommittee on investigations to act as that subcommittee's special counsel in the dispute between Senator Joseph R. McCarthy of Wisconsin and the Army. Jameson announced his decision after consulting with the ABA's board of governors, several of whom felt that the association represents attorneys of many and frequently conflicting views.

William James Jameson was born in Butte, Montana on August 8, 1898 to Annie (Roberts) and William J. Jameson, a lawyer. He has one sister, Mrs. Lucille J. Armsby. William was graduated in 1915 from Roundup High School in Roundup, Montana where he had been on the debating team. He continued his debating activities at Montana State University in Missoula while majoring in economics and sociology. He was also president of the student body and the senior class, a member of Phi Delta Phi and Alpha Kappa Psi, and, during 1918, he served in the Students' Army Training Corps. He received the A.B. degree in 1919 and three years later fulfilled the requirements for the LL.B. degree.

On admission to the Montana bar in 1922, Jameson was employed by the law firm of Johnston, Coleman & Johnston in Billings; he became a member of the firm in 1925. The young attorney served in the Montana legislature from 1927 through 1930. He had accepted in 1929 a partnership in his law firm which became known as Johnston, Coleman and Jameson. The firm specializes in surrogate court matters, and corporation, public utility and insurance law; its name was changed in 1940 to Coleman, Jameson and Lamey.

Interested in the activities of professional societies, Jameson served as president of the Montana Bar Association in 1936 and 1937 and was selected to represent that association in 1936 in the ABA's house of delegates which was established in that year to act as a policy-making board. Its members, who meet biannually, are elected by individual states or chosen by state associations and affiliated legal organizations.

From 1938 to 1943 Jameson was a state delegate to the house of delegates; in 1943 he became a member of the board of governors, which executes policy while the house of delegates is not in session. He was an assembly delegate from 1936 to 1953.

The diamond jubilee of the association was held in Boston in August 1953 and was attended by about 4,000 lawyers and judges. Jameson was elected seventy-seventh president for a one year term by the 227-member house of delegates on August 24, 1953, the first of his state to fill this post. He dedicated his presidency to "the preservation of representative

JAMESON, WILLIAM J.—*Continued*

government in the United States, the protection of individual liberties along with national security, improving the administration of justice, the bringing of legal services within the means of every citizen, and the maintenance of high standards of legal education and professional conduct" (*Christian Science Monitor,* August 29, 1953).

The retiring ABA president, Dean Robert G. Storey of Southern Methodist law school, announced a $50,000 grant by the Ford Foundation to assist a special association committee headed by Supreme Court Justice Robert H. Jackson to undertake a five years nationwide study of the administration of criminal justice.

Action by the house of delegates at the meeting included adoption of a declaration that Communist lawyers should be disqualified to practice; authorization of a special committee on Communist tactics, strategy and objectives; a declaration that "a license to practice confers no vested right but is . . . revocable" for cause; and a decision to aid the Attorney General's committee studying anti-trust laws. After a controversial discussion concerning the Bricker amendment to restrict the treaty-making powers of the President, the house of delegates endorsed the amendment despite a speech in opposition to it delivered by Secretary of State John Foster Dulles.

Meeting in Atlanta, Georgia in March 1954, the ABA house of delegates voted to support statehood for Hawaii but not for Alaska. Loyd Wright of Los Angeles was nominated for election in August as the seventy-eighth president of the ABA.

The ABA presidency is, for all practical purposes, a full-time, unsalaried office. The president visits state and local bar associations, sometimes speaking five times a week; he presides at the four meetings of the board of governors held during the year and is also president of the American Bar Foundation, which has built the American Bar Center in Chicago. The building, costing $2,000,000, is on land donated by the University of Chicago, and opened August 1954. It houses the national headquarters of the ABA and affiliated organizations.

Jameson has contributed articles to the *Montana Law Review* and *Dicta.* He is a member of the Yellowstone county and Montana law associations, National Conference of Commissioners on Uniform State Laws, American Law Institute, and American Judicature Society. He is also a Mason and an American Legionnaire.

Active in community work, the attorney has served in the American Red Cross, Billings Chamber of Commerce, Lions International, and board of school trustees of Billings. Presently, he is a member of the governing bodies of the First Methodist Church of Billings, Billings Deaconess Hospital, Billings Young Men's Christian Association, and Endowment Foundation of Montana State University.

On July 28, 1923 Jameson married Mildred Lore. They have a daughter, Mary Lucille (Mrs. Walter Honaker), a son, William James, Jr., and two grandchildren. Jameson is five feet ten inches tall, weighs 180 pounds, and has gray eyes and hair. In politics he is a Republican. He is a director of the Montana Coal and Iron Company and Montana Power Company. Montana State University conferred on him the honorary LL.D. degree in 1952.

References

A B A Jour 39:292+ Ap '53 por
America's Young Men, 1938-39
Who's Who in America, 1954-55
Who's Who in Law, 1937
Who's Who in Methodism (1952)
World Biography (1948)

JAYNES, CLARE (pseud. of MAYER, JANE and SPIEGEL, CLARA)

Mayer, Jane Dec. 30, 1903- Author
Address: b. c/o Random House, 457 Madison Ave., New York 22; h. 614 Sheridan Rd., Glencoe, Ill.

Spiegel, Clara Dec. 6, 1904- Author
Address: b. c/o Random House, 457 Madison Ave., New York 22; h. 180 Beech St., Highland Park, Ill.

Reprinted from the *Wilson Library Bulletin,* May 1954

Clare Jaynes is brown-haired, brown-eyed; she is five feet three inches tall, and is of German-American ancestry. She was born in Kansas City, and again the following year in Chicago. She attended Vassar for one year, and was graduated after completing a four-year course at Vassar. And, although she already had a husband whom she married in 1923, she was again lawfully married in 1927. She has two children, also three, and her home is in two of Chicago's northshore suburbs about a mile apart. She has traveled widely in Europe, and has often appeared simultaneously in two places. She both likes and dislikes skiing, tennis, riding, music, and raising camellias.

Impossible? Not at all. Clare Jaynes is two people—Jane Mayer and Clara Spiegel, who use Clare Jaynes as the *nom de plume* for their work together: four novels all published by Random House, as well as stories in several English publications, and in leading magazines in the United States.

Jane Mayer was born on December 30, 1903 in Kansas City, Missouri, the only daughter in a family of three. Her parents were Louis P. Rothschild and Nora Westheimer. She attended Sunset Hill School in Kansas City, Missouri, and earned a B.A. at Vassar where she majored in English.

August Gatzert and Isabel Florsheim had one son, and Clara Spiegel was their only daughter, born December 6, 1904 in Chicago, Illinois. She attended first the Faulkner School in Chicago, then Vassar. It was there that Jane Mayer and Clara Spiegel met, and began the friendship which, beginning with their collaboration in 1936, has produced novels, articles, and short stories. One of the latter, "The Coming of Age," originally published in *Story*, was included in the *O. Henry Memorial Award Prize Stories of 1942*.

Their first novel, *Instruct My Sorrows* (1942) told of Jessica Drummond's first year of widowhood, and of how she finally achieved happiness and mental peace. F. H. Bullock in *Books* felt that "written with competence but without distinction, *Instruct My Sorrows* is calculated to hold the attention of every woman and, I should think, most men, from start to finish. It would seem to be difficult for an author, or in this case a pair of authors, to be glib and penetrating at the same time; yet *Instruct My Sorrows* is exactly that." Warner Brothers liked it so much that they made it into a motion picture which was released under the title *My Reputation*.

In 1944 *These Are the Times* was published: the story of a lovely, possessive woman, Judith Kenyon, who tried unsuccessfully to keep her husband from joining a medical unit for duty overseas. The Boston *Globe* said, "Matters medical are pretty sure-fire fascination for the layman, and if white coats and stethoscopes make you prick up your ears, *These Are the Times* is the book for you. Clare Jaynes is the pen name of two talented gals, who have turned out above average fiction on a subject it's pretty easy to make melodramatic or sentimental."

This Eager Heart (1947) was the story of a twelve-year-old marriage, which was brought to the breaking point by an Easterner who bought the ranch adjoining Kay and Mac MacFarland's ranch. Mary Ross wrote in the New York *Herald Tribune:* "Both Montana country and very real and likeable people who lived in it are shown skillfully in this straightforward and appealing story of a marriage that didn't end up on the rocks."

The Early Frost (1952) was a character study of Lann Saunders, the child of divorced parents. It is the story of her last year at boarding school, and traces her lonely way to the threshold of a better future. Of this book M. M. Ahern in the New York *Times* states, "*The Early Frost* might have been a mere catalogue of miseries and humiliations, bound up in a bright, skillful picture of a girls' school; but Lann is saved. . . . Clare Jaynes has set forth the image of loneliness with so steady but so light a hand, and we have felt for Lann so intensely that we are likely to accept her new maturity (as she accepts her improbable job in a kennel) out of sheer relief." On March 25, 1953 this book received the certificate of honorable mention from the Friends of American Writers.

In addition to the books and stories written under the pseudonym Clare Jaynes, Jane Mayer has published under her own name *Betsy Ross and the Flag* (1952), and is now working on "Dolly Madison."

Although their life as Clare Jaynes occupies much of their time, both writers have full private lives. Jane Mayer is married to David Mayer, a businessman, and has three children David III, Mary Jane, and Philip. Mrs. Mayer is of the Jewish faith. She weighs 115 pounds, and her favorite recreation is vacationing in Aspen, Colorado.

JANE MAYER

CLARA SPIEGEL
"Clare Jaynes"

Clara Spiegel is a divorcée. She has two sons, F. William, Jr., and Andrew G. She prefers traveling to staying in one spot, and has seen most of the United States, Europe and North Africa. She is fond of the theatre and sports. Of the latter her favorites are riding, hunting, and skiing, and these interests may explain why she weighs only 112 pounds.

As different as are their personalities, Jane Mayer and Clara Spiegel in combination make Clare Jaynes, a sensitive, understanding and successful writer.

References

Warfel, H. R. American Novelists of Today (1951)
Who's Who in America, 1954-55

JENKINS, RAY H(OWARD) Mar. 18, 1897- Lawyer

Address: b. Bank of Knoxville Bldg., Knoxville 2, Tenn.; h. Nash Hall, Knoxville, Tenn.

Widely known in Tennessee as an able trial lawyer who has handled some 600 criminal cases as well as civil suits during his thirty-year practice, Ray H. Jenkins has become known to millions of television viewers since the Army v. McCarthy hearings began on April 22, 1954. During the course of the investigations which have been held in the Caucus Room of the Senate Office Building in Washington, D.C., Jenkins has been both criticized and ac-

Wide World

RAY H. JENKINS

claimed for his "hammering, dogged tenacity" in eliciting answers from witnesses.

Three Democrats and four Republicans of the permanent investigating subcommittee of the Senate Committee on Government Operations voted unanimously to employ Jenkins as special counsel after they were assured that Jenkins, a Republican, had no public record of support of or opposition to the Wisconsin junior Senator, Joseph R. McCarthy.

The hearings closed on May 26. On July 27 Jenkins sent to each member of the Senate subcommittee a summary of the testimony and a brief of the evidence. He reduced the 7,000 pages to a 447-page summary (New York *Times,* July 28, 1954).

Ray Howard Jenkins was born on March 18, 1897 in Unaka, North Carolina, a Cherokee county village in the Great Smokies near the Tennessee border. His birthplace is no longer in existence as it was submerged during the building of one of the dams of the Tennessee Valley Authority in 1933. His father, C. S. Jenkins, was a country doctor and his mother, the former Amanda Nicholsen, was born in Union county, Georgia. (Now eighty, she lives in Tellico Plains, Tennessee. His father was killed in a railroad accident in 1923.)

The family moved to Tellico Plains in Western Tennessee while Ray and his two sisters were small children. Ray attended the public schools there and worked his way through the preparatory school at Maryville, Tennessee, and the University of Tennessee Law School where he won first prize for scholarship three straight years. He was admitted to the bar in 1919. Jenkins did a stint along the Mexican border as an Army top sergeant and was champion wrestler of his company. He served in World War I as a Navy seaman (*Time,* April 19, 1954).

After the war he opened a law office in Knoxville, Tennessee where he has practiced ever since. He has appeared in some 600 criminal cases, usually as a trial lawyer defending the accused and "he is naturally very proud that none of his clients has ever gone to the electric chair" (New York *Post,* May 2, 1954).

His first murder case set the pattern of his career. He represented a moonshiner, charged with the brutal murder of his wife. By vigorous cross-examination Jenkins impressed the jury, and the moonshiner got life imprisonment instead of the death penalty which the prosecution had demanded. The late Ed McNew, a Knoxville professional bondsman, asked Jenkins to defend him in a felonious assault case. McNew was charged with shooting at a Knoxville photographer who took his picture of McNew in the act of firing as documentary evidence. Jenkins took the case and, demonstrating that McNew was both mentally and physically ill, and had been harassed and goaded into firing the shot by the prying photographer, got his client off with a light fine and a sixty-day workhouse sentence (New York *Times,* April 11, 1954).

"He's the sort of lawyer who completely dominates a case and a court. Rising with square jaw set and fire in his eyes, he'll unbutton his collar, loosen his coat, untie his tie, and go to work. The gestures of his hands are almost as gripping as his oratory" (New York *Post,* May 2, 1954).

Described as a "staunchly conservative Republican," Jenkins managed the Tennessee campaigns of Wendell Willkie for President in 1940, Howard Baker (now Representative from the Second District, then running for the Senate) and Arthur Bruce for governor. All three candidates lost. Jenkins ran for the G.O.P. nomination for Congress in a special election in 1939, but lost to Representative John Jennings. In 1950 he backed Howard Baker who defeated Jennings. He actively supported Robert A. Taft for President in 1952, but at the Republican Convention he urged (unsuccessfully) the Tennessee delegation to switch to Eisenhower. "Let's get behind somebody who can win," he is reported to have said. Jenkins' law partner, Erby Jenkins (not related to him) is chairman of the Knox county Republican committee and his private secretary, Charles Maner, is vice-chairman.

Jenkins was recommended by Senator Everett M. Dirksen of Illinois as special counsel for the Senate permanent investigations subcommittee temporarily headed by Senator Karl E. Mundt of South Dakota. Dirksen described him as "just about the best trial lawyer in East Tennessee." His appointment was approved on April 7, 1954. He succeeded Samuel P. Sears of Boston who resigned as special counsel after a five-day tenure when it was decided that Sears was not impartial because of "his past expressions of approval of Senator McCarthy."

The Tennessee lawyer stated that he had "no preconceived notions with respect to Senator McCarthy or what has been termed mccarthyism," and he told the subcommittee that he had "no preconceived notions on the merits of this controversy. I have no prejudice, no bias, my mind is completely open." The committee went to some lengths to assure itself that Jenkins had no public record of support or opposition to the Wisconsin junior Senator. It checked carefully with both Knoxville, Tennessee newspapers and with a number of Tennessee officials, including ten judges (*Christian Science Monitor,* April 8, 1954). Mayor George Dempster of Knoxville, a Democrat, said: "Jenkins will conduct an investigation in a fair and impartial manner and I know he'll reflect credit on the committee."

Senator Estes Kefauver (Democrat) of Tennessee said, when asked about Jenkins, "I know him as a capable, hard-hitting trial lawyer and a staunch Republican" (Washington *Post and Times-Herald,* April 8, 1954).

Although Jenkins did not seek the appointment he accepted because, as he told the Nashville *Tennessean,* April 11, 1954: "The issues are so sharply drawn and seem so distinctly impossible to reconcile that a full public investigation seems necessary. I will do my best to see that both sides are given full opportunity, facing each other, to present their cases." However, he also stated that he regarded it as "most regrettable that the need for such an investigation ever arose. Indeed, it would be a marvelous thing if the respective parties could get together and compose their differences to the satisfaction of the public."

His first job, as Jenkins saw it, was to get both the Army and Senator McCarthy to specify their charges. He held meetings in a two-room suite on the second floor of the Senate Office Building with Army Secretary Robert T. Stevens and his counsel, Joseph Welch, and then with McCarthy's aides, Roy Cohn and Francis Carr. Jenkins asked each side for a bill of particulars and a list of witnesses and a resumé of what each witness was expected to prove.

The controversy centered around the charge by the Army that "Senator McCarthy and his staff made the Army a special target for investigation in reprisal for the Army's refusal to grant either a commission or a special assignment to Private G. David Schine" [a former special unpaid consultant to the Senate permanent investigations subcommittee]. The countercharge—by Senator McCarthy—was that "the Army used Schine as a 'hostage' as part of an effort to 'blackmail' the Senator into calling off his Army investigation" (New York *Times,* May 2, 1954).

Reporters covering the hearings described Jenkins' voice as "a deep, roaring Tennessee drawl", "a tiger-like roar" which earned him the nickname the "terror of Tellico" in the courts of Tennessee. Jenkins has a simple definition of the problem he was hired to untangle: "Apparently everybody can't be telling the truth" (*Time,* May 3, 1954).

The Tennessee lawyer's most characteristic mannerism during cross-examination of witnesses is to "lean toward the table, hunch up his shoulders, and shoot forth his queries like a Boston bulldog poised for attack" (William V. Shannon, New York *Post,* May 2, 1954). When asked by CBS commentator Eric Sevareid, "Mr. Jenkins, some people say you are badgering witnesses. Would you like to comment on this?" Jenkins replied: "Sometimes it is necessary to make a rigid cross-examination —sometimes mild cross-examination—in order to elicit facts."

Described as a big (six feet three inches tall, 195 pounds) "rawboned, thickly set" man with a "jutting chin" and "closely cropped reddish-brown hair," Jenkins is a renowned storyteller. "His flair for oratory, his sense of the dramatic, his ability to feel out a jury and witnesses, win him case after case" (New York *Times,* April 11, 1954). He was married in 1924 to the former Eva Nash, "daughter of a socially prominent Knoxville physician." Mrs. Jenkins founded the Knoxville chapter of the D.A.R. They live in an "elegant Georgian mansion" furnished with mirrors, vases and art objects purchased by the Nash and Jenkins families in Europe over the years.

Jenkins owns, and operates as a hobby, a 500-acre cattle farm in the Tennessee River Valley. He has one daughter, Mrs. Alexander Cunningham, Jr., and a granddaughter, nineteen-months-old Evalyn. He enjoys an occasional game of golf, is a member of the American Legion and the Sons of the American Revolution. He summarized his views: "I am opposed to Communism, Socialism, and all other isms except Americanism."

References

N Y Post Mag p2 My 2 '54 por
N Y World-Telegram p3 Ap 21 '54 por
Newsweek 43:17 Ap 19 '54; 43:27 Ap 26 '54 por; 43:30 My 3 '54 por
Time 63:18+ My 3 '54; My 17 '54 por
U S News 36:12 Ap 16 '54
Martindale-Hubbell Law Directory, 1952

JIMÉNEZ, MARCOS PÉREZ *See* Pérez Jiménez, M.

JORDAN, SARA M(URRAY) Oct. 20, 1884- Physician

Address: b. c/o Lahey Clinic, 605 Commonwealth Ave., Boston, Mass.; h. Foster St., Marblehead Neck, Mass.

The director of the department of gastroenterology at the Lahey Clinic in Boston for thirty-two years, Dr. Sara M. Jordan has also served many professional organizations in an official capacity and was the first woman elected to the board of directors of the Boston Chamber of Commerce. She is the author of numerous articles on gastroenterological subjects and co-author of *Good Food for Bad Stomachs.* For her contributions to medicine she has received the Elizabeth Blackwell Citation and the Julius Friedenwald Medal.

Dr. Jordan was born Sara Murray in Newton, Massachusetts on October 20, 1884 to Patrick Andrew and Maria (Stuart) Murray. Her early life, until she entered Radcliffe College in Cambridge, Massachusetts, was spent in Newton. Graduated from Radcliffe with an A.B. degree in 1905, she enrolled at the University of Munich in Germany where she studied philology and received the Ph.D. degree in 1908.

(Continued next page)

Boris—Boston

DR. SARA M. JORDAN

Her marriage to Sebastian Jordan took place on January 14, 1913, and it was not until after their daughter Mary Stuart (now Mrs. Thomas H. Logan, Jr.) was born and the marriage terminated that Mrs. Jordan entered Tufts College Medical School at Medford, Massachusetts. She received the M.D. degree in 1921.

While Sara Jordan was a medical student she wrote an article with A. B. Yates which was published in a series called *Rhythm in Industry* by the United States Public Health Service. She was an intern at the Memorial Hospital in Worcester, Massachusetts and later was engaged in special work with Dr. Bertram Sippy. Dr. Jordan became director of the department of gastroenterology at Lahey Clinic in 1922.

At the annual session of the American Medical Association held in Dallas, Texas in April 1926, Dr. Jordan addressed the assembly for the section on gastroenterology. The speech, "Calcium, Chloride and Carbon Dioxide Content of Venous Blood in Cases of Gastroduodenal Ulcer Treated with Alkalis" was published in the December 4, 1926 issue of the *Journal of the American Medical Association.* She was a representative to the scientific exhibit of the A.M.A. section on gastroenterology and proctology.

The physician participated in the war effort as chairman of the woman's committee on procurement and assignment of the War Manpower Commission. Interested in the work of the professional medical societies, she served as president of the American Gastroenterology Association from 1942 to 1944, secretary of the section of gastroenterology of the A.M.A. from 1941 to 1944, vice-chairman of the section from 1946 to 1947, and chairman from 1947 to 1948.

Dr. Jordan was unanimously elected a member of the board of directors of the Boston Chamber of Commerce in 1948. At that time, the president of the chamber stated that Dr. Jordan was the first woman to hold a directorship. She served in this post for three years.

Sara Jordan contributed the section entitled "Abdominal Pain" to the book, *Signs and Symptoms, Their Clinical Interpretation* (Lippincott, 1947, 1952), a treatise on the duodenum ulcer. Persuaded by the late Harold W. Ross, editor of the *New Yorker,* while he was a patient at the Lahey Clinic, to write a cookbook for the layman, Dr. Jordan departed from the technical field to collaborate with Sheila Hibben on *Good Food for Bad Stomachs* (Doubleday, 1951). The book contains 500 recipes for sufferers from ulcers and other digestive disturbances. In a foreword, Dr. Jordan explains that she considers it the responsibility of the physician to make it possible for a patient to enjoy food through a varied but wise choice in diet.

The New York *Times* (August 26, 1951) in a review of the book commented: "In a world more calculated than ever before in its history to bring on ulcers and nervous indigestion, it is difficult to imagine a book that is more timely." The *New Yorker* (August 18, 1951) said that the authors had "succeeded by culinary legerdemain, in devising dishes that will be thoroughly acceptable to the unafflicted" as well as to the "sufferer from chronic queasiness. . ."

Dr. Jordan was one of five prominent American women physicians to receive the Elizabeth Blackwell Citation on January 28, 1951 for their contributions to the practice and teaching of medicine. She was also awarded the Julius Friedenwald Medal in 1952 for outstanding achievement in gastroenterology.

The *New England Journal of Medicine* (May 21, 1953) published the full text of the annual oration presented by Dr. Jordan at the Massachusetts Medical Society annual meeting held in Boston on May 19, 1953. In this address, "Medicine and the Doctor in Word and Epigram," Dr. Jordan referred to her premedical interest in philology and said, "In medicine as in statecraft and propaganda, words are sometimes the most powerful drug we can use." She suggested that medical pundits had exchanged certain monosyllabics for "painfully constructed polysyllabics," thus depriving the medical language of some of its vitality.

In an article, "Postpone Your Obituary" (*Rotarian,* August 1953), Dr. Jordan cited a Latin text of the year 1607 on health management: "Use Three Physicians still—first Dr. Quiet, next Dr. Merryman, and Dr. Dyet," and pointed out that the need for relaxing avocations, frequent vacations and careful diet is even wiser advice today. She expressed her belief that arbitrary age retirement should be reconsidered in the light of evidence that older people continue to demonstrate their mental and physical soundness. She emphasized that experts in geriatrics advise elderly people to keep well-nourished and mentally and physically active for as long as possible as the practical way to postpone an obituary.

Dr. Jordan was elected a life trustee of Tufts College on April 29, 1951. She is a trustee of the Boston Museum of Science, a member of the state commission for the study of alcoholism, and an associate editor of *Gastroenterol-*

ogy, the official journal of the American Gastroenterological Association. In addition to her work at the Lahey Clinic, she is a staff physician of the New England Baptist Hospital and the New England Deaconess Hospital.

A fellow of the American College of Physicians, Sara Jordan is also an honorary member of the American Therapeutic Society, American Proctologic Society, a member of Phi Beta Kappa, Phi Beta Kappa Associates, College Club in Boston, and Cosmopolitan Club in New York. The physician has received the honorary Sc.D. degree from Smith College in 1935, Tufts College Medical School in 1943 and Wilson College in 1946.

She married Penfield Mower, a Boston broker, on September 26, 1935. Dr. Jordan is a tall, slender woman with gray hair and blue eyes, and it has been said that her spirit of earnest helpfulness, a fundamental of her character, has marked her distinguished career. By way of recreation, she is an active golfer.

References

N Y Times p16 Ja 6 '48 por
American Medical Directory, 1950
Directory of Medical Specialists (1951)
Who's Who in America, 1952-53
Who's Who in the East (1953)

JOUHAUX, LÉON July 1, 1879-Apr. 28, 1954 French labor leader; was re-elected president of the French Republic's Economic Council on the day of his death, having been re-elected each year since 1947; won Nobel Peace Prize (1951); was elected secretary general of the General Confederation of Labor (1909); delegate to the First International Labor Conference at Washington, D.C. (1919); delegate to the League of Nations (1925-1928); interned by Nazis; resumed leadership of General Federation of Labor (1945) but split with its Communist majority (1947) to establish a non-Communist Workers Force; founded a review *Fighting Democracy* which was criticized as Communist-dominated in 1952 by AFL; stoutly maintained his anti-Communist position. See *Current Biography,* (Jan.) 1948.

Obituary

N Y Times p31 Ap 29 '54

KAPELL, WILLIAM Sept. 20, 1922—Oct. 29, 1953 Pianist; awarded scholarship to study at Philadelphia Conservatory of Music under Olga Samaroff; received a fellowship at Juilliard Graduate School of Music; made Town Hall debut in 1941; appeared with New York Philharmonic Symphony Orchestra, Philadelphia Orchestra, and Boston Symphony Orchestra; toured United States, South America, Australia, and Europe; well-known for his performances of Khachaturian's *Piano Concerto* and other modern works; won youth contest of Philadelphia Orchestra and Town Hall Endowment Series Award (1942). See *Current Biography,* (May) 1948.

Obituary

N Y Times p48 O 30 '53

KECK, MRS. GEORGE FRED *See* Keck, L. L.

KECK, LUCILE L(IEBERMANN) Jan. 3, 1898- Librarian; library association official
Address: b. 1313 E. 60th St., Chicago 37, Ill.; h. 5551 University Ave., Chicago 37, Ill.

The president for the year 1953 to 1954 of the Special Libraries Association is Mrs. Lucile L. Keck, whose election was announced in June 1953 at the association's annual meeting, held that year in Toronto, Canada. Founded in 1909, the Special Libraries Association, with headquarters in New York City, has twenty-nine chapters in the United States and Canada and comprises at present approximately 5,000 members from countries in many parts of the world. In June 1954 Miss Gretchen Little was made president-elect, to succeed Mrs. Keck in June 1955.

Since 1932, while employed as librarian of the Joint Reference Library of Public Administration Clearing House in Chicago, Mrs. Keck through a number of committee and administrative offices has contributed notably to the purpose of S.L.A. as set forth in its slogan "Putting Knowledge to Work."

The daughter of Albert B. and Flora (Bellack) Liebermann, Lucile Liebermann was born on January 3, 1898 in Watertown, Wisconsin. Reared in Watertown, she was graduated in 1915 from the local high school, where her chief activities outside of classes were in the glee club and the yearbook. With English as one of her major subjects at the University of Wisconsin in Madison, she devoted part of her free time to writing for the university's literary magazine. She also specialized in library science, a field in which her interest was especially stimulated by Mary Emogene Hazeltine, preceptor of the library school of the University of Wisconsin.

Leaving the university in 1920 with a B.A. degree, a Phi Beta Kappa key, and a certificate from the library school, Miss Liebermann spent over a year in New York City. She was employed first as circulation assistant in the New York Public Library and then for a time during 1921 as an indexer of the *Readers' Guide to Periodical Literature,* a publication of the H. W. Wilson Company.

The young librarian was married on November 26, 1921 to George Fred Keck, the architect, whom she had known during her childhood in Wisconsin. About a year after her marriage, Mrs. Keck accepted the post of library researcher for the book section of Marshall Field and Company in Chicago. This position, which she held until 1924, was regarded in an article about Mrs. Keck in *Special Libraries* (July-August 1953) as the beginning of her special library work. For three years (from 1928 to 1931) she was librarian of the Institute for Research in Land Economics and Public Utilities at Northwestern University in Chicago.

During 1931 she organized the Lawson Young Men's Christian Association library in Chicago and the following year undertook the

Shelburne

LUCILE L. KECK

task of reclassifying and cataloguing of the public library in River Forest, Illinois.

After the establishment of the Joint Reference Library of Public Administration Clearing House in Chicago, Mrs. Keck was appointed in May 1932 as its first librarian. Since that time the Joint Reference Library, which began as a cooperative effort among several associations in related fields, has grown to provide service for seventeen public administration organizations. Meanwhile, during the summers of 1936, 1938 and 1941 the librarian lectured at the graduate library school of the University of Chicago. She has also been consultant on organization to various social science libraries and has conducted surveys of different types of libraries, among them, in collaboration with Walter Kaiser in 1942, a survey of the American Hospital Association library.

As a member of the S.L.A., which she joined in 1932, Mrs. Keck first became prominent in the Illinois chapter, where she was president from 1935 to 1937 and director from 1937 to 1939. In the national organization, meanwhile, she was elected a vice-president in 1937 and then was made chairman of the nominating committee from 1939 to 1940. Other positions she has held in S.L.A. are member of the joint committee to survey the special library field (1939 to 1941), group liaison officer (1943 to 1944) and member of the committee to study affiliation between S.L.A. and the American Library Association (1946). Prior to assuming the S.L.A. presidency for the 1953 to 1954 term, she served as director in 1951 and vice-president and president-elect in 1952.

In a greeting to S.L.A. members Mrs. Keck spoke of the diversity and similarity in interests between the S.L.A. and the A.L.A. "In S.L.A.," she pointed out, "we are banded together as specialists to foster analytical service in particular subject fields. But certain of our interests as librarians fall only within the broader scope of librarianship as a whole . . . for instance, intellectual freedom, as the focus on the 'burning of the books' at this moment in history attests" (*Special Libraries,* July-August 1953).

Mrs. Keck is a co-editor of *Public Administration Libraries; A Manual of Practice* (Public Administration Service, 1948), an undertaking of S.L.A.'s social science division. She is also the author of "The Work and Publications of the Organizations Operating the Joint Reference Library" (in *Public Documents,* A.L.A., 1937). With Margaret Elizabeth Egan she presented before the library institute of the University of Chicago a paper which was entitled "Fugitive Materials" and was published in *Library Buildings for Library Service* (A.L.A., 1947).

Among her articles on matters relating to library science are "Public Health Material" (*Library Journal,* June 15, 1938), "Periodicals" (S.L.A. *Proceedings.* 1939) and "Joint Reference Library of Public Administration Clearing House" (*Illinois Libraries,* May 1947). Many of her book reviews have appeared in the *Library Quarterly.*

Lucile Keck also belongs to the A.L.A. (member of the board of education for librarianship, 1944 to 1948), American Society for Public Administration and American Political Science Association. Her civic organizations are National Housing Conference, Hyde Park-Kenwood Community Conference and the American Association for the United Nations. The librarian, whose political affiliation is "independent, usually Democratic," is a member of the American Civil Liberties Union and Americans for Democratic Action.

In appearance, she has blue eyes and graying ash-blonde hair; she is five feet four inches in height with a weight of 130 pounds. Fond of travel, she has made several trips to England and the Continent. She also finds enjoyment in music and art.

References

Who's Who in Chicago and Illinois (1945)
Who's Who in Library Service (1943)

KEE, ELIZABETH (FRAZIER) June 7, 1899- United States Representative from West Virginia

Address: b. 1016 New House Office Bldg., Washington, D.C.; h. 301 New Jersey Ave., S.E., Washington, D.C.; Woodland Dr., Bluefield, W.Va.

The first woman Representative in Congress from West Virginia, Mrs. Elizabeth Kee has represented that state's fifth district since the death of her husband, former Congressman John Kee, (Democrat) on May 8, 1951.

First elected by a special election to fill his unexpired term, Mrs. Kee campaigned for reelection in the 1952 general elections and won with a plurality of 36,000 votes over her Republican rival, topping the margin received by any other West Virginia Congressman. She also won the 1954 Democratic primary as a candidate for re-election in November.

Elizabeth Frazier was born in Radford, Virginia, June 7, 1899. While she was still "too young to remember" her family moved to Roanoke where her father, J. W. Simpkins, was in the real estate business. During her childhood, the family lived in Vinton. After attending Roanoke's public schools, she obtained her first job, during World War I, as secretary to the late W. E. Thomas, business manager of the Roanoke *Times*. She later worked as a court reporter for the firm of Hart and Morris. In 1925 she moved to Bluefield, West Virginia. She became administrative assistant to her husband, John Kee, a lawyer, in 1932 when he was first elected to Congress.

For several years she wrote a weekly column from Washington for a chain of West Virginia newspapers. She discontinued this when her husband became chairman of the Foreign Affairs Committee, so that she could devote more time to assisting with his increased correspondence and office work.

As a candidate for her husband's office after his death, Mrs. Kee was endorsed by the United Mine Workers. She wrote letters and toured the seven counties of the Fifth Congressional District—Greenbrier, Mercer, McDowell, Monroe, Summers, Wyoming, and Mingo. The district, with a population of approximately 329,584, contains the Pocohantas coal fields. Elected on July 17, 1951 (with 58 per cent of the voters in the mining district casting votes), she was sworn into office on July 26, 1951.

Congressman John Kee was known as a progressive Democrat, and Mrs. Kee's voting record in the Eighty-second Congress followed a similar pattern. She voted against cuts in economic aid for Europe and for the $7,500,000,000 foreign assistance bill. She opposed a 10 per cent cut in Federal jobs, the tidelands oil bill, the end of consumer price controls by June 30, 1952, the end of Federal rent controls September 30, 1952, and the use of the Taft-Hartley law to halt the steel strike.

In the Eighty-third Congress she supported $4.4 billion for foreign aid appropriations (1953) and over $5 billion for foreign aid in 1954. In that year she voted against extending the Trade Agreements Act for one year, against building the St. Lawrence Seaway, and against a bill amending the Atomic Energy Act of 1946. She favored social security expansion and supported the bill making it a felony to be a Communist.

A member of the House Committee on Veterans' Affairs, she serves on a special subcommittee charged with investigation of Veterans' Administration hospitals. She feels that "more attention should be devoted to the welfare of this country's veterans. . . . To begin with, they (veterans' hospitals) just aren't getting the appropriations they need from Congress. . . ." Consequently, in her opinion, there is inadequate hospital personnel. "You just can't economize at the expense of the veteran. And I know the American people—regardless of how much they want Government spending cut—I know they feel that way."

In addition to her concern for domestic problems, Mrs. Kee maintains her husband's interest in foreign affairs. The Congresswoman took a self-financed 16,000-mile air trip through seven South American countries in the latter part of 1952, fulfilling what had been her husband's life-long dream.

Chase Studios
ELIZABETH KEE

The Representative has established and sponsored a library for the physically handicapped at the Woodrow Wilson Rehabilitation Center at Fisherville, Virginia. In addition, she serves as vice-regent of the Woodrow Wilson Birthplace Foundation at Staunton, Virginia.

Her son James, a former foreign service officer in South America, now serves as her administrative aide. Her daughter Frances also helps voluntarily on occasion despite partial disability caused by poliomyelitis.

Mrs. Kee is a member of the Christ Episcopal Church in Bluefield, and is active in Episcopalian organizations. She regularly attends weekly Congressional prayer breakfasts on Capitol Hill. "Legislation, if it is to serve its real purpose, must be spiritually motivated—and that is the purpose of this breakfast club," she explains.

Representative Kee is active in Red Cross work. She is a member of the American Newspaper Women's Club, the English-Speaking Union, Bluefield Country Club, and Daughters of the American Revolution. Blue-eyed, brown-haired Elizabeth Kee is known for her vitality and determination.

References

Ind Woman 30:311 O '51; 32:36 F '53 por
Roanoke Times F 15 '53
Washington (D.C.) Post Je 20 '51
Congressional Directory (1952)

KEE, MRS. JOHN *See* Kee, E. (F.)

KELLY, EMMETT Dec. 9, 1898- Clown
Address: c/o Ringling Brothers, Barnum and Bailey Combined Shows, Inc., 10 Rockefeller Plaza, New York 20

The stock in trade of a clown is laughter. But Emmett Kelly, who has played a clown in American and British circuses for more than twenty years and who has been called "one of the world's leading creators of laughter," has created a character more famous for his mournful demeanor and melancholy pantomime than for boisterous, rollicking humor.

EMMETT KELLY

"Weary Willie," a pathetic little hobo in a ragged suit and battered hat who wanders quietly around the arena of the Ringling Brothers, Barnum and Bailey Circus, staring thoughtfully at the audience, was first conceived by Kelly as a cartoon subject. In 1933 Kelly brought him to life, and and he is now a familiar figure to thousands of circus-goers. In 1952 Willie reached an even wider audience in his movie debut in Cecil B. De Mille's circus extravaganza, *The Greatest Show on Earth.* Sorrowful-eyed Willie was the guiding spirit behind Kelly's autobiography *Clown,* written in collaboration with F. Beverly Kelley, and published by Prentice-Hall on March 31, 1954.

Unlike many circus performers who follow the circus as a family profession from one generation to the next, Kelly stumbled into circus life almost accidentally. He was born December 9, 1898 in Sedan, Kansas, where his father worked as a section foreman for the Missouri-Pacific Railroad. A staunchly nationalistic Irish immigrant, his father named his son Emmett for the Irish patriot Robert Emmet. Kelly's mother was of Bohemian descent. He has one younger sister.

While Emmett was still a little boy, his father retired from the railroad and bought a farm near Cabool, Missouri. There he grew up, helping with all the farm chores, and attending a one-room frame school house. Kelly never went beyond the eighth grade, but at school he first discovered his talent for drawing. With his mother's encouragement he sent away for a correspondence course in cartooning. In 1917 Kelly set out for Kansas City to become a professional cartoonist. He soon discovered that a young country boy with some rudimentary training in cartooning had little to offer the major newspaper syndicates. But he managed to earn his way at a variety of jobs such as sign painting and managing a side show in a carnival.

Meanwhile Kelly had made his debut as an entertainer by giving "chalk-talks"—comic illustrations and caricatures—for church suppers and other informal groups. His first professional job was with the Frisco Exposition Shows in Kansas City where, for $20 a week, he did a cartoon-talk, in white-face clown make-up, and a trapeze act. ("The tent was so low," he recalls in his autobiography, *Clown,* "I could almost touch the ground when I hung upside down.")

Such employment, Kelly discovered, was temporary. When the show closed, he took other jobs—working on farms, in an oil refinery. Back in Kansas City he found a job as a cartoonist with an advertising film company. Here Kelly first created his hobo cartoon character whom he describes in *Clown* as "a forlorn and melancholy little hobo who always got the short end of the stick and never had any good luck at all, but who never lost hope and just kept on trying."

Kelly gave up his cartoon job to rejoin the circus—this time Howe's Great London Circus—as trapeze artist and clown. In 1923, while traveling with John Robinson's Circus he met and married Eva Moore, also a trapeze artist. They worked together in a double trapeze act until two months before their first son, Emmett, Jr., was born. They continued to travel with the circus during summers and in the winters they returned to his family's farm where he did odd jobs.

Because of the world depression of the early 1930's, the Sells-Floto Circus with which Kelly and his wife were then working, closed down. Unable to secure a position as a trapeze artist, Kelly accepted a job as a general clown with the Hagenbeck-Wallace Circus in 1931. Realizing in the season that followed that his future was in clowning, Kelly says: "I did some serious thinking, and decided that if I were going to have to spend all my time in Clown Alley, I would not be just another clown, but would try to create something special."

The "something special" he created was his cartoon hobo Willie. Unlike the traditional white-face clown, Willie bears a grotesque but distinct resemblance to a real life person. In place of the riotous splash of colors of the clown suit and the bright, painted grin, Willie wears an incredibly tattered and baggy but conventional suit. His face is made up with a growth of beard, his hair hangs in wisps from beneath his hat, and except for a bright pink bulbous nose, he is a totally pathetic picture.

His routines consist mainly of sweeping the ring with a frayed broom and chasing the elusive spotlight, munching on bread or a cabbage leaf while he stares mournfully at a member of the audience, or trying to crack a peanut with a sledge hammer.

Kelly himself finds it difficult to analyze Willie's humor. "I don't feel funny when I'm this hobo character. I'm a misfit, a reject. Life is passing me by. Maybe it's Willie's attempt at a little dignity in spite of everything that tickles folks. Incongruity, they say, is one of the main ingredients of humor. Maybe it's because everybody can feel superior to me. Or maybe when I stare at 'em it's just nervousness. I honestly don't know." Clowning, he explains, is nothing one can study for. "It's got to be inside you, a way of feeling about things that comes out somehow if you get the opportunity."

The artist Loren MacIver painted a famous portrait of Kelly as Willie in 1947 which is regarded as "one of the world's best-known clown studies." Her comment on Willie's appeal is that "he combined the grand manner with complete humility." (The portrait was reproduced in *Life* magazine for July 21, 1947). In 1937 Kelly was invited to go to London to appear with the Bertram Mills Circus. His engagement was so successful that he returned in 1938 and again in 1939. He returned to the United States when World War II broke out and toured the country playing night club engagements. In 1940 he appeared on Broadway in the musical comedy *Keep Off the Grass,* which starred Jimmy Durante.

Since 1942 Kelly has been a member of the Ringling Brothers, Barnum and Bailey Circus. In July 1944 Kelly played an important part in the rescue work during the tragic Hartford, Connecticut circus fire, when the outdoor tent in which the circus was playing caught fire, with a toll of 168 lives. Kelly, who was in make-up in the dressing tent at the time of the fire, joined in the rescue operations and helped prevent panic by directing people out of the burning main tent. A news photographer snapped a dramatic photograph of Kelly, in his clown's costume, rushing toward the fire carrying a water bucket, and the catastrophe is vividly described by him in his book, *Clown.*

When the war ended, Kelly played a return engagement with the Mills Circus in England. He has played before distinguished audiences abroad, before Winston Churchill, the Queen of Spain, the Duke and Duchess of Gloucester, Duke of Windsor, and Emperor Haile Selassie. In 1950 he went to Hollywood for his first motion picture role, that of a murderer, in *The Fat Man.* Because the role was a villainous one, Kelly refused to play it in the make-up of his hobo clown who was such a sympathetic figure. Instead he devised a white-face clown's make-up, and Willie was spared. But it was as Willie that he appeared in *The Greatest Show on Earth.*

Kelly and his first wife were divorced in 1935, a year after the birth of their second son, Thomas Patrick. In 1944 he married Mildred Ritchie, also a circus performer, and after their wedding, they went through another ceremony for the benefit of the press in Madison Square Garden. They were divorced several months later. According to John Kobler, writing in *Cosmopolitan* for June 1953, Kelly leads a lonely, solitary life. He travels with the circus and devotes most of his time to studying and improving his character of Willie. By nature, like Willie, he is melancholy. "I've always taken a serious view of things ever since I can remember. I worry all the time." He is five feet nine inches tall, wears his greying hair long, and, Kobler writes, "he seems older and shorter because he is stooped and paunchy." Like his character Willie, however, an outward sadness conceals an inward serenity. He has said: "I couldn't say that life with the circus is the softest deal in the world, but I would rather live out my life in Clown Alley than in a marble palace."

References

Am W p10+ Mr 21 '54 por; p8+ Mr 28 '54 pors
Christian Sci Mon Mag p13 Je 26 '43
Cosmopolitan 134:52+ Je '53 pors
Life 23:45+ Jl 21 '47 pors
Pathfinder 60:30+ Jl '53 pors
Kelly, E. (with F. B. Kelley) Clown (1954)

KENNON, ROBERT F(LOYD) Aug. 21, 1902- Governor of Louisiana; former judge

Address: b. State Capitol, Baton Rouge, La.; h. Governor's Mansion, Baton Rouge, La.

After victory in a hotly-contested runoff primary, Robert F. Kennon, in May 1952, took office as Governor of Louisiana for a four-year term, ending "at least, temporarily, the twenty-four-year dominance of Louisiana politics by the Longs" (New York *Herald Tribune,* February 21, 1952). He succeeded Earl K. Long, brother of the late Huey P. Long.

Kennon, at twenty-three, had been the state's youngest mayor on record, holding that office in Minden, and has served on the Supreme Court of Louisiana. On July 14, 1954 the U.S. Governors' Conference, meeting in Bolton Landing, New York, elected Kennon as its president to succeed Dan Thornton of Colorado.

In its account of Kennon's victory in the second primary, the *Christian Science Monitor* (February 21, 1952) described him as "a tall, lanky country boy with a warm handshake and a friendly drawl, whose Lincolnesque approach captivated voters.... He did it all in a straightforward homespun manner, a grass-roots approach which left some seasoned campaigners baffled." *Time* (January 28, 1952) called him "no rabble-rouser, but a neat and solid citizen."

Robert Floyd Kennon was born on August 21, 1902, near Minden, Louisiana, the son of Laura (Bopp) and Floyd Kennon. After being graduated from Minden High School in 1919, he studied at Louisiana State University, where he received an A.B. degree in 1923, and an LL.B. in 1925. At the university he was active in ROTC, becoming captain of his company. In sports, he earned letters in football and ten-

Sylva-Dyer Studio
ROBERT F. KENNON

nis. He received the best grades in the freshman class and also the best grades in the university.

Admitted to the bar of Louisiana in 1925, Kennon was associated with G. K. Kitchens in the practice of law in Minden, from 1925 to 1941. He was elected to the mayoralty of Minden in 1925. During his two-year term of office, he established a modern city court; reorganized the government through legislative act; installed a modern fire alarm system; and improved Minden's fiscal condition. Before he left this post he was elected vice-president of the Louisiana Municipal Association.

Elected district attorney for the Bossier-Webster district in 1930, Kennon was re-elected in 1936 without opposition. During this period he was also elected vice-president of the Louisiana District Attorney's Association. In September 1940 he became a judge of the Court of Appeal for the Second Circuit of Louisiana.

Kennon organized a National Guard company in Minden in 1925, and remained its captain for fifteen years. In January 1941, the company was called into active service. Kennon attended the Command and General Staff School at Ft. Leavenworth, Kansas, and later served with the XIII Corps, Ninth Army, in Europe. He was discharged as a lieutenant colonel in June 1945, and now holds the rank of colonel in the Reserve.

After the war he was appointed to Louisiana's Supreme Court, to fill the unexpired term of the late Associate Justice Archibald T. Higgins, from October 1945 to January 1947. In 1948 Kennon ran in the Democratic primary for the governorship, and came in third. The primary was won by Earl K. Long. Later that year Kennon again entered the Democratic primary for nomination as U.S. Senator; he was defeated by Russell B. Long, son of Huey, who carried the primary by about 10,000 votes, and was thus assured of election in this traditionally Democratic state.

Judge Kennon again entered the Democratic primary for Governor in January 1952. Chief among the eight others in the race were former Judge Carlos G. Spaht of Baton Rouge, the candidate backed by outgoing Governor Earl K. Long who, by law, could not succeed himself, and U.S. Representative Thomas Hale Boggs, endorsed by Russell B. Long.

The New York *Times* (February 17, 1952) commented that although Kennon lacked solid organizational backing, he "kept intact his support among veterans and independents, and added enough votes from those disgruntled with the factional line-up to emerge second man in the primary." Spaht ran first, by 10,000 votes. A runoff primary between Spaht and Kennon was necessary, by law, as the former had not received a majority. Some observers believed that the results of the primary election were due to a splitting of the Long followers between Boggs and Spaht.

The remaining seven candidates gave their support to Kennon in the runoff primary. On February 19, 1952 Kennon defeated Spaht by approximately 200,000 votes, and was thus assured of election. His campaign platform included a two-cent reduction in gasoline taxes, states' rights, economy in state government, decreasing the power of the Governor's office, and a determination to send an uninstructed Louisiana delegation to the Democratic national convention in July. At the election on April 22 he defeated the Republican candidate, Harrison Bagwell. He took office in May. His inaugural parade included ninety-one bands and forty floats.

In March Kennon backed Senator Richard B. Russell of Georgia for the Democratic nomination for president. At the national convention, Kennon led his state's delegation, which refused to take the "loyalty pledge" to the national party's candidates. After the convention he said that there was "considerable uncertainty" concerning the South's support of Adlai E. Stevenson, the Democratic presidential nominee. Kennon opposed the Democrats' endorsement of a fair employment practices act, and feared that they would urge Federal ownership of tidelands oil, which he maintains belongs to the states, and contains "wealth for . . . schools, roads and improvements for the coming generations" (New York *Times,* September 7, 1952).

When Louisiana's Democratic central committee voted on August 20, 1952 to pledge its ten electors to Stevenson, six of the electors resigned. On September 6 Kennon announced his endorsement of General Dwight D. Eisenhower for the Presidency. Eisenhower, stated the Governor, "appears to have the courage . . . to end the Truman era of mink coats, deep freezers, pay-offs, and rackets" (New York *Herald Tribune,* September 7, 1952).

Announcing plans for a "Democrats for Eisenhower" meeting, Kennon stated, "I am not having any part of the Republican setup in

KENNON, ROBERT F.—*Continued*

Louisiana, but I am cooperating with the Democrats in this state who feel that the traditional Democratic principles are best stated in the Republican platform" (New York *Times,* September 13, 1952). Louisiana, which had not gone Republican in a Presidential election since 1876, remained in the Democratic column in 1952, although with 651,952 votes cast, only 38,102 votes separated the two candidates. Governor Kennon was among prominent southern Democrats, including Senators Spessard L. Holland (Florida) and Harry F. Byrd (Virginia), and Governors James F. Byrnes (South Carolina) and Allan Shivers (Texas), who failed to attend a national Democratic conference, held in September 1953, because of enmity with the party's national leadership.

On July 12, 1952 Kennon signed a bill which provides that Louisiana's public welfare rolls will be made public. Louisiana's welfare rolls include about one-twelfth of the state's population. Two years later he signed a bill outlawing the closed shop in Louisiana. After the U.S. Supreme Court ruled, on May 17, 1954, that racial segregation in public schools was unconstitutional, Kennon stated that Louisiana's Legislature would provide a public school system "which will include segregation in fact."

He later said that state laws would be "sufficient" to maintain segregation despite Federal actions, if a proposed amendment allowing the state to use its "inherent police powers" for enforcement, is approved by the state voters in November (New York *Times,* October 3, 1954).

Kennon married Eugenia Sentell on June 30, 1931; they have three sons, Robert Floyd, Charles Sentell and Kenneth. The Governor is a member of the Louisiana Bar Association, and of the American Legion. He has been president of the Minden Lion's Club, and in 1936-1937 was Grand Master of Masons, state of Louisiana. In 1946-1947 he was president of the Assembly Men's Council of the Presbyterian Church in the United States.

At the Southern Governor's Conference on November 3, 1953, Kennon stated that the principle of state sovereignty is more important than grants of Federal money to the states. "Whatever the cost, let's bear the burdens of state responsibility, use political courage. . . . Washington is worse than busted and owes more money than anyone . . . in human history. The poorest business people are in Washington and we are asking them to handle our money" (New York *Times,* November 4, 1953).

On the other hand, an emergency created by the diversion of 30 per cent of the Mississippi River to the little Atchafalaya River has caused Louisiana's Governor to seek Congressional approval of a great river control project to prevent New Orleans from losing her trade and industries (*Senior Scholastic,* September 15, 1954).

References

Martindale-Hubbell Law Directory, 1952
Who's Who in America, 1954-55

KHRUSHCHEV, NIKITA S(ERGEYEVICH) (kroo'shchĕv nē-kĕ'tȧ sĕr-gā'yĕ-vyĭch) Apr. 17, 1894- Soviet Communist party official

Address: b. Office of the Central Committee, Communist party of the Soviet Union, Moscow, U.S.S.R.

Nikita S. Khrushchev is the First Secretary, or chief executive officer, of the Communist party of the Soviet Union, holding the post from which the late Joseph Stalin for thirty years exercised his control of that country. Long a powerful figure in the Ukraine, which is the agricultural center of the Soviet Union, he has been since 1949 the party's foremost spokesman on farm matters. Khrushchev assumed his new position in September 1953 and has been directing the government's drive to increase agricultural output.

Because of his control of the party bureaucracy Khrushchev is considered by many observers to be in a position to contend for sole dictatorial leadership of the U.S.S.R. He is one of the nine members of the presidium of the central committee of the Communist party of the Soviet Union. He is the deputy from Moscow's Kalinin district to the Soviet of the Union, one of the two chambers of the Supreme Soviet, the U.S.S.R.'s bicameral "legislature."

Nikita Sergeyevich Khrushchev was born April 17, 1894, the son of a mine worker, in the village of Kalinovka, near Kursk, close to the Ukrainian border. In his early years he worked as a shepherd, and later as a locksmith in the factories of the Ukraine. During World War I he was drafted into the Czarist Army, but in 1918, after the Bolshevik revolution, he joined the Communist party and fought in the ranks of the Red Army on the southern front.

At the end of the Civil War in 1921, Khrushchev returned to the Ukraine to work in the mines. He attended one of the high schools established by the party; until then his schooling is said to have been very limited. After being graduated he was assigned to direct the work of the party first in Stalino, an important coal mining center, and later in Kiev, the capital of the Ukraine. The Communist party's general secretary of the Ukraine at that time was Lazar Kaganovich. In 1929 Khrushchev was assigned to take courses at the Industrial Academy in Moscow, and became the secretary of the school's party committee. He completed his two-year course and advanced rapidly in the Moscow party organization, which was then in the throes of a purge directed by Kaganovich.

Khrushchev was assigned in 1931 as party secretary of the Bauman district in Moscow, and later moved to the Krasnaya Presnya district. From 1932 to 1934 he graduated in quick succession from second secretary to first secretary of the party's city committee, and then to second secretary of the Moscow regional committee. At the end of this period he was elected to the central committee of the Communist party of the Soviet Union, and

Sovfoto

NIKITA S. KHRUSHCHEV

finally in 1935 he succeeded Kaganovich as first secretary of the Moscow regional committee.

Here, he was responsible for carrying out the industrialization program of the second five-year plan, and the construction of the Moscow subway. For his part in building the subway he was awarded the Order of Lenin. In 1937 he was designated a member of the Supreme Soviet by the Krasnaya Presnya district of Moscow.

In January 1938 the party transferred Khrushchev back to the Ukraine as first secretary of that republic's party, and named him a candidate member of the All-Union party's political bureau (a predecessor of the present central committee presidium). For his success in bolstering Ukrainian agricultural production, Khrushchev was in 1939 awarded the Order of the Red Banner of Labor. The party official was advanced by the central committee of the All-Union party to a full member of the political bureau, and he also became a member of the presidium of the U.S.S.R. Supreme Soviet.

When the German Army invaded the Ukraine in 1941, the leader of the Ukrainian Communist party was charged with organizing and coordinating the guerrilla defense of the republic, and with establishing contact between it and the Red Army. Khrushchev was given the rank of lieutenant general and received the Order of Suvorov. After the Soviet retreat from the Ukraine in the first year of the war, he headed the political department of the Red Army on the southern front which included Stalingrad.

After the enemy was driven from the Ukraine, Khrushchev in February 1944 took over the additional post of chairman of the Ukrainian republic's Council of Ministers, and started to restore order, destroying the alleged traitors who had collaborated with the Germans, and rebuilding the economy of the region upon which all Russia is largely dependent.

The Ukraine suffered a devastating drought in 1946, and from March to December of 1947 Khrushchev was replaced as secretary of the republic party by Kaganovich but remained in the Ukraine as the head of the government. When a successful harvest had been brought in, Khrushchev resumed his party responsibilities.

He was transferred from the Ukraine back to his former post of first secretary of the Moscow regional committee in December 1949, and also became a member of the secretariat of the All-Union party's central committee. His return, it developed, was to launch a drastic reorganization of agriculture. In a speech in January 1950 Khrushchev called for the amalgamation of smaller collective farms into larger enterprises. At the same time he suggested that the scattered peasant settlements which dot the collective farms should be broken up and their families concentrated in centralized "farm cities" (New York *Times,* March 6, 1950).

The amalgamation of farms was rapidly effected, and within six months the 6,000 collective farms in Moscow province had been cut to 1,668. In a year the 252,000 collective farms in the Soviet Union had been reduced to 123,000. Another part of this program was the collectivization of many private cows "which brought a wave of resentful slaughter of these animals" (*Saturday Night,* March 6, 1954).

The proposal to break up peasant settlements, however, was thrown open for discussion in the party. The conclusion of the discussion was negative. The idea of "farm cities" was dropped, and Khrushchev later admitted it had been a mistake.

For the nineteenth Congress of the Communist party of the Soviet Union in October 1952, Khrushchev was called upon to draft new party statutes, and to organize disciplinary action against unworthy party members. It was at this time that the Communist party replaced the politburo and orgburo with the presidium.

When Stalin died on March 5, 1953, Khrushchev was named the chairman of the commission to arrange the funeral. In the government reorganization after Stalin's death he was relieved of his duties as secretary of the Moscow regional party organization to devote his full time to affairs of the central committee.

At a special meeting of the central committee on March 14, 1953, Malenkov resigned as a central committee secretary. In the new list of secretaries, Khrushchev's name appeared first. However, he was not given the formal title of First Secretary until the central committee met again on September 13, 1953. Khrushchev thus became the actual head of the Communist party of the U.S.S.R. which, by the constitution of December 5, 1936, is the only listed party. Its highest organ is the All-Union party Congress which elects a central committee. The committee functions through a presidium of nine members a secretariat of four members and a committee of party control.

At the time of his appointment Khrushchev reported on the agricultural situation in the Soviet Union and asserted that agricultural production "does not fully satisfy the population's increasing need for food, or light industry's need for raw materials" (New York *Herald Tribune,* September 20, 1953).

The long and intense concentration of effort to build the industry of the Soviet Union had created economic imbalances, Khrushchev stated. He called for shifting the bulk of government and party efforts from industrialization to agriculture. His report and the program he detailed were approved by the central committee, and the program was launched immediately.

Edward Crankshaw believes that this constitutes "an admission that the Soviet Union cannot maintain its great industrialization program unless agricultural production is radically increased" (New York *Herald Tribune,* September 20, 1953). Willson Woodside (*Saturday Night,* March 6, 1954) commented: "The Soviets are recognizing material incentives because they need a bigger farm yield in a hurry. But once they 'get over the hump' again they are bound to defy experience and attempt again to socialize the countryside."

As part of the effort to strengthen Soviet agriculture, Khrushchev visited Kazakhstan republic in central Asia in May 1954 to inspect the progress of the campaign to increase Soviet grain production by bringing 35,500,000 acres of virgin land under cultivation. Kazakhstan was assigned the task of getting 16,250,000 acres tilled.

Walter Duranty, author of *Stalin & Co.,* says that Khrushchev's standing in the party "is no doubt partly due to his profound knowledge of the age-old feelings of the Ukrainian people in relation to Russians on one side and Poles on the other." In the Ukraine after the war Khrushchev took strong action against Ukrainian nationalists, many of whom were bitterly anti-Polish and anti-Russian.

Marshall MacDuffie, a New York lawyer, interviewed Khrushchev in November 1953 and reported in *Collier's* (March 19, 1954) that Khrushchev told him he had "many daughters" and a son studying engineering. An older son, he said, was an air force pilot killed during the war. MacDuffie described Khrushchev as a stocky man with a powerful wrestler's physique, and an appearance reminding one of an American political boss. He is, MacDuffie said, "a man with a great deal of warmth and charm—confident, relaxed and fairly reasonable. But he showed a shocking rigidity in his thinking about the West—an apparent willingness to swallow the propaganda he himself has helped create. Furthermore, I couldn't forget for a moment that a man has to be very tough and very ruthless to climb as high in the Soviet Union as Khrushchev has." On his sixtieth birthday the First Secretary was named a "Hero of Socialist Labor" and was the recipient of the Order of Lenin and the Gold Hammer and Sickle Medal.

According to Harrison E. Salisbury, Khrushchev wears light gray or brown suits, sometimes "with an embroidered Ukrainian shirt." In the summer he uses a "light yellow Panama hat with a thin black silk band or a fawn-colored light fedora" (New York *Times,* August 16, 1954).

Harry Schwartz of the New York *Times* (April 29, 1954) stated: "The swift rise of Nikita S. Khrushchev in the last year seems to have reached a new high" with his appearance before the Soviet of the Union in a role equal with that of Malenkov who addressed the Soviet of the Nationalities. While Khrushchev's earlier speeches were in the main confined to agriculture, in this speech he discussed all the problems which confront Soviet leaders, including foreign policy. An editorial in the New York *Times* (June 2, 1954) observed that "one has only to read *Pravda* and *Izvestia* day after day to be sure that there is elbowing and rivalry at the top of the Soviet pyramid of power."

"For the West, Khrushchev might be a far more dangerous adversary than Stalin was," commented the Associated Press, August 11, 1954 in the *Christian Science Monitor,* "just because of his realism . . . by presenting a reasonable face to the world he could go a long way toward dissipating suspicion of aggressive intentions. If he has his way, further Communist expansion will be as free as possible of direct risks to the Soviet Union."

References

Collier's 133:25+ Mr 19 '54 pors
N Y Herald Tribune II p 1 S 20 '53 por
N Y Times Mag p60 F 2 '47; p10 Ap 4 '48
Time 61:29+ Ja 12 '53 por; 62:28+ N 30 '53 por
International Who's Who, 1953
World Biography (1948)

KIAM, OMAR 1894-Mar. 28, 1954 Fashion designer; changed name from Alexander to Omar; began his career in a St. Louis millinery concern as a stock boy; obtained work in New York City in a retail fur company; started his own dress and suit designing firm and in 1935 was called to Hollywood to design clothes for motion picture stars Janet Gaynor, Loretta Young, Ruth Chatterton, Merle Oberon, and others; returned to New York in 1941 as chief designer for Ben Reig Corporation, a wholesale dress, suit and coat establishment; kept that post until his death; was a staunch champion of American-designed fashions; won Nieman-Marcus fashion award (1942), *Life* honor list (1945); designed costumes for stage stars Lynn Fontanne and Ina Claire; had exhibitions of his designs at Metropolitan Museum of Art (1941 and 1945). See *Current Biography,* (Dec.) 1945

Obituary

N Y Times p27 Mr 30 '54

KINER, RALPH (MCPHERRAN) Oct. 27, 1922- Baseball player

Address: b. c/o Cleveland Indians, The Stadium, Cleveland, Ohio; h. Palm Springs, Calif.

Ralph Kiner, formerly "Mr. Home Run" of the Pittsburgh Pirates, in 1954 completed his first full season with the Chicago Cubs. He did not succeed, however, in winning back his former home run record. From 1946 through 1952 he led or tied the National League in home runs, and is second only to the late George Herman (Babe) Ruth in the all-time listings.

Wide World

RALPH KINER

Kiner tops all right-handed hitters in circuit clouts, and holds other batting records. He was traded to Chicago on June 4, 1953, after seven years with Pittsburgh. In November 1954 Kiner moved to the Cleveland Indians and will play left field and be a reserve first baseman for the team.

Ralph McPherran Kiner was born on October 27, 1922 in Santa Rita, New Mexico to Beatrice (Grayson) and Ralph Macklin Kiner. He is of Pennsylvania-Dutch, Irish and Scotch ancestry. His father died when Ralph was four years old, and Mrs. Kiner moved to Alhambra, California.

She worked as a nurse to support them while Ralph sold newspapers and magazines and delivered groceries to buy baseball equipment. The boy showed so much interest in baseball that his mother wondered if he was being raised properly. When she asked Ralph about it he replied: "I'll be getting a major league salary while other guys are stuck in offices."

In high school Ralph played baseball, football and basketball and he was also a member of the baseball team of the Alhambra Merchants. On his high school team he was a successful pitcher, but his batting ability overshadowed his hurling and he was sent to the outfield. Young Kiner soon attracted offers from the Yankees, Pittsburgh and the Hollywood Stars.

A bonus offered by the Pirates was eagerly accepted by Ralph and his mother, and the strapping youth began his baseball career in Albany, New York. He played two years there, in the Eastern League, batting .279 and .257, hitting a total of twenty-five home runs. He then went to Toronto, but war interrupted his baseball within a year. He became a Navy pilot specializing in anti-submarine work out of Hawaii.

Lieutenant Kiner flew 1,200 hours in the air. He gained weight and strength in that period, weighing 200 pounds when his service ended. When he joined the Pirate team in the 1946 spring training, he showed such hitting power that Frank Frisch, the manager, put him in left field. Except for a brief session at first base, Kiner played left field until he left Pittsburgh in mid-1953.

In his first year as a Pirate, Kiner became the National League home-run king, with twenty-three home runs. This was not a high record, nor was it even close to Ruth's sixty homers in 1927, so Kiner set about raising it. In this effort he received valuable aid from Henry (Hank) Greenberg.

In 1947 Ralph Kiner became a member of an exclusive baseball group, the Fifty (homer) Society, whose members then included Babe Ruth, Johnny Mize, Jimmy Fox, Lewis (Hack) Wilson, and Hank Greenberg. He hit fifty-one that year tying for the lead in the National League, with a batting average of .313. One day Babe Ruth watched him in New York's Polo Grounds. The Bambino said, "that boy is just learning to hit." The Babe himself led both leagues in homers from 1926 through 1931.

Kiner has made other records: he was the only major leaguer to hit four consecutive homers twice in his career; the first National Leaguer to hit forty or more home runs for five straight years; he tied for the grand-slam homer record of four in one season, and the National League record for most home runs on the road in one season, with twenty-five. He is the only man in baseball history, Ruth included, to knock 257 balls out of the park in his first six major seasons. He holds the National League mark for sixteen homers in one month. Kiner leads all sluggers in homer average, per year, with 42 in seven years, Ruth having 39.4 homers in eighteen years.

In 1948 Kiner hit forty home runs tying for the lead in his league, his batting average was .265; in 1949 he hit fifty-four homers, leading his league, and his batting average was .310; in 1950 he hit forty-seven homers, leading his league, with a batting average of .272; in 1951 he hit forty-two homers, again leading his league, and had a batting average of .309; in 1952 he tied for the lead with thirty-seven homers and had a batting average of .244; and in 1953 he hit thirty-five homers with a batting average of .279.

In addition, Kiner is perennially among the leaders in bases on balls. He has received at least 100 a year in his last six seasons, averaging 108.8 per year during his career. In 1953 Kiner walked 100 times. His high mark was 137 in 1951 when he led the league, as he did in 1949 (117) and in 1952 (110).

In baseball, homers can make history. Fans speak of the Yankee Stadium as the "park that Ruth built", for the Babe's home-run hitting brought the admission fees that made the stadium possible. In somewhat the same way, Kiner's slugging brought new life to the Pittsburgh team. The fans poured through the turnstiles not so much to see the Pirates win, (they lost more often than not) but to see the big out-fielder drive one out of the park.

Heavy hitting brought Kiner an excellent salary. In 1953 he was paid a reported $75,000, (second only to Stan Musial of the St. Louis Cardinals) and the opportunity to invest his money. For this purpose he set up the Kiner & Prince Enterprises, which handles Kiner's non-playing interests. Running it are his partners, Bob Prince, a Pittsburgh radio sports announcer, and Abram Friedman, a New York attorney. The enterprises included a television show, newspaper columns, oil wells, natural gas wells, other investments, and the signing of endorsements. Kiner has made, it is reported, about $25,000 a year on these activities. He has also endorsed a health bread, milk, razor blades, and the Ralph Kiner bat. He is a partner in a sports-goods store in Alhambra, and runs a gift shop in Palm Springs.

In his early baseball years Kiner won a reputation as a model performer. Manager Billy Meyer said of Ralph that "there never was a time that Kiner didn't do anything I asked him for the general good of the ball club". Few players were so generally admired by his Pittsburgh teammates as was Kiner, and "there isn't a selfish bone in his body" said catcher Clyde McCullough. Kiner's appointment as National League player representative to deal with owners on the pension plan was an evidence of the respect afforded him.

On June 4, 1953 it was announced that Kiner was sold by the Pittsburgh Pirates to the Chicago Cubs. The details of the transaction revealed that the Cubs were to get Kiner plus pitcher Howie Pollet, catcher Joseph Garagiola and outfielder-infielder George Metkovich; the Pirates to receive a reported $100,000 plus pitcher Robert Schultz, catcher Maurice (Toby) Atwell, outfielders Gene Hermanski, Preston Ward and Bob Addis, and an option on George Freese of the International League.

Ralph Kiner and Nancy Chaffee, the tennis star, were engaged to be married in June of 1951. At a "wedding shower" given by fans, the couple received many gifts. Kiner requested that all cash presents be turned over to the Children's Hospital of Pittsburgh, and he sent the hospital a check for the value of the gifts. On October 14, 1951 their marriage took place in Santa Barbara, California. After a honeymoon in Acapulco, Mexico, the couple moved into a ranch home Kiner had designed at Palm Springs, California. In July 1953 a boy, Ralph Michael, was born.

The baseball player is over six feet tall and weighs about 190 pounds; he has blue eyes and brown hair. Tom Meany described Kiner as a "handsomely rugged chap who resembles a professional football player. At the plate, Ralph straddles, feet extremely far apart and hits almost flat-footed, scarcely striding at all. It takes physical power to hit sixty home runs. All the timing, the keen sight and the rhythmic swing aren't worth a nickel unless the possessor of these attributes has a powerful frame. Ralph has youth and he has the physique." During the off-season the player lifts weights and studies movies of himself and of other hitters in order to improve his home run power. His hobbies include golfing, tennis and the theatre.

References

Baseball Stars 1:18+ N 2 '50 por
Collier's 121:6 Mr 27 '48
Sat Eve Post 222:32+ Jl 2 '49 pors; 224:22+ D 15 '51 pors
Scholastic 56:24 My 17 '50 por
Sport 12:35+ Je '52 pors; 14:10+ Mr '53 pors
Sports 1:61 F '53 pors
Time 54:30 O 3 '49 por

Meany, T. Baseball's Greatest Hitters (1950)
Stump, A. J. Champions Against Odds (1952)
Waldman, F. ed. Famous American Athletes of Today (1951)

KINSEY, ALFRED C(HARLES) June 23, 1894- Zoologist

Address: b. c/o Institute of Sex Research, Inc., Indiana University, Bloomington, Ind.; h. 1320 E. First St., Bloomington, Ind.

With the publication in 1948 of *Sexual Behavior in the Human Male* and in 1953 of *Sexual Behavior in the Human Female,* Dr. Alfred C. Kinsey and his colleagues completed the first two progress reports on a projected several-volume investigation which has been described as the most extensive survey of its kind ever undertaken. Kinsey's statistical best-selling books, based on interviews with thousands of men and women, have caused him to be compared with Sigmund Freud and Havelock Ellis as a pioneer in the field of sex research. Profits from the sale of these books do not go to Dr. Kinsey, but to the Institute for Sex Research, affiliated with Indiana University.

Professor of zoology at Indiana University since 1929, Kinsey was known as an authority on gall wasps before beginning his studies on human behavior in 1938. While some critics have condemned his highly controversial work as "dangerous" and "useless," others have acclaimed his achievement in increasing candor and knowledge of human relationships.

Alfred Charles Kinsey, the son of Alfred Sequine and Sarah Ann (Charles) Kinsey, was born on June 23, 1894, in Hoboken, New Jersey, where his father taught at the Stevens Institute of Technology. During his boyhood, most of which was spent in nearby South Orange, he prepared his first study based on the activities of birds in the rain, which was published in a nature journal. "This early

Dellenback

ALFRED C. KINSEY

ornithology foreshadowed the two main drives of his life—love of nature and passion for explicit details" (*Time,* December 15, 1952).

Following his graduation in 1916 from Bowdoin College with a B.S. degree, Kinsey entered Harvard University, where in 1917 and 1918 he was an assistant in zoology, in 1918 and 1919 an assistant in botany, and in 1919 and 1920, a Sheldon traveling fellow. He received the Sc.D. degree at Harvard in 1920 and became an assistant professor of zoology at Indiana University. Two years later he was advanced to associate professor and in 1929 to professor.

As a Waterman research associate in 1931 and 1932 and in 1935 and 1936, Kinsey directed biological exploration, in Mexico and Central America, of the habits of the gall wasp. His researches, begun at Harvard, have been called "a landmark in the world of entomology" (*PM,* November 21, 1947). According to an estimate given by *Time* (December 15, 1952), "Kinsey traveled 80,000 miles collecting gall wasps, and he measured, catalogued and preserved 3,500,000 specimens to demonstrate their individual variations. Under a microscope he took and recorded 28 different measurements on each wasp."

The results of these investigations were presented in a number of Indiana University publications: *Studies of Some New and Described Cynipidae (Hymenoptera)* (1922), *The Gall Wasp Genus Neuroterus (Hymenoptera)* (1923), *The Gall Wasp Genus Cynips: A Study in the Origin of Species* (1930), and the supplementary *The Origin of the Higher Categories in Cynips* (1936).

During his first twenty years at Indiana University Dr. Kinsey was also the author of several scientific volumes published by J. B. Lippincott Company, some of which have been used as high school textbooks, notably: *An Introduction to Biology* (1926), *New Introduction to Biology* (1933, revised 1938), *Workbook in Biology* (1934), and *Methods in Biology* (1937). In collaboration with M. L. Fernald, he wrote *Edible Wild Plants of Eastern North America,* in 1920, published by Idlewild Press in 1943.

While engaged in teaching a course in marriage problems in the 1930's, Professor Kinsey became concerned with the paucity of scientific knowledge on human sexual behavior. His turning from insect taxonomy to his new field of research has been described by Kinsey as "a natural step." "If we could study the life habits of insect populations, why not of human populations?" he told Albert Deutsch (*PM,* January 7, 1947). "I always had been interested in people, was struck by the fact that a large area of living had not been studied on a broad, objective basis, and started out to do so."

In the summer of 1938 the zoology professor began interviewing his friends on their sex experiences and working out a statistical method to tabulate his findings. When the university authorities learned of his project, Kinsey was given assurance of "the right of a scientist to do objective research" (New York *Times,* March 14, 1948). Kinsey, who had been financing his investigations with his own savings, appealed in 1940 to the National Research Council and succeeded in obtaining modest assistance from the council's committee for research on problems of sex.

Later, through the N.R.C., Kinsey was granted $40,000 annually for at least three years by the Rockefeller Foundation. These groups, jointly with Indiana University, have continued to sponsor his work. Covering all aspects of human sex behavior, the survey is expected to be recorded in nine or ten books which by 1968 will cover information compiled from interviews with 100,000 men and women.

The first report on the project, *Sexual Behavior in the Human Male,* appeared in January 1948 and was based statistically upon 5,300 case histories gathered by Kinsey and his chief colleagues, psychologist W. B. Pomeroy, and statistician C. E. Martin. Much of the tabulation, as well as the actual gathering of material, was done by the author, since all recording of information is made in a code devised by Kinsey and known only to him and his chief associates.

A technical book designed for use by professional workers in medical, sociological and allied fields, the 804-page *Sexual Behavior in the Human Male* was published by W. B. Saunders Company, publishers of medical books, with a first printing of 5,000 volumes. The Kinsey Report, as it came to be called, was a best seller immediately, has sold 275,000 copies (at $6.50 each), and received extensive discussion in the national press, on radio programs and in meetings of scientific organizations. Public interest also gave rise to several derivative books: *Sex Habits of American Men* (1948), edited by Albert Deutsch, and *American Sexual Behavior and the Kinsey Report* (1948) by Morris Ernst and David Loth.

Through their questioning of people from every part of the United States on every social-economic level, the interviewers observed that there was a correspondence between the individual's sex habits and the educational and occupational group to which he belonged, and that there was a notable difference in sex patterns between one group and another. One of the conclusions of the report which received considerable attention was that actual sex practices deviated from those established by the laws and conventions of society. The New York lawyer, Morris Ernst, regarded the report as "the single greatest contribution of science to the rule-making part of law during my lifetime" (New York *Times,* December 31, 1949).

Many readers who objected to Kinsey's book argued that it encouraged immorality by citing statistics. Kinsey was both criticized and praised for his efforts to avoid social and moral interpretations of his findings; his work was both challenged and defended in regard to the soundness of his sampling methods. At a conference of the American Social Hygiene Association, anthropologist Margaret Mead expressed her view that his impersonal handling of the subject was "extraordinarily destructive of interpsychic and interpersonal relationships" (New York *Times,* March 31, 1948).

The Indiana group, which had been joined by anthropologist Paul H. Gebhard, continued after its initial publication to gather material in preparation for a comparable book on women. Kinsey lectured without fee to women's organizations in different parts of the country in order to find subjects on various social levels who would submit to answering between 300 and 500 questions in an average interview of two and a half hours.

The second survey, also published by Saunders, was fifteen years in preparation and was based on interviews with 5,940 women.

Among the important conclusions of *Sexual Behavior in the Human Female,* as pointed out by anthropologist Clyde Kluckhohn (New York *Times,* September 13, 1953), is that "the range of variation in the female far exceeds the range of variation in the male" and that "females are not conditioned as much as males by the attitudes of the social groups in which they live." The New York *Herald Tribune* (August 21, 1953) stated that the Indiana scientists regarded the pattern of female sexual behavior as a "composite between innate biological drives, social restrictions and pressures and psychological attitudes instilled by social mores."

In the Chicago *Tribune,* Kinsey was denounced as a "real menace to society" (*Time,* August 31, 1953) and Representative Lewis B. Heller of New York termed the survey "the insult of the century against womanhood" (New York *Herald Tribune,* September 1, 1953). Defending the availability of books such as Kinsey's, which soon became a best seller, novelist Fanny Hurst (*Life,* August 24, 1953) wrote, "This is the best measure we ever had. The Kinsey statistics, like cereal shot from a gun, are not frightening, but nourishing."

Royalties from the sale of the two books (which are averaging $50,000 a year) are used to further the work of the Institute of Sex Research, Inc. which was incorporated in April 1947 and operates on a budget of about $100,000 annually.

The third volume in the Kinsey project is expected to deal with sex laws and to contain a comparative study of the relevant laws of the forty-eight states. Other forthcoming volumes include examinations of sex education, sexual adjustments in institutional populations and marital adjustment.

Professor Kinsey is a member of the American Association for the Advancement of Science, Entomological Society of America, Indiana Academy of Science, Cambridge Entomological Club, American Society of Geneticists, American Society of Naturalists (secretary since 1941), American Zoological Society, American Iris Society, and New England Botanical Club. His Greek-letter societies are Zeta Psi, Phi Beta Kappa and Sigma Psi.

The scientist was married on June 3, 1921 to Clara Bracken McMillen, then a graduate student in chemistry at Indiana University. They have three children: Anne McMillen (Mrs. Warren Corning), Joan McMillen (Mrs. Robert M. Reid) and Bruce McMillen Kinsey, a postgraduate student at Indiana University. A second son, Donald McMillen is deceased. The zoology professor is tall and heavy-set, with bluish hazel eyes and sandy hair. He has been characterized as "out-going" in manner, a man of "patience," "forebearance," and "sincerity." With many interests outside his work, he turns most often for recreation to the theater, music, hiking, gardening, and pottery.

According to *Time,* August 24, 1953, Kinsey's "only concession to the social amenities is to hold Sunday-evening record recitals. But he is no relaxed amateur. He is a relentless musicologist, and his soirees are an exacting ritual. He plans a carefully balanced program and gathers material for commentary. Guests arrive on the stroke of 8 and are seated in a hieratic U pattern with the high-fidelity player and the master's chair at the open end of the U. All talk is hushed as Kinsey picks up the first record and announces why he thinks it worth playing."

References

Harper 195:490+ D '47
Life 25:87+ Ag 2 '48 pors
Look 11:106+ D 6 '47 pors; 15:81+ My 8 '51 pors
N Y Herald Tribune p44 Ap 11 '48
N Y Post p4 My 10 '50 por
N Y World-Telegram My 14 '48
Newsweek 40:68+ Ag 24 '53 pors
New Yorker 24:19+ Mr 27 '48
PM p24 Ja 7 '47; p24 Ja 8 '47; p11 N 20 '47; p5 My 9 '48
U.S. News 35:40+ N 6 '53

American Men of Science (1949)
National Cyclopædia of American Biography, Current vol H (1952)
Who Knows—And What (1949)
Who's Who in America, 1952-53

KIRKUS, VIRGINIA Dec. 7, 1893- Literary critic; author

Address: b. 317 W. 4th St., New York 14; h. 38 Bank St., New York 14; h. Poverty Hollow, Redding Ridge, Conn.

NOTE: This biography supersedes the article which appeared in *Current Biography* in 1941.

Subscribers to the Bookshop Service originated by Virginia Kirkus have called her "the Kiplinger of the book world." They depend upon her advance evaluations of new books to tell them what to order for their customers and readers. Her terse predictions for or against the dollar-and-cents success of forthcoming books are regarded by booksellers and librarians as about 85 per cent accurate. Established in 1933 with ten subscribers, the service is now used by over 1,500 bookstores and libraries. Some ninety publishers supply Miss Kirkus with galleys or page proofs of each year's books on which she gives capsule criticisms in her bi-monthly *Bulletin*.

With the aid of four assistants she reports on some 4,000 titles annually. Her informal and impartial comments are also a check on what she calls "the natural enthusiasm of publishers' blurbs." She is credited with "discovering" many unknown authors by calling attention to the merits of their books long before the magazine and newspaper reviews appeared. Among the 1954 books which Miss Kirkus has highly recommended are *Of Whales and Men* by R. B. Robertson and *The Magnificent Bastards* by Lucy Crockett. Her favorites in 1953 included Theodore White's *Fire in the Ashes* and *Battle Cry* by Leon M. Uris.

She is also well known as a lecturer and as an author of magazine articles and *A House for the Week Ends*. In January 1953 she received nationwide acclaim for uncovering a case of plagiarism which she detected in time for the publisher to stop publication.

Virginia Kirkus is the daughter of Dr. Frederick Maurice Kirkus, an Episcopal minister, and Isabella (Clark) Kirkus. She was born in Meadville, Pennsylvania on December 7, 1893 and spent most of her childhood in Wilmington, Delaware. At the age of eight she told her father that when she grew up she wanted to "make books." She attended the Misses Hebbs School in Wilmington, and then the Hannah More Academy at Reisterstown, Maryland. She received the A.B. degree from Vassar College, Poughkeepsie, New York in 1916, and then took some courses at Teachers College, Columbia University.

After three years of teaching English and history at the Greenhill School in Delaware she went to New York and obtained a job as assistant fashion editor for the Pictorial Review Company. This was followed by an editorial position at *McCall's* and some free-lance writing for Doubleday, including her first book, *Everywoman's Guide To Health and Personal Beauty*, in 1922. For Doubleday, she edited *Robert Bacon, Life and Letters* by James Brown Scott in 1923. She became in 1925 the head of the children's book department of Harper & Brothers where, during the next seven years, she was responsible for the success of many new books and for the abridgment of many old ones.

When the depression started and publishers began to retrench, Harper decided to discontinue its juvenile book department in May 1932. Miss Kirkus was offered a job in another department but she was not certain that she wanted to do that kind of work. She decided to go to Bavaria on an eight weeks vacation and to visit her father who was rector of the American church in Munich.

On the voyage back to the United States, the idea for her service to booksellers came to her in the middle of the night. The plan, as she worked it out in detail, would provide "bookstores with brief, informal and impartial reports of books, based on actual reading, several weeks in advance of publication, to help the stores in buying. Its working depended, of course, on the willingness of publishers to furnish her with galley proofs of their books far in advance" (*Publishers' Weekly*, March 27, 1943).

The business as it subsequently developed has differed very little from her original scheme. To get the Virginia Kirkus' Bookshop Service started, she presented her plan to twenty publishers who agreed to furnish advance proofs of their books, and soon she was sending bulletins to ten subscribers who paid $10 a month for the service. (Today, however, stores pay from $3 to $10 a month, depending on their volume of business.)

Two years after the establishment of the service for bookstores, it was also made available to libraries. Libraries with book budgets under $4,000 pay a fee of $19 a year for the service, whereas larger libraries pay $24.50 to $32. Book clubs, and radio and television stations pay $50 per year.

Publishers agree that Virginia Kirkus' judgments on books are right about 85 per cent of the time. She herself admits she has been mistaken on a few titles, such as *Anthony Adverse* ("I fell down on that simply because I didn't believe that the public would take such a lengthy book"), but on the other hand she very frequently spots "sleepers"—books destined to have a great success in the future. She was once twitted by a group of librarians for her dismissal of Thomas Wolfe's book, *Of Time and the River* as "snob appeal." "How many of you have read it?" she asked. Only five of the hundreds who attended had.

She has personally read more than 16,000 books since she launched the service in 1933, and among the "dark horses" which later became best sellers which she enthusiastically hailed "must promote" have been *Tortilla Flat, Time Out of Mind, Mister Roberts, Cry, the Beloved Country, Cheaper by the Dozen, Death Be Not Proud,* and *The Caine Mutiny*. Her service was hailing George Orwell as far back as 1933 and Joyce Cary in 1936.

Her phenomenal memory stood her in good stead on the day after Christmas of 1952 when she made a discovery which startled the book world. As she was reading the galley proofs of *Position Unknown* by Robert E. Preyor, Jr. shortly to be published by Little, Brown & Company, she found it "a haunting experience." As she read, she kept saying to herself: "I know what happens next. . . . I know what happens next." Looking through her files, she discovered that in 1944 Viking Press had published *Island in the Sky* by Ernest K. Gann, with precisely the same plot and characters. The book had been copied word for word except for the title.

Research proved that this was one of the most flagrant cases of plagiarism on record, but since Preyor was already serving a sentence in the Ohio State Penitentiary for burglary, no legal action was taken against him. "I understand he bought an electric typewriter with most of the $600 advance given him by Little, Brown," Miss Kirkus recalls.

Miss Kirkus is aided by four assistants in her office in Greenwich Village, New York. Her aim, she has said, is to be informal, colloquial and readable—and not literary. Always, she tries to keep in mind questions likely to come up in the minds of buyers. While the bi-monthly *Bulletin* (which is mimeographed) had but a dozen pages when the service started, today it averages thirty-five pages with special supplements.

Here are a few samples of her opinions, (authors and titles omitted): "For me this completely missed fire." "A cheap bit of fustian, written by a movie bit actor." "Slender little story, rather starry-eyed, strictly for the rental market." "This man can write but he has no sense of plot. Shows promise but unlikely to produce much fanfare." Of a well-known author's new book: "Tripier than usual." From time to time Miss Kirkus encounters the opinion that her service is run by the publishers, but nothing could be further from the truth.

Every year Miss Kirkus takes several trips around the country to find out what people are thinking. She reads the local papers, talks to the porters, taxi drivers, and waitresses. She visits bookshops and the public libraries, and tries to find out how much people are reading and what books they like. This personal attention also improves her relationship with her subscribers and gives them a greater faith in her.

Her opinions are so valued that she is in demand as a lecturer on literary subjects. Writing in *Book Previews* (January-February, 1952), Miss Kirkus gave an indication of the methods she uses in choosing books. "What are some of the tests I apply in final selections? Those who demand high standards of literary judgment will quarrel with my insistence that the creative artist must still have something the reader seeks, not simply beauty of literary form. . . . On another level I'd choose a book that excited my anticipation for what an author might do in subsequent work, as against a finer piece of craftsmanship that showed little originality." The service obtains outside opinions for specialized or technical books.

In an end of 1951 summary of "top" books, Miss Kirkus listed her preferences under such

VIRGINIA KIRKUS

descriptive headings as "First-Rate Storytelling—in Perceptive Analysis," "The Past Comes Alive Through These," and "These Challenged Established Thinking."

Virginia Kirkus was editor, with Frank Scully, of *Fun in Bed for Children* and *Junior Fun in Bed* (Simon & Schuster, 1935). She wrote *A House for the Week Ends* (Little, Brown, 1940) which described her experiences in remodeling an old house in Redding Ridge, Connecticut. She finds much pleasure in gardening, cooking, collecting antiques, and working around this house.

She was married on June 4, 1936 to Frank Glick, a personnel director. She is an Episcopalian and a Democrat. She has blue eyes, gray hair, weighs 129 pounds, and is five feet, three and a half inches tall. She belongs to the Vassar Club of New York; American Booksellers Association; Woman's National Book Association; Civics Club of Redding, Connecticut; and is on the board of West Redding's Mark Twain Library, an institution in which she takes great pride and interest. She reads with remarkable speed and says that it is no strain on her eyes to read about 700 books a year.

In selecting books for children Miss Kirkus advised: "I'd take for granted that it was better to reach above their level of understanding . . . and as they grow older I'd give access to books about people who had made a mark in the world, whether a heroic mark or not; I'd give them history and politics and social problems not prettied over for the tender-minded. These young people will inherit the world we've made. Let us give them tools for understanding that world" (*Publishers' Weekly*, August 31, 1946).

She believes that the level of the public's taste in reading is definitely higher than it was twenty years ago and "is steadily rising be-

KIRKUS, VIRGINIA—*Continued*

cause most people who can read are more aware than ever that they cannot run from anything any more and accordingly, are relating themselves not only to their environment but to the larger social expression." However, she thinks that the level of reprint publication tends to lower the quality of original books which are aimed at the reprint trade.

References (see also references listed in 1941 biographical sketch)

Newsweek 41:100 Ja 19 '53 por
Pub W 143:1342+ Mr 27 '43 por; 150: 994+ Ag 31 '46
St Louis Post-Dispatch p3D Mr 18 '53 por
American Women, 1939-40
Who's Who in New York, 1947

KNOPF, MRS. HANS *See* Vanderbilt, A.

KRAUTTER, ELISA BIALK *See* Bialk, E. (WLB) Yrbk '54

KREBS, H(ANS) A(DOLF) (krĕbs) Aug. 25, 1900- Biochemist; university professor

Address: b. c/o University of Sheffield, Sheffield 10, England; h. 19 Kingsley Park Ave., Sheffield 7, England

For his "discovery of the citric acid cycle," Dr. H. A. Krebs of the University of Sheffield in England was awarded the 1953 Nobel Prize in physiology and medicine jointly with Dr. Fritz Lipmann of Harvard Medical School. Krebs's "brilliant" and "ingenious" contribution was the cyclical "wheel of fortune," his explanation of how the body converts food into energy, while Lipmann discovered co-enzyme A, an "organic catalyst" in the Krebs cycle.

British Inf. Services
DR. H. A. KREBS

Dr. Goran Liljestrand, secretary of the Nobel medical committee, described the doctors' work as being "of the utmost theoretical significance and very likely to have great practical importance in understanding diseases and similar disturbances."

The son of a surgeon, Hans Adolf Krebs was born to Georg and Alma (Davidson) Krebs on August 25, 1900 in Hildesheim, Germany. He studied medicine at the universities of Göttingen, Freiburg, Munich, and Berlin, and received his M.D. degree from the Universität Hamburg in 1925.

After a year's graduate study of chemistry at the University of Berlin, Dr. Krebs entered the Kaiser-Wilhelm-Institut as an assistant in the department of Professor Otto Heinrich Warburg. (Warburg, a physiologist, was later awarded the 1931 Nobel Prize in medicine for his work on the "assimilation and oxidation" of various substances in the body.) According to an Associated Press account, the work of both Krebs and Lipmann "elaborates an idea first suggested by Dr. Warburg many years ago." (Lipmann was at the institute when Krebs was there, but in the department of Professor Otto Meyerhof.)

Krebs studied with Dr. Warburg from 1926 to 1930 and then became an assistant at the Municipal Hospital in Hamburg. He later lectured at the medical clinic of the University of Freiburg and studied under Professor S. J. Thannheuser. "With the advent of the Hitler regime," Krebs wrote, "I was forced to leave Germany because of my Jewish descent."

Invited to Cambridge University, he arrived in 1933 with "virtually nothing but a sigh of relief and a few books." Krebs studied from 1933 to 1934 at Cambridge as a Rockefeller research student, and worked there for two years under Sir Frederick Gowland Hopkins, professor of biochemistry, who was a co-winner of the 1929 Nobel Prize in physiology and medicine for his pioneer work on vitamins. Krebs was a demonstrator in biochemistry from 1934 to 1935 and was awarded an M.S. degree in 1934.

The following year, he became associated with the University of Sheffield where he lectured in pharmacology from 1935 to 1938. Krebs was appointed lecturer in charge of the Sheffield department of biochemistry in 1938, and according to *Nature,* a British scientific magazine, [he] "attracted to his department research workers from both Europe and America." A British citizen, naturalized in 1939, he contributed to wartime research on problems of diet and nutrition and was largely responsible for the national whole meal loaf, described by the British Information Service as "the economical and healthful stand-by of a bread-short nation."

In 1945, when Dr. Krebs was appointed professor of biochemistry and director of the medical research council unit for research in cell metabolism, *Nature* commented, "The University of Sheffield has conferred on Dr. H. A. Krebs the title and status of professor of biochemistry in recognition of his eminence in the world of science. . . . His main contributions to biochemistry," the journal continued, "are in the field of intermediary metabolism. He showed that the synthesis of urea in the mammalian liver is catalysed by ornithine. This observation led to the formulation of the 'ornithine cycle,' according to which ornithine, citrulline, and arginine are intermediate stages in the synthesis of urea. His work on the oxidation of carbohydrate in muscle showed that this metabolic process, too, is a cyclic one (known as the 'Krebs cycle'), where a series of organic acids arises periodically."

Basically, Krebs was investigating the way the body changes food into energy. The urea referred to is the end product of the metabolism of nitrogen, from protein food. Seeking to ascertain the process by which sugar is converted into other compounds, liberating energy, Dr. Krebs "manipulated the formulas" of twenty or thirty organic acids related to sugar, in order to find which of them was capable of making a series of transformations by itself. Lactic and pyruvic acids both met these specifications, and eventually he used pyruvic acid for his experiments in the metabolic process.

When the pyruvic acid was oxidized, it formed a "go-between" chemical named acetyl co-enzyme A, and carbon dioxide was given off. Other acids were formed with the oxidation and the whole process continued until another molecule of co-enzyme A was rejuvenated. Energy is released by this process.

According to Fieser and Fieser in *Organic Chemistry* (Heath, 1950), "the Krebs cycle accounts for the fact that glutamic acid, aspartic acid, and alanine, and only these amino acids, are oxidized rapidly in muscle, since they are convertible by [the process of] transamination into keto acids, that are intermediates in the cycle."

Krebs believes that the basic principle can be applied also to other foodstuffs, such as fatty acids. He is credited with forming many scattered findings on the subject into one unified theory.

In a sense, the work of Dr. H. A. Krebs and Dr. Fritz Lipmann, of Harvard Medical School and Massachusetts General Hospital, is complementary. Since Lipmann's co-enzyme A makes it possible for energy to be produced in the body cells, the substance has been called "the entrance to the Krebs mill." Although the biochemists worked separately the faculty of the Caroline Institute of Medicine awarded the 1953 Nobel Prize in medicine and physiology to the two jointly. The two scientists shared a prize in Swedish crowns equal to $33,840.

After the announcement of the Nobel Prize came another, one of the five Lasker awards in public health of the American Public Health Association was given to Dr. Krebs who was cited as "the discoverer of the urea and citric acid cycles which are basic to the understanding of vital biological processes in normal metabolism and in disease." (The selection had been made in June 1953). The scientist came to the United States to accept the award which consisted of $1,000, a hand-illuminated leather-bound citation, and a gold statuette of the Winged Victory of Samothrace.

Krebs was made a fellow of the Royal Society in 1947. His writings have appeared in such scientific journals as the *Annual Review of Biochemistry, Biochimica et Biophysica Acta, Lancet, Enzymologia,* and *Biochemical Journal.* He has written numerous articles for *Nature,* among which are "Metabolism of Acetoacetic Acid in Animal Tissues" (with L. V. Eggleston) (August 12, 1944) and "Urea Synthesis in Mammalian Liver" (June 14, 1947). His article, "Tricarboxylic Acid Cycle", appeared in the *Harvey Lectures* in 1950.

He is five feet eight inches tall, weighs 154 pounds, and has brown eyes and brown hair. He was awarded an honorary Doctor of Science degree by the University of Chicago, 1954.

The biochemist is described as a quiet, reserved man who is fond of reading, music and walking. He was married in 1938 to Margaret Cicely Fieldhouse of Wickersley, Yorkshire, and they have two sons and a daughter. Of his work he has said, "One cannot have a definite aim in metabolism research. The field is endless."

References

N Y Herald Tribune p5 O 23 '53
N Y Times p21 O 23 '53 por
Newsweek 42:86 N 2 '53 por
Time 62:104 N 2 '53 por
Who's Who, 1953

KROHG, PER (LASSON) (krôg) June 18, 1889- Artist

Address: h. Halvdan Svartesgate 48, Oslo, Norway

Associations with two artists, one French and one Norwegian, were strong formative factors in the development of the Norwegian painter, Per Krohg. The "heated brushstrokes of fauvism", as taught him by Henri Matisse, and the "colder, less lyrical realities" of his father's paintings, are evident in his *genre* scenes, figure studies, portraits and landscapes.

Per Krohg's work was introduced to the American public in a retrospective show which toured the United States in the spring and summer of 1954. The exhibition spanned a period of over forty years, and demonstrated why Krohg has achieved a reputation in Norway as one of its greatest contemporary artists. He is acknowledged as a pioneer in monumental mural painting, and his frescoes are an outstanding feature of many public buildings in Oslo. He is also a distinguished scenic designer for Scandinavian theatrical productions. In 1952 he executed a large mural for the Security Council Chamber in the United Nations Conference building in New York City.

Per Lasson Krohg was born on June 18, 1889, in Åsgårdstrand, Norway. His father, Christian Krohg, was a famous Norwegian writer and painter of the realist school. (In 1936, a faithful copy of the elder Krohg's *Leif Ericson Discovers America,* made by Per Krohg, was placed in the Capitol in Washington, D.C.) Per's mother, Oda or Ottilie (Las-

Louise Dahl-Wolfe

PER KROHG

son) Krohg, was likewise an artist. His godfather was Edvard Munch, widely regarded as Norway's greatest painter.

The Krohg family settled in Paris when Per was seven years old, and spent the summer months in Brittany in the company of such friends as Georg Brandes, Auguste Rodin, and Per's uncle, the landscape painter Fritz Thaulow. At an early age Per began to draw, and he made his debut at ten in a children's exhibition held at the Petit Palais. During the day, he studied at the Lycée Michelet, and in the evenings, from 1903 to 1905, attended his father's classes in sketching and life drawing at the Académie Colarossi. As Per's first teacher, his father gave him a solid foundation in the fundamentals of drawing and design. Young Krohg completed his general education by obtaining a diploma from the University of Oslo. His works were shown for the first time in his native country at the annual state exhibition in Oslo in 1907.

Returning to Paris, Krohg joined the group of talented young Norwegian painters (including Jean Heiberg, Henrik Ingvar Sörensen, and Axel Revold) who studied with Henri Matisse, at the Académie Matisse between 1907 and 1909. From Matisse he gained an understanding of certain basic artistic principles, and to some degree was influenced by the French master's decorative fauvist style.

Krohg was briefly preoccupied with concepts of depth and the dynamics of movement. For a time he was interested in the experiments of the cubists, but unlike them, he was dominated by the desire to create figures in which there should be nothing static, and sought to restore the sense of space that surrounds individuals and objects in the unposed immediacy of real life. Among his important prewar canvases are the *Portrait of Sven Elvestad* (c. 1911) and *An Accident* (1912). He exhibited his work at the Salon des Indépendants from 1909 to 1914, and later sent pictures to the Salon des Tuileries and the Salon d'Automne.

The outbreak of World War I found Krohg in Scandinavia. Unable to return to Paris, and without resources, he earned his living by traveling from city to city selling his drawings. In the evenings, he and his first wife, Lucy, often performed dance numbers in various music halls and small circuses. He made many sketches of backstage life and circus animals at that time. By 1916 he succeeded in returning to France as an ambulance driver in the Red Cross.

After the war, Krohg gained the reputation of being one of the most original younger artists of the Ecole de Paris. His portrait and figure studies, *Woman on the Staircase* (1925), *Guy and Serge* (1927), *Maurice Bedel* (1927), *Guy, or "The Voyages of Thought"* (1927), and *The Pearl Dealer* (1928) revealed a flair for dramatic characterization. Krohg's concern with capturing movement and spontaneous gesture was reflected in *The Bullfighter* (1926), *Dogfight* (1927), *The Blacksmith* (1929), and the numerous impressions of life in bars and cabarets (*Welcome Bar, The Accordion Player*).

Entirely different in subject matter was the impressive series dealing with fishing on the Islands of Lofoten, off the northwest coast of Norway, which he visited in the winter of 1928-1929. He had earlier made trips to Italy and North Africa (where he painted the well-known *Camels in Nefta* of 1924).

Some critics of Krohg's work during this period found an almost baroque expressionism in his predilection for fanciful and grotesque subject matter and in his twisting forms, attenuated figures and swirling bravura brushwork. His palette was usually limited to three dominant but skillfully modulated tones. "When I exaggerate a line, I do so in order to make it appear normal," the artist has stated. "A line must not be submerged in color; it should serve to accentuate design and movement."

After spending the first part of his adult life in France, he decided in 1932 to return to Norway permanently. Among his canvases depicting the Norwegian scene are *Hoarfrost* (1933), *Rain in Bergen* (1938), and *Frogner* (1940). During the German occupation of Norway in World War II, he served in the Resistance and spent a year in a concentration camp.

The first one-man show of Krohg's easel paintings in the United States took place at the Galerie St. Etienne, in New York, in April 1954. It comprised forty-two oils dating from 1912 to 1953, and was later exhibited in Philadelphia, Washington, D.C., Seattle, and San Francisco. In reviewing the show, Stuart Preston wrote: "Krohg is a realist with strong overtones of sentiment and satire. He will give us a lyrical impression of the Norwegian landscape . . . and then turn to illustrating the lives of his friends and neighbors, mostly with good humor but occasionally with indignation" (New York *Times*, April 2, 1954).

Krohg has made notable contributions to the development of mural painting in Norway which began with decorations by Munch for the concert hall of the University of Oslo during World War I. However, it was the generation of artists following Munch—led by Krohg, Axel Revold, and Alf Rolfsen—that revived the true fresco technique, demonstrated the close relation of mural painting to architecture and established a modern style of monumental painting in Norway. Oslo has since become known as the city of murals, and Norway's output in this sphere is said to be equalled only by Mexico.

Krohg did his first murals in 1913 for the Chat Noir cabaret in Oslo. His designs won second prize in the competition in 1918 for the decoration of the Bergen Stock Exchange. His first major undertaking was the fresco paintings for the Merchant Marine Academy (1921-1924) in Ekeberg opposite Oslo, where he used for his motif the young man's longing to see the world. These frescoes, with their imaginative blending of realism and symbolism, are still considered among his most impressive achievements.

In 1927, Krohg executed two other murals in Oslo: three panels in fresco for the Ullevål Hospital; and *Nature,* for the Hersleb Public School, which shows a close-up of all sorts of insects engaged in their dramatic life cycle, while in the background people, automobiles, and towns are scaled down to insect size. Other commissions followed, and between 1928 and 1932 Krohg executed murals at the Grand Hotel in Oslo; the Restaurant Prunier and Le Bar des Vikings in Paris; a forty-foot fresco, *Electricity,* for the municipal Light Works building and the ceiling of the new House of Artists in Oslo.

Since Krohg settled in Norway, he has received a number of important public commissions including the fresco *Ragnarok* for the library (1933) and the new science building (1935) of the University of Oslo; a panel, *Midsummer Night* (1938) for the Norwegian-American liner *Oslofjord.* This ship was sunk during World War II, and for the new liner of the same name, which was launched in 1949, he did a mural called *Tempest of the Sea.* During the 1940's, Krohg's major task was the vast fresco paintings for the ceiling and walls of the East Gallery of the new Oslo Town Hall. More recently, he has undertaken three large oil murals for the Folks Theatre in Oslo.

The most notable example of Krohg's monumental style outside of Norway is the twenty-seven by eighteen foot canvas panel he painted in oils (1952) for the Security Council Chamber of the United Nations Headquarters in New York, which was commissioned by the Norwegian government as part of its gift of furnishings for the U.N. In the center is a huge phoenix rising from the ruins of war, painted in sinister shades of bright green, rust and steel-blue. The remainder of the canvas, which depicts symbolical figures entering the new ordered community of nations, is in the form of a polyptych, divided into rectangular and medallion-shaped areas, and painted in light, bright colors, with ascending lines. "Mankind is thronging into the new world to join the phoenix," explains the artist. "All meet openhanded and with outstretched arms. There are no clenched fists. Equality is symbolized by a group weighing out grain so that all share alike."

Per Krohg has designed the scenery for several theatrical productions, including *Le Diable dans le beffroi,* a ballet presented at the Paris Opéra; *Volpone* (1930) and *Green Pastures* (1933), for the National Theatre in Oslo; and Ludvig Holberg's *Jeppe på Berget* (1934). He has also executed a few sculptures, of which *The Drinkers,* a bas-relief, is perhaps the best-known. Krohg himself is the author of *Foredrag om malerkunst i Brakke 12* (*Lectures on the Art of Painting in Barrack 12*), published by J. W. Cappelen in 1945, and he has illustrated several books.

As a teacher, Krohg served in 1926 as a professor at the Académie d'Art Scandinave, founded in Paris. In Oslo, he taught free-hand drawing at the State Arts and Crafts School in 1934, and since 1946 has been a professor at the State Academy of Art. He was chairman of the board of the Association of Painters from 1937 to 1940. In 1948 he received the Prince Eugen Medal.

One-man shows of Krohg's paintings have been held in Oslo, Bergen, Paris, Copenhagen, Stockholm, Berlin, and Brussels. His works are represented in the art museums in Oslo, Bergen, Stockholm, Göteborg, Copenhagen, Paris, San Francisco, and Washington, D.C.

The Norwegian artist was married to his second wife, Ragnhild Helene Andersen, in 1932. When Krohg visited the United States in 1951, an interviewer described him as a "tall, spare white-haired" man, "with the keen blue-eyed look of his Viking forebears." His studio is in Oslo, but after World War II he built a small wooden house by the edge of the sea he loves so well.

References

Art Digest 28:21 Ap 15 '54
Art N 53:41 My '54
Washington (D.C.) Post Mag p23 Je 27 '54
Dictionnaire Biographique des Artistes Contemporains, 1910-1930
Hvem er Hvem ? (1950)
Langaard, J. H. Per Krohg (1947)

KUCHEL, THOMAS H(ENRY) (kē'kul) Aug. 15, 1910- United States Senator from California

Address: b. Senate Office Bldg., Washington 25, D.C.; h. 315 S. Caludina St., Anaheim Calif.

Describing himself as "a middle-of-the-road Eisenhower Republican," Senator Thomas H. Kuchel, former state controller of California, now occupies the senatorial seat left vacant by Vice-President Richard M. Nixon. When Kuchel was appointed by Governor Earl Warren, now Chief Justice, the *Christian Science Moni-*

Keeley

THOMAS H. KUCHEL

tor commented: "It seems doubtful that (Warren) could have picked any man more widely acknowledged as politically wise and practically serviceable as Mr. Kuchel." It was an interim appointment until the 1954 elections.

On June 8, 1954 Republican voters, under California's cross-filing procedure, gave Thomas H. Kuchel 785,254 votes at the primary election for the Senatorial seat; his opponent, U.S. Representative Samuel W. Yorty (Democrat) polled 77,335 Republican votes. Kuchel lost the Democratic nomination to Yorty by 332,190 to 550,193 votes. On November 2, 1954 Kuchel was elected to the Senate for the term ending in January 1957.

Thomas Henry Kuchel was born in Anaheim, California, on August 15, 1910, the son of Henry and Lutetia (Bailey) Kuchel. His grandparents had helped found the city in 1859. For forty-eight years Henry Kuchel owned and edited the Anaheim *Gazette,* which remains in the Kuchel family today. While attending school, Tommy worked as a printer's devil.

Young Kuchel received his B.A. degree *cum laude* from the University of Southern California in 1932. He was on the track team, joined Phi Kappa Psi fraternity, and was elected to the general honor society, Phi Kappa Phi. After receiving his law degree in 1935, he was admitted to the California bar. He practiced law in his home town for eleven years, and won election to the state Assembly from Orange county in 1936 and in 1938. Kuchel ran successfully for the state Senate in 1940. Chosen chairman of the Republican state central committee, he was one of the youngest men ever to hold this post.

After the attack on Pearl Harbor, Kuchel requested active naval duty, and served as a lieutenant until released to inactive reserve status in 1945. During this period, he was re-elected to the state Senate. On February 11, 1946 Governor Earl Warren appointed Kuchel state controller, a choice confirmed at the polls that November by the largest vote ever received by a candidate for that office.

As state controller, Kuchel was responsible for the income and outgo of California's billion-dollar budget. That official draws warrants on the treasury for supplies and services and is responsible for seeing that expenditures are consistent with all provisions of the laws; he is also an ex-officio member of the board of control and board of equalization. In 1950, Kuchel won both Republican and Democratic nominations (a common practice in California) and received approximately 3,000,000 votes for re-election as controller.

The *Christian Science Monitor* reported in 1952 that Kuchel had "made himself particularly well known . . . for auditing reforms and modernization of procedures in the State Controller's office, and . . . as outspoken critic of government fiscal trends contrary to local responsibility for expenditures."

After Senator Richard Nixon was elected Vice-President, the Governor designated Kuchel on December 22, 1953 to fill the Senate vacancy. In accepting this appointment, Kuchel took a salary cut from $16,000 a year to $12,500.

Senator William F. Knowland, the senior Californian in the upper chamber, was also a Warren appointee, leading the New York *Herald Tribune* to remark: "If Senators were to be regularly appointed, Governor Warren of California would seem to us the best possible man to appoint them. . . . Thomas H. Kuchel, forty-two years old, shows every evidence of being one of those younger men who give to the Republican party the promise of a bright future . . . Governor Warren's faith in Mr. Kuchel is a good reason to believe that both the party and the country will benefit."

One of Senator Kuchel's first actions after signing the Senate register on January 2, 1953 was to put his name as co-sponsor on two major bills. He was one of sixty-four senators who co-sponsored the Bricker amendment which provides that no treaty which conflicts with the Constitution shall become effective, that treaties should come into force as domestic law only by regular legislation, and that all executive and other agreements with foreign powers or international organizations should be regulated by Congress. Kuchel's name was also on the list of sponsors of the tidelands oil bill vesting in the separate states the title to the "submerged lands" within their "historic boundaries."

When the Republicans organized the Senate, Kuchel's committee assignments were to interior and insular affairs, which deals with public lands, natural resources, and Indian affairs, and to public works.

Amid reports of a Nixon-Knowland rivalry over patronage, Kuchel stated that both Senators from California would make recommendations to the President for Federal jobs in their own state and that Nixon's recommendations would receive the same "serious consideration" given those of the Governor, other state Republican leaders, and "any interested citizens."

Senators Kuchel and Knowland jointly introduced a number of bills authorizing public works in California, recommending certain uses of public land and other local matters. Kuchel voted for cutting the foreign aid ceiling by $1,000,000,000, and favored a foreign aid bill amendment which would allow surplus farm crops to be sent abroad. He voted against adding $30,000,000 to airport funds and against $400,000,000 to Air Force funds for jet bombers. He favored the across-the-board 5 per cent cut in all major budget items and selling government-owned rubber plants. On the question of standby economic controls, he supported the Byrd amendment limiting presidential imposition of controls to a declaration of war or a Congressional resolution. Kuchel favored the ratification of a treaty by which United States forces stationed in North Atlantic Treaty nations could be tried in foreign courts. He voted for the confirmation of the nomination of Charles E. Bohlen as Ambassador to Russia and of Charles E. Wilson as Secretary of Defense.

Kuchel opposed allowing a simple majority of either house to disapprove a presidential reorganization plan and he voted against disapproving Eisenhower's reorganization of the Department of Agriculture. He did not favor the establishment of Federal ownership of the submerged offshore lands beyond the three-mile limit and was against appropriating Federal revenues from offshore mineral resources to state education.

In the second session of the Eighty-third Congress, Kuchel voted for U.S. participation in building the St. Lawrence Seaway, and the Atomic Energy bill. He favored granting statehood to Hawaii and Alaska, and outlawing the Communist party.

Addressing the annual meeting of the Conference of California Cities on October 19, 1953, Kuchel said that the strength of the U.S. in the fight against Communism "rests in our local governments." He urged citizens to guard against allowing the powers now vested in the "cities, towns and states" to become concentrated in the Federal government.

Senator Kuchel is described as "a slight, friendly man." According to the Los Angeles *Daily News*, "the newspaper boys can't get over calling him Tommy." Married to Betty Mellenthin in June 1942, Kuchel has a daughter, Karen Christine. His church is the Episcopal, and he belongs to the Elks, American Legion, Sutter Club in Sacramento, and Native Sons of the Golden West.

References

Christian Sci Mon p1 D 24 '52
N Y Herald Tribune p1+ D 23 '52 por; II p1 D 28 '52 por
N Y Times p1+ D 23 '52 por
Time 61:10+ Ja 5 '53
Washington (D.C.) Post p1+ D 23 '52 por
Congressional Directory (1953)
Who's Who in the West (1951)

KUEKES, EDWARD D(ANIEL) (kē'-kĕs) Feb. 2, 1901- Cartoonist

Address: b. c/o Cleveland Plain Dealer, Cleveland, Ohio; h. 6180 Columbia Rd., Olmsted Falls, Ohio

For about thirty years Edward D. Kuekes has been creating notable cartoons for the Cleveland (Ohio) *Plain Dealer* and since 1949 he has been chief editorial cartoonist. The newspaper, established in 1845, has published more than 200 pictorial sketches by Kuekes on its front page, in addition to a large number of his cartoons on the editorial, motion picture and comic pages. On four occasions the artist has received Freedoms Foundation awards, and in 1953 he won the Pulitzer Prize for the best newspaper cartoon of the year.

Edward Daniel Kuekes, the son of Otto and Elizabeth (Lapp) Kuekes, was born on February 2, 1901 in Pittsburgh, Pennsylvania, where his father operated an employment agency. Kuekes recalls no evidence of artistic talent in his family, but states that his parents ". . . suspected that I might have some talent. . . I was about eight years of age, and I started snipping at a piece of paper with a scissors. Two birds and a horse fell out" (Cleveland *Plain Dealer*, May 5, 1953).

Wishing to encourage the boy, his parents sent him to a private art teacher with whom he studied draftsmanship and design, sketching and water color. At the age of nine, his water color of a bird was exhibited in a city exposition. His other boyhood interest was in becoming an amateur magician.

When Edward was twelve years of age, his father moved with the family to Berea, Ohio, where he opened a general store named for his own initials, the "O. K. Store." Edward attended public schools, and at intervals did art work for their newspapers. He also helped in his father's store, and says: "[I] drew a lot of cartoons when I was supposed to be cleaning . . . and making deliveries" (Cleveland *Plain Dealer*, May 5, 1953).

Graduated from Berea High School in 1918, Edward entered Baldwin-Wallace College in the same town. "I never entertained any notion of doing anything except editorial cartooning," he has stated, "and my studies were in that direction." After completing his work at the college, he took art courses at the Cleveland School of Art (now called the Cleveland Institute of Art) and at the Chicago Academy of Fine Arts. To help meet his expenses, he played the drums in a dance orchestra.

Kuekes began his career as a newspaper artist and cartoonist in 1922 and handled general art for the Cleveland *Plain Dealer*. Since newspaper photographers at that time did not have the use of fine grain film and flash bulbs, the artists on a newspaper could frequently produce better illustrations and Kuekes was often assigned to illustrate news events. Beginning in 1926, he substituted whenever the newspaper's senior cartoonist was ill or on vacation.

Entering the comics field, Kuekes produced with Olive Ray Scott a feature strip "Alice

EDWARD D. KUEKES

in Wonderland" which was distributed as a weekly colored supplement by the United Feature Syndicate. It appeared in twenty newspapers in the United States and in a number of publications in Europe. The two collaborators developed another syndicated feature, "Knurl the Gnome," a mischievous elf. For the *Plain Dealer,* Kuekes composed "Funny Fables" from 1935 to 1937. This group was published as a book, *Funny Fables; Modern Interpretation of Famous Fabulists* (Foster and Stewart, 1938), which included Kuekes' pictorial interpretation of such stories as the goose that laid the golden egg.

Kuekes acquired the idea for one of his best-known animal characters, "the Kernel," from a magicians' convention he covered for the *Plain Dealer* in Kenton, Ohio in 1942. This rabbit caricature became his trademark until 1949, and appeared in the newspaper as a one-column strip. "I put 'the Kernel' into one of my cartoons just to add a little life and humor," he stated, "and the thing attracted more attention than the cartoons. So, for a long time, I had him make some remark about the cartoon in which he appeared" (Cleveland *Plain Dealer,* May 5, 1953).

A movie page feature "Closeups," in which Kuekes collaborated with W. Ward Marsh, and a weekly editorial cartoon called "All in a Week" brought the artist acclaim in the late 1940's. Another popular feature which was published on the Sunday editorial page of the *Plain Dealer* was "Cartoonist Looks at the News." Kuekes seldom asks his friends for comments on his work, believing that this would lead to "false praise or unfounded criticism."

Kuekes was appointed the chief editorial cartoonist of the Cleveland *Plain Dealer* on June 13, 1949 to succeed the late Hal Donahey. In that year he won the first of four awards he has received from the Freedoms Foundation for his original cartoons advancing the American way of life. His winning sketch in 1949 was called "The Qualifying Steps," and portrayed honesty-integrity, vast experience, and freedom from political bias as the three stairs leading to a United States Federal court office.

At Valley Forge, Pennsylvania, General Dwight D. Eisenhower presented Kuekes with the award, the foundation's first prize of $2,000, and a medal. The following year, the artist earned the organization's second-place award and a cash prize of $300 which were given to him by General Omar N. Bradley.

The cartoonist produced such forceful pictorial editorials in the *Plain Dealer* in 1951 as "It's the Cornerstone of Our Great Nation" (February 6, 1951), which warned that "those who serve the public must not betray the public"; and the "New Deal Candle" (October 9, 1951), showing the country's economy being consumed at one end by the "quest for new sources of taxes," and at the other by the "increase in non-essential spending".

His work won the 1951 Freedoms Foundation Distinguished Service Award which was presented to him at Valley Forge, Pennsylvania by the late Robert Millikan. The artist again was honored by the foundation in 1952 with a Distinguished Service Scroll "for outstanding achievement in bringing about a better understanding of the American way of life as recognized by Freedoms Foundation Awards for the years 1949-1950-1951."

The most coveted award in his profession was won by Edward D. Kuekes in 1953 when he received the Pulitzer Prize and $1,000 for his drawing "Aftermath," judged the best newspaper cartoon of the year. In this sketch he pictured two soldiers in Korea carrying a third on a stretcher. One asks: "Wonder if he voted?" and the other replies "No—he wasn't old enough." Kuekes claims the drawing was inspired by thinking of his older son who had been unable to vote while he was overseas in World War II. At the time he drew "Aftermath," the artist states he thought it was "just another cartoon." A *Plain Dealer* editorial (May 6, 1953) describes it as "a simple cartoon, with few lines but terrific impact."

The cartoonist was the recipient of the American Newspaper Guild Award in 1947 and the Certificate of Honor from the National Safety Council in 1949. Other honors he has received include an award of $100 in 1937 for a safety cartoon which won a national contest sponsored by the Citizens' Investment Trust Foundation, the Disabled American Veterans' award, the Silver "T" Square of the National Cartoonists Society in 1953, and the Baldwin-Wallace College alumni merit award in 1953.

The cartoonist is the president of the Berea (Ohio) Kiwanis Club and of the Baldwin-Wallace College Alumni Association. Organizations in which he holds membership include the Admiral American Airlines Flagship Fleet, National Cartoonists Society and Lambda Chi Alpha fraternity. His church affiliation is Methods. Kuekes has stated that a good drawing should be like a good golfer—"the fewer the strokes the better" (Cleveland *Plain Dealer,* June 14, 1949).

The Pulitzer Prize winner married Clara Pearl Gray on April 23, 1922, and their two sons are Edward Grayson and George Clive.

Kuekes has hazel eyes and light brown hair. He stands five feet nine inches tall and weighs 148 pounds. His hobbies include raising orchids, taming wild ducks, doing pastels and etchings, and playing a set of twenty-five to thirty musical bells.

References

Cleveland Plain Dealer Je 14 '49 por; p15 Mr 16 '52 pors; p1+ My 5 '53 por
N Y Times p24 My 5 '53 por

KURUSU, SABRO 1888(?)-Apr. 7, 1954 Japanese diplomat who was negotiating with Cordell Hull, Secretary of State, when Japan attacked Pearl Harbor; entered foreign service, 1910; served as Japanese consul in Chicago (1913-1919) and in Manila (1921); first secretary, Japanese Legation, Chile (1922-1925), and at Japanese embassy in Italy (1925); was made consul general in Hamburg, Germany (1927) and Minister to Peru (1928); appointed director commerce bureau of Foreign Office (1932-1937); Ambassador to Belgium (1937); Ambassador to Germany (1939-40); signed pact which brought Japan into the Axis, Sept. 28, 1940; and signed protocols for adherence to the pact by Hungary, Romania, Slovakia; sent from Tokyo November, 1941 to assist Japanese Ambassador Nomura in negotiations with United States for peaceful settlement of differences (U.S. refused to consider "joint overlordship" in Pacific area and Japanese "special interests" in China); was instructed by Tokyo to submit a note to Secretary Hull at 1 P.M., December 7, 1941 after destroying all secret documents and code machines in Japanese embassy; submitted note at 2:20 P.M. after the White House had received word at 1:50 P.M. that Pearl Harbor had been attacked; was interned and later exchanged for American diplomats interned in Japan; insisted that he knew nothing of Premier Hideki Tojo's secret plan to bomb U.S. naval base at Hawaii, but was excoriated by Secretary Hull in his memoirs; retired from public life (1945). See *Current Biography,* (Jan.) 1942.

Obituary

N Y Times p27 Ap 8 '54

LACY, DAN (MABRY) Feb. 28, 1914- Publishing association executive

Address: b. c/o American Book Publishers Council, Inc., 2 W. 46th St., New York 36; h. 52 W. Clinton Ave., Irvington, N.Y.

In naming Dan Lacy as the managing director of the major trade association in the United States book field, the American Book Publishers Council chose a man outside the publishing industry whose interest in books has marked every phase of his career. At the time of his appointment in March 1953, Lacy had just resumed his duties as deputy chief assistant librarian of the Library of Congress after a year-and-a-half service as chief of the Division of Overseas Information Centers, for which he had been "borrowed" by the Department of State.

He had earlier held important positions with the Historical Record Survey of the Work Projects Administration, the wartime Committee on Conservational Cultural Resources and the National Archives. He is the author of numerous articles and reviews in historical and library periodicals.

Dan Mabry Lacy, a descendant on both sides of his family from pre-Revolutionary Virginia residents, was born in Newport News, Virginia on February 28, 1914. His father, Tolbert Hardy Lacy, was employed as special attorney for the Atlantic Coast Line Railroad and his mother, Ann Electa (Boatwright) Lacy, was a teacher. His brother is Dudley Balthrope Lacy.

In Rocky Mount, North Carolina, where he spent his boyhood and youth, Dan Lacy attended the local public high school, graduating in 1929 at the age of fifteen. He then entered the University of North Carolina and under a university scholarship studied history as the major subject in his curriculum for the B.A. degree, which was granted *cum laude* in 1933. During his undergraduate years he was a member of the staff of the campus newspaper and, continuing his high school interest in debating, became president of the university's debating council. He was a Phi Beta Kappa student, and belonged to Tau Kappa Alpha, Epsilon Phi Delta and Sigma Delta societies.

For a few years after his graduation Lacy remained at the University of North Carolina as a teaching fellow in history (1934-35) and as an instructor in history (1935-36). Meanwhile, having taken graduate courses in United States history, he presented the thesis *The Beginnings of Industrialization in North Carolina, 1865-1900* and received his M.A. degree with distinction in 1935. He later completed residence requirements at the university for a doctorate in American history, but did not take a degree.

Lacy left his teaching post in 1936 to become assistant State supervisor for North Carolina of the Historical Record Survey. This was an undertaking of the Work Projects Administration directed by Luther H. Evans, which prepared guides to unpublished historical sources in the United States and made inventories of early American imprints. After his promotion to State supervisor for North Carolina, Lacy also held the position of regional supervisor for the Southeastern States (June 1939-April 1940), with offices in Raleigh, North Carolina. He then moved to Washington, D.C., to serve until December 1941 as assistant national director of the project. For the North Carolina Historical Commission, he edited with C. C. Crittenden the three-volume *Historical Records of North Carolina.*

When the United States entered World War II, Lacy was appointed executive secretary of the Committee on Conservational Cultural Resources, an inter-departmental Federal committee of the National Resources Planning Board, which initiated plans for the protection of cul-

The Library of Congress
DAN LACY

tural resources of the United States (such as libraries, museums, art galleries, archives and historical buildings) in the event of air attack and other hazards of war.

Beginning in July 1942, while working part time with the Committee on Conservational Cultural Resources, Lacy took on the additional duties of assistant to the executive officer of the National Archives. Through subsequent promotions he became assistant to the archivist (spring of 1943), director of operations of the National Archives (December 1943) and assistant archivist of the United States (January 1947). His special responsibilities in the two last-named posts were to develop and execute a program for the planned retirement of the records of the wartime agencies of World War II.

Lacy's employment with the Library of Congress began in July 1947 when he was made assistant director of the processing department in charge of acquisitions. For part of 1948 he was also acting chief of the division of manuscripts. Later advancing from assistant director in charge of cataloguing (1949-50) to deputy chief assistant librarian, he was given supervision of planning and formulating policy for the library and its international activities. In the article "International Cultural Cooperation" (*Scientific Monthly,* May 1948), he discussed the cooperative effort of American and foreign libraries—in particular the work of the American Book Center and its successor, the United States Book Exchange—to bring about an interchange of information and a "widespread pooling of knowledge," especially on scientific matters.

He also wrote "The Library of Congress: A Sesquicentenary Review," which appeared in the July and October 1950 issues of *Library Quarterly.* In this series of two articles he undertook "to describe some of the forces that have formed the Library and continue to shape its growth; to discuss the character and the significance of certain aspects of its relationship to librarianship and scholarship; and to assess . . . [its] future development." He was the author as well of a number of contributions to the *Library of Congress Information Bulletin,* two of them on the cooperative acquisitions project.

"On loan" from the Library of Congress to the Department of State, Lacy was appointed on September 18, 1951 chief of the Division of Overseas Information Centers and later made assistant administrator for the Information Center Service of the International Information Administration. As director of the State Department's overseas library and book activities, he was responsible for the work of 145 United States information centers in sixty-nine foreign countries.

While in this office he wrote, in collaboration with Paul Hill, "An Enduring Monument" (*Wilson Library Bulletin,* December 1952), which discussed the establishment of the American Memorial Library in Berlin. "In its role as a channel for the flow of ideas and information among nations," the library was pictured as continuing "through the years to contribute to those very ends of international understanding for which its existence stands."

Discussing the controversy over the State Department's overseas libraries in the *Library Quarterly,* April 1954, Lacy recommended that the book program be very much larger; that "administratively, the use of books be intimately associated with the educational exchange service and with the Technical Assistance Program. Its isolation from these two programs is a major obstacle to the possible success of all three"; that institutes like that at Salzburg, be sponsored in foreign universities "as a means of assuring the continuing association of intellectual leaders from many free countries in the consideration of the major common problems of free society."

About a month after Lacy had returned to the Library of Congress as deputy chief assistant librarian, he was chosen, on March 23, 1953, to succeed Theodore Waller as managing director of the American Book Publishers Council in New York City. Members of this cooperative association of United States publishers, which was established in 1946 to deal with problems confronting the industry in the postwar world, represent about 85 per cent of the dollar volume of trade book sales, including all categories other than textbooks. In its operations in the significant areas of distribution and promotion, the rights of publisher and author, and service functions to aid the business of publishing, the Council has facilitated resumption of many "of the valuable programs which the National Association of Book Publishers, formed after the first World War, had been forced to drop" during the depression (*Publishers' Weekly,* January 6, 1951).

One of the important interests of the American Book Publishers Council is "to provide adequate safeguards for the freedom to publish and the rights stemming from that basic freedom" (*Publishers' Weekly,* January 6, 1951). At a conference concerned with books and intellectual freedom, held in Rye, New York in May 1953, Lacy was a member of a committee which drafted a document entitled "Freedom to Read." This manifesto, praised in a New York *Times* editorial (June 27, 1953) for "the nobility and courage of its expression," was issued as a joint declaration of principles by the Council and the American Library Association at the latter's annual meeting in Los Angeles in June. "It is in the public interest," the document read in part, "for publishers and librarians to make available the widest diversity of views and expressions, including those which are unorthodox or unpopular with the majority. . . . Ideas can be dangerous, but the suppression of ideas is fatal to a democratic society" (quoted in the New York *Times,* June 26 and 27, 1953).

The Book Publishers Council's committee on reading development held a two-day conference in June 1954 to discuss ways of encouraging reading habits among teen-agers that would last a lifetime. The twenty-two educators, publishers and librarians discussed with Lacy a program to expand community and high school libraries "so that books of all sorts are available to high school students. These experts also emphasized the important role played by teachers in exciting youngsters' appetites for reading" (New York *Herald Tribune,* June 27, 1954).

Lacy's contributions to the work of the U.S. Overseas Information Centers won for him the Superior Service Medal of the Department of State, conferred in 1952. He belongs to the American Library Association and the Academy of Political Science. His church is the Unitarian and his political party the Democratic.

By his marriage on December 14, 1946 to Hope Lenore Leiken, formerly an archivist, Dan Lacy is the father of Philip Tolbert, Dudley Boatwright and Elizabeth Hardy.

The council's director is over six feet tall and weighs 200 pounds; he has blue eyes and brown hair. Besides reading, he enjoys hiking, baseball and the theatre.

References

Library Q 20:203 Jl '50; 24:178 Ap '54
Pub W 160:1400 S 29 '51
Directory of American Scholars (1951)
Phi Beta Kappa Directory, 1776-1941
Who's Who in America, 1954-55

LA GORCE, JOHN OLIVER (lȧ-gôrs)

Sept. 22, 1879- Editor; association official

Address: b. c/o National Geographic Society, 16th St., N.W., Washington 6, D.C.; h. 2120 Kalorama Rd., N.W., Washington, D.C.

The National Geographic Society's newly elected president and its magazine editor, John Oliver La Gorce, is a man whose contributions to geographic knowledge during the past forty-nine years have been in a large measure responsible for the society's development as a world-renowned educational and scientific organization. Succeeding on May 5, 1954 to the offices long held by Gilbert Grosvenor, La Gorce heads a society of more than 2,000,000 members and edits a magazine reaching over 8,000,000 readers. Its success is attributed to the fact that it combines scholarship with popular appeal, and continues to "satisfy the human thirst for accurate information about people, places and things" (*Time,* May 17, 1954).

Many honors have been conferred on La Gorce, including the title of Postmaster of Little America, Antarctica. He began work for the National Geographic Society in 1905, after some years of experience as a skilled telegrapher and feature writer for newspapers and magazines. Since then he has written frequently for the *National Geographic Magazine,* has shared in such advancements as its innovations in the use of natural color photography, and has had a direct part in sponsoring the society's numerous geographical expeditions.

"The National Geographic Society is the product of many men and women," Grosvenor said when he retired from the presidency and became chairman of the board, but "without the powerful assistance of John Oliver La Gorce's personality, its gratifying progress would have been impossible" (Washington *Post,* May 9, 1954).

John Oliver La Gorce, who was born on September 22, 1879, is a native of Scranton, Pennsylvania and the son of Colonel Gabriel Hauteville and Elizabeth Cecilia (Oliver) de la Gorce. On his mother's side of the family two of his forebears had been Union Army telegraphers during the War Between the States, and others had been associated with the pioneering work of Western Union. From his mother, who as a girl had worked in a railroad telegraphic office, John learned the Morse code and became an expert telegrapher by the age of fourteen.

Most of his childhood was spent in Washington, D.C. He returned to Scranton to take his first important job as a press telegrapher and in time was sent to various parts of Pennsylvania wherever significant news stories required skilled code operators. Transferred subsequently to Washington, D.C., La Gorce held the position of Western Union manager on Capitol Hill for two Congressional sessions. Beginning in 1903 he wrote feature articles on geography, history and the natural sciences for newspapers and magazines, and soon became the author of a syndicated column on geography that appeared in seventeen United States papers.

The work of the young newspaperman attracted the attention of Gilbert Grosvenor, editor of the *National Geographic Magazine.* Hired by Grosvenor at a salary of $60 a month, La Gorce became assistant secretary of the society in 1905. A clerk was the other member of a staff of three, which in 1954 numbers some 900 persons.

In explaining why he was willing to accept a position at less than half his accustomed salary, La Gorce has said, "From childhood I have been interested in how people work and

National Geographic Society
JOHN OLIVER LA GORCE

play—and where they are. This interest coincided with what Dr. Grosvenor calmly outlined as to the possibilities and work of the society. I was unmarried then and didn't need much to live on" (Washington *Post,* May 9, 1954.).

When La Gorce joined the staff of the National Geographic Society, it was an enterprise still in an experimental stage, comprising about 10,000 members. Currently it has a membership of 2,150,000, the largest in its history. Since its establishment in 1888 when Gardiner Greene Hubbard, one of the founders, became its first president, the society has had as its purpose "the increase and diffusion of geographic knowledge."

Its magazine was first published in 1899 with an issue of 900 copies. In 1910 it offered an issue containing twenty-four pages of natural color photographs. "No magazine had ever printed so much color in one issue," Grosvenor has stated (Washington *Post,* May 6, 1954). "From that day to this the *National Geographic Magazine* has led all periodicals in the quality and number of its color illustrations," and has over 8,000,000 readers.

During his forty-nine years with the society La Gorce served from 1905 to 1907 as assistant secretary of the association, from 1907 to 1911 as assistant editor of the magazine, and as vice-president and associate editor until 1954. He has also been a life trustee of the society. On May 5, 1954 he was elected to succeed Grosvenor, who had been editor of the magazine since 1899 and president of the society since 1920.

The National Geographic Society has sent out more than 100 scientific expeditions in all parts of the world including many to the south-western part of the United States. At present it is sponsoring twelve explorations, including the raising of a Roman galley sunk in 200 B.C. In cooperation with the California Institute of Technology, it is preparing at Palomar a photographic map—the first sky atlas—of the heavens. La Gorce announced in May 1954 that the society and the Royal Ontario Museum of Geology and Minerology are sponsoring an expedition to see whether a water-filled crater in Labrador was caused by a meteorite. The society and the Royal Museum had organized an expedition in 1951 to explore Chubb Crater, in Quebec's Ungava Peninsula, the earth's largest known crater.

One of the notable achievements of the society was the discovery on January 16, 1939, of the oldest work of man in the Americas—a slab of stone in Mayan characters with a date of 291 B.C. The expedition was sponsored jointly by the society and the Smithsonian Institution, and the stone antedates by 200 years anything heretofore dated, and reveals a great center of early American culture, previously unknown. The society granted $25,000, and $75,000 was contributed by some of its members, to help preserve for the American people the finest of the giant sequoia trees in Sequoia National Park, California.

A recognized authority on fresh-water and salt-water fishes, La Gorce is editor of the society's *Book of Fishes,* revised in 1939 and 1952. Hundreds of color portraits and photographs illustrate information on food and game fishes of the coastal and inland waters of the United States. He has written numerous articles for the magazine during his years of work for the society, which has taken him on trips to many parts of the world, often living in tents and caves with native tribes to collect material.

La Gorce's contributions in the field of geography have brought him many honors. Mount La Gorce, a lake and a glacier in Alaska are named for him, as are a golf course in Miami Beach, Florida and a mountain range and peak in the Antarctic. The First Byrd Antarctic Expedition set up the La Gorce Meteorological Station and in 1933 the editor was appointed to the office of Postmaster of Little America, Antarctica.

As a delegate of the U.S. government, La Gorce attended the Third Pan American Scientific Congress in Lima, Peru in 1925. That year he was named an honorary member of the Geographic Society of Peru. He is also an honorary member of the Argentine Geographic Society, a fellow of Great Britain's Royal Geographical Society and a chevalier of the French Legion of Honor.

He was awarded the Henry Grier Bryant Medal of the Geographic Society of Philadelphia in 1948. His honorary degrees include the M.A. from Georgetown University; Litt.D. from George Washington University; and D.Sc. from the South Dakota School of Mines, the University of Tampa and the University of Miami.

The explorer-editor is chairman of the board of the Champion International Company, a trustee of the Corcoran Gallery of Art in Washington and of the University of Miami, and director of the Riggs National Bank in Washington. In Florida, where he spends winter vacations, he is chairman of the Miami Beach Committee of One Hundred and a member of that city's Surf Club.

Among his other clubs are Washington's Alfalfa Club (president 1953-1954), the Cosmos, National Press, University, Army and Navy, and Overseas Writers. He belongs also to the Chevy Chase Club of Maryland, the Blue Ridge Rod and Gun Club in Harpers Ferry, West Virginia and the Armor and Arms Club of New York.

His wife, the former Ethel Davis Witaker of Washington, shares his adventures in international travel. Their children are Gilbert Grosvenor La Gorce of Washington, D.C., and Mrs. Eleanor W. Newell of Alexandria, Virginia.

La Gorce is a man of stocky build and gregarious personality. His hobbies include his interest in sunken and buried treasures in the Americas and his collection of arms and armor. A variety of weapons, ranging from a primitive stone club to a World War II Commando dagger, line the paneled walls of his office, along with mementos of his travels. "In port cities," *Time* (May 17, 1954) reveals, "La Gorce makes straight for the pawnshops, often finds valuable trinkets that sailors have pawned."

References

N Y Times p35 My 6 '54 por
Newsweek 43:57 My 10 '54
Time 63:95 My 17 '54 por
Washington (D.C.) Post p1+ My 6 '54; p12C My 9 '54; p30 My 17 '54
Who's Who in America, 1954-55
Who's Who in Commerce and Industry (1953)

LAMBERT, JANET (SNYDER) Dec. 17, 1894- Author

Address: b. c/o E. P. Dutton & Co., 300 Fourth Ave., New York 10; h. Brant Beach, N.J.

Reprinted from the *Wilson Library Bulletin,* Oct. 1954

In the immediate family background of Janet Lambert are representatives of the professions (army, judicial and medical) as well as farming and insurance. She is the author of twenty-two books for girls.

Janet Snyder was born in the city of Crawfordsville, Indiana on December 17, 1894 to Mabel Lee (Galey) Snyder and Francis L. Snyder. "As so many records will tell, Crawfordsville, the 'Athens' of Indiana," says Mrs. Lambert, "was known for its authors. General Lew Wallace often talked to me under the beech tree where he wrote *Ben Hur.*" There, too, she made the acquaintance of Booth Tarkington and George Ade.

There were poets, as well, in the child's ken and at the age of six she wrote her own poetry. But her first love was the stage. "I was taken to all good plays by my father," she recalls. "He trotted me backstage to meet famous actors and actresses such as Otis Skinner, Maude

JANET LAMBERT

Adams, even Eva Tanguay whom I constantly imitated, and many others."

After being graduated from the Crawfordsville High School in 1912, Janet went to Ferry Hall at Lake Forest, Illinois. Its location had attracted her because it was near Chicago where she could see more plays.

Mrs. Lambert's own description of the way she obtained her first part is pointed and amusing: "My dream was to play with Walker Whiteside and with the confidence of youth I waylaid him backstage (he was playing in *The Typhoon* in Indianapolis then) and told him I thought his ingenue was very poor. Apparently he thought so, too, for I got the part." Thus begun, the young Janet, well chaperoned, came East to do a part in still another play, and to spend hours in a New York hotel writing when not acting. A year in Northampton, Massachusetts with a stock company followed, and then, still dramatic, there was a marriage. The boy from home, Kent Craig Lambert, who had meantime qualified for the United States Army, appeared in New York in the winter of 1917, a captain in uniform soon to go overseas.

They were married January 1, 1918, the bride with the mental reservation that it would be only a temporary interruption to her stage career. It was longer. She never went back. The birth of Jeanne Anne, in the spring of 1919, changed everything. After the war her husband remained in the army and for twenty-odd years they lived on army posts. Mrs. Lambert says: "Because I had decided to write, I constantly tried, but army wife and author rarely go together. It took nineteen years, to the point where we were stationed in New York—on Governors Island—before I found myself as a writer." The foundation had been laid in the endless bedtime stories told to Jeanne and the necessity to provide most of her reading when they spent two years in Poland. The tales became serials, with daily installments. They became books, later.

The initial success of that new career was almost a fictional story itself. "I finished *Star Spangled Summer* on a Thursday and the E. P. Dutton Company bought it the next day." The new career had been launched with the ease and suddenness of her earlier career in the theatre. To date Mrs. Lambert has written twenty-two books published by Dutton. They have been well received and watched for anxiously by girls who follow the fortunes of their popular heroines. There are six titles now in the Penny Parrish series, which Mrs. Lambert's first book introduced. Six others have been written about Penny's sister Tippy. There are three stories about Candy Kane, three about the Jordon family, and two about the Draytons of Pennsylvania. *Star Dream* and *Summer for Seven* introduce Dria Meredith.

Mrs. Lambert's novels cover a wide variety of subjects interesting to teen-age girls. Of *Star Spangled Summer* (1941), a story of army post life, the New York *Times* said: "A thoroughly pleasant story for girls of the early teen age." *Dreams of Glory* (1942), set in West Point, had, as the *Christian Science Monitor* commented, "good characterization, story interest, a romance, plus a picture of life at the Academy." Of *Glory Be* (1943), which was announced as the final Parrish story but wasn't, as it proved, the Springfield *Republican* said, "Warm, brisk and timely, stands high in the list of juveniles for a difficult-to-please age of readers." The scene of *Just Jenifer* (1945) is Florida and the story concerns a teen ager who takes over the rearing of her eight younger sisters and brothers. Ellen Buell said of it: "Young girls, uncomfortably aware of their own shortcomings, may wish that Jenifer owned at least one fault, but she and her family are so gay, so genuinely youthful, that only the most determinedly unsentimental will cavil about that." *Don't Cry, Little Girl* (1952) is a story of tragedy, the loss of Tippy Parrish's first love to the war in Korea. The *Times'* reviewer found that the story lacked depth, but commented that "the plot moves smoothly along a course of junior college life and West Point parties, with adroitly woven counterpoint of relationships with friends and family in the background." *Rainbow after Rain* followed in 1953.

Mrs. Lambert is a Republican in politics and a Christian Scientist in church affiliation. She is blonde and hazel-eyed, is five feet five inches tall, and weighs 138 pounds. She and her husband (now a retired army colonel) live on Long Beach Island, Brant Beach, New Jersey. She lists her favorite sport with an exclamation mark—fishing! And she proudly states that she has three grandchildren, her daughter being married to an army colonel.

The authors she likes best are John P. Marquand, Robert Browning, Henry Wadsworth Longfellow, and William Shakespeare, but the Hoosier authors she knew in her childhood, and her parents, she admits, exerted the most influence on her in her choice of writing as a career.

LANE, SIR ALLEN (LANE WILLIAMS) Sept. 21, 1902- Publisher

Address: b. c/o Penguin Books, Ltd., Harmondsworth, Middlesex, England; h. Silverbeck, Stanwell Moor, Middlesex; 19 Whitehall Court, London, S.W. 1, England

The New Year honors list announced by the British government on January 1, 1952 contained the award of a knighthood to Allen Lane, founder and managing director of Penguin Books, Ltd., the first concern to publish paper-backed books successfully in Britain. Publishers are not often recipients of such an honor, but, in the words of *Newsweek*, "Allen Lane was knighted by King George VI for his service to letters." Of him R. J. Minney wrote in the *Recorder*: "In a few years he has changed the reading habits and taste of the public. I feel he has done for reading what the wireless has done for good music."

Since the Penguin books first appeared in 1935 the company has published numerous series including Pelicans, King Penguins, Penguin Shakespeares, Puffins, Porpoises, Penguin Classics, Penguin Poets, Penguin Bound Editions and others. Its total sales have now reached 150,000,000 books.

On July 30, 1954 Penguin Books, Ltd. published Penguin Number 1000. Publication date coincided with the nineteenth anniversary of the first Penguin, and the new book has been designed by Edward Young, who in 1935 designed the now-famous Penguin cover for Number 1. The 1000th Penguin title is *One of Our Submarines*.

The publisher was born in Bristol, September 21, 1902, as Allen Lane Williams, eldest son of Allen Gardiner Williams, an architect who was deputy city surveyor of Bristol at the time. His mother, Camilla Matilda, was a cousin of the famous British publisher, John Lane, who had launched many successful authors on their careers, and had published the literary quarterly, *Yellow Book*.

Allen began his education in Bristol at a private school, which he left at fourteen for a short period to work as a junior clerk in the rates department (municipal taxation) of the Bristol Corporation. However, John Lane had other ideas for the boy. Childless himself, he suggested that Allen continue his schooling for a few years and then be taken into the firm of John Lane, The Bodley Head, Ltd. He also thought it desirable that Allen Gardiner Williams should change his name to Lane. This was done, by the legal process of deed poll, in 1919.

Allen attended Bristol Grammar School between 1916 and 1919, when he joined the firm in Vigo Street, London. He began by delivering parcels, then clerking and bookkeeping, and later did commercial traveling. In time he joined the publicity department, and in 1927 became advertising manager.

The next move was to the editorial side, and here Allen Lane was responsible for the publication of James Joyce's *Ulysses* in England. Havelock Ellis was another author whose work he published, and he introduced the American cartoonist Peter Arno to the British public. This last was an early example of the insight ("I can only describe it by the overworked word, 'flair'," says Lane) which has been one of the main factors in the success of Penguin Books.

The board of The Bodley Head would not approve the Arno book, so Lane offered to underwrite the venture. This was agreed upon. Aided by the dramatist, Benjamin Travers, Lane selected the pictures. The book came out in 1933 as *Peter Arno's Circus,* and had a modest success.

Meanwhile, Lane, in association with his brothers Richard and John, had thought of making good literature available in inexpensive, paper-backed form to the public. The auguries for paper-covered books were not good. "The argument," wrote Edmond Segrave in *Penguins, A Retrospect,* "was as clear and constant as the North Star. The British public did not care for paper-bound books and never would care for them."

"The books would get tattered," he continued, "and torn and dusty, and would simply add to the bad stock with which every bookshop was already most unpleasantly full. Unorthodox book production had been tried out before and on every occasion the book-buying public had turned down its thumb or thumbed its nose with promptness and vigor. In short, it was perfectly clear . . . that Penguin Books, London, as a publishing project, was doomed before it began."

Nevertheless, Lane and his brothers went ahead. In the summer of 1935 Allen Lane traveled through the country with a specimen "dummy" of Eric Linklater's *Poet's Pub.* "The Lane brothers," wrote Segrave, "estimated that they would break even when the sales of each title reached 17,500 copies." When Lane returned, his total orders for ten projected titles were less than 7,000. He then went to Woolworth's, and Clifford Prescott, their buyer, gave Lane a large order.

The first ten Penguins were issued on July 30, 1935. (The name was the invention of Joan Coles, Lane's secretary at the time.) The first book was André Maurois' *Ariel, the Life of Shelley,* and the other authors represented were Ernest Hemingway, Eric Linklater, Susan Ertz, Dorothy L. Sayers, Agatha Christie, Beverley Nichols, Emily Hilda Young, Mary Webb, and Compton Mackenzie. According to *Everybody's Weekly,* the test Lane applied in selecting the titles was to ask himself: "Is this a book which, had I not read it, and were I to see it on sale for sixpence, would make me say: 'This book I have always wanted to read; I will get it now.' "

The format was small enough, four by seven inches, to slip easily into a pocket or handbag. The price was 6d. (12 cents). The cover was simple and striking: a bright color (red for novels, green for detective stories, blue for biography, etc.) with a white panel on front and back, bearing title and author in Gill Sans type, and a small black-and-white penguin also on front and "spine". "Edward Young's formula for the Penguin cover, good in 1935, is still good today," wrote *Design.*

Carlton, London

SIR ALLEN LANE

To these four factors—choice of title, format, price, and design—Lane added a fifth important one. In contrast to the flimsy covers of the average French book, the Penguin has a solid paper cover which enables it to stand up squarely on the shelf without tattering or dog-earing.

Within a few days of the first issue the Woolworth concern placed a heavy reorder. In October 1935 the second ten titles appeared. They included Samuel Butler's *Erewhon,* Norman Douglas's *South Wind,* and Victoria Mary Sackville-West's *The Edwardians*—all books for the discriminating. These twenty books were distributed by The Bodley Head, but at no time was its board responsible for the series.

On January 1, 1936, the three Lane brothers formed their own company, Penguin Books, Ltd., with a capital of £100 (approximately $500). The bold choice of good (though never dull) literature continued. After sixteen years, Lane was able to tell the *Weekly Telegraph* (October 6, 1951): "We are a little proud of the fact that every book on our list is by a topflight author."

The Penguin company's first warehouse was the crypt of Holy Trinity Church, Euston Road, London. Two empty tombs were fitted with metal doors, and served for the storage of ledgers and petty cash. Early in 1937 The Bodley Head went into voluntary liquidation (it has since been resuscitated under other management).

Penguin Books took offices in Great Portland Street, but Lane wanted a one-floor building. Finding nothing in the London district within his resources, he bought three acres of land at Harmondsworth, in Middlesex. There, just opposite London Airport, and on a major road-traffic artery, he built the one-story building which he still occupies. Early in 1954 Sir Allen approved plans by architect Ralph Tubbs,

LANE, SIR ALLEN—*Continued*

F.R.I.B.A., for a new and larger building to be constructed on the site.

Following the Penguins, Lane began in May 1937 a sister series, called Pelican Books, which have "a definite educational impulse behind them." Early authors were George Bernard Shaw, Julian Huxley, Eileen Edna Power, Sigmund Freud, and Virginia Woolf.

The next step was the launching of Penguin Specials. Unlike the two earlier series, these were not reprints of works which had appeared in other forms, but texts written especially for Penguin Books. The first three were Edgar Ansel Mowrer's *Germany Puts the Clock Back,* G. T. Garratt's *Mussolini's Roman Empire,* and Geneviève Tabouis's *Blackmail or War.* They have since covered such varied subjects as mass observation, bacteriology, food, theology, hydroponics, and fruit growing. According to Segrave, "the publication of new books, as opposed to reprints, now forms more than half of the entire Penguin Books output."

In some cases, the Penguin Specials have been republished with cloth covers by other firms, thus reversing the usual procedure. In 1951 Penguin Books began publishing the same book simultaneously in cloth-bound and paper-bound editions.

Other series include Penguin Shakespeares (started in 1937), King Penguins (an illustrated series, begun in 1939), Puffin Picture Books for children (1940-), Puffin Story Books (1941-), Puffin Cut-Out Books (1943-), Penguin Music Scores (1949-), Penguin Buildings of England (1951-), Penguin Modern Painters, Porpoise Books, and Penguin Poets. For King Penguins, Lane appointed R. B. Fishenden, a leading authority on color printing, as technical editor. In 1947 Jan Tschichold, an outstanding Swiss typographer, was brought in for three years' service in that capacity.

During the Second World War Lane's brothers, Richard and John, volunteered for the Royal Naval Volunteer Reserve, and John was killed in November 1942 at the Allied landings in North Africa.

Sir Allen habitually spends from four to six months of every year abroad. A typical trip was that made in 1945 to Argentina, Brazil, Chile, Peru, Colombia, Mexico, and Cuba, which spread trade all over South America. Commonwealth offices were established at Melbourne, Australia, Cape Town, South Africa, and at Montreal, Canada. Penguin's American office is in Baltimore, Maryland.

Another venture was that of issuing on one day 1,000,000 copies of ten books by one author. The series, called the Penguin "Millions", began with a set of George Bernard Shaw's plays in celebration of the writer's ninetieth birthday. Other authors in this series are H. G. Wells, Agatha Christie, Evelyn Waugh, and D. H. Lawrence.

Sir Allen is a believer in the capacity of the modern reader to absorb even "difficult" books. His publication of new translations of Sophocles, Xenophon, Molière, Chaucer, Chekhov, Dante, and Homer began in 1946 in the Penguin Classics series.

Still another series is the Pelican History of Art, under the direction of Nikolaus Pevsner. These are large illustrated books, written by distinguished European and American scholars. The series began with four volumes in 1953, and is planned for forty-eight volumes covering ten years. Guide books, reference books and periodicals are other activities of the publishing firm.

There is little time for relaxation, but occasionally Sir Allen manages to assist at some digging up of the past (for archaeology is his main preoccupation apart from his work). He has a small yacht, which gives him much pleasure when he has time to sail it. The publisher has served on the council of the Royal College of Art and is presently on the board of the London & Lancashire Insurance Company, Ltd. and is chairman of the cooperating body for mass communication of UNESCO. Bristol University awarded him an honorary M.A. degree in 1948.

On July 9, 1941 he married Lettice, daughter of Sir Charles Orr, former Governor and Commander-in-Chief of the Bahamas. They have three daughters. Lane's London club is the Travellers', and either there or at his London apartment he meets most of those with whom he has literary and business dealings.

Sir Allen is of medium height and build and of great good looks. *Newsweek* speaks of his "piercing blue eyes, and youthful unlined face." He is a nonsmoker. He is said to have a lively sense of humor.

References

Bookseller Ag 23 '45; S 6 '45; S 13 '45
Newsweek 42:80 Jl 6 '53 por
Who's Who, 1953

LANIEL, JOSEPH Oct. 12, 1889- Former Premier of France; industrialist

Address: Hotel Matignon, 57 Rue Varennes, Paris, France; Château de Villers, Glos, France

After serving for one year as Premier of the nineteenth Cabinet to be formed in France since the end of World War II, Joseph Laniel resigned on June 12, 1954. He was succeeded by Pierre Mendès-France.

Joseph Laniel has a long record of public service. As early as 1919 he was mayor of Notre-Dame-de-Courson and general councillor for Calvados, and from 1932 to 1940 he represented Lisieux in the Chamber of Deputies.

An expert on economic and financial affairs, he was Under-Secretary of State for Finance in the 1940 Cabinet of Premier Paul Reynaud. During the German Occupation, he was one of the founders of the National Council of Resistance.

The confirmation of Laniel as head of the Cabinet on June 26, 1953 was not regarded as an emphatic endorsement but simply as an interim compromise until the election of a new President by the Assembly in December 1953 and the subsequent customary resignation of the government. Premier Joseph Laniel, accompanied by Foreign Minister Georges Bidault, represented France at the conference in Bermuda with President Eisenhower and Prime Minister Churchill from December 4 to 8.

Laniel endorsed Eisenhower's proposals to the United Nations in December 1953 for the internationalization and use of atomic energy for peaceful purposes. Describing the plan as "an intelligent and generous initiative," he stated that "it is time one of the greatest discoveries of modern times should inspire hope in mankind and not fear."

In the December elections Laniel was a candidate for the Presidency, but he failed on the eighth ballot to obtain the required majority by twenty-two votes. After the tenth ballot he withdrew his name, and René Coty was elected President of France on the thirteenth ballot, with 477 votes, on December 23. Laniel planned to resign as Premier in January 1954, but was persuaded to remain and was given a substantial vote of confidence by the National Assembly on January 6, 1954.

Joseph Laniel was born in Vimoutiers in Normandy on October 12, 1889, the son of Henri and Melle (Cayrou) Laniel. Since the time of his great-grandfather, his family had been linen manufacturers, and were once the purveyors of household linen for the courts of European monarchies. His father managed the family textile mills in Vimoutiers and Lisieux while representing the department of Calvados in the Chamber of Deputies from 1896 to his death in 1932. When Joseph was eight he left his father's nineteenth-century Château de Villers to attend the Ecole Gerson and later the Lycée Janson-de-Sailly. He obtained the degrees Sc.B. and Litt.B. and in 1910 assumed his duties in the family's textile firm.

Mobilized on August 2, 1914 for World War I, he fought first at the front as a sub-lieutenant of cavalry, then as an artillery officer; by 1919 he had attained the grade of captain commanding a group of three batteries. He was decorated as a Chevalier of the Legion of Honor, and received the Croix de Guerre.

After the war Laniel returned to the textile industry and also made his first entries in the arena of politics. He was elected mayor of the town of Notre-Dame-de-Courson and general councillor of Calvados in 1919. He was persuaded to run for his father's parliamentary seat (at the latter's death in 1932) and was elected to represent Lisieux (Calvados).

In Parliament Laniel specialized in economic and financial questions, and was re-elected to his seat in 1936. In the 1940 ministry of Paul Reynaud he was appointed Under-Secretary of State for Finance. When Reynaud's government fell that June, Laniel was one of the eighty Deputies who refused to grant full powers to Marshal Pétain. He became vice-president and one of the principal founders, with Georges Bidault, its president, of the Council of National Resistance (an "underground" organization).

Rather than run his factories for the Germans, Laniel voluntarily exiled himself to his large Bellerive-sur-Allier farm which he made an important Resistance headquarters. When Paris was liberated in 1944, he descended the Champs-Elysées at the side of General de Gaulle. He was later honored with the Resistance medal, with officer's rosette.

French Embassy Press & Inf. Div.

JOSEPH LANIEL

While a member of the Provisional Consultative Assembly in 1944, Laniel sat on the Financial, Agricultural and Reconstruction Commissions. The next year, on October 21, 1945, he was elected to the first National Constituent Assembly which also elected him its vice-president. He was a member of its finance commission and *rapporteur* on the budget of reconstruction.

He helped to found the Rightest political party, the Parti républicain de la Liberté (P.R.L.) and was re-elected on June 2, 1946 from Calvados to the second National Constituent Assembly, for which he again served as vice-president, budget *rapporteur* and member of the finance commission. Laniel was elected to the National Assembly in November 1946 and was named its vice-president in January 1947. He resigned the vice-presidency in order to become the president of the parliamentary group of his party, serving as the spokesman of the P.R.L. party in economic and financial questions.

Laniel was one of the principal writers of the law of March 21, 1948 which called for the establishment of the Caisse Autonome de la Reconstruction (a special fund to finance reconstruction), of which he became president. He acted as Secretary of State for Finance and Economic Affairs in the brief (July to August 1948) government of André Marie, was Minister of Posts, Telegraphs and Telephones in René Pleven's Cabinet from August 1951 to September of that year when Pleven appointed him Minister of State, which portfolio he held through the dissolution of the Pleven ministry in January 1952 to the fall of the succeeding government of Edgar Faure in February 1952.

(Continued next page)

LANIEL, JOSEPH—*Continued*

After the government of René Mayer fell on May 21, 1953, President Auriol invited seven Deputies to form a government. Four had accepted the mandate, but none of these (Reynaud, Mendès-France, Bidault, and Marie) had been able to muster enough support from the Assembly. President Auriol then called on Joseph Laniel, who was strongly encouraged by moderates and conservatives of the Assembly.

Laniel's status as a wealthy landowner and industrialist rendered him favorable to the conservative parties; his wartime Resistance record won him the respect of all sections of the chamber, especially the De Gaullists; and his record of generous pay and social benefits for his employees made him attractive to the leftists, according to Barrett McGurn in the New York *Herald Tribune,* June 26, 1953.

Seeking the confirmation of his nomination, Laniel presented a short outline of his program in a speech before the National Assembly. The Deputies' eagerness to end the crisis was evident by their frequent applause and by their shouts for a vote as soon as he had finished. Yet the applause indicated also, said Joan Thiriet in the *Christian Science Monitor* (June 26, 1953) that "His listeners were clearly paying tribute to a man who, relatively unknown to the general public, has a fine record of public and private integrity."

Laniel promised that his foreign policy would "continue to be characterized by fidelity to our Atlantic Alliance." He favored a "Big Four" meeting with Russia if the Soviets would first give "tangible proof of good will." He would seek an early end to the Indo-Chinese war. He would support the European Defense Community. *Time* (July 6, 1953) called it a "maybe-yes maybe-no" program presented "with all the tight-fisted caution of a Norman farmer."

The National Assembly confirmed Laniel's nomination by a vote of 398 to 206 on June 26, 1953. Since only a majority of 314 was needed, it seemed probable, said Lansing Warren (New York *Times,* June 27, 1953), "that his government would last through the summer, and perhaps until the voting for a new President in Parliament at the end of this year."

On June 30, Premier Laniel obtained the Assembly's approval of his Cabinet by a vote of 386 to 212. No fewer than six former Premiers were selected for the new Cabinet: Georges Bidault, Foreign Minister; René Pleven, Defense Minister; Paul Reynaud and Henri Queuille, Deputy Premiers; Edgar Faure, Minister of Finance; and André Marie, Minister of Education. The Cabinet represented seven political parties, and ten members of the twenty-two were retained from the previous ministry.

The Laniel government was sustained in its first major proposal on July 11, when the National Assembly, by a majority vote of 313, restored provisions for new taxes on gasoline and alcohol, on its second and final reading, after the Council of the Republic had attempted to mutilate the bill.

The Assembly, in its supporting vote, gave Premier Laniel broad authority not only to cut budgets during the summer parliamentary recess, but to transfer appropriations "from unproductive to productive use." "No post-war Cabinet has ever enjoyed such powers and, as Charles Barange, *rapporteur* in the Assembly, assured M. Laniel, 'the power to act is not so important as the decision to use that right'" (New York *Times,* July 12, 1953).

Under these new powers, Laniel and his Cabinet set out to balance the national budget and to create full employment. The Communist and non-Communist trade unions became fearful of certain government economy proposals which involved pensions and discharges of civil personnel, and called a "warning" strike in August 1953. The strikes involved postal, telegraphs, and telephone workers as well as those in mines, railroads, municipal departmental, government, gas, electric services and private industry.

By August 21, the non-Communist unions agreed to end the strike and the government agreed to consult the unions before applying the decrees affecting pensions and to help obtain higher salaries for workers in both civil service and industry. The Cabinet then continued its economic reforms: it reduced "essential" living costs by cutting prices in food and manufactured goods from 5 to 15 per cent; it raised wages for about 300,000 low-paid government workers; and it began a program to find and elicit payment from income tax evaders. When the National Assembly reconvened in October 1953, it rejected Communist and Socialist censure motions involving Laniel's economic actions by 390 to 222, and 299 to 242 votes.

In an attempt to end the seven-year war in Indo-China, Premier Laniel early in July offered the Associated States of Indo-China (Viet-Nam, Cambodia and Laos) further consolidation of their independence within the French Union. The "Laniel-Navarre plan" provided for a further strengthening of French arms and troops in prosecution of the war against the Communist guerillas, transference of power from French to Indo-Chinese officials, and development of a native Indo-Chinese army.

Laniel was successful in obtaining promises of more American aid for the war in Indo-China: the National Security Council recommended to President Eisenhower that in addition to the $400,000,000 already appropriated, an extra $385,000,000 should be granted for the war. In October, the National Assembly voted 315 to 251 to support in principle the French Cabinet's plan for the Associated States and expressed its hope for the achievement of a "general peace in Asia."

On November 27, 1953 the National Assembly, although not actually voting for the European Defense Community, supported Laniel in his policy for European unity. Passed by 275 to 244 votes, the Assembly resolution asked that "the continuity of the policy of building a United Europe be assured." With this vote of confidence, Laniel and Foreign

Minister Bidault could go to the meeting of the British, French and American heads of government at Bermuda in early December "with a mandate to represent France to keep the idea of the European Defense Community and of Europeanization as a whole in being" (New York *Times*, November 28, 1953).

Prime Minister Churchill, President Eisenhower and Premier Laniel attended the Bermuda conference which began December 4. After four days of confidential talks, the three men "confirmed the unity of purpose of our three countries," agreed to accept the Kremlin's proposal for a meeting of foreign ministers in Berlin, and decided to continue the strengthening of the military defenses of the Western world.

In Indochina, meanwhile, the Communists increased their pressure. Bidault represented the Laniel government at the Geneva conference in the spring of 1954, and tried to reach a settlement on the war.

Premier Laniel resigned in June 1954 after the National Assembly, by a vote of 306 to 293, refused to give him a vote of confidence on his policy in the Indochina War.

Laniel married Lucienne Fougerolle, a member of an old family from the Creuse region of France, on April 20, 1920. They have two children, a boy and a girl; the son and son-in-law now manage the family textile plants, although the Premier still supervises the accounts. Reputed to be the fifteenth wealthiest man in France, Laniel, in addition to his French factories and real estate, has a large construction firm in Morocco that is at present building the giant dam of Bin el Quidane. He is now a member of the Independent Republican party whose members come from other rightist groupings and include Paul Reynaud and Antoine Pinay.

Laniel is president of the Societies of Mutual Assistance. For relaxation he reads political economy, finance and history, is an expert shot (he derives an income from the sale of the hundred or more rabbits killed daily on his estate and shipped to the Paris food markets), and has a fine collection of French butterflies. He has a reputation as a gourmet. The only excess he permits himself is smoking: he enjoys two packs of cigarettes, ten pipes and three or four cigars daily. He is respected as a farmer; the story is current in Paris that he can spot the age and weight of a heifer from thirty paces. The Premier is six feet tall and weighs 198 pounds; he is stocky and has a ruddy, "apple-cheeked" complexion.

References

N Y Post Mag p2 Jl 12 '53 por
N Y Times p1 Je 27 '53 por
Newsweek 42:33+ Jl 6 '53 por
Time 62:24+ Jl 6 '53 por
U S News 35:50+ Ag 28 '53 por
Dictionnaire Biographique Français Contemporain (1950)
International Who's Who, 1953
International Yearbook and Statesmen's Who's Who, 1953
World Biography (1948)

LASSER, J(ACOB) K(AY) Oct. 7, 1896-May 11, 1954 Tax authority; after becoming a certified public accountant, established J. K. Lasser & Company (1923); was chairman of Institute on Federal Taxation at New York University (1942-1951) and of Pennsylvania State College Institute on Taxation (1947-1950), and director of the Tax Institute in Princeton, New Jersey (1944-1951); wrote numerous books including *Your Income Tax* (1939), revised edition (1946) sold 7,000,000 copies; and *How to Run a Small Business* (1950). See *Current Biography,* (May) 1946.

Obituary

N Y Times p31 My 12 '54

LEE, DORIS (EMRICK) Feb. 1, 1905-
Artist

Address: b. c/o Associated American Artists, 711 Fifth Ave., New York 22; h. Woodstock, N.Y.

The paintings of Doris Lee might not be so well-known, the artist believes, had it not been for an "astounding day" in 1936 when she received two letters. One was from the United States Treasury Department which notified her that she had won a competition to do a mural, *Rural Postal Delivery,* in the new post office at Washington, D.C.; the other letter was from the Art Institute of Chicago congratulating her upon winning the annual Logan Award for her painting *Thanksgiving Dinner.*

The award set off a controversy that started the "Sanity in Art Movement." Her style has been variously described as "primitive", "modern", "whimsical" although at the beginning of her career, she had concentrated on nonrepresentational abstract painting. Today, her work appears in some of the leading art museums in the United States. She has received nine awards and honors, has illustrated seven books and has done the paintings for three picture essays for *Life* magazine.

The artist's father, Edward Everett Emrick was a merchant and banker. Her mother, Nancy May (Love) Emrick was a country school teacher before her marriage. Doris, the fourth in a family of six children, was born in Aledo, Illinois on February 1, 1905. Her ancestors—Irish, English and German—were early pioneers in Illinois. A great-grandfather, an engineer, came from England to build a bridge across the Mississippi at Keithsburg, near Aledo, and Doris recalls the bridge as a scene which her grandfather often painted. Her grandmothers and great aunts also painted, and did embroidery, quilting and the carving of frames and bed posts.

Doris Emrick was sent to Ferry Hall, a boarding school in Lake Forest, Illinois from which she was graduated in 1923. She then entered Rockford College, Rockford, Illinois. Although she had a natural aptitude for mathematics, she decided to major in art and philosophy. She would have preferred art school rather than college, but college was more important to her family. She saved whatever money she could and after being graduated in

DORIS LEE

1927, she began traveling and studying in Paris and Italy.

Upon her return to the United States, she attended the Art Institute in Kansas City, Missouri, but soon went back to Paris to study under André Lhote and other semi-abstractionists. When she returned home again, she was painting abstractions, but dissatisfaction with her work led her to San Francisco for further study at the California School of Fine Arts.

Arnold Blanch was a teacher at the California school. He suggested that she paint subjects that appealed to her, or paint from nature and use its variety to make whatever shapes she wanted. Harry Salpeter illustrated his article, *Arnold Blanch: Bohemian* (*Esquire,* March 1938), with a reproduction of *Portrait of Doris Lee* which Blanch had painted in 1933, and said that her development as a painter was shaped by Blanch. "He [commended] Doris Lee," Salpeter wrote, "as a combative student who helped make teaching interesting by entering into disputes with her teacher and expressing differences of opinion."

After studying in California, Doris Lee moved to Woodstock, New York, in 1931, and has lived there ever since. "It was a great advantage for me as a young painter to live in Woodstock," she has written, "and to know so many artists working [there]."

The years between 1931 and 1936 were devoted to painting in Woodstock and in New York City and to museum study in Europe. Miss Lee had exhibited at different museums before she won the Federal mural competition and the Logan Award ($500). Mrs Frank Logan, patron of the Chicago Art Institute, used such words as "atrocious" and "insanity" because the Logan prize had been awarded to Miss Lee by the jury for her *Thanksgiving Dinner,* and sponsored the "Sanity in Art Movement," which sought to abolish modern art in its various forms. The institute, however, "acted with courage and integrity" regardless of Mrs. Logan's protests. The controversy became a source of amusement to Doris Lee and helped establish her reputation as an important American painter.

For four successive summers, Miss Lee was a guest artist at the Colorado Springs Fine Arts Center. She won second prize at the Worcester Art Museum in the "American Painters Today" exhibit (1938), and spent several winters painting in Mexico, South Carolina and Key West, Florida. There were exhibits at the Whitney Museum, the Walker Gallery, New York, and at both World's Fairs, in San Francisco and in New York.

She was a guest artist at Michigan State College, Lansing in 1943 and 1944, and in 1943, she won a prize at the Carnegie Institute for her painting, *Siesta,* now owned by Henry Luce. In the same year, she was awarded the Jennie Sesnan Landscape Medal at the Pennsylvania Academy of Fine Arts in Philadelphia for *Shore Leave,* a painting subsequently purchased by Anita Wechsler.

Life magazine commissioned Doris Lee to do a series of paintings in Hollywood, California, and in Central America in 1945 and 1946. These were reproduced in the magazine with descriptive essays. Some of her paintings also appeared in Metro-Goldwyn-Mayer's motion picture, *The Pirate.*

Her lithograph, *Country Wedding,* was given a Library of Congress purchase prize in 1943 and her canvas of the same title was exhibited in the "Artists for Victory" show at the Metropolitan Museum of Art in New York and is now at the Albright Art Gallery in Buffalo, New York.

In the *Encyclopaedia Britannica Collection of Contemporary American Painting* (1946), Grace Pagano wrote, "For the same reason that a bird sings—sheer joy of living—Doris Lee paints her exuberant and subtly humorous legends of the rural scene. . . . Her pictures have that rarest of all gifts, charm, plus the fairy godmother of enthusiasm. She may sacrifice some detail of authenticity, but she will replace it with a very beautiful and special kind of 'imagining' which is far more satisfying."

Illustrations of Miss Lee's *gouache* paintings appeared in Arnold Blanch's book, *Methods and Techniques for Gouache Painting* (American Artists, 1946) with her comment, "*Gouache* is the best medium for experimentation and invention, and as sketch preparation for larger oil paintings."

Other books illustrated by Doris Lee are *The Great Quillow* by James Thurber (Harcourt, 1944); *Hired Man's Elephant* by Philip Duffield Stong (Dodd, 1939); *Painting for Enjoyment* by the painter and Arnold Blanch (Tudor, 1947); *The St. Johns* by James Branch Cabell and A. J. Hanna (Farrar, 1943); *Mr. Benedict's Lion* by Walter D. Edmonds (Dodd, 1950) and the *Rodgers and Hart Song Book* by Richard Rodgers (Simon and Schuster, 1951). The last named has her full-page color reproductions of scenes from some of the Rodgers and Hart musicals with her portrayal of Richard Rodgers and the late Lorenz Hart at work as a frontispiece.

In similar vein, the artist has painted scenes from Rodgers' and Hammerstein's *Oklahoma!* Of these paintings, Carlyle Burrows, in the *Christian Science Monitor* of July 8, 1944, wrote ". . . it is Miss Lee's exuberant gaiety and humor related to her deft and knowing use of the painter's brush that count for most in the build-up of human interest appeal."

Under the title "An Artist in Africa," *Life* magazine published a series of picture essays (November 10, 1952) subtitled, "Doris Lee paints Arab World on Trip from Tangier to Tunis." To do this work, Miss Lee and her husband, Arnold Blanch, made a tour of North Africa in 1951. All impressions were jotted down in a voluminous series of pencil sketches, annotated with color reminders. On her return to the United States, she incorporated the sketches into "stylized, whimsical" paintings. *Artist's Eye-view of North Africa,* a map panorama in colors, included impressions of arrival at Tangier, the sultan's palace at Rabat, the port of Casablanca, the journey inland to Marrakech, to Fez, eastward to Algiers, to Tunis and Carthage, and south to Kairouan, and was centered by a large African sun. The smaller pictures, including *Snake Charmer, Parade of Passers-by* and *Garden in Carthage,* followed a pattern of native activities.

Many of Doris Lee's paintings are in private collections, including those of Oscar Serlin and Leland Hayward. Others are in thirteen permanent public collections including the Metropolitan Museum of Art, the Chicago Art Institute, the Library of Congress, the University of Arizona and the Florida Gulf Coast Art Center at Clearwater, Florida where she has been guest artist at intervals from 1949 to 1951. In 1946 and in 1950 she won the New York Art Director Award of Merit. She worked at the Research Studio in Maitland, Florida in 1950. She has also made many visits to Key West, Florida and painted numerous scenes there.

The artist has been known as Doris Lee since her marriage to Russell Werner Lee in 1927. They were divorced in 1939. She married Arnold Blanch, well-known painter and teacher, in 1941. They make their permanent home—between travels—at Woodstock, New York, where she has been active in the Woodstock Artists' Association, for which she served as president in 1951.

Miss Lee is fond of traveling, likes to read and sew, and her special hobby is collecting shells and butterflies. She has brown hair and eyes, is five feet five inches tall and weighs 130 pounds. She is a Presbyterian and a Democrat. In 1949, Rockford College conferred upon her the honorary degree of Doctor of Laws.

References

American Artists Group. Doris Lee (1946)
Pagano, G. The Encyclopaedia Britannica Collection of Contemporary American Painting (1946)
Who's Who in America, 1952-53
Who's Who in American Art (1953)

LEMAY, CURTIS E(MERSON) Nov. 15, 1906- United States Air Force officer

Address: b. c/o Headquarters, Strategic Air Command, Offutt Air Force Base, Omaha, Neb.

NOTE: This biography supersedes the article which appeared in *Current Biography* in 1944.

A pioneer in the concept of strategic bombardment, General Curtis E. LeMay is commander of the Strategic Air Command, which is responsible for long-range bombing operations in the event of war. He previously had commanded U.S. Air Forces in Europe during the period of the Berlin airlift. In World War II, General LeMay headed the 305th Bombardment Group of the Eighth Air Force, based in England, and personally led the Regensburg raid and other important missions.

Later he was transferred to the Pacific theater of operations to head the 20th and 21st bomber commands and directed raids against Manchuria and Japan. He was chief of staff of the Strategic Air Forces when the first atom bombs were dropped on Hiroshima and Nagasaki. He became a "four star" general in October 1951 in a recess appointment made by President Harry S. Truman.

Curtis Emerson LeMay was born to Erving and Arizona Dove (Carpenter) LeMay in Columbus, Ohio on November 15, 1906, and was brought up in his native city where his father, an ironworker of French-Canadian descent, was employed. He liked to "spend his leisure [time] building crystal 'wireless' sets or prowling through the hills of southern Ohio with a gun and a bowie knife" (*Time,* September 4, 1950).

Young LeMay's ambition, after his graduation from South High School, was to attend the U.S. Military Academy at West Point, New York, but he did not get the appointment from his Congressman. He enrolled in the School of Engineering at Ohio State University in Columbus and became a member of the Reserve Officers' Training Corps. In 1928, he was commissioned a second lieutenant, Field Artillery Reserve, and went on active duty with the 62nd Field Artillery Brigade at Camp Knox, Kentucky. LeMay received the B.C.E. degree from Ohio State University in 1932, when Army duty at Columbus enabled him to complete the requirements.

According to an article on LeMay by William Bradford Huie in *Coronet* (October, 1950), "it was Lindbergh's flight to Paris which caused... [LeMay] and his best friend, Francis H. ('Butch') Griswold, to put in for flying cadet school." These two future Air Force generals, who enlisted together in the Regular Army on September 28, 1928, were fellow students at the Air Corps Primary Flying School, March Field, California, and were graduated together the following June. "While his classmates swooped off for weekends in Los Angeles," wrote *Time* (September 4, 1950), "he often hung back to take engines

U. S. Air Force

GEN. CURTIS E. LEMAY

apart, work at machine guns, [and] pore over weather charts and navigation logarithms."

From March Field LeMay went to the Air Corps Advanced Flying School at Kelly Field, Texas, where he was commissioned a second lieutenant in the Air Reserve on October 12, 1929. He was put on active duty the following day, and became a second lieutenant, Air Corps, in the Regular Army on January 6, 1930.

His first service as an officer in the Regular Army was with the 27th Pursuit Squadron at Selfridge Field, Michigan. Except for two periods of detachment (as assistant engineer and operations officer at Norton Field in Columbus, Ohio from September 1931 to March 1932, and as a student in advanced navigation at Langley Field, Virginia from October to December 1933), he was stationed at Selfridge Field until October 1934, when he was transferred to the 18th Pursuit Group at Schofield Barracks, Hawaii. LeMay was promoted to the rank of first lieutenant on June 1, 1935, and was recalled to the Air Force General Headquarters at Langley Field in January 1937 to serve as operations and intelligence officer of the 49th Bombardment Squadron and as one of the first navigator-pilots of the B-17 heavy bomber.

In 1937, according to *Generals of the Army and the Air Force* (February, 1954), LeMay took part in a good-will flight of B-17 fortresses to South America. After a second good-will tour the following year, the group of which LeMay was a member was awarded the Mackay Trophy for superior achievement in aviation. In one of his flights, LeMay "navigated . . . 600 miles out to sea—a famous and daring feat in 1937—and came out of the overcast over his objective, the Italian liner, *Rex*" (*Time,* August 13, 1945).

After taking a three-month course at the Air Corps Tactical School, Maxwell Field, Alabama in 1939, LeMay rejoined the 49th Bombardment Squadron in August as a B-17 airplane commander. Promoted to captain on January 6, 1940, LeMay was transferred a month later to the 41st Reconnaissance Squadron at Langley Field as operations and intelligence officer. In January 1941 he was assigned to the 34th Bombardment Group, first as commander of the 7th Bombardment Squadron at Langley Field and then as group operations officer at Westover Field in Massachusetts.

Having been promoted to the rank of major in March 1941, LeMay was selected "because of his extensive experience in long-range over-water navigation . . . to pioneer the ferry routes to Africa via South America and the South Atlantic, and to England via the North Atlantic" (*Generals of the Army and the Air Force*). He made landings at what were described as "fourteen strange airports . . . in general too small for successful operation of the B-24 airplane" in the citation accompanying the award to Major Curtis LeMay of the Distinguished Flying Cross in December 1941.

Advanced to lieutenant colonel on January 5, 1942 and to colonel on March 1, 1942, LeMay was transferred in April 1942 to Muroc, California as commanding officer of the 305th Bombardment Group. He trained the group and led it to England in the autumn of 1942—it was part of the Eighth Air Force and was one of the first USAF bombardment units to enter combat in World War II.

For "exceptionally meritorious achievement" as the pilot of a B-17 on five combat missions over Europe in late 1942, LeMay was awarded the Air Medal in February 1943. (He also received the Silver Star.) The most celebrated of these missions was one directed at the German-held French port of Saint-Nazaire. Deciding that "too many of his B-17's were missing enemy targets because they zigzagged" to avoid flak, LeMay "clamped a cigar in his jaw, led the next raid over Saint-Nazaire, [and] held his plane on course up to the bomb drop through murderous ack-ack for a grim seven minutes" (*Time,* September 4, 1950).

The next day he issued an order that there should be "no more evasive action on the final bombing run," and while these revolutionary daylight bombing tactics were widely criticized as "suicidal," the "efficiency of a straight-in bomb run" was "demonstrated beyond all doubt." Under LeMay's command, furthermore, the 305th Bombardment Group was "the first to put into tactical use a combat formation utilizing eighteen aircraft per group arranged so the formation's firepower could be fully exploited against fighter attacks from any angle," a type formation which is still in use today (*Generals of the Army and the Air Force*).

On August 17, 1943, Colonel LeMay "led the famous shuttle mission of Flying Fortresses from England to the target at Regensburg, Germany, landing at the end of the mission in North Africa." This was "the first such mission ever flown." For his heroism in the attack on Germany's principal Messerschmitt plant, LeMay was awarded the Distinguished Service Cross in December 1943.

LeMay was advanced to the rank of brigadier general on September 28, 1943. Confirmed as a major general on March 2, 1944, he became, at the age of thirty-seven, one of the youngest men in the U.S. Army to hold this rank. He continued with the Eighth Air Force in England as commanding general of the Third Bombardment Division through June 1944. (He received the Distinguished Service Medal in December for his work in England.)

On August 13, he was assigned to the China-Burma-India theater of operations to head the 20th Bomber Command. Under LeMay, China-based B-29 "Superfortresses" made three attacks on Anshan and other Manchurian industrial centers in July and September.

Taking over from Brigadier General Haywood S. Hansell, Jr., the leadership of the 21st Bomber Command in January 1945, LeMay made "a courageous decision" to sponsor a low-level night-time incendiary attack on Tokyo with his full force of B-29's, the planes having been depleted of gunnery to make way for extra bomb loads (*10 Eventful Years*). "Some 300 planes," wrote Hanson W. Baldwin in the New York *Times* (April 1, 1945), "coming in at 5,000-foot levels below effective range of Japanese anti-aircraft batteries, poured 2,500 tons of firebomb clusters into a ten-square-mile area in the heart of the city."

The General continued to head the 21st Bomber Command when it became the 20th Air Force, and was awarded an Oak Leaf Cluster to his Distinguished Service Medal on July 31, 1945. The following day he yielded the B-29 command to Major General Nathan F. Twining and became chief of staff to General Carl Spaatz of the U.S. Strategic Air Forces. There he took a major part in planning the atomic bombing of Hiroshima and Nagasaki.

Recalled to the United States after the Japanese surrender, LeMay piloted a B-29 on a record-breaking non-stop flight from Japan to Chicago. Governor Frank Lausche of Ohio offered the returning hero the seat in the U.S. Senate vacated by Harold H. Burton, who had been appointed to the Supreme Court, but this honor was declined. "I want to stay in the Air Force," asserted LeMay.

Temporarily assigned to Air Force Headquarters at Washington, D.C., LeMay was named special deputy to the AAF Air Matériel Command at Wright Field, Ohio on October 26, 1945. In December he was recalled to Washington to become deputy chief of air staff for research and development. (For a full description of the work of this office, see LeMay's article, "AAF's War of Research," in *Flying,* June 1946.)

After the Air Force became an independent service under the National Security Act of 1947, LeMay was assigned to command the U.S. Air Forces in Europe, with headquarters at Wiesbaden in Germany. Curtis E. LeMay was responsible from June 26 to September 30, 1948 for the direction of the Berlin airlift, and himself occasionally took the pilot's seat in one of the transport planes employed in that operation. Among his many decorations is the Medal for Humane Action, qualification for which was "at least 120 days of service" in supplying "necessities of life to the people of Berlin."

The General has been the commanding general of the Strategic Air Command (SAC) since October 1948. The headquarters of SAC at Offutt Air Force Base, near Omaha, Nebraska, has been described as a "nerve center."

Baldwin noted (October 22) that the command firmly believed that "it provides the nation's best deterrent to war" because of its "power of retaliation," while the planes at its disposal had increased greatly in both number and quality since 1950. John G. Norris, who toured the North Africa bases early in 1954, was struck by the perfection of aerial refueling to the point where it is considered "routine" (as of September 1954, an air refueling operation by SAC aircraft takes place somewhere around the globe every four and a half minutes, twenty-four hours a day), and by the feat of moving the entire 301st Medium Bomber Wing from Louisiana to French Morocco in a single mass non-stop operation (New York *Post,* March 7, 1954).

As part of their mobility training, all SAC combat units deploy overseas as a group once each year to gain operational experience in forward areas such as England, North Africa, or the Far East. On one such deployment in March 1954, the 22d (B-47) Bomb Wing executed the longest mass jet bomber flight on record by flying 5,860 miles from England to California non-stop, using air refueling. In June 1954, a group of three B-47's flew non-stop from California to Japan, a distance of 6,700 miles, again using air refueling. While not engaged in overseas training exercises, all SAC combat units practice simulated combat missions over "targets" in the United States on a twenty-four hour a day all weather schedule.

Among the foreign awards which LeMay has received are the Legion of Honor (France), the Croix de Guerre with palm (Belgium), the Order of the Southern Cross (Brazil), the Distinguished Flying Cross (Great Britain), and the Order of the Patriotic War (Russia). He is a commander in the Moroccan Order of the Ouissam Alaouite Cherifien. Aviators Post 743 of the American Legion presented LeMay with its General William Mitchell Memorial Trophy in May 1954. He is a life trustee of the National Geographic Society.

Curtis LeMay was married on June 19, 1934 to Helen Estelle Maitland; they have one daughter, Patricia Jane. He likes "ham" radios. He also enjoys building sports cars and hunting. He is five feet eight inches tall.

References (see also references listed in 1944 biographical sketch)

Life 25:88 N 1 '48 por; 36:132+ Je 14 '54 pors
Newsweek 33:24+ Ap 18 '49 por
U S News 25:40+ Jl 30 '48 por; 32:62+ Mr 14 '52 por
Who's Who in America, 1954-55

LIBBY, W(ILLARD) F(RANK) Dec. 17, 1908- University professor; chemist

Address: b. c/o U.S. Atomic Energy Commission, Washington 25, D.C.; h. 3101 Hawthorne St., Washington 8, D.C.

An "atomic clock" technique for determining the age of ancient mineralogical, archaeological and prehistoric plant and animal remains was invented by Dr. W. F. Libby, professor of chemistry at the University of Chicago and on the staff of that university's Institute for Nuclear Studies. In recognition of his outstanding achievements in chemistry, Dr. Libby was the recipient of Columbia University's Chandler Award in February 1954. In addition

Wide World

DR. W. F. LIBBY

to his discovery of "radiocarbon dating" of radioactive isotopes of carbon in ancient materials, he has also made a notable contribution to the technique of measuring faint radioactivity in all living matter. He participated in the development of atomic energy during World War II, and was a member of the general advisory committee of the United States Atomic Energy Commission.

On September 15, 1954 the summer White House at Denver, Colorado announced that President Eisenhower is naming Dr. W. F. Libby to replace Dr. Henry DeWolf Smyth (who is returning to Princeton University) to serve as a member of the Atomic Energy Commission. The appointment is subject to confirmation by the U.S. Senate.

Dr. Libby spoke at the annual meeting of the American Chemical Society, held in New York City September 13-17, 1954, on the subject of cosmology. He reported his findings concerning tritium, triple-heavy-weight hydrogen, in the upper atmosphere by cosmic rays from somewhere out in space. He demonstrated that, because tritium has a half-life of twelve and one-half years, it is now possible to determine the age of water by measuring the amount of radioactivity it contains and calculating this in relation to the known age of tritium. According to Robert K. Plumb in the New York *Times* (September 19, 1954), studies can now be made on underground water supplies.

Willard Frank Libby was born on December 17, 1908, to Eva May (Rivers) and Edward Ora Libby in Grand Valley, Colorado. His father was a farmer. The family moved to a ranch near Santa Rosa, California about 1913. Willard attended a two-room country grammar school, and was graduated from Analy Union High School, Sebastopol, California, in 1926. He entered the University of California at Berkeley in 1927 and majored in chemistry. He received the B.S. degree in 1931 and the Ph.D. degree in 1933.

Beginning his career as an instructor of chemistry at the University of California in 1933, Dr. Libby remained with the university until 1941, engaging in teaching and research, and attaining the rank of associate professor. Many of his studies of the chemistry of radioactive elements, the behavior of neutrons, and of elements in the gaseous state were published. He served with the Columbia University division of war research (1941-1945), assisting in the development of the gaseous-diffusion process for the separation of the isotopes of uranium. This was a fundamental problem in the development of the atomic bomb.

In 1945 Libby joined the faculty of the University of Chicago as a professor of chemistry and has since been active in research work with that university's Institute for Nuclear Studies.

Dr. Libby's postwar work with a radioactive isotope of carbon (called radiocarbon or Carbon-14) followed his earlier studies of the detection and measurement of faint radioactivity. In 1946 he published a paper in which he discussed the production of radiocarbon in the upper atmosphere as a result of the activity of cosmic rays. Previous studies by other workers had indicated that one of the results of cosmic radiation was the production of neutrons in the upper air. Laboratory experiments had shown that while the effect of such neutron bombardment on oxygen is negligible, nitrogen, which constitutes about four fifths of our atmosphere, is readily affected by neutrons which penetrate its nucleus and change it into radiocarbon.

These facts were collated by Libby who advanced, in his paper, the theory that since neutrons are known to exist in our upper atmosphere, the reaction which had been produced in the laboratory also occurred in nature. He then hypothesized that such carbon would be oxidized into carbon dioxide which in turn would become mixed with the ordinary carbon dioxide in the air, and through the process of photosynthesis (by which plants remove the carbon from the dioxide), would become a tiny but measurable part of all plant life and thence of all living matter. Libby predicted that all living matter would become faintly radioactive from this source.

Actual measurements taken by Libby and his associates in 1947 not only established that radioactivity was present in living things, but also confirmed his estimate of the amount of radiocarbon present. It was further shown that radiocarbon is uniformly distributed in nature, and that during the lifetime of living matter its specific radioactivity remains at a fairly constant level, an equilibrium being established between the natural gain and loss of radiocarbon.

Since the process of radioactive disintegration proceeds at a regular rate, unaffected by chemical or physical change, and since the intake of carbon ceases at death, this observation suggested to Libby that the age of a dead sample might be determined on the basis of the naturally diminishing radioactivity of its carbon content.

These experiments attracted the attention of the American Anthropological Association and the Geological Society of America, and in 1948 these groups organized an advisory committee on Carbon-14 which worked with Libby in his further researches, with financial assistance from the Wenner-Gren Foundation for Anthropological Research.

Libby then began intensive research and experimentation in order to determine the "half-life" of fresh radiocarbon as exactly as possible, because it would be on the basis of a comparison of the specific radioactivity of a given sample with the known rate of disintegration of radiocarbon that an age could be assigned to a given sample. Once this had been established provisionally (the final figure was not arrived at until 1949), Dr. Libby tested his hypothesis against samples the age of which could be established by historical chronology.

One of these tests was to measure a piece of the funerary boat of King Sesostris III of Egypt (from the Chicago Natural History Museum). Professor Libby chopped the precious board into kindling, threw the kindling into an electric furnace, burned it down to charcoal, ground up the charcoal and then applied a Geiger counter to it. The radiocarbon dating gave a date of 3,621 years for the Egyptian ship, which was only 3.5 per cent off the known age of 3,750 years. After further tests of objects of known ages, Libby undertook to determine the approximate date of samples of objects of which the age is not known. This new science of chronology is regarded as "the hottest development to hit antiquarian circles since Howard Carter opened up King Tut's tomb, and is far more significant than all of Tutankhamen's golden trappings" (*Saturday Evening Post,* March 14, 1953).

Since September 5, 1949, when the first successful results were announced at a meeting of the ninth International Congress of Americanists in New York City, Libby and his associates have been able to clarify several important dates. One of the more notable is the final period of the Ice Age in North America which was established as having been 10,000 rather than 25,000 years ago as previous estimates had placed it. Dr. Libby made the complete specifications of his process available to all interested geologists and archaeologists. In the summer of 1954 Indian copper vessels found in Wisconsin were dated 1,000 years older than the first Egyptian pyramids.

As a corollary to his researches in radiocarbon, Libby has studied another reaction between neutrons and nitrogen which he had noted as early as 1939. In this reaction the nitrogen nucleus is likewise invaded, but instead of being changed to radiocarbon, it is split into normal carbon (Carbon-12) and tritium, the isotope of hydrogen three times as heavy as ordinary hydrogen, which has come into prominence because of its use in the hydrogen bomb. The period of significant radioactivity of this isotope is short (half-life is twelve and a half years); he has proposed that this short period may be utilized in drawing conclusions concerning the vertical mixing of ocean waters, since a comparison between the specific radioactivities of surface waters and deep waters might prove whether the waters of the ocean mixed from top to bottom within the period of measurable activity of the tritium content. Libby is also urging the introduction of courses in radioisotopes into high schools and colleges.

Libby was a Guggenheim Memorial Foundation fellow in 1941 and in 1951. In the latter year he also won the Research Corporation Award. He is a member of the American Chemical Society, American Physical Society, American Association for the Advancement of Science, and National Academy of Sciences. He also belongs to the American Institute of Physics, American Philosophical Society, and American Academy of Arts and Sciences. He has written *Radiocarbon Dating* (University of Chicago Press, 1952) in which he details his researches and his procedures. His fraternities are Pi Mu Epsilon, Alpha Chi Sigma, and Sigma Xi.

The scientist is six feet, two inches tall, has reddish hair and blue eyes. On August 9, 1940 he married Leonor Lucinda Hickey, a teacher. They have twin daughters, Susan Charlotte and Janet Eva. Dr. Libby credits Professor G. N. Lewis and Professor Wendell M. Latimer of the University of California with having influenced his professional career. His extracurricular interests are watching baseball games, reading and listening to music.

References

Christian Sci Mon p10 S 24 '54
N Y Times p29 S 6 '49; p9 F 27 '52; p 1+ S 16 '54 por
Newsweek 44:29 S 27 '54 por
Sat Eve Post 225:36 Mr 14 '53 por
Science 105:576 My 30 '47; 109:227 Mr 4 '49; 113:111 F 2 '51
Time 60:57 Ag 18 '52
Washington (D.C.) Post Mag p24 S 19 '54 por

American Men of Science (1949)
Libby, W. F. Radiocarbon Dating (1952)
Who's Who in America, 1954-55

LIBERACE, (WLADZIU VALENTINO) (lĭb″ĕr-ä′chē) May 16, 1919- Pianist; television personality

Address: b. c/o Guild Films, 420 Madison Ave., New York 17; h. Sherman Oaks, Calif.

"Well, I'm an entertainer and concert pianist—although certain music critics have disagreed about the latter," says Liberace, often called television's first genuine matinee idol. In the two years since he began distribution of his filmed television series he has become the center of a lively national controversy between his critics and his loyal and vociferous fans.

His over 180 sponsors (savings banks, beer and paper manufacturers, automobile companies, and undertakers) credit him with bringing them over $50,000,000 worth of new business in one year. *Life* magazine reported him in 1953 to be "the biggest solo attraction in U.S. concert halls" and "one of the biggest sellers of record albums." His concert in Madison Square Garden in New York City in May 1954 drew a capacity audience.

Referring to much adverse criticism from music critics and television columnists, Liberace has remarked, "Wisecracks. . .lifted my income from $150 a week to more than $1,000,000 a year—so why should I resent them?" (*Parade,* July 18, 1954). He likes to say that he and his brother George cry all the way to the bank and to dedicate his theme song, *I Don't Care,* to his critics.

Wladziu Valentino Liberace was born in West Allis, Wisconsin on May 16, 1919, one of the four children of Salvatore and Frances Liberace, and grew up in nearby West Milwaukee with his brothers George and Rudy and his sister Angelina. "In our house, music was as much a part of us as our conversation," Liberace related in *American Weekly* (July 18, 1954). His father, a native of Italy, played the French horn and later became a member of the Milwaukee Philharmonic Orchestra. His Polish-born mother was also of a musical family.

When Walter (as he was generally called in childhood) was four years old he played the piano by ear and at seven he began to study music with Florence Bettray Kelly. At first the elder Liberace discouraged his son's desire to be a pianist, but approved after Ignace Jan Paderewski, Poland's great pianist and statesman, had visited the Liberaces and praised Walter's playing. He later followed Paderewski's advice to make Liberace his legal name, although for some years in night club work he was billed as Walter Busterkeys.

The depression of the 1930's was a time of anxiety for the Liberaces. To keep her children in school Mrs. Liberace operated a grocery store and vegetable market in which Walter worked as a delivery clerk. The pianist still expresses gratitude to his mother for having treated and saved his hand when at sixteen a serious infection brought the threat of amputation.

After having played for the patrons of a Milwaukee ice cream parlor, seventeen-year-old Liberace was given the opportunity to perform with the WPA symphony orchestra, and won a scholarship to Wisconsin College of Music. He auditioned for the late Dr. Frederick Stock, conductor of the Chicago Symphony Orchestra; when the orchestra came to Milwaukee Dr. Stock arranged to have Liberace appear as piano soloist. In 1939 at a recital in La Crosse, Wisconsin, having learned that informality can entertain an audience, he played *Three Little Fishes* as an encore, with winks and smiles, and there, according to *Look* (June 29, 1945), he caught from the applause "an idea on how to make piano playing pay." He discovered that the majority in his audiences wanted "comfortable middle-music, not cramping culture. . . People never asked for the classics or high jazz, but always for the sweet, sentimental numbers like *O Promise Me*" (*Collier's,* September 17, 1954).

From $35-a-week entertaining jobs in Milwaukee, Liberace went to New York City in 1940, where Mae Johnston, his agent, booked him as an intermission pianist at the Persian Room of the Hotel Plaza. Virginia Forbes of the New York *Sun* (July 5, 1945), thought him "gifted" and "brilliant," and wrote: "His entertainment has a firm foundation in classical music, yet this remarkable young pianist's own sense of showmanship keeps his program as sprightly as it should be for dinner and supper entertainment."

By 1947, when he again performed in the Persian Room, he had his own piano, an oversized Bluthner grand, insured for $150,000. On the top of the piano was the lighted candelabra that has been his trademark since he borrowed the idea from the film about Frédéric Chopin, *A Song to Remember.* Besides classical selections, he played *Mairzy Doats* in the various styles of Mozart, Chopin, Bach and Strauss. "There is no doubt about his being an accomplished pianist," commented New York *Herald Tribune* critic Bert McCord (October 15, 1947), "and he has the personality to sell his playing to a night club audience."

During World War II Liberace volunteered for military service, but was rejected because of a spinal injury. After the war his brother George, who had served with the Seabees, became his business manager as well as orchestra conductor and violinist. They appeared together for the next few years at many night clubs across the nation, Liberace developing his own interpretations of *September Song,* which he sang as well as played, and *Clair de Lune.*

In Los Angeles, California, where Liberace had moved with his mother and brother after his parents had agreed on a divorce, he was given his television debut in January 1952 by Don Fedderson, general manager of Station KLAC. His first sponsor, a month later, was the Citizens' National Bank which was deluged with new accounts started by people "just because we like Liberace." His concert appearance in April 1952 brought him $4,400 at the

Philharmonic Auditorium and $5,000 a few months later at the Hollywood Bowl.

"Still no national sponsor wanted me," Liberace wrote in *American Weekly* (July 18, 1954). "It took an advertising man named Reub Kaufman to make me a national figure. He got the idea that my program could be put on film, sent to any station, and sponsored by any local business concern." The Liberace show is filmed by Guild Films before a "live" audience at KLAC-TV's Music Hall Theatre. By recent count (*Collier's*, September 3, 1954) his weekly half-hour program is seen on 192 stations, more than the very popular *Dragnet* and *I Love Lucy*. During his first year on TV (1952) Liberace was awarded two TV Academy "Emmies," for the best entertainment program and outstanding male personality.

Deciding to concentrate on concert work, Liberace toured with an orchestra under the direction of his brother George. "In just a little over a year of concertizing Liberace has developed into one of the strongest concert attractions around today," *Variety* reported on September 23, 1953. For his thirty-three concerts during 1953 he drew $410,000 (*Pictorial Review*, May 23, 1954).

On September 25, 1953, he played to a capacity audience at New York's Carnegie Hall. In a review of Liberace's varied program, the New York *Times* critic found that the pianist "disclosed good fingers and prodigious skill at faking 'brilliant' runs up and down the keyboard. He has two styles of playing—fast, loud and energetic; and slow, with sentimentally exaggerated retards and accelerandos." Liberace also sang. "It was perhaps not great vocalism," the *Times* reviewer continued, "but the majority of concert pianists do not even try. Liberace tells jokes, too; family-humor sort of thing."

Liberace's well publicized concert triumph was his performance on May 26, 1954 at Madison Square Garden when his audience of more than 16,000 (13,000 women; 3,000 men) topped the box office record set by Paderewski in 1932. Liberace said, "Paderewski played for the masses and that's what I want to do." His several costumes for the concert reportedly cost him $3,500. One of them, a dress suit of white silk mohair, is familiar to his TV fans.

The "phenomenal" sale of his records accounted for over $100,000 of Liberace's 1953 income, *Ave Maria* being his most popular single record. According to *Time*, by early June 1954 his fans had bought some 400,000 albums, more than the number of Eddie Fisher records sold. His contract with Columbia Records is handled by Gabbe, Lutz & Heller, the firm that also manages his concert engagements.

Discussing Liberace's recordings, New York *Times* critic Howard Taubman noted that the pianist's version of Beethoven's *Moonlight Sonata* took less than four minutes to play (Horowitz needs the whole side of a long-playing record for it). "Compression is obviously one of Liberace's neatest tricks," he concluded (New York *Times Magazine*, March 14, 1954).

Liberace owns 51 per cent of the stock of International Artists, Ltd., an entertainment

LIBERACE

promotion corporation which supervises the distribution of his recorded programs to 150 or more radio stations, and which is managed by his lawyer, John R. Jacobs, Jr. Guild Films Company, Inc., produces and distributes his television films. Liberace Enterprises is a partnership composed of Liberace and his brother George.

Women comprised 81 per cent of his Madison Square Garden audience, "and most of them were over twenty-one," observed Paul V. Beckley in the New York *Herald Tribune* (May 27, 1954). Liberace has sought to show that he also has a sizable male following by asking the men in his audience to yell "hey" during a piano break.

The object of many satirical jokes and much parody on other TV shows, Liberace is said to take criticism good-humoredly. In January 1954 he appeared on a Jack Benny program that made fun of some of the pianist's stage devices.

As quoted in *Parade* (July 18, 1954), Liberace attributes much of his appeal to his love for people. "When I was a little boy I wanted to be a priest. Now, when I do a show, I exude love. This is something people like. I think every woman appreciates it. I'm interested in the way they dress, prepare a meal, decorate a home. . . . When I work I try to sparkle."

The pianist's religious bent is a dominant part of his personality. "Of all the vibrant people of the stage, Liberace is certainly one of the most deeply moved by human misery, and the most intensely convinced that he can somehow help the sick and the confused" (*Collier's*, September 3, 1954). He is said to be especially generous in his gifts to polio fund appeals.

Near Hollywood, in California's San Fernando Valley, Liberace lives with his mother in a $100,000 home, which he had a large personal share in designing and decorating. He has a piano-shaped swimming pool and a collection of

LIBERACE—*Continued*

miniature pianos given to him by fans and friends. Among his hobbies are cooking and painting.

"Lee," as the TV star is known to his friends, is six feet tall and weighs 175 pounds. He has dark brown eyes and black wavy hair that is becoming streaked with gray.

His aim, reportedly, is "to be to the piano what Bing Crosby is to the voice." Another goal he expresses in these words, "I'll never be satisfied until I can make people happy on an international scale."

Selected References

Am W p4+ Jl 18 '54 pors; p7 Jl 25 '54
Collier's 134:29+ S 3 pors; 72+ S 17 '54 pors
Life 35:88+ D 7 '53 pors
New Yorker 30:23+ Je 5 '54
Newsweek 43:96 F 22 '54 por
Radio-TV Mirror 41:41+ D '53 pors
Time 62:51 O 5 '53 por; 63:50 Je 7 '54

LINDBERGH, CHARLES A(UGUSTUS, JR.) Feb. 4, 1902- Aviator

Address: h. Scott's Cove, Darien, Conn.

NOTE: This biography supersedes the article which appeared in *Current Biography* in 1941.

Holder of the Wright Brothers Memorial Trophy "for significant public service of enduring value to aviation in the United States," Charles A. Lindbergh established his place in history in May 1927 when he made the first successful flight across the Atlantic in the Ryan monoplane "Spirit of St. Louis."

He is the author of the current bestseller *The Spirit of St. Louis* (Scribner, 1953). He has been awarded the Congressional Medal of Honor and the Distinguished Service Cross, and has contributed much valuable research and exploratory work to the United States Air Force.

Colonel Lindbergh was advanced to the rank of Brigadier General, Air Force Reserve, on April 6, 1954. He was awarded a Pulitzer Prize on May 3 for a "distinguished American biography." He also won the 1953 Daniel Guggenheim International Aviation Award "for pioneering achievements in flight and air navigation."

Born in Detroit, Michigan on February 4, 1902, Charles Augustus Lindbergh, Jr. was the only child of the late Charles Augustus Lindbergh and the former Evangeline Lodge Land. He is of English, Irish and French ancestry on the maternal side. His father was born in Stockholm, Sweden and his paternal grandfather was a member of the Swedish Parliament and secretary to the King of Sweden.

At the age of two months Charles Lindbergh was brought to a farm near Little Falls, Minnesota, where his father (who had become a naturalized citizen) practiced law. The family lived there until 1907, when the elder Lindbergh, a Republican, was elected from the Sixth District of Minnesota to the United States House of Representatives. He remained a member of Congress until 1917 and frequently expressed his isolationist sentiments.

When Charles was eight, he entered the Force School in Washington, D.C.; thereafter, he attended a number of schools, both public and private, before being graduated from the Little Falls High School in 1918. His main preoccupations at that time were with motorcycles, automobiles, pistol shooting and machinery. In 1920 he entered the University of Wisconsin in Madison, Wisconsin where he became a member of the Reserve Officers Training Corps and of the rifle and pistol teams, but admittedly found studying irksome.

Fascinated by aviation since his first glimpse of an airplane near Washington, D.C. in 1912, Lindbergh decided to make flying his vocation, and in 1922 left the university to enter the flying school conducted by the Nebraska Aircraft Corporation in Lincoln, Nebraska.

The young trainee made his first airplane flight on April 9, 1922 as a passenger in a Lincoln Standard plane. In the ensuing month, after less than eight hours of instruction, he served as mechanic and helper to another aviator, E. G. Bahl, on a "barnstorming" trip through southern Nebraska on which they took passengers for five or ten minute flights at five dollars apiece. In June he teamed with the "stunt" flier, Charles Harden, and made his first double parachute jump.

After additional exhibition trips in partnership with H. J. Lynch, Lindbergh bought a surplus wartime plane from the United States government for $500 and took his first solo flight in April 1923. On March 19, 1924 he enrolled at Brooks Field, Texas as a flying cadet in the United States Air Service Reserve. About one year later, when his training was completed, he was commissioned a second lieutenant in the United States Air Service Reserve, and subsequently became a captain. In November 1925 he was commissioned a first lieutenant in the Missouri National Guard and later was advanced to a colonel. After more barnstorming, Lindbergh took his first flight as an Air Mail Service pilot on the Chicago-St. Louis route on April 15, 1926.

In the autobiographical book entitled *"We"* (Putnam, 1927), Charles A. Lindbergh has recorded that it was during a night air mail flight in the autumn of 1926 that he first seriously considered attempting to win the $25,000 prize offered by Raymond B. Orteig in 1919 for the first non-stop flight from New York to Paris.

After many difficulties and much discouragement, Lindbergh secured from a group of civic-minded St. Louis, Missouri, businessmen sufficient financial backing to purchase and condition a Ryan monoplane with a single radial air-cooled engine. Christening this craft the "Spirit of St. Louis," he "took off" from the factory at San Diego, California on May 10, 1927 and after a stop-over at St. Louis, reached Curtiss Field, Long Island, New York on May 12. By this flight, Lindbergh established a new transcontinental record of twenty-one hours and twenty minutes.

On the misty, rainy morning of May 20 at 7:52 A.M. Lindbergh, carrying only sandwiches for food, left Roosevelt Field, Long Island on the flight which ended at Le Bourget airport near Paris on the following day, after a coverage of an estimated 3,610 miles in thirty-three hours, twenty-nine minutes and thirty seconds.

Lindbergh's pioneer achievement, which is treated briefly in *"We"* but is very fully described in the subsequent *The Spirit of St. Louis,* fired the imagination of the world, and brought the flier the honors of official governmental receptions in Paris, Brussels and London, and decoration as *chevalier* of the Legion of Honor in France, the Order of Leopold in Belgium, and the Royal Air Cross in Great Britain.

In an official greeting at Washington, D.C. the young flier was awarded the Distinguished Flying Cross and promoted from captain to colonel in the Air Corps Reserve.

The aviator was given enthusiastic receptions in numerous other American cities including St. Louis and New York (where he received the State Medal for Valor). Decorations and awards later conferred on Colonel Lindbergh have included the Congressional Medal of Honor (by special Act of Congress), the Langley Medal of the Smithsonian Institution, the Hubbard Medal of the National Geographic Society, and the Cross of Honor of the United States Flag Association.

The air tour of the United States which Lindbergh made after his return from Paris was accomplished under the auspices of the Daniel Guggenheim Foundation for the Promotion of Aeronautics and took the flier and his now world-famous monoplane to some seventy-five cities. In his numerous addresses Lindbergh spoke of "the limitless future of the sky" and urged the construction of airports and the expansion of commercial aviation.

At the invitation of President Plutarco Calles of Mexico, Lindbergh made in December 1927 a non-stop flight from Washington, D.C. to Mexico City, covering the 2100 miles in twenty-seven hours and ten minutes. He extended his air tour to cover "good-will" visits to Central America, the West Indies and Cuba, and in recognition of this, was awarded the Woodrow Wilson Medal and $25,000. At a reception given in Mexico City by United States Ambassador Dwight W. Morrow, Lindbergh met the latter's daughter, Anne Spencer Morrow, who became his wife on May 27, 1929.

Colonel Lindbergh became associated with the Transcontinental Air Transport Company (he later became chairman of its technical committee) and also served as technical adviser to Pan American Airways. "He helped," Lauren D. Lyman has noted in the *Saturday Evening Post* of April 4, 1953, "build greater safety into equipment and flying procedures. He surveyed new domestic and Latin American air routes. He explored and pioneered the Alaskan route to Asia, and the Labrador-Iceland route to Europe which is in use today." Mrs. Lindbergh accompanied her husband on many

W. C. Persons

BRIG. GEN. CHARLES A. LINDBERGH

of these flights—to Mexico, to the Orient, and to the countries bordering the Atlantic Ocean.

The young couple's happiness was shattered in 1932 by the kidnapping and death of their first child, Charles Augustus Lindbergh III. A carpenter, Bruno Richard Hauptmann, was convicted for the crime which led to the enactment of the "Lindbergh law."

Federal laws passed in 1932 and 1934 prescribed severe penalties for interstate abduction, with the death sentence for cases in which the victim had been harmed or not returned before the sentence was passed, and providing that the Federal Bureau of Investigation may create a presumption that a kidnapping case involves interstate transportation seven days after the act has been committed.

In December 1935, after the trial and conviction of Hauptmann, the Lindberghs went to live in England, and later moved to France where Lindbergh resumed work with the scientist Dr. Alexis Carrel whom he had first known at the Rockefeller Institute in New York in 1930 and for whom Lindbergh had designed a perfusion pump which greatly aided Carrel with his scientific experiments. As a result of further collaboration between the two men, their book, the *Culture of Organs* was published by Harper's in 1938.

At the suggestion of Major Truman Smith, the United States military attaché in Berlin, Hermann Goering, at that time commander-in-chief of the *Luftwaffe,* invited Lindbergh to Germany to view the development of the German air force. The flier and Smith wrote reports which gave the American government much valuable information on the strength and condition of the *Luftwaffe.* Lindbergh made surveys of air power in France, the U.S.S.R., and England.

Returning to the United States in the spring of 1939, Colonel Lindbergh went on active duty

LINDBERGH, CHARLES A.—*Continued*

with the Air Corps and remained in uniform until the outbreak of World War II in Europe in September. A member of the America First Committee, he returned to reserve status in order to engage in a speechmaking campaign in which he urged his country to avoid involvement in the war.

"When President Roosevelt made a remark at one of his press conferences which, Lindbergh felt, carried the implication that his conduct was treasonable," states *Newsweek* (December 5, 1949), "he resigned his commission as a colonel in the reserve." This was in April of 1941, but after the Pearl Harbor attack in December, Lindbergh again offered himself for active service, asserting that "now that war has come, we must meet it as united Americans, regardless of our attitude in the past."

Applying to the War Department, he was told that this statement was "not enough," and that he must completely recant his earlier pronouncements, a condition with which he was unable conscientiously to comply (*Saturday Evening Post,* April 4, 1953). The flier then offered his services in a civilian capacity to both the United Aircraft and the Wright Aeronautical corporations, but when these companies "sought Washington clearance" they were "told that employing Lindbergh would be frowned upon" (*Newsweek,* December 5, 1949).

Henry Ford, however, risked White House disapproval and engaged Lindbergh as a consultant at the Willow Run plant near Detroit. By 1943 the "Lone Eagle" was also working with the United Aircraft Company and was specializing there in perfecting the Navy's "Corsair" fighter.

In the following year, Lindbergh went to the Pacific theater of operations as a civilian technician. In the course of a six months stay, he flew some fifty missions and became unofficially credited with having shot down a Japanese plane.

After the capitulation of Germany he spent two months in that country with a United States Navy mission sent to study enemy developments in jet aircraft, rocket and guided missile warfare. With the conclusion of the war in the Pacific against Japan, Lindbergh retired to private life. Lindbergh later issued a statement reiterating his belief that "we could have prevented the war in Western Europe" and that he had been right in advocating that "England, France and America build their strength but refrain from war while Nazi Germany and Communist Russia fought out their totalitarian ideas" (New York *Times,* April 15, 1947).

At his new home in Darien, Connecticut Lindbergh wrote *Of Flight and Life* which was published by Scribner's in 1948 and was condensed in the *Reader's Digest.* This brief, provocative book coupled reminiscences of wartime with what a New York *Times* reviewer characterized as "an often savage attack on scientific materialism, a doctrine to which he once subscribed."

It was disclosed in August 1948 that Lindbergh was working without compensation as a research consultant for the Air Force on "high altitude and 'cruise control' flight problems affecting heavy bomber engines" and that he had "already given . . . invaluable help in stepping up the efficiency of engines and cutting gasoline consumption in heavy bombardment aircraft" (New York *Times*).

"For more than two years," states Lauren D. Lyman in the *Saturday Evening Post* of April 4, 1953, "he visited air bases all over America, in Alaska, Japan, Europe and the Philippines. He flew the new jet fighters and went with bomber training missions over the polar wastes. His work since the war is a story in itself, but not one of which much can be told now, because so much of it is still in the secret category."

When the Wright Brothers Memorial Trophy was awarded to Lindbergh on December 17, 1949, he referred in his speech of acceptance to having "misgivings about today's reliance on scientific achievements." "I am convinced," he asserted, "that man cannot thrive indefinitely in the hothouse atmosphere we are creating. I believe that for permanent survival we must balance science with other qualities of life, qualities of body and spirit as well as those of mind. . . ."

On the twenty-fifth anniversary of his solo flight from New York to Paris, the flier's boyhood home in Little Falls, Minnesota was dedicated as a part of Lindbergh State Park.

The "Lone Eagle's" fourth book, described as his "autobiography up to 1927" appeared in ten installments in the *Saturday Evening Post* under the title "33 Hours to Paris." It was renamed *The Spirit of St. Louis* when published in book form by Scribner's in September, 1953 when it was a Book-of-the-Month Club selection.

This work, also condensed in the October 1953 number of the *Reader's Digest,* recalls in great detail the aviator's thoughts and emotions during his history-making flight, with revealing "flashbacks" to his boyhood and early years as a "barnstormer" and airmail pilot. The book covers much the same ground as the earlier *"We"* but has a different emphasis and a considerable difference in style.

Academic honors conferred on Charles Lindbergh have been the degree of Master of Aeronautics from New York University in 1928, the LL.D. degree from both Northwestern University and the University of Wisconsin in the same year, and an honorary M.S. from Princeton University in 1931.

The Lindbergh's have five children: Jon Morrow, Land Morrow, Scott, Reeve, and Anne Spencer. Lauren D. Lyman, who has known Lindbergh since 1927 states that the flier has changed little in the past twenty-six years. "His hair has thinned a bit in front and shows a trace of gray," Lyman has written, "but his tall figure is still a hard, lean 175 pounds. His distance vision is still far keener than normal. He has no objection to others smoking and drinking, but has always abstained from both himself—as a matter of taste but not principle, he says." He is studious and well-read, enjoys talk, music and books, and with his family, delights in long walks in the country.

Selected References (see also references listed in the July 1941 biographical sketch)

Aero Digest 64:18+ My '52 pors
Am Mag 127:16+ Ap '39 pors; 132:106+ Ag '41 pors
Collier's 117:11+ F 16 '46 por; 117:26+ F 23 '46 por; 119:18+ My 3 '47 por
Life 11:65+ Ag 11 '41 pors
N Y Times Mag p14 Ja 23 '49 por
New Yorker 6:26+ S 20 '30; 6:30+ S 27 '30
Newsweek 34:23+ D 5 '49 pors
Sat Eve Post 213:12+ D 28 '40 pors; 213:27+ Je 21 '41 pors; 224:26+ Mr 8 '52 por; 225:22+ Ap 4 '53 pors-to and including 225:36+ Je 13 '53 por
Time 27:34+ Ja '36 por; 31:40+ Je 13 '38 por; 33:15+ My 8 '39; 37:17+ My 5 '41; 52:70+ S 6 '48 por; 62:116+ S 14 '53 por
U S News 36:8 F 26 '54

America's Young Men, 1938-39
Fife, G. B. Lindbergh, the Lone Eagle (1927)
Fraser, C. C. Famous American Flyers (1944)
Haines, L. and D. Lindberghs (1931)
International Who's Who, 1953
Lindbergh, A. M. Listen! the Wind (1938)
Lindbergh, A. M. North to the Orient (1935)
Lindbergh, C. A. Spirit of St. Louis (1953)
Lindbergh, C. A. "We" (1927)
Mussey, V. T. H. Flying Adventures of Lindbergh (1933)
National Cyclopædia of American Biography, Current Volume E (1937-38)
O'Brien, P. J. Lindberghs (1935)
Snyder, E. E. Biology in the Making (1940)
Stone, I. and Kennedy, R. eds. We Speak for Ourselves (1950)
Who's Who in America, 1952-53
Who's Who, 1953
World Biography (1948)

LIPMANN, FRITZ (ALBERT) June 12, 1899- Biochemist; university professor

Address: b. c/o Biochemical Research Laboratory, Massachusetts General Hospital, Boston 14, Mass.; h. 100 Revere St., Boston 14, Mass.

For his "discovery of co-enzyme A and its significance in the intermediary metabolism," Professor Fritz Lipmann of Harvard Medical School and Massachusetts General Hospital was awarded the 1953 Nobel Prize in physiology and medicine jointly with Professor H. A. Krebs of England. Educated in German universities, and for seven years engaged in biological research work in Copenhagen, Lipmann has made significant contributions to the understanding of the life processes which occur in human cells.

Harvard Univ. News, Walter R. Fleischer
DR. FRITZ LIPMANN

The members of the Nobel Prize committee for medicine selected Lipmann because he "isolated and identified co-enzyme A in 1945 as a crucial element in providing usable energy for the body-building process" and contributed in demonstrating how "co-enzyme A brought forth the construction of such things as fatty acids and steroids necessary to the body's renewal and growth" (New York *Times,* October 23, 1953).

Fritz Albert Lipmann, the son of Leopold and Gertrud (Lachmanski) Lipmann, was born June 12, 1899 in Königsberg, Prussia (since 1946, Kaliningrad, U.S.S.R.). Beginning his medical education at the universities of Königsberg, Berlin, and Munich from 1917 to 1922, he received his M.D. degree from the University of Berlin in 1922. Planning a career in biochemistry, Dr. Lipmann returned to Königsberg for four years of graduate study and received a Ph.D. degree in chemistry at Berlin in 1927.

He then became a research assistant at the Kaiser-Wilhelm-Institut in the laboratory of Otto Meyerhof (Meyerhof was co-winner of the 1922 Nobel Prize in medicine for his work on the lactic acid transformation in muscles). At the institute, Lipmann began investigating the mechanism of fluoride effects; his first paper showed that under anaerobic conditions, lactic acid does not disappear in muscle tissue in the presence of sodium fluoride. During the next two years he established that the oxidation quotient of lactic acid is greatly reduced by fluoride, and that in frog muscle no resynthesis of lactic acid occurs in the presence of the fluoride ion.

From 1930 to 1932, Fritz Lipmann was Dr. Albert Fischer's assistant in tissue culture at the Kaiser-Wilhelm-Institut in Berlin. Having

LIPMANN, FRITZ—*Continued*

won a Rockefeller fellowship, Lipmann came to New York in 1931 and began to work on phosphorus mechanisms at the Rockefeller Institute for Medical Research in the laboratory of Dr. P. A. Levene. Returning to Europe in 1932, the biochemist went to Copenhagen, where he spent the next seven years as research associate with Dr. Albert Fischer in the Biological Institute of the Carlsberg Foundation.

In 1939 Lipmann came to the United States as the world war threatened Denmark's neutrality. Nearly penniless when he arrived, he found that licensing and immigration restrictions limited the possibilities of finding employment. However, he obtained a research fellowship in the biochemistry department of Cornell University Medical College.

Since 1941, Dr. Lipmann has been the senior biochemist at the Massachusetts General Hospital. He became an associate professor at the Harvard Medical School in 1946 and since 1949 has been a full professor of biological chemistry there. During the war, Professor Lipmann was a civilian scientist with the Office of Scientific Research and Development.

The noted biochemist, Dr. Carl Neuberg, stated in 1937 that Dr. Lipmann observed that a transphosphorylation, brought about by cocarboxylase, is essential to pyruvate oxidation. This started Lipmann on a series of investigations, during which he developed the ideas of phosphate bond energy and energy rich phosphate bond energy. The ordinary ester linkage has a bond energy of 3,000 calories while 11,000 calories are liberated during the hydrolysis of energy rich phosphates, such as creatine-phosphoric acid, adenosine-polyphosphates, and acyl-phosphates.

Lipmann has listed his chief research interests as energy metabolism, metabolic function of B vitamins, flocculation of iron hydroxide soles, and the fluoride effect on glycolysis and fermentation. Summarizing Lipmann's work at the time he received the Carl Neuberg Medal of the American Society of European Chemists and Pharmacists in 1948, Neuberg related that Lipmann studied the phosphoric acid linkage in phosphoproteins and determined its position in the hydroxylated amino acids. He isolated serine phosphoric acid, whose product, phosphoglyceric acid, plays a dominant role in carbohydrate metabolism.

Dr. Lipmann in 1940 proved the existence of acetyl phosphate; he isolated it in 1942 and in 1944 he and his co-workers were able to synthesize it and establish a method for its determination. He developed the "metabolic dynamo" in 1941. His later work includes research into the structure of cancer cells and investigations into pantothenic acid. He isolated co-enzyme A in 1945 and identified it as a key element in providing useful energy in the body in part by "converting phosphate bond energy into other useful forms of chemical energy."

Most recently, he has been investigating the mode of action of the energy-regulating thyroid hormone and has written of this work: "Our recent limited success with the thyroid hormone makes us now hopeful that sooner or later the biochemist may be able to break open the hormone field in a fashion similar to the opening up of the vitamin field."

Lipmann's investigation and isolation of the co-enzyme which aids the chemical reactions by which energy is released in the cells of the body, supplements the information on Kreb's cycle of the transformation of food into physical energy in human cells. Although Lipmann and Krebs worked independently, the Caroline Institute of Medicine chose to award the 1953 Nobel Prize in physiology and medicine to both biochemists.

Interviewed after the announcement of the Nobel award, Fritz Lipmann said of his research methods: "You have to follow your nose; you don't map it out. You try one experiment, then another, and bring some sense into it."

The University of Marseille awarded Lipmann an honorary M.D. in 1947; he received an honorary M.A. from Harvard in 1949 and an honorary Sc.D. from the University of Chicago in June 1953. Lipmann received in 1948 the Mead Johnson and Company award for outstanding work on Vitamin B-complex. He is a fellow of the Danish Royal Academy of Sciences and the New York Academy of Sciences. He is a member of the National Academy of Sciences, American Chemical Society, Harvey Society, American Association for the Advancement of Science, Society of Biological Chemists, Biochemical Society, Society for General Microbiology, Society of American Bacteriologists, and Society of General Physiologists.

Dr. Lipmann has written over 160 articles in such scientific journals as the *Journal of Biological Chemistry, Journal of the American Chemical Society, Annual Review of Biochemistry,* and *Federation Proceedings.*

Among the articles which Dr. Lipmann has written for *Nature* are: "Coupling Between Pyruvic Acid Dehydrogenation and Adenylic Acid Phosphorylation" (February 18, 1939), "Coloured Intermediate on Reduction of Vitamin B_1" (November 13, 1937), and "Fermentation of Phosphogluconic Acid" (October 3, 1936). His later articles include: "Biosynthetic Mechanisms" (*Harvey Lectures,* 1950) and (with G. D. Novelli) "Catalytic Function of Co-enzyme A in Citric Acid Synthesis" (*Journal of Biological Chemistry,* January, 1950).

Married to Elfreda M. Hall of Defiance, Ohio on June 21, 1931, Lipmann has a son, Stephen Hall. He became a naturalized U.S. citizen in 1944. Brown-haired and brown-eyed, he lists music as his favorite recreation. Fritz Lipmann has been described as an "intense, dedicated scientist" who is "unaffected and friendly."

References

Chem and Eng N 26:860 Mr 22 '48
N Y Herald Tribune p5 O 23 '53
N Y Times p15 O 21 '53; p21 O 23 '53 por
N Y World-Telegram p1 O 22 '53 por
Newsweek 42:86 N 2 '53 por

American Men of Science (1949)
Chemical Who's Who, 1951
Who's Who in America, 1952-53
World Biography (1948)

LOCKE, ALAIN (LE ROY) Sept. 13, 1886-June 9, 1954 Educator; author; received education at Harvard University, Oxford University (Rhodes Scholar), and University of Berlin; was assistant professor of philosophy and education (1912-1916) and professor of philosophy (1917-1953) at Howard University; he was exchange professor, Fisk University (1927-1928); Inter-American Exchange Professor to Haiti (1943); was visiting professor to University of Wisconsin (1945-1946), and New School for Social Research (1947); author of numerous books about the Negro race, its culture and relations with other races, including *The New Negro* (1925) and *The Negro in Art* (1941); was recently a contributing editor to *Survey Graphic*. See *Current Biography,* (Jan.) 1944.

Obituary

N Y Times p31 Je 10 '54

LODER, JOHN DE VERE *See* Wakehurst, J. de V. L., 2d Baron

LODGE, HENRY CABOT, JR. July 5, 1902- United States Government official; former United States Senator from Massachusetts

Address: b. c/o United States Mission to the United Nations, 2 Park Ave., New York 16; h. 275 Hale St., Beverly, Mass.

NOTE: This biography supersedes the article which appeared in *Current Biography* in 1943.

The United States Representative to the United Nations and Representative in the Security Council (which carries the rank of Ambassador) is Henry Cabot Lodge, Jr., who believes that the United Nations is America's "best hope" for peace. Succeeding Warren R. Austin to this post in January 1953, Lodge has been the spokesman for the U.S. Department of State's policy that the Communist regime in China should not be recognized by the United Nations since it was an aggressor in Korea and does not represent the will of the people.

For thirteen years Lodge was a United States Senator (Republican) from Massachusetts; previously he had been a reporter on the Boston *Transcript* and later on the political news and editorial staff of the New York *Herald Tribune*. His military service in World War II and world events led to his belief that America's only hope for survival is in unified efforts for peace through an international governing agency, pledged jointly to unite to combat aggression.

Born at Nahant, Massachusetts on July 5, 1902, Henry Cabot Lodge, Jr. is the elder son of George Cabot and Mathilda Elizabeth Frelinghuysen (Davis) Lodge, and the grandson of Henry Cabot Lodge, U.S. Senator from Massachusetts, who served continuously from 1893 to 1924. George Cabot Lodge, who was a poet and his father's secretary, died in August, 1909.

HENRY CABOT LODGE, JR.

Thereafter Henry Cabot, his younger brother John Davis (now Governor of Connecticut), and their sister Helena were brought up by their mother and her father-in-law, at whose home they "sat on the knee" of two presidents, Theodore Roosevelt and William Howard Taft. Young Cabot Lodge was prepared for college at the Middlesex School in Concord, Massachusetts, from which he was graduated in 1920.

During this period Senator Henry Cabot Lodge fought successfully against ratification by the United States of the Covenant of the League of Nations. "My grandfather contended that the League of Nations Covenant should not be linked with the Versailles Treaty," his namesake observed in *Life* (September 14, 1953. "The greatest point at issue" was Article X of the Covenant which would have pledged the United States "to give aid in the preservation of the territory and political independence of all League members." The elder Lodge's position was that all military action on the part of the United States should first be approved by Congress.

Young Lodge entered Harvard University where he completed the requirements in three instead of the usual four years. He rowed as captain for his class crew, took part in the dramatic productions and contributed to the *Harvard Advocate*. "Above all," wrote his Harvard contemporary, John Mason Brown, in the *Saturday Review* (July 18, 1953), "he liked to talk . . . Bull sessions were his meat, political arguments his delight."

Having been told by his grandfather that journalism was "at least the equal of the law as training for political life," young Lodge became a reporter for the Boston *Transcript* in the summer of 1923. He waited until 1924 to receive the B.A. degree, *cum laude,* with his own class, and then joined the staff of the New York *Herald Tribune.*

Lodge reported on the political conventions of 1924, 1928 and 1932. One of his assignments

LODGE, HENRY CABOT, JR.—*Continued*
was the Coolidge Commission's "restoration of orderly government" in Nicaragua. He also covered the London Naval Conference in 1930, interviewed Benito Mussolini, and subsequently visited Malaya, the East Indies and the Philippines "to observe the different methods of government" in British, Dutch and American dependencies.

Lodge's article "The Meaning of the Kellogg Treaty" in *Harper's* for December 1928 was critical of that pact as tending to make Europeans believe that the United States was prepared to cooperate in League of Nations sanctions against any aggressors. His article, "Our Failure in the Philippines," in *Harper's* (January 1930) assailed the Jones act of 1916 and advised the United States to heed European (and particularly Dutch) experience in colonial administration.

Later, Lodge became an editorial writer for the New York *Herald Tribune*. After a leave of absence from the paper, he completed his book, *Cult of Weakness* (Houghton, 1932). In the book he relates how pacifist groups had hampered U.S. foreign policy since World War I.

In 1932 Lodge became a Republican candidate to represent his district in the lower chamber of the General Court of Massachusetts. He was elected after a door-to-door campaign which took him out of what John Mason Brown characterized as the "protected . . . society of Beacon Hill and Nahant" and into the homes of average Americans. During his four years in the Massachusetts House of Representatives he served as chairman of the committee on labor and industry and has been credited with "putting through" legislation which liberalized the Massachusetts workmen's compensation law. He was re-elected in 1934.

For thirteen months before the senatorial race of 1936 Lodge toured the state in an attempt to secure the Republican nomination. "The reason I won," he stated, "was that I went into farmhouse kitchens and sat and talked with the men who were going to be delegates." "Little Boy Blue", as his adversary Governor James Michael Curley called him, defeated Curley by 135,000 votes in November 1936. Lodge was the only Republican at that time to win a Senate seat away from the Democrats.

Only thirty-four when he entered Congress, the "boy wonder" proved in domestic matters far less hostile to the New Deal than most of the Republican minority. He went on record for the Wagner act, Wages and Hours Act, and in 1939 he sought to amend the Social Security Act to increase old age assistance payments.

His views on foreign policy were generally in accord with the isolationists. In May 1940 he opposed aid to Britain. He argued against American responsibility for the protection of the Philippines and he wrote of the suicidal character of the "theory of starting a war to stop a war" as manifested in the "desire for American membership in the League of Nations." On the other hand, the Senator supported strengthening the national war potential by voting for naval expansion in 1938, selective service in 1940 and Lend-Lease in 1941. He proposed that we keep sales of airplanes to foreign purchasers from interfering with Navy deliveries.

A member of the Army Reserve since 1924, Senator Lodge had reached the grade of captain when on August 1, 1941 he went on "extended active duty." In the following year he was sent to Libya with several tank detachments on active combat duty with the British Eighth Army. Promoted to the rank of major, Lodge witnessed the retreat from Tobruk to El Alamein. In July 1942, after Major Lodge reported on his mission to the Armed Forces, Secretary of War Henry L. Stimson denied his request for further service, stating that "skilled legislators who fully comprehend the requirements of military service are as important to the Army as soldiers in combat."

Accordingly, Lodge resumed his legislative duties until February 1944 when he resigned from the Senate in order to go on combat duty in the Army, being the first U.S. Senator since the Civil War to leave the Senate in order to go to war. (Lodge had been re-elected in November 1942, and in the summer of the following year had been one of five Senators who made a 41,000-mile tour of the war fronts).

Lodge served the Fourth Corps as deputy chief of staff in Italy in 1944 and was made chief of the Combat Liaison Section of General Jacob L. Devers' southern group of armies in France and Germany. When his duty ended on December 2, 1945, he held the rank of lieutenant colonel and for his war service he received the Bronze Star and Legion of Merit. His foreign awards were the Legion of Honor (rank of chevalier), Croix de Guerre (with palm) and Order of Polonia Restituta.

In the *Saturday Review* John Mason Brown observed that "the Lodge who came back [from the war] . . . was not the Lodge who had gone overseas." This was made clear in February, 1946, when Lodge addressed the Minneapolis Foreign Policy Association. "The ideal of a provincial nation . . . has given way to the realization that we have become the world's greatest power," he declared. In approving the United Nations organization, he pronounced it "our best hope" and asserted that "we must give it things to do, so that its muscles will grow strong with exercise" (*Time,* February 11, 1946).

After being re-elected to the Senate in November 1946, he became a member of the Senate Foreign Relations Committee and Rules and Administration Committee. During the first session of the Eightieth Congress he offered amendments to the Greek-Turkish aid bill which would require those governments to establish a tax program based on ability to pay, and to appoint a Senate-approved administrator for the program. He voted in favor of the Greek-Turkish aid bill and confirmation of the Italian peace treaty.

In the Eightieth Congress, the Senator concurred in the Taft-Hartley bill and the move to override the President's veto of that bill, although he opposed inclusion in the new labor law of proposals to permit injunctive action by private employers against jurisdictional strikes and to outlaw the union shop.

In the first session of the Eighty-first Congress, he supported ratification of the North Atlantic Treaty and he co-sponsored the Lodge-Gassett constitutional amendment to do away with the electoral college. This eventually passed the Senate in 1950 by 64 votes to 27 but was defeated in the House by 210 to 134.

In an article "Modernize the G.O.P." (*Atlantic,* March 1950), the Senator suggested a domestic program which included a revision of the tax laws "to reward those businesses which lower prices, increase production . . . and keep their people at work even though they are old" and to "ease the taxes on young people who are starting new business ventures," eliminate the poll tax, make lynching a Federal offense, and end racial segregation in the armed forces and in housing projects and educational aid projects financed by the Federal government. In regard to health problems the Senator recommended action to increase the number of young doctors with inducements "so that they will practice in places where they are most needed" and lowering hospital bills by "using public funds for hospital construction and for . . . the care of the indigent."

The Senator was appointed by President Harry S. Truman in August, 1950 as an alternate delegate to the fifth General Assembly of the United Nations. In his first major speech before that body he answered Soviet charges of American warmongering so effectively that Andrei Y. Vishinsky was said to have "turned brick red as he listened."

In the Senate debate in July 1951 on defense appropriations, Lodge urged an Air Force of 150 groups, as against the ninety-five group force for which funds were asked. Later in the year he was credited with being "the first to charge publicly" that the "North Atlantic Treaty Organization was getting only one-fifth of the aid promised by the United States."

Lodge was named manager of a "Draft Eisenhower Movement for President" in November, 1951, and manager of the Eisenhower campaign after the general had finally agreed to permit the entering of his name in certain state primaries. While furthering the Eisenhower candidacy, Lodge neglected the repairing of political fences at home, where in seeking a third term to the Senate he was defeated by Congressman John F. Kennedy by 1,207,956 votes to 1,138,896.

On November 9, 1952 President-elect Eisenhower announced that he had appointed Lodge his "chief liaison officer on all government matters except the budget." Later it became known that the outgoing Senator from Massachusetts would, on the inauguration of the new Administration, assume the post of head of the United States Mission to the United Nations. In this office Henry Cabot Lodge, who holds the rank of Ambassador is one of the Administration's principal advisers in the formulation of foreign policy and, thus, attends Cabinet meetings.

Ambassador Lodge spoke to the General Assembly Political Committee in April 1953 on an American plan for the evacuation of Chinese Nationalist troops from Burma. On August 18, 1953 he presented the U.S. position on the exclusion of all nonbelligerents from the projected political peace conference on Korea. The Ambassador stated that "a large conference attended by many nations in which unanimity on all decisions is required would be a sure way not to get results" (New York *Herald Tribune,* August 19, 1953). The final vote on August 27 indicated that the move to include India had failed to secure the necessary two-thirds majority.

The Korean phase of the Geneva Conference on Far Eastern Affairs began on April 26, 1954. It was attended by eighteen nations that had participated in the Korean conflict as well as the U.S.S.R. On June 15 the U.N. Allies broke off the Korean discussions because the Communists had rejected "every effort to obtain agreement."

The purposes of the U.N. are, according to Lodge, "to maintain international peace and security; to develop friendly relations among nations based on the equal rights and self-determination of peoples and to take other appropriate measures to strengthen peace; to achieve cooperation in solving international economic, social, cultural, and humanitarian problems. . . .

"When the United Nations was founded, it was assumed that the great allies of World War II would stay together to keep peace. But the Soviet Union became hostile to the free world and, by its abuse of the veto, caused the Security Council to become less and less active, with the result that the General Assembly has become the busy place. (A veto-proof method has at last been evolved for bringing a collective defense program into being by recommendations passed by a two-thirds vote of the General Assembly. . . .)

"In the modern world there is already a growing knowledge that countries have many common *practical interests.* But the growth of a common sense of *justice* seems to come more slowly . . . the essential first step is a world forum where issues can be debated and put to a vote, and where *world public opinion* can develop. The General Assembly is thus a place where they 'talk and vote' . . . it is by talking and voting that you sometimes avert war, and it is by talking and voting that you build a world sense of right and wrong" (*The Reference Shelf; The UN Today,* H. W. Wilson Co., 1954).

In his article "An Answer to Critics of the U.N." (New York *Times Magazine,* November 22, 1953), Lodge asserted that the "United Nations stands between us and World War III." The Ambassador pointed to several of the U.N. projects oriented toward peace, among which is "The United Nations Technical Assistance Program [which] has put 1,500 experts of more than sixty nationalities to work helping to drain the swamps, irrigate the deserts, eliminate disease, and increase the food

LODGE, HENRY CABOT, JR.—*Continued*

supply in underdeveloped areas. This program has nothing to do with handouts, it is real sharing.

"The United States, with only one-sixth of the world's population but with much of the world's wealth, has a great deal to gain by furthering the United Nations efforts to raise living standards in underdeveloped areas because persons in these areas . . . will be able and eager to protect . . . themselves when their way of life is threatened."

In the New York *Herald Tribune* (October 8, 1954 Lodge reported on U.N. activities since the Eisenhower Administration took office. He stated in part: "On the Korean War the United Nations General Assembly noted with approval the armistice agreement. . . . By this agreement the Communist aggressors had gained not one square inch of territory, and many thousands of former soldiers in the Communist armies were given the right to choose freedom. . . . On Guatemala, in two meetings . . . of the . . . Security Council, we decisively defeated a Soviet attempt to perpetuate Moscow's domination of the Guatemalan government. . . .

"On world Communism we have stepped up our efforts in the United Nations, with a world audience listening, to remind free peoples of the evils of the Communist system . . . the Communist attempt to seat Red China has been voted down twenty-three times. . . . President Eisenhower . . . appeared . . . before the . . . General Assembly and made a bold proposal—an international agency to develop the peaceful uses of atomic energy for all mankind."

Henry Cabot Lodge, Jr. and Emily Esther Sears, the daughter of a Boston physician, were married on July 1, 1926. They have two sons, George Cabot and Henry Sears, and three grandchildren. Their permanent home is the "French provincial mansion overlooking Massachusetts Bay" in Beverly. "The Army, in which he now holds the rank of brigadier general, is Cabot's one and only hobby," wrote Leigh White (*Saturday Evening Post,* May 31, 1952). "He enjoys singing barbershop melodies with his sons . . . and he amuses his office staff by the way he whistles at his work." The diplomat has light blue eyes and is over six feet tall and keeps in trim by following a "rigorous diet" and doing "setting-up exercises."

Selected References (See also references listed in 1943 biographical sketch)

Collier's 119:20+ Ja 18 '47 pors
Coronet 35:115+ F '54 por
N Y Post Mag p24 Ap 25 '53 por
N Y Times p5 F 5 '44; p63 N 30 '52
N Y Times Mag p10+ O 26 '52 pors
Sat Eve Post 224:18+ My 31 '52 pors
Sat R 36:9+ Jl 11 '53 por; 36:9+ Jl 18 '53 por
Time 58:21+ D 17 '51 por; 60:19 S 29 '52 por; 60:22 D 8 '52 por
U S News 33:58+ Ag 22 '52 por; 33:77 N 14 '52 por; 33:63+ N 21 '52 por
America's Young Men, 1938-39
Biographical Directory of the American Congress, 1774-1949 (1950)
Congressional Directory (1952)
International Who's Who, 1953
International Yearbook and Statesmen's Who's Who, 1953
Who's Who in America, 1952-53
Who's Who in the United Nations (1951)
Who's Who in United States Politics (1952)
World Biography (1948)

LOWE, JACK. *See* Whittemore, A. and Lowe, J.

MACARTHUR, DOUGLAS, 2d July 5, 1909- United States Government official; diplomat

Address: b. c/o Department of State, Washington 25, D.C.; h. 3400 N St., N.W., Washington 7, D.C.

A Foreign Service officer of the United States' Department of State for nearly twenty years, Douglas MacArthur, 2d, is experienced in many phases of international relations. In March 1953 he was appointed Counselor of the department. In his wide background of diplomatic service he has had assignments in Belgium, Canada, France, Italy, and Portugal. From October 1949 to January 1951 he was deputy director of the office of European regional affairs, in which unit the planning and development of the North Atlantic Treaty Organization (NATO) was begun.

Early in 1951 MacArthur became adviser on international affairs to General Dwight D. Eisenhower, at that time the Supreme Allied Commander of Supreme Headquarters, Allied Powers Europe (SHAPE). He subsequently served under General Eisenhower's successor, General Matthew B. Ridgway.

Douglas MacArthur, 2d, who is the nephew and namesake of General Douglas MacArthur, was born in Bryn Mawr, Pennsylvania on July 5, 1909, the son of Arthur and Mary Hendry (McCalla) MacArthur. Douglas was graduated from Milton Academy, Milton, Massachusetts in 1928, and continued his studies in New Haven, Connecticut at Yale University. He majored in history and economics and played football. After receiving the B.A. degree in 1932, MacArthur spent a few months as a merchant seaman.

In 1933 he was commissioned a first lieutenant in the Officers' Reserve Corps, and served for two and a half years. Meanwhile MacArthur had passed the Foreign Service examinations for diplomatic service, and on October 3, 1935 he received his first assignment in the U.S. Foreign Service, an appointment as vice-consul in Vancouver, Canada.

MacArthur's next appointment brought him to Europe when fascism was threatening world peace. In 1937 he assumed his new post as vice-consul in Naples, Italy. Later he was sent to France as a secretary of the U.S. Embassy in Paris. After the outbreak of World War II, MacArthur was temporarily assigned, in July 1940, to the Embassy in Lisbon, Portugal.

He later returned to France to serve as a secretary at Vichy. With the capitulation of Pierre Laval's Government in France to the Nazi invaders, diplomatic relations with the United States were severed, and MacArthur, in November 1942, attempted to return to the United States.

The Vichy Government, however, interned MacArthur and other diplomats at Lourdes from where they were handed over to German authorities. Released after sixteen months of confinement, MacArthur, who had suffered a severe loss of weight, was brought back to the United States on the Swedish liner *Gripsholm* on March 15, 1944. At the time he exclaimed: "It's swell to be back home—but even better would be the opportunity to get on the job back there."

His appointment as assistant political adviser at Supreme Headquarters, AEF (SHAEF) came in July 1944. With the liberation of France and the subsequent recognition of the French Provisional Government by the United States, MacArthur was assigned to Paris, in October 1944. Four years later he was transferred to the Embassy at Brussels, Belgium as first secretary.

In March 1949 MacArthur was named chief of the Department of State's division of western European affairs, and in October he became deputy director of the office of European regional affairs, the agency which planned and developed NATO. MacArthur was designated in early 1951 as adviser on international affairs to General Eisenhower at SHAPE, where he was regarded as one of Eisenhower's "brain trusters". At this time he also served as counselor of the Paris Embassy.

With his appointment in March 1953 as Counselor of the State Department to succeed Charles E. Bohlen, MacArthur also became the department's senior staff officer on the National Security Council, a position to which he can "bring the full weight of his training in national security to bear on almost all external policies affecting the nation's welfare" (New York *Times Magazine,* April 26, 1953).

After becoming Counselor of the Department of State, MacArthur went with Harold E. Stassen, head of the Mutual Security Agency, George M. Humphrey, Secretary of the Treasury, and John Foster Dulles, Secretary of State, in April 1953 to the first meeting of Eisenhower Cabinet members with representatives of NATO. On May 8, 1953 MacArthur joined the U.S. party headed by Dulles and Stassen for a tour of twelve Near East and South Asian countries in order to obtain information to help in drafting a new policy with respect to that part of the world.

Accompanying Dulles and Senators H. Alexander Smith of New Jersey and Michael J. Mansfield of Montana, MacArthur attended a three-day conference in Manila which ended on September 8, 1954 when eight nations, the United States, Great Britain, France, Australia, the Philippines, New Zealand, Pakistan, and Thailand, signed the Southeast Asian Collective Defense Treaty to maintain and develop their individual and collective ability to resist armed attack, to cooperate in economic and technical aid programs, and to establish a council for military matters and the implementation of the treaty. Formosa was excluded from the treaty region, defined as "the general area of Southeast Asia . . . not including the Pacific areas north" of 21 degrees 30 minutes latitude north. The treaty will become effective when it is ratified by a majority of the signatories, and it will be in force indefinitely.

E. G. Malindine

DOUGLAS MACARTHUR, 2d

The nations also signed a protocol extending the protective and economic benefits of the treaty to Cambodia, Laos and south Viet-Nam, and a Pacific Charter by which the signatories pledged to strive "by every peaceful means to promote the self-government and to secure the independence of all countries whose people" desired it and were "able to undertake its responsibilities."

On August 21, 1934 MacArthur married Laura Louise Barkley, daughter of (former) Vice-President Alben W. Barkley. They have one daughter, Laura.

In appearance MacArthur is described as having the trim athletic build and sloping shoulders of a light heavyweight. He is five feet, ten inches tall and weighs 170 pounds. His eyes are hazel, and he has brown hair. It is said that MacArthur looks very much like his uncle, General MacArthur.

References

N Y Times Mag p56 Ap 26 '53

Who's Who in America, 1954-55

MCBRIDE, MARY MARGARET Nov. 16, 1899- Radio commentator; author

Address: b. c/o American Broadcasting Company, 7 W. 66th St., New York 23; h. 230 Central Park South, New York 19

NOTE: This biography supersedes the article which appeared in *Current Biography* in 1941.

The first woman to bring newspaper techniques to radio interviewing and to make daytime broadcasts profitable, Mary Margaret McBride observed in May 1954 her twentieth year as an "ad lib" radio commentator. Her annual fan mail exceeds a quarter of a million letters. She first appeared on Mutual Broadcasting System's station WOR in 1934 and remained there for six years; she was with Columbia Broadcasting System from 1937 to 1941, with the National Broadcasting Company from 1941 to 1950, and she has been with the American Broadcasting Company since 1950. On May 15, 1954 she relinquished her six-day, hour-long radio broadcasts. On September 27 she started a new Monday through Friday commentary series over NBC radio from 3:00 to 3:05 P.M.

Her "seemingly aimless technique is really a rich mixture of experience and skill" (*American Mercury*, January 1949) and her homey voice with the folksy twang has become familiar to millions of American housewives.

Before turning to radio, Miss McBride was a successful newspaper reporter and one of the highest paid magazine writers in the United States. She is also the author of several books and the recipient of world-wide awards. Since October 1953, in addition to her ABC radio program, she has been writing a daily newspaper column entitled "Mary Margaret McBride Says" for the Associated Press syndicate.

Mary Margaret McBride was born in Paris, Missouri, on November 16, 1899, the only daughter and the oldest of four children of Thomas Walker and Elizabeth (Craig) McBride. From a grandfather who was a Baptist preacher, Mary Margaret acquired an abhorrence of "the smallest white lie," which marks her unique treatment of products: she accepts and advertises on her radio program only those she personally finds acceptable. Her father, a farmer, was, she recalls, a "born trader," who kept the family moving as he rapidly turned in one prairie farm for another. The "McBride temper," says the radio commentator, "was a family trait celebrated and respected throughout the county."

Mary Margaret obtained some of her early education in the local one-room schoolhouse. "My best friends in childhood," she declares, "were the people in books loaned by a grandfather who from the time I was five taught me Latin and poetry and encouraged me in my ambition to write" (*Scribners*, March 1931). She adds: "I was sure I could write, though it was the only thing I was at all confident about. . . . I was abnormally unsophisticated and serious even for my time."

In 1906 she entered William Woods College, a private boarding school endowed by a great-aunt whose ambition was to educate Mary Margaret to head the institution. Enrolling at the University of Missouri in 1916, she announced her intention of majoring in journalism and becoming a writer, thereby losing her great-aunt's financial support.

Faced with the necessity of earning her own college expenses, Miss McBride worked part time as a cub reporter on a local newspaper. She says: "I worked my way through college because I imagined a writer had to have a college education" (*Scribner's*, March 1931).

After she received her Bachelor of Journalism degree from the University of Missouri in 1919, Mary Margaret began her newspaper career as a reporter for the Cleveland *Press*. Her ability to see human values in any story brought her feature assignments and she worked one year as the paper's special correspondent in Washington, D.C. Asked to cover a religious convention of the Interchurch World Movement, she displeased the editor of the *Press* by writing an uncritical report but it won the admiration of the movement's publicity director. He offered her a job as his assistant in New York. She accepted, established herself in Greenwich Village in 1920 and worked in the church organization's office where she met Estella Karn, who is now her radio program manager. "Things come to me by accident," Miss McBride says.

Deciding to return to newspaper work, after eight months with the church group, Miss McBride was first in line to apply for a first-rate reporter's position at $40 a week on the New York *Evening Mail*. She was interviewed personally by the editor, Henry Luther Stoddard, who asked if she could cover fires. "Just give me a chance," she replied. Three days later her colorful report of a Bronx fire appeared on the front page of the paper and Miss McBride has said, "I felt that I had arrived" (*Saturday Review of Literature*, March 1, 1947).

She stayed with the *Evening Mail* until 1924. In addition to her reporting assignments, she began to write articles for such magazines as *Pictorial Review*, *Cosmopolitan*, and *Good Housekeeping* and soon became one of the most successful women magazine writers in the country. With Paul Whiteman she collaborated on a four-part serial, *Jazz*, which appeared in the *Saturday Evening Post* and in book form in 1926 (published by Sears). "I'll never know such a thrill again," declares the radio commentator.

Between 1929 and 1932, Miss McBride wrote four travel books in collaboration with Helen Josephy: *Paris is a Woman's Town* (Coward-McCann, 1929), which became a best seller; *London is a Man's Town* (Coward-McCann, 1930); *New York is Everybody's Town* (Putnam, 1931); and *Beer and Skittles* (Putnam, 1932). She also collaborated with Alexander Williams on the book *Charm* (Rae D. Henkle, 1927), and alone wrote the *Story of Dwight Morrow* (Farrar, 1930), called "a well told story of a well filled life" by *Christian Century* (December 24, 1930).

With the onset of the depression in the early 1930's and the resulting decreased market and payment for her writings, Miss McBride turned to radio in 1934. Little expecting to get the position, she auditioned for a woman's program on WOR. She says, as quoted by Bennett Cerf in the *Saturday Review of Literature* (March 1, 1947): "I was the only one of fifty applicants who made no salary demands." Her homey Missouri twang won her the job and soon earned her a radio audience which liked her friendly, casual approach. Under the pseudonym of "Martha Deane", she posed as a helpful grandmother giving household hints. One day she announced in the middle of a broadcast: "From now on I'll just tell you about myself—the places I've been and the people I meet" (*American Mercury*, January 1949). Audience reaction strongly supported her decision, and admirers wrote "I feel as if I knew you well."

Concurrently with her radio broadcasts, during 1934 and 1935 Mary Margaret was editor of the woman's page of the Newspaper Enterprise Association of New York City. From 1937 until late 1940, she not only appeared as "Martha Deane" on Mutual Broadcasting System's station WOR for 45 minutes, but also broadcast for 15 minutes five days a week under her own name over Columbia Broadcasting System. In her dual role, she earned from $50,000 to $100,000 a year and on her program used the "ad lib" technique. In celebration of her fifth year on radio, in 1939 her admirers packed New York City's Grand Central Palace.

Mary Margaret McBride discontinued her broadcasts over WOR in the fall of 1940, retaining only her program on CBS. Beginning in 1941 the National Broadcasting Company drew Miss McBride from CBS to its studio with a chance to return to a 45-minute program.

Three years later 125,000 of her admirers requested tickets to the Madison Square Garden celebration of her tenth year on radio. Mrs. Eleanor Roosevelt, one of Miss McBride's favorite program guests, flew from Washington, D.C. to attend.

During World War II, when the United States government asked for scrap paper, Miss McBride contributed more than three million fan letters stored in a warehouse. She worked indefatigably selling war bonds with great success at bond rallies, and at the end of hostilities flew to London to broadcast her program from Europe. The Army placed a B-29 at her service and allowed her to go into Germany as the first civilian reporter.

By 1948 approximately six million housewives were listening to Mary Margaret McBride broadcast at 1 p.m. over NBC. Shortly after Labor Day she made her first appearance on television for a period of thirteen weeks Tuesday evenings, then announced: "I plan to wait until a lot more television sets are sold . . . then I'm going right back into television" (*Woman's Home Companion*, April 1949). She flew to the opening of Norway's government radio station in 1948 upon that country's invitation and received from King Haakon a medal for notable broadcasts. The next year an audience larger than the usual baseball gate crowded New York's Yankee Stadium to observe Miss McBride's fifteenth radio anniversary and to see the woman they admired.

MARY MARGARET MCBRIDE

Miss McBride left the National Broadcasting Company in 1950 and moved to the American Broadcasting Company. The "first lady of radio" broadcast the coronation of Queen Elizabeth II from London's BBC station, where British radio engineers came in to study her expert handling of commercials. Among the later books which Mary Margaret McBride has written are *Here's Martha Deane* (Garden City, 1936); *How Dear to My Heart* (Macmillan, 1940), an autobiography of her childhood; *America for Me* (Macmillan, 1941); and *Tune in for Elizabeth* (Dodd Mead, 1945). Of *How Dear to My Heart,* the reviewer for the New York *Times* (December 22, 1940) writes ". . . it has a pleasant human quality," expressed "with ingratiating candor and simplicity." *America for Me,* in the words of the *Christian Century* reviewer (December 24, 1941), gives "vivid and concrete pictures of experiences which fortify the conviction that an American can properly and proudly say, 'America for Me!'" A vocational story for girls about a radio interviewer, *Tune in for Elizabeth* is called "interesting, honest and convincing, [offering] no short cut to fame and fortune" (*Saturday Review of Literature,* January 19, 1946). Miss McBride is the editor of *How to Be a Successful Advertising Woman* (Whittlesey House, 1948).

Miss McBride's annual fan mail now exceeds a quarter of a million letters and she ranks among America's master salesmen. Hers is "one of the shrewdest minds in radio," wrote

MCBRIDE, MARY MARGARET—*Cont.*

Barbara Heggie (*Woman's Home Companion,* April 1949).

In *Successful Women,* Isabella Taves quotes Miss McBride: "When I am on the air, I imagine that I am talking to a young married woman with a couple of children. A woman who at one time had a job and is still interested in the jobs of other people, the business world. So I talk about people who do things, the world at large. I try to give her the vicarious thrill of going places and meeting people. When I describe a restaurant where I had dinner. . . I try to look at it as she might . . . and to share her enthusiasm."

Among her world-wide awards are Haiti's National Order of Honor and Merit; a special medal of honor from the City of Vienna; special recognition from the Virgin Islands; and the One World Award (1950). Her clubs include the Authors' League, Women's City, New York Newspaper Woman's, Query, and Heterodoxy. She also belongs to Kappa Alpha Theta and Theta Sigma Phi.

Miss McBride has gray hair and keen brown eyes, and is of stocky build. When she conducts her broadcasts from her apartment she likes to wear black silk pajamas and an oriental housecoat. She frequently punctuates her broadcasts, like an understanding Dutch uncle, with the word "Now. . ." and says of her work "I love it!" Her interests include books, the theatre, gardens, and flying.

References (See also references listed in 1941 biographical sketch.)

Am Mercury 68:7+ Ja '49
Life 17:47+ D 4 '44
New Yorker 18:27+ D 19 '42
Sat R of Lit 30:4+ Mr 1 '47
Woman's Home C 76:36+ Ap '49
America's Twelve Master Salesmen (1952)
Who's Who in America, 1952-53

MCCARDELL, CLAIRE May 24, 1905- Fashion designer

Address: b. c/o Townley Frocks, Inc., 550 7th Ave., New York 18; h. 151 E. 79th St., New York 21

"Claire McCardell's name is always up on top in any discussion of creative United States designers," wrote Evelyn Hayes in the *Washington Post* (August 15, 1954). For more than twenty years, as designer for Townley Frocks, Inc., New York City, Miss McCardell has been creating casual and popular-priced styles for American women. She introduced the classic "Monastic" dress in 1938, the versatile "Popover" house dress in 1942, and the "Diaper" bathing suit in 1943. *Life* (August 23, 1954) reported that hers is "the busiest drawing board in the U.S. fashion industry."

The fashion designer became a vice-president and partner of Townley Frocks in 1952. During a reorganization of this firm in 1939 and 1940, she worked as a designer for Hattie Carnegie. Currently, she is a curriculum critic and member of the advisory board of the Parsons School of Design, her alma mater, in New York City.

Claire McCardell was born in Frederick, Maryland, on May 24, 1905, the daughter of Adrian Leroy and Eleanor (Clingan) McCardell. She has three brothers. Her father was president of the Frederick County National Bank and at one time a Maryland state senator. Claire received her early education in her native town. As a small child, she cut out and dressed paper dolls from her mother's discarded fashion magazines. As quoted by Beryl Epstein in *Fashion is Our Business,* she recalled, "My fingers cut the silhouette of the moment, and my eyes began their training."

During her teens, she enjoyed sports, and obtained a knowledge of what constituted durable and comfortable sportswear, which she now employs in designing active sports clothes. In high school, she favored her sewing class, and when at home often remodeled clothes. "I didn't sew very well," she admits, "but I managed to get 'an effect'."

After her graduation from high school in 1923, she entered Hood College in Frederick. However, she found most subjects, except sewing, distasteful; after two years, she left college to attend the Parsons School of Design. She planned to become a fashion illustrator after she discovered that "manufacturers then were not employing designers directly." Residing at the Three Arts Club in Manhattan, she became, with other members of this girls' club, a recipient of dresses discarded by wealthy women. Many of these were French imports, which introduced Claire to the careful work and delicate styling of French dressmakers. In 1927 she went to study at the Paris division of the Parsons School of Design.

While studying in France, Miss McCardell worked part time during the rush style season tracing the drawings of accomplished fashion artists for a firm that sold sketches of Paris models. Of this experience, she is quoted in *Fashion is Our Business* as saying: "I was learning important things all the time—the way clothes worked, the way they felt, where they fastened."

Miss McCardell completed her final year at the Parsons School of Design in New York in 1928. Unable to obtain a position as a fashion illustrator, she accepted work painting floral designs, on lamp shades. For a few weeks she worked as a model in the French Room of B. Altman's department store.

Her instructors at the Parsons School of Design recommended her for a sketching position with Emmet Joyce in a fashionable dress shop in Manhattan, where she remained for about four months at a salary of $20 a week. "I felt I was at last actually on the inside, working in a dress shop," she declares. Late in 1929, however, she accepted a post as assistant and designer with a knit goods manufacturer in New York City. She discovered her experience was inadequate for this position, and eight months later she was discharged.

A chance meeting with the dress designer Robert Turk, who became her friend and teacher, opened a post for her as his assistant in late 1930. When his firm, Robert Turk, Inc., was disbanded, and he became designer for Townley Frocks, Inc., in 1932, Miss McCardell went with him as his assistant. Modeling and sketching under his supervision, she gathered valuable experience in fashion design. Following his death a few months later, she received the assignment to complete his designs for the season.

After the first showing of her own dress designs in 1932, Claire McCardell was appointed a designer with Townley Frocks. With her new assignment, Miss McCardell began to visit the style showings in Paris twice a year. Unlike other designers, who sketched the Paris models to copy for the American trade, she decided to modify them to fit the ordinary woman's purse and demand for comfort as well as fashion. Stanley Marcus of the Neiman-Marcus Company said: "She is one of the few truly creative designers this country has produced, borrowing nothing from other designers. She is to America what Vionnet was, and now Grès is, to France."

The designer's idea is that clothes should fit the individual and the occasion, and should be comfortable as well as handsome. The color and line should flow naturally with the body. Miss McCardell first wears her most daring creations herself. When her designs first came on the market, only the more venturesome women wore her clothes. She invaded the popular field during "the separates movement" in 1934 with her five-piece wool jersey casual combination of halter, culottes, slacks, skirt and jacket. "Slightly sloppy to begin with, her clothes never get that wilted look. . . And indifferent to fashion's whims, they never seem to go out of style" commented *Look* (May 19, 1953).

The McCardell "Monastic" dress, sometimes referred to as the "American classic," had its origin in 1938. *Flair* described it as "a free flow of cloth, held to form by a belt, a band, a girdle." Beryl Epstein stated: "Almost overnight American women wanted it. . . It swept through the entire dress market." And, the writer added, many of Miss McCardell's styles became successes in the same way: "She designed something she liked or felt the need of for herself" and discovered that "it answered the wants and necessities of other women, too."

During World War II, in 1942, the designer conceived the idea for her popular "Popover" wrap-around house dress for women whose maids were leaving them for factory and defense work. It was adapted in 1948 as a lined camel's hair coat, and in 1951 as "a dress, coat, beach wrap, [and] bathrobe" (*Look*, May 19, 1953). During the war she used colorful patches for dress sleeves and pockets in order to make patches smart and help conserve material.

Miss McCardell has introduced in women's clothes many details from men's clothing, such as large pockets, shirtsleeve shoulders, stitching on blue jeans, and trouser pleats. She matched up ballet slippers as dress accessories. In 1943 she brought out her famous "Diaper" bathing suit, with brass fishing boot hooks up the side.

CLAIRE MCCARDELL

Addressing an audience of women fashion experts on March 7, 1944, the designer informed them that the American woman has "a posture all her own; she is neither erect nor queenly" (New York *Times*, March 8, 1944). She also stated: "The field of design is big enough to hold both New York and Paris as fashion centers."

In the winter of 1946 Miss McCardell featured her "Empire" collar, and in the fall of 1949, she introduced her "Bandana" neckline. In addition to designing coats, suits, dresses and playclothes, Claire creates "top-to-toe ideas" for shoes, raincoats, hats, gloves, jewelry, and "even eyeglasses" (*Life*, August 23, 1954). The New York *Herald Tribune* reviewer for a fashion show held by the designer in 1954 wrote: "Subtle colors are part of the McCardell look" (January 29, 1954). She herself declares: "I do not like glitter... I like comfort in the rain, in the sun, comfort for active sports, comfort for sitting still and looking pretty. Clothes should be useful."

One of her most popular 1954 designs for "glamourous casual living" is a pair of boned, high-waisted Persian wool challis tapered slacks, with a black wool jersey top.

Among the honors Claire McCardell has received are the Mademoiselle Merit Award (1943), American Fashion Critics Award (1944), Neiman-Marcus Award (1948), and the Women's National Press Club Award, presented to her in 1950 by United States President Harry S. Truman. At the Frank Perls Gallery in Beverly Hills, California in April 1953, she held a retrospective exhibition of her clothing styles from 1933 to 1953. The designer gave a Claire McCardell Gold Thimble Award to an outstanding student at the Parsons School of Design in 1954.

Claire McCardell married Irving Drought Harris, an architect, on March 10, 1943. She

MCCARDELL, CLAIRE—*Continued*
is five feet seven inches tall, weighs 130 pounds, and has blue eyes and brown hair. Her political party is Republican and her church affiliation is Protestant. Her manner is unaffected, cordial and pleasant. For recreation, she enjoys cooking garlic stews in an iron kettle over the fireplace in her farmhouse at Frenchtown, New Jersey, or going skiing. "I'm not a good skier," she says, "but I love it."

References

Collier's 117:16+ Ja 19 '46
N Y World-Telegram Ag 3 '49
Washington (D.C.) Post p13 Ag 15 '54
Epstein, B. Fashion is Our Business (1945)
Who's Who in America, 1954-55
Who's Who in Commerce and Industry (1953)

MCCARRAN, PATRICK A(NTHONY) Aug. 8, 1876-Sept. 28, 1954 United States Senator (Democrat) from Nevada; lawyer; was graduated from University of Nevada (1901); served in state legislature (1903) and as district attorney for Nye county (1907-1909); practiced law in Nevada; was associate justice of state Supreme Court (1913-1917) and chief justice (1917-1918); served in U.S. Senate since 1933; for most part opposed administrations of presidents Franklin D. Roosevelt and Harry S. Truman; supported remonetization of silver; favored aiding Nationalist government in China and the Franco regime in Spain; author of Internal Security Act (1950) and co-author of legislation establishing Civil Aeronautics Authority (1938) and of McCarran-Walter Immigration and Nationality Act (1952). See *Current Biography,* (July) 1947.

Obituary

N Y Times p 1+ S 29 '54

MCCLELLAN, HAROLD C(HADICK) Aug. 20, 1897- Manufacturers' organization official

Address: b. c/o National Association of Manufacturers, 2 W. 48th St., New York 36; Old Colony Paint and Chemical Co., P.O. Box 2152, Terminal Annex, Los Angeles 54, Calif.; h. 2220 Orlando Rd., San Marino, Calif.

Long active in the affairs of the National Association of Manufacturers, Harold C. McClellan was elected president of that organization on December 3, 1953 for a period of one year. President of the Old Colony Paint and Chemical Company, of Los Angeles, California, McClellan is the first Pacific Coast businessman ever to head the group. He succeeded Charles R. Sligh, Jr., who became chairman of the board of the association. In addition to holding executive positions in paint industry associations, McClellan is widely interested in civic and educational problems in the Los Angeles area.

Interviewed on the National Broadcasting Company television program *Meet the Press* on July 4, 1954, McClellan said that long-range business conditions appeared "very good." He said that except for the "bulge" from mid-1952 to mid-1953, the economy was now about as strong as it had been since the end of World War II. He stated that he was disturbed by the rise in unemployment, but believed the fact that 60,000,000 were employed was more important in the over-all picture. He has declared on several occasions that the NAM is in accord with the objectives of President Eisenhower's program.

Harold Chadick McClellan was born in Crow's Landing, California, on August 20, 1897, one of the three sons of the Reverend Edward Leander Barker and Ada (Small) McClellan. Recalling his childhood, Harold C. McClellan says: "We were not well off. And my mother was ill a good deal."

"Chad" attended the schools of Colton, California. The family later moved to Los Angeles, where McClellan was graduated from Lincoln High School. He entered Occidental College in Los Angeles, but his studies were interrupted when he enlisted in the Navy in 1918. McClellan served overseas in the Medical Corps, after which time he returned to Occidental College, majored in English, and received the B.A. degree in 1922.

In order to maintain himself while at college (where he was assisted by several scholarships), he worked as a college janitor, and devised a method of saving the college 10 per cent on cleaning expenses. He was made head janitor. Young McClellan earned additional money packing and inspecting cantaloupes from sixteen to twenty hours a day, and by cooking in his fraternity (Sigma Omicron) house. He was also a distance runner on the track squad and president of the glee club, in which he sang baritone.

Upon finishing college McClellan was employed by the Crescent Creamery Company in Los Angeles. Although he wished to be a salesman, he had been hired to promote better relations among the firms in the dairy industry. Borrowing a company car without permission, McClellan entered a "tough" territory, where selling had been difficult, and proved that he could really sell. He was then given the most difficult and challenging sales problems.

After becoming sales manager in 1923, he continued in that post until he decided to form his own business in 1927. He studied business reports, becoming convinced that paint companies "had the most advantages for small enterprise, in earnings, expansion possibilities and ability to compete with the big companies." Although he had never been inside a paint factory until he was ready to buy one, McClellan purchased the Remolite Company in Los Angeles with $10,000.

It had one girl in the office, two men in the plant, and one salesman, with a monthly gross sale of only $900. McClellan changed the name of the business to the Old Colony Paint and Chemical Company.

Emphasizing quality products, because he felt the small paint firm could compete with the big paint companies only on a quality basis, and believing it to be good business to price a product for not more than moderate profit, McClellan managed the company so well that it had outgrown its plant by the end of the first year. In 1937 he purchased two acres and constructed a new building. Today the Old Colony Company occupies more than four acres. The company also has a warehouse and a branch sales staff in San Francisco, and its products are distributed as far east as Denver, Colorado.

It operates on a dealer-only sale basis, having shifted from a consumer-sale basis a few years after McClellan organized the company. McClellan has stated: "In twenty-six years we have lost fewer dealers to competitors than there are fingers on your hand." He has also said: "We've never had any use for chiseling or chiselers." His company, which now employs 150 people, has steadily increased its sales, and had a gross profit of about $2,500,000 in 1953.

McClellan first became prominent in the National Association of Manufacturers when he successfully concluded an argument between a West Coast segment and the parent organization. He became regional vice-president, and has also served the NAM as director, chairman of the employee benefits committee, chairman of the inter-association relations advisory committee, and a member of the executive and educational advisory committees. When he assumed the presidency of the NAM, McClellan declared: "I'm optimistic about the general outlook. All elements for further economic expansion are present. We should keep expanding if business does its part and we have sound government" (*Christian Science Monitor,* December 7, 1953).

On October 29, 1953 the board of NAM had unanimously resolved that "it is impracticable for the association to generalize in the national interest on a matter such as tariffs, which is so specific to the divergent points of view of its more than 20,000 members and their employees" (*World,* January 1954).

The NAM announced on January 3, 1954 that it advocated the amendment of the Labor-Management Relations Act of 1947 to provide stronger guarantees of freedom of speech for employers, a ban on strikes to compel union recognition, a tighter definition of union responsibility for the actions of union members, and more effective clauses to outlaw featherbedding (New York *Times,* January 4, 1954).

In the spring of 1954 McClellan visited Yugoslavia on an official invitation of Marshal Tito. In Paris he spoke to the American Club, a group of American business and professional men. He said, in part: "In American business the flood stage is over and business and employment seek a more normal level. The transition is moving well. . ." He predicted that the United States population would reach 221 million by 1975, and the needs of people will increase proportionately. He also stated that new products are invading the market and business experts are working out new sales techniques. Costs are being brought under better control. All of industry is up on its toes" (Washington *Post,* May 21, 1954).

HAROLD C. MCCLELLAN

McClellan is a former president of the Los Angeles Paint, Varnish and Lacquer Association, and is former regional vice-president of the National Paint, Varnish and Lacquer Association. He was an industry member of the regional War Labor Board and Wage Stabilization Board. In 1949 and 1950 he was president of the Merchants and Manufacturers Association of Los Angeles, and is a member of the board of the Los Angeles Chamber of Commerce, and chairman of the Chamber's metropolitan traffic and transit committee.

He is a member of the board of the Haynes Foundation, Los Angeles, and a member of the Los Angeles Metropolitan Transit Authority, having been appointed by Governor Earl Warren. The executive has served on an advisory committee on industrial relations at the University of California, Los Angeles, and is president of the board of Occidental College.

Americans should travel, McClellan believes. Spending abroad should be twice the billion dollars it was in 1953, he declared. Dollars spent on such trips enable nations to buy more American products, and they are willing and anxious to buy more of them. Since we cannot live alone, we should get better acquainted with our neighbors, he advised.

"Chad" McClellan, as he is known to his friends, married Katherine Elizabeth Stone of Sycamore, Illinois, on June 29, 1923. They have one daughter, Martha Louise (Mrs. Gunther Looser). He and Mrs. McClellan make a joint hobby of collecting oil paintings, especially those of the American impressionist school. McClellan, an energetic man of strong physique and graying hair, enjoys golf and gardening. He grows some fifty or sixty varieties of camellias, some plants ten feet tall.

(Continued next page)

MCCLELLAN, HAROLD C.—*Continued*

McClellan makes his home in San Marino, California, where he is a member of the City Council and chairman of the finance committtee. He is a member of the Pasadena Presbyterian Church. His clubs include the California, Jonathan, and San Gabriel Country.

The NAM president spoke to the teachers assembled in June 1954 in New York City for the 92nd annual convention of the National Education Association. He said that industry "is greatly disturbed over the meagerness of teachers' salaries." He insisted that ways must be found to increase substantially the money spent on schools. He called upon localities, states and individuals to meet the need for better schools and better-paid teachers "because we know that our own and the nation's progress depends on education" (New York *World-Telegram and Sun,* June 23, 1954).

References

Bsns W p34 D 5 '53
Christian Sci Mon p18 D 4 '53; p14 D 7 '53
Time 62:104 D 14 '53

MCCORMICK, ANNE O'HARE 1882-May 29, 1954 Foreign correspondent; member of the New York *Times* editorial board; interpreted news in her thrice-weekly column "Abroad"; reared in Columbus, Ohio; educated at the College of St. Mary of the Springs; was associate editor of *Catholic Universe Bulletin,* Cleveland; as the wife of Francis J. McCormick, an engineer and importer, traveled extensively; began writing occasional articles for the New York *Times* in 1921 on the rise of fascism in Italy; became correspondent in 1922; interviewed many leading personalities including Hitler, Stalin, Mussolini, Churchill, Roosevelt, Truman, Eisenhower; appointed to the *Times* editorial staff, 1936; won the Pulitzer Prize (1937) for European correspondence; among awards were the Gold Medal of the National Institute of Social Science, 1942; Theodore Roosevelt Distinguished Service Medal, 1950; Women's National Press Club Achievement Award, 1945; received honorary degrees from many universities and colleges including Columbia, Fordham, Smith, and Wellesley; author of *The Hammer and the Scythe* (1928). See *Current Biography,* (Yrbk.) 1940.

Obituary

N Y Times p 1+ My 30 '54

MCCORMICK, MYRON Feb. 8, 1908-
Actor

Address: b. c/o Actors Equity Assn., 45 W. 47th St., New York 19

When the Rodgers and Hammerstein musical play *South Pacific* closed on January 16, 1954 after 1,925 performances, the record showed that Myron McCormick (who played the role of Luther Billis, a Seabee) was one of three featured members of the cast who had been in the Pulitzer Prize play since its opening in April 1949.

Now appearing in motion pictures, McCormick, who has also performed on radio and television, has appeared in over thirty plays on Broadway, including *Yellow Jack, Winterset, The Wingless Victory, Thunder Rock, The Damask Cheek,* and *State of the Union.* He made his professional debut in 1930 as a member of the University Players.

Myron McCormick was born in Albany, Indiana on February 8, 1908, the son of Walter Perlee and Bess (Eviston) McCormick. As a child, according to Helen Ormsbee in the New York *Herald Tribune* (January 2, 1944) he was associated with Bartone's Wonder Show, a medicine show operated by neighbors of the McCormicks. "One summer, when I was about eleven," he has recalled, "my parents let me travel with the company for three weeks, and I was completely happy. I took tickets, ran errands and sometimes did a walk-on."

He went to high school in Muncie, Indiana, where he was active in school plays. At the New Mexico Military Institute, which he attended next, he majored in economics and studied dramatics under Paul Horgan, the playwright and novelist. He then entered Princeton University, where he was elected to Phi Beta Kappa, and where he performed in Triangle shows with José Ferrer, James Stewart, and other subsequently famous Hollywood and Broadway personalities.

McCormick made his first appearance on the professional stage at West Falmouth, Massachusetts, in June 1930, with the University Players. The group, which had been organized in 1928 by Bretaigne Windust of Princeton, and Charles Leatherbee of Harvard, was eventually to include such famous theatrical figures as Margaret Sullavan, Henry Fonda, Joshua Logan, Kent Smith, and James Stewart. McCormick has said of his association with the group: "I consider the years I spent with the University Players of incalculable value to me in my profession." A history of the five years (1928 to 1932) of the University Players by Norris Houghton was published in 1952 by William Sloane under the title *But Not Forgotten.*

On October 29, 1932 McCormick made his debut on the New York stage as James Campbell in *Carrie Nation,* a play which failed. He next appeared in *Goodbye Again* (1932), the play which gave him his "first big break in the theater," and subsequently in *I Was Waiting for You* (1933), *Yellow Jack* (1934), *Small Miracle* (1934), *On to Fortune* (1935), *Paths of Glory* (1935), *Substitute for Murder* (1935), *How Beautiful with Shoes* (1935) and *Hell Freezes Over* (1935).

In February 1936 he portrayed his most important role to that date, that of Trock in Maxwell Anderson's *Winterset.* At the end of that year he performed in another Anderson drama, as Ruel McQuestion in *The Wingless Victory.* There followed appearances as James Freeman in *In Clover* (1937) and as Dan Grimshaw in *How to Get Tough about It* (1938).

During July and August 1938 he played in summer theatres in *Charles and Mary* and *High Tor*. Under the auspices of the Group Theater he performed the role of Streeter in *Thunder Rock* the following year. After appearing in *The Cream in the Well* (1941), he played the role of Shorty in *Lily of the Valley* (1942). Neither the New York *Times* critic Brooks Atkinson nor the New York *Herald Tribune* critic Richard Watts admired this Ben Hecht fantasy, but both were favorably impressed by McCormick's acting.

Atkinson wrote in the *Times*: "Myron McCormick is a conspicuously gifted actor. As the militant longshoreman, he is vigorous and sharpminded"; and Watts observed in the *Herald Tribune* that McCormick's part was "well-played." Atkinson also complimented McCormick's "dry-humored" performance as Jimmy Randall in *The Damask Cheek,* by John van Druten and Lloyd Morris.

In January 1944, McCormick appeared at the Belasco Theatre in another Anderson drama, playing the role of Sergeant Peter Moldau in *Storm Operation.* The critics wrote admiringly of McCormick's acting, even though he was handicapped by joining the cast two weeks after the play had been in rehearsal.

Variety's reviewer wrote: "Myron McCormick is excellent in the long, trying part of the Yank sergeant. . . Without giving the appearance of driving, he manages to keep the action moving, even though the part offers little dramatic scope and only a single scene of real conflict or stress."

Howard Barnes remarked in the *Herald Tribune* that McCormick's "steady playing [sustained] the action and mood of the play at all times." In *PM,* Louis Kronenberger applauded McCormick for giving "a generally straightforward performance." Reviewing the play for the *Times,* Lewis Nichols wrote: "Myron McCormick, as the top sergeant, carries an air of authority which is excellent." In Ward Morehouse's opinion, McCormick got "fire and feeling" into his role.

Rose Franken's play *Soldier's Wife,* which opened in October 1944 and ran for 255 performances, furnished McCormick his next role, that of John Rogers, a discharged Army captain who experiences difficulty in readjusting to civilian life. The play received mixed notices, but McCormick's acting was again generally admired. Kronenberger described his performance as "excellent" and Morehouse as "restrained, likeable and believable."

The actor's next role was his best, until he appeared in *South Pacific.* As Spike McManus, the brash reporter in the Howard Lindsay-Russell Crouse Pulitzer Prize-winning play, *State of the Union,* which opened in November 1945 and ran for 765 performances on Broadway, McCormick won unanimous praise. "Many of the laugh lines," wrote *Variety,* "come from Myron McCormick . . . he's an actor who knows timing." Ward Morehouse in the New York *Sun* described him as "a high-powered newspaper man who makes you feel he has actually been one." The opinion of Howard

MYRON MCCORMICK

Barnes was that McCormick performed his role "with immense effect."

After his triumph in *State of the Union,* McCormick appeared as J. Newton McKeon, a cynical publicity man, in the Allan Scott play, *Joy to the World* in 1948. Although the play did not make a favorable impression generally, McCormick's performance did, even in a role that was becoming familiar for him. Barnes wrote: "Myron McCormick . . . fills the place with the wry humor which makes it so rewarding a burlesque. His dead-pan remarks about the whole system of picture-making are some of the best aspects" of the play. The reviewer of the *World-Telegram* commented: "Myron McCormick plays with deft ingenuity. He adds nuances and an uncanny tempo to an amusing role. . ."

April 7, 1949 marked the opening of one of the most successful productions in American theatrical history, *South Pacific,* the musical play written by Richard Rodgers and Oscar Hammerstein II from James A. Michener's Pulitzer Prize-winning book of stories, *Tales of the South Pacific.* In the role of Luther Billis, an enterprising Seabee, McCormick won unreservedly warm praise.

"After wasting his talents on stereotyped parts for several years," wrote Brooks Atkinson, "Myron McCormick has a good one as a braggart, scheming Seabee, and plays it with great comic gusto." According to *Variety,* McCormick took "advantage of the best role of his career as a tough, angle-playing, laughable Seabee." Barnes remarked: "As the brash and eventually heroic Billis, who manufactures grass skirts for his companions in arms, he [McCormick] adds lusty and earthy accents to the show."

After playing in the role two years, McCormick replied to what had become a standard question: "Why quit a fat part? Billis runs

MCCORMICK, MYRON—*Continued*

through the whole show, and he's an interesting guy to play. Some parts, you go crazy; you stand around on the stage with nothing to do. . . This is different. Billis is busy all the time. I've been more tired in some shows after three weeks than I am in this one after two years."

Besides his stage work, McCormick has been active on radio and in motion pictures. Among the pictures he has appeared in are *Winterset, One Third of a Nation*, and *China Girl*. On the radio, he has performed in Archibald MacLeish's *Fall of the City, American School of the Air, Joyce Jordan, Second Husband*, and numerous other programs.

Myron McCormick married Martha Hodge in 1940; the McCormicks have a nine-year old daughter named Gaea. "We found the name Gaea in a dictionary of mythology," McCormick told William Hawkins. "It means 'Earth as a Goddess born out of chaos.' I thought that was particularly appropriate for an actor's daughter." McCormick is five feet eight inches tall, weighs about 150 pounds, and has blue eyes and thinning reddish blond hair. "I love the theatre," he has written, "and the people in it."

References

N Y Herald Tribune IV p1 Ja 2 '44; IV p2 Ap 8 '45
Theater Arts 34:54+ My '50
Who's Who in the Theater, 1953
Houghton, N. But Not Forgotten (1952)

MCCOY, FRANK R(OSS) Oct. 29, 1874-June 4, 1954 Former United States Army officer and organization official; served forty-five years (1897-1938) in U.S. Army, retiring as major general; was graduated from U.S. Military Academy, West Point, New York (1897); was wounded in the Battle of San Juan Hill (1898); served as military aide to President Theodore Roosevelt; as aide-de-camp to Major General Leonard Wood in Cuba; fought against outlaws in the Philippines; was secretary of Moro Province (1905); was General Staff secretary in World War I of A.E.F. in France and later commanded the "Rainbow Division" (New York's "Fighting 69th"); represented U.S. at the Pan American Conference in Washington (July, 1928); on League of Nations Commission (1932) to inquire into Japanese occupation of Manchuria; was commanding general of Governors Island, New York (1936); served with Justice Owen J. Roberts to investigate responsibility for the Pearl Harbor disaster (1941); headed military commission (1942) for the trial of eight Nazi spies and saboteurs who had been landed on the Atlantic coast from submarines; served as chairman of the Foreign Policy Association (1939-1945) and of the Far Eastern Commission (1945-1949). See *Current Biography*, (Nov.) 1945.

Obituary

N Y Times p17 Je 5 '54

MACDONALD, MALCOLM (JOHN) 1901- Commissioner-General for the United Kingdom in Southeast Asia

Address: Mallaig, Gallop Rd., Singapore

The Right Honorable Malcolm MacDonald, Commissioner-General for the United Kingdom in Southeast Asia, is "a firm believer in eventual self-government for the Asiatic colonies" of North Borneo, Brunei, Sarawak, the Federation of Malaya, and Singapore. Although he has no direct influence in the administration of local affairs in these areas, he makes recommendations to the Colonial Office which affect British policy in all of the Far East. MacDonald is the chairman of a joint coordination committee which is recommending a plan for the unification of Malaya and Singapore.

Malcolm John MacDonald was born in Lossiemouth, Scotland, in 1901, one of the two sons and five children of the late James Ramsay and Margaret Ethel (Gladstone) MacDonald. The relationship between Malcolm and his father, who was four times Prime Minister of Britain, was very close. Malcolm went to Passmore Edwards Kindergarten School in London, and then entered the City of London School. He spent so much time studying he was nicknamed "the philosopher." As a small boy, he had a talent for dancing.

After his mother's death when he was eleven years old, Malcolm went to Bedales School in Petersfield, Hampshire, where he remained until he was eighteen. When he left Bedales to enter Queen's College, Oxford University, he held the position of "head boy" (*Living Age*, November 1938).

With his college tutor, Godfrey Elton (now Lord Elton), MacDonald "shared a common enthusiasm for reading, politics, old furniture, glass, pewter, first editions, and historic documents" (*Living Age*). During his last years in college, 1923 and 1924, MacDonald entered the general elections as a Labour party parliamentary candidate for the Bassetlaw division of Nottinghamshire. He lost the election both years.

After MacDonald received the B.A. degree from Oxford University, he worked as a journalist on a weekly London periodical, and wrote articles, travel series, and industrial reviews. He is quoted by *Living Age* as saying the piece he most enjoyed writing was an affirmative point of view on "Has Jazz Come to Stay?" He joined the Oxford University debating team on a world tour, and served on the London County Council from 1927 to 1930.

Contesting for parliamentary representative for the Bassetlaw division of Nottinghamshire again in 1929, MacDonald won on the Labour party ticket. The following year, at the London Naval Conference he served as secretary to his father, then Prime Minister. At the Imperial Conference of 1930 and in 1932 in Ottawa at the Imperial Economic Conference, he was the British delegation's press officer. "He brought to his job," reported the London *News Review* (May 30, 1946), "a youthful, almost undergraduate open-mindedness, enjoying arguments with his advisors, capable of his own decisions and sometimes obstinate, but feeling all the time for the inescapable facts and the practicable issue. . . ."

After the Labour government collapsed in England in August 1931 and MacDonald's father resigned to become Prime Minister in the National (coalition) government (since economic conditions had become so serious as to demand unity among the different parties), MacDonald became Under-Secretary of State for Dominion Affairs. He was elected as a National Labour representative to the House of Commons for the Bassetlaw constituency in October, and was again appointed Under-Secretary in his father's new Cabinet.

Malcolm MacDonald served in this position until June 1935, when he became Secretary of State for the Colonies under the late Prime Minister Stanley Baldwin. In the same year he lost the parliamentary election for the constituency of Bassetlaw and as a result, he sought election from the Ross and Cromarty he sought election from the Ross and Cromarty division on the National government ticket in 1936. He defeated his opponent, Randolph Churchill, after a difficult fight, and represented this division in Parliament until 1945.

As Secretary of State for Dominion Affairs from November 1935 to May 1938, MacDonald effected a treaty satisfactory to both countries in the Eire-British trade war. In May 1938, he returned to the office of Secretary of State for the Colonies, and served until May 1940. Concurrently, from October 1938 to January 1939, he filled the post of Secretary of State for Dominion Affairs. His leading problem was Palestine; after a visit to the Holy Land to confer with both Arabs and Jews, he announced that he had worked out a zoning plan restricting Jewish land purchases in Palestine. A motion of censure by the Labour party in the House of Commons against a bill encompassing this proposal was defeated.

As Minister of Health in Britain from May 1940 to February 1941, MacDonald served on the home front early in World War II. Appointed High Commissioner for the United Kingdom in Canada in February 1941, he succeeded Sir Gerald Campbell. The London *Observer* (May 26, 1946), commenting on his success in this post, stated: "His gift of unaffected democratic 'equality' endeared him to Canada."

In April 1946, MacDonald became the first Governor-General of the Malayan Union and Singapore. His job was to co-ordinate the interests and policies of the territories, and to help repair the unsettled conditions in Malaya, where there were frequent armed clashes between the Malays and the Chinese.

By raising the living standards and the efficiency of the Malays, Indians and Dyaks through education, MacDonald hoped to increase their ability to compete economically with the Chinese and to co-operate with them in building an independent Malayan state (*Christian Science Monitor,* September 14, 1946). He was appointed Governor-General of Malaya and British Borneo in July 1946.

British Inf. Services
MALCOLM MACDONALD

When Great Britain joined his post with that of Special Commissioner of Southeast Asia in 1948, MacDonald was appointed to the new post of Commissioner-General for the United Kingdom in Southeast Asia. During the Communists' attempt to seize power in Malaya, he said in a radio broadcast from Singapore in July 1948 that "there will be no security in Malaya until the Communists are smashed" (New York *Times,* July 8, 1948). He announced at a press conference on September 5, 1949 that the Communist movement in Malaya and Thailand was almost wholly Chinese.

MacDonald sponsored in 1950 the British-backed proposals to open citizenship in the Federation of Malaya to many non-Malay residents, including Chinese and Indians, as a means of advancing the country toward democratic statehood and promoting racial harmony. Three years later, he said that progress against the Communist terrorists was being matched by political progress and that the number of Chinese who had severed their ties with China and regarded themselves as citizens of Malaya was increasing (London *Times,* September 14, 1953).

He became chairman of the joint coordination committee which was established on May 11, 1953, and was described as "the first step toward the unification of the Federation of Malaya and the colony of Singapore" (New York *Times,* May 12, 1953). Its function is advisory, to co-ordinate the interests and policies of the two governments, and to recommend changes in their existing constitutions.

In order to carry out Britain's policy of friendship and assistance toward Southeast Asian countries, MacDonald spends much of his administrative time traveling. He enjoys particularly going into Borneo in a "native canoe for a brief sojourn . . . [among] the

MACDONALD, MALCOLM—*Continued*

headhunter people." When MacDonald appeared at an evening concert in Singapore without a dinner jacket, many people disapproved. Tillman Durdin, however, wrote in the New York *Times* (June 29, 1952): "The Asians generally applauded . . . MacDonald's costume as another evidence of the disregard for colonial conventions by a man who has declined to join Singapore's old-line British clubs because they exclude Asian members."

In his article "Malaya and Her Neighbors" (*The Straits Times Annual,* 1953), MacDonald wrote: "It can be said confidently that none of the peoples of southeast Asia are by nature inclined to Communism." As quoted in the London *Times* (April 18, 1953), MacDonald stated in his pamphlet *Healing Thoughts* that "what is being overthrown in Asia is the economic, social and political system called feudalism . . . and one of the most important tasks of statesmanship today is to avert the division of east and west into two mutually suspicious . . . camps."

In his book *Down North* (Oxford, 1943), reprinted as *Canadian North* in 1945, MacDonald describes two airplane trips from Ottawa to the Arctic Ocean. *The Birds of Brewery Creek* (Oxford, 1947) is a "month-to-month record of his observations" of birds in this Ottawa region in 1945.

The British diplomat holds an M.A. degree from Oxford University and honorary LL.D. degrees from McGill and Queen's universities in Canada. He was a Rhodes trustee in 1948, and is a chancellor of the University of Malaya. His clubs are the Athenæum and Brooks's in London.

Malcolm MacDonald married Mrs. Audrey Fellowes Rowley, a Canadian widow with one son and one daughter, on December 9, 1946. They have one daughter, Fiona. He enjoys looking for rare Chinese porcelain in the antique shops of Singapore, and has a "fine collection of Asian paintings and *objets d'art.*" Occasionally he plays golf or goes swimming. He has been described as a "hard-working, clear-headed, lucid-speaking" diplomat and as "a man of tact and imagination." Thomas E. Dewey wrote in *Journey to the Far Pacific* that MacDonald has "an easy, spontaneous grin and a nature which makes him like people for their own sake."

William H. Stringer (*Christian Science Monitor,* June 6, 1949) wrote: "It has been said that MacDonald holds the most vital and responsible position of any British colonial official since Warren Hastings. It is doubly fortunate that Britain has a man of such spontaneous friendliness, such modesty and good humor, in this crucial position amidst the harried colonial peoples."

References

Life 31:73 D 31 '51 pors
London Calling F '54
Time 35:23+ Mr 18 '40 por
International Who's Who, 1954
Who's Who, 1954

MACGREGOR, ELLEN May 15, 1906-
Author; librarian

Address: b. c/o Whittlesey House, 330 W. 42nd St., New York 36; h. Hotel Allerton, Chicago 11, Ill.

Reprinted from the *Wilson Library Bulletin* April 1954

Bulletin: Ellen MacGregor died on March 29, 1954

Ellen MacGregor has been recognized as the first writer of science fiction for younger children. Mention Miss MacGregor's name to an eight-year-old or to his mother or father, and they beam and immediately talk about Miss Pickerell, whose name and experiences they know as well as those of President Eisenhower.

The creator of the popular Miss Pickerell was born in Baltimore, Maryland, May 15, 1906

ELLEN MACGREGOR

to the late Charlotte Genevieve Noble MacGregor and the late Dr. George Malcolm MacGregor. Her parents met when they became the faculty of two of the high school in a small Wisconsin town, but did not marry until shortly before George MacGregor was graduated from Johns Hopkins Medical School. During his years at Johns Hopkins, Charlotte Noble was traveling from one Wisconsin town to another, setting up libraries.

After living in Baltimore, the MacGregors returned briefly to Wisconsin, then moved with their three children (the younger two were boys) to the state of Washington. Here, they lived first in Garfield, then in Kent, where Ellen MacGregor went to high school. The many happy summers of her childhood were spent at Woodmont Beach on Puget Sound. She majored in science at the University of Washington, earned a B.S. in Library Science in 1926, and in 1931 she did postgraduate work in science at the University of California.

Dr. and Mrs. MacGregor were influential in their daughter's choice of careers, both as a librarian and as a writer. Her parents "had an exquisite sense of fun, with a lovely feeling for the ridiculous. There was much laughter in our home. Also there was much, much reading aloud. . . . Nevertheless it was with a slight lack of personal enthusiasm that I fell in with their plans for my career." She felt that she would be a librarian until something more interesting came along. "What I didn't know then, was that my training as a librarian was to be the key to many interesting jobs, to many enriching experiences, and to many happy associations."

Some of these interesting jobs included serving as librarian for the elementary schools of the Central Hawaii School district and as cataloger in the Hilo (Hawaii) Library; supervising the people who compiled the Union Catalog of Art in Chicago; serving as librarian of the Naval Operating Base in Key West; organizing and administering the library for the Naval Air Technical Training Center. She has done research in children's literature for Scott, Foresman and Company; has served as serials librarian of the Chicago Undergraduate Division of the University of Illinois; and as editor of the Illinois Women's Press Association's monthly bulletin, *Pen Points*.

It was not until 1946 that Ellen MacGregor began to write. At that time a story that she submitted for a class at the Midwestern Writers Conference was published as the book *Tommy and the Telephone*. Miss Pickerell's first appearance was in a short story, "Swept Her into Space," published in *Liberty* in 1950. This short story became in 1951 *Miss Pickerell Goes to Mars*, a science fiction book about Miss Pickerell, who in trying to protect her cow, was inadvertently whisked off on a history-making flight to Mars. The critics loved this fantasy filled with correct scientific facts. Typical of the reviews was that of Virginia Kirkus, "A lively novelty. Fact and fancy in a new venture for this age group." It was recently named the initial selection of the new Weekly Reader Children's Book Club.

Since these auspicious beginnings, Miss MacGregor has sold many stories to such magazines as *Story World, The Instructor, Christian Home*.

Miss Pickerell and the Geiger Counter was published in 1953. Critics again praised this story of Miss Pickerell, who—on the way to get a check-up for her cow—got into trouble with the owner of a steamboat and eventually discovered an unexpected source of uranium. Marjorie Fischer in the New York *Times* wrote: "Once again Ellen MacGregor has written a fine, funny story, a combination of science and science fiction which remains integrated and entertaining throughout."

In *Miss Pickerell Goes Undersea* (1953) her heroine dons the latest in underwater equipment and goes under the sea. Of this book, the Chicago *Tribune* said: "Trust Miss Pickerell to find the wreckage, learn all about undersea diving, atomic powered submarines, and underwater photography before she brings the adventure to a conclusion highly satisfactory to herself and her youthful admirers, who are sure to increase with this newest exploit."

Ellen MacGregor's latest book is *Miss Pickerell Goes to the Arctic*, which will be a Junior Literary Guild selection in 1955.

Miss MacGregor is Protestant in religion and independent in politics. She belongs to the Society of Midland Authors, Children's Reading Round Table, and Authors League. She is brown-haired and brown-eyed; is five feet seven inches tall (she weighs 150 pounds). Her hobbies include tennis, swimming, sewing, and of course she likes all kinds of books, but her favorites are those in which the ridiculous is treated seriously, as in the *Peterkin Papers*.

Reference

Chicago Sch J 32:sup29 My '51 por

MCGREGOR, G(ORDON) R(OY) Sept. 26, 1901- Organization official; aviation executive

Address: b. c/o International Air Transport Association, International Aviation Bldg., Montreal, Quebec, Canada; Trans-Canada Air Lines, International Aviation Bldg., Montreal, Quebec, Canada; h. 3526 Grey Ave., Montreal, Quebec, Canada

One of Canada's distinguished aviators in World War II, G. R. McGregor has been the president of Trans-Canada Air Lines since 1948. The air line, owned by the Canadian government and incorporated by an act of Parliament in 1937 as a subsidiary of Canadian National Railways, has expanded its routes from an original 122 miles to more than 18,000. In addition to serving all parts of Canada, it serves the United States and Mexico, and operates overseas flights to Bermuda, the West Indies, Great Britain, Ireland, France, and Germany.

McGregor was chosen president in 1952 of the International Air Transport Association, a group which is composed of sixty-two air lines which together carry 95 per cent of the world's scheduled international air traffic.

Gordon Roy McGregor was born September 26, 1901 in Montreal, Canada, the son of Dr. Thomas Daniel McGregor, a dentist, and the former Florence May Morris. He attended the Montreal High School and St. Andrew's College before entering McGill University where he studied engineering. At the age of twenty-two, he joined the engineering department of the Bell Telephone Company in Montreal. He was advanced to division engineer in Ottawa in 1929, and in 1932 was promoted to district manager and transferred to Kingston, Ontario.

"It was in Kingston," Ken Johnstone has written in *New Liberty* (November 1951), "that Gordon McGregor became deeply interested in flying. He joined the Kingston Flying Club on the year of his arrival there and three years later captured the coveted Webster Trophy for amateur flyers. He repeated the feat in 1936

Dwight E. Dolan, Montreal

G. R. MCGREGOR

and 1938. . ." McGregor spent six years at Kingston and in 1938 returned to Montreal to become the telephone company's district manager there.

Having joined Auxiliary Squadron No. 115 of the Royal Canadian Air Force in 1938, McGregor was commissioned a flight lieutenant in No. 1 Squadron after Canada entered World War II in September 1939, and was stationed at Northolt, England.

Transferred in January 1941 to the command of the 402d Squadron, McGregor participated in many air sweeps over France and won promotion to Wing Commander at the Lincolnshire station of the RCAF in the following April. From October 1941 to May 1942, McGregor served as director of the Air Staff, RCAF Headquarters Overseas; from May 1942 to February 1943 he was commanding officer of the Canadian X-Wing based at Anchorage, Alaska, and later of the Canadian air force station at Patricia Bay. British Columbia.

He was reassigned in January 1944 to the staff headquarters of the 83d Group, 126th Wing, of the Second Tactical Air Force. This group was assigned to provide air coverage for the British Second Army in the coming invasion of France. McGregor planned with such thoroughness and efficiency that on "D-Day plus four" aircraft of the 126th Wing were able to operate from airstrips prepared by its own ground forces in the Orne River valley in Normandy.

He commanded the 126th Wing on the European continent from July 1944 to October 1945, when he was returned to Canada for demobilization with the rank of group captain. For his wartime services, which included shooting down five Nazi planes, McGregor was decorated with the Order of the British Empire, the Distinguished Flying Cross, the Czechoslovakian War Cross, and the French Croix de Guerre. He was made a commander of the Order of the Orange Nassau of the Netherlands.

Among those who had found McGregor's organizational work for the Normandy invasion particularly noticeable was H. J. Symington, president of Trans-Canada Air Lines. The air line had been incorporated by an act of the Canadian Parliament in April 1937 as a "publicly owned company" and began its first commercial air service between Vancouver (British Columbia) and Seattle (Washington) in September 1937. It inaugurated the first Canadian transcontinental passenger service (Montreal to Vancouver) on April 1, 1939. The air line extended its service to the Maritime Provinces in 1940 and began its first transatlantic flights in 1943.

H. J. Symington persuaded McGregor to join TCA in December 1945 as a "special representative" and a month later McGregor was promoted to general traffic manager. In the immediate postwar period, many ex-service personnel were trained as pilots, mechanics, radio operators, and other specialists in the air line and a new twin-engine fleet of twenty-seven DC-3 aircraft was established. In 1946 1,212 miles of new routes were inaugurated with service between cities in Canada and the United States.

Twenty Canadian-built four-engine "North Stars," patterned on the Douglas DC-6 and powered with Rolls-Royce engines, were first put into service in 1947 on a transatlantic route between Canada, Ireland and Great Britain.

In August 1947 McGregor, whose work as TCA's general traffic manager had led to an intensive study of all traffic problems confronting the air transportation industry, went to Petrópolis, Brazil and officiated as chairman of the traffic conference of the International Air Transport Association and later as chairman of the entire conference.

When H. J. Symington retired as president of Trans-Canada Air Lines, G. R. McGregor succeeded him on February 2, 1948 and was appointed to the seven-member board of directors. The air line is considered to have made noteworthy advances under McGregor's administration. In 1949 its fleet carried 685,000 passengers, and while the North Atlantic operations were not profitable largely owing to the competition of British, Dutch and French overseas air lines, economies and efficiency held the deficit to $4,000,000.

For 1950, however, McGregor was able to report "a surplus for North American operations and a reduced deficit for overseas operations, approximately half that of 1949," while "the total revenue mileage flown by the company increased by 6 per cent over 1949, with 5 per cent fewer employees and with a fleet that remained unchanged in size."

McGregor was a passenger on the Avro jet liner which covered the 365 miles between Toronto and New York City in 59 minutes and 56 seconds on April 18, 1950. This Avro liner was the first turbojet transport plane ever flown in the United States. Although McGregor then predicted regular commercial jet schedules in from two to five years, he stated about two months after the initial jet flight that TCA had no immediate plans for using jet-propelled air liners.

By 1950 Trans-Canada air routes had been established between Canada and Tampa, the Bahamas, Bermuda, Jamaica, Barbados and Trinidad; in 1951 its transatlantic service was extended to Paris; and by 1954 the air line had routes to Düsseldorf, Germany and to Mexico. It was serving forty communities in Canada, and nineteen outside Canada, and was operating routes totalling more than 18,000 miles.

Elected president of the International Air Transport Association in the autumn of 1952, McGregor has taken an active part in IATA conferences. At the ninth general assembly held in Montreal in October 1953, he stated that Trans-Canada had ordered eight new American Lockheed Super Constellations for its North Atlantic and transcontinental air routes, and fifteen British-built Viscount turbine-propeller ("turbo-prop")-powered air liners for medium-range, coast-to-coast flights in North America. McGregor added that ties of sentiment played no part in final decisions for either order, because, in view of the world competitive situation, "no air line could possibly afford such a luxury" (New York *Herald Tribune*, October 9, 1953).

McGregor keeps his private flying license regularly renewed and is an honorary member of Canadian Air Lines Pilots Association. He maintains membership in the Air Force Veterans Association, the Wartime Pilots and Observers Association, and the RCAF Association in Montreal, where he is Honorary Wing Commander of 401 Squadron, and Honorary President of the 306th Maple Leaf Wing.

He serves on the board of governors of the Canadian Corps of Commissionaires, is a life governor of the Montreal General Hospital and is on the executive committee of the aviation section of the Montreal Board of Trade. The air line executive is a Presbyterian in faith, and is a Mason (Scottish Rite)

McGregor belongs to the Kingston, Lethbridge, Montreal and Winnipeg flying clubs; the Kanawaki and Royal Ottawa golf clubs, the Mount Bruno Country, Mount Royal, United Services, and Royal St. Lawrence Yacht clubs, Wings (New York), Buck's (London), and Forest and Stream. He plays golf in the low 90's, enjoys trout and deep sea fishing, and yachting.

He was married on June 29, 1928 to Alexandra May Ramsay of Montreal. He is five feet ten inches tall, weighs about 185 pounds and has brown hair and eyes. "His business associates and the press," Ken Johnstone has written, "know McGregor as . . . cautious and . . . precise. . . . But his friends know another McGregor—a gregarious, genial and very witty type."

References

Sat Night 68:23+ Ap 23 '52 por; 68:6+ N 1 '52 por

Business Executives of America (1950)
Who's Who in America, 1952-53
Who's Who in Canada, 1951-52

MACY, GEORGE May 12, 1900- Publisher; editor

Address: b. 595 Madison Ave., New York 22; h. 1185 Park Ave., New York 28

Twenty-five years ago, in the spring of 1929, George Macy conceived the idea of establishing an unusual publishing enterprise, the Limited Editions Club, which was to make him, as Sir Francis Meynell has said, "the world's leading impresario of the fine book." In his subsequent "daring concoctions" (to use Bennett Cerf's words) in the field of book printing and distributing, he has organized the Heritage Club, the Junior Heritage Club and the Readers Club. Since its founding in 1935 he has been president of the Heritage Press and since 1936 managing director of London's Nonesuch Press.

To celebrate its silver jubilee on May 11, 1954, the Limited Editions Club, whose de luxe reprints of past and present classics have become internationally famous, appropriately honored twenty-five American authors, illustrators and book designers for achievements "most likely to endure as the classics of our time."

A native New Yorker, George Macy was born on May 12, 1900 to Harris and Rose (Fedder) Macy. His high school was the De Witt Clinton in New York, from which he was graduated in 1917 with general honors. While achieving the high scholastic rating that earned him the title of valedictorian of his class, he also gave his attention to a number of extracurricular activities as editor-in-chief of school publications, president of the honor society and student member of the board of governors.

Macy entered Columbia University in 1917 and before graduating in 1921 took part in the United States World War I effort in the rank of second lieutenant. He was secretary of Columbia's student board of governors, a member of the Sigma Delta Chi and Pi Delta Epsilon honor fraternities, and three-times-winner of the Gold King's Crown. He also belonged to Zeta Beta Tau social fraternity, of which he later (1923-28) served as secretary.

As editor-in-chief of both the *Columbian Jester* and the *Columbian*, Macy may be said to have cut his editorial teeth at the university. He was still a student when he published selections from Franklin P. Adams' *The Conning Tower* (a newspaper column in *The World* to which Macy was a frequent contributor). He sold some 11,000 copies of this anthology of light verse.

In 1924 Macy founded the publishing house of Macy-Masius, and four years later (1928) he sold this firm to become head of the Vanguard Press, a connection which proved to be his last association with "ordinary" trade book publishing.

The nation's prosperity was at a peak in the spring of 1929 when Macy followed the suggestion of Colonel Harold Riegelman (Republican nominee for mayor of New York City in 1953) to approach a stock-broker friend, Jack O. Straus, for support of a publishing

Portrait by Norman Rockwell

GEORGE MACY

project. Learning that Macy needed $40,000 to finance his enterprise, (according to Bennett Cerf in *Saturday Review of Literature,* July 4, 1942), Straus went to the floor of the Stock Exchange and shortly returned with twenty checks for $1,000 and a $20,000 check of his own. "Someday," the broker is quoted as saying to the young publisher, "you must tell me what the project is."

Macy's new idea, for which its backers have since regularly received a 10 per cent dividend on their investment, was to form a limited editions club. Each month 1,500 copies of an elaborate illustrated edition of a classic were to be printed for sale to enrolled members at $10 a copy (later $12) or at $108.00 paid in advance for the year's series. Macy limited the edition to 1,500 because additional copies would show some loss in the precision of the hand-set type and hand-wrought lithographs.

When its first selection, a handsome reprint of *Gulliver's Travels,* illustrated by Alexander King, (*The Travels of Lemuel Gulliver,* first edition printed by Motte in 1726, was followed) was ready for distribution, the club had 1,100 subscribers. Copies were mailed on October 23, 1929—the "Black Wednesday" of the stock market collapse. During the years of the depression that followed, the club nevertheless flourished, filling its membership ranks by 1932 and forming a waiting list.

From the beginning, 70 per cent of the members of the Limited Editions Club have been men, many of them in professional, educational and military fields. Its members include a large number of well-known Hollywood stars like Humphrey Bogart and Tyrone Power, and Government figures like Oveta Culp Hobby and Ambassador Clare Boothe Luce. Among other subscribers are housewives, a coal miner and a drop-forge operator.

The careful devotion that the club's organizer gives to producing a fine book may be seen in his article in the *Hornbook* (May 1940), "Arthur Rackham and *The Wind in the Willows,*" in which he relates calling on the English artist in the summer of 1936 and planning the details which resulted in the Limited Editions Club's reprint of the Kenneth Grahame classic.

The most significant achievement of the club is probably its edition of the writings of William Shakespeare, designed by Bruce Rogers and edited by Herbert Fargeon, in the original First Folio spelling. The thirty-seven volumes, published in 1939-40, are illustrated by thirty-seven painters from fifteen different countries, with four-color end-papers reproducing a wall-painting found in the home of John Davenant, where Shakespeare is believed to have lodged.

The Club's publications are "interesting as exhibits of international bookmaking," (*Time,* December 19, 1935) to which artists, scholars and craftsmen of a number of countries have contributed. Volumes have been printed in twenty different countries; for example, Dante's writings in Italy, *Don Quixote* in Spain, *Anna Karenina* in the U.S.S.R., *Confucian Analects* in China and Lafcadio Hearn's *Kwaidan* in Japan.

In selecting the most appropriate illustrator for a particular classic, Macy has engaged such well-known artists as Grant Wood, Rockwell Kent, John Steuart Curry, Henri Matisse, Pablo Picasso and Jacob Epstein. The publisher makes an effort to choose bindings that will conform to the spirit of the book; for example, sailcloth was used to bind *Robinson Crusoe* and deerskin to bind Cooper's *The Prairie.*

Several of the 260 volumes appearing during the past twenty-five years under the club's imprimatur, ranging chronologically from Homer to Hemingway, have become collectors' items. The autographed edition of James Joyce's *Ulysses* now brings up to $75 on the open market, and *Alice in Wonderland,* with new woodcuts of the original Tenniel drawings, sells for $50.

The monthly promotion letter that Macy writes for his club's members "reads as though he were selling some rare, international compounded medicine instead of reprinted classics" (*Time*). His basic point of view is that "no object of art so completely represents the cultural tastes of a nation as does a fine illustrated book, for in a fine book one reads a classic of the nation's literature and studies illustrations representative of the nation's taste in art, all printed on a paper of such a quality and bound in materials of such a quality that they represent the nation's taste in the crafts as well."

Expanding his publishing activities, Macy in 1935 organized the Heritage Press, of which he is president, for the creation and distribution of "semi-luxe" books, and the following year became managing director of the Nonesuch Press of London, founded by Sir Francis Meynell. To satisfy book-lovers who for some reason could not join the Limited Editions Club, he founded in 1937 the Heritage Club, which offers subscribers twelve monthly selections for $27.00 a year. By 1942 its membership had exceeded 9,200 and three of its selections (also purchasable in book stores), *Lust for Life, Song of Songs* and *Mother Goose,* had each sold more than 20,000 copies.

In 1940 Macy organized his third group, the Readers Club, which reached some 40,000 members with its first selection, E. H. Young's *William,* distributed in March 1951. The publisher founded his new enterprise on the idea that a large number of good books had never won their deserved popularity and that reprints of twelve such books could be sold to subscribers each year at a dollar a copy. As members of his first board of judges to make book selections, Macy chose four distinguished literary men: Clifton Fadiman and Carl Van Doren, and the late Alexander Woollcott and Sinclair Lewis.

All of Macy's publishing enterprises, including the Junior Heritage Club, which he established in 1943, were combined in 1944 as units of the George Macy Companies, Inc., in New York City.

The Limited Editions Club's "silver jubilee" selection in May 1954 of twenty-five Americans whose achievements seem destined to endure as "classics" included the following: writers Van Wyck Brooks, Rachel Carson, Carl Sandburg, Samuel Eliot Morison, William Faulkner, Bernard De Voto, Robert Frost, Ernest Hemingway, John Steinbeck, and H. L. Mencken; illustrators Boris Artzybasheff, Ludwig Bemelmans, T. M. Cleland, Fritz Eichenberg, Reginald Marsh, Fyodor Rojankovsky, Lynd Ward, and Edward A. Wilson; designers W. A. Dwiggins, Bruce Rogers, and Carl P. Rollins; and printers Elmer Adler, Joseph Blumenthal, Edwin Grabhorn, and the Lakeside Press of Chicago.

Macy is the author of *The Collected Verses of George Jester,* a Heritage publication. In 1943 he edited Heritage's *A Sailor's Reader* and *A Soldier's Reader,* each volume containing "four hundred thousand words of select literary entertainment" for members of the American armed services.

One of the many tributes paid to Macy was a special exhibition in 1948 of his books in Salle d'Honneur of the Bibliotheque Nationale in Paris, France, an honor never before accorded to a living publisher. In the fall of the following year the President of France conferred on him the title of Chevalier of the Legion of Honor.

In England during 1952, Macy was honored when he was chosen as the first living publisher to be given a special exhibition of his books in the King's Library of the British Museum in London. The American Institute of Graphic Arts named the publisher its 1953 medalist, "the highest honor that the institute can give." He has been presented with the Plaque for Distinguished Achievements by the De Witt Clinton Alumni Association (1939) and with the Zeta Beta Tau fraternity Man of the Year Trophy (1953).

Macy, who married Helen Kaplan in 1927, is the father of a daughter, Lucinda Harris, born in 1932, and of a son, Jonathan George, born in 1937. The blue-eyed, brown-haired publisher is five feet nine inches tall and weighs 160 pounds. He belongs to the Columbia and the Lotos clubs and for recreation he is likely to turn from making books to playing tennis. In politics, he is independent.

References

Pub W 156:2145 N 19 '49
Sat R Lit 25:28+ Jl 4 '42
Time 32:55 D 19 '38 por
Who's Who in the East (1953)

MAHADY, HENRY J(OSEPH) July 1, 1916- Veterans organization official; lawyer

Address: b. c/o Amvets, National Headquarters, 1710 Rhode Island Ave., N.W., Washington, D.C.; h. 701 Spring St., Latrobe, Pa.

The American Veterans of World War II, in convention in September 1953, elected Henry J. Mahady, Pennsylvania lawyer and real estate broker, as national commander for the year 1953-1954. With a membership of approximately 100,000, Amvets is the largest of the organizations for veterans of World War II and now includes veterans of the Korean campaign as well. Besides devoting its efforts to securing improved housing, medical care and other benefits for these veterans, it is concerned with problems of world peace and national security.

Since joining Amvets in 1946, after having completed his World War II service as an officer in the United States Navy, Mahady has held several local, state and national posts in the organization. Among these was commander of the Pennsylvania department in 1950.

Like his parents, James Joseph and Katharine (O'Neill) Mahady, Henry Joseph Mahady is a native of Pennsylvania. He was born in Latrobe on July 1, 1916. He had nine brothers and sisters, seven of whom are living: James J., Regis F., Paul W., Robert E., Thomas R., Katharine O., and Jane O. The elder Mahady, who conducted a real estate business in Latrobe, was able to make a college education available to all his children.

During his high school years in Latrobe, Henry was active in dramatics, football, basketball, and the school publications. He was graduated with the class of 1933, entered the University of Pennsylvania and received the A.B. degree in 1937. To help meet part of his educational expenses he took a number of odd jobs, including dishwashing, working in a laundry and modeling. While in college he also represented the New York *Times.*

Having decided to make law his career, Mahady studied at the Harvard Law School for the LL.B. degree, which was conferred in 1940. Since his admission to the bar he has practiced law with the firm of Mahady & Mahady, of Latrobe and Greensburg (Pennsylvania), with four of his brothers and a sister. He has taught law as associate professor at

HENRY J. MAHADY

Latrobe's St. Vincent College and has acted as solicitor for Unity and Derry townships and for the Pleasant Unity Volunteer Department. In Latrobe he has also been treasurer of the Westmoreland Federal Savings and Loan Association.

Not long after he had begun his law practice, Mahady in March 1942 joined the U.S. Navy and was commissioned a lieutenant (j.g.). He served in the American and European theaters of war before his discharge in December 1945 as a lieutenant commander, a rank that he retains in the Naval Reserve.

Mahady became a member of Amvets in 1946 and after occupying various positions in Latrobe Post 38, was chosen Pennsylvania department commander in 1950. For the year 1952-1953 he held the chairmanship of the Amvets' Americanism committee. He was elected national commander on September 6, 1953 at the organization's ninth annual convention, meeting that year in Indianapolis, where a close balloting made him the successor to Marshall E. Miller of Illinois.

Amvets was formally constituted in December 1944 from some twenty smaller groups of World War II veterans and received its charter from Congress on July 17, 1947. By a vote of the organization's national executive committee on July 18, 1950, veterans of the Korean War and of any future wars would be eligible to become members. In 1952 its members had increased to 85,000, about 10,000 more than the previous year. *The World Almanac* (1954) estimates its current membership at 100,000.

Three major objectives of Amvets are: "To promote peace, to preserve America's way of life, and to help veterans help themselves." In pursuing these aims the organization supports programs designed to attain improved housing, better social security and medical care for veterans, as well as policies assuring adequate national defense. Among its public services are funds for the Arlington Memorial Carillon and scholarships for war orphans. It has also established a number of awards, one of which, the Harold Russell Award, is named after the motion picture actor and former Amvets commander.

The September 1953 convention that elected Mahady to the Amvets' top executive post adopted a set of resolutions dealing with questions of national and international importance. Opposing cuts in defense expenditures and reduction in the civilian defense program, it urged that military power be maintained at a high level and that the Selective Service Act be strictly enforced. It further presented a series of arguments against admitting Communist China to the United Nations and endorsed President D. Eisenhower's opposition to the proposed Bricker amendment limiting presidential treaty-making powers.

Among the six arguments cited by the Amvets delegates against the admission of Red China were that the Peiping Government was intervening "aggressively and unlawfully" in the Indochina conflict, and that as a permanent member of the Security Council Peiping would be "unrepresentative of the peoples of Asia."

At the convention which elected Mahady its national commander the delegates urged the Republican and Democratic parties to join in a non-partisan approach to foreign relations.

In handling the problem of Allied prisoners of war accused of collaborating with Communists in Korea, the convention recommended that such prisoners "be treated adequately, that any special treatment or stigmatization be avoided. Special study is required for this new problem and this should be approached positively, but with no undue publicity" (New York *Times*, September 6, 1953).

Mahady was succeeded in August 1954 by Rufus H. Wilson as national commander, 1954-55.

In other efforts to further veterans' welfare, Mahady has been secretary of the Pennsylvania Joint Veterans Commission and legislative director of the Pennsylvania Joint Veterans Council. He has served as a trustee of the Veterans of Foreign Wars and is a member of the American Legion. He belongs to the Ancient Order of Hibernians, the Westmoreland County Volunteer Firemen's Association, and to the American, Pennsylvania and Westmoreland County bar associations. A Catholic, he is affiliated with the Knights of Columbus, in which he has filled the office of financial secretary, and of the Holy Name Society of the Holy Family Church. He is a Democrat.

He was married on November 29, 1941 to Dorothy Poulin, a secretary. They have four children: Patrick Henry, Suzanne, Sarah Jane, and John. Mahady has blue eyes and brown hair, stands six feet one inch tall, and weighs 200 pounds. Sports are his favorite recreation: he enjoys watching football, basketball and baseball games.

References

N Y Times p13 S 7 '53

Martindale-Hubbell Law Directory, 1952

MALCOLM, GEORGE A(RTHUR) (măl'kŭm) Nov. 5, 1881- Author; former Justice of the Supreme Court of the Philippine Islands

Address: h. 4947 Marathon St., Hollywood 29, Calif.

Characterizing himself as the only American to have made a career of colonial service, George A. Malcolm, former Philippine Supreme Court Justice, has drawn from his experiences and studies the materials for his legal textbooks and articles. During an eighteen-year tenure as Associate Justice and ultimately Presiding Justice of the Civil Division of the Supreme Court of the Philippine Islands, Malcolm handed down approximately 3,300 opinions for the court. In the course of his career, Malcolm has said, he has been called "young and radical", "liberal", and "an orthodox conservative" (*Rotarian,* April 1954).

A founder and first dean of the College of Law at the University of the Philippines, Malcolm counts among his former students many Filipino leaders who charted their nation on the course of independence and democracy, including three Presidents, three Speakers of the House, many Cabinet members, and ten Justices of the Supreme Court. He discussed the historical, legal and economic aspects of the Philippine Islands in his book *First Malayan Republic, the Story of the Philippines* (Christopher, 1951). "A government may be one of laws," Malcolm believes, "but fundamentally it is the character of the men who administer the government that determines its success" (*Far Eastern Review,* July 1938).

George Arthur Malcolm was born of Scottish ancestry on November 5, 1881 in Concord, Michigan to Carrie A. (MacKenzie) and Byron D. Malcolm. Educated at public schools in Ann Arbor, Michigan, George was graduated from high school in the year 1900 and won the oratorical competition. Continuing his studies at the University of Michigan in Ann Arbor, he was active on the debating teams, was chosen class orator, and was a founder of Acacia fraternity. He obtained the B.A. degree in 1904. On receiving the LL.B. degree in 1906, he went to Manila, arriving there on the Army transport *Logan.* "I was a callow graduate of the University of Michigan," he recalls, "with a law degree to be sure, but no job awaited me and less than ten dollars jingled in my pockets."

His first job, a temporary clerkship at seventy-five dollars a month, was one which "no one else wanted" in the Bureau of Health. He then became an assistant in the editing of the Philippine *Reports,* and taught evening classes in the Philippine Normal School. By 1910 he had attained the position of assistant attorney general in the Bureau of Justice.

Malcolm had proposed that a school of law be instituted at the University of the Philippines but his suggestion was not accepted by the authorities. "With the audacity of youth," Malcolm recollects, he organized law courses at the Y.M.C.A. of Manila. One year there-

JUDGE GEORGE A. MALCOLM

after the University of the Philippines instituted its College of Law, appointing Malcolm its first dean. Dean Malcolm taught his students "to dig for the law and the facts with untiring industry, to think and reason for themselves, and to understand democracy in all its phases." In a textbook, *Philippine Civics* (D. Appleton, 1919) written with Maximo M. Kalaw, Malcolm sought to encourage a love of country on the part of law students.

History, Malcolm believes, has demonstrated that government is necessary. It stems from the fact that the individual often puts self-interest first and therefore must be controlled by an outside force. "We should, therefore," Malcolm concludes, "want to understand the nature of government in order to protect our rights and not disturb the rights of others" (*Philippine Civics*).

President Woodrow Wilson in 1917 appointed Malcolm to the Supreme Court of the Philippines. The appointment was nonpolitical; the President had not inquired into Malcolm's political affiliation but selected the new Justice on his fine record and reputation.

In a case which involved the charge of criminal falsification of certain documents, Judge Malcolm, speaking for the court, made a distinction between mere error, ineptitude, or stupidity on the one hand, and criminal responsibility on the other. "It is a serious matter," he said, "to be responsible for sending the accused to prison for long terms. All reasonable doubt intended to demonstrate error and not crime should be indulged in to the benefit of the prisoners at the bar. If the inculpatory facts and circumstances are capable of two or more explanations, one of which is consistent with innocence of the accused of the crime charged and the other consistent with their guilt, then the evidence does not fulfill the test of moral certainty and is not

MALCOLM, GEORGE A.—*Continued*

sufficient to support a conviction" (*People v. Pacana* et al., [1924] 47 Phil. 48).

He wrote: "Being susceptible to little restraint, the court could cut through technicalities to do justice. Being a court which had to piece out the meaning of legislation, it judicially legislated. . ." (*The Commonwealth of the Philippines*, Appleton-Century, 1936).

The function of constitutional law, according to Malcolm, is to define the "political center of gravity" of the state. It is the product of men's effort to promulgate "standards through which the fundamental stability of the state and its organs is legally regulated and protected. A constitution," Malcolm continues, "has three main objects. One is to establish and maintain a frame of government under which the work of the state can be efficiently carried on. Another is to provide due security for the rights of the individual citizen. The third object is to hold the state together" (*The Constitutional Law of the Philippine Islands*, Lawyers Cooperative, 1920).

In *The Commonwealth of the Philippines*, Malcolm examines the government and economic conditions of the islands. Theodore Roosevelt, Jr., Governor General of the Philippines in 1932 and 1933 commented, "Justice Malcolm genuinely cares for the people but he is not blinded by his affection. He sees their virtues . . . and the inevitable future that lies before them when they face the stormy years of Asian politics. . . ." (*Saturday Review of Literature*, May 23, 1936). Another critic wrote: "This book is one of those rare volumes that successfully combine popular appeal with genuine scholarly worth. . . . He has always been notably sympathetic with the people among whom he has lived and worked, yet has never lost his sturdy Americanism" (*American Political Science Review*, August 1936).

After the inauguration of the Commonwealth of the Philippines, November 15, 1935, Malcolm retired from the court. At this time the people of the Philippines assumed the entire operation of government under the leadership of Manuel L. Quezon. The establishment of the Commonwealth, Malcolm has indicated, was one part of the American policy which has permitted the development of the democratic institutions of the Philippines. The United States maintained its sovereignty over the Philippines during the period of the Commonwealth which terminated July 4, 1946 at which time the Republic of the Philippines was established. Malcolm remained in the Philippines as a member of the staff of the U.S. High Commissioner from 1936 until 1940. On February 12, 1940 he was appointed attorney general of Puerto Rico. He served in this position until November 1942.

In commenting on Malcolm's book, *First Malayan Republic*, Howard P. Linton of the East Asiatic Library, Columbia University has written: "His career and intimacy with leaders qualify him to speak with authority on the history of government, politics, law, and international relations of a country which is really little known and yet of great importance to us" (*Library Journal*, June 1, 1951).

General Carlos P. Romulo described the book as "a panoramic presentation of the Philippines . . . a kaleidoscope that aims frankly at nothing more ambitious than variety and comprehensiveness. . . . It is perhaps inevitable that some trivia should creep into such an exhaustive summing-up" (*Saturday Review of Literature*, September 1, 1951).

Included among his many books are *The Government of the Philippine Islands; Its Development and Fundamentals* (Lawyers Cooperative, 1916), *Revised Ordinances of the City of Manila* (Manila Bureau of Printing, 1908, 1916, 1927), with M. M. Kalaw *Philippine Government; Development, Organization and Functions* (Heath, 1923), *Legal Ethics* (Oriental Commercial, 1923), and *Legal and Judicial Ethics, adapted for the Republic of the Philippines* (Lawyers Cooperative, 1949). He also prepared for enactment *The Charter of the city of Baguio . . . and the Revised Ordinances of the city of Baguio* (1934). Among the numerous periodicals in which Malcolm's articles have appeared are the *American Law Review, Far Eastern Review, Political Science Quarterly,* and *Rotarian.*

Malcolm is a member of the American Bar Association (past president of the Philippine branch), Philippine Bar Association (past president). Puerto Rican Bar Association, Philippine Society of Southern California (past president). He served as the first Rotary Club governor of the Philippines and is a past president of the Rotary Club of Manila. His memberships also include the Masons and Elks. Honorary degrees have been conferred upon him by the University of Michigan (1921), (Hogaku Hakushi) Imperial University, Tokyo (1922), University of the Philippines (1949) and the National University in Manila (1949).

On December 13, 1932 Malcolm married Lucille Margaret Wolf; the couple has a daughter, Mary MacKenzie Malcolm. The white-haired judge has blue eyes and is five feet eleven inches in height and weighs 140 pounds. Among his favorite recreations is traveling, and he has completed about a dozen world trips. He is an independent Republican.

After his long career in the Philippines Malcolm wrote: "It has been a worth-while adventure. From a front row in the audience, but privileged occasionally to prompt the actors, I have seen a great drama unfold. . . ." (*Rotarian*, April 1941).

References

Malcolm, G. A. First Malayan Republic (1951)
Who's Who in America, 1954-55
Who's Who in Law, 1937
Who's Who in the West (1954)

MALLAKH, KAMAL EL *See* El Mallakh, K.

MARCANTONIO, VITO Dec. 10, 1902-Aug. 9, 1954 Former United States Representative from New York; lawyer; educated at New York University; served as secretary and campaign manager of the late Fiorello La Guardia, and as U.S. assistant district attorney (1930-1931); was U.S. Congressman between 1935-1937 and 1939-1951, first as Republican-City Fusion representative and later as American Labor party member; often accused of espousing Communist causes and the Soviet Union's foreign policy, he always denied that he was a Communist. See *Current Biography,* (Feb.) 1949.

Obituary

N Y Times p1+ Ag 10 '54

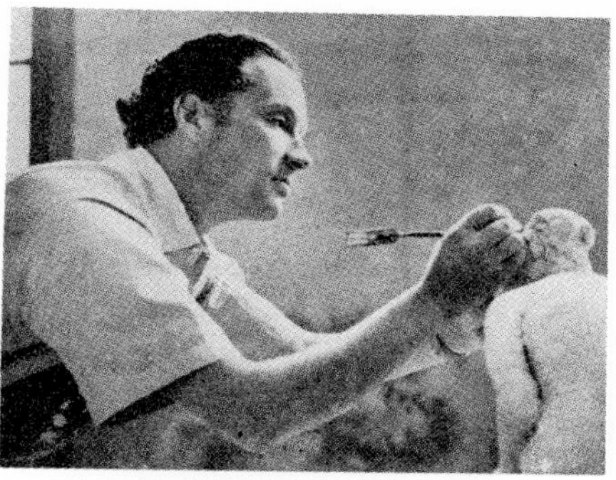

MARINO MARINI

MARINI, MARINO Feb. 25, 1901- Sculptor; painter

Address: b. Piazza Mirabello, Milan 2, Italy

Italian sculptor Marino Marini has studied the great art of his country, both classical and Renaissance, and Egyptian and Chinese art. To these rich elements he has added the viewpoint of a perceptive modern artist. Recognized as one of the finest portrayers of our times in bronze and in stone, Marini is best known for an eloquent series known as the Horsemen, fraught with feeling and symbolic of the tragedy of mankind. Recently, his paintings have received equally favorable criticism.

His work has been exhibited at the Museum of Modern Art and the Buchholz Gallery in New York City, the M. H. de Young Memorial Museum in San Francisco, the Institute of Contemporary Art in Boston, the Cincinnati Art Museum, and in other American cities as well as in leading galleries abroad. His most recent show was held at the Curt Valentin Gallery in New York City which included besides sculpture, painting, drawing and lithography, and served "to confirm his stature to a greater degree," according to art critic Howard Devree in the New York *Times* (November 1, 1953).

Marino Marini was born on February 25, 1901 to Guido and Bianca (Bonacchi) Marini in the town of Pistoia, Tuscany, famed in the fourteenth century for its Romanesque sculptors. At the age of fourteen Marino enrolled at the Academy of Fine Arts in Florence with the intention of becoming a painter. At the end of the course, spent among old anatomy casts, he came out a seeming product of traditional studies in an old academy, not unlike Picasso, Morandi and Modigliani who had attended the same classes ten years earlier. As a pupil he was introspective and without a show of virtuosity. The most precious memory of his youth was a meeting with the sculptor, Auguste Rodin, who stopped in Florence in 1915 on his return from Rome where he had finished the portrait bust of Benedict XV.

Marini's early years, especially the formative period from 1928 to 1938, were devoted to extensive traveling, the study of painting and visiting Paris galleries. He first entered an art competition in 1929, and thereafter, was represented in every national and international exhibit in Italy. From 1929 to 1940 he taught at the School of Art of Villa Reale in Monza. In 1935 he took first prize in sculpture in Italy's *Quadriennale,* top exhibit for Italian artists held every four years in Rome. He exhibited his works in Paris and in 1937 won the Grand Prix. In 1940 he received high honors on his sculptures from the Academy of Sculpture of Brera in Milan. Marini worked assiduously and evolved the Horsemen into a series, the prototype of which was first struck in 1936.

Quickly discerning Marini's talents early in the horesmen series, a French critic, Paul Fierens, (XXe *Siècle,* July 1938) declared: "Marini shines like a star of the first magnitude. His *Horse and Rider* is an original and brilliant idea. In the horseman and other figures we are able to see an image and almost a symbol of faithful and authentic humanity. . . . Marino Marini gets . . . away from mannerisms . . he is modern yet above vogue, he is Italian without need of leaning upon his Italianity, and without further imitation of the Romans and Etruscans."

His work was influenced by the war years and reflects the shock of death and destruction upon him. This experience is evident in the feeling of suffering humanity within the massive forms of his sculpture. His deepest impression was that of the fleeing peasants of his adopted Lombardy.

He illustrated *Il Fiore delle Georgiche* by Salvatore Quasimado (1942). Returning to Milan in 1946, he resumed teaching at the Academy of Sculpture of Brera where he is still an instructor. Now matured and freed of academism, he permits his students the utmost stylistic liberty. His studio is in the courtyard below his apartment. He models in plaster, and only occasionally carves. He finds it hard to work in Rome where its vast cultural accrual is omnipresent, preferring Milan because his intense working schedule fits into the energetic life and industry of that city.

His works did not reach the United States until 1948. Since then he has had a number of exhibits. His first presentation to America was at the twentieth-century Italian art exhibit at the New York Museum of Modern

MARINI, MARINO—*Continued*

Art in 1948. His sculpture was included in the international sculpture exhibit in Philadelphia the following year.

He had his first one-man show at the Buchholz Gallery in February 1950 in New York and for this occasion he made his first voyage to America. *Newsweek* wrote (February 27, 1950): "The show amply demonstrated that Marini, one of Italy's most promising young artists, confines his penetrating simplicity to few subjects. He is deeply preoccupied with the equestrian arrangements."

Italian art critic Lamberto Vitali has said that Marini "combines the assurance of a plastic artist with all the curiosity of a psychologist, and he has all the Tuscan's quick intuition, irony, and malicious astuteness."

In this country, as in Europe, the Horsemen series made the greatest impression on the art critics. Aline B. Louchheim (New York *Times*, February 19, 1950) described the horse as the symbol of the most helpless, terrified, and lost of living creatures, the rider tragically letting himself be led, his arms in resigned agony. In other versions of the horseman, she wrote, the rider is more hopeful, lifting his hands to the sky to welcome life. She concluded, "these horses and riders and female torsos are not individuals but part of the universe."

Carlyle Burrows wrote (New York *Herald Tribune*, February 19, 1950): "This is work of moderation, with a lyrical and human sensibility, not unreminiscent of the abstract expressions of Henry Moore. And it is closer in sympathy with Chinese and Egyptian art than to the resolute fantasies of American and north European sculptors who have chosen to explore abstract form more vigorously."

On the other hand, *Time* (February 27, 1950) reported that the riders looked like oversized babies mounted bareback on Mongolian ponies —scared not proud, and going nowhere, and the statue of a girl showed she obviously suffered and survived. But, it concluded, "those whose taste in sculpture had been formed by that of the Greeks and Renaissance Italians would find such works hard to take."

Marini himself thinks of his work as the "new renascence of sculpture in Italy, the new humanism, the new reality" (New York *Times*, February 19, 1950). He nods to futurism in sculpture but considers his work essentially Italian in tradition. Futurism, he says, was a mighty force of liberation from the past and outmoded styles but because it created an impression rather than a definite form it was not lasting, and speaks disparagingly of accidental rather than wholly intentional effects. The Italian temperament, he believes, is eternally grounded in the definitive, in a sense of the definite almost in an architectural concept; and here it seems, after discarding futurism, is Marini's point of departure from Massaccio and Donatello and earlier Romanesque masters.

In the United States, Marini is represented in the Detroit Museum and the Museum of Modern Art in New York. In his own country, Marini's works are included in the Galleria d'Arte Moderna (Rome), and the Galleria d'Arte Moderna of Florence, Turin, Trieste, and Milan. He is also represented in the Museé du Jeu de Paume (Paris), the Academy of Albertina (Vienna), as well as a museum in Basel (1936) and in Zurich. In 1950 the *Biennale* international exhibit in Venice had a Marini room of sculptures, repeated the following year at the Palais des Beaux Arts (Brussels). Marini exhibited in Zurich (1940), Basel (1944), Madrid and Stockholm (1948).

In May, 1951 Marini had an exhibition at the Hanover Gallery in London, England, and in July, 1951 at the Frank Perls Gallery in Beverly Hills, California. In 1953 a group of his sculptures and paintings was exhibited in Boston, San Francisco and other cities of the United States. His numerous exhibitions have included a series known as Marini's "Gallery of Heads."

Commenting on Marini's show in the fall of 1953 at the Curt Valentin Gallery, Howard Devree wrote in the New York *Times*: "There are horses which make one think of ancient Chinese pieces and there are small bronzes which have about them something of the dignity of Etruscan figures . . . there are large bronzes such as *Juggler* and *Dancer* in which Marini succeeds in evoking his own mystery—enigmatic forms embodying a curious fatalism of their own. He has evoked color, too, in touches of gilt and rusty red in some figures." He has received awards from the Royal Academy of Monaco, the Royal Academy of Fiamminga and the Royal Academy of Stockholm. The sculptor was married to Marina Pedrazzini on December 12, 1938. He is five feet six inches tall, weighs 164 pounds, and has black hair and brown eyes. His religion is Catholic.

References

Life 28:99+ My 22 '50
Newsweek 35:74 F 27 '50
Sat R 32:64 D 3 '49
Time 55:45 F 27 '50

Dictionnaire des Peintres, Sculpteurs, Dessinateurs et Graveurs vol 5 (1952)
Enciclopedia Italiano (Trecane) (1948)
Italia e gli Italiano de Oggi (1947)
Marini M. Marino Marini, Scultore (1948)
Vitali, L. Marini (1946)

MARSH, REGINALD Mar. 14, 1898-July 3, 1954 American painter, illustrator and etcher; graduated from Yale University (1920); first worked as artist for magazines and New York *Daily News;* taught painting at Art Students League and Moore Institute; his paintings, noted for their portrayals of the modern American girl and city life, are in Metropolitan Museum of Art and Library of Congress; received gold medal from the National Institute of Arts and Letters (1954) and other awards; designed theatre curtains for *Greenwich Village Follies;* curtain and sets for *Fashion;* a curtain for Otis Skinner's *Sancho Panza;*

designed several curtains for John Murray Anderson's *Almanac;* his pictures were shown at Weyhe, Valentin, Marie Sterner, and Rehn galleries; his murals are in Washington, D.C. Post Office and New York City customs house; an opponent of modernism in art. See *Current Biography,* (Sept.) 1941.

Obituary

N Y Times p31 Jl 4 '54

MARSHALL, THURGOOD July 2, 1908-
Lawyer

Address: b. c/o National Association for the Advancement of Colored People, 20 W. 40th St., New York 18; h. 409 Edgecombe Ave., New York 32

As special counsel for the National Association for the Advancement of Colored People (NAACP), Thurgood Marshall has appeared before the Supreme Court of the United States and has successfully presented his position on fourteen separate occasions. The brief presented to the court which resulted in the May 17, 1954 opinion that racial segregation in the public schools manifestly failed to fulfill constitutional mandates was prepared under the direction of Marshall who also argued the case.

He contended that segregation, in any form, is unconstitutional, and that the Fourteenth Amendment was intended "to proscribe all forms of state-imposed racial distinctions" (New York *Times,* May 18, 1954). Marshall earlier said that the doctrine of "separate but equal" facilities laid down by the Supreme Court in the case of *Plessy v. Ferguson* in 1896 had been used since that time to perpetuate unconstitutional practices and should now be set aside (New York *Times,* December 10, 1953).

Called "America's outstanding civil rights lawyer," Marshall has established constitutional precedents within the last fifteen years. His major Supreme Court victories include *Smith v. Allwright,* establishing the rights of Negroes to vote in the Democratic primary elections in Texas; *Morgan v. Virginia,* declaring unconstitutional the state's segregation law as applied to interstate bus passengers; *Sweatt v. Painter,* requiring the University of Texas to admit Sweatt to its law school; and *Shelley v. Kraemer,* rendering state enforcement of racial restrictive housing covenants a denial of the rights guaranteed by the Fourteenth Amendment.

Thurgood Marshall was born in Baltimore, Maryland, on July 2, 1908, the son of William Canfield and Norma A. (Williams) Marshall. His great-grandfather was brought to Maryland as a slave from the African Congo, and later won his freedom because of his independent spirit (*Survey,* January 1949). His mother was a teacher in a primary segregated public school in Baltimore, where Thurgood attended elementary and secondary schools. His father was a country club steward.

After being graduated with honors from Douglas High School in Baltimore, Marshall attended Lincoln University in Chester County, Pennsylvania, earning his tuition as a grocery clerk, dining car waiter and baker. However, he found time to be a member of the debating team. He received the A.B. degree *cum laude* in 1930, and then enrolled as a law student at Howard University in Washington, D.C., where he says "for the first time, I found out my rights" (*Time,* December 21, 1953).

Wide World
THURGOOD MARSHALL

Awarded the LL.B. degree *magna cum laude* from Howard in 1933, Thurgood Marshall was admitted to the Maryland bar the same year. He was engaged in private practice in Baltimore from 1933 to 1938, and also served as counsel for the NAACP Baltimore branch. Specializing in civil rights cases, which, according to James Poling (*Collier's,* February 23, 1952), "seldom earned a lawyer anything but respect," Marshall "built up the largest law practice in Baltimore and still couldn't pay his rent."

The attorney successfully attacked segregation in the public schools in 1935, when a suit against the University of Maryland Law School resulted in compelling that school to admit a Negro law student. He became an assistant to the late Charles Hamilton Houston, special counsel to the NAACP, in 1936. When Houston retired to private practice in 1938, Marshall succeeded him as the national organization's special counsel, with headquarters in New York City.

As special counsel to the NAACP Marshall prepared the brief for the Lloyd L. Gaines suit against the University of Missouri's discrimination policy. He also protested to James V. Allred, then Governor of Texas, the exclusion of a Negro in Austin from jury duty, and without litigation won gubernatorial support for defense by the state of jury rights of Negroes.

The lawyer was admitted to practice before the U.S. Supreme Court in 1939. In his efforts to obtain civil, political and educational rights

MARSHALL, THURGOOD—*Continued*

for Negroes, he has appeared in state and federal courts of many southern states. Federal Judge William H. Hastie, of the U.S. Third Circuit Court of Appeals, Philadelphia, stated: "Certainly no lawyer, and practically no member of the bench has Thurgood Marshall's grasp of the doctrine of law as it affects civil rights" (New York *Times,* April 6, 1951).

Marshall defended, in 1941, W. D. Lyons, of Hugo, Oklahoma, a Negro handyman accused of murder and arson. Fought to the Supreme Court, this was one of the two cases Marshall lost before that court. In the suit of Herman Marion Sweatt, a Houston Negro seeking admission as a law student to the University of Texas in 1947, Marshall questioned the equal facilities of a "temporary" segregated law school provided by the university board of regents. The suit reached the Supreme Court, and the court ordered the state to admit Sweatt to its university.

Referring to governmental exclusion of American citizens of Japanese origin from the West Coast during World War II, in his article on "The Supreme Court as Protector of Civil Rights: Equal Protection of the Laws" (*Annals of the American Academy of Political and Social Science,* May 1951), Marshall wrote: ". . . in determining the permissible reach of constitutional safeguards with respect to civil rights, military judgment must be subjected to as searching an analysis as any other type of governmental interference." He affirmed that the Supreme Court in the past decade "has done considerably more than any other arm of the federal government to secure, preserve and extend all civil rights."

Marshall went to Japan and Korea in 1951 to investigate for the NAACP complaints by Negro soldiers convicted by U.S. Army courts-martial that they received unfair trials. In arguing appeals, he had sentences reduced for twenty-two of forty convicted men. He reported that the general practice was one of "rigid segregation" in Korea, and charged "the rule of segregation was most glaringly apparent at the headquarters of the Far East Command, to which no Negroes" were assigned (New York *Times,* April 6, 1951).

When arguments began in the U.S. Supreme Court in 1952, on whether racial segregation in the nation's public schools violated the Federal Constitution, Marshall opened the argument on the Clarendon county case of South Carolina, where segregation is mandatory. "Slavery is perpetuated in these statutes," he declared. "We (NAACP) are asking only that state-imposed segregation be taken off" (New York *Times,* December 10, 1952). His opponent in this case was John W. Davis, noted constitutional lawyer.

On May 17, 1954 the U.S. Supreme Court unanimously held that racial segregation in the public schools violates the Constitution. The decision was presented in two separate rulings, one in cases involving South Carolina, Virginia, Kansas and Delaware and the other involving the District of Columbia. In the former, it was held that school segregation deprived Negroes of "the equal protection of the laws guaranteed by the Fourteenth Amendment." In the case of the District of Columbia, the court held that segregation denied Negroes "the due process of law guaranteed by the Fifth Amendment."

The opinion of the court stated: "To separate Negro children . . . solely because of their race generates a feeling of inferiority as to their status in the community that may affect their hearts and minds in a way unlikely ever to be undone. . . We conclude that in the field of public education the doctrine of 'separate but equal' has no place. Separate educational facilities are inherently unequal" (*Time,* May 24, 1954).

Howard University awarded Marshall its Alumni Award in 1944, and he was the recipient of an LL.D. degree from Lincoln University in 1947, from Virginia State College in 1948, Morgan State College in 1952, Grinnell College and Howard in 1954. In 1946 he was given the Spingarn Medal for his advancement of rights for Negroes. His name appears on the honor roll of race relations, Schomburg Collection, New York City, and he won the Negro Newspaper Publishers Association's Russwurm Award in 1948. Two years later he received the Afro-American National Honor Roll Award.

Marshall is a member of the National Bar Association, New York County Lawyers Association, American Civil Liberties Union, and Alpha Phi Alpha. He is a Democrat and an Episcopalian. James Poling wrote in *Collier's* (February 23, 1952): "Marshall seems to have gained the respect and admiration of the legal fraternity as much for his honesty and high sense of ethics as for his cleverness, eloquence and extreme skill in logic and argumentation."

The attorney married Vivien G. Burey in 1929. He is six feet one and one-half inches tall, weighs 200 pounds, and enjoys listening to phonograph recordings, watching football, and reading detective stories. Marshall has said: ". . . it's only by law suits and legislation that we'll ever teach reactionaries the meaning of the Fourteenth Amendment" (New York *Post,* May 12, 1947). He opposes the idea of a "disobedience movement" on the part of Negroes in the South and their white allies, saying this would result "in wholesale slaughter with no good achieved" (New York *Times,* November 23, 1946).

Attending the (sixty-second) annual meeting of the American Psychological Association in September 1954 in New York, Marshall stated that white and Negro children traditionally play together in the South, and that "the only time they are segregated is in school and in church" (New York *Times,* September 5, 1954).

References

N Y Times p30 Je 23 '46; p17 Je 29 '46
Survey 85:18+ Ja '49
Who's Who in Colored America, 1950

MARTIN, WALTER B(RAMBLETTE) Jan. 16, 1888- Physician; organization official
Address: b. c/o American Medical Association, 535 N. Dearborn St., Chicago 10, Ill.; 521 Wainwright Bldg., Norfolk, 10, Va.; h. 7520 North Shore Rd., Norfolk, Va.

"The physician should be interested in and responsible for the total health of his community. He should be active in his professional society, in his place of worship, and in his community welfare agencies." Such is the "basic concept of a physician's duties" expressed by Dr. Walter B. Martin, the president of the American Medical Association.

At the annual convention of the A.M.A. held at San Francisco, California in June 1954, Dr. Martin was inaugurated as the 108th president of the association. He was elected to that position one year previously by the more than 147,000 members. He succeeded Dr. Edward J. McCormick of Toledo, Ohio, and serves for one year ending June 1955. A specialist in internal disorders, Dr. Martin has practiced in Norfolk, Virginia, for over thirty years. He served in the Army Medical Corps in both World Wars, and received several decorations. He was elected first vice-president of the American College of Physicians in 1953.

In August 1954 the A.M.A. denied the American Legion's charges that it was engaged in an "anti-veteran crusade," stating that "the great preponderance of physicians in the United States are themselves veterans."

Of Scots-Irish ancestry and the descendant of American Revolution forebears, Walter Bramblette Martin was born on a farm near Pulaski, Virginia, on January 16, 1888. He was the ninth in a family of seven girls and three boys, born to David Hall Martin and the former Louisa Rachel Sutton.

David Martin moved his family to Glade Springs, Virginia, when his son Walter was three, in order that his daughters might attend the Southwest Virginia Institute.

Because of lack of available schools in the locality at this period, the three elder girls tutored their younger brothers and sisters. Thanks to their efforts and to his father's books, Walter Martin qualified for admission at the age of fourteen, to Emery and Henry College nearby. However, after about a year and a half of attendance, because of illness in his family he left, and worked as a night clerk in a country hotel. Later he was employed by two railroad construction companies and still later in a chemical manufacturing plant.

He entered the Virginia Polytechnic Institute at Blacksburg, Virginia at the age of seventeen. Although he worked his way through V.P.I., he found time to participate in college track and class football. He also became editor-in-chief of the V.P.I. *Bugle,* and was elected president of the student body, of the junior class, and of one of the debating societies. He was graduated in 1909 with a B.S. degree in analytical chemistry.

For three years beginning in 1909 Martin taught chemistry and mathematics at Norfolk

Joseph Merante
DR. WALTER B. MARTIN

Academy, a day school for boys in Norfolk, Virginia. During this period he organized and became scoutmaster of one of the country's first Boy Scout troops. Entering The Johns Hopkins University Medical School at Baltimore, Maryland in 1912, he worked his way through a four-year course by teaching in night school. He was elected to Phi Beta Kappa as well as to the Alpha Omega Alpha honorary fraternity. Martin's other Greek letter society is the Nu Sigma Nu.

For a year following the award of his M.D. degree in June 1916, Dr. Martin was a resident house officer at The Johns Hopkins Hospital. On June 13, 1917 he joined the Medical Corps of the U.S. Army for World War I service. Commissioned a first lieutenant, he was assigned as assistant divisional surgeon of the 14th Division, and was called upon to cope with the influenza epidemic which decimated the division, causing its departure for France to be cancelled.

Released from the service in 1919 holding the rank of captain, Dr. Martin returned to Norfolk to begin private practice as a specialist in the treatment of internal disorders. Within two years he began to contribute papers to medical magazines and wrote on such subjects as epidemic encephalitis, the pathology of diabetes, acute and sub-acute endocarditis, and hospital and sickness insurance. (A majority of Dr. Martin's professional papers in this period were published in the *Virginia Medical Monthly;* others appeared in the *Southern Medical Journal, Southern Medicine and Surgery, American Journal of Clinical Pathology,* and the *Annals of Internal Medicine.*)

In 1935 Dr. Martin was a prime mover in organizing the Tidewater Hospital Service Association, a non-profit group selling hospital and medical care insurance. He also helped in

MARTIN, WALTER B.—*Continued*

the passage of a city ordinance providing for the pasteurization of milk.

He began his long service to A.M.A. as a member of the House of Delegates in 1936, and was elected president of the Medical Society of Virginia for the year 1941. He is also a past president of the Norfolk County Medical Society and the Seaboard Medical Association; a fellow and a former regent of the American College of Physicians; a diplomate of the American Board of Internal Medicine; and a member of the Southern Medical Association, American Society of Clinical Pathologists, American Clinical and Climatological Association, American Association for the Study of Allergy, and the American Association for the Study of Rheumatism.

Volunteering for active World War II service, Dr. Martin rejoined the Army Medical Corps on May 8, 1942 as a lieutenant colonel. He was assigned in September to the Percy Jones Hospital, Battle Creek, Michigan, as chief of medicine, where he served until the fall of 1943 when he was made a medical consultant to the Fifth Service Command. His fourteen months of overseas duty began in July 1944 when he was assigned as medical consultant with the 10th Army and spent a portion of his time attending General Joseph ("Vinegar Joe") Stilwell. With two other medical officers, Colonel Martin toured collecting stations and other medical installations on such Pacific islands as Saipan and Peleliu, and was often "under air attack and artillery bombardment."

He was awarded the Bronze Star Medal for meritorious service on Okinawa during a period when he often went without sleep for thirty-six hours serving the 6th Marines. (Other decorations conferred on him were three battle stars and a commendation ribbon for superior service at the Percy Jones Hospital.)

Colonel Martin's wartime observations were recorded in papers on such subjects as psychoneurosis, relapsing malarial infections, snake bites, and dengue-like fever, published in the *U.S. Army Medical Department Bulletin* and elsewhere. He was one of three men assigned, after the cessation of hostilities in the Pacific, to tour Army hospitals in Germany and make recommendations for a training program.

In 1945 Dr. Martin began five years of membership in the A.M.A.'s Council on Medical Service. He became a member of the A.M.A.'s board of trustees in 1946, and was a member of its executive committee from 1950 to 1953. He went to England as chairman of an A.M.A. committee assigned to study medical care under the National Health Act. (Their report may be found in the August 19, 1950 number of the *Journal of the American Medical Association.*)

In September 1951, Dr. Martin was spokesman for the A.M.A. at hearings held in Washington by the House of Representatives' Interstate and Foreign Commerce Committee on the bill sponsored by Congresswoman Frances P. Bolton of Ohio to provide $47,000,000 in Federal aid annually for the training of nurses. He criticized the measure as "an intrusion of the Federal government into the field of education," and argued for a substitute bill approved by the A.M.A. which would have limited a grant-in-aid to five years and to the training of advanced nurses. "The real bottleneck," he declared, "is qualified teachers." (Mrs. Bolton's measure was tabled in committee).

At Norfolk, where he returned to practice after the war, Dr. Martin was for several years the chief of medicine at the St. Vincent de Paul Hospital, and is now its medical consultant. He is also the attending specialist in internal medicine at the U.S. Public Health Service Hospital in Norfolk, civilian consultant to the Army Air Force, honorary consultant to the Navy Medical Corps, and a member of the Hoover Commission's Medical Task Force. He is a past president of the Norfolk Community Chest as well as of the Norfolk Hospital Association. In the early 1950's he "saved" the Community Hospital of Norfolk, an institution for Negroes administered by Negroes, by accepting chairmanship of a commission which made a detailed report recommending changes and improvements. In his private medical work, Dr. Martin is associated with Drs. John Franklin and Robert B. Gahagan; a fellow practitioner has remarked on his "uncanny ability to absorb information and evaluate it instantaneously."

On June 4, 1953, in the concluding sessions of the A.M.A.'s 102nd annual convention held in New York City, Dr. Martin was chosen as president-elect. Representing his association at hearings held by the House of Representatives' Veterans Affairs Committee in July 1953, Dr. Martin urged Congress "to curtail sharply free Federal care of veterans suffering from maladies which have no connection with their military service" (New York *World-Telegram and Sun,* July 13, 1953).

In January 1954, at hearings by the House Interstate and Foreign Commerce Committee, he testified to A.M.A. support of the Eisenhower health program with the exception of his $25,000,000 health reinsurance measure on "catastrophic illness." (This bill was defeated in the House of Representatives in July 1954 by a vote of 238 to 134.)

In August 1954 the A.M.A. received criticism from two quarters: the *Yale Law Journal* published a report based on a two-year study by a group of Yale Law School students charging that the A.M.A. wields "excessive power" and blocks progress in solving medical-economic problems by low-cost health plans (New York *Herald Tribune,* August 3, 1954). On August 26 Arthur J. Connell, national commander of the American Legion, accused the A.M.A. of waging "an anti-veteran campaign," attacking the Legion's desire for compensation for non-service-connected disabilities for veterans, and opposing Federal insurance. The A.M.A. contends that it opposed the Federal insurance plan because it was unnecessary and was an intrusion of Federal power.

Taking office as A.M.A. president on June 22, 1954, Dr. Martin emphasized the need for doctors to "reach back further than the disease" in treating patients. ("Medicine is a healing art," he declared. "It must deal with individuals. . . . The tendency of modern medicine is to separate the patient further and further from the physician.") The 147,000 members of what has been described as "the world's largest and most diversified medical organization" elected Dr. Elmer Hess of Erie, Pennsylvania to succeed Dr. Martin in June 1955.

He has long been a deacon in the First Presbyterian Church of Norfolk, and since 1953 has been an elder. In politics Dr. Martin is a Democrat. His principal hobby is reading Confederate history, but "for relaxation before sleep he reads western stories and mystery yarns." For exercise he enjoys duck shooting, horseback riding, camping, canoeing, hiking, skating, and golf, which he recently substituted for tennis. He married Lucretia Reid de Jarnette, daughter of a Norfolk broker in commercial fertilizers, on September 18, 1917. They have two daughters, Lucretia de Jarnette and Nancy Patton, a married son, Walter Bramblette, Jr., and one grandson.

His professional associate, Dr. Franklin, has described Dr. Martin as "a man of indomitable energy and a demon for work." Others have mentioned his "disdain of sartorial splendor," his dislike of "fanfare," his dry humor, and his gift for verse, both serious and humorous.

References

N Y Herald Tribune p10 Je 5 '54
Who's Who in America, 1954-55
Who's Who in the South and Southwest (1952)
World Biography (1954)

MARTÍNEZ TRUEBA, ANDRÉS 1884-
Uruguayan Government official; banker
Address: b. Legislative Palace, Montevideo, Republic of Uruguay

Wide World
ANDRÉS MARTÍNEZ TRUEBA

Frequently referred to in the North American press as "one of the few truly democratic countries in Latin America," Uruguay is governed by a nine-man National Council. The chairman, Andrés Martínez Trueba, relinquished his position as President of the Republic in 1951 when a new constitutional amendment was voted (and made effective March 1, 1952) which supplanted the presidency with a National Council of nine members, six of them belonging to the several wings of the strongest political party, and three to the dominant group in the leading minority party. Modeled directly on the Swiss form of government, this Council has been watched by the outside world as "an unprecedented experiment in democracy" (New York *Herald Tribune,* February 24, 1952).

Uruguay, the smallest independent country in South America (population, 2,500,000), long known as a "buffer state" between Argentina and Brazil, has always been a popular place for tourists because of its wide beaches, modern hotels, democratic government, and stable economy. Martínez Trueba, who has been active in public office for many years, was elected to the presidency in 1950 by the *Colorados,* Uruguay's majority party. A friend and disciple of the late President José Batlle y Ordóñez, Martínez Trueba would have held this office until March 1955, but he campaigned vigorously to have the constitutional amendment passed which would eliminate his own office.

Although the presidency of the National Council rotates annually among the six majority-party members (in order to prevent one man from having too much power), it was, nevertheless, provided that Martínez Trueba should hold the Council's presidency as long as he would have been President of the Republic, i.e., until March 1955. Prior to his election he was president of the Bank of the Republic. His four-year Presidential term has been marked by free elections, social legislation, but has been hampered by inflation, curbs on wool exports, and loss of tourist revenue from nearby Argentina.

The eighth session of UNESCO is being held in Uruguay's capital city of Montevideo November 12-December 11, 1954.

Andrés Martínez Trueba was born in 1884, the son of Andrés Martínez Delgado and Narcisa Trueba Gainza. He was educated in the city of Montevideo at the University of Montevideo, where he studied chemistry. At an early age he settled in the small city of Florida, in the department of Florida. Later he was several times elected to the lower house of the national legislature, the Chamber of Deputies, as one of the representatives of the department of Florida (Uruguay is divided into nineteen departments). In 1903, when he was nineteen years old, he joined the followers of Batlle, a leader of the Colorado party who was elected to the

MARTÍNEZ TRUEBA, ANDRÉS—*Cont.*

Presidency in that year. Martínez Trueba remained a friend and intimate collaborator of Batlle's until the latter's death in 1929. Batlle's followers are traditionally dedicated to progressive social measures.

Several times before 1934 (when a new Constitution went into effect), Martínez Trueba was elected to the National Administration Council, one of the two branches of the executive under the Constitution of 1919, which provided for a President and a National Administration Council, modeled after Switzerland's political system. (The Swiss Federal Council has seven members; Uruguay's National Administration Council had nine members.) The adopting of the Constitution of 1919 was largely the work of Battle. By the 1934 Constitution the dual-executive was replaced by a President, who selected his own Cabinet. (This system of government was in force until 1951.)

Among the political accomplishments ascribed to Martínez Trueba in these years was the law creating the Banco Hipotecario. This law laid the groundwork for agricultural reform in Uruguay, particularly for the distribution of land and work implements which helped to create the highly developed agriculture in which the Uruguayans today take pride. Martínez Trueba was president, from 1928 to 1932 and from 1942 to 1946, of the Banco Hipotecario, a state institution charged with the distribution of land to farmers, and with the planning and construction of housing for workers and white collar employees in the cities. There is no income tax in Uruguay, and revenues are obtained through indirect taxation, mainly from customs duties. Old-age pensions and wages are higher than in other Latin American countries.

Martínez Trueba is credited with being the author of the electoral law that is said to be one of the factors responsible for Uruguay's political stability. During a study of constitutional reform in 1942, he took a leading role in obtaining the incorporation of advanced social principles, particularly concerning labor, into the constitution which was approved that year. These laws remain in force in Uruguay today.

Elected Intendant of Montevideo in 1946, Martínez Trueba gave up that post in order to accept the position of president of the Bank of the Republic which exercises the functions of a central bank, issuing money and regulating the economic and financial activities of the nation. In May 1950 he resigned from the presidency of the Bank in order to accept the candidacy for President of the nation.

In the elections of 1950, as explained in Russell H. Fitzgibbon's book, *Uruguay: Portrait of a Democracy* (1954), three Colorado candidates ran for the presidency. Andrés Martínez Trueba received 161,262 votes; César Mayo Gutierrez, 150,930; and Eduardo Blanco Acevedo, 120,949. The Nationalist (or Blanco) candidate, Luís Alberto de Herrera, won 254,834 votes, or 93,572 more than the highest of the three Colorado candidates. About 70 per cent of Uruguay's adult population (including women) voted. Since the three Colorados were running under the same *lema* (motto, or party ticket), the total of all their votes was consequently given to Martínez Trueba, the leading Colorado, which gave him a substantial plurality over Herrera.

The Uruguayan electoral system can best be described as "the double simultaneous vote." This means that each voter votes at one and the same time for the candidate and for the party of his choice. Each of the parties, operating in an election, lists its candidates under a *lema.* The *lema* is the legal property of a party organization which can grant or refuse its use to the candidates. The terms "Colorado" and "Blanco" meaning "red" and "white", were first used in 1836 in the Battle of Carpintería on September 19, when followers of Manuel Oribe wore white hatbands and adherents of José Fructuoso Rivera wore red hatbands as marks of distinction. Thus were born Uruguay's two longest-lived political parties.

During the 1950 campaign Martínez Trueba had preached Batllista social reform. At various meetings he was termed the "candidate of the poor," and the "candidate of hope." He called for the participation by workers in profits and in the management of business. On the international scene he promised to continue Uruguay's traditional policy of support to the democracies. The Blanco opposition, according to a *Christian Science Monitor* correspondent (December 26, 1950), stood for more conservative and nationalistic-isolationist policies.

In his inaugural address on March 1, 1951, the new President reaffirmed Uruguay's international stand: "The position of Uruguay is and will be with the democracies, just as it was with the democracies in the struggle against Nazism" (*Christian Science Monitor,* March 17, 1951). He pointed out that in the election the Communists had lost their only seat in the Senate and three out of five seats which they had held in the Chamber.

Later, in a United Press interview, he expressed the conviction that communism would not be a problem to his administration: "Progress already has been made by our legislation favoring workers; and the voters' confidence that we shall continue along the same road will not permit ideologies and tactics in conflict with our concepts to flourish." In the same interview Martínez Trueba indicated that he already had plans that would eliminate his position before his term of office was completed. Constitutional reform, he said, could not be postponed. "The fundamental concern of my party will be to achieve a collegiate executive form of government." Such a government would mean the replacement of the President by a Council.

Martínez Trueba believed the establishment of a true council government would not only check potential dictators, but would also give the major political groups more participation in the government. By August 1951 the Uruguayan President had completed plans for a nine-man Council, in which the Blancos, the strongest minority party, would fill three seats, and the several groups among the majority Colorados would fill six. Both houses of the Uruguayan legislature approved the plan unanimously. In addition, a constitutional amendment submitted to a popular plebiscite in December 1951, was passed by the voters (New York *Times,* December 17, 1951). In March 1952 the Council was installed, and Martínez Trueba, the retiring President, was named chairman or President of the National Council.

"In its first months of operation the new collegiate government," wrote Russell H. Fitzgibbon, "the first full-dress experiment of the sort ever tried in the New World, seemed to work reasonably well. An initial honeymoon between the two old rival parties, born of their cooperation in getting the 1951 constitution adopted, tended to wear off as 1952 passed. Party maneuvering for advantage gradually returned. . . . The Cabinet is fixed constitutionally at nine members. At present they head the ministries of the interior, foreign relations, national defense, public instruction and social welfare, industries and labor, stock raising and agriculture, public works, public health, and finance."

Nine months after the new government was inaugurated Martínez Trueba took stock of its accomplishments and expressed satisfaction with its efficiency according to Sam Pope Brewer (New York *Times,* December 18, 1952). The Council's first problem had been a series of strikes beginning during its first month in office. According to Brewer, "The Governing Council acted firmly in each case, and kept the situation in hand." Martínez Trueba commented that a President acting in the same way risked accusations of dictatorial tendencies and the possibility of Congressional repudiation of his measures for political reasons.

Another advantage of the Council, he pointed out, was continuity in government. There is never a complete break, even if the majority shifts to another party. The party coming into power has had representatives on the Council and, when it takes over, is fully aware of the prevailing problems.

An article in the New York *Times* (January 6, 1954) stated that Uruguay's biggest headache was increasing inflation. To counteract this, Martínez Trueba and the Council sharply restricted imports. This led Uruguay to "a near-record favorable trade balance of almost $100,000,000" for 1953. While exports increased, imports were kept at a low level. The Uruguayan economy suffered from the world-wide decline in wool prices. (Wool and meat are the staples of Uruguayan sales abroad.) During 1953 Uruguay had a tariff dispute with the United States. The U.S. Treasury decided that preferential exchange treatment by Uruguay of wool top exports was tantamount to a subsidy, and a compensatory duty on such imports was mandatory.

Since the United States is Uruguay's most important customer (one fourth of all its exports go to the United States), and since nearly 75 per cent of the country is devoted to agriculture, Martínez Trueba realizes that Uruguay must sell more of its wools, hides and skins in order to have enough dollars to buy U.S.-made machinery and equipment (New York *Herald Tribune,* June 13, 1954). Both U.S. and European capital is heavily invested in Uruguay, since its constitution does not discriminate between citizens and foreigners. For example, three of its four large meat-packing concerns are Swift, Artigas and Anglo.

Martínez Trueba is especially proud of Uruguay's cultural development as witnessed not only by its National Museum of Fine Arts, its National Historical Museum, its monuments and other museums in Montevideo, but by its National Library which dates back to 1816, is the country's largest, and has a collection of 250,000 volumes. The National Congress Library contains 90,000 volumes. The International American Institute for the Protection of Children, with headquarters in Montevideo, has a specialized library of some 15,000 volumes, notable as one of the best collections in the world.

The silver-haired President was married to Maria Serra on January 5, 1911. Their children are Cesar and Silvia Martínez Serra.

The supporters of Uruguay's President have said: "Andrés Martínez Trueba has dedicated almost all his life to public activity, fighting always within the program of the Batllismo . . . (faction) for the most absolute respect for free and democratic institutions, for the nationalization of enterprises of general interest, and for advanced social legislation that has as its fundamental tenet the protection of the worker within a framework of peaceful relations between capital and labor."

References

Américas 4:3 Ja '52
Christian Sci Mon p5 Mr 17 '51
N Y Herald Tribune II p2 F 24 '52
N Y Times p13 D 1 '50; p12 Mr 2 '52 por
Fitzgibbon, R. H. Uruguay: Portrait of a Democracy (1954)

MARTLAND, HARRISON STANFORD
Sept. 10, 1883-May 1, 1954 Pathologist; educator; served as Newark pathologist (1908-1953), as Essex County medical examiner (1925-1953), and as professor of forensic medicine at New York University (1935-1950); discovered and diagnosed radioactive poisoning in humans; designed protective devices for employees at Oak Ridge, Tennessee nuclear laboratories; reported the lethal effects of beryllium poisoning; was known for his scientific analyses in criminal cases; wrote numerous scientific papers. See *Current Biography,* (Nov.) 1940.

Obituary

N Y Times p88 My 2 '54

MAVERICK, MAURY, SR. Oct. 23, 1895-June 7, 1954 Lawyer; former Congressman from Texas and former Mayor of San Antonio; a colorful figure in Democratic politics for many years; was graduated from the University of Texas (1916); admitted to the Texas bar (1916) and California (1917); commissioned a first lieutenant in the A.E.F., and received the Silver Star for "gallantry in action" and the Purple Heart for his wounds during the Argonne Battle; became an ardent New Dealer and was elected to Congress in 1935 as a Representative from the 20th Texas District; fought the local Ku Klux Klan; led the House fight for TVA, slum clearance and strengthening the armed services; advocated fairer treatment for "little businessmen;" became the leader of a liberal group in Congress that called itself "Mavericks" (a term meaning an unbranded calf); supported anti-trust and anti-lynching legislation; elected Mayor of San Antonio (1939); headed the government division of the War Production Board (1941-1944) and was chairman, Smaller War Plants Corporation (1944); author of *A Maverick American* (1937), his autobiography, and *In Blood and Ink* (1939); credited with coining the word "gobbledy-gook" to describe verbose official language. See *Current Biography,* (Mar.) 1944.

Obituary

N Y Times p27 Je 8 '54

MAYBANK, BURNET R(HETT) Mar. 7, 1899-Sept. 1, 1954 United States Senator from South Carolina; received B.S. degree from the College of Charleston where he played varsity football; served in the Naval Militia in World War I; entered cotton exports business; was mayor of Charleston (1931); re-elected (1935); won the Democratic nomination for Governor (1938); and was elected; worked for hydroelectric power in his state; aided cotton farmers; elected to the U.S. Senate to finish unexpired term of James F. Byrnes (1941) re-elected (1942, 1948); considered one of the leaders for Federally aided low-cost housing; was chairman of Senate Banking and Currency Committee. See *Current Biography* (April) 1949.

Obituary

N Y Times p21 S 2 '54

MAYER, JANE *See* Jaynes, C.

MAYO, CHARLES W(ILLIAM) July 28, 1898- Surgeon

Address: b. c/o Mayo Clinic, Rochester, Minn.; h. "Mayowood," Rochester, Minn.

NOTE: This biography supersedes the article which appeared in *Current Biography* in 1941.

One of America's most distinguished surgeons, Dr. Charles W. Mayo represents a family renowned in the field of medicine for many generations. He has recently become prominent also for his work in the field of international relations. As one of the governors of the Mayo Clinic in Rochester, Minnesota he directs the services of the world-famous clinic founded by his father and uncle.

Speaking for the United States as alternate delegate to the eighth General Assembly of the United Nations in 1953, Dr. Mayo refuted Communist charges that his country had used bacterial weapons in the Korean War. The methods employed by Chinese and North Korean Communists to obtain false confessions of germ warfare from American flyers were comparable, he told the U.N. political committee, to Soviet experiments on dogs and rats. In February 1954 Dr. Mayo was elected president of the American Association for the United Nations.

The Mayo family has been outstanding in American medical progress since the mid-nineteenth century when William Worrall Mayo, a young chemist who had studied under John Dalton, moved from England to America where he took his degree in medicine. The general practice that he established in Rochester, Minnesota was later carried on by his two sons, William James and Charles Horace Mayo. His grandson, Charles William Mayo, was born to Charles Horace and Edith (Graham) Mayo in Rochester on July 28, 1898.

Charles William's mother, a nurse graduated from the Woman's Hospital in Chicago, reared her own six children as well as two foster children. A leader in civic affairs, she helped to organize the Civic League in Rochester, the local Y.W.C.A, the Rochester Magazine Club and the Mayo Clinic Women's Club. In 1940 she was chosen American Mother of the year by the Golden Rule Foundation.

After five years (1912-17) of preparatory training at the Hill School in Pottstown, Pennsylvania, Charles entered Princeton University, where he took his B.A. degree in 1921. During 1917-18 he served in the Students' Army Training Corps. He was granted his M.D. degree by the University of Pennsylvania in 1926 and the following year interned at the Robert Packer Hospital in Sayre, Pennsylvania.

For the next four years (1927-1931) he held a fellowship in surgery in the Mayo Foundation. He received the M.S. in surgery from the University of Minnesota in 1931. (Since 1933 Dr. Mayo has taught surgery at the Mayo Foundation, a part of the Graduate School of the University of Minnesota, becoming a professor in 1947).

Recognized as one of the world's great medical centers, the Mayo Clinic, of which Dr. Mayo is a governor, had its beginning shortly after the tornado of 1883 had claimed many victims in Rochester. Seeing the need of a hospital, Dr. William Worrall Mayo, in cooperation with the Mother Superior of the Sisters of the Order of St. Francis, established St. Mary's Hospital in 1889. From this nucleus he and his two sons (Charles W. Mayo's father and uncle) founded the Mayo Clinic. The brothers in early 1915 set up the Mayo Foundation for Medical Education and Research at Rochester, which became a department of the graduate school of the University of Minnesota. Since 1951 Dr. Charles W. Mayo has been a member of the university's board of regents, which directs the funds and resources of the foundation.

Just as doctors from all over the world have gathered at the Mayo Clinic to observe the surgical procedures employed, so also have patients come from near and distant places to benefit from the variety and quality of the clinic's services. It is estimated that the town of Rochester, with a population of 30,000, provides for some 200,000 transients annually. About 130,000 of these are people in need of medical care and the remainder are relatives of patients. The clinic bases its fees upon each patient's ability to pay and its facilities are never denied to those who are without funds.

After the death of his brother, Dr. Joseph Mayo, in an automobile accident in 1936, Charles W. Mayo continued to carry on the name of his family in "brilliant and dedicated work" at the clinic. During World War II he saw active duty in the Pacific as lieutenant colonel (later colonel) in the Army Medical Corps at the 233rd Station Hospital and at other Mayo Clinic affiliated units. He was commanding officer of the 237th Station Hospital in New Guinea.

In March 1950, Mayo testified at hearings of the House Expenditures Committee against a reorganization bill which would combine all government medical facilities under one agency. He is a member of the national medical advisory board of the American Legion.

As a surgeon Dr. Mayo has specialized in diseases of the colon. He is editor-in-chief of *Postgraduate Medicine*, to which he has contributed a number of papers, among the more recent, "Diverticulitis of Colon" (November 1950), "Diagnosis and Treatment of Ileitis" (June 1951) and "Gallstone Obstruction of the Small Intestine" (November 1952, with E. F. Routley). Articles by Dr. Mayo on abdominal surgery and related subjects have appeared in other medical journals, including *American Journal of Surgery, Surgical Clinics of North America, Journal of the American Medical Association* and *Collected Papers of the Mayo Clinic and Mayo Foundation.*

In accordance with its practice of appointing a professional man to its United Nations delegation each year, the United States in July 1953 accepted the recommendation of Senator Edward J. Thye, a Minnesota Republican, who proposed Dr. Mayo on a non-partisan basis. Mayo has related in a *New Yorker* interview (November 21, 1953) that his appointment as alternate delegate to the eighth U.N. General Assembly came to him unexpectedly. On two occasions when Senator Thye telephoned to give him the news, the surgeon was performing abdominal operations and could not take the calls.

"When I finally talked with the Senator," Mayo explained, "he told me I was to become an alternate delegate, and here I am. My wife, Alice, has long been interested in the United Nations. I began to do a great deal of reading. . . . I read everything I could lay my hands on about the United Nations. . . . And when I came here and saw the reality of the situation, the place itself, and the people, I obtained still another understanding of the problems. What had been academic in the books suddenly became real. I am fascinated, and consider it a wonderful sabbatical from the clinic."

DR. CHARLES W. MAYO

It was "with a surgeon's precision" (*Time*, November 2, 1953) that Dr. Mayo answered Communist accusations that the United States had waged germ warfare during the fighting in Korea. Appearing before the General Assembly's political committee on October 26, 1954, he described in scientific detail "Russian-directed" attempts to extort "confessions" from American flyers regarding bacterial weapons.

The picture presented by Dr. Mayo of the methods of torture and interrogation used by Chinese and North Korean Communists was "one of human beings reduced to a status lower than that of animals; filthy; full of lice; festered wounds full of maggots; their sickness regulated to a point just short of death . . . bullied incessantly, deprived of sleep and browbeaten into mental anguish."

The Communist interrogators, Mayo continued, made perverted use of the conditioned reflex experiments of Ivan Petrovich Pavlov. Then, calling attention to evidence that some of the prisoners did not yield, he said, "Such testimony seems to teach us that the spirit of man can run deeper than the reflexes of Pavlov."

Earlier in October Dr. Mayo had rejected Soviet charges that the United States Government profiteered by exploiting European refugees for slave labor. On his Minnesota farm, he told the General Assembly's social, humanitarian and cultural committee, that he employed four refugees at a salary of more than $100 monthly in addition to board and lodging, thus refuting Russian allegations.

(Continued next page)

MAYO, CHARLES W.—*Continued*

Speaking before the meeting of the American Library Association in Minneapolis on June 25, 1954, Dr. Mayo noted that the University of Minnesota libraries' report for 1952-53 showed that library patrons had used 11,465 documents pertaining to the U.N., and called the figure "a most encouraging index of public opinion."

He stated that "the United Nations, with the looming shadow of the hydrogen bomb and atomic warfare on the horizon, is the best and possibly the last sound hope of civilization. But the United Nations can be no stronger than the expressed interest and intelligent public opinion of the peoples of those sixty nations who are members of the United Nations." Success of the U.N., he believes, depends upon the same qualities as does success in individual projects. "Each nation need not and should not be the image of another. The necessary factors are mutual understanding, tolerance, patience and effort."

Commenting in July 1954 on the United States' position regarding admission of Communist China to the U.N., he cautioned against his country's withdrawal from the world organization. Such withdrawal, according to Mayo, would permit Communists to "fall heir to the leadership which now belongs to this country and the whole free world" (*New York Times*, July 13, 1954).

Professional organizations of which he is a member include the American Medical Association, American Surgical Association, Western Surgical Association, Minnesota State Medical Association, Minnesota Surgical Association, Alumni Association of the Mayo Foundation, Association of Resident and Ex-Resident Physicians of Guthrie Clinic and Robert Packer Hospital, and the Surgeons' Club. He also belongs to the American College of Surgeons (fellow), Minnesota Society for the Control of Cancer, Minnesota Public Health Association (board of directors), American Board of Surgery (founders' group), Minnesota Academy of Medicine, International Society of Surgeons, and Society of Medical Consultants of World War II. Since 1953 he has been medical adviser for Northwest Airlines and since 1951 a member of the board of directors of the Mutual Benefit and Accident Association of Omaha. He became a trustee of Carleton College, Northfield, Minnesota in 1940.

He is an honorary fellow of the Seaboard Medical Association of Virginia and North Carolina, and also holds honorary memberships in the Mississippi Valley Medical Society and the Societieta Italiana di Chirurgia in Rome. Other honors conferred on him are the Order of the Crown of Italy and commander, Order al Merito of Chile. Among his honorary degrees are the LL.D. from St. Lawrence University (1947) and the D.Sc. from Franklin and Marshall College (1949).

Dr. Mayo is a Mason (Knight Templar) and a member of the Rotary Club, of which he was president in 1934-35. He belongs to Sigma Xi, Nu Sigma Nu, Quadrangle Club (Princeton University), Princeton Club (New York) and the University clubs in Rochester, St. Paul, and Chicago. He belongs to the Episcopalian church.

Married on June 25, 1927 to Alice Varney Plank, Dr. Mayo is the father of six children: Mildred, Charles Horace 2d, Edward Martin, Joseph Graham, Edith Maria and Alexander Steward. His brother Joseph's two sons, David Graham and William James Mayo were his wards until they became twenty-one. Among his hobbies are farming, fishing, and horseback riding. A *New Yorker* interviewer has pictured him as "short, easygoing, possessed of a gay and twinkly smile."

References

N Y World-Telegram p7 O 31 '53 por
New Yorker 29:35 N 21 '53
Rotarian 85:31 Ag '54 por
Time 62:27 N 2 '53 por
U S News 35:10 N 6 '53

American Men of Science (1949)
Directory of Medical Specialists (1953)
Who's Who in America, 1954-55
World Biography (1954)

MEANY, GEORGE Aug. 16, 1894- Labor union president

Address: c/o American Federation of Labor Bldg., Washington 1, D.C.

NOTE: This biography supersedes the article which appeared in *Current Biography* in 1942.

Chosen to head the 8,000,000-member American Federation of Labor on November 25, 1952, George Meany has been a prominent labor organization official since 1939. He was named by the AFL executive council to succeed the late president William Green and was confirmed as president on September 25, 1953 by the unanimous vote of the delegates to the federation's seventy-second annual convention held in St. Louis, Missouri.

A journeyman plumber before he became a union official, Meany was president of the New York State Federation of Labor from 1934 to 1939, when he was made secretary-treasurer of the national organization. He served on the National Defense Mediation Board and the War Labor Board and recently was instrumental in revoking the AFL charter of the International Longshoremen's Association.

Born August 16, 1894 in Manhattan to Michael Joseph Meany, a plumber who became the president of a local union, and Anne (Cullen) Meany, George Meany is of Irish-Catholic ancestry. He grew up in the Bronx in New York where he attended public schools and distinguished himself in interscholastic baseball.

Young Meany became a plumber's apprentice in 1910 and a journeyman in 1915 the year in which he was admitted to the plumbers' union. A frequent speaker at union meetings, Meany was elected in 1922 as the business agent of local 463 of the union. After twelve years in this post, he was selected to be president of the New York State Federation of Labor which represents approximately 1,000,000 members.

At the age of forty, he was the youngest man since Samuel Gompers to hold this office. In the course of his five years tenure he also served on the New York State Industrial Council and the State Advisory Council on Unemployment Insurance. The New York state federation's president was responsible for increasing the membership despite adversities resulting from economic depression. He was also a labor spokesman at Albany when a considerable number of labor laws were enacted including an unemployment insurance act.

When Frank Morrison, the veteran secretary-treasurer of the AFL decided in 1939 not to run again for this post, George Meany was strongly backed to succeed him. At the October convention in Cincinnati, Ohio, Meany was the unanimous choice of the delegates. Taking office on January 1, 1940, the new secretary-treasurer began to concentrate on public relations by using such techniques as federation sponsored news broadcasts.

Meany was one of four union officials appointed in March 1941 by President Franklin D. Roosevelt to the new National Defense Mediation Board, which in November rejected by a 9 to 2 vote a demand by John L. Lewis of the United Mine Workers of America for a "closed shop" in the so-called "captive" coal mines. Because of the decision, the Congress of Industrial Organizations' members, Philip Murray and Thomas Kennedy, resigned from the board. Meany, who had recommended that the closed shop be effected, stated: "The majority has spoken and in the interests of national defense the parties should abide by the decision."

A strong advocate of *rapprochement* between the AFL and the CIO, Meany was mentioned in January 1942 as a possible compromise president for an amalgamation suggested by John L. Lewis. Meany served as a member of the War Labor Board from 1942 to 1945.

The AFL named the secretary-treasurer to represent it at the British Trades Union Congress convention of 1941. At the convention Meany warned that Russia was trying to make use of the World Federation of Trade Unions as a fifth column to undermine the democratic nations. He asserted: "The so-called Russian trade union movement . . . has denied to the workers of Soviet Russia the basic freedoms that American workers hold prerequisite to a free nation" (New York *Times Magazine,* December 21, 1952). In the following year he was appointed by President Harry S. Truman to represent U.S. labor at the American States conference of the International Labor Organization held in Mexico City.

Speaking for the federation in a nationwide broadcast on May 23, 1947, he assailed as "an insult to the intelligence of the American worker" the "attempt of reactionary big business and its Congressional collaborators to sell" the idea of the then pending Taft-Hartley law.

Nevertheless, at the AFL convention held at San Francisco in November 1947 he made a stinging speech on the subject which led to the defeat of a bid by John L. Lewis for a place on the executive council and the second withdrawal of the United Mine Workers from the

Hessler

GEORGE MEANY

federation. "The issue," according to the New York *Times* of November 26, 1952, "was whether the members of the . . . executive council should sign non-Communist affidavits under the law. Mr. Meany thought the affidavits should be signed, Mr. Lewis thought they should not."

Meany was the first leader of Labor's League for Political Education in 1948. In the following year he received a recess appointment to the Economic Cooperation Administration's public advisory board. At the annual AFL convention of that year at a hotel in Houston, Texas, Meany forced the admission of two Negro delegates. He declared: "Either they get in or we all get out."

During that year the British Trades Union Congress and a French labor organization withdrew from the World Federation of Trade Unions on the ground that it had become dominated by the Communists. Both the AFL and CIO assisted their British and French colleagues in the formation and financing of the International Confederation of Free Trade Unions. Meany was chosen a member of its executive board in 1951 after participating at a conference in Mexico City called to organize a regional inter-American division of the confederation.

When the labor official revisited Europe in November 1951, he was disappointed by the apathy he encountered at the sessions of the I.C.F.T.U. executive committee at Brussels. "There is no real cooperation in Europe on the issue of Communist unions," he reported on his return (New York *Times,* December 26, 1951).

The labor members of the Office of Defense Mobilization's Advisory Committee dramatically resigned early in 1951 because they felt the administration had stripped union officials of any real voice in the conduct of the preparedness program. Meany was the "strongest pro-

MEANY, GEORGE—*Continued*

ponent of the walk-out idea" (*Fortune*, May 1951).

Furthermore in April when President Truman summoned AFL and CIO leaders to the White House and urged them to reassume their positions in the defense structure, Meany insisted on and obtained a definite understanding in regard to the rights of labor. He was appointed to the National Advisory Board on Mobilization Policy, and in the following January became a member of the government Contract Compliance Committee.

His prestige in labor circles in recent years increased to such an extent that prior to the AFL convention of October 1952, "there was some thought of retiring [president William] Green to the president-emeritus status, with Meany as the most likely candidate to succeed him" (*Business Week*, November 29, 1952). Green was, however, re-elected by acclamation for a twenty-eighth term which was prematurely terminated by his death on November 21, 1952. Four days later the AFL executive council named Meany to serve as president until the 1953 convention.

Meany's "first major act as A.F.L. president was to announce the revival of an A.F.L. committee set up in 1950 to discuss reunification with the C.I.O." (*Time*, December 8, 1952).

In regard to the Labor-Management Relations Act of 1947, the labor president has explained that the AFL was not demanding the complete repeal of the law, but sought "simultaneous enactment of a new law, fair to labor and management alike" (*Newsweek*, January 12, 1953). Shortly before the resignation of AFL leader Martin P. Durkin as President Eisenhower's Secretary of Labor, Meany charged on June 5, 1953 that President Eisenhower had failed to keep a campaign pledge to work to make the Taft-Hartley law more acceptable (New York *Herald Tribune*, June 6, 1953).

At the AFL seventy-second convention in St. Louis, Missouri on September 25, 1953, Meany was unanimously re-elected as president. The convention expelled the "racket-ridden" International Longshoremen's Association from the federation "for failure to purge its ranks" of gangsters, and decided to establish a rival union. In a representative election conducted by the National Labor Relations Board in December 1953 the I.L.A. won by 9,060 votes against the new AFL union's 7,568 with 4,405 uncounted challenged ballots (New York *Times*, December 25, 1953).

During the voting period three supporters of the new union were hospitalized with stab wounds and a fourth suffered a gash over his eye received in fights near the polls. The AFL announced on December 25, 1953 that it would attempt to persuade the board to invalidate the election because of intimidation and Meany charged that the balloting had been conducted "under circumstances of . . . violence by known criminals to a degree without precedent in a representative election" and that the board had rushed the vote to provide maximum advantage to "the racket union and the crooked employers who for years have maintained a profitable partnership" (New York *Times*, December 25, 1953). The NLRB ruled in August 1954 that the election of the ILA was legal.

At the beginning of 1954 the labor leader recommended that public policy encourage "better housing; wider and increased social security and broader distribution of purchasing power to support expanding business activity through a widened ability to consume." He also stated that "lasting economic prosperity requires acceptance of collective bargaining and more stable relations between management and labor" (Washington *Post*, January 4, 1954).

At a press conference debate on minimum wage law changes, held in Miami, Florida during the mid-winter meeting of the AFL executive council, Meany differed with Secretary of Labor James P. Mitchell who stated that the present time is not appropriate for such changes. "Now is the time to increase minimum wage standards," Meany declared.

After sixty-five affiliates of the AFL and twenty-nine affiliates of the CIO signed a cease-fire contract on June 9, 1954, Meany in a joint statement with Walter Reuther, president of the CIO, said they will now work for "a merger of the two major labor federations into a single, united labor movement" (New York *Times*, June 10, 1954).

Meany, who has been an editor of the *American Federationist* and has contributed many articles to it, has said that he is "intensely interested in world affairs and international labor matters, and is an active opponent of totalitarianism." The Pennsylvania Council of Public Employees, an AFL affiliate, presented him with the "man-of-the-year" award in 1945. He is a member of the board of governors of the American Red Cross.

Married to Eugenia A. McMahon on November 26, 1919, Meany has three daughters, Regina Clare, Eileen and Genevieve. The AFL president has blue eyes and gray hair, is slightly under six feet in height and weighs over 200 pounds. He is described as "very powerfully built and the owner of a voice that makes the chandeliers shake." Meany is a Roman Catholic and a Democrat.

For relaxation he enjoys reading, listening to music, golf, duck shooting, fishing, watching baseball, football and prize-fights, dancing, poker and gin rummy. Except for "a penchant for pearl-gray or cocoa-brown vests," Meany dresses conservatively. An associate believes that "the secret of his effectiveness in any situation is his appetite for acquiring every bit of relevant information."

Selected References (See also references listed in the January 1942 biographical sketch)

Commonweal 57:304+ D 26 '52
Eng N 149:29+ D 4 '52 pors
N Y Herald Tribune p49 N 22 '52; II p1 N 30 '52 por
N Y Times p42 N 22 '52 por; p14 N 26 '52

American Catholic Who's Who, 1952-53
Who's Who in America, 1952-53
Who's Who in Commerce and Industry (1953)

MECHEM, EDWIN L(EARD) July 2, 1912- Governor of New Mexico

Address: b. State Capitol, Santa Fe, N.M.; h. Las Cruces, N.M.

Upsetting an eighteen-year precedent in the traditionally Democratic state of New Mexico, Edwin L. Mechem was elected to the governorship in 1950 and reelected in 1952. He campaigned on a reform program advocating the removal of various commissions from politics and placing the appointments of many state employees on a merit system instead of on patronage. The Governor announced his candidacy in 1954 for the United States Senate seat now held by Clinton P. Anderson, Democrat, and at the May primary he was unopposed for the Republican nomination. Anderson defeated Mechem on November 2, 1954.

Mechem had previously practiced law in Las Cruces for eight years and had served with the Federal Bureau of Investigation. In April 1954 he attended a conference of Governors of the "dust bowl" area held at the White House to discuss soil and crop conservation problems, and recommended that loan and credit facilities be used to give maximum benefits on a long-range basis to farmers and ranchers in the southwestern states affected by drought and by dust storms.

Edwin Leard Mechem was born in Alamagordo, New Mexico on July 2, 1912. He is the youngest of the three sons of Eunice (Leard) and Edwin Mechem, a lawyer, and the nephew of former Governor of New Mexico, Merritt Cramer Mechem. His parents are both of English descent.

Young Mechem attended school in Alamogordo until the family moved to Las Cruces, New Mexico in 1924. There he studied at Union High School from which he was graduated in 1930. Enrolling in the New Mexico College of Agriculture and Mechanic Arts, Mechem majored in government for a year. He left school to become a land surveyor for three years with the U.S. Reclamation Service. Deciding to practice law, Mechem studied at the University of Arkansas School of Law which granted him the LL.B. degree in 1939. In that year he was admitted to the bar.

After practicing law in Las Cruces from 1939 to 1941, he served with the Federal Bureau of Investigation for two years. During that time he was assigned to regional offices in Dallas, Little Rock, San Francisco, and San Antonio. In 1944 he returned to the private practice of law in Las Cruces and decided to enter politics. He recalls that as youngsters, the children in his family "were encouraged to take an interest in politics and government."

For some time Mechem had been convinced that there was a need to free the state government from the entrenched Democratic political machine. To accomplish this was a formidable task. The six eastern counties of New Mexico, populated by many former Texans to whom the word "Republican" was anathema had long delivered a regular vote to the Democrats. In the central section of the state, the people of Spanish descent held the balance of power between

Hanley Marks

EDWIN L. MECHEM

the two major parties. Originally they had voted Republican but with the advent of the New Deal, the Spanish-American vote shifted to the Democratic party, and New Mexico became staunchly Democratic.

In 1950, Mechem's best chance to win the governorship was to run on a ticket which stressed reform rather than the Republican party. His opponent was the incumbent, John E. Miles, a Democrat, but in the primaries Miles ran against Judge David Chavez, brother of Senator Dennis Chavez, and defeated him. That, in effect, lost Miles the support of the Spanish-Americans with whom the Chavez family is very popular. Another probable advantage to Mechem was that the people of New Mexico had expressed their dislike of the old patronage system.

Mechem promised to put the state's purchasing systems and insurance on a basis of competitive bidding instead of patronage; to appoint police on a merit system; to place liquor control with a state board; to make state court judgeships nonpolitical offices; to overhaul and consolidate the Public Service Commission and State Corporation Commission; to remove the State Highway Commission from politics and to establish a ten-year-pay-as-you-go highway construction program, and to reduce gasoline taxes. He promised thus to save at least $1,500,000 by eliminating waste and payroll padding. He defeated Miles by a majority of about 13,000 and was the only Republican elected in 1950. In 1952, however, New Mexico went Republican except for Senator Dennis Chavez who won in the controversial Senate race between him and Patrick Hurley.

At the time of Mechem's first victory he was the youngest in New Mexico's long list of 105 governors (colonial, territorial, and state) dating from 1598 when the Spanish colony was

MECHEM, EDWIN L.—*Continued*

established under Juan de Oñate. He was the fourth Republican governor in the history of New Mexico. He explained his astonishing victory as a "protest of the people against political machines." At the time of Mechem's inauguration the Democrats sponsored or submitted for legal drafting most of his proposals.

Shortly before his inauguration Mechem stated: "I think the legislature will go along with most of the recommendations I will make since they will not be Republican or Democratic suggestions at all. All of us are interested in seeing that the state makes rapid progress."

Speaking on January 1, 1951, he "stressed civilian defense, in view of the proximity of Los Alamos, atomic installation . . . and the White Sands rocket proving ground" (New York *Times*). In 1952 he urged that the world's first atomic bomb crater, near Alamagordo, be preserved as an historical site.

At a meeting in Albuquerque, New Mexico in November 1953, Governor Mechem was the official host to ten western Governors, including the Governor of Hawaii. The state executives resolved at that time that the Indian service should be discontinued as soon as consistent with the rights of Indian citizens; that the U.S. Tariff Commission and Congress should end excessive imports of certain western metals; that Congress should pass the bill giving statehood to Hawaii; that the Forest Service permits on weight of trucks should conform to loads permitted by state standards on state roads; and that surplus seed stocks should be used to reseed western ranges.

During April 1954 the Governors of all the states attended a three-day White House conference. At a panel discussion on the drought situation, Governors Johnston Murray of Oklahoma, Dan Thornton of Colorado, Allan Shivers of Texas, Edward F. Arn of Kansas, and Mechem recommended to the President that: $15,000,000 be made available to the agricultural conservation program to combat the dust and wind problem in the drought area of the Southwest; loan and credit facilities of the Federal government be used to give maximum benefits on a long-range basis to ranch owners and farmers in disaster areas.

Mechem married Dorothy Ellen Heller of Pueblo, Colorado on December 30, 1932. They are the parents of one daughter, Martha, and three sons, John, and Jesse and Walter, twins. Mechem is a Protestant and a member of the American Bar Association.

In January 1951 Governor Mechem directed Dr. Reginald Fisher, art director of the Santa Fe Museum of New Mexico, to hang paintings of New Mexican artists in the governor's office. Since then the exhibits have been changed about every three months. The collections have included works by Peter Hurd, Ernest Blumenschein and Kenneth Barrick.

References

Martindale-Hubbell Law Directory, 1952
Who's Who in America, 1954-55

MENDERES, ADNAN 1899- Prime Minister of Turkey; political leader

Address: c/o National Assembly, Ankara, Turkey

The Middle East's "strongest anti-Communist bastion" is Turkey, where Prime Minister Adnan Menderes is a key figure in the development of his country into a bulwark for the free world in the strategic Mediterranean area. Menderes, a lawyer and progressive farmer, was appointed to the Premiership by Turkey's President Celâl Bayar after the elections of May 1950 when the Democratic party defeated the long-dominant Republican People's party. He was renamed Prime Minister after the May 1954 elections and has been active in fostering collective measures for military security of the Balkan countries and also through the North Atlantic Treaty Organization (NATO).

The overwhelming victory of the Democratic party in the 1954 general election has been regarded as a clear endorsement of the policies of the Menderes' government during the past four years to encourage private enterprise at home and to cooperate with the Western powers in international affairs. At the invitation of the U.S. government, the Turkish Prime Minister visited the United States in June 1954 for conferences on American aid to Turkish military and economic growth. The fostering of close Turkish-American relations in collective security undertakings, Menderes has said, is based upon "the mutual trust and identity of viewpoint" which exists between the two countries.

Adnan Menderes was born in a small town near İzmir (Smyrna), Turkey in 1899. Following his graduation from the American College in Izmir, he studied at the University of Ankara, where he received a degree in law. He then returned to his family farm and introducd modern methods of agriculture.

While working as a political organizer in his district, Menderes came to the attention of Kemal Atatürk, who in 1923-1924 had created the Republic of Turkey on the ruins of the Ottoman Empire and had become President of the new state. Elected to the National Assembly in 1930, Menderes took part in the government controlled by Atatürk's Republican People's party, a totalitarian political organization which sought to extend Turkey's Westernizing revolution through a system of state capitalism.

Sixteen years later, in 1946, Menderes joined Celâl Bayar and other political associates in organizing the Democratic party, thus introducing a genuine two-party system into the country. For the next four years he was one of the leaders of the opposition in the National Assembly. A speech by him in 1947, charging fraud in certain elections to the assembly, made him the center of a free-press controversy. The trial which followed publication of his speech in several newspapers vindicated freedom of the press. As Menderes' new party gained in popularity, it attracted the support of the Turkish peasantry.

Claiming political descent from Atatürk (who had died in 1938), the Democrats remained attached to the reforms instituted by the beloved national hero, at the same time that they advocated a system of free enterprise to replace the state-owned business operations of the Republican People's party. This difference in objectives was the chief issue between the two political groups in the general election of May 14, 1950.

The sweeping victory of the Democratic party candidates for the National Assembly brought to an end the twelve-year tenure of President Ismet Inönü, Atatürk's successor. Soon after he was named President of Turkey by the assembly, Celâl Bayar appointed Menderes as Prime Minister. The new party program that Menderes announced to the assembly on May 29 included granting workers the right to strike, passage of a liberal press law, curtailment of government expenditures, transfer of state-controlled industries to private enterprise, and encouragement of foreign investments in developing the country's resources. In the by-elections of 1951 the Democratic party won eighteen out of twenty contested seats in the National Assembly.

Because of a dispute over internal matters in March 1951, Menderes submitted the resignation of his Cabinet, but was at once asked by President Bayar to form a new government. The Associated Press stated at this time that Menderes' administration had been criticized for presenting a deficit budget and for failing in its election promise to reduce the cost of living. An unfavorable attitude toward what it considered the inflationary policies of Menderes' government has also reportedly been held by the International Bank for Reconstruction and Development, whose mission in Ankara was closed in March 1954 on the demand of Turkey (New York *Times,* March 21, 1954).

The Democratic party's first four years in power saw the standard of living in Turkey reach a point hitherto never achieved. In an interview with Joseph Fromm of the *U.S. News & World Report* (December 7, 1951) Menderes discussed his party's goal of securing the development of free enterprise and of transferring state-owned industrial plants to private business. "I am convinced that free and private enterprise," the Prime Minister emphasized, "is the only system which can give the greatest impetus to economic development."

As part of its program to encourage private initiative the Menderes government provided facilities and guarantees for the investment of foreign private capital in Turkey; it also passed a law permitting foreign groups to share in the development of the country's petroleum resources. Through financial, economic and technical aid from abroad—especially from the United States—Turkish agricultural production and mineral output have been increased and new roads have been built throughout the nation. Turkey is now the fourth largest wheat exporting country in the world.

Consistent with its policy of cooperation with the West, soon after the outbreak of the Korean War Menderes' Cabinet decided to send Turkish troops to Korea to fight with United Nations forces. Menderes believes that "those who fought in Korea for the security of the free world were also defending their homelands. . . . The struggle in Korea has shown that the great principles behind the United Nations are something more than mere words."

Turkish Inf. Office

ADNAN MENDERES

Turkey's application for admission to NATO in the summer of 1950 was also viewed by some observers as evidence of the government's greater initiative in matters of military preparedness and collective security. Reviewing Turkish foreign policy of the past four years, Fuat Köprülü, Minister of Foreign Affairs in Menderes' Cabinet, disclosed in February 1954 that the United States had given Turkey $954,-000,000 in military aid since 1950 and $237,000,-000 in economic grants. He also announced that NATO had approved expenditures of $135,458,000 for building military bases and installations in Turkey during the next few years.

"The real directing force behind the Democratic party"—these are the words used by Welles Hangen of the New York *Times* (May 2, 1954) to describe the Prime Minister's political power. "He is uncontested master of the party today," Hangen continues, "although he has won many enemies by his ruthless suppression of opposition." Menderes was criticized at home and abroad in 1952 for proposing a bill to protect his Cabinet ministers from insult by making adverse criticism punishable by law.

The National Assembly in March 1954 adopted a measure prescribing prison sentences and fines for newspaper reporters whose published statements "could be harmful to the political or financial prestige of the state." Defending the bill, the Prime Minister, who denied an attempt to curb freedom of the press,

MENDERES, ADNAN—*Continued*

maintained that restraint was necessary against excessive vilification of officials.

The general election of May 2, 1954 returned the Democratic party to power with 58.4 per cent of the votes cast. In the National Assembly, which will remain in session until 1958, the Democrats gained 503 seats, while other parties won a total of thirty-eight. (The Communist party, outlawed in Turkey, is not represented in this group.) Menderes, who was renamed Prime Minister, interpreted the election results primarily as an endorsement of his government's foreign policy.

An important aspect of this policy has been Menderes' efforts to improve collective measures for peace and security. On a visit to Greece in May 1952 he stopped at the island of Spetsai, once a stronghold of resistance against the Ottoman Turks. "The suave Turkish leader," reported the *Christian Science Monitor* (May 3, 1952), "won all hearts, when, speaking in excellent Greek he told the islanders he brought 'greetings, love and friendship from Turkey to Greece. . . .' "

Since strengthening Turkey's ties with Greece and Yugoslavia through the Balkan "friendship and collaboration" pact of February 28, 1953, Menderes has been interested in integrating the Balkan agreement with NATO, thus militarily allying Italy and Yugoslavia in common defense. "Collective security," the Prime Minister said, "can be effective only when it presents a continuous front without gaps" (New York *Times,* June 6, 1954).

An editorial in the Washington *Post* (June 4, 1954) has expressed the view that if Menderes "is able to lay the groundwork for a Trieste settlement he will have established his country as the diplomatic as well as the military leader of the Mediterranean area." On August 9, 1954 a twenty-year treaty was signed by the foreign ministers of Turkey, Greece and Yugoslavia, agreeing that an act of aggression against one or more of them would be considered against them all, and providing for political and military cooperation and mutual aid. This treaty had the effect of linking Yugoslavia indirectly with NATO of which both Turkey and Greece are members. *Time* magazine (August 23, 1954) commented: "The new Balkan pact, in effect, closes the last gap in NATO's ring around Europe, which begins in Iceland and extends to Mount Ararat."

With another neighbor, Pakistan, in early April 1954, Turkey signed a mutual defense and economic cooperation pact, in an attempt to create a collective security system in the Middle East. Menderes and Mohammed Ali, Prime Minister of Pakistan, met at Ankara in June to discuss measures to "widen the scope" of the treaty—"presumably by adding such neighbors as Iraq and Iran" (*Newsweek,* June 21, 1954).

The Turkish statesman made his first trip to the United States in early June 1954 when he was invited to confer with government officials on American aid for Turkey's future economic and military development. Maintenance of a large defense force, it has been pointed out, imposes an economic burden upon the country that it cannot bear without external assistance (Turkey has a standing army of about 450,000). At the end of Menderes' four-day visit in Washington it was announced that the United States would grant Turkey about $200,000,000 in military aid during the coming year and about $70,000,000 in economic aid, and would speed up movement of $500,000,000 worth of military equipment "in the present pipeline" (New York *Times,* June 6, 1954).

Prime Minister Menderes is married and is the father of a son, Aydin, and two other children. He is said to be an eloquent speaker, with great personal power over political and governmental affairs. A New York *Herald Tribune* editorial (June 2, 1954) describes him as "a Liberal in the old tradition and a doughty champion of his own principles."

References

N Y Herald Tribune p22 Je 2 '54; II pl Je 6 '54 por
N Y Times p17 My 2 '54; p26 Je 1 '54
Reporter 10:22 Ja 19 '54
International Who's Who, 1954

MENDÈS-FRANCE, PIERRE (mĕn'dĕz frăns) Jan. 11, 1907- French Premier; lawyer; economist

Address: Hotel Matignon, 57 rue Varennes, Paris VII, France

Upon the resignation of the Laniel Government in June 1954, President René Coty of France called on Pierre Mendès-France, a Radical Socialist, to assume the premiership. A brilliant lawyer, economist and the mayor of Louviers, Mendès-France has long been known as "the pitiless gadfly of French politics", frequently criticizing the policies of various Cabinets of the Fourth Republic.

Believing France's position in world affairs depended upon her withdrawal from the war in Indochina and the renovation of her antiquated economy, Mendès-France made these two issues the cornerstone of his policy. He also placed emphasis upon establishing peace and security in North Africa, and upon giving the Western powers France's answer on the European Defense Community (EDC).

EDC, designed to rearm West Germany within a European army, was rejected by the French National Assembly on August 30, 1954 by a vote of 319 to 264 to postpone indefinitely further debate. After the vote, Premier Mendès-France said that he had "long warned . . . friends and allies" that there was no majority for the treaty in the Assembly, and that "new solutions should be studied rapidly" (New York *Times,* August 31, 1954).

At the nine power conference in London held shortly afterwards, Mendès-France and other Western leaders signed, on October 3, 1954, the Final Act of London which is designed to integrate Germany politically and militarily in Western Europe. On October 13 the National

Assembly gave Mendès-France a vote of confidence to continue negotiations to carry out the Final Act.

Pierre Mendès-France was born on January 11, 1907 in Paris to a dress manufacturer who was descended from a long line of Sephardic Jewish dealers of cloth. His mother was the former Palmyre Calin. His maternal grandmother, a devout Orthodox Jew, was responsible for Pierre's religious training. There are several theories about the origin of Mendès-France's hyphenated name. A cousin believes that it derives from Mendoza, and that upon expulsion from Spain in 1492, the French branch of the family added "France" to differentiate themselves from those who settled elsewhere. Pierre Mendès-France believes that his name originates from an alliance between the Mendès and Franco families in either Spain or Portugal prior to the fourteenth century.

Young Mendès-France attended public schools and the College Turgot. Later he matriculated simultaneously at the Faculté de Droit and the Ecole des Sciences Politiques of the Université de Paris. At the age of eighteen he received the doctor's degree in law, first in a class of 800. He also received a diploma in political science.

During his student days he was the leader of a group at the Faculté de Droit, which became involved in a street fracas with Royalist students, from which he emerged with a misshapen nose. By passing his bar examinations at the age of twenty-one, he became the youngest lawyer in France.

At sixteen, Mendès-France had enrolled in the Radical Socialist party (comprised of conservative business men) to which his father belonged. He established residence in Louviers, with a view to entering politics when he became legally eligible for office. He wrote an economic study, *L'Oeuvre Financière du Gouvernement Poincaré* (published in 1928), which favorably impressed then Premier Raymond Poincaré. Besides practicing law, Mendès-France wrote other economic studies, including *La Banque Internationale; Contribution à l'Etude du Problème des Etats-Unis d'Europe* (1930); *Le Mouvement des Cartels et la Crise* (1931). In 1934 he was elected mayor of Louviers, a post which he still holds.

Running on the Radical Socialist ticket in 1932, he became the youngest member of the Chamber of Deputies. When Léon Blum formed his second Popular Front ministry in 1938, the young Radical Socialist was named Under Secretary of State to the Treasury, a position which brought him into contact with Georges Boris, Blum's chief of cabinet, who is today Mendès-France's closest adviser. After four weeks of tenure, the Cabinet fell when a measure for economic mobilization prepared by Mendès-France was rejected. (He has consistently been a member of the French parliament, except through the World War II period.)

In September 1939 the politician entered the French air force as a lieutenant, and was assigned to Syria. On leave in Paris when the Germans entered the city in June 1940, he ac-

French Embassy Press & Inf. Div.

PIERRE MENDÈS-FRANCE

companied his family to Bordeaux, and then went to North Africa. There he was arrested (on a charge of desertion from the French Army) by officials of the Vichy Government, and sentenced to six years in prison. He escaped by climbing down a rope of bed sheets and took refuge in Grenoble. Later he joined General Charles de Gaulle's Free French forces in London, and participated in raids over Germany and France.

Summoned to Algiers by General de Gaulle in November 1943, Mendès-France was named commissioner of finance of the Committee of National Liberation. In its behalf he signed the Franco-British monetary agreement of February 1944. Six months later, he headed the French delegation to the Bretton Woods Monetary Conference. He represented France on the board of governors of the International Monetary Fund, and also served as an alternate governor of the International Bank for Reconstruction and Development.

Following the liberation of Paris, Mendès-France in September 1944 was appointed Minister of the National Economy, in de Gaulle's Provisional Government, a post he held until January 1945, when the rejection of his economic plan—stringent rationing, suppression of the black market, ceilings on wages and prices, limitation of paper money, capital levies on profits, and blockage of bank accounts—caused him to resign. Mendès-France's anti-inflationary policies were in conflict with the inflationary measures of René Pleven, the Finance Minister. De Gaulle at first sought to make peace between them, and refused Mendès-France's resignation, but ultimately, in April 1945 accepted it.

For a long period Pierre Mendès-France refused offers of ministerial posts, and confined himself to opposing the inflationary policies of successive Cabinets and to serving on technical

MENDÈS-FRANCE, PIERRE—*Continued*

missions for the French government, as delegate to the 1946 Savannah monetary conference, and as member of the French delegation to the United Nations Economic and Social Council from 1947 to 1950.

When it became apparent that the disorganized French economy and the drain on it by the war in Indochina required a new policy, Mendès-France in June 1953 was invited to form a Cabinet, but upon presenting his program to the National Assembly, he missed the necessary approval by a margin of only thirteen votes—301 to 119, with 205 abstentions. When Premier Joseph Laniel resigned on June 12, 1954, Mendès-France, as the foremost opponent of the outgoing ministry, was asked by President René Coty to form a new Cabinet. Six days later, he achieved the necessary majority vote of 419 to 47 with 143 abstentions. Although he had categorically refused to accept the premiership if it depended upon Communist votes, he received ninety-five ballots from Communists. These votes were not needed to give him the required number of supporters.

Genêt in the *New Yorker* (July 10, 1954) declared that "the poorer class, and the topmost educated class, are the most enthusiastic about him, the middle class the least." He created a new portfolio for Moroccan and Tunisian affairs, and, deciding to retain the foreign affairs ministry for himself, called upon relatively young and new men for his twenty-nine member Cabinet "instead of playing musical chairs as other postwar premiers have done" (*Business Week,* June 26, 1954). He also required rigorously efficient methods for the operation of his staff, and put a stop to the traditional practice of leaking Cabinet secrets to the press prematurely.

Immediately after accepting the premiership, Mendès-France went to Geneva to discuss the essential points of a cease-fire agreement in Indochina with Chou En-lai, Premier and Foreign Minister of Communist China. He again went to Geneva in July to pursue the major part of the negotiations, in which Great Britain's Foreign Minister Anthony Eden also participated (U.S. Under Secretary of State Walter Bedell Smith was present at the request of the French Premier). Mendès-France had, said *Commonweal,* "a unique factor of strength behind him: the remarkably united support of the French people." France, Viet-Nam, Laos, and Vietminh signed an agreement effective July 22, while Cambodia signed a separate agreement effective July 23. In reporting to the French Assembly the Premier said: "I have no illusions . . . as to the contents of the agreements. Their text is sometimes cruel . . . but the best we could hope for under the circumstances" (*Christian Science Monitor,* July 23, 1954).

The agreement, approved by a 462 to 13 vote of the National Assembly, provided for the division of Viet-Nam roughly along the seventeenth parallel, thus leaving the city of Hanoi and the port of Haiphong in the Communist area, for the free passage to the South of any of the northern area's 12,000,000 inhabitants who preferred not to remain under Communist rule, for general elections in 1956, and for supervision of the implementation of the truce by Canada, India, and Poland. Hanson W. Baldwin of the New York *Times* characterized the truce as "a personal triumph for the French Premier but also a national defeat."

Turning slightly more than a week later to what he called "the next act of the drama," Mendès-France "flew to Tunisia, and this, together with his offer of a program of genuine internal autonomy to the Tunisians . . . had the appeal of the spectacular." On July 30, his Cabinet had approved the Premier's plan to turn over the administration of all internal affairs to the Tunisians, while the control of defense and foreign affairs would remain under French jurisdiction.

Approved by the Tunisian Bey Sidi Mohammed al-Amin and the interned leader of the nationalist Neo-Destour party, Habib Bourguiba, the Tunisians immediately began formation of a Cabinet to negotiate the details of the autonomy which they had demanded since 1947, all negotiations to be contingent, as Mendès-France had specified, on the restoration of order and suppression of the prevailing terrorism against French colonists in the region.

To recoup France's perilous economic condition, the Premier on August 10 presented what he characterized as his "New Deal" to the National Assembly, which by a vote of 361 to 90 thereupon granted him extensive economic powers, effective until March 31, 1955. Based primarily on the necessity for modernizing France's antiquated industrial plants, the long-range plan also provided for the elimination of unnecessary subsidies, the liberalization of foreign and domestic trade, agricultural reforms, reorganization of the social security system and of nationalized industries, increased housing, diminished protectionism, freer competition, elimination of marginal businesses, and establishment of governmental funds for the aid of relocated workers.

Toward the middle of August, the Premier undertook the solution of the long-existent deadlock in the Assembly on ratification of EDC which had already been ratified by the parliaments of four other nations. Visiting Brussels at that time, Mendès-France laid before the representatives of Western Germany, the Netherlands, Belgium, Luxembourg, and Italy a number of modifications which would be more acceptable to the National Assembly. The proposals included a veto for each nation in the administration of the European army, the right of France to maintain its own separate army in addition to its forces in EDC, and the denial of such a right to Germany.

Rejection of his modifications by the five ministers led the Premier to fly to England on August 23 in order to obtain Sir Winston Churchill's assurance that Great Britain would join EDC or an alternate organization as well as France; this, too, met with rejection. When the matter came up for debate before the French National Assembly on August 28, the

Premier disassociated the vote on the measure from one on confidence in his Government. In his three-hour speech to the Assembly that day, Mendès-France, who maintained his personally objective attitude to the problem, pointed out that failure to approve the EDC provisions for a supranational army would require an alternative vote to approve the Bonn treaty, which would allow sovereignty to Western Germany.

The New York *Times* (August 31, 1954) called the defeat of EDC by the National Assembly "the greatest postwar triumph for Soviet policy," and stated that "the primary responsibility" must rest on Premier Mendès-France, "who refused to fight for the Community project." However, the New York *Times* pointed out that the Premier "has recognized that neither German sovereignty nor German rearmament can be delayed indefinitely." Three of his Cabinet members resigned before the Brussels conference and three more have resigned since the vote on EDC.

Nine powers—Belgium, Canada, France, German Federal Republic, Italy, Luxembourg, Netherlands, Britain, and United States—signed the Final Act on October 3, 1954.

The agreement provides that the occupation of the German Federal Republic will be ended, the Brussels treaty will be expanded to include Germany and Italy and its signatory powers will establish an agency for control of armaments on the Continent for its members, and the eight members of the North Atlantic Treaty Organization that were present agreed to recommend that Germany be invited to become a member of NATO. Britain gave assurances that she will maintain four divisions and a tactical air force on the Continent.

The Final Act was considered by many observers a victory for the French Premier. It received the implied approval by the National Assembly on October 13, 1954 by a vote of confidence that will enable the Mendès-France Government to complete the negotiations in accordance with the agreement of October 3. The vote was 350 to 113 with 152 abstentions.

Mendès-France, who was rapporteur on financial matters to the Radical Socialist Congress in 1932, has given courses in that field at the Ecole Nationale d'Administration in Paris. Besides specializing in the practice of corporate law in Paris, he has been an advocate at the Court of Appeals. Honors which he has received include the Legion of Honor, War Cross, Medal of the Resistance, Medal of Escaped Prisoners, and Order of Leopold (Grand Officer).

On December 26, 1933 Mendès-France married Lily Cicurel, a talented portrait painter; they have two sons, Bernard and Michel. He is said to have few amusements, other than skiing and playing the piano; he rarely goes to the theatre or a concert, and is seldom seen in Paris society.

Theodore H. White described Mendès-France as a "short, stocky, heavy-set man, jet-black of hair, broad of nose, and blue-black of jowl, who looks far more like one of the blue trousered workers in the Paris Metro than one of the most eminent and scholarly intellectuals in French life" (*Reporter*, December 22, 1953).

According to Theodore H. White, Mendès-France believes that the first duty of the French government is to choose what shall be given up, for only by abandoning part of its claim to global greatness now can France withdraw, regroup its forces and energies for counterattack, and then return to its rightful power.

References

Le Monde p2 Je 18 '54
Life 37:84 Jl 19 '54
N Y Herald Tribune II p3 Je 20 '54; II p2 Je 27 '54
N Y Times p2 Je 18 '54
N Y Times Mag p10 Je 27 '54
N Y World-Telegram p7 Je 26 '54
Time 63:27+ Je 28 '54 por
U S News 37:47+ Jl 2 '54 por

Dictionnaire Biographique Français Contemporain (1954)
Who's Who in France, 1953-54
Who's Who in the United Nations (1951)
World Biography (1954)

MERZ, CHARLES (mûrs) Feb. 23, 1893-
Newspaper editor; author

Address: b. c/o New York Times, 229 W. 43d St., New York 36; h. 10 Gracie Sq., New York 28

Presiding over an editorial page second to none in its influence on American thinking, Charles Merz, editor of the New York *Times*, believes that careful documentation, reasoned argument and firsthand information have replaced "mere rhetoric, invective and sheer rant" of the "thundering editors in the old days of American journalism." The editorial page has changed, he believes, and for the better, since it is now created "out of the aggregate experience of the whole staff of a newspaper."

Since 1938 he has been the chief interpreter of the news for the *Times*, utilizing the specialized knowledge of sixty different editors and reporters, as well as many other experts in their fields. He came to the *Times* in 1931, after seven years on the staff of the New York *World*, as an associate editor and as an overseas correspondent, and earlier as Washington correspondent for the *New Republic* and a frequent contributor to *Harper's Magazine*.

Merz is the author of several books including *The Great American Band Wagon* (John Day, 1928), a whimsical study of fads and foibles in the age of jazz, soda fountains, the silver screen, the open road and the bathing beauty; *The Dry Decade* (Doubleday, 1931) a study of the Prohibition era; and editor of *Days of Decision* (Doubleday, 1941) a book of New York *Times* editorials. He holds four honorary D. Litt. degrees.

Born in Sandusky, Ohio on February 23, 1893, Charles Merz is the only son of the late Dr. Charles Hope Merz and the former Sakie Emeline Prout. For twenty-eight years his

CHARLES MERZ

father edited and contributed extensively to a Masonic bulletin, and wrote four books on Masonry. He practiced medicine in Sandusky until his eighty-sixth year. Charles's grandfather, Karl Merz, was a professor of music at the College of Wooster in Ohio. His mother's family came from Connecticut and settled in Ohio in the early 1800's. Charles attended high school in his native city, edited the school paper, and was graduated in 1911. His extracurricular activities included baseball and track.

He entered Yale University, New Haven, Connecticut in the fall of 1911, and majored in English. He joined the Elizabethan Club, Wolf's Head Society and Zeta Psi, and was elected to Phi Beta Kappa. At Yale, reports *Time* (November 28, 1938), "he was editor of the rowdy *Record* while his classmate Archibald MacLeish conducted the more pontifical *Literary Magazine.*" Merz, who acquired the nickname "Doc" in college, was graduated in 1915 and immediately joined the staff of *Harper's Weekly,* becoming its managing editor in the same year. The publication was sold in 1916 and Merz became the Washington correspondent for the *New Republic* (1917-1918).

When the United States entered the first World War in 1917, Merz was commissioned a first lieutenant, AEF, in the Military Intelligence. He was sent to France and later became assistant to the American Commission to Negotiate Peace which met in Paris. After the Armistice he was successively a member of the editorial staff of the *New Republic* (1919-1920), staff correspondent of the New York *World* in Europe and Asia (1921-1923), and associate editor (1924-1931). Merz worked for the New York *World* during "the seven lean years before its demise." From 1920 to 1923 he wrote many articles as a free-lance writer for *Century, Atlantic Monthly* and *Collier's.*

His first book, *The Great American Band Wagon,* published in 1928, contained articles on the American scene, some of which were reprinted from *Harper's Magazine,* The *Outlook* and *The American Sketch.* It was completed following a motor trip through the Middle West, on the open road "of pop-stands, gas tanks, hot dogs, ukeleles, kewpie dolls and chocolate almond bars that has become the broad and pulsing artery of a nation." Arthur Krock, reviewing the book in the New York *Times* (February 5, 1928) remarked that "the fine flavor of satire in this particular piece of reporting rises like laughing gas."

Mark Van Doren in the *Nation* (February 22, 1928) noted that "the edge of his satire is sheathed in good humor," and that the author "gives a vigorous presentation of such American idiosyncrasies as jazz, bathing beauty contests, radio programs . . . and the blare of murder trials and prize fights."

His second book, *The Dry Decade,* published in 1931, also received favorable reviews. The *World Tomorrow* (August 1931) commented: "His book, written without animus and very little bias, recommends itself as an invaluable piece of history . . . of the successes and failures of prohibition enforcement."

He joined the editorial staff of the New York *Times* on May 18, 1931. In November 1938 Merz succeeded Dr. John H. Finley (who had become editor in 1937) to the editorship of the *Times,* and Dr. Finley was made editor emeritus. "Merz' new, sober post will probably not dim his quick wit," observed *Time.*

Merz does not approve of the "ivory tower" seclusion in which editorial writers have tended to lock themselves, and he encourages his staff of ten "regulars" to "get out into the field as much as possible," thereby helping them to write more authoritatively and interestingly on their respective subjects. Reporters and department heads (such as the science editor, education editor, automobile editor, aviation editor, and the real estate editor) come to his desk to submit editorials. These are given as careful consideration as any of those written by the regular members of the editorial staff.

One of his colleagues describes Merz in these words: "Charlie is the kind of editor who gets things done by kindness. He is always willing to listen to your opinion, and is ready to be convinced if you can present your point of view logically and factually. He gets things done because you're ashamed not to do your best for him." His working day, writes an associate, "begins about 10:30 every weekday morning. (He keeps in constant touch with the paper, even when not in his office). Taking off his gray Homburg hat, he enters his beige-walled, green-carpeted office and seats himself behind a broad walnut desk. . . . When his desk is cleared up, he confers with editors and after lunch settles down to writing his almost daily editorial. He swivels his chair around, and while a cigarette burns he writes on lined yellow pads with a soft lead pencil. Afterwards he reads all the evening papers and makes up the editorial page for the next morning."

In an article entitled "The Editorial Page" in the *Annals of the American Academy of Political and Social Science* (January, 1942), Merz wrote: "If he is alive to his responsibility, the editor studies the news more carefully than any possible reader of his paper. He puts together items that are seemingly not linked, and looks for trends that are not always evident on the face of the day's news. He reads a good many books, talks with as many informed people as he can, uses his personal contacts for enlightenment. . . . He can set himself against the trend of the moment when he thinks that trend is wrong. He can do his best to precipitate discussion in a democracy. Only by following his conscience and his best judgment can he have or deserve influence."

In the article Merz pointed out the trends in the evolution of the modern editorial page. These include the trend toward interpretation of "the increasingly complex character of the news itself," the trend toward specialization, using experts to help clarify situations and events; the trend toward independence (since issues frequently cross party lines, and political labels have lost their meaning), and the trend toward social reality (appealing to the moral nature of his readers as well as to the intellectual nature). He tries "to make them see the good or bad results, from his point of view [after weighing evidence], of the things that people, individually or collectively, are doing or not doing."

Although the New York *Times* has steadfastly avoided becoming a political party organ, it had in general supported the Democratic Party up to 1940. In 1940, however, the *Times* editorial pages favored Franklin D. Roosevelt's foreign policy, but disapproved of his domestic policy, and opposed the third term. After the *Times* announced its support of President Roosevelt in the 1944 campaign, according to columnist Leonard Lyons in the New York *Post* (October 21, 1944), "Charles Merz, the Times' editor who wrote the Roosevelt editorial, knew that a large number of letters and telegrams would be waiting for him. Merz walked into his office and, as he expected, a man-size pile of messages covered his desk. This was the reaction of America's intellectuals, he mused. This was Public Opinion responding to one of the most important editorials in the history of one of the great newspapers of all time. Merz seated himself at his desk and, with trepidation, opened the first telegram. It read: 'Cheerio. Glad you're with our side.' It was signed Frank Sinatra."

The *Times* is an "independent" newspaper, and Merz has pointed out that it is no longer a journalistic sensation when a "Democratic" newspaper bolts a Democratic candidate or a "Republican" newspaper attacks the Republicans in Congress. "On all the important issues of the day—foreign policy, national defense, regulation of the market, social reform, and labor legislation—there is less sheer partisan regularity than there has ever been at any other time in the whole history of the press."

"A good page," he has stated, "while it values consistency, does not make a fetish of it. And since the editorial page no longer claims to be written on Olympus by men who are omniscient, it can afford to alter its position when facts or changes in conditions show it to be wrong. . . . What is evolving is a genuinely cooperative editorial page, built on the experience of the whole organization. The *Times* may have experimented more in this direction than most other newspapers, since it has a larger-than-average staff to draw upon. But the trend toward specialization is a general trend, arising from the very nature of the problem of interpreting many kinds of news."

Ward Morehouse, in an interview with Merz which was published in *Editor and Publisher,* April 15, 1944, commented: "Mr. Merz has often been at his desk at 3 A.M., writing a last-minute editorial, made necessary by a development in war or world news. 'There is always the danger,' said Mr. Merz, 'that an editorial page will freeze too early in the day. Ours is kept open until the last possible minute. I don't think we've missed coverage on any important after-midnight event. . . .' "

He is a systematic man without ever seeming to be. "In my long and happy association with Merz," (on the New York *World*), Walter Lippmann recalled, "I came to regard him as the indisputable master in journalism of the art of keeping and looking at the record." The New York *Times* staff sometimes consults Merz' own files, accumulated over the years, when the "morgue" fails to provide them with the information they require.

Ever one to enjoy making the best of a bad situation, Merz likes to recall that he met his future wife (Evelyn Scott) after encountering her on the opposite fairway, following a poor golf shot. They were married on June 30, 1924. They live at Gracie Square. His wife is a trustee of the China Institute in America. Merz is a member of The Century Association and the Yale Club in New York City. He is a trustee of the Guggenheim Foundation and the Russell Sage Foundation, and since 1943 has been a member of the board of managers of the Seamen's Church Institute of New York.

The *Times* editor is six feet one inch in height, weighs 180 pounds, has brown eyes and brown, graying hair. Two of his favorite forms of relaxation are fishing and traveling. He and his wife spend their summer vacations on Cape Cod. He is something of an expert in solving crossword puzzles and double crostics. His enthusiasm for puzzles reached such a peak that he tried his hand at making them. He also made several in collaboration with Arthur Hays Sulzberger, president and publisher of the *Times,* which were published in the Sunday Magazine section. He has shown a gift for writing light verse. In politics he is independent, and in religion his church affiliation is Episcopalian. Ward Morehouse described Merz as "a man of modesty and unfailing courtesy. He is quick and terse in speech."

Among his honors are the order Al Merito in the rank of Commander, conferred by the

MERZ, CHARLES—*Continued*

Chilean Government in 1949. In his speech of acceptance at the Chilean Embassy (January 13), Merz said: "We all recognize the close and the lasting friendship between North and South America and will always try to strengthen that friendship." He was given the fifteenth award of the Montclair, New Jersey "Yale Bowl", a tribute from Yale University alumni in that area to a distinguished graduate. Honorary Doctor of Literature degrees have been conferred on Merz by Yale University (1942), Columbia University (1944), Colgate University (1939) and College of Wooster (1939).

Although the *Times* gets numerous requests for reprints of its editorials, it seldom complies, but in several cases the demand was so overwhelming that reprints were made. Two of these by Charles Merz were "I Am An American", published on May 17, 1942 and "The Cause For Which We Fight", published on January 5, 1945.

"I am an American," he wrote. "It is a friendly way of life, with room for the opinions of the man across the street. . . . It is an alert way of life, on guard day and night against impairment of the rights that a free people cherish: the right to think for themselves and to vote as they please, to choose their own church, to read a free press, to name their own leaders in a free election; the right to discuss, to disagree, to try new roads, to make mistakes and to correct them; the right to be secure against the exercise of arbitrary power. . . ."

References

Ed & Pub 77:12+ Ap 15 '44 por
Newsweek 12:28 N 28 '38
New Yorker 30:35 Jl 31 '54 por
Time 32:43 N 28 '38

Who's Who in America, 1954-55

MILLIKAN, ROBERT A(NDREWS) Mar. 22, 1868—Dec. 19, 1953 Physicist; educator, philosopher and humanitarian; studied at Oberlin College, Columbia University and at the universities of Berlin and Göttingen; member of physics staff of University of Chicago (1896-1921); director of Norman Bridge Laboratory and chairman of executive council of the California Institute of Technology (1921-45); U.S. representative to League of Nations' Committee for International Cooperation (1922-32); known throughout the world for his work in physics and notably on the cosmic ray, electrons, photo-electric effect, behavior of "field currents," light polarization, and rocket and jet propulsion development; won Nobel Prize in physics (1923); author of many books and frequent contributor to scientific publications; wrote *Autobiography* (1950); received honorary degrees from many American and foreign colleges and universities. See *Current Biography,* (Jan.-June) 1940 and (June) 1952.

Obituary

N Y Times p1+ D 20 '53

MITCHELL, JAMES P(AUL) Nov. 12, 1900- United States Secretary of Labor

Address: b. c/o United States Department of Labor, Washington, D.C.; h. Upland Terrace, N.W., Washington, D.C.; 214 S. Blvd., Spring Lake, N.J.

Described as a personnel executive who "feels that trade unions are here to stay and that business should . . . view them as a challenge" (*Christian Science Monitor,* October 9, 1953), James P. Mitchell was sworn in as United States Secretary of Labor on October 9, 1953, succeeding Martin P. Durkin who resigned on the previous September 10. For four months prior to his appointment to the Cabinet post Mitchell was Assistant Secretary of the Army in charge of manpower and reserve forces affairs.

The Secretary has had more than twenty years' experience in personnel administration and in management-employee relations, both in private industry and government service. He is on leave of absence as vice-president of Bloomingdale Brothers department store in New York City, where he has been in charge of labor relations and operations since 1947. His views toward labor organizations are considered "middle-of-the-road" (New York *Times,* January 4, 1954).

James Paul Mitchell was born in Elizabeth, New Jersey, on November 12, 1900, the son of Peter J. and Anna C. (Driscoll) Mitchell. His uncle, Thomas Mitchell, the actor, was brought up with him. James attended St. Patrick's Parochial School and in the evenings and on Saturdays ran errands for a grocery store.

After his graduation from Battin High School in 1917, he went to work for fifteen dollars a week in this store. Within a year he was promoted to manager. Leaving his employer, he opened his own store in Rahway, New Jersey and in 1921 set up a second store in Elizabeth. Both failed in 1923. Mitchell recalls: "I was young and inexperienced, and vastly overextended myself" (New York *Post,* November 8, 1953).

Following two years of employment as a truck driver and salesman, Mitchell in 1926 became an expediter in the Western Electric Company plant in Kearny, New Jersey, and was soon transferred to the personnel department. He secured a position in 1931 with the New Jersey relief administration to direct its program in Union county, and later returned to Western Electric.

Mitchell left that company in 1936 to take charge of labor relations in the New York City division of the Works Progress Administration, headed by the then Colonel Brehon Somervell. At a time when left-wing factions were attracting the unemployed, Mitchell found his task as "trouble-shooter" difficult, and says: "I have a recollection . . . of always having to cross a picket line to go to work in the morning" (New York *Post,* November 8, 1953).

When Somervell went to Washington, D.C., in 1940 to head the Army's construction program, he requested Mitchell to go with him as chief of the labor relations division. The next year, Mitchell became director of the civilian personnel division for the Services of Supply of the War Department. He was also a member of the National Building Trades Stabilization Board, the Joint Army-Navy Personnel Board, an alternate for the Under Secretary of War on the War Manpower Commission, and head of a program of special cooperation between the Army, War Manpower Commission and the War Production Board to supply workers where they were needed.

Mitchell supported preinduction training in the high schools ". . . to provide trained manpower that will not only produce the weapons for the Armed Forces, but provide them with men who know how to keep the weapons rolling and keep them fighting" (*Science News Letter,* November 14, 1942).

Returning to private industry in 1945, Mitchell became director of personnel and industrial relations for R. H. Macy and Company in New York City. The personnel expert helped to settle the strike at Macy's store in 1946, allowing full pay to employees who did not remain on the job and triple pay to those who did.

Mitchell became vice-president in charge of labor relations and operations at Bloomingdale Brothers in 1947. He is credited with stabilizing the store's "chaotic labor situation" by putting supervisory methods on a basis of "consent" and "communication" rather than authoritarian procedures (New York *Post,* November 8, 1953). A unionist remarked that Mitchell "never took a mechanical view of a contract, but was able to realize that it concerned human beings and not just commodities" (New York *World-Telegram and Sun,* October 12, 1953).

At the U.S. Army's request, Mitchell went to Germany in 1948 to study the military government's civilian employment program, and after the outbreak of the Korean War, he examined and reported on combat pay problems. After working on a research project for the Citizens Committee for the Hoover Report, the personnel manager headed a group of the Citizens Committee in 1951 to encourage public and Congressional recognition for the need of modernizing personnel policies.

President Dwight D. Eisenhower designated Mitchell in April 1953 as the Assistant Secretary of the Army, in charge of manpower and reserve forces affairs. On a leave of absence from Bloomingdale Brothers, Mitchell filled this position from May 4 until October 9, 1953. During this period he called the Administration's defense policy a "sensible long-range program" (New York *Times,* May 17, 1953).

Nominated as Secretary of Labor by President Eisenhower on October 8, 1953, Mitchell took office the following day. The President said his choice was based more upon Mitchell's "character and interest in other people than his broad experience in the labor relations field" (Washington *Post,* October 9, 1953). The appointment was unanimously confirmed by the Senate on January 19, 1954.

The Department of Labor was created March 4, 1913 and is charged with enforcing statutes "designed to advance the public interest by promoting the welfare of the wage earners of the United States, improving their working conditions, and advancing their opportunities for profitable employment." Included under its jurisdiction are the bureaus of standards, labor statistics, veterans' re-employment rights, employment security, wage and hour and public contracts division, and the women's bureau.

JAMES P. MITCHELL

The New York *Times* (October 25, 1953) commented that "there are more Government functions and employes outside the department dealing with labor than there are in the department . . . the department has nothing to do with the Taft-Hartley Law except to receive union financial reports. It has nothing to do with the Railway Labor Act or with the mediation of labor-management disputes." Mitchell has said that he wants to see "the department strengthened and broadened."

On November 13, 1953, he told the National Council of Negro Women that he welcomed the banning of racial discrimination, effective November 16, 1953, in all contracts made with the District of Columbia government and that he was "particularly gratified" with progress toward ending racial segregation in the armed forces (New York *Times,* November 14, 1953).

Addressing the convention of the Congress of Industrial Organizations in Cleveland, Ohio, the Secretary recommended widening the national wage structure which leaves 63,000,000 working people without safeguard of a minimum wage and advocated "an increase in the present 75-cents-an-hour minimum" legal wage (New York *Times,* November 19, 1953).

Mitchell claimed that the Administration's policy "of leaving to labor and management the solution of their own labor relations problems" had resulted in a "smaller loss of man-hours" and led to "more genuine collective bargaining" (Washington *Post,* January 3, 1954).

(Continued next page)

MITCHELL, JAMES P.—*Continued*

In a speech before the New Jersey Republican Committee, Mitchell asserted: "Good industrial relations cannot be created by laws. At best, the Government can only provide the framework in which labor and management operate. Employers and employes themselves must develop better relationships at the plant level and settle their own differences without dictation from Washington. The Government's sole interest is that of protecting the public" (New York *Times,* January 14, 1954).

Secretary Mitchell urged the enactment of the fifteen revisions suggested by President Eisenhower to the Labor-Management Relations Act of 1947. One request of the Administration was for Federal polls of strikers. The other proposed changes included relaxation of the ban on the secondary boycott prohibition in certain instances, prohibiting of an election immediately after a strike called for economic reasons was effected, providing a union and an employer to make a contract before employees are hired and legalizing the right of such a contract to require employees to become union members in the construction, amusement and maritime industries, and a non-Communist oath for employers until Congress adopted substitutes for dealing with Communist infiltration generally. (In August 1954 Congress passed a bill outlawing the Communist party. The proposal was approved by the President.)

Secretary of Labor Mitchell conferred with George Meany, president of the American Federation of Labor on February 4, 1954 at the AFL executive council meeting in Miami, and discussed minimum wage law changes. Both men were agreed that the wage should be raised from its present 75-cent an-hour-level, time. Mitchell said the changes should be made but major disagreement was on the question of "at the appropriate time" and that "this is not the proper time". He said he looked for a rising trend in the national economy by the end of the year. He termed the "present so-called recession a temporary inventory readjustment" (Miami *Herald,* February 5, 1954).

On August 26, 1954 President Eisenhower created the Committee on Migratory Labor, and named Mitchell chairman of the committee.

Predicting that by 1975 half the nation's adult population will be forty-five years old or older, Mitchell said that prejudice toward hiring older workers must end or these workers will be "condemned to a life of economic uselessness."

The Secretary of Labor has served as a special mediator of the New York State Board of Mediation, as chairman of the employee relations committee of the National Retail Dry Goods Association and of the executive committee of the Retail Labor Standards Association of New York, and has been a member of the executive committee of the National Civil Service League. He is a Republican and a Roman Catholic. Fordham University conferred the honorary doctor of laws degree on the Secretary of Labor in 1954.

Married to Isabelle Nulton of Roselle Park, New Jersey in 1923, Mitchell has one daughter, Elizabeth. He is six feet tall and weighs 196 pounds. *Time* describes him as a man with "deep-set blue eyes, . . . huge shoulders and bristling hair." Among his hobbies is deep-sea fishing.

References

N Y Times p10 Je 11 '51 por; p14 O 9 '53
N Y World-Telegram p22 O 12 '53
Time 62:27 O 19 '53
U S News 35:16 O 16 '53
Washington (D.C.) Post Mag p2 N 8 '53
Who's Who in America, 1952-53

MOHAMMED, GHULAM Aug. 29, 1895-
Governor-General of the Dominion of Pakistan
Address: b. Governor-General's House, Karachi, Pakistan

The third Governor-General of the Dominion of Pakistan within the British Commonwealth of Nations is Ghulam Mohammed who was appointed in October 1951 by the late King George VI on the advice of a Constituent Assembly which functions as a provisional legislature. Distinguished as an economist and fiscal expert, he had served Pakistan as Finance Minister since Pakistan was carved out of northern India and its name first appeared on the map of the world on August 15, 1947. Strongly anti-Communist, Pakistan, described as "a bastion of the free world," supported the United Nations' decision to stop Communist aggression in Korea. It has consistently voted in the U.N. with the Western democracies and against the Soviet bloc (*Scholastic,* January 13, 1954).

Ghulam Mohammed's outstanding contributions as Finance Minister were his work in organizing the Ministry of Economic Affairs, arranging for the release of Pakistan currency, and establishing the state and national banks of Pakistan. He also played a major role in implementing the Six-Year National Development program of his country, the Agricultural Finance Corporation, the Industrial Development Corporation, and the Industrial Finance Corporation.

Pakistan—next door to neutral India, on the doorstep of Russia in Asia—has signed a one-year mutual defense agreement with the United States. The pact, as finally drawn and signed in May 1954, has safeguards in which Pakistan pledges that it will not undertake any act of aggression against any other nation. Under its terms the United States will furnish arms, equipment, and a military mission to help build up Pakistan's defense forces, but there is no provision for the establishment of American military bases in Pakistan. The country has a population of nearly 80,000,000 including 300,000 trained troops.

The two parts of Pakistan—East and West Pakistan—lie as far apart as Massachusetts and Missouri. East Pakistan is flat and well-watered; its inhabitants' main food is rice. West Pakistan is mountainous and arid; its residents' chief food is wheat. The Pakistanis adhere to the Moslem faith, which distinguishes them from the people of India who adhere to the Hindu faith. The Indian peninsula was partitioned into two separate countries—one Hindu and the other Moslem. There has been a mass migration in both directions, but there are still sizable minorities in India and Pakistan.

Ghulam Mohammed was born on August 29, 1895 in Lahore, India. His ancestors were devout Moslems. He received his advanced education at the Mohammedan Anglo-Oriental College at Aligarh in the United Provinces (now called the Aligarh Muslim University) and acquired both the M.A. and the LL.B. degrees.

Successful in a competitive examination for appointment to the Indian Audit and Accounting Service, Ghulam Mohammed joined the Indian Audit Department in 1920. In 1932 he became a commissioner of development to Bhopal, a state in Central India and a dependency of Great Britain. After two years in this Moslem principality, Ghulam Mohammed returned in 1934 to the Indian government's civil service as deputy director of finance, posts and telegraphs, and as financial adviser on communications.

Six years later (1940) he was advanced to the position of controller-general of purchase, and in 1941 was appointed additional secretary in the Department of Supply. For his loyal service and impressive record in economics he received in 1941 the title of Companion in the Order of the Indian Empire.

In 1942 he was appointed Finance Minister to the Nizam (ruler) of Hyderabad, one of India's princely states; he filled this position with distinction until 1945, when he retired and was elected a director of the iron and steel enterprise known as Tatas, Ltd.

Not long after the end of World War II, the Labor government of Prime Minister Clement Attlee dispatched a Cabinet Mission to India to study the future status of the peninsula. The All-India Moslem League, headed by Mohammed Ali Jinnah and with Liaquat Ali Khan as general secretary, was dedicated to the aim of establishing a separate government for the predominantly Moslem areas of India. On the other hand, the Hindu Congress party, led by Jawaharlal Nehru, urged a united India.

In the spring of 1946 the Cabinet Mission rejected as unfeasible the idea of separate Hindu and Moslem states, which caused some bitterness among the Mohammedans. Ghulam Mohammed, however, avoided any display of acrimony, and indeed accepted (June, 1946) the honor of being knighted. He retained his title of Sir Ghulam Mohammed until 1947, even though a number of prominent members of the Moslem League had renounced their British titles in July 1946, as a "first installment of non-cooperation" with the plan for a united India.

A few months later, however, the Moslem League decided to adhere to the Cabinet Mission's recommendations for the setting up of an all-India interim government and aided in establishing it. Tension within the interim government mounted, however, and at a conference with both Hindu and Moslem leaders at London in December 1946, the British government reversed its previous position and decided that a partition should take place.

Harris & Ewing

GHULAM MOHAMMED

A Partition Council was formed in 1947, and in August, certain terms of the Independence of India Act went into effect. According to this act, the new Dominion of Pakistan was created—West Pakistan (311,406 square miles; population 33,600,000) and East Pakistan (54,501 square miles; population 42,200,000) separated by about 1000 miles of Indian territory. The Sind seaport of Karachi was chosen as the capital.

One source tells that the name *Pakistan* was first used in 1930 by a group of Moslem students who composed it from the initial letters of Punjab, Afghania, Kashmir, and Sind, adding *stan,* meaning land. Another source explains that *Pakistan* is a Hindustani term meaning the "land of the pure."

Mohammed Ali Jinnah accepted the appointment as the dominion's first Governor-General; Liaquat Ali Khan became Prime Minister, and Ghulam Mohammed was appointed Minister of Finance and Economic Affairs. Pakistan was accepted as the fifty-seventh member of the United Nations on September 30, 1947.

Despite the peculiar problems of the newly established and predominantly agricultural state, Pakistan's first Finance Minister was conspicuously successful. During his first twenty months in office he gave his country "two balanced budgets with a prospective surplus, contrary to almost all expectations" and was able to cite as indications of a promising future a new currency, a favorable bal-

MOHAMMED, GHULAM—*Continued*

ance of trade and a liberal import policy, as reported by Robert Trumbull in the New York *Times* (May 8, 1949). Trumbull also noted that Ghulam Mohammed was "among the large body of Asiatic economists who believe that the way to keep out Communism is to raise the standard of living of the masses." The Finance Minister was convinced, however, that "no Asiatic government can accomplish this unaided."

Already serving as president of the International Islamic Economic Organization, Ghulam Mohammed became in 1950 the governor for Pakistan of the International Bank for Reconstruction and Development and the International Monetary Fund, and in that year obtained substantial grants for his country from both bodies and also negotiated for a $450,000,000 loan from the United States.

Following the death of Mohammed Ali Jinnah in September 1948, the Bengali political leader Khwaja Nazimuddin became Pakistan's second Governor-General and functioned as such until October 1951, when the four-year-old dominion was confronted with a serious crisis through the assassination of Prime Minister Liaquat Ali Khan. Khwaja Nazimuddin resigned the Governor-General's post to become the new Prime Minister.

The late King George VI of Great Britain appointed Ghulam Mohammed in 1951 as the third Governor-General of Pakistan. On November 16, 1951, when the Constituent Assembly had met for a new session, the new Governor-General delivered an address in which he not only called upon the Indian government of Nehru to agree to an "impartial plebiscite" in Kashmir, but also expressed the hope that the Anglo-Egyptian dispute over the Suez Canal and the Sudan would be "amicably settled through wise statesmanship." (This dispute was settled by an agreement signed by Premier Abdel Nasser of Egypt and Great Britain in July 1954, the withdrawal of British troops from the Canal to be completed within twenty months.) A month later Ghulam Mohammed himself was called upon to exercise "wise statesmanship" in the province of Sind, where he temporarily suspended constitutional rule following a corruption scandal in the local government.

The new federal government of Khwaja Nazimuddin did not command the same confidence as that of Liaquat Ali Khan, and Ghulam Mohammed was forced in 1953 to dissolve the Cabinet and to call on Mohammed Ali to form a new government. In an article, "Pakistan: The Divided Dominion", in *Current History* (December, 1953), Carl Leiden wrote: "Nazimuddin reluctantly acquiesced.... Though ousted, [he] still retained control of the Moslem League, the only major party in Pakistan. . . . It is still hard to justify Ghulam Mohammed's action on constitutional grounds."

That Ghulam Mohammed will probably be the last Governor-General of Pakistan was indicated on December 22, 1952, when the Basic Principles Committee of the Constituent Assembly recommended a constitution which would make Pakistan, like India, a republic. It would, however, remain within the British Commonwealth of Nations. According to the proposed constitution, a two-chamber federal legislature would be established.

A further development occurred in November 1953 when the Constituent Assembly, still considering the proposed constitution, decided over the protests of the Hindu minority that Pakistan would be known as an "Islamic" republic. "Under the terms of that decision," noted the New York *Times,* "the propagation of the Moslem faith is enjoined upon the state; only Moslems are eligible for the post of chief of state; and no law can be passed repugnant to the spirit of the Koran."

After Ghulam Mohammed's visit to the United States in November 1953 for medical treatment there were rumors that Pakistan had offered the United States the use of its air bases in exchange for American aid in equipping Pakistan's volunteer army of over 300,000 well-trained men.

India's Prime Minister Jawaharlal Nehru warned the United States that a military pact with Pakistan would have far-reaching consequences. However, Pakistan's Prime Minister Mohammed Ali and Governor-General Ghulam Mohammed denied that Pakistan's military bases had been offered to any country.

"As long as the quarrel with India continues," wrote William Clark in *The Reporter* (June 8, 1954), "Pakistan will be a weak ally whose attention is mainly directed to its frontiers with India, rather than to the outside. Nevertheless, by association with the western world Pakistan may become less hypnotized by the quarrel, more prepared to recognize its larger interests. In particular by association with its Middle Eastern neighbors, Pakistan may gradually lose some of its isolationism, and may become relatively a source of strength to those weak and divided states."

On September 21, 1954, by four amendments to the Government of India Act of 1935 as adopted for Pakistan, the Constituent Assembly removed from the Governor-General his broad independent powers.

Ghulam Mohammed declared a state of emergency in Pakistan on October 24, 1954 and dissolved the Constituent Assembly (new elections would be held soon). Mohammed Ali formed a new Cabinet.

The Governor-General is a member of the executive council of Aligarh Muslim University and a member of the courts of that university and of the University of Delhi. He is married and has two children.

References

Illus Lond N 219:663 O 27 '51 por
International Who's Who, 1953
International Year Book and Statesmen's Who's Who, 1953
Nalanda Year-Book and Who's Who in India and Pakistan, 1951-53
Who's Who, 1954
Who's Who in America (Sup. D '52)

MOLOTOV, VÎACHESLAV M(IKHAILOVICH) (mô'lŭ-tŏf vyĭ-chĕ-slâf' myĭ-kī'lŭ-vyĭch) Mar. 9, 1890- U.S.S.R. Foreign Minister; Communist party leader

Address: b. c/o Soviet Foreign Ministry, Smolenskaya Square, Moscow, U.S.S.R.

NOTE: This biography supersedes the article which appeared in *Current Biography* in 1940.

The Western world knows Vîacheslav M. Molotov primarily as the chief spokesman for Soviet policy during World War II, and during the postwar period when Communist expansion in eastern Europe and parts of Asia led to growing deterioration in East-West relationships. As Commissar (later Minister) for Foreign Affairs from 1939 to 1949, and since early 1953, Molotov attended most of the important international meetings of the time, including the Conference on International Organization in San Francisco in 1945 to establish the United Nations.

He is the member of longest standing in the presidium of the Central Committee of the Communist party (formerly the politburo) and is one of the few leaders in the U.S.S.R. today who had a major part in the Bolshevik Revolution of 1917. For more than thirty years he was considered the man closest to Joseph Stalin, as the chairman of the Council of the People's Commissars (Premier) from 1930 to 1941 and deputy chairman (Vice-Premier) since 1941.

In Berlin in early 1954 Molotov conferred with the western Foreign Ministers on problems relating to Germany and Austria which remained unsolved almost ten years after World War II and which continued unsolved at the end of these talks.

Later at the Geneva conference, convened on April 26, 1954, Molotov, reiterating the position of Chinese Communist Premier and Foreign Minister Chou En-lai, asserted that the "peoples of Asia have the full right to settle their affairs themselves." A New York *Times* editorial (April 30, 1954) noted: "Unfortunately the Asian peoples who have thrown off foreign rule . . . to become free and self-governing are not yet strong enough to resist by their own forces the new imperialism that threatens to engulf them in the name of communism. They need the help of the older democracies to save them from being submerged in the totalitarian flood."

The Soviet Foreign Minister on May 11, 1954 bitterly attacked the Southeast Asian defense pact proposed by the United States, and also denounced the United Nations as a "belligerent" in Korea. His attack was answered by Paul-Henri Spaak, Foreign Minister of Belgium, who declared: "We cannot allow the justifiable intervention of the United Nations in Korea to be depicted as an act of aggression."

Born Vîacheslav Mikhailovich Skrîabīn on March 9, 1890, Molotov is a native of the village of Kukarka in the Vyatka (now Kirov) region. His father, Mikhail Skrîabīn, a shopkeeper, was able to afford music lessons and some formal education for his children. When the boy was about twelve years old he left school in Nolinsk to attend a Czarist secondary school in Kazan, where he joined a students' Marxist group and took part in the revolution of 1905. As a member of the Bolshevik wing of the Russian Social Democratic Labor party, he became a leader in a Kazan Marxist youth organization in 1906. Still in his teens, the young Bolshevist was arrested by Czarist police and deported to Vologda in north European Russia. Here he proceeded to organize railway workers. During his years of exile, jailings, escapes and re-arrests, he used a number of pseudonyms, one of which, Molotov (hammer), he came in time to adopt permanently.

Wide World

VIACHESLAV M. MOLOTOV

His two-year sentence of exile in Vologda completed in 1911, Molotov entered the Polytechnical Institute of St. Petersburg (later Leningrad). While carrying on underground activities in St. Petersburg schools, he continued studying the theories of Marx, Engels and Lenin. He contributed to the Bolshevik journal *Zvezda* and in May 1912 became part-founder, with Stalin, of *Pravda,* an official party paper illegally published in St. Petersburg.

After being expelled from the city for his political activities, he conducted party work from the suburbs and in Moscow. Molotov was exiled to Irkutsk in Siberia in 1915, but the following year he escaped and returned to St. Petersburg to become a member of the Russian Bureau of the Bolshevik Central Committee. While many party leaders were in exile in Siberia or abroad, Molotov took a prominent role in directing preparations at home for the November 1917 Revolution which brought the Bolsheviks to power.

In 1917 he became a member of the executive of the Petrograd (Leningrad) Soviet and, with Stalin, of the military revolutionary committee. After decrees had been issued for nationalization of industry, he was made chair-

MOLOTOV, VIACHESLAV—*Continued*

man in 1918 of the People's Economy Council, northern region. During the next two years he was sent to various parts of the country, to direct restoration of areas conquered by the Red Army and devastated by civil war.

Molotov's political duties increased in 1920 when he was chosen secretary of the central committee of the Communist party of the Ukraine. Upon becoming a member of the Central Committee of the Soviet Union a year later, he was named by Lenin as the committee's responsible secretary (Stalin was general secretary of the secretariat). At the age of thirty-one (1921) he was also admitted as a candidate member of the party's politburo (political bureau), influential in formulating Soviet government policy. In December 1925, he gained full membership on the politburo, the youngest member this body has ever had.

In the struggle for party leadership after Lenin's death, Molotov sided with Stalin against Trotsky, worked in Leningrad in 1926 against the Zinovievists (Trotsky supporters) and in Moscow in 1928 against Bukharin and Rykov. Some of his titles at this time were member of the central executive committee of the Russian Soviet Socialist Republic (1927), member of the presidium of the central executive committee of the U.S.S.R., and member of the executive committee of the Communist International (1928-1934).

With Stalin's control of the party secure, Molotov in 1930 succeeded Rykov as chairman of the Council of People's Commissars of the U.S.S.R., thus becoming Premier at the age of forty. "The secret of Molotov's success," wrote Walter Duranty (*Stalin & Co.,* 1949) "was that every step up the ladder, he left behind him the record of a difficult task efficiently performed." The new head of the government spoke proudly in his acceptance speech of the guidance he had received from Stalin.

As Premier he was largely concerned with the industrial and agricultural phases of the Five Year Plans, "helping Stalin to force the country through its industrial revolution and to crush all domestic opposition" (New York *Times Magazine,* February 11, 1951). In 1935 he served on the committee for drafting reforms to the constitution. Early in the same year he made his first important speech on foreign affairs when he addressed the All-Union Soviet Congress, soon after Russia had joined the League of Nations.

In May 1939 Molotov succeeded Maxim M. Litvinov as Commissar for Foreign Affairs. His first important act in this office was the signing in August 1939 of the Russo-German nonaggression pact. While the Nazis subsequently overran the democracies in central and western Europe, the Soviet Union absorbed the Baltic Republics and engaged in war with Finland. In a continuing effort to remain at peace with Germany, the Russian diplomat visited Berlin in November 1940 for consultation with Nazi leaders, reportedly on his first trip outside his own country.

When Germany invaded the U.S.S.R. in June 1941 Molotov turned his efforts to negotiating a mutual-aid pact with Great Britain, in which both nations agreed not to make a separate peace with Germany. After a visit to England in the summer of 1942, he flew to Washington, where he arranged for an increase in lend-lease aid from the United States. The Soviet Foreign Commissar at this time also occupied the position of vice-chairman of the Council of People's Commissars, Stalin having taken over the premiership from him in May 1941. Molotov became as well in 1941 a member of the five-man State Committee of Defense (with Stalin, Malenkov, Beria and Voroshilov) formed to prosecute the war.

The Soviet official had an important part in the international conferences among Allied leaders during and immediately after World War II, including the historic meetings at Tehran, Yalta and Potsdam. In 1945 he headed the Soviet delegation to the Conference on International Organization in San Francisco. Here and at subsequent early sessions of the U.N. General Assembly first appeared the differences between the U.S.S.R. and the West.

While failing to reach agreement with Western powers on many details of the treaties affecting the defeated nations of World War II and on other world problems such as control of atomic energy, Molotov was able to conclude a series of trade and nonaggression pacts with eastern European nations. The satellite countries became in 1947 participants in the Council for Economic Mutual Assistance (Molotov plan). This program to integrate Soviet and eastern European economies was effected after the June 1947 Paris conference, where Molotov rejected the Marshall plan.

"The stalling, obstructionist tactics Molotov employed at the Italian peace treaty parley in 1946 and at every council of foreign ministers which he has attended are also characteristic," wrote Donald Robinson (*The 100 Most Important People*). "By long-winded speeches impugning the democracies' motives, devious parliamentary maneuvers calculated to stall the sessions, and by an adamant refusal to compromise a single point, he either has gotten . . . what he has wanted or has seen to it that no agreement of any kind was reached."

Molotov's was "the dominant Soviet voice in the East-West debate" during the years between the end of World War II and 1949 (Anne O'Hare McCormick in New York *Times,* July 25, 1951). Not merely Stalin's mouthpiece, he came to be regarded "more than any other man" as responsible for Soviet aggressiveness (New York *Times Magazine,* February 11, 1951). The announcement on March 4, 1949 that he had been replaced by Andrei Y. Vishinsky as Foreign Minister gave rise to speculation in the West as to Molotov's future role in Russia. One conjecture was that he was preparing to assume the premiership in the event of Stalin's death. A report from Formosa in March 1952 stated that from a base in Siberia he was directing operations for an expanded Communist underground in the Far East.

After the death of Stalin on March 5, 1953, Molotov resumed his position as Minister of Foreign Affairs. Georgi M. Malenkov, who became Premier, is believed to be a member of a committee dictatorship which supplanted the one-man rule. According to the *U.S. News & World Report* (February 26, 1954), some experts say that Molotov urged the rule by committee and is an influential member of the group.

Time (April 20, 1953) reported that the British Foreign Office sees four objectives in present Communist foreign policy: "(1) the breakdown of NATO, (2) the neutralization of Germany, (3) the end of Nationalist China, and (4) a break between the United States and her foreign allies." When the big-four Foreign Ministers met in Berlin in early 1954, Molotov attacked the European Defense Community (EDC) and NATO as a course to another world war and proposed a collective security treaty for European countries that would exclude U.S. participation. At the Berlin conference, which failed to produce agreement on issues relating to Germany and Austria, the ministers decided to meet again, in late April in Geneva, to discuss problems of Korea and Indochina. The Chinese Communist government was invited to take part at the Geneva meeting on a basis that would not imply U.S. recognition of that government.

On two occasions (January 30 and February 13) during their stay in Berlin, Molotov and Secretary of State John Foster Dulles met in secret sessions to talk about President Dwight D. Eisenhower's proposal of an international pool of atomic energy for peacetime uses.

Molotov is the author of a number of publications (in Russian): *The Party's Policy in the Villages, Elections to the Soviets, On the Lessons of Trotskyism, On the Success and Difficulties of Socialist Building, Fighting for Socialism* and others. Among his writings available in English translation are *The Communist Party of the Soviet Union* (Modern Books, 1929), *Food for All; the Abolition of the Bread Card System in the Soviet Union* (International Publishers, 1934) and *Stalin and Stalin's Leadership* (Foreign Languages Publishing House, 1950).

Many attempts have been made by Western observers to evaluate the position of the Soviet Foreign Minister, who is also a member of the Supreme Soviet of the U.S.S.R. John Gunther expressed his opinion in *Inside Europe* that Molotov "is by no means a mere figurehead, but a man of considerable intelligence and influence." To E. Crankshaw (New York *Times Magazine,* February 11, 1951) he is a "dangerous man . . . because of the limitations of his thought and imagination." Partly because Lenin reportedly called him "the best file clerk in Russia," Molotov has been the butt of some humorous and disparaging comments in his own country and abroad. His career, as W. Duranty has pointed out, belies any idea of him as a "dull, unenterprising fellow, a plodder, who could be trusted to do a job competently but would never set any stream on fire."

In 1922 he married Polina Karpovskaya, a "handsome woman noted for her charm as a hostess." She is a Ukrainian-born Jewess who worked in the Communist party of the Ukraine under the name of Zhermchuzhina (pearl) Semyanovia.

While director of the Soviet perfume and cosmetics trust, she visited the United States in 1936 to study American methods. She later (1937-1939) served as Commissar of the fish industry. The Molotovs have a daughter, Svetlana, and an adopted daughter, Sonia. The diplomat received the Order of Lenin in 1940, 1943, 1945, and 1946. He also holds the Hammer and Sickle Gold Medal and the title of Hero of Socialist Labor, among other honors.

The Soviet leader is a scholarly looking figure, a stockily built man who wears a pince-nez and has a round face, broad forehead and trimmed mustache. He plays the violin, is interested in the arts and literature, and in the past enjoyed tennis and skiing. In manner he is methodical, precise and somewhat pedantic. Sir Winston Churchill (*Time,* April 20, 1953) once said of him, "He was above all men fitted to be the agent and instrument of . . . an incalculable machine."

According to Donald Robinson in *The 100 Most Important People,* Molotov is "a very suspicious man. When he stayed at Winston Churchill's country home, he kept a loaded revolver by his bedside. He brought his own food when he stayed with President Roosevelt at the White House. He did sneak off on a secret trip to see the sights of New York. And he has no antipathy to vodka."

References (see also references listed in 1940 biographical sketch)

N Y Herald Tribune II p3 O 24 '43 por; p5 Mr 5 '53 por
N Y Times p10 Mr 6 '53; p6 Mr 9 '53
N Y Times Mag p12+ S 22 '46; p8+ F 2 '47; p5+ F 11 '51 por
Newsweek 43:34+ F 8 '54
P M p9 Jl 9 '41 por
Time 61:34 Mr 16 '53; 61:32+ Ap 20 '53 por

Coates, W. P. and Z. K. A Biographical Sketch in Soviet Peace Policy (1941)
Duranty, W. Men Who Make Your World (1949); Stalin & Co. (1949)
Steel, J. Men Behind the War (1942)
Who's Who, 1954
Who's Who in America, 1954-55
World Biography (1948)

MOODY, (ARTHUR EDSON) BLAIR

Feb. 13, 1902-July 20, 1954 Former United States Senator (Democrat) from Michigan; newspaperman; was graduated from Brown University (1922); worked for Detroit *News* (1923 to 1951) as sports writer, Washington, D.C. columnist, and war correspondent; appointed in 1951 to fill the unexpired term of the late Senator Arthur H. Vandenberg; sought election in 1952, but was defeated; conducted radio and television program, *Meet Your Congress;* supported a bipartisan foreign policy in Congress, and the adoption of a civil rights plank in Democratic platform of 1952; wrote *Boom or Bust* (1941). See *Current Biography,* (Sept.) 1951.

Obituary

N Y Times p27 Jl 21 '54

MOORE, GARRY Jan. 31, 1915- Comedian
Address: b. c/o Columbia Broadcasting System, 485 Madison Ave., New York 22; h. Manursing Way, Rye, New York

As one of television's most popular stars, Garry Moore can persuade millions of women to drop their housework in the middle of the morning, sit down in front of a TV set, and watch his show. The diminutive, crew-clipped, bow-tied comedian received his early training in radio, beginning as a continuity writer for a Baltimore station in the mid-1930's. After a three-year stint with *Club Matinee*, which established his reputation along Radio Row, he started his own morning show, *Everything Goes*, in 1942.

Moore became Jimmy Durante's radio partner in 1943 and was teamed with him until 1947, when he was made master of ceremonies of *Take It or Leave It*. The Columbia Broadcasting System first starred him in the *Garry Moore Show* in 1949, and the next year the program went on television. By 1951 this weekday afternoon show was CBS-TV's second biggest source of revenue. On May 17, 1954 he celebrated the 1000th telecast of his Monday through Friday show. Since June 19, 1952 he has also been seen in the television program, *I've Got a Secret*.

Born of a well-to-do socially prominent family in Baltimore, Maryland, on January 31, 1915, Garry Moore was christened Thomas Garrison Morfit. His father, Mason P. Morfit, was a lawyer. At an early age Thomas resolved to become a writer. When he was eighteen and a senior in high school, he joined the Vagabonds, an amateur theatrical group, and was assigned to write the sketches for a revue. The songs were contributed by Zelda Fitzgerald, the wife of the famous novelist, F. Scott Fitzgerald, who was so favorably impressed by Morfit's sketches that they collaborated on some one-act plays patterned after the Grand Guignol French melodrama. "Nobody bought them," Morfit recalled.

Through his association with Fitzgerald, Morfit got a job as a continuity writer with Baltimore's radio station, WBAL. He went on the air when a comedian failed to appear. "I was astonished to find people laughing at my jokes," he has admitted. The station manager hired him permanently for the show.

In 1938, full of ambition to be a serious writer, Morfit went to St. Louis as a news announcer and sports commentator for Station KWK. But before long word got around about his previous experience as a comedian, and he was promptly shifted to a spot as station humorist. After seven months he quit. According to the New York *Times* (September 12, 1948), it was only after a casual stranger in St. Louis called him "the funniest feller on the air" that Morfit finally accepted the fact that his talents were in comedy.

He entered network radio in 1939 as a comedian and writer on *Club Matinee*, a five-afternoon-a-week variety show originating in Chicago via the National Broadcasting Company's Blue Network. The show was headed by Ransom Sherman, who helped establish a school of comedy that acknowledged its audience "had a mind and could use it." Morfit, who once described Sherman as "the man who taught me everything I know," alternated with him as master of ceremonies of *Club Matinee*, and wrote about half the show. In 1940 he decided to change his name, since he found that "Morfit" was frequently mispronounced. A contest was held to select a new name, and a Pittsburgh woman won $50 and a trip to Chicago for suggesting "Garry Moore."

In the summer of 1942, NBC brought Moore to New York to launch an early morning weekday show called *Everything Goes*, similar in format to *Club Matinee*. "As an emcee, Moore is just another likeable guy with a knack for gags," was the opinion of *Time*'s reviewer.

By the following year Moore had made sufficient impression upon early risers to be slated for the summer replacement of the Abbot and Costello show. But Costello got sick in March 1943, and Moore was rushed in ahead of schedule for his first stand on a night-time cross-country hookup. Since the sponsor (R. J. Reynolds Tobacco Company) was unwilling to trust its show to the youthful comic alone, he was co-starred with Jimmy Durante. *Variety*'s reviewer thought the team's première broadcast "proved anything but a rousing click," but added that the show contained "just enough solid moments of entertainment to take it over the hurdles."

The *Durante-Moore Show* eventually developed into one of the most popular programs on the air. It built up a radio audience numbering an estimated 4,000,000 listeners a week and was voted nationally second only to Fibber McGee and Molly as ranking radio raters. In October 1943, the team moved to CBS and two years later a new sponsor (United Rexall Drug Company) signed them to a five-year contract. Moore's salary was said to be $2,000 a week, and the show was reportedly the only one in radio at that time owned jointly by its two stars and the director (Phil Cohan).

Moore wrote most of his own material and exhibited a breezy type of humor, characterized by rapidly delivered gags, droll monologues, zany antics, and erudite vocabulary which proved an ideal foil for Durante's malapropisms. Durante fondly referred to him as "Junior," and so often exclaimed "Dat's m'boy!" that some listeners thought Moore was his son. Moore's "screwball" verses, stories, and songs were grouped under the general title "Culture Corner," and made into a record in 1946.

During this period, Moore was also under contract to movie producer David O. Selznick for two years, but he never appeared in a film. In the summer of 1945, he spent ten weeks on a USO tour of the Pacific as head of a seven-man variety unit that entertained American soldiers.

After four years with Durante, Moore decided to strike out on his own, and in September 1947 succeeded Phil Baker as master of ceremonies and quizmaster of Eversharp's *Take It or Leave It* on NBC. He remained on that Sunday night give-away program, which originated in Hollywood, for two years. In May 1948, after Tom Breneman's sudden death, Moore stepped into his place as host of *Breakfast in Hollywood* for two months, also continuing his regular stint on *Take It or Leave It.*

Against the advice of everyone except Arthur Godfrey, Moore went back to daytime radio. CBS gave him the chance to build his own variety show along the lines of the old *Club Matinee,* and he changed his approach from that of "the smarty who knows all the answers" to the likeable guy who gets "humor from human things." The *Garry Moore Show* began in September 1949 as a sixty-minute, five-day-a-week sustaining program broadcast from Hollywood. After its debut, Harriet van Horne wrote in the New York *World-Telegram and Sun* that it was the only daytime show to offer "real comedy," and *Variety* called it "a refreshing hour's interlude with a loosely-constructed format that accents music and Moore's comedy byplay."

In 1950 CBS suggested that Moore come to New York and work out a new series of the *Garry Moore Show* for its television network. The half-hour show made its initial appearance in June at seven in the evening (E.D.T.), five nights a week. Two months later, Moore began an hour-long video version of the show as a summer replacement for *Arthur Godfrey and His Friends* on Wednesday evenings. That fall CBS placed the hour's show as a sustaining program on an early afternoon spot, every weekday.

"Moore is setting a high standard for daytime television" commented John Crosby (New York *Herald Tribune*). "The *Garry Moore Show* is a very loose, relaxed, tuneful, and entertaining operation." By the fall of 1951 Moore had seven sponsors, and *Variety* announced that he was CBS-TV's second biggest source of revenue, responsible for gross earnings to the network amounting to $6,000,000 on an annual basis. Moore received the Baltimore Ad Club's annual award as "the outstanding television personality" of that year.

The comedian and his permanent cast were also seen on a sponsored half-hour *Garry Moore Evening Show* on alternate Thursdays, beginning in October 1951. The following June he became moderator of a TV panel show called *I've Got a Secret.* While Arthur Godfrey was in the hospital in the spring of 1953, Moore substituted for him one night a week on the *Talent Scouts* program.

Differences arose between Moore and CBS in 1952. *Newsweek* reported that the network wanted to drop Moore's daytime television program and have him "emcee", (act as the master of ceremonies of) a less expensive "gimmick" type of show. The comedian refused, and was backed in this decision by one of his sponsors (Stokely-Van Camp). The network finally acquiesced. On the air Moore told his listeners what had happened and asked them to write thank-you notes to the sponsor. Within a week 14,000 letters were received. With this evidence of Moore's faithful audience following, CBS began to sell the show.

CBS-TV

GARRY MOORE

In September 1952, Moore signed a new contract with the network to continue the *Garry Moore Show.* It was mutually agreed at that time to cut the program from an hour to thirty minutes. By October 1953, the show had a waiting list of nine would-be sponsors. Two months later, the show was extended to an additional half-hour on Tuesdays and Thursdays.

The format of the *Garry Moore Show* is flexible, varied, and informal. It has been described by Elizabeth Pope (*Woman's Home Companion,* September 1953) as follows: "He [Moore] sings a little, dances a little, plays the drums. He tells jokes, acts in comedy skits, does take-offs. He talks about whatever strikes his fancy (the talk is likely to be serious), reads mail, answers questions from his audience. He plays host to unusual birds and animals, recites poetry (some of it original), and welcomes guests—all with the able support of singers Denise Lor and Ken Carson, announcer-actor Durward Kirby, and Howard Smith and his band."

The comedian has noted, however, that a successful ad lib format is one which only *looks* spontaneous; in actuality, it has to be carefully plotted. Approximately thirty per cent of the show is done from script, including the comedy sketches which Moore prepares with the assistance of three writers. He observed in *Theatre Arts* (August 1952): "Above and beyond everything else, we're selling a mood, not formalized entertainment." He avoids humor at someone else's expense. "We believe in kindliness," he said.

The television star receives innumerable gifts from his listeners and an average of 500 fan letters a day. One day in September 1954 Moore suggested to his estimated 3,000,000 televiewers that they each send a Michigan housewife, Mrs. Margaret Deibel, (a visitor

MOORE, GARRY—*Continued*

with her husband to the CBS studio) a nickel. Within a week she had received nickels totaling $7,000 from Moore's loyal fans.

On June 5, 1939, Moore married Eleanor Little, and they have two sons—Mason, and Garry, Jr. The comedian, who stands five feet seven inches tall and weighs 145 pounds, has brown hair and hazel eyes. His trademarks are a crew haircut, a brash bow tie, and a "Puckish" grin. According to Richard Gehman (*Cosmopolitan,* July 1953), he is "a happy, well-adjusted, and genuinely modest man." His income is said to be in "six substantial figures." Moore lists his hobbies as sailing, golf, raising tropical fish, and collecting old and rare jazz records. One of the reasons he prefers daytime television is because it enables him to maintain a schedule of normal business hours. He commutes daily to New York from his home in Rye, and catches the 5:29 commuter's train in time to spend his evenings at home with the family. He spends his weekends on his yawl *Red Wing* cruising Long Island Sound.

References

Cosmop 135:26+ Jl '53 pors
Cue 23:13 Jl 17 '53 por
N Y Times II p7 My 9 '43; II p5 N 18 '45; II p9 S 12 '48; II p11 Mr 7 '54
Newsweek 29:54 Ap 7 '47
Radio-TV Mirror 37:30 Ja '52; 38:38 Je '52 pors; 41:64 D '53 pors
TV Guide 1:5 Ap 17 '53 pors
Time 61:47 F 2 '53 por

MOORE, HENRY (SPENCER) July 30, 1898- Sculptor; painter

Address: Hoglands, Perry Green, Much Hadham, Hertfordshire, England

British sculptor Henry Moore's work may be seen in churches, parks and public squares as well as in museums. Although influenced by Egyptian, African Negro and Mexican sculpture, he has developed a highly individualistic style of his own. His creations in stone and wood and marble "with tiny heads, massive torsos and gaping holes" seem to have a pent-up energy. He tries to achieve in his sculptures the undulating rhythms of rocks, trees and shells, and his human figures, although bizarre, "are somewhat shocking, but in most cases the shock has been highly agreeable" (*Life,* January 20, 1947).

Moore is best known for his semi-abstract figures of women, and of group compositions of mother and child. His drawings and watercolors depicting Londoners in underground air-raid shelters during World War II have been widely praised. His reputation has grown steadily since his first one-man show in London in 1928, and he has come to be generally recognized as "England's outstanding modernist sculptor." Examples of his work are in the Museum of Modern Art in New York, the Tate Gallery in London, and in leading galleries of Europe.

Moore won first prize of $500 for sculnture at the International Exhibition of Arts and Architecture at São Paulo, Brazil on December 16, 1953 in which thirty-eight countries were represented.

The seventh child of Raymond Spencer and Mary (Baker) Moore, Henry Spencer Moore was born on July 30, 1898, at Castleford, a small mining town in the West Riding of Yorkshire, England. For several generations the men on both sides of his family had been either farmers or miners. At an early age young Henry decided to become a sculptor, and he recalls the vivid impressions left on him by certain eleventh century carvings he had seen as a boy in the Methley Church in Yorkshire.

In 1910, he won a scholarship from elementary school to Castleford Grammar School, to train to be a teacher, and there he met with encouragement from his art instructor, Alice Gostick. By September 1916, he was occupying a post as student teacher in his old elementary school. Joining the British Army as a private in the 15th London Regiment, Civil Service Rifles, he went to France early in the summer of 1917. In the following November he was gassed in the Battle of Cambrai and was invalided back to England.

On his demobilization as a corporal in February 1919, Moore resumed teaching at the Castleford Elementary School, but in September he obtained an education grant as an ex-serviceman and went to the Leeds School of Art. He soon became dissatisfied with the school's conventional academic training in sculpture but was grateful to have access to the notable collection of contemporary art belonging to Sir Michael Sadler, then chancellor of the University of Leeds. It was there for the first time that Moore examined paintings by Gauguin and van Gogh. In the reference library at Leeds he read Roger Fry's *Vision and Design* and first learned of African Negro and pre-Columbian Mexican sculpture, which were to exercise a profound influence on his early work.

In 1921 Moore entered the Royal College of Art in London where modelling in clay rather than carving in stone and wood was encouraged. However, Moore believed that the real tradition of sculpture demanded "the hard control and the energy of direct carving," which he practiced on his own. He spent most of his week-ends in the sculpture galleries and ethnological sections of the British Museum, studying Egyptian, archaic Greek, and Sumerian sculpture, Etruscan sarcophagus figures, and paleolithic carvings, as well as primitive art from North and South America, Africa, and the Oceanic Islands.

Moore won a travelling scholarship in 1925 which took him abroad for several months. He went to Italy determined not to be captured by the Renaissance. He sought the "simple, monumental forms of life." In Florence, he was greatly impressed by Masaccio's frescoes in the chapel of Santa Maria del Carmine.

On his return to London, he was appointed to a post at the Royal College of Art, where he taught sculpture two days a week for the next six years. He began visiting the Natural History Museum to study life in its natural forms and framework, from cells to skeleton and found "principles of form and rhythm from the study of natural objects such as pebbles, rocks, bones, trees, and plants."

In 1928 Moore had his first one-man show at the Warren Gallery in London, and in the same year the architect Dr. Charles Holden commissioned him to execute one of the decorative panels for the façade of the headquarters of the London Underground Railway, at St. James's Park. Moore's relief figure of the *North Wind* has been called his "first fully mature work." The success of the commission encouraged him to attempt figures on a larger scale.

According to James Johnson Sweeney's monograph, Moore left few sculptor's materials unexplored during the years from 1928 to 1940—working in stone, terracotta and concrete, wood, and metal.

Moore's sculpture of the early 1930's showed the influence of Picasso and his "evocations of strange sub-human creations" and "featureless pinheads" have prompted certain critics to find surrealist elements in his later works of this decade. Between 1937 and 1940 he executed a number of abstract "stringed figures," made of lead and wire or wood and string, and inspired by some mathematical models he had seen in a science museum.

He carved "opened-out sculpture," in which he disrupted the volumes of his figures by introducing holes, cavities, and concavities. (A hole can have as much meaning as a solid mass, he believes.) Throughout this decade from 1931 to 1939, he served on the staff of the Chelsea School of Art. The sculptor feels that "all good art has contained both abstract and surrealist elements just as it has contained both order and surprise, intellect and imagination, the conscious and the unconscious." In his art he strives primarily toward a liveliness of form rather than a lifelikeness of form (James Johnson Sweeney's monograph: *Henry Moore,* 1946).

By the end of the 1930's, Moore had established himself as a leader in contemporary sculpture. After the outbreak of World War II, when sculptural materials became unobtainable, Moore moved back to London from his studio in the country and began filling a notebook with sketches of the huddled masses sleeping in the tube shelters during the air-raids. These drawings came to the attention of the War Artists' Advisory Group, which commissioned him to do a series of such underground shelter scenes, and this task occupied him through most of 1941. (He served as sergeant in the Home Guard until the end of the war.) Art critic Eric Newton has called Moore's shelter sketches "a synthesis of the whole emotional atmosphere of the blitz," and in the opinion of Sir Herbert Read, constituting "the most authentic expression" of the special tragedy of World War II—"its direct impact on the ordinary mass of humanity."

Moore returned to his home town in 1942, made his first descent into the coal mines, where he spent some two or three weeks sketching the miners.

Impressed by the "spiritual quality and deep humanity" of Moore's shelter drawings, Canon

British Inf. Services
HENRY MOORE

Walter Hussey, Vicar of St. Matthew's Church, in Northampton, commissioned him to carve a monumental stone *Madonna and Child* (1943-44) for that church. The result, according to Sweeney, was "a work of sculptural dignity and hieratic impressiveness . . . without any concessions to vague emotionalism, or sentimentality." It was pointed out at the unveiling that this was the first time for a hundred years that the Church of England had employed a sculptor who worked in a contemporary style.

After the war, Moore received such important public commissions as the *Memorial Figure* (1945-46), for the grounds of Dartington Hall, in South Devon; *Three Standing Figures* (1947-48), presented by the Contemporary Art Society to the London County Council and placed in Battersea Park; and another *Madonna and Child* (1947-49), for St. Peter's Church, at Claydon, in Suffolk.

In an article for *Magazine of Art* (May 1951), Sir Kenneth Clark observed that the chief development in Moore's work since the end of the war has been his greatly increased use of metal as a medium of expression. Among the important, large-scale works designed to be executed in bronze are the *Family Group* (1944-49), commissioned for Barclay School, in Stevenage; *The Striding Man* (1950); and *The Reclining Figure* (1950-51), commissioned by the Arts Council of Great Britain for the 1951 Festival of Britain.

A. D. B. Sylvester has stated that since the war Moore has attempted to combine the principles of opened-out sculpture with a conception which is fundamentally naturalistic. For example, Moore completed in 1952 a large sculptural screen for the façade of the new *Time* and *Life* Building in London. And it has been announced that he has designed the scenery and costumes for Sir William Wal-

MOORE, HENRY—*Continued*

ton's opera, *Troilus and Cressida,* to be premiered at Covent Garden.

"For me a work of art must first have a vitality of its own . . ." Moore has written (in *Unit One,* Cassell, 1934), ". . . independent of the object it may represent. When a work has this powerful vitality we do not connect the word Beauty with it. Beauty, in the later Greek or Renaissance sense, is not the aim of my sculpture. Between beauty of expression and power of expression there is a difference of function. The first aims at pleasing the senses, the second has a spiritual vitality which for me is more moving and goes deeper than the senses."

The principal London exhibitions of Moore's sculpture and drawings include those at the Leicester Galleries in 1931, 1933, 1936, 1940, 1946, and 1948, the Zwemmer Gallery in 1935, the Mayor Gallery in 1939, and the Berkeley Galleries in 1945. His works have been shown at exhibitions in Venice and Berlin (1929); Stockholm (1930); Zurich (1931); Hamburg (1932); and Paris (1945).

Important retrospective exhibitions of his work were held at the Temple Newsam, in Leeds, in 1941; the Museum of Modern Art in New York (reportedly the largest exhibition ever given in America for a living British artist, fifty-eight pieces of sculpture), in 1946-47; the State Galleries of Australia, in 1947-48; the Venice Biennale of 1948 (where he was awarded the 500,000-lire International Sculpture Prize); in Manchester, Wakefield, Brussels, and Paris (1949); Amsterdam, Hamburg, Düsseldorf, and Bern (1950); Athens, Berlin, Vienna, Stockholm, and at the Tate Gallery in London (1951).

In New York City his sculptures were exhibited during 1954 at the Curt Valentin gallery. His work has been the subject of two documentary films (listed in the Educational Film Guide, 1953). His *Shelter Sketch-Book* was published by Nicholson and Watson in 1944, and in 1945 he illustrated Edward Sackville-West's *The Rescue,* based on Homer's *Odyssey.* He has also made designs for hand-screened linen print fabrics.

Examples of Moore's work are represented in many important private collections throughout the world, as well as in the permanent collections of the Tate Gallery, Victoria and Albert Museum, and the Whitechapel Art Gallery, in London; the public galleries in Leeds, Wakefield, Manchester, and other provincial English cities; the Museum of Modern Art, the Albright Art Gallery (Buffalo), Washington University (St. Louis), and other museums in the United States and Europe.

The sculptor attended the International Conference of Artists, sponsored by the United Nations Educational, Scientific, and Cultural Organization (UNESCO), in Venice, in September 1952, where he delivered a paper on "The Sculptor in Modern Society." Honorary Litt.D. degrees have been bestowed upon him by Leeds University (1945)) and the University of London (1953). A member of the Royal Fine Arts Commission since 1947, he has served as a trustee of the Tate Gallery from 1941 to 1948 and was re-elected in 1949 for a further term of seven years.

He is an honorary associate of the Royal Institute of British Architects, a member of the Art Panel of both the British Council and the Arts Council, and a corresponding foreign member of the Royal Flemish Academy of Sciences, the Belgian Academy of Letters and Fine Arts, and the Royal Academy of Fine Arts in Stockholm. His club is the Savile in London.

On July 27, 1929, Moore married the Russian artist Irina Radetsky. They have a daughter, Mary Spencer. The sculptor, who stands five feet four inches tall and weighs around 150 pounds, has blue eyes and brown hair. One critic has described him as "a smallish, tough, elemental man," with a "gentle, steady, unhurried, unaffected voice." He lives in a Hertfordshire village and in his garden, Moore has a home-made furnace where he casts his own statues.

References

Life 22:77+ Ja 20 '47 por
N Y Times Mag p22 O 15 '46

Argan G. C. Henry Moore
Grigson, G. Henry Moore (1943)
International Who's Who, 1952
Read, H. Henry Moore, Sculptor (1934); ed. Henry Moore: Sculpture and Drawings (1949)
Sweeney, J. J. Henry Moore (1946)
Who's Who, 1953
Who's Who in America, 1952-53
World Biography (1948)

MOORE, RUTH July 21, 1903- Author

Address: b. c/o William Morrow & Co., Inc., 425 4th Ave., New York 16; h. Bass Harbor Head Rd., McKinley, Me.

Reprinted from the *Wilson Library Bulletin,* Nov. 1954

Gott's Island, three miles long, lies in the open Atlantic about a mile and a half off the shore of Mt. Desert Island, Maine. It was settled in the 1780's and people lived there continuously until 1927. Among those hardy pioneers were the forebears of Ruth Moore, who was born on the island July 21, 1903, to Philip and Lovina Ethel (Joyce) Moore.

Miss Moore considers her novel *The Weir* (1943) her first real success. A long poem called "The Voyage" which appeared in the *Saturday Review of Literature* in the spring of 1929 was her first publication, followed later by several short stories in the *New Yorker* and *Harper's Bazaar.* The thread of those future successes, including the novels written since *The Weir,* can be traced far back to those island beginnings. Her mother's people were Joyces from Dublin and Hinckleys from Cape Breton Island. The Gott's Islanders had always been seagoing men, with the mackerel and Grand Banks fleets. It has been only natural that the sea and the hardy fine stuff of character it developed should one day be brought to life in novels by a woman who knew it in its glorious days before two World Wars.

As Miss Moore describes her home and childhood: "The Island was a small, self-contained community of farmer-fishermen's families, some eighty-five people; we had two churches, and a grade school where my brother and two sisters and I went for all eight grades. Although we were separated from the mainland and at times in the winter completely cut off by ice or bad weather, I do not recall that we ever underwent much hardship such as the 'poor fishermen's hut' sort of misery which crops up occasionally in fiction and which even now visitors to our coast seem puzzled not to find. In addition to a herring weir my father ran a 'gang' of lobster traps, farmed sixteen acres of land and kept general store and post office. It is true that we seldom had much cash in the house but cash wasn't a commodity. You lived off the bounty of the land and never, in all my travels across the United States, have I seen a place where the land supplied a more bountiful living. Our house cost, to build, around seven hundred dollars. It had double gables enclosing fourteen rooms, had a woodshed, big barn, and outhouses. It was put up in 1850 by a man who salvaged the lumber from the Union River, boards that had floated down from the big wasteful mills at the head of Blue Hill Bay. There was a good deal of it in those days. Lumber is scarcer, now."

After finishing those eight grades on the island, Miss Moore attended the high school at Ellsworth, Maine, from which she was graduated in 1921. In Albany at New York State College for Teachers (B.A. 1925) an interest in writing first became apparent, at least to her public, when she became editor of the *State College Quarterly*. There followed a variety of activities which included a year of teaching, secretarial work in New York and California, and the management of a fruit and nut ranch there, for five years. On her return to New York in 1941, Miss Moore became an editorial correspondent and later an associate editor for *Reader's Digest*. It was during this editorship that *The Weir* was published (by Morrow).

Of this book, Rose Feld, writing in the New York *Times* said, "Miss Moore writes in language that captures the sound and heart of her characters and tells her tale with the restraint and salty humor that is their own." The Springfield *Republican* commented, "*The Weir* will make a lot of people mad, including the summer visitors who like to see the island through a rosy haze. But Miss Moore ought not to care. She has done a magnificent job, honest and single-minded."

In 1946 *Spoonhandle* was published and it had perhaps the most spectacular success of all her books. It was not only the choice of the Dollar Book Club, but the following year Twentieth Century Fox purchased the screen rights and released a picture called *Deep Waters,* based on the book, in July 1948. Reviewers disagreed about the characters in this novel, some calling them conventional, or commonplace, but there was agreement on the

RUTH MOORE

writing. In *Saturday Review of Literature,* George Dangerfield called it "a serious novel and a surprising novel. It is so sturdy, forthright and kindly and at the same time so deeply pessimistic."

The Fire Balloon (1948) was chosen by the Family Book Club. The *New Yorker* said, "The elements have as usual the more enduring and attractive qualities. The trials of a fisherman's two high-school age children become a bit soppy before very long. Plenty of sturdy coastal characters, all the salty dialect you could ask for, and good detail on the locale."

Candlemas Bay was published in 1951, and in 1952, *Jeb Ellis of Candlemas Bay* was drafted from it, for the older teens, by Morrow Junior Books. The adult book was chosen by Literary Guild that year and Mary Ross, writing in the New York *Herald Tribune,* commented, "A good story in the outward sense of excitement, suspense and humor. It is more than that in giving you, with beautiful explicitness of time and place and individuals, a quickened sureness of the importance of human beings."

A Fair Wind Home (1953) was a choice of the Dollar Book Club. John Gould, a staunch State-of-Mainer himself, wrote in the New York *Times,* "Of the many Maine residents who have set pen to paper, Miss Moore catches the feel of the state and the spirit of the people as well as any and better than most."

Miss Moore's hazel eyes have the far look which distinguishes people who live close to the sea. Her generous smile is enigmatic. She says she is not working on a new book at the moment. She lives now in a house she herself helped to build at McKinley, Maine, where she manages her farm and rests between books.

References

Warfel, H. R. American Novelists of Today (1951)
Who's Who in New England (1949)

MORSE, WAYNE (LYMAN) Oct. 20, 1900- United States Senator from Oregon; lawyer; farmer

Address: b. Senate Office Bldg., Washington 25, D.C.; h. Edgewood Farm, Route 3, Box 124, Eugene, Oregon

NOTE: This biography supersedes the article which appeared in *Current Biography* in 1942.

The only member of the U.S. Senate without party allegiance is Wayne Morse of Oregon, who was elected to Congress on the Republican ticket in 1944 and re-elected in 1950. He withdrew from the Republican party during the Presidential campaign of 1952, and, while supporting the candidacy of Democrat Adlai E. Stevenson, declared himself to be an Independent. Since that time he has become, as described by Richard L. Neuberger (*American Magazine,* April 1953), "the most fiery and persistent critic of the Eisenhower Administration anywhere in the nation." Senator Morse's current term in Congress expires in January 1957.

Senator Morse was a spokesman for the Democrat Senators who attacked President Eisenhower's peacetime atomic energy bill as a "give-away to big business", and led the "filibuster" in the Senate from July 14 to 27, 1954. He spoke for twenty-six hours and fifty minutes in three speeches against the measure (which was passed on July 27 by a vote of 57 to 28, but with some major amendments "aimed at guaranteeing that public power bodies shall share in the promise of electrical energy from the atom", New York *Times,* July 28, 1954). It was the first major revision of the Atomic Energy (McMahon) Act of 1946 and will enable private enterprise to develop peacetime uses of atomic power.

The Senator, who in 1953 was denied the assignments he had earlier held on the Senate's labor and armed forces committees, regards himself as a liberal fighting alone to symbolize America's need for political realignment. A highly unpredictable figure to many Washington observers, he insists upon voting, he has said, according to the merits of the issue without concern for party expediency.

In his pre-Senate career Morse, dean and professor of law at the University of Oregon from 1931 to 1944, had been nationally known as one of the country's foremost labor arbitrators, serving for two years on the National War Labor Board. Earlier he had won distinction for his work in studying criminal law procedures and conditions in penal institutions.

Wayne Lyman Morse, (like Samuel F. B. Morse, the inventor of the telegraph) is a descendant of John Morse (Moss), who moved from England to America in 1639 and helped found the town of New Haven, Connecticut. He was born on a farm in Madison, Wisconsin on October 20, 1900 to Wilbur Frank and Jessie (White) Morse. In his boyhood he raised Shetland ponies and poultry, and later earned some of his college expenses by breeding laboratory animals.

It has been suggested that Morse's skill in argumentation had a beginning in family political debates. He won the Vilas Medal in debating at the University of Wisconsin, where he majored in labor economics. After taking a Ph.B. degree in 1923, he was an instructor in argumentation and coach of the university debating team while studying during 1924 for his M.A. degree. At the university he also completed in 1923 an advanced four-year military training course.

As assistant professor in argumentation Morse taught and studied at the University of Minnesota from 1924 to 1928, when he was granted his LL.B. degree. He then accepted, in 1928, a year's teaching fellowship at Columbia University. The fourth J.D. degree ever awarded by Columbia was conferred on Morse in 1932. His doctoral thesis, "A Survey of the Grand Jury System" is regarded as an authoritative study of the subject. It was published in 1931.

Morse meanwhile had in late 1929 become assistant professor of law at the University of Oregon. The next year he was promoted to associate professor, and, in 1931, was made full professor of law and dean of the School of Law. Then thirty-one years old, he was the youngest dean of any standard law school in the country. "Under his deanship," stated the *National Cyclopædia of American Biography* (1946), "the school's scholastic standing was raised and it achieved national recognition." In addition, in 1932, Morse was appointed dean and director of law of the Oregon state system of higher education.

Apart from his educational work, the young lawyer undertook a survey of crime in Oregon which resulted in the publication, with Ronald Beattie, of *The Administration of Criminal Justice in Oregon* (1932). On leave from the University of Oregon he became in 1936 special assistant to the U.S. Attorney General and administrative director for the Attorney General's survey of release procedures. In this capacity he supervised a staff of some 2,000 employees in making a study of criminal law administration throughout the United States. He was editor-in-chief of the five-volume *Attorney General's Survey of Release Procedures* (1939).

At the same time, Morse began to serve as an arbitrator in labor disputes. The first of these, according to Margaret Thompson (*Saturday Evening Post,* October 20, 1945), concerned a small Oregon lumber company case which he helped settle in 1935. From 1938 to 1942, under appointment by Secretary of Labor Frances Perkins, he served as Pacific Coast arbitrator of disputes between the shipowners and the International Longshoremen's and Warehousemen's Union. He was chairman in 1940 of the wage and hour hearings for the converted paper products industry.

By 1941 Morse had become one of the country's most prominent arbitrators. He was made a member of a special commission of the National Defense Mediation Board to study the Douglas Fir Lumber Industry, and was chairman of the Railway Emergency Board. In late

1941 he was alternate public member of the National Defense Mediation Board and was appointed in January 1942 as public member of the newly created National War Labor Board.

Three principles on which Morse insisted during his two years with the WLB were "that decisions rest only on evidence; that complainants keep on working while arbitration was under way; and that all parties accept WLB decisions as constituted authority until the courts tested them" (*Saturday Evening Post*, October 20, 1945). He resigned from the board in 1944 in protest against what he considered unwarranted concessions to John L. Lewis and the coal miners' union.

Back in Oregon in 1944, Morse, although tending to have New Deal sympathies, won the Republican nomination for a seat in the U.S. Senate from Senator Rufus Cecil Holman. In the following November election he defeated his Democratic opponent by carrying more counties than any previous Oregon candidate for the Senate. Among his supporters was the CIO Political Action Committee, whose proffered campaign funds he refused to accept.

Oregon's junior Senator, who took his oath of office in January 1945, was assigned during his first term to Senate committees on Education and Labor, Armed Services, Mines and Mining, Claims, Public Buildings and Grounds, and Post Offices and Post Roads. He co-sponsored a bill for a fair employment practices commission, introduced a resolution to study operations of the Army and Navy courts-martial systems, and introduced a resolution under which the United States accepted compulsory jurisdiction of the International Court of Justice.

Before the end of his second year in the Senate, Morse was described as "a significant national figure as the spokesman and strategist of such opposition as exists within Republican ranks to the reigning monarchs of the party" (*American Mercury*, July 1947). His voting record included, in 1945, his backing of the Democratic appointments of Henry A. Wallace and Aubrey Williams.

His action on legislative measures during his first term shows that in foreign affairs he supported the United Nations Charter (1945), Bretton Woods agreement bill (1945), Greek-Turkish aid bill (1947), European recovery bill (1948), North Atlantic Security Pact (1949), allocations for the Marshall plan (1950), and opposed the $100,000,000 loan to Spain (1950). On domestic issues the Senator voted against the Taft-Hartley bill (1947), for Federal aid to education (1948, 1949) and for the (Alben W.) Barkley anti-filibuster ruling (1949).

Certain possible inconsistencies were noted in Senator Morse's record. John Gunther, for example, pointed out in *Inside U.S.A.* (1947), "On the other hand—progressives say—Morse voted to take controls off dairy and meat products; his attitude in the fight on public vs. private power is uncertain and he has never taken a strong line on lumber conservation; he is the only Northwest Senator not committed to the idea of a Columbia Valley Authority."

Wide World

WAYNE MORSE

After his re-election as a Republican member of the Senate in November 1950, Morse voted in the Eighty-second Congress against a number of economy measures generally favored by his party. During 1951 he opposed cuts in reclamation funds, soil conservation funds, and economic aid to Europe. The following year he voted "nay" on proposed reductions in foreign aid and in river-harbor appropriations.

Although Morse had been one of the first in his state to support publicly Dwight D. Eisenhower, in the 1952 Presidential campaign, he later denounced the Republican candidate and supported Adlai E. Stevenson. The Senator has explained his action in "My Personal Declaration of Independence" (*New Republic*, July 6, 1953), where he characterized as "reactionary" the platform adopted at the 1952 Republican convention. "I was shocked by the failure of the Eisenhower group to make a fight on the platform," Morse said.

When Morse formally resigned from the Republican party in October 1952, he did not join the Democratics, but became an Independent. As a consequence, he was removed in the Eighty-third Congress from his place on the Senate Armed Services Committee and Labor and Public Welfare Committee, and was offered assignments on the less important District of Columbia Committee and Public Works Committee.

The death of Republican Robert A. Taft in the summer of 1953 and the subsequent appointment of a Democrat, Thomas A. Burke, to fill part of the unexpired term, left Morse with the opportunity to exercise a possible controlling vote should the Democrats seek committee power in the Senate. The Oregon legislator made it clear, however, that he felt "an ethical obligation to vote with the Republicans on Senate organizational issues. The people of

MORSE, WAYNE—*Continued*

the nation in the election of 1952 voted the Republicans into power and I shall abide by that mandate on the Republican control of the Senate" (New York *Times,* August 1, 1953).

On legislative programs Morse's point of view is that he should judge the merits of issues regardless of political considerations and that by voting as an Independent he "can best challenge the political expediencies of both major parties" ("My Personal Declaration of Independence").

Speaking for "a little band of liberals," the Oregon Independent in April 1953 delivered the longest continuous oration in the history of the Senate when he talked for twenty-two hours and twenty-six minutes in demonstration against the pending offshore oil bill giving title to the states. In a television interview in February 1954, Senator Morse, as quoted by the New York *Times* (February 10, 1954), charged Eisenhower with failure to provide a breakdown as to security dismissals in publicizing the firing of 2,200 Government employees. The Republicans, he maintained, were seeking to give the impression that Communists had "honeycombed" the government under Democratic Administration.

Appointed to the Senate District of Columbia Committee in May 1953, Morse "attended more committee meetings than most members, has taken a sharp lawyer's look at all District bills and made his influence felt on many." He helped the judges to win their fight against mandatory prison terms for first offense felons, and became the "chief needler for action on a District home rule bill" (Washington *Post,* July 18, 1954).

His voting record in the first session (1953) of the Eighty-third Congress indicates that he favored admitting 209,000 refugees from behind the Iron Curtain, and that he opposed using foreign aid to cut farm surpluses, pressuring France to free Indochina, selling government-owned rubber plants, and penalizing nations trading with Communist China.

In the following session (1954), he voted against the (John W.) Bricker amendment, the anti-court packing amendment, and the housing bill authorizing the building of 140,000 public housing units. He favored the authorization of the St. Lawrence seaway, and statehood for Hawaii and Alaska.

The Senator, in a New York speech of March 1954, expressed his view that "the answer to McCarthyism is not to be found in personal attacks on the Senator," but in correction of faulty procedures. As further reported by the New York *Times* (March 10, 1954), he spoke in behalf of a bill that he had introduced to change Congressional investigating committee rules and pointed out that "the substantive rights of the American people can never be better than procedural rights. Under Communism and fascism, the individual is without guarantee of procedural rights."

In his speech on May 12, 1954 before 1,500 delegates to the fortieth convention of the Amalgamated Clothing Workers of America, CIO, Senator Morse accused the Republican party of "fast becoming a war party" and an "anti-labor party." He asserted that he would support the President "no matter who he may be" but he stressed that until national policy was made clear he felt free to fight it" (New York *Times,* May 13, 1954).

Before his election to the Senate, Morse had been active in the Association of American Law Schools as chairman of the criminal law council in 1937 and of the committee on tenure in 1942. He had been chairman as well, in 1934, of the Pacific Coast Institute of Law and Administration of Justice and was associated with the Social Science Research Council of America, National Conference of Family Relations, and American Council of the Institute of Pacific Relations. Morse belongs to the Federal, American, Oregon, and Lane county bar associations, American Judicature Society, and American Law Institute.

Morse's Greek-letter societies are Delta Sigma Rho, Gamma Eta Gamma and Pi Kappa Alpha. He belongs to the Order of the Coif, Scabbard and Blade, Rotary Club, Masonic Order (Scottish Rite and Shriner), Eagles and Moose. Honorary LL.D. degrees were awarded the Senator by Cornell College (Mt. Vernon, Iowa) in 1946, by Drake University and the College of South Jersey in 1947, and Centre College (Danville, Kentucky) in 1952. He attends the Congregational Church.

His speeches are said to be used by teachers in the Northwest as models of argument, logic and effective factual presentation. His chief interest aside from politics is in horses and he has won a number of exhibition trophies with thoroughbreds that he keeps on land which he rents in Poolesville, Maryland, where he likes to spend his weekends. On his farm in Eugene, Oregon, he raises registered horses, sheep and goats.

Wayne Morse's wife is Mildred (Downie) Morse, formerly an instructor in home economics whom he married on June 18, 1924. The couple's three children are Nancy Faye, Judith Mary and Amy Ann. The legislator is a man of medium height and weight, with green eyes, thick black eyebrows and dark hair. A teetotaler who prides himself on keeping physically fit, he believes that Washington cocktail parties are a great waste of energy. One of the Senator's dominant characteristics, in the opinion of John Gunther, is courage.

References

Am Mag 155:27+ Ap '53 por
Collier's 131:20+ Ap 4 '53 por
Time 61:23 My 4 '53 por

Biographical Directory of the American Congress, 1774-1949 (1950)
Congressional Directory (1954)
Gunther, J. Inside U.S.A. (1947)
International Who's Who, 1954
International World Who's Who (1949)
National Cyclopædia of American Biography Current Vol G (1946)
Who's Who in America, 1954-55
Who's Who in United States Politics (1952)
World Biography (1954)

MOSES, ROBERT Dec. 18, 1888- Public official

Address: b. 270 Broadway, New York 7; Belmont Lake State Park, Babylon, Long Island, N.Y.; h. One Gracie Sq., New York 28

NOTE: This biography supersedes the article which appeared in *Current Biography* in 1940.

In more than thirty years of public service to the City of New York and New York state, Robert Moses has achieved an unparalleled record in building highways, bridges, parks, and recreation areas. As city park commissioner and as head of several construction authorities and civic committees, he has worked under four consecutive administrations for improvements in Manhattan and its environs. His concern has been with problems of traffic and slum clearance, as well as with the projects for which he is nationally known, such as Jones Beach and the Triborough Bridge.

When Mayor-elect Robert F. Wagner, Jr., in November 1953 asked Moses to remain with the city government, the appointment was widely applauded in the press. The New York *Times* commented that "no single action [Wagner] could take would assure more benefit for the city and its people."

On March 7, 1954 Moses was appointed chairman of the New York State Power Authority which is directing the state's share of the New York-Canadian St. Lawrence River hydroelectric project now under construction.

The man who is said to have done more than any other individual to change the appearance of New York City, came to live in Manhattan as a boy from New Haven, Connecticut, where he was born on December 18, 1888 to Emanuel Moses, a department store proprietor, and Bella (Cohen) Moses. In his book, *Robert Moses: Builder for Democracy* (1952), Cleveland Rodgers relates that the boy preferred his native city to New York and studied diligently so that he could return to New Haven as a student at Yale University.

Besides distinguishing himself at Yale by election to Phi Beta Kappa and membership in the senior council, young Moses was president of the University Swimming Association and secretary and treasurer of the Intercollegiate Swimming Association. He also edited the Yale *Courant* and with a classmate, Carl Thurston, compiled *Yale Verse* (Yale Publishing Association, 1909). After receiving the A.B. degree in 1909, he went to England to enroll at Oxford University (Wadham College), where he took his B.A. degree in 1911, with honors in jurisprudence, and his M.A. degree in 1913. At Oxford he captained the swimming and water polo teams and was the first American student to become president of the Oxford Union, a debating society. Returning to New York, he was granted the Ph.D. degree from Columbia University in 1914. His thesis was *The Civil Service of Great Britain* (1914).

From 1913 to 1918, Moses was associated with New York City's bureau of municipal research, concerned with improvement in administrative service. During World War I he was also employed by the United States Shipping Board. As counsel for the National Federation of Federal Employees in 1919 he prepared a plan, later adopted by Congress, to regulate salaries of government employees.

ROBERT MOSES

Governor Alfred E. Smith appointed Moses in 1919, chief of staff of the New York state reconstruction commission to provide a program for streamlining the state government. Most of the proposals of this commission became law by constitutional amendment in 1924. From 1921 to 1925 Moses was secretary of the New York State Association, a civic organization, and edited its journal, the *State Bulletin*.

As a principal adviser to Governor Smith, Moses presented a plan in 1920 for state-wide improvement of parks and highways. When the New York state council of parks was established in 1924, he was named president of the council and chairman of the Long Island state park commission, positions to which he was subsequently reappointed by Governors Franklin D. Roosevelt, Herbert H. Lehman and Thomas E. Dewey. Thus, Moses supervised the program for the unified state park system covering the entire state from Buffalo to Long Island.

Meanwhile, he was a member of the state fine arts commission (1924-1927), secretary of state (1927-1928), a member of the state reorganization commission (1927-1928), chairman of the committee of public improvements (1927-1928), a member of the Moreland commission to investigate the state banking department (1929), the New York state commission for the Chicago World's Fair, and chairman of the state emergency public works commission (1933).

After having declined the Fusion mayoralty nomination and having been defeated in 1934 as Republican candidate for Governor of New York, he was appointed by Mayor Fiorello H. La Guardia to be the new city commissioner of

MOSES, ROBERT—*Continued*

parks. His task was the administration of New York's park and parkway systems and coordinating them with the state and suburban systems. As park commissioner, a post to which he has been reappointed by all succeeding New York city mayors, Moses receives at present a salary of $25,000 annually, the only one of his public offices for which he accepts remuneration.

Under La Guardia's administration, Moses reorganized the park commission system to bring the five boroughs under one head and set out to build Long Island's Grand Central Parkway and Jones Beach which was completed in the face of much opposition from owners of Long Island estates. Since 1933 he has been chairman of the Jones Beach State Parkway Authority and Bethpage Park Authority. After the establishment of the Triborough Bridge Authority to create and administer a structure connecting Manhattan, Queens and the Bronx, the commissioner was appointed a member of the authority in 1934, chairman in 1936, and since 1946 he has been chairman of the Consolidated Triborough Bridge and City Tunnel Authority.

Commissioner Moses also directed the construction of the Henry Hudson Parkway, Marine Parkway and the Belt Parkway around Brooklyn and Queens. He was named in 1938 as the sole member of the New York City Parkway Authority which absorbed the Henry Hudson Parkway and Marine Parkway Authorities and built Cross Bay Parkway Bridge and shore front improvements in the Rockaways. Under his administration the number of playgrounds in the city have increased from 117 to 600. In the introduction to Cleveland Rodgers' book, *Robert Moses,* radio commentator H. V. Kaltenborn estimated that Moses had supervised the spending of over a billion dollars of public money.

He was chief consultant on public works for the Commission on Organization of the Executive Branch of the Government (Hoover commission) in 1948. He has also been a consultant on bridge and highway construction and municipal planning in Pittsburgh (1939), Portland, Oregon (1943), Baltimore (1944), New Orleans (1946), Caracas, Venezuela (1948), Hartford, Connecticut (1949), São Paulo, Brazil (1950), and New Britain, Connecticut (1951).

The park commissioner was a delegate to the state constitutional convention in 1938. In 1943 he acted as coordinator of a survey on congested war production areas for the Army and Navy Munitions Board. He served as chairman of the state committee on postwar employment in 1942, was a member of the state postwar public works commission and chairman of the mayor's committee for a permanent world capital. After the war he went to Germany for the Department of War to report on economic conditions.

While serving as park commissioner Moses has been a member of the city planning commission (since 1942), city construction coordinator (since 1946) and chairman of the mayor's slum clearance plans committee (since 1948). His name is associated with the East River Drive, Whitestone Parkway, Flushing River Bridge, Hutchinson River Parkway, saving the lighthouse at Washington Bridge, Brooklyn Battery Tunnel, and the airline terminal at First Avenue. He was largely responsible for the improvement of Central Park including the landscaping, the cafeteria, baseball diamonds and playgrounds, salvaging an old-time carousel, and the zoo.

He is presently occupied with plans for a new beach on Staten Island, slum clearance and thirteen new housing developments, building of a convention and exhibition hall on New York's Columbus Circle, creation of a park in the Jamaica Bay area, improvement of Jones Inlet, and completion of the Captree Causeway Bridge which connects Jones Beach with the mainland.

Commissioner Moses, who has described himself "by tradition, instinct and temperament an independent Republican" (*Life,* October 20, 1952), favored Dwight D. Eisenhower in the 1952 Presidential election. As in previous mayoralty years, he declined in 1953 a bid to become the Republican candidate for the mayor of New York City.

The author of *Theory and Practice in Politics* (Harvard University, 1939) and *Tomorrow's Cars and Roads,* Moses has also expressed his ideas concerning politics and civic improvement in government reports and articles in newspapers and magazines including the *American City, Saturday Evening Post, Atlantic Monthly,* New York *Times Magazine,* and *Recreation.* In an address at the centennial of the University of Michigan's College of Engineering, he expressed his view that "the most respected faculty, instead of the most neglected faculty, in an engineering institution should be the department of English" (New York *Times,* October 24, 1953). His biographer, Cleveland Rodgers, finds that he is "at his best in the almost lost art of letter writing" and that in his addresses and articles "there is more poetry—or superior prose—than statistics."

In June 1953 he won the first national award of $25,000 in the General Motors Better Highways Contest for submitting the best essay of about 44,000 entries. The essay is entitled "How to Plan and Pay for the Safe and Adequate Highways We Need." He has also received awards from the Hundred Years Club (1935), American Scenic and Historic Preservation Society (1937), St. Nicholas Society (1937), Fairmount Park Art Association (1938), Garden Club of America (1938), National Institute of Arts and Letters (1941), American Institute of Steel Construction (1941), Kiwanis Club (1942), Rotary Club (1943), Nassau County Bar Association (1945), National Sculpture Society (1945), National Institute of Social Sciences (1946), New York Academy of Public Education (1950), Greater New York Civic Center Association (1951), College of the City of New York (1951), and New York Councils of Police Department (1953).

Among his honorary degrees are the LL.D. from Union College (1938), Princeton University (1947), Hofstra College (1948), Columbia University (1952), Yale University (1952), Harvard University (1953); and the Eng. D. from New York University (1950) and the University of Michigan (1953). Moses has lectured at Duke University (1939), Harvard University (1939), Princeton University (1940), and Miami University (1946). He is a trustee of Hofstra College.

At the dedication of the Triborough Bridge (1936) Moses stated, "Enterprises such as this are too big for personal enmities . . . objectives seem to be more important than personalities." Although there are some city planners who desire decentralization Moses "accepts the city, believes wholeheartedly in its future, and seeks to strengthen a 'magnetic core' which he expects to retain its magnetism for a long time to come" (New York *Times Magazine,* December 13, 1953).

He has stated, "Public works are necessary not only to satisfy the demands of the great rank and file of citizens, but also to maintain and enhance land values and to provide an incentive to private capital to keep up with progress and expand its investments" (*American City,* October, 1953).

On Moses' sixty-fifth birthday (December 18, 1953) the New York *Times* commented editorially: "He has been the strong man under all . . . Mayors, always looking far ahead of the current visible objectives, impatient with those who disagree with him but free of bitterness when the battle is over, a master of the ridicule that leaves an opponent hanging in tatters, but back again the next week, with the past forgotten, appealing in the public interest for support to bring some fine new dream to reality."

Robert Moses and his wife, Mary Louise (Sims) Moses, who were married on August 28, 1915, have two children: Barbara (Mrs. Richard J. Olds) and Jane (Mrs. Frederic A. Collins). The commissioner finds recreation in swimming and fishing. Raymond Moley has described him as "a big man, with a quick, infectious smile."

A short story enthusiast, Moses admits in an article in *Saturday Review,* December 19, 1953, that his favorite story is Anatole France's "The Procurator of Judea."

References

(See also references listed in 1940 biographical sketch)

Cue 10:3 Ag 16 '41 por
N Y Herald Tribune II p3 Ag 3 '47 por
N Y Sunday News Mag p7 F 1 '53 por
N Y Times p1+ Ap 3 '47; p10 Je 24 '47
N Y Times Mag p13 Je 29 '41 por; p14 Ag 10 '52 por; p12+ D 13 '53
New Yorker 28:21+ Ag 16 '52
Sat Eve Post 227:36+ S 25 '54 pors

International Who's Who, 1952
Moley, R. 27 Masters of Politics (1949)
National Cyclopædia of American Biography Current Vol F (1939-42)
Rodgers, C. Robert Moses: Builder for Democracy (1952)
Who's Who in America, 1952-53
Who's Who in New York, 1952

MUMFORD, L(AWRENCE) QUINCY

Dec. 11, 1903- Library administrator; library association official

Address: b. Library of Congress, Washington 25, D.C.

In nominating L. Quincy Mumford as the eleventh Librarian of Congress, President Dwight D. Eisenhower on April 22, 1954 selected a man whose name was on the list of candidates recommended for the post by the American Library Association (which is composed of 21,000 members). Mumford was elected, in 1953, first vice-president (president-elect) of the A.L.A. to be installed as president in June 1954.

Highly regarded for his experience in reference and research libraries and for his skill in library administration, Mumford has been director of the Cleveland Public Library since 1950. Previously (1929-1945) he filled a number of positions with the New York Public Library, from which he took a leave of absence in 1940-1942 to reorganize the processing division of the Library of Congress.

In selecting Mumford to succeed Luther H. Evans (who resigned July 5, 1953), President Eisenhower chose a man who would be the first professionally trained librarian to hold the country's highest librarianship (New York *Times*). The nomination was confirmed by the U.S. Senate on July 29, 1954.

Lawrence Quincy Mumford, who is a native of Ayden, North Carolina, was born to Jacob Edward and Emma Luvenia (Stocks) Mumford on December 11, 1903. He studied at Duke University where he was elected to Phi Beta Kappa and received the B.A. degree *magna cum laude* in 1925. Three years earlier he had joined the staff of Duke University Library, where in 1926-1927 he was head of the circulation department and then acting chief of reference and circulation. He resigned in 1928 when he was graduated from Duke with the M.A. degree in English.

While studying at the Columbia University School of Library Service for his B.S. degree, which was conferred in 1929, Mumford held a student assistantship in the university's library. He went to the New York Public Library in 1929 as a reference assistant, was made general assistant in charge of the director's office (1932-1935), and subsequently executive assistant and chief of the preparation division (1936-1943). During his last two years with the New York Public Library (1943-1945) his titles were executive assistant and coordinator of the general service division, responsible for administration, including personnel in the main library, and the general reference service, stacks, main reading room, theatre collection and photographic service.

Archibald MacLeish, then Librarian of Congress, appointed Mumford the director of the processing division of the Library of Congress in Washington, D.C., to reorganize that division. On leave from the New York Public Library, Mumford supervised the work of over 300 employees in the revision of assignments, development of a work program, improvement of procedures and methods, and temporary

L. QUINCY MUMFORD

classification of duties for the appointment and promotion of personnel.

After the completion of this assignment in January 1942, Mumford's work was praised by Luther H. Evans, then Acting Librarian. "He has discharged this weighty and delicate responsibility with such conspicuous success," Evans said, "that the Librarian [MacLeish] has described his achievement as 'a minor—perhaps a major—miracle'" (*Library Journal,* October 1, 1945).

A survey made of the Library of Congress in 1940 was one of three similar projects in which Mumford participated. In 1943-1944 he was a member of the committee for survey of the Army Medical Library and in 1944 assisted in examining the technical processes of the Columbia University Library. During his period of employment with the New York Public Library he was associated for several months in 1944-1945 with the American Library in Paris. As organizer of that library's New York office he was concerned with matters of fund raising and publicity.

Upon leaving the New York Public Library in 1945, Mumford became assistant director of the Cleveland Public Library, one of the largest public library systems in the United States. He served as director from 1950 to 1954. In an interview with the Washington *Post and Times-Herald* (April 13, 1954) L. Quincy Mumford discussed, as his principal accomplishment in Cleveland, the extension of services to young adults and aged persons in the city. The library seeks to bring together in small groups persons who share common interests. It has organized the Live Long and Like It Library Club, comprising approximately 800 members over the age of sixty.

For almost a year the office of the Librarian of Congress had stood vacant following the resignation in July 1953 of Luther H. Evans, who became general director of the United Nations Educational, Scientific and Cultural Organization. On April 22, 1954 Mumford, whom Senator John W. Bricker had recommended for the post on the basis of his professional record, was nominated by President Eisenhower as Librarian of Congress. Earlier in the month, when the likelihood of the appointment became known, a New York *Times* editorial (April 6, 1954) applauded the selection: "Under the direction of Mr. Mumford we feel sure that the Library of Congress will continue to maintain its cultural leadership among the libraries of the world. We congratulate the President on his choice and salute Mr. Mumford as a worthy successor to the great practicing librarians who preceded him."

Mumford was one of six qualified candidates for the position of Librarian of Congress suggested to President Eisenhower in 1953 by a special committee of the American Library Association, the nation's largest organization for librarians, with a membership of 21,000. At that time Mumford was first vice-president and president-elect of A.L.A., having been installed at the association's seventy-second annual conference, held in Los Angeles in June 1953. After serving a year in this office, he succeeded Flora B. Ludington as president in June 1954, when the librarians met in Minneapolis.

During more than twenty years as an A.L.A. member, he has been chairman of the library administrative committee (1941-1944), photographic reproduction of library materials committee (1944-1946), Federal relations committee (1950-1952), and audio-visual board (1952-1953). He was president of the Library Club of Cleveland and Vicinity in 1947, Ohio Library Association in 1947-1948, a member of its executive board in 1949, and local chairman of the 1950 A.L.A. conference in Cleveland.

A frequent contributor to library publications, Mumford is the author of "An Account of the Reorganization of the Processing Department at the Library of Congress" (A.L.A. *Cataloger's and Classifier's Yearbook,* 1941), "Cataloging Problems and Research Libraries" (*College & Research Libraries,* March 1942), "Wartime Adjustments and Economies in the Large Reference and Research Library" (*Library Journal,* January 1, 1943), "Weeding Practices Vary" (*Library Journal,* June 15, 1946), "History of Copyright" (*A.L.A. Bulletin,* February 1952) and "Libraries in Educational Television" (*A.L.A. Bulletin,* February 1953).

He lectured at the School of Library Science of Western Reserve University (beginning in 1945); and was a member of the library committee of the Ohio Postwar Planning Commission (1947-1948), library advisory committee to the U.S. Office of Education (1950) and executive committee of the Cleveland Occupational Planning Commission (1950-1951). He has been a director of the Film Council of America and the Great Books Foundation and a member of the American Association for Adult Education.

Other groups with which he has been associated are Cleveland's Welfare Federation (member of the executive committee), Chamber of Commerce (member of the committee on education) and Real Property Inventory (director). He has belonged to that city's Mid-Day Club, Cheshire Cheese and Men's City Club.

Mumford, who married Permelia Catharine Stevens, a librarian, on October 4, 1930, has a daughter, Kathryn. His church affiliation is the Methodist and his political party the Republican.

Agreeing with the A.L.A. statement of principles on the freedom to read, the librarian opposes banning from public or government libraries books which uphold political philosophies different from those popular in the United States. As quoted by the Washington *Post and Times-Herald* (April 13, 1954), Mumford believes that "the function of a library is to have material on both sides of an issue and that people should have the right to choose what books they want to read."

The Washington *Post and Times-Herald* commented editorially (April 28, 1954) on President Eisenhower's nomination of Mumford: "This is manifestly a merit selection by the President and deserves the warmest public approbation. The Library of Congress is, in respect of the number of volumes it embraces, the world's greatest library today. It ranks among the great libraries of the world by every other standard as well. . . . Keeping it free from politics and placing it under the expert and scholarly direction of a professional librarian constitutes an expression to the world of the respect which Americans have for this place of learning."

References

A.L.A. Bul 47:325 Jl '53 por
Coll & Res Lib 12:290 Jl '51 por
Library J 70:901 O 1 '45 por
N Y Herald Tribune p17 Ap 23 '54 por
N Y Times p13 Ap 3 '54; p28 Ap 6 '54; p28 Ap 23 '54 por
Washington (D.C.) Post p22 Ap 13 '54 por
Who's Who in America, 1954-55
Who's Who in Library Service (1943)
Who's Who in the East (1951)

NASSER, GAMAL ABDEL (nä'sẽr) Jan. 15, 1918- Egyptian Premier; Army officer
Address: Cairo, Egypt

The leader of the military junta that has ruled Egypt since the bloodless *coup d'état* of July 23, 1952 is Lieutenant Colonel Gamal Abdel Nasser. He succeeded Major General Mohammed Naguib as Premier in April 1954. At that time, leaving Naguib in the ceremonial post of President, he took title to the power that he had in fact exercised behind the scenes after the dethronement of King Farouk I, and the establishment of the Revolution Command Council. Nasser, who is said to have a remarkable capacity for leadership and planning, spent ten years selecting and training other young Army officers to take part in the overthrow of the monarchy.

Since Nasser assumed control of the government, Egypt has gone far toward accomplishing two of the revolution's major goals: social reform and settlement of the Suez Canal Zone dispute with Great Britain. The initialing in July 1954 of the Anglo-Egyptian agreement, of which Nasser was Egypt's principal negotiator, has been described in a New York *Herald Tribune* editorial as "one of the more important diplomatic feats of the postwar period."

On August 21, 1954 Premier Nasser publicly declared that Egypt was ready to accept United States military aid, and warned Egyptians that any Soviet attack on Turkey would be a threat to Egypt. A communiqué from his Revolution Command Council on September 2 to foreign correspondents made it clear that "Egypt stands in every respect with the West" but that a formal defense pact with the Western powers now would only provide the Communists with fuel to stir up "the still suspicious minds of the Arabs" (reported by the Associated Press in the *Christian Science Monitor,* September 2, 1954).

The oldest of four sons of an Upper Egypt middle-class family, Gamal Abdel Nasser was born on January 15, 1918 in the small town of Beni Mor in Asyût Province. The senior Nasser, who is of Arabian stock, was a post office civil servant (he is now retired). After the death of his first wife in 1926, he remarried and is the father of eleven children. Illustrative of Gamal's early rebellious traits is the story that at the age of seven when forbidden to dig in the garden, he dug a hole so large that his father fell into it.

Young Nasser is said to have been closely attached to his mother, the daughter of an Alexandrian building contractor. Her death increased the contemplative tendencies of the eight-year-old boy, who was then living in Cairo, where his father had sent him to be educated.

In his early schooling Gamal was an indifferent pupil, preferring American motion pictures to his classes. At the age of sixteen, he organized and led the students of Cairo's Al Nahda Al Misria School in a demonstration against British domination in Egypt. Soon becoming a serious student, interested especially in law and in biographies of the great men in history, he was awarded his secondary school certificate with distinction.

While attending the Royal Military Academy, which he entered in 1937 as one of forty applicants chosen out of 400, he was known for his outspokenness against colonialism. After his graduation at the age of twenty, Nasser joined the Third Rifle Brigade and was sent to Mankabâd in Asyût, where he served as an infantry platoon commander. "The senior officers were very bad," *Life* (March 8, 1954) quotes him as recalling. "I organized all the junior officers into a group against [them]."

About this time the young officer came to know some of the men who were later to be his political colleagues. At the Asyût barracks he met Anwar Al Sadat and Zakaria Mohie El Din (now members of the Revolution Command Council), and Ahmed Anwar (now chief of the military police). In 1939, while stationed in Alexandria, he met Abdul Hakim

GAMAL ABDEL NASSER

Amer (now a member of the Revolution Command Council and Commander-in-Chief, armed forces of Egypt).

Nasser was transferred in 1942 to El Alamein. He soon returned to Alexandria for a brief period of duty as lieutenant with the Fifth Infantry Brigade, and was then sent to the Sudan, where he served in Jabal El Awlia with Abdul Hakim Amer. In the same year he received an appointment as a teacher at the Royal Military Academy.

In Cairo he also studied at the Army Staff College, from which he was graduated with honors. As part of his instruction there, states an Egyptian Embassy biographical sketch of Nasser, he learned how to protect the capital city and its approaches from ground and air enemy forces, information which he put to use when he undertook the *coup d'état* that dethroned King Farouk.

For several years Nasser had been distressed by conditions in the Army, widespread inefficiency in the government, and the ferment throughout Egypt arising from opposition to British influences. While closely observing the tension of the period, he began clandestinely to organize a group to plan for revolution, hand-picking each member from the men he met in the Army. "I was patient and never despaired," he later told James Bell (*Life,* March 8, 1954). "I chose them one after another and tested them without their ever knowing it."

Sent to Palestine in 1948 to fight against Israel, Nasser became more than ever determined to overthrow the Farouk regime, which had failed to supply adequate munitions for the Army. His heroism in battle brought him a shoulder wound and the nickname "Tiger of Faluja."

It was at Faluja that he called the first meeting of his Free Officers Movement, an organization described by *Newsweek* (April 26, 1954) as "a masterpiece of secrecy." Men from this group, whose total membership of 700 is known only to Nasser, infiltrated the government and King Farouk's palaces as well as the military high command to gather information to aid underground preparation for the Army revolt. Realizing that the public would be reluctant to accept seizure of power by young, inexperienced revolutionists, the Free Officers chose for the movement's "front man" Major General Mohammed Naguib, a highly respected hero of the war in Palestine.

The coup that Nasser had been planning for ten years was staged on July 23, 1952. It forced the abdication of King Farouk (his seventeen-month-old son was made King) and set up a ruling military junta, with Naguib taking over the Premiership in September. In a move ending the reign of Farouk's son, King Ahmed Fuad II, Naguib in June 1953 proclaimed Egypt a republic and formed a new cabinet.

Lieutenant Colonel Nasser at that time became Deputy Premier. He was also named Minister of the Interior, with control over internal security, a key post that he held until October 4, 1953. Another of Nasser's titles was secretary general of the Liberation Rally, a quasi-political mass organization established and directed by the young officers (in May 1954, he assumed leadership of the rally's high council). He was the dominant figure in the Revolution Command Council (R.C.C., the Army junta), and the chief policy maker of the Naguib regime.

Growing dissension between Naguib and Nasser came to a climax on February 25, 1954 when Naguib was charged with demanding "absolute and autocratic power" and was forced to resign as Premier, President, Military Governor of Egypt, and chairman of the R.C.C. By March 15, 1954 the popular general had been restored to all his offices; and Nasser had relinquished the post of Premier that he had temporarily filled. On April 18 Nasser again replaced Naguib as Premier. This time Naguib, whose prestige with the people Nasser was regarded as having previously underestimated, retained the Presidency—now largely a figurehead position. Nasser reshuffled his twenty-two man cabinet, which includes eight members of the junta, apparently to oust ministers who had sided with Naguib.

On November 14, 1954 Major General Naguib was deposed from the Presidency by the junta, thus ending the struggle for power between Nasser and Naguib.

One cause of conflict between the two rival factions was over the question of how long the "transition period" from monarchy to full democracy should last. Naguib and his supporters advocated an early parliamentary election and the return of the government to civilian rule. Nasser maintained that the junta should remain in power until it had accomplished its aims of bringing social justice to Egypt's workers and peasants and of freeing the Suez Canal Zone from British occupation. After having rescinded Naguib's promise to restore parliamentary government, the junta announced in May 1954 that the National Consultative Assembly, when elected, would have only an advisory role.

"The Nasser government's most important measure so far," according to an article in the *New Republic* (June 14, 1954), "has been the resumption of land reform." The Premier has estimated that some 620,000 acres of land confiscated from wealthy landowners have been distributed among the fellahin (peasants). It is expected that in time about a quarter of Egypt's agricultural workers will be given farms of their own.

Following the coup of July 1952 Colonel Nasser was Egypt's chief negotiator in efforts to settle the long-standing dispute with Great Britain over the Suez Canal. In general he pursued a policy of compromise, with violence as a last resort, and is credited with having done much to clear the ground for eventual accord. On July 27, 1954 Egypt and Britain representatives initialed an agreement embodying the general principles for withdrawal of British forces and supplies from the Canal Zone within twenty months—thus bringing to an end Britain's seventy-two-year-old occupation. In case of an attack on Egypt, any other member of the Arab League or Turkey, Great Britain would be permitted, according to the agreement, to put the base on a "war footing" and would consult with the Egyptian government on other steps to be taken.

The settlement of the Suez dispute was viewed in the United States press as a personal victory for Nasser and a triumph for the moderate leadership he has given Egypt. To Nasser the Anglo-Egyptian agreement was "the turning point in the history of Egypt." He spoke also of "a new era of friendly relations based on mutual trust, confidence and co-operation [opening] between Egypt and Britain and the Western countries" (quoted in *Manchester Guardian,* July 28, 1954). Political observers expected that removal of Egypt's resentment toward the West would result in increased military collaboration between Egypt and the free world and would pave the way for foreign economic aid needed to finance the social reforms of the Nasser administration.

The Philosophy of Revolution, a seventy-three page booklet published in the spring of 1954, is Colonel Nasser's record of his impressions of the Egyptian revolution, telling of the hopes, ideals, disillusionments and struggles of the young officers before and after their ousting of King Farouk. Nasser attributes some of the problems that they have faced since the coup to the fact that Egypt is undergoing two revolutions simultaneously: one political and the other social..

Nasser's publication also clearly reflects the personality of the man who now rules about 21,000,000 Egyptians. He writes of his apprenticeship in revolution, when violence and political assassination "blazed" in his mind, and of the gradual change in his thinking. "I did not feel at ease within myself to consider violence as the positive action necessary for the salvation of our country's future" (quoted in *Christian Science Monitor,* June 3, 1954).

Egypt's Premier is married and has two sons, Khaled and Abdul Hamid, and two daughters, Huda and Mona. The family occupies an unpretentious house in the Army compound at the Abbasia military district of Cairo. In his personal habits and manner of living he avoids any show of luxury that might invite comparison with Farouk. *Newsweek* (April 26, 1954) pictures him as "a lean six-footer with a hawk-like profile." He has black hair. His sports are squash, tennis and swimming. Nasser, who is a Moslem, has made a number of pilgrimages to Mecca, most recently in August 1954 when he also attended a conference with other Arab leaders on international matters.

Peter Lisagor of the Chicago Daily News Service wrote: "If Nasser is indeed a dictator, as some Western observers claim, he seems to be the most benign, mild-mannered, and soft-spoken one going today" (Washington *Post,* August 3, 1954). Naguib has been quoted as saying, "Gamal, that strong mind, that abnormal determination—Gamal, who doesn't relax a second in doing his duty" (*Time,* May 4, 1953).

The Nasser government withdrew Egyptian citizenship from five leaders of the anti-Western Moslem Brotherhood on September 23 and from Mahmoud Abdul Fath, owner of a suspended Cairo newspaper. They were accused of "treasonous actions abroad harmful to Egypt's prestige and strength" (New York *Times,* September 25, 1954).

References

N Y Times p 1+ Mr 30 '54; p 1+ Ap 18 '54
N Y Times Mag p12+ S 19 '54 pors
N Y World-Telegram p7 Jl 31 '54 por
Time 63:30 Mr 8 '54 por; 63:38 Ap 26 '54
U S News 34:44+ My 22 '53 por; 36:16 Mr 5 '54 por
World Biography (1954)

NEWELL, HOMER E(DWARD), JR.

Mar. 11, 1915- Physicist; mathematician

Address: b. c/o The Rocket Sonde Branch, Naval Research Laboratory, Washington 25, D.C.; h. 4401 Westbrook Lane, Kensington, Md.

As director of the United States Navy's rocket-sonde research program, Dr. Homer E. Newell, Jr., heads a group of physicists endeavoring to solve the riddles of the upper atmosphere by sending rockets carrying delicate instruments over 100 miles up into the air. He belongs to the Upper Atmosphere Rocket Research Panel which coordinates the complete program of rocket research that is being conducted in this country. Since 1951 he has resumed his lectures in mathematics at the University of Maryland where he had taught from 1940 to 1944.

His book, *High Altitude Rocket Research* (Academic Press, 1953), is a study of rocket research from its beginnings in 1945 at the White Sands Proving Grounds in New Mexico

HOMER E. NEWELL, JR.

to the experiments carried out in 1953. He has also written articles concerning the purely mathematical problems of differential equations, and techniques employed in propagating radio waves in order to study upper atmosphere phenomena from the ground.

Homer Edward Newell, Jr. was born in Holyoke, Massachusetts on March 11, 1915, the son of Homer Edward Newell, an electrical engineer, and Annie Abigail (Davis) Newell, a professional organist and pianist. Homer graduated first in his class from Holyoke High School in 1932. He entered Harvard College, Cambridge, Massachusetts, in the fall of 1932 to study mathematics and held a scholarship during each year of his undergraduate studies. His principal extracurricular activity was rowing. Newell graduated *magna cum laude* in 1936 with an A.B. degree and was elected to Phi Beta Kappa. He then entered the Graduate School of Education at Harvard, and was granted the master's degree in teaching and mathematics in 1937.

Continuing his postgraduate work, Newell became, in 1937, a graduate assistant in the mathematics department of the University of Wisconsin in Madison. He remained at the University until 1940 when he received a Ph.D. degree in mathematics. During his last year there he held a fellowship. In September 1940 he was appointed an instructor of mathematics at the University of Maryland in College Park.

After the entrance of the United States into World War II, Newell became a ground instructor in navigation for the Civil Aeronautics Administration, and was also a lecturer in astronomy at National Park College, Forest Glen, Maryland. In addition, he continued his association with the University of Maryland where he was promoted to an assistant professorship in mathematics in 1943.

Dr. Newell left his teaching post in 1944 to become a theoretical physicist and mathematician at the Naval Research Laboratory, working as a special assistant to the head of the communication security section. Newell was appointed to head a theoretical analysis subsection of what has become the Rocket Sonde Branch of the Naval Research Laboratory in 1946. He was made an associate section head of the Rocket Sonde Branch in that year and became its head in 1947. The suffix, "-sonde," is the French word for "sounding." Rocket Sonde is, therefore, a new way to take "soundings" of the upper air to determine atmospheric conditions. It supplements work with balloonsondes, soundings by balloon-borne instruments, and the more recent radiosondes, and balloon-borne radio transmitters.

The Naval Research Laboratory is one of several government agencies that began to experiment at the White Sands Proving Grounds in New Mexico with German V-2 rockets captured at the end of the war. The experiments carried on by these groups fall into three general categories: general experimentation with the actual performance of the rocket; the use of the rocket as a military weapon; and the investigation of upper-air phenomena. Dr. Newell directs the Naval Research Laboratory's program that deals with the third category, upper-air phenomena.

In an article appearing in the June 1947 issue of the *Scientific Monthly,* Newell describes the importance of the rocket as a research tool for investigating the nature of the upper atmosphere. For the first time in history portions of the atmosphere above 32 kilometers (19.8 miles) are accessible to direct observation. Before the invention of the rocket, knowledge of the atmosphere beyond the range of balloons was obtained through indirect methods such as the study of meteors, the aurora, and the propagation of radio and sound waves.

The rocket does not replace these methods, but merely supplements them. The principal advantage of the rocket is that despite its relatively short period aloft, it actually gets into the region under study and thus answers some of the questions that indirect methods had not answered for scientists in the past. One disadvantage is that a rocket may be used but once as it is not yet possible to "land" them. In order to avoid the total loss of the instruments or, at least, the record of their observations, through the force of the impact of the entire rocket hitting the earth at velocities up to one mile per second, a small bursting charge is placed in each rocket so that shortly before it is to strike the earth it may be exploded, the recorded observations of the instruments being collected out of the scattered debris.

Describing the launching of a rocket, Newell wrote, "The thrill which the sight of such a launching brings can hardly be expressed in words. . . . At the moment of take-off the jet exerts just enough force to lift the missile which rises gently and gracefully. The full thrust of 28.3 tons is turned on . . . , the missile starts to move . . . and within a few seconds the speed of the missile exceeds that of sound" (*Scientific Monthly,* June 1947). Rockets which have soared into the stratosphere and the ionosphere have measured temperature, pressure, density, winds, cosmic and solar radiation, and magnetic fields at these high altitudes.

The role played by the rocket in disproving the theory that there was no change in temperature above the troposphere is told by Newell in an article in the *Compendium of Meteorology,* a publication of the American Meterological Society. According to measurements taken in rockets the temperature falls steadily up to an altitude of 15 kilometers and then rises abruptly until an altitude of 50 kilometers is reached. At this point the temperature begins to fall again, but starts to increase at a height of 80 kilometers. Measurements taken in rockets above 80 kilometers show a continual rise in temperature.

Research conducted under Newell's direction has led to many changes in the concept of the stratosphere. The wide discrepancies among the different temperatures, densities and pressures that have been ascribed to the atmosphere above the stratosphere are being resolved by rocket measurements with their on-the-spot recordings.

The Naval Research Laboratory has made some original contributions to the knowledge of the solar spectrum. Since the earth's atmosphere is remarkably opaque to all but the visible wave lengths of sunlight no spectrogram taken from the ground can be complete. Rockets penetrate regions where sunlight has experienced very little absorption and have taken the most complete pictures of the spectrum that have ever been recorded. However, many questions concerning solar radiation remain.

One of these riddles, Newell points out in an article in the *Journal of the American Rocket Society* (January-February, 1953), is determining at what altitudes the different wave lengths are absorbed and measuring the incident intensities before an absorption has occurred. Another phenomenon that is being investigated by Newell's group is cosmic radiation. The balloon is still a superior vehicle for the instruments used in this area of research because of its greater stability and longer period of flight.

The German V-2 was the only rocket used in the early years of research conducted at White Sands because it was the best rocket available at the time. However, experts have learned that the V-2 had definite deficiencies. It had been designed primarily as a weapon of war and carried a ton of explosives. It was necessary to add dead weight to the V-2 in addition to the research instruments which were placed inside to make it stable.

The Viking rocket was developed for upper-air research under the direction of Newell's group. As explained by Willy Ley in *Rockets, Missiles, and Space Travel* it followed the general design principles of the V-2, but it embodies a great many improvements over the older rocket. The Viking can operate while carrying a far smaller load and, thus, has been able to reach heights never achieved by the V-2.

Newell's book *High Altitude Rocket Research* includes some very technical material and, also, background material to help the layman in understanding the meaning of recent discoveries concerning the upper atmosphere. He points out the extensive information that has been gathered about temperature, pressure and density at altitudes higher than 240 kilometers. Most of the interesting phenomena in the high atmosphere such as the formation and behavior of the ionosphere, the variation of the earth's magnetic field, and a satisfactory theory of the aurora are yet to be fully explained.

Dr. Newell became the Naval Research Laboratory's representative on the Upper Atmosphere Rocket Research Panel in 1947. This panel is composed of representatives from the various government agencies engaged in rocket research and serves the purpose of directing and correlating the over-all program of upper-air research with rockets.

He belongs to the American Mathematical Society, Washington Academy of Sciences, American Geophysical Union and Sigma Xi. Newell is a fellow of the American Association for the Advancement of Science.

Newell married Janice May Hurd on February 12, 1938. Their children are Judith Deborah, Sue Ellen, Jennifer Dianne, and Andrew David. Dr. Newell is five feet nine inches tall and weighs 150 pounds. He has light brown hair and blue eyes. His favorite forms of recreation are swimming, dancing, playing the piano, reading, and spectator sports. Newell's political affiliation is Republican and he is a member of the Christian Science Church.

In an article that appeared in the *Transactions* of the American Geophysical Society. Newell made this statement about rocket research: "The fair amount of success enjoyed thus far in the rocket upper atmosphere program is gratifying. Nevertheless, the past years must be regarded as a beginning phase. The ultimate potentialities of the rocket, and perhaps some day the satellite vehicle, are yet to be realized."

References

American Men of Science (1949)
High Altitude Rocket Research (1953)

NORGAY, TENZING *See* Hunt, Sir (H. C.) J.; Hillary, Sir E. (P.); and Tenzing Norkey

NORODOM SIHANOUK, KING OF CAMBODIA (nō-rō-dŭm' sĭ-hănŭk) Oct. 31, 1922-

Address: Royal Palace, Pnompenh, Cambodia

The ancient and once-powerful kingdom of Cambodia, in southeastern Asia, has been a virtual dependency of France for the past ninety years. Today, it is governed by thirty-one-year-old King Norodom Sihanouk, who came to the throne in 1941. Established over a thousand years ago by Khmer warriors from India, Cambodia is one of the three associated states—Viet-Nam and Laos are the others—which now comprise Indochina and which are incorporated in the French Union.

During 1953, King Norodom Sihanouk gained from the French government additional prerog-

French Embassy Inf. Div.

NORODOM SIHANOUK, KING OF CAMBODIA

atives of independence from colonial rule. "By what must seem like a miracle of politics," wrote Lucien Bodard in *World* magazine (December, 1953), "Sihanouk has, in effect, won independence for Cambodia—and without losing the financial support of France and the United States. . . . He has succeeded in giving the United States the assurance of a theoretical anti-communism, and he has succeeded in obtaining continued military assistance from the French without even pledging military cooperation in return."

In late December 1953 the King demonstrated his anti-Communist sentiments by launching a military drive to rid his kingdom of Communist guerrilla bands entrenched in the Cardamom mountains. He announced over the national radio that "in order to give tangible proof that I am not seeking personal power . . . I ask permission to . . . transfer this power to the people, in whom I have confidence." He urged the leaders of political parties to form a democratic government.

In Geneva General Henry Deltiel, representing the French forces, and Colonel Ta Quang Buu, Vietminh Minister of Defense, signed agreements on July 21, 1954 which provided for the cessation of hostilities in Viet-Nam and Laos. Several hours later, Ta Quang Buu and General Nhiek Tioulong, Cambodian Minister of Defense, signed a similar agreement for Cambodia. This agreement satisfied Cambodian protests against concentration areas for Communist troops in Cambodia and against limitations on Cambodian military forces.

Cambodia became a protectorate of France in 1863. Its area of 69,480 square miles has a population of approximately 3,500,000 inhabitants, the preponderant part of which adhere to the Buddhist faith. Cambodia was technically an absolute monarchy until late in 1947 when a constitution was promulgated by the King.

Norodom Sihanouk was born on October 31, 1922, the great-grandson of King Norodom and the grandson of King Sisowath, who ascended the throne in 1904. (The royal title is not strictly hereditary; the King is either nominated by his predecessor, or elected by a royal council from among the Brah Vansa, members of the royal family within the fifth degree.)

Norodom Sihanouk was sent by his mother, the Princess Suramarith, to French schools at Saigon, Cochin China, and Paris. He was only eighteen when on April 26, 1941 he was elected by the royal council to the Cambodian throne. The young sovereign was encouraged by the French colonial rulers to continue the royal ceremonies and traditions. His name with titles is Preah Bat Samdach Preah Norodom Sihanouk Varman Reach Harivong Uphato Sucheat Visothipong Akamohaboras Rat Nikarodom Mohareacheathireach Baromaneat Baromabopit Preah Chau Anachak Kampuchea.

The German-dominated Vichy government of France authorized the troops of Germany's ally, Japan, to enter Indochina. Under the Japanese occupation the young king was virtually a prisoner while the "real power in Cambodia was exercised by a . . . Japanese puppet named Son Ngoc Thanh" (*Time,* July 21, 1952). During this period strong nationalist movements developed in Indochina.

After the war British and Chinese troops occupied the area and restored order. The French reassumed control on March 4, 1946. After the adoption of the new French constitution of October 1946 which established the French Union, negotiations between Cambodian and French officials began in order to redefine the relations of the two countries.

The king disclosed in February 1947 that he expected in the near future to establish a constitution which would convert Cambodia into a limited monarchy and would provide for a bicameral legislature. Such a constitution was actually effected on May 6, 1947. Under it the sovereign exercises his executive power through a council of ministers and the legislative power rests with an elected assembly.

At this time the young ruler alluded to the Issarak (Free Cambodia) movement as "mere banditry" and stated that it would be "ridiculous" to break with Paris. "No one is more desirous of complete independence than I," he stated, "but we must look facts in the face. We are too poor to support or defend ourselves. We are dependent upon some major power to give us technicians and troops. If not France, it would be some other great nation" (New York *Times,* February 13, 1947).

Elections held in Cambodia late in 1947 helped to pave the way to conclude negotiations by a treaty with France on November 8, 1949 whereby Cambodia became one of the three "associated states" of the Indochinese federation along with Viet-Nam and Laos.

The aftermath of the first "free election" in Cambodia was such that the King was forced to dissolve the Assembly in 1950 and to resume rule by decree. However, he remained a believer in representative government and called for a new election in 1951 in which he himself actively participated.

As a result of this election the Democratic party (which advocated complete independence from France) took 54 of the 80 Assembly seats, and its leader, Huy Kanthoul, became Premier. The King found the Premier "more interested in plaguing the French" than in taking strong measures against "some 1,800 guerrillas" led by the puppet Premier of the Japanese occupation, Son Ngoc Thanh (*Time,* June 23, 1952).

Accordingly, he dismissed the Kanthoul Cabinet on June 15, 1952 and supplanted it with a National Union government in which he himself took the Premier's portfolio. Nearly all of the other Cabinet posts were filled by princes. The King promised to "clean up the kingdom within two years and bring about greater independence within three years," after which he would be prepared to "answer for his actions" at a popular tribunal and in the presence of representatives of six foreign countries. In September and October of 1952 King Norodom Sihanouk personally led his troops in two jungle campaigns against the Issarak rebels.

Cambodia's export trade in rice, pepper and fish suffered severely from the recurrent guerrilla warfare; for this and other reasons the domestic situation deteriorated. The Kanthoul-dominated Assembly continued to meet, however, until January 13, 1953 when its failure to take action to curb a series of disturbances brought about the dissolution of the legislature and the arrest of ten Democratic leaders as "Issarak collaborators" (New York *Herald Tribune,* February 13, 1953).

Some weeks later the King began a world tour to interest as many governments as possible in Cambodia's case for "greater independence." He visited New York City on April 18, and in an interview warned that unless such independence was granted "within the next few months" there was "real danger" that his subjects could not be induced to oppose a Communist invasion. "They do not want to die for the French, and help them stay," he said.

The monarch cited as one domestic grievance that "Cambodian police cannot touch the French." "In economic matters," he continued, "they have our hands tied; we cannot import and export freely and we have no freedom of taxation."

At Paris about a month later French officials conferring with Cambodian representatives, completed a series of protocols which, it was said, would assure Cambodia full judicial competence and economic adjustments. The King was "reaffirmed" as commander of the Cambodian Army, but "the French High Command in Indo-China would still retain direction of military operations" (New York *Times,* May 10, 1953).

Unsatisfied with these concessions, Norodom Sihanouk continued to demand complete sovereignty for his country, but at the same time advocated giving France the right to maintain military bases in Cambodia. "My people want complete independence," he reiterated at Pnompenh on May 25, 1953, "but my country cannot stand alone. If France gives us independence, we will give preference to France in all things" (New York *Times,* May 26, 1953).

In a move which was "intended to force a showdown," he crossed into neighboring Thailand and transferred power to Premier Pen-Nouth in June 1953. He claimed to be a political refugee. "I want to remain faithful to France," he declared, "but the people . . . have asked me to permit them to revolt" (*Newsweek,* June 22, 1953). Thailand granted the Cambodian monarch personal asylum, but denied him the right to engage in political activity.

About a week later he returned to Cambodia, and established residence, not at the capital, but at Siemréap, a town in northwest Cambodia.

Units of the Cambodian Army, presumably at the royal command, on June 29 seized all the official buildings at Pnompenh. The King however maintained his "voluntary exile" at Siemréap. At the beginning of July the French proposed new talks on the future status of all three of the Indochinese "associated states." Viet-Nam and Laos accepted this bid, but the reply of Norodom Sihanouk (released by the French government on July 25) was that Cambodia would agree to adhere to a French Union only if it "enjoyed a status at least equal to that of India" in the British Commonwealth.

The King's continued insistence on equal sovereignty, as well as the general critical situation in Indochina, were factors in prompting a statement (August 8) by French officials at Pnompenh that France would grant Cambodia full independence in 1954, "reserving only military authority in the area threatened by the Communist-led Vietminh forces" (New York *Herald Tribune,* August 9, 1953).

On August 29, 1953 there was signed at Pnompenh a French-Cambodian agreement transferring to the Cambodians "full sovereignty" over their own police and judiciary. On October 17 a further agreement was concluded whereby King Norodom Sihanouk was given "territorial command of all troops stationed in Cambodia, including French forces." The King ended his "voluntary exile" and resumed residence in the royal palace.

Pen-Nouth, who had incurred royal disfavor, resigned as Premier and on November 16 the King's private councilor, Chan Nak, was named Premier of a reshuffled National Union Cabinet. One of his duties, it was announced, would be to organize new general elections in 1954.

After leading a drive which was reported to have liberated an area that had been in Vietminh hands since 1949, the King announced early in January 1954, that he planned an immediate total attack on increasing rebel activity in the eastern areas of his kingdom. In this new campaign he stated that he expected to rely heavily on French air support.

The King has been described as "a plump young man with a handsome round face, bright intelligent brown eyes under heavy black brows, and an air of easy authority." He is "alert, sensitive, stubborn" and has many interests. He plays the saxophone in his own jazz band and is a composer, having written military marches and songs. His *Miniature Suite* was performed

NORODOM SIHANOUK—*Continued*

by the Air Force Symphony Orchestra in Washington. With his friends he has produced and acted comedy roles in slapstick films such as *Two Murders in the Maginot Line*. He enjoys horseback riding, swimming, painting and playing Monopoly and war games with soldiers. The monarch is an enthusiastic driver of fast sports cars and an accomplished linguist.

In his role of temporal and spiritual leader of his people, he is said to be highly conscientious, a mystic, and accustomed to receive each week five hundred of his subjects in audience. Buddhist priests are believed to have "won him away from playthings of the West to champion Cambodia's holy destiny." Although he has never married, he has, according to the custom of his country, concubines and mistresses, and several children (*World*, December 1953).

On September 29, 1954 the United States and France adopted a plan—after consultation with representatives of Cambodia, Laos and Viet-Nam—to save Indochina from further Communist aggression. The United States agreed to provide $700,000,000 annually and the French agreed to keep military forces in southern Viet-Nam, and to train native troops to contribute to the security of the area.

References

Life 34:116+ F 9 '53 pors
N Y Herald Tribune II p1 Je 21 '53 por
N Y Times Mag p9+ N 8 '53 pors

NORWICH, ALFRED DUFF COOPER, 1ST VISCOUNT Feb. 22, 1890-Jan. 1, 1954 British statesman, author; educated at Eton and Oxford; served in Grenadier Guards in World War I; member of House of Commons (1924-1929, 1931-1945); financial secretary to War Office (1928-1929, 1931-1934), and to Treasury (1934-1935); Secretary of State for War (1935-1937); First Lord of Admiralty until 1938 when he resigned over Munich agreement; Minister of Information (1940-1941); Ambassador to France (1944-1947); author of nine books including *Talleyrand* (1932), *Haig* (1935-1936), *How to Supervise People* (1952), and *Old Men Forget* (1953); received D.S.O. (1919); knighted (1948); made 1st Viscount of Aldwick (1952). See *Current Biography*, (Aug.) 1940.

Obituary

N Y Times p11 Ja 2 '54

NYBORG, VICTOR H(UGO) Nov. 27, 1905- Association executive

Address: b. c/o Association of Better Business Bureaus, Inc., 723 Chrysler Bldg., New York 17; h. Stuyvesant Ave., Rye, N.Y.

Considered one of the leading business-consumer relations authorities in the United States, Victor Nyborg has been president of the Association of Better Business Bureaus since 1946. A strong advocate of the American free enterprise system, he has stated that "it is only when business fails to prove its good faith, that government answers the complaints of the public and steps in to remedy the situation" (Indianapolis *Star*, September 28, 1951). To meet the numerous requests for his views on business self-regulatory and trade practice procedures, he travels extensively throughout the United States and Canada.

The duties of the Better Business Bureau, Nyborg has explained, "are to help wipe out bad business and to help make good business better . . . the business man of today is concerned with the ideals and conduct of all business. He knows that the attackers of our system of enterprise get substance for their attacks from the machinations of the dishonest fringe in business."

Born in Providence, Rhode Island on November 27, 1905, Victor Hugo Nyborg is the son of Knut Julius and Dagmar Constance (Rente) Nyborg and is of Swedish and Norwegian ancestry. He grew up in Providence and attended public schools there. As a boy, he enjoyed baseball and football, swimming and gardening. While in grammar school, he participated in the liberty gardens popular in World War I. His outside interests during high school included reading books concerned with business procedures on the one hand and with musical studies on the other.

After leaving high school, Nyborg believed that his main interest was music, and from 1926 to 1928 he took private singing lessons and opera class studies with Arthur and Vincent Hubbard at the Hubbard Studios in Boston, Massachusetts. He commuted from Providence to Boston, and in his spare time earned money as an apprentice house painter and employee in a jewelry shop. During this period, he met the assistant manager of the Providence Better Business Bureau, who aroused in him an interest in the bureau's activities. Together they discussed individual cases and problems of the organization and how they might be worked out. When the bureau executive went to Hartford, Connecticut in 1928 to take charge of the Better Business Bureau of that city, he asked Nyborg to accompany him and to accept the position of investigator. Victor concurred and relinquished his music studies in Boston shortly afterward.

In his first year as investigator for the Hartford Better Business Bureau, Nyborg helped to reveal "questionable" advertising solicitation practices of groups representing nearly 100 nonexistent publications and organizations that were collecting large sums from local business men. His competent work soon earned him promotion to the office of assistant manager of the bureau.

In 1931 he uncovered artful schemes used by unscrupulous individuals to capitalize on the public's interest in contributing to charities. To the readers of pseudo-financial literature and prospective victims of stock swindles, he advised in 1933: "Investigate before you invest" (Hartford *Courant*, March 2, 1933). He was frequently called upon to address schools, parent-teachers groups, and clubs in the community, and found time outside his active career to sing in the Hartford Choral Club. Advancing his education, he took United States Army extension courses in various military subjects from 1933 to 1935.

Nyborg developed a lecture course on fabrics in the spring of 1936 for employees of retail stores, cleaners and laundries in Hartford. Going to Buffalo (New York) in 1936 as assistant manager of the Better Business Bureau, he aided that city's furniture trade in formulating an eighteen-point pact of standards for advertising and selling practices.

Joining the Buffalo Junior Chamber of Commerce, he became an instructor in its speakers bureau in 1938. Although he had started to study in one of the speech classes, he ended by being the teacher. In 1939 Nyborg was elected a director of the Junior Chamber of Commerce, and in 1940 was unanimously chosen vice-president. He prepared and broadcast the "racket buster" program over Buffalo's local radio station.

Appointed general manager of the Cincinnati (Ohio) Better Business Bureau in November 1940, Nyborg was elected its president and a member of the board of governors in the following year. Nyborg was also named to the offices of governor and treasurer of the National Association of Better Business Bureaus in 1942.

In June 1945, he became president of the association which at that time had about eighty bureaus in the United States and five cooperating bureaus in Canada. Concurrently, he served for two terms as president of the Ohio Better Business Bureaus, Inc. In the local Cincinnati community, he was chairman of the speakers bureau of the Advertisers Club, a member of the city's Charity Solicitations Commission, a special consultant to the OPA, and a trustee of the Legal Aid Society.

As chairman of the important merchandise committee of the National Association of Better Business Bureaus, Nyborg helped develop a revised "Guide for Retail Advertising and Selling." Attacking "blue-sky schemers" attempting to defraud the public, and particularly veterans, of World War II savings estimated at $170,000,000,000, Nyborg has declared that business cheats were costing the [general] public $650,000,000 a year" (New York *Times,* December 13, 1945).

At the annual conference of the National Association of Better Business Bureaus in June 1946, the organization voted to change its name to the Association of Better Business Bureaus, Inc., and to establish headquarters in New York City. In September, the board of governors elected Victor H. Nyborg president and executive secretary. Nyborg assumed his duties as head of the new association on October 15, 1946, and he stated two weeks later that its program would include closer coordination among business bureaus in different cities and greater cooperation with public schools in an educational plan to combat "an anti-business element which was attempting to cast a bad light on all business" (Fort Worth *Press,* October 29, 1946).

In June 1949 President Harry S. Truman sent Nyborg a letter which expressed his best

VICTOR H. NYBORG

wishes to the annual conference of Better Business Bureaus and commended their "impressive record of service and protection to the American consumer."

In the summer of 1950, Nyborg announced that the Association of Better Business Bureaus was ready to set up voluntary machinery for helping business to adjust to anticipated new credit and installment regulations under the national mobilization program. A few months later he advised that the association was joining with subscription book publishers in an effort to obtain ethical sales practices and voluntary registration of sales people. This is another "practical demonstration" of how business houses are taking "voluntary action to work in the public interest," he declared (New York *Times,* October 2, 1950).

"Collectivism and private enterprise cannot operate together," Nyborg affirmed, speaking to the Indianapolis Better Business Bureau on September 27, 1951 (Indianapolis *Star,* September 28, 1951). The following year, he told the Washington Better Business Bureau that "it would be a crime against our country and its people if we allowed ourselves to be lured into an acceptance of any form of state collectivism on the false philosophy that because there are some leeches in business, enterprise in this country is no longer entitled to freedom. . . ." (New York *Herald Tribune,* May 20, 1952).

He affirms that the "indications of a new climate for business under the present Administration in Washington, D.C. place additional responsibility on the Better Business Bureaus to help businessmen solve their problems and serve the interests of the public without asking Government to take a direct hand."

In a "Consumer Education Study" program, Nyborg states, the Association of Better Business Bureaus, Inc. is cooperating with the National Association of Secondary School Prin-

NYBORG, VICTOR H.—*Continued*

cipals in financing and developing teaching units and materials currently used in more than 5,000 of the nation's high schools to interpret the American enterprise system. On the adult level, the association is educating the public to an understanding of economic processes through the distribution of "Fact Booklets" on merchandise, securities, and similar topics.

Nyborg put into effect in 1952 the Better Business Bureaus' new Research and Education Foundation which, he says, had been "in the dream stage" in the minds of bureau executives for about "fifteen years." Chartered under the laws of New York State, the foundation will make available scholarships and fellowships in colleges and universities for research studies in the fields of business administration and finance.

"New tools and methods must be developed for organized programs of study and research," Nyborg said in relation to the work of the foundation. "The broadest possible dissemination should be made of published findings."

In November 1953 the association which Nyborg heads had expanded its 1945 membership to a total of ninety-eight business bureaus. Of this number, one bureau was in Hawaii, seven bureaus were in Canada, and ninety were in cities throughout the United States. On a membership basis, 65,000 business firms support this organization which received from the public more than 2,000,000 inquiries in 1953. The Better Business Bureaus issued a bulletin on December 14, 1953 urging cigarette advertisers to avoid questionable and confidence-destroying medical and health claims.

Nyborg is the author of several articles on business-consumer relations, including "Quacks of the Electronic Age" (*American Magazine,* March 1951). The Buffalo Junior Chamber of Commerce honored him with a merit award in November 1940 for his services as director and vice-president. In 1950 Nyborg received a certificate of appreciation from the Lions Club of Fort Worth, Texas. He is a member of the Advertisers Club, of which he was governor in 1946. He is a Republican and a Congregationalist.

Nyborg married Tyra Hawkinson on October 12, 1929. He is described by a business associate as "a conscientious, level-headed and sincere leader." The business executive has blue eyes and wavy graying blonde hair, is five feet eleven inches tall, and weighs 185 pounds. His hobbies include music, boating, fishing and home movies. Nyborg's hope is that American enterprise will voluntarily accept its responsibilities for the future so that "we may avoid a philosophy or way of thinking that will lead to restrictive legislation or government competition with business."

References

Buffalo News N 13 '40
Roanoke Times F 1 '47
Who's Who in America, 1952-53
Who's Who in Commerce and Industry (1953)

ODRÍA (AMORETTI), MANUEL A(POLINARIO) (ō-thrē'ä) Nov. 26, 1897- President of Peru; army officer

Address: Presidential Palace, Lima, Peru

Within six years "strong man" President Manuel A. Odría of Peru has carried out promised social reforms, has had schools, hospitals, highways and housing developments built, and has found favor with a large group of the population. This is the opinion of Robert M. Hallett (*Christian Science Monitor,* October 27, 1953) and other reporters who have been observing Odría's regime, which began after a bloodless coup in 1948. Odría was elected to a six-year term as constitutional President on July 2, 1950.

A career Army officer, Odría was appointed Chief of Staff by President José Luis Bustamante y Rivero in 1946. A year later, he was named Minister of the Interior. Bustamante's policies caused Odría to resign from the Cabinet in July 1948. Since assuming the presidency in October 1948 he has abolished many state controls on Peru's economy, and encouraged foreign capital to invest in his country.

Manuel Apolinario Odría Amoretti was born in Tarma, Department of Junín, Peru on November 26, 1897, son of Arturo Odría y Alvarez and Zoila Amoretti de Odría, and the grandson of Colonel Manuel Odría, a nineteenth century war hero. His father died during Manuel's childhood, and his mother, who became a dressmaker, managed to finance his early military education. He entered the Escuela de Oficiales de Chorrillos (Military School) in 1915, and was commissioned a second lieutenant in 1919. He remained as an instructor at the school until he advanced to the rank of captain.

In 1927, he entered the Escuela Superior de Guerra (War College) from which he was graduated in 1930; he was promoted to the rank of major. Later he studied at the Escuela Superior de Guerra Naval (Navy School).

The officer was made a lieutenant colonel in 1936 and became chief of staff of the Fourth Division stationed at Cuzco. He served as chief of the third section of the Army General Staff and chief of staff of the First Division at Piura. This was near the unmarked boundary between Peru and Ecuador, which has been in dispute for more than a hundred years. During a skirmish, Odría distinguished himself in action and was made a full colonel. Returning to the Escuela Superior de Guerra, he became assistant director. Later, as director of the college, he made a study tour in the Panama Canal Zone and the United States.

The legislature confirmed Colonel Odría's promotion to the rank of brigadier general in 1946, and he was made Chief of Staff of the Army. President Bustamante appointed him Minister of Interior and chief of police in January 1947, when the country was stirred by the assassination of Francisco Graña Garland, publisher of *La Prensa,* one of Lima's newspapers.

At this time the country was undergoing a period of inflation which *Newsweek* (November 16, 1953) attributed to state controls and severe restrictions placed on imports and exports. The government of Peru was heavily in debt and printing-press money flooded the country. General Odría urged Bustamante to outlaw the Allianza Popular Revolucionaria Americana (Apra), whose members, the Apristas, Odría blamed for the country's economic crisis. General Odría resigned as Minister of Interior because of his disagreement with official policy in regard to this issue.

An uprising against the government by the Apristas in Callao on October 3, 1948 was quickly defeated by the Army, after which Apra was outlawed. A second uprising began in the Army garrison at Arequipa on October 27. General Odría assumed command and requested Bustamante to resign because of the danger of seizure of the government by radical elements. *Time* (November 8, 1948) reported that the President "waited stubbornly" until escorted to Limatambo airfield. He went into exile in Argentina.

General Odría flew to Lima on October 31 and was greeted by a military band and cheering crowds. The revolution, called the "Restoration Movement," was without bloodshed. Odría promptly dissolved the legislature, established an all-military government and was proclaimed provisional President by the Army, pending a constitutional government. He said he would remain in power only long enough "to call an election and install a truly democratic government" (*Newsweek,* November 22, 1948). Víctor Raúl Haya de la Torre, leader of Apra, took refuge in the Colombian Embassy in Lima, and was forced to remain there until April 1954 when negotiations between Colombia and Peru permitted him to seek asylum in a foreign country.

President Odría promised to re-establish the economy of the nation and its credit abroad but the prospect seemed remote, since the country was said to be on the verge of bankruptcy. One of his first acts was to hire Klein and Saks, a U.S. firm of economic consultants. Recommendations of the economists were put into effect by special decree on November 11, 1949.

Business Week (December 31, 1949) reported that the decree released the sol, the Peruvian monetary unit, from the official exchange, removed state subsidies except those for the import of wheat, granted increases in wages, and cancelled price controls except on fuel and breadstuffs. The government was ready with restraining orders if industry jumped prices. Odría also repealed a law that required exporters to surrender dollars for sols, and instituted a mining code eliminating taxes on minerals for a period of twenty-five years.

Most business executives felt that Odría had cleared the way for a stable government. A hydroelectric works and two large irrigation projects were built. U.S. companies invested about $90,000,000 in oil, metal industries and agriculture. Further investments were thought risky until a constitutional government was established.

General Odría resigned as provisional President on June 1, 1950 to become a candidate for

Wide World

MANUEL A. ODRÍA

the presidency in the national elections of July 2, when many seats in parliament were to be filled. During the interim, General Zenón Noriega was President. Odría's only opposition candidate was General Ernesto Montagne. Robert K. Shellaby (*Christian Science Monitor,* June 27, 1950) reported that on June 11 the electoral tribunal disqualified Montagne as a candidate after his petitions were declared fraudulent.

This was followed by uprisings of students at the Arequipa and San Marcos universities. Order was restored by government troops on June 15, and General Montagne and leaders of the outlawed party, Apra, were arrested.

Odría and his followers won the election, with two minority parties—Socialist and Independent—trailing in the parliament. General Odría assumed the office of President on July 28, 1950 for a six-year term. In his inaugural speech, he said that health, education and labor were the principal concerns of the government and announced plans for new hospitals, schools, low-cost housing and social insurance. A public works program called for a highway system and completion of irrigation projects.

The New York *Times* (January 4, 1952) reported that foreign trade increased 50 per cent during the first half of 1951 over the same period in 1950. Production of minerals had increased 20 per cent during 1951, and the American Smelting and Refining Company was engaged in preliminary work in copper deposits.

Reader's Digest (April 1954) noted that in the Sechura Desert, there are hopeful indications of oil deposits. The government has invited investors in that area on the basis of a fifty-fifty split in earnings and forty-year renewable concessions. "As a result, Peruvian, Canadian and U.S. firms have begun large-

ODRÍA, MANUEL A.—*Continued*

scale operations. Peru may become a major source of oil for the Western Hemisphere."

Arrangements for Le Tourneau del Peru, Inc., a subsidiary of Le Tourneau Institute of Longview, Texas, to build a colony called Tournavista on a 1,000,000-acre tract in the jungle of the Pucalpa area was approved by the Peruvian Senate on January 22, 1954. In return, Le Tourneau del Peru will build thirty-three miles of paved highway connecting the colony with the Trans-Andean Highway, a water supply, sewage disposal and other public services.

During a good-will visit to Brazil in August 1953, President Odría issued with the late President Getulio Dornelles Vargas of Brazil, a declaration of their joint determination to defend democratic and Pan-American principles. The two nations signed five agreements to strengthen their trade and economic relations. Odría has stated that "political cooperation among the American nations also requires economic cooperation" (New York *World-Telegram and Sun,* January 9, 1954).

Odría married Maria Delgado de Odría in 1927. They have two sons, Cesar and Manuel. The family is Roman Catholic. The President is of average build "with a weatherworn face . . . and a steady gaze." He has sandy hair and blue eyes. For relaxation, he enjoys chess, bullfights and the opera. He has been decorated by the governments of Argentina, Nationalist China, Ethiopia, Spain, and Venezuela as well as Peru. *Time* (November 8, 1948) quoted General Odría as saying: "Party politics poisons the hearts of the people and sickens their minds."

References

Time 52:40 N 8 '48 por
New Century Cyclopedia of Names (1954)
World Biography (1954)

O'MALLEY, WALTER F(RANCIS) Oct. 9, 1903- Baseball executive; lawyer

Address: b. c/o Brooklyn National League Baseball Club, 215 Montague St., Brooklyn 2, N.Y.; h. 318 Ocean Ave., Amityville, Long Island, N.Y.

The president and one of the principal stockholders of the Brooklyn National League Baseball Club, better known as the Brooklyn Dodgers, is Walter F. O'Malley. He attained the presidency in October 1950 when he and Mrs. John L. Smith, widow of one of his old friends, purchased the 25 per cent interest held by Branch Rickey and thereby came into control of 75 per cent of the organization's stock.

O'Malley first entered the Brooklyn baseball scene in 1932 as a director. He later became the club's legal representative. An attorney by profession, he practiced law for approximately twenty years. In addition, he is active in numerous business and civic enterprises.

The son of Edwin J. O'Malley, former New York City commissioner of public markets, and Alma (Feltner) O'Malley, Walter Francis O'Malley was born in the Bronx, New York, on October 9, 1903. He attended Jamaica High School and Culver Military Academy in Indiana, where he played on the baseball team until his nose was broken in a game. Graduated in 1922, he entered the University of Pennsylvania and became a battalion commander in the Reserve Officers' Training Corps.

O'Malley was commissioned a second lieutenant in the Chemical Warfare Service (serving in the Reserve from 1926 until 1936). He was president of his class and a member of the council on athletics and the baseball committee. After receiving the A.B. degree with honors in 1926, he entered the School of Law of Columbia University. He changed to the law school at Fordham University, which he attended at night, while he worked in the daytime as an assistant engineer for the Riley Drilling Company.

Following his admission to the New York bar in 1930, O'Malley established his own engineering firm and earned more than $50,000 in his first year. He became a director of the Brooklyn Borough Gas Company in 1932, and in the same year, a director of the Brooklyn Dodgers. According to Arch Murray of the New York *Post* (November 5, 1950), it was at that time that O'Malley's "romance" with the Dodgers began.

After becoming the Dodgers' legal representative in 1943 (succeeding the late Wendell L. Willkie), O'Malley in November 1944, helped to organize a syndicate consisting of Branch Rickey (who was then general manager and president of the Dodgers and is now with the Pittsburgh Base Ball Club), the late John L. Smith and himself. The syndicate purchased 25 per cent of the Dodger stock and less than a year later it bought 50 per cent of the additional stock.

In accordance with a previous pooling arrangement, O'Malley and Mrs. John L. Smith acquired Rickey's stock in October 1950 and O'Malley became president. At the time the transaction was announced, the New York *Herald Tribune* (October 27, 1950) remarked: "O'Malley, a shrewd legal brain, has taken on a not-insignificant task of running a major-league ball club." An indication of the dimensions of this task may be seen in the fact that the Dodgers have six minor league clubs and have working agreements with nine others. The baseball executive discontinued his practice of law in 1951.

Shortly after assuming the presidency, O'Malley announced the appointment of Fresco Thompson, former director of Brooklyn's farm system, and Emil J. ("Buzzy") Bavasi, former manager of an affiliated Montreal team, as vice-presidents. Joe Williams of the New York *World-Telegram and Sun* (October 7, 1953) noted that the Dodgers' president "has proved a pleasant surprise. A lawyer-banker who got the knack pretty quick. . . . [He] has surrounded himself with knowing, enthusiastic baseball men. . . . They give the job a full-time wrestle. Their scouts are active and competent; they have a comprehensive instructional program. In short, they run a sound baseball operation."

At the end of the 1953 baseball season, after the Dodgers had won the National League pennant for the second successive year but lost to the New York Yankees in the World Series with Charles (Chuck) Dressen as manager, O'Malley became the center of a controversy when he did not rehire Dressen. The Dodgers' president explained that although he was satisfied with Dressen's performance (which had been the best managerial record in the team's history), he was opposed on principle to changing the Dodger's policy of granting administrative contracts for only one year. Dressen had stated that he would not accept less than a two-year contract (New York *Times,* October 15, 1953). Speculation concerning the identity of Dressen's successor ended with the appointment of Walter Alston, the relatively unknown former manager of a Brooklyn farm team in Montreal.

In November 1953 when the United States Supreme Court upheld the controversial "reserve clause" written into professional baseball contracts, thus reaffirming the thirty-one-year-old decision that the game is a sport, not a business, and therefore, outside the scope of laws restricting monopolies, the president of the Dodgers commented: "I am pleased that the integrity of baseball has been reaffirmed by the Supreme Court. But the decision does not mean that baseball will go along with the horse and buggy days. We must clearly recognize the changing conditions and particularly the possibility of territorial expansion. For too long now baseball has been an open target for those who could profit easily by attacking it through litigation" (New York *Times,* November 10, 1953).

Despite his many heavy responsibilities, O'Malley has managed to preserve his sense of humor about the Dodgers. In answer to a suggestion that the name "The Bums" should be abandoned, because it has an adverse psychological effect on the players, O'Malley replied: "I cannot lend myself to any squeamish campaign which has as its objective the demise of The Bum. So far as we in Brooklyn are concerned, the lovable little fellow is here to stay. Besides, most of us take ourselves too seriously. It's good for our souls to be lampooned now and then. And one of these days The Bum will have the laugh on everybody. . . ." (New York *World-Telegram and Sun,* November 13, 1953).

Early in December 1953 O'Malley disclosed that plans for a new stadium to replace Ebbets Field were well advanced, and that the stadium, to cost about $7,200,000 and to have a seating capacity of 52,000 (Ebbets Field seats 32,000), might be completed within the next five years. He stated that "the Dodgers will own it but it also will be constructed to accommodate other enterprises."

During World War II O'Malley was director of the Kingsbury Ordnance Plant in Indiana and of Todd and Brown, Inc., supervisors of the planning and building of New York's Rockefeller Center and Virginia's Old Williamsburg. He is owner of the New York Subways Advertising Company; part owner of J P. Duffy,

Barney Stein

WALTER F. O'MALLEY

Inc., a building materials concern; president of the Ebbets-McKeever Exhibition Company, the real estate adjunct of the Brooklyn baseball club; and director of John F. Trommer, Inc. and Todd Associates, Inc.

Shortly after becoming president of the Dodgers, he was made a member of baseball's executive council, an unusual honor for a "freshman" club president. He is an executive officer of several minor league clubs and in 1949 was vice-president of the New York Football Yankees. That year he was also general chairman of the United Hospital Fund of Brooklyn. Among other civic activities, he is a director of Brooklyn's Swedish Hospital and chairman of the board of Froebel Academy.

He belongs to the Brooklyn Bar Association, Catholic Lawyers Guild, Cathedral Club, Swedish Engineers Society, and Scabbard and Blade; his fraternity is Theta Delta Chi. He is a Roman Catholic and a Democrat. O'Malley's clubs are the Metropolitan, New York Athletic, Brooklyn (of which he is a director and vice-president), and Unqua Corinthian Yacht.

The baseball executive was married to Kay Hanson on September 5, 1931. The O'Malleys have a daughter, Terry, and a son, Peter. Baseball and fishing are the favorite forms of recreation of the Dodgers' president, who organized and is a member of the annual U.S. Atlantic Tuna Tournament. Arch Murray has characterized O'Malley as a man who, "with the lilt of Irish laughter in his eyes and on his lips . . . combines the warmth and gregariousness of the born mixer with the shrewd hard head of the successful business man."

References

N Y Herald Tribune III p1 O 11 '53
N Y Post Mag p18 N 5 '50 por

Martindale-Hubbell Law Directory, 1952
Who's Who in America (Suppl. N '53)
Who's Who in New York, 1952
Who's Who in the East (1951)

ÖTÜKEN, ADNAN 1911- Director of Turkish National Library

Address: b. c/o Turkish National Library, Yenişehir, Ankara, Turkey; h. Gazi M. Kemal Bulvari 23, Ankara, Turkey

In the recent progress in library service that has been a part of Turkey's rapid development as a modern nation, one of the most significant achievements was the founding in 1948 of Milli Kütüphane, the Turkish National Library. Much of the credit for the establishment of the library and for its subsequent growth belongs to its director, Adnan Ötüken, who is also acting general director of fine arts of the Ministry of Education. Ötüken teaches

ADNAN ÖTÜKEN

librarianship at the University of Ankara and is the author of an important two-volume introduction to library science and bibliography.

Adnan Ötüken was born in Manastir, Turkey in 1911, the son of Ali Nasit and Lütfiye. He was educated at the lycée of Istanbul (he was graduated in 1931), and at the University of Istanbul, where he majored in Turkish and French literatures and languages, with special work in Turkish proverbs. After leaving the university in 1935, he was sent to Germany by the Turkish Ministry of Education to study library science. He remained in Germany until 1939. He took his degree in librarianship at the Preussische Staatsbibliothek in Berlin and engaged in study and practical work in German libraries, among them, the Deutsche Bücherei in Leipzig.

When he returned to Turkey he was employed for a time in 1940 as an assistant in the Turkish language and literature department of the University of Istanbul and then became lecturer of library science at the University of Ankara. Ötüken's work in this field has been discussed in American professional journals by Lawrence S. Thompson, who made a study of Turkish libraries for the United States Department of State. Thompson pointed out in an article in *Library Quarterly* (July 1952) that Turkish librarianship was handicapped by lack of facilities for professional training and stressed the importance of Ötüken's pioneer undertaking in organizing a basic course in library science.

Meanwhile, not long after his return from Germany, Ötüken was made director of publications of the Ministry of Education, a post that he filled for five years. In 1946 the Ministry of Education assigned him the task of founding the Turkish National Library in Ankara. Preliminary work for the institution was begun on April 15, 1946 and two years later, on August 16, 1948, it was ready to open its doors to the public.

At this time the library was in possession of some fifteen years' accumulation by the Ministry of Education of copyright copies of Turkish books, newspapers, and periodicals. By 1950 it had collected about 132,000 volumes and employed a staff of thirty persons. Four years later it had 200,000 volumes while its staff had grown to fifty-six members. Ötüken has estimated that by 1956 the library would own a million volumes.

Discussing the establishment and operations of the library in "The Youngest National Library in the World" (*Libri, International Library Review,* 1950), Ötüken has listed eight categories of material which the library is charged with collecting. In addition to copies or microfilms of all manuscripts in the country, these include maps and atlases, phonograph records, films, scientific publications in foreign languages, musical scores and books on music. One of its special collections will be all Turkish works published in the Arabic script (from 1729 until the adoption of the Latin alphabet in 1928).

Under Ötüken's direction, the young Turkish National Library has become "one of the best administered and most rapidly growing" libraries in the world ("Books Are Basic Beyond the Bosphorus," *American Library Association Bulletin,* June 1952). The library, which is used daily by an average of 400 readers, has its own bookbinding department and has been designed as a library school and as a center for concerts, motion picture presentations and conferences.

In 1951 it took over from the Turkish Copyright Office the responsibility for distributing copyright material and also assumed the task of publishing *Türkiye Biblyografyasi,* a national bibliography of all Turkish private and official publications; informational articles; and a monthly library bulletin. Other projects that Ötüken has furthered are providing library facilities for young people, with special exhibits for Children's Book Week, and building up a collection of books for home use.

Ötüken's contributions to professional literature in library science are especially valuable, as L. S. Thompson has reported, because of the scarcity of Turkish books in that field. Among the librarian's published works are *Library Science and Bibliography* (1940), *Bibliography of the Publications of the University* of *Istanbul* (1941), *Establishing the National Library* (1946), *Bibliography of the Publications of the University of Istanbul, 1933-45* (1947, with Acaroglu), and *Bibliography of Classical and Modern Works Translated and Published by the Turkish Ministry of Education, 1940-48* (1947), with a second revised edition (1950).

Particularly useful in the training of young librarians has been Ötüken's two-volume manual of library science and bibliography, published in Ankara in 1947-1948. The descriptive cataloging code presented in this introduction to librarianship, derived largely from the Prussian *Instruktion,* is being adopted in many Turkish libraries.

Since little uniformity exists among Turkey's 497 libraries in policies of cataloging and classifying and in other practices, it is thought that the National Library might provide leadership in establishing wide cooperation. Ötüken is a member of the working committee of the Turkish Libraries Association and for more than a decade has given talks on books over Radio Station Ankara.

Formerly (1952-1953), the Turkish librarian was associate general director of higher education of the Ministry of Education. He is currently the ministry's acting general director of fine arts. In this office he is concerned with the operations of the Ankara State Conservatory (theatre, opera, music and ballet), Istanbul Academy of Fine Arts, Izmir State Conservatory, Ankara Presidential Philharmonic Orchestra, Museum of Painting and Sculpture in Istanbul, and Gallery of Painting and Sculpture in Izmir. As an incentive to young artists the department arranges an annual exhibition at Ankara of painting and sculpture in which hundreds of Turkish artists apply to have their work represented.

The widely traveled director of the Turkish National Library speaks German and French in addition to his native language. While visiting in England, France, Switzerland, Italy, the United States, and Iraq, he has studied the chief libraries of those countries. He is a member of the working committee of the Turkish national commission of the United Nations Educational, Scientific and Cultural Organization, and is a member of UNESCO's international consultative committee on bibliography. He represented Turkey at the Bibliographical Congress of UNESCO, held in Paris in 1950.

In 1937 Ötüken married Sabiha, a student at the University of Istanbul who is now a children's librarian. Their two daughters are Deniz and Yildiz. A man of sturdy build, he stands about five feet ten inches in height and weighs over 200 pounds; he has green eyes and brown hair. Apart from books, which are also a hobby, his recreational interests are soccer and cooking. The librarian's warm smile and friendly, outgoing manner are as impressive to people who meet him as his intellectual acuteness.

References

Lib Q 22:270+ Jl '52
International Who's Who, 1953

OWEN, RUTH BRYAN *See* Rohde, R.B.O.

PACHECO E CHAVES, JOÃO (pă'shâ-cô shä'vâs jä'ô) Jan. 27, 1916- Brazilian Government official; agricultural engineer

Address: b. c/o Instituto Brasileiro do Café (Brazilian Coffee Institute), Rio de Janeiro, Brazil; h. Rua Roberto Moreira 97, São Paulo, Brazil

When João Pacheco e Chaves was appointed president of the Instituto Brasileiro do Café (Brazilian Coffee Institute) in September 1953, the world demand for coffee had become greater than the supply. This condition was attributed to the drought, and to the frost which had damaged the crops in Paraná and São Paulo, two of Brazil's richest coffee producing states. The consequent rise in coffee prices in the United States, which some authorities believed was caused by speculation, became a serious problem for Pacheco e Chaves.

The price of coffee to American consumers dropped following the announcement in August 1954 of relaxation of foreign exchange controls in Brazil. Pacheco e Chaves is pessimistic about the 1954-1955 crop, which he estimates will be only 13,454,000 bags, by far the lowest Brazilian crop in years. Formerly Brazil supplied 60 per cent of the world's coffee, but since 1948 it has decreased its output, and in 1953 only 43 per cent came from Brazil.

The *Brazilian American Survey* (1952) called coffee "the paving on the two-way trade route between Brazil and the United States." One of the aims of the institute, a government agency, is to keep the paving smooth. By way of doing this, Pacheco e Chaves invited four representative housewives of the United States to visit Brazil in February 1954 at the expense of the institute to see the extent of the damage by frost on many coffee trees.

As an agricultural engineer, Pacheco e Chaves has been active in Brazil's apprenticeship service in his home state of São Paulo. He was elected to the state legislature in 1950, and later served as state secretary of agriculture. He is the author of several pamphlets on coffee problems.

The name Pacheco e Chaves goes back in the history of São Paulo for ten generations. João, the son of Jorge and Jane Conceição Pacheco e Chaves, was born on January 27, 1916 in São Paulo. He attended private schools and at an early age entered the Escola Superior de Agricultura "Luiz de Queiroz" da Universidade de São Paulo. He was graduated with the degree of Engenheiro-agrônomo (agricultural engineer) in 1936. For a few years, young Pacheco e Chaves studied modern methods of cultivation on his father's coffee plantation, and was concerned with the shortage of skilled labor.

Brazil, in 1942, had not recovered from the disastrous over-production year of 1933,

JOÃO PACHECO E CHAVES

when millions of tons of coffee had rotted, or were burned or dumped into the sea, as a result of overproduction during the world depression. New planting had been reduced to a minimum, but a more satisfactory reserve storage system had been established. Therefore, when coffee consumption increased during World War II, the demands were met while production was being increased. Since it takes five years for coffee trees to mature sufficiently to bear a crop, the reserves were exhausted by the end of the war.

During this period Pacheco e Chaves entered São Paulo's apprenticeship service, a system of on-the-job training to assist in the development of native industries. He soon became an instructor and, in 1949, was named director general of the service. Elected deputy to the state assembly of São Paulo in 1950, he served for one year. He was made state secretary of agriculture in November 1951. In September 1953 he was appointed the head of the Brazilian Coffee Institute by Getulio Dornelles Vargas, the late President of Brazil.

The institute was established by President Vargas in December 1952 and replaced the National Coffee Department of Brazil. The organization conducts research on soil conservation, cultivation methods, transportation improvements, and regulates price supports linked to foreign competitive levels.

Pacheco e Chaves became the second president of the institute at a time when a crisis in the coffee market was inevitable. World demand since 1945 had kept the storage reserves low, and more recently growers, fearing a depression, had failed to plant a sufficient number of new seedlings. A drought in January 1953 inflicted damage in some areas and the frost in July in Paraná and São Paulo reduced the crop by 20 per cent. The government was concerned with the effect of the shortage on its best customer, the United States, where coffee supplied the dollars for Brazil to pay for its overseas purchases.

A few weeks after Pacheco e Chaves became president of the Coffee Institute, he visited New York and observed the New York Coffee and Sugar Exchange and other activities centered on the coffee market. He then went to Boca Raton, Florida, in November 1953, to attend, with representatives from other coffee-producing Latin-American countries, the National Coffee Association convention. His speech to the convention was later published under the title of *A Posição do Café Brasileiro em Face do Mercado Norte-Americano* (The Position of Brazilian Coffee in Relation to the North American Market). In another pamphlet *Problemas do Café* (Coffee Problems) he presented his program for promoting the aims of the institute.

The first international coffee congress was held in Curitiba, Paraná, Brazil, from December 11 to 19, 1953, prior to the opening of a coffee exhibition in the same city. Coffee experts from thirty-seven countries heard Pacheco e Chaves analyze a twenty-year table of coffee statistics, which indicated that the 1954 exportable crop was estimated at less than 14,000,000 bags, as compared to the 1953 estimate of 17,000,000 bags. He announced that a billion-dollar expansion program for increased coffee production was under way.

The coffee shortage became apparent in the United States early in January 1954 when retail prices began to mount rapidly. The immediate result was a charge by Senator Guy M. Gillette of Iowa that "gambling and speculation" had caused the price rise (New York *Times,* January 27, 1954) The Brazilian government was said to be a "party to the scheme to force prices upward." A housewives' boycott was proposed, and the Federal Trade Commission began a study of the coffee market.

Pacheco e Chaves issued an invitation to members of Congress, publishers and representative housewives to visit Brazil and see for themselves. On behalf of the Coffee Institute, he offered a "ten-day expense-paid tour" to four "typical" American housewives. This was accepted by the General Federation of Women's Clubs, and four of their officers from different parts of the country were selected. According to the New York *Herald Tribune* (February 17, 1954) the women were "amazed and distressed" on seeing the extent of frost damage to the coffee crop. Drought had caused premature and uneven ripening of the berries. They saw no evidence of coffee being "held back in Brazil for purposes of forcing up the price."

The FTC on July 29, 1954 issued a report of its probe to determine the cause or causes of spiraling coffee prices, in which blame was scattered in the direction of both Brazilian and U.S. crop estimators and coffee speculators, the New York Coffee and Sugar Exchange, and U.S. importers, roasters and retailers. The FTC charged that "when it became evident that the shortage in the frostbitten Paraná area would be largely offset by increased production in frost-free Brazilian areas and in other countries, speculation had already disrupted the exchange market. . . ." The report also accused "U.S. restaurants of jacking retail prices far above the point of increased costs" (*Business Week,* August 7, 1954). The report stated that government controls over coffee trading would be the only effective safeguard against unreasonable increases in coffee prices. The charges of the FTC were denied by the New York Coffee and Sugar Exchange and by the Brazilian coffee growers through the Coffee Institute.

Mrs. Theodore S. Chapman, who headed the committee of four women representing the General Federation of Women's Clubs which went to Brazil in February to study the cause of the coffee price rise, differed sharply with the FTC report. "We saw hundreds of miles of just dead trees, so I know there is a shortage," Mrs. Chapman said. "The Federal Trade Commission made no study in Brazil" (New York *Times,* July 31, 1954). An official of the Brazilian Coffee Institute in New York declared that coffee reserves were low and that a "return to normal" could not be expected before July 1955, and not then, unless weather conditions were favorable.

João Pacheco e Chaves was married on June 11, 1940 to Ruth Seng. The couple has three children: Maria Cristina, Miguel Francisco and Mercedes. The family's religion is Roman Catholic. Pacheco e Chaves is a member of the Partido Social Democrático. He is tall, well-built and has black hair and eyes.

PARKES, HENRY BAMFORD Nov. 13, 1904- University professor; historian

Address: b. c/o New York University, Washington Sq., New York 3; h. 439 E. 86th St., New York 28

A professor of history at New York University since 1949 and a faculty member since 1930, Henry Bamford Parkes came to the United States in 1927 to do graduate work at the University of Michigan after he had received his Bachelor of Arts degree at Oxford. An author, he has written eight books, and numerous magazine articles. His most recent book, *The United States of America* (Knopf, 1953), has received many favorable reviews.

Born in Sheffield, England on November 13, 1904, Henry Bamford Parkes was the son of James Frederick and Rosa (Burrows) Parkes. He is descended from a line of Methodist ministers which extends back almost to the founding of the church in the eighteenth century. His father was a clergyman, as were both his grandfathers. Since the English Methodist Church had the system by which ministers were moved to a different church every three years, the childhood of Henry Parkes was spent in many parts of England, but mostly in and around London.

This period ended in 1915 when he entered the Kingswood School, a Methodist institution near Bath which was noted for its high scholastic standards and for its simple life. The teachers at this school encouraged his interest in history which had been kindled at six by a child's history of England partly written by Rudyard Kipling. The eight years he spent at the school had, according to Parkes, a greater influence upon his mental and social development than any other experience, including the four years which he spent at Oxford University (Queen's College) where he majored in the classics and history. He took a "second class" in the final examination at Oxford and received his B.A. in 1927.

He chanced to hear of the Frances Riggs Fellowship which was offered to English students for a year of postgraduate work at the University of Michigan in Ann Arbor. Winning this fellowship "which few people knew about and for which there was therefore little competition", he entered the university in 1927.

Impressed by a sense of "limitless opportunity, of a civilization still in the making" in the United States, he decided to make it his permanent home. He started an intensive study of America and particularly of its religious background and heritage. This reading, encouraged by his professors, C. H. Van Tyne and U. B. Phillips, stimulated his interest in many fields of learning. He received a grant from the University of Michigan for his second year of study.

For his third year, he received a Lloyd Fellowship (a grant from the University of Michigan) and studied in libraries in New York and New England. His researches, along with his doctor's thesis on "The Great Awakening in New England" earned him a Ph. D. degree in 1929, and a year later, he joined the faculty of New York University as an instructor in history.

Soon moving to Staten Island the teacher divided his time between commuting to Washington Square, tending a large garden, and contributing articles and book reviews to magazines which included the *New England Quarterly, Hound and Horn, Symposium, New Republic, Nation, New Freeman, Scrutiny* and the *Southern Review.*

His first book, *Jonathan Edwards; the Fiery Puritan* (Minton, 1930) presented "the great Puritan in relation to his time" (*Bookman,* October 1930).

Supplementing his research with a trip to Mexico in 1936 under the auspices of the Committee on Cultural Relations with Latin America, he wrote *A History of Mexico* (Houghton, 1938, 1950). Maurice Halperin called the book "... a remarkably well balanced and sound interpretation. . ." (*New Republic,* January 4, 1939).

When his book on Communist theory, *Marxism; an Autopsy,* was published in 1939 by Houghton Mifflin, *Time* (October 23, 1939) wrote that "as an effort at disinterested, civilized social blue printing, [it] is head and shoulders above any documents of the right, left, or centre for a long time back."

Parkes wrote *Recent America* (Crowell, 1941), *Pragmatic Test* (Colt, 1942), and *World*

Blackstone Studios

HENRY BAMFORD PARKES

After War (Crowell, 1942). Reviewing the last-mentioned book, Hugh Gibson noted that this study of the problems of maintaining peace in the postwar world was "a valuable contribution to clear thinking" (*Saturday Review of Literature,* March 20, 1943) and F. R. Flournoy wrote that it was ". . . a penetrating criticism of two exceedingly dangerous types of postwar planning: (1) that which provides for a peace of force without justice; and (2) that which provides for a peace of justice without force" (*Social Education,* February 1943).

American Experience, an interpretation of the history and civilization of the United States as shown by the people themselves in their writings, manners and customs, was published by Knopf in 1947. G. W. Johnson (New York *Herald Tribune Weekly Book Review,* December 28, 1947), called it ". . . shrewd, penetrating."

Joseph Henry Jackson (*San Francisco Chronicle,* January 11, 1948), commenting on the book, wrote that Parkes is "quite as willing to point out the faults and weaknesses of the left as he is willing to note those of the right. . . He is . . . against the encouragement of class conflict in America—something both right and left would like to see."

His latest book, *The United States of America* (1953), covers both the social and political history of America. Reinhold Niebuhr, reviewing it in the *New Republic* (July 27, 1953, wrote: "Such a total survey is a masterpiece both of scholarship and of a wisdom which transcends scholarship." Parkes summarizes American achievement in all fields including the arts, industry, education, science and sociology, and integrates them into the whole social picture. He concludes that if Americans looked back "over the amazing story of their own past development . . . how one advance after another had been made through faith in the principles of freedom . . . they could feel confident that the problems ahead were capable of solution."

Parkes became an assistant professor at New York University in 1941; in 1945 he became an associate professor. In the summer of 1943, he was an editorial writer and a foreign policy analyst for the Baltimore *Evening Sun.* A newspaper concerns itself with day-to-day news interpretation; Parkes likes to "take longer views" and he found the *Sun's* requirements confining.

He returned in the winter to his work as teacher, student and writer of history and resumed contributing articles and book reviews to such periodicals as the New York *Herald Tribune Book Review, Sewanee Review, Partisan Review,* and *Saturday Review of Literature.*

In 1949 Parkes became a full professor at New York University. He has been the chairman of the American civilization group at the graduate school there since 1944. The historian extended his teaching at the university with lectures at the New School for Social Research in New York City from 1946 to 1950. He was also a visiting professor at the summer session of the University of Wyoming (1948) and of the University of Washington (1949).

Parkes has written that "my primary interest, as I have gradually realized, is in the history of civilization as a whole, particularly in literature, art and philosophy as expressions of social trends, and in the influence of ideas. . . . Although most of what I have published so far has dealt with the United States, I have been concerned for many years with the general development of Western civilization since the Greeks and expect to spend the rest of my life working on it."

Parkes married Mollie Brown, who was running a bookstore in Hartford, Connecticut when he met her, in 1931. They have two daughters, Nancy Rosa and Alison Rosemary Parkes. The historian has blue eyes and brown hair; he is five feet eleven inches tall and weighs 160 pounds.

Parkes is a Democrat and was a supporter of Adlai Stevenson in the last presidential election. He has written that he finds "much to agree with in both intelligent conservatism and intelligent liberalism". He served in 1952 and 1953 as chairman of the New York chapter of the American Studies Association, and is a member of the American Historical Association and the Academy of Political Science.

The professor enjoys traveling (usually by rail, except in Mexico where he likes to board a bus and mingle with the population) particularly in western United States and in Mexico. When not traveling, he enjoys tennis and swimming, and likes to read literary and aesthetic criticism.

References

Directory of American Scholars (1951)
Who's Who in America, 1952-53
Who's Who in New York, 1952

PASCAL, GABRIEL June 4, 1894-July 6, 1954 Film director; brought George Bernard Shaw's plays to the screen; was born in Hungary, became a British subject; joined the Imperial Theatre Company of Vienna; served in Hungarian Army in World War I; worked for movie studios in Germany, Scandinavian countries, France, and Italy; directed *Popoli Morturi* and *Narcotic* (1925); overcame Shaw's hostility to movie treatments of his plays; produced *Pygmalion* (1938), *Major Barbara, Caesar and Cleopatra,* and *Androcles and the Lion.* See *Current Biography,* (Jan.) 1942.

Obituary

N Y Times p31 Jl 7 '54

PELTZ, MRS. JOHN DEWITT See Peltz, M. E. (O.)

PELTZ, MARY ELLIS (OPDYCKE) May 4, 1896- Journalist; author

Address: b. c/o Metropolitan Opera Guild, 654 Madison Ave. New York 21; 2. 340 E. 72d St., New York 21

MARY ELLIS PELTZ

The publications director of the Metropolitan Opera Guild is Mary Ellis Peltz, who has also been editor of *Opera News* since 1936, and who has helped immeasurably to widen the circle of opera lovers in America. Of the nine books about opera which she has written, co-authored or edited, the most recent, *Accents on Opera* (1953), on which she collaborated with Boris Goldovsky, is currently being offered as a prize for listeners who submit questions on music to a panel of experts who answer them during the intermissions of the Saturday afternoon radio broadcasts from the Metropolitan Opera House.

In the last eighteen years nearly a quarter of a million students have attended the opera matinees given by the Guild at reduced prices. The Guild also serves to link opera lovers of the vast radio audience in a common fellowship. Every member of the Guild (and there are more than 50,000) receives *Opera News,* issued weekly during the opera season.

Mary Ellis Opdyke was born May 4, 1896 in New York City to Edith (Bell) and Leonard Echstein Opdycke. Her father, a lawyer, was a philanthropist, political reformer, translator and scholar. Her brother, Leonard Opdyke, is a professor of fine arts at Harvard University. Mrs. Peltz expressed her literary inclination early, editing the school yearbook of Miss Spence's School in New York City where she completed her secondary education in 1915. Her elementary education was in Miss Chapin's School.

At Barnard College (Columbia) where she majored in English and music, she edited the monthly undergraduate magazine, was student manager of the glee club and wrote the music for the Greek Games. She received her baccalaureate in 1920 *cum laude* and with honors in both her major fields.

Immediately following her graduation, Miss Opdyke joined the staff of the New York *Sun* (now combined with the *World-Telegram*) as assistant music critic, a position she held until the year of her marriage (1924). In the tradition of her father's humanitarian interests, Mrs. Peltz had worked in the American Red Cross during her student days (World War I), and after her marriage she became dramatic critic of the *Junior League Magazine,* the publication devoted to the social welfare activities of members of the Junior League of New York. In 1928 Mrs. Peltz was elected president of the league, a post she held until 1930, when she became arts and interests director of the parent organization, the Association of Junior Leagues of America.

During the Thirties Mrs. Peltz wrote articles and poems for a variety of publications. Some of her poems were published in *Harper's, Vogue* and *Poetry.* Her articles appeared in *The Churchman, New Republic, Town and Country, Musical America* and *Musical Courier.*

The inevitable decline of opera subscriptions in the season of 1931-32 (due to the economic depression) led Gatti-Casazza, the general manager, to "succumb to the overtures of the National Broadcasting Company, and on Christmas Day, 1931, the first Metropolitan performance was broadcast: a matinee of *Hänsel und Gretel.*" Nevertheless, as Mrs. Peltz wrote in her book *Behind the Gold Curtain,* "In spite of the continued support of the Juilliard Foundation and the commercial sponsorship of the broadcasts, the Metropolitan again found itself hard put to it to meet rising expenses and the waning resources of its subscription public."

Furthermore, the brilliant Giulio Gatti-Casazza retired in the spring of 1935 and his successor, Herbert Witherspoon, collapsed from a heart attack. His successor, Edward Johnson, who took office five days after Witherspoon's death, found only a handful of singers under contract

PELTZ, MARY ELLIS—*Continued*

for the following year and manifold financial problems. Mrs. August Belmont, the first woman member of the Metropolitan Board, who already had a reputation as a fund raiser, came to the new manager's assistance with the organization of the Metropolitan Opera Guild, composed of laymen who worked to broaden interest in and support of the Metropolitan from coast to coast.

The first innovation sponsored by the Guild shortly after the founding, was the publication of a small weekly newspaper covering news of the opera in general and the Metropolitan in particular. *Opera News* began publication in May 1936 and was placed under the editorial supervision of Mrs. Peltz. Since its inception, she has not only assumed full responsibility as editor, but has written all the unsigned articles in the magazine—several hundred of them since 1936. In addition she has also been responsible for all the publicity material for the Guild.

She participates frequently in the discussions with other music experts during the intermissions of the opera broadcasts.

In an article on the activities of the Metropolitan Opera Guild in *Theatre Arts,* December, 1953, Mrs. Peltz described the series of opera matinees presented for the students of public, private and parochial schools in and near New York at greatly reduced prices. The Guild holds various art and music contests and works with teachers in co-ordinating group projects with the operas to be performed. "To build an audience for the future that will know more of scores than stars, to open the eyes of the younger generations to a live, dynamic, operatic tradition that flows on from one golden age to another, gathering new currents in its course—these are among the most important functions of the Opera Guild."

During the period of her editorship of *Opera News* Mrs. Peltz has written, edited or co-authored nine books: *Opera Primer* (1936); *Metropolitan Operagrams* (1937); *Metropolitan Opera Guide* (With Robert Lawrence) (1939); *Spotlights on the Stars* (1943); *Metropolitan Opera Milestones* (1944); *Your Metropolitan Opera* (1944); *Opera Lover's Companion* (Ziff-Davis, 1948); *Behind the Gold Curtain* (Farrar Straus, 1950) and *Accents on Opera* (with Boris Goldovsky, Farrar Straus, 1953) which contains a series of essays stressing known and little-known facts, with vital statistics on operatic premières. These books are directed generally to the listeners to the Saturday afternoon broadcasts from the "Met".

The San Francisco *Chronicle* criticized *Behind the Gold Curtain* as being too eclectic to be valuable as a work of reference on the history of the Metropolitan and frowned on its tendency to glorify the opera company. The *Saturday Review of Literature,* however, noted that it contained "the highlights for those who do not want all the detail to be found in more elaborate works on the subject." *The Opera Lover's Companion* was praised by the *Saturday Review* for its wealth of valuable information.

Mrs. Peltz has brown hair and "grey-green" eyes. She is five feet five-and-a-half inches tall. She married John DeWitt Peltz on June 6, 1924. Her husband is a social worker with the American Red Cross. The Peltzes have three children: John DeWitt, Jr., Mary Ellis and Henry Stevenson. Mrs. Peltz enjoys needlework, writing poetry and "mild mountain climbing." She is a Protestant Episcopalian. Her clubs are the Colony in New York and the Bar Harbor Club in Maine where she has a summer home. During World War II Mrs. Peltz worked 500 hours as a nurse's aide for the Red Cross.

She is an honorary member of the Junior League of New York. Mrs. Peltz acknowledges the guiding influence of Professor Minor W. Latham (of Barnard College), the late Richard Ward Greene Welling and Mrs. August Belmont in the shaping of her career.

References

Opera N Ja 14 '46
Who's Who in New York, 1938
Who's Who in the East (1951)

PÉREZ JIMÉNEZ, MARCOS (pā'râs hē-mă'nĕs măr'cōōs) Apr. 25, 1914- President of Venezuela

Address: Palacio Miraflores, Caracas, Venezuela

The President of Venezuela, a country containing rich sources of oil and iron ore, is Colonel Marcos Pérez Jiménez, who ruled as provisional president from December 1952 to April 1953, and as constitutional President since that time. A career soldier, Pérez Jiménez rose to military leadership during the 1945 revolution (when President Medina Angarita was deposed), and was one of the Army officers who ousted the Acción Democrática government in 1948, establishing military rule under a three-man junta. As a member of the triumvirate, Colonel Pérez Jiménez was Minister of Defense.

Since the 1948 *coup d'état* the government has spent two billion dollars on national improvements. "Dedication Week" was celebrated in December 1953, after which the new public works began operating. In March 1954 Caracas, the capital of Venezuela, was the site of the Tenth Inter-American Conference.

The city's population has grown during the past ten years (since oil was discovered within its boundaries) from 300,000 to nearly 1,000,000. The royalties from oil and iron ore have made it possible to finance many of the public works programs introduced by President Pérez Jiménez.

"The new prosperity," reports *Life* (September 13, 1954) "has enabled many Venezuelan workers, whose average wages have doubled in ten years, to replace their rope-soled sandals with shoes, buy canned goods in new supermarkets and satisfy a craving for chicken and ice cream. . . The dictatorial rule of 'P.J.', as President Pérez Jiménez is referred to by Americans, has some definite advantages."

Marcos Pérez Jiménez was born on April 25, 1914 in the state of Táchira, Venezuela, the son of Juan Pérez Bustamente and the former Adela Jiménez. He was educated at the Colegio Gremios Unidos in Cúcuta, Colombia; Escuela Militar de Caracas in Venezuela (comparable to West Point); and the Superior War School in Lima, Peru. He was commissioned a second lieutenant in the Venezuelan Army in 1934. The young officer served with the technical service at Maracay, and later was a member of the faculty of Escuela Militar.

During the presidency of General Isáias Medina Angarita (1941-1945), Captain Pérez Jiménez became section chief of the general staff, and received the rank of lieutenant colonel. Dissatisfied with the Medina Angarita regime, the Acción Democrática party and several young army officers, including Pérez Jiménez, joined in a *coup d'etat,* overthrowing the government on October 18, 1945. They installed Rómulo Betancourt, a leader of Acción Democrática, as provisional president. Pérez Jiménez became Army Chief of Staff.

Professor Robert J. Alexander (New York *Herald Tribune,* December 30, 1952) wrote that one of Latin America's most liberal constitutions was enacted in 1947. It provided for popular election of the President and legislature, as well as universal suffrage. Rómulo Gallegos Freire, well-known novelist, was elected President under this constitution in December 1947. The New York *Times* (November 14, 1950) commented that this was Venezuela's first democratic election. During its 124-year history, virtually every government has taken office by military *coup* and remained in power as long as the dominant faction in the Army supported it.

The Acción Democrática government began a program of economic development. Most observers believed the new government was attempting to institute democratic rule, although the New York *Times* (December 3, 1952) commented that the Gallegos regime "proved inefficient, harsh and on the dictatorial side." *Fortune* (May 1949) noted: "The program of Acción Democrática imperiled the status of the military. It became clearer and clearer to the young officers that the government recognized for them . . . only a mundane everyday mission to support the elected government. Moreover there were intimate links between Army factions and conservative merchants and landowners who were duly horrified at the developing social revolution."

Gallegos was overthrown on November 24, 1948 in a military *coup* led by Lieutenant Colonel Carlos Delago Chalbaud, the Minister of Defense. Delago Chalbaud established a three-man junta with Lieutenant Colonel Luís Felipe Llovera Páez and Pérez Jiménez, who became the new Minister of Defense. The Acción Democrática party was outlawed on December 9, 1948. On January 21, 1949 the United States granted diplomatic recognition to the military regime but said the *de facto* recognition "does not imply any judgment whatsoever as to the domestic policy" of Venezuela.

Delgado Chalbaud was assassinated on November 13, 1950. Dr. Germán Suárez Flamerich, a civilian, succeeded him, but according to

Wide World

MARCOS PÉREZ JIMÉNEZ

Herbert L. Matthews (New York *Times,* April 28, 1951), Pérez Jiménez was "the real power in Venezuela." He was credited with sponsoring the long promised "electoral statute" that provided for a constituent assembly to determine a new form of government, and the organization of a pro-junta political party, Frente Electoral Independiente (F.E.I.). In 1951 Pérez Jiménez received the military rank of colonel.

Ex-Venezuelan Ambassador to the United States, Dr. Antonio Martín Araujo, a member of the original junta Cabinet, charged in a New York *Times* interview November 22, 1952 that the junta conducted a "reign of terror," assassinated army officers and others opposed to the government, and jailed "approximately 4,000 citizens, including women and children."

These charges were vigorously denied by the Venezuelan Ambassador to the United States, César González, who has said: "The present constitutional government respects human rights."

An election was held on November 30, 1952. *Time* (December 8, 1952) reported that 2,000,000 Venezuelan voters went to the polls from "jungle clearings and Caracas villas." Early returns gave the lead to a minority party Union Republicana Democrática (U.R.D.). The New York *Times* (December 3, 1952) reported that censorship obscured election news in Venezuela until December 2, when the Supreme Electoral Council said that of 1,193,240 votes counted F.E.I. had 570,123, the U.R.D., 473,880, and Copei (Christian Socialists), 138,003.

Sam Pope Brewer of the New York *Times* reported on January 28, 1953 that the opposition U.R.D. polled 1,000,000 votes to 350,000 each for the pro-government candidates and the Copei party. Pérez Jiménez and his group "issued figures that would show victory for the

PÉREZ JIMÉNEZ, MARCOS—*Continued*

government's backers . . . [and] Dr. Jovito Villalba and six other U.R.D. leaders were forced to leave Venezuela."

The junta presented its resignation to the Army on December 2, 1952, and ranking Army officers named Colonel Pérez Jiménez provisional President. The national Constituent Assembly confirmed him in that position on January 9, 1953, pending the re-establishment of a "constitutional government."

The Assembly approved a new constitution which was signed by the President and promulgated on April 15, 1953. It provides for the direct election of a President and members of the lower house of Congress and contains a Bill of Rights. Eight transistory measures were appended to the main text, one of which empowered the Constituent Assembly to form a new government for the initial five-year constitutional period beginning April 19, 1953. Accordingly, the Constituent Assembly elected Pérez Jiménez as constitutional President on April 17, 1953. With the installation of the Congreso Nacional on April 19, the Constituent Assembly was dissolved.

On January 20, 1953 the Associated Press reported that Venezuela had imposed tight censorship on outgoing news. Pérez Jiménez has stated that censorship does not exist to defend the government's political actions but "to protect against any abuse of freedom of the press which incites against the interests of the nation" (New York *Times,* December 14, 1953).

During the years of military regime, Venezuela has spent two billion dollars on government improvements. These were opened to the public during "Dedication Week" early in December 1953. *Time* (December 14, 1953) described the superhighway from Caracas to the sea as "Venezuela's most daring piece of engineering," and "more expensive per mile than any other in the world."

Other completed projects were apartment houses that replaced forty-five blocks of Caracas slums, 107 water systems, thirty-nine electric plants, sixty-three schools, thirty-two hospitals and clinics, and an underground station that houses 600 buses. In Caracas, Centro Bolívar (comparable to Rockefeller Center), Hotel Tamanaco, a 400-room hotel, and the "finest officers' club in the world" were built.

Sydney Gruson (New York *Times,* December 18, 1953) wrote that "oil is the backbone of the booming Venezuelan economy; it supplies approximately 65 per cent of the government's annual revenues of about $700,000,000; [this is] 98 per cent of the Central Bank's foreign exchange requirements and 90 per cent of the country's total foreign exchange needs." There is a fifty-fifty split of oil profits between the government and the oil companies. About 73.6 per cent of the total oil imported to the United States comes from Venezuela. In turn, 72 per cent of Venezuela's imports, all paid in cash, are from the United States.

In an effort to develop other industries, Venezuela has encouraged U.S. Steel's endeavors to mine iron ore. On January 9, 1954 U.S. Steel's first shipment of iron ore was transported through a newly constructed channel designed to let iron ore ships reach mines on the Orinoco River.

Bethlehem Steel began its operations in 1941, building rail lines and river ports. A law requires that 75% of the workers in all mines be native Venezuelans. According to *Life* (September 13, 1954), the United States now has its biggest private foreign investment ($2 billion) in Venezuela, and one of its largest overseas civilian colonies (23,000).

After it was announced that the Tenth Inter-American Conference would take place in Caracas in March 1954, President José Figueres Ferrer of Costa Rica declared that his country would not be represented at the conference because of the lack of civil rights in Venezuela. All of the other twenty nations, however, were represented.

At the conference, the United States sponsored a resolution which was adopted by a 17 to 1 vote (Guatemala against, Argentina and Mexico abstaining) which declared that the "control of the political institutions of any American state by the international Communist movement" was "a threat to the sovereignty and political independence of the American states." and would call for "consultation and appropriate action in accordance with existing treaties."

Pérez Jiménez married Flor Mariá Chalbaud; they have three children. The President is a corresponding member of the International Institute of American Ideals, and an honorary lieutenant colonel of Ecuador. He has received the General Urdaneta Medal, Military Order of Ayacucho, Grand Cross Cóndor de los Andes (Bolivia), Orden Militar de Qyacucho (Peru), Grand Cross of Order del Sol (Peru), National Honor al Mérito (Haiti), Orden del Quetzal (Guatemala), Medalla Abdon Calderon (Ecuador), Grand Cross of Leon Nederlandes, Legion of Honor (France), and Grand Cross, Order of Leopold II (Belgium).

John Crosby (New York *Herald Tribune,* December 11, 1953) who visited Venezuela during "Dedication Week" described the President as "a hard working, very capable and benevolent despot" and commented that almost everything about Venezuela was "faintly incredible."

President Pérez Jiménez has stated: "Venezuela . . . suffers from a shortage of capital and . . . technical assistance, necessary factors for the development of its natural riches and for industrialization. . . . Thus, my country can do no less than look with satisfaction upon the inflow of foreign capital . . . after a short time Venezuela will be able to finance the greater part of its own development with resources derived from the national income" (*U.S. News & World Report,* June 26, 1953).

References

Life 37: 122+ S 13 '54 por
International Who's Who, 1953
Who's Who in Latin America (1951)
World Biography (1954)

PER KROHG *See* Krohg, P. (L.)

PETERS, ROBERTA May 4, 1930- Singer
Address: b. c/o Hurok Attractions, Inc., 711 Fifth Ave., New York 22

Periodically, on the great stage of New York's Metropolitan Opera House, a real-life Cinderella story is enacted—a young, pretty, previously unknown American girl makes her debut, is accorded an ovation from the audience, wins the approval of the press and overnight becomes a star. Such is the story of Roberta Peters, who substituted for an indisposed singer on November 17, 1950, in the role of Zerlina in Mozart's opera *Don Giovanni*. Since then she has become the Metropolitan's "most celebrated pinch-hitter" as well as a singer with a rare *sopra acutissima* (very high coloratura) voice who has mastered twenty roles.

Among her recent roles were Susanna in *Marriage of Figaro* (January 28, 1954) and Rosina in *The Barber of Seville* (March 1, 1954); of the latter, music critic Louis Biancolli wrote: "It was a pleasure to hear that delightful new Rosina, Roberta Peters, again—to follow her nimble flights into the vocal stratosphere. The line was smooth and warm with a fetching blend of word and note. Her spoken Italian was just as beautiful, and so was she" (New York *World Telegram and Sun*, March 2, 1954).

She was born Roberta Peterman on May 4, 1930, the daughter of Ruth (Hirsch) and Solomon Peterman. Her parents are of Austrian stock and live in the Bronx, New York City. Her father is a shoe salesman and her mother is a milliner. Roberta attended Public School 64 and Wade Junior High School from which she was graduated in 1943.

Seven years of intensive study preceded Roberta's engagement by the Met. She was in junior high school when Jan Peerce sighted her as potential opera material. He suggested to her family that she study with William Herman, Patrice Munsel's teacher and coach for numerous opera stars. Herman found the thirteen-year old girl's voice promising and accepted her as a pupil. He outlined the grueling program for the years ahead. Roberta promised to adhere to it and her parents agreed to finance it.

As her musical education progressed, Roberta's voice attracted more and more attention. Without a date on her official calendar, she mastered three complete concert programs. Eventually, she turned down offers from the Trapp Singers, from the producers of *Lute Song* and *Street Scene*, holding back for the greatest prize of all, the Met contract.

There were private tutoring lessons in French, German and Italian, instruction in dramatics and ballet. There were long months of exercises and scales, practice and more practice, before actual operatic roles could be tackled. Now, Roberta commands twenty of them, practically the entire coloratura repertory, from Carolina in *Il Matrimonio Segreto* to Adele in *Die Fledermaus*.

ROBERTA PETERS

To strengthen her diaphragm and keep in excellent physical form, she underwent rigorous physical training with a professional teacher and "made" *Life* magazine with the caption "Diva With Muscle", plus photos of her 175 pound trainer balancing on her operatic diaphragm, a ten pound bag of gravel on top of her head and other muscle and lung-toning techniques.

After six years of concentrated study, Roberta's dream began to take form. On November 9, 1949, she sang for Sol Hurok, veteran manager of many successful artists. Hurok was sufficiently impressed to do what he had done only once before in his long career as an impresario. He signed the neophyte to a contract and made careful plans for Miss Peters. His first step was to arrange an audition in New York's Town Hall for his booking representatives throughout the United States. Miss Peters made a sensational impression.

On January 23, 1950 there was another audition. This time, at the Metropolitan, she sang for musical secretary Max Rudolf who accompanied her at the piano. In the darkened auditorium Roberta sang the difficult "Queen of the Night" aria from Mozart's *The Magic Flute*. At the close, conductor Fritz Stiedry wandered in and Max Rudolf asked her to start all over again. A second time, she repeated the aria. Two days later, there was another audition—this time, before Rudolf Bing, the opera's general manager, as well as Stiedry, Max Rudolf, and conductor Fritz Reiner. The outcome of these auditions was a coveted Met contract.

Now, Roberta was on the Met's payroll but no roles were assigned to her. First, she became one of the small group of young Metropolitan artists enrolled in the Kathryn Turney Long opera courses. She received advanced professional training in acting, stage deportment, foreign languages, and vocal interpreta-

PETERS, ROBERTA—*Continued*

tion, in classes taught for the most part by members of the Metropolitan staff, right in the opera house. These courses are made possible by a fund left in bequest to the opera in 1942 by Mrs. Kathryn Turney Long, a member of the original board of the Metropolitan Opera Guild. In the group, Roberta was being groomed for a January 1951 debut as Queen of the Night in *The Magic Flute*.

Then the call came, two months ahead of time, which skyrocketed her into the front ranks of America's young operatic singers. Roberta's rise to stardom came on the night of November 17, 1950. She was twenty years old then and had never sung on any professional stage before. She had never had a rehearsal with an orchestra. Five hours before curtain time the opera management called her to substitute for Nadine Conner in the lead of Mozart's *Don Giovanni*, the role of Zerlina, with an all-star cast before a sold-out house. The Met was gambling on a completely unknown singer but one the management knew to have been meticulously schooled. Whirlwind rehearsals with stage director Herbert Graf in cues, and stage business and assistant manager Max Rudolf, artistic administrator, and final instruction an hour before curtain call from conductor Fritz Reiner, were her only immediate preparation for her debut.

But Roberta was ready. Critics reported that her singing and acting showed the ease of a veteran; her voice, in the big house, bright, focused, as clear as a bell; her performance, smooth, charming; her command of Italian, polished. Audience applause was thunderous, and thus Roberta Peters was established as the Met's brightest new coloratura and youngest prima donna.

Of her debut Fritz Reiner said after the performance: "She was wonderful. A really gifted girl. Her fine preparation should be a lesson to other young American singers. When the chance came, she was qualified" (New York *Herald Tribune*, November 18, 1950). During her first season, Roberta scored again as Rosina in *The Barber of Seville*. She sang the Queen of the Night in *The Magic Flute* and Gilda in *Rigoletto*. In July 1951 she sang in the revival of Balfe's *The Bohemian Girl* at London's Royal Opera House, Covent Garden, Sir Thomas Beecham conducting.

The "Met" had fostered Roberta's career. It was to foster her romance as well. On March 30, 1952 she was married to baritone Robert Merrill, a fellow star of the opera. Jan Peerce sang at their wedding before a gathering of 1,000 guests and 2,000 sidewalk well-wishers. However, several months later they announced their intention of ending their marriage (they were divorced in Juarez, Mexico on June 26, 1952.) The couple made headlines on June 7, 1952 when they sang duets to a crowd of 17,000 attending the fourth annual *Music Under the Stars* benefit program at Ebbets Field, Brooklyn, and again when they sang on July 12 before 9,000 at the Lewisohn Stadium in New York. So well did Merrill and Miss Peters serve their art on this occasion that critic Louis Biancolli of the *World Telegram and Sun* was moved to comment on "their marvelous singing all through the program," and of Roberta in particular, "Miss Peters came through like an Olympics winner."

Hearing of the critical acclaim Miss Peters won for her initial Metropolitan Opera performance, a Hollywood company offered her a contract to do her own Cinderella story in a picture called *Debut* but negotiations were never completed. It was very much to Miss Peters' satisfaction that she waited to make her screen bow in 20th Century Fox's *Tonight We Sing*, a film based on the life story of her manager Sol Hurok, the impresario, which had its premiere at the Radio City Music Hall, in February 1953.

In January 1954 Miss Peters substituted for Nadine Conner and sang the role of Susanna in Mozart's *Marriage of Figaro*. She had never sung the opera and had not studied it for five years but "she called in a relay of coaches, who put her through the plot, brushed her up on the endless chatter of Italian recitatives," reported *Time*, (February 8). At 5:30 she was eating a pre-performance steak and at the end of the two and a half hour performance she displayed "the kind of confidence and musicianship that critics like to call aplomb . . . she skipped through the role without blowing a cue, delivered herself of some of the sweetest-sounding high notes to be heard anywhere."

Other last-minute substitutions made by the young singer were as Gilda in *Rigoletto*, and as Adele in *Die Fledermaus* replacing other sopranos. She also appeared on a television version of James Thurber's fairytale with music, *The Thirteen Clocks*, in the role of the Princess. She has a voice of exceptional purity and with Lily Pons singing less often, and Patrice Munsel dividing her time between the Met and her child, young Roberta is carrying a veteran's load of soubrette and coloratura roles (*Time*, February 8, 1954).

As Rosina in *The Barber of Seville* young Miss Peters "achieved a new standard of performance" (*Christian Science Monitor*, February 27, 1954). "Her brilliant account of the coloratura role was enhanced by her assumption of the original music for the lesson scene . . . a proving ground of vocal art. Her negotiating of its difficult passages brought her new distinction."

Roberta Peters weighs 119 pounds, is five feet, two inches tall, is blue-eyed and has brown hair.

She enjoys sports, and hopes to find time to improve her tennis game. She likes parties but does not drink or smoke. Her only fear is that when she's onstage at the Met she might sometime trip over something and fall. In the summer she likes to paint seascapes at Provincetown. She hopes some day to return to school to study philosophy. She likes to keep a diary of her impressions of people and events.

References

Life 31:97+ O 8 '51
Mus Am 70:13 D 1 '50 por
Newsweek 36:78 N 27 '50 por
Time 56:38 N 27 '50; 63:40 F 8 '54 por

PICKEN, MARY BROOKS Aug. 6, 1886-
Author; sewing authority; teacher

Address: b. c/o McGraw-Hill Publishing Co., 330 W. 42nd St., New York 36; 11 E. 73rd St., New York 21; h. Arcadia, Quaker Hill, Pawling, N.Y.

Countless millions of women in all areas of the world have learned home sewing and decorating from the ninety-four books written by Mary Brooks Picken, one of America's best-known authorities on dress, fabric, design, and sewing for over thirty years. Her latest book is *Advanced Sewing* (Fawcett, 1954), and her most widely distributed is *The Singer Sewing Book* which was selected in 1949 by the Book-of-the-Month Club for special promotion. A revised edition, released in 1953 by the McGraw-Hill Publishing Company, has increased the total number of copies sold to over 1,000,000. The book has been translated into six languages and is being sold in eighty-seven countries.

Mrs. Picken is the author of *The Language of Fashion* (Funk, 1939), the first dictionary ever compiled by a woman (a new edition is scheduled for 1955). She believes that "Fashion is a living, vital force that tells more about the people of any age than any other one thing."

Young people have a vigorous ally in Mrs. Picken; she has aided and encouraged countless students and newcomers to the fashion world, and helped them to get a start in business. Her own experience has included the vice-presidency of the Woman's Institute of Domestic Arts and Sciences at Scranton, Pennsylvania (1916-1925); fashion and dressmaking editor for *Pictorial Review* (1925-1927); director of her own fashion and fabric school (1939-1950) in New York City, organizer of fashion clinics for home economists, and instructor at Columbia University in "economics of fashion." She is the only woman trustee of the Fashion Institute of Technology, and is a founder of the Fashion Group.

Mary Brooks was born on a farm near Arcadia, Kansas on August 6, 1886, daughter of Christopher Columbus Brooks and Mattie E. (Buchanan) Brooks. She attended a country school near Arcadia. At home, her pioneer grandmother taught her to card wool, spin and weave fabrics and carpets, and to sew and mend. At eleven, Mary made a complete layette for her baby brother and in her twelfth year made seventeen shirts for her father and brothers. She sewed dresses, copied from a pattern book, for her mother, sisters and herself.

After a dressmaking course in Kansas City, Mary went to Boston and studied designing, cutting, fitting and tailoring. After Miss Brooks's marriage to Harold Orlando Picken on November 8, 1906, she lived in Kansas City. Eager to share her knowledge of sewing, Mrs. Picken taught evening classes at the Y.W.C.A. She also taught sewing to women prisoners at Leavenworth Penitentiary.

MARY BROOKS PICKEN

Following the death of her husband in 1911, Mrs. Picken became an instructor at the American College of Dressmaking in Kansas City, Missouri. She was later made supervisor of a large staff of teachers who taught residence classes and correspondence courses. To shorten the process of making a single garment, she experimented and discovered new methods which simplified both dressmaking and tailoring.

The opportunity to write textbooks came in 1914 when she was engaged by the Woman's Institute of Domestic Arts and Sciences at Scranton, Pennsylvania to prepare complete courses in sewing and dressmaking for correspondence instruction. She spent two years writing the sixty-four books that were grouped and published by the institute in twelve volumes. The school opened in February 1916 and Mrs. Picken was named vice-president and director of instruction. In the nine years that followed, 253,000 students enrolled for home instruction in sewing, dressmaking, designing, millinery and cooking. Mrs. Picken had a staff of 300 teachers. The school was the most extensive project in the study of household arts that had been undertaken up to that time in the United States.

The courses became so well known that in 1919, the Singer Sewing Machine Company asked Mrs. Picken to write a series of books featuring machine sewing. These were followed by *The Secrets of Distinctive Dress* (1918) and *Sewing Materials* (1924), published by the institute. *Inspiration and Fashion Service,* the institute's magazine, was edited by Mrs. Picken from 1920 to 1925, and she contributed many articles to farm and home magazines.

Moving to New York in 1925, she became fashion and dressmaking editor of *Pictorial Review.* During her two years there she conducted a department of dressmaking instruction, wrote articles for the magazine's asso-

PICKEN, MARY BROOKS—*Continued*

ciated publications and covered the Paris fashion openings.

She decided in 1928 to establish her own studio and offer classes in fashion and fabric styling for employees of department stores and fabric manufacturers. Graduates of these classes later obtained top positions with leading stores. She was asked by manufacturers of threads, fabrics and patterns to write books and articles to promote home sewing. These included a series for the Dennison Manufacturing Company on home decorating, a series for Spool Cotton Company, and a book on crochet and needlework for Cartier-Bresson. An extension course, "economics of fashion," was conducted by Mrs. Picken at Columbia University from 1931 to 1933.

The Mary Brooks Picken School at 285 Madison Avenue, New York, was established in 1939, and as a special feature, Mrs. Picken organized a series of fashion clinics. Manufacturers' representatives met with hundreds of home economists, state supervisors, teachers, and students and supplied fashion ideas, charts, materials and a wealth of information designed for classroom use.

In September 1941, Mrs. Picken spoke at the New York Library Association conference at Lake Mohonk, New York. Her address, "Fashion's Story," appeared in the June 1942 *Wilson Library Bulletin.* She cited the novels of Edith Wharton, Gertrude Atherton, James Hilton, Daphne du Maurier, Jane Austen, George Eliot, John Galsworthy, and Louisa May Alcott as especially descriptive of the fashions worn in various historical periods "which present an authentic picture of the styles of yesterday . . . and an excellent background of fashion history."

Observing the need for a book which would define all the words and phrases of fashion, she collected material and assembled it in *The Language of Fashion.* Described as a "dictionary and digest of fabric, sewing and dress," the book contains approximately 8,000 words and 600 line-drawings associated with wearing apparel and accessories, and includes the origin and history of fashion phrases.

She also wrote *Modern Dressmaking Made Easy* (Funk, 1940), *Sewing for the Home* (Harper, 1941) and *Mending Made Easy; the ABC and XYZ of fabric conservation* (Harper, 1943) which was used as a textbook in Great Britain during World War II.

Many of Mrs. Picken's articles have appeared in national magazines under various pseudonyms: Martha Buchanan, Marilyn Madison, Eleanor McCleary, Mary Sumner and Jane Warren Wells. A popular series of "how-to . . ." articles by Mary Brooks Picken has been published at intervals since 1944 in *Better Homes and Gardens.* Mrs. Picken closed her school in 1950 to devote more time to writing.

She accepted the post of fashion and homemaking editor for *Everywoman's Magazine* in 1950 but resigned in August 1953. Her book *Sewing Magic* (McGraw-Hill) was published in 1952, and *Simplified Sewing* (Fawcett) a large-sized, paper-bound book appeared in 1950, and was reissued in 1953.

An honorary D.Litt. degree was conferred upon Mrs. Picken in 1948 by Albion College, Albion, Michigan. She was president of the Fashion Group from 1934 to 1936, an international organization which she helped to found, and has served continuously on the advisory council. She is one of five original directors of the Costume Institute, now part of New York City's Metropolitan Museum of Art; a member of the board of the School of American Craftsmen, Rochester Institute; and of the fashion advisory board of Stephens College, Columbia, Missouri. Governor Thomas E. Dewey appointed Mrs. Picken, in November 1951, as the first woman trustee of the Fashion Institute of Technology, the only needle-trade college in America comparable to trade colleges for women in Europe.

She married G. Lynn Sumner, an advertising executive, on November 21, 1931. She and her husband originated the idea for the highly successful DuBarry Success School in 1939 and planned the promotion campaign. Since Mr. Sumner's death on April 7, 1952, Mrs. Picken has maintained a studio in her town house at 11 East Seventy-third Street in Manhattan.

She has a week-end home in Pawling, New York where she has acquired a reputation as a hostess, entertaining celebrities at festive dinner parties in her home on Quaker Hill. The guests often include her neighbors, Mr. and Mrs. Lowell Thomas, Governor and Mrs. Thomas E. Dewey, and Judge Charles E. Murphy of the New York Supreme Court "the lone Democrat," she notes, "among the Republicans on Quaker Hill."

Mrs. Picken, a Protestant, is a member of the Christ Church (nonsectarian) at Quaker Hill. She is a Republican and has engaged actively in several campaigns. She has a youthful, dynamic appearance, white hair, brown eyes, and is of medium height. She believes that young women who are able to sew have a better chance for a happy and successful marriage, and always have earning power in their finger tips.

References

N Y World-Telegram p7 Jl 2 '41 por
Who's Who in America, 1954-55

PIERSON, WARREN LEE Aug. 29, 1896-
Organization official; lawyer; banker
Address: b. 630 5th Ave., New York 22; h. 655 Park Ave., New York 21

NOTE: This biography supersedes the article which appeared in *Current Biography* in 1941.

A leader in the field of international economics for twenty years, Warren Lee Pierson is chairman of the United States Council of the International Chamber of Commerce which acts as spokesman for American businessmen on world-wide problems of trade and finance. Pierson, who assumed this post in January

1953, is also chairman of Trans World Airlines, Inc., has been director of a number of corporations with foreign connections, and has acquired broad experience in international fiscal affairs through his nine years (1936-1945) as president of the Export-Import Bank of Washington, D.C., and his participation in various Inter-American conferences. From 1951 to 1953, in the rank of Special Ambassador, he represented the United States on the Tripartite Commission on German Debts.

Warren Lee Pierson is the son of Louis W. and Hilda (Pearson) Pierson, who a few years after their child's birth in Princeton, Minnesota, on August 29, 1896, moved to California, where the boy was reared and educated. His graduation from the University of California in 1917 was followed at once by enlistment in the American Ambulance Corps serving with the French Army. Joining the American Expeditionary Force in 1918, young Pierson attended the Saumur Artillery School and received a commission as first lieutenant. Until the end of World War I he fought in the 101st Field Artillery of the 26th Division of the U.S. Army.

When he was released from military service in 1919, Pierson entered Harvard Law School to prepare for his LL.B. degree, which he received in 1922. In the same year he was admitted to the bar of the State of California and until 1933, practiced law in Los Angeles, first as a member of the firm of O'Melveny, Milliken, Tuller & Macneil and later independently. While his practice was largely in corporation law, he acted as counsel for several irrigation districts and took part in cases concerning water rights.

Called to Washington, D.C., in 1933, Pierson was engaged for a year as special counsel for the Reconstruction Finance Corporation. Appointed in 1934 general counsel of the Export-Import Bank, he took office within two years in the dual post of general counsel and president, a position that he held until April 1945. The Export-Import Bank, a government-owned institution which in 1939 became a unit of the Federal Loan Agency, was established in 1934 to finance imports, exports, and exchanges of commodities between the United States and foreign countries.

During World War II Pierson, who was regarded as a key man in Latin American affairs in Washington, took a direct part in a number of negotiations for loans to Central and South American countries, which by 1941 had borrowed almost $232,000,000 of the $700,000,000 provided to the Bank by Congress. He made many trips to Latin America, especially to Brazil, to discuss credit operations, investigate new sources of war materials and speed up the production of material for which the United States had contracted.

On other government service, Pierson was a member from 1934 to 1936 of the National Emergency Council, from 1938 to 1944 of the Executive Committee on Commercial Policy, and from 1940 to 1945 of the Inter-American Financial and Economic Advisory Committee.

Fabian Bachrach

WARREN LEE PIERSON

He visited Rio de Janeiro in January 1942 as advisor to the U.S. delegation at the third Meeting of the Ministers of Foreign Affairs of the American Republics. In a similar capacity he attended the United Nations Monetary Conference in Bretton Woods, New Hampshire, in July 1944 and the Inter-American Conference on Problems of War and Peace, meeting in Chapultepec in 1945.

As Special U.S. Ambassador, a rank conferred on him by President Harry S. Truman in June 1951, Pierson served as American representative on the Tripartite Commission on German Debts, which had been established at a meeting in 1950 of the foreign ministers of France, Great Britain, and the United States. "The commission," stated Lawrence Farrant, financial writer of the New York *World-Telegram and Sun* (December 20, 1952), "has worked out a plan for settlement of German prewar external debts, made doubly confusing by two world wars." After a series of intergovernmental agreements (designed to settle these debts) entered into force on September 16, 1953, Pierson resigned.

He assumed office as chairman of the association which represents American businessmen in the International Chamber of Commerce on January 1, 1953, to serve for a two-year term in succession to George A. Sloan. The International Chamber of Commerce has been described by Ralph Hendershot of the New York *World-Telegram and Sun* (December 19, 1952) as "a world-wide organization of businessmen. They meet from time to time to help find solutions to the more pressing economic problems of the world. They usually pass their recommendations along to the officials of their respective governments, helping in that way to smooth over some of the rough spots in this highly important field."

(Continued next page)

PIERSON, WARREN LEE—*Continued*

When announcement was made of Pierson's nomination as head of the United States Council in December 1952, he proposed the setting up of a citizens' commission to advise the U.S. government on international economic policies. He urged at this time the establishment of a long-range foreign economic program, which he later discussed in a speech before the Council of World Affairs of Greater Kansas City, Missouri on January 24, 1953.

Among Pierson's recommendations was the administration by one agency of all government activities in such matters as investments, currency, technical and military assistance, and export-import trade. He further suggested that the United States open her market to more foreign producers, that private foreign investments be facilitated, and that convertibility of major currencies be encouraged.

During the year the new chairman made numerous other speeches and public statements on the world economic situation, international trade, and U.S. tariff policies. He told the San Francisco Commonwealth Club that the foreign economic policy of the United States was "centered too much on Western Europe to the exclusion of Asia." His program for a new American tariff policy included reduction in tariff rates, limiting the use of import quotas, and simplification of customs procedures and "red tape."

These views were also voiced in an address in Washington, D.C., before a meeting of the Chamber of Commerce of the United States, where Pierson said that the United States had "inherited the role of unifier to the non-Soviet orbit" and that its "greatest single obstacle" to accepting leadership was its "deep-seated protectionist traditions."

Meeting in May 1953 in Vienna, Austria, some 1,000 businessmen representing fifty countries attended the fourteenth biennial Congress of the International Chamber of Commerce. Pierson, who headed the U.S. delegation, spoke at the plenary session on the benefits of international trade, expressing his view that American trade policies would gradually become more liberal. Action, however, by the United States alone, he noted, would not solve "all the world's economic ills," since "Europe's industries are handicapped in their efforts to enter foreign markets" by hurdles such as trade barriers within the continent, government restrictions, and cartels. He characterized the International Chamber of Commerce as "the only world body of wide membership which has for its aim the promotion of freer trade and payments and the prosperous growth of world economy."

Since April 1947 Pierson has been chairman of the board of directors and of the executive committee of one of the major airlines of the United States, Trans World Airlines, Inc., which at the time of his election was undergoing a change in administrative personnel because of a net loss the previous year of $14,000,000. For 1953, TWA reported the highest gross revenue ($187,220,806) in its history, with a net income of $5,064,392. Gross revenues for the first half of 1954 amounted to $93,343,000, and net income was $1,945,000. The company had net earnings of $9,031,000 after taxes and all charges for the first nine months of 1954.

Pierson was president from 1945 to 1947 of All America Cables and Radio, Inc., Mackay Radio & Telegraph Company, Inc., and the Commercial Cable Company. He is currently a director of these business organizations as well as of E. R. Squibb & Sons, Pressed Steel Car Company, Inc., International Telephone & Telegraph Corporation, Fruehauf Trailer Company, Vertientes-Camaguey Sugar Company of Cuba, Wah Chang Corporation, and American Security & Trust Company. He is also a member of the executive council of United States Associates and of the national advisory committee for CARE, Inc. (Cooperative for American Remittances to Everywhere), a director of the Foreign Trade Council, and a trustee of The Pan American Society, Inc.

A past president of the International Air Transport Association (1950-1951), he wrote a short article entitled "Mission of the IATA" for *United Nations World* (October 1950). By promoting air transportation, he pointed out, IATA members are achieving a greater purpose, because "every international traveler is a contributor toward world understanding." Pierson is the author also of "Europe and East-West Trade," which appeared in *Foreign Policy Bulletin* (August 1, 1953).

Speaking at the Executives Club of Chicago on November 5, 1954, Pierson advised that the United States should develop a consistent, more liberal import policy. "We should not insist that friendly nations shut off trade with Iron Curtain countries unless we are willing to assist them in finding alternate markets," he declared.

The business diplomat, as Pierson has been called, is the recipient of several foreign decorations: officer in the Legion of Honor (France) and Order of the White Rose (Finland); commander in the Order of Southern Cross (Brazil); Order of Aztec Eagle (Mexico); Order of the Star of Italian Solidarity; and Order of Christ (Portugal). His clubs are the University and Links in New York, the Chevy Chase in Maryland, the Metropolitan in Washington, D.C., and Travellers' in Paris. He belongs to the Masonic Order, and to the Phi Delta Theta society.

Pierson married Eleanor Shelton Mehnert on August 12, 1927. His church is the Episcopal and in politics he favors the Democratic party. Sports have been his most frequent form of recreation, particularly swimming, tennis, and golf.

References (see also references listed in 1941 biographical sketch)

N Y Times p28 My 12 '47; III pl S 6 '53
Newsweek 40:62 D 22 '52 por
National Cyclopædia of American Biography, Current Volume F (1942)
International Who's Who, 1954
Who's Who in America, 1954-55
World Biography (1954)

PLESMAN, ALBERT Sept. 7, 1889-Dec. 31, 1953 Netherlands airlines official; attended Royal Military Academy at Breda; became manager, managing director and then president of K.L.M. (Royal Dutch Airlines); created an Officer in the Order of Orange Nassau (1931); decorated by Denmark, Belgium, Sweden, Czechoslovakia, Greece, Lebanon and Syria; credited with having established Holland as one of the four leading nations in civil aviation. See *Current Biography,* (Mar.) 1953.

Obituary

N Y Times p23 Ja 1 '54

POOLE, LYNN Aug. 11, 1910- Public relations executive; university official

Address: b. c/o Johns Hopkins University, Baltimore 18, Md.; h. 112 W. University Parkway, Baltimore 10, Md.

The success of the *Johns Hopkins Science Review* program, which is classed as educational and is operated at far less cost than commercial programs, but which has managed to meet commercial competition since 1948, is in large part due to its originator, Lynn Poole, who has become "this country's most unintentional television personality." Originally, according to Robert M. Yoder in the *Saturday Evening Post* (August 21, 1954), he had planned to stay off-camera, but about the third show his scientist guest balked, and insisted that Poole join him before the television cameras. So Poole became the master of ceremonies, the host and a fixture on the show.

"Also," reports Yoder, "Poole is peculiarly picture-minded. He may forget the text of a book, but he remembers the illustrations vividly, and he is unhappy unless he has seen what he is talking about. This feeling sometimes gets him into precarious spots. In London, so that he could describe the world's tallest television tower, he climbed it. This same urge to see first-hand induced Poole to go along on 86,000 miles of bombing missions in the Pacific, when he was PRO [Public Relations Officer] for the 7th Bomber Command. . . . He had made a name for himself publicizing the Air Force, especially with a traveling show called *Wings Over America.* After the war he wanted a new job, something new to show off and display." In 1946 he became the director of public relations for Johns Hopkins University.

He felt that a television show should be a part of the university's public relations program. Educators were missing a chance, he thought, to use what he believed was "a superb instrument for mass education." Many others agreed, but "Poole's distinction is that he pushed and promoted the idea." He recruited the "talent" from among the university's brilliant scientists who are carrying on investigations in a dozen or more fields. The first program, he admits, was a little too all-encompassing. It was presented on March 19, 1948 on Baltimore's station WMAR and the subject was "All About the Atom." When Baltimore's second station (WAAM) was started in November, the *Review* was made a weekly feature, and in 1949 it was carried on the whole Du Mont network. On Sunday, December 26, 1954 it completes its 293d broadcast. The *Science Review* program received the George Peabody Award in 1950 and again in 1952.

LYNN POOLE

Lynn Poole was born in Eagle Grove, Iowa on August 11, 1910, the son of Harry George Poole and Laura Jane (Buellis) Poole. He grew up in the Midwest, and then in the East, where he attended New Rochelle High School, in New Rochelle, New York. After his graduation in 1930, he matriculated at Western Reserve University in Cleveland, Ohio. During his undergraduate days, he worked at a part-time job in the education department of the Cleveland Museum of Art and could spare no time for collegiate extracurricular activities.

While at the museum, he met Dr. Thomas Munro who influenced him greatly in his choice of educational activities as a lifework. He earned his A.B. degree *magna cum laude* in 1936, and continued graduate studies for the M.A. degree, which he received in 1937. Immediately upon graduation, he held a Rockefeller Travelling Fellowship for study in Europe.

Poole's first professional assignment was with the Walters Art Gallery of Baltimore, Maryland, where he was the director of the education department from 1938 to 1942. Profiting from his contacts with Dr. Munro, and with Dr. Robert W. G. Vail, director of the New York Historical Society in New York City, he originated and developed a museum program for adult education. At the same time, he correlated the general museum program with that of the public schools so that the Walters Art Gallery became a living institution in Baltimore.

After the attack on Pearl Harbor on December 7, 1941, Lynn Poole was commissioned a

POOLE, LYNN—*Continued*

first lieutenant in the U.S. Army Air Force. He served through the war with distinction as a public relations officer, and when the war ended, had attained the rank of major. Following his discharge, he became director of public relations at Johns Hopkins University.

In 1946 television was still in its infancy, but Poole foresaw its possibilities as a mass education medium. In order to learn as much as he could about it, he spent many hours in television studios and control rooms. He observed and talked with cameramen, producers, and directors, and absorbed a considerable amount of technical information.

At that time, Baltimore had no television studio, although one was under construction. Poole approached the new station's program men with the idea of having the Johns Hopkins University professors entertain people with visually dramatic and absorbing facts on science, medicine, and engineering. The new station (WMAR) agreed to try out Poole's suggestion (station WAAM later took over the program).

Perseverance, aided by his imagination and months of observation in TV studios, enabled Poole to develop the *Science Review* into a popular sustaining show. Today it is seen on the Du Mont network on Sunday afternoons. One of his major difficulties was the reluctance of faculty men to appear before the camera. Their comment usually was that they could not act. Poole persuaded them to try, with the result that they are now eager to participate. Poole has explained the value of their appearance on the show by stating: "There's an immediacy and actuality about these guys. Mrs. Jones, watching Dr. Ralph Witt, head of the Johns Hopkins plastic research laboratory, can see how he tests and does his research. He's not a polished actor; he is a pipe-smoking research man who knows what he's doing, and Mrs. Jones knows it."

As a matter of convenience, the show still originates from station WAAM, in Baltimore, the home town of Johns Hopkins University. In a show, abstract science becomes clarified through imaginative visualization. For instance, a 1950 program dealt with the vacuum tube. The problem was to demonstrate electrons "bouncing off a hot wire and hitting the plate that actuates the tube." Lynn Poole described the solution: "We took a large, round glass jar and filled it one-third full of puffed wheat. Through a hole in the bottom we pumped air and the puffed wheat jumped around. Then we stepped up the air flow. The puffed wheat shot up through another hole in the top. The camera was right over that hole. We got our dramatic finish when the puffed wheat hit the lens" (New York *Herald Tribune,* January 7, 1951). A Chicago, Illinois teacher wrote a letter thanking Poole for the demonstration of the vacuum tube and asked for permission to use the puffed wheat idea in his classroom demonstrations.

From his experience with the *Science Review* program, Lynn Poole has suggested certain rules for successful educational shows: (1) Learn as much as possible of TV and find the common denominator of successful operation between TV presentation and education; (2) Television is essentially show business, in other words, a program competes for attention; (3) If you cannot show it, don't talk about it; (4) Present it honestly and respect the audience's intelligence; and (5) Don't be afraid of tackling subjects, but do it with good taste.

The *Johns Hopkins Science Review* received the American College Public Relations Association Annual Award for outstanding achievement in 1951. Poole received the Award for Distinguished Service in Public Relations from the American Public Relations Association in January 1953. He has written several articles on public relations and television, and he summarized his work on the *Science Review* in his book, *Science via Television,* published in 1950 by the Johns Hopkins Press. He is also the author of *Today's Science and You* (McGraw-Hill, 1952) and *Your Trip into Space* (McGraw-Hill, 1953), and *Science the Super Sleuth* (McGraw-Hill, 1954), all of which were written for teen-age readers.

In *Science the Super Sleuth,* Poole outlines the achievements of science in crime detection, records actual cases, and describes microscope tests and other laboratory procedures. He has developed with the Porter Chemical Company, a Super Sleuth Science Kit containing tools and materials with which boys and girls can experiment.

He belongs to the Johns Hopkins clubs of Baltimore and New York. He is a founding member and former secretary-treasurer (1947-1951) of the American Society of Aesthetics, a member of the board of directors of the American College Public Relations Association, a founding member and past president of the Baltimore Public Relations Council, and a member of the Public Relations Society of America and the American Public Relations Association.

Lynn Poole is five feet seven inches tall and weighs 130 pounds. He has blue eyes and white hair. His tremendous energy enables him to carry through his weekly science TV show, as well as his other duties as director of public relations of Johns Hopkins University. He is an Episcopalian, and in politics, a Republican. On January 1, 1941, he married Gray Johnson, a free lance writer.

He said on a recent television program that the urgent problem in science today is to have on tap a supply of competent scientists. The high school graduates of 1954 may become the prominent scientists of 1961. It requires seven years to train a young man or woman to be a scientist and he urged high school science teachers to encourage students to enter this field, and to qualify for the Westinghouse science scholarships for college education offered annually to outstanding high school pupils majoring in scientific subjects.

References

Johns Hopkins Mag 3:8+ Mr '52 pors
N Y Herald Tribune V p5 Ja 7 '51
Sat Eve Post 227:30+ Ag 21 '54 por
Who's Who in America, 1954-55

POTTER, CHARLES E(DWARD) Oct. 30, 1916- United States Senator from Michigan

Address: b. c/o Senate Office Bldg., Washington 25, D.C.; h. Cheboygan, Mich.

The voters of Michigan elected Charles E. Potter, on November 4, 1952, to fill the unexpired term of the late Senator Arthur H. Vandenberg, and to the full Senate term ending January 3, 1959. Potter has brought to this position his experience as a U.S. Congressman between 1947 and 1952, and earlier as a social worker and vocational rehabilitation advisor. He is a member of the Senate permanent subcommittee on investigations and the Government Operations, Rules and Administration, and Interstate and Foreign Commerce committees. In World War II Potter served with the 28th Infantry Division in France where he was severely wounded.

Potter gained national headlines in December 1953 with his investigation of alleged Communist atrocities during the Korean conflict. The evidence which he collected from witnesses who survived the ordeal prompted him to request the United Nations to condemn the Communists and punish "the criminals responsible." In an article for *Parade* (March 7, 1954) he charged the Communists with holding many U.S. servicemen, listed as missing, and asked for a U.N. committee to investigate and report on the status of missing prisoners of war.

During the course of the thirty-six-day Army-McCarthy hearings which ended on June 17, 1954, Senator Potter, on several occasions pleaded for greater dispatch in order to bring the hearings to a conclusion. When the hearings ended Senator Potter expressed the hope that the American people would not get the idea that the government was overrun by disloyal people.

Charles Edward Potter, was born October 30, 1916 on a farm in Lapeer, Michigan, to Fred and Sarah Elizabeth (Converse) Potter. He has a sister, Frances, and a brother, James. The family is of English, Scotch and Irish descent.

Potter attended a Mayfield township grade school in Lapeer, Michigan, and Lapeer High School, from which he was graduated in 1934. He was a halfback on the football team, and a high jumper. In 1934 he entered Michigan State Normal College at Ypsilanti, and during the four years of attendance supported himself with jobs in a sawmill, a cannery and an automobile plant. His major study was social science and during his senior year he applied his training to a part-time job as a social worker in Ypsilanti. After receiving the B.A. degree in 1938, Potter became the administrator of the Cheboygan county bureau of social aid.

In May 1942 he enlisted in the U.S. Army. He completed the officers' training course at Fort Benning, Georgia, was commissioned a second lieutenant, in December 1942, and was assigned to the 28th Infantry Division, as a platoon leader. While stationed in England he was promoted to the rank of first lieutenant.

Miller of Washington

CHARLES E. POTTER

Potter's first battle action was at St. Lô, France. He joined the troops marching into Paris and then his division moved through northern France, into Luxembourg, and the Siegfried Line. At the battle of Hürtgen Forest, Potter's battalion commander was killed and Potter assumed command and was given a battlefield promotion to captaincy. Although wounded in the shoulder, Potter remained with his forces and later, in the Battle of the Bulge, he again stayed with his troops in spite of a wound to his upper lip. During an attack in the Colmar Pocket in France, on January 31, 1945, Potter landed on a German land mine and his legs were irreparably damaged, necessitating amputation.

Potter remained at the Walter Reed Hospital in Washington, D.C. for a year, from July 1945 to July 1946. On leave from the hospital he attended Congressional debates. In the *Saturday Evening Post* (April 11, 1953), Potter described the experience as "the best therapy possible." He was discharged from the Army on July 10, 1946, with the rank of major. Potter was awarded the Silver Star, Bronze Star, Croix de Guerre with Silver Star, and Purple Heart with two clusters.

After his discharge he became a vocational rehabilitation representative for the U.S. Department of Labor's retraining and reemployment administration. In June 1947 he resigned in order to enter the contest for the seat of the late U.S. Congressman Frederick V. Bradley. In the course of the campaign, Potter traveled about 5,000 miles through Michigan's Eleventh District. On August 26, 1947 the vote was 2 to 1 in his favor. He was re-elected in 1948 and 1950.

His voting record indicates that while he was serving in the House of Representatives he favored aid to Austria, China, France, and

POTTER, CHARLES E.—*Continued*

Italy; restoration of wartime curbs on installment buying; registration of Communist and Communist-front organizations; the anti-poll tax bill; and increasing the minimum wage.

In 1952 he voted to override the Presidential veto of the McCarran-Walter immigration act. In that year he also favored invoking the Taft-Hartley act to enjoin steel workers from striking.

When a bill was introduced, in 1949, to give a ninety-dollar monthly pension to all veterans over the age of sixty-five, Potter vehemently opposed the proposal, declaring: "I hate to see the veterans of this country used as political pawns. . . ." However, in 1950, he suggested that a bonus of five dollars a day be given to infantry men serving in combat.

In 1950 he became a member of the House Committee on Un-American Activities. In this capacity, he was instrumental in reopening the investigation of Communist infiltration in the Hollywood film industry, and conducted hearings on similar infiltration into labor unions in Detroit, Michigan. Congressman Potter was also a member of the Education and Labor Committee.

In the spring of 1952 Potter entered the four-way race in the Michigan Senatorial primary election, occasioned by the death of Senator Arthur H. Vandenberg. He won the Republican nomination and, in the November election, defeated the Democratic candidate, the late Blair Moody (who had been appointed as interim Senator), by a margin of more than 47,000 votes.

As a member of the Senate Interstate and Foreign Commerce Committee, the Senator has advocated a treaty between the United States and Canada which would restrict shipping between Great Lakes ports to vessels owned and operated by citizens of the two countries. He has also urged the strengthening of the American Merchant Marine for defense through government subsidies to shipbuilders.

During the spring of 1954 the Senate permanent subcommittee on investigations conducted hearings on whether Senator Joseph R. McCarthy of Wisconsin, Roy M. Cohn and Francis P. Carr used the investigating arm of the Senate in an effort to secure preferential treatment for G. David Schine, (a private in the Army), and whether Secretary of the Army Robert T. Stevens and his counsel, John G. Adams, attempted to use Schine as a means to halt or deter investigation of the Army by the subcommittee.

Senator Potter said that the statements of witnesses "for both sides" should be studied by Attorney General Herbert Brownell, Jr., because of the possibility of perjury, and he recommended "dismissal of those employees who played top roles on both sides" since they "demonstrated a failure to understand" their obligations to the government (New York *Times*, June 18, 1954). With the conclusion of the hearings, Potter signed the majority (Republican) report, and also issued one of his own (reported fully in the New York *Times*, September 1, 1954).

In the 1953 session of Congress Potter voted for the offshore oil bill (May), a controls bill amendment that would require a declaration of war or a concurrent resolution by Congress before the President could impose a stand-by ninety-day freeze on prices, wages and rents (May), and an amendment to the foreign aid authorization bill to send surplus farm crops abroad (July). He opposed increasing Federal grants to states for hospital construction (July), a small business exemption amendment to the excess profits tax extension bill (July), and a provision (to a Constitutional amendment assuring equality under the law to men and women) which would sustain benefits already granted to women by law.

During the second session of the Eighty-third Congress (1954) Senator Potter favored the authorization of the St. Lawrence seaway (January), the (John W.) Bricker amendment to limit executive power in regard to foreign relations (February), the anti-court packing amendment (May), and the eighteen-year-old vote amendment (May). He voted against adding $35,000,000 to the Rural Electrification Administration's loan authority (June), an amendment to add $350,000,000 to the defense bill (June) and against substituting a three-year reciprocal trade agreements act for the Administration's one-year extension bill (June).

In 1951 Potter received a plaque for distinguished service from the Michigan Department of the Veterans of Foreign Wars, an award from the United Veterans Council of Kent county, Michigan, and he was chosen by the U.S. Junior Chamber of Commerce as one of the ten outstanding young men of the United States. He is a member of the American Legion, Disabled American Veterans, Veterans of Foreign Wars, AMVETS, Eagles, Elks, and Kiwanis International. The Senator is also a member of the Battle Monuments Commission of the American Legion. Michigan State Normal College awarded him the honorary LL.D. degree in 1954.

The Senator was married on November 25, 1939 to Lorraine Esther Eddy. He has "a firm jaw, regular features, brown eyes, horn-rimmed spectacles and receding black hair." Potter moves about on his artificial legs with the help of two canes made of transparent plastic, with battery and flashlight built in the handles. At night the canes aid the Senator in crossing streets. He says they are "wonderful for hailing taxicabs."

References

N Y Herald Tribune p3 Ap 4 '54 por
Newsweek 30:18 S 8 '47; 40:29 N 3 '52
Sat Eve Post 225:36+ Ap 11 '53
Biographical Directory of the American Congress, 1774-1949 (1950)
Who's Who in America, 1954-55

PRATT, MRS. HARRY ROGERS *See* Rothery, A. (E.)

PRIDE, ALFRED M(ELVILLE) Sept. 10, 1897- United States Naval officer

Address: b. c/o Department of the Navy, Washington, D.C.; h. Dover-Foxcroft, Me.; 2330 S. Meade St., Arlington, Va.

"I think they can start it, but I don't think they can finish it. We know we can stop them." These words, referring to a threatened Chinese Communist attack on Formosa, were spoken in August 1954 by Vice Admiral Alfred M. Pride, commander of the United States Seventh Fleet, charged with the defense of the island held by the Chinese Nationalists.

On September 13, 1954 the Seventh Fleet was also instructed, through the Joint Chiefs of Staff and the office of the Chief of Naval Operations, to give "full logistic support" to the Chinese Nationalists in their defense of the island of Quemoy. In effect, this means all aid short of American ground troops.

Admiral Pride assumed command of the Seventh Fleet, which consists of several aircraft carriers as well as cruisers, destroyers and other vessels, in December 1953, succeeding Vice Admiral J. J. Clark, who retired. A pioneer in carrier operations, he assisted in the outfitting of the U.S. Navy's first "flattop" in 1921. He commanded the carrier *Belleau Wood* in World War II, and from 1947 to 1951 was chief of the Navy's Bureau of Aeronautics. He began his naval service as a machinist's mate in World War I, and is "the first line officer to rise from the enlisted ranks to the three-star rank and [the] Navy's highest ranking ex-gob" (Washington *Post,* October 13, 1953).

Alfred Melville Pride, the son of Alfred Morine and Grace (White) Pride, was born at Somerville, Massachusetts on September 10, 1897. He was graduated from Somerville High School in 1916, and then studied at Tufts College, Medford, in the engineering school.

He enlisted in the U.S. Naval Reserve Force in March 1917 and served as a machinist's mate, second class, aboard the USS *Wild Goose I*. He was reassigned in October 1917 to the enrolling office of the First Naval District at Boston, and was promoted to chief quartermaster in March 1918. Being keenly interested in aeronautics, he was given duty with the naval aviation detachment at the Massachusetts Institute of Technology. He was later transferred to Florida.

After his formal flight training was completed in Miami, he was designated Naval Aviator Number 1119, commissioned an ensign in the U.S. Naval Reserve, and sent to France. He was serving at the U.S. Naval Air Station at Montchic-Lacanau when the Armistice was signed on November 11, 1918. The World War I Victory Medal was the first of the many decorations he has received.

During a tour of duty in 1919 as ordnance officer at the Naval Air Station at Chatham, Massachusetts, Ensign Pride was promoted to lieutenant, junior grade, in the Naval Reserve Corps. He underwent training in land machines at Carlstrom Field at Arcadia in Florida, after

U. S. Navy

VICE-ADM. ALFRED M. PRIDE

which he had alternate duties in the Atlantic Fleet Ship Plane Division, Mitchell Field, Mineola, New York, and aboard the USS *Arizona.* He was promoted to the rank of full lieutenant in the Naval Reserve on July 1, 1920.

While assigned to the aviation detachment of the USS *Langley* in 1921, he developed an arresting gear which was installed on the *Langley* (the former collier *Jupiter,* then being refitted for "her new role as the first aircraft carrier in the United States Navy"). Pride was transferred to the regular Navy with the rank of lieutenant on November 28, 1921; he joined the converted *Langley,* and with other junior officers, carried out experimental takeoffs and landings in October 1922, on the carrier's deck.

Detached from the *Langley* in May 1924, Lieutenant Pride reported to the Navy's postgraduate school at Annapolis, Maryland for a year's course in aeronautical engineering, followed by further study at the Massachusetts Institute of Technology in 1926. He then had duty in connection with the fitting out of the USS *Saratoga,* after which he had similar duty on the USS *Lexington,* and served aboard that aircraft carrier (1927-1929) as watch and division officer and pilot. In September 1931, as officer in charge of experimental duty at the Naval Air Station at Hampton Roads, Virginia, Pride personally piloted a naval autogyro plane in its initial landing tests aboard the *Langley.* His leg was badly injured in a plane crack-up in the mid-30's.

In June 1934 Pride began a two-year tour of duty in charge of the flight test section at the Naval Air Station, Anacostia, D.C. In 1936 he was with the Engineering Division, Material Branch, of the Navy's Bureau of Aeronautics at Washington. He served as air officer aboard the USS *Wright* (1937-1938), and was

PRIDE, ALFRED M.—*Continued*

stationed at San Diego, California, as chief of staff and operations officer of Patrol Wing I (1938-1939). Recalled to Washington for duty with the Aeronautical Board of the Bureau of Aeronautics, he was there at the time of the Pearl Harbor attack of December 7, 1941. After sea duty in 1942 as executive officer aboard the carrier *Saratoga,* Pride was ordered to duty in charge of the fitting out of the USS *Belleau Wood.* He assumed command, with the rank of captain, on its commissioning in March 1943.

"Under his command," states Pride's Navy biography, "the *Belleau Wood* participated in the occupation of Baker Island and the raid on Tarawa, Gilbert Islands, in September 1943; the raid on Wake Island in October 1943; the occupation of Makin Island, Gilbert Islands, in November 1943; and the raid on Kwajalein Island, Kwajalein Atoll, Marshall Islands in December 1943." The carrier also participated in raids on Taroa Island, Maleolop Atoll, Marshall Islands in January 1944; the occupation of Kwajalein in January and February 1944; and the raids on Truk Islands, Saipan, and Tinian in February 1944.

For his personal "distinguished service... in action during the operation against the Japanese bases at Tinian, Saipan and Guam in the Marianas on February 22, 1944" Captain Pride was commended by Admiral Chester W. Nimitz, Commander-in-Chief of the Pacific Fleet, and authorized to wear the Commendation Ribbon. To the USS *Belleau Wood* a Presidential Unit Citation was awarded "for extraordinary heroism in action against enemy Japanese forces in the air, ashore and afloat."

Promoted to the rank of rear admiral in March 1944, Pride was ordered to the Fourteenth Naval District headquarters at Pearl Harbor, Hawaii, where he commanded the Naval air center and Naval air bases. In April 1945 he assumed command of the air support control unit of the Amphibious Forces, Pacific Fleet, and during the capture of Okinawa, he rendered "valuable assistance to the assault troops" and "planned and directed the activities of the Combat Air Patrol." The quoted words are from the citation accompanying the award to Rear Admiral Pride of the Legion of Merit with Combat "V."

For his World War II service Admiral Pride has also been awarded the American Defense Service Medal, Fleet Clasp; the Asiatic-Pacific Campaign Medal with Silver Star (representing five engagements); the World War II Victory Medal; the National Defense Service Medal; and the Philippine Liberation Ribbon.

Admiral Pride's first postwar assignment was to the office of the Assistant Secretary of the Navy in Washington; he served there from January to December 1946, as officer in charge of the Material Control Branch of the Material Division. He subsequently commanded Carrier Division 6 and Carrier Division 4.

On May 1, 1947 Rear Admiral Pride became chief of the Bureau of Aeronautics, where he served for four years. At hearings by a House of Representatives Armed Services Committee subcommittee about five weeks later, Pride emphasized the need for haste in constructing a proposed jet testing laboratory at Trenton, New Jersey. On June 26, in support of a request for a $34,000,000 appropriation for a naval test range for guided missiles at Point Mugu, California, he disclosed that his bureau was "already spending 40 per cent of its resource . . . on this work" and predicted that missiles would eventually be equipped with atomic warheads (New York *Times*).

By the early months of 1950 guided-missile development was costing the country more than $100,000,000 annually, and (stated Pride) had already "disclosed applications far beyond the scope of original planning." *U.S. News & World Report,* March 31, 1950, commented that these "presumably" included "long-range supersonic missiles . . . that will seek out enemy submersibles" and "antiaircraft missiles to protect fleets at sea."

On the other hand, in an article in the Washington *Post* (April 16, 1950), John G. Norris noted that "top Navy airmen, like Rear Admiral A. M. Pride" were "convinced that at least for the immediate future, the turbine propeller plane is the best suited for such key naval roles as carrier attack craft." (Five months later, at Patuxent River in Maryland, what C. B. Allen of the New York *Herald Tribune* characterized as "the world's most powerful turbo-propeller aircraft engine yet flown" was publicly demonstrated for the first time.)

When Pride's four-year tour of duty as chief of the Bureau of Aeronautics came to an end in May 1951, he assumed command of Carrier Division 2. In May 1952 he became commander of the Naval Air Test Center at Patuxent River, continuing until his current assignment as commander of the Seventh Fleet in late 1953. (He had been advanced to the temporary rank of Vice Admiral in October 1953.)

The Seventh Fleet became a center of international attention in August 1954 through the Chinese Communists' renewed threat to undertake the "liberation" of Formosa from Generalissimo Chiang Kai-shek and the Nationalists, and not to stop "until this objective is attained." At his press conference on August 17 President Dwight D. Eisenhower (who in 1953 had reaffirmed President Truman's 1950 order to the Seventh Fleet to protect Formosa from a mainland attack) was quoted as saying that "if the Chinese Reds intend to take Formosa they would have to run over the United States Seventh Fleet to do so" (New York *Times*).

In a news conference at Manila, Admiral Pride declared that "we will repel the Communists if they attempt to attack." On August 21 he took over from the First Fleet three aircraft carriers (which at one time had been part of the Seventh Fleet), thus becoming commander of the entire Pacific Fleet naval forces operating in the Philippine area and the South China Sea (New York *Herald Tribune,* August 22, 1954).

Admiral Pride's "superiors, equals and subordinates in the Navy, largely Annapolis-trained," states the Washington *Post and Times-Herald* (September 26, 1954), "concede that we couldn't have a better man in the crucial Cold War post. 'He's sound and sensible,' they say, 'always fair, always tactful, but always firm.' "

He married Helen Nickerson Burrell of Somerville, Massachusetts on June 1, 1921. They have one daughter, Carol, the wife of Ensign Andrew Anthony Lemeshewsky of the U.S. Navy, and one son, Alfred Morine, a Navy lieutenant (j.g.). He enjoys hunting and fishing, reading mysteries, and he plays weird musical instruments such as the sweet potato and the kazoo.

References

N Y Herald Tribune p25 O 11 '53
Washington (D.C.) Post p2 O 13 '53 p 1 B S 26 '54
Register of Commissioned and Warrant Officers of the United States Navy and Marine Corps (1954)
Who's Who in America, 1954-55

JOSEPH PULITZER, 2d

PROCOPÉ, HJALMAR JOHAN Aug. 8, 1889-Mar. 8, 1954 Finnish diplomat; statesman; began practicing law (1915); Minister of Commerce and Industry (1920, 1924); delegate to International Hague Conference (1922); Finnish Foreign Minister (1924-1925, 1927-1931); Minister to Poland (1926-1927); delegate to World Economic Conference (1933); general manager of the Finnish Paper Mill Association (1931-1938); and Minister to United States (1939-1944). See *Current Biography,* (Apr.) 1940.

Obituary

N Y Times p27 Mr 9 '54

PULITZER, JOSEPH, 2d (pŭl'ĭt-sẽr) Mar. 21, 1885- Editor; publisher

Address: b. c/o St. Louis Post-Dispatch, 1111 Olive St., St. Louis 1, Mo.; h. Ladue, Mo.

Following the policy of militant journalism set for it by Joseph Pulitzer, its founder, the St. Louis *Post-Dispatch,* under the leadership of Joseph Pulitzer 2d, has continued to expose corruption and injustice, to campaign for reform, and to present news in a colorful style, rich in visual detail. The newspaper has won five Pulitzer Prizes for Meritorious Public Service, and six members of its staff have been awarded Pulitzer Prizes. Its circulation is nearly 400,000 on weekday evenings, and about 475,000 on Sunday mornings. Pulitzer has been its editor and publisher since 1912, and is president of the Pulitzer Publishing Company, which owns the affiliated radio and television stations in St. Louis, KSD and KSD-TV.

Serious students of American journalism have long ranked the "rich, rambunctious and opinionated *Post-Dispatch* among the top four or five dailies of the nation . . . its news coverage of the entire country is superb; its editorials hit hard and speak plain . . . its cartoons (by the celebrated D. R. Fitzpatrick) are famed for draftsmanship and power; its photographs and features compare favorably with the best in the leading national magazines.... But what really makes the *Post-Dispatch* great is the deadly thoroughness and generally high purpose with which it fights. . . . The *P-D*—as St. Louisans call it—is frankly a crusading paper" (Roger Butterfield in *Collier's,* December 16, 1950).

The second of the three sons of Joseph and Kate (Davis) Pulitzer, Joseph Pulitzer 2d was born in New York City on March 21, 1885. His father, an Hungarian immigrant, had founded the St. Louis *Post-Dispatch* in 1878 by merging two afternoon newspapers. The elder Pulitzer was also the publisher of *The World* in New York City, which he purchased in 1883.

After preparatory schooling at St. Mark's in Southboro, Massachusetts, young Pulitzer entered Harvard University in 1904. At the end of two years' study he withdrew from college, and was sent to St. Louis in 1907 with a letter of introduction from his father to George S. Johns, editor of the editorial page of the *Post-Dispatch*: "Dear Mr. Johns, This is my son Joseph. Will you try to knock some newspaper sense into his head?"

"Although Joseph, Jr., started his apprenticeship on the business side," wrote James W. Markham in his biography of O. K. Bovard (managing editor of the *Post-Dispatch*), "he soon became fascinated with the news and editorial departments. . . . Bovard gave him reporting assignments, and trained and tested him with practical problems in the news. In time young Pulitzer's suggestions and the stories he brought in became valuable contributions to the paper. Joseph set down his impressions in a diary, which went to his father as a sort of

PULITZER, JOSEPH, 2d—*Continued*

daily report" (now in "Pulitzer Papers" at Columbia University).

On October 29, 1911, the elder Joseph Pulitzer died. In his will he set up a trust to operate his newspapers, decreeing that three-fifths of the annual dividends should go to his youngest son, Herbert, one-fifth to his oldest son, Ralph, one-tenth to Joseph, and the remaining one-tenth to various editors and executives. The three Pulitzer brothers, however, were given equal votes in the family trust. Herbert and Ralph promptly gave Joseph full authority in St. Louis, making him editor and publisher in 1912.

"It is one of the celebrated ironies of newspaper history," wrote Roger Butterfield in *Collier's* (December 23, 1950), "that the two more favored Pulitzer sons, who took charge of *The World*, failed to maintain either its prestige or its profits and sold it in 1931. . . . Joseph Pulitzer 2d, who stayed with the *Post-Dispatch* . . . has fully realized his father's ideal of a powerful, honest and national-minded newspaper, which is constantly fighting vigorous and worthwhile battles, and also making a great deal of money."

In World War I Pulitzer was accepted in September 1918 for ground service in Naval aviation and assigned to training at Hampton Roads, Virginia. He was commissioned an ensign in November, the month that the fighting ended.

After the outbreak of World War II, Pulitzer sent staff correspondents to nearly all parts of the world in an effort to assure accurate reporting. The publisher himself joined a number of other American editors and publishers in 1945 in inspecting and reporting on German concentration camps. During this trip, from April 25 to May 4, which was made at the invitation of General Dwight D. Eisenhower, he wrote daily accounts of his observations for the *Post-Dispatch* (these articles were later collected and published in *A Report to the American People*, 1945). Back in the United States, Pulitzer made it known that American newspapers had not exaggerated German atrocities. "I am for a just but very severe peace as far as the Germans are concerned," he said (New York *Times*, May 9, 1945).

Much of the national prominence of the *Post-Dispatch* is due to its editor's adherence to the "platform" written by his father in 1907 and printed each day since November 1911 at the head of the editorial page: ". . . always fight for progress and reform, never tolerate injustice or corruption, always fight demagogues of all parties, never belong to any party, always oppose privileged classes and public plunderers, never lack sympathy with the poor, always remain devoted to the public welfare, never be satisfied with merely printing news, always be drastically independent, never be afraid to attack wrong, whether by predatory plutocracy or predatory poverty."

With these principles as the guide in his newspaper career, Pulitzer has taken a large personal role in initiating campaigns such as those which have earned the paper five Pulitzer awards for public service. The publisher is a member of the advisory board on Pulitzer Prizes of Columbia University's Graduate School of Journalism. Whenever the *Post-Dispatch* is a candidate for an award, he does not take part in decisions and, as *Newsweek* (December 14, 1953) has stated, he "has on occasion withdrawn his paper from competition rather than risk suspicion of favoritism."

The first Pulitzer Prize received by the *Post-Dispatch* was for its exposure in 1936 of vote registration frauds in St. Louis.

Other awards have been made in 1941 for its campaign to eliminate smoke in St. Louis; in 1948 for an investigation of the mine disaster in Centralia, Illinois; in 1950 for disclosure of newspapermen on the Illinois state pay roll (with the Chicago *Daily News*); and in 1952 for revealing corruption in the United States Bureau of Internal Revenue.

Six staff members of the *Post-Dispatch* have also been given Pulitzer awards: cartoonist D. R. Fitzpatrick (1926); reporters John T. Rogers (1927), Paul Y. Anderson (1929), and Edward A. Harris (1946); correspondent Charles G. Ross (1932); and editorial writer Bart Howard (1940).

Among other notable crusading endeavors was the newspaper's investigation of the Teapot Dome scandal in the 1920's and the publication of a special rotogravure section prepared at Pulitzer's direction in 1937 to present arguments against President Franklin D. Roosevelt's Supreme Court "packing" proposal. The *Post-Dispatch*, according to *Collier's* (December 23, 1950), has "the most far-ranging and best-informed crime staff of any newspaper in the country; it was one of the prime movers in setting up the [1950] Senate subcommittee to investigate interstate crime and . . . supplied that committee with some of its basic data." The politically independent paper tends to support the Democratic ticket in national elections, but backed Alf Landon in 1936 and Thomas E. Dewey for President in 1948.

During the 1948 Presidential campaign, when Pulitzer decided, after much intramural debate, that the paper should support Governor Dewey, only one of his six editorial writers was on his side in this argument. The other five wrote editorials on other subjects, while the sole Dewey adherent wrote column after column. Thus, wrote Roger Butterfield, the *P-D*'s editorial writers "may be counted among the freest hired brains on earth." *P-D* reporters send back Christmas gifts from hopeful politicians and top *P-D* executives do not join civic boards and committees for fear their judgment of future news stories might be impaired. *P-D* baseball writers pay their own railroad fares and hotel bills while traveling with the Cardinals (National League).

The newspaper is a pioneer in censorship of advertising, rejecting proffered ads that are offensive or deceptive or harmful to health. Its radio station has led in eliminating "plug-ugly" commercial announcements. Pulitzer has actively pushed campaigns for better housing.

Celebrating its seventy-fifth anniversary in December 1953, the *Post-Dispatch* published a special thirty-two-page supplement containing more than thirty articles by leaders in various fields of activity, such as history, medicine, art, labor, politics, and international relations. *Newsweek* (December 14, 1953) reported, "Today the *P-D,* with its radio and television stations, is a $24,000,000-a-year business, employing 1,600 persons and has netted somewhat in excess of $1,000,000 in its best years. It . . . has an influence far beyond its home area." Pulitzer purchased the newspaper assets of the *Star-Times* in 1951, so that the *Post-Dispatch* is now the only evening newspaper in St. Louis.

For his distinguished service to journalism, the editor was presented in 1947 with an award from the University of Missouri's School of Journalism. The citation read: "Joseph Pulitzer, in recognition of his accomplishment in sustaining and perpetuating one of the greatest names and traditions in journalism; his wise and competent direction of the St. Louis *Post-Dispatch,* one of the great American newspapers, for the past thirty-five years; and his broad interests, professional skill and understanding heart." He received an honorary LL.D. degree from Columbia University in 1952.

On October 1, 1954 Joseph Pulitzer 2d participated in a ceremony in City Hall Park, New York City, observing National Newspaper Week, in which a plaque was dedicated to his father. The Pulitzer building which housed *The World* on Park Row is soon to be demolished. Pulitzer recalled that as a boy of four he had laid the cornerstone in 1889.

Pulitzer's first wife, Elinor (Wickham) Pulitzer, whom he married on June 1, 1910, died on March 13, 1925. He married Elizabeth Edgar on April 7, 1926. The publisher has two sons, Joseph 3d (now associate editor and vice-president of the *Post-Dispatch*) and Michael Edgar (a lawyer), and two daughters, now Mrs. Elwood R. Quesada and Mrs. Louis H. Hempelmann. His church is the Episcopal.

Like his father, Pulitzer suffers from failing eyesight and is required for reasons of health to spend much of his time outdoors. For several months of the year he enjoys yachting at his summer home in Bar Harbor, Maine, duck hunting in Arkansas and Illinois or fishing for salmon in Canada's Restigouche River. At all times he keeps in close touch with his editors and has the newspaper read to him for many hours each day. He is well poised, reserved and modest, according to Roger Butterfield, and considers himself "an active everyday newspaperman."

An estimate of Joseph Pulitzer 2d was given by Silas Bent in *Newspaper Crusaders*: "To but one of his sons did the elder Pulitzer transmit the strong sense of social justice and civic responsibility, the courage, and the high order of intelligence essential to a crusader. . . . It was under his hand that honest elections were restored finally to the city [St. Louis]. . . . His services to the press have been marked, as well as his services to his city and his state. The [*Post-Dispatch*] has been a benison on occasion, when civic causes called, a builder as well as a scourge and a discipline."

References

Collier's 126:27+ D 16 '50; 126:30+ D 23 '50 por
Newsweek 42:56+ D 14 '53 por
Time 45:62 Mr 26 '45 por

Bent, S. Newspaper Crusaders (1939)
Markham, J. W. Bovard of the Post-Dispatch (1954)
Who's Who in America, 1954-55
World Biography (1948)

PURCELL, EDWARD M(ILLS) Aug. 30, 1912- Physicist

Address: b. c/o Department of Physics, Harvard University, Cambridge, Mass; h. 5 Wright St., Cambridge 38, Mass.

"To see the world for a moment as something rich and strange is the private reward of many a discovery," said Dr. Edward M. Purcell in his Nobel Prize address in 1952. The physicist, who has been associated with the Harvard University Physics department since 1936, is recognized as one of America's most distinguished younger atomic scientists. He has made several important contributions to the knowledge of nuclear phenomena which have significance in such widely diverse fields as astronomy and physical chemistry. His specialized work has been done in microwave phenomena, nuclear magnetism and radio-frequency spectroscopy.

He received the Nobel Prize in physics in 1952 for his discovery of the nuclear resonance method of measuring certain nuclear properties. He shared the prize with Professor Felix Bloch of Stanford University whose method was similar to that of Professor Purcell, but was arrived at independently. During World War II he was associated with microwave work at the Massachusetts Institute of Technology. In 1945 he returned to the Lyman Laboratory of Physics at Harvard University, and there made his discovery on magnetic absorption effects.

In discussing the work for which he won the Nobel Prize, the physicist said: "We are dealing not merely with a new tool but with a new subject, a subject I have called simply nuclear magnetism. If you think of the history of ordinary magnetism, the electronic kind, you will remember that it has been rich in difficult and provocative problems and full of surprises. Nuclear magnetism, so far as we have gone, is like that, too" (*Science,* October 16, 1953).

Edward Mills Purcell was born in Taylorville, Illinois, on August 30, 1912, to Edward A. and Mary Elizabeth (Mills) Purcell. He distinguished himself at Purdue University in Lafayette, Indiana, receiving his B.S. degree in physics in 1933.

He spent the following year as an exchange student at the Technische Hochschule,

Wide World

EDWARD M. PURCELL

Karlsruhe, Germany. He did post-graduate work at Harvard University and completed his requirements for the M.A. degree (1936) and Ph.D. degree (1938). He has been associated with Harvard ever since (except for his wartime work supervising the Fundamental Studies Group at the Massachusetts Institute of Technology Radiation Laboratory, 1941-45) in the capacity of instructor (1938-40), associate professor (1946-49) and professor of physics from 1949 to date.

After his war work, Dr. Purcell turned his attention to the problem of the behavior of atomic nuclei in magnetic fields for the light these phenomena can shed on the structure and relationships of the heart of the atom. The effect of magnetic fields on the elements as manifested in the appearance of displacement and splitting of their lines in the spectroscope was first detailed and explained as the reactions of what we now know to be electrons to the field around them by the Dutch physicists, Pieter Zeeman (1865-1943) and Hendrick Antoon Lorentz (1853-1928), who shared a Nobel Prize for their work in the "Zeeman effect" in 1902.

Further work in the field of magneto-optics under increasingly refined experimental conditions had revealed the existence of the so-called "hyperfine" spectral lines which the Austrian scientist Wolfgang Pauli demonstrated (1924) to be the effects of nuclear reactions to the magnetic field. Practical limits of spectrographic resolution of these fine lines in the presence of the larger electron lines prevented analysis of the magnitude of the nuclear forces revealed by this technique. In view of these limitations, Dr. Bloch concluded, "one is led to values of nuclear magnetic moments with an accuracy of a few per cent at best."

It was for the purpose of seeking means of more fully elucidating the nuclear reactions to a magnetic field that both Professor Felix Bloch and Professor Purcell began seeking new ways to analyze these phenomena, following up the work of others whose attempts had thus far been unsuccessful. It is because of the purpose rather than because of any mechanical analogy to the spectroscope that their procedures are sometimes called "radio-frequency" spectroscopy.

Toward the end of his war service in 1945, Professor Purcell, in his spare time, working at night with borrowed radio equipment and the big electromagnet at Harvard's Lyman Laboratory of Physics, began to apply the knowledge derived from his work in the development of radar to this problem of nuclear paramagnetism. Paramagnetism is the property by virtue of which objects in a magnetic field tend to align themselves with the magnetic lines of force. When the object is rotating, as does a proton in the nucleus of an atom, the axis of rotation is affected. By introducing a second field at right angles to the magnetic field, the axis of the proton is caused to wobble (precess) just as the axis of the earth wobbles (as noted in the "precession of the equinoxes") by virtue of the different gravitational pulls of the sun and the moon.

The frequency of this precession can be detected. In Professor Purcell's method this is done by the manifestation on an oscillograph of changes in impedance in a coil (of a radio-frequency bridge) which surrounds the sample in the magnetic field, the phenomenon of resonance being responsible for the changes once the frequency in the coil has been adjusted experimentally so that it conforms to the frequency of the nuclear precession. The oscillograph tracings can then be analyzed in terms of proton precession frequencies.

The frequencies for the proton of a given atom are found to vary with the chemical composition of the material in which the atom is found. Thus a proton of hydrogen gas will manifest itself in a way different from a proton of hydrogen in the water molecule, the influence of the magnetic fields of the surrounding electrons and protons with which it is combined modifying its precession frequency. These "chemical shifts," as Professor Purcell calls them, in his Nobel Prize address, while a nuisance to the experimenter in nuclear phenomena, "are interesting to the physical chemist because they reveal something about the electrons that partake in the chemical bond."

His first experiment was performed by putting a lump of paraffin wax contained in a resonant cavity into a magnetic field and observing the change of the Q-value when the magnetic field, H, passed through the resonance point. He found the absorption effect to be intimately connected with the mechanism by which the spin system transfers energy to the crystal lattice. The method is also of great sensitivity and has been used for measuring the proton magnetic moment of hydrogen gas. "Since the first observation, many papers have been published by Professor Purcell and others on details of great importance, such as line shapes and the use of the method for structural studies of crystals" (*Nature,* November 29, 1952).

Professor Purcell's experiments had been completed by 1949, and by the time he had received the Nobel Prize for his work in nuclear phenomena (November 1952), he had already completed the fundamental research in the new radio telescope which has been built at Harvard under the direction of Professor Bart J. Bok and Dr. Harold I. Ewen, the latter having been granted his doctorate for his work with Professor Purcell on the preliminary investigations. This "telescope" is able to "see" by means of radio-detection techniques the invisible radiations from the sun, the stars, and the great clouds of hydrogen which occupy the interstellar space in the Milky Way.

He has recently been directing experiments in the effects of electron beams as they are reflected off a diffraction grating, a fine-ruled plate at which the stream is directed. "There is nothing practical about this," said Professor Purcell in an interview reported in the *Christian Science Monitor* on August 25, 1953, "it is just a simple idea that occurred to me, and I put a student to work on it. . . . It's like running a stick along a picket fence," Dr. Purcell explained. "We shoot a beam of electrons across this grating and it gives off monochromatic light." The *Monitor* commented on the atmosphere of unhampered freedom at Harvard from restrictions of secrecy and from the demand for practical results which, it believes, has fostered the work of scientists like Purcell.

The scientist has been a contributing author to the Harvard *Radiation Laboratory Series* in 1949 and 1950 and is the author of numerous papers in his fields of specialization. In 1948 he was associate editor of the *Physical Review.* He is a member of the National Academy of Sciences, the American Physical Society, and, since 1949, has been Senior Fellow of the Society of Fellows. His fraternities are The Society of the Sigma Xi, (honorary science research), Tau Beta Pi (engineering), and Phi Kappa Sigma (a social fraternity).

Professor Purcell married Beth C. Busser on January 22, 1937. They have two children, Dennis and Frank. Concerning his work he said in his Nobel Prize address:

"Professor Bloch has told you how one can detect the precession of the magnetic nuclei in a drop of water. Commonplace as such experiments have become in our laboratories, I have not yet lost a feeling of wonder, and of delight, that this delicate motion should reside in all the ordinary things around us, revealing itself only to him who looks for it. I remember, in the winter of our first experiments, just seven years ago, looking on snow with new eyes. There the snow lay around my doorstep—great heaps of protons quietly precessing in the earth's magnetic field" (*Science,* October 16, 1953).

References

Christian Sci Mon p3 Ag 8 '53
N Y Herald Tribune p 1, 36 N 7 '52
N Y Times p 1, 21 N 7 '52
Who's Who in America, 1954-55

QUINTERO, JOSÉ (BENJAMIN) (kēn-tĕ'rō hō-sā') Oct. 15, 1924- Stage director

Address: b. c/o Music Corporation of America, 598 Madison Ave., New York 22

In the comparatively short span of its existence—between 1950 and 1954—Circle in the Square, of which José Quintero is the director, has already made a lasting contribution to the American theatre scene. Quintero has gained a reputation as a skillful and imaginative expert in arena-staging. He has also received praise from the Broadway drama critics for his sensitive direction of a proscenium-staged play, *In The Summer House,* by Jane Bowles which starred Judith Anderson at the Playhouse from December 1953 to February 1954.

The Circle in the Square was compelled, on March 22, 1954, to discontinue its use of the building on 5 Sheridan Square because of New York City fire department regulations. Its play, *The Girl on the Via Flaminia,* was then moved to the Forty-eighth Street Theatre where it closed on May 29 after 111 showings.

The young director cast Geraldine Page in the Circle in the Square production of Tennessee Williams' play *Summer and Smoke* in 1952 which chalked up a record-breaking run of 355 performances, and which was instrumental in "uncovering the bright and shining talent" of Miss Page, who went on to Broadway stardom. He also revived Truman Capote's play *The Grass Harp,* John Steinbeck's *Burning Bright* and Jean Giraudoux' *The Enchanted* and directed an original play, *American Gothic* by Victor Wolfson which was presented from November 10, 1953 to January 24, 1954. His direction of Alfred Hayes's play *The Girl on the Via Flaminia,* which opened at the arena theatre on February 9, 1954 received favorable comment. Recently, Quintero directed *Portrait of a Lady* starring Jennifer Jones. The play which was under the production of L. Austin and T. Noyes opened at the American National Theatre and Academy Playhouse in December 1954 and closed after five performances.

José Benjamin Quintero was born in Panama City, Panama on October 15, 1924, the son of Carlos Rivira and Consuelo (Palmorala) Quintero. He has two older brothers, Louis and Ernesto, and a younger sister, Carmen. His father who was born in Spain, is in the cattle and brewery business and in Panamanian politics. While José was attending LaSalle Catholic High School (from which he was graduated in 1943) he discovered that he had a talent for decorating altars, and through some of the priests who were his instructors, he began to read the *Lives of the Saints, Quo Vadis,* and other books.

This might have led him into the priesthood except that he happened to see a motion picture in which Bette Davis was starred, and thereafter he determined to become an actor. He saw all of Miss Davis's pictures that came to Panama City. Having persuaded his father to send him to Los Angeles City College, he studied there for two years. Only an average

Paula Horn

JOSÉ QUINTERO

student, he admits that he spent much time watching movies, and studying the technique of acting.

"I never saw a play until I reached Los Angeles," he recalled. "I went to see *Life with Father.* I didn't understand a word of English except God. I was intensely religious at the time, and the slangy use of the word depressed me" (*Cue*, January 23, 1954). When his English had improved somewhat, he saw Emlyn Williams' *The Corn Is Green.* He saw it every night for its entire two weeks' run in Los Angeles.

Transferring to the University of Southern California, Quintero took drama courses and acted in plays by modern playwrights. He received his B.A. degree in 1948. Although his father wanted him to become a doctor, he agreed to pay his son's expenses at the Goodman Theatre Dramatic School in Chicago, Illinois. It was there that he met Geraldine Page, then a novice player, and admired her acting in a school production of *The Sea Gull.*

In the summer of 1949 Quintero and some other drama students went east and established a summer theatre at Woodstock, New York. Their first production was *Alice in Wonderland.* Quintero soon discovered that he was more interested in directing than in acting. He directed *The Glass Menagerie* by Tennessee Williams and *Riders to the Sea* by J. M. Synge. The group managed to show a profit by the end of the summer and with their savings decided to continue in New York City as the Loft Players.

One of their number, Ted Mann, their business manager, searched for a suitable place where arena productions could be staged. He learned that the Greenwich Village Inn near Sheridan Square was vacant, and the group rented it. Each member of the cast received ten dollars a week and eked out a livelihood by taking part-time jobs so that they could devote a part of every day to acting. They arranged the seats in the arena style around the dance floor of the inn. Since their plays usually have scenery at one end, most of the productions have been on a horseshoe-shaped rather than a circular stage.

Among the co-founders with Quintero were Emilie Stevens, Jason Wingreen and Ted Mann. Their first play was a revival of the Berney-Richardson musical fantasy *Dark of the Moon,* which opened on February 5, 1951. It ran for eight weeks, was praised enthusiastically by every critic who saw it and won four awards for off-Broadway theatre. Among the plays directed by Quintero in that first year were *The Bonds of Interest* by Jacinto Benavente, *The Enchanted* by Jean Giraudoux, adapted by Maurice Valency, and *Yerma,* by Federico García Lorca. In this play Geraldine Page played the role of an old pagan crone who lived in the hills with her fourteen children.

In the spring of 1952 the Loft Players presented John Steinbeck's *Burning Bright* which ran for three months. When the group decided to revive *Summer and Smoke* by Tennessee Williams, Quintero selected Geraldine Page to portray the role of Alma Winemiller. The Broadway drama critics, by that time knowing of the group's work, saw the play and went back to their typewriters to write the most glowing set of notices received by an unknown young actress in years. Much credit was given to Quintero for his imaginative direction of the play.

Following the Williams play (which ran for over a year), Quintero revived Truman Capote's *The Grass Harp,* and again the production ran longer than the earlier Broadway presentation, and the critics praised the direction as well as the acting. After 183 performances, this play closed, and the group presented, in November 1953, *American Gothic,* a dramatization by Victor Wolfson of his novel *The Lonely Steeple.* This production, which ran until January 24, 1954, was the first original play, and it represents the attainment of a goal toward which Circle in the Square has striven since its inception.

Opinion was divided in regard to Quintero's direction of *American Gothic.* Walter F. Kerr in the New York *Herald Tribune* (November 11, 1953) commented: "Indeed, director José Quintero has drawn quietly intelligent performances from every one. . . His own style seems to me to have grown in variety and dramatic force. After the infinitely sensitive, and enormously successful *Summer and Smoke,* the director turned—with *The Grass Harp*—to a theatre of somewhat tortured pause, searching for nuance where none existed and letting the excitement go hang. With *American Gothic* he is attending to the over-all shape of the play again, and the evening moves firmly and confidently forward."

Brooks Atkinson, on the other hand, wrote in the New York *Times* (November 11, 1953): "As a director, José Quintero has two mannerisms that are disillusioning. In the climactic moments he sets his actors shouting in a harsh frenzy that his little theatre can hardly contain. The shouting is ham: it is more of a performance trick than an expression of character. Mr. Quintero is also overfond of silences. Those are his trademarks, and they should not be permitted to divert attention from the fact that he also has insight into a script and a gift for organizing a performance. . . On the whole, the production and the performance are admirable."

"I do not like a fast-paced show," Quintero said. "I prefer subtlety and atmosphere. And particularly silences. Silence is as eloquent as words. Characters without some silences tend to be too secure, just people mechanically reciting lines."

When Oliver Smith and The Playwrights' Company called in José Quintero to direct *In The Summer House* in December 1953, the play by Jane Bowles had already been in rehearsal for five weeks but it was not shaping up to the satisfaction of the producers. Quintero said that he had just three weeks to get it ready for the Broadway opening, scheduled at the Playhouse Theatre on December 29. He admits that at first he felt strange directing a proscenium production after all his experience in arena staging.

"They asked me to take it, and I was frightened," he relates, "the play was stuck somewhere. But it turned out to be the most exciting, harassing experience you can imagine. Everything else will seem pale from now on." He and Mrs. Bowles rewrote the whole second act in two weeks.

The director said that he greatly enjoyed working with Judith Anderson and with Mildred Dunnock—"real professionals" (who both received enthusiastic reviews on their performances). Walter F. Kerr wrote, "director José Quintero has linked together the evening's more incisive flashes with gentler moods, lovingly sustained" (New York *Herald Tribune*, December 30, 1953). In the New York *World-Telegram and Sun* critic William Hawkins stated: "José Quintero has directed with ingenuity and authority."

Judith Anderson, when interviewed by drama critic Henry Hewes (*Saturday Review*, January 23, 1954), said that Quintero "is particularly good at creating a mood and a movement that expresses what a character is thinking and feeling." As an example, Miss Anderson pointed to the moment when, after she says "Mr. Solares is a solid manageable man," Quintero suggested that she mold the ball of wool she is holding.

After being hailed as a distinguished and imaginative play, *In the Summerhouse* was closed on February 13, 1954.

The dramatization of Alfred Hayes's novel *The Girl on the Via Flaminia,* directed by Quintero, opened at the Circle in the Square Theatre on February 9, 1954. Among the many favorable reviews received for the playwright, the actors and the director were those by Brooks Atkinson who wrote: "Put this down as one of José Quintero's most genuine jobs of direction. It has qualities of flow, spontaneity and emphasis without artfulness" (New York *Times,* February 10, 1954) and William Hawkins in the New York *World-Telegram and Sun*: "It is unlikely that anyone in the business understands more about how to keep an arena-style play moving in believable and natural fashion."

Quintero is six feet tall, of slight build, and has brown hair and eyes. He has no hobby except "reading and seeing plays." The kind of plays he likes to see, he told a *Current Biography* writer, are *The Madwoman Of Chaillot, A Streetcar Named Desire* and *Autumn Garden.* He is always seeking original plays of this *genre* to direct. When asked what actress he would like to direct if he had the opportunity, he answered readily: "Geraldine Page. She is the most inventive actress I know."

Reference

Cue 23:17+ Ja 23 '54 pors

RAAB, JULIUS (räb) Nov. 29, 1891-
Chancellor of Austria

Address: b. Ballhausplatz 2, Vienna 1, Austria; h. 6 Sauerburggasse, Vienna 19, Austria

Although little known outside Austria before becoming Chancellor in April 1953, Julius Raab has been prominent in both the prewar and postwar economic and political life of his country. An engineer-architect by profession, he is a founder of Austrian trade and industrial organizations and has special influence in the industrial section of the People's party, which he helped to establish in 1945 and of which he is national chairman.

Like his predecessor, Leopold Figl, Chancellor Raab heads a coalition government of the People's party and Socialists, in a nation which nearly a decade after World War II is still occupied by troops of the United States, France, Great Britain, and the Soviet Union. During his first year in office he has urged repeatedly the conclusion of negotiations for an Austrian state treaty which would restore the country's sovereignty and eliminate the restrictions which the occupation has imposed.

Descended from an old Austrian family of architects, Julius Raab was born to Julius and Franziska (Wohlmyer) Raab on November 29, 1891 in St. Pölten, Lower Austria. He attended elementary school in St. Pölten before entering the classical grammar school in Seitenstetten. For his professional training he studied at the Technische Hochschule in Vienna, where he specialized in aboveground and underground construction, and was graduated with an engineering degree.

Raab fought in World War I from 1914 to 1918 as a lieutenant in the Austro-Hungarian Sapper Second Battalion. Turning to politics in the late 1920's he became a member of the Heimwehr, and a supporter of Ernst Rüdiger, Prince von Starhemberg who helped establish the government of Engelbert Dollfuss. Raab was a member of the town council of St. Pölten from 1927 to 1933, and was sent by the constituency of St. Pölten in 1927 as a deputy

Fayer, Vienna

JULIUS RAAB

to the Nationalrat (the lower chamber of the Austrian Parliament), in which he retained membership until the assembly's dissolution in 1934.

At about this time, influenced by Nazi pressures, Austria was becoming divided by internal antagonisms. Raab in 1934 was instrumental in establishing the Federation of Austrian Tradesmen, which has been described as "the first uniform and legal organization of Austrian trade." Representing Trade, a professional corporation, he served for four years as a member of the Federal Economic Council, before being named in January 1938 as Minister of Commerce and Transportation in the government of Chancellor Kurt von Schuschnigg. In this Cabinet, Raab was responsible for "aligning Austria's economy with Germany's rearmament plan" (*Time,* April 13, 1953).

When the German occupation of Austria in March 1938 brought about a suspension of Raab's political and economic activities, he accepted employment as an engineer for a road-building firm and was so occupied during all of World War II. This enterprise, stated an official biographical release on the statesman, he "developed [in]to a harbor of refuge for political and racial persecutees."

On his return to public service following the liberation of his country in 1945, Raab contributed to the founding of the Austrian People's party (Österreichische Volkspartei), which on November 25 of that year won a victory in the first postwar national elections. Raab was later made chairman of the party in the national legislature (1945), as well as chairman of the national party organization (1951) and head of the party's Lower Austrian branch. The middle-class, conservative People's party is predominantly Catholic, although not officially associated with the Church, and is composed largely of industrialists, peasants, and members of the Farmers League and the League of Employees and Clerks.

For a brief period in the provisional government set up on April 27, 1945 under Karl Renner, Raab filled the post of Secretary of State for Public Works and Reconstruction. "When proposed as a minister in Austria's first post-liberation government," noted John MacCormac of the New York *Times* (March 23, 1953), "his name was vetoed by the Russians in the Allied council," apparently because of his earlier close association with the "authoritarian" government of Schuschnigg.

During the reorganization of Austrian economy following the war, Raab founded and became president of the Economic Federation (Wirtschaftsbund), a political organization of businessmen which was later influential in determining Austria's economic policy. He was also president until 1953 of Austria's Federal Chamber of Commerce. In politics, meanwhile, he won election in October 1949 and in February 1953 to the Nationalrat.

Since 1945 the Austrian government had been headed by a coalition Cabinet of the People's party and the Socialists under Chancellor Leopold Figl, a People's party leader. While subject to certain restrictions by the Allied powers, which had divided the country into four zones of occupation, the government had general authority in passing legislation and administering laws throughout Austria. After the February 1953 elections, in which both parties gained an almost equal number of votes, Figl found himself unable to set up a new Cabinet, mainly because of Socialist opposition to Cabinet representation of members of the neo-Nazi Union of Independents.

Raab, who was called upon by Austrian President Theodor Körner to form a government, was sworn in on April 2 as head of a coalition Cabinet much like the one Figl had led. The new Chancellor yielded to the Socialists in excluding the Independents, but insisted that policy decisions be made by Parliament, where the People's party could generally rely on support from the Independent party. The program agreed upon by the two dominant parties, which had earlier been in conflict over Socialist objection to Figl's anti-inflationist views, included measures to increase foreign trade and to combat growing unemployment through government investment.

"Socialists respect Raab for being a man of his word and for speaking it frankly," reported *Time* (April 13, 1953), "but detest his politics." In this connection the Catholic periodical *America* (April 18, 1953) pointed out that the Socialists picture Raab "as a 'Fascist,' who never suffered under the 'Fascist' regimes in Austria from 1933 to 1939, as did some of the Socialist Cabinet members, who were imprisoned at that time. Actually, Dr. Raab was (and still is) a leading member of the Catholic Students Organization, which spearheaded a fierce fight during that period against Nazism and pan-Germanism."

The opening of the fourteenth Congress of the International Chamber of Commerce, held in Vienna in May 1953, was the occasion of a speech in which the new Chancellor, who is a member of the Austrian Council of the I.C.C., protested against the continued occupation of Austria by American, French, British and Russian troops. "The liberation of our country was declared formally by the Allies to be one of the aims of the war," Raab said. "This promise, however, has not been fulfilled—eight years after the end of the war. . . . We say humbly and without arrogance that, without Austria's freedom and independence, the existence of the whole free world is threatened" (New York *Herald Tribune,* May 19, 1953).

Prolonged delay in the restoration of Austrian sovereignty arose from the failure of Russia and the Western powers to agree fully on all fifty-nine of the articles of the proposed state treaty drawn up in 1949. An abbreviated treaty presented by the West in March 1952 was rejected by the Russians because it restricted Soviet rights regarding former German assets in Austria. Throughout 1953 Raab continued to press for the re-establishment of Austrian independence and, as reported by Gordon Graham of the *Christian Science Monitor* (August 19, 1953), urged Prime Minister Jawaharlal Nehru of India to offer a solution of the treaty problem to the United Nations.

A few weeks after Great Britain in September 1953 announced her intention of withdrawing two-thirds of her occupation troops from Austria, Raab visited Paris to discuss with French officials the terms of the state treaty, reduction of French occupation forces, and eventual inclusion of Austria in the European Coal and Steel Community. The Chancellor expressed his hope that the January 1954 conference of the Big Four Foreign Ministers in Berlin would bring agreement on Austria's treaty. He told a People's party convention in January that the government would undertake an "iron campaign" to obtain independence.

While speaking in favor of strengthening Austria's economic, cultural and political ties with Western Europe, Raab later said that his government was against undertaking any military alliance with either the East or the West. His government would be willing, however, to accede to certain Soviet economic demands in order to induce the Soviet Union to sign the peace treaty. The foreign ministers, at the Berlin meeting, became deadlocked once again over the treaty negotiations.

Another pressing issue confronting Raab has concerned demands of the Conference on Jewish Claims for compensation for heirless property of Jewish victims of Nazi persecution. He made clear in December 1953 the government's position that determination of whether or not the property was heirless must await enforcement of the state treaty and that claims for indemnity could be presented up to six months after the treaty became effective. Later, however, he stated that Austria was willing to acknowledge her obligations and to "give what is right and reasonable" on the claims (New York *Times,* February 13, 1954).

Twice awarded the Military Merit Cross, Austria's Chancellor also holds the Great Silver Medal for Valor for Officers, Great Silver Medal for Valor for Men, Military Merit Medal, and Commander of the Papal Order of St. Gregorius. His wife is the former Hermine Haumer, whom he married on January 14, 1922.

Time has described Julius Raab as a "blunt, tough-talking engineer." During an interview with the Chancellor in 1953, the late Anne O'Hare McCormick of the New York *Times* found him to be a "simple, taciturn, publicity-shy man . . . an industrialist on a modest scale, an indefatigable worker and a person of quick, positive decisions. He is happier behind the scenes than out in front."

References

America 89:66+ Ap 18 '53
N Y Times p14 Mr 23 '53; p8 Ap 3 '53; p28 Ag 19 '53
Time 61:37 Ap 13 '53 por
International Who's Who, 1953
Österreicher der Gegenwart (1951)
Wer is Wer in Österreich, 1951

RAEDLER, DOROTHY (FLORENCE)

(rād'lẽr) Feb. 24, 1917- Theatrical producer; director

Address: b. 30 Rockefeller Plaza, New York 20; h. 505 E. 82nd St., New York 28

"A dedicated Gilbert and Sullivan impresario," is the way Dorothy Raedler was described by drama critic Brooks Atkinson in the New York *Times.* She is the founder and director of the American Savoyards, the only professional Gilbert and Sullivan company currently in the United States. Her group is recognized as "a worthy counterpart of the famed D'Oyly Carte Company" of the Savoy Theatre, London, England. She organized her singers in March 1939, as the Masque and Lyre Light Opera Company, reorganized in November 1948 with a semiprofessional, nonunion cast, and in 1952 gave them their present name when the members became an Equity company.

Following two seasons on tour throughout the United States in 1952 and 1953, and a summer theatre engagement at Monmouth, Maine, the Savoyards made their Broadway debut. They were the first American company to present ten Gilbert and Sullivan operas in one season, playing at the President Theatre on West Forty-eighth Street in Manhattan in the spring of 1954. The group made a highly successful appearance at the Brooklyn Academy of Music from October 11 to 16, 1954.

Dorothy Florence Raedler was born in New York City on February 24, 1917 to Florence Elizabeth (Radley) and Conrad Charles Raedler, an inspector for the city's department of transportation. She is of French, German, Austrian and English ancestry. Her paternal grandmother was Baroness von Sparr zu Graefenberg. Dorothy has one sister, Florence, a speech correctionist in the Los Angeles, California school system.

After graduating from Bryant High School in Long Island City, New York, in 1934, where she had been secretary of the playwrights' club

J. Abresch

DOROTHY RAEDLER

and had participated in the glee club and operettas, Dorothy Raedler entered Hunter College, New York City. She attended the evening session, majoring in biology, and worked during the day, first as an insurance claims adjuster, then as a researcher for *Life* magazine. She wrote and produced her first musical comedy at the age of seventeen. Glee club was an extracurricular activity, together with an interest in operetta, while she was in college. Hunter College awarded her an A.B. degree in 1942.

She began directing an amateur Gilbert and Sullivan group "for fun" in March 1939, calling it the Masque and Lyre Light Opera Company. Early meetings were held in members' homes; later a rehearsal hall was provided by the local Police Athletic League. The first public performance was at the First Presbyterian Church, Jamaica, Long Island.

Miss Raedler reorganized the troupe in November 1948, established a permanent repertoire, and engaged a semi-professional cast. She opened a four-week season at the Good Citizenship League building in Flushing, Long Island, in February 1949. The company also gave many benefit performances, at the Heckscher Theatre in Manhattan, the Young Men's Hebrew Association, the Seamen's Church Institute of New York, and for soldiers on Army piers and at veterans' hospitals.

In July 1949 the director moved her group to the church basement of Jan Hus House at 351 East Seventy-Fourth Street, New York City, where leading drama and music critics journeyed, and wrote highly favorable reports of the group. They became the first "Off-Broadway" theatrical troupe to operate on a year-around basis in the same theatre for more than three and a half years, with a record run of 575 performances. (Neither DeWolf Hopper's nor Winthrop Ames's highly successful productions in America had such long runs.) Of the productions at the Jan Hus House, Douglas Watt (*New Yorker,* February 16, 1952) wrote: "The voices were fresh, the players were young yet experienced (the company has been singing together about three years), and they had been excellently directed."

A principal reason for the growing popularity of her productions, Dorothy Raedler said (New York *Herald Tribune,* November 6, 1949), was her adherence to W. S. Gilbert's original librettos and staging instructions. Regarding any modern interpretation or interpolation she promised: "That will never happen with our group. Other G.&S. companies have tried it, and where are they now?"

"Customers accuse us of modernizing the lines," Miss Raedler told Henry Hewes (*Saturday Review,* May 8, 1954). "But we never change a word. It's just that Gilbert *is* so modern. For instance, there's a line in *Ruddigore* (1887) in which Sir Ruthven announces that he has made a false income tax return. Somebody thought that we had added that, but it's right there in the original."

From starting at the Jan Hus House with a treasury of thirty dollars and sets valued at six dollars, the Masque and Lyre, operating on a cooperative basis, within three years progressed to newspaper and radio advertising, ownership of a station wagon, and building its own sets. Its twenty-five young members, the majority of whom were college graduates, owned shares, assisted with the theatre chores and held part-time positions outside of the company. Beginning with Thursday through Saturday evening performances, the group soon added a Saturday matinee. The audience was invited to meet and talk with the members of the company backstage after each production.

What impressed the critics the most was that the chorus work was "clean, every word distinguishable." The youthful members of the cast (the age of the girls averages twenty-three and the men twenty-seven) are cognizant that the operas are a satire on the manners of Victorian society and on the stuffiness of the conventional operas of the period. Her group gives "just the right touch of dry, mischievous formality in the acting," commented Brooks Atkinson.

To advance the authenticity of her company's productions, Dorothy Raedler went to England and Scotland in June 1952, accompanied by the troupe's leading soprano, Sally Knapp, and her brother Rue Knapp, leading comedian, for some weeks of Gilbert and Sullivan research. The following November, she directed her group, renamed the American Savoyards, in a ten-week cross-country tour under the auspices of Charles L. Wagner. The comic operas *The Mikado* and *Patience* were restaged for the road.

For the first time the repertory company had a full-scale orchestra instead of just a piano accompaniment as in their early productions. The financing for their tour came from the sale of stock to Gilbert and Sullivan enthusiasts. Their successful 1952 road season was followed by another tour the next year under their present manager, Charles E. Green.

Miss Raedler opened her first summer season in Monmouth, Maine, a village of about 1,600, in 1953 and operated a profit. The audience came from neighboring towns, and at one matinee four hundred were refused admission. Popular demand extended the expected nine-week season to ten weeks. This success was repeated during the summer of 1954.

The American Savoyards then moved to the 284-seat President Theatre on West Forty-eighth Street, New York City, in the spring of 1954. They opened their ten-week repertory of ten operettas presented in weekly sequence with *The Mikado.* "Doing the shows in repertory at one theatre is ideal," commented Miss Raedler. She obtained the cooperation and concessions of theatrical unions, which permitted her to operate with a maximum weekly expense of $4,800 and revenue of $4,800, and also required the elimination of scenery and of all orchestra except a piano and an electric organ.

Brooks Atkinson wrote: "Eliminating bogus scenery gives the performers and the costumes the importance they deserve" (New York *Times,* April 4, 1954). Of the missing orchestra, he said, ". . . the overtures especially need the pure and sustained tone that only an orchestra can provide. . . . Miss Raedler thoroughly understands the genius of the Savoy operas and the performances make the happy compromise between gaiety and ritual that conveys the essence of Gilbert and Sullivan" (New York *Times,* April 4, 1954).

The chorus for the performances was limited to ten or twelve. "Either singly or in ensemble, they sing the words precisely and articulately," stated John Beaufort (*Christian Science Monitor,* March 27, 1954). In the opinion of Brooks Atkinson, the reduced chorus enunciated the lyrics "rather better than the D'Oyly Carte choruses" (New York *Times,* April 4, 1954).

Miss Raedler auditions many accomplished singers, selecting those who can coordinate the Gilbertian gestures with Sullivan's music—a feat, she says, about as difficult as rubbing one's stomach and patting one's head at the same time.

After seeing *The Mikado,* William Hawkins (New York *World-Telegram and Sun,* March 24, 1954) wrote: "This youthful company tends more toward freshness than professionalism. They are light without being coy." He termed their performance of *H. M. S. Pinafore* "one of their best" (May 19, 1954).

Discussing the rarely seen *The Sorcerer,* the *Christian Science Monitor* reviewer wrote on May 29, 1954: "Once more, Dorothy Raedler has staged a production distinguished by its style, discipline and charm."

Miss Raedler is the author of an article, "Here Is A Case Unprecedented," in *Blueprint for Summer Theatre* (John Richard Press, 1949) by Richard Beckhard and John Effrat.

Estelle Jackson (Washington *Post,* June 16, 1954) wrote that Miss Raedler hopes to establish Gilbert and Sullivan residence repertory theatres through the United States, having members of her company as supervisors. The producer-director is an honorary member of the New York Gilbert and Sullivan Society.

Dorothy Raedler has hazel eyes and brown hair, weighs 165 pounds and is five feet nine inches tall. She describes herself as a "Christian," but "not a church member," and her political affiliation is Republican. In 1951 she was named the best off-Broadway director by *Show Business,* and in 1954 she received the Show Business Award. She lists her favorite recreations as horseback riding, dancing, photography, and cooking foreign foods. Her pets, two English pugs, travel with her on tour.

References

N Y Herald Tribune IV p3 N 6 '49
Sat R 37:25 My 8 '54
Washington (D.C.) Post p46 Je 16 '54

RAMA RAU, LADY (BENEGAL) *See* Rau, D. (H.) R.

RAU, SIR BENEGAL NARSING Feb. 26, 1887—Nov. 30, 1953 International lawyer, Indian statesman; began civil service career in 1910; joined Legislative Department of Government of India (1934); headed revision of Indian Statute Book (1935) and committee for codification of Hindu law (1940-41, 1943-46); Prime Minister of Jammu and Kashmir (1944-45); adviser to Indian and Burmese Constituent Assemblies (1946); on United Nations' International Law Commission and chairman of atomic energy subcommittee (1948); named India's permanent delegate to UN (1949); urged immediate atomic energy control and tried to help find a settlement of Korean war; judge of International Court of Justice since 1952. See *Current Biography,* (Dec.) 1951.

Obituary

N Y Herald Tribune p3 N 30 '53

RAU, DHANVANTHI (HANDOO) RAMA (rou dônvăń thē rä'mä) May 10, 1893- Organization official

Address: h. 5 Carmichael Rd., Bombay 26, India

Often called the "Margaret Sanger of India," Dhanvanthi Rama Rau is the founder and president of the Family Planning Association of her country and is chairman of the International Planned Parenthood Federation. For over thirty-five years Lady Rama Rau (who acquired her title when her husband was knighted in 1939) has been a leader in women's political and social welfare movements in India. On a lecture tour sponsored by the Planned Parenthood Federation of America in the fall of 1953, she addressed audiences in thirty-four cities of the United States on the subject of "India's Social Revolution."

She appeared on such radio and television programs as *Author Meets the Critics* with

DHANVANTHI RAMA RAU

Mrs. Eleanor Roosevelt, on the New York *Times* Youth Forum, on programs for the United Nations radio station and for the Voice of America. The Indian welfare leader is a member of the advisory panel on health of the National Planning Commission of India, and serves on her government's family planning programs and research committee.

Dhanvanthi Handoo was born on May 10, 1893, in the village of Hubli in southwest India, the daughter of Rup Krishna and Bhagvati (Shah) Handoo. She was reared in a family of six brothers and five sisters in a modest home, with the emphasis on simplicity and character-building. Her father had a civil service position with the government-owned railways, and her mother, a progressive in her ideas, expressed her support for equal rights for women in magazine articles. "Self-sacrifice, hard work—that was the way my parents educated my brothers and sisters and me," Lady Rama Rau has recently stated (Richmond *Times*, October 23, 1953).

Instead of having the customary tutors, Dhanvanthi received her early education at St. Mary's School in Hubli. When she completed her courses there, she stood first among the girl students. Taking a radical step for a young woman of her caste, she asked her parents to send her to college. With their consent, she entered co-educational Presidency College at Madras University in the south of India. Her break with tradition brought daily protests from male students, who called her a "traitor" to her caste.

"When I was young," Lady Rama Rau recalls, "girls were betrothed at nine and married at fourteen; a bride went to live in her mother-in-law's house and wasn't supposed to play a musical instrument, or eat with her husband, or go out alone . . . most young brides, even those from the best of families, couldn't read or write" (*Glamour*, November 1953). She affirms: "From as far back as I can remember, I knew that I wanted—if I could—to break these terrible bonds."

In college she was further inspired toward the struggle for women's independence by the campaign efforts in Madras of Margaret Cousins, Irish suffragette, to secure women's rights. Another strong influence was Mrs. Sarojini Naidu, who urged social reforms, and filled Dhanvanthi with what she describes as "a desire to play some small part in any movement that was being organized for the amelioration of the many social ills the community suffered from."

In spite of her extracurricular activities to promote the social rights and privileges of women, Dhanvanthi Handoo took a number of scholastic awards. She received the matriculation Mahaden Parmanand Prize, the intermediate Sattianathan Gold Medal, and the graduate level Griggs Gold Medal. After receiving the M.A. degree from the University of Madras in 1917, she obtained the post of lecturer in English at Queen Mary's College of her alma mater. Before accepting such an unorthodox position for a woman, she sought and secured, with the strong support of an older brother, the approval of her parents, whose authority she deeply respected.

While Dhanvanthi Handoo was teaching from 1917 to 1919 at the University of Madras, she became one of the pioneer workers in the Indian women's movement. At a time when women did not go to public gatherings, she went to them in their homes. "We held drawing-room meetings," she says, "and it was a contest between the squalling babies on the floor and the speaker. One never knew who would win the contest" (*Christian Science Monitor*, November 9, 1953).

Gradually, she states, the women accepted ideas about the need for educating their daughters, for more knowledge and facilities on health matters, for social and legal reform, and for participation in national affairs. Many women even began to promote social reforms and to become legislators. By 1927, Lady Rama Rau said, they were ready for national organization, and the All-India Women's Conference was formed in Poona. But there has been "no anti-man feeling," no real feminist movement in the women's reforms, she declares (Richmond *Times*, October 23, 1953).

Dhanvanthi Rama Rau actively participated in the campaign to pass the Sarda Act of 1930 in India, raising the legal age of marriage for girls to fourteen years. While living in England from 1929 to 1938, she took an interest in the women's movement in Great Britain, addressed audiences in that country, and contributed to Indo-British understanding. In London, she met Margaret Sanger and, as a result, turned her attention to family planning. "I firmly believe," she says, "that family planning is essential to substantial and lasting improvements in the living standards and general welfare of the people of all nations."

When the Bijapur famine in India was causing suffering in 1943, Lady Rama Rau, then president of the Bombay Women's Committee for Famine Relief, organized the collection of funds and clothing and supervised their distribution on frequent trips to the famine area.

The Indian social leader has supported the "Skippo Van" project for bringing free medical aid to isolated Indian villages. This has been the major practical contribution to village welfare of the All-India Women's Conference, of which she was vice-president from 1939 to 1946 and president in 1947.

After World War II, Lady Rama Rau lived in Washington, D.C. with her husband, who was India's Ambassador to the United States. She made herself familiar with what the Economic and Social Council of the United Nations was doing, and learned that her country's pressing population problem was common to the whole world. Upon her return to India in 1949, she founded and became president of the Family Planning Association of India. She is recognized as largely responsible for India's including a birth control program in its government plans.

On the invitation of the Family Planning Association of India, the Third International Planned Parenthood Conference met in Bombay in November 1952. At this conference, attended by 500 delegates from fourteen nations, the International Planned Parenthood Federation was formed, and Lady Rama Rau was named co-president with Margaret Sanger. Less than a year later, in August 1953, the new constitution was adopted at the Fourth International Planned Parenthood Conference in Stockholm, and Dhanvanthi Rama Rau was elected chairman. "I feel," she says, "that the work of the International Planned Parenthood Federation is vital to world peace, as overpopulated countries, where starvation is rampant, are targets for communism" (Richmond *Times,* October 23, 1953).

Lady Rama Rau explained that the purpose of her coast-to-coast lecture tour of the United States in the fall of 1953 was to "stimulate interest among researchers" to help India find a safe and simple birth control device, which would not require medical supervision (Los Angeles *News,* October 29, 1953). She also expressed an interest in obtaining expert help in organizing effective methods of mass communication.

Referring to the family planning program of establishing birth control clinics in India, Lady Rama Rau states: "We hope it will ease India's public health and unemployment problems and other side effects of overpopulation" (Washington *Post,* December 5, 1953).

Speaking on the New York *Times* Youth Forum on December 26, 1953 on the Dumont television network, Lady Rama Rau pointed out the need for better information among American youth about ways of life in Asia to help bring about better understanding before East-West problems can be solved. She also said that her country was pursuing a neutral course and she denied that the Indian government was "soft" toward communism. She said that it was just as wrong to make such a charge because the legal Communist party had strength in some Indian districts as it would be to assume the United States was pro-Communist on the basis of "Communist and subversive activities disclosed every day."

Lady Rama Rau in an article "Women of India" in the *Atlantic Monthly* (January 1954) wrote: "The women of India showed their political awareness and power in India's first free election, for which they turned out in record numbers to vote with their men—though not necessarily for the same candidates. At the moment, they are conducting a great fight against orthodoxy and conservatism by demanding that the ancient Hindu laws governing marriage, divorce, and inheritance be overhauled and made more equitable. Many thousands of women have now taken jobs of one sort or another, ranging from government service to positions as salesgirls in shops or hostesses on planes. India has women in its foreign service all the way up to the rank of ambassador. There are women in Parliament and in the Cabinet. There are women lobbyists, women on the National Planning Commission, women presidents of colleges. Almost all of them owe their jobs, their power, and their position to the rights that Indian women's movement has established for them through twenty-five years of work."

For her outstanding social work, Lady Rama Rau was awarded the Kaiseri-Hind Gold Medal by the British government. On December 10, 1953 she received from Barnard College a citation and from Columbia University a bicentennial medallion, in honor of her "contribution to the advancement of women's rights and the general welfare of India." Bard College, at Annandale-on-Hudson, New York, awarded her a Doctor of Humane Letters in December 1953.

She has served as chairman of the United Nations Save the Children Committee, as a member of the major committee on women's rights for India's five-year-plan, and as head of the Bombay Women's Association. She established the only children's orthopedic hospital in Bombay.

A fellow countryman states that Lady Rama Rau has "a practical . . . genial, optimistic and robust temperament . . . and . . . a definite philosophy of life which is attuned to the deepest spiritual values. . . ." On May 3, 1919, she broke prevalent Indian custom by marrying a man from a different state, (Sir) Benegal Rama Rau, at present governor of the Reserve Bank of India. Their children are Premila and Santha. The Indian woman leader is five feet six inches tall, weighs 160 pounds, and has brown eyes and gray hair. For relaxation, she likes to cook. "To me," she says, "the family is of utmost importance—it represents security and stability" (Richmond *Times,* October 23, 1953).

References

Cleveland Plain Dealer p21 O 13 '53
Detroit Times O 11 '53; O 20 '53
Glamour p129 N '53
Newsweek 42:82+ 28 '53

RAU, LADY (BENEGAL) RAMA *See* Rau, D. (H.) R.

RAWLINGS, MARJORIE KINNAN Aug. 8, 1896—Dec 14, 1953 Author; for ten years a reporter for Louisville (Kentucky) *Courier-Journal* and Rochester (New York) *Journal*; winner of *Scribner's* story contest (1931); "Gal Young Un" won the O. Henry Memorial Prize (1933); for the *Yearling* she received the Pulitzer Prize (1939); her other works include *South Moon Under* (1933), *Golden Apples* (1935), *When the Whippoorwill* (1940), *Cross Creek* (1942), *Cross Creek Cookery* (1942) and the *Sojourner* (1953). See *Current Biography,* (July) 1942.

Obituary

N Y Times p35 D 16 '53

REESE, EVERETT D. Jan. 15, 1898- Organization official; banker

Address: b. c/o American Bankers Association, 12 E. 36th St., New York 16; c/o Park National Bank of Newark, 32 N. Park Pl., Newark; Ohio; h. 299 Merchant St., Newark, Ohio

When the American Bankers Association held its seventy-ninth annual convention in September 1953 in Washington, D.C., the more than 6,000 banking executives attending the meeting elected Everett D. Reese as their president. He has been president and a director of the Park National Bank of Newark in Ohio since 1926, and was vice-president of the A.B.A. during 1952 and 1953. The A.B.A., which was founded in 1875, represents 98 per cent of all the banks in the United States.

Reese was a pioneer during the late 1940's in furthering the small business clinic and in developing the techniques and services offered by the A.B.A. commission on small business. He is also a teacher of banking in several universities and a director of business and industrial concerns in central Ohio.

Of Welsh descent, Everett D. Reese, who was born in Columbus, Ohio on January 15, 1898, is the son of David T. and Sarah R. (Davis) Reese. He was educated in Columbus, where he "worked his way through grade and high school selling papers, through Ohio State peddling milk and fraternity jewelry. . ." (*Time,* October 5, 1953).

Before his graduation in 1919 with a B.S. degree from Ohio State University, Reese attended Field Artillery Central Officers Training School at Camp Taylor in Louisville, Kentucky. For the academic year 1919 to 1920, he taught at Ohio State University as an instructor in the school of commerce. He then accepted an instructorship at the Georgia Institute of Technology in Atlanta, but left after a year to become a part-time instructor at Denison University in Granville, Ohio, a position he held in 1922 and 1923, and again in 1939 and 1940.

Meanwhile, in 1921, Reese began his long association with the Park National Bank of Newark, Ohio. When he became president and a member of the board five years later, the Park National, which had been established in 1907, had resources of $1,576,000 and was the smallest of five banks in Newark. Deciding "to do something about selling the bank's services," according to *Burroughs Clearing House* (September 1953), the young president secured new accounts by calling on prospective customers among the merchants and farmers throughout the area. At the same time he gained useful information about the needs of the county for banking credits and services.

Assets of the bank increased under Reese's administration to $3,700,000 by 1936 and by 1953 reached more than $19,000,000. Together with its branches in Hebron and Kirkersville, the Park National serves approximately 20,000 customers out of a county population of about 70,000.

The banking executive, who had been president of the Ohio Bankers Association in 1942 and 1943, became prominent in the American Bankers Association through his activities during a three-year term (1943 to 1946) on the executive council and simultaneously on the federal legislative council. A member of the A.B.A.'s small business credit commission from its inception in 1944, he held the chairmanship of the group from 1948 to 1952 and was a member of the credit policy commission for the years from 1949 to 1952.

At the A.B.A.'s seventy-eighth annual convention, held in Atlantic City, New Jersey, in October 1952, Reese was elected vice-president. The following year on September 23, during the association's meeting in Washington, D.C., he was advanced to the presidency in succession to W. Harold Brenton. Arthur Krock commented in the New York *Times* (September 25, 1953) that the bankers convention in Washington "was enveloped in an atmosphere of partnership with the Administration." Among the resolutions endorsed by the group were the government's monetary policy, the objective of a balanced budget, and the extension by Congress of the trade agreement act of 1934. The convention also resolved that the nation should "continue to open its markets increasingly to foreign goods" (New York *Times,* September 24, 1953).

Soon after Reese had taken office as A.B.A. president, the association announced that a new plan had been worked out whereby banks would have a wider role in the financing and servicing of Commodity Credit Corporation price support loans. The arrangement "is based on a nationwide pool of loans against which certificates of interest will be issued and offered to banks for investment and on changes in loan servicing procedures." Reese pointed out that the banks' support of this program would "reduce to a minimum the Commodity Credit Corporation's use of Treasury funds" (New York *Times,* October 14, 1953).

Known as an expert on small business credit, Reese has urged the practice of holding small business conferences in conjunction with local educational institutions. Two such conferences in which he took part were sponsored in 1949 and 1951 by Newark bankers and Denison University. His experience in the problems of small business was made available during 1951 and 1952 through his service as a member of the National Voluntary Credit Restraint Committee and of the Small Business Advisory Committee to the Secretary of Commerce. As quoted by *Banking* (October 1953), A.B.A.'s president believes, "We should so effectively serve the interests of small business that the demand for Government credit or guaranty of loans will be meaningless."

Reese has developed a seven-point program of recommendations that he made in addresses before many state bankers' organizations in various parts of the United States. Among his suggestions is: "Back up those in Government who are trying to reduce expenses, cut taxes, eliminate bureaucracy, and foster a democratic form of government" (*Banking*, October 1953). His program stresses the role of the bank as spokesman to the public for the system of free enterprise.

About a month after his election to the A.B.A. presidency, he sent a letter to banks regarding a series of advertisements on the advantages of free enterprise in the United States. Banks, in Reese's view, are among the business interests that must be resourceful in finding ways to continue a high level of production and distribution in the event of curtailment of defense preparations. If the nation tried to achieve a higher standard of living by improving roads, by giving better medical and dental care, and by providing greater educational and research opportunities, Reese believes more jobs would be created and in this way, the "challenge to our entire economic system" could be met. On October 20, 1954 the A.B.A. elected Homer J. Livingston to succeed Reese as its president.

The banking executive returned to the classroom in 1949 as a member of the faculty of the Graduate School of Banking, where he lectured in the field of credit. This school, of which the A.B.A. is the parent organization, is conducted at Rutgers University and has an enrollment of over 1,000 bank officers. Reese also lectures on the public relations of the small bank at the Central States Conference School of Banking, University of Wisconsin. He has resumed his association with Denison University as a trustee of the school and of its research foundation, and is a trustee also of the development fund of Ohio State University.

Reese is president and director of the First Federal Savings and Loan Association in Newark, and vice-president and director of North High Savings and Loan Association in Columbus, Ohio. Among Reese's other business affiliations in Columbus are his directorships in Suburban Motor Freight, Inc., Commercial Motor Freight, Inc., and Midland Mutual Life Insurance Company. He is treasurer and director of the Kennedy Manufacturing Company of Van Wert, Ohio. In Newark he was formerly president of the Chamber of Commerce.

The A.B.A. president is a Mason, Elk, American Legionnaire, a member of Sigma Chi and Alpha Kappa Psi societies, of the Moundbuilders Country and Rotary clubs in Newark,

Fabian Bachrach

EVERETT D. REESE

and of Columbus and Rocky Fork Hunt and Country clubs in Columbus, and University Club of New York City. His church affiliation is Presbyterian.

Everett D. Reese and his wife, the former Martha Grace Miller, who were married on September 4, 1924, are the parents of four children: John Gilbert, Phoebe Lang (Mrs. John D. Lewis), Thekla Alice and David Everett. As his favorite recreations the Ohio banker names tennis, horseback riding, reading, and the theatre. Reese has said that "a successful banking career must be based upon a genuine liking of people" (*Banking*, October 1953).

References

Banking 46:44+ O '53 pors
Burroughs Clearing House 37:36+ S '53 pors
Newsweek 42:63+ O 5 '53 por
Time 62:102 O 5 '53
Who's Who in America, 1952-53
Who's Who in Commerce and Industry (1953)

REID, WHITELAW July 26, 1913- Editor; publisher

Address: b. c/o New York Herald Tribune, Inc., 230 W. 41st St., New York 36; h. Ophir Farm, Purchase, N.Y.

In succeeding to the editorship of the New York *Herald Tribune* upon the death of his father, Ogden Mills Reid, in January 1947, Whitelaw Reid became the fifth editor of that major United States newspaper since its founding by Horace Greeley more than a century ago as the New York *Tribune*. In 1953 he was named president of the corporation which publishes the *Herald Tribune*, having served six

N. Y. Herald Tribune, James Kavallines

WHITELAW REID

years as vice-president. He succeeded his mother, Mrs. Helen Rogers Reid, who became chairman of the board. During World War II Reid served for four years as a U.S. Navy aviator and saw action in the Pacific theater.

The *Herald Tribune* won the Pulitzer Prize in 1942 for Meritorious Public Service, and since 1917 twelve of its editors or reporters have won individual Pulitzer Prizes. In 1954 the newspaper won the F. Wayland Ayer cup award for excellence in typography, make-up and printing. Permanent possession of the first Ayer cup went to the *Herald Tribune* with awards in 1939, 1941 and 1945. There were 829 newspapers competing for the 1954 cup. On April 8, 1953 the *Herald Tribune* introduced numerous changes in its make-up, restyling its headlines and format to insure greater readability.

Whitelaw Reid was named after his grandfather who had followed Horace Greeley as editor and principal owner of the New York *Tribune* and had died in 1912 while he was U.S. Ambassador to the Court of St. James (Hart Lyman was editor of the paper at that time). "I missed seeing this distinguished relative of mine by several months," the grandson said many years later, "but the more I study him and the more I am confronted with newspaper problems, the more I realize he was a great editor, equipped with a fine mind" (New York *Times,* November 18, 1948). Whitelaw Reid's father became editor of the newspaper in 1913 and in 1918 his mother (the former Helen Miles Rogers) became associated with the *Tribune's* advertising department.

Whitelaw Reid was born on July 26, 1913. He had a sister, Elizabeth, who died in childhood, and a younger brother, Ogden, who is now president of the European edition of the *Herald Tribune.* The boy was reared at his birthplace, the Reid estate, Ophir Cottage, Purchase, New York, and for his early education was sent to Lincoln School in New York City (1918-1927) and to St. Paul's School in Concord, New Hampshire (1927-1932).

While studying for his B.A. degree at Yale University, New Haven, Connecticut, where his major subject was sociology, he belonged to the freshman swimming team, the Yale Political Union, Delta Kappa Epsilon fraternity, and Book and Snake. He was also publicity manager of the Yale dramatic association and assistant business manager of the *Yale Daily News.* After his graduation in 1936, Reid and six of his classmates sailed a small schooner, *Vagabond,* from Norway to the United States. He helped to get a reporter's job on the *Herald Tribune* for one of his Yale swimming team companions, John Crosby, who now is one of the newspaper's most widely read columnists.

To further his training for a profession in publishing Reid took a course in printing at the Rochester Athenaeum and Mechanics Institute (now called the Rochester Institute of Technology). He later received instruction in typesetting at the Mergenthaler Linotype Company in Brooklyn, where he was taught how to take apart and fit together a Linotype machine. Starting work in the mechanical department of the New York *Herald Tribune* in 1938, he became more directly acquainted with the many operations involved in the publication of a newspaper. He was employed briefly also in the paper's business department and in 1939 directed the *Herald Tribune's* facsimile exhibit at the New York World's Fair.

As a reporter on the paper's New York City staff, which he joined in January 1940, Whitelaw Reid covered all types of stories. In June he was assigned to the *Herald Tribune's* bureau in London, England. He filed eye-witness accounts of the London "blitz" by Nazi aircraft and the shelling of Dover, and saw the war also as a passenger of a Royal Air Force plane in a flight over enemy territory and of an English Channel trawler on an invasion patrol.

The young newspaperman, impressed by his experiences of the German aerial bombardment of the British Isles, returned to the United States in 1941 to lecture for Colston Leigh on the battle of Britain. In April of that year Reid, who was over age for cadet flight training, took private lessons in flying and in August received his commission as a Naval aviation lieutenant for ground duty. For the next few months as a member of the New York Naval Aviation Cadets Selection Board, he visited colleges for purposes of recruitment and also spent some time in Washington, D.C., at the Bureau of Naval Personnel. He then received refresher flight training at the Naval air station in Corpus Christi, Texas, and after the United States had entered World War II, he was made a Naval aviator.

In the early 1940's Reid was stationed at Floyd Bennett Field in Brooklyn with Squadron VRF-1 and given the duty of ferrying single-engine Navy planes from New York to

Florida and the West Coast. After being assigned to multi-engine training, in June 1945 he piloted across the Pacific a four-engine Privateer with a crew of twelve men and from a station on Iwo Jima commanded the patrol bomber on flights to the shores of Japan.

Squadron VPB-116, to which Lieutenant Reid was then attached, cooperated with the U.S. fleet in final action against the enemy in 1945. After the war he served for a time as personal pilot to Admiral Marshall Raymond Greer, chief of Fleet Air Wing 18 on Tinian. He also piloted his father and Wilbur Forrest, assistant editor of the New York *Herald Tribune,* from Guam to Tokyo on a tour of the Pacific theater which the two men made as guests of the Department of the Navy and the War Department.

Whitelaw Reid returned to the New York *Herald Tribune* as assistant to the editor (his father) in February 1946. The following month he was made chairman of the *Herald Tribune* Forum for High Schools and in the fall of 1946 presided at the session on atomic energy of the *Herald Tribune* Forum on Current Affairs. Addressing the third session, "Atomic Power for Peace," in November, he spoke of atomic energy as having "the potential for being either the biggest boon or the greatest curse for human beings everywhere. Which of these two it will be is the major challenge of our times" (New York *Herald Tribune,* November 3, 1946). He opened later forums and forums for high schools dealing with topics like "The Force of Free Economy," "Problems Confronting Europe in the World We Want," and "What Kind of Government Ahead?"

Shortly after the death of Ogden Mills Reid, the thirty-three-year-old son on January 13, 1947 was appointed editor of the New York *Herald Tribune* and vice-president of the corporation that publishes the newspaper. Helen Rogers Reid was named president of the corporation. Her son succeeded her in that office on May 14, 1953, when she became chairman of the board.

The New York *Herald Tribune,* which received its present name in 1924 when the Reid interests bought the New York *Herald* and merged it with the *Tribune,* is an independent Republican newspaper. Its daily circulation is about 328,892 and its Sunday circulation is approximately 548,331. It publishes in Paris the New York *Herald Tribune European Edition,* which was suspended for part of World War II.

During the eleven-day strike in late 1953 of AFL photoengravers against New York City's newspapers, the *Herald Tribune,* which was not directly involved in the strike, discontinued publication for nearly a week in sympathy with other publishers. On September 14, 1954 it was announced that the *Herald Tribune* had resigned from the Publishers Association of New York City, to which twelve other newspapers belong for business, labor and informational purposes. Mrs. Reid, chairman of the board, said that the newspaper had "decided to negotiate directly with its employes through their authorized representatives because we feel this procedure will help us to keep in closer touch with our own people and their problems."

The *Herald Tribune* has a quality of warmth and liveliness of style that distinguishes it from some of the other leading newspapers of the country. Further readability is achieved by its typographical excellence, for which it has won twenty national awards.

Outlining the aims and policies of his paper for *Editor and Publisher* (April 10, 1948), Reid spoke of efforts to attain the best possible news coverage: "Get special articles as they come along . . . plan ahead and make the information count as much as possible. We will play our part in making the country realize how grim the situation is and do everything we can to back national action. We have a twin problem—at home, to preserve civil liberties and yet protect our institutions from subversive activity; and to make it possible for the European countries to stay independent."

A project of special interest to Reid has been the *Herald Tribune*'s Fresh Air Fund, of which he became president in April 1946—a service giving underprivileged children of the city the opportunity to vacation for several summer weeks in the country. He has also been vice-president and director of the Reid Foundation, established by Ogden Reid, which awards grants for study abroad to journalists and editors of other newspapers. In 1947 the *Herald Tribune* editor was named a member of an advisory commission of experts to review information services at the United Nations and in June of the following year headed a subcommittee which offered recommendations for improving coverage of U.N. activities.

Reid presided at the twenty-third annual *Herald Tribune* Forum held October 18-19, 1954, which dealt with the topic "Progress of Freedom in the United States."

Reid is a member of the Metropolitan Club in Washington, D.C., and of the Manursing Island Club and St. Regis Yacht Club in New York. Other organizations with which he is associated are the River Club, Century Association, Yale Club, Sigma Delta Chi fraternity, Union Club and Silurians. He belongs to the Episcopal Church and in politics is an independent Republican.

The New York publisher, who married Joan Brandon on July 24, 1948, is the father of Brandon and Carson Reid. He has blue eyes and brown hair and is five feet eleven inches tall. An active sportsman, he finds his recreation in tennis, swimming, horseback riding, sailing, and skiing.

References

Ed & Pub 81:65 Ap 10 '48 por
N Y Herald Tribune p1+ Ja 14 '47
N Y Sun p10 Ja 14 '47
N Y Times p27 Ja 14 '47; p20 Mr 22 '48; p45 Jl 25 '48
Stewart, K. and Tebbel, J. Makers of Modern Journalism (1952)
Who's Who in America, 1954-55
Who's Who in Commerce and Industry (1953)

RICE, GRANTLAND Nov. 1, 1880-July 13, 1954 Sports writer; poet; born in Tennessee, was graduated from Vanderbilt University; joined staff of Nashville *Daily News* (1901); worked on *Forester Magazine,* Atlanta *Journal* (1902-1904), Nashville *Tennesseean* (1906-1910), New York *Evening Mail* (1911-1914), and New York *Tribune* (1914-1930); since 1930 his column "The Sportlight" was syndicated through North American Newspaper Alliance; served as first lieutenant in U.S. Army (1918-1919) and wrote for *Stars and Stripes;* was president of Grantland Rice Sportlights (motion pictures); won an Academy Award ("Oscar") in 1943 for best one-reel picture; coined phrase "the four horsemen" to describe quartet of Notre Dame football backs; during World War II toured Army training camps as lecturer on sports; wrote books on golf, *The Duffer's Handbook* and *The Winning Shots;* to mark his fiftieth anniversary as a sports writer in 1951 an anonymous donor established Grantland Rice fellowship in journalism at Columbia University; among his books of poetry are *Songs of the Stalwart* (1917); *Songs of the Open* (1924); *Only the Brave* (1941). See *Current Biography* (Sept.) 1941.

Obituary

N Y Times p27 Jl 14 '54

RICHARDS, WAYNE E. Nov. 19, 1910- Veterans organization official; businessman
Address: b. c/o Veterans of Foreign Wars, 610 Wire Bldg., Washington 5, D.C.; h. 1102 N. 4th St., Arkansas City, Kan.

America's second largest veterans' organization, the Veterans of Foreign Wars of the United States, elected Wayne E. Richards as its commander in chief for the 1953-1954 term at the fifty-fourth annual encampment in August 1953.

Since the end of World War II, in which he fought as an Air Force pilot, Richards has advanced steadily in V.F.W. administrative responsibility and has combined leadership in civic and V.F.W. affairs with his business activities as owner of an Arkansas City enterprise dealing in automobiles and farm machinery.

The V.F.W. drew wide attention in February 1954 when its post in Norwalk, Connecticut, headed by Albert A. Beres, stated that members "followed to the letter the turning in of names" of persons suspected of being Communists to the Federal Bureau of Investigation (New York *Times,* March 1, 1954). Commander in Chief Richards defended Beres' action, despite strong criticism from many V.F.W. posts and the public. He denied, however, that his organization encouraged "vigilante committees" and "witch hunts." In August 1954 Richards was succeeded as commander in chief by Merton B. Tice.

Wayne E. Richards is a native of Oklahoma —he was born in Newkirk in the northern part of that state on November 19, 1910. In his early childhood, his parents, John Arthur and Effie (Anstine) Richards, made a home for the family in Arkansas City, Kansas, just across the state line, twelve miles from Newkirk. Richards was reared and educated in Arkansas City, where in high school he was chosen a member of the student council. Later as a student at the Arkansas City Junior College, from which he was graduated in 1930, he continued playing football and baseball, the sports that had been his favorite in high school.

Before joining the U.S. armed services in World War II, Richards was affiliated from 1933 to 1941 with the Kanotex Refining Company of Arkansas City. He enlisted in the Air Force in July 1942 and the following year, on October 16, received his commission as an airplane pilot. During the rest of the war he was stationed chiefly in the Pacific, where for eighteen months he saw active duty in New Guinea, Australia, the Philippines, Biak, Okinawa, and Japan. Richards, who retains his rank as an officer in the Air Force Reserve, received his discharge from the service on February 20, 1946. For his contribution to the war effort he was awarded the Air Medal, Philippine Liberation Medal with two battle stars, and the Asiatic-Pacific Campaign Medal with four battle stars.

While still overseas in 1946, the combat pilot joined the Veterans of Foreign Wars and on his return home later in that year transferred his membership to the Spencer-Ralston Post 1254 in Arkansas City. He advanced from junior vice-commander of that post (1946-1947) to senior vice-commander (1947-1948) and then to commander (1948-1949). After a year (1949-1950) as junior vice-commander of the department of Kansas, Richards served in 1950-1951 as department commander before being elected junior vice-commander in chief of the national organization at the 1951 V.F.W. encampment in New York. The following year when V.F.W. members met in Los Angeles they made him their senior vice-commander in chief.

In the course of carrying out his duties in the national V.F.W. administration, Vice-Commander in Chief Richards traveled in nearly every state in the country. With Commander in Chief James W. Cothran, he went to Europe in September 1952 to attend the dedication of an American monument at Suresnes Memorial Cemetery in France, and on that trip also visited military installations in Germany, Italy, France, and England.

Richards was elected to succeed Cothran as V.F.W. commander in chief at the national encampment in Milwaukee, Wisconsin on August 7, 1953. During that encampment V.F.W. members adopted a number of resolutions which included approval of the proposed Bricker amendment to restrict the treaty-making powers of the president and the request for a Congressional investigation of alleged atrocities committed during the Korean conflict. The encampment recommended increased government medical care for veterans, and urged that hospitalization, without regard for ability to pay, be provided for veterans suffering from chronic disabilities.

For more than fifty years—since its development from three societies of overseas veterans formed in 1899—the V.F.W. has conducted a nationwide program to further its objectives in regard to the welfare of disabled veterans and their dependents, care of widows and orphans of veterans, national defense, and the preservation of the principles expressed in the Bill of Rights. V.F.W. activities include maintenance of a 640-acre national farm and home in Michigan to provide for needy dependents of veterans. As prescribed by the organization's constitution and by Congress, which granted a charter in 1936, the purposes of the V.F.W., with its current membership of more than a million veterans, are "fraternal, patriotic, historical and educational" (*Encyclopedia Americana*).

On a tour of the Far East in October 1953 Commander in Chief Richards was present at an Independence Day mass meeting in Formosa, where he heard Generalissimo Chiang Kai-shek urge his people to redouble their efforts to defeat communism and to retake the mainland of China. During his stay in Formosa, the V.F.W. leader presented Chiang with a citation in recognition of his "long and courageous resistance to communism" (New York *Times*, October 12, 1953).

For defense against communism in his own country, Richards announced in November 1953 that the V.F.W. in cooperation with other organizations was planning an anticommunist assault which might include the appointment of a staff with headquarters in Washington, D.C. Among the objectives of the drive, as summarized by the New York *Times* (November 27, 1953), were "the outlawing of the Communist party, a thorough review of schoolroom texts, alerting the public to the dangers of communism and removing the books of communist authors from overseas servicemen's libraries."

His views on methods of ferreting out communists as a part of V.F.W. policy have been challenged by Illinois State Commander Joseph Carnella, Chief Justice Charles S. Dougherty of the Criminal Court (Chicago), chairman of the V.F.W.'s Americanism committee, and by other V.F.W. officials in Iowa and California. Richards explained his point of view on a National Broadcasting Company television program, *American Forum,* on February 28, 1954 when he discussed "Are Citizens Competent to Investigate Communism?" in which he denied that V.F.W. members used vigilante methods, but as individuals were simply being patriotic in reporting suspected subversives.

Richards told the House veterans' committee that the Norwalk incident brought the domestic situation "to a head" and perhaps would lead to Federal legislation outlawing the Communist party in the United States. On August 24, 1954 a bill embodying this proposal became a Federal law.

The V.F.W. commander in chief presented President Eisenhower with a cap bearing his Abilene, Kansas membership number, a life-

WAYNE E. RICHARDS

time membership card and a diamond-studded lapel pin at a ceremony attended by 105 national and state leaders on February 16, 1954.

In his home community of Arkansas City, Richards is the owner and operator of Farmers' Enterprise, Inc., a firm dealing in automobiles and farm machinery. His affiliations in the business field are with the Junior Chamber of Commerce, the Retailers' Association of his city, the National Federation of Independent Businessmen, and the Western Retail Implement Dealers' Association. He is a director of the Arkansas City Chamber of Commerce.

Other organizations to which the V.F.W. head belongs are the Kansas Peace Officers' Association, Air Force Association, and the American Legion. Richards is a member of the Kansas Veterans' Commission. He is active in the Shrine, a 32nd degree Mason of Midian Temple, Wichita (Kansas) Consistory and a member of Crescent Lodge 133 in Arkansas City. He attends the Presbyterian Church.

Richards married Edith Lewis on February 14, 1941. The couple had a daughter, now deceased. In an article in *V.F.W. Magazine* (September 1953) Brian Coyne quotes a number of comments made by V.F.W. members about their new commander. "Wayne is a typical, Midwestern American—friendly, unassuming and always himself," one veteran said. "He makes no pretense of being a silver-tongued orator. He just speaks from his heart. You know he means what he says."

A resolution presented by Richards denouncing the Federal Government and Congress for their "growing and cynical disregard" for the welfare of veterans and their families, was adopted by the V.F.W. delegates at the National Encampment in August 1954.

Reference

V.F.W. Mag 41:18+ S '53 por

RINEHART, STANLEY M(ARSHALL), JR. Aug. 18, 1897- Publisher
Address: b. c/o Rinehart & Co., Inc., 232 Madison Ave., New York 16; h. 1115 5th Ave., New York 28

As the publishing house of Rinehart & Company enters its second quarter century, its president, Stanley M. Rinehart, Jr., can look back with pride on many notable books which appeared under its imprint. The firm's biggest success has been *Anthony Adverse,* a 1224-page historical novel by Hervey Allen, which was published on June 26, 1933 and which has sold over 1,800,000 copies in all editions and in fifteen languages. Other successful books published by Rinehart (it was Farrar & Rinehart from 1929 to 1946, and Rinehart & Company since then) were Elizabeth Page's *The Tree of Liberty,* Charles Jackson's *The Lost Weekend,* Frederic Wakeman's *The Hucksters,* and Norman Mailer's *The Naked and the Dead.*

STANLEY M. RINEHART, JR.

Rinehart's popular "Rivers of America" series was inaugurated in 1937 and has since published forty-seven titles; all published units are still in print. Other successful series (wherein the books are independent of each other) have included "Battle Reports," which has extended to six volumes and which covers the U.S. Navy's operations from Pearl Harbor through the Korean war; the Medical Series; Murray Hill Mysteries; Rinehart Editions (paperback editions of seventy classics); a series in the field of music, on applied electricity, and labor histories.

The firm was set up in June 1929 in the Murray Hill area of New York City, at 12 East 41st Street, and its first four titles that fall included books by DuBose Heyward, Herbert Gorman, Myron Brinig and Mary Roberts Rinehart. In 1953 the firm published 160 titles and 210 reprints. Stanley Rinehart's talents for choosing best sellers and for promoting sales were developed during ten years with Doran & Company (later, Doubleday, Doran), and as advertising manager of *The Bookman.*

Stanley Marshall Rinehart, Jr., is the eldest son of a specialist in tuberculosis, the late Dr. Stanley Marshall Rinehart, and the noted novelist, Mary Roberts Rinehart (the former Mary Ella Roberts, a nurse). He was born in Pittsburgh, Pennsylvania on August 18, 1897. Stanley and his two brothers, Frederick and Alan, were sent to Eastern private schools, and spent their holidays at the family home in Sewickley, Pennsylvania, and their long vacations at their mother's ranch in Wyoming, or on excursions to the West Indies, Mexico, Central America, or Europe.

Stanley entered Harvard University, Cambridge, Massachusetts as a member of the class of 1919. He made "A's" in mathematics but did not excel in English literature. He worked on the *Harvard Lampoon.* In the fall of 1917 he enlisted in the U.S. Army as a private. He did not return to college after the war.

By the time Rinehart went overseas with the Eighty-third Division of the AEF he was a sergeant. While attached to the British Eleventh Division, he was commissioned a second lieutenant and assigned to teach at an officers' training camp in the south of France. The inactivity bored him. Anxious to see his mother, who was then at the front covering the war for the *Saturday Evening Post,* Rinehart wired General John J. Pershing: "Please may I go to the front to see my mother?" His request was ignored.

After his demobilization from the Army in 1919 with the rank of second lieutenant, Rinehart entered the advertising department of George H. Doran Company, publishers, where he solicited advertising for Doran's magazine, *The Bookman.* When John Farrar took over its editorship about a year later, Rinehart's friendship and collaboration with Farrar began. In time Rinehart was made advertising manager, secretary and a director of Doran and Company, while Farrar became an editor. After the merger of Doran with Doubleday, Page and Company in 1927 to form Doubleday, Doran and Company, both young executives were named directors of the new concern, and Rinehart directed its sales.

The publishing house of Farrar & Rinehart was incorporated June 4, 1929 by Stanley and Frederick Rinehart and John Farrar. They bought stock from Doubleday, Doran & Company of Hervey Allen's book *Israfel: The Life and Times of Edgar Allan Poe,* and acquired the right to look at Allen's future work (which included a long novel later titled *Anthony Adverse*). In spite of the Wall Street stock market crash, the new firm thrived, and five months after its incorporation had grossed $46,000. By May 1931 they moved to larger offices at 9 East 41st Street.

In 1934 the growth of the company caused another removal, this time to 232 Madison Avenue, where Farrar & Rinehart leased two floors. Many members of the staff were chosen, says Edith M. Stern (*Saturday Review of Literature,* March 21, 1942), "under Farrar & Rinehart's distinctive brand of nepotism, which gives preference to young people who have grown up in a literary and publishing atmosphere on the theory that they make good book-business personnel." Only two special departments were maintained by the firm: college and juvenile. In the former, emphasis was on English, psychology, and social science publications, while the children's book list included the stories of Elizabeth Enright, Newbury Prize Medal Winner.

On Farrar & Rinehart's general trade list were authors of diversified appeal: Allene Corliss, Faith Baldwin, Katharine Brush, Myron Brinig, Elizabeth Page, and Hervey Allen. (Allen's 530,000 word best seller (at $3.00 a copy), *Anthony Adverse* (1933), brought the company a large profit, which was channeled into the development of the college department.) Of Americana, "F & R" has published the "Rivers of America" series, and of Pan-Americana, Ciro Alegría's *Broad and Alien is the World,* which won first prize in a contest jointly sponsored by Farrar & Rinehart, *Redbook Magazine,* and the Pan-American Union. Mystery novel contests were occasionally promoted by the firm, and in this manner, Elizabeth Daly and Frank Gruber were added.

In 1930 Farrar & Rinehart was one of the first publishing concerns to bring out dollar fiction. However, the field became so overcrowded that the publishers dropped the experiment later. Farrar & Rinehart's acquisition of the Cosmopolitan Book Corporation from William Randolph Hearst in 1931 proved to be very profitable, for it brought such authors as Faith Baldwin, Louis Golding, Rex Beach, Peter B. Kyne and Ruth Suckow into the company. A college textbook department was started in 1934 and is now one of the firm's main sources of income.

The advertising for Farrar & Rinehart has been handled by Franklin Spier since the firm was started in business in 1929. From Doran's, Stanley Rinehart and John Farrar had brought a keen sense of promotional values, which was demonstrated in prohibition days by their mix-your-own-drink party in honor of the publication of their *Art of Drinking.* On another occasion, when one of Rex Stout's Nero Wolfe stories appeared, the publishers bestowed orchids on all the feminine book reviewers in New York.

Upon the United States' entry into World War II, John Farrar joined the OWI. His partner devoted his spare time to the Council on Books in Wartime, of which he was a member of the executive committee. The dissolution of their sixteen-year-old partnership was announced at the end of the war, and John Farrar formed his own firm (later Farrar, Straus & Young). On January 1, 1946, the letterhead of Farrar & Rinehart became Rinehart & Company. The two Rinehart brothers, Stanley and Frederick, remained as president and vice-president of the organization, while Stanley also retained the presidency and directorship of Murray Hill Books, Inc.

In 1951 Rinehart & Company bought control of the basic publishing operations (not including editorial and selling) of A. S. Barnes and Company, publishers of sports books. In 1952 the firm pioneered by publishing the first book by the Higonnet-Moyroud photographic type-composing machine (called Photon). The book was Albro T. Gaul's *The Wonderful World of Insects.*

Among its failures, which Rinehart readily admits, were the publication of *Speculation: The Wall Street Gamebook* (1929). "The book," commented John T. Winterich in *Publishers' Weekly,* September 4, 1954, "was the publishing non-sensation of the day. . . . The account books show that 5,000 copies were printed and 5,500 were returned—a mystery now unlikely ever to be solved. But all was not lost. Every copy of *Speculation* had been provided with a pencil in a slot [and these] were sold to a stationery jobber." In an unwise moment the firm brought out *Napoleon's Letters to Marie Louise.*

By his first marriage to Mary Noble Doran (George Doran's daughter), on May 24, 1919, the publisher has two children, Mary Roberts Rinehart 2d (now Mrs. C. H. Huvelle), and George H. Doran Rinehart. His first marriage was ended by divorce in 1930. Rinehart was married to Francis Alice Yeatman on July 28, 1933. By this marriage he has one son, Stanley Marshall Rinehart 3d. Rinehart adheres to the Republican and Episcopalian traditions of his family, and is a member of the Harvard Club and the Dutch Treat Club, both of New York. From 1936 to 1938 he was president of the National Association of Book Publishers.

The publisher is six feet two inches tall, and weighs 185 pounds. His hair is black and his eyes are brown. He lists his hobby as photography and his sports as fishing (active) and baseball (spectator). His brother Frederick is a vice-president of the firm, and his brother Alan is a director.

References

Pub W 145:1292+ Mr 25 '44; 166:826 S 4 '54
Sat R Lit 25:11+ Mr 21 '42
Who's Who in America, 1954-55

RODINO, PETER W(ALLACE), JR.

(rō-dēn'ō) June 7, 1909- United States Representative from New Jersey; lawyer
Address: b. c/o House Office Bldg., Washington 25, D.C.; Metro & Rodino, 1060 Broad St., Newark 2, N.J.; h. 205 Grafton Ave., Newark 4, N.J.

The Representative of the Tenth District of New Jersey, Peter W. Rodino, Jr., a Democrat, has served three terms in Congress. A captain during World War II, and a lawyer by profession, he has been active on the Veterans' Affairs and the Judiciary committees of the House. He also maintains an active in-

Wide World

PETER W. RODINO, JR.

terest in the work of welfare and civic groups. Rodino won re-election on November 2, 1954 after being opposed by a Republican, William E. McGlynn of Kearny, New Jersey, an attorney.

One of three children of Peter and Margaret (Gerard) Rodino, Peter Wallace Rodino, Jr., was born in Newark, New Jersey, on June 7, 1909. His maternal grandfather was the first clerk of court in Newark, and his father is employed by the Hyatt Bearings Division of General Motors. Young Rodino received his early education at the McKinley Grammar School and Barringer High School in Newark. He attended the University of Newark and the New Jersey Law School, and received the LL.B. degree in 1937.

Rodino had earlier, from 1930 to 1932, taught public speaking and citizenship classes at the Young Men's Christian Association and Federation of Clubs of Newark, and in 1934 and 1935 had been the managing editor of the *Jersey Review.* Admitted to the New Jersey bar in 1938, he entered general law practice with the firm of Metro & Rodino, in Newark, with which he remains associated. He was an unsuccessful candidate for the New Jersey House of Assembly in the 1940 election.

Among the first professional men to volunteer for military service in World War II, Rodino joined the Army on March 10, 1941, and was trained at Fort Dix, New Jersey. In 1942 he was a member of one of the earliest contingents to be sent overseas, serving with the First Armored Division and later with the Military Mission Italian Army. Rodino was among the first enlisted men to be commissioned overseas. After he had taken part in all the Allied North African and Italian campaigns, he was assigned to coordinating operations of British and American troops for the organization, training and equipping of the Italian Army. He was also active in the drive against communism in the Italian elections of April 18, 1948, and organized the good-will mission of former U.S. servicemen to tell the Italian people about democracy.

Upon his discharge from the Army with the rank of captain in April 1946, Rodino returned to campaign on the Democratic ticket for election to the U.S. House of Representatives from the Tenth District of New Jersey. He was defeated in the 1946 election by Republican Fred A. Hartley, Jr., whose vacated seat Rodino won two years later.

The Tenth District is composed of parts of Essex and Hudson counties (with a population in 1950 of 312,306).

He was re-elected to the Eighty-second Congress by more than 20,000 votes over his Republican opponent, William Rawson, and also scored a victory in the election of November 4, 1952. His committee assignments have been to the Veterans' Affairs and the Judiciary committees.

Rodino's voting record in the first session of the Eighty-first Congress (1949) shows him supporting extension of the Trade Agreements Act to 1951 (February), extension of rent controls (March), the repeal of Federal taxes on oleomargarine (April), extension of the Marshall plan (April), and the anti-poll tax bill (July). He voted "nay" on a proposal to cut European arms aid by 50 per cent (August). In the session of the following year he favored economic aid to Korea and Formosa (February), and opposed a cut of $600,000,000 in Federal spending (May). On other proposals regarding government expenditures in 1950, he approved an increase of two billion dollars in farm price supports (June) and a measure to cancel an economy cut in postal services (August).

While the Federal Communications Commission was holding hearings on the license renewal application of a Los Angeles radio station in June 1950, Rodino, in a speech in the House of Representatives, demanded an inquiry to investigate "scurrilous and defamatory" statements about Italian Americans made by a former newscaster of the station (New York *Times,* June 22, 1950).

After a three-day inspection, in September 1950, of Army induction and training processes at Newark and Fort Dix, Rodino and Representatives Hugh J. Addonizio and Charles R. Howell of New Jersey, made a report of their impressions to the Armed Services Committee, which was then studying induction methods. Among Rodino's recommendations was a change in literacy tests, which he believed were too severe. "Certainly a man who drives a truck or cooks in civilian life can drive a truck or cook in the Army, even if he can't pass the present literacy tests" (New York *Times,* September 16, 1950). Another suggestion was that military stores serving the armed forces be granted tax-free privileges so that soldiers, proportionately lower paid, would not have to buy at civilian prices.

After accepting a challenge from a Newark supermarket to work behind its meat counter, the Congressman wrote an article describing consumer reaction to high prices. "It was a heart-rending experience," he stated, "and I only wish 400 other Congressmen would go behind meat counters to learn how people feel. There'd be no question of a real price control bill being voted this week" (New York *Herald Tribune,* July 9, 1951). He urged housewives individually to let their Representatives know their attitude toward price rollback legislation.

After U.S. President Harry S. Truman had nominated Republican Richard Hartshorne for a New Jersey Federal judgeship in October 1951, Rodino and Addonizio called the action the "Pearl Harbor" of the Democratic party. They charged that it was done "without any consultation with the leadership of the Democratic party and the National Democratic Club of New Jersey" (New York *Times,* October 19, 1951).

On key issues presented in the Eighty-second Congress, the legislator voted in favor of the draft-extension—universal military training bill (April 1951), and against an amendment to the Defense Production Act which would provide for reasonable profits under price ceilings (July 1951). He opposed an amendment limiting public housing to 5,000 units (March 1952), a proposal to use the Taft-Hartley act to stop the steel strike (June 1952), an amendment to the Defense Production Act to end Federal rent controls on September 30 (June 1952), and he favored sustaining the President's veto of the McCarran-Walter immigration bill (June 1952).

Voting with the Republican majority in 1953, Rodino voted to admit Hawaii to statehood (March), to support President Dwight D. Eisenhower's reorganization plan for the Department of Agriculture (June), and to continue the excess profits tax for six months (July). The 1954 roll call indicates that the Representative voted "yea" in regard to increasing the personal income tax exemption from $600 to $700 (March), the wire tapping bill for court cases involving treason and espionage (April), an amendment to the wire tapping bill prohibiting interception of messages except with the approval of a Federal judge (April), the authorization of the St. Lawrence seaway (May), the expansion of social security (June), and an amendment making it a felony to be a Communist (August).

An active interest in community welfare work has marked Rodino's career. He was a leader in a movement in New Jersey for the rehabilitation of delinquent boys. At the end of World War II he was one of the principal speakers of the United Nations appeal crusade for aid to children in war-striken areas. He has held the Middle Atlantic chairmanship of the Veterans Housing Committee. Other organizations with which he is associated are the American Veterans of World War II, National UNICO Club, Fellowship of United States-British Comrades, American Legion, and Veterans of Foreign Wars. He belongs to the Loyal Order of Moose, Elks, and Essex County Bar Association. The Congressman is a knight of the Sovereign Order of Malta, and has received a papal decoration, the Italian War Cross and Bronze Star. He is also a Knight of the Order of the Crown of Italy.

By his marriage, on December 27, 1941, to Marianna Stango, formerly a supervisor in the Prudential Insurance Company, Rodino is the father of Margaret Ann Rodino. The brown-eyed, black-haired Congressman weighs 170 pounds and stands five feet seven inches tall. He attends the Catholic Church and is a member of the Holy Name Society.

References

Congressional Directory (1954)
Who's Who in America, 1954-55
Who's Who in the East (1953)
Who's Who in United States Politics (1950)

ROHDE, MRS. BORGE *See* Rohde, R.B.O.

ROHDE, RUTH BRYAN OWEN Oct. 2, 1885-July 26, 1954 Former United States Minister to Denmark; eldest daughter of William Jennings Bryan; attended the University of Nebraska; married Major Reginald Altham Owen (1910); after his death in 1927 became a popular lecturer and advocate of women in politics; was a member of Congress from 1929 to 1933 and the first woman sent to Congress from Florida; appointed U.S. Minister to Denmark in 1933 by President Franklin D. Roosevelt; resigned from the foreign service (1936) and married Captain Borge Rohde of the Danish Royal Guards; author of *Leaves from a Greenland Diary* (1935), *Denmark Caravan* (1936), *The Castle in the Silver Wood and Other Scandinavian Fairy Tales Retold* (1939), *Look Forward, Warrior* (1942), and *Caribbean Caravel* (1949); appointed alternate U.S. delegate (1949) to the General Assembly of the United Nations; was chairman of the executive committee of the Speakers Research Committee of the United Nations; received Distinguished Service Medal from King Frederik of Denmark in July 1954. See *Current Biography,* (Dec.) 1944.

Obituary

N Y Times p21 Jl 27 '54

ROMANO, UMBERTO (rŏ-mȧ'nô o͞om-bĕr'tō) Feb. 26, 1905- Artist; teacher

Address: b. c/o Associated American Artists Galleries, 711 5th Ave., New York 22; h. 162 E. 83rd St., New York 28; Gallery-on-the-Moors, E. Gloucester, Mass.

In the world of art Umberto Romano stands on a lofty but lonely peak, somewhere between modern painting in the manner of the French expressionist schools and painting in the great tradition of the Renaissance. Among his best-known works are *Ecce Homo* and a portrait of

UMBERTO ROMANO

Sara Delano Roosevelt. His first important show, held in 1928 when he was only twenty-three years of age, brought him the acclaim of leading art critics.

Since then, the years have been crowded with paintings, murals and portraits which have emphasized the middle ground which Romano chose for himself. He is acknowledged as an outstanding painter by both critics and collectors, and as a disciplined craftsman of great assurance and sound academic proficiency.

Umberto Romano was born on February 26, 1905 in the town of Bracigliano, near Salerno, Italy, the son of Andrea and Rafaella (Cerrate) Romano. As a boy of nine he came to America with his parents and settled in Springfield, Massachusetts where he was reared. He has five brothers, two of whom are musicians, and three sisters.

Since the age of five, Romano was interested in drawing and he started painting at the age of nine. By the time he had graduated from the Classical High School in Springfield, he had won enough prizes and scholarships to enable him to spend four years at the National Academy of Design. He was awarded the Suydam Silver Medal of the academy, the Pulitzer Traveling scholarship and the Tiffany Foundation fellowship. The young artist then studied at the American Academy in Rome during 1926 and 1927. Here he concentrated on the styles and techniques of the Italian primitives and Renaissance painters, particularly the Florentines and Venetians.

His first one-man show, in 1928, was held at the Frank K. M. Rehn Galleries in New York City. Despite his youth, the debut won widespread attention. Following his initial exhibit the young artist was invited to participate in the major national art shows, including those at the Carnegie Institute, Toledo Museum of Art in Cleveland, Chicago Art Institute, Anderson Galleries, Corcoran Gallery of Art, Cincinnati Art Museum, and Pennsylvania Academy of the Fine Arts.

During the ensuing decade Romano's work continued to receive much laudatory comment. However, in 1938, he was criticized by William Germain Dooley of the Boston *Transcript,* who could see little development and no new direction in the young artist. Dooley said that Romano was a "classical modernist," adding he did not know what that meant unless one considers it "an admixture of aloof antiquity and contemporary expressionism" (*Art Digest,* November 15, 1938).

Tracing the "classical modernist" title to Dooley himself in an article on Romano a few years earlier, Romano replied, "No matter under what title my work is classified, it will always remain a sincere personal experience, emotionally felt and intellectually controlled . . . I have a conception of what I want to do in my lifetime sufficiently intense to keep me independent of the fads of the prevailing French influence or of erotic surrealism or of the Red Barn School" (*Art Digest,* November 15, 1938).

In 1944 Edward Alden Jewell, the late art critic of the New York *Times,* wrote of Romano's show of paintings of the war which were exhibited at the Associated American Artists Galleries: "Something amazing and glorious has happened to Romano. His is an art transfigured; an art that has grown to majestic stature. Romano has long been recognized as an accomplished American artist. He herewith ascends to greatness. . . . *Ecce Homo* is one of the masterpieces of our time." *Art News,* reviewing the same show, commented: "So much power of feeling has seldom appeared in American painting" (October 15-31, 1944).

When the Associated American Artists Galleries exhibited another group of paintings by Romano at the end of 1946, Jewell wrote that the artist "paints with burning, often savage indignation. . . . Even when the mood is of a gentler, more patiently brooding sort, as in the picturing of clowns, tragic implications are stressed with the same unremitting zeal that marks the socially pointed religious subjects and those that have more simply to do with aspects of war and peace" (New York *Times,* November 3, 1946).

Umberto Romano's exhibition at the André Weil Galleries in Paris in 1949 was not well received; John Devoluy reported in the New York *Herald Tribune* (March 28, 1949) that "his painting was typical of the kind the French do not like." Jewell, however, evaluated Romano's growth with praise.

The artist has studied and has been affected by different periods of art. From 1928 to 1933 his work was strongly influenced by the Italian primitives. During the period of 1933 to 1940 he showed a kinship with the Renaissance painters. In the decade from 1940 to 1949 he displayed greater freedom, but was still linked to the styles of Rembrandt, Goya, Daumier, and Rouault. More recently, after a trip to Italy in 1949, his canvasses revealed the influence of early Etruscan and prehistoric art forms which use grotesque exaggerations and distortions of human form to exemplify ideas.

Among the murals executed by Romano, the best known is at the Springfield, Massachusetts Post Office, and depicts *Three Centuries of New England History.* A large mural, *Spirit of Freedom,* contributed during the war by Romano to the United Service Organizations' chapter in Trenton, fell under the unexpected censorship of the local USO. The mural represented the might of the U.S. Air Force by a winged and nude Junoesque figure with drawn sword high in the sky, hovering over the havoc of war.

In the field of portraiture, Romano has painted a gallery of official portraits of public figures and of persons prominent in society. He has combined a classical technique with an insight into the character of the sitter. *Art Digest* (March 15, 1942) commented that he is a "capable portrait painter, combining fine likenesses with distinctive touches."

His portrait *Mrs. Sara Delano Roosevelt,* mother of the late President, shows a "gentle American mother thoughtfully studying her son Franklin's baby picture in the family album." Mrs. Roosevelt sat twice for the portrait and it was finished after her death from the artist's sketches. The portrait hangs in the library collection at Hyde Park, New York.

Romano was commissioned to paint the portrait of Fredric March who portrayed the role of Major Joppolo in the stage presentation of *A Bell for Adano.* In the third act of the play, the townspeople present the portrait to the major as a token of their gratitude. This portrait of Fredric March is reproduced on the jacket of the published version of *Bell for Adano* by Paul Osborn, who dramatized John Hersey's novel.

His works are included in the Conger Goodyear, Stephen Clark and Henry Kaiser collections, as well as in the permanent collections of the Tel-Aviv Museum of Fine Arts, Fogg Art Museum (Cambridge, Massachusetts), Worcester Art Museum, Springfield Museum of Fine Arts, Baltimore Museum of Art, Rhode Island School of Design, Smith College, Mount Holyoke College and University of Georgia museums, Encyclopædia Britannica collection, the Addison Gallery of American Art (Andover, Massachusetts), Pennsylvania Academy of the Fine Arts (which bought *Ecce Homo* in 1953) and San Diego Fine Arts Gallery.

The distinguished artist, Umberto Romano, has received many honors including the Peabody Prize of the Chicago Art Institute for *My Granduncle Gaetano* which was widely reproduced; Art Guild Medal for the best work in the annual show of the Louis Comfort Tiffany Foundation; first prize and portrait prize of the Springfield Art League; Crowninshield award; Lewis Prize of the North Shore Arts Association; Atheneum Prize of the Connecticut Academy of Fine Arts; and Carnegie award of the National Academy Annual Exhibition (1951). He illustrated an edition of Dante's *Divine Comedy* (Doubleday, 1947) with drawings and paintings. Of this series *I Too Have Suffered* and *Purgatorio* were included in a retrospective exhibit at the Associated American Artists Galleries in 1950.

For the past twenty summers the artist has headed the Romano Summer School at East Gloucester, Massachusetts and, since 1941, an art school in New York City. He was formerly head of the Worcester Art Museum School from 1934 to 1940.

Umberto Romano was married to Clorinda Corcia of New York on June 12, 1941. He is five feet six inches in height, weighs 150 pounds and has brown hair and black eyes. The painter was naturalized in 1926. He is a member of the national board and an officer of the New York chapter of the Artists Equity Association, a member of the North Shore Arts Association, Rockport Art Association, and Cape Ann Society of Modern Artists.

References

Art Digest 8:17 F 1 '34
Who's Who in America, 1952-53
Who's Who in American Art (1953)
Who's Who in the East (1951)

ROSEN, AL(BERT LEONARD) Mar. 1, 1925- Baseball player

Address: b. c/o Cleveland Indians, The Stadium, Cleveland, Ohio; h. Kemper Rd., Cleveland, Ohio

"A right-handed blockbuster who churns the insides of baseballs and of people who pitch them," Al Rosen of the Cleveland Indians was unanimously voted the Most Valuable Player (MVP) in the American League in 1953. He led the league in home runs, forty-three; in Runs Batted in (RBI's), 145; and his batting average was .336 as against Mickey Vernon's .337.

His batting average in the 1954 season was 300. He was given a trial as first baseman, and this, in addition to several injuries, hampered him. Nevertheless, after he returned to his former position at third, he aided his team in breaking the Yankees' long lease (five years) on the American League pennant. The Indians lost the World Series in four straight games to the New York Giants.

The life of Al Rosen has to date fallen into a three-way pattern. He has always set a definite but difficult goal, has found in his path tremendous obstacles, and has overcome them through persistence and hard work. He wanted to be a baseball player since he was five, yet he had asthma until he was about sixteen.

In the minor leagues, he was a powerful hitter, but was called a "nose fielder" or a "chest fielder" because of his own odd way of stopping a hard grounder. Year after year his batting average was balanced against poor fielding; year after year he practiced to end his awkwardness until in 1950 he won a regular job with the Indians. He developed into such a good defensive player, that when he was shifted to first base in 1954, no one doubted his ability to take care of that position.

(Continued next page)

AL ROSEN

Albert Leonard Rosen was born on March 1, 1925, in Spartanburg, South Carolina, the son of Louis and Rose (Levine) Rosen. His father was a salesman. When Al was eighteen months old, the family moved to Miami, Florida, where another son was born. During the depression, the Rosens were divorced and Mrs. Rosen went to work in a dress shop while Al took a newspaper route and did odd jobs. According to Gordon Cobbledick (*American Weekly,* May 2, 1954), Mrs. Rosen soon discovered that Al was "a very determined boy." A friend also commented that Ai never ran out of goals.

The chief goal was baseball. Al earned the name "The Flipper" or "Flip" from the way he pitched a softball. When he was thirteen, he won an infield job in a night softball league. For his first games he was paid $2 each (his 1954 salary is reported to be $40,000). He attended Riverside Elementary School and Ada Merritt Junior High School in Miami. At this period his nose was broken for the first of nearly a dozen times.

A story is told which illustrates the boy's "do-or-die" determination. One evening a hurricane hit Miami; Al was up at four the next morning getting out his bicycle for his paper route. His mother protested, but he replied that his customers would "want to find out about the storm," and went through with his mission.

When Al was fourteen, he toured Florida with a softball team, and acquired a reputation that won him a scholarship at Florida Military Academy in St. Petersburg. He entered as a cadet in 1939, and did well at boxing, football and baseball. In the spring of 1941, he met Roger Peckinpaugh, then manager of the Cleveland Indians. Peckinpaugh suggested that Al report to a minor-league team, a farm for Cleveland, at Sumter, South Carolina. At his tryout, he had to bat against Allie Reynolds, now with the New York Yankees, and Steve Gromek, now with the Detroit Tigers. Rosen struck out four times.

Despite this inauspicious beginning, according to Frank Gibbons in the Cleveland *Press* (December 2, 1953), Rosen was offered $75 a month to play with Thomasville, in the North Carolina State League. However, Al refused, graduated from the academy, and enrolled in the University of Florida at Gainesville. He waited on tables to pay his way.

In the spring of 1942, Al received a criticism of his baseball playing which made him more than ever determined to make good. He was given a tryout by a Class C team in Danville, Virginia, at the request of Herb Pennock. The manager looked him over, then told him to go home, get a job and a lunch pail, and forget baseball. Rosen said his critic would regret his words. He then went back to Thomasville, got a third-base job, and did well that summer: he batted .307 and hit seven home runs.

After one year at the University of Florida, Rosen transferred to the University of Miami at Coral Gables, Florida. When the Navy introduced its V-12 program there in 1942, Rosen became an apprentice seaman. In 1944 he began midshipman training at Plattsburg, New York, and that year received a commission. After amphibious training he was assigned to the U.S.S. *Procyon,* an attack transport. On D-Day he was at Okinawa in charge of an LCM (Landing Craft Mobile). In April 1946, he was discharged from the Navy.

He reported to the Indians and was assigned to Pittsfield, Massachusetts, at $175 a month. Pittsfield was a Class C team in the Canadian-American League. Rosen batted well, .323, but made thirty-four errors.

The next year Bill Veeck at Cleveland promoted Rosen to a Class AA team, that of Oklahoma City in the Texas League. There Rosen hit "like a wild man," .349 with twenty-five home runs, but also made a record—for him—with forty-two errors. He was named the Texas League's player of the year. In the fall of 1947 he played at Yankee Stadium for the Cleveland Indians. He faced pitcher Joe Page, took three swings and went back to the bench. A few more games like that, and he was optioned to Kansas City.

During these minor-league years Al kept fighting his greatest weakness—fielding ground balls. When other players banged the ball in batting practice, Rosen would forego his turn at bat, and induce the coaches to bang balls at him for many dreary hours. He tried to get the grounders in front of his legs instead of between them. During this period, he received a degree in business administration from the University of Miami.

After the 1948 season with Kansas City, Rosen was named the American Association's rookie of the year. He batted .327, hit twenty-five home runs, but made thirty-six errors. When the Cleveland player Don Black was hurt, Rosen was brought in for the World Series with the Boston Braves. He was given one chance, as a pinch hitter, and popped up. But he got a share of World Series money.

Again, in 1949, Rosen went to a minor-league team, San Diego. He hit well (.319) and made sixteen errors. In 1950 the Indians' third baseman, Ken Keltner, was slowing up, and Rosen was kept in Cleveland. General manager Hank Greenberg finally decided that new blood was needed on the team, and Rosen became the regular third baseman. That year Al led the American League with thirty-seven home runs, and made only fifteen errors.

The next winter Rosen found himself another "goal". He wanted to marry a girl named Terese (Terry) Ann Blumberg. He had batted only .287 in 1950, however, and decided that he would not propose until that figure passed .300. Terry did not care about that idea, and Rosen himself weakened when 1951 brought him only .265. In March 1952 he finally proposed. Later they were married in Terry's home town of Dothan, Alabama, and honeymooned at Acapulco, Mexico. A boy, Robert, was born in January 1954.

At the end of the 1952 season, Rosen's batting average had topped his .300 goal and reached .302. He won the RBI title in the league with 105, and led in total bases with 297. He hit twenty-eight home runs.

Rosen's 1953 season was his best to date. In 1954 he was switched to first base when another good hitter, Rudy Regalado, joined the team as a third baseman. When the change was announced, the Cleveland manager, Al Lopez, said: "Al Rosen at first base for us is no makeshift or temporary arrangement" (New York *World-Telegram and Sun,* May 1, 1954). However, this proved to be a temporary arrangement when Rosen was later assigned to third base.

Al Rosen's interests are varied. He enjoys going to movies, watching prize fights, fishing, and reading books—usually pocket-sized reprints of best sellers. He smokes a pipe, and occasionally a cigar. He weighs 185 pounds, and is five feet eleven inches tall. He has gray hair. He has been described as a "gregarious, personable guy" and a "ready, nimble conversationalist."

Experts say that Rosen's batting success is due to a strong pair of wrists and a knack of whipping into the ball at the last possible second. He has been commended for his ability to take and utilize advice. When baseball is over, Rosen, according to Tim Cohane in *Look* (July 15, 1952), plans to become a baseball announcer. He has had a radio-TV job in Cleveland, and also works for an investment banking firm.

Speaking at the annual meeting of the National Conference of Christians and Jews in Washington, D.C. in November 1953, Rosen said that color and religion don't mean a thing in baseball and that the only concern of baseball is "Can you produce?" He pointed out that the Cleveland roster includes Negroes, Cubans, Mexicans, Catholics, Jews, and Protestants and that "you will never find any discrimination among any of the players" (*Christian Science Monitor,* November 11, 1953).

Al Rosen polled 1,452,736 votes among the 4,272,470 votes cast by baseball fans throughout the nation for the Major League All-Star game held in Cleveland, Ohio on July 13, 1954.

References

Am W p18+ My 2 '54 pors
Cleveland Press N 29-D 5 '53; D 7-D 12 '53; D 14-D 16 '53
Collier's 133:72+ My 28 '54 pors
Look 16:73+ Jl 15 '52 pors
Pathfinder 57:50+ S 6 '50 por
Sat Eve Post 224:25+ Ag 11 '51 pors
Baseball Register (1953)
Reichler, J. Inside the Majors (1952)
Turkin, H. and Thompson, S. C. Official Encyclopedia of Baseball (1951)

ROSENSTOCK, JOSEPH Jan. 27, 1895-

Conductor; pianist; composer

Address: b. c/o New York City Center of Music and Drama, Inc., 130 W. 56th St., New York 19; h. 549 Riverside Dr., New York 27

After four years as "the dynamic and precise" conductor of the New York City Opera Company, Joseph Rosenstock was named general director of the musical group in 1952 and has continued its highly-praised policy of presenting new operatic works and reviving forgotten ones and of featuring young American singers. He was conductor and director of various opera houses in Austria and Germany during the 1920's and until the rise of Adolph Hitler in 1933. A pianist as well as a conductor, he has composed various musical works including a sonata, a concerto, and choral pieces.

During the fall of 1953 Rosenstock directed the first performance in the United States of Gottfried von Einem's opera *The Trial,* based on Franz Kafka's novel, of which Virgil Thomson wrote in the New York *Herald Tribune* (October 23): "The musical direction and the orchestra, under the fine hand of Joseph Rosenstock, were impeccable." Of his direction of Rossini's opera *La Cenerentola,* Howard Taubman wrote in the New York *Times* (October 9): "Rosenstock deserves immense credit for the way he has kept the performance musically fresh."

Joseph Rosenstock was born in Cracow (Poland) on January 27, 1895, the son of Bernard and Sabine (Gelberger) Rosenstock, and spent his boyhood in Vienna. After completing his education at the Vienna Academy of Music and the University of Vienna, he became the assistant conductor of the Vienna Philharmonic Choir in 1918. He was also a professor at the Academy of Music in Berlin. He served as the conductor of the Stuttgart Opera House from 1921 to 1922; he then went on to become general music director of the Darmstadt State Opera House, where he remained five years. The Wiesbaden State Opera House secured his services as music director in 1927 and after two years there he made his first visit to the

G. D. Hackett

JOSEPH ROSENSTOCK

United States, for a brief period conducting the German wing of the Metropolitan Opera.

On his return to Europe in 1930 Rosenstock was made the general music director at the Mannheim National Theatre, but he was forced to leave this post three years later by Hitler's anti-Jewish regulations. As an Austrian citizen, he was not in such immediate danger as the German Jews and went to Berlin in 1933 to work with the Jewish Cultural Association. Conditions worsened, however, and in 1936 he accepted an invitation from the newly organized Nippon Philharmonic Orchestra in Tokyo, Japan to become its head; he also was appointed musical director of the Japanese Broadcasting Corporation. Rosenstock said (in the *New Yorker,* October 4, 1952), "A lot of Western music is played in Japan, and Japanese audiences respond just like Western ones. The Nippon Philharmonic is just like European and American orchestras . . . [although] it *may* be better disciplined."

With Japan's entry into World War II Rosenstock resigned as conductor and took no part in that country's musical life, and it was not until Allied forces landed that he again took up the leadership of the Tokyo orchestra, scheduling some Sunday concerts for the troops. In 1946 he left Japan to conduct orchestras in Havana, Palestine, and Vancouver (he is still the conductor of the Vancouver orchestra, commuting to the Canadian city every two weeks).

Rosenstock joined the New York City Opera Company in 1948 and made his debut as conductor with the new production of *Figaro* presented on October 14 in English. The New York *Times* praised the "spirit and taste and commanding style" of Rosenstock's performance ". . . [he] revealed himself not only as an excellent musician and leader, but as a . . . sensitive artist, one who understood the traditions of the opera and the essence of the score."

Selected as the music director for the annual music festival at Aspen, Colorado in 1949, Rosenstock has filled the post since that time. Commenting on the high quality of the musical presentation at the 1950 festival, the New York *Times* (July 23) said, "The audience were indebted for this principally to Dr. Joseph Rosenstock, who, in selecting the music demonstrated not only scholarship and refreshing artistic curiosity, but fine taste, perspective and sense of balance." On June 27, 1951 Rosenstock ended a six week tour of Japan with an engagement as guest conductor of the Nippon Philharmonic Orchestra at Tokyo City Hall.

The New York City Opera Company selected Rosenstock as the general director of the company in January 1952 to succeed Laszlo Halasz. He outlined his plans in an interview in *Cue* (March 8, 1952): "Most important," he said, "we must build an American repertory. . . . I plan to present more and more works by Americans, known and unknown."

He stated that the United States has "an incredibly rich reservoir of good voices" and that the City Opera Company is largely composed of young American singers. Contrasting his group with the Metropolitan Opera Company, he said, "We stress more opportunities for the young. . . . We offer fresh, streamlined productions on a budget . . . for a $3.60 top. It's something the customer cannot get elsewhere."

The board of the New York City Center, of which the City Opera Company is a part, voted in May 1952 to renew Rosenstock's contract as general director, complimenting him on the artistic success of his first season. New productions presented under his leadership in the spring and fall seasons of 1952 were Berg's *Wozzeck,* Bartok's *Bluebeard's Castle,* Ravel's *L'Heure Espagnole,* and Gian-Carlo Menotti's *The Consul* and *Amahl and the Night Visitors.* In two performances of *Madame Butterfly* given in October 1952 the cast was composed of twenty-one Japanese and three American singers. Rosenstock cited the admiration for Japanese musical talent which he had gained during his stay in that country as the reason for his "naturalistic casting."

Returning as an honored guest to Japan in the summer of 1952, Rosenstock spent a month there conducting twenty-two concerts and broadcasts in Tokyo, Osaka, Nagoya, and Kyoto (the orchestra which he formerly led insisted on paying for his vacation and providing a house for him during his stay). As reported in an interview in *Musical America* (February 1953), the conductor found that the entire range of Western music is performed and appreciated in Japan, although the older generation adheres firmly to the traditional forms associated with the country's classical drama. Rosenstock feels that a synthesis of the two types of music is now going on and that a new art form embodying the spirit of the traditional in the language of more modern composition may well emerge.

During the New York City Opera Company's spring season of 1953 a revival of Rossini's *La Cenerentola* was presented. The imaginative staging and production of the opera were greeted with critical enthusiasm, and Virgil Thomson commented, "Orchestrally the execution was all delicacy and sparkle under Joseph Rosenstock's precise hand" (New York *Herald Tribune*, March 27, 1953).

Rosenstock's musical compositions include *Piano Sonata* (1918), *Symphonic Concerto for Piano and Orchestra* (1919), *Overture*, and *Variations for the Orchestra* (1945), and songs and choral works. He is a member of the American Federation of Musicians and honorary music director of the Japanese Broadcasting Corporation.

On August 7, 1952, the conductor married Herta Glaz, an opera singer. He has blue eyes and brown hair, is five feet three inches tall and weighs 140 pounds. An article in *Theater Arts* (May 1952) describes him as a "slight, soft-spoken . . . man who looks more like an overworked school teacher than an impresario capable of rapping the errant second violinist over the knuckles with his baton or outscreeching a diva reaching for C sharp."

References

Cue 21:13 Mr 8 '52 por
Mus Am 73:21 F '53 por
New Yorker 28:25 O 4 '52
Who is Who in Music (1951)

ROSTAND, JEAN Oct. 30, 1894- Biologist; author

Address: 29 rue Pradier, Ville d'Avray, Seine et Oise, France

"In my frogs," says Dr. Jean Rostand, noted French biologist, "I see the entire universe." During the last quarter of a century the scientist has been absorbed in the study of artificial parthenogenesis (reproduction by means of chemically fertilized eggs) in thousands of frogs and toads, in hereditary and acquired anomalies deriving in these batrachians from both natural and artificial reproduction, in the predetermination of sex and in the actions of cold on the development of an egg. His work and that of his colleagues has a potential decisive effect on the future determination of hereditary differences and developments in human beings, the philosophical and moral implications of which deeply disturb Rostand as a philosopher.

He has written extensively in the field of genetics and the origin of species, but of his fifty published volumes, a number reflect the literary heritage of his father, the distinguished author of the poetic plays, *Cyrano de Bergerac, L'Aiglon* and *Chantecler*. Rostand's literary output includes novels and collections of maxims and philosophical works.

In his article "Biology and the Burden of Our Times," published in the *Bulletin of the Atomic Scientists*, August 1952, Dr. Rostand discusses the "almost inevitable consequences of the natural evolution of biology," which considers the prolongation of life, the voluntary determination of sex, virginal procreation, compulsory eugenics, and what Rostand calls "the therapy of the spirit." This, he regards, as "the most worrysome consequence of the progress of biology." The chemical compounds such as hormones exert powerful influence on the psychic traits of man. . . . "There is only one step to the discovery of hormone-like substances that could make a person more intelligent, more inclined to be good to others, or to be more courageous. What would be the worth of an artificial virtue, brought about by chemical means . . . or modifications of personality that could result from adroit surgical intervention or from chemical or electrical treatment of the brain?" He concludes, however, that we should not reproach science for the difficulties it has created for us. "All increase in knowledge . . . and human capabilities complicates the moral life, since it imposes the duty to choose between use and abstention."

Jean Rostand was born in Paris, Oct. 30, 1894, the son of Edmond and Rosemonde Gerard Rostand. His father, (1868-1918), the poetic dramatist, wrote *Les Romanesques* in the year of Jean's birth and his masterpiece, *Cyrano de Bergerac,* three years later. His mother (a granddaughter of Count Etienne Gerard, a Marshal of France during the Napoleonic wars) was a playwright and poetess, a member of the jury for the Prix Femina for many years. Jean had one brother, François, born in 1891, who has since acquired a considerable reputation of his own as dramatist, novelist and poet, being the author of *Le Proces de Oscar Wilde* (1935) and *Catherine Empereur* (1937), among other successful plays.

Ill-health forced Jean's father to seek a more pleasant climate than Paris, and the family moved to Cambo-les-Bains in Southern France, where Jean spent his youth. When he was ten, at his father's urging, when "children are learning their first fairy tales, I read [Darwin's] *Origin of Species,"* as he told Andre Lang (*Jean Rostand, Annales Politiques et Littéraires,* Mar. 15, 1930). "Then I naturally dreamed of writing, and at the age of thirteen I began to write some sentences which led me (eventually) to write *La Loi des Riches."* His interest in experimental biology also manifested itself; he set up a small laboratory at one end of his father's estate where he began examining whatever biological life presented itself. "Of a family where the rarest gifts were common currency," Rostand qualified for his college matriculation when he was fourteen. He wrote to the great entomologist Jean Henri Fabre and a correspondence ensued. At fifteen he wanted to solve all the mysteries of life, he told Claude Yelnick recently ("Une Heure Avec Jean Rostand," *France Illustration,* Jan. 17, 1953). "Today he is content to work in his highly specialized field."

He studied in the Faculty of Sciences of the Sorbonne and from 1915 to 1918 served with the French Army in the anti-typhoid vaccination laboratory. After the war, armed by what he calls "a stock of frightful naïveté . . . three ways tempted me, . . . political action, science and simply living my life. . . ." While assidu-

JEAN ROSTAND

ously and slowly pursuing his biological studies, he published, after long hesitation, a series of reflective novels in which the emphasis was more on the philosophical idea or the epigram than on action or character.

His first book (*La Loi des Riches,* Paris, 1919) "was a record of bitter and long-stifled thoughts, written in a plain and labored style which permitted no comparison with his father." The next year came *Pendant qu'on souffre.* Of *Ignace ou l'Ecrivain* (Paris, 1923), Yvonne Sarcey said (*Annales Politiques et Littéraires,* Sept. 2, 1923), "I would willingly believe, for my part, that this book, both bitter and idealistic—and what I consider a small masterpiece—will find its natural place in all the choice libraries." . . . In *Deux Angoisses: la mort, l'amour* (Paris, 1924), Rostand presented two essays on love and death, of which Henri Bidou wrote (*Annales Politiques et Littéraires,* Feb. 17, 1924), "The two successful studies in the volume which M. Rostand publishes, although formed from diverse subjects, have each a continuity, a design, a character. The appearance is a collection of maxims (e.g., 'Who loves violently knows at the time the irritation of loving too much and the remorse of not having loved enough'), the reality is a small analytic novel in which the persons are not described but in which their attitudes are neatly traced." Other analytical novels in this *genre* were *Valere, ou l'Exapérè* (1927) and *Julien ou Une Conscience* (1928).

Meanwhile, Rostand had settled down, in 1922, in a small white house with a large garden and "much shade, silence and simplicity" at Sevres-Ville d'Avray, not far from Versailles. There he has lived ever since, except for periodic forays to marshes in Normandy, Brittany and the Mediterranean area to collect more frogs and toads for his innumerable experiments in parthenogenesis. Although Eugene Bataillon was the first biologist to obtain fatherless offspring from female frogs, in 1910, Rostand has since then been the most notable specialist in the field.

Methods of parthenogenesis, he wrote (*Mes Recherches, France Illustration,* Jan. 17, 1953), have since that time "been varied and perfected, and it is now easy, with the toad at any rate, to obtain a great quantity of subjects of parthenogenetic origin. They are as vigorous as those born of two parents, on the condition that the egg has been submitted to prolonged refrigeration, which has the effect of doubling the number of maternal chromosomes."

Observing in nature certain toads and frogs with variations from the normal five toes, he discovered after intensive investigation that these anomalies were hereditary and "in a pattern of Mendelian character," and that he could reproduce these variations in toads but not in frogs. Is the cause of these anomalies a "physico-chemical factor present in the milieu or an infectious agent or virus?" he asked. "The first hypothesis seems very improbable, for we actually know no inorganic factor capable of producing such effects. If the second hypothesis is verified . . . the study, made more profound by anomalies, whether hereditary or acquired, in toads or frogs, in one way or another may profit the study of human anomalies."

The philosophical side of Rostand is preoccupied with the problem of human parthenogenesis, since many invertebrate animals such as sea urchins and silk worms, and vertebrates such as frogs, toads and rabbits have been parthenogenetically reproduced by Rostand in the laboratory. "As a scientist, Dr. Rostand naturally holds aloof from moral implications," commented *Time* (September 1, 1952), "but as a Frenchman, he is sure that, once parthenogenesis is possible, some women will want to try it. And that really scares him. 'It is thus inevitable that a new kind of human being (according to our present knowledge, they will all be girls) will appear in society and will be aware of their extraordinary origin. . . . Realization of the fact that the male has ceased to be necessary for propagation will not fail to exercise a profound effect on the relations between men and women'" (quoted by *Time* from *Bulletin of the Atomic Scientists,* August 1952).

Of Rostand's fifty published volumes, the majority are on scientific subjects and have been emerging in a steady stream since the publication, in 1928, of *Les Chromosomes, artisans de l'hérédité et du sexe.* Among other works are: *L'Aventure Humaine* (three volumes studying the physiological development of man from the germ stage through old age) (1932-35) and *La Vie des Crapauds* (1933).

In addition Rostand has published numerous experimental research reports in the *Comptes Rendus de la Société de Biologie, Le Bulletin de la Société Entomologique* and *Annales Politiques et Littéraires,* among others. He has also continued to publish from time to time collections of reflective essays: *Les Familiotes et autres essais de mystique bourgeois* (1925), *De la Vanité* (1926), *Le Mariage* (1927), *Jour-*

nal d'un caractère and *Pensées d'une biologiste* (1929) and *Nouvelles Pensées d'une biologiste* (1947). His trenchant, characteristically French individualism and Olympian personality are somewhat reflected in epigrams he has written, such as these from the *Nouvelles Pensées*: "Science has made us gods before we even merit being men"; "To be adult is to be alone"; "The true work is to know how to wait."

The biologist has stated: "There is no metaphysical explanation of the problems of life: nothing but facts and a series of logical reasonings which follow from these facts. Animal forms come into being by chance, progressively, according to a confused process. There is no predetermination."

Rostand is a member of many scientific societies; among these are the Société de Biologie and L'Academie Internationale d'Histoire des Sciences (he is a corresponding member of the latter). He has been awarded the Grand Prix Littéraire de la Ville de Paris, le Prix de l'Academie des Sciences and the Prix du Palais de la Découverte, among others. He is the director of collections for Gallimard editions of the following series of scientific publications: Avenir de la Science, Historie Naturelles and Grandes pages de la Science.

Rostand married Andrée Mante, a sculptress, in 1920; they have one son, François. The biologist stands five feet six inches tall and weighs 150 pounds. He has grey hair and brown eyes, partly obscured by his thick horn-rimmed glasses. He is afraid his eyesight will not outlast his passion for biology, the last science, he believes, in which one can work like an artist, absolutely alone. He sports a walrus moustache and has "the ungarnished cranium of the thinker."

Rostand has said, "When I create literature I can't forget that I'm a scientist. But when I am in my modest laboratory, I completely forget literature." He disavows contact with the modern world, the future of which he may so profoundly affect.

He seldom leaves his home except to go to the theatre when the work of his father or brother is presented. Each Saturday night he goes to the little railroad cafe in Ville d'Avray and plays chess, his only recreation. He believes his gifts are modest ones: "I am absolutely incapable of realizing—I don't even dream of it—that which has been accomplished by . . . Fabre and Maeterlinck," but he does believe that "one should be able to credit me with much patience and a great faculty of concentration."

References

Ann Politiques et Littéraires 94:288 Mr 15 '30
France Illus no379:92 Ja 17 '53
Time 60:33 S 1 '52 por
Dictionnaire Biographique Français Contemporain (1954)
Dictionnaire National des Contemporains (1939)
International Who's Who, 1954
Who's Who in France, 1953-54
World Biography (1954)

ROTHERY, AGNES (EDWARDS) 1888-Aug. 11, 1954 Author; began her career in 1909 after graduating from Wellesley College; on editorial staff, *Ladies' Home Journal;* became literary editor, Boston *Herald* (1910-1914); conducted column (1912-1916), *Christian Science Monitor;* married Professor Harry Rogers Pratt (1917); author of many books on travel, homemaking and gardening, including *New York Today, The Joyful Gardener, Rome Today;* was decorated by King Christian X of Denmark in 1946 for her cycle of books on the five countries of modern Scandinavia including *Denmark, Kingdom of Reason* (1937); also wrote books on Latin America; two autobiographies, *Family Album* (1942) and *A Fitting Habitation* (1944); four novels including *Balm of Gilead* (1946); contributor of articles and stories to leading periodicals. See *Current Biography,* (Yrbk) 1952.

Obituary

N Y Times p25 Ag 12 '54

RUBATTEL, RODOLPHE (rōō'bă-tĕl") Sept. 4, 1896- President of Switzerland; Minister of the Department of Public Economy; lawyer

Address: b. Palais Fédéral, Berne, Switzerland; h. 33 Humboldtstrasse, Berne, Switzerland

In Switzerland, a country that has been described as "astonishingly prosperous, politically stable, and quite satisfied with its way of life," Rodolphe Rubattel is the president for 1954. This office rotates among the seven members of the Federal Council, the executive branch of the Swiss government. Since 1948 Rubattel has been a Federal Councillor, and has also been the head of the Department of Public Economy, a position he continues to hold while President. He had served previously in the Federal and cantonal or state governments, and had been an editor and director of various newspapers.

Rodolphe Rubattel was born on September 4, 1896 in Villarzel, a town between Berne and Lausanne in Switzerland. He is the son of Ernest Rubattel, a landowner and Councillor of State, and Lucie (Chuard) Rubattel, the niece of Ernest Chuard, who was a Federal Councillor from 1920 to 1928. Rodolphe attended the *collège* and the classical Gymnasium in Lausanne. He then began to study law and went to the universities in Paris and Vienna, and the University of Lausanne, from which he received the LL.D. degree.

In his thesis, which was published by the Imprimerie Commerciale in 1922 under the title *Contribution à l'étude de la Réglementation du Travail agricole,* he analyzed the reasons why the rural population in Switzerland was diminishing in favor of the urban, and what could be done to improve the working conditions of the farm laborer. He felt that because of the varying needs of different farms and farmers, general Federal legislation would be ineffective.

(Continued next page)

RODOLPHE RUBATTEL

While spending several months at the Secretariat of Farm Workers at Brugg, he sent questionnaires to 400 Swiss farmers. From the 333 replies he received, he concluded that satisfactory rural working conditions could be established if a farm employer and employee signed an individual contract stipulating wages, the employee's hours, length of service, holidays, and insurance and sickness benefits.

While attending the University of Lausanne, according to Lillian Ross in the *New Yorker* (December 12, 1953), Rubattel acquired a reputation as a debater, and it was predicted that he would become a politician. His fellow students used to tease him by singing "Someday we shall all be brothers and Rubattel will be Federal Councillor" to the tune of the "Internationale." When his friends, who are staunch city fathers, see him now, they still greet him with their old song.

In 1920 he began his career in publishing, and became the editor of such newspapers as the *Feuille d'Avis de Montreux,* the *Tribune,* and the *Feuille d'Avis de Lausanne.* These papers, politically neutral, are concerned primarily with cantonal news. Rubattel began his association with the Department of Public Economy in 1930 and held an administrative post there until 1932. In that year he became the director of *La Revue de Lausanne* (now *La Nouvelle Revue de Lausanne*). This newspaper supports the Radical-Liberal party, of which Rubattel is a member.

The Radical-Liberal party, according to the *Political Handbook of the World* (1954), is "a progressive, middle-class party" which helped to obtain the Swiss Constitution of 1874. It now favors strengthening the country's national defenses. It advocates reform legislation, including social measures and factory laws, and the use of the revenue from alcohol and tobacco taxes for social welfare.

He became, in 1933, the president of a section of the Federal military administration's commission on appeals which hears cases involving soldiers. In that year, he began his political career as a member of the legislative council of the canton of Vaud. He held this position until 1939, when World War II began in Europe.

During the war he served as a judge of the Supreme Penal Court of the War Economy. This court was established to enforce the rules and legislation which were made for rationing food and materials and for regulating the exports and imports of materials and products by Swiss industries. He was director of the cantonal university hospitals from 1939 until December 1944 when he was elected to the executive council of the canton of Vaud. There he directed the department of agriculture, industry, and commerce. He became president of the council in 1946.

The seven members of the Swiss Federal Council are elected for a four-year term by the Federal Assembly (the two houses of the Swiss Parliament, the Council of States and the National Council, meeting in joint session). On December 11, 1947 this assembly elected Rubattel to the Federal Council to succeed Walther Stampfli in 1948 (Rubattel was re-elected in 1951). Every Federal Councillor is put in charge of an administrative department of the republic, and Rubattel was made head of the Department of Public Economy.

The Federal Assembly elects a member of the Federal Council to be the President of Switzerland for one year, and also elects a vice-president who usually succeeds the President. Having served as vice-president of the Confederation in 1953, Rubattel succeeded Philipp Etter as President of Switzerland on January 1, 1954, after being elected the preceding December 22 by a majority of 185 out of 189 valid votes. He assumed office without ceremony.

As head of state, Rubattel receives foreign ambassadors and speaks over the radio to the Swiss people on New Year's Day and on August 1st, a national holiday commemorating the birth of the Confederation in 1291. He prepares the agenda for Federal Council meetings and presides over them. As a councillor he receives a salary of 48,000 francs (about $11,000) a year, and in the presidential post, receives an extra 3,000 francs (about $700) a year.

The Department of Public Economy, of which Rubattel is the director, has a reputation for being the most complex and difficult of the Federal departments to administer. It is concerned with agriculture, industry, foreign trade, price controls (which exist on various commodities and on rents), and the federal old-age insurance fund. According to the provisions of old-age legislation, every Swiss worker contributes 2 per cent of his wages to the insurance fund, and when he retires after the age of sixty-five, he is entitled to an average of about twenty-five dollars a month.

The prosperity of Switzerland has often caused wonder among the many tourists who flock there summer and winter. The country (which remained politically neutral during both world wars) is completely landlocked and has almost no natural resources. Its arable land amounts to only 6 per cent of its total 15,944 square miles. Yet its per capita gold holdings ($306) are larger than those of all other countries—the per capita holdings in the United States are $138—, and its unemployment rate in June 1953 was 0.3 per cent—the rate in the United States was 2.4 per cent (*Newsweek*, June 14, 1954). When asked how the Swiss are able to do it, Rubattel said: "The answer is that Switzerland's principal asset is labor... and the manufacture and export of goods of high value from imported raw materials."

These exports included machines (which earned $242.3 million in 1953), instruments and tools ($82 million), textiles ($141.7 million), chemicals ($129.4 million), and most important of all, watches ($258 million). (The tourist trade earned $116.5 million in 1953.) The watch industry has about 2,500 manufacturers and employs about 50,000 workers. Under the Reciprocal Trade Agreement of 1936, the American tariff on Swiss watch movements was cut from 82.6 to 37 per cent. Recently, such U.S. manufacturers as the Hamilton, Waltham and Elgin companies, which do not use Swiss watch movements (in comparison to Longines-Wittnauer, Gruen, Bulova, and Benrus), asked for an increase in import duty on watches.

On May 28, 1954 the six-man nonpartisan U.S. Tariff Commission recommended the increase, and about a month later, Rubattel appealed to President Dwight D. Eisenhower to prevent the "deep injustice" of increased U.S. duties on Swiss watches, which represent one-half the value of Swiss exports to the United States. He said that the Swiss watch industry "has no desire or claim to secure a monopoly of the American market" and that it "intends only to exercise with the American watch factories that free and loyal competition which is the strength of the American and Swiss economies alike" (New York *Times*, June 26, 1954).

President Eisenhower, however, on July 27, 1954, on recommendation of the Federal Tariff Commission, raised the tariff rates up to 50 per cent on imports of watch movements of seventeen jewels or less. In a news conference on July 28, he said that he had accepted the Tariff Commission's recommendation because U.S. watchmakers' jobs should be protected and because, in the interest of national defense, watchmaking and precision skills should be maintained.

When the U.S. Department of Justice filed an anti-trust suit against twenty-four American and Swiss concerns in October 1954, Michael L. Hoffman wrote that the Swiss were "seething with anger" at what they regarded as the "latest U.S. move against the Swiss watch industry" (New York *Times*, October 21, 1954).

Rodolphe Rubattel married Marthe Moulin on May 20, 1926 and has one daughter, Claire. He has gray hair and wears spectacles. He speaks French and German, and has traveled in Italy, France and Austria, as well as in every canton in Switzerland. He is a major in the Swiss infantry.

The walls of Rubattel's office at the Palais Fédéral are dark brown and on them hang several oil paintings which the Swiss government bought as part of its program to encourage Swiss artists.

References

New Yorker 29:100+ D 12 '53
Annuaire des autorités fédérales, 1953
International Who's Who, 1954
International Yearbook and Statesmen's Who's Who, 1954
Who's Who in Switzerland, 1950-51

RUSSELL, ANNA Dec. 27, 1911- Comedienne; singer

Address: b. c/o Eastman Boomer, 113 W. 57th St., New York 19

Canadian-born Anna Russell, a comedienne in the concert and entertainment field, began her career as a serious opera singer. As a result of a curious accident which elicited hilarious laughter from her audience, she decided to become a comic vocalist. During the past five years, she has become widely known as a satirist of opera stars, a lampooner of oratorios and salon music, and a "gifted and irreverent" mimic of folk singers and concert pianists.

Miss Russell's latest New York concert appearances were on November 27, 1953 at Carnegie Hall and on November 27, 1954 at Town Hall. She gave thirteen sold-out concerts in London, England in the fall of 1954. In addition to doing concert work, the comedienne has appeared on Broadway and on radio and television shows. In one season she has performed before more than 100,000 persons in the United States and Canada. All of her recordings have reached the best seller lists. Anna Russell plays the voice of the witch in *Hansel and Gretel*, a 3-D movie which uses electronic puppets. In this role she made her debut at the New York City Opera Company on April 3, 1954; she is now a permanent member of this company.

Claudia Russell-Brown was born in London, Ontario, Canada, on December 27, 1911, the only child of Colonel Claude Russell-Brown and Beatrice Magdalen (Tandy) Russell-Brown. For three generations every male on her father's side of the family served in the British Army; a grandfather, Colonel F. D. M. Brown, won the Victoria Cross and her father was awarded the C.B. and D.S.O. Her mother received the M.B.E. (Member of the Order of the Britsh Empire) for doing rehabilitation work in Hong Kong. Claudia's great-great-grandmother was Mrs. Hannah Cowley, author of the play *The Belle's Stratagem* (1781).

When she was six months old, her father moved from the Royal Military College in Canada where he had been a teacher and took the family to London, England. "I was thoroughly *done* as I grew up," Miss Russell stated in an interview (New York *Times*, September 6, 1953). "I was presented at court in 1934. I was a debutante. I was exposed to all the

ANNA RUSSELL

likely looking young men in the hope that one of them would marry me."

For four years, she attended the Royal College of Music in London where she studied piano, theory, harmony, cello, voice, and composition with such teachers as the composer Ralph Vaughan Williams. Upon graduating Claudia Russell-Brown embarked upon a serious singing career.

Her first engagement was with the British Broadcasting Company, to give folk song recitals. During this period, she shortened her name to Anna Russell. The young singer performed in Spanish, French and German, in addition to appearing throughout England in oratorios and operas.

It was while she was on tour with a British company and singing in *Cavalleria Rusticana* that the incident occurred which made her begin to think of changing from serious to satirical singing. Playing opposite her was a tenor much smaller than Miss Russell. During the duet he was unable to hurl her to the ground according to the stage directions in the script. In her effort to assist the diminutive singer, Miss Russell turned her ankle and went spinning across the stage and into the "prop" church, and the whole set came tumbling down. The audience roared, and even the orchestra laughed so much that the performance was ended. "So was my career," says Miss Russell. "My life's work was shattered, after five years of hard preparation. . . . But I got over it."

Before the Second World War Anna Russell and her mother returned to Toronto where the former began singing English music hall songs on a Toronto radio station. The entertainer wrote her own material, a practice which she has continued, because, as she explains, "such horrible things [were] shot at me that I decided to sit down and write stuff myself." Her appearances before women's clubs, on Army camp shows and on various radio programs enabled her to establish a reputation as a satirical vocalist. She gave many concerts in Toronto before she came to New York in 1947.

"In New York I lived at the Rehearsal Club and kept going around to the producers and agents, but I was never the girl they needed," Miss Russell relates. She finally was assigned to the part of playing Lady Bracknell in *The Importance of Being Earnest* on television.

Anna Russell first appeared at Town Hall on February 10, 1948. Describing herself as the "former leading soprano of the Ellis Island Opera Company," Miss Russell gave "skillful mimicry of the affectations and mannerisms of *lieder* singers, fading operatic artists and pianists of varying types." A reviewer for the New York *Sun* (February 11, 1948) found: "Miss Russell combines and coordinates a number of talents. She is a fine actress . . . her voice is better than average. Binding these elements together is a fundamental sense of humor and keen observation that make it possible for her . . . to organize her material in a demoralizingly effective manner. The audience had a wonderful time."

A capacity hall greeted Anna Russell on November 27, 1951 when she returned to Town Hall. A reviewer in the New York *Herald Tribune* (November 28, 1951) wrote: "Arias such as . . . 'Ah, lover!' from the operetta *The Prince of Philadelphia* evoked howls of merriment, while the lieder *Schlumph* (for singers with tremendous artistry and no voice) . . . reduced the audience to near hysteria."

Other reviewers were equally enthusiastic, and by 1953, Miss Russell was able to state that she'd made in total "about six appearances at Town Hall" (New York *World-Telegram and Sun,* August 26, 1953). In the 1952 to 1953 season, the sharp-witted lampooner appeared before more than 100,000 spectators in thirty-seven cities across the nation and Canada in addition to making frequent telecasts with *The Fred Waring Show* over CBS-TV from October 19, 1952 to the spring of 1953. She has also appeared on the *Toast of the Town* (CBS), *The Garry Moore Show* (CBS) and the *Kraft Television Theatre* (NBC).

The operatic comic has recorded for Columbia Records, Inc. Her album entitled *Anna Russell Sings?* held best seller rank for eighteen weeks in the "art" category. Her next album, *Anna Russell Sings! Again?,* released late in 1953, has proved very popular with musical sophisticates. Her latest, *Anna Russell* released October 1, 1954, has outsold all her other records.

Anna Russell and Her Little Show opened at the Vanderbilt Theatre on September 7, 1953, under the production auspices of Eastman Boomer, Miss Russell's manager, and Arthur Klein. A master of ceremonies, a magician and a troupe of Haitian dancers were included in addition to Miss Russell's repertoire.

However, the production did not do well at the hands of the drama critics; only several were favorable toward it. Ward Morehouse of the New York *World-Telegram and Sun,* (September 12, 1953), spoke for a majority of the critics when he said: "In her burlesque of songs and singers and pianists she is fairly overpowering and seems frequently on the verge of tearing down the theater . . . in her first brush with the Broadway stage she meets a defeat." In the New York *Journal-American,* (September 8, 1953), John McClain reported: "Miss Russell has assayed to write the material, the music and arrangements. She has abundant energy, unqualified gifts of comedy and timing. . . ." The revue closed on September 19, 1953.

On the other hand, the music critics were laudatory in reviewing her concert appearance at Carnegie Hall on November 27, 1953. The New York *Times* commented: "With acid wit she satirizes coloraturas . . . . barrel-chested singers of German lieder; people who sing madrigals; people who do not sing madrigals; Bach cantatas; antique operas; modern operas; drawing-room ballads; flamenco singers; and anything else that swims within her somewhat jaundiced ken. It is all done very deftly, with a light touch. . . ."

Musical America (December 15, 1953) reported: "A jam-packed house was on hand to confirm the wisdom of Miss Russell's decision to forego the intimacy of Town Hall for the added prestige, and seating capacity, of Carnegie Hall. . . . Much of her program also was entirely new . . . . and there were the familiar regrets that she had to drop several of her old standby bits for reasons of time. It came as no surprise, however, that the fresh material was a harvest of delight. . . . Miss Russell's inimitable analysis of the Ring cycle . . . [is a] comic masterpiece."

"No one in the world of music is safe from the satire of Anna Russell," orchestra leader Fred Waring once said. "She tears them apart from Brünnehilde's meaty bellows to the lacey coloratura. From the torch singers like Edith Piaf to the handkerchief waving of Hildegarde —she is the authority on what not to do on the concert stage—unless you want to risk the Russell barbs."

Anna Russell has appeared as a soloist with such symphony orchestras as the Cincinnati, New Orleans and Toronto, and at the musical festivals in Aspen (Colorado), Brevard (North Carolina), Tanglewood, and Chicago. The National Federation of Music Clubs chose her as the featured artist for their biennial convention and she appeared as guest artist with the National Concert Managers Association convention. She is an honorary member of the music faculty of the Aspen Institute.

The comedienne's first marriage, to John Dennison, ended in divorce. In 1954 she was divorced from Charles Goldhamer, an artist. Miss Russell is five feet eight inches tall, has blue eyes and blonde hair and is described as "hearty and likeable." She enjoys gardening and making soup.

References

N Y Herald Tribune IV p1 S 6 '53 pors; IX p25 O 25 '53 por
N Y Times II p3 S 6 '53 por
N Y World-Telegram p24 Ag 26 '53

SALK, JONAS E(DWARD) (sawlk) Oct. 28, 1914- Epidemiologist; physician

Address: b. c/o School of Medicine, University of Pittsburgh, Pittsburgh, Pa.; h. 5633 Bartlett St., Pittsburgh, Pa.

In testing a new anti-polio vaccine on nearly 1,000,000 children during 1954, the National Foundation for Infantile Paralysis utilized the serum discovered by Dr. Jonas E. Salk, and announced by him in the spring of 1953. Reports on the new vaccine, which preliminary tests have shown to be effective and safe, have given rise to the belief, as expressed by Leonard Engel in the New York *Times Magazine* (May 31, 1953) that "the total conquest of polio through immunization is in sight." The mass-testing of Dr. Salk's new weapon of science in the battle against the crippling poliomyelitis is being financed by contributions to the foundation's March of Dimes appeal, and cost over $7,500,000.

Evaluation of the test was expected to be completed in April 1955. "Taking a calculated risk," as its president, Basil O'Connor, explained in October 1954, the National Foundation contracted to purchase $9,000,000 worth of Salk's vaccine. The additional 25,000,000 cc. of vaccine thus obtained, together with the 2,000,000 cc. that the foundation had on hand, would be used to inoculate 9,000,000 persons in 1954, should the vaccine prove to be effective.

Largely through his skill in putting to use technical achievements of many scientists, Dr. Salk developed the anti-polio vaccine at the School of Medicine of the University of Pittsburgh, where he has been a research professor of bacteriology and director of the Virus Research Laboratory since 1947.

He is known also for his work with influenza vaccines, on which he experimented while at the University of Michigan from 1942 to 1947. In April 1953 he announced that tests of his new influenza serum on 20,000 persons had given some of them protection against the disease for about two years.

The eldest of three sons, Jonas Edward Salk was born to Daniel B. and Dora (Press) Salk on October 28, 1914 in upper Manhattan. His father, who was employed in the garment district of New York City, soon afterward moved his family from Manhattan to a home in the Bronx, where Jonas went to grade school. He graduated from Townsend Harris High School, which was then a secondary school for exceptional students. He has been described as a studious youth who "read everything he could lay his hands on, tried to be a perfectionist in school work . . . and earned high grades" (New York *Times,* October 11, 1953).

While preparing for his B.S. degree (conferred in 1934) at the College of the City of New York, Salk spent his summers working as a counselor at a boys' camp and was also employed for a time as a laboratory technician. Assisted by fellowships in chemistry and experimental surgery, he studied medicine at the New York University College of Medicine. After being granted his M.D. degree in June 1939, he remained for a brief period at the university as a fellow in bacteriology. He then

Wide World

DR. JONAS E. SALK

interned for two years at New York's Mount Sinai Hospital.

A fellowship in epidemiology from the National Research Council enabled Dr. Salk to attend the University of Michigan in 1942 for research on the influenza virus, a subject in which he had become interested while a medical student. At Michigan, in collaboration with the virologist Dr. Thomas Francis, Jr. (under whom he had studied at New York University), Salk helped to develop commercial vaccines against influenza.

He became a research fellow in the department of epidemiology of the university's School of Public Health in 1943, a research associate there in 1944, and was advanced to assistant professor of epidemiology in 1946.

When the University of Pittsburgh expanded its program for virus research in 1947, Dr. Salk joined the staff. Since that time he has been director of the Virus Research Laboratory of the School of Medicine and was promoted in 1949 from associate research professor of bacteriology to full research professor. While he continued his work on influenza vaccines, he grew increasingly interested in the search for an effective preventive against poliomyelitis.

Operating with funds from the March of Dimes of the National Foundation for Infantile Paralysis, Dr. Salk became one of the directors of a three-year study of the "typing" of polio virus, undertaken by the universities of Pittsburgh, Utah, Kansas, and Southern California. This project showed that polio in the United States is caused by one of three strains of virus (types I, II and III; then called Brunhilde, Lansing and Leon) and that a vaccine—to be effective—must immunize against all three.

Further progress toward an anti-polio vaccine was made when Dr. Salk used a new technique, reported in 1949 by Dr. John F. Enders of Harvard University, for growing polio virus in cultures of non-nervous tissues. After cultivating the virus in the kidney tissues of monkeys, Dr. Salk killed it with formaldehyde.

Another step toward his goal was his finding a way to increase the stimulation of antibodies by the virus. As related by Leonard Engel in the New York *Times Magazine* (May 31, 1953), "Dr. Salk . . . tried a trick for enhancing vaccine potency discovered by Dr. Jules Freund of the New York City Health Department in 1942. . . . This was whipping the vaccine into a creamy emulsion with a small amount of a specially purified mineral oil."

"Dr. Salk's prescription," according to *Time* (March 29, 1954), "calls for the Mahoney strain (Type I), MEF-1 strain (Type II) and the Saukett [Sarkett] strain (Type III). . . ."

When he had tested his vaccine on over 100 children and adults, Dr. Salk announced his results in the *Journal of the American Medical Association* (March 28, 1953) and at a press conference arranged by the National Foundation for Infantile Paralysis. The vaccine, while experimentally successful, did not mean that the "desired objective" had been attained, the scientist cautioned. It was pointed out that techniques needed to be perfected and that the vaccine would have to be extensively tested for effectiveness and safety before being made available to the general public.

Press comments on Dr. Salk's announcement called attention to the difference between the new vaccine and gamma globulin, an expensive blood derivative containing antibodies that for some people minimize the effects of polio for about six weeks. A vaccine, if effective, would prevent the disease, which during the epidemic of 1952 killed 3,300 of the 57,626 persons stricken.

At a conference of the American Academy of Pediatrics in Miami, Florida on October 9, 1953 Dr. Salk reported that more than 600 persons had been inoculated with the new vaccine. "It now becomes possible to determine whether or not—and to what extent—the incidence of naturally occurring paralysis may be influenced," he told the conference (New York *Times*).

The National Foundation for Infantile Paralysis also disclosed at this conference that it was making plans for large-scale testing of Dr. Salk's vaccine. The following month (November 1953) the foundation announced that by midwinter some 5,000 children in western Pennsylvania would be inoculated and that beginning in the spring of 1954 mass field trials would be started in which from 500,000 to 1,000,000 children, with the approval of their parents, would receive vaccination.

In the $7,500,000 test each child would be given three injections with serum checked for safety by pharmaceutical manufacturers, Dr. Salk and the United States National Institutes of Health. Dr. Salk, who tested the vaccine on his wife and children as well as himself, has sought on several occasions to dispel any question regarding its safety and gave assurance in a speech in New York City in November 1953 that he would be "personally responsible" for it.

The purpose of the foundation's test is to determine whether the vaccine will prevent paralytic polio and how long the immunity will last. "If the vaccine fulfills the hope that at last a way has been found to cope with poliomyelitis as effectively as public health officers cope with smallpox or typhus," observed Waldemar Kaempffert of the New York *Times* (November 22, 1953), "Dr. Salk will have scored one of the greatest triumphs in the history of medicine."

After about 5,000 children in the Pittsburgh area had been vaccinated, it was stated in an article in *Time* (March 29, 1954) that Dr. Salk has had no "unfavorable reactions with his vaccine. . . . If any unfavorable reactions develop, they are likely to be minor, and if serious, as rare as the one case in 10,000 that reacts badly to diphtheria vaccine."

Because of "unwarranted attacks" on the safety of the polio vaccine, the New York State Health Commissioner, Dr. Herman E. Hilleboe, reaffirmed his confidence in Dr. Salk on April 8, 1954, and stated that every safeguard known to medical science has been employed to protect the children's health and that the vaccine has passed all safety tests.

A decision on the effectiveness of the new polio vaccine during one season "must await Dr. [Thomas] Francis' report [an evaluation of the tests] a year from now. Dr. Salk has high hope that his vaccine will lead the way to lifelong immunity; proof of this will take more years."

Shortly after reporting his anti-polio vaccine, Dr. Salk announced in the *Journal of the American Medical Association* (April 4, 1953) a new vaccine giving long-lasting protection against influenza. The flu vaccine, on which experiments were conducted among some 20,000 persons (soldiers at Fort Dix, New Jersey, and medical personnel and foundlings at the Roselia Foundling Home), owes its effectiveness to the same kind of mineral oil emulsion used in the anti-polio vaccine.

The findings of Dr. Salk and his associates on polio and influenza virus research have appeared frequently in scientific papers in a number of professional periodicals other than the A.M.A. *Journal;* among them are the *Journal of Immunology, American Journal of Public Health,* and *Proceedings of the Society for Experimental Biology and Medicine.* He has also contributed articles to magazines like *Science* and *Parents' Magazine.*

Since 1944 Dr. Salk has been a member of the commission on influenza of the United States Army epidemiological board, until 1947 as consultant in epidemic diseases to the Secretary of War and from that time consultant in the same field to the Secretary of the Army. He has served since 1948 on the consulting staff of the Municipal Hospital for Contagious Diseases in Pittsburgh, and since 1949 on the consulting staff of the Presbyterian Hospital in Pittsburgh. He is also a consultant on virus diseases to the World Health Organization.

He belongs to a number of professional associations: American Epidemiological Society, American Association of Immunologists, American Society for Clinical Investigation, Central Society for Clinical Research, Society for Experimental Biology and Medicine, Allegheny County Medical Society and American Association of University Professors.

He is a fellow of the American Public Health Association and the American Association for the Advancement of Science, an honorary member of the Mississippi Valley Medical Society and past president (1949 to 1950) of the Allegheny branch of the Society of American Bacteriologists. His Greek-letter societies are Alpha Omega Alpha, Sigma Xi and Delta Omega.

Dr. Salk and his wife, Donna (Lindsay) Salk, a former social service worker whom he married on June 9, 1939, are the parents of three children—Peter, Darrell and Jonathan.

According to an article in *Time* (March 29, 1954), it is not unusual for Dr. Salk "to work a sixteen-hour day six days a week, though he tries to take most of Sunday off to be with his boys. Golf and tennis are only memories."

Time also reported a story about Dr. Salk's "concentration, and . . . his humor. . . . [Mrs. Salk] was talking to him about family matters and could tell by his faraway look that his thoughts were back in the lab. 'Why, Jonas,' she protested, 'you're not listening to me at all.' Grinned Dr. Salk: 'My dear, I'm giving you my undevoted attention.'"

References

N Y Times Mag p11+ My 31 '53; p7+ Ja 10 '54 por
N Y World-Telegram Mag p11 Ap 11 '53 por
Time 63:56+ Mr 29 '54 pors
American Men of Science (1949)

SAMUEL, BERNARD Mar. 9, 1880-Jan. 12, 1954 Former mayor of Philadelphia; Republican member of city council of Philadelphia (1923-1939); served as finance committee chairman of city council; elected president of city council (1939); succeeded Mayor Robert E. Lamberton upon the latter's death (1941); elected as mayor (1943) and re-elected (1947); returned to brokerage business after not seeking a third term. See *Current Biography,* (Sept.) 1949.

Obituary

N Y Times p32 Ja 13 '54

SARACOGLU, SÜKRÜ 1887(?)-Dec. 27, 1953 Former Prime Minister of Turkey; received law degree from University of Lausanne; Nationalist deputy to Ottoman Parliament (1919); deputy (Mustafa Kemal Pasha's People's Party) of first Kamutay (National Assembly); appointed Minister of Finance; served as Minister of Justice (1932-1938); as Foreign Minister (1938-1942) maintained Turkey's neutrality; served as Prime Minister (1942-1946); in February 1945 declared war on Germany and Japan. See *Current Biography,* (June) 1942.

Obituary

N Y Times p21 D 28 '53

SAUD, KING OF SAUDI ARABIA (sōō-ōōd) Jan. 15, 1902-
Address: Royal Palace, Riyadh, Nejd, Saudi Arabia

When Crown Prince Saud Ibn Abdul Aziz became King of Saudi Arabia following the death of his father in November 1953, he succeeded to a throne that during the rule of the late King Ibn Saud had come to be regarded as the wealthiest and most powerful in the Middle East. Trained since the age of thirteen for public life and desert warfare, Saud had been made the King's heir in 1933, and as commander in chief of the Saudi Arabian Army and later as Premier had gradually assumed increased governmental authority.

Wide World
SAUD, KING OF SAUDI ARABIA

American political observers have called attention to the importance of King Saud's friendly attitude toward the West. The significance of his succession was commented on by the New York *World-Telegram and Sun* (November 14, 1953): "For on the ultimate course followed by the new King hangs a $700,000,000 investment by the American oil companies, and Saudi Arabia's strategic air bases form a shield against the ever threatening Russians."

Saud Ibn Abdul Aziz al Faisal al Saud (whose name means Saud, the son of Abdul Aziz of the family of Faisal of the house of Saud) was born on January 15, 1902. In the year 1901 his father, known to the Occident as Ibn Saud, whose family had been deposed as rulers of the kingdom of Nejd and had sought refuge in Kuwait, succeeded in recapturing the Nejd city of Riyadh, which he then made the center of his expanding realm.

Saud, the third of Ibn Saud's many sons, was educated in Kuwait and during his youth took part in his father's campaigns against the Ottoman Turks. At the age of thirteen the young prince was sent to the Sheikdom of Qatar to capture a political refugee. In 1919 he took a prominent role in the victorious fighting against the Utaibah tribe and in subsequent battles joined his father to complete the conquest in 1924 of the Hashimite rulers of Hejaz. After Abdul Aziz had established himself in 1927 as King of Hejaz, Nejd and dependencies, there was further warfare to subdue the unruly Bedouin tribes and consolidate monarchial power throughout the oasis towns and vast deserts of the Arabian peninsula.

Emir Saud made his first pilgrimage to Mecca in 1924. It was on a later visit to the Islamic holy city that the prince saved his father's life by intercepting the stab of an assassin's dagger. The Arabian kingdom of some 927,000 square miles with a population of about 6,500,000 had meanwhile, in 1932, been given the name of Saudi Arabia. The following year, on May 11, 1933, the prince, who had proved his statesmanship in his rule of various provinces, was designated successor to the throne by the Consultative Assembly. Through this decision, later supported by royal decree, King Ibn Saud secured for his eldest surviving son an inheritance which under Arab custom he would not automatically have received.

Having been appointed commander in chief of the Army in Asir and Najran in 1934, a few years later (1939) Crown Prince Saud became deputy commander of the Saudi Arabian Army and some time afterward commander in chief of all troops in the kingdom. Another of his titles was Viceroy of Nejd. As the representative of King Ibn Saud, who seldom traveled abroad, he made a trip to the Netherlands in 1935, attended the coronation of the late King George VI of England in 1936, visited Iraq in 1937 and later a number of European countries. He was present at the Enshas conference in Egypt in 1946.

At the invitation of President Harry S. Truman, Saud spent more than a month in 1947 in the United States. He paid an official call at United Nations headquarters on January 21 and spoke of his awareness of the great sacrifices needed to realize the goals of the U.N. in establishing world peace. "The Arabs in general and Saudi Arabia in particular," he gave assurance, "are determined to bear the brunt of the burden which befalls them in that respect and to serve the cause of these ideals" (*United Nations Bulletin*, January 28, 1947).

The kingdom of Saudi Arabia has been of growing economic importance to the United States since 1933 when King Ibn Saud granted concessions to the Standard Oil Company of California to explore what was later discovered to be possibly the richest oil deposits in the world. In 1945 he concluded a contract with Aramco (the Arabian American Oil Company owned by the Standard Oil Company of California, Standard Oil Company of New Jersey,

Socony-Vacuum Oil Company, and Texas companies), by which, under a later renegotiation, Saudi Arabia received 50 per cent of the company's annual profits of $150,000,000.

Crown Prince Saud shared in the direction of a program of modernization initiated by his father, including the building of highways across the deserts and the completion in 1951 of the Saudi government railroad. In early 1953 he announced a number of projected domestic improvements such as administrative changes in government and the building of roads, schools and hospitals.

By a decree issued on October 10, 1953 establishing the first regular Saudi Arabian Cabinet, the critically ill King Ibn Saud named the Crown Prince as Premier, with direct authority over all ministries and with power, subject to the King's veto, to pass on any contract or agreement made by the ministries. This decree foreshadowed the death of Ibn Saud a month later, on November 9, and Saud's immediate accession to the throne.

"It is rare in Arabian history," noted Harry B. Ellis of the *Christian Science Monitor* (November 10, 1953), "that tribal loyalty has been transferred permanently from a ruler to his son, and the burden of proof is expected to be on the new King in the task of persuading tribal sheiks that he is a worthy successor of one of the greatest desert warriors of all time."

One of the foremost problems confronting the monarch was economic unrest among Aramco's oil workers and among the nation's middle-class businessmen. In a policy statement of December 5, 1953, King Saud made known his plans to use the country's revenues from oil to accelerate utilization of her other resources. He spoke particularly of development of "agricultural resources by adopting modern methods, providing water for irrigation through construction of dams and canals, and connecting the agricultural areas of the country with other parts of the kingdom by modern communication facilities" (New York *Times*, December 6, 1953). Plans also call for the improvement of the ports of Jidda and Dammam, which will be linked with Riyadh by an extension of the Saudi railroad.

The New York *Times* of December 12, 1953 commented on the "forward-looking leadership" of the new King and on the challenge before him of overcoming vested interests in order to create a progressive state. "The constitutional arrangements of the country, which has only recently begun to emerge from feudalism, offer difficult barriers. The royal household of almost 10,000 people consumes 16 per cent of the state revenues, while tribal leaders require subsidies which are a further heavy drain."

Like his father, King Saud has welcomed investment of American capital. After Saud's accession, the U.S. Military Assistance Advisory Group in Saudi Arabia elaborated plans for a military training program to expand and equip the kingdom's ground troops and to create a small air force. With the assistance of the public health section of the U.S. point four mission, King Saud was building a quarantine center, said to be the largest in the world, to handle the annual visits of thousands of pilgrims to Mecca and other shrines in the country.

However, on October 17, 1954, it was announced that the United States had closed its foreign aid mission in Saudi Arabia in accordance with Arabian demands.

In early 1954 the King visited nearly every community and Bedouin encampment in north and central Arabia in order to renew ties of loyalty with his independent-minded people, and distributed gifts of silver, clothing, etc.

The new Saudi Arabian King holds honors conferred by foregn countries; Knight Grand Cross of the British Empire; chevalier of the Legion of Honor; Grand Cordon of the Crown of Italy; Grand Cordon of Orange-Nassau of the Netherlands; Grand Cordon of Léopold I of Belgium; and Grand Cordon of Al-Istiklal of Jordan. On his visit to the United States he received the Legion of Merit from President Truman, to whom he presented a jeweled sword and dagger.

A strict adherent of the Mohammedan Wahhabi sect, as was his father, King Saud abstains from tobacco and alcohol. He follows the late King's practice of furthering alliances among Arabian tribes by contracting many marriages—taking in accordance with Koran rule not more than four wives at a time—and is the father of twenty-two sons. The new Crown Prince is not one of Saud's sons, but rather his brother Emir Faisal Ibn Abdul Aziz, Saudi Arabia's chief delegate to the United Nations.

King Saud's stature almost equals his father's six feet four inches and like the late King he wears glasses for nearsightedness. He also shows Ibn Saud's fondness for some of the luxuries of Western civilization such as air conditioning, neon lighting and Cadillac cars. He employs an American steward for his Waldorf-Astoria-inspired kitchen, reportedly stocked with large supplies of food imported from the United States.

In January 1954 King Saud "suggested . . . that the Arab nations should sacrifice up to 10,000,000 of their 50,000,000 people, if necessary, to wipe out Israel." He asserted that "Israel, to the Arab world, is like a cancer to the human body, and the only way of remedy is to uproot it just like a cancer" (New York *Times*, January 10, 1954).

References

Christian Sci Mon p9 Ap 27 '53; p6 N 10 '53 por
Life 35:66+ D 21 '53 por
N Y Herald Tribune p5 O 11 '53; p1+ N 10 '53 por; II p1 N 15 '53 por
N Y Times p14 N 10 '53; p12 D 11 '53
N Y World-Telegram Mag p14+ N 14 '53 pors
U N Bul 2:73+ Ja 28 '47
Washington (D.C.) Post p41 D 9 '53
International Who's Who, 1953
Who's Who in Egypt and the Near East, 1953

SAWYER, HELEN (ALTON) Artist; teacher

Address: b. 4823 Harry Higel Ave., Sarasota, Fla.; h. 3482 Flamingo, Sarasota, Fla.; "Five Elms," North Truro, Cape Cod, Mass.

Although Helen Sawyer is best known for her paintings of circus clowns, acrobats and bareback riders, her own interest in subject matter encompasses landscapes, marines, flowers, and portraits as well. Since her first one-man show was held at the Milch Art Gallery in 1940 in New York City, she has exhibited widely in America and in Europe and was elected a full painter member of the National Academy of Design in 1950. She was chosen in 1953 president of the Florida Artist Group for a one-year term.

She is represented in many private collections as well as in national museums and has shown a great versatility and "controlled harmony" in her paintings. In spite of much study and travel abroad, she has kept close to the American scene. Her Florida and Cape Cod landscapes have been exhibited at The Art Institute of Chicago, The Pennsylvania Academy of the Fine Arts, and the Metropolitan Museum of Art.

Lucia

HELEN SAWYER

"Unquestionably, Helen Sawyer is one of America's most gifted painters," wrote Ernest W. Watson in the *American Artist* (September, 1949). "Always she paints to express a mood rather than to record a specific scene," Watson commented, "—spring rather than an orchard; the threat and fury of sea and sky rather than a particular place in time of storm. She is one of very few contemporaries who really paints the sky convincingly. She absorbs the world she paints into something both personal and endowed with the rhythmic quality of nature."

Helen Alton Sawyer, known to her friends as "Henka," was born in Washington, D.C., the daughter of Wells Moses Sawyer and Kathleen (Bailey) Sawyer. She had one brother who served in the Royal Air Force in World War II and was killed. Her mother is of English and Irish descent, and her father of Scotch and Spanish ancestry. She is a descendant of New England seafaring families on both sides of her family.

"I grew up in an atmosphere of painting and painting talk," she has said. Her mother was interested in music, and her father was a professional artist. "Music, painting and a great interest in the natural world formed the background of my childhood and my growing-up years. I had the friendships of grown-up people who were richly endowed with wide interests in many fields—scientists, naturalists and musicians as well as painters."

While her parents lived at Scarboro-on-the-Hudson, she attended Yonkers High School in Yonkers, New York for several years, and later went to The Masters School at Dobbs Ferry, New York, from which she was graduated in 1918. Her artistic talent was obvious as a young girl, and was encouraged by her father whose paintings of Mexico, Spain and Africa have been exhibited at the Ferargil and Milch galleries. With her parents she spent several years in Spain, then returned to the United States and studied at Charles W. Hawthorne's school on Cape Cod. Later she took art courses at the Art Students League and at the old Academy school in New York City.

"When I started to paint," she recalls, "my father taught me to study thoroughly the background for any type of creative effort. He showed me how to think of the visual world in terms of form and color and inner significance in relationship to life as a whole. The last line in Thoreau's *Walden,* 'The sun is but a morning star,' and its implication seems to have been with me since the age of memory."

Her first one-man show was held at the Milch Art Gallery in New York. "Rarely does one come on a debut exhibition as deeply satisfying as that of Helen Sawyer's paintings," wrote the art critic in the New York *World-Telegram* (November 23, 1940). There can be no question of the maturity of her talent. . . . Strongly evident are the warmth of her colors, her poetic approach, and the vigor and breadth of her technique. Whether she does a work like the large, strong, richly pigmented *Bouquet with Bronze Sunflowers,* or the expansive yet compactly organized landscape she calls *My Dog Jeffer,* or the rhythmically designed *Valley Farm,* or the crisp and incisive *Winter in the Village,* her oils have that combination of vital energy, sensibility and textual warmth which are the mark of the true artist."

She is represented in the Whitney Museum of American Art with her still-life *Florida,* and at The Pennsylvania Academy of the Fine Arts with *Sailors Take Warning* which she painted on Cape Cod during a three-day northeaster in January. "She parked the car on the cliff a hundred feet above the Atlantic," wrote Ernest W. Watson (*American Artist,* September 1949), "where the gale tossed the old car about like a small boat."

Asked to describe her experiences in painting this canvas which shows the Cape Cod Lighthouse, one of the great beacons of the Atlantic coast, Miss Sawyer said: "Drawing the detailed red and white trusses of the radio beacon and construction of the tower was difficult with my large canvas billowing like a square sail.... I made a few detail drawings as I went along. I decided to finish the canvas in the old station wagon, though there I had to work on my knees. I tried to suggest the presence of the unseen ocean beyond the drop of the lighthouse buildings."

"When I paint a landscape," she has written, "it is never a literal representation, but I paint what I feel about what I see. Imaginative concepts have paralleled translations of nature and people. . . . Color and paint quality have great value as significant manifestations of the world in our crowded times. . . . Leave the terms and the meanings to the brilliant critics and the scholars. The artist cannot be self-conscious in his work. He can only paint. I like to paint the great and the small" (Sarasota *Herald-Tribune*).

Regional landscapes by Helen Sawyer were shown at the Milner Gallery of the Illinois State Normal University in February 1943, following a retrospective show in January at the University of Illinois. Dr. Gladys L. Bartle, reviewing the show for Bloomington's *Pantagraph,* wrote that Miss Sawyer's "view of Wellfleet, Massachusetts entitled *Trees by the Turn* has directness, dignity and . . . shows the true worth and depth of feeling of the people through the dominance of vertical tree forms, firmly modeled and decisively outlined."

Miss Sawyer married, on August 26, 1925, Jerry Farnsworth, an artist whom she met on Cape Cod where both were students in one of Charles W. Hawthorne's painting classes. Together, they now conduct art classes in their studio in North Truro on the Cape during the summers, and in the winter months they have a large school in Sarasota, Florida. They do their own painting in a second floor studio of their home, designed and largely built by her husband, on a Florida bayou. Here they can enjoy sailing, fishing, and "hunting fossils."

Since Sarasota is the winter quarters of the Ringling Brothers circus, Helen Sawyer spends much time among the wagons and tents of the "Big Show", sketching and painting the circus folk in action. The clowns and acrobats also come to pose in her studio for their portraits.

She is included in *Twenty Painters and How They Work* (Watson-Guptill, 1950), written by Ernest W. Watson, editor-in-chief of the magazine *American Artist.* She is the author of the article "Living Among the Modern Primitives" which appeared in *Scribner's Magazine* (November 1927) and was part of a journal she kept while living in France.

One of her Florida landscapes, *Morning on the Beach,* was selected for the "American Painting Today" competition in 1950 at the Metropolitan Museum of Art in which over 6,000 artists competed and some 300 of whose works were chosen for exhibition. (A portrait by Jerry Farnsworth, her husband, was also included among the 300.)

Her paintings which hang in the Carnegie Institute (Pittsburgh, Pennsylvania) include: *Florida Landscape, Halloween Still-Life, Castaway at Noon, Carnival,* and *Mardi Gras.* The Toledo (Ohio) Museum of Art owns her *Valentine Still-Life,* and the Indianapolis (Indiana) museum, her *Still-Life with Staffordshire.* The Miami University of Oxford, Ohio has her *Arrangement on a Chair,* and the Chesapeake & Ohio Railway Company, her *Spring in the Blue Ridge.* Other of her paintings are owned by the International Business Machines Corporation, the Vanderpoel Collection, Chicago, and the John and Mable Ringling Museum of Art in Sarasota. The Library of Congress owns some of her lithographs.

Her awards include first honorable mention for landscape in the Forty-seventh Annual American Exhibit of The Art Institute of Chicago (1936); first prize for landscape (1935) and portrait (1936) in the Hudson Valley Art Association exhibitions; honorable mention for figure, Southeastern exhibit, Atlanta, Georgia, in 1946 and 1947; the Barry Award for the best painting in the Circus Subjects Art Show at the Ringling museum in Sarasota; and the Sarasota *Herald-Tribune* prize for a landscape (1951). Her lithograph, *Amanda,* is included in *Fine Prints of the Year* (1937). Her painting *Circus Girl* was reproduced in full color on the cover of *This Week Magazine* (April 11, 1948).

She had a one-man show at the Miami (Florida) Art Center in 1953. She has had two-man shows with her husband at the Speed Memorial Museum, Louisville, Kentucky, and at the New Britain (Connecticut) Institute; two-man shows with her father, Wells Sawyer, at the Babcock and Ferargil galleries; and a one-man show at the Grand Central Art Galleries (New York).

Her paintings were exhibited at the Century of Progress Fair, Chicago; New York World's Fair; San Francisco World's Fair; Montclair (New Jersey) Women Painters of America exhibit; the Corcoran Gallery of Art (Washington, D.C.); and the Audubon Artists Group shows. She is a member of the Sarasota (Florida) Art Association, Provincetown (Massachusetts) Art Association, and the National Arts Club in New York City.

Helen Sawyer is slight, dark-haired, and "endowed with a warm, out-giving personality." She has hazel eyes, is five feet two inches tall, and weighs 120 pounds. Although usually Republican, she states that she is an independent voter. She generally attends the Congregational or Presbyterian church. Among her hobbies are "reading," "animals" (she has a wire-haired terrier, "Pompey"), "birds," and "camping."

References

Am Artist 13:32+ S '49 por
Who's Who in America, 1954-55
Who's Who in American Art (1953)

SCHERMAN, THOMAS (KIELTY) Feb. 12, 1917- Conductor

Address: b. c/o The Little Orchestra Society, Inc., 35 W. 53rd St., New York 19; h. 154 W. 57th St., New York 19

During eight seasons of concerts at The Town Hall in New York City, and at other auditoriums, Thomas Scherman has been acclaimed for his conducting and direction of The Little Orchestra Society, which presents "a balanced program of contemporary music and unjustly neglected works of earlier periods." In 1952 he received Columbia University's Medal for Excellence "for introducing new performers and compositions," and, in May 1954, he received from the National Association for American Composers and Conductors a citation "in recognition of his seven-year contribution to orchestral concerts in New York where he has presented at least ten American works annually, a record not equalled by any other established orchestra of first rank in this city." In addition to his series at Town Hall, Scherman also conducts two other subscription series—the Young People's Concerts and the Public Dress Rehearsals.

THOMAS SCHERMAN

The Book-of-the-Month Club inaugurated in the fall of 1954 "Music Appreciation Records", which feature classical music, played by world-famous orchestras on one side of each record, and, on the other, a lucid analysis of the various themes written and narrated by Thomas Scherman. In a few weeks after the series was announced, more than 65,000 members had subscribed.

Scherman, who founded The Little Orchestra Society in 1947, had previously been the conductor of *Let's Go to the Opera,* a radio show, and assistant conductor to Otto Klemperer at the New School for Social Research. He has served as guest conductor to other orchestras, and is also director of the Colonial Little Symphony Society, which is sponsored by Drew University, Madison, New Jersey.

Thomas Kielty Scherman was born on February 12, 1917 in New York City, the son of Harry and Bernardine (Kielty) Scherman. Well known as the founder of the Book-of-the-Month Club, Inc., and its president for many years, his father is at present the chairman of the board. His mother is an author, columnist and editor, and his sister, Katharine Scherman Rosin is also a professional writer. Young Scherman grew up in New York City and attended the Horace Mann School and Lincoln High School.

After his graduation in 1933, he entered Columbia University and selected mathematics as his major interest; extracurricular activities at college included track and serving as accompanist of the glee club. He received his B.A. degree in 1937, and remained at Columbia for one year of postgraduate study in music. He studied piano at the Mannes School of Music in New York City with Frank Sheridan and Isabelle Vengerova, composition and theory with the late Hans Weisse, and conducting with Carl Bamberger. He also studied piano at the Juilliard School of Music in New York, and conducting with Max Rudolf.

In 1939 Scherman became assistant conductor to Otto Klemperer at the New School for Social Research in New York City and filled this position until 1941. In June of that year he entered the United States Army as a private in the infantry, and served in the European Theater. He was discharged from the Army in February 1946 with the rank of captain in the Signal Corps. In the same year he conducted *Let's Go to the Opera,* a series of operatic arias presented in English by radio station WOR. He spent the summer of 1947 in Mexico City as assistant conductor at the Opera Nacional.

The conception of The Little Orchestra Society had been with Scherman since his school days, and after the war he decided to put his plan into effect. He arranged a series of programs for a small orchestra and brought his suggestion to radio station WQXR; the directors of the station were impressed but unable to institute the project because of a limited budget. Scherman thereupon decided to organize the group himself and The Little Orchestra Society came into being in 1947, backed by funds which the conductor and his friends provided. The orchestra was designed to present music requiring from eight to forty players. Brochures were mailed describing the proposed season of eight concerts at The Town Hall in New York City. Six months before the series was scheduled to begin it was completely subscribed.

The purpose of The Little Orchestra Society is to present works by modern composers and revive worthwhile but neglected masterpieces of the past. Another characteristic is the appearance of well-known soloists performing works not included in their customary repertoires. During the first series compositions by David Diamond, Norman Dello Joio, Weisse, Ottorino Respighi, and Alexander Tcherepnin were presented. Soloists who appeared included Benny Goodman, Claudio Arrau, Dorothy Maynor, and Joseph Szigeti. The night following each of the concerts the same program was given at the Brooklyn Academy of Music.

"A wholly delightful concert," wrote Olin Downes in the New York *Times* of The Little Orchestra Society's debut on October 20, 1947. "The orchestra . . . is an aggregation of exceptionally accomplished musicians." Scherman "conducted as a man who obviously knew his business well, and gloried in his task."

During the 1948-1949 season of The Little Orchestra Society, interpretations of works by Walter Piston, Giovanni Battista Pergolesi and Alexei Haieff were produced. The series ended with a concert performance of Christoph Willibald Gluck's opera *Orfeo ed Euridice,* with the late contralto Kathleen Ferrier and the Westminster Choir, which was regarded by the critics as the greatest achievement of the orchestra's season. In the summer of 1950 Scherman served as guest conductor for the Orchestre de la Suisse Romande in Geneva, and conducted the Vienna Symphonic Orchestra in Vienna.

An observance of the seventieth birthday of Ernest Bloch and the 200th anniversary of Johann Sebastian Bach's death opened The Little Orchestra Society's fourth season. They "have made themselves invaluable contributors to the New York musical scene," wrote Howard Taubman (New York *Times,* October 24, 1950). The following year was marked by two noteworthy performances: George Frederick Handel's *Acis and Galatea* and Hector Berlioz' *L'Enfance du Christ.*

In addition to its regular Town Hall concerts, in the 1952-1953 season The Little Orchestra Society was heard in three Carnegie Hall presentations of operas and oratorios. Shortly before Christmas, *L'Enfance du Christ* was repeated. The performance of this work (which tells the story of the flight of the Holy Family into Egypt) during the Christmas holidays has become a tradition with the Society. In January 1953 Carl Maria von Weber's *Euryanthe,* last heard in New York at the Metropolitan Opera House in the 1914-1915 season, was presented in concert form.

Scherman has pioneered in bringing neglected operas to the concert stage. In 1951 he introduced an April festival of Mozart operas at The Town Hall including *Abduction from the Seraglio, Cosi Fan Tutte,* both in English, and *Idomeneo.* In March 1954 he conducted Richard Strauss's opera *Ariadne auf Naxos* and received audience and critical acclaim. An accomplished pianist himself, Scherman has, on occasion, laid aside his baton to conduct from the keyboard. For example, on December 14, 1953 he assisted Ethel Bartlett and Rae Robertson in playing Bach's three-piano *Concerto in C Major.*

On several nights before its Monday performances at The Town Hall, the orchestra holds a dress rehearsal at Hunter College Assembly Hall. Scherman is thus enabled to gauge audience reaction to his selections. If soloists are required for any piece, young, unknown artists are chosen to perform, while at The Town Hall concert a famous artist appears. Admittance fees to the Hunter series are low, and the assembly hall's 2,200 seats have been filled on subscription each season and a number of memorable debuts have resulted.

The conductor instituted the Young People's Concerts for children in the 1948-1949 season; these are given at Hunter College, at Newark, New Jersey and Greenwich, Connecticut. Extended tours have been undertaken by the society after the close of the regular season. The orchestra has also recorded numerous works for Decca and Columbia Records. The recording of *L'Enfance du Christ* (SL 199) was greeted by the New York *Herald Tribune*'s critic as "charming music, superbly performed by a fine orchestra," and by the *Saturday Review* as "an enchanting tone-portrait" because of "the emotional persuasiveness of Scherman's reading."

To find the material which his society will present the following season, Scherman spends the late spring and early summer studying scores in libraries in the United States and abroad and examining the latest published music. He also enlists the help of contemporary composers whenever possible, to obtain an authoritative interpretation.

The seventh concert of its seventh season which was given at The Town Hall on February 15, 1954 included the New York première of Aaron Avshalomoff's *Buddha and the Five Planetary Deities.* During the summer of 1954 Scherman conducted five concerts at the Lewisohn Stadium in New York.

In what spare time the conductor has he enjoys tennis, bridge, poker, swimming, cooking, and reading.

Scherman has brown eyes, is five feet seven and one-half inches tall and weighs 165 pounds. Irving Kolodin of the *Saturday Review* has stated, "Scherman shows agreeable symptoms of providing for New York what another Thomas (Beecham by name) did for London—musical experience above and beyond the call of institutional duty."

References

N Y Herald Tribune II p5 O 12 '52
N Y Times II p7 N 16 '47; II p7 S 27 '53
Theatre Arts 35:43+ F '51

SCHNEIDER, ALMA K(ITTREDGE) Aug. 21, 1901- United States Government official

Address: b. c/o United States Mint, Colfax at Delaware, Denver, Colo.; h. 2040 Nelson St., Denver 15, Colo.

A housewife who measures hard cash by the barrel and who has learned to shoot a pistol as part of her duties in guarding some $6,000,-000,000 of Uncle Sam's gold, is Mrs. Alma K. Schneider. As superintendent of the United States Mint at Denver, Colorado, she holds one

Chase Photo
ALMA K. SCHNEIDER

of the important posts in the Republican Administration. After thirty years of volunteer work for the Republican party, Mrs. Schneider was appointed to this salaried position in January 1953 by President Dwight D. Eisenhower. She heads a staff of 281 technicians and guards of the mint which turns out over $20,000,000 in pennies, nickels, dimes, quarters, and half dollars each month. She purchases gold, silver and copper from Rocky Mountain miners, and the storage of gold at the Denver mint ranks second to that at Fort Knox, Kentucky.

Alma Kittredge was born in Denver on August 21, 1901, and grew up with her two brothers and a sister in the state capital. Her father, Charles Marble Kittredge, a descendant of early (1640) New England colonists, helped his father to build the first cantilever bridge across the Niagara River before turning to a long career in banking and real estate in the West. In Colorado he developed many subsections near Denver, including the town of Kittredge, which was named for him. Since his death in 1940, his widow, the former Anna Frederica Von Myrbach, has also been active in real estate; their daughter, Mrs. Schneider, still holds a license to sell real estate.

Alma Kittredge began studying to become a concert pianist at the Blanch Dingley Matthews School of Music while a student at East Denver High School, only to discover when facing an audience at her first public recital that she trembled and almost fainted with shyness. In order to conquer that handicap, she followed the advice of a friend and entered politics. She began to work as a precinct official in the 1920 election. On June 2, 1926 she married Daniel Jacob Schneider, a young pharmacist.

Four years after her marriage, Mrs. Schneider began to write for county newspapers with such success that she was asked to accept a position as managing editor of the *Jefferson County Sentinel*. Her strong Republican sympathies, however, led her to decline this offer to work for a Democratic paper. In 1930 she became precinct committeewoman for Morrison, Colorado; she held this office until 1950.

She also served her party as vice-chairman of the Jefferson County Republican Committee (1934-1942), vice-chairman of the State Central Committee (1942-1948), delegate to the Republican National Convention (1944), and assistant director of the women's division of the Republican National Committee, an appointive office which took her in 1945 to Washington, D.C. She found the climate there detrimental to her health and she remained only two months. At this time, however, she helped to write the first handbook on political organization to be published by the Republican National Committee.

Mrs. Schneider returned to Colorado, and subsequently joined the speakers' bureau of the Republican National Committee and attended meetings all over the country. From 1948 to 1953 she was Republican National Committeewoman from Colorado, and in 1952 she was vice-chairman of the Republican National Committee.

Mrs. Schneider has sought to win for women a place of equality with men in the Republican organization. "Even . . . [in 1945]," she has said, "women were not accepted politically on an equal basis with men. While the men had to admit that there were certain things in a political campaign that women could do as well, or better, than men, their fundamental attitude was that, as a group, women were a necessary evil to be tolerated and sometimes appeased but never wholeheartedly accepted" (*Independent Woman,* July 1953).

Mrs. Schneider has recalled her dread at making her first "big" political speech, and the sympathy her husband showed for her and her career at that time. "I was terribly nervous . . . ," she said. "It even got to bothering Dan [her husband]." Eventually she mastered her shyness and has learned to speak easily in public.

"Dan" Schneider intervened once in the career of his energetic wife; he pointed out to her that politics, as a hobby, was consuming a disproportionate share of the family budget. "He was entirely right, of course," says Mrs. Schneider, but rather than abandon her work, she started selling real estate. "All the money I made went for my political expenses, and when I'd run out of money, I'd go back to selling real estate again. . . ."

Mrs. Schneider believes that in order to overcome male prejudice against women, she and other women in responsible positions must prove themselves more efficient than men. "This is one of the few government jobs in the upper salary bracket [$10,800] open to women," she said. "Women have not yet gained equality in politics." Her advice to women who want to enter the field is: "Take things as they come. If you're slighted, don't pout. Just work all the harder. . . ."

As part of her duty in guarding the mint, Mrs. Schneider does regular target practice with a revolver in the sub-basement. She also keeps a gas gun in the drawer of her office desk and knows how to use it. "The mint is an extremely complex as well as important division of the government," Mrs. Schneider said. "It is operated with beautiful efficiency, and is possibly the only government agency that makes money for the government literally as well as figuratively." Except for her predecessor, Mrs. Gladys Morelock, a Democrat, Mrs. Schneider is the first woman to run a mint.

She has been described as a quiet, friendly woman—tall, blonde, hazel-eyed, and slender. Much of her free time is spent with her husband, who is now a banker, in their home in Denver. She still finds time to sew, cook, garden, arrange flowers, fish, and watch football and baseball games.

She belongs to the Daughters of the American Revolution, the Colorado and Jefferson County Women's Republican clubs, and the Lincoln Club. For twenty-five years she has been American Red Cross chairman in her area and has worked on town fund raising. She served on the board of control of the State Industrial School for Girls for many years (she was chairman of the board from 1950 to 1953), and on the advisory board of the Child Welfare Bureau. She took extension courses in journalism, pharmacy, banking and dress design at the University of Denver in 1936 and 1949.

Of her new job she said, "I've had so much fun . . . as a volunteer that I never dreamed of any other reward. But of course it's wonderful, and I cherish it."

References

Washington (D.C.) Post p27 Je 17 '53
Who's Who in America, 1954-55
Who's Who in United States Politics (1952)

SCHNEIDER, MRS. DANIEL JACOB *See* Schneider, A. K.

SCHORR, FRIEDRICH Sept. 2, 1888-Aug. 14, 1953 Singer; noted for Wagnerian baritone roles; was born in Hungary; studied law at University of Vienna; joined Philadelphia-Chicago Opera Company of Andres Dippel (1912); Berlin State Opera (1923), made debut February 14, 1924 at Metropolitan Opera Company in Tannhäuser; was especially acclaimed for his portrayal of Wotan in *Ring* cycle, and of Hans Sachs in *Die Meistersinger;* sang at Bayreuth festivals; retired from Metropolitan Opera (1943); thereafter taught singing at Hartt School of Music, Hartford, Connecticut and Manhattan School of Music; New York City Opera Company artistic counselor for German operas (1950-1951). See *Current Biography,* (July) 1942.

Obituary

N Y Times p15 Ag 15 '53

SCHREIBER, (KARL RUDOLF) WALTHER June 10, 1884- Mayor of Western Berlin

Address: b. c/o Rudolf-Wilde-Platz, Berlin-Schöneberg, Germany; h. Wernerstrasse 14a, Berlin-Grunewald, Germany

Elected to serve in one of the most challenging mayoralty posts in the world, Dr. Walther Schreiber succeeded the late Ernst Reuter as governing Lord Mayor of Western Berlin. Schreiber assumed the leadership of the city—"the last outpost of democracy behind the Iron Curtain"—on October 22, 1953.

Although he has been described as a "number two" man who lacks Mayor Reuter's "fine soaring optimism", Schreiber has been praised for his ability to get along with others, for his disbelief in "narrow party politics", and for his opposition to totalitarianism—whether Nazi or Communist.

Active in Berlin politics and in the administration of the Christian Democratic Union since 1945, Schreiber has been deputy mayor of Western Berlin for the last three years. He had served in the Prussian Diet and as Prussian minister of state, and minister for trade and commerce until 1933 when the Nazis' rise to power in Germany caused his abrupt dismissal.

Karl Rudolf Walther Schreiber was born on June 10, 1884 in Pustleben, a town in the southern part of the Harz Mountains in Prussia. His father, Adolf Schreiber, a Prussian landowner and gentleman farmer, was the son of a privy councillor for commerce, and his mother, Margarethe Rockstroh, was the daughter of a district judge and was related to Franz Krüger, the artist.

Walther Schreiber attended a *gymnasium* in Weimar from 1897 to 1903. He then studied jurisprudence and political economy at the universities of Grenoble (France), Munich, Berlin, and Halle-an-der-Saale, and passed his junior barrister examination in 1906.

While he was a university student, Schreiber has stated, he came under the influence of Friedrich Naumanns, the founder and first president of the National Socialist party (a pre-Weimar liberal party which had no connection with the one later developed under Adolf Hitler). Schreiber became interested in the leftist liberal movement in Germany and supported the advanced liberals in the Reichstag elections of 1907.

After receiving his doctorate from the university of Halle in 1910, he passed the state law examination in 1911. He began to practice law in Halle in March of that year and also served as court clerk. When war was declared in August 1914, Schreiber volunteered for military service. Beginning September 1, 1914, he served in the Sixth Regiment, fought in most of the important battles of the war, and became an officer in June 1915. What gave him the most satisfaction, he states, was his unanimous election by the other officers and men of his regiment as their trusted spokesman in November 1918 and his position as his Army division's representative to the German High Command. There it was his duty to advise the high com-

WALTHER SCHREIBER

mand in political questions and to prepare for the Congress of German Soldiers which took place at the beginning of December 1918 in Bad Ems.

The soldiers at the Congress decided that a German national meeting should be held as soon as possible and cleared delegates, including Dr. Schreiber, to the Congress of German Workers and Soldiers which was to be held in Berlin at the end of December 1918. Schreiber was one of the few non-socialists who attended the Congress.

The war over, Schreiber returned to Prussia and entered the German Democratic party (which was mainly supported by the liberal bourgeoisie). He represented his party for the districts of Merseburg and Erfurt at the Prussian Constituent Assembly in 1919. He became a member of the Prussian Diet in 1920 and soon was responsible for the business affairs of the Democratic party in the legislature.

When Wolfgang Kapp and other reactionary members of the *Vaterlandspartei* attempted to overthrow the Weimar Republic in March 1920, Schreiber was thrown into jail in Halle because of his democratic beliefs. He was released after the uprising had failed and was named civil commissioner.

Continuing his service in the Prussian Diet until 1933, Schreiber served as chairman of the Democratic group from 1924 to 1925. He finally became the preferred candidate of his party for the legislative elections, and in the March 1933 Reichstag elections, he was the chosen candidate of his party for the Berlin district.

In February 1925 Schreiber had been named minister of state, and minister of trade and commerce for Prussia. Outside his political duties, he was responsible for the supervision of business activities, communications, electrical works, mining (Prussia was then the largest mineral-producing state in Germany), and technical training programs.

Schreiber was ousted from his position in March 1933 after Hitler had become Chancellor of the German Reich and after Franz von Papen was named Federal commissioner for Prussia. Schreiber told the Nazis: "You think you have conquered us, but you are wrong. We will be here long after you are gone."

Without work for a year and a half, Schreiber finally established a private law practice in Berlin, but was not permitted to appear before the law courts.

After the Second World War he resumed his law practice and also returned to an active political life. He helped found the Christian Democratic Union in July 1945. This party, derived from the Catholic Center party of the Weimar Republic, was composed of both Catholics and Protestants who hoped to settle current problems through the application of Christian principles.

Schreiber served as second chairman of the party until December 19, 1945. He tried to organize the CDU in East Germany and spoke against the Russian land reforms and the "Sovietization" measures which were being carried out there. "What you and your government are doing is wrong," he stated. The U.S.S.R.'s Marshal Georgi K. Zhukov ousted him on December 21, 1945.

Becoming a member of the City Assembly of Berlin in 1946, Schreiber soon led the Democratic group there and until the end of 1948 served as deputy chairman of the council. From March 1947 to April 1952 he was chairman of the Christian Democratic Union for the Berlin district, and from January 1950 to March 1951 he was the chairman of the party.

In the 1951 election, Schreiber was his party's candidate for mayor of Western Berlin and opposed the incumbent, Ernst Reuter, a Social Democrat. According to its constitution of October 1, 1950, Western Berlin became a state of the Federal Republic of Germany (although it was not yet formally incorporated) as well as a city. The city government was, therefore, reorganized in 1951. The City Assembly became the House of Representatives with 200 seats (seventy-three were reserved for Eastern Berlin delegates). The House would elect the mayor who would head the Senate, the executive branch of the government.

In the vote taken by the House of Representatives, on January 12, 1951, Schreiber and Reuter tied for the office of mayor. Schreiber withdrew his candidacy and on January 18, Ernst Reuter was re-elected as mayor of Western Berlin. Schreiber was named Deputy Lord Mayor and by this solution of the problem, it was believed that Western Berlin would continue to be ruled by the "great coalition" of the Social, Christian, and Free Democratic parties for another four years. Schreiber served as Berlin's representative to the West German Republic's Bundesrat.

When Mayor Ernst Reuter died on September 29, 1953 Schreiber became the acting mayor until an election could be held in the House of Representatives. Schreiber was a candidate for the mayoralty post and was opposed by the Social Democrat, Dr. Otto Suhr, the chairman of the House of Representatives. On October 22, 1953 Schreiber was elected with a majority of five votes through the support of the so-called "right-wing" parties, the Christian Democrats and the Free Democrats.

Despite pressure from the Allied powers to maintain the "great coalition" and despite Schreiber's desire to form a three party coalition government in the Senate, the Social Democratic party decided to go into active opposition. This was the first time since the Western Berlin government was formed in 1948 that the three parties did not unite to form a Cabinet.

Besides the political problem of working without a large majority in the House of Representatives, Schreiber faces certain basic economic difficulties in Western Berlin. In November 1953 there were 207,000 persons registered as unemployed out of a total population of about 2,200,000. Moreover, there is a constant stream of refugees from Eastern Germany which must be cared for until they become incorporated into Berlin's economy or sent into West Germany.

Although increased industrial production figures, greater retail business and a stabilized budget show that the city's economic position is gradually improving, the Federal Republic of Germany and the United States still must give Western Berlin considerable financial aid. The city can only be described, Don Cook has written, as "doing well . . . in relation to the size of the [economic] problem—one might almost say, the hopelessness of the problem. . ." (New York *Herald Tribune,* November 20, 1953). Mayor Schreiber must also strive to give the people of his city the leadership which was considered Ernst Reuter's greatest asset in keeping Western Berlin "a symbol of the free world's struggle against Communist tyranny."

Schreiber was awarded an honorary degree in political science from the Wirtschafts-Hochschule in Berlin in 1927. He has written *Revolution in Halle* (1920) and numerous political articles for German newspapers and periodicals.

He married Margarete Rüffer on March 16, 1911. By this marriage he had two children: a daughter, Waltraut, and a son, Klaus-Dietrich, who was killed during the Second World War. His second marriage took place on September 13, 1947 to Ada Lewin-Traeger. His religion is Protestant. Formerly an expert tennis player, Schreiber now enjoys riding, hunting and shooting. He has been described as a "calm, kindly, unselfish and courageous" man who has been "a genuine liberal, in the European sense of the word" all his life.

References

N Y Herald Tribune II p1 O 25 '53; p8 N 21 '53

N Y Times p1+ O 23 '53 por; p14 O 24 '53

Time 62:32 N 2 '53 por

International Yearbook and Statesmen's Who's Who, 1953

Wer ist Wer? (1951)

SELASSIE *See* Haile Selassie I, Emperor of Ethiopia

SERRATOSA CIBILS, JOAQUIN Sept. 5, 1884- Organization president, business executive

Address: b. 18 de Julio 1110, Esquina Paraguay, Montevideo, Uruguay; c/o Rotary International, 35 E. Wacker Dr., Chicago 1, Ill.; h. 1430 Rio Branco, Montevideo, Uruguay

A prominent business executive of the Republic of Uruguay was elected president of Rotary International for the year 1953-54. He is Joaquin Serratosa Cibils, who has been a member of Rotary for thirty-two years and has held high offices in the organization.

Rotary International consists of 7,867 Rotary clubs in eighty-eight countries and geographical regions, whose members total an estimated 374,000. Rotarians hope to advance international understanding "through a world fellowship of business and professional men united in the ideal of service." Serratosa was succeeded as president by Herbert J. Taylor, of the United States, on July 1, 1954.

Joaquin Serratosa Cibils was born in Montevideo, the capital of Uruguay, on September 5, 1884. As is sometimes the custom in Latin America he added his mother's maiden name, Cibils, to his father's surname, Serratosa. His father, Dr. Antonio Serratosa, founded the School of Medicine in Montevideo and was one of the Republic's most distinguished physicians. His maternal grandfather pioneered in the meat industry and was a prominent director of Uruguay's banks and railroads.

He was educated at the University of Uruguay, and for many years was active in cattle raising and agriculture. In 1914 he established the company he now heads, the firm of Serratosa and Castells, representatives in Uruguay for the Goodyear Tire and Rubber Export Company, Westinghouse Electric International Company, General Motors, and other North American and European companies. He is also a director of the Italian Bank of Uruguay.

The Rotarian leader's civic activities have ranged from delegate for Uruguay to the International Olympic Committee to chairman of the Uruguayan Commission against Tuberculosis and Cancer. He has also served as a director of the League of Cultural Relations between Uruguay and the United States, chairman of the Import and Export Commission of Uruguay, president of the Commercial Association of Uruguay, and member of the Inter-American Commission of Commerce and Production.

Serratosa's Rotarian work began in 1921 when he became a member of the Rotary Club of Montevideo. He was later president of that club, vice-president of Rotary International, a District Governor (Rotary International representative for a particular area embracing many clubs), and member and chairman of many committees. As Governor in 1937-38 of District 63 of Rotary, Serratosa Cibils spurred an extension program that resulted in the formation

JOAQUIN SERRATOSA CIBILS

of twenty-eight new Rotary clubs in Argentina, Paraguay and Uruguay.

He has been described in the *Rotarian* (September, 1953) as having "great tact and diplomacy . . . so keen is his sense of fair dealing that it was instrumental in settling a frontier controversy in 1941 between Ecuador and Peru . . . three Rotarians worked together at Serratosa Cibils' home and formulated a solution for the boundary problem . . . which had existed for a century and a half and attempts to reach a settlement had all been unsuccessful."

The nominating committee of Rotary International meeting in Chicago in January 1953, chose Serratosa a candidate for president for 1953-1954. By the time Rotary International met in Paris in May for its forty-fourth annual convention two other nominees had been put forward by their local clubs. Serratosa won the election at the convention, succeeding president H. J. Brunnier of California as of July 1, 1953. Present at the convention were some 10,300 Rotarians, including their wives and children, from seventy-six countries and geographical regions, making it the largest ever held outside the United States, and the most internationally representative in Rotary's history.

After his election Serratosa Cibils told the gathering: "Here in Paris forty years ago I knew my greatest sorrow when on a visit here with my beloved father I lost him. He died in this beautiful city. Here in Paris today I have received the greatest honor and joy of my life —the elevation to the highest office in our Rotary." He added that his "first goal" in his new post would be to "encourage in all Rotarians here, there and everywhere, a deeper understanding of each other and a deeper loyalty to each other and to Rotary. More and more closely united, we shall thus be better able to carry forward our world-wide program inspired by the ideal of service." He urged also that members work for more clubs, "for hundreds more. Let us dream of and strive for . . . 5,000 and 10,000 more. . . For the more clubs we have, the more friends we have; and the more friends, the greater our opportunities for service."

Rotary's official object is "to encourage and foster the ideal of service as a basis of worthy enterprise, and, in particular to encourage and foster: 1. The development of acquaintance as an opportunity for service. 2. High ethical standards in business and professions, the recognition of the worthiness of all useful occupations, and the dignifying of each Rotarian of his occupation as an opportunity to serve society. 3. The application of the ideal of service by every Rotarian to his personal, business, and community life. 4. The advancement of international understanding, goodwill and peace through a world fellowship of business and professional men united in the ideal of service." Rotary's International Student Exchange Committee meets each year to select some 100 young men and women to receive Foundation Fellowships for travel abroad. The 1953-1954 awards brought the total Foundation expenditure for this purpose to about one and a quarter million dollars.

President Serratosa began in his new post by leading the first sessions of the new Rotary International Board of Directors at an interim meeting in Paris in June. In July he visited Rotary's International Headquarters in Chicago, and in August he and his wife sailed from New York aboard the S. S. *United States* for a three month trip to take him to Rotary clubs in France, Luxemburg, Portugal, Switzerland, Italy, Greece, Israel, Lebanon, Egypt, India, Pakistan, Vietnam, Hong Kong, the Phillipines, Japan and Hawaii. In September he met in Zurich, Switzerland with Rotary's European, North African and Eastern Mediterranean Advisory Committee. Traveling with him was the new "first lady" of Rotary International, Mrs. Serratosa Cibils, a talented linguist, the former Sofia Stajano, to whom he was married May 18, 1912.

Reference

Rotarian 82:45 Mr '53; 83:34+ S '53

SHAFER, PAUL W(ERNTZ) Apr. 27, 1893- Aug. 17, 1954 United States Representative from Michigan; began his career as a reporter on an Elkhart (Indiana) newspaper; later became editor and publisher of the Bronson (Michigan) *Journal;* admitted to Michigan bar after taking correspondence courses from the Blackstone Institute (Chicago); was municipal judge of Battle Creek (1929-1936); Republican member of U.S. Congress since 1936; served on House Military Affairs Committee (later the Armed Services Committee); active in proposing legislation on synthetic rubber. See *Current Biography,* (July) 1952.

Obituary

N Y Times p29 Ag 18 '54

SHAHN, BEN(JAMIN) Sept. 12, 1898-
Artist

Address: b. c/o Downtown Gallery, 32 E. 51st St., New York 22; h. Roosevelt, N.J.

More American in his choice of subject matter than many artists born in the United States, Russian-born Ben Shahn was selected by the Museum of Modern Art as one of two artists whose works represented contemporary America at the 1954 Venice, Italy Biennale Exhibition of International Art. He also won the $800 award offered by the Museum of São Paulo, Brazil in 1954. One of his best known murals is in the main corridor of the Social Security Building in Washington, D.C. (now housing the Department of Health, Education and Welfare). His story-telling pictures stress the contrasts of man and his surroundings, and depict the life of workers in factories and on farms in both poetic and realistic terms.

Through frequent activity as a graphic-arts propagandist for Government bureaus and labor organizations, Shahn has expressed his "tangible humanism." Art critic James Thrall Soby has appraised Shahn's contribution to contemporary art: "He is one of the most authentic and powerful of American humanists, an artist who translates the American scene into a strikingly personal statement of sympathy for mankind."

Selden Rodman's biography of Shahn, *Portrait of the Artist as an American,* was published in 1951 by Harper. A retrospective exhibit of Shahn's work was given at the Museum of Modern Art in 1947, and at the Downtown Gallery in 1949 where, in the winter of 1954-55, a show covering twenty-five years of his work is scheduled.

Benjamin Shahn was born on September 12, 1898 in Kaunas, Russia, one of five children of Hessel Shahn, a carpenter and wood carver, who belonged to the Misnagdim Jewish sect, which put special emphasis on the virtue of craftsmanship. Ben emigrated with his parents to Brooklyn, New York when he was eight years old. They lived in two rooms in a cold water flat. His mother, Gittel Lieberman, is from Lithuania. At the age of fifteen he was apprenticed to a lithographer. He knew early the privations of poverty and "the separateness of Jewish family life." Always he clung to his goal—to be a painter and to really know the America he wanted to paint. He took courses at night at City College, New York University and the National Academy of Design.

Following his marriage to Tillie Goldstein in 1922, Shahn saved up enough money to go to Europe where he saw for the first time the great art galleries. He made another trip in 1929, spending much time in Paris. He attended the Grand Chaumière. He was influenced to some degree by Georges Rouault, but Europe strengthened his decision to tell the story of America with emphasis on social commentary, and with realistic architectural details. At the same time that Shahn took new directions in his painting he met a personal crisis

Studio Associates, Inc.
BEN SHAHN

which resulted in the separation and subsequent divorce from his wife, Tillie.

In 1932 he completed twenty-three satirical *gouache* paintings on the trial of Nicola Sacco and Bartolomeo Vanzetti, convicted in 1921 of a murder of a shoe factory paymaster and guard. (Doubt of their guilt led to widespread support and world-wide protests; they were electrocuted August 23, 1927. Many believed that the conviction had been influenced by the men's reputation as political radicals. However, a special committee appointed by Governor Alvin Fuller of Massachusetts to review the case found the trial fair and both men guilty.) Shahn's paintings were exhibited by Mrs. Edith Halpert at the Downtown Gallery, and Shahn received fame and recognition. In 1933 Shahn completed fifteen paintings on Tom Mooney, the labor leader who was convicted and sent to prison.

While enrolled with the New York City Public Works Art project Shahn painted eight tempera pictures on the Prohibition era.

Diego Rivera admired Shahn's work and employed him as his assistant on the ill-fated frescoes in the RCA building in Rockefeller Center in 1933. (The mural, *Man at the Crossroads,* became a *cause célèbre* when it was apparent that the labor leader in a vignette showing a May Day demonstration of marching workers with red banners bore an unmistakable likeness to Lenin. Rivera refused to substitute a portrait of an unknown man for the head of Lenin; he was subsequently paid, but ordered to stop work. The mural was eventually chipped from the wall.)

The Federal Relief Administration commissioned Shahn in 1934 to prepare murals for the Riker's Island Penitentiary, but the Municipal Art Commission rejected them.

(Continued next page)

SHAHN, BEN—*Continued*

Shahn obtained work with the Farm Security Administration as artist, designer, and as photographer from 1935 through 1938. His final assignment for this agency was a wall fresco for the community center of a housing project for garment workers at Roosevelt, New Jersey. The mural shows immigrants arriving from Eastern Europe and their march forward to economic freedom. Labor unions, sweatshops, the Triangle Shirtwaist Company fire, labor and civic leaders, all form part of the dramatic saga of the growth of the garment workers' union. This mural led to another commission in 1938 for the Bronx Central Annex post office. The mural, which was executed by Shahn and his second wife, Bernarda Brysen, has thirteen panels giving a comprehensive picture of American life in its cities and on its farms.

The Treasury Department's Section of Fine Arts awarded Shahn the sum of $19,980 in 1940 (in competition with 375 artists) to depict on the walls of the Social Security building the story of that agency's progress in aiding the American people. In every way, Shahn recalls, painting these murals was an exhilarating experience. He brought together on one wall such figures as a boy on crutches, two girls surveying an accident, a boy with a baseball bat, a family dispossessed.

In 1943 Shahn worked for the OWI, designing war posters. In 1944 he was chief artist for the CIO Political Action Committee, working for a nominal salary for a cause he believed in. Simultaneously with his mural and poster work Shahn carried on his easel work which resulted in eleven of his paintings being included in the Museum of Modern Art's "American Realists and Magic Realists" exhibition of 1943 and in a one-man show at the Downtown Gallery in 1944. A retrospective one-man show of his paintings, drawings, mural studies and photographs was given at the Museum of Modern Art in 1947.

Many of his pictures carried a message such as *Death of a Miner* (1947), which seemed to say: "Here is tragedy. What is being done to prevent its happening again?" Other story-telling paintings of great poignancy are *The World's Greatest Comics* (1946), *The Violin Player* (1947) and *East Twelfth Street* (1947).

A critic from the New York *Times* commented, "Often Shahn seems bent upon telling us that this is a terrible and a cruel and a heart-breaking world. Yet there are the stimulatingly swift and keen imaginative flights. And his color can be such as an angel might use." James Thrall Soby, director of the exhibition, wrote: "In recent years Shahn has emerged as one of the most lyric of living American artists, his pictorial invention steadily more varied and rich, his technical fluency and warmth more and more impressive."

The United States pavilion at Venice, Italy, where the important biennial art exhibitions are held, was bought in 1954 by the Museum of Modern Art, which offered the works of only two painters—social realist Ben Shahn and abstract-expressionist Willem De Kooning. "A two-man affair by deliberate museum decision," commented *Time* (June 28, 1954), "it made for a forceful though far from representative showing. Shahn, whose work had its roots in proletarian fury, has now become fashionable. . . . At peace with the world in recent years, he has been overtaken in his later work by his weakness for arty picture-making of an allegorical sort."

Thirty-four of Shahn's paintings were included at the twenty-seventh Venice Biennale. Among these were his war-haunted *The Red Stairway* (1944), the "wryly idyllic" *Spring* (1947) and *Composition with Clarinets and Tin Horn* (1951) symbolizing the conflict of the creative mind in the world today, and "the loud empty noises made by passing idols in the contemporary scene," the artist says. "Where the Shahn of 1939 painted the windows of *Looming Wall* in realistic drab colors," commented *Life* (October 4, 1954), "the Shahn of 1953 arranges windows in a bright [stained glass] pattern to point up the drabness of a factory town."

Once Shahn's paintings were considered too photographically realistic; more recently they have displayed a growing reflectiveness, expressed in vivid colors. Now, "instead of bitter protests against oppression, his colorful and strongly composed work is more characterized by bittersweet portrayals of men, women and children who stand alone and lost and sad" (*Life,* October 4, 1954).

Shahn now lives with his second wife and three children at Roosevelt, New Jersey. From 1945 to 1948 he was a city councilman. Rodman describes his physical appearance as "burly," with thinning iron-gray hair and mustache, "glittering blue eyes whose expression varies depending on whether his quizzical intellect or his great capacity for physical enjoyment happens to be in command."

References

Art N 46:41+ O '47 por; 48:20+ My '49 por
House & Garden 90:209 D '46 por
Life 37:96+ O 4 '54 pors
Look 14:70+ Jl 18 '50 pors
Time 63:74 Je 28 '54
Rodman, S. Portrait of the Artist as an American; Ben Shahn (1951)
Who's Who in American Art (1953)

SHAY, FRANK Apr. 8, 1888-Jan. 14, 1954 Author and authority on sea chanties; proprietor Shay's Book Shop (Provincetown, Massachusetts); lumberjack; merchant seaman; book auctioneer; originated Caravan Theatre and Frank Shay's Traveling Bookshop; wrote about forty-five books including *American Sea Songs and Chanteys, From the Days of Iron Men and Wooden Ships* (1948), *The Bos'n's Locker, Folklore of American Sailormen* (1949), *Sailor's Treasury* (1951), and *Tall Ships Flying* (1953). See *Current Biography,* (Yrbk) 1952.

Obituary

N Y Times p19 Ja 15 '54

SHELLABARGER, SAMUEL May 18, 1888-Mar. 21, 1954 Author; educator; English instructor (1914-1916) and assistant professor (1919-1923) at Princeton University; was headmaster of Columbus (Ohio) School for Girls (1938-1946); wrote the best-selling historical novels *Captain from Castile* (1945), *Prince of Foxes* (1947), *King's Cavalier* (1950), *Lord Vanity* (1953), and numerous books; used also pen names John Esteven and Peter Loring. See *Current Biography,* (May) 1945.

Obituary

N Y Times p27 Mr 22 '54

SHIMKIN, LEON Apr. 7, 1907- Publisher

Address: b. c/o Simon & Schuster, Inc., 630 5th Ave., New York 20; h. 8 E. Dr., Larchmont, N.Y.

Graphic Arts, John Albert

LEON SHIMKIN

If anyone can be said to have the golden touch in the publishing business it is Leon Shimkin, who started as a twenty-five dollar-a-week bookkeeper in the publishing house of Simon & Schuster in 1924, and today is its executive vice-president and treasurer, and is often spoken of as this firm's "Third 'S' ". He is also president of Pocket Books, Inc. which has sold 400,000,000 copies of over 1,000 titles since the company was organized in 1939.

The twenty-five top-selling Pocket Book titles to date have included *The Pocket Book of Baby and Child Care* by Dr. Benjamin Spock, *The Merriam-Webster Pocket Dictionary, The Pocket Cook Book* by Elizabeth Woody, *How To Win Friends And Influence People* by Dale Carnegie, *Nana* by Emile Zola, *See Here, Private Hargrove* by Marion Hargrove, *Tales of the South Pacific* by James A. Michener and a number of mystery novels by Erle Stanley Gardner.

Born in Brooklyn, New York on April 7, 1907, Leon Shimkin is the son of Fannie (Nickelsberg) and Max Shimkin, who was in real estate. Both his mother and father were born in Russia. Leon attended Alexander Hamilton High School in Brooklyn, where he was president of the Congress Literary Society and the Spanish club, and won the Rothschild Medal for the highest average. After graduating in 1923 he entered the School of Commerce, Finance, and Accounts of New York University.

During the summer vacation after his freshman year, he obtained a job with Boni & Liveright, the publishers, as bookkeeper-credit manager-stenographer-switchboard operator. When news of his ability reached the newly-formed publishing house of Simon & Schuster he was offered a better position. Shimkin accepted and continued his studies at New York University at night. He was elected to Delta Mu Delta, an honorary society, and received the B.C.S. degree in 1926. The following year he spent his evenings studying at Brooklyn Law School.

Shimkin was soon promoted to Simon & Schuster's business department. The new firm at first had marked success with its crossword puzzle books (which it introduced in 1924), but after the vogue for puzzles subsided and the depression deepened, it soon reflected the general downward trend in book sales. Meanwhile Shimkin had been studying secondary rights of books, and brought public attention to Simon & Schuster when he sold the right to the title "Inner Sanctum Mysteries" to a Hollywood studio.

In 1936 he had another inspiration. The complexities of the income tax were beginning to be a real burden; he asked the late J. K. Lasser to compile an easily-understood manual entitled *Your Income Tax*, which sold for a dollar. It was immediately successful, and a revised edition has been issued every year since by Simon & Schuster.

By this time Shimkin was business manager of the firm. One day in 1937 he enrolled for a course called "Cultivating Human Relationships"; the instructor was Dale Carnegie. Fascinated by Carnegie's simple formulae for attaining success he suggested that Carnegie write a book. Dale Carnegie replied that he already had had two books rejected by Simon & Schuster, but Shimkin brushed this aside and told him his book should contain just what he had been saying in his lectures. With Shimkin editing and advising, Dale Carnegie wrote *How to Win Friends and Influence People* (1937). There were seventeen editions of the book within the first months after it was introduced and to date it has sold about four million copies in standard and pocket editions.

Shimkin genuinely admires inspirational self-help material such as the Carnegie book. He once declared that a chapter entitled "The Affirmative Mental Attitude" in Elmer E. Ferris' *Developing Sales Personality* was an important factor in his advancement. Benjamin Franklin's *Autobiography* is another of his favorite books. The selection of Dale Carne-

SHIMKIN, LEON—*Continued*

gie's *How to Win Friends and Influence People* was an instance of Shimkin's conviction that "publishing can help people solve their problems."

Simon & Schuster's next major project was Pocket Books, Inc., undertaken in conjunction with publisher Robert F. de Graff in 1939. For a great many years publishers, concerned over the high cost of books, had considered paper-covered editions, but all experiments in that direction had failed. A new approach was tried by Simon & Schuster. For six months before actual publication large quantities of a circular outlining its plan were sent out, in which were listed a wide selection of possible titles, and people were invited to write in and tell which ones they would like to buy. As a result, one of the first titles was Pearl S. Buck's *Good Earth.* The first printing was distributed only in the New York area.

The public's response gave the partners of Simon & Schuster, M. Lincoln Schuster, Richard Simon and Leon Shimkin, and de Graff the encouragement they needed. Wallis Howe was hired as sales manager, and very soon Pocket Books were on sale throughout the United States. From the very first the books had as their trade-mark a small kangaroo, known as "Gertrude", holding one book in her paws, and another in her pouch.

Realizing that there were not enough bookstores in the country to make such a mass-production project profitable, Shimkin and de Graff made arrangements with wholesale magazine distributors, and Pocket Books began appearing in supermarkets, filling stations, subway stations, and remote country stores. In its first decade, Pocket Books sold more books than the combined total of all the best-selling books since 1880, and to date approximately 400,000,000 copies of over 1,000 titles have been sold, and the little "Gertrude" (since redrawn by Walt Disney) is now known all over the world.

About 25,000,000 Pocket Books were shipped overseas during World War II by the Army, Navy, Red Cross and other welfare organizations. Shimkin became president of Pocket Books on January 31, 1950 after serving from that company's inception as treasurer.

During the war Shimkin started the People's Book Club, in association with Sears Roebuck and Company, the mail-order house, and Consolidated Book Publishers of Chicago. Shimkin called on George Gallup to poll representative groups, who were given copies of proposed books to read. Again the idea of providing the customer with what he wanted resulted in large sales. This club was designed for Sears Roebuck's rural customers, and it turned out later that between them, Shimkin and Gallup had secured the audience they wanted, for 85 per cent of the subscribers lived in towns with less than 2,500 persons.

Many of the more conventional publishers were, at this time, inclined to be critical of Shimkin's methods of book distribution. Twenty-five cent books would never have any prestige, they said, and the idea of ordering books from a catalogue along with house dresses and farm supplies, was entirely unorthodox. Equally unconventional were racks of books in supermarkets. However, Shimkin was reaching a vast number of people who had never had the opportunity to buy books before, and in recent years it has been said that he has tremendously expanded the number of readers. Another criticism of the paper-bound book publishers has been from the authors who feel their royalty rights should be considerably increased.

Interviewed by Clip Boutell in the New York *Post* (August 17, 1944), Shimkin said: "Some book publishers seem to think of their business as a large cake of ice. I like to think of it as a tree with its roots deep in people's desire for knowledge... the difference between thinking of publishing as a cake of ice or a tree, is the difference between a restricted and an expanding universe. The ice-cake connotes melting or depleting assets. Some publishers even feel that each new means of book distribution has chipped a piece from the private cake. The concept of the tree has branches reaching out in many different directions. It carries with it the idea of growth and vitality."

After developing the People's Book Club into a highly successful concern, Simon & Schuster sold its interest in it in 1946 for a handsome profit. Equally profitable have been Simon & Schuster's "Little Golden Books," a juvenile version of the Pocket Book idea. These are also sold in almost every type of store, and were an instantaneous success.

Interested in education, Shimkin organized a series of lectures at New York University in 1943 concerning "The Practice of Book Publishing." He was one of the organizers of the Larchmont Forum of Public Opinion, and is a member of the advisory board of the New York University Press. Shimkin has been a trustee of Bard College, Annandale-on-Hudson, New York, since 1950.

The publisher has served as vice-president and a director of the American Book Publishers Council. Interested in welfare work, he is chairman of the book publishers division of the Federation of Jewish Philanthropies in New York City and chairman of the book publishers division of the United Jewish Appeal. He is a director of the Quarrie Corporation.

Married to Rebecca Rabinowitz, a teacher, on August 17, 1930, Shimkin is the father of two children, Emily and Michael. He is a Republican and a member of the Temple Israel of New Rochelle, New York. His clubs are the Rockefeller Luncheon, Metropolitan Country and Beach Point.

The publisher has brown eyes and black hair, is five feet six inches in height and weighs 172 pounds. He has been described as "a cross-between Babbitt, Houdini and Count Metternich" (Bennett Cerf in *Saturday Review of Literature,* February 11, 1950). Cerf appraised Shimkin: "A soft-spoken, mild-mannered executive . . . a deceptive placidity conceals the feverish activity of his thoughts. Business is life and breath to him. He takes his problems home with him and broods over them half the night. . . . His conversation is peppered with rather high-sounding platitudes and pleasantries that you feel he has used often before. He can say 'no' so adroitly that the suppliant is sometimes halfway down the elevator before he realizes he didn't get a single thing he had come for. The entire executive board of Simon & Schuster has an infallible solution for every knotty problem: 'You will have to take that up with Mr. Shimkin.' Mr. Shimkin loves it."

References

N Y Post p29 Ag 17 '44 por
Sat R Lit 33:4+ F 11 '50
Who's Who in America, 1952-53
Who's Who in Commerce and Industry (1953)

KATHERINE B. SHIPPEN

SHIPPEN, KATHERINE B(INNEY) Apr. 1, 1892- Author

Address: b. c/o Harper & Bros., 49 E. 33rd St., New York 16; c/o Viking Press, 18 E. 48th St., New York 17; h. 45 Christopher St., New York 14

Reprinted from the *Wilson Library Bulletin,* Oct. 1954

There are history-makers in Katherine B. Shippen's ancestry, which may account for her keen sense of history. One was the first mayor of the city of Philadelphia. Edward Shippen was a chief justice of Pennsylvania Colony and there was William, member of the Continental Congress and one of the founders of the College of New Jersey which later became Princeton University. These men, with roots in Yorkshire, England, have gone on bequeathing their gifts to American school children through Katherine Binney Shippen who was born to their descendant, Francis Shippen, and his wife, the former Ellen Wheeler Kellogg, in Hoboken, New Jersey on April 1, 1892.

She studied languages at Hoboken Academy where she was graduated in 1910 and later majored in history and economics in Bryn Mawr College, with time out there for the glee club and water polo. She went on to earn an M.A. degree from Columbia University in history in 1924.

During the period of studying for her M.A., Miss Shippen taught history at Miss Beard's School in Orange, New Jersey, from 1917 to 1926. In that year she came to New York to teach history at the Brearley School. Then, in 1936, she became headmistress of Miss Fine's School in Princeton, leaving there in 1941 to become curator of the social studies division at the Brooklyn Children's Museum.

These years of teaching were fruitful for the author-to-be. Holidays were spent in study and travel to Germany, France, and Italy and there were longer visits to England, Scotland, Switzerland, Canada, and China. There was also exploration of the United States. Of those journeyings Miss Shippen writes: "My family came to the New World in the first half of the seventeenth century, but, so far as I know, not one of them ever stepped into a covered wagon or felt the least inclination to pull up stakes and go west, north, or south. So it remained for my sisters and me to do the family's exploring. Some years ago we took a Ford and set out across America. Of course, in these days of good roads and automobiles many people have explored the United States, each in his own way."

Out of Miss Shippen's travels came her first book, *New Found World* (1945, Viking) for high school young people. Virginia Kirkus said, "A colorful book about South America, explaining the varied races who make up this nation. Excellently written." This, and her next two books were Junior Literary Guild selections.

The questions asked by the children of Brooklyn when she was giving her popular lectures at the museum, showed Miss Shippen the need of the information which became *The Great Heritage* (1947). She said of it: "I wanted to tell everybody that the United States is bigger, stranger, and more beautiful than most of us dream. People who spend their lives in one part of the country know little about other parts."

In 1949 Miss Shippen wrote two books for younger children; one of these was *Bright Design,* a story of the development of electricity. The New York *Times* said, "The subject matter of this book is unusual, the approach challenging and the style pleasing." The other was a biography of Moses (published by Harper).

In February 1950 Miss Shippen resigned her work in Brooklyn after nine years of talking to children at the museum and answering their probing questions. It was her intention to give all her time thereafter to writing. She said, "I'm very used to talking to young people and writing isn't very different . . . carrying on a habit." *Lightfoot,* published in September of that year, is a story of an Indian boy who grew

SHIPPEN, KATHERINE B.—*Continued*

up at the height of power of the Iroquois League. "I wanted to show," said the author, "that the Iroquois were people like everybody else . . . not cruel savages who spent their lives with tomahawks in their hands . . . that the Iroquois disliked fighting so much that they organized the League to keep the peace." *Lightfoot* was well received. *Saturday Review* said, "Like all Miss Shippen's books, it is told in crystal-clear prose, and it has dignity and authenticity."

Also published in 1950 was *Passage to America,* which received the Boys Clubs of America medal that year. This is a story of the three-century migration of people to America. *Horn Book* said, "The narrative moves easily and smoothly and the book should arouse the interest of anyone over twelve or thirteen who looks into it." Her *Leif Eriksson* (1951) was praised in the New York *Herald Tribune* as "a distinguished book for junior high school libraries."

Of *A Bridle for Pegasus* (1951), a history of aviation spanning the time from the mythical winged horse to the first flight to the stratosphere, the *Horn Book* said, "Miss Shippen has the gift of direct approach to young readers and true selective sense in dealing with a wealth of research." Reviewers were equally enthusiastic about *Mr. Bell Invents the Telephone* (1952, Random House) and *Big Mose* (1953), a collection of tall tales about a legendary New York Bowery boy who performed feats that were Bunyanesque on and around Manhattan Island.

In *Big Mose,* according to *Horn Book* (April 1953), "each chapter captures the zest of the waterfront with its sailing ships, or of Broadway with its horse cars, or of life in the Bowery. Mose, in his red volunteer-fireman's shirt, blowing a blue cloud from his two-foot cigar, is a fabulous figure. . . ."

I Know a City (1954) is a history of New York from 1625, when the first Dutch fort was built at the tip of Manhattan, to modern times. The New York *Times* wrote, "The book is for anyone, New Yorker or not, who has watched a fire engine racing to a fire or has seen the street lights go on at dusk. It will be of special value in social studies projects." *The Pool of Knowledge* (1954) is a story of the way in which United Nations share their skills. The *Christian Science Monitor* described it as "a deeply thrilling book, stirring the imagination far more than a mystery novel."

In addition to her books, Miss Shippen has had some adult verse published and has written a number of short stories for children's magazines.

She is tall and slender with blue eyes. She has two sisters with whom she shares two homes, a Greenwich Village apartment and a country house in Rockland County, where she enjoys gardening when not busy at her desk. She is currently at work on a history of biology.

References

Sat R Lit 33:34 N 11 '50 por

SILLCOX, LEWIS K(ETCHAM) Apr. 30, 1886- Mechanical engineer; organization official

Address: b. c/o New York Air Brake Co., 230 Park Ave., New York 17; Starbuck Ave., Watertown, N.Y.; h. 241 Clinton St., Watertown, N.Y.

At the seventy-fourth annual meeting of the American Society of Mechanical Engineers in December 1953, Lewis K. Sillcox was elected president for the year 1954. He began his career in the railroad industry at the age of seventeen as a shop apprentice and worked his way through various engineering jobs to become in 1927 first vice-president of the New York Air Brake Company, of which he is now honorary vice-chairman of the board.

During the past twenty-five years, according to *Mechanical Engineering* (September 1953), Sillcox has been instrumental in the development of many "improved methods of railway-power application and the control of railway trains." He has received honorary degrees from several universities, has lectured widely on railway practices, holds memberships in many technical and professional societies, and has received several important awards.

Lewis Ketcham Sillcox was born in Germantown, Pennsylvania, on April 30, 1886, the son of George Washington Sillcox and Georgiana (Parker) Sillcox. He spent his early years in New York City and attended Trinity School, from which he was graduated in 1901. He also studied for a year at l'Ecole Polytechnique in Brussels, Belgium.

Upon his return to the United States in 1903, Sillcox began a four-year apprenticeship in the shops of the New York Central Railroad at High Bridge, New York. Later he worked as a foundry apprentice with the McSherry Manufacturing Company in Middletown, Ohio, for two years. From 1909 to 1912, he was shop engineer for the Canadian Car and Foundry Company, Turcot Works, Montreal, and from 1912 to 1916 he was mechanical engineer, Canadian Northern Railway, Toronto. He then spent two years as mechanical engineer with the Illinois Central System and from 1918 to 1927 he was general superintendent of motive power for the Chicago, Milwaukee and St. Paul Railway at Chicago.

The American Railway Association named Sillcox chairman of its mechanical division for the year 1926-1927 and in 1927 he became first vice-president of the New York Air Brake Company at Watertown, New York. These two events marked his entry as an authority in his chosen field.

His best known achievements have been the development of "the brake-cylinder release valve which eliminates hand-bleeding retained air in standing freight cars, improved sanding methods for rail conditioning, the brake-pipe flowmeter which registers brake-pipe pressure in freight and passenger trains irrespective of main supply pressure, and basic brake types (freight, passenger and locomotive)." He also sponsored "the designing of several types of aircraft hydraulic pumps now found on practically all current military aircraft and the latest commercial aircraft."

For many years Sillcox has lectured on engineering at Purdue University, and on applied mechanics at Clarkson College of Technology, the Massachusetts Institute of Technology and Yale University. He has also lectured on transportation at Princeton, Northwestern, Ohio State and Syracuse universities, and on economics and transportation at the Harvard Graduate School of Business Administration. He has been a member of the visiting committee of the department of mechanical engineering, Massachusetts Institute of Technology, honorary curator of the Baker Library (Transportation) at Harvard University and a member of the New York State Citizens' Advisory Council, New York Board of Regents. He is also chairman of the mechanical engineering advisory committee, School of Engineering, Princeton University.

Sillcox' lecture entitled "Speed, More Speed in Transportation," delivered at Princeton on November 14, 1939, and subsequently published by Brackett Lecturers, attracted widespread attention. Sillcox keynoted the lecture with the statement, "Space is real and time is arbitrary"—an indication of his concern with the philosophical as well as the technological aspects of transportation.

He wrote a chapter in *Engineering Opportunities* (Appleton-Century, 1939) edited by R. W. Clyne, in which he outlined the functions and needs of the railway equipment industry, which is "normally a billion dollar enterprise, employing one man for approximately every four on the nation's railway payroll."

In a more recent lecture delivered at Northwestern University on the coordination of rail and highway transportation (New York *Times*, March 8, 1953), Sillcox warned that unless railways make the most of the growing practice of carrying thirty-two-foot standard semitrailers on flatcars operated on freightcar timetables, toll-operated super highways would be built and the railways might lose much of their traffic.

Six of Sillcox' best known lectures, given at M.I.T. between 1936 and 1940, were adapted for a book called *Mastering Momentum* (Simmons, Boardman, 1941). The book, revised in 1946 and 1953, contained discussions of modern transportation trends and their influence upon the equipment of American railroads.

In recognition of his contributions to the field of transportation, Sillcox received an honorary D.Sc. degree from Clarkson College of Technology in 1932, D.Eng. degrees from Cumberland University in 1941 and Purdue University in 1951, and an LL.D. degree from Syracuse University in 1948.

From 1934 to 1936 Sillcox was chairman of the mechanical advisory committee of the Federal Coordinator of Transportation. In 1942 he was designated permanent chairman of the Metals Engineering Handbook Board of the American Society of Mechanical Engineers, and in 1943 was awarded the society's Gold Medal for distinguished service to engineering and science.

LEWIS K. SILLCOX

For the excellence of his paper, "Power to Pull," on a method for appraising the relative performances of steam and Diesel locomotives, Sillcox was awarded the Gold Medal of the Institution of Locomotive Engineers of Great Britain on June 5, 1946. In 1949 he received the Salzberg Memorial Award from Syracuse University.

At the eighth Pan-American Railway Congress in 1952-1953 Sillcox served as chairman of the paper committee. He is a life member of the board of trustees of Clarkson College of Technology and, as of January 1954, a term trustee of Norwich University. He became executive vice-president of the New York Air Brake Company in 1949 and vice-chairman of the board of directors and member of the executive committee in 1952. In 1953 he was elected honorary vice-chairman of the board. He is a director of the Agricultural Insurance Company and the Empire State Insurance Company.

Sillcox has been a member of the American Society of Mechanical Engineers since 1916, and is now an honorary member as well as its 1954 president. He succeeded Frederick S. Blackall, Jr., to the presidency; his successor for 1955 will be D. W. R. Morgan. The American Society of Mechanical Engineers was established in 1880. It has a membership of 39,520.

He is an honorary member of the Railway Fuel and Traveling Engineers Association, New England Railroad Club and the Navy League. He is a fellow of the American Physical Society, the American Institute of Electrical Engineers and the Royal Societies for the Encouragement of the Arts, Manufactures and Commerce (London).

Among Sillcox' numerous other professional affiliations are the American Society of Traffic and Transportation, American Institute of Chemical Engineers, American Institute of

SILLCOX, LEWIS K.—*Continued*

Mining and Metallurgical Engineers, Society of Automotive Engineers, American Association for the Advancement of Science, and Franklin Institute. His London memberships include the Engineering Institute of Electrical Engineers, Institute of Transport, and Newcomen Society of England. He belongs to the Sigma Xi and Pi Tau Sigma fraternities.

Despite his crowded professional life, Sillcox finds time for his hobby—reading—and membership in such organizations as the Audubon Society, the University clubs of New York and Chicago, the Seigniory of Montebello, Quebec, and the Adirondak Loj of Lake Placid, New York. He is a 32nd degree Mason (Knight Templar) and a Shriner and attends the Episcopal Church. Politically, he is a Republican.

Lewis K. Sillcox was married to Edna May Harris in Toronto, Canada on September 14, 1918. They have four daughters and one son—Robert Lewis. The daughters are Elsie Winifred (Mrs. Donald G. Bridge), Esther Harris (Mrs. Stanley L. Whittemore), Enid Burnham (Mrs. Peter Darlington) and Edith May (Mrs. Frank A. Kelly). Sillcox has gray hair and eyes, is five feet, six inches tall and weighs 151 pounds. He has been described as a "preeminent learned technologist—lover of wisdom—inspirer of men."

References

Mech Eng 75:755 S '53 por
Who's Who in America, 1954-55
Who's Who in Commerce and Industry (1953)
Who's Who in Engineering, 1948
Who's Who in Railroading, 1946

SIMON, EDITH May 18, 1917- Author

Address: b. c/o G. P. Putnam's Sons, 210 Madison Ave., New York 16; h. 7 Rosebery Crescent, Edinburgh, Scotland

Reprinted from the *Wilson Library Bulletin,* Feb. 1954

There is no greater symbol of the lofty heights to which man's genius can rise than the medieval cathedral. The twentieth century tourist coming upon such a building, often in the heart of a noisy, bustling European city, is caught suddenly in the web of the past, and for a moment at least he is transported into another era when human art and labor and ingenuity combined in one of the noblest achievements of religious faith. Such a moment came for the novelist Edith Simon during a visit to Norwich Cathedral. Three years (and seven versions) later, her novel, *The Golden Hand* (1952), the story of the building of the purely fictitious cathedral of St. Hand, was finished. Like the great cathedrals themselves, it was a labor of love. In addition to the vast amount of research involved in recreating a fourteenth century English town and its inhabitants, Miss Simon actually drew an imaginary map of the district and filled a notebook with sketches of

EDITH SIMON

the cathedral in different stages of building, of its woodwork, sculpture, paintings, etc. The result is an historical novel of unusual vividness and verisimilitude, one which the New York *Herald Tribune* found "a spacious and carefully wrought novel, thought-provoking and rewarding," and Orville Prescott of the New York *Times* called "one of the finest historical novels I have read in recent years."

Edith Simon was born in Berlin, Germany, May 18, 1917, the daughter of Walter Frederick and Grete (Goldberg) Simon. She has one younger sister who is also a novelist, writing under the name I. Goodwin. Miss Simon's early interests in painting and writing were encouraged at school (the Fuerstin Bismarck Schule). In 1931 the family settled in London where she studied painting at the Slade School of Art and later lithography at the Central School of Arts and Crafts, with the intention of becoming a professional artist. It was a busy life. In addition to the art—and she was now exhibiting paintings and doing book illustrations and jacket designs for publishers—there was always reading and writing stories and essays "for private consumption."

In 1938 she translated Arthur Koestler's first novel, *The Gladiators,* from German into English. Her own first novel, *The Chosen,* appeared in 1940. Although it received favorable reviews, it was destined for oblivion. The first edition was destroyed by fire bombs, and the book has never been reprinted. Nothing daunted, Miss Simon published three more—*Biting the Blue Finger* (1942), *Wings Deceive* (1944), *The Other Passion* (1948)—none as yet published in the United States.

Meanwhile, in August 1942, she married Dr. E. C. R. Reeve, a research geneticist. He has always been sympathetic with her writing ambitions, and she is duly grateful for his encouragement and "the obvious pleasure with which he will lay aside a textbook of mathematics in order to discuss a technical problem which is holding me up." The Reeves moved from London to Edinburgh in 1947 when he was appointed to the Edinburgh University Agricultural Research Council. There their two children were born—Antonia Mary in 1950 and Simon Raynold in 1952. There too Miss Simon has written the two novels by which the American reading public knows her—*The Golden Hand* and the more recent *The House of Strangers* (1953)—both published by Putnam. The latter is a contemporary novel, the story of a young widow who joins a colony of archaeologists uncovering a prehistoric village in Scotland and in the tensions of communal life makes her own emotional adjustments and finds her place. The book is full of solid detail. Some reviewers indeed, like V. P. Hass of the Chicago *Tribune*, found the detail excessive: "Fine writing and intelligent probing are not enough. The reader must be given something in which he is willing to invest his emotions." But Nancie Matthews, in the New York *Times*, commented: "Beneath Miss Simon's deliberately ponderous style there is an intensity of feeling and an undercurrent of suspense that makes reading *The House of Strangers* an immensely gripping experience."

The distractions of a multiple career are real for Miss Simon. The writing of *The House of Strangers* was interrupted by the births of the two children, and much of it was done during five months in the hospital. Miss Simon says: "Treating writing as a serious job while bringing up small children and running a house is not altogether easy, but I wouldn't leave my children in anyone else's hands, and I find the constant contact with them rewarding and endlessly instructive." She does much of her writing in the evenings and while the children are napping, but it is rapidly becoming a family project. "The French windows of my study open on the garden, so the children can run in and out. Antonia has a little desk next to mine, where she paints on the back of discarded manuscripts, decorates typewriter spools with plasticine, drops beads, and frequently asks questions."

For recreation Miss Simon paints (and occasionally designs book jackets), swims, reads, and enjoys taking the children walking along Edinburgh's enchanting Princes Street. She likes to travel and says that her most memorable trip abroad was a visit to the cave paintings of Lascaux in the Dordogne, "which inspired some of the feeling in *The House of Strangers*."

SIMON, JOHN ALLSEBROOK SIMON, 1ST VISCOUNT Feb. 28, 1873-Jan. 11, 1954

Former Lord Chancellor of England; attended Wadham College, Oxford; called to bar (1899); became known as one of England's outstanding lawyers; elected to Parliament (1906); Solicitor General (1910-1913); Attorney General (1913-1915); Secretary of State for Home Affairs (1915-1916, 1935-1937); as Secretary of State for Foreign Affairs (1931-1935) attempted negotiations with Germany; Chancellor of the Exchequer (1937-1940); Lord Chancellor (1940-1945); knighted (1910); raised to peerage as Viscount Simon of Stackpole Elidor (May 13, 1940). See *Current Biography,* (July) 1940.

Obituary

N Y Times p23 Ja 12 '54

SIMPSON, HARRIETTE LOUISA *See* Arnow, H. S.

SINGER, KURT D(EUTSCH) Aug. 10, 1911- Author; lecturer

Address: b. c/o Max Pfeffer, International Literary Agency, 45 W. 45th St., New York 36; Funk & Wagnalls Co., 153 E. 24th St., New York 10; h. 5645 Netherland Ave., Riverdale 71, New York; 1322 N. Havenhurst Dr., Hollywood 46, Calif.

The world of espionage has fascinated Kurt D. Singer for over two decades, and among the twenty-six books which he has written, twelve are concerned with international spies, ranging from Mata Hari to Dr. Klaus Fuchs. A Viennese by birth, Dr. Singer became an American citizen in 1946. He has lectured widely throughout the United States, warning America to be alert against enemies within its boundaries. An ardent foe of both Fascism and Communism, he has actively participated in exposing their foreign agents. His articles on treason and counterespionage were incorporated in the official report of the Atomic Energy Commission, entitled *Atomic Espionage* (1951). He has been a consultant for Allied military and civilian governmental agencies, and a special speaker for the United Nations.

"The modern spy," Dr. Singer has said, "is an emissary from one world to destroy another. He is a diplomat, a scientist, a man of knowledge. It is more important for any espionage system to get the latest industrial and laboratory secrets of a nation than to kidnap an *émigré* general." Microfilms and short wave transmitters have replaced secret inks and disguises, but Singer points out that the work of spies is as important as military power in today's struggle between the democracies and the totalitarian countries. "America has lost her two-ocean protection with the coming of the jet plane and the H-bomb," he emphasizes, "but we are newcomers in the field of international intrigue."

He was the editor of *Mitteilungsblätter,* an underground anti-Hitler weekly, in Berlin, Germany. The Nazis put a price on his head, held his wife as a hostage, and Singer escaped to Sweden in 1934 where he worked in the Scandinavian underground. Among his biographies are *Göring,* published in England in 1940; *Carl von Ossietzky; Martin Niemöller; The Story of a Hypnotist* (with Franz J. Polgar); and *The Laughton Story,* a biography of the actor

KURT D. SINGER

Charles Laughton (published in the fall of 1954 by the John C. Winston Company).

Kurt Singer was born in Vienna, Austria on August 10, 1911 of Czech parents, Ignaz Deutsch and Irene Singer. He took his mother's maiden name as a pen name. Kurt's father, who was a steel importer and exporter, dealing with Krupp and Thyssen, died when Kurt was fourteen. Moving to Berlin, he attended the Kaiser Friedrich Schule and was graduated in 1929. He then attended Handels Akademie in Berlin and later the Eidgenössische Technische Hochschule and the University of Zurich in Zurich, Switzerland.

When Singer was fourteen he met Artur Schnabel, the great pianist, who told him to "find the beauty in life, in art, in the past and in the future." "When I was seventeen," Singer recalled, "I wanted to write biographies like Emil Ludwig. George Bernard Shaw, Nietzsche and Schopenhauer were my silent teachers. Without my mother opposing my writing efforts (she burned my first poems), I would never have become a writer. I had to show her that I could." His mother advised him to learn a trade. "To be a writer means to starve," she said. Accordingly, he became an apprentice in a railroad car factory, building tank cars and learned to repair them in Quedlinburg, Germany.

His first book, a collection of poems, was published when he was eighteen. The German radio stations bought his poems, "but I don't think they were any good," he said. "Revolutions and inflation in Europe made me believe service was more important than profits," he told a *Current Biography* writer. "Hitler and Stalin convinced me that everyone had to defend democracy against such political cancers. Sweden and America taught me real democracy."

Singer published one of the earliest German underground newspapers. His wife, Hilda Tradelius, whom he had married on December 24, 1932, is an X-ray technician. After he had escaped to Sweden when the Nazis indicted him for high treason, she was held as a hostage, but was finally released. In Sweden, he founded the Ossietzky Committee which secured the release of Carl von Ossietzky, the German pacifist and writer, from a concentration camp (Ossietzky was awarded the Nobel Peace Prize for 1935).

A Swiss newspaper, *Berner Tagwacht,* made him its correspondent in Sweden. "War clouds over Europe threw me into the field of counter-espionage," Singer said. "Stockholm was a spy center [after Hitler came into power]. I could not be neutral as Sweden was. I teamed up with the British (first) in 1939, after the invasion of Norway and Denmark, with the Norwegian Secret Service, and was later consulted by most United States intelligence agencies...."

"Sixty-six members of my family were killed by the Nazis and the Communists from 1939 to 1945," Singer has stated. "I never saw my mother after I left Germany. . . . She was gassed to death in a Nazi concentration camp in 1941."

He was secretary of a refugee committee in Sweden, and foreign correspondent for half a dozen European newspapers while he completed his Ph.D. degree in 1938 at the ABF (Labor) College. In July 1940 Singer came to the United States, and with his wife and five-month-old baby, was detained on Ellis Island. The detention, however, did not discourage him. "I knew I was safe," Singer wrote. "I had escaped both the Nazis and Communists." He brought with him $1,500 he had earned from his books, but this was used to post a bond.

On being released, Singer visited one of the largest publishing firms in New York, whose president asked him, "Why do you want to write? Everyone wants to write. Why don't you go into business and get a job?" He did not follow this advice and has continued to write books. He has also written many articles on his favorite subject—espionage—for the *Saturday Evening Post, American Mercury, American Weekly, Christian Science Monitor,* the North American Newspaper Alliance, the Bell Syndicate, and the United Feature Syndicate.

"I write my books mostly from 8:00 A.M. until I am exhausted," Singer says. "I never write at night. I need daylight and plenty of it. I type my own books, my secretary retypes them. Only lately have I used a dictaphone which I even plug into my car if necessary to complete a chapter. After I have finished a book, it is a closed chapter to me—I start on a new one."

"I started out with the hope of becoming a Steinbeck, Werfel or Theodore Dreiser," he related, "but now I know my limitations—I'm a journalist. . . . I wish I . . . had the language command of my idols, but I don't, I never will. I speak eight languages, but none really 100 per cent."

He attended Indiana University and in 1942 received a Ph.D. degree in psychology (the Swedish government paid his tuition for one year). He began to lecture on the psychology of espionage, and has become so popular that he now gives 250 lectures each year in the United States. "Lecturing to me is an adventure," Singer stated. "I don't mind the cremated chicken and green peas circuit—it is to me the symbol of free speech—and I love my audiences."

In his lectures he describes the constant work of conniving spies throughout the world, classifies them, and agrees with J. Edgar Hoover (whose work he greatly admires) that "the Communist party is a Fifth Column better organized than anything the Nazis ever had." He has made guest appearances on all the major radio networks, including CBS (*We, the People*) and the Mutual Broadcasting Company (*Martha Deane*).

In 1951 Singer completed one of his most widely read books: *The World's 30 Greatest Women Spies,* published by Wilfred Funk. These included the "case histories" of women like Tokyo Rose, Judith Coplon, Ruth Greenglass, Ethel Rosenberg, Velvalee Dickinson (the lady with the dolls), as well as Mata Hari, and her daughter, Banda McLeod (the latter spied for the democracies).

Leo Lania in the *Saturday Review of Literature* (December 1, 1951) commented: Singer "has always been on the right side, a fighter for democracy. His excursions and raids into the jungle of the totalitarian underworld were undertaken only to defend and promote the cause and struggle of free men. . . . Each of the thirty case histories not only reads like a first-class thriller but gives the reader a clearer understanding of the forces behind the events that make headlines." The book's sales in 1954 in the United States reached 47,000; it was published in pocket editions in Canada and England, and in hard covers in twenty-five countries, and has been translated into sixteen languages. Some of Singer's stories of espionage have been dramatized on radio, television, and in motion pictures, the most recent being *The Daughter of Mata Hari,* which is being filmed on location in Indochina by United Artists.

Kurt Singer explained to a *Current Biography* writer that he is "not the Kurt Singer who was a medical doctor in Germany and conducted the opera choir," and he is "not a Kurt Singer from Czechoslovakia who is a Communist because I hate the Commies." "God has been very, very good to me," he said. "I love the United States of America which presented me with her greatest gift—citizenship."

In Singer's opinion, the real danger for the democracies is from brilliant scientists such as Dr. Klaus Fuchs, Dr. Allan Nunn May, or a cosmic ray specialist like Dr. Bruno Pontecorvo—top men in their specialized fields—but "children in politics." They were at home in the rarefied atmosphere of their specialties, but they were "lost in the chaos of a terrifying outside world. And so the Communists got them."

When not on lecture tours, Dr. Singer lives at Riverdale, New York, with his wife and two children, Marian Alice and Kenneth Walt (who has taught his father something about baseball). Singer belongs to the Weowna Yacht Club and the International Platform Association (of which he was once vice-president). His hobby, besides reading, is boating on the Hudson River, which he regards as "the most beautiful river in the world, and I told this to my friends in the Rhineland."

He has dark brown hair and brown eyes, is five feet eight inches tall, weighs "a solid 200 pounds" and so must "diet permanently." He is "half-Catholic and half-Jewish," admires the Quakers, and joined the Unitarian church. In politics he says that he "votes for the best candidate and statesman." He is an honorary member of the Rotary Club, and he was made an Indian Chief of the Black Hill Sioux tribe in 1949.

Commenting on Kurt D. Singer's collection of sketches of espionage agents, both Nazi and Communist, entitled *The Men in the Trojan Horse* (Beacon, 1953), in the *Saturday Review,* Merle Miller wrote: "Singer handles the language better than most natives. . . . He is a man of fierce integrity and of refreshing good sense. In a superb last chapter, 'Can We Trust the Ex-Communists?' . . . Singer concludes: 'Democracy must not forget that it can never be sure how many ex-Communists may still be on the pay roll of the Soviet secret service.' "

References

Tomorrow 10:12 S '50
Who's Who in the East (1953)

SISAVANG VONG, KING OF LAOS
July 14, 1885-

Address: Royal Palace, Luangprabang, Laos

Laos (formerly Lane Xang, "the kingdom of the thousand elephants and the white parasol") in French Indochina is governed by His Majesty King Sisavang Vong. A protectorate of France since 1893, Laos became, with Cambodia and Viet-Nam, in 1950 an Associated State within the French Union. Crowned King of Luangprabang in northern Laos in 1905, Sisavang Vong has ruled almost continuously for forty-nine years. In October 1953 Laos was recognized by France as "fully independent and sovereign" while continuing in the French Union and agreeing to contribute "all possible means to its common defense."

The small country of Laos has an area of 89,320 square miles and a population of nearly 1,200,000, most of whom are Laotians (racial kindred of the Thais) and adherents of Buddhism. Rice forms the chief item of agriculture. The tin mines have recently resumed operation.

Like Cambodia and Viet-Nam, Laos has been the scene of Communist military operations since 1945, and several attempts have been made by Vietminh Communist troops to capture the capitol at Luangprabang. Their advance in February 1954 was halted when they found a region of scorched earth, where villagers had burned their settlements and destroyed crops in order to stop the aggressors. France then

French Embassy Press & Inf. Div.

SISAVANG VONG, KING OF LAOS

asked to have the Indochinese war included in the program for the Far Eastern conference opening on April 26 at Geneva. Laos thus became a crucial factor in discussions on Asian problems.

After Pierre Mendès-France was confirmed by the French National Assembly as Premier on June 18, 1954, negotiations began for a truce in Indochina. Armistice agreements ending the seven-and-a-half year war were signed in Geneva on July 21, 1954.

Sisavang Vong was born on July 14, 1885 to King Zakarine and Queen Tiao Thongsi. While he was still a small boy the Siamese, who had occupied the central part of Laos, struck northward to attack Luangprabang. Laos accepted the protection of France in 1893, and Siam was compelled to cede the annexed territory.

The Laotians, whom Lucien Bodard in *World* magazine (December, 1953) described as "gentle, good-natured people", were satisfied to be *protégés loyaux* of France, if this would deter depredations by Siam.

The French established an administrative capital at Vientiane on the Mekong River and merged into twelve provinces the various *muongs* or local principalities of which Laos was then comprised. A French *résident supérieur* at Vientiane thenceforward supervised the administration of the twelve provinces by local *commissaires* acting with the advice of the native nobility.

Contact with the protecting power was indeed so irregular and infrequent that when Sisavang Vong ascended the throne of Luangprabang in 1905, he knew no French. (He still does not speak the language with ease). Caucasian visitors other than French civil servants were few, although a zoological expedition headed by Harold J. Coolidge of Harvard University passed through Luangprabang in 1928 and 1929.

Lucien Bodard has characterized Sisavang Vong as "a product of Ancient Asia. . .beloved by his people," a man of "piety, dignity and respect for old traditions." One such tradition attaches to the Prabang, an eleven-hundred-year-old golden statue of Buddha, housed in a pagoda facing the royal palace. The legend of the Prabang relates that "as long as it remains in its sanctuary, neither king nor kingdom will come to any harm."

The monarch's benevolent rule, in which during the period between the World Wars he was ably assisted by a brother, Prince Phetsarah, continued unimpaired until the Vichy Government invited Germany's ally, Japan, to use Indochina as a stepping stone to Singapore. The status of the kingdom was not substantially altered until March 1945 when the Japanese decided to declare French protection "abrogated". A month later, presumably in accordance with the policy of Tokyo, Sisavang Vong declared his country "independent".

After the Japanese capitulation the task of disarming the enemy in Indochina north of the sixteenth parallel, and of preparing the country for return to French administration, was allotted to Chinese troops, some of whom were by no means in sympathy with the latter objective. In mid-September those which occupied Luangprabang encouraged a "Lao-Issarak" ("Free Laos") party, similar to the Vietminh movement in Viet-Nam. Sisavang Vong and the Crown Prince Tiao Savang Vattana were forced to abdicate in 1945 and to declare the Lao-Issarak regime the "legitimate" government of the kingdom.

"About half the people of Indochina either want the French back or feel that they cannot yet get along without them," wrote George Weller (*Saturday Evening Post*, November 30, 1946). "This half includes Laos and Cambodia." Thus when early in 1946 paratroops under Colonel Jean-Marie Crèvecoeur were airlifted to the middle Mekong and struck northward to Luangprabang they found a majority of Laotians resigned and even friendly to their return. The "Free Laotians" under Prince Souhanou Vong (a distant relative of Sisavang Vong) fled to the mountains along the Chinese border after defeat in a series of battles, and by midsummer of 1946 Sisavang Vong had been recognized by the French as King not of Luangprabang alone but of the whole of Laos.

An agreement was signed on August 27, 1946 by France and Laos which confirmed the unity and independence of Laos and formulated a new democratic political structure. Deputies for a National Constituent Assembly were elected in the following January. In May 1947 King Sisavang Vong proclaimed the constitution which made Laos a parliamentary monarchy with a unicameral Assembly elected every four years and meeting for a two months session in alternate Novembers, and a consultative Royal Council three of whose nine members were to be chosen by the people.

By a treaty concluded at Paris on July 19, 1947, Laos became an "Associated State within the French Union," and exactly two years later a further agreement assured Laos of "full internal sovereignty." These agreements were ratified in Paris as of February 2, 1950.

King Sisavang Vong played a quietly heroic role in the spring of 1953, when Vietminh troops invaded his country. "His government begged him to leave the city," Lucien Bodard has written. "The French, too, urgently advised him to seek refuge. But Sisavang Vong declared he would not move; he would share the fate of his people in the city of his ancestors. With a sublime faith that the enemy would be repelled, he stayed in bed." There was no panic, and a few days later, in accordance with the prophecy of a celebrated soothsayer known as the "Blind Priest", the invaders suddenly withdrew when only a few miles from Luangprabang.

By the end of May, Sisavang Vong felt that Laotian security was sufficiently restored for him to travel to Vittel, France for his annual mineral water treatments for his rheumatism and gout. He arrived at Vittel in mid-June and in the course of the summer discussed with French officials the treaty which he signed with President Vincent Auriol on October 22, 1953.

Barrett McGurk of the New York *Herald Tribune* noted that Sisavang Vong promised that his country would continue to contribute "all its means" to the common defenses of the French Union wherein Laos was pledged to remain a permanent member with internal autonomy. Under the treaty the French president would coordinate the contributions of French Union members, and could presumably call on the Laotian regular army of about 11,000 men.

In January 1954, Siam approached both Cambodia and Laos with the suggestion that a "group of Buddhist countries, including Cambodia and Laos, would make the best barrier against the penetration of the Vietminh [Communist] troops toward the West, notably India." A Siamese spokesman hinted that his country would soon "sign commercial agreements" with Cambodia and Laos.

Tillman Durdin, writing in the New York *Times* on January 17, 1954, noted that these overtures were made just after Vietminh forces operating from Communist-held areas had cut through to the Mekong River near Thekong, dividing Laos in two and presenting a direct threat to Siam. The New York *Times* reporter believed it "unlikely . . . that either Cambodia or Laos" would "want to embrace Thailand too closely" but did foresee "the development of mutually beneficial, friendly relations."

It is understood that anti-French "Free Laos" nationalists who had originally joined with Ho Chi Minh, Viet-Namese Communist leader, have subsequently withdrawn and have made their peace with the French. King Sisavang Vong issued a proclamation calling for the mobilization of Laos in a patriotic war against the Vietminh, and reminding his countrymen of their debt of gratitude to France. It is his task to try to reconcile those who seek total independence from colonial rule, for without France, he knows that they may fall prey to the Communists.

The United States and France adopted a plan on September 29, 1954, after consulting with officials of Laos, Viet-Nam and Cambodia, by which the United States will provide $700,000,000 annually to the three Indochinese states and France will maintain military forces in southern Viet-Nam and will train native troops in order to enhance the security of the area.

On his periodic visits to Vittel, accompanied by his senior wife and queen, Sisavang Vong "affords the outside world brief glimpses of a round, cheerful face and a stumpy figure clad in the Laotian's baggy silken pantaloons," observes Lucien Bodard, who also notes that "according to custom" the Oriental monarch "has many wives."

The French journalist further mentions some of the "wonderful projects" for Laos envisioned by the Occidental-minded Crown Prince, who rules during his father's absences. "He hopes to make Luangprabang an international resort, world-famed for its art treasures, palaces and native entertainment." Prince Savang further believes that "Laos can become a major producer of caviar" since the roe from the sturgeon in their rivers is as tasty as that from Russia.

References

Sat Eve Post 219:18+ N 30 '46
Time 61:31 My 11 '53 por
World 1:22+ D '53 pors

SLAVENSKA, MIA 1917- Ballet dancer; choreographer

Address: b. c/o Betty Smith, 18 E. 60th St., New York 22; h. Demarest, N.J.

Since she was a child star in her native Yugoslavia, prima ballerina Mia Slavenska has endeavored to combine a flair for the dramatic with her classic ballet training. She has made worldwide tours with the Ballet Russe de Monte Carlo and with her own companies, for which she was also the choreographer.

However, it was not until she formed the Theater Ballet Company with Frederic Franklin in the summer of 1952, and commissioned Valerie Bettis to create a ballet based on the Tennessee Williams play, *A Streetcar Named Desire*, that she found the perfect role for her talents. In this ballet the dancer made a highly successful tour of the United States and Canada.

During the summer of 1954 Mia Slavenska was prima ballerina of *Arabian Nights* at the Jones Beach Marine Theatre on Long Island, New York. She is presently engaged as *première danseuse* with the Metropolitan Opera Ballet for the 1954-1955 season.

Mia Slavenska was born Mia Corak (pronounced Chorak) in Slavonski-Brod, Yugoslavia in 1917. When she was two, her family moved to Zagreb, a larger city with an opera and ballet company. Her dance studies began when she was four years old, at the school of a former Viennese ballet mistress, Josephine Weiss. She also studied musical composition.

In 1922 Mia took lessons with Margarete Froman of the Zagreb National Opera and made her professional debut in an opera ballet at the age of five. At six, she became child

MIA SLAVENSKA

soloist of the opera's dance company, and three years later two ballets were composed especially for her. "In that part of the world," she recalls, the audiences "either carry you on their shoulders after a performance, or throw tomatoes at you. I was lucky" (Washington *Post,* November 19, 1953).

She remained with the opera until she was twelve, when she went to Vienna and saw a performance by modern dance originator Mary Wigman. Attracted by the freedom of expression offered by the modern form, the young star took lessons in "expressional dance" with Gertrud Kraus and Lilly von Wieden. She began to compose her own dances, making up one program in classic ballet form (except for a Debussy number with classic footwork and free body movement), and another comprised entirely of modern dances. With these programs she made her concert debut at the age of twelve in Zagreb, and the following year at the Zagreb National Opera. She made two subsequent tours through Yugoslavia in 1930 and 1933.

At seventeen, Miss Slavenska went to Paris to study simultaneously with three famous dance teachers, Preobrajenska, Egorova and Kchessinska. She believes this was advantageous because she escaped being stamped with the mannerisms of any one instructor. At this time she appeared as soloist with the Opera Russe in Paris, and then joined the Ballet Russe de Monte Carlo as a soloist for three months in 1934. At Monte Carlo she worked with Mme. Bronislava Nijinska and other dancers.

As prima ballerina of the Zagreb Opera House from 1934 to 1936, Miss Slavenska worked with a dance corps of fifty. She gave a concert in memory of Pavlova in 1936.

At the international Dance Olympics held in Berlin in 1936, in which fourteen nations participated, Miss Slavenska represented Yugoslavia. She received one of the three top prizes, the others going to dancers Mary Wigman and Harald Kreutzberg. Up to this point she had performed under the name Mia Slavenska Corak, but she then dropped her family name.

As a result of the Olympics award, Miss Slavenska received many offers from ballet companies throughout the world. She selected Arnved Meckler, manager of other noted dancers, as her agent, and made her Paris debut with Serge Lifar in *David Triomphant* in 1936. After a tour of France, she made a world tour and in London in 1938, she appeared with Anton Dolin as her partner.

Returning to Paris, Miss Slavenska co-starred with Yvette Chauviré in a film called *La Morte du Cygne* in 1938. Released in the United States as *Ballerina,* picturing the development of a dancer's career, the film was well received, and the ballerina was praised for her acting ability.

The success of the movie brought her an offer to make a concert tour of the United States, but because of her manager's death, it was not carried out. She returned reluctantly to the Ballet Russe de Monte Carlo, with which she toured until 1940.

When Miss Slavenska appeared at the Metropolitan Opera House in New York City in *Coppelia* in the afternoon, and as Giselle in the evening, John Martin wrote in the New York *Times* (October 28, 1940) that she was much better in the first ballet, in which as Swanilda she "danced and mimed broadly and tellingly," and in which she was "extremely decorative."

Tired of touring, she decided to settle down to create some new dances. "I took my mother, my dog and my cat," she told a reporter, "and drove to Hollywood because I had liked it when the ballet had played there once." She stayed a year, working on new dances and developing a ballet company of her own and a repertoire.

Miss Slavenska returned for a year to the Ballet Russe de Monte Carlo as prima ballerina. In 1944 the dancer formed a company of her own, which opened in New York City early in January, and then gave twelve performances in Canada en route to the Pacific Coast. In Ottawa, her company gave a benefit for Yugoslav War Prisoners. Late in March 1944, Miss Slavenska returned to New York to teach at the Institute of Arts and Sciences in Brooklyn.

After a second American tour with her company the following year, she appeared in a musical film, *Song Without Words.* During the year 1946 she taught in her own studio in Hollywood, and then formed her own group again, which she called Slavenska Ballet Variante.

In addition to the classic ballets Miss Slavenska has appeared in *Vienna—1814, Seventh Symphony* and *Ghost Town,* the last a dance on an American theme. Among works she has choreographed for her group are *Balkan Sketches,* to music by Tajtchevitch, *Concerto Romantique* to music by Liszt, and *Trilogy* to music by Chopin.

In the summer of 1952 Miss Slavenska and Frederic Franklin formed a company called Theater Ballet, in which Alexandra Danilova was featured as guest dancer. The group commissioned Valerie Bettis to create a dance version of Tennessee Williams' play, *A Streetcar Named Desire.* Mia Slavenska danced the role of the ill-starred Blanche Du Bois in the ballet which translates the emotion-charged atmosphere of the play in terms of contemporary dance. She was acclaimed by the critics for her acting as well as her dancing. Walter Terry referred to "the uncommon brilliance and dramatic force" that marked her delineation of Blanche (New York *Herald Tribune,* December 10, 1952).

The role of Blanche brought Miss Slavenska the opportunity she has long awaited, to find a good dramatic part, a difficulty she has met throughout her career. She has had two strong desires, to act and to choreograph.

After an extended New York engagement in December 1952, the company toured the United States and then flew to Japan, where the Tennessee Williams play had already become a favorite of theatre-goers. The ballet was highly successful, and Miss Slavenska returned to the United States in July to dance and act the leading role in the musical comedy *On Your Toes* in Chicago. During the summer of 1953 she appeared with her company at the Lewisohn Stadium in New York City, and played to a capacity audience.

While enjoying a successful nation-wide tour, the Slavenska-Franklin Ballet Company, had *Streetcar* as the featured work. Miss Slavenska found that it was more popular in larger cities than in small. She told Eileen Summers in an interview in the Washington *Post,* November 19, 1953, that she thinks ballet is beginning to take hold in America outside the big cities, but that the ballet tradition cannot be built up "unless a national ballet company is founded, subsidized by the Government and with its own training school, as it is in many European countries." She does not believe that nationalization of ballet would lead to stultification. "Great artists—and dancers—develop in spite of insecurity, not because of it," she said.

After a four-week engagement at the Century Theatre in New York, the Franklin-Slavenska company was dissolved early in 1954.

The ballerina was married to Dr. Kurt Neumann at Sherman Oaks, California on September 13, 1946. They have a daughter, Maria, and they live when not on tour, in a house in New Jersey with a hundred acres where they raise chickens. Dr. Neumann was manager of the Slavenska-Franklin company. Miss Slavenska has red hair and gray eyes. She has her country's official title of Etoile des Théâtres Nationaux de Yougoslavie.

Her advice to those aspiring to be ballerinas is "Just remember that there is very little room at the top, that the odds will be sharply against you in combining marriage with your career, that your dancing days will be numbered by the time you're 45, and that you'll make very little money out of it."

References

Washington (D.C.) Post N 19 '53

Chujoy, A. ed. Dance Encyclopedia (1949)

Music & Dance in New York State (1951)

SLYE, MAUD Feb. 8, 1879-Sept. 17, 1954 Pathologist; educated at the University of Chicago and Brown University; taught pathology from 1919 to 1944 at the University of Chicago; known for her work on cancer and her theory that the disease can only be eliminated in humans by breeding it out of the race; received gold medals from the American Medical Association and American Radiological Society; published technical brochures and two volumes of poetry, *Songs and Solaces* (1934) and *I in the Wind* (1936). See *Current Biography,* (Yrbk) 1940.

Obituary

N Y Times p15 S 18 '54 por

SMATHERS, GEORGE A(RMISTEAD) Nov. 14, 1913- United States Senator from Florida; lawyer

Address: b. Senate Office Bldg., Washington, D.C.; Alfred I. duPont Bldg., Miami 32, Fla.; h. 1410 W. 24th St., Sunset Island 3, Miami Beach, Fla.

An advocate of friendlier relations with Latin America, United States Senator from Florida, George A. Smathers, also favors stimulating a healthier and freer world trade. He was elected to the Senate on November 7, 1950, having previously defeated Claude Pepper, Senator since 1936, in the race for the Democratic nomination. For four years prior to his election to the Senate, he had served as a member of the House of Representatives from Florida's Fourth District, and in the early years of his career, had practiced law.

The son of Judge Frank Smathers and the former Lura Jones, George Armistead Smathers was born in Atlantic City, New Jersey on November 14, 1913. His brother, Frank, is now manager of the Miami Beach Trust Department of the First National Bank; his sister is Mrs. Phillip Myers. His father had served as chairman of the Atlantic county delegation to the New Jersey Democratic convention that nominated Woodrow Wilson for governor, and later managed Wilson's presidential campaign in southern New Jersey. Because he suffered from arthritis, Judge Smathers moved with his wife and children to Miami, Florida in 1919, hoping that the climate would prove beneficial.

George received his early education in the public schools of Dade county, Florida. He distinguished himself in athletics at Robert E. Lee Junior High School and at Miami Senior High School, where he was president of his class, played football and baseball and captained the high school basketball team that won the state championship in 1931.

At the University of Florida at Gainesville, Smathers was captain of the basketball team and president of the student body. He won the southern intercollegiate oratorical contest, was chosen the "best all-around man" in school and earned a B-plus scholastic average. In 1936 he received the B.A. degree. Remaining at the University of Florida for two additional

Wide World

GEORGE A. SMATHERS

years, Smathers earned his LL.B. degree in 1938. During the same year he was admitted to the Florida bar and began to practice law. At present, he is a member of the firm of Smathers, Thompson, Maxwell & Dyer.

The young lawyer was chosen state president of the Junior Chamber of Commerce in 1940, and, through the influence of Senator Claude Pepper, was appointed an assistant U.S. district attorney for Dade county. He handled the La Paloma white slavery case, sending a former county solicitor to Federal prison.

In May of 1942 Smathers enlisted in the Marine Corps. Graduating as a first lieutenant from the reserve officers training school at Quantico, Virginia, he served in the Pacific theater with the First Marine Bomber Squadron.

Discharged from the Marine Corps as a major in October 1945, Smathers was appointed special assistant to the U.S. Attorney General and was assigned to cases in his home state. He remained in this position until January, 1946, when he resigned in order to run for Congress. In his campaign he was supported by a committee of thirty young men who adopted the appellation, "Goons of 1946", applied to them by the opposing candidate. On November 5, 1946, Smathers was elected to the Eightieth Congress as Democratic Representative from Florida's Fourth Congressional District which includes Dade, Collier, and Monroe counties.

In Congress Smathers served on the committees on Foreign Affairs and House Administration and on a special committee on Reconstruction of the House Roof and Skylights and Remodeling of the House Chamber. His voting record in the first session of the Eightieth Congress indicates that he favored the Greek-Turkish aid bill (1947), overriding the veto of the Taft-Hartley bill (1947) and extension of rent controls (1947). In the second session he voted for six billion dollars foreign aid authorization (1948), the Mundt-Nixon bill (1948) and to override the veto on a bill to permit railroads to enter into rate agreements without being liable to prosecution under the anti-trust laws (1948).

The roll call of the Eighty-first Congress shows that the Congressman voted for the extension of the Trade Agreements Act to 1951 (1949), the shelving of a bill to pay pensions of ninety dollars a month to veterans of both World Wars when they reach the age of sixty-five (1949), for the long-range housing bill which included the public housing section (1949), for the Lodge-Gossett constitutional amendment (1950), and against voluntary compliance of FEPC (1950).

Early in 1950 Smathers had begun campaigning for the Democratic nomination to the Senate. His opponent, senior Senator Claude Pepper, had formerly been his political colleague. In 1938, Smathers, then studying at the University of Florida, had managed Pepper's campaign on the campus, and Pepper had subsequently aided him to obtain the posts first of assistant U.S. district attorney for southern Florida and later of Democratic Representative to the House.

By the time of the senatorial campaign, however, the two men were in fundamental disagreement on important political matters. Smathers made Communism and Negro relations the main issues of his campaign, and declared that the Fair Employment Practices Commission supported by Pepper was a Communist-inspired plan to break down Southern segregation.

Other issues of the campaign were the Truman compulsory health insurance proposal and the Townsend plan for pensions, both supported by Pepper and attacked by Smathers, and the Taft-Hartley act and practice of filibustering in the Senate; the latter two were advocated by Smathers and opposed by Pepper. While labor unions, Negroes and politicians allied to the state party machine gave their support to Senator Pepper, university classmates, business men represented in the Junior Chamber of Commerce, many Republicans, and all but two of the Florida daily newspapers, rallied around Smathers.

On May 2, 1950, Smathers defeated Pepper for the nomination by a majority of approximately 64,000 in the largest vote ever cast in the state, and accordingly won his seat in the Senate on November 7, 1950.

As a Senator, Smathers sponsored a resolution in January 1952 to amend the Constitution by replacing national political conventions by national primaries to be held in all forty-eight states during June of a presidential election year. Together with other Senators he introduced a six-point "clean government act" to place the entire tax-collecting system under Civil Service.

During the presidential campaign, the Senator from Florida supported Adlai E. Stevenson, although he declared himself in disagreement with the Democratic candidate on civil rights, his stand for Federal control of tidelands oil, advocacy of anti-filibuster and repeal of the Taft-Hartley law. At the same time Smathers warned that Florida might have a Republican majority in 1952.

On February 15, 1953 he said in an interview on the American Broadcasting Company television program *Junior Press Conference* that a Supreme Court decision outlawing segregation would "set the situation in the South back fifty years." He said the South had made "tremendous progress" in providing better education for Negroes, but he felt that further moves should be left to the local communities. "I don't like bigotry and intolerance, but they do exist and I don't think you're going to get them out by passing laws," Smathers said. He felt that as long as Negro schools were equal to white schools, the Southern states were fulfilling their duty.

(The U.S. Supreme Court ruled unanimously on May 17, 1954 that racial segregation in public schools is unconstitutional.)

The Senator believes that education is fundamentally a matter of state concern, he nevertheless advocated Federal aid to the states for education. He insisted, however, that there should be "complete state control of funds" to prevent Federal domination of schools (New York *Times*, October 18, 1953). He supported the Hill amendment to the continental shelf bill to devote Federal revenues from offshore mineral resources to a program of aid for education.

When the issue of Alaskan statehood neared the voting stage in the Senate, Smathers made a motion which temporarily shelved it. His motion, adopted on a 45 to 44 vote, proposed that the bill be returned to the Senate Committee on Interior and Insular Affairs with instructions to study the possibility of a constitutional amendment to give "commonwealth status" to both Alaska and Hawaii. On June 22, 1953 Smathers demanded a Congressional inquiry into the possible increase of Communist influences in Hawaii, and he spear-headed the fight in the Eighty-third Congress against statehood for the territory. This bill was also tabled.

The Eisenhower administration's plan to reduce foreign aid was not entirely supported by Senator Smathers. On October 26, 1953 he told a United Press reporter that the United States should give "more selective" aid to countries like Greece and Turkey "where we get some return in mutual security." He also urged that our obligations to bolster mutual security in Latin America be kept.

On July 30, 1954 the Senate approved an amendment, sponsored by Smathers, to the foreign aid bill. By this motion the Senate appropriated an additional $10,000,000 for technical assistance in Latin America. The foreign aid bill was signed by the President at the end of August.

Smathers praised President Eisenhower's report to Congress in January 1954. "The President is exactly right in saying that friendship with our good neighbors in the south is the cornerstone of our entire foreign policy," said Smathers. "He is also correct in saying there must be a healthier and freer system of trade all over the world. I think personally this is something we must accomplish if any nation is to live long" (Miami *Herald*, January 8, 1954).

Expressing his views in regard to universal military training, Senator Smathers stated on NBC's television debate, *American Forum of the Air*, on December 20, 1953, "I favor UMT to build up a reserve for America's defense. Youth today has a solemn obligation to protect our basic liberties as did the Minute Men of 1776. It will strengthen the moral fibre of the youth of our nation to be prepared to defend it in time of danger."

Presently, the Senator is a member of the Senate Committee on Finance and Committee on Interstate and Foreign Commerce. His voting record as a member of the upper chamber indicates that he favored an increase in taxes of five and a half billion dollars (1951), a reduction of government payrolls by 10 per cent (1951), cutting TVA appropriations by $46,000,000 (1952), a motion that the President use the national-emergency provisions of the Taft-Hartley act to halt the steel strike (1952), extending the Defense Production Act which continued economic controls (1952), tabling the move to curb Senate filibusters (1953) and boosting soil conservation payments (1953). He was against penalizing foreign aid recipients carrying on trade with Red China (1953).

In 1954 Smathers voted for authorization of the St. Lawrence seaway (January), the (John W.) Bricker amendment limiting executive control of foreign relations (February), a one-billion-dollar excise tax reduction (March), authorization of 140,000 public housing units (June), an amendment to add $350,000,000 to the defense bill (June), an amendment to extend the trade agreements act for three years (June), the atomic energy bill (July), and an amendment to make membership in the Communist party a crime (August).

He opposed ratification of the mutual security pact with the Republic of Korea (January), a constitutional amendment permitting eighteen-year-olds to vote (May), and an amendment (to a bill providing for pay raises to Federal employees) which would increase postal rates (August).

George A. Smathers was married on March 19, 1939 to Rosemary Townley whose father had opened Miami's first drugstore in the early days of the city. The Smathers have two children, John Townley and Bruce. The Senator is on the board of the Junior Chamber of Commerce and is vice-president of the Dade County Bar Association. He is an Elk, a member of the Kiwanis Club, and is affiliated with the Methodist Church. Six feet three inches tall, dark-haired Smathers is ruggedly built and possesses a "rich speaking voice" He is one of the Senate's better golfers.

References

N Y Herald Tribune II p3 Ap 30 '50
N Y Times p26 My 3 '50
Sat Eve Post 222:32+ Ap 22 '50 pors
Congressional Directory (1952)
Who's Who in America, 1954-55

SMITH, (OLIVER) HARRISON Aug. 4, 1888- Editor; publisher

Address: b. c/o The Saturday Review, 25 W. 45th St., New York 36; h. 9 E. 63rd St., New York 21

Since Harrison Smith became president and associate editor of the *Saturday Review of Literature* in 1938 when it was a struggling literary weekly, he has seen it grow into a firmly established publication of great prestige which reports on all of what he calls "the arts of communication" for more than 120,000 subscribers. Beginning on January 5, 1952 it became simply *The Saturday Review,* since it is no longer restricted to the world of books but now also surveys opera, records, radio, television, politics, education, travel and many other fields of public interest.

Active in the publishing business since 1911, Smith worked for Harcourt Brace and Company (1919-1928) when the firm published Sinclair Lewis's novels; with Jonathan Cape (1929-1931); and with Doubleday Doran & Company (1936-1938). In addition to writing literary criticism, essays and editorials for the *Saturday Review,* he has contributed articles to general magazines, many of them on the subject of modern women and their careers. He believes that the one inexhaustible theme for literature is "woman in a man's world, or in a world mismanaged by men," and "women's war to assume a sure place in society."

Feeling the compulsion to answer what he called "a full-fledged anti-feminist campaign" which began after the Second World War, Smith wrote numerous articles defending career women, and pointing out numerous discriminations against women in medicine, law, politics, and industry. "What we all need now is women who will be willing to assume all the burdens that can be placed on them," he wrote, "who will want to take their due place in the social, economic, and political world. The new feminism must be based, not on a jealousy of men and an attempt to be their rivals, but on full partnership with men in all the . . . responsibilities of life" (*Independent Woman,* December, 1947).

His first political editorial, "Let the Eagle Scream," which he wrote for the March 15, 1947 issue of the *Saturday Review,* was reprinted in newspapers over the country, and in the July 1947 *Reader's Digest.*

The son of Oliver Cotton Smith, a Hartford, Connecticut physician and surgeon, and Clarabel (Waterman) Smith, Oliver Harrison Smith was born on August 4, 1888. His uncle, Winchell Smith, was a playwright. His paternal grandfather (William Brown Smith) was a nephew of old John Brown of Osawatomie. Of his youth in Hartford he chiefly recalls that he read everything he could lay his hands on, at home, in his friends' homes and in the public library. At Yale he was influenced by "Professor Billy Phelps's [William Lyon Phelps] ardor for Shakespeare and the nineteenth-century writers."

Graduating in 1911 with a B.A. degree, Smith took his M.A. in 1914, the same year in which his father was awarded an honorary degree by Yale University. In New York he worked on the editorial staff of *Century* magazine (1911-1913); as a textbook salesman for the Century Company (1913-1915); then an editor in the trade department (1915); and a reporter on the New York *Tribune* (1917-1919).

He roomed with George Soule, who later became an editor of the *New Republic.* Soule introduced Smith to Sinclair Lewis of whom he wrote: "I thought of Red Lewis as a beardless, younger Shaw, or another Wells, perhaps, and suddenly I knew that I had met my first genius."

Shortly after this, Smith recently recalled, he fell in love with a Scotch girl named Claire Spencer but fearing that matrimony would hamper his freedom, he convinced the managing editor of the (then) New York *Tribune* that he should investigate the Russian Revolution, at his own expense. Thus, as an accredited correspondent, he embarked for Russia.

After a series of hairbreadth escapes he returned to the United States by way of Siberia and Japan, and now prides himself as "being one of the few journalists who did not write a misleading or any other kind of book about the Russian Revolution." Shortly after his return he decided that matrimony was now in order, and in 1918, married Claire Spencer, who later became a novelist.

Obtaining a position in 1919 as an editor with Harcourt Brace and Company, Smith stayed with this publisher until 1928. During this period the firm published many of Sinclair Lewis' greatest novels, as well as works by important British writers. Eventually Smith decided to start his own publishing house, and so founded Jonathan Cape & Harrison Smith, Inc. His first list (1929) included William Faulkner, with whom Smith worked for the next ten years, and many other authors of note, but the depression was disastrous, and this publishing firm was succeeded by Harrison Smith, Inc., and then Harrison Smith & Robert Haas, Inc., which was finally absorbed by Random House where he was a partner of the firm.

At this time Smith decided that he needed experience with mass publishing, and from 1936 to 1938 he worked on the editorial staff of Doubleday Doran & Company, one of the largest publishing firms.

Then, at the end of 1938 Smith left to take charge of the *Saturday Review of Literature.* This was a good deal of a gamble, he has since admitted, for it was in a very shaky position. He had the idea, however, that while book advertising alone could never provide a sound economic base for this publication, if its coverage were expanded to include all of the arts of communication, it could become a profitable enterprise. When Norman Cousins accepted the editorship of the magazine and J. R. Cominsky became its advertising and business manager, Smith had no doubt of its future as a national literary magazine.

Accordingly, while book reviews and general literary comment continued to fill many of its pages, the *Review* shortly acquired John Mason Brown as critic of Broadway plays (and later Henry Hewes), Irving Kolodin to review operas and concerts as well as new issues of recorded music. The dance, motion pictures and radio also began to receive regular attention. Later, television and travel were added to the other features, with experienced critics reporting regularly on each field. Bennett Cerf, president of Random House, publishers, began his popular weekly column "Trade Winds".

The magazine has also benefited from the leadership of Dr. Henry Seidel Canby, chairman of the editorial board; Amy Loveman, associate editor; Christopher Morley (who, although no longer on the editorial board, writes occasional pieces); the late William Rose Benét who conducted the poetry column "The Phoenix Nest," and Norman Cousins, editor. Cousins' editorials are more often concerned with the destiny of man and the dangers of the atomic and hydrogen bombs than with the literary scene. Harrison Smith, on the other hand (who writes about every third editorial) functions as a sort of allayer of the fears conjured up by Cousins and other editorial writers.

Although Smith and Cousins frequently take differing points of view, in an editorial signed with both their initials they agreed in defining their magazine's general purpose: "We are against cults which profess to hold the exclusive keys to the literary kingdom. We are against cultural snobbery. We are against the mutual benefit and admiration society approach to criticism and literature under which members enjoy special privileges and immunities and write blurbs and prefaces for each other and review each other's books. . ." (December 31, 1949).

Smith says that he is called "the office optimist", but his own explanation of his point of view is hardly that simple. "The U.S. has never been a country of despair," he says, and in his editorials he has scolded writers for writing only of "the sins of American society," and for "producing an aggressively negative literature. . ."

In an editorial, "Wanted: New Novelists", in the *Saturday Review*, July 31, 1954, he pointed out that "the astonishingly rapid improvement in racial relations over the last decade has already outdated many subjects. . . The novel of moral or social protest has . . . become suddenly antiquated. War is horrible . . . poverty and juvenile depravity are dreadful to contemplate, but . . . we are attempting to alleviate them. The United States is a confusing nation to write about."

"Hal" Smith, as he is known to his friends, rushed to the defense of modern woman in the January 18, 1947 *Saturday Review*, following the publication by Harper of *Modern Woman: the Lost Sex* by Ferdinand Lundberg and Marynia Farnham. Smith's editorial, "Woman is the Scapegoat" brought him a great deal of mail, all agreeing with him, and he was invited to appear on several radio talks at Town Hall. So profitable was Smith's defense of modern woman that *Publishers' Weekly*, in a lighthearted comment on his activities, (June 21, 1947), quoted the advertisement: "Never underestimate the power of a woman." Smith has also lectured on contemporary literature at clubs and colleges throughout the country.

HARRISON SMITH

"It is no wonder that the most powerful and inexhaustible theme in our fiction is the American woman," wrote Smith in "The Greatest of All Stories" (*Good Housekeeping*, July 1947). "Four major factors determined the present impregnable position of women in American society," he wrote: "The First World War, in which they got their taste of freedom; the depression, in which they discovered that if a man faints by the wayside, a woman can pick him up and go on; the Second World War, in which women discovered that, however encumbered by babies and absent husbands, they have special talents, highly paid for and invaluable to modern industry; and, finally, the knowledge that American women, through insurance policies and their husbands' bequests, own nearly half the wealth of America."

Recently, he says, he has discovered that feminism of the old school is "as dead as a doornail. Now that we have a suburban civilization and an astounding rise in the birthrate I expect some day to take up the cudgels for the millions of young women who 'have so many children they don't know what to do' about those twenty or more years of their lives when husband and children have departed and whatever talents they have had have been lost forever."

As a result of his intimate friendship with Sinclair Lewis, Smith edited a volume of his letters not long after his death, which were published in 1952 by Harcourt Brace under the title *From Main Street to Stockholm*, and he is at present collecting material for a full-length biography of Lewis. Previously, in 1945, under the name Oliver Smith, he had written a pamphlet, "Sinclair Lewis", also published by Harcourt Brace.

(Continued next page)

SMITH, HARRISON—*Continued*

His only other published book was *North America,* one of the *Century Geographical Readings* which appeared in 1914, three years after he left Yale. It was reprinted in 1926. Smith wrote a number of the pieces in this collection, calling himself variously "Oliver Harrison", and "Harrison Smith."

Smith is a Republican, a Congregationalist, a member of the Yale Club and the Overseas Press Club of New York, and Psi Upsilon fraternity. He is five feet nine inches tall, weighs 140 pounds, and has brown eyes and gray hair. He finds his chief relaxation in sailing about Long Island Sound in his sloop "Venture". He belongs to the City Island Yacht Club in New York. In addition to his New York apartment, he maintains a country home at Farmington, Connecticut. Smith was divorced in 1934. His children are Harrison Venture Smith, now an officer in J. P. Morgan & Co., and Patricia Smith. The name "Venture," he explains, was discovered in his study of American Revolutionary history. Venture Smith was the skipper of his own small sailing craft in Stonington, Connecticut. He was hit by a cannonball and was, Harrison Smith believes, the first Negro to be killed by the British.

In an article "Speak Up For Your Country" in *Good Housekeeping,* April 1948, Smith urged that patriotism be revived. "We do not need Fourth of July orations to convince ourselves that [America] is great and that in us, the strongest and wealthiest nation on earth, there is neither arrogance nor any deep hatred of any other country. It is known that we have the qualities of mercy and compassion, that we are generous beyond the average of mankind. . . . Let us recognize and calmly analyze our faults, so that in time we may correct them. But let us also, and with humility, list the proofs of our strength."

References

Pub W 151:3027 Je 21 '47
Who's Who in America, 1954-55
Who's Who in the East (1953)

SNOW, C(HARLES) P(ERCY) Oct. 15, 1905- Author; physicist

Address: b. c/o The Macmillan Company, 60 5th Ave., New York 11; h. Nethergate House, Clare, Suffolk, England

Reprinted from the *Wilson Library Bulletin,* Jan. 1954

Although he has always wanted to be a creative writer, C. P. (Charles Percy) Snow has been able to combine two successful and distinct careers: novelist and scientist. He has completed the fourth in a cycle of novels which picture English life between 1920 and 1950. It is entitled *The New Men.* The first three volumes to be published—*The Light and the Dark, Time of Hope, The Masters*—have been greeted with increasing critical acclaim.

Lotte Jacobi

C. P. SNOW

C. P. Snow was born in Leicester, England, October 15, 1905. (The childhood of his character, Lewis Eliot, in the novel, *Time of Hope,* is in part autobiographical.) His father was William Edward Snow, an unsuccessful businessman, and his mother, Ada Sophia (Robinson) Snow. He has three brothers. Since he was born poor, Snow has said, "I first made my way in the most practicable career open to me, as a professional scientist. Getting through the university (University College, Leicester) on scholarships, I did research in physics at Cambridge (Ph.D. 1930), became a Fellow of Christi College (Cambridge) and continued in scientific work and college administration through the thirties. At this time I had published my first works." Snow tutored at Christi from 1935 to 1940 and from 1938 to 1940 was editor of *Discovery.* He was also editor of Cambridge Library of Modern Science.

During World War II, Snow was the chief of scientific personnel for the Ministry of Labor and was rewarded with the C. B. E. (Commander of the British Empire) in 1943. Immediately after the war, in 1945, he was appointed civil service commissioner, a post he still holds. He has also been physicist-director of the English Electric Company.

Snow's first book to appear in the United States was a humorous detective story, *Death Under Sail,* in 1932. In 1935 *The Search* appeared. The *New Statesman and Nation* described it as "the story of a scientist, a well-known crystallographer, of his rise from indigence to eminence and of his decline from scientific eminence to hard-won matrimonial felicity." The novel was generally well received with special praise for its characterization of the scientific world but with some criticism of the weakness of its characters.

Beatrice Sherman wrote, in the New York *Times*, that it was "a meaty, stimulating novel which deserves and demands a careful reading," and the late William Rose Benét found it "superior to the average modern novel in that it deals more with the intellectual and less with the purely emotional and physical."

Although the idea for the ten-novel series was first consciously conceived by Snow as early as 1935, he did not actually begin writing until after the Second World War. During this period, the novel-sequence matured in his mind. He conceived of the series as separate but interrelated novels. The first to be published in the United States, *The Light and the Dark* (1948), is a character study of a young Cambridge don who attempts to curb his dark moods by promiscuity, alcohol, concentration on his studies, and religion. He joins the Royal Air Force at the outbreak of the war and is killed in action. The New York *Times* expressed the general opinion of the critics: "Several of the minor characters come alive; some of the incidents, such as the forming of academic cliques within the college, are vivid. But the dominant characters are essentially sterile. They move like puppets, with the handler behind the platform exhorting us to consider the unique qualities and problems of his actors." The *Spectator* characterized the novel as "the work of a civilized, sensitive author who writes for readers like himself."

The second novel in the series, *Time of Hope*, was published in the United States in 1950. In this volume, the narrator of *The Light and the Dark*, Lewis Eliot, relates the story of his own childhood and youth, his training in law, and his unhappy marriage. Harrison Smith in the *Saturday Review of Literature* wrote that "the pages illuminating Eliot's inner nature . . . can stand with the finest examples of the novelist's or the biographer's art; one unconsciously thinks of Rousseau and Emma Bovary. . . ."

James Hilton wrote: "*Time of Hope* is a good novel, clearly the work of a good writer. But I did not find it as intellectually and emotionally exciting as *The Search*. . ." (New York *Herald Tribune Book Review*).

The Masters, published in the United States in 1951 has won the best critical reception. The narrator is still Lewis Eliot and this time he describes the conflicting forces aroused in the faculty over the election of a new master in one of the Cambridge colleges. The *New Yorker* declared: "Mr. Snow's writing is slow, sure and shrewd, and powerful enough to draw the reader entirely into his closed, almost airtight world of scholars and their families." The London *Times Literary Supplement* concluded its review thus: "There can be no doubt that *The Masters* gives an excellent account of at least one side of university life, upon which Mr. Snow is to be warmly congratulated." *The Masters* was chosen as the English Book Society Fiction Choice for July 1951.

The New Men (1954) shows the problems faced by Lewis Eliot and his brother, a physicist, with the development of nuclear fission.

C. P. Snow has blue eyes, fair hair, is six feet tall and weighs 175 pounds. On July 14, 1950 he married the well-known English novelist and critic, Pamela Hansford Johnson. They have one son, Philip Charles Hansford Snow. They live in Clare, Suffolk, in eastern England. He has neither political nor church affiliations. Although he does not disclose his present hobbies, he was a distinguished cricketeer in secondary school and at University College. He is a fiction reviewer for the London *Sunday Times*.

References

Author's and Writer's Who's Who (1948-49)
International Who's Who, 1953
Who's Who, 1954

SNYDER, JANET *See* Lambert, J. (S.)

SPERRY, WILLARD L(EAROYD), REV. DR. Apr 5, 1882-May 15, 1954 Former university dean; author; was ordained (1908); Rhodes scholar; pastor, Central Congregational Church, Boston (1914-1922); lecturer and professor, Andover Theological Seminary (1917-1925); dean, Harvard University Divinity School (1930-1953); author; worked on revision of Old Testament for Revised Standard Version of Holy Bible. See *Current Biography,* (May) 1952.

Obituary

N Y Times p87 My 16 '54

SPIEGEL, CLARA *See* Jaynes, C.

STARK, LOUIS May 1, 1888-May 17, 1954 Editorial writer and former labor reporter for the New York *Times;* born in Hungary; was educated in New York City schools; spent four years in the advertising and publishing fields; was a general assignment reporter for the New York City News Association (1913-1917) and briefly on the New York *Sun;* joined the New York *Times* (1917); covered coal and textile strikes (1920's) and the rise of the CIO; assigned to the Sacco-Vanzetti case (reprinted in the book by *Times* reporters: *We Saw It Happen* in 1938); won the Pulitzer Prize (1942); author of articles on management-labor relations in *Atlantic Monthly, New Republic,* etc.; retired from the *Times* Washington Bureau (1951) where in eighteen years he won the respect of colleagues, union and government officials for his accurate and impartial treatment of labor news. See *Current Biography,* (June) 1945.

Obituary

N Y Times p29 My 18 '54

STARR, CHAUNCEY Apr. 14, 1912-
Physicist

Address: b. c/o North American Aviation Company, Los Angeles 45, Calif.

Electricity from atomic power is a present-day possibility in the opinion of Dr. Chauncey Starr, director of the atomic energy research department at North American Aviation Company's plant at Downey, California. The physicist directed the design, development and completion in 1952 of a low power nuclear reactor —a junior-size atomic energy plant small enough to fit into a garage—and suitable for test and research by industrial firms, universities and scientific groups.

A specialist since 1935 in the physics of metals at high pressures, Dr. Starr recommends the building of a large pilot plant to test the production of electricity by means of a reactor, which, when tapped by a metal (such as sodium) is piped to a conventional steam boiler and then coupled to a turbine-generator. Designs for this experimental power plant were announced by North American Aviation Company in May, 1953.

Speaking before the San Joaquin Valley Council of the California Chamber of Commerce in April 1952, Dr. Starr said that the major problems of harnessing atomic-energy for peace-time use are now solved, and that it is up to the initiative of private enterprise to develop this power practically.

"The problems faced by any industrial group entering this field are many," he explained. "A large capital investment somewhere between $25,000,000 and $30,000,000 would have to be made, the return from which would be dependent upon a government agreement both for the supply and purchase of fissionable materials. . . The atomic-power field must now involve the primary participation of private capital or alternatively drift into the shape of a government monopoly" (*Christian Science Monitor*, April 19, 1952).

Chauncey Starr was born in Newark, New Jersey on April 14, 1912. As a boy he was actively interested in science, experimenting at home, and becoming increasingly absorbed in the study of metals. He entered the Rensselaer Polytechnic Institute at Troy, New York, from which he was graduated in 1932. Continuing his post-graduate studies in the same institution, he earned a Ph. D. degree in physics in 1935.

During the next two years, from 1935 to 1937, he was Charles A. Coffin fellow and research fellow in phvsics at Harvard University, Cambridge, Massachusetts. Working with Dr. P. W. Bridgman, he studied the behavior and the thermal conductivity of metals under high pressure.

Upon completion of his researches at Harvard, Dr. Starr joined the electronics firm of P.R. Mallory & Co., Indianapolis, Indiana, as research physicist in 1937. His familiarity with metals aided the improvement of Mallory-designed instruments ranging from dual automobile ignition systems to professional radio and electronic apparatus. He also helped to bring up to date the technical tables and manuals which Mallory publishes periodically as aids to engineers and electricians.

In 1938 Dr. Starr left the Mallory firm and entered the Rogers Laboratory of Massachusetts Institute of Technology as research associate in physical chemistry. His specialities were the magnetic susceptibilities of metals and compounds at low temperatures, and the production of liquid hydrogen. These two fields were quite allied since liquid hydrogen brings the temperatures of metals toward absolute zero wherein the crystals of metallic molecules polarize and become susceptible to magnetic attraction.

In the early part of World War II, between 1941 and 1942, he was physicist for the U.S. Navy Bureau of Ships at the D. W. Taylor model basin. Dr. Starr experimented with electronic devices for the study of transients in ship structure, which again involved metals.

In 1942 Dr. Starr entered the then secret, rapidly growing atomic energy field. His initial work was at the University of California Radiation Laboratory in Berkeley, where the pioneer atom-smashing machine, the cyclotron, had been developed. He was soon transferred to the Tennessee Eastman Corporation of Oak Ridge, Tennessee as senior physicist, and in the period of 1943-46, he was a member of the Manhattan District Project, working in the Oak Ridge Clinton Laboratories operated by Monsanto Chemical Corporation of St. Louis, Missouri.

His knowledge of metallurgy and the physics of metals under extreme temperatures and pressures was important enough to make him a member of the Manhattan District Technical Committee on Inspection and Control of Atomic Energy in 1945.

When North American Aviation Company of Los Angeles, entered the atomic energy field in 1946 for the eventual production of atom-powered airplanes, it chose Dr. Chauncey Starr as section chief of special research in its nuclear plant at Downey, California. Dr. Starr now faced a different problem. In the Manhattan District Project at Oak Ridge, he had been working with the sudden release of energy, in staggering quantities, as in the atom bomb. Now he was confronted with the task of utilizing the atom's storehouse of tremendous energy for industrial purposes—in other words, the slow and controlled burning of fissionable fuel.

California's first atomic energy plant was opened in the summer of 1952 at the North American Aviation company's Downey plant. The "baby reactor" water boiler is now being used to further development of reactors and associated projects. "While small in comparison with reactors for producing fissionable materials," according to *Iron Age* (September 4, 1952), "it will give information of value in improving reactor design. The water boiler is part of a facility for making reactor physics measurements to enlarge basic atomic energy information." This boiler neutron source will supply the neutrons, minute particles of matter, needed for measurements.

Early delivery of the million-dollar "baby" Starr reactor was credited, in large part, to Dr. Starr's knowledge of metals. He said that the reactor has a built-in safety factor. "In addition to the usual automatic devices to shut down the reactor, the design of the core is such that as its temperature rises, the neutron production goes down." (Neutron production is necessary to sustain any chain reaction—without neutrons there is no atomic fire or explosion.) (*Aviation Week,* November 19, 1951).

Pointing out that a lot of important research could be done on the West Coast with short-lived isotopes, the major product of the reactor he designed, Dr. Starr explained that two classes of experiments are possible with the reactor. The "in pile" type used the neutron flow within the reactor; in the second class, a neutron beam is led through a port in the shield and used to irradiate objects outside the reactor. . . . The shape of the reactor is octagonal; it is eleven feet high, nineteen feet wide, and grosses about 450 tons. (*Aviation Week,* November 19, 1951).

The exterior of the low power reactor is shielded by a housing of two-feet thick concrete blocks each weighing 1,000 pounds, forming a structure about the size of a single car garage. The concrete surrounds a cylindrical graphite reflector five feet in diameter and six feet high, formed by stacking graphite bars horizontally inside a steel tank. The reflector surrounds the reactor core, a stainless steel sphere one foot in diameter. Production of atomic energy takes place inside this sphere which contains Uranium 235 enriched uranyl nitrate solution. It is from the nuclear fission of this material in a water solution that the reactor derives its power—and its name "water boiler" (*Automotive Industries,* October 1, 1952.)

In Dr. Starr's projected large piiot plant, which will be the forerunner of the engine for North American Aviation's future atom-powered airplanes, the key energy-producing item is the standard nuclear reactor. It will convert uranium into fissionable plutonium by trapping and slowing down the flight of neutral sub-atomic particles, neutrons. Tremendous heat is the by-product. It is usually wasted in the reactor manufacturing plutonium for the atom bomb but is used for the atomic trigger of the hydrogen bomb.

The scientist has designed pipes which circulate a metal-like sodium through the reactor, absorbing the tremendous heat. The molten metal will be piped through a water boiler, producing steam, which in turn will drive a conventional turbine-generator. The end product will be electricity.

In planning and building an atomic furnace various materials are of necessity tested to determine their ability to contain the tremendous heat of fissionable material while at the same time protecting researchers from radioactivity. Similar tests are continuing under Dr. Starr's direction. In May, 1953 North

CHAUNCEY STARR

American Aviation, Inc. announced that designs had been completed for an experimental power plant that is ready to be tested for the generation of useful commercial power.

Dr. Starr's practical experience has made him widely recognized as an authority in the development of atomic energy by private enterprise. At the same time he has not lost sight of the economic problems involved in such a pioneer undertaking. In his July 6, 1953 speech before the Joint Congressional Committee on atomic energy, he said of the projected North American Aviation atomic energy production of electricity: "It is our belief that a reactor program which would provide pilot plant experience would require approximately five years and have a total cost of about $10,000,000, including the cost of development. . . . Following such a program, it would then be proper to consider the construction of a full-scale plant which could reasonably be expected to compete with the cost of power from conventional plants at that time. . . ." (New York *Times,* July 7, 1953).

He acknowledged that the cost of producing electricity by nuclear reactor would initially be considerably higher than electrical production by coal or water power. He predicted however that through research with the pilot plant, more effective methods of power production from atomic energy could be developed and the cost correspondingly lowered.

Like Great Britain's Cumberland atomic-power station, North American's pilot plant would be able to produce atomic fuel (plutonium) as well as electricity. Dr. Starr estimates that his proposed plant would generate 8,000 kilowatts of electric power, enough to supply 2,000 average homes with electricity. Even now, the physicist looks beyond the initial power plant to a more efficient one, in which ten pounds of fissionable material would

STARR, CHAUNCEY—*Continued*

produce power equal to the ultimate capacity of Hoover Dam.

Besides researches into the physics of metals at extreme pressures and temperatures, and metallurgy connected with atomic energy, Dr. Chauncey Starr has also experimented with semiconductors, gas discharge phenomena, the physics of the solid state and the mechanics of jet propulsion.

Dr. Starr and Doris Evelyn Debel of Troy, New York were married in 1938. They have a son, Ross M. Starr, and a daughter, Ariel. The scientist is a member of the American Physical Society and the Society of Sigma XI. His chief hobby is painting.

References

Christian Sci Mon p6 Ap 19 '52
N Y Times p5 Ap 10 '52; p35 My 27 '53; pl Jl 7 '53
American Men of Science (1949)

STAUDINGER, HERMANN Mar. 23, 1881- Chemist

Address: b. c/o Forschungsinstitut für Makromolekulare Chemie, Lugostr. 14, Freiburg im Breisgau, Federal Republic of Germany

The winner of the $33,840 Nobel Prize for chemistry in 1953 was Dr. Hermann Staudinger, professor emeritus of the University of Freiburg in Germany, and director of the Research Institute for Macromolecular Chemistry. In a half century's activity in organic chemistry, he has published some 500 books and papers in the field. It was his pioneer work with "giant molecules," begun some thirty years ago, which laid the theoretical basis for subsequent developments in plastics, synthetic fibers, and various branches of industrial chemistry.

DR. HERMANN STAUDINGER

Hermann Staudinger was born in Worms, Germany on March 23, 1881, the son of Professor Franz Staudinger and Auguste (Wenck) Staudinger. He received his early training at the local *gymnasium,* from which he was graduated in 1899. He pursued advanced studies at the universities of Halle and Munich, and at the Technische Hochschule in Darmstadt. At first he was drawn to the study of botany, but in the belief that in order to understand plant life one must first master the basic principles of chemistry, he changed his field of major interest.

He received the Ph.D. degree from the University of Halle on August 3, 1903, and continued his studies at the University of Strasbourg until 1907 when he became qualified to teach and was made an extraordinary professor at the Fridericiana Technische Hochschule at Karlsruhe. He remained there until 1912 and worked in association with the noted scientist Fritz Haber.

Called to the chair of chemistry at the Eidgenössische Technische Hochschule of Zurich, Switzerland in 1912, Staudinger succeeded the Nobel prize winner Richard Willstätter. In the same year he published his first important book, *Die Ketene* (Enke), a work which is still considered standard. At Zurich, where he remained for fourteen years, he attracted students from all over the world.

According to Willem Quarles, "They all came under the spell of this tall German who, with his curt nervous gestures and whispering voice, penetrated into the mysteries of the carbon atom and kindled a love for the strange organic world."

Staudinger's next appointment, which became effective in April 1926 and lasted for twenty-five years, was at the University of Freiburg im Breisgau as professor and director of the chemical laboratory. In 1940 he became director of the Research Institute for Macromolecular Chemistry.

He worked in association with two students, Leopold Ruzicka and Tadeus Reichstein, both of whom have since been Nobel Prize winners. With the former, he investigated pyrethrin, an insecticide, and succeeded in developing an artificial pepper. With Reichstein, he found a compound which synthesized the flavor of coffee and which was widely manufactured during World War II.

He began to concentrate on the study which has occupied him ever since, the field of macromolecular chemistry. Professor Arthur Lüttringhaus wrote that Staudinger published 400 contributions in this field alone: "Thus arose in Freiburg the chemical principles of this increasingly significant branch of the natural sciences."

Working in what is known as "high polymer chemistry," Staudinger is credited with "establishing that the molecules of synthetics . . . have their atoms in long chains" (*Science News Letter*, November 14, 1953). "Either by natural processes or by the skill of the chemist's reactions, big molecules are made out of little ones by a process called polymerization. This is fundamental to many fields of industrial chemistry today, with products that gross many millions of dollars."

At first Staudinger's account of polymerization evoked the opposition of his fellow chemists. "When he started his work," *Time* (November 16, 1953) has related, "many organic compounds were known to contain large groups of atoms, but these were considered mere mechanical clumpings of smaller molecular groups. Dr. Staudinger showed [when he succeeded in putting together the first long-chain synthetic fiber in 1927] that they are true molecules, their thousands of atoms hooked together in definite patterns. Out of this discovery grew such great modern industries as plastics and artificial fibers, as well as new understanding of the way that nature builds the complex compounds in living organisms." In 1930 Staudinger reported another discovery of great importance, that there is a relationship between viscosity and molecular weight.

Heinrich Hopff, a German chemist, wrote on the occasion of Staudinger's seventieth birthday in 1951 that the vast majority of chemists engaged in synthetics now think in concepts which Staudinger established experimentally and developed further. During a recent interview Staudinger's wife declared that her husband's discoveries were not only of great technical importance, but even more, have led to far-reaching conclusions about the nature of organic life. "My husband's work," she stated, "has taught us that we must pay closer attention to the vital principle, and our age needs this insight. Every individual is a unique work of art, even in the chemical sense."

Staudinger himself considers the decade from 1920 to 1930 his "heroic" period, when he demonstrated to those who had opposed him that his theories were correct. "I might not have worked so hard at the matter," he has asserted, "if I had not been so vehemently attacked."

Professor Lüttringhaus has written that in Staudinger's personality and career two basic traits are manifest: intuitive artistry and combativeness. "Staudinger's accomplishments arise from the finest sensitivity for matter. For that reason his thought has always raced far forward. It is hence not remarkable that his insights were at first sharply opposed. This opposition, however, made him strong."

The day after the Nobel award was announced, several hundred students from the University of Freiburg im Breisgau celebrated Staudinger's nomination by holding a torchlight procession in his honor. Professor Lüttringhaus saluted him as a model for students. In accepting these tributes Staudinger acknowledged his deep indebtedness to the cooperative efforts of his research associates and to the inspiration of his students.

Staudinger is a member of the scientific academies of Göttingen, Heidelberg, Halle and Munich; of the Frankfurt and Zurich physical societies; and of the Royal Physiographical Society of Lund (Sweden). He is an honorary member of the Union of Finnish Chemists and a corresponding member of the Society for Natural Research of Zurich.

In 1930 he was awarded the Emil Fischer Medal by the Society of German Chemists; in 1931, the Leblanc Medal by the Chemical Society of France; and in 1933 the Cannizzaro Prize of the Royal Academy of Rome. In 1950 the Fridericiana Technische Hochschule of Karlsruhe conferred upon him the honorary degree of doctor of engineering; the following year the University of Mainz awarded him the honorary degree of doctor of natural science.

Among his many books are *Anleitung zur Organischen Qualitativen Analyse* (Springer, 1923), which had reached a fifth edition by 1948; *Tabellen zu den Vorlesungen über Allgemeine und Anorganische Chemie* (Braun, 1927; fifth edition, 1947); *Organische Kolloidchemie* (Vieweg, 1940; third edition, 1950); *Makromolekulare Chemie und Biologie* (Wepf, 1947); and *Vom Aufstand der Technischen Sklaven* (Chamier, 1947). Since September 1947 he has been publisher of the technical journal, *Die Makromolekulare Chemie.* The scientist's wife, the former Magda Woit (daughter of Dr. Oskar Woit, special Envoy and Minister of Latvia, 1920-1932), who is a biologist and botanist, has been for decades his colleague.

References

Badische Zeitung p3 N 6 '53 por
J Chem Ed 28:120+ Mr '51
Newsweek 42:86+ N 16 '53 por
Sci N L 64:307 N 14 '53 por
Washington (D.C.) Post p9 N 5 '53 por
International Who's Who, 1953
Wer Ist Wer? (1951)

STINE, CHARLES MILTON ALTLAND Oct. 18, 1882-May 28, 1954 Organic chemist; was educated at Gettysburg (Pennsylvania) College and Johns Hopkins University; started career teaching chemistry at Maryland College for Women (1904); named at E. I. du Pont de Nemours & Company as staff member (1907), chief technical adviser (1924), and member of board of directors, executive committee member and vice president (1930); his researches aided in the development of American weapons, nylon, American dye industry, better explosives for use in coal mines, and low-freezing dynamite. See *Current Biography,* (Jan.-Jun.) 1940.

Obituary

N Y Times p15 My 29 '54

STRAUS, OSKAR Apr. 6, 1870-Jan. 11, 1954 Composer; studied with Hermann Grädener, Adolph Prosniz and Max Bruch; wrote over fifty operettas including *Die Lustigen Nibelungen* (1904), *Waltz Dream* (1907) *The Chocolate Soldier* (1908), *The Little Friend* (1911), *All Around Friend* (1914); many serious works, and music for several Hollywood pictures; toured U.S. as conductor (1942); awarded Order of Merit by Austrian government (1930) and French Legion of Honor. See *Current Biography,* (Mar.) 1944.

Obituary

N Y Times p23 Ja 12 '54

STREET, JAMES (HOWELL) Oct. 15, 1903-Sept. 28, 1954 Author; studied at Southwestern Theological Seminary and Howard College; was a Baptist minister for several years; was news editor for Pensacola (Florida) *Journal,* correspondent for the Associated Press, columnist on New York *American,* and reporter for New York *World-Telegram;* wrote many best-selling books, including *Oh Promised Land* (1940), *The Biscuit Eater* (1941), *In My Father's House* (1941), *Tap Roots* (1942), *The Gauntlet* (1945), *The Velvet Doublet* (1953), and *The Civil War* (1953); his dog stories were well-known. See *Current Biography,* (Yrbk) 1946

Obituary

N Y Times p31 S 29 '54

SULLIVAN, MRS. JOHN B(ERCHMANS) *See* Sullivan, L.(A.)K.

SULLIVAN, LEONOR (ALICE) K(RETZER) United States Representative from Missouri

Address: b. 1313 House Office Bldg., Washington 25, D.C.; h. 2303 Minnesota Ave., St. Louis, Mo.

The first woman ever sent to Congress from Missouri is Leonor K. Sullivan, who was elected in November 1952 to represent the Third District (composed of part of St. Louis) in the Eighty-third Congress. Mrs. Sullivan, who is a Democrat, is the widow of John Berchmans Sullivan, who represented the former Eleventh Congressional District of Missouri in the Seventy-seventh, Seventy-ninth, and Eighty-first Congresses, and, briefly, in the Eighty-second Congress.

Congresswoman Sullivan is a member of the House Merchant Marine and Fisheries Committee. Since taking office she has proposed legislation to extend the authority of the Federal Food and Drug Administration, and has advocated tax relief for widows and working mothers. Mrs. Sullivan won re-election in November 1954.

Leonor Alice Kretzer, one of the nine children (six girls and three boys) of Frederick William and Nora (Jostrand) Kretzer, was born in St. Louis. After studying in public and private schools, she attended the evening session of Washington University in St. Louis for training in vocational psychology. She devised new finger dexterity, coordination, and mechanical ability tests for use in selecting students.

For several years, Miss Kretzer taught business arithmetic and accounting, and for a period was the placement director of the St. Louis Comptometer School. She later became the director of the St. Louis Business School. Prior to her marriage on December 27, 1941 to Congressman John Berchmans Sullivan, a lawyer and World War I veteran, she was employed by a manufacturing company.

LEONOR K. SULLIVAN

While her husband served in Congress, Mrs. Sullivan was his administrative assistant, and his campaign manager in five primary and election campaigns. After her husband's death on January 29, 1951, Mrs. Sullivan continued her career in Washington by becoming the administrative aid to Representative Leonard Irving of the Fourth Congressional District of Missouri. She resigned in May 1952 and returned to St. Louis to campaign for the Democratic nomination in the Third Congressional District. (In the reapportionment of the House of Representatives on the basis of the 1950 census, Missouri lost two of its former thirteen seats, and the old Eleventh District, which had been represented by Congressman Sullivan, became the Third.) Mrs. Sullivan won the primary in which she was opposed by seven candidates. On November 4, 1952 she unseated the incumbent, Claude I. Bakewell, by a vote of 2 to 1. (Bakewell had been elected on March 9, 1951 to complete John B. Sullivan's unexpired term.)

In the first session of the Eighty-third Congress, she joined other Missouri representatives in sponsoring a bill to authorize Federal assistance in developing the St. Louis river front as a Lewis and Clark memorial. She was the author of a bill to amend the Federal Food, Drug and Cosmetic Act to provide Food and Drug Administration inspectors with "unqualified authority for inspection of factories where food, drugs, cosmetics or devices are manufactured."

"In the closing hours before adjournment," she reported in a newsletter to her constituents, "Congress passed a factory inspection bill containing the provisions of the bill I introduced."

Representative Sullivan sent another newsletter to her constituents in April 1953, in which she stated: ". . . every week day of 1952 the inspectors of the Food and Drug Administration seized and destroyed nearly twenty-seven tons of filthy or decomposed foods which would otherwise have gone on sale in markets throughout the country." She continued: "...the Food and Drug Administration has a total staff of only 205 inspectors to check... over 77,000 manufacturing plants and warehouses. Because of this very limited personnel and a shortage of funds, only a small fraction of 1 per cent of the total production of food, drugs and cosmetics can actually be examined by the inspectors. . . . This is one of the situations to be remedied. . . ."

At the invitation of the U.S. Army and the Atomic Energy Commission, Congresswoman Sullivan witnessed the firing of the first atomic cannon in Nevada in May 1953. On June 16, 1953 she appeared before the House Ways and Means Committee to urge that the income tax law be amended to allow widows and working mothers to make deductions for the care of children. She also requested the "total deduction of medical and dental expenses for dependents over the age of sixty-five."

The Congresswoman joined twenty-three other members of the House in urging the formation of a permanent House committee to study consumer protection. In 1953 she spoke on the floor of the House against cutting the budget for the Women's Bureau of the Department of Labor, and in opposition to decreasing the appropriation for veterans' medical and dental care.

During the first session of the Eighty-third Congress, Mrs. Sullivan voted in favor of statehood for Hawaii (March), maintaining the nonpartisan character of the Tariff Commission (June), increasing air force funds (July), extending the excess profits tax for six months (July), a 4.4 billion dollar foreign aid appropriation (July), admitting 217,000 refugees, many from Iron Curtain countries (July), and lifting the public debt limit from 275 billion dollars to 290 billion dollars. She voted against the offshore oil bill (May), and opposed a bill to permit private power companies to construct additional power facilities on the Niagara River (July).

Her voting record for 1954 indicates that she favored the general tax revision bill giving approximately 1.4 billion dollars in tax relief (March), raising the personal income tax exemption from $600 to $700 (March), the motion picture tax relief (March), the construction of 140,000 public housing units (April), a bill to stimulate home building and rehabilitation through government aids (April), a bill making evidence obtained through wire tapping admissible in court cases involving treason (April), an amendment to the wire tapping bill which prohibits interception of telephone messages without approval of a Federal judge (April), authorization of the St. Lawrence seaway (May), a one year extension of the reciprocal trade agreements act (June), social security expansion (June), a 3.3 billion dollar foreign aid bill (July), and an amendment to the anti-Communist bill making it a felony to be a Communist (August).

She voted against a sliding-scale farm support program (July), the atomic energy bill (July), and a bill to provide immunity for witnesses before Congressional committees and grand juries (August). In the August 1954 Democratic primary in her District, Mrs. Sullivan was unopposed.

After the Federal Trade Commission issued its report on the coffee shortage on July 29, 1954, Mrs. Sullivan stated that the report indicated that coffee drinkers in this country had taken a "merciless beating" on the basis of a "phony shortage that never existed." She added that the House Agriculture Committee "for some mysterious reason" had bottled up efforts to meet the situation through legislation (New York *Times,* July 31, 1954).

The Congresswoman is a member of the League of Women Voters and the Auxiliary of the American Legion. Her faith is the Roman Catholic. Mrs. Sullivan has green eyes and brown hair, is about five feet five inches tall, and weighs 132 pounds. Her hobby is making hooked rugs. Bowling, swimming and riding are her favorite forms of exercise. She does her own cooking and housework, and shares an apartment with her mother in Washington, D.C. Another interest of Representative Sullivan is her radio interviewing program, "Women in Government" which she conducts over the St. Louis station, KWK.

References

Ind Woman 32:35 F '53 por
Washington (D.C.) Star p12B D 10 '52 por
Congressional Directory (1954)
Who's Who in America, 1954-55
Who's Who in the Midwest (1954)

SUMNER, (BERTHA) CID RICKETTS

Sept. 27, 1890- Author

Address: b. c/o Bobbs-Merrill Co., 468 4th Ave., New York 16; h. Duxbury, Mass.

Reprinted from the *Wilson Library Bulletin,* Dec. 1954

"Tall, gracious with luminous hazel eyes and a smile that lights up her face, she is beautiful and consistently charming. She is a happy combination of logic and fair-mindedness, too, but I think of her primarily as a person of warm and deep understanding. It is a quality that reflects the inner radiance of her mind, one that enables her to write or talk discerningly of the controversial without being controversial herself."

This is a description of Mrs. Cid Ricketts Sumner by her son-in-law, John Henry Cutler, a description which has been readily confirmed by those who know her. Her readers, who have followed the fortunes of the characters in her novels from *Ann Singleton* to *The Hornbeam Tree,* feel that she must be just that kind of person, or she could not write about people so understandingly and intelligently.

Bertha Ricketts (such a calm baby that her family called her Placid, then shortened it to Cid) was born on September 27, 1890 in Brookhaven, Mississippi, the only girl in a family of three children. She is of English and Scottish

CID RICKETTS SUMNER

descent with a dash of Irish. Her father, Robert Scott Ricketts, taught in colleges in Mississippi for over forty years, and her mother, the former Bertha Burnley, was a music school teacher.

Bertha was tutored at home, then attended Jackson, Mississippi, High School and Millsaps College where she majored in chemistry and English and received the B.S. degree in 1909. An excellent student, she won the D.A.R. essay medal, the scholarship prize at the end of her first two years, and the senior essay medal. She received a master's degree in English and psychology at Columbia University in 1910, then taught English at Jackson High School. She returned to Columbia for a year and then transferred to the Cornell University Medical School. She left in 1915 to marry Dr. James Batcheller Sumner, (who won the Nobel Prize for chemistry in 1946).

Mrs. Sumner has taught both English and French, the latter in Millsaps College. Her first love, however, is writing. She has published poetry and short stories, but her most important work has been her novels. *Ann Singleton* (1938), first published as a serial, is the story of a young woman scientist appointed to a laboratory position in a little southern town, and the gossip she incites because of her self-sufficiency. Of it, the New York *Times* said: "Ann and Dexter are ably characterized and the interest of the story is in general well sustained."

Quality (1946), which was called "Pinky" in its motion picture adaptation, was the story of the problems of an educated Negro girl who returned to her Southern home after passing as white in the North. Of this book, which was a Negro Book Club choice, S. I. Hayakawa said in *Book Week*: "Mrs. Sumner, white, and born in the South, has written a book of genuine human insight and social perception. I hope it becomes a best seller."

Tammy Out of Time (1948) tells of Tammy who, after having spent her seventeen years on a Mississippi houseboat, found a different life and love at Peter Brent's plantation home near Natchez. Of this Peoples Book Club choice, Anne Whitmore said in the *Library Journal* that there is "nothing original in this 'poor, uneducated girl meets and catches college educated son of a snobbish family' theme, but the conversation is original. . . Recommended."

But the Morning Will Come (1949) a Fiction Book Club choice, is the story of a Southern white girl and her reactions when she discovers that her coming child will inherit Negro blood. W. K. Rugg said in his review in the *Christian Science Monitor,* "Grace in the writing, warm appreciation of the emotional involvements, and of the relationship between background and action are impaired only by the disturbing impression that Bentley, telling her story in the first person, is viewing herself from the outside."

Sudden Glory (1951), a Peoples Book Club selection, is the story of Rhoda Lee Dalton, who is a charming fifteen-year-old when the book begins, and when it ends a few years later is a very grown-up young lady. This novel of family life in Mississippi in the years after the Civil War was praised in the Chicago *Sunday Tribune* by Henry Cavendish, who said, "The fluent writing is tightly woven, the characters are real, and for my money *Sudden Glory* is a fresh breath of clean atmosphere blowing through the mildewed pages of other period pieces long since gone sour."

Mrs. Sumner's latest book, *The Hornbeam Tree* (1953), is the story of the decision Miss Eva Iveson makes when at fifty, freed from the family responsibilities that had kept her from the adventures and romances she had secretly longed for, she falls in love. Of this story of New England small town life, Hubert Creekmore in the New York *Times* said, "Cid Ricketts Sumner, in her story of Miss Eva Iveson has achieved only a moderate success. But she has managed the plotting with skill and sprinkled the story with humorous touches."

Now, Mrs. Sumner is working on a musical and is writing poetry. This versatile woman is five feet seven inches tall, weighs 140 pounds, and has hazel eyes and gray hair. She is a Protestant and, as she puts it a "variable Democrat." She is an excellent cook, plays the piano and harp, paints, and sews.

Although she writes mostly about the South, she has spent half of her life in New York and Massachusetts (now in Duxbury), and loves Capri and Scotland.

She was divorced from Dr. Sumner in 1930. She is the mother of four children: Roberta Rand (Mrs. John Henry Cutler), Prudence Avery (Mrs. Edward Gamard), James Cosby Ricketts Sumner and Frederick Burnley Sumner.

References

Warfel, H. R. American Novelists of Today (1951)

Who's Who in America, 1954-55

SUMNER, MRS. G. LYNN See Picken, M. B.

SVEDA, MICHAEL (svā' da) Feb. 3, 1912- Chemist

Address: b. c/o E. I. du Pont de Nemours & Co., Wilmington 98, Del.; h. 116 Duncan Ave., McDaniel Heights, Wilmington, Del.

A specialist in the fields of silicon and sulfur chemistry, Dr. Michael Sveda is always searching for raw material out of which marketable compounds may be created. In the course of his researches he has discovered a number of commercially successful compounds. For example, while experimenting with sulfamides (compounds of nitrogen, hydrogen, oxygen and sulfur), he accidentally discovered sodium cyclohexyl sulfamate, which he synthesized in 1939 while working for his doctorate at the University of Illinois. This compound is now produced by Abbott Laboratories under the trade name Sucaryl, and it has proved to be a non-fattening sweetening agent which may be cooked in foods, and it retains its full sweet flavor even in coffee, tea, and other boiling solutions.

Outstanding among Dr. Sveda's contributions to the rapidly growing list of synthetics are a group of waxes and lubricants derived from silicon (a constituent of sand). One of these is Ludox colloidal silica, an aqueous floor wax which is antislip and still hard under foot. He also invented the process for the production of pyrosulfuryl chloride and thionyl chloride and the process for vapor-phase sulfonation hydrocarbons with sulfur trioxide. While working on the process for producing DDT, he discovered a means for separating chemically the two chief forms of this pesticide. He holds ten patents in the field. Since 1952 Dr. Sveda has been the product manager at the Grasselli chemicals department of the E. I. du Pont de Nemours & Company in Wilmington, Delaware.

Michael Sveda was born in West Ashford, Connecticut on February 3, 1912. He is the only son of Michael and Dorothy (Druppa) Sveda. His father, a farmer, was of Czechoslovakian ancestry. Michael and his two sisters grew up in Toledo, Ohio where his family moved during his boyhood. He attended Woodward Technical High School in that city and was graduated in 1928.

Entering the University of Toledo in Ohio, he majored in chemistry, and won the Paul Block scholarship. From 1931 until his graduation with a B.S. degree in 1934, he was a teaching assistant. Immediately after graduation he went to the University of Illinois in Urbana on a teaching fellowship. In 1936 and 1937, he held a graduate teaching assistantship, and in 1938, the Eli Lilly research fellowship, majoring in inorganic chemistry. He assisted Dr. Ludwig F. Audrieth, an editor of the annual, ***Inorganic Synthesis,*** not only in the university laboratory, but also in the preparation of technical manuscripts. He received the Ph.D. degree in 1939.

Willard Stewart, Inc.

MICHAEL SVEDA

In the course of his graduate work Sveda experimented with organic aquo-ammono-sulfuric acids and their derivatives. These compounds are combinations of carbon, sulfur, and ammonia. One day, while his bench was cluttered with reagents, he lit a cigarette without stopping to wash his hands. He was surprised to find that the cigarette had a very sweet taste. Realizing that the sweetness was due to one of the chemicals he had been working with—none of which was a sugar—he quickly tasted everything on the bench. He soon tracked down the sweetening agent which proved to be sodium cyclohexyl sulfamate.

The compound was adopted by the Abbott Laboratories of Chicago, Illinois. After many years of exhaustive tests it was introduced in 1950 under the trade name of Sucaryl Sodium. After two years of its own intensive tests, the U.S. Food and Drug Administration passed the sulfamate with high recommendation. Its stability under heat and abuse made it a natural noncaloric sweetener for soft drinks, canned foods and preservatives now sold in food shops. Its one disadvantage had been its sodium base which precluded its use by people on salt-free diets and those with kidney ailments. Recently, however, a calcium-based form of Sucaryl was developed for that trade.

In 1939 Sveda had joined the staff of the Grasselli chemicals department of E. I. du Pont de Nemours & Company in Cleveland, Ohio as a research chemist. From 1945 to 1947 he was a research supervisor, and in 1948 Sveda became a sales development supervisor at the du Pont division in Wilmington, Delaware, concentrating on developing markets for silica products. He supervised research on silicon which resulted in two commercially significant compounds. One of them is Ludox colloidal silica, a concentrated liquid product containing

SVEDA, MICHAEL—*Continued*

silicon—a component of sand—in colloidal suspension. As the base of a floor wax, it gives a hard and yet nonslip surface. Another product was a finely divided form of solid silica (which is sand itself) now being used as a component of high-temperature lubrication grease, so important in modern high-compression engines and in jet engines.

Dr. Sveda's further work with silicon led to the first polymerization of the element, that is, the atoms of a silicon compound molecule arranged in line like artificial rubber, nylon and dacron. This silicon compound can be cold-drawn into thin filaments which become the raw materials of fabrics and other commercial products. These silicon products have not as yet reached the commercial stage.

With Dr. Audrieth, Sveda patented the cycloaliphatic sulfamic acids in March 1942. They have also written several articles together: "Mandelamide" (a white crystal compound) which appeared in *Organic Syntheses,* Volume 20; "Pyrosulfuryl Chloride" in the 1950 edition of *Inorganic Syntheses;* and "Demonstration of Cold Light" in the *Transactions of the Illinois State Academy of Sciences,* Volume 29.

On August 23, 1936, Sveda married Martha Augusta Gaeth, a high school teacher. They have three children: Sally Anne, Michael Max, and Marcia Lynne. Dr. Sveda is six feet tall and weighs 180 pounds. He has brown eyes and brown hair turning gray. He enjoys playing golf, and is an avid football fan. His hobbies are cabinet making, music, and three-dimensional photography.

The chemist is a member of the Alpha Chi Sigma, Sigma Xi, Phi Kappa Phi, and Phi Lambda Upsilon. He belongs to the American Chemical Society, American Association for the Advancement of Science, Chemical Specialities Manufacturers Association, and American Society for Testing Materials. The University of Toledo named him its outstanding alumnus for 1954.

References

Read Digest 63:118 D '53
Time 55:43 Je 5 '50

American Men of Science (1949)
Who Knows—And What (1954)

SWINGS, PAUL *See* Swings, Polidore (F. F.)

SWINGS, POL(IDORE, F. F.) Sept. 24, 1906- Astrophysicist; university professor

Address: b. c/o Institute of Astrophysics, University of Liége, Sclessin, Belgium; h. 20 Av. Léon Souguenet, Esneux, Belgium

Among the international group of scientists probing the composition of the upper atmosphere to facilitate the conquest of space by rockets and guided missiles, is Dr. Polidore Swings. One of the world's foremost astrophysicists, Dr. Swings of Belgium is responsible for many outstanding discoveries in the physical constitution of stars and comets. He has contributed over 300 papers to scientific periodicals. Since 1949 he has been a consultant on upper atmosphere research for the Naval Ordnance Test Station at Inyokern, California.

For the past twenty-two years he has been director of the Institute of Astrophysics at the University of Liége, in Sclessin, Belgium, where he has concentrated his own and his pupils' study on molecular optics and applied spectroscopy. He is also a research associate of the University of Chicago and visiting professor at the University of California. In 1953 he organized his fifth astrophysical symposium at Liége.

Polidore F. F. Swings was born at Ransart, Belgium, on September 24, 1906, the only child of Jean B. Swings and Marie Antoinette Swings (née Bils). Although his father was a machinist and electrician, the family had been engaged in horticulture for centuries, and Swings's uncle continues the tradition today. His childhood associations were with farmers, coal miners and workers from the glass factories near his home. He attended grammar school in Ransart and secondary school at the Athenée Royal, Charleroi, where he studied science. He had to earn part of his living by tutoring other students.

The first World War and the subsequent German occupation of Belgium created further hardships, since it necessitated his walking eight miles daily, often in wooden shoes, to attend classes. In early youth he was considering a career in agronomy or forest work, but at the age of fifteen he read Camille Flammarion's book *Astronomie Populaire,* which he had won as a school prize. This book was decisive in persuading him to dedicate his life to astronomy.

Swings matriculated at the University of Liége in 1923. Although he received all available scholarships, he still found it necessary to tutor, and thus he had no time to participate in extracurricular activities. For his Ph.D. degree in mathematics (1927) he wrote a thesis on celestial mechanics which won him a special citation from the examining jury. He spent the next year as voluntary astronomer at the Paris Observatory in Meudon, directed at that time by the noted astronomer, Deslandres. There he decided to specialize in astrophysics, the science that deals principally with the composition of the celestial bodies. Since 1928 he has been associated with the Faculty of the University of Liége, as assistant in astronomical research and astrophysics to 1931, assistant professor from 1931 to 1937, and professor since that time occupying the chairs of optics, astronomy, astrophysics and spectroscopics.

Since early in his career, Dr. Swings has held the view that astrophysics depends essentially on spectroscopic evidence. The spectroscope is essentially a prism which disperses any celestial light into a rainbow of colors ranging from red to violet according to the intensity of the wave lengths brought into focus. Careful analysis of the spectrum of a star or comet can reveal the chemical and physical composition of those bodies. Since the University of Liége could not place at his disposal the necessary instruments for continuing his investigations in this complex new branch of science, Dr. Swings spent a considerable part of the next seven years (after 1927) studying in such foreign universities as Paris, Warsaw, Uppsala, Stockholm, Amsterdam, Oslo, Munich, Cambridge, Oxford and Munich.

At Professor Pienkowski's Institute of Experimental Physics of the University of Warsaw (1928-30), he concentrated on molecular spectroscopics. He soon distinguished himself by the elaboration of a method which enabled him to undertake the spectral study of the resonance of molecule S_2 in a more complete manner than had ever previously been achieved. This study, published in his thesis on molecular spectra, earned him the degree of D.Sc. in physics from Liége in 1931.

Dr. Swings first came to the United States in 1931, when he was appointed advanced fellow at the Yerkes Observatory of the University of Chicago for the academic year. Then and later (1934-35 and as visiting scientist in 1939-40) he was closely associated with Dr. Otto Struve, who later became director of the Yerkes Observatory and founder in 1934 of the McDonald Observatory in the Davis Mountains of Texas. This collaboration resulted in nine very important scientific papers on the Peculiar Stars. They advanced theories on certain phenomena found in the atmosphere of these stars not explainable by classical laws of radiation, ionization, dissociation or excitation.

Returning to Liége in 1932, Dr. Swings was finally able to organize a research laboratory in molecular optics. He focused his attention and that of several of his students on the study of cold stars. They succeeded in finding a correct solution to the theoretical problem of the equilibrium of dissociation in the stellar atmospheres (propounded in a paper by Yvonne Cambresier, his pupil, and Professor L. Rosenfeld of the University of Liége). The scientific treatises produced under Swing's direction at the Institute include over 120 publications, credited to some thirty students.

In 1934 and again in 1938, with Professor B. Edlen of the University of Lund, Sweden, he undertook researches on the spectra of ionized metals. After two years of repeated experiments, they produced an analysis of the third spectrum of iron, which is very abundant in the stars. This analysis permitted astrophysicists to interpret numerous stellar rays not previously identified.

In 1941 Dr. Swings announced at a Conference at the Yerkes Observatory that he had noted three sharp lines in the spectrum of distant stars, signs of a very thin gas, previously unidentified. The New York *Times* (November 16, 1941) reported that the gas, a combination of one atom of carbon and one of hydrogen, had been reproduced in the laboratory of the University of Saskatchewan by Drs. A. E. Douglas and Gerhard Herzberg and identified as the same because it produced the same kind of spectrum. This molecule, CH, played a decisive role in inducing Dr. Swings's theory on interstellar environment, published as *Considerations Regarding Cometary and Interstellar Molecules* (1942).

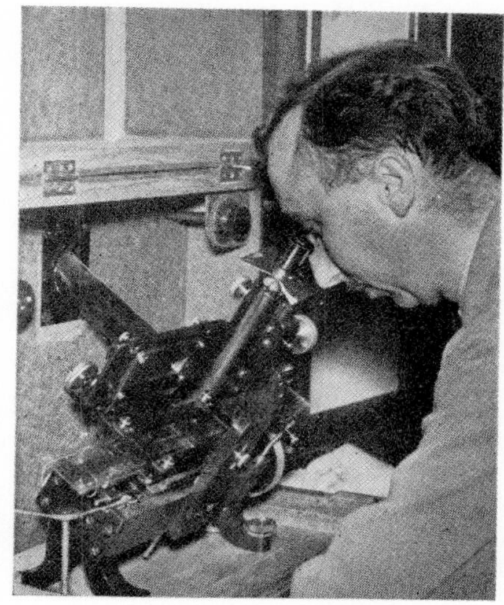

Herman M. Appel

POL SWINGS

While the Alexander Morrison research associate at the Lick Observatory of the University of California in 1941, Dr. Swings prepared a monumental study on the interpretation of cometary spectra (*Complex Structure of Cometary Bands,* Lick Observatory Bulletin 19, 1941), which showed in a direct fashion the preponderance of fluorescent phenomena in the spectra and thus solved a riddle which had long puzzled astronomers.

During the war, the astrophysicist was on the faculty of the University of Chicago, as assistant professor of astrophysics (1940-41), associate professor (1941-42) and professor (1942-43). He has been a research associate there since 1947. From 1943 to 1946 he was employed as research director of the Ray Control Company of Pasadena, an optical company, where he designed a high-speed spectrograph and optical instruments for use by the Navy and the Bureau of Ships.

Elaborate studies are now being made by scientists and engineers at the China Lake, Inyokern, California, Naval Ordnance Test Station, of the composition and physical state of the earth's atmosphere. These researches, principally undertaken to facilitate knowledge of conditions that rocket weapons will face there, will also aid long-range weather forecasting and radio communications, and are divided into three investigations: light emitted by the upper atmosphere (night glow), the lower atmosphere and the polar aurora (*The Rocketeer,* January 28, 1953). Dr. Swings, who has been consultant at the Station for the last four years, has undertaken the polar study, in cooperation with Dr. C. T. Elvey, head of the

SWINGS, POL—*Continued*

Geophysical Institute of the University of Alaska, where he makes on-the-spot observations of the polar aurora.

Swings believes that in such studies of the atmosphere, astronomy, physics and meteorology are closely allied. He has promoted the utilization of astrophysical discoveries for research in other sciences such as chemistry and metallurgy. In 1933 he instituted a course in applied spectroscopics under the technical faculty at Liége and inaugurated there spectrochemical researches with a view to applying them to industrial sciences. He published in the industrial *Revue Universelle des Mines et de la Metallurgie* several articles.

Speaking before the Astronomical Society of the Pacific in March 1953, Dr. Swings reported that the advice of European astronomers has resulted in major advances in many heavy industries which had been devastated by the war but are now reorganized. Industrial physicists borrow the latest equipment and techniques of the astronomical observatories in their quest for better steels, plastics and synthetic chemicals. He said that the problems involved in studying a molten alloy in an industrial furnace are basically similar to those of determining the (discussed in David Dietz' Scripps-Howard newspaper column, Cleveland *Press,* March 13, 1953).

In 1951 Professor Swings was visiting professor at the California Institute of Technology and received a similar appointment from the University of California in 1952. He has also been visiting professor in Poland (1939), France (1951), Italy (1952) and the Netherlands (1953). His technical papers have appeared mainly in the *Astrophysical Journal* and the *Bulletin of the Belgian Royal Academy.* He has also published a book, *Spectroscopie Appliquee* (Hermann and Co., Paris, 1935) and several booklets on spectroscopic and astrophysical topics.

The astrophysicist was awarded the Francqui Prize, the highest scientific accolade in Belgium, in 1948. Previously he had won various prizes from the Belgian Academy, the University of Liége and the Alumni Foundation, including the Prix Mailly and the Prix de Potter. He has also received two decorations from the Belgian government: Officer of the Order of the Crown (1947) and Officer of the Order of Leopold (1950). Dr. Swings has been a member of the Belgian Royal Academy since 1947. During each of the five years from 1949 to 1953 he organized an international symposium on astrophysics in Liége. Swings's memberships in scientific societies include the American Society for the Advancement of Sciences, the British Royal Astronomical Society, the American Geographical Society, the American Association of University Professors, the Dutch Astronomical Society, the Société Astronomique de France, the Astronomische Gesellschaft (Germany) and many Belgian scientific societies. In 1952 he was vice-president of the International Astronomical Union, President of its Commission on Physics of Comets and of its sub-committee on molecular bands; formerly (1948-52) he was President of its Commission on Stellar Spectra.

Since 1932 Dr. Swings has been married to Christiane M. Swings (née Borgerhoff), who has a Ph.D. in philology and has taught high school; they have one son, Jean Pierre. Dr. Swings has blue eyes, gray-brown hair somewhat receded from the forehead, weighs 150 pounds and is five feet ten inches tall. He is a Roman Catholic. He has no political affiliation. His favorite relaxations are hiking, reading, some gardening and some amateur moviemaking. His non-scientific clubs include a tennis club, faculty club, alumni club, Association for Benelux and the Association for the Intellectual Progress of Wallonia.

Dr. Otto Struve, a long-time associate of Swings and now chairman of the astronomy department of the University of California, wrote in *Sky and Telescope* (September 1950): "Professor Swings combines in a remarkable manner the qualifications of an experimental and theoretical physicist with those of an astrophysicist. . . . Unquestionably [he] possesses today the greatest accumulation of expert knowledge in the study of the Fraunhofer lines" of the spectroscope.

References

N Y Times II p8 N 16 '41; IV p9 O 25 '42; IV p9 Ap 1 '45
N Y World-Telegram p12 Mr 21 '53
American Men of Science (1949)
International Who's Who, 1954

TAYLOR, JOHN W(ILKINSON) Sept. 26, 1906- Educator; television director

Address: b. c/o Chicago Educational Television Association, 38 S. Dearborn St., Chicago, Ill.

A leader in the field of utilizing educational techniques in meeting prevailing problems, Dr. John W. Taylor was named on September 14, 1954 as executive director of the educational television station planned in Chicago for Channel 11. The station is being sponsored by the Chicago Educational Television Association, a nonprofit corporation.

Dr. Taylor, who is widely known in educational circles, served from January 1951 to July 1953 as Deputy Director-General of UNESCO (United Nations Educational, Scientific and Cultural Organization).

He believes that by raising the level of productivity through technical education the world may "rekindle the will for peace and replace the creeping resignation to the inevitability of war."

He resigned as president of the University of Louisville, Kentucky after serving there for three and a half years, to take on the challenging work of UNESCO, the "specialized agency" established by the United Nations "to contribute to peace and security through science, education and culture."

Taylor headed the educational and religious division of the military government under General Lucius D. Clay and helped to de-

Hitlerize the German school system during and immediately following World War II.

Born in Covington, Kentucky on September 26, 1906, John Wilkinson Taylor is the only son of the late John Wesley Taylor, a businessman, and the former Ethel Wilkinson, and is of Scotch, English and Irish descent. (He has one sister, now Mrs. Walter Williams.) His mother was a native of Tennessee and a schoolteacher before her marriage.

Young Taylor was graduated from the Peabody Demonstration School at Nashville, Tennessee, in 1924; he then attended Vanderbilt University in Nashville for one academic year (1924 to 1925) before leaving the United States for the first time in 1925 for a year of travel in Germany, Austria, France, Denmark, England, and Norway.

On his return, Taylor resumed work for a degree at Columbia University in New York City and from 1927 to 1929 served as an assistant at Teachers' College. He received his A.B. degree in 1929 and was awarded an Earl scholarship. He taught for a while at the Demonstration Elementary School of the Parker School District in Greenville, South Carolina, before receiving his M.A. degree from Columbia in 1930.

During the summer of 1930 Taylor taught comparative education at Teachers' College, and in October returned to Europe to teach English for one year in the Kaiser Friedrich Real Gymnasium at Berlin-Neukölln and to do postgraduate work at the universities of Berlin and Vienna. From 1931 to 1932 he taught science and modern languages at the Broughton High School in Raleigh, North Carolina (he described his classes in an article in *Progressive Education,* March, 1932).

In 1932 he was engaged as educational adviser to the president of the John Day Publishing Company in New York City. He again crossed the Atlantic in 1933 for courses at the University of London (he has also studied at the Alliance Française in Paris). He was appointed in 1934 an assistant in education and director of foreign studies at Columbia and from 1935 to 1937 served as assistant to the chairman of New College (an "experimental offshoot" of Teachers' College).

Michael Horton in the Paris edition of the New York *Herald Tribune* of January 13, 1951 wrote that Taylor "shepherded groups of New College students to Europe for the year's study that was part of the curriculum. He would deposit his charges in Paris, Florence, London and other cultural centers and shuttle around from one group to another—always dropping in on local schools."

Again in Berlin in the late summer of 1935, Taylor completed his Ph.D. thesis, *Youth Welfare in Germany,* which discussed the Hitler Youth Movement. It was published in 1936 and was prepared under the direction of Dr. Richard Thomas Alexander, of the International Institute of Teachers' College. Taylor has written that Dr. Alexander greatly influenced him in his choice of education as a career.

JOHN W. TAYLOR

After receiving his Ph.D. degree, he spent an additional year at New College as chairman of the admissions, scholarship, curriculum and personnel-guidance committees. Dr. Taylor then moved to Louisiana State University in Baton Rouge, Louisiana as associate professor of comparative education and as administrative assistant to the president. Appointed in 1940 the director of L.S.U.'s Bureau of Educational Research, he collaborated with Clarence P. Dunbar on the bureau's 1942 monograph entitled *Manpower Planning for Victory.*

Taylor took a leave of absence from L.S.U. in 1942 to serve as executive secretary of the committee named by the American Council of Education to "survey" the University of Illinois, and was co-author of the council's report.

Beginning his World War II service in 1942 as a civilian he went to Tizi-Ouzou, North Africa, to become assistant director (and later director) of studies at the Military Government School and Holding Center established for British and American officers and men by NATOUSA (North African Theater of Operations, United States Army).

Commissioned a captain in the Army of the United States in 1943, he was advanced to major in 1944 and reassigned as chief of the education and religious affairs branch of the projected United States Military Government for Germany. In England he joined the "planning unit," and before the Normandy landings, "spent months . . . looking at microfilmed copies of 268 pre-Hitler textbooks" in order to determine the best books to use in the de-Nazification program.

While the battle for Germany was still under way, Michael Horton reported, "Taylor, then a lieutenant-colonel, moved into newly-fallen Aachen and had the twelve textbooks [which he selected] hurriedly printed up on whatever paper was available. A preface was added to each book, stating that it was a gen-

TAYLOR, JOHN W.—*Continued*

uine German textbook, used in pre-Hitler Germany, and that not one word had been changed or deleted." As head of the operational unit at Berlin from 1945 to 1947, and United States representative on the Quadripartite Education Committee for Germany, he "dredged up names of teachers with democratic backgrounds, had them tracked down, and put to work" in a reorganization of the German school system.

For his wartime services, Taylor was awarded the United States Legion of Merit in 1946. He was decorated with the riband of *chevalier* of the French Legion of Honor by Ambassador Henri Bonnet at Washington on May 27, 1949.

Elected in December 1946 to succeed Dr. E. W. Jacobsen as president of the University of Louisville in Kentucky, Dr. Taylor took up his new appointment in May 1947 after his contract with the government expired. He established two (later four) "Neighborhood Colleges" (one for Negroes) in branches of the Louisville public library. (The cost to students seeking credit for a degree was $100 a semester. Classes were held three hours a night, five nights a week.) He proposed that colleges "hire" their football teams "just like professors," but the only other institution to endorse the idea was the University of Kansas City.

In 1948 the University of Louisville combined with radio station WHAS to offer a "radio-assisted correspondence course" in which lectures were given on the air, while the university provided textbooks, written assignments and examinations at $30 per credit. In the second semester of 1949-1950 Dr. Taylor pioneered by offering a university "course for credit" in English literature through television station WAVE-TV.

Always accessible, (he put a sign on his office door reading "Please Enter Without Knocking"), President Taylor was personally popular and proved a successful raiser of money and endowments (the alumni fund more than trebled in his three-and-a-half-year administration, while salaries were increased and the budget more than doubled). He was also instrumental in bringing about the repeal of Kentucky's school segregation law.

Dr. Taylor succeeded Dr. Walter Laves as Deputy Director-General of UNESCO in January 1951. The organization was established (according to the Constitution adopted on November 4, 1946) "to contribute to peace and security by promoting collaboration among nations through education, science and culture in order to further universal respect for justice, for the rule of law, and for the human rights and fundamental freedom which are affirmed for the peoples of the world, without distinction of race, sex, language or religion by the charter of the United Nations."

While he was in office an international copyright convention was concluded by UNESCO; Spain, Libya and Nepal were admitted as UNESCO members; and a conference of German and American historians was sponsored for the purpose of improving history instruction in both countries. A CARE-UNESCO program for the distribution of books and periodicals was continued.

After Dr. Jaime Torres Bodet resigned as Director-General of UNESCO on November 22, 1952, Dr. Taylor was named acting Director-General and functioned as such until the next annual conference at Paris when Dr. Luther H. Evans, Librarian of Congress, was elected as the new permanent Director-General. Taylor, as Deputy-Director had gone on UNESCO missions to Ecuador, Peru, Panama, Brazil, Iran, Iraq, India, Thailand, the Philippines, Japan, Egypt, Liberia, and Germany.

Dr. Taylor's professional memberships include the American Council on Education, the National Education Association and the American Academy of Political and Social Science. He was a member of the United States Commissioner of Education's Council of Advisors from 1950 to 1952 and since 1950 has been on the advisory panel of the Comptroller of the Army.

He is a Rotarian, American Legionnaire, and belongs to the Phi Delta Kappa, Kappa Delta Pi, Phi Kappa Phi and Omicron Kappa Delta fraternities. His club memberships include the Executives, Arts, Salmagundi and Pendennis (Louisville) and the Allied Circle (London). His church is the Presbyterian. Dr. Taylor and the former Katherine Willis Wright were married in 1939 and have one son, Walter Bradford. They were divorced in 1951. On December 23, 1952 he married Mrs. Helen Hutchinson Greene.

The educator is six feet one inch in height and 180 pounds in weight, and he has brown eyes and gray hair. He reads detective stories for relaxation and mentions golf and badminton as his favorite sports. He is "very fond of animals" and has had as pets "many dogs, mice, Siamese cats and ducks."

References

Christian Sci Mon p11 N 22 '50
N Y Herald Tribune p5 D 2 '52 por
N Y Herald Tribune Paris ed. Ja 15 '51
N Y Times p8 D 2 '52 por
Time 50:67 S 1 '47 por; 51:53+ F 23 '48 por
Directory of American Scholars (1951)
Leaders in Education (1948)
Who Knows—and What (1949)
Who's Who in America, 1952-53
Who's Who in the United Nations (1951)

TELLER, EDWARD Jan. 15, 1908- Physicist; university professor

Address: b. c/o Radiation Laboratory, P.O. Box 808, University of California, Livermore, California

The hydrogen bomb, achieved in 1952 by the United States, a few months before the Russians fired a hydrogen weapon of their own, was the product of many minds. Because of Dr. Edward Teller's dedication to the possibilities of a thermonuclear weapon, while many other scientists concentrated on the A-bomb and atomic fission, he has been credited with being "the principal architect of the H-bomb" (*Newsweek,* August 2, 1954). He himself disclaims the main credit, and pointed out, when interviewed by William L. Laurence, that "it took scores of brilliant, highly skilled workers, all members of the Los Alamos Laboratory, the only one of its kind in the United States, to translate theory into a practical weapon" (New York *Times,* July 4, 1954).

Expressing his views on the morals of making the H-bomb, Dr. Teller stated in *Newsweek,* August 2, 1954: "There's no doubt that we are engaged in an arms race with Russia.... In regard to the argument that development of the H-bomb was immoral, I felt only that there must be a clear-cut distinction between scientific and technical questions on the one hand, and questions of morals and politics, on the other. . . . However, I feel that questions about whether these weapons should be made . . . and used . . . are up to every citizen in a democracy, and in the case of secret work, up to their representatives and proper government agencies. Like anyone else, I would rather work on defense than on aggressive weapons."

One of the early proponents of the atomic bomb, along with Drs. Enrico Fermi and Leo Szilard, Teller urged Army officials to begin work on the bomb in 1939. He was one of the six scientists who persuaded Dr. Albert Einstein to write his now famous letter in 1939 to President Franklin D. Roosevelt which resulted in the establishment of the atomic-bomb-development program (this came under the direction of the Manhattan Engineer District——"Manhattan Project"——on June 18, 1942).

The son of well-to-do Jewish parents, Max and Ilona (Deutch) Teller, Edward Teller was born on January 15, 1908 in Budapest, Hungary. His formal education began at the Institute of Technology in Budapest. Although Teller demonstrated a precocious gift for mathematics, he took a degree in chemical engineering at the Institute of Technology at Karlsruhe, Germany in 1928. Inspired by the discovery of quantum mechanics in 1926, he specialized in physical chemistry and went to Munich for further study. There, at twenty, he lost his right foot in a street car accident; today, Teller walks with a slight limp.

Having been granted the Ph.D. degree from the University of Leipzig, Germany in 1930, Teller became a research associate in physical chemistry to Professor Fritz Eucker at the University of Göttingen, Germany from 1931 to 1933. Awarded a Rockefeller fellowship, he traveled to Copenhagen in 1934 for additional study under Dr. Niels Bohr. After the Nazis took power in Germany in 1933, Teller went to England and became a lecturer at the University of London.

In 1935 Teller accepted the invitation of Dr. Cloyd Heck Marvin, president of George Washington University, Washington, D.C., to come to the university as a visiting professor. Teller taught molecular and atomic physics and collaborated on research work with Dr. George Gamow. During these years Teller contributed

Wide World

EDWARD TELLER

to discussions which led to Dr. Hans Bethe's explanation of solar energy. This explanation anticipated basic H-bomb concepts.

Teller left George Washington University in 1941 and became affiliated with the group of scientists at Columbia University doing atomic energy research headed by Dr. Enrico Fermi. From 1941 to 1946 Teller worked on the atomic bomb; he continued with the uranium pile project when it was transferred to the metallurgical laboratory at the University of Chicago; he joined Dr. J. Robert Oppenheimer's theoretical studies group at the University of California at Berkeley; he later moved to the Los Alamos Laboratory, Los Alamos, New Mexico.

While there, Teller became a member of Dr. Hans Bethe's theoretical physics division. Later he was transferred to Dr. Fermi's division and was encouraged, among other things, to pursue investigation on the feasibility of the H-bomb.

As early as the summer of 1942, Teller, Bethe, Oppenheimer, Konopinski, and others had collaborated at Berkeley on the thermonuclear problem. At the end of 1945 Teller told Oppenheimer he would stay at Los Alamos if the laboratory could either test a dozen fission weapons each year, or initiate a complete thermonuclear program. Neither of these alternatives proved feasible at that time.

Accordingly, Teller left Los Alamos in 1945 and became a member of the Institute for Nuclear Studies and the department of physics of the University of Chicago. He was named professor of physics in 1946 and advocated lifting restrictions on atomic research. After the 1946 atomic test on Bikini, Teller predicted how the United States would be endangered if 100,000 or a million atomic bombs were dropped and how radioactive gases would endanger our survival even though a single bomb had not

TELLER, EDWARD—*Continued*

been dropped within our national boundaries.

Named chairman of the committee of American scientists who traveled to England in 1949, he met with British and Canadian specialists to discuss safeguards for atomic reactors. Teller became a member of the Atlantic Union organization and supported the Acheson-Lilienthal report which is the basis of the "Baruch Plan," an attempt to control atomic power internationally. Convinced that the best insurance against war was adequate armaments, Teller returned to work at the Los Alamos Laboratory in 1949.

Russia's atomic explosion in September 1949 caused top-level military officials to urge the immediate development of an H-bomb. At that time Teller participated in discussions on the Los Alamos Laboratory program directed toward work on the thermonuclear bomb. The Laboratory under the direction of Dr. Norris Edwin Bradbury advocated a vigorous program.

During the winter of 1949-1950, "momentous debates" ensued among the members of the AEC over whether to proceed with a "crash program" to develop and prepare the H-bomb with all possible haste. Opponents of the program felt that the H-bomb was an immoral weapon and believed the program would be a drain on nuclear supplies important in the A-bomb program. President Harry S. Truman made the final decision to go ahead with the "crash program" in January 1950 after Dr. Klaus Fuchs had confessed that he had been spying for the Russians and had supplied them with detailed information for the making of atomic bombs.

The group working on the development of the H-bomb included Edward Teller, John Wheeler, Lothar Nordheim, Stanislaus Ulam, John Von Neumann and Frederic de Hoffmann. During the initial months of the development, severe doubts arose as to the ultimate feasibility. Later, due to the pooled effort of the group working at Los Alamos, alternative methods proved more hopeful.

After a successful initial test in 1951, a meeting was held at the Institute for Advanced Study in Princeton, New Jersey attended by members of the Atomic Energy Commission, by Oppenheimer, Wheeler, Nordheim, Bradbury, Bethe, Fermi, and others. At this meeting Teller summarized the results obtained at Los Alamos, which amounted to a new approach to the thermonuclear question. After that meeting the development went forward rapidly. Teller had little to do in the actual building of the H-bomb as he is primarily an "idea" man.

On November 1, 1952 the hydrogen bomb was shipped to Eniwetok in the Pacific, and was exploded with a force equal to five megatons (million tons) of TNT. (In December 1953 President Dwight D. Eisenhower, in his address to the United Nations, revealed that the uranium bomb had been refined to a weapon with twenty-five times the force of the bomb dropped on Hiroshima.)

In the fall of 1952 a new hydrogen bomb laboratory costing $11,500,000 was established by the AEC at Livermore, California, as an adjunct of the University of California's radiation laboratory, and Dr. Teller was placed in charge. He is also teaching theoretical atomic physics to graduate students at the University of California at Berkeley, and assisting on theoretical problems in connection with "still more and newer weapons."

Teller's main scientific contributions are in the fields of chemical physics and nuclear physics. He and Dr. Francis Owen Rice collaborated on *The Structure of Matter,* which was published in 1949. Recently he worked with Montgomery Johnson on the forces holding together the atomic nucleus.

When Teller testified before the AEC's Personnel Security Board (the Gray board) in the Oppenheimer case in April 1954, he stated that he considered Dr. J. Robert Oppenheimer a loyal American, but believed the U.S. Government would be "wiser not to grant [him] clearance" to work on security projects. The H-bomb could have been developed in 1947, he stated, if Dr. Oppenheimer had given his "moral support" (Teller's testimony is recorded in the New York *Times,* June 17, 1954).

The Hydrogen Bomb (written by James Shepley and Clay Blair, Jr. and published by the David McKay Company), considered the most controversial book to be published this year, has strong words to say about the "delay" in the development of the H-bomb, and makes Dr. J. Robert Oppenheimer, wartime Los Alamos director, the "villain" of the story, while Dr. Teller is the "hero." Dr. Teller, asked to comment on the book, disclaimed any "shred of any responsibility for any part" of the book, and stated that the authors "did not have any corroborative evidence from me." He expressed admiration for the accomplishments at Los Alamos, and hoped that scientists would be able to work on the big job ahead "without being interrupted by irrelevant discussions" (*Newsweek,* October 18, 1954).

A highly intuitive person, Teller uses only a slide rule and a blackboard when he works. He speaks rapidly in a pleasant voice with a slight Hungarian accent. His complexion is dark; his thick bushy eyebrows frame blue eyes. For relaxation, Teller enjoys playing the piano and chess. He became a naturalized American citizen in 1941.

He married Augusta Harkanyi on February 26, 1934; they have two children Paul, and Susan Wendi, to whom he enjoys reading Lewis Carroll's *Alice in Wonderland* and C. S. Forester's Horatio Hornblower stories. Friends report that Teller has a "gorgeous sense of humor," and is by nature a cheerful and gregarious man.

References

Life 37:60+ S 6 '54 pors
Newsweek 44:23+ Ag 2 '54 por
N Y Times p58 Ja 31 '54; p17 Je 3 '54; p 1+ Je 16 '54; p 1, 22 Je 17 '54 por; p13 Jl 4 '54 por

American Men of Science (1949)
Who's Who in America, 1954-55
World Biography (1954)

TENZING NORGAY *See* Hunt, Sir (H. C.) J.; Hillary, Sir E. (P.); and Tenzing Norkey

TERRELL, DANIEL V(OIERS) Oct. 5, 1886- Engineering association official; college dean

Address: b. c/o University of Kentucky, Lexington, Ky.; h. 227 Catalpa Rd., Lexington 30, Ky.

"We must strive to overcome the idea that registration as a professional engineer signals the end of the need for professional training and judgment." Daniel V. Terrell, dean of the College of Engineering of the University of Kentucky, has patterned his own career after this precept which he explored in his inaugural address as president of the American Association of Civil Engineers on October 21, 1953.

As an educator Terrell organized successful graduate and undergraduate highway educational programs at the University of Kentucky; as a practicing engineer he designed a university stadium; and as a researcher he directs the university's engineering experiment station and the Kentucky state highway department's research laboratory.

The son of George W. and Mariah (Chandler) Terrell, Daniel Voiers Terrell was born on October 5, 1886 in Bedford, Kentucky. Graduated from the University of Kentucky in 1910 as a Bachelor of Civil Engineering, he was employed for one year with the Santa Fe Railway and another year with the Louisville & Nashville Railroad.

Terrell returned to the university in 1912 as a professor of engineering and received the degree of civil engineer in 1914. During this period he established and conducted road conferences at the university and developed a plan for state aid to counties which formed a permanent foundation for the Kentucky state highway department.

Becoming professor of civil engineering and head of the department in 1917, he was also appointed acting dean of civil engineering for 1917 and 1918. In the latter position, he was instrumental in consolidating three separate colleges into a College of Engineering. He remained professor of civil engineering and head of the department until 1942.

As a special service, Terrell was engineer of design and construction for the University of Kentucky stadium in 1924 and 1925. Since that time he has served as general consultant on campus planning and construction. In 1935 the university called on him to be acting dean of the College of Engineering. He was assistant dean of the College of Engineering and head of the department of civil engineering from 1942 to 1946. In 1946 the engineer was appointed to his present posts of dean of the College of Engineering and director of the university's engineering experiment station.

During the period that Daniel V. Terrell has been associated with the University of Kentucky, he has also served with the state government of Kentucky. From 1917 to 1928 he was part-time engineer of tests and then part-time research engineer from 1928 to 1931 in the highway department. He has published articles on his research work.

DANIEL V. TERRELL

In 1942 he became director of the state highway research laboratory, a position which he still holds today. He was active in the early good-roads movement in Kentucky, and later supported the program for greater industrial development through research and more effective use of the state's natural resources. The engineer was a member of the governor's Postwar Advisory Planning Commission. Since 1946 he has been a member of the State Board of Examiners and Registration of Architects, and also of the State Board for Registration of Professional Engineers. Dean Terrell received a certificate of service and a thirty-five-year pin from the Kentucky Department of Highways in 1949.

The civil engineer has contributed to federal projects as the Kentucky state representative on local controls surveys for the United States Coast and Geodetic Survey from 1933 to 1934; as his university's representative on the Engineering, Science, Management, War Training Program from 1940 to 1945; as administrator of the Engineers School, Enlisted Specialist Branch from 1942 to 1943; and engineering administrator of the Army Specialized Training Program from 1943 to 1945.

Interested in the work of professional engineering societies, Dean Terrell is a charter member and former president (1938) of the Kentucky section of the American Society of Civil Engineers and in 1921 he organized the University of Kentucky student chapter, one of the society's early chapters. He joined the national organization in 1919 and became a full member in 1926.

After serving as a director from 1947 to 1950 and as a vice-president during 1951 and 1952, Dean Terrell became president of the

TERRELL, DANIEL V.—*Continued*

American Society of Civil Engineers for one year, succeeding Walter L. Huber of San Francisco, California. When he took office in October 1953 the new president stated: "Professional as well as technical training should be continuous throughout a man's career." William R. Glidden succeeded Terrell as president in the fall of 1954.

Dean Terrell also holds membership in the Kentucky Society for Professional Engineers, American Society for Engineering Education, American Society for Testing Materials, Tau Beta Pi, Sigma Xi, Triangle, University of Kentucky Research Club and Newcomen Society. He has been the recipient of certificates of achievement from the Louisville and Lexington Automobile Clubs. The engineer is a Mason (Shriner) and a Rotarian.

Daniel V. Terrell married Lula Bitterman on June 19, 1914; they have two children, Daniel V. Jr. and Claude B. Terrell. The dean is a Democrat and a Methodist. His special fields of interest include concrete and highway materials, sanitary engineering, ready-mix concrete, and field control of concrete. For relaxation he enjoys camping, hunting and fishing.

References

Civil Eng 16:553 D '46 por; 20:49 O '50 por; 23:66 Jl '53
N Y Times p16 S 23 '53 por
American Men of Science (1949)
Leaders in Education (1948)
Who's Who in America, 1952-53
Who's Who in Engineering, 1948

TERRELL, MARY CHURCH Sept. 23, 1863-July 24, 1954 Author; educator; lecturer; was graduated from Oberlin College (1884); served on District of Columbia Board of Education (1895-1906) and as first president of National Association of Colored Women (1896-1901); attended International Congress of Women in Berlin (1904), International Peace Conference (1919), and other world conferences; advocated civil and political rights for women, and equality for the Negro race; wrote *A Colored Woman in a White World* (1940). See *Current Biography,* (June) 1942.

Obituary

N Y Times p23 Jl 29 '54

THIMAYYA, K(ODENDERA) S(UBAYYA)- Mar. 31, 1906- Indian Army officer

Address: c/o Indian Army Headquarters, New Delhi, India

The adoption of a plan resolving the prisoner of war repatriation problem which had deadlocked the Korean truce discussions for over a year, resulted in India's soldier-statesman, Lieutenant General K. S. Thimayya, becoming a world figure in 1953. The agreement, signed on June 8, 1953, provided that both sides engaged in the Korean conflict would turn over to the custody of a Neutral Nations Repatriation Commission, headed by an Indian representative, those prisoners of war who did not wish to return to their own countries.

The most unusual feature of this plan was that during the period while the prisoners were under the commission's custody each side could send "explainers" to their reluctant soldiers to exhort them to return to their own country.

Prime Minister Jawaharlal Nehru selected Thimayya to head India's difficult international assignment. India not only chaired the commission but also furnished about 6,000 troops to guard over 22,000 prisoners in the Korean buffer zone. Nehru realized that he was entrusting a large part of India's reputation abroad to the manner in which General Thimayya discharged this ticklish truce job (New York *Times,* October 26, 1953).

Kodendera Subayya Thimayya was born in Coorg, India on March 31, 1906. After his early education at Bangalore, he became one of the first Indian boys to enter the Prince of Wales' Royal Indian Military College at Dehra Dun in 1922. He was also one of the first Indians to attend Sandhurst Royal Military College, Britain's West Point. He received his army commission following graduation from Sandhurst in 1926.

A normally varied Army career, with many assignments followed for Thimayya. He served with the Hyderabad Regiment in Iraq and Quetta from 1936 to 1939, and he was adjutant of the Fifth Battalion (Madras), University Training Corps from 1939 to 1941. In 1944 he was assigned to Arakan. The officer distinguished himself in the Battle of Kangaw and was awarded the D.S.O. Thimayya became the first Indian officer to lead a brigade in action, commanding both the 51st and 36th Indian brigades.

As a representative of the Indian Army, Thimayya was present at the formal surrender of the southern armies of Japan to Admiral Louis Mountbatten, Supreme Allied Commander, South East Asia, at Singapore in September 1945. In 1946 Thimayya went to Japan as commander of the 268th Indian Brigade, which formed part of the British and Indian occupation forces. He was a representative of the Indian Army at the celebrations when the Philippines became independent on July 4, 1946. In December of that year, he assumed duties on the Armed Forces nationalization committee in New Delhi.

Later, Thimayya became a member of the Armed Forces reconstitution committee, following which he had a tour of duty with the Punjab Boundary Force. When these forces were dissolved he assumed command of the 4th Indian Division. He was responsible for the restoration of law and order in East Punjab after the partition of India and Pakistan in 1947, and arranged for the two-way movement of millions of refugees between the two countries. During the fighting between India and Pakistan Thimayya commanded an infantry division in Kashmir and won a tank battle on terrain 13,000 feet high. Tanks had never been used at that altitude before (*Life,* November 30, 1953). From 1948 to 1950 Thimayya was commander of Indian troops in Kashmir.

He was commandant of the National Defense Academy in 1950 and 1951. Later in 1951 Thimayya became quartermaster general at the Indian Army Headquarters. About a year and a half later, he became general officer commanding, Western Command, from which post he was selected on July 21, 1953 to be the chairman of the Neutral Nations Repatriation Commission.

Thimayya's concern for his men has been commented on by *Newsweek* (November 16, 1953): "He's a stickler for neatness and military bearing, as his carriage and carefully trimmed mustache suggest. But he is informal and friendly even with subalterns, and his care for his juniors has extended to changing the uniform regulations so that a more comfortable type of crepe-soled shoes would pass muster."

When Thimayya arrived in Korea in September 1953 he encountered a wall of suspicion and mistrust. Later, he admitted that he, as well as most of his aides, suspected that a large number of U.N.'s Chinese and North Korean prisoners were being forcibly prevented from returning home (*Life,* November 30, 1953).

Despite U.N. criticism, Thimayya refused to withdraw the repatriation commission's ground rules according to which explanations to the prisoners were to be conducted. He termed the U.N. charge of favoritism to the communists "unfair" and insisted that the rules were in line with the provisions of the armistice agreement.

In the development and implementation of these rules, Thimayya established what was to become the characteristic pattern of his chairmanship. In official communications he sometimes took positions which seemed to favor the communist side. Yet the execution of the rules gave the prisoners full freedom of choice—the chief U.N. concern. As his pattern became apparent, the attitude of the U.N. Command and the free world in general changed from distrust of Thimayya to one of respect.

The general sought to allay the U.N. fears of the results of the explainers' talks by saying that, according to the commission's rules, prisoners would have to go to the explanation centers "but how do you make a man listen?" (*Time,* October 19, 1953). Thimayya was criticized for treating the Soviet satellites on the commission, Poland and Czechoslovakia, the same as Sweden and Switzerland. He did so, apparently, in order to make it possible for the commission to function at all.

When the "explanations" to the prisoners finally began in mid-October 1953, the Koreans refused to leave their compounds to face the explainers, but General Thimayya broke a fifteen-day deadlock by personally persuading them to go and listen. "I advised the P.W.s to trust me," Thimayya said, "and I would see they were treated with fairness and integrity" (*Time,* November 9, 1953).

On one occasion the general intervened to end an interview in which a communist explainer "threatened" a prisoner of war. "This is absurd," said Thimayya as he went into the explanation center. "It's got to stop" (*Time,* November 16, 1953). He consistently tried to satisfy "the desires of the boys" (as he called the prisoners) and at the same time accord both sides the rights they claimed under the terms of reference. "Above all," he said, "I know there must be some consideration for the individual" (New York *Times,* November 11, 1953).

Gov't. of India Inf. Services
LT. GEN. K. S. THIMAYYA

When, after a breakdown, the communists resumed explanations but dragged them on interminably, General Thimayya again intervened. He would not permit the explanations to continue unless the communists stopped long interviews with individual prisoners. He threatened that if necessary the Indian troops would take over the job of screening the Chinese and North Korean prisoners of war.

Prior to the deadline for the end of the explanations, Thimayya made every effort to aid the U.N. appeal to the prisoners captured by the communists, including twenty-two Americans who had refused to return home. He made a personal appeal to the former American GI's to give their countrymen a chance to explain to them why they should return home. Yet Thimayya recognized that there was little chance he could budge them when the mother of one of them had failed (New York *Times,* December 15, 1953).

When the explanations terminated on December 23, 1953, the Indians were faced with the problem of disposing of the prisoners. The U.N. Command insisted that the armistice agreement called for their assumption of civilian status thirty days later. The communists opposed this interpretation. Thimayya was instrumental in getting Prime Minister Nehru, who leaned toward the communist position, to agree to the return of the prisoners.

Thimayya recognized that he had neither sufficient troops nor legal authority to hold the prisoners after their scheduled release date. He believed the prisoners could be held in the compounds only by force which he was re-

THIMAYYA, K. S.—*Continued*

luctant to apply. When the general convinced Nehru that the prisoners could not be held after the deadline he helped formulate a compromise designed to please the U.N. in substance and the communists in form, while absolving India of any failure to discharge her obligations (New York *Herald Tribune,* January 16, 1954).

This compromise was to restore the prisoners to the side that had held them prior to the date of Indian custody. By this move India would not be responsible for the release of the prisoners nor the declaration of their civilian status. The communists used this compromise to claim that the armistice terms were broken. By the same token the U.N. Command's main aim—that the prisoners be free to go where they wanted to—was preserved.

From January 20 to January 22, 1954 the prisoners were returned to the North and South Korean sides; General John E. Hull, Commander in Chief of the U.N. Forces, released the anti-communist prisoners at one minute after midnight on January 23, 1954. After the successful termination of its duties, the Neutral Nations Repatriation Commission went out of existence on February 22, 1954.

General Thimayya's policy of dead-center neutrality won approval from the American press. As the New York *Times* (January 21, 1954) summed it up: "India not only resisted Communist pressure to use force on the prisoners but also turned these men over to the United Nations . . . for fulfilling the substance if not the letter of the armistice agreement, India deserves the thanks of free men."

In Korea, Thimayya conducted "a scientific, internationally visible, laboratory test on Communism's success as a way of life. . . . And because of Thimayya's cold impartiality not even the Communists can say that the test tube was doctored" (*Life,* November 30, 1953).

Lieut. General Thimayya returned from Korea to New Delhi on March 4 and told an Associated Press reporter that he opposed voluntary repatriation of war prisoners as a "conversion of the mind" that "puts a premium on voluntary desertion" (New York *Times,* March 5, 1954).

The general, called "Timmy" by his friends, is a rugged, husky, 200 pound six-footer. In New Delhi he and his wife, the former Mina Caripa whom he married in January 1935, have a one-story home which is furnished in western style. The couple have a sixteen-year-old daughter, Mira. Thimayya is a Hindu.

He "likes polo, shooting, ballroom dancing, military history." While in Korea he did daily calisthenics on the skin of a panther which he had bagged himself. Soft-spoken, personally affable, frank, and casual, Thimayya "handled the prisoner of war repatriation process courageously and imaginatively."

References

Newsweek 42:40 N 16 '53 por
Time 62:42+ O 19 '53 por
U S News 36:16 Ja 8 '54 por
Hindustan Year-book & Who's Who, 1954

THOMAS, CHARLES S(PARKS) Sept. 28, 1897- United States Secretary of the Navy

Address: b. c/o Department of the Navy, Washington 25, D.C.; h. The Westchester, 4000 Cathedral Ave., N.W., Washington, D.C.

"We must be strong in the military sense as a deterrent to war," said Secretary of the Navy Charles S. Thomas in July 1954, "and strong in spirit so that we can meet the challenge if it comes." Sworn in as Secretary of the Navy in May 1954, Thomas succeeded Robert B. Anderson who became Deputy Secretary of Defense after Roger M. Kyes had resigned from that post in April 1954.

Since the Eisenhower Administration took office in January 1953, Thomas, who is a Republican, had served successively as Under Secretary of the Navy and Assistant Secretary of Defense in charge of supply and logistics. He was a naval aviator in World War I, and was a special assistant to Secretary of the Navy James V. Forrestal in World War II. Thomas was president and a director of Foreman & Clark, Inc. (a chain of retail clothing stores with headquarters in California) from 1937 until 1953.

Although the state of California has been his place of residence for most of his life, Charles Sparks Thomas is a native of Independence, Missouri. He was born to Charles Rogers and Della (Rouse) Thomas on September 28, 1897. His parents moved in 1911 to Los Angeles, California, where Charles completed his secondary schooling. He was enrolled for one year (1915-1916) at the University of California at Berkeley and then transferred to Cornell University in Ithaca, New York. In his junior year he joined the U.S. Naval Reserve for World War I service as a Naval aviator.

At the conclusion of his active service in 1919, he joined an investment house, the George H. Burr Company, in Los Angeles. He became a partner and vice-president of George H. Burr, Conrad & Broom, Inc. in 1925, and was placed in charge of the company's affairs in southern California, Arizona and New Mexico. In 1932 he became vice-president and general manager of Foreman & Clark, Inc., retail merchants of men's and women's wearing apparel, and (stated Kimmis Hendrick in the *Christian Science Monitor,* February 13, 1953) "rescued" the firm from the depression. Thomas became president and a director of Foreman & Clark in 1937.

In 1942, after the United States had entered World War II, Thomas was called to Washington, D.C. as a special civilian assistant to Artemus L. Gates, Assistant Secretary of the Navy for Air. A year later he became special assistant to the Secretary of the Navy.

"In that capacity," Charles S. Thomas told the Senate Armed Services Committee in February 1953, "I set up the Navy's inventory control program and represented . . . [Forrestal] in the Navy's logistics program. . . ."

Thomas was also concerned with the procurement of aircraft. He is credited with initiating "incentive-type contracts providing bonuses for savings on costs." In one instance, he "brought the cost of horizon-indicating instruments in planes down from $300 each to $65" (according to Douglas Larsen in the New York *World-Telegram and Sun,* March 27, 1954). He also developed a program for assigning trained negotiators to assist the Navy's contracting officers.

Technically, his duty with the Department of the Navy came to an end in December 1944, but a few months later, at the special request of Forrestal, he made a 30,000-mile "morale and recreational survey" of the Navy's Pacific bases. On his return, he suggested the establishment at Guam of a Navy newspaper for servicemen, and recommended a variety of improved entertainment facilities. For his "outstanding service" in the field of Navy procurement and logistics, Thomas was decorated with the Distinguished Civilian Service Award by Forrestal on April 4, 1945, and was awarded the Presidential Medal for Merit on January 31, 1947.

Back in Los Angeles in 1945, Thomas resumed his duties as president and director of Foreman & Clark. He bought stock and assumed directorships in the Lockheed Aircraft Corporation, the Pacific Finance Corporation, the Broadway Department Store, and the Byron Jackson Company, pump manufacturers. He was airport commissioner for Los Angeles from 1945 to 1950, and also served as the president of the eleventh region of the Navy League and vice-president of the Los Angeles Chamber of Commerce.

His active participation, as a Republican, in local, state and national politics began in this period. "In Washington," noted *Time* magazine (August 5, 1946), "he was astonished by the small calibre of some of the political big guns he met. It occurred to him that this was something of his own fault—'At home I hardly knew who my Congressman was,' [he admitted]."

In 1945 Thomas organized a "Campaign Operations Group" for Republicans in the strongly Democratic Los Angeles county, and personally brought to the Pacific Coast an enterprising advertising man, Ross Barrett, to work out a plan to "sell" Republicanism and to take "the $2,000 to $5,000" income group away from the Democrats. The plan was so successful that the local Republicans "could count on spending $175,000 in the 1946 campaign," as against $15,000 a year previously (*Time*).

From 1949 through 1952, Thomas was chairman of the California Republican Finance Committee; he has also been a member of the National Finance Committee. He was one of the first Californians to urge Dwight D. Eisenhower to seek the U.S. presidency, and under Thomas' leadership, California Republicans contributed $468,000 to Eisenhower's successful 1952 campaign.

After taking office, President Eisenhower named Robert B. Anderson as Secretary of the Navy, and nominated Thomas as Under Secretary of the Navy. At the hearing held by the Senate Armed Services Committee on February 4, 1953, his confirmation was quickly recommended. (Thomas testified that he had already

U. S. Navy
CHARLES S. THOMAS

resigned the presidency of Foreman & Clark, although he was retaining his stock. He further made it clear that he was resigning his other directorships and disposing of most of his other securities, including his Lockheed Aircraft stock.) The Senate confirmed his nomination and Thomas took office on February 9, 1953. He was advanced to Assistant Secretary of Defense in charge of supply and logistics on July 28, 1953.

When the Department of Defense reported to Congress in 1953 that "79 per cent of strategic materials scheduled for stockpiling in the event of war had been obtained or was on order as of June 30," Thomas, giving specific figures, stated that "$4,184,307,550 worth of the seventy-five stockpile materials was on hand and another $1,469,101,166 was on order" and that the program called for a total of "$7,167,084,716 worth of strategic and critical materials normally obtained from overseas" (New York *Times,* September 5, 1953).

During an interview in October 1953, Thomas stated that since the new administration took office, the Department of Defense had studied and catalogued thousands of concerns, listing the capabilities and potentialities of each, and that in the event of an emergency, the United States could "get into production almost overnight" (New York *Times,* October 26, 1953). He informed the Senate small business subcommittee in late March 1954 that the Department of Defense had a "vigorous and effective" policy of giving small business a "fair chance" on defense contracts which had already "more than paid off in money saved" (New York *Herald Tribune,* April 1, 1954).

At the time of his nomination, on March 11, 1954, to become Secretary of the Navy, Thomas held a press conference in which he stated that one of his "major projects" had been "to start a single catalog of all the equipment and mate-

THOMAS, CHARLES S.—*Continued*

rials used by the three armed forces" in order to improve efficiency and eliminate duplication. He explained that "an estimated 4,500,000 items are listed in the catalogs compiled separately by the armed forces" and that it "might be possible to reduce the list by half in a single catalog by 1956" (New York *Times,* March 12, 1954). He was sworn in as Secretary of the Navy on May 3, 1954. Toward the end of the same month, he started for Quonset Point, Rhode Island, "within minutes" of hearing about the fire aboard the U.S.S. *Bennington.*

At the time he became Secretary of the Navy, it was reported in the New York *Times* (May 4, 1954) that one of the factors in his promotion was his work for racial equality as a member of the Government Contract Committee (which works to prevent racial discrimination on any project involving the government). After he became Secretary, Thomas answered a charge by Lester Granger, who resigned as a Navy consultant on racial problems, that the Navy had failed to recognize the "urgency" of eliminating racial segregation in its ranks. Thomas stated that "the Navy has been the leader" in securing racial equality. He pointed out that "complete integration" has been carried out in the Navy and Marine Corps, and that segregation among civilian workers has been eliminated in southern Navy yards (New York *Herald Tribune,* July 29, 1954).

On October 23 the Navy announced that a contract had been awarded to the Quincy, Massachusetts shipyard of the Bethlehem Steel Company for the construction of two destroyers, and on October 28 the Navy placed $700,000,000 worth of contracts with the aircraft industry. Secretary Thomas said that "the Navy has a continuing interest in preserving the essential skills and facilities for combatant ship [and plane] construction. . . ."

Charles Sparks Thomas and Julia B. Hayward of Los Angeles were married on April 15, 1920 and are the parents of three sons and a daughter. The sons are Hayward Thomas (who was an officer in the Naval Reserve in World War II), Ensign Charles Rogers Thomas of the Naval Reserve, and Comstock Archer Thomas; their daughter, Julia Louise, is now Mrs. Frank Alexander.

Thomas belongs to the Psi Upsilon fraternity; his clubs are the Country and California in Los Angeles, the Chevy Chase in Maryland, and the Maryland-Kansas City Country in Kansas City, Missouri. He belongs to the Episcopal Church. Secretary Thomas has been called "one of the nattiest dressers" in the Pentagon. He shoots golf in the middle 70's. "The game is his major hobby," wrote Douglas Larsen. "He's a sociable but quiet man who prides himself on never losing his temper."

References

N Y Herald Tribune p8 Ja 20 '53; p5 Mr 12 '54 por
N Y Times p14 Ja 20 '53; p 1+ Mr 12 '54 por
N Y World-Telegram p7 Mr 27 '54 por
Who's Who in America, 1954-55

THORNTON, DAN(IEL I. J.) Jan. 31, 1911- Governor of Colorado; cattleman

Address: b. State Capitol, Denver, Colo.

After building up a famous herd of registered Herefords, from a start on borrowed money in 1937, which sold for $875,940 in 1947, Dan Thornton turned from cattle breeding to politics. He was chosen to replace the Republican candidate five weeks before the election and was elected Colorado's governor in 1950, one of the youngest state executives in the nation. He was re-elected in November 1952.

Daniel I. J. Thornton was born in Hall County, Texas on January 31, 1911 to Ida (Fife) and Clay C. Thornton, a share cropper. They moved to a 177-acre farm near Slaton in 1920, where Dan, with the rest of the children in his family picked cotton, did farm work and attended Posey Community School.

Although under age, he joined the 4H Club when he was ten years old and soon became a leader. He was a featured guest at the Chicago international livestock show and was president of the 4H Club congress of Texas in 1927. At thirteen he won a declamation contest by reciting Lincoln's Gettysburg address.

After graduation from the Lubbock High School, Dan became a student at the Texas Technological College and at the University of California at Los Angeles in 1933, where he played football. Young Thornton left college and worked at various jobs, as a bit player for Warner Brothers, at $250 per week, a gas station operator and a "roughneck" and derrick man on the Wilmington oil fields.

Preferring ranching, in 1937 he borrowed $37,000 from his father-in-law and bought a ranch in Arizona, and began breeding Herefords. He was often called to judge cattle shows and on seeing the "Western Slope" of Colorado he decided to move his herd to Gunnison, Colorado in 1941. He purchased a 4,000 acre ranch and soon his initial investment was paid off, and it was costing about $100,000 a year to operate the business. Thornton kept a Beechcraft plane in which he flew some 100,000 miles a year, buying, selling and spreading the fame of his Triumphant Type Herefords. At a Denver Stock show in 1945 he sold two bulls at the same sale for $50,000 each. The plush rugs of the Brown Palace Hotel were rolled back to put the great white-faced creatures on display in the lobby.

A crowd of 6,000 from forty-six states and several foreign countries gathered in 1947 at Thornton's ranch for a dispersal sale (*Time,* October 6, 1947). The auction went on for two days. In twenty hours of selling, buyers bought an average of $729.95 worth of cattle a minute. One three-year-old heifer, TT Zato Heiress, brought a record price of $35,000.

In 1948 he was elected state senator and served a term of two years. Roscoe Fleming (Washington *Post,* January 7, 1951) reported that "he once got up on a GOP senatorial caucus and said he hadn't heard anything for two hours but how to obstruct and discredit the Democrats, and he'd be back when his fellow-Republicans wanted to start doing something for Colorado."

Commenting on his experience in the legislature, he said, "I should say the Republicans are going to have to live closer to the people, put on overalls, and mix with the crowd. . . . The party must toss away its high hat" (*Christian Science Monitor,* April 10, 1951).

By the end of the legislative session, he was ready to leave politics and return to the ranch, but that year, 1950, Ralph Carr, a Republican, who was running for governor of Colorado, died five weeks before election. Thornton was selected to succeed him, although few expected to see him elected.

During his short campaign Dan Thornton relaxedly went up and down the state smoking his pipe, promising to do his best and being himself. However, he made 303 talks in 201 scattered towns; he won at the polls on November 7, 1950. Murray Snyder, in the New York *Herald Tribune* (September 2, 1951) wrote that Thornton won largely because some 2,500 volunteers, mostly political amateurs, founded an organization, the Republican Associates, in Denver County, and captured this key county. Previously Colorado had gone Democratic in several state and national tests.

Brass bands and 5,000 citizens were out to greet Thornton's return to Gunnison a few days later. He took the oath of office on January 9, 1951 on the steps of the State House, and within one year, Thornton had undertaken four major legislative reforms.

He succeeded in securing passage of legislation to control the contagious Bang's cattle disease; to effect workmen's compensation; and a fair employment practices act in regard to state government hiring. The governor failed in his attempt to enact a bill to scale truck license fees on the basis of distance as well as weight. Thornton was selected as an executive of the National Governors Conference, an honor seldom bestowed on a governor during his first term of office.

He was one of the earliest of the western governors to support General Eisenhower's candidacy for President. Although Senator Eugene D. Milliken was the titular head of the Colorado Republican party and a supporter of Senator Robert A. Taft, the governor, who led the faction for General Eisenhower in the Colorado Republican convention, obtained fifteen of the state's eighteen votes. At the Republican national convention, Thornton made a floor speech for the amendment barring contested delegates from voting on their own contest. Throughout the campaign he worked vigorously for Eisenhower.

His prospects for a Federal post were discussed nationally but on July 21, 1952 he announced that he would run again for governor, and he was re-elected November 4, 1952, and inaugurated on January 13, 1953.

The governor successfully established a severance oil tax; developed civil defense; secured the enactment of comprehensive legislation to finance the schools; raised the exemption of surtax on intangibles from $200 to $600; put penal and charitable affairs under a board of state institutions headed by a paid director, started a state advertising program; and conducted an aggressive and successful campaign to eliminate gambling. He also organized an efficient patrol administration; obtained raises for all state employees; promoted mining in the state; secured a complete revision of the coal mining laws; reorganized the State Highway commission and formulated long range highway plans (he is now working on a highway safety program); he has offered measures to protect national resources and has balanced the budget. His fiscal policy requiring departments to place 10 per cent of their appropriations in reserve each year has resulted in a saving of $813,000 in the general fund.

Lainson Studio

DAN THORNTON

His herd of registered Herefords was again for sale on February 28, 1952, because Thornton found the business was too "personalized" to conduct while carrying out his gubernatorial duties, but he continues to own the Gunnison ranch, which is known as a model of its kind so far as soil conservation is concerned. He keeps the place for a summer home, while he rents a house in Denver.

The governor still finds time from state affairs to take a prominent part in conferences all over the nation, and on August 6, 1953, he was elected, for one year, chairman of the National Governors Conference. In October he was chairman of a special meeting of governors from twelve drought-stricken states at which it was recommended that a joint Federal-state program be established for obtaining hay for emergency relief, the Federal government to pay half the transportation costs, while the states procure and distribute the hay. On December 12 Governor Thornton was elected president of the Council of State Governments, succeeding Governor Allan Shivers of Texas. The council is an organization of officials of the states serving as a clearing house for the exchange of information.

Speaking at the Indiana Republican Editorial Writers Association meeting in Indianapolis on

THORNTON, DAN—*Continued*

October 31, 1953 Governor Daniel Thornton declared that the Democrats were "trying to use your tax dollar and mine" to buy the political support of farmers. "Today they have the farmers' vote on the auction block . . . tomorrow the labor vote; day after tomorrow, the business vote, and the following day catastrophe for all the free people of this nation" (New York *Times,* November 1, 1953).

Thornton supports Eisenhower's farm program and has recommended "cost-of-production supports, designed to protect farmers against disaster but not to guarantee them a profit. The government would prop prices at a level to cover average production costs" (*Christian Science Monitor,* December 7, 1953).

In an article, "I Believe" in *Country Gentleman,* November, 1953, Governor Thornton wrote: "Let's plan to keep agriculture strong. . . . Any country where the land is abused, or the people on the land are pushed into substandard living, is headed for trouble. . . . I believe we must find an agricultural program that encourages farmers to improve their land to help themselves, instead of leaning so heavily on the government." The Governor was not a candidate for re-election in 1954.

He was married in 1934 to Jessie Willock, who had been a student at the University of California in Los Angeles and whose father was Curtis M. Willock, founder of the American Steel Package Company of Defiance, Ohio.

Texas Technological College awarded Governor Thornton an honorary degree in 1953. Thornton, who is six feet tall, has used his pipe, ten-gallon hat and finely wrought high-heeled cowboy boots as colorful trademarks.

References

Christian Sci Mon II pl Ap 10 '51
Country Gent 123:13+ N '53
Denver Post Ja 17 '48; p44 N 14 '50; p3 Ja 9 '51; p1 Ag 6 '53
Denver Post Mag O 26 '47; Ja 7 '51
N Y Herald Tribune II p3 S 2 '51; II p3 Ja 20 '52
Rocky Mountain News S 29 '50; p11 N 14 '50; Jl 21 '52; Ag 19 '52; My 22 '53; pl Ag 7 '53
Time 50:90+ O 6 '47 por

TILLICH, PAUL J(OHANNES), REV. DR. (tĭl'lĭk) Aug. 20, 1886- Theologian

Address: b. c/o Harvard University Divinity School, Cambridge, Mass.

One of the great contemporary Protestant theologians, Paul J. Tillich was dismissed from his post as professor of philosophy at the university in Frankfurt am Main, Germany in 1933 because of opposition to the Nazi regime. In that year he emigrated to the United States, where he served as a member of the faculty of Union Theological Seminary from 1933 to the summer of 1954. On July 1, 1954 he was appointed to the faculty of Harvard University Divinity School, Cambridge, Massachusetts.

Through his teaching and writings he has helped to clarify the meaning of the Christian faith in relation to the needs and dilemmas of modern man. He is the author of approximately twenty-five books expounding his ideas on the relation of religion to politics, art, sociology, philosophy, and depth psychology. A group of noted theologians and philosophers have compiled their views of Dr. Tillich's important contribution to religious thinking in a book, *The Theology of Paul Tillich,* published in 1952 by Macmillan. In 1953 he delivered the Gifford lectures on theology at the University of Edinburgh.

Dr. Tillich believes that "the Protestant principle" is the power to call men to an awareness of God's infinite nature and their own limitations. It is "the protesting voice of the prophet outside the temple calling the people back to God. . . ." According to Professor Walter Marshall Horton of Oberlin College, Dr. Tillich's philosophy has "furnished a dwelling place for multitudes of homeless modern minds . . . [contributing] to the reform of the modern Church and the reintegration of modern culture."

Paul Johannes Tillich was born in Starzeddel, Kreis Guben, Prussia, on August 20, 1886, the son of Johannes and Mathilde (Dürselen) Tillich. His father, a Lutheran pastor, became diocesan superintendent of a group of parishes in eastern Brandenburg.

His Lutheran family and church community had decisive influences upon his life and work. He has written, "It is the experience of the 'holy' which was given to me at that time as an indestructible good and as the foundation of all my religious and theological work." He also encountered the love of true philosophy, learned from his father, which enabled him to free himself from Protestant orthodoxy. Tillich suggests that, "It is this painful break-through to autonomy which has made me immune against any system of thought or life which demands the surrender of this autonomy."

He attended humanistic gymnasiums in eastern Brandenburg and later in Berlin. After studying theology at the universities of Berlin, Tübingen and Halle, he received the Ph.D. degree from the university at Breslau in 1912 and the degree of Licentiate of Theology from Halle. The subject of his theses for both degrees was Schelling's philosophy of religion.

Tillich was ordained as a minister of the Evangelical Lutheran Church in 1912. He served as a chaplain in the German forces from September, 1914, to September, 1918. Early in the war he became convinced that the conflict would ruin Europe, and he saw class antagonisms persisting in Germany which finally brought revolution in 1918. Yet as a chaplain he found a profound response among the soldiers to his affirmations of the ultimate meaning of life. In sympathy with the revolution in Germany at the close of the war, he felt that it was his Christian duty to participate in the struggle for justice. Dr. Tillich attacked both the otherworldliness and individualism of traditional church piety and the secular utopian illusions of the political left. He saw religious dignity in the proletarian struggle, despite his rejection of certain Marxist views.

Following the war Dr. Tillich was *privatdozent* of theology at the university of Berlin from 1919 to 1924, professor of theology at the university in Marburg from 1924 to 1925, university in Dresden from 1925 to 1929, Universität Leipzig from 1928 to 1929 and professor of philosophy at the university in Frankfurt am Main from 1929 to 1933. During this period he produced his major German writings.

In those years of chaos, the "religious center," i.e., the ultimate concern presupposed in every sphere of human activity, became for Tillich the starting point for a "theology of culture," which he developed in one of his best known books, *Die Religiöse Lage Der Gegenwart* (Ullstein, 1926). A translation, *The Religious Situation,* was published by Holt in 1932.

When the Nazi regime came to power, it not only destroyed Tillich's hopes for Germany's immediate future but it drove him from his native land. Because of his opposition to national socialism he lost his professorship at Frankfurt in 1933. "I had the great honor and luck," he said, "to be about the first non-Jewish professor dismissed from a German university" (New York *Post,* May 1, 1940).

In the summer of 1933 Tillich was asked to come to the Union Theological Seminary by Reinhold Niebuhr, one of the seminary's professors. "It was Union," he writes, "that took me in as a stranger, then as visiting, associate, and full professor."

In his open and searching manner he has continually discussed philosophy and theology with liberal Protestant and secular thinkers and has won their respect for his erudition and insight. John Herman Randall, Jr., professor of philosophy at Columbia University, wrote: "Paul Tillich seems to me not only the ablest Protestant theologian of the present day, but also by far the most persuasive exponent of the philosophy of existentialism, and a real contributor to the present-day revival of metaphysical inquiry. His is a first-rate philosophical mind."

The theologian delivered the Tailor lectures (1935) and Terry lectures (1950) both at Yale University. On May 24, 1953, he lectured on "Religion and Art" at the National Gallery in Washington, D.C. In 1953 he was asked to deliver the Gifford lectures on theology at the University of Edinburgh, an honor extended to only four other Americans in the history of this lectureship.

In 1948 and in 1951 he lectured at German universities and found the spiritual situation surprisingly open to his ideas. Many of his English writings are now being translated and published in Germany. "This way of returning to Germany is the best I could imagine," he writes, "and it makes me very happy."

Tillich is the author of many articles for such periodicals as the *Journal of the History of Ideas, Religion in Life, Journal of Religion, The Christian Century, Christianity and Society, American Journal of Sociology,* and *Social Research.*

REV. DR. PAUL J. TILLICH

The professor has written five books in this period: *The Interpretation of History* (Scribner, 1936), *The Protestant Era* (University of Chicago Press, 1948), *The Shaking of the Foundation* (Scribner, 1948) wherein he is at one with the skeptical, the lonely, the empty-hearted contemporary man, and yet he speaks out of the assurance of faith, *The Courage to Be* (Yale University Press, 1952) a collection of the Terry lectures of 1950, and *Systematic Theology* (University of Chicago Press, 1951) his major work upon which he has been laboring for nearly three decades. Tillich is at present working on a second volume to *Systematic Theology.*

Protestant theology can, he believes, "without losing its Christian foundations, incorporate strictly scientific methods, a critical philosophy, a realistic understanding of men and society, and powerful ethical principles and motives."

Actively interested in the psychoanalytical movement, he wrote: "I do not think it is possible today to elaborate a Christian doctrine of man, and especially a Christian doctrine of the Christian man, without using the immense material brought forth by depth psychology."

Dr. Tillich believes that man is a creature part animal and subject to fate, yet also a being which takes thought and has certain powers over itself in freedom. The religious basis of human life he regards as inescapable, it is that which concerns man ultimately as the center of his existence. God is the unconditional fulfillment *intended* in every ambiguous fulfillment in history. The religious is not one compartment of life alongside others. It is the "sacred depth" of every aspect of life and its unifying center. "The confidence of every creature, its courage to be, is rooted in faith in God as its creative ground."

The scholar has been chairman of the Self-Help for Emigrees from Central Europe, an organization supported entirely by refugees, giving help and advice to refugees abroad and in

TILLICH, PAUL J.—*Continued*

America. He has served on the executive committee of the American Committee for Christian Refugees, as vice-chairman of the Center for German and Austrian Art and Handicraft, and as provisional chairman of the Council for a Democratic Germany.

In 1950 he was a member of a special commission, appointed by the Federal Council of the Churches of Christ in America, which made a study on "The Christian Conscience and Weapons of Mass Destruction." The report concluded that the use of military force, even of nuclear weapons, may sometimes be less evil than surrender to tyranny; that Christian conscience must oppose atrocities and all unnecessary killing and destruction; and that because modern wars are so catastrophic, the supreme issue is the avoidance of war altogether without surrender to tyranny.

A man of medium height and build, Tillich is reserved in manner, yet direct, simple, and warm in relation to others. He has a great love for nature, especially the sea. In the American West he has admired the desert and the California redwood trees. In 1924 he married Hannah Werner; they have a daughter, Erdmuthe, and a son, Rene.

Dr. Tillich is a minister of the Evangelical and Reformed Church and in 1940 became a citizen of the United States. He is a member of the American Academy of Arts and Sciences, American Philosophical Association—East, and American Theological Association. Honorary degrees were conferred upon him by the universities of Halle (1926), Yale (1940) and Glasgow (1951).

References

N Y Post p13 My 1 '40
N Y Times 6:1 Je 4 '50
Time 60:69 O 20 '52

Directory of American Scholars (1951)
Kegley, C. W. and Bretall, R. W. eds. The Theology of Paul Tillich (1952)
Tillich, P. The Interpretation of History (1936)
Tillich P. The Protestant Era (1948)
Wer ist Wer? (1951)
Who's Who in America, 1952-53
Who's Who in New York, 1952

TOSCANINI, ARTURO (tôs-kä-nē'nê är-tōō'rô) Mar. 25, 1867- Conductor

Address: h. Riverdale-on-Hudson, New York

NOTE: This biography supersedes the article which appeared in *Current Biography* in 1942.

The dominant position that Arturo Toscanini has held in the world of music for more than half a century has been accorded to few musicians. In Carnegie Hall on Sunday evening, April 4, 1954, the Maestro conducted his last concert with the National Broadcasting Company Symphony Orchestra, thereby ending a seventeen-year association. The capacity audience of invited guests and the millions of radio listeners did not know until after the concert that the eighty-seven-year-old conductor was relinquishing his baton. Of his farewell concert Jack Tait in the New York *Herald Tribune* (April 5, 1954) wrote: "Every measure of it bore the crest of Toscanini's greatness. . . . He is the musical universe's central star and by his light we have learned to see."

Toscanini made his podium debut in Rio de Janeiro in 1886. Beginning in 1896, and extending at intervals over a period of many years, the Maestro was the outstanding leader of operas and symphonies, many of them premières, at La Scala Opera House in Milan, Italy. In the United States, he conducted at the Metropolitan Opera House (1908-1915), and was with the New York Philharmonic orchestra (1926-1936). In the 1930's Toscanini served as a guest conductor of famous orchestras in France, Austria, Italy, and Germany. He led the newly-formed Palestine Symphony Orchestra at Tel Aviv during the 1936-1937 season.

The broadcasts of Arturo Toscanini as conductor of the NBC Symphony Orchestra have been among the most exciting musical events in America since 1937. His RCA Victor recordings rank high in popularity in the classical record field. His recording of Beethoven's monumental *Missa Solemnis* was released by RCA Victor in March 1954.

Arturo Toscanini was born in Parma, Italy, on March 25, 1867, the son of Claudio and Paola (Montani) Toscanini. He was impressed early with the democratic ideas of his father, a tailor, who was an ardent supporter of the Italian patriot, Giuseppe Garibaldi. Arturo entered the Parma Conservatory of Music at the age of nine, although his youthful ambition was to draw patterns on cloth to be cut for clothes.

Within two years he won a scholarship in a cello class and received the nickname "genius" among his schoolmates. His interest in music aroused, he secretly organized an extracurricular band for which he and his schoolfellows were punished. In order to buy music scores which he could not afford, he often sold his food.

After graduating from the Conservatory of Music of Parma in 1885 *con lode distinta* (with distinguished praise), Toscanini was engaged as a cellist with various touring Italian orchestras. His nearsightedness made it necessary for him to memorize every note and marking on a score. As a cellist with an opera company, he went to Brazil in 1886.

The company was in Rio de Janeiro when the conductor quit, and the singers beseeched Toscanini to conduct in his place. The women in the chorus, fearing to be stranded penniless in South America, said, "He will save us! He knows all the operas by heart!" The young cellist leapt to the podium amid shouting and jeering from the audience. He led the performance of Verdi's *Aïda* and the audience gave Toscanini an overwhelming ovation. After the final notes were sung, someone noticed that the score of the opera was still opened to page one. This performance was on June 25, 1886.

On his return to Italy in the fall of 1886 Toscanini made no attempt to capitalize on his success in Rio de Janeiro. He returned quietly to the cellist's place. But the singers of the company spread word of his talent and soon he received engagements to conduct small opera companies throughout Italy. In one season he conducted nineteen operas.

Toscanini was invited to conduct Alfredo Catalani's opera *Edmea* at Turin which led to his strong friendship with the composer. For the world première of Verdi's *Otello,* Toscanini returned to the cellist's chair. During rehearsals he met Verdi for the first time. His admiration for Verdi the man, and Verdi the composer, has been a guiding light of Toscanini's career.

The young musician conducted the world premières of Leoncavallo's *I Pagliacci* in Milan in 1892 and of Puccini's *La Bohème* in Turin in 1896. Making his first appearance at La Scala, he conducted four symphonic programs there in 1896. The year before he had introduced Wagner's *Götterdämmerung* in Italy. Word of his astounding ability to learn operas in a short time and conduct them from memory reached across the musical world. He also established a reputation as a symphonic conductor and led forty-three concerts at the international fair held in Turin in 1898.

He directed *Die Meistersinger von Nürnberg* at La Scala, his first opera performance there, on December 26, 1898. Thus began his association with the famous opera house as chief conductor and artistic director from 1898 to 1903. During these five years, he introduced new operas and symphonic works. His refusal to permit encores led to his resignation in 1903, and for the next three years he led orchestras in Buenos Aires, Rome, Bologna, and Turin.

Toscanini returned to La Scala in 1906 and conducted there until 1908. A new chapter in his life was opened when Giulio Gatti-Casazza, director of La Scala, left to become associated with the Metropolitan Opera Company in New York and brought Toscanini with him. He conducted Verdi's *Aïda* on November 16, 1908 and was hailed as "a unique genius." He served as conductor for seven seasons, during which he conducted what musicians consider some of the most memorable performances of opera ever given, although there were some who objected to his "lordly expenditure of extra rehearsal time and his adamantine sense of discipline." Once, when he thought the cellists looked too relaxed and self-satisfied, he told them, "When I played the cello for Guiseppe Verdi, I had water on my face. I don't see any water on your faces!"

Following the outbreak of World War I Toscanini left the Metropolitan and returned to Italy where he offered his services to the government, and conducted orchestras at benefit performances for war sufferers. A staunch Italian patriot, he nevertheless played German music in Italy, even when the war fever was at its highest.

After the war he built up a new orchestra and with it toured the United States from 1920 to 1921. He made his first orchestral records at the Victor studios in Camden, New Jersey. Returning to Italy, he helped rebuild La Scala and conducted there for several years. In 1926 he accepted the post of guest conductor with the New York Philharmonic Orchestra. When

ARTURO TOSCANINI

this orchestra merged with the New York Symphony Society orchestra to form the New York Philharmonic-Symphony Orchestra in 1928, he became the principal conductor.

During 1930 he took the orchestra on a European tour. In the 1930's he filled engagements as guest conductor at the Wagner festivals at Bayreuth (Germany), a Debussy memorial celebration in France, the Salzburg festivals in Austria, and concerts with the British Broadcasting Company orchestra in London.

Having resigned as conductor of the New York Philharmonic-Symphony Orchestra in 1936, Toscanini conducted the Palestine Symphony Orchestra for a year. When he considered retiring from conducting, he was induced by David Sarnoff (president of RCA and director of the National Broadcasting Company) and Samuel Chotzinoff to return to the United States in 1937 as director of the newly-formed NBC Symphony Orchestra. His broadcasts with this orchestra—originally from Radio City and more recently from Carnegie Hall—were attended by holders of reserve tickets secured months in advance. Aiding the Federal government in the promotion of Pan-American good will, Toscanini made a 13,000-mile tour with the orchestra in South America in 1940.

In the early 1940's, the Maestro led the NBC Symphony Orchestra in works by Mendelssohn, Haydn, Tchaikovsky, and Brahms, and convinced music critics that "as an artist he never stands still" (New York *Times,* December 22, 1940). Olin Downes wrote: "When Toscanini accomplishes one of these revelations of a work of the past one is aware of the unpayable debt we owe this master who successfully fights the annihilation by Time of beauty" (New York *Times,* April 6, 1941). As guest conductor, the Maestro led concerts of the Philadelphia Orchestra and of the New York Philharmonic-

TOSCANINI, ARTURO—*Continued*

Symphony Orchestra in 1942. In 1941 he rejected an offer of $250,000 to make a Hollywood movie.

During World War II, the conductor led the NBC Symphony Orchestra in a series of concerts to promote the sale of war bonds. He also volunteered his services to the Red Cross and other war benefits, and aided the Office of War Information by conducting for the film, *Hymn of the Nations.*

The Maestro marked the fiftieth anniversary of Puccini's *La Bohème* by conducting the NBC Symphony Orchestra in this work in 1946. Olin Downes commented: "The vision of a sovereign interpreter has not dimmed; his power has not waned" (New York *Times,* February 4, 1946). Answering those critics who remark on his absence of attention to contemporary music, Toscanini said: "I am the man who did Wagner when Wagner was new; who produced all the moderns from Strauss and Debussy to Malipiero and Sibelius. Now let the other young men do what I did when I was young" (New York *Times,* March 22, 1942). His conducting of Verdi's *Otello* in 1947 was called by many people the greatest operatic performance they had ever heard.

His transcontinental tour of the United States in 1950 with the NBC Symphony Orcestra brought out large audiences in twenty cities. Although generally dignified in manner and fastidious in dress, on this tour he was "like a boy let out of school," and permitted photographs of himself in Sun Valley on the ski lift in shirt sleeves (*Newsweek,* May 29, 1950).

Following a knee injury, Toscanini cancelled some of his concerts with the NBC Symphony Orchestra in 1950. The next year he returned and honored the memory of Verdi by conducting the composer's Requiem Mass fifty years after his death. In 1952 he was guest conductor of the London Philharmonic Orchestra.

Works in which Toscanini conducted the NBC Symphony Orchestra during the 1953-54 season included Strauss' *Don Quixote,* and *Don Juan,* Beethoven's "Pastorale" Symphony, Mendelssohn's "Italian" Symphony, and Verdi's *Te Deum* and *Un Ballo in Maschera.* On April 4 he concluded his seventeen years as leader of that group. "One of the most distinguished audiences to gather in recent years on any artistic occasion in this city assembled to pay him homage," wrote Olin Downes in the New York *Times* (April 5, 1954). "At the last moment, Mr. Toscanini had made a change in the program . . . to the Overture and Bacchanale from *Tannhäuser* (Paris version). . . . It is a long excerpt, and it ends with the softest sonorities, echoing as from the distance, of which strings are capable." He ended the program with the Prelude to *Die Meistersinger.*

"With the last chord," continued Downes, "the master hand which has so long and gloriously held the baton, dropped it to the floor, as Toscanini, almost before the sound of it had stopped, stepped from the podium, left the platform and never returned to the stage. . . . There has never been a more gallant and intrepid champion of great music, or a spirit that flamed higher, or a nobler defender of the faith. . . . For the moment, at least, he chose to leave. But we need not have heard the last of Toscanini and his phenomenal interpretive powers, unless he himself decides so."

Following the final radio concert under the baton of Toscanini, David Sarnoff announced the Maestro's retirement and made public an exchange of letters between Toscanini and himself. Toscanini's letter, dated March 25, on his eighty-seventh birthday, stated in part: "Year after year it has been a joy for me to know that the music played by the NBC Symphony Orchestra has been acclaimed by the vast radio audiences all over the United States and abroad. . . . And now the sad time has come when I must reluctantly lay aside my baton and say good-bye to my orchestra and in leaving I want you to know that I shall carry with me rich memories of these years of music making and heartfelt gratitude to you and the National Broadcasting Company for having made them possible."

When RCA Victor issued all nine of Beethoven's symphonies with Toscanini conducting the NBC Symphony Orchestra, music critic Ernest Newman wrote: "These records, indeed, are a joy to the connoisseur and an education to all musicians, even to those of us . . . who flattered ourselves that we already knew and understood our Beethoven pretty thoroughly" (*Saturday Review,* April 25, 1953). The Maestro, hesitant about listening to a tape recording of his music for the first time, said: "No, no, I am afraid to listen" (*Time,* November 16, 1953). When he hears what he considers a flaw, his first impulse is to discard the tape.

In March 1954 RCA Victor released Toscanini's recordings of the four Brahms symphonies in a long-playing album of which music critic Neville Cardus of the *Manchester Guardian* wrote: "Toscanini raises the blood pressure of Brahms; his own vitality dominates softer qualities. . . . How tired Toscanini must be of his uncritical public! He, the restless searcher after the truth, is treated like the prima donna who said that praise was good enough for her. We can bow to his genius, gratefully and humbly, with freedom to say that his veracity compels us frequently to crave for a yielding touch, an indulgent *rallentando* . . . for a sign of mortal fallibility of touch" (*Saturday Review,* March 27, 1954).

James G. Deane in *High Fidelity* magazine (March 1954) wrote that he had witnessed the recording of Beethoven's *Missa Solemnis* by Toscanini for RCA Victor in March 1953: "Between a concert and a recording session there is for Toscanini little difference. . . . He conducts from memory. Usually the score is within reach on a music stand at the left of the podium but almost invariably it is shut. . . . This is a prodigious fact. . . . His musicians anticipate, catch and treasure his every slightest cue. . . . I and others present marveled that Toscanini should be the one participant whose energy appeared least to flag, whose dedication seemed only reinforced by the advancing hour hands.

"Preparing to descend the stage at Tuesday night's recording session, he quickly but plainly made the figure of a cross against his breast. And at the final rehearsal . . . the old man, seeking to inspire in his singers the feeling essential to communicating Beethoven's reverent 'Sanctus,' said gently in Italian: 'This must go slowly and mysteriously, as if coming from Heaven.'"

Through the years Toscanini has been uncompromising in his refusal to accept political dictatorship. In 1931 he was physically attacked in Bologna, Italy for his refusal to play the Fascist hymn. He left Bayreuth, where he had directed the Wagner festivals, because of Hitler's dictatorship. He left Salzburg for the same reason. When asked to return to La Scala Opera House in Milan, he waited to accept until after the Mussolini regime ended. "I shall be happy to return among you as a citizen of a free Italy," he declared (New York *Times*, May 5, 1945).

Stories are legion about Toscanini's temperament, his lusty humor, his fabulous memory and his amazing vitality. It is sometimes difficult to distinguish between the true stories and the apocryphal, but Milton Katims, who was given his first opportunity to conduct the NBC Symphony Orchestra by Toscanini, wrote in the New York *Times Magazine* (November 8, 1953): "People are always asking me about the temperamental outbursts of Toscanini. For my part, these reports have always been overemphasized. Naturally, he becomes impatient and stormy if he feels any player is 'letting down'—he constantly gives the utmost of himself, and expects the same from every man. Whenever he has 'blown up', he has always had good reason—and it is always a musical reason.

"One night," recalled Katims, "as Toscanini came off-stage, he mopped his brow, and returned several times to the podium to acknowledge an ovation. As he was ready to ascend the stairs to his dressing room he put his arm around me. 'Young conductor,' he asked, his voice moist with emotion, 'do you get nervous, too?'" Katims remembered the day when Toscanini was rehearsing Debussy's *La Mer*. He wanted to achieve a highly evanescent effect in one spot, and "at a loss to describe what he wanted, he took from his breast pocket a large, white silk handkerchief. He threw it high into the air and every man in the orchestra was hypnotized as it floated softly, sensuously to the floor. 'There,' the Maestro smiled happily, 'play it like that.'"

Once he was raging in Italian at a cellist who had made a mistake when he suddenly realized the musician had not understood a word. Trying to express his anger in English, he finally burst out: "You bad, bad, bad man!"

Arturo Toscanini married Carla dei Martini in 1897. She died in June 1951. Their children are Walter, Wally and Wanda. The conductor is short in stature, of slight build, and has brown, alert eyes, an iron-gray mustache and white hair. He is an Italian citizen. His hobby is watching prize fights and wrestling on television.

Once when a reporter used the word genius, Toscanini echoed, "Genius? Not I, my dear fellow; the composer. I am only a conductor." In the words of music critic Louis Biancolli (New York *World-Telegram and Sun*) Toscanini has "always put music first. . . . Never [does] he allow anything or anybody to interfere with this unwavering commitment, and a true humility."

After Toscanini's retirement, the National Broadcasting Company discontinued the NBC Symphony Orchestra. However, the group refused to be disbanded and organized itself as the Symphony of the Air. As a tribute to the Maestro it decided not to invite a permanent conductor during his lifetime. Its "conductorless" concert at Carnegie Hall on October 27, 1954 was praised by the critics.

Selected References (See also references listed in 1942 biographical sketch)

Mus Am 73:13 N 15 '53
N Y Sunday News p14+ N 15 '53 pors
N Y Times p1+ Ap 7 '46
N Y Times Mag p9+ N 8 '53 por; p10 D 27 '53 por
N Y World-Telegram p29 Ap 6 '54 pors
Newsweek 35:74 My 29 '50 por
Read Digest 51:74+ Ag '47
Time 51:54 Ap 26 '48 por; 62:88+ N 16 '53 por
Ewen, D. Story of Arturo Toscanini (1951)
Sargeant, W. Geniuses, Goddesses and People (1949)
Taubman, H. Maestro; the Life of Arturo Toscanini (1951)
Thompson, O. ed. International Cyclopedia of Music and Musicians (1949)
Who's Who, 1953
Who's Who in America, 1952-53

TRABERT, MARION ANTHONY *See* Trabert, T.

TRABERT, TONY (trā'bẽrt) Aug. 16, 1930- Tennis player

Address: 1531 Franklin Ave., Cincinnati 37, Ohio

The United States national tennis champion for 1953, Tony Trabert, secured the national singles title by defeating Victor Seixas. Twenty-three-year-old Trabert astounded tennis observers by his nationals victory in September 1953 since his absences from tournament play to serve in the United States Navy were considered a possible impediment to his victory. The net star has served on the Davis Cup team for several years.

In May 1954 he lost to Enrique Morea of Argentina in Italy's international tennis tourney, but won the Count Godomen's Trophy of the international lawn tennis tournament in Spain and the French international men's singles title. He teamed with Seixas in Paris to defeat Australia's Lewis Hoad and Ken Rosewall in the final game of the international men's doubles tourney.

(Continued next page)

N. Y. World-Telegram & Sun, Bill Greene

TONY TRABERT

Trabert's one-year reign as national champion ended on September 4, 1954 when he was defeated in the Forest Hills (Long Island) Stadium of the West Side Tennis Club by Rex Hartwig.

Marion Anthony Trabert was born on August 16, 1930 in Cincinnati, Ohio. His father, Archibald Wilson Trabert, a sales engineer for the General Electric Company, is of Scotch origin; his mother, Bernice (Roach) Trabert, is of Swedish ancestry. Their two elder sons are Douglass Wilson and John Marcus. Because the family lived near a playground when he was small, Tony Trabert began to play tennis at the age of six.

He received his schooling in Cincinnati and was graduated from the Walnut Hills High School there in 1948. He was vice-president of the junior class, was cocaptain of the school's basketball team in 1948, and captain of the tennis team in 1946, 1947, and 1948. Subsequently Trabert matriculated at the University of Cincinnati. He became a member of the university's tennis and basketball teams, was elected president of the junior class, and was chosen for membership in Sigma Sigma and Sigma Chi fraternities.

His school and club tournament record brought his name to the attention of the United States Lawn Tennis Association and he entered amateur national matches.

With the aid of Bill Talbert, Trabert began to work out the "bugs" in his tennis game in 1950. He won the Paris doubles (May 7) with Talbert and the French doubles (June 4); he lost the National Clay doubles (July 24); won the Pacific Southwest doubles (September 18), and the national hard-court doubles (September 24). By the end of 1950 he was the twelfth ranking player on the national listings.

Time, on August 6, 1951, reported Trabert as saying that Talbert was "like a brother. My tour of Europe in 1950 with Bill did much to raise my game. I learned so much that I couldn't absorb it all. Now it is sinking home. . ." Trabert opened the 1951 tennis season by taking the tristate championship from Talbert, the clay-court title from Art Larsen, the intercollegiate from Earl Cochell, and the southern from Jack Tuero.

In July 1951 Trabert teamed with Talbert to beat a Japanese doubles team in the second round eliminations of the American Zone play for the Davis Cup competitions. Then he repeated his clay-court victory over Larsen on the Southampton, Long Island, Meadow Club turf-court, and came through to the finals there to down Herbie Flam—a significant win, wrote *Time,* "because all top tournaments are played on grass courts."

At Montreal in August 1951 he took a singles victory in the American Zone finals for the Davis Cup from Canada's Lorne Main. Late that month he defeated Gardnar Mulloy for the Middle Atlantic grass-court championship in Baltimore. He was turned back by Frank Sedgman of Australia in the quarter-finals of the national tennis championships held at the West Side Tennis Club in Forest Hills, Long Island. Trabert next competed in the Pacific Southwest tournament in Los Angeles.

Although called from the reserves to service with the U.S. Navy in September 1951, Trabert was granted a ninety-day leave of absence from boot training to compete in the 1951 Davis Cup matches; until his discharge in June 1953, he was frequently given other leaves for international tourneys. With partner Ted Schroeder he came through the doubles final in the New South Wales competition in late November 1951, but they were defeated by Australians Frank Sedgman and Ken McGregor in the finals.

The same pair of American players routed an Australian doubles pair in the Victoria final at Melbourne. In single play Trabert beat Swedish contender Sven Davidsson, only to go down again in the doubles final of the Davis Cup competition with partner Schroeder to Sedgman and McGregor, with the cup going to Australia for the second year in succession. "Trabert ended the year [1951] by becoming America's best young player," reported *Sport Stars.*

When the 1951 tennis rankings were announced by the United States Lawn Tennis Association (USLTA) early in 1952, Trabert was named third in the United States, below Victor Seixas and Richard Savitt. Trabert was given leave in May 1952 to compete in the French tennis championships, from which he was eliminated in an unexpected upset by the Philippine player Felicisimo Ampon.

Going from Paris to Brussels to compete in the Belgian international tournament, Trabert secured a singles victory there over Australian Mervyn Rose, and with Budge Patty, a doubles over Rose and McGregor. Despite a long absence from tournament play due to his sea duty, Trabert was selected for the 1952 Davis Cup team and returned to Australia that December for the matches. The American team lost to the Australians in 1952.

After playing in the California State championships in May 1953, Trabert two months later won the annual tristate singles championship at Cincinnati. In Vancouver, he gained a victory for the American Davis Cup team by defeating Japanese Kosei Kamo in the first round of American Zone eliminations. Late in July he lost to Seixas for the Pennsylvania State turf-court championship, after what Allison Danzig of the New York *Times* called "a magnificent fight in the opener."

After taking the Middle Atlantic crown at Baltimore in August 1953 by defeating Bernard Bartzen, Tony Trabert went to South Orange, New Jersey for the eastern grass-court matches, where his playing showed signs of his lack of practice. "If he regains his 1951 touch," predicted chairman Alrick Man of the Davis Cup Committee, "he could whip everybody." At the Newport, Rhode Island invitation tournament on August 16, 1953, Trabert took the final singles round from Seixas, and then teamed with him in the doubles to defeat their opponents, Bill Talbert and Hamilton Richardson.

Seixas and Trabert were contestants in the national doubles championship at the Longwood Cricket Club in Massachusetts and were defeated at the rackets of Australians Mervyn Rose and Rex Hartwig on August 22, 1953. In the 1953 nationals, Trabert was second-seeded player, below Seixas. On September 7, in a one-hour match that finished in "as stunning a final-round reversal as Forest Hills has seen in many years," Trabert scored 6-3, 6-2, 6-3 to wrest from Seixas the national tennis crown.

"In his powerful serving and deadly play in the forecourt and in his speed in bringing off one amazing recovery after another for spectacular winners, Trabert was a foe for the best to reckon with," reported Allison Danzig in the New York *Times*. "But his ground strokes were what broke Seixas' resistance and turned the match into something of a rout in the second set."

Following his relatively poor showing in the Pacific Southwest tournament later in September, Trabert took the Pacific Coast men's tennis championship from Seixas by a 7-5, 6-3, 6-2 decisive match. In October at Mexico City he teamed with Gardnar Mulloy to win the Pan American doubles title, and took the singles from Danish contender Kurt Nielsen. The USLTA ranking for 1953, issued in December, named Tony Trabert the No. 1. U.S. player.

Trabert, who returned to Australia in December 1953, paired with Davis Cup captain Bill Talbert to take a doubles match from Belgian contenders in the interzone finals, in which he also won a singles victory over Belgian contender Jacques Brichant. With Seixas, he downed Australian team Hoad and Hartwig at Melbourne before being defeated by Hoad in the singles challenge round (the Australians in 1953 retained the Davis Cup for the fourth successive year).

The partners Trabert and Seixas were beaten in the South Australian doubles in January 1954, but Trabert alone took the singles title. For the national Australian championship, he was beaten in the semifinals by veteran Jack Bromwich. Upon his return to the United States, Trabert re-entered the University of Cincinnati and continued as a member of the basketball team.

Trabert thinks basketball is a perfect game for tennis players. "It taught me change of direction and wide court coverage," he said (*Scholastic*, May 12, 1954). The coach of the University of Cincinnati basketball team, George Smith, commented: "Not only is Tony in great shape all the time, but he could be great in any sport he attempted." In the February 1954 national indoor tennis matches, Trabert almost lost to Frank Shields before going down to Bill Talbert in the quarter-finals.

He was defeated in the semi-finals at Wimbledon in 1954 by Ken Rosewall, but won the men's singles championship of the Pan-American tennis tournament in October 1954.

Trabert and Seixas regained the Davis Cup for the United States in December 1954 by their singles and doubles victories over the Australian team of Hoad and Rosewall.

The tennis player likes to rise very early and skip rope. "While most of the other fellows are sleeping until noon, I'm conditioning myself. When I get into a five-set match, I'll have enough strength to beat anyone," he told Zander Hollander (*Scholastic*, May 12, 1954). He told an Associated Press reporter (April 27, 1954) that his biggest ambition is to turn professional. "There's no use trying to kid anyone," Tony said. "I want . . . to get some money before it's too late. That's why I'm leaving school shortly. You can't concentrate on two things at once, and from now on, it will be strictly tennis with me. I want to find out if I'm good enough to play professional tennis. If I am, I'll turn pro. Jack Kramer's tour is just about ripe for another new face."

He has received the Governor's Award of Ohio and an award from the Cincinnati Junior Chamber of Commerce. He holds a lifetime membership in the Cincinnati Tennis Club. He is a Republican. He is six feet tall, and weighs 185 pounds; he is freckled, has blue eyes, and wears his brown hair in a crew cut. He was married on October 26, 1953 to Shauna Dean Wood who was "Miss Utah" of 1953.

References

Scholastic 64:23 My 12 '54 por
Time 58:48+ Ag 6 '51 por

TRUEBA, ANDRÉS MARTÍNEZ *See* Martínez Trueba, A.

TUOMIOJA, SAKARI (SEVERI) (tōō"-ŏmī-ō'yȧ sâ'kâ-rê) Aug. 29, 1911- Former Premier of Finland; banker

Address: b. c/o Bank of Finland, Helsinki, Finland; h. Merikatu 7A, Helsinki, Finland

Finland's "caretaker" Cabinet, formed in November 1953, was headed by Premier Sakari Tuomioja, who was chosen to lead the government until parliamentary elections could be held in 1954. A non-party economic expert of independent and liberal views, Tuomioja has been governor of the Bank of Finland since 1945 and has directed important ministries in Finnish postwar governments.

Sakari Tuomioja is also known outside his country as the representative of Finland in the International Bank for Reconstruction and Development and the International Monetary Fund and as a prominent negotiator of the Finnish-Soviet five-year trade pact of 1950.

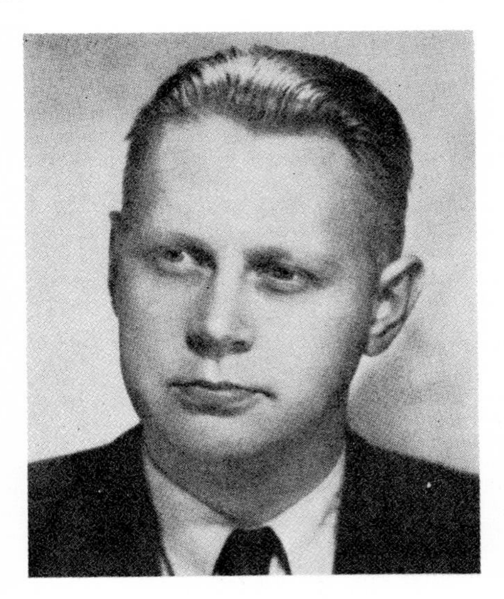

SAKARI TUOMIOJA

On May 5, 1954 after Premier Tuomioja had sought to resign, a coalition Cabinet was formed, headed by Ralf Toerngren.

Sakari Severi Tuomioja, the son of Walto Wihtori and Laina Sofia (Boman) Tuomioja, was born in Tampere in southwest Finland on August 29, 1911. Like his father, a lawyer who became chief editor of *Helsingin Sanomat,* Sakari Tuomioja prepared for his career by studying law. He was graduated from the University of Helsinki in 1936 with the B.C.L. degree and in 1937 received his Master of Civil and of Canon Law degree. Three years later he was called to the bar.

Indicative of the course his lifework was to take, Tuomioja's first employment after he left the university was as secretary of the financial committee of the Diet (Finnish parliament). At the end of two years (1938 to 1940) in this post, he became permanent secretary of the Ministry of Finance, a position that he filled until 1944. During World War II he also took on other public offices, some of which he retained in the postwar period: secretary to public auditors (1939 to 1940); referendary councillor of the Ministry of Finance and chief of the budget department (1940 to 1944); member of the state committee for public salaries (1941); member of the board of treasury office (1943); trustee of the Central Cooperative Relief Fund (1943); trustee of Cooperative Warehouse Elanto (1944), and member of the War-Indemnity Commission (1944).

At the conclusion of the Soviet-Finnish armistice in 1944, Tuomioja served as assistant Minister of Finance before being called upon to head that Ministry in 1945. He has been chiefly active in the economic postwar life of his country as governor of the Bank of Finland, an office which he accepted in 1945 and which he still holds. Concurrently he has been chairman of the board of management of the Post Savings Bank (since 1945), chairman of the state licensing board (1945 to 1949), chairman of the Finnish Foreign Trade Association (1945 to 1949), and chairman of Tervakoski Osakeyhtiö (since 1946).

The Finnish economic expert has represented his country abroad as a governor of the International Bank for Reconstruction and Development from 1948 to 1950 and since 1948 has been a governor of the International Monetary Fund. A specialized agency of the United Nations, the fund was established in Washington, D.C., in 1945 "to promote international monetary cooperation and the expansion of international trade; to promote exchange stability; to assist in the establishment of a multilateral system of payments in respect to current transactions between members" (*Information Please Almanac*).

Under the leadership of Premier Urho K. Kekkonen, a Finnish coalition Cabinet of three bourgeois political parties dominated by the Agrarians was formed on March 17, 1950. Tuomioja, who had agreed with the Agrarian party in its objection to the Social Democrats' wage policy, was named Minister of Commerce and Industry, and later served as Assistant Minister of Foreign Affairs. The following year in Kekkonen's third Cabinet, established on September 20, 1951, he held the portfolio of Minister of Foreign Affairs.

In keeping with the 1948 friendship and mutual assistance pact between Finland and the Soviet Union, Kekkonen's government had in 1950 entered into trade discussions with Russia which resulted on June 13 in a five-year trade and reparations agreement between the two nations covering the years from 1951 through 1955. Tuomioja was in charge of the negotiations for Finland. The agreement provides for the exchange of Soviet oil for Finnish houses, wooden ships, barges, and metal products.

After a year as Minister of Foreign Affairs, Tuomioja in September 1952 submitted his resignation to Finnish President Juho Kusti Paasikivi and when this resignation took effect he returned to his duties as governor of the Bank of Finland. As reported by the New

York *Times* (September 28, 1952), the Minister's "financial policy was criticized during the budget debate and at a meeting of the state bank by members of Parliament sitting on the bank's board of control. They said that the bank, which ought to be fully independent, was assuming more and more the character of the Cabinet's bank."

Sakari Tuomioja was formally installed in the office of Premier on November 17, 1953, after Kekkonen's Cabinet on November 4 had lost a parliamentary vote of confidence on his program to subsidize industrial construction. As head of a fifteen-member "caretaker" government of a number of political parties, the new Premier was appointed to hold office until the general elections of March 1954.

He named to his Cabinet four members of the Conservative party (which had directed the government during World War II and, which had not previously been represented in any postwar Cabinet). Members of the new government "agreed to forswear political affiliations and work as 'independents'" (*Christian Science Monitor,* November 18, 1953).

In a broadcast statement soon after his Cabinet came to power, Premier Tuomioja gave assurance that Finland would continue her policy of friendship "with all nations and especially the Soviet Union" (New York *Times,* November 18, 1953). A month later he announced that his government was about to begin negotiations in Moscow for a Soviet gold loan and also disclosed that Finland would ask that her surplus trade balance with Russia be paid in Western currencies or gold.

Like the preceding minority Agrarian government, Tuomioja's Cabinet faced pressing domestic problems of economic decline, rising unemployment and the threat of increased inflation. The budget that was submitted to the Diet in November recommended a cut from 1953's $888,000,000 to $658,000,000 for 1954 by reducing expenditures for welfare benefits, agricultural subsidies, education, and state employees.

The Diet defeated this economy program as it had earlier rejected Kekkonen's austerity budget. "The first task of the new government," reported the *Christian Science Monitor* (November 18, 1953), "is to boost exports by lowering prices of many of Finland's staple products." In this effort the country must look to Russia and eastern Europe, where since World War II her foreign trade has greatly expanded, as well as to Great Britain, Western Germany and the United States, which in 1953 held second, third and fourth place, respectively, in Finnish trade.

Tuomioja is a member of the board of several industrial enterprises: Veitsiluoto Oy, Oulu Oy, Outokumpu Oy, and Enso-Gutzeit Oy. For his achievements in public service he has been decorated commander of the Order of the Finnish Lion (1942), of the French Legion of Honor (1948) and of the Order of the White Rose of Finland (1948) and with the Swedish Grand Cross of the Order of Vasa (1952).

Married on March 18, 1939 to Vappu Illike Wuolijoki, daughter of the Finnish playwright, Hella Wuolijoki, Tuomioja has two children: a daughter, Tuuli Anneli, and a son, Erkki Sakari. The gray-eyed, fair-haired Finnish statesman stands about six feet tall and weighs about 200 pounds. His church is the Evangelical Lutheran.

References

N Y Herald Tribune p3 N 17 '53
International Who's Who, 1953
Who's Who in America, 1952-53
Who's Who in the United Nations (1951)
World Biography (1948)

UNDERHILL, RUTH M(URRAY) Aug. 22, 1884- Anthropologist; author

Address: h. 2623 S. Clayton St., Denver, Colo.

A deep interest in people and in social organizations carried Ruth Underhill through many experiences, many countries, and many university classrooms, but it was not until she was in her forties that she discovered anthropology where her scholarly, humane, poetical abilities found a useful outlet in studies of the Southwest Indians which brought her national recognition. Her many informative books interest not only specialists in her field but also the general public. She has also written several books to teach Indian children about their own background and culture.

In her latest book, *Red Man's America* (University of Chicago Press, 1953) Miss Underhill treats the Indians of the United States by regional divisions—the Southeast, Northeast, Great Lakes and Mississippi valley, the Plains, California and the Northwest, and the Southwest. She traces the history of the Stone Age hunters and the South American Indians as well. "The author includes brilliant selections from ethno-history. The result is a wonderfully packed storehouse of information" (*United States Quarterly Book Review,* September, 1953).

Ruth Murray Underhill was born in Ossining-on-the-Hudson, New York, on August 22, 1884. Her father, Abram Sutton Underhill, was a lawyer who practiced three days a week in New York City. Her mother was the former Anna Taber Murray. There were two younger sisters, Margaret and Elizabeth, and a younger brother, Robert. The Underhills traced their ancestry back to 1636 to the Indian fighter, Captain John Underhill. Ruth's grandfather, Robert Lindley Murray, owned a country house on Murray Hill in New York City where Madame Murray had entertained the British officers, thus aiding General Israel Putnam to escape. Their farm, Bellevue, was given to the city for a hospital. Later Robert Murray wrote one of the early grammars.

Ruth studied at the Ossining School for Girls and the Preparatory School for Bryn Mawr. She had the run of her father's large library, where there was much material on Darwin and the "new thought", and she began the study of

Glogau

RUTH M. UNDERHILL

Greek at the age of fourteen. At sixteen, she took a trip to Greece and saw the ancient ruins at Athens with an uncle, Augustus Murray, who was a professor of Greek.

She attended Vassar College, at Poughkeepsie, New York, majoring in English and winning a prize with an essay on Shakespeare. She was elected to Phi Beta Kappa, and her A.B. degree was conferred in 1905. She went to work in Boston as agent for the Massachusetts Society for the Prevention of Cruelty to Children. A year later, a trip abroad added to her knowledge of languages, of which she later spoke five fluently: French, German, Spanish, Italian, and Papago, the tongue of the Indians of southern Arizona. She took courses at the London School of Economics and at the University of Munich. She often lists mountain climbing as her favorite hobby, and at this time she tried her skill in the Austrian Tyrol.

After two years in Europe, she returned home to do social work at the Charity Organization Society in New York City (1913-1914). During the first World War she worked with the American Red Cross and did social service in Italy.

While in New York she visited Columbia University and inquired of the departments of economics, philosophy, and sociology, "What do you teach about the human race and how it got this way?" The answers seemed to her "very routine" until she met Professor Ruth Benedict (author of *Patterns of Culture*) in the anthropology department who welcomed her searching questions. And so began a long friendship which was "very valuable."

While studying for her doctorate at Columbia, Miss Underhill acted as assistant in anthropology to Dr. Gladys Reichard at Barnard College. In the summers, and for half a winter, she had fellowships from the Columbia Humanities Council to study two tribes of Indians in the Southwest, the Papago and then the Mohave. In 1935, when her thesis was printed, Columbia awarded her the Ph.D. degree.

In the course of her work on the fellowships, she was brought into close contact with the Indian Service, and she decided to enter government service. From 1933 to 1934 she was with the U.S. Department of Agriculture as soil conservationist. From 1934 to 1948 she worked for the U.S. Indian Service, the educational division of the U.S. Bureau of Indian Affairs, as consultant in anthropology, with the title of associate supervisor of Indian Education, and later supervisor (from 1942 to 1948).

She traveled to many Indian reservations and resided with the tribes for months at a time. Living in their midst and speaking their tongue enabled Dr. Underhill to establish her place as a friend within the tribes and to observe their ceremonies and government. These observations were passed on in reports to the Indian Service.

Striving to capture the poetic quality of the Indian's own literature at its best, Dr. Underhill wrote study books for Indian children giving them information of their heritage and helping them to understand the present. Dr. Underhill soon became an outstanding authority on Indian life. Her *Autobiography of a Papago Woman* was printed in the Memoirs of the American Anthropological Association, Number 46, 1936, her *Ethnobiology of the Papago Indians* (with C. F. Castetter) was in the University of New Mexico Bulletin in 1936, and *A Papago Calendar Record,* in the same publication in 1938.

With the appearance of *First Penthouse Dwellers in America* (The Pueblo Indians), brought out by J. J. Augustin, New York, in 1938, Dr. Underhill came to the attention of the general public. Oliver La Farge praised her work:

"Miss Underhill has been able to avoid the dry literalness which is the habitual scientific affectation . . . her work of equal merit has been put out in an unfrightening, attractive form" (*Saturday Review of Literature,* July 2, 1938).

Her translation of Indian songs, *Singing for Power,* was published the same year by the University of California Press, and in the July 2, 1938 issue of the *Saturday Review of Literature,* Oliver La Farge wrote, "It is a stroke of luck that a sound scientist, possessed of a genuine literary gift, should have come in contact with this delightful body of poetry. . . . There have been few scientists who added to their deep understanding of Indian poetry, their true sense of its background and purport, the ability to retain its literary worth in English. . . . There is a nice balance between her delightfully written explanations and the poems themselves."

Hawk over Whirlpools was brought out in 1940 by J. J. Augustin, New York, and the November 17, 1940 New York *Herald Tribune's* review concludes, "Ruth Underhill has a scholarly and humane intellect which is obviously saturated with Indian facts and lore. In this book she has taken a long step forward in literary skill as well."

By 1948, although her interest in Indians had not waned, she was weary of the endless traveling involved in her government position, so she resigned to become professor of anthropology at the University of Denver. She built a charming log home, with a mountain view, in the vicinity, and indulged in her love of gardening. She retired from active teaching in 1952, becoming professor emeritus of the department, in order to give more time to writing and to take a trip around the world. In 1953 she gave a number of lectures at the university.

In *Red Man's America* (1953) Dr. Underhill discusses the Indians who leave the reservations, who are interested in retaining their ancient cultures. To help them adjust to off-reservation life, she asks the white men to "help redeem their ancestors' mistakes by showing extra brotherhood and understanding to those Indians passing, one by one, into the new lifeway." She sees no end to "the Indian problem" today but "the amalgamation of white men and red, both racially and socially . . . here is a responsibility, not for the government, but for the average citizen."

Her writings not already mentioned, (in addition to articles and book reviews) comprise *The Papago Indians and their Relatives, the Pima* (U.S. Indian Service, 1940); *Indians of Southern California* (1938); *The Northern Paiute Indians,* (1945); *Pueblo Crafts* (1944); *Workaday Life in the Pueblos,* (1945), (published by the Haskell Institute, Lawrence, Kansas); *Indians of the Pacific Northwest, Social Organization of the Papago Indians* (Columbia University Press, 1939); *Papago Indian Religion* (Columbia University Press, 1946); *Ceremonial Factors in the Greater Southwest* (1948), and a section on Indians for the *World Book Encyclopedia,* 1946.

She is a member of the American Anthropological Association, American Association for the Advancement of Science, American Folklore Society, Society of American Archaeology, Society for Applied Anthropology, the Denver Women's Press Club, The Westerners (Denver), and is the present president of the Western Folklore Society.

Dr. Underhill is five feet six inches tall, weighs 140 pounds, has gray eyes and white hair. She is a Democrat and a Quaker.

References

Denver Clarion Ja 25 '49

American Men of Science (1949)
American Women, 1939-40
Directory of American Scholars (1951)
International Directory of Anthropologists (1940)

VANDENBERG, HOYT S(ANFORD) Jan. 24, 1899-Apr. 2, 1954 Air force officer; commissioned a second lieutenant in the U.S. air corps (1923) and rose to general (1947); served as assistant chief of staff of air force (1940-1941), chief of Northwest African Strategic Air Force (1942-1943), deputy commander in chief, A.E.F. (1944), commanding general U.S. 9th Air Force (1944); attended Quebec, Cairo and Teheran conferences; director of Central Intelligence (1946); chief of air staff, A.A.F. (1947); vice-chief of staff, U.S.A.F. (1947); chief of staff (1948-1953); advocate of a stronger and larger U.S. air force. See *Current Biography,* (Mar.) 1945.

Obituary

N Y Times p1+ Ap 3 '54

VANDERBILT, AMY July 22, 1908-
Author; journalist

Address: b. c/o Doubleday and Company, 575 Madison Ave., New York 22; h. "Daisyfields," Valley Forge Rd., Westport, Conn.

Amy Vanderbilt's Complete Book of Etiquette has been described by the author as "a guide to gracious living rather than a rulebook," and one which recognizes the increasing casualness of modern social life. Since Miss Vanderbilt's book was published by Doubleday in October 1952, it has sold more than 120,000 copies. She has contributed to newspapers and magazines since the early thirties.

Believing that there is nothing old-fashioned about good manners and good taste, Amy Vanderbilt has stated that changes in etiquette come about because of inventions, wars, political upheavals, legislation, and economic developments. Since the era of Mrs. Grundy, the bustle, and the Prince Albert beard ended a long time ago, she asserts that it is "patently ridiculous to live by rules laid down by . . . people of another century." The great houses, replicas of French châteaux, staffs of liveried servants, gala balls, and the formalities of endless course dinners are "as a dream that is told."

A fifth generation Staten Islander, Amy Vanderbilt is a descendant of the first Vanderbilt to settle in America, Jan Aoertsen van der Bilt, and of a first cousin of Commodore Cornelius Vanderbilt, the shipping and railroad magnate. Her great-great-grandfather was one of the founders of the Bank of Manhattan and her grandfather, Joseph L. Vanderbilt, invented the figure-eight stitch on baseballs. Born on July 22, 1908 to Joseph Mortimer Vanderbilt, an insurance broker, and Mary Estelle (Brooks) Vanderbilt, she is of Dutch, Irish and French stock.

"When I was a child," Miss Vanderbilt recalls, "Staten Island was a literary community. My parents knew many writers of the nineteenth century; among them were the poet Edwin Markham, George William Curtis (editor of *Harper's Weekly*), the Funks (who compiled the dictionary) and others." While attending Curtis High School, she worked on the newspaper, Staten Island *Advance,* as a society and feature writer. Later she became assistant advertising and publicity director of H. R. Mallinson Company, silk manufacturers. She was also a columnist for the International News Syndicate.

After studying home economics at the Institute Heubi in Lausanne, Switzerland, she attended Packer Collegiate Institute, Brooklyn, and New York University, the latter for two

Editta Sherman

AMY VANDERBILT

years (1926-1928) as a special student in journalism.

Miss Vanderbilt became the business manager of the *American Spectator* (a literary magazine) in 1933; home service director for Tower Magazines in 1934; from 1935 to 1939 she occupied herself with advertising, serving at one time as an account executive; and from 1939 to 1945 she was first vice-president and then president of Publicity Associates, Inc., a public relations firm in New York City whose clients included seventeen publishers.

When Doubleday asked her to write an etiquette book, she built herself a rustic office on the grounds of her home, "Daisyfields," in Westport, Connecticut. "I knew that it was going to be a four-year job," she said, "but I also knew that I wasn't going to let the prospect of that much steady writing and research get me down. And so it proved! What could possibly be more lively, while writing a book, than having two children born to keep our first active youngster company! While the babies slept, I wrote."

She said, "I feel living has changed so that it's almost silly to go into such things as the traditional formal dinner for thirty-four with a butler and several footmen." However, her publishers insisted that people like to read about such things, so she finally included chapters devoted to such traditional items as when to turn down a calling card, how to address the younger sons of a duke, and the proper uniform for a chambermaid. These subjects are outweighed in the book by discussions of contemporary problems and even a chapter on elopements and civil ceremonies.

"My great interest in children led me naturally to include, in my finished book," said Miss Vanderbilt, "an entire chapter on the family and social education of children." Other chapters are devoted to adoption of children, teen agers and their problems, and community relations.

She believes that "women are getting more and more into worthwhile community activities as their home lives are becoming simplified and informal. Fifty years ago it was important to have a maid on front door duty for afternoon callers." Now, the lady doesn't languish at home waiting for a caller but is "more likely to be found at some meeting of a community organization and doing some good."

The 700-page indexed volume is addressed "more to men than most etiquette books," since, the author observes, "men have a much better time of it socially in this more informal age." The author has stated that "the basis of good manners is kindness. I have no use for people who exhibit manners" (New York *Herald Tribune,* October 26, 1952).

In its review, *Time* (October 13, 1952) commented that Miss Vanderbilt writes with an "un-verbenaed frankness" and has "pushed the horizon of social propriety out to include such goings-on as divorce proceedings, the entertainment of problem drinkers, and appearances on television. She has not only viewed etiquette as a cradle-to-the-grave proposition, but turned out advice (most of it highly sensible) on every conceivable aspect of life."

Miss Vanderbilt has contributed to the *New Yorker, McCall's, Collier's, This Week, Better Homes & Gardens, American Home,* the *Christian Science Monitor* and the Los Angeles *Times.* She has written book reviews and feature stories for the New York *World-Telegram and Sun,* and has contributed to the *Book of Knowledge.*

She told an interviewer in the New York *Herald Tribune Books* (October 26, 1952): "I hate big parties. I like simplicity in people and in entertaining. . . . I have met all kinds of people, I like to talk to and hear them talk."

She was married to photographer Hans Knopf in 1945. This marriage ended in divorce in 1954. She has three sons, Lincoln Clark (by a previous marriage), Paul Vanderbilt Knopf and Stephen John Knopf. Miss Vanderbilt has "adopted" four more children in war-ravaged countries under the Foster Parents' Plan of which she is a sponsor. Active in various social work organizations, she has been an officer of the Westport Weston Mental Health Group.

Her hobby is collecting early American glass, on which she is an authority. She also collects old etiquette books and has for the past twelve years been "entertaining and etiquette director" for Royal Crest Sterling. She plans to keep her etiquette book constantly up to date. Meanwhile, her publishers, Doubleday, are syndicating parts of it to newspapers throughout the country for their women's pages.

The author is five feet three and a half inches tall, weighs 145 pounds, has gray eyes and blonde hair. Her political affiliation is Democrat and she belongs to the Protestant Episcopal church. She is a member of the Overseas Press Club of America. She has traveled abroad many times and has visited in almost every state in the Union, speaking on the radio and in person at clubs. Miss Vanderbilt speaks French fluently, and has a working knowledge of four other foreign languages. She has been known to prepare dinner for as many as eighteen guests who might include anyone from a British Lord to an Arab sheik. For relaxation she enjoys gardening and likes to fish. The well-stocked Saugatuck River passes through her property in Connecticut.

A cosmopolitan herself, Amy Vanderbilt speaks feelingly about manners in the larger sense. "Now that this country is host to the United Nations," she said, "we have broader opportunity for making people of different countries and traditions feel at home. We need to be aware of their social customs, which are often very strict, if we are to play the part of host gracefully."

References

Christian Sci Mon p12 O 9 '52
Denver Post O 25 '53
N Y Herald Tribune Book R p2 O 26 '52
American Women, 1939-40
Who's Who in New England (1949)

VAN HORNE, HARRIET May 17, 1920-

Radio and television critic

Address: b. c/o New York World-Telegram and Sun, 125 Barclay St., New York 7; h. 53 E. 75th St., New York 21

"Television has effected devastating changes in the entertainment industry," wrote Harriet Van Horne, radio and television critic of the New York *World-Telegram and Sun*. It has changed "the pattern of America's leisure, the character of its political campaigns. It has given small boys such new heroes as the spaceship pilot." As one who must spend the better part of her days and evenings watching the television screen, Miss Van Horne, with a newspaper background of more than fifteen years, twelve of which have been on the *World-Telegram*, reports to readers of her column (Monday through Friday) what she sees and hears over the air waves and coaxial cables.

Readers have come to expect from her trenchant, hard-hitting and often witty criticism. She has crusaded for educational programs which utilize showmanship in order to compete successfully with the professional entertainment programs. Her newspaper column and her articles in *Theatre Arts, House & Garden, Collier's, Holiday, Reader's Digest,* and other national magazines have attracted a wide following. Jack Gould, TV critic on the New York *Times,* described Miss Van Horne as "a young lady of charm, pulchritude and perceptive pen," who occupies "a unique niche in the ranks of . . . critics of the broadcasting arts."

She served her apprenticeship in journalism on newspapers in Rochester, New York and Greenwich, Connecticut, and in 1942 joined the staff of the New York *World-Telegram* as a radio columnist. In 1947 she conducted her own television show of interviews and "chatter." "In those days," she recalls, "it was about 110 degrees under the lights and the crewmen wore pith helmets. I feel that I was a pioneer in the medium." More recently she has appeared as a guest on several TV "panel" shows—among them *Meet the Girls* and *What's the Story?*

Harriet Van Horne is the youngest of the three daughters of Victor Cornelius Van Horne, a businessman now retired, and Gertrude Theall Van Horne. The family is of Dutch-English colonial ancestry. She was born on May 17, 1920 in Syracuse, New York, and was raised in that city and in Rochester and its suburbs. She attended high school in Syracuse, and, having been "bitten early by the journalism bug," she began work on a small weekly there and did reporting, proofreading, headline writing and miscellaneous tasks.

Since she was sixteen, Harriet Van Horne has said, "I have never been without a byline." Entering the College for Women of the University of Rochester in 1936, she majored in government and history and also took every drama course offered, plus some courses at The Eastman School of Music. She edited the college newspaper, *The Tower Times,* and was campus correspondent of the Rochester *Democrat and Chronicle.* During the summer she worked full time for the paper and tried her hand at society reporting. In addition to these activities during her undergraduate years, she wrote plays, worked on the college literary magazine, and served on the student government council.

After receiving the B.A. degree in 1940, Harriet Van Horne took a job on the Greenwich (Connecticut) *Time* as society editor. Now and then she covered fires and crimes. She also wrote features for the paper and once a week took her turn writing a column "about almost anything." One of her "scoops" was a story with photographs of one of Tommy Manville's weddings which took place in Greenwich. She was the only reporter-photographer on the scene, and her story was picked up by the wire services and sent across the country.

Determined to "crash the big city newspaper game," she sent "fistfuls of clippings" to Lee Wood at the *World-Telegram* and waited hopefully. He finally asked her to come in for an interview, and she was hired in September 1942 and assigned to write the radio column. Her work involved mainly reviewing radio programs, but she also discussed general trends in radio entertainment and interviewed radio personalities.

From the beginning, her column has been lively and outspoken. Frequently her comments have provoked controversy and criticism. In a column written for the New York *World-Telegram,* July 17, 1943 she listed as some of her special complaints: "women's chatter programs," talkative disc jockeys, "the vulgar outpourings of the soap opera," and the "bad taste" of commercials. In the same column, however, she praised some of the local stations which feature recordings of classical music, news reports, and announcements of civic and cultural events around New York.

(Continued next page)

HARRIET VAN HORNE

Some of these complaints were expanded in an article which Miss Van Horne wrote for *Vogue* (February 1944) entitled "Things I Hate in Radio" (reprinted in the *Reader's Digest,* June 1944). She listed a number of the clichés of radio entertainment—quiz programs, garrulous lady commentators, the affected pronunciation of news commentators and announcers, etc. Her article provoked *Variety* into publishing an editorial (February 2, 1944) called "'Hit and Run' Criticism" which protested that she presented only one side of the case and failed to cite the positive, "good" features of radio.

That Harriet Van Horne was, however, fully aware of her responsibility to offer constructive criticism of radio entertainment was shown in her article in the *Saturday Review of Literature* (February 19, 1944): "It is later than Radio Thinks: There Is Still only a Nodding Acquaintance with the World of Ideas." Here she again enumerated some of the ailments of radio. She argued that radio must "lift the level of the average taste." It must replace its "faith in the almighty dollar" with "a faith in the intelligence and integrity of the people." If this is done, she hopefully concluded, the radio listener can look ahead to great developments in international broadcasting—international forums, concerts, comedy programs, and dramas.

By 1947 Harriet Van Horne was supplementing her radio reports with news of the new medium, television. As television has come to dominate the home entertainment scene, she has devoted more and more space to it, although she continues to review radio shows and is by no means pessimistic about the future of radio. In May 1952 she wrote an article for *Theatre Arts* magazine called "Radio Grows Up," in which she reported that during the 1951-1952 season she found a number of programs that were intellectually "on a higher level." She wrote: "All in all, it looks as if radio is growing up. Or could it be that the nation is growing up, and radio, like everything else in this great land, is simply reflecting the nature and the whims of the people?"

With television as with radio, Miss Van Horne's standards are high. She has been outspoken in her condemnation of crime shows, violent melodramas, slapstick comedy, old movies, daytime soap operas and quizzes. "Are we a nation of morons?" she wrote indignantly in *Theatre Arts* (June 1952). "Do we all have mean little souls, beguiled by bloodshed, bored by beauty? To judge by the entertainment set before us these evenings, the television industry gives a strong affirmative in reply."

Again, however, as with radio a few years earlier, Miss Van Horne finds signs of many hopeful trends. "I like Sid Caesar and Imogene Coca," she told an interviewer in 1953, "the *Fred Waring Show,* the *Philco-Goodyear Playhouse,* the *Music Show,* and *Author Meets the Critics,* although I wish they'd discuss more fiction. I like Herb Shriner, but I'd like to see him in something other than that quiz show which I think demeans him. I like *Mr. Peepers* [Wally Cox], *Kukla, Fran and Ollie,* and *Zoo Parade,* excerpt for the snakes. I'm sure people would rather watch monkeys. I know I would. I like Bob and Ray and I think Edward R. Murrow's *See It Now* is a great show."

"There is no doubt about it," wrote Miss Van Horne in *House & Garden,* December 1952, "the home has been obliged to suffer many fools and mountebanks since the advent of TV. But the mail received by this critic-on-the hearth indicates that viewers are becoming increasingly show-wise; they can tell honest showmanship from exhibitionism. Credit for survival of certain quality programs can be laid directly at the door of the splendid citizens who state their feelings in writing to the networks and to the TV critics." She lists among the dramatic programs that have won and held audiences *I Remember Mama,* starring Peggy Wood; *Colgate Comedy Hour;* and the *Kraft Theater* (the grandsire of "live" dramatic shows).

Although TV is a long way from fulfilling its promise, she feels that audiences enjoy "programs on which public officials fight it out with the press and with each other, and the panel games where wits clash and ladies bare their shoulders. There is much to be said for the large piece of furniture in your living room."

An admirer of Katherine Mansfield, whom she considers "the finest short story writer of this century," she collects her books and in August 1953 discussed Miss Mansfield's work on the CBS radio program *Invitation to Learning.*

Miss Van Horne lists her recreations as reading and decorating. She candidly admits that she hates sports. An expert cook, she is now writing a cook book. She loves the theatre but rarely attends movies. She is five feet three and one-half inches tall and weighs ninety-eight pounds. Her colleague, William Peper, on the *World-Telegram and Sun* described her as "small and slender, has fragile good looks.... Along with her delicate white skin and soft blond hair there is a sardonic smile and an air of self-assurance indicating she is more than capable of holding her own in a rough business in the toughest city in the world" (*Scripps-Howard News,* December 1953).

She does most of her work at home in her Manhattan apartment. She views and listens to the shows, writes her column, and mails it to the newspaper by special delivery in the early hours of the morning. She is a member of the New York Newspaper Women's Club.

Since the advent of television her mail has greatly increased. TV addicts, it seems, are a vociferous lot and violent in their opinions. Her column has stirred up "some lovely storms." When she "panned" the Ford Anniversary Show some readers accused Miss Van Horne of being dyspeptic and frustrated. To this she sweetly replied, "I have never had an ulcer and I am very happy."

Employees on the *World-Telegram*'s copy desk say "she's a nice kid", "she can spell and her literary allusions are right."

Reference

Scripps-Howard N 8:3+ D '53 pors

VARGAS, GETÚLIO DORNELLES Apr. 19, 1883- Aug. 24, 1954 President of Brazil; joined Army (1899); received LL.B. degree from the University of Pôrto Alegre (1907); practised law privately (1908-1923); served in various capacities in Rio Grande do Sul state government and in Federal government; became provisional president of Brazil (1930) after a military *coup,* permanent president (1933); ruled until 1945 as virtual dictator; introduced many economic and political reforms; joined Allies in World War II; re-elected president of Brazil (1950); was unable to deal successfully with certain government problems and agreed to take a leave of absence in August 1954. See *Current Biography,* (May) 1951.

Obituary

N Y Times p1+ Ag 25 '54

VICTOR, SALLY (JOSEPHS) Feb. 23, 1905- Millinery designer

Address: b. 18 E. 53d St., New York 22; h. 1230 Park Ave., New York 28

The creator of many "firsts" in hat fashions, Sally Victor has been called "the dean of American millinery design." Among the best known of her designs are the baby bonnet, the collapsible straw hat, the Flemish sailor, war workers' turban, the Grecian pillbox the accordion and Chinese lantern silhouettes, and the airwave hat. She has been Mrs. Dwight D. Eisenhower's favorite milliner for many years, and eight designs in her 1954 collection were selected by the First Lady for spring headgear.

She received the Fashion Critics' Millinery Award in 1943. Mrs. Victor has always advocated making American fashion design first in importance in the world, whether it be in the field of dresses or hats, and she has contributed an important share in maintaining New York City's position as fashion center of the world. She is a frequent lecturer at fashion schools and on television programs and her "imaginative and inventive" collections always receive enthusiastic reviews in the press. The *New Yorker* (February 27, 1954) called her "a magnificent sculptress of straws and felts, [who] masks the basic mathematical precision of her hats with touches that are feminine without being unruly."

One of eight children, Sally Josephs was born on February 23, 1905 in Scranton, Pennsylvania. At the age of two Sally and her family moved to New York City where she has made her home ever since. Under her mother's guidance Sally learned to sew her own clothes and help with her sisters'. It was during one of these sessions that experimentation with thirty cents worth of hatbraid led to her becoming the hatmaker for the family. She continued to increase her skill in design and her knowledge of the technical side of hat-making during the hours she spent after school in her aunt's millinery shop.

Despite her gift for hat designing, Sally Victor decided to become a school teacher. However, her plans did not materialize. She took a "summer job" at the age of eighteen as stockgirl in Macy's millinery department, and at the end of the summer had become head stock-girl. Her salary had been increased from twenty-five to forty dollars in four weeks.

In a year she had become assistant millinery buyer at Macy's, and from there, in 1926, she moved to Newark, New Jersey's department store, L. Bamberger's (not at that time associated with R. H. Macy's) to become head millinary buyer at the then unusually high salary of a hundred dollars a week.

On March 4, 1927 she married Sergiu F. Victor, head of the wholesale millinery house of Sergé. By 1932 she had become the chief designer of her husband's firm, and twenty of the best known retail stores in the country sold hats under her label—Sally Victor. In the same year her hats attracted the attention of Miss Dorothy Shaver of Lord & Taylor's, who sponsored her as that store's first Young American Designer.

Sally Victor opened her own retail millinery salon in September, 1934, at a time when the millinery industry was suffering acutely, due to the economic depression and mechanical improvements which had displaced many handworkers. Her shop catered to prominent members of society and of the entertainment world. Her prices for her original creations at that time started at $16.50. Today, they are upwards of fifty dollars.

Six months after the opening of her own store Mrs. Victor employed two assistant designers and thirty-five workers. At that time *Fortune* magazine said of her: "The name of Sally Victor stands with Lilly Daché and John Frederics at the very top of U.S. style leaders although her modernistic, white retail salon in New York's East 50's has been open only since September. . . . Since she has been in the

SALLY VICTOR

U. S. millinery business longer than Daché and John and Frederic, Sally Victor can be called the dean of the smartest U. S. [millinery] designers and a bright prospect in the retail field . . . based on her cunning as a designer and her own easy informality."

Because of her combination of originality and talent and her shrewd business sense, the Sally Victor salon has always prospered. She has met conditions of the times as a challenge. When materials used in hat manufacture were scarce during World War II, she did not depend on textile manufacturers but experimented with fabrics, often dying and weaving them in her own establishment to get the effects she wanted.

It was the revival of the sailor hat which brought Sally Victor her first fame. American design was coming into its own. Clare Potter was making a name for herself by creating the casual dresses which were the beginning of the American look, and Sally Victor was defying the dictates of Paris at a time when French modistes were promoting top-heavy hats for women.

During World War II, when Paris lost its style leadership, Sally Victor pressed vigorously for the strengthening of the position of American fashion design. To this end, in 1942 she and two other prominent figures in hat design, Lilly Daché and Mr. John of John Frederics sat down together at the request of the millinery industry, to create fall and winter trends in hats. The hats they inspired were labeled "Millinery Fashion Inspiration, Inc." This idea followed the tradition of the great Parisienne modistes who had in the past collaborated to create fashion trends.

During the war she designed a beret for the U. S. Cadet Nurse Corps, and for General Electric Company she created a flattering denim work hat to which was attached an adjustable snood of self-fabric to confine the long hair of women workers so as to prevent accidents.

In the 1952 Presidential campaign she designed a popularly priced "I like Ike" hat for women. It was a light blue faille pillbox beret with a red faille cockade to which an "I like Ike" button could be attached. It was sponsored by the Wilton, Connecticut committee for Eisenhower and was modeled at the Hotel Statler by Mrs. John Davis Lodge, wife of the Governor of Connecticut. Mrs. Victor also designed her successful airwave hat especially for Mrs. Eisenhower at this time.

Mrs. Victor, who has designed hats for Mrs. Eisenhower for many years, said that an increasing number of her customers ask, "What's Mamie getting?" before making their own selections. They may buy a design similar to one ordered by the First Lady, Mrs. Victor explained, "but never a duplication, because each of her hats is made to order."

The designer has frequently gone to museums for inspiration and she has borrowed from periods in American history which have never before been used in hat creation. The Louisiana Purchase and the western Mormon Empire have both been subjects for Sally Victor hats, the latter having inspired the still popular baby bonnet (taken from the demure bonnets of Brigham Young's wives).

Speaking at a "Fashion is an Art" luncheon given in May 1953 in behalf of the costume collection of the Smithsonian Institution in Washington, D.C., Mrs. Victor said: "Museums have helped me so much, I want to do anything I can to help them. . . ."

Visitors to the Brooklyn Museum in the spring of 1942 were startled to see, alongside ancient headgear, an exhibit of modern hats created by Sally Victor and inspired by the museum's own treasures. For example, Mrs. Victor contrived a black net dinner hat edged in jet beads and draped in black maline which took its inspiration from a century-old Formosa wooden hunting hat. Another Victor-designed hat had an up-flung brim lined in a design of flat, bright feathers, suggested by a thousand-year-old Tiahuanaco headdress in the museum's collection and once worn by a Peruvian Inca priest.

Because the year 1954 commemorates the 700th anniversary of the birth of Marco Polo and the 500th anniversary of the capture of Constantinople, Sally Victor designed hats inspired "by the rich splendor of Constantinople's mosaics, the gold and silver pillars of its churches, the opulence of Cathay, Byzantium, India, Persia and Arabia." Her 1954 designs include hats shaped like Chinese lanterns, Oriental fans, geisha bonnets, Chinese pinwheels, and Ali Baba "topknots." Her choice of colors also reflect her interest in the Far East: she has named them "Bagdad Blue", "Sinbad Red," "Arabian Nights Pink", "Damsel" and "Aladdin." She even designed a hat "Garden of Eden", complete with apple and serpent.

To Mrs. Victor, fashion flair is a sixth sense. She explains: "[It is] a vision that translates harmony of line and color into the practical channel of daily use. Logic, precision, and a healthy technical knowledge are all absolutely essential." Her school-teaching ambitions were partly realized when, for several years, she conducted a class in millinery design at New York University.

She also conducts forums and is a consultant for Hollywood film companies. Her hats have been carried by Patterns of the Times, American Designer Series, making it possible for women to cut and sew their own Sally Victor hat, plus weskit and handbag. She has lectured before women's clubs, girls' schools and other groups interested in millinery and in hat-making.

Sally Victor has received from leading New York fashion critics such accolades as "Sally, the magician"; "the inventive Mrs. Victor"; "sensible, entertaining, brilliant, thanks to a little thing called genius which apparently Mrs. Victor has"; "the Frank Lloyd Wright of millinery" and [creator of] "beauty with function."

Many of the stars of stage and screen are her customers. Irene Dunne, Helen Hayes and Merle Oberon are among those who regularly wear Sally Victor hats. For the inauguration of Dwight D. Eisenhower on January 20, 1953 Mrs. Eisenhower wore Miss Victor's "Airwave" hat, in grey felt to match her grey suit. This design was described as 'a ripply, cut-out treatment of felt. The lining of green felt showed through the cut-outs."

Once she was asked about the right of a husband to criticize a woman's taste in hats. "Criticizing a hat", she replied, "is a psychological outlet . . . it's a way he has for letting off steam" (New York Close-Up, New York *Herald Tribune,* April 30, 1951).

There is a keen need for creative young designers in millinery, Mrs. Victor believes. Her advice to young girls with talent is to forget about copying, to look ahead and not backward. "So long as you make hats that become women, that make them look prettier than they really are, the world is yours," she said. She thinks the best way to start on a hat designing career is to get into a department store. There a young woman will find not only ready fields for her talent but also good experience in business, facts and figures (*Successful Women,* by Isabel Taves).

A brunette of medium height, Mrs. Victor likes to paint, and to collect miniature pieces of silver and furniture. She has one son, Richard Michael Victor, born in 1932, and now a student at Columbia University.

References

Collier's 103:15 Mr 11 '39 por
Ind Woman 21:109 Ap 42 por
N Y Herald Tribune p9 Ap 30 '51
N Y Times p33 O 16 '50
N Y World-Telegram p16 Ja 8 '54
Washington (D.C.) Post p14 My 30 '53
Taves, I. Successful Women (1943)
Who's Who In America, 1952-53
Who's Who in Commerce and Industry (1948)

VISCARDI, HENRY, JR. May 10, 1912- Social service organization official; manufacturer

Address: b. Just One Break, Inc., Bellevue Hospital, 411 First Ave., New York 10; Abilities, Inc., 59 Railroad Ave. East, West Hempstead, Long Island, N.Y.; h. 307 Steamboat Rd., Kings Point, Long Island, N.Y.

Instead of parades, pensions and pity, handicapped people want the opportunity to live productive lives and to support their families in dignity—this is the credo of Henry ("Hank") Viscardi, Jr., executive director of Just One Break, an organization formed at Bellevue Hospital in New York City to find employment for amputees and victims of polio and cerebral palsy. He is also the president and manager of Abilities, Inc., an electronics manufacturing enterprise which employs only severely handicapped persons. Viscardi himself must be included in that classification; he walks on artificial limbs.

As a special Red Cross officer in World War II, he did much to restore the morale of hospitalized servicemen, especially the more seriously injured of Air Force pilots. Viscardi's autobiography, *A Man's Stature,* was published by the John Day Company in 1952 and contains a foreword by Bernard Baruch.

The only boy in a family of five children, Henry Viscardi, Jr., was born on May 10, 1912 in New York City to his Italian-born parents, Henry and Anna (Esposito) Viscardi. Young "Hank" was born without feet or knees; he spent the first seven years of his life in hospitals, where he underwent a series of operations which made it possible for him to move about "on two short stumps encased in padded boots that resembled boxing gloves" (Lois Mattox Miller in the *Reader's Digest,* July, 1952).

Because Hank's arms reached almost to the ground as he propelled himself along, the neighborhood children called him "Ape Man"—but a good disposition and intelligence enabled him to laugh at his nickname.

He completed both primary and secondary schooling in eight years. Despite his handicap, Hank Viscardi was keenly interested in sports, and at the Newtown High School in Queens, New York was made manager of the basketball team.

Henry Viscardi, Sr. died while his son was still in high school; the boy helped his elder sister in the support of the family by earning money as a basketball referee and as a reporter on school athletics for the New York *Times.* After graduation from Newtown High School in 1930 he entered Fordham University, earning tuition and living expenses by both manual and office work. He majored in science and made honor grades, but left Fordham without taking a degree, having obtained a full-time job in the taxation division of the Home Owners Loan Corporation. He also attended night courses at the Law School of St. John's University in Brooklyn.

When Viscardi was twenty-six, an elderly German craftsman named George Dorsch solved the difficult problem of fitting him with

Sanderson-Almquist, Inc.

HENRY VISCARDI, JR.

artificial legs; and, after persistent practicing under Dorsch's tutelage he learned to walk with only a slightly perceptible limp and even learned to dance. Viscardi borrowed the money to pay for the limbs which raised his stature by fully twenty-four inches, but when he broached the matter of a fee to Dr. Robert R. Yanover, whose patient he had been since childhood, the orthopedic surgeon shook his head. "There is no bill, Hank," Lois Mattox Miller quotes Yanover as saying. "But some day, when you get the chance, do something to help other cripples. Then our account will be settled." (Viscardi himself has named Dr. Yanover as the first of the four individuals who most greatly influenced him in making his lifework the service of handicapped persons; the others are Bernard M. Baruch, Mrs. Eleanor Roosevelt and Orin Lehman.)

Thus when the United States entered World War II, Viscardi eagerly sought an opportunity to assist in the rehabilitation of amputees; and after rejection by the Army, Navy and Marines for any type of service, was accepted by the Red Cross as a special field-service officer. At Fort Dix, New Jersey, where he underwent the regular basic training, his ability to drill and march attracted such attention that he was sent to the Walter Reed Hospital in the District of Columbia. Here he achieved his objective of working with amputees and by encouragement and example did much to restore the morale of the permanently injured, particularly among pilots of the Army Air Forces.

Nevertheless, certain officials were critical of his activities and sought his removal. However, Colonel Howard A. Rusk, the medical officer in charge of the Army Air Forces convalescent training centers, protested and brought the Viscardi matter to the attention of General H. H. ("Hap") Arnold, commanding general of the AAF. As a consequence of Arnold's intervention, Viscardi was retained in the service as a "special consultant on problems of employment of disabled veterans," and as an "adviser" to both the surgeon general of the Air Forces and the director of the War Production Board.

During the latter part of the war he spoke frequently at industrial plants and before civic groups, in the interests of the handicapped veteran. "To prove that a properly rehabilitated cripple could work competitively with other men," states Lois Mattox Miller, "he often signed on for a job in a shop or factory. Then, having proved himself, he would reveal to his bosses that he was a legless man." For two years Viscardi worked as assistant director of special events and sports for the Mutual Broadcasting Company, and in 1947 became personnel director of Burlington Mills, Inc.

When the New York University-Bellevue Institute of Physical Medicine and Rehabilitation was established, the director, Colonel Howard A. Rusk, found it difficult to find work for his discharged patients. In 1949 the JOB ("Just One Break") Committee (later Just One Break, Incorporated) was formed with Bernard M. Baruch, Bernard F. Gimbel, Mrs. Eleanor Roosevelt, and others as an advisory board. Orin Lehman, a nephew of former Governor Herbert H. Lehman, and himself a World War II amputee, was made president. Dr. Rusk offered Viscardi the position of executive director, which entailed considerable personal financial sacrifice for Viscardi, since it meant giving up his $15,000 a year position at Burlington Mills. Remembering his promise to Dr. Yanover to help the disabled, he assumed the direction of JOB in January, 1950.

The placement campaign was developed by Viscardi on the assumption that the correct approach to industry was not an appeal to compassion but a better understanding by employers of the abilities of the handicapped by fitting the right man to the right job. One of his earliest successes was the placing with a New York hotel of a Navy veteran who had lost a hand, and whose steel-hook replacement proved not a liability but an asset in removing glasses from steam sterilizers without danger of scalding.

The Hilton Hotel Corporation was one of the earliest concerns to cooperate with JOB; others include Lever Brothers, Metropolitan Life Insurance Company, Sperry Corporation, Ford Instrument Company, and International Business Machines. Nevertheless, for the first two years it was difficult to obtain the cooperation of industry, as evidenced by an address made by Viscardi to a National Office Management Association conference on October 21, 1951 in which he stated that government agencies were showing greater interest than private industry in the placement of the physically handicapped.

However, by the end of 1952 JOB had assisted in the employment of "several thousand" partially incapacitated persons (including deaf and blind individuals and victims of polio and cerebral palsy as well as amputees) in productive work. Many of these persons had been on relief or languishing in hospitals for years. The organization had also established JOB committees in twelve cities outside of New York.

It was to provide employment for certain more difficult cases that Abilities, Inc. was established at West Hempstead, Long Island in 1952 with Viscardi as president and general manager. In an article in *Office Executive Magazine,* Viscardi has characterized this venture as not "another charity" but "a legitimate American business, operating in free and open competition, perpetuating its existence on its ability to operate at a profit."

The plant, which was designed by Jeff Friend, process layout engineer with the Sperry Gyroscope Corporation, specializes in making electronic equipment, and is "geared" to accommodate fifty workers. The first five employees to report had, states Viscardi, "but one usable leg among them and eight arms in all." Nevertheless "this same unit of workers in a week's time was producing a harness wiring assembly" for the automatic firing mechanism of Sabre jets used in the Korean War.

Viscardi has served on an Office of Defense Mobilization Task Force Committee under Charles E. Wilson, and is a member of the President's Committee on the Employment of the Physically Handicapped. Organizations of which Henry Viscardi, Jr. is a member include the New York Personnel Management Association, Office Executives Association, National Rehabilitation Association, and National Office Management Association. He is also a faculty member of the New York University College of Medicine. He has contributed articles to several periodicals.

When the elder statesman Bernard Baruch was named Citizen of the Year in June 1953 by the Junior Order, United American Mechanics, he accepted the sheepskin scroll and gold medal which go with the honor, but directed that the $5,000 award be given to Viscardi for his work in making useful citizens out of handicapped persons.

For the second straight year the Advertising Men's Post 209 of the American Legion presented in May 1954 Viscardi with $5,000 to help rehabilitate disabled veterans.

Mrs. Viscardi, a cartographer before her marriage on November 16, 1945, is the former Lucille Darracq; the Viscardis have three daughters, Nina, Donna and Lydia. Viscardi, who stands at five feet eight inches on his artificial limbs, weighs around 180 pounds; his eyes are brown, his hair black. He is a Roman Catholic. For recreation he enjoys sailing on Long Island Sound.

"If we can only get more people thinking along the lines of *ability* rather than *disability,*" wrote Viscardi. "All of us are physically limited. It is just a matter of degree. Steeled in the crucible of suffering, many of the disabled have developed compensatory qualities to offset the extremes of physical makeup."

References

Collier's 126:22+ Ag 19 '50 pors
N Y World-Telegram p31 Je 8 '53
Viscardi, H. A Man's Stature (1952)

VOGEL, HERBERT D(AVIS) Aug. 26, 1900- United States Government official; engineer

Address: b. c/o Tennessee Valley Authority, New Sprankle Bldg, Knoxville, Tenn.

In a widely praised nonpolitical appointment, President Dwight D. Eisenhower in August 1954 named Brigadier General Herbert D. Vogel of the Army Corps of Engineers, as chairman of the board of directors of the Tennessee Valley Authority. Vogel took office on September 1, immediately after his retirement from the Army, for a term that will expire in 1963. During his career of thirty years in the Army Engineers, he had won a high reputation as an expert on water problems and flood control, and is credited with having introduced into the United States large-scale experimental hydraulics. He was promoted to the rank of brigadier general on January 16, 1954.

TVA, a subject of political controversy since its inception in 1933, has been a central part of the current national debate over public-versus-private power. Generally believed to favor a cooperative or partnership approach to the problem, Vogel was described in *Time* and the *Christian Science Monitor* as a "caretaker" of TVA who would assure its efficient operation without diminishing or expanding it.

Herbert Davis Vogel was born to Lewis P. and Pearl M. (Davis) Vogel on August 26, 1900 in Chelsea, Michigan where he grew up, and was graduated from the local high school in 1918. After a two-year course (1918-1920) at the University of Michigan in Ann Arbor, he entered the U.S. Military Academy, from which he holds a B.S. degree.

He was sent to Fort Belvoir, Virginia for three years, where in 1925-1926 he attended the Army's Engineer School. In 1927 Vogel enrolled at the University of California, and upon receiving his M.S. degree in engineering in 1928, studied under an exchange scholarship at the Berlin Technical University in Germany for his Dr. Ing. degree, granted in 1929. He returned to the University of Michigan a few years later for a course in experimental hydraulics and received a C.E. degree in 1932.

"Academic knowledge," Vogel was to say many years later (1952), "is of value only when it has the ultimate application in the service of humanity" (New York *Times,* August 3, 1954). He was given the opportunity to make such application of his technical training in 1930 when he was appointed director of the Waterways Experiment Station in Vicksburg, Mississippi. Charged with designing, constructing and operating the station, he introduced the technique of open channel experimentation and developed its procedures and science.

"Vogel did some of the most important work of his life at Vicksburg," reported *Time* (August 16, 1954), "on his knees with a grapefruit knife in his hand, digging out the first scale models of American rivers. He recalls that many top engineers ridiculed the project, and Vogel for making 'mud pies,' but the Vicksburg scale models now allow the engineers to

BRIG. GEN. HERBERT D. VOGEL

predict and combat great river floods with amazing accuracy." It was Vogel's experimental laboratories that were used in 1952 to chart the course of the Missouri River flood.

Leaving Vicksburg in 1934, Vogel studied at the Command and General Staff School at Fort Leavenworth, Kansas until 1936. He was sent to Hawaii for two years as adjutant with the Third Engineers at Schofield Barracks. Later as an instructor at the Fort Belvoir Engineer School (1938-1940), Vogel taught river and harbor engineering, flood-control engineering and public speaking. During the period from 1930 to 1940 he also contributed a number of technical articles on experimental hydraulics to professional journals.

After serving as assistant to the district Army engineer in Pittsburgh, Pennsylvania (1940-1942), he was appointed district engineer in 1942, and was responsible for constructing ten large flood control dams, and operating the navigation systems of the Ohio, Monongahela and Allegheny rivers. He was also engaged in the building of war facilities, including TNT plants, airfields, cantonments, and industrial plants during the early years of World War II.

By 1942 Vogel had advanced to the (temporary) rank of colonel. Following a course at the Army and Navy Staff College, he was sent to the Pacific in 1944, where he held logistical commands in Australia, New Guinea, the Philippine Islands, and Japan. His first postwar assignment was the position of district Army engineer in Buffalo, New York (1945-1949) where he was concerned with the building of flood control dams, and with the maintenance and development of all harbors on Lake Erie and Lake Ontario.

Next stationed in the Panama Canal Zone, he served as engineer of maintenance for the Canal in 1949-1950, and in 1950 was appointed lieutenant governor of the Canal Zone. From 1950 to 1952 he was also director and vice-president of the Panama Canal Company, a corporation that operates and maintains the Panama Railroad and Panama Steamship Line (of which Vogel had been a director and vice-president in 1949-1950), the Panama Canal, and ten commissaries. It provides as well for all public utilities and for such facilities as hotels, printing plants and restaurants.

When Vogel left the Canal Zone, he went to Dallas, Texas to become in June 1952 division engineer of the Southwest division of the Army Corps of Engineers. He had charge of districts at Fort Worth, Albuquerque, Galveston, Tulsa and Little Rock, carrying out civil and military construction in eight states of the Southwest. As described in *Engineering News* (August 7, 1952), "the military construction program in the division is one of the largest in the United States and the civil works program covers a variety of coastal and river basin projects."

Vogel, who had earlier been a member of the Beach Erosion Board (1947-1949), was also made a member of the Mississippi River Commission (1952-1954) and of the Board of Engineers for Rivers and Harbors (1952-1954). He was a representative as well of the Department of the Army on the International Boundary and Water Commission for the Rio Grande.

For two years (1952-1954) he held the chairmanship of the Arkansas-White-Red Basins Interagency Committee, which comprises Federal and state agencies engaged in developmental soil and water projects affecting one-eleventh of the United States. "Our job," he told the committee in 1952, "is . . . primarily to help the people make better use of their soil and water resources, and secondarily to give to those who follow us . . . the value of experience we gain here" (*Engineering News,* August 7, 1952).

Brigadier General Vogel was named by President Eisenhower on August 2, 1954 to the three-man board of directors of the Tennessee Valley Authority. It was announced that after Senate confirmation of the nomination, the President would designate the Army engineer to succeed Gordon R. Clapp as TVA chairman for a nine-year term at a salary of $15,000 annually. The other two TVA board directors are Dr. Harry A. Curtis, vice-chairman, and Dr. Raymond R. Paty.

Testifying for several hours before the Senate Public Works Committee on August 9 and 10, Vogel repeated earlier statements that he believed in the "wisdom and feasibility" of TVA. The Senate approved Vogel's nomination on August 11. Earlier, in the Public Works Committee, Senator Wayne Morse of Oregon had opposed the appointment, primarily because he objected to naming a military officer to a high civilian post. Vogel took his oath of office as chairman of the TVA board of directors on September 1, the day after his retirement from military service.

The Tennessee Valley Authority, which was established in 1933, is a Federal project serving seven Southern States. "Its purpose, first and foremost," a *Christian Science Monitor* editorial recently emphasized, "was to rehabilitate a washed-out, farmed-out valley." It handles problems of flood control, river navigation, land conservation and generation of electrical power. About half of its power output at present is used to supply atomic energy installations and other government undertakings connected with national defense. It is estimated that 75 per cent of its output will go into defense production by the middle of 1956.

According to a TVA report issued in August 1954, during the last twenty years the authority has spent $1,555,009,825 in the purchase of machines, services and raw materials, and has built twenty dams at a cost of $760,000,000. The completion in 1956 of six steam plants now under construction will make TVA the world's largest integrated power supply system.

On September 3, 1954 Vogel and Major General K. D. Nichols, general manager of the Atomic Energy Commission, declared jointly that a "meeting of the minds has been reached on all the fundamental issues" of the proposed (Edgar H.) Dixon-(E. A.) Yates contract. According to the New York *Herald Tribune* (September 4, 1954) the proposed contract provides for the construction, by the Dixon-Yates combine (Middle South Utilities, Inc., and the Southern Company), of "a 600,000-kilowatt plant in Arkansas. . . . The power from this plant would be fed into the TVA system, which serves Memphis among other places, to replace power sold by TVA to the AEC for its plants in Kentucky."

On November 11, 1954 the contract was signed by the Atomic Energy Commission and the Dixon-Yates combine. The final draft provides for a limit on the earnings of the private company of $600,000 a year and "possible recapture" of the plant by the government within three years after the contract becomes effective.

Vogel, a registered professional engineer in New York and Texas, belongs to the American Society of Civil Engineers, and the Society of American Military Engineers. He is an honorary member of Scabbard and Blade of the University of California, and his clubs are the Army and Navy in Washington, D.C., and the Downtown in Dallas.

Married on December 23, 1925 to Loreine Elliott, Vogel is the father of two sons, Herbert D. Vogel, Jr., and Richard E. Vogel. He has black hair, brown eyes, stands five feet nine inches tall and weighs 170 pounds. His church is the Episcopal. He is the recipient of the Legion of Merit and the Distinguished Service Medal. In welcoming his appointment to the TVA board, American press editorials referred to the engineer as "an able and experienced citizen" and as "an administrator of integrity."

References

N Y Herald Tribune p 1+ Ag 3 '54; II p 1 Ag 8 '54; II p3 Ag 15 '54 por
N Y Times p 1+ Ag 3 '54; p19 S 2 '54
Time 64:19 Ag 16 '54

American Men of Science (1949)
Who's Who in America, 1954-55
Who's Who in Engineering, 1948

WAGNER, ROBERT F(ERDINAND), JR. Apr. 20, 1910- Mayor of New York City

Address: b. City Hall, New York 7; h. Gracie Mansion, New York 28

As New York City's 102d mayor, Robert F. Wagner, Jr., fills one of the most difficult and important executive posts in the United States. He was elected to the mayoralty from his position as president of the Borough of Manhattan in November 1953, after having held various municipal offices since 1947 and earlier a seat in the Assembly of New York State.

Wagner's election was generally viewed in the press as a victory for the liberal wing of the Democratic party, since the new mayor's political ideas are similar to those expounded by his father, the late Robert F. Wagner, for many years a prominent U. S. Senator, sponsor of New Deal legislation and judge of the Supreme Court of the State of New York.

Commenting on New York's mayoralty election, the *Christian Science Monitor* wrote: "It is a gigantic task to initiate the governmental reforms New York City must make to function efficiently. . . . Mr. Wagner knows too well that the complex problems of this city of 8,000,000 inhabitants with its $1,500,000,000-a-year expense budget, will be up to his administration . . . But such a feat is required . . if his long-cherished ambition to succeed to the senatorial mantle worn so successfully by his father is to be realized" (December 7, 1953).

The only child of Robert F. and Margaret (McTeague) Wagner, Robert Ferdinand Wagner, Jr., was born on April 20, 1910, in Manhattan's Yorkville, a district that his father had earlier (1905-08) represented in the New York State Assembly. His mother having died when he was nine years old, the boy was reared largely by his father, with whom he traveled in Europe during summer vacations, often to Nastatten, Hesse-Nassau, in Germany, the elder Wagner's birthplace. As a result of these trips he learned to speak French and German. Young Robert also accompanied his father, who served in the U.S. Senate from 1927 to 1949, on his campaigns and at the age of six was his page in the state Senate. Growing up in an atmosphere of liberal political thought, he acquired many of his views about social reform that later marked his career in government.

Robert Wagner, Jr., attended public school in Yorkville, St. Ignatius Loyola School, and later the Taft School in Watertown, Connecticut. His sports in preparatory school were football and basketball, while public speaking and debating also held his interest. He entered Yale University where he played lacrosse and basketball and was manager in his senior year of the university baseball team. After graduating from Yale in 1933 he studied at the Yale Law School for the degree of bachelor of laws (1936) and Harvard University for bachelor of business administration (1937). He also spent a summer (1934) at the School of International Relations in Geneva, Switzerland, where he gave his attention mainly to labor relations.

(Continued next page)

ROBERT F. WAGNER, JR.

"Young Bob," a nickname given him by Senator Wagner's colleagues, was elected in 1937 at the age of twenty-seven to the New York State Assembly from the Sixteenth Assembly District, which his father had once represented. In the Albany legislature, to which he was twice re-elected, he introduced a Democratic bill for a long-range housing program and offered legislation relating to compulsory health insurance and improved labor relations.

Some years later, acknowledging that his father's reputation had been an influential factor in his career, Wagner stated "my father helped me get started in politics and his name still helps. Although I want to stand on my own record and my own two feet, my father's record sets a pretty high standard" (New York *Times,* October 17, 1953).

With the outbreak of World War II, Wagner was the first member of the Assembly to resign his seat to volunteer for war service. He entered the Eighth Bomber Command as a lieutenant in 1941, was attached for a time to SHAEF in Europe and was discharged in 1945 as a lieutenant colonel with six battle stars and the Croix de Guerre.

About a month after leaving the armed forces, Wagner was appointed by New York City's Mayor William O'Dwyer, in January 1946, as a city tax commissioner. In December of that year he was made commissioner of housing and buildings to supervise the city's 700,000 buildings and as such advocated a strict enforcement of multiple-dwelling laws. "We need an educational program to bring this slum condition to the attention of all the people," he stated. "If the people knew more of the facts, there would be a great clamour to do more about it" (New York *Post,* January 20, 1947).

Relinquishing his post as commissioner of housing and building, Wagner became chairman of the city planning commission. Two years later he made a successful bid as the Democratic-Liberal candidate for the Manhattan borough presidency, defeating Oren Root, his Republican-Fusion opponent, by a vote of 353,644 to 143,898. His four-year term as president of the Borough of Manhattan, an office giving him two votes on New York's board of estimate, expired in December 1953. Wagner's first political defeat came in August 1952 when he sought the Democratic nomination for a seat in the United States Senate, from which his father had recently retired. He lost the nomination to John Cashmore of Brooklyn.

As the candidate of the liberal faction of the Democratic party in New York City, Wagner won the nomination for mayor in the September 15, 1953 primary election by a plurality of 169,199 votes over incumbent Mayor Vincent R. Impellitteri. In his campaign for the November election, Robert Wagner had the endorsement of many national leaders of the Democratic party.

His program was outlined in an address before the state convention of the Congress of Industrial Organizations in September. (The candidate was endorsed by the state CIO, the New York City CIO Council and the AFL Central Trades and Labor Council of Greater New York.) Pledging himself to strict law enforcement, appointment of expert administrators, he also promised establishment of a civil rights commission, reorganization of the civil service commission, encouragement of both low-rent and middle-income housing, creation of a city traffic control board and traffic advisory committee and strengthening of the water front police squad.

On the question of city finances he urged abolition of existing nuisance taxes and redistribution of the taxing powers between the city and the state. In a later compaign speech Wagner said that he would be a "fighting mayor" who would protest in Washington against the Labor-Management Relations Act of 1947 and the Immigration and Nationality Act of 1952 and in Albany against increases in rent and transit fares.

An appraisal of Wagner's qualifications for Mayor made by the non-partisan Citizens Union in October 1953 pointed to his "consistent interest in the problems of housing, education, labor and public health." This report read "he has shown initiative in inviting public cooperation, particularly in the establishment of district planning boards throughout the Borough of Manhattan. His conduct in office has demonstrated general party regularity, with some independence, and the circumstances of the recent primary have left him in an unusually good position to disregard pressures from discredited elements within his party" (New York *Times,* October 7, 1953). However, the morning newspapers (New York *Times* and New York *Herald Tribune*) did not support Wagner's candidacy chiefly because he had the endorsement of Tammany Hall.

In an election on November 4, 1953, regarded as a victory for the New Deal-Fair Deal wing of the Democratic party, Robert F. Wagner, Jr., was voted mayor of New York by a plurality of 360,078 over his Republican opponent Harold Riegelman. The other two contenders for the mayoralty were Rudolph Halley, Liberal-Independent candidate, and Clifford T. McAvoy of the American Labor party.

Before taking office on January 1, 1954 Wagner announced the appointments of Henry Epstein as deputy mayor; Nathan Straus as chairman of the newly organized mayor's advisory council, with Averell Harriman as honorary chairman; Dr. Luther H. Gulick, director of the mayor's committee on management survey, in the new office of city administrator; Abraham D. Beame as budget director and Robert Moses as city park commissioner and city construction coordinator. He also designated Joseph E. O'Grady as the head of a new city agency, the department of labor, Dr. Leona Baumgartner as commissioner of health, Magistrate Anna M. Kross commissioner of correction, and ex-Mayor Vincent Impellitteri a justice of the court of special sessions.

Mayor Wagner's non-political affiliations include the Elks, the American Legion, Grand Street Boys, Knights of Columbus, and National Conference of Christians and Jews. He attends the Catholic Church. Married on February 14, 1942 to Susan Edwards of Greenwich, Connecticut, he is the father of two boys, Robert F. Wagner 3d and Duncan Wagner.

The black-haired, brown-eyed Mayor is stocky in build and stands five feet eight inches tall. Swimming, golf and squash are his diversions and he enjoys his boat on Great South Bay, Islip, Long Island. He thinks of his career in politics as a public service and believes, "There should be more people in government who don't have to consider it a livelihood—people who don't have to worry about taking a stand they believe is right even if it is unpopular, because they don't have to worry about re-election or keeping their jobs" (New York *Times*, October 17, 1953).

References

N Y Herald Tribune p1+ O 22 '46 por; III p3 Je 19 '49 por; p1+ Ag 20 '52 por; p6 Jl 23 '53; p1+ S 16 '53; IX p55 O 25 '53; p18 N 4 '53
N Y Sun p9 Ja 3 '48 pors
N Y Times p1 Ag 20 '52; p1 Jl 23 '53; p17 O 17 '53; p16 N 4 '53

WAKEHURST, JOHN DE VERE LODER, 2D BARON Feb 5, 1895- Governor of Northern Ireland

Address: Government House, Hillsborough, County Down, Northern Ireland; 31 Lennox Gardens, London S.W. 1, England

The Governor of Northern Ireland, the Right Honorable Lord Wakehurst, was Captain John de Vere Loder before inheriting his title in 1936. He was appointed to his present post in 1952. He is the Prior of the Order of St. John of Jerusalem and was chairman of the English Speaking Union from 1946 through 1951, and Governor of New South Wales, Australia from 1937 to 1946, after having served as a member of the House of Commons in London for approximately ten years. The widely traveled Lord Wakehurst is the author of several books.

The Sydney *Sun* praised Lord Wakehurst's service as Governor: "It is a job which could only have been done by a man as conscientious and earnest as Lord Wakehurst, a man of culture, dignity, integrity, tolerance, and firmness of character with a mind of wide horizons."

He is the second Baron Wakehurst, that title having been assumed by his late father, Gerald Walter Erskine Loder, on elevation to the peerage in 1934 after a distinguished career as a barrister, Conservative Member of Parliament, and chairman of the Southern Railway. His mother is the former Lady Louise de Vere Beauclerk, eldest daughter of the tenth Duke of St. Albans.

John de Vere Loder was born in London, England, on February 5, 1895, the only boy in a family of five (his sisters are the Honorable Mrs. Jocelyn Lewis Palmer, the Honorable Mrs. Alan Rees Colman, Lady Strathcona and Mount Royal, and the Honorable Mary Irene Loder). He attended Eton College, Berkshire from 1908 to 1914.

After the outbreak of World War I, Loder became a captain in the 4th Royal Sussex Regiment in 1914. He served for about five years in Gallipoli Peninsula, Egypt and Palestine, and was mentioned in dispatches. For the two years preceding the Armistice, he was attached to the Intelligence Corps.

Following the war, Captain Loder was a clerk in the Foreign Office from 1919 to 1921. His first book, *The Truth About Mesopotamia, Palestine & Syria* (G. Allen), was published in 1923. It was favorably reviewed in the London *Times Literary Supplement*. In the foreword, Lord Cecil of Chelwood observed that Loder "admirably accomplished" his purpose "to state the facts." *Contemporary Review* (January 1925) published Captain Loder's article, "On the Roof of the World in Peru," after he had made a voyage to South America in 1924.

Loder was secretary of the British Institute for Adult Education when in the summer of 1924 he was chosen by the Conservatives of the east Leicester constituency as their candidate for Parliament. Victorious in the October 1924 election, Loder served for about five years. A three-cornered contest, splitting the anti-Labor party vote, resulted in the loss of Loder's east Leicester seat at the election in 1929.

Fifteen thousand miles of travel in Russia in 1929 and 1930 resulted in another book, *Bolshevism in Perspective* (G. Allen, 1931). The London *Times Literary Supplement* (January 14, 1932) noted Loder's prediction that the five-year plan would "succeed in part and thereby free Communist attention for a more vigorous campaign against Western capitalism."

At the general election in October 1931 Captain Loder was returned to the House of Commons as a Conservative member for the Lewes division in Sussex. In Parliament in April 1933 he advocated trade relations with the Soviet Union, and in February of the following year

British Inf. Services

LORD WAKEHURST

spoke with considerable force on the subject of imperial defense.

Captain Loder was re-elected member for Lewes in 1935, the year following his father's elevation to the peerage as the first Baron Wakehurst. (Baron Wakehurst took his title from his Sussex manor home, Wakehurst Place.) John de Vere Loder became the second Baron Wakehurst on the death of his father on April 30, 1936, and took his seat in the House of Lords.

In 1937 the news was released that the King had "been pleased to announce the appointment of Lord Wakehurst to be Governor of New South Wales" in Australia, and in that year Lord Wakehurst was designated a Knight Commander of St. Michael and St. George. He remained Governor of New South Wales, until 1946, and was made an honorary colonel of the University of Sydney Regiment and honorary air commodore of the 22nd (City of Sydney) Squadron of the Royal Australian Air Force.

As Governor, Lord Wakehurst was very popular. His term of office, more than once extended at the request of the state government, would have been extended again in 1945, but for the desire of Lord and Lady Wakehurst to return to England. Collections of Lord Wakehurst's wartime speeches were published by Angus under the titles *Our Second Chance* (1944) and *Preparations for Peace* (1945).

Long a member of the English Speaking Union of the Commonwealth, he was chairman for five years beginning in 1946. In June 1948 he was installed as Prior of the Order of St. John of Jerusalem, sponsor of the St. John's Ambulance Brigade, after having returned from the United States, where he addressed a capacity audience at the Museum of Natural History in New York City. (Lord Wakehurst has made, and widely exhibited, color films of life in both Australia and Great Britain.) In the course of a nation-wide speaking tour of the United States in 1952, Lord Wakehurst delivered a major address to members of the National Geographic Society in Washington. He resigned the chairmanship of the English Speaking Union when he was appointed to the British delegation to the United Nations General Assembly in Paris.

On December 3, 1952 Lord Wakehurst was sworn in as Governor of Northern Ireland, succeeding Lord Granville (who resigned because of ill health) for a term of six years. The executive power of Northern Ireland is vested in the office of the Governor on behalf of the Sovereign. By the Government of Ireland Act (1920) the Governor, on the advice of Ministers responsible to Parliament, summons and dissolves Parliament, and gives or withholds the Royal Assent to bills passed by both Houses.

The Parliament consists of a popularly elected House of Commons of fifty-two members and a Senate of twenty-six, chosen by the House of Commons with the exception of the Lord Mayors of Belfast and Londonderry, who are ex officio members. This parliament has extensive local powers, although certain legislative and fiscal powers are reserved to the United Kingdom. Northern Ireland, which consists of the counties of Antrim, Armagh, Down, Fermanagh, Tyrone, and Londonderry in the former province of Ulster, has an area of 5,238 square miles and a population of approximately 1,400,000. The inhabitants are 65 per cent Protestant and the majority are strongly loyalist in sentiment. Thus, at the general election in October 1953, the voters gave 38 of the 52 House of Commons seats to the Unionist party of Prime Minister Lord Brookeborough, which opposes merging with the Republic of Ireland. Northern Ireland is represented by twelve members in the House of Commons in London.

The Governor of Northern Ireland and Lady Wakehurst revisited the United States in January 1954, their tour encompassing New York City, Richmond, Philadelphia, Providence, and Washington. Lord Wakehurst brought with him two films, one dealing with the Order of St. John of Jerusalem and the other with Northern Ireland, for exhibition to various private groups, and on January 5 spoke over the CBS radio network. This was not, however, a "state" visit.

Among the articles which Lord Wakehurst has written are "Tangier, Morocco and the Strait of Gibraltar" (*Fortnightly Review,* August 1923), "The Changing Soul of China" (*World Today,* November 1924), and "Egypt During and Since the War" (Edinburgh *Review,* July 1928). He wrote (with Robert John Graham Boothby and other Members of Parliament) *Industry & the State, A Conservative View* (Macmillan, 1927), and *Colonsay and Oronsay in the Isles of Argyll; Their History, Flora, Fauna and Topography* (Oliver, 1935).

Lady Margaret Wakehurst is the daughter of the late Sir Charles Tennent; she was married to Lord Wakehurst in the Church of the

Holy Trinity, Sloane Square, London, on June 3, 1920. The Wakehursts have one daughter, Henrietta Marguerite (Mrs. John Wilmot Reader-Harris), and three sons, John Christopher de Vere, James David Gerald, and Robert Beauclerk. Lord Wakehurst is a trustee of the Royal Opera House, Covent Garden since 1949, and a governor of the Sadler's Wells Ballet. His clubs are the Carlton and Travellers' in London. He mentions golf and tennis as his favorite recreations. Lord Wakehurst has collaborated with a friend in writing secret service "thrillers" under a pseudonym.

References

The Times of London Election Suppl. p4 O 31 '24; p18 My 1 '36; p12 Ja 7 '37; p6 S 12 '52 por
Author's and Writer's Who's Who (1948-49)
Burke's Peerage, Baronetage and Knightage (1953)
International Who's Who, 1954
International Year Book and Statesmen's Who's Who, 1954
Kelly's Handbook to the Titled, Landed and Official Classes, 1951
Who's Who, 1954
Who's Who in America, 1954-55
World Biography (1954)

WALLER, FRED(ERIC) Mar. 10, 1886-May 18, 1954 Inventor of Cinerama; invented first automatic photographic printer and timer; first water skis; produced title illustrations and short films for Famous Players Lasky (now Paramount Pictures) (1919-1922); was with Paramount (1924-1926, 1929-1936); made films for New York World's Fair; among his 160 inventions is Waller gunnery trainer which was used by U.S. armed forces and British Admiralty; received Academy of Motion Picture Arts and Sciences award (1954) for Cinerama which won U.S. Camera Achievement Award (1952). See *Current Biography,* (Feb.) 1953.

Obituary

N Y Times p31 My 19 '54

WAN (WAITHAYAKON), PRINCE Aug. 25, 1891- Minister of Foreign Affairs of Thailand

Address: b. Ministry of Foreign Affairs, Bangkok, Thailand; h. 16 Sai Namphung Lane, Bangkapi, Bangkok, Thailand

The first chairman of the conference of nineteen nations assembled at Geneva in April 1954 to discuss the problems of Indochina and Korea was Prince Wan, Foreign Minister of Thailand. The diplomat has served his country on a wide variety of assignments for nearly four decades. He entered the foreign service in 1917 as secretary to the Siamese delegation at Paris. Thirty years later he was appointed Thailand's first Ambassador to the United States.

When Thailand was admitted to the United Nations in 1946, Prince Wan, who had been associated with the League of Nations, became Thailand's permanent delegate to the international organization. He held both posts for five years, until his appointment in 1952 as Foreign Minister of Thailand. In addition to being a diplomat, he has been a college professor and administrator.

Prince Wan told the Geneva conference in his ten-minute speech on April 30, 1954 that the new colonialism [proposed by the North Koreans] is even more to be feared than the old. He also said, "Thailand has yet to learn that in order to be a good Asian one has to be exclusively Asian. Peace is world-wide—it is one and indivisible" (New York *Herald Tribune,* May 1, 1954).

Prince Wan Waithayakon Krommün Naradhip Bongsprabandh was born in Bangkok, Siam on August 25, 1891. His grandfather was Maha Mongkut, King Rama IV, the central figure of the book *Anna and the King of Siam* by Margaret Landon and of the Rodgers and Hammerstein musical based on it, *The King and I.*

His father, Prince Naradhip Prabandhbongse, Deputy Minister of Finance, was in the railway and tramway business, and was also a dramatist; his mother, Mom Luang Tuan Montrikul, was a composer. Prince Wan is a cousin of King Rama IX. Raised in Bangkok, he attended King's College there from 1902 until 1905, and Marlborough School in England from 1905 to 1910. In 1914 he was graduated with honors in history from Balliol College, Oxford and received the M.A. degree from that college in 1927.

The Prince pursued advanced studies at the Ecole des Sciences Politiques of Paris, becoming Lauréat in 1917; his thesis was entitled "La Jurisdiction Consulaire au Siam." In that year he was appointed secretary to his country's legation at Paris.

After occupying his initial diplomatic post for two years, he served successively as private secretary and chief of cabinet to the Minister of Foreign Affairs until 1924. From 1924 until 1926 he was Under Secretary of State for Foreign Affairs; the next four years he held the post of Envoy Extraordinary and Minister Plenipotentiary to London, Brussels and The Hague. During that period, from 1927 until 1930, he was Siam's permanent delegate to the League, a member of the copyright conference in Rome (1928), a deputy member of the League's supervisory committee (1929), vice-president of the conference on revision of the statute of the Permanent Court of International Justice (1929), and a member of the Geneva conference on bills of exchange (1930).

Prince Wan was professor of history at Chulalongkorn University in 1931 and two years later he became acting dean of the university's faculty of law. In 1934 he taught international law at the University of Moral and Political Sciences at Bangkok.

For more than a decade, from 1933 until 1947, he was an acting member of the Civil Service Commission; from 1933 until 1946 he was an advisor to the Prime Minister and the Minister for Foreign Affairs; and from 1934

PRINCE WAN

until 1946 he was an advisor to the council of foreign ministers.

During this period he also served, from 1934 until 1941, as a member of the Permanent Court of Arbitration at The Hague; in 1946 he was his country's chief delegate to the conference called at Washington, D.C. to settle a territorial dispute between Thailand and France; and in 1946 and 1947 he was a member of the Thai Senate.

In March 1947 the United States and Thailand raised their diplomatic missions to the rank of embassies; Prince Wan was appointed his country's first Ambassador Extraordinary and Plenipotentiary to the United States. On April 28, 1947, Thailand, which had been unanimously elected the fifty-fifth member of the United Nations (December 16, 1946), was formally welcomed into the organization.

Prince Wan, who had guided Thailand's application for admission, commented: "It is a very good thing the United States is a member of the United Nations, for that makes all the difference. There seems to be a real determination to bring about a lasting peace settlement, and compared to the League of Nations the United Nations has started off much more energetically" (New York *Herald Tribune,* December 15, 1946).

From 1947 until his appointment as Foreign Minister in 1952 he held the posts of Ambassador to the United States and permanent representative to the United Nations. At the United Nations he was vice-chairman of the legal committee during the third regular session of the General Assembly in 1948, vice-chairman of the trusteeship committee in 1949, chairman of that committee the following year, chairman of the economic and financial committee in 1951, and chairman of the legal committee in 1952.

In March 1952 he was named Foreign Minister of Thailand. Elizabeth Maguire (Washington *Post,* April 6, 1952) commented: "Washington has grown to love the popular Prince and his gentle Princess. Hospitably inclined, they have entertained at countless embassy galas." While serving his country as Foreign Minister, he remained its permanent delegate to the United Nations; in September 1953 he was a leading candidate for the presidency of the General Assembly, the post which was won by Madame Vijaya Lakshmi Pandit of India.

In April 1954 he presided, as one of three rotating co-chairmen, over the first meeting of the Geneva conference on the problems of Korea and Indochina; the two other co-chairmen were British Foreign Minister Anthony Eden and Soviet Foreign Minister V. M. Molotov. The New York *Times* noted: "Although he and his country are stalwart supporters of the United States, Prince Wan has practiced the old-fashioned diplomatic virtues during his long and successful career as a delegate to the United Nations and has avoided the harsh language customary in East-West debates. These qualities will be useful to him in presiding every third day over the discussions of the Korean question" (April 27, 1954).

In September 1954 Prince Wan was again a candidate for the presidency of the General Assembly. Although he was supported by the United States, he withdrew his name "in the interest of harmony" and Dr. Eelco van Kleffens was elected to that post on September 21.

Prince Wan is an honorary member of the Rotary club; he belongs also to the Siam Society and the Académie Diplomatique of Paris. In 1944 Chulalongkorn University awarded him the honorary degree of Doctor of Letters, and in 1953 Thammasat University conferred on him the degree of Doctor of Diplomacy.

He holds a number of decorations from his native country, being Knight Grand Cross of the Most Illustrious Order of Chula Chom Klao (1939); Knight Grand Cordon of the Most Noble Order of the Crown of Thailand (1940); Knight Grand Cordon of the Most Exalted Order of the White Elephant (1941); and Knight of the Most Illustrious Order of the Royal House of Chakri (1943).

His foreign decorations are the Order of the Orange Nassau of the Netherlands (1925), Dannebrog (1926), Order of the Sun of Peru (1926), Isabella the Catholic of Spain (1926), Crown of Italy (1927), St. Olaf of Norway (1927), Leopold of Belgium (1938), Grand Cross of the German Eagle (1938), Imperial Order of the Rising Sun (1939), Legion of Honor of France (1940), Order of the Brilliant Star (Jing Hsing) Special (1948), and Civil Merit of Spain (1953).

The diplomat was married in May 1921 to Momchao Phibun Kitiyakara; the marriage ended in divorce a year later. He married Proi Bunnag, in November, 1930. He has two children, Wibun Worawan, a son born of his first marriage, and Wiwan Worawan, a daughter born of his second marriage, who is a student at Wellesley College. The Foreign Minister is a Buddhist. He has black hair and eyes and is about five feet six inches tall and weighs 160 pounds.

The Prince's hobby is reading, and in his research he has discovered the origin of the name Siam. The people have always referred to their country as Thailand, "Land of the Free", and the name was officially changed to Thailand in 1949. Prince Wan explains that the Thai people came originally from China but their language is written in Hindu characters; the name Siam was derived from Sanskrit and was borrowed by Portuguese navigators.

References

N Y Herald Tribune II p1 My 2 '54 por
N Y Times p5 Mr 27 '54 por
N Y Times Mag p62 O 25 '53 por
U N Bul 9:408 O 15 '50 por; 11:402 N 15 '51 por; 13:388+ N 1 '52 por
Washington (D.C.) Post p9S Mr 19 '50
International Who's Who, 1953
Who's Who in the United Nations (1951)

WARREN, EARL Mar. 19, 1891- Chief Justice of the Supreme Court of the United States

Address: United States Supreme Court Bldg., 1 First St. NE, Washington, D.C.

NOTE: This biography supersedes the article which appeared in *Current Biography* in 1944.

Sworn in on October 5, 1953 as the fourteenth Chief Justice of the United States, Earl Warren was appointed by President Dwight D. Eisenhower to succeed the late Chief Justice Fred M. Vinson. Self-described as a "progressive conservative," Warren is the only man to have been elected to the governorship of California for three successive terms, and in 1948 was the Republican party's nominee for the vice-presidency of the United States.

On May 17, 1954 Chief Justice Warren read the United States Supreme Court's unanimous decision which held that racial segregation in the public schools of the country is unconstitutional.

Earl Warren was born on March 19, 1891 in a five-room frame house in Los Angeles, California to Methias H. and Crystal (Hernlund) Warren. He has a sister, Ethel (now Mrs. Vernon Plank). His father, whose surname was originally Varran, was brought as an infant to this country from Stavanger in Norway, his mother was born in Sweden and spent most of her girlhood in Minnesota.

Methias Warren was a master car builder for the Southern Pacific Railroad and became a member of the pioneering American Railway Union (founded by Eugene V. Debs). He settled near Bakersfield, California where his son attended the Kern County High School.

Earl "earned pocket money as a newsboy, later as a cub reporter for the Bakersfield *Californian*. He spent summers as a call boy waking up railroaders for the Southern Pacific, did odd jobs as a freight hustler and farm hand, learned to play the clarinet in the school band. He still carries a card in the musicians' union" (*Time*, April 12, 1948).

In *Earl Warren, a Great American Story*, Irving Stone wrote that Warren's "determination" to be a lawyer dates back before his high school days when he listened to criminal cases at the Kern County courthouse. Successful real estate ventures by his father made it possible for Earl to enter the University of California at Berkeley, where he majored for three years in political science before entering the university's school of jurisprudence.

Having received his B.L. degree in 1912 and his J.D. degree in 1914 (he was admitted to the California bar on May 14 of the latter year), Warren joined the legal department of the Associated Oil Company at San Francisco, then moved to Oakland to become a law clerk with the firm of Robinson and Robinson.

In 1917 the lawyer applied for admission to the Army Officers' Training Corps, but by the time he had recovered from a minor operation the A.O.T.C. had been filled; and in August, accordingly, Warren enlisted in the Army as a private. Assigned to Company I, 363rd Infantry, 91st Division, he took basic training at Camp Lewis, Washington and was advanced to first sergeant within four weeks.

On January 5, 1918 he was accepted as an officer candidate and commissioned a second lieutenant in the following May. He served at Camp Lee, Virginia, where he trained recruits, and Camp MacArthur, Texas, where he instructed at the central infantry officers' training camp. Discharged on December 11, 1918 as a first lieutenant, Warren was appointed to a captaincy in the Officers' Reserve Corps early in the year following, and retained this commission until 1935.

A chance meeting between Warren and California Assemblyman Leon Gray of Oakland, who was a former member of the firm of Robinson and Robinson, led to the appointment of Warren in 1919 as clerk of the judiciary committee of the California Assembly. When the legislature adjourned, Warren hung out his shingle at Gray's law office in Oakland, but before he had secured a single client was invited by the Oakland city attorney to become his deputy. Warren accepted and served in this position from 1919 to 1920.

The young lawyer attracted the attention of Ezra Decoto, the district attorney of Alameda County, and on May 1, 1920 he was appointed a deputy in the latter's office. Three years later (1923) he was advanced to chief deputy, and in addition was made legal counsel to the Alameda County Board of Supervisors. After Decoto resigned in 1925 Warren succeeded him as district attorney and broke a serious "log-jam" in the court calendar and destroyed a notorious bail-bond racket. When he ran for a regular four-year term as Alameda County district attorney in 1926, he was elected by an overwhelming majority.

Immediately after his election, Warren began a campaign to rid Alameda County of crime. He was re-elected in 1930 and again in 1934 as district attorney.

(Continued next page)

Wide World

CHIEF JUSTICE EARL WARREN

He also served as chairman of the board of managers of the State Bureau of Criminal Identification and Investigation, and was a research associate of the Bureau of Public Administration, University of California.

Warren was elected president of the District Attorneys' Association of California for the term of 1931 and 1932. Warren was secretary from 1932 through 1938. In 1934 he received the United States Flag Association's medal for outstanding work in the field of law enforcement.

"As a prosecutor," Robert Coughlan commented (*Life,* April 24, 1944), "Warren has been accused of high-handedness in his methods . . . but his legal rectitude is indicated by the fact that in 13 years and in thousands of cases ranging from murder to window-breaking, he never had a conviction reversed by a higher court." Warren has stated: "I never heard a jury bring in a verdict of guilty but that I felt sick at the pit of my stomach."

Named an alternate delegate to the Republican national convention in 1928, Warren became a full delegate in 1932, chairman of the Republican state central committee from 1934 to 1936, and Republican national committeeman from 1936 through 1938. When, however, he sought election as attorney general of California in the latter year, he cross-filed (as permitted by the state law) in the primaries for the Democratic and Progressive, as well as the Republican nomination. Promising a nonpartisan regime, he was elected as the nominee of all three parties.

Successful prosecutions by Warren put a quietus on the state's race track racketeering, and gambling on board the luxury ship *Rex,* operating off Long Beach, was halted in a spectacular raid. As attorney general of California at the time of the outbreak of World War II, he was the principal author of the Uniform Sabotage Prevention Act, commonly known as the Warren act. He was, however, criticized in many quarters for an affirmative opinion on the legality of the action of military authorities in removing Japanese and Japanese-Americans from their homes located near defense plants and installations and sending them to what were described as "prepared camps."

The attorney general represented California in a dozen cases before the United States Supreme Court; and testified before Congress on state title to tidelands oil.

In announcing his candidacy for governor in 1942, he declared: "I am a Republican, but . . . I shall seek the support of people of both parties. I can do this honorably because I am an independent, and therefore in a position to serve the people fairly, regardless of their politics or mine." At the primaries, he won the Republican nomination with ease, and lost the Democratic by 110,000 votes out of a total of approximately 919,000. At the November 3 election he carried every county in the state, defeating the incumbent Culbert Olson, a Democrat, by 342,000.

After taking office in January 1943 he kept his campaign promises of independence, especially in the matter of appointments. "He went into both major parties for good men," Robert Coughlan has observed, "and even beyond the parties into the nonpolitical world of civil service." The governor eliminated the spoils system from the Department of Public Works and reorganized the state guard and the Department of Industrial Relations to expedite the disposition of workmen's compensation accident claims.

Legislation adopted during this term reduced the state sales tax, raised old age pensions from $40 to $50 a month, (in 1947 to $60), and provided $43,000,000 for postwar development. Unemployment insurance coverage was widened to include employees of small establishments, and appropriations were made for child-care centers.

When the Republican national convention opened in June, 1944, Governor Warren was installed as temporary chairman and made the keynote speech. A "favorite son" nominee for the presidency, he released his California delegation to Governor Thomas E. Dewey of New York who strongly urged him to seek the vice-presidential nomination but Warren declined.

Warren's popularity remained strong and in 1946 he received both the Republican and Democratic nominations for governor. With the November balloting a mere formality, Warren became the first Californian governor in thirty-two years to win a second term, and the third in the state's history to be re-elected.

As early as November 1947, Governor Warren announced that in the coming year he would again be a candidate for the presidency of the United States, and began to express more positively his views on world affairs. He urged firm support for the United Nations (to the organizational conference of which he had made the welcoming address at San Francisco in 1945), the Marshall Plan, statehood for Hawaii, and universal military training.

In the federal fiscal field he was for a balanced budget, debt retirement, lower taxes (in that order). He endorsed the Taft-Hartley law, but with reservations as to the clause requiring loyalty oaths only from union officers. ("If it is to be in the law at all," he averred, "it ought to apply mutually to both sides.")

At the Republican national convention of 1948 Warren held the California delegation until the final ballot, thus playing the decisive role in swinging the presidential nomination to Dewey. Prevailed upon to accept the vice-presidential candidacy, Warren was nominated by acclamation but he was subsequently defeated in November.

He was re-elected in 1950 as California's first third-term governor, defeating the Democratic candidate James Roosevelt by nearly two to one.

As a member of the board of regents of the University of California, he "sided with the minority in voting against the dismissal of professors who refused to sign a special loyalty pledge," holding that "they had already subscribed to the California constitutional oath given to all state officers" (New York *Times* Magazine, October 11, 1953). Nevertheless, he approved a new California law requiring a similar oath from all state, county and municipal employees.

Warren was "one of the first to oppose the doctrine of 'inherent powers' under which President Truman seized the steel plants in 1952 and he challenged the 'paramount rights' theory, on which the Federal government based its claim of control over coastal oil bearing tidelands" (New York *Herald Tribune,* October 4, 1953).

Again a candidate for the presidential nomination at the Republican national convention of July, 1952, Warren received eighty-one votes on the first and only ballot, and held seventy-seven of these ballots after the changes in vote which led to the nomination of General Eisenhower.

He has proclaimed his belief in the wisdom of leaving the administration of affairs so far as possible to "the states and their local subdivisions." A declared friend of social progress, Warren is opposed to socialism which means abolition of the free competitive system. He has stated "in government, as in all other affairs of life, it is not so much the size of the steps that determine progress as it is the directions in which the steps are taken."

On September 30, 1953 President Eisenhower announced to a press conference his intention "to designate Governor Earl Warren as Chief Justice of the United States" in succession to the late Fred M. Vinson because he "wanted a man whose reputation for integrity, honesty, middle-of-the-road philosophy, experience in government, experience in the law, were all such as to convince the United States that he was a man who had no ends to serve except the United States."

The press of the country united in praising the nominee's character and capability, though some editorials noted that while Warren was admittedly skilled as a prosecutor and administrator, he had no direct experience as either a state or federal judge. On October 5 Earl Warren was sworn in as Chief Justice by Associate Justice Hugo Black.

On May 17, 1954 the Chief Justice read two opinions that put the stamp of unconstitutionality on school systems in twenty-one states and the District of Columbia where segregation is permissive or mandatory. The court, taking cognizance of the problems involved in the integration of school systems concerned, put over until the October term the formulation of decrees to effectuate its 9-0 decision. The opinion set aside the "separate but equal" doctrine laid down by the Supreme Court in 1896 (New York *Times,* May 18, 1954).

"In the field of education," Chief Justice Warren said, "the doctrine of 'separate but equal' has no place. Separate educational facilities are inherently unequal."

An article, "Affirmative Opinion on Justice Warren" by Professor John P. Frank of Yale Law School in the New York *Times Magazine* on October 3, 1954 commented on the decisions handed down by the Court during Warren's first year as Chief Justice. He quoted Warren as follows: "I conceive of this Court as the balance wheel of this government. Its function is to keep us from swinging too violently to one extreme or another.

"To the extent that anyone indiscriminately charges individuals or groups of individuals with dishonesty or subversion or whatever it might be that would destroy reputation, that is, in my opinion, not in the American tradition and should not be encouraged."

Among notable speeches made by Warren during 1954 was that at the dedication of the American Bar Association Center in Chicago on August 19 and the College of William and Mary at Williamsburg, Virginia on September 25.

Academic distinctions conferred on Warren include an honorary D.C.L. from Union College in New York, the degree of Doctor of Political Science from the University of Alaska, and honorary L.L.D.'s from the University of Redlands, College of the Pacific, University of Southern California, Santa Clara University, Mills College, Occidental College, Cornell College in Iowa, and Jewish Theological Seminary.

He was president of the National Association of Attorney Generals in 1940 and 1941 and is a member of the American Bar Association, (vice-chairman of the criminal law section since 1938) and the bar associations of California, and Alameda and Sacramento Counties.

A Mason, he belongs also to the Elks, Native Sons of the Golden West, Oddfellows, Moose, Phi Delta Phi and Sigma Phi. His clubs are the Olympic, Commonwealth, and Bohemian in San Francisco, the Athens Athletic and the Exchange at Oakland, the Jonathan in Los Angeles, and the Sutter at Sacramento.

Earl Warren was married at Oakland, California on October 14, 1925 to the widowed Mrs. Nina (Palmquist) Meyers, whose young son James he legally adopted. They have five other children, Earl, Jr., Robert, Virginia, Dorothy and Nina. He is six feet and one inch tall,

WARREN, EARL—*Continued*

and weighs about 207 pounds. Warren "greets visitors with a crushing handshake, and has a frequent booming laugh" (New York *Times*). His eyes are blue, his once blond hair is now silvery.

A Baptist, Warren regularly reads his Bible before going to bed and first thing in the morning. He is well read in the field of contemporary affairs but cares little for fiction. For outdoor recreation he "likes to hunt deer and ducks or watch football and baseball."

Selected References (See also references listed in 1944 biographical sketch)

Am Mag 155:22+ Je '53 pors
Am Mercury 66:535+ My '48 por
Christian Sci Mon p13 S 30 '53; p14 O 10 '53 por
Collier's 117:20+ Je 8 '46 pors; 121: 65+ Je 26 '48 por; 129:18+ Ja 19 '52 pors
Life 15:106+ S 6 '43 pors; 16:100+ Ap 24 '44 pors; 24:137+ My 10 '48 pors
N Y Herald Tribune II p4 D 19 '43 por; p1 S 29 '53; II p1 O 4 '53 por
N Y Times Mag p18 F 22 '48 por; p10 O 11 '53 por
New Repub 109:514+ O 18 '43 por; 126: 11+ Je 23 '52 por
Sat Eve Post 216:22+ Ag 7 '43 pors; 223:17+ F 3 '51 pors
Scholastic 52:9 Ap 19 '48; 53:6A O 6 '48 por
Time 51:22 Ap 12 '48; 52:19+ S 27 '48 por; 62:19 O 12 '53
U S News 21:60+ N 1 '46 por; 28:34+ Je 23 '50 por; 31:41+ N 23 '51 por
International Who's Who, 1953
National Cyclopædia of American Biography, Current Volume H (1952)
Salter, J. T. ed. Public Men In and Out of Office (1946)
Stone, I. Earl Warren; A Great American Story (1948)
Who's Who, 1953
Who's Who in America, 1952-53
Who's Who in United States Politics (1952)
World Biography (1954)

WELCH, JOSEPH N(YE) Oct. 22, 1890- Lawyer

Address: b. c/o Hale and Dorr, 60 State St., Boston 9, Mass.; h. Walpole, Mass.

An Iowa-born Boston attorney, Joseph N. Welch, who has practiced law principally in the civil field for over thirty-five years, was appointed in April 1954 by Defense Secretary Charles E. Wilson as special counsel to handle the Army's case in the dispute between Senator Joseph R. McCarthy of Wisconsin and Secretary of the Army Robert T. Stevens. The hearings opened on April 22 before the permanent subcommittee on investigations of the Senate Committee on Government Operations in the Caucus Room of the Senate Office Building in Washington, D.C., and closed on June 17.

In the course of the hearings before acting committee chairman Karl E. Mundt, (Republican Senator from South Dakota), Welch became a familiar figure to television audiences viewing the proceedings. Reporters commented on the Army counsel's "quiet irony," "his gentlemanly calm in the midst of bedlam," his "honeyed fluency" and "legal cunning." "He has brought some tension-snapping humor and incisive questioning to the ponderous showdown sessions," wrote Frederick Guidry in the *Christian Science Monitor* (April 29, 1954).

Joseph Nye Welch was born in Primghar, Iowa on October 22, 1890 to William and Martha (Thyer) Welch. Both of his parents were English-born. Joseph is the youngest of their seven children. The Welches were poor, and Joe worked hard. Even as a young boy his great pleasure was "to slip down to the courthouse and watch the trials. . . . After two years of clerking in a real estate office, he entered Grinnell College [Grinnell, Iowa] with $600 he had saved. Summers, he stored up money for more education by selling maps from door to door" (*Time*, May 17, 1954).

He was graduated from Grinnell in 1914 with an A.B. degree, a Phi Beta Kappa key and a $600 scholarship at Harvard Law School, where he received his LL.B. degree in 1917. When the United States entered World War I he attended Army officer candidate school but the war ended before he had received his commission as a second lieutenant. Admitted to the Massachusetts bar in 1918, he steadily specialized in trial practice and tried cases in state courts in Massachusetts, New Hampshire and New York, and in the Federal courts of Massachusetts and New York. He has been a partner in the firm of Hale and Dorr in Boston since 1923.

Careful preparation of a case is a trade-mark for Welch, according to *U.S. News & World Report*, April 23, 1954. "His practice has been mostly in civil law, not criminal, and he admits rather wryly that he lost one of the biggest cases he ever handled—a seven-million-dollar tax matter for the Chicago stockyards that he carried all the way to the Supreme Court."

One of his Harvard Law School classmates said of Welch, "I attribute his success in the law practice to his knowing when not to act as much as his colorful and skillful action. You'll find that he is polite and genial, but he won't miss many points" (*Christian Science Monitor*, April 29, 1954).

The attorney nearly turned down the job as special counsel for the Army because, as he said, "I don't know anything about television or newspapers." After his appointment on April 2 he said in an interview at the Pentagon that he intended to develop "the pertinent facts whether they help or hurt" either side of the controversy. Assistant Defense Secretary Fred S. Seaton, who announced Welch's appointment, said that the lawyer and his two assistants from his Boston office, Frederick G. Fisher, Jr., and James D. St. Clair, would do the work without compensation, either in salary or expenses (New York *Herald Tribune*, April 3, 1954). "They are just doing a public service," Seaton said.

Welch is a registered Republican. Asked by a reporter "Are you pro-McCarthy?" Welch replied, "I'm just for the facts. I certainly have an impression that I have an interesting case."

Two weeks after his appointment as special counsel Welch filed with the Senate subcommittee, as requested by the subcommittee's counsel, Ray H. Jenkins, twenty-nine charges, chiefly that Senator Joseph McCarthy and his aide, Roy M. Cohn "had improperly pressed the Army to promote Private G. David Schine" (*U.S. News & World Report,* April 23, 1954).

During the televised hearings the public came to be fascinated by Welch's "varied expressions and his beaming eyes." He has been described as "the watchdog of time"; he used a stop watch when interrogating witnesses to be certain that he took advantage of the ten minutes made available to him.

"He is not one who seeks attention through shouts and table-pounding," commented Alvin Shuster in the New York *Times,* May 3, 1954. "Rather, the sixty-three-year-old Boston [lawyer] appears to the television audience and committee room observers as a gentleman viewing bedlam with calm . . . disagreement . . . cool silence. . . . This is not to say he is 'dead pan.' At times his eyes beam. A dubious smile often creeps across his face when testimony is not to his liking. When the time comes to speak, however, he often provides some of the brighter moments in long, hard days of hearings."

A New York *World-Telegram and Sun* (May 3, 1954) reporter described Welch as "the calm but colorful attorney who always seems to get at the heart—and the humor—of things in the McCarthy-Army hearings." A widely quoted example of this is the incident when Welch was not satisfied with the answers given by a witness as to how he came into the possession of a disputed photograph. Welch asked him, "Did you think this came from a pixie?" McCarthy interrupted to ask for a definition of pixie. Welch replied: "I should say, Mr. Senator, that a pixie is a close relative of a fairy. Shall I proceed, sir? Have I enlightened you?"

The Boston lawyer was married to Judith Hampton Lyndon of Washington, Georgia on September 20, 1917. The couple has two sons, Joseph N., Jr., and Lyndon, both of whom are engineers, and three granddaughters. Associates of Welch report that he likes to work in his Boston office standing at a high, old-fashioned clerk's desk. He speaks "with honeyed fluency and a meaningful grin that hints of legal cunning" (*Time,* May 3, 1954). They fear that the sitting down in the committee room "might cramp his style, but those who have enjoyed the 'Welchisms' cannot believe this" (New York *Times,* May 3, 1954).

Welch and his wife live in a 150-year-old eleven-room Colonial house in Walpole, Massachusetts. He has "shied away from joining clubs because he would rather entertain friends and clients at home." He keeps a pair of radios at his bedside—"one a short-wave set for listening to foreign broadcasts and amateur operators. He also has a set of earphones to keep the radio from annoying Mrs. Welch. Scattered strategically around the house are barometers. . . . There are indoor and outdoor thermometers, and combinations of them" (*Christian Science Monitor,* April 29, 1954).

Wide World

JOSEPH N. WELCH

He enjoys fishing and cribbage, is a crack shot with a rifle, detests gardening, and "owns more than 150 bow neckties."

"He loves coming home and changing into slacks and a sport shirt," said his wife, in describing their "very quiet life", "and sitting [in his favorite armchair] and reading. . . ." She said that her husband "loves to do trial work."

He is a member of the American College of Trial Lawyers, American Bar Association, and Massachusetts Bar Association.

In the July 26, 1954 issue of *Life* Welch made the point that the opprobrious epithet, "Fifth Amendment Communist", seems to lump the Constitution and communism into equal condemnation. He agreed that many "rascals have resorted to the Fifth Amendment" but he emphasized that "no matter who invokes the amendment, it stands in our Constitution as one of the guardians of our liberties."

"On television," commented *Life* (May 17, 1954) "Welch looks almost ethereal, a most gentle gaffer straight from the musty pages of Dickens. In real life he is a big raw-boned man who once weighed over 200 pounds and even now, after three years of dieting, hits 180. . . . He has the old-shoe manner of such courtroom greats as Clarence Darrow. His elaborate politeness and gentility mask a highly active, well-disciplined, bear-trap mind."

Welch received an honorary Doctor of Laws degree from his alma mater, Grinnell College, in October 1954.

References

Life 36:47+ My 17 '54 pors
U S News 36:12 Ap 23 '54
Martindale-Hubbell Law Directory, 1952

WENTE, CARL F(REDRICK) Mar. 27, 1889- Banker

Address: b. 300 Montgomery St., San Francisco 20, Calif.; h. 537 Marina Blvd., San Francisco 23, Calif.

From September 1952 until March 27, 1954, as the president of the Bank of America, Carl F. Wente headed the largest privately owned bank in the world. On March 27, his sixty-fifth birthday, he retired and was succeeded by Seth Clark Beise. Wente retains his seat on the board and some of his committee posts.

The bank, whose net profit in 1953 totaled $55,461,617, has 535 branches, resources over $8 billion, and deposits of about $7.2 million. Wente was a protégé of A. P. Giannini, founder of the world-wide Transamerica Corporation, a vast banking empire which once had as a subsidiary the Bank of America.

Moulin Studios

CARL F. WENTE

From 1937 to 1943 Wente served as president of the Central Bank of Oakland, California and from 1943 to 1949 as senior vice-president of the Bank of America. After having retired from most of his active duties in May 1949, he was recalled to become president of this bank on September 10, 1952.

The son of Carl Heinrich and Barbara (Trautwein) Wente, Carl Fredrick Wente was born March 27, 1889, on a farm near Livermore, California. His father, a farmer and wine producer, had emigrated from Hanover, Germany, in 1879. Paternal advice led Carl to enter the banking field after one year at the Livermore Union High School, while his two younger brothers, Ernest and Herman, remained on the farm in the wine business.

Carl, who had taken care of his father's accounting books, took a position in April 1907 at the lowest rung of the banking ladder, as messenger boy at the Oakland, California Central Bank. After working at this job for five months, he returned to his home town of Livermore, to become assistant cashier at the First National Bank, in which his father owned an interest. He remained with this institution until 1918.

Wente meanwhile had become interested in the business methods of Amadeo Peter Giannini, who was then building his giant banking system. On February 1, 1918 Wente took a position at the Madera branch of Giannini's Bank of Italy (later to become the Bank of America National Trust and Savings Association). His first duties were as senior teller and pro-assistant cashier. Some personnel changes caused him to advance on July 9, 1918 to the post of assistant cashier, and a few weeks later he became, at the age of twenty-nine, the manager of the branch.

Wente served in this capacity in several of the bank's other California branches: in 1921, in Modesto; in 1924, in Visalia; in 1925, Merced; and in 1926, in Stockton. He was promoted in 1927 to assistant vice president of the central mortgage loan department in the bank's San Francisco headquarters, and two years later became vice president. By 1932 he was executive vice president in charge of credits for northern California, and in 1934 he became supervisor of credits for the entire Bank of America system.

During the depression years, Wente was chosen by Giannini as a trusted aide in a personal inspection of the 411 branches of the Bank of America. The two bankers traveled 25,000 miles in this five-and-a-half month tour of 243 communities.

Shortly after the completion of this trip, the Governor of Nevada appealed to Giannini to assist the banks of his state.

Giannini sent Wente, who became on June 14, 1934, chairman of the board of the First National Bank of Reno, Nevada, and president in August 1934. During his three years of leadership, he increased deposits from $7,000,000 to $25,000,000 and did not hesitate to ride horseback over the ranges to inspect cattle offered as collateral for loans.

On September 1, 1937, Wente became president of the Oakland Central Bank, where he had worked as a messenger thirty years previously. He remained at this post until July 1943, when "A.P." asked him to become senior vice president of the Bank of America. In May 1949, having reached the age of sixty, Wente retired from all duties, retaining only a seat on the bank's board of directors and memberships on various committees, with the title of vice-chairman of the general executive committee.

On August 19, 1952, after the death of Lawrence Mario Giannini, the founder's son, the presidency of the Bank of America became vacant; and Wente, out of "duty and loyalty" accepted the offer to fill this position. He is the first person not in the Giannini family to serve in this capacity for more than a short period of time. Wente, who will reach the bank's age of retirement in 1954, has stated that his biggest job will be to pick a successor.

Wente's policies closely resemble those of A. P. Giannini—"banking services for all people." Wente testified in October 1949 when the Federal Reserve Board had charged that Giannini's holding company, the Transamerica Corporation, was a "credit monopoly" in violation of the Clayton Act. The Court of Appeals for the Third Circuit ruled on July 16, 1953 that the board had not proved a "tendency toward monopoly", but on October 14, 1953 the Department of Justice asked the Supreme Court to review the decision.

When Henry Ford proposed that tariff barriers around American business be discarded, Wente approved and commented: "If you are going to give these countries aid, why give it to them outright; why not trade with them and get your money that way?" (*Christian Science Monitor,* March 2, 1953).

In addition to heading the Bank of America, Wente holds posts in many other organizations: director of the First National Bank of Portland; director of the California State Chamber of Commerce; chairman of the water resources committee of the California State Chamber of Commerce; committee member of the California Fish and Game Commission; member of the Forest Service Advisory Council, California Region; Northern California chairman of the Savings Bond committee of the American Bankers Association; chairman of the board of trustees of the San Francisco Bureau of Governmental Research; member of the San Francisco Chamber of Commerce; member of the Los Angeles Chamber of Commerce, member of the executive committee of the Grand National Livestock Exposition; committee member of the investors panel of the Transportation Association; committee member of the San Francisco Arbitration Panel of the New York Stock Exchange; and director of the Marina Improvement Association.

This banker is a member-at-large of the national council of the Boy Scouts of America, and is a member of the regional executive committee of this organization. Wente is a member of the San Francisco Stock Exchange Club; the Bohemian Club (San Francisco), the Commercial Club (San Francisco); the Rotary Club (San Francisco), of which he is a member of the business counsel committee; the St. Francis Yacht Club; the Masons and the Shriners.

Carl Wente and Jessie Huldah Orelup, a former Livermore school teacher, were married on January 19, 1915. He is president of the Duck Hunters Association, and is a member of Ducks Unlimited. He is also fond of woodworking. In religion he is a Protestant; in politics a Republican. He has brown eyes and brown hair; is six feet tall, and weighs two hundred pounds. *Time* describes him as a "gusty and hustling" man who talks the farmer's language. Wente's most frequent injunction to underlings is "Give 'em action!"

References

N Y Herald Tribune p1+ S 11 '52 por
Time 60:93 S 22 '52 por
Who's Who in America, 1952-53
World Biography (1954)

WHITE, FRANCIS W(ILFORD) July 22, 1893- Business executive

Address: h. 15 Wolcott Ave., Andover, Mass.

A leading figure in New England's textile industry for the past twenty years, Francis W. White was president of the American Woolen Company from April 1950 to May 1954, when he resigned and was succeeded by Joseph B. Ely.

Described by *Time* magazine as "the world's largest woolen and worsted manufacturer," this company owns mills throughout New England, in New York State and in several southern states. Before being elected president White had been associated with the company for eleven years as a designer, and seven years in administrative positions. During 1953 he launched a program to meet increasing taxes, higher wages and foreign competition in the woolen business.

In March 1953 White told stockholders at the fifty-fourth annual meeting that the management of the American Woolen Company was "embarked on a program of diversification in synthetic fibers, accompanied by a liquidation of 'excess capacity' in woolens and worsteds" (New York *Times,* March 25, 1953).

Francis Wilford White was born in Plymouth, Massachusetts on July 22, 1893, the son of Leo L. and Mary M. (Sampson) White. At the age of seventeen he began his career in the textile industry as an apprentice in designing worsted fabrics for the Standish Worsted Company of Plymouth. Four years later, in 1914, he became a designer for Puritan Mills, a division of the American Woolen Company, and he remained in that post until 1925, with the exception of a period of military service overseas in World War I as a captain.

He moved to Ohio in 1925 to assume the post of head designer of the Cleveland Worsted Mills; two years later he became manufacturing superintendent, and in 1928 general superintendent. Returning to New England in 1936, he was appointed superintendent of the A. D. Juilliard's Atlantic Mills in Providence, Rhode Island. His next move, ten years later, marked a return to the American Woolen Company when he became resident manager of its Wood Mills in Lawrence, Massachusetts. He rose to a vice-presidency in 1949, in charge of the company's worsted division, and on April 26, 1950, he succeeded Moses Pendleton as president.

The American Woolen Company received its first charter in March 1899. According to the *Magazine of Wall Street,* the firm possessed in 1951 assets of more than $126,000,000; it operated twenty-five mills in New England, New York and Kentucky, and employed some 25,000 persons. Its mill in Lawrence, which is three blocks long, is the largest worsted mill in the world.

At the time of White's promotion to the presidency, *Time* reported that his "next big job" would be "designing a new look for American Woolen's profits, which plummeted from $16,472,393 in 1948 to $2,194,451 last year [in 1949]." Less than a year later, in Feb-

FRANCIS W. WHITE

ruary 1951, the *Christian Science Monitor* reported that the company's net income had risen to $5,309,630 in 1950, and that unfilled orders had increased from $29,000,000 to "some $55,000,000." At the same time White announced that the company had accepted increasingly large contracts and that a large part of its production was devoted to turning out Government orders.

At the annual meeting in March 1951 he informed stockholders that unfilled orders had reached a record high of $217,000,000. A proposal was made at this meeting to investigate a decline of earnings, efficiency of present operations, directors' attendance at board meetings, policies with respect to adoption of synthetic fibers, and the possibilities of retiring the preferred stock. "Although no general rebuttal of the charges implied in the group's resolution was made . . . Mr. White praised the management policies of the late Moses Pendleton" and said that "he personally was devoting full time 'seven days a week' to bettering the interests of the company" (New York *Herald Tribune*, March 28, 1951).

In the beginning of 1952 as reported in the *Christian Science Monitor* (February 15, 1952), the woolen-worsted industry in New England was in "the worst depression" since 1933, with many mills either closing or moving to the South. Addressing an audience which included both management and labor leaders at an annual dinner of the Greater Lawrence Chamber of Commerce in January 1952, White announced that the American Woolen Company was seriously considering the removal of all its operations out of New England. "We have, at present," he asserted, "every intention of removing a great deal more of our machinery from this area. Whether any of it will remain here depends entirely on whether we and our workers can operate mills in this city, and in New England, on a competitive basis with the mills and the workers of the South" (New York *Times*, January 18, 1952).

Although the company had netted a profit of $11,851,082 in 1951, he added, the year would have been "one of the worst" in the company's history without Government contracts. The difference between North and South, he explained, is in the high New England state taxes, unstable wool prices and the cost of labor; Southern workers on the other hand, "produce fabrics at lower unit costs, and the products of their labor can be sold from 30 to 50 cents a yard cheaper than we can sell them." The Textile Workers' Union of America (CIO), which had already agreed not to ask for wage increases in 1952, responded to White's remarks by stating that there was nothing in the union's contract to prevent an increase in work loads when new production machinery was put into use or new fabrics produced.

White told company stockholders in March 1952 that the worst of the textile depression of 1951 appeared to be over, but repeated that unless unit costs could be substantially lowered, the company would have to move the bulk of its manufacturing operations out of New England. Speaking before the National Association of Woolen and Worsted Overseers in Boston in November 1952, he paid tribute "to New England textile workers for their cooperation during the year in accepting new work assignments in the struggle to meet outside competition," but warned management leaders against the growing threat of foreign competition. He announced in March 1953 that the American Woolen Company had launched a program of "diversification in synthetic fibers" recognizing the trend toward the wider use of lighter weight materials and new synthetics.

In May 1953 a neutral arbitrator for the Textile Workers Union of America and the American Woolen Company denied a company request for a 20 per cent wage cut for 16,000 employees in sixteen Northern mills. The company had applied for the wage reduction of thirty-one cents in the present average of $1.55 an hour in January, soon after its annual report had disclosed a $6,000,000 loss [for 1952] (New York *Times*, May 20, 1953).

On October 22, 1953 a net loss of $6,000,000 was reported by the American Woolen Company for the nine months ended September 30.

The textile company executive married the former Katherine Hickey, a teacher, on July 12, 1922. They have five children, Katherine A., Francis W., Mary E., John R., and Ann. The Lowell Textile Institute conferred upon him an honorary Master of Science degree in June 1951. He is a member of the Algonquin Club of Boston and the American Legion. White is a Republican and a Catholic. *Time* describes him as "a rockbound New Englander who still believes that 'the best thing in New York is the 5 o'clock train to Boston.'"

References

Time 55:87 My 8 '50
Who's Who in America, 1952-53

WHITTEMORE, ARTHUR Oct. 23, 1916-
Pianist

Address: b. c/o Columbia Concerts, Inc., 113 W. 57th St., New York 19; h. Quogue, Long Island, N.Y.

LOWE, JACK Dec. 25, 1917- Pianist
b. c/o Columbia Concerts, Inc., 113 W. 57th St. New York 19; h. Quogue, Long Island, N.Y.

New York City's venerable Town Hall ushered onto the musical scene, in 1940, a new two-piano team, Arthur Whittemore and Jack Lowe. Here were two personable young men destined to make their mark not only as technically brilliant musicians, but also as innovators in concert programing. Since that time their Carnegie Hall concerts have doubled the previous box-office records of any other duo-pianists.

They also appear frequently on nationwide television programs and give about eighty concerts throughout the United States and Canada each season.

Since their first record was released in 1942 more than a million disks have been sold. A recent addition to their RCA Victor catalogue is the LP release of the Ralph Vaughan Williams *Concerto for Two Pianos* with Golschmann conducting. Their best-seller *Two Grand,* has been reissued. They have personally arranged nearly 200 works for two pianos.

Their success, aside from winning personalities, has been due in large part to their daring to straddle the formidable gap between serious and popular music. They are protagonists of musical "Americana" in both categories, with accent on the melodious; they attend properly to the classics, give pronounced attention to new works from any source, package the whole with finish and élan, and thereby stretch their audience appeal to divergent groups. Critics rap them for their lighter moments, but the public flocks, and recording companies approve their selections. The pianists' reason for this unorthodox programing, they feel, is sound. They had found themselves handicapped by the limited literature composed originally for two pianos. Having solved this problem in their own individual fashion, they like the wider audience their programs attract.

Bender

ARTHUR WHITTEMORE

Bender

JACK LOWE

Whittemore and Lowe began their partnership quite by chance. Although they both come originally from the West, they did not meet until college days were over and they had come East for advanced study. Arthur Whittemore, better known as "Buck", was born in Vermillion, South Dakota, October 23, 1916, where his father, Arthur H. Whittemore, was a football coach at the University of South Dakota. His mother, Helen Pickett (Austen) Whittemore, had been a voice student at the university. "Buck" Whittemore Senior held the distinction of having been named an All-American guard during his own college days at Brown University.

Buck's music lessons began when he was five years old. Athletics were barred to him as a precaution against injuring his hands. He studied piano and organ, and when only twelve years old became organist for the Congregational Church. At fourteen, he was appointed organist and choir master of the Methodist Church.

In college, Buck was a favorite soloist with the university symphony orchestra. When he graduated from the University of South Dakota in 1934, he was named to the university's Hall of Fame, an honor bestowed upon six students each year, and a teaching fellowship at the Eastman School of Music, in Rochester, New York. At the Eastman School, his original compositions attracted the attention of the

WHITTEMORE, A. and LOWE, J.—*Cont.*
broadcasting networks. After he had won his Master's degree he was appointed director of music at the University of Rochester's College for Men. It was here that he met Jack Lowe.

Jack Lowe's home town was Aurora, Colorado, now a part of "Greater Denver". He was born December 25, 1917. His father, Curtis W. Lowe, was a postal inspector and his mother, Beatrice (Hargiss) Lowe, was a singer who appeared with local choral societies. Jack started his musical career on a toy violin from a mail order catalogue, from which he drew music of sufficient notice to win for himself a good violin. Soon, he was appearing in local concerts as a child prodigy. By the time he was sixteen, he was a member of the Denver orchestra. At graduation from high school, he won a scholarship and enrolled in Colorado's state teachers' college, where he turned from the violin to piano and organ. He worked as an entertainer in resort hotels. He, too, composed, submitted some of his works to the Eastman School of Music, and was awarded a scholarship, which took him through his Master's studies.

Jack was appointed, in 1935, assistant to the director of music (Arthur Whittemore) at the University of Rochester's College for Men.

Thus, their partnership began, but not yet as a piano team. They trained the Rochester Glee Club which won the national competition for university glee clubs over 145 other groups.

At the end of the first year of their teaching collaboration, Whittemore's aunt, living in Puerto Rico and active in local music circles, invited her nephew to spend his vacation there. To insure an invitation for Jack, too, Buck wrote her that they were already a well-known duo-piano team. They reached Puerto Rico to find that Whittemore's aunt had arranged a concert for them. With only eighteen days to prepare themselves for the concert, with practically no music available in the island's shops, they created their own two-piano arrangements, and made their debut on schedule with nineteen compositions. The success of this concert and ensuing radio engagements encouraged Whittemore and Lowe to decide upon a joint career.

First, however, they returned to their jobs at the Eastman School, and during the next few years prepared an extensive repertoire. In preparation for a New York debut, they toured the mid-West, acting at first as their own managers, publicity agents, ticket printers, and box-office men.

Their quick and promising rise to popularity was interrupted when both men enlisted in the Navy in January 1942 after the attack on Pearl Harbor. For four years, they were stationed at the Brooklyn Naval Receiving Station busy at desk jobs and giving occasional concerts for the sailors. Then followed a seventy-eight day tour of Naval hospitals, multiple broadcast appearances and a tour of the Pacific as the first Navy entertainment unit—a total of 700 performances at Navy bases before more than half a million service men.

When they were discharged from service in 1946, Whittemore and Lowe returned to the concert stage and played 110 engagements within the first eighteen months—individual concerts, with major orchestras from coast to coast and summer stadium appearances. Then came television and a proposition to find a format by which serious music could be made palatable on sponsored TV programs—a reversal of their concert approach breaking the precedent of standard programs with lighter musical fare. WOR-TV's *Music in Silhouette* was the answer—five nights a week of music ranging in taste appeal from the compositions of Richard Rodgers and Cole Porter, to Franz Schubert and Maurice Ravel.

Their twenty finger tips command practically the entire two-piano literature and have transcribed more than 200 compositions not originally composed for this medium, ranging from the classics to the best of today's semi-classical music. In their search for new material, they have commissioned works from contemporary composers including Manuel Rosenthal, Ernst Krenek and Morton Gould.

To date Whittemore and Lowe RCA Victor records have sold over the million mark. Their recorded albums include Stravinsky, Ravel, Poulenc, Bax, Bartok, Copland, Brahms, Vaughan Williams, Saint-Saens, Dvorak, Bach, Kreisler, and popular compositions. They cater to the juke boxes with such old favorites as *Third Street Rumba* and *Begin the Beguine*—which was on their Town Hall debut program, with critics somewhat aghast. Their album *Two Grand* with the RCA Victor Orchestra accompanying, best selling album of popular tunes of all time, includes such hits as *Brazil, Still of the Night* and *Falling in Love with Love*. When they appear with New York's Philharmonic Symphony, they deftly switch to the serious composers.

Whittemore and Lowe make their home at Quogue, Long Island. Here, they practice, swim, sail, and follow their individual hobbies—Whittemore collects rare recordings, Lowe paints, and the two enjoy a joint hobby, their two record stores, the "House of Music". From Quogue, they set out in a Cadillac convertible for their nationwide tours, never under eighty engagements per season. Their car, which they drive themselves, bears the license number 88 WL—for the number of keys on the piano and the first letters of their own last names. They cover thousands of miles each season, followed by a truck carrying their two matched concert grand pianos.

Critic Cecil Smith has called Whittemore and Lowe "the most versatile team in the business." The New York *Times* survey-list of classical records recommends their recordings for a basic collection. But, probably, one of their most cherished honors has been the citation bestowed upon Whittemore and Lowe by the University of Rochester on the occasion of its centennial, as two of the institution's thirteen most distinguished alumni.

References

Christian Sci Mon p15 Ag 13 '52
Look 19:76 S 17 '46
Newsweek 40:56 D 1 '52

WILDE, LOUISE K(ATHLEEN) July 18, 1910- United States naval officer

Address: b. c/o United States Department of the Navy, Bureau of Naval Personnel, Washington 25, D.C.; h. 2500 Q St., N.W., Washington, D.C.

Appointed the director of the women's branch of the Navy in April 1953, Captain Louise K. Wilde is the fourth woman to hold this position since the WAVES (Women Appointed for Volunteer Emergency Service) was established in 1942. Captain Wilde has risen steadily to her new assignment: she has served as public relations officer of the Navy, as assistant to three former directors of the WAVES and as assistant director of the shipping control division in California. Before entering military service, Miss Wilde had been director of publicity for Mount Holyoke College in Massachusetts and freshman dean at Rockford College in Illinois.

Louise Kathleen Wilde was born on July 18, 1910 in Concord, New Hampshire. The only child of George William Wilde, a businessman, and the former Jane Louise O'Donoghue, she is descended on both sides from English ancestors. Brought up in Concord, New Hampshire, Louise Wilde attended the Concord High School where she was class president.

After her graduation in 1927, Miss Wilde attended Mount Holyoke College in South Hadley, Massachusetts, and majored in French. Active in the student government, she was elected an officer of her class and chairman of the college judicial board. Although she was a member of the college glee club and of the varsity soccer team, she also found time for newspaper work on the college press bureau and as a campus correspondent for various newspapers. She was graduated from the college in June of 1931.

Miss Wilde returned to Mount Holyoke in the fall of 1931 as assistant director of the press bureau, a position she held until 1934. She then worked as the education reporter for the Springfield *Union* in Springfield, Massachusetts. Miss Wilde became the director of publicity and public relations for Mount Holyoke in 1935 and had the responsibility of directing the public relations program for the celebration of the college's one hundredth anniversary in 1937.

Becoming very interested in college administrative work through the influence of Dr. Mary E. Woolley of Mount Holyoke, Miss Wilde accepted the position of assistant to the president of Rockford College in Rockford, Illinois in 1938. She helped with public relations, publications, fund raising, and teaching in addition to her general college administrative duties.

After two years at the college, Miss Wilde attended Columbia University where she had received a scholarship. In 1941 she was awarded a master's degree in personnel administration. Miss Wilde returned to Rockford College in 1941 and served as freshman dean and assistant to the president.

After the outbreak of World War II, Miss Wilde decided to enter military service. She

CAPT. LOUISE K. WILDE

was one of the first women commissioned after Congress had authorized the creation of the WAVES on July 31, 1942. Enlisting in the women's division of the naval reserve with the rank of lieutenant (junior grade), she served as a public relations officer at the United States Naval Reserve Midshipmen's School in Northampton, Massachusetts.

Assigned to Washington, D.C. in January 1943, Lieutenant Wilde was assistant to the first director of the WAVES, Captain Mildred McAfee (later Mrs. Douglas Horton), and was coordinator of public relations for the women's reserve. She was advanced to the rank of lieutenant commander.

Her interest in military service having been stimulated by her association with Captain McAfee, the naval officer decided to remain in the service after the war was over. She became the district director of the women's reserve in the fourteenth naval district (Hawaii) in August 1945. Her duties were both administrative and concerned with personnel. During the postwar demobilization period, when the WAVES decreased from a complement of 86,000 to a little over 2,000, she was responsible for this district. Lieutenant Commander Wilde was soon promoted to the rank of commander (in December 1945).

Named deputy director of the WAVES in June 1946, she assisted Captain Jean T. Palmer, director of the WAVES, and was primarily concerned with administrative and personnel planning problems.

When Captain Joy B. Hancock succeeded Captain Palmer as director of the WAVES in 1946, Commander Wilde became assistant director for plans of the women's division of the Navy and worked on the legislation which would provide for the WAVES to become a permanent part of the regular Navy and the Naval Reserve. The Women's Armed Services Integration Act, signed by President Harry S.

WILDE, LOUISE K.—*Continued*

Truman on June 12, 1948, authorized the direct assimilation of women into the naval services up to 2 per cent of the total authorized strength. Commander Wilde then helped to work on the plans to implement this legislation.

When Captain Hancock was named, under the new act, as assistant to the chief of naval personnel for women, Commander Wilde continued to act as her administrative assistant, and was given the permanent rank of commander in the regular Navy on January 1, 1950.

Commander Wilde left Washington, D.C. in 1952 to serve on the staff of the commander of the western sea frontier as assistant director of the shipping control division in San Francisco, California. She remained in this post until April 10, 1953 when she was named to succeed Captain Hancock as assistant chief of naval personnel for women.

Captain Wilde received the Secretary of the Navy Commendation Ribbon in 1945 for her wartime service and the Bronze Star in 1946 for her work in Hawaii. She also holds the American Area Service Medal, the Asiatic-Pacific Area Service Medal, and the World War II Victory Medal. Mount Holyoke awarded her a citation at the Convocation in Science and Human Values in 1952 for her distinguished work in human relations.

Captain Wilde is a member of the Mount Holyoke Club of Washington, D.C., the American Association of University Women, and Pi Lambda Theta.

The director of the women's division of the Navy has hazel eyes and dark brown hair. She weighs 125 pounds and is five feet four inches tall. Her church affiliation is Catholic. Her hobbies include golf, tennis, riding, flying and reading. Known as "Billie" to her friends, Captain Wilde has been described as a woman with "poise and astuteness ... [and] ... effervesent charm. . . ."

References

Ind Woman: 32:348+ O '53

WILGRESS, (LEOLYN) DANA Oct. 20, 1892- Diplomat

Address: b. c/o Canadian Delegation to the North Atlantic Council, 3, rue André Pascal, Paris 16, France; h. 371 Mariposa Ave., Rockcliffe Park, Ottawa, Ontario, Canada

A career diplomat with a background of forty years of service in Canada's Department of Trade and Commerce and in the Department of External Affairs, Dana Wilgress was named his country's permanent representative to the North Atlantic Council and to the Office of European Economic Cooperation in June 1953. He had served since June 1952 as the Canadian Under Secretary of State for External Affairs.

His duties took him to diplomatic posts in Moscow, where he was Canada's diplomatic representative between 1942 and 1947; at Berne, Switzerland, where he was Minister from 1947 to 1949; and in London where he was High Commissioner for Canada in the United Kingdom from 1949 to 1952. He has represented Canada on many international bodies, including the contracting parties to the General Agreement on Tariffs and Trade (GATT), of which he was chairman from 1948 to 1951, and was re-elected chairman on October 24, 1953. He is a strong opponent of all forms of discrimination in international trade. He was a delegate to the North Atlantic Council of Deputies in 1950, 1951 and 1952.

Leolyn Dana Wilgress was born October 20, 1892, in Vancouver, British Columbia, to Henry Trollope and Helene Maud (Empey) Wilgress. His father was employed by the Canadian Pacific Steamship Company, and young Wilgress, raised in China, Japan and Canada, received his early education at Queen's School, Vancouver, British Columbia, the Modern School, Yokohama, Japan, and University School, Victoria, British Columbia.

He entered McGill University, Montreal and won the Mackenzie Exhibition Scholarship in 1912 and 1913. When he was graduated in 1914, he received honors in economics and political science.

Wilgress became a junior trade commissioner in Canada's Department of Trade and Commerce in 1914. At that time the department was placing its trade commissioner service on a career basis for the first time, with a view to securing and training able men who would make it their life work. Wilgress was one of the first recruits to the service, on the recommendation of the late Professor Stephen Leacock of McGill University.

After two years in Ottawa, Wilgress was assigned to Omsk in Russia. That area, undergoing extensive development of its natural resources, was of interest to Canada at that time as a potential market for mining machinery and similar equipment, and as a territory which, because of its geographical position, faced problems similar to those of Canada. Stationed there for two years, Wilgress made extensive trips and gained a knowledge of the Russian language and culture.

The diplomat was transferred in 1918 to the Russian Pacific port of Vladivostok and investigated trade openings in southern China. In the following year, he was a member of a Canadian economic mission to Siberia. Named trade commissioner to Bucharest, Romania, in 1920, he explored trade possibilities in southeast Europe. During 1921, Wilgress served as trade commissioner in London. He was posted to Hamburg, Germany in 1922 and remained there for ten years as Canadian trade commissioner. In this period, he paid two visits to Russia, in 1921 and in 1923.

Designated as acting director of the commercial intelligence service of the Department of Trade and Commerce, Wilgress returned to Ottawa in 1932 to assume the duties of that post; his confirmation in the position of director followed in April 1933. Among his first tasks was the work of preparing for the imperial economic conference, held in Ottawa in 1932, at which he was one of the advisers to the Canadian delegation.

Wilgress acted in the same capacity at the World Economic Conference, held in London in 1933. He accompanied the Prime Minister, Richard Bedford Bennett, to London to the Silver Jubilee of King George V in 1935. During this period a series of trade agreements between the United States and Canada, and a Canadian-United Kingdom pact were signed. In the House of Commons, the next Prime Minister, Mackenzie King, specifically named Wilgress as one of three members of the public service who had had the responsibility of working out the details of the agreements (*Saturday Night,* March 15, 1941).

Appointed Deputy Minister of Trade and Commerce in 1940, his services were required on the committee advising the Cabinet on economic policy, on the Foreign Exchange Control Board, on a sub-committee on Canadian shipping of the advisory export control committee, and on the Wartime Prices and Trade Board. He was a member of the Canadian trade mission to South America in 1941.

After two years' service in this post, Wilgress entered the Department of External Affairs with his appointment as Canada's first Minister to the Union of Soviet Socialist Republics in 1942. Raised to the rank of Ambassador in 1944, he continued to represent his country in Moscow until 1947. While filling this position he was called on to act as a special adviser to the Canadian delegation to the San Francisco Conference in 1945, and to act as chairman of the Canadian delegation to the Preparatory Commission of the United Nations, held in the same year in London. His work with the United Nations was continued in 1946 as a Canadian delegate to the General Assembly, and in 1948, when he presided over the Committee of Five at the third session of the General Assembly in Paris.

In the meantime the diplomat in 1947 had been named Minister to Switzerland, but he retained his personal rank of ambassador. He went to London to be High Commissioner for Canada in the United Kingdom in 1949. While in these two diplomatic posts he represented his country at international meetings including the World Trade Conference in Havana, Cuba, in 1947 (where he led the Canadian delegation), and the 1947 conference on trade and employment in Geneva, Switzerland.

Here he was chairman of the committee working on the text of the general agreement on tariffs, and was credited by New York *Times* reporter Michael L. Hoffman with preventing a breakdown of the conference by his persistent efforts to avoid an imminent Anglo-American rift (October 17, 1947). He was elected chairman of successive meetings of the contracting parties to the Geneva agreement, known as the General Agreement on Tariffs and Trade (GATT).

In his speech opening the firth session of the group, Wilgress stated: "These sessions have become the sole existing international forum for the discussion of commercial policy questions on a world-wide basis" (New York *Times,* November 3, 1950).

Early in 1952 it was announced that Wilgress had been appointed Under Secretary of State for External Affairs, to succeed A. D. P. Heeney, and in June of that year he took up

National Film Bd. of Canada
DANA WILGRESS

his duties in Ottawa as administrative head of the department. *Saturday Night* (May 7, 1952) remarked: "No man in Canada's history has brought to this job a wider knowledge of the world or a more varied experience of foreign service. . . . The Department of External Affairs will be in very good hands."

On June 9, 1953, Secretary of State for External Affairs Lester B. Pearson announced that Wilgress would become Canada's permanent representative to the North Atlantic Council and the Office of European Economic Cooperation. Having been Canada's deputy to NATO's Council of Deputies for three years, Wilgress was credited with knowing as much about the details of NATO as "any man alive."

The career diplomat is a member of the Canadian Institute of International Affairs and of the Civil Service Professional Institute; when he was trade commissioner in Hamburg, he was a member of the Cosmopolitan Club (president, 1930-1931) and chairman of the British Board of Commerce there in 1931-1932.

He is five feet eight and one-half inches tall, weighs 160 pounds; his hair is gray, his eyes, blue. On June 4, 1919, he married Olga Buergin. They have three children, Victor Jura, Diana Sonia and Edward Dana. His church affiliation is with the Church of England. In Ottawa he belongs to the Rideau Club and the Country Club. His recreations are golfing and skiing.

References

Maclean's Mag 56:18 F 1 '43
Montreal Gazette Jl 26 '52
Sat Night 56:21 Mr 15 '41; 60:2 Ap 28 '45; 67:7 My 17 '52 por
International Who's Who, 1953
Who's Who, 1953
Who's Who in Canada, 1951-1952
Who's Who in America, 1954-55
Who's Who in the United Nations (1951)

WILKINS, J(ESSE) ERNEST Feb. 1, 1894- United States Government official; lawyer

Address: b. c/o Department of Labor, Washington 25, D.C.; 180 W. Washington St., Chicago, Ill.

The first Negro to occupy a sub-Cabinet post in the United States Government is J. Ernest Wilkins, a Chicago lawyer, who is Assistant Secretary of Labor in charge of international affairs. The appointment was made in March 1954 by President Dwight D. Eisenhower, who in 1953 had named Wilkins a public member and vice-chairman of the President's Committee on Government Contracts, concerned with the problem of civil rights.

Early in the tenure of his new office Wilkins scored a number of diplomatic victories when in June 1954 as head of the United States delegation at the International Labor Organization conference, he won support for his country's policies by his skillful manner in handling world labor issues.

The son of a Baptist minister, Jesse Ernest Wilkins was born to Henry Byrd and Susie Olivia (Douthit) Wilkins in Farmington, Missouri on February 1, 1894. He attended the Farmington primary school and took preparatory work at Lincoln Institute (now Lincoln College) in Missouri. He then entered the University of Illinois, where he was elected to Phi Beta Kappa. He specialized in mathematics, writing a thesis on an algebraic numbers theory, and was granted a B.A. degree with special honors in 1918. In the fall of that year, following his enlistment in the United States armed forces, he was sent to France for World War I service as a supply sergeant in the 809th infantry.

After the war Wilkins worked his way through law school at the University of Chicago and upon taking his J.D. degree in 1921 was admitted to the Illinois bar. He then established a private law practice in Chicago, where he won distinction as an attorney and a civic leader and was elected president of the Bar Association of Cook County, Illinois, for the year 1941-42.

Wilkins, a Republican, first came to nationwide attention in 1953 when, on August 15, President Eisenhower appointed him vice-chairman of the newly established President's Committee on Government Contracts. This panel, of which Vice-President Richard M. Nixon was named chairman, was set up by an executive order to augment enforcement of the government policy against discrimination in hiring or promoting because of race, creed or national origin in any establishment engaged in government business. Non-discrimination clauses are embodied in all government contract work.

At the first meeting of the fifteen-member committee, on September 14, 1953, Wilkins, acting as spokesman for the group, told reporters that wherever possible the committee would seek voluntary compliance and would give much of its attention to an educational campaign.

The following year, on October 25, Wilkins made a report for the New York *Herald Tribune* on the way that the Eisenhower Administration has handled problems of race discrimination. Reviewing the accomplishments of the Committee on Government Contracts, he wrote, "We have been successful because we have concentrated first on limiting discrimination in those areas where the Federal government has authority and responsibility. Instead of seeking more legislative authority now, we are using effectively the power we already have. . . . We have demonstrated that it is not legislation, but determination that will end discrimination."

Impressed by Wilkins' work on the anti-bias committee, Nixon, according to the New York *Times,* suggested to Eisenhower that the Chicago lawyer was deserving of a high position in the Republican Administration. Subsequently, on March 4, 1954 the President named Wilkins to succeed Spencer Miller as Assistant Secretary of Labor in charge of international affairs, at a salary of $15,000 a year.

His nomination to the sub-Cabinet post was confirmed by the Senate on March 12. The new Assistant Secretary of Labor said of his appointment: "I consider this an honor not to Wilkins individually but to my race in general. I think that this is an answer more eloquent than anything I could say to those who say that the American government is not fair to all of its citizens." Since he had never been affiliated with a labor union, the lawyer remarked, he would have an open mind on labor problems.

Chiefly concerned with foreign affairs for the Department of Labor, Wilkins represents the United States government at international labor organization meetings and labor conferences abroad. During a press interview on March 4 he stated that three-fourths of the people of the world belong to other than the white race and that his being a Negro would aid his work at international conferences. *Business Week* (May 29, 1954) observed that Wilkins "converts what has always been a U.S. weak point in international meetings dealing with social affairs—the American race problem—into a point of strength."

In the first important assignment of his office, the Assistant Secretary headed the five-member United States delegation to the thirty-seventh annual general conference of the International Labor Organization conference, held in Geneva, Switzerland in June 1954. He was one of two representatives of the government; other members of the delegation represented workers and employers. The ILO, originally a part of the League of Nations and later incorporated within the structure of the United Nations, had been boycotted by the Soviet Union since 1939. The Russian decision to return, with its satellite countries, to the labor organization, made the 1954 ILO session one in which the main issue was what role the Communist nations should take in the U.N. agency.

One of the principal figures in the debate over this issue was the United States chief representative. At the opening session of the labor conference, on June 2, Wilkins expressed opposition to Soviet efforts immediately to secure influential positions on important ILO committees. "It is the interest of the United States," he made clear, "that nations of chief industrial importance be recognized as such and receive a place on the Selections Committee.... [But] we all should come here not with the idea of saying ours is the greatest nation in all the world, but with the idea of building this organization into the great organ for peace it should be" (New York *Times,* June 3, 1954).

The restraint of Wilkins' statement compared to the "imperiousness" of the Russian demand, commented a New York *Times* editorial (June 4, 1954), won considerable praise for the United States stand and brought the American delegate a notable "diplomatic achievement" in his first appearance at a world conference.

To Wilkins' personal credit also was the victory gained by the United States when the conference by a vote of 133 to 48 agreed to allow Nationalist China to keep its voting rights in the conference. The ILO constitution bars from voting any country that owes more than two years' dues. Wilkins could argue that while Nationalist China had not paid its full dues in five years, it had recently paid $50,000 toward its debt of $883,000 to the ILO and that in 1952 and 1953 the conference had allowed the Nationalists to retain their vote.

"Wilkins' forceful but moderate speech," reported William H. Stoneman, "delivered in a resonant, clearcut tone, was regarded by the other delegates as a deciding factor in swinging the vote to the American side" (Washington *Post and Times Herald,* June 29, 1954).

He was active too in the unsuccessful protest made by the United States and other free nations against seating Communist worker and employer delegates at the conference. The "monolithic" Soviet system, Wilkins told a press conference, did not allow independent employer and worker representation as the ILO constitution requires, since all Communist delegates would merely represent their government.

The Assistant Secretary of Labor was honored in August 1954 by the National Association of Colored Women, which presented him an award of merit for pioneer service in the advancement of the colored people. Speaking at the twenty-ninth biennial convention of that organization, Wilkins pointed out that "with new gains in civil rights come new responsibilities." Since the U.S. Supreme Court's recent decision on racial integration in public schools has given new freedom for all Americans, he said, "we must help prepare our children to take their place in a world not bound by the old horizons" (Washington *Post and Times Herald,* August 2, 1954).

Wilkins is a prominent layman in the Methodist Church, having been a member of the commission on world service and finance from 1942 to 1948, and of its executive committee from 1944 to 1948. Since 1948 he has served on the judicial council and in 1953 was elected council secretary. On May 7, 1954 he gave a speech in Chicago entitled "Labor and Social

J. ERNEST WILKINS

Relations" before the board of social and economic relations of the Methodist Church. After discussing general economic conditions in the United States and developments in the economic status of Negroes, he made suggestions on what the Church can do in the field of economics.

He belongs to the National Bar Association, the American Judicature Society and the University of Chicago Alumni Association. His Greek-letter societies are Sigma Pi Phi and Kappa Alpha Psi. He is a Mason, a Knight of Pythias and a member of the City and Illini clubs of Chicago. In 1941 he was awarded an honorary LL.D. degree from Lincoln University in Jefferson City, Missouri. He was a member (1942-1952) and is treasurer (since 1952) of the board of trustees of Provident Hospital in Chicago and is also a director of the Hyde Park-Kenwood Community Conference.

Wilkins' wife, the former Lucile Beatrice Robinson, whom he married on November 23, 1922, is recording secretary of the women's division of Christian Service, a Methodist organization. The Wilkinses have three sons: Julian B., who is a law partner of his father in Chicago; J. Ernest, Jr., an industrial physicist; and John R., a lawyer employed by the Department of Justice.

Observers have commented on the even temper and natural modesty of the sturdily built lawyer. He is a teetotaler with a special fondness for iced tea.

References

N Y Herald Tribune p3 Mr 5 '54; p10 Mr 6 '54
N Y Times p52 Ag 16 '53
Time 63:20+ Mr 15 '54
Washington (D.C.) Post p19 Je 29 '54
Who's Who in America, 1952-53

WILLIS, FRANCES E(LIZABETH) May 20, 1899- United States Ambassador to Switzerland

Address: b. Department of State, Washington 25, D.C.; h. 503 W. Highland Ave., Redlands, Calif.

The senior woman officer in the foreign service and the first American woman to attain the rank of class one as a career diplomat is Dr. Frances E. Willis. She was nominated by President Eisenhower on July 11, 1953 to the post of Ambassador to Switzerland to succeed Minister Richard C. Paterson, Jr. In assuming her new assignment in August, 1953, Dr. Willis became the first United States Ambassador to Switzerland. (In March 1953 the Swiss Government gave permission for the raising of the Legation at Berne to Embassy status.) A former social science instructor at Goucher and Vassar Colleges, the Ambassador has had twenty-six years of experience in the foreign service. Her immediately preceding assignment was that of counselor of the American Legation in Helsinki, Finland.

FRANCES E. WILLIS

Frances Elizabeth Willis was born in Metropolis, Illinois, on May 20, 1899, one of the three children of John Gilbert and Belle Whitfield (James) Willis. She is of Scotch, English, Irish, and Dutch ancestry. When Francis was six years old, the family moved to Memphis, Tennessee and several years later to Kenosha, Wisconsin. She attended the school of the Sisters of St. Mary (Episcopal), and the Kemper Hall High School in Kenosha, graduating in 1916. Her extracurricular activities included basketball and dramatics.

Continuing her education at Leland Stanford University in California, she majored in history and was a reader in political science, taking an interest in student government and the Y.W.C.A. Her recreations during her college years were diving and horseback riding. Miss Willis was elected to Phi Beta Kappa and received the A.B. degree in 1920. The recipient of a CRB Fellowship, she did postgraduate work for one year at the Université Libre de Bruxelles in Belgium, and for two years at Leland Stanford where she received the Ph.D. degree in political science in 1923.

Dr. Willis entered the profession of teaching, serving as an instructor at Goucher College, Baltimore, Maryland, from 1923 to 1924. At Vassar College she was an instructor and assistant professor of political science from 1924 to 1927; she spent the summer of 1926 in public health work and teaching for the International Grenfell Association in Labrador.

Believing that a better understanding of her subject would be obtained by actual experience in government, Dr. Willis took the foreign service examination, and entered the service in 1927. She found the work so challenging that she did not return to teaching, and having attended the foreign service school, she received her first foreign assignment in 1928 when she was appointed vice-consul at Valparaiso, Chile.

The next appointment for the young diplomat was a vice-consular post in Santiago, Chile, in 1931, followed in the same year by a transfer to Stockholm, Sweden, where she held the rank of third secretary. Two years later, in 1933, she was transferred to the same post for Belgium and Luxemburg, and in 1937 was advanced to the position of second secretary. With the advent of war, Dr. Willis escaped internment, but for two months she and her colleagues in the American Legation at Brussels were completely cut off from contact with the outside world.

As consul and second secretary, the diplomat assumed her duties in Madrid, Spain, in 1940, becoming first secretary and consul in 1943. The following year she returned to the United States and was appointed assistant to the Under Secretary of State in Washington, D.C., a post held until 1947, when Dr. Willis became assistant chief, division of Western European affairs.

Her next appointment was as first secretary and consul to England. When she and Kathleen Molesworth, also of the service, were presented at the Court of St. James in 1947, they were the first women diplomats to have that honor, and the English newspapers commented that it was the first time United States officials had curtsied to the King.

Promotion to class one in the diplomatic service came with President Truman's nomination of Frances E. Willis to legation counselor at Helsinki, Finland in 1951. The diplomat was the first American woman to attain that rank as a professional diplomat; only the permanent rank of career Minister has a higher rating. In her new position, she took over the responsibilities of the Minister, Jack K. McFall, whenever he was away, serving as deputy chief of mission.

The appointment of Dr. Willis to the post of Ambassador to Switzerland aroused speculation as to the suitability of the choice, inasmuch as Swiss women do not have the right to vote. According to the New York *Times* of April 15, 1953, foreign diplomats in Berne, though not Swiss themselves, predicted "unfavorable repercussions in Switzerland because of the country's opposition to women's participation in politics;" however, the New York *Times* stated that "the business-like attitude of the Swiss" was "likely to ignore such reasoning." In the New York *Times* of the following day, a dispatch from Geneva quoted a spokesman for the Swiss Federal Government as saying that "he had no reason to believe that the fact that Dr. Willis was a woman would influence the Federal Council's decision" in accepting the appointment.

Frances E. Willis' appointment to the Ambassadorship of Switzerland was unanimously confirmed by the Senate on July 20, 1953 and on August 10 she was sworn into her new office. This marks the third appointment of an American woman to the position of an Ambassador. Dr. Willis stated that this distinction "brings pride and humility" and that she would assume her duties with "a prayer that I may be given wisdom and skill to serve my country worthily" (New York *Times,* August 11, 1953).

Ten months after assuming her new post, Miss Willis was interviewed by Jean Libman Block, (*This Week,* June 27, 1954), who wrote: "Many people, both in Switzerland and the United States, were aghast when Miss Willis was appointed. Wouldn't a woman ambassador in a land of disenfranchised women cause resentment? Miss Willis was a little troubled herself. But her friendly, direct manner soon put all apprehension to rest. She captured the Swiss by simply being herself."

Miss Willis said, "The basis of diplomacy today is to be tactful and sincere at the same time. We don't want to hurt people's feelings, either nationally or individually. But we do want to be honest."

On October 21, 1954 Foreign Minister Max Petitpierre summoned Ambassador Willis to his office to inform her that "successive measures" against the Swiss watch industry by the U.S. Government could not fail to have a bad effect on Swiss-American relations.

The number of women in the foreign service has increased ten fold since the beginning of World War II (*Independent Woman,* February 1952). There were twenty-one "lady diplomats" in the field in 1952. An average of 30 per cent of the appointees to diplomatic posts are made from outside the personnel of the foreign service; the others, like Ambassador Willis, have risen within the ranks. Foreign service officers rarely remain in one country for more than two years. Their work entails the issuing of passports or visas, disseminating information on American policies, handling extradition cases, and analyzing and reporting political, social and economic conditions of the particular country, in addition to promoting and protecting our foreign trade.

The Ambassador has stated that the foreign service is "no easy life," yet she believes she has had "as interesting a life as it is humanly possible to have." Like most professional women, she wants the service to consider her as a person who does a job, not as a woman. For her, the major reward is the feeling of being able to contribute to the solution of some of the problems of the world, no matter how small that contribution may be.

In Dr. Willis' home, almost every piece of furniture, silver and china, carries an association with a country in which she has carried on diplomatic work. The Ambassador is a member of the American Red Cross, the Sulgrave Club, and the Redlands Golf and Tennis Club. Blue-eyed, with graying brown hair, she is five feet eight inches in height and weighs 135 pounds. She has been described as combining sincerity and enthusiasm with a sense of humor. Fond of swimming, bridge, picnics, music and classical literature she lists under hobbies, as the principal one, a well-run home.

References

Christian Sci Mon p2 Ag 10 '53
Ind Woman 31:43 F '52; 32:306 S '53 por
N Y Herald Tribune p25 My 6 '51; p15 Jl 12 '53 por; II p1 Jl 19 '53
N Y Post Mag p2 Ag 2 '53 por
N Y Times p1 Ap 15 '53; p5 Ap 16 '53; Jl 12 '53 por; p24 Jl 13 '53
Time 62:12 Jl 20 '53
Washington (D.C.) Post Jl 12 '53 por; p19 Ag 11 '53 por
Who's Who in America, 1954-55
Who's Who in the West (1951)

WILLISTON, SAMUEL (wĭl'ĭs-tŭn) Sept. 24, 1861- Legal scholar; university professor emeritus; lawyer

Address: b. c/o Baker, Voorhis & Co., 25 Broad St., New York 4; h. 17 Berkeley St., Cambridge, Mass.

The dean of the American legal profession and one of the most beloved professors in the history of Harvard Law School is Samuel Williston. He was honored by many of his former students at the diamond jubilee meeting of the American Bar Association held in August 1953, for his part in the development of the Law School where he was associated from 1890 to 1938.

Williston is the author of the four-volume *The Law Governing Sales of Goods at Common Law and Under the Uniform Sales Act* (Baker, Voorhis, 1909, 1948), which has become a standard text, and the nine-volume *The Law of Contracts* (Baker, Voorhis, 1922-1927, 1936-1938), which has taken its place among the great reference books of Anglo-American law. Under the sponsorship of the National Conference of Commissioners on Uniform State Laws, Williston drafted uniform laws of sales, warehouse receipts, bills of lading, and certificates of stock which have been generally adopted. His contributions were also important

SAMUEL WILLISTON

in the preparation of the *Restatement of the Law of Contracts* (1932) for the American Law Institute. For many years Williston was retained as counsel in the Boston law firm of Hale and Dorr, and by many lawyers in the United States.

Dorothy Canfield Fisher has written in *American Portraits:* "It was as a great personality of the poised, equable classic kind that he made his finest contribution to American life. Prolonged personal contact with a noble intelligence and a serenely lofty character changes the lives of young people more than any words. . . ."

Samuel Williston was born on September 24, 1861 to Ann Eliza Safford (Gale) and Lyman Richards Williston, a high school principal. His father, orphaned at an early age, was adopted by Samuel (1795-1874) and Emily Graves Williston, the founders of the Williston (Seminary) Academy, Easthampton, Massachusetts. Young Samuel Williston attended Harvard College, and received the A.B. degree in 1882. He was an instructor at Shortlidge's Academy in Media, Pennsylvania, in the year following his graduation. Entering Harvard Law School in 1885, he served on the first board of editors of the *Harvard Law Review,* and was the first recipient of the Harvard Law School Association Prize for his "History of the Law of Business Corporations Prior to the Year 1800." In 1888 he received the A.M. and LL.B. degrees, graduating at the head of his class. He then served for a year as secretary to Justice Horace Gray of the U.S. Supreme Court. He was admitted to the bar of Massachusetts in 1889.

During that summer Williston assisted Professor James Bradley Thayer of Harvard in collating and drafting materials for a constitution for the new states being formed in the Northwest. Williston recalls in his autobiography, *Life and Law* (Little, 1940): "The constitution thus prepared was ultimately presented to the constitutional conventions in North and South Dakota at least, and considerable portions of it, I believe, were adopted."

Williston was retained as a law clerk by Hyde, Dickinson and Howe from October 1889 to October 1890, and for five years after his clerkship he was associated with this firm on a part-time basis. In 1890 he became an assistant professor of Harvard Law School, which then had 285 students. For nearly fifty years, all during the emergence of that school into an important institution of America, he taught there. This included that period in which Christopher Columbus Langdell's case method replaced the earlier approach of teaching law by means of treatises and lectures. Harvard's success in the case method made it a leader in its field.

After 1910, under the influence of Dean Ezra Ripley Thayer, Dean Roscoe Pound and then Professor Felix Frankfurter, the basis of legal education at Harvard expanded in accordance with the view that "law must be dealt with as one of the social sciences, and that all inquiries bearing on the adaptation to society of rules enforced by governmental agencies are pertinent subjects for legal scholars and teachers" (*Life and Law; An Autobiography*).

Williston became a professor in 1895; in 1903 he was named Weld professor, a position previously filled by Oliver Wendell Holmes; and in 1919 he became Dane professor. In 1910 he served as acting dean, and early in his teaching career he was made secretary of the Harvard faculty.

Following a strenuous program of teaching, writing, practicing law, and reading in fields other than law, Professor Williston suffered a nervous breakdown in the fall of 1895. He was incapacitated for several years and received a series of leaves, on salary.

In his autobiography Williston acknowledged his debt: "I am glad . . . that both President [Charles William] Eliot and Dean [James Barr] Ames lived long enough to see that my renewal of successful work justified, in some degree, their tolerance of my years of incapacity. I have subsequently had the satisfaction of contributing to the university in cash at least the amount of unearned salary that I received in my years of absence, but my sense of obligation is undiminished."

Between 1903 and 1912 Professor Williston suffered two or three shorter attacks. This malady reoccurred in 1923. It was with great perseverance that he was able to conquer this illness and slowly return to his rigorous schedule which bore fruits so helpful to the legal profession.

On May 4, 1938 Williston's resignation from the faculty of Harvard was announced, and he assumed the title of professor emeritus. In the foreword to Williston's *Life and Law,* Justice Learned Hand wrote of his former teacher: "For, while this Socrates of ours never coerced our assent, like his prototype he did not let us alone until we had peered into the corners of our minds, and had in some measure discovered the litter they contained."

Austin Wakeman Scott, Dane Professor of Harvard Law School said: "No one could sit in the classroom under Professor Williston, as I did thirty-four years ago, without realizing at once that here was a great teacher. The students were not merely interested; they were roused. . . . Many of us realized for the first time the real joy of intellectual combat" (*Harvard Law Review,* December 1940).

In 1902 the National Conference of Commissioners on Uniform State Laws selected Professor Williston to prepare a draft of a statute which would make uniform the law of sales among the several states. The first draft was prepared by Williston in 1902-1903 and distributed to law teachers, textbook writers and lawyers with a request for criticism. After several revisions a proposed statute was adopted and recommended by the commissioners in 1906. In the Uniform Sales Act, Williston provided a model which was followed by the legislatures of many of the states. It was the first thoroughgoing codification of one important area of the common law.

At the request of the commissioners, Williston also prepared acts to make uniform the law of warehouse receipts, bills of lading and certificates of stock. These, also, have been generally adopted. In this manner Professor Williston helped American business law develop to meet the needs of a vast new commerce. From 1910 to 1929 Professor Williston served as Massachusetts Commissioner on Uniform State Laws. It was during these years that the greatest progress toward the unification of American commercial law was made.

Retained by the American Bankers Association, Williston worked with Thomas B. Paton, general counsel of the A.B.A., in drafting and promoting the enactment of a Federal bills of lading act which would render a uniform system for bills of lading in interstate commerce, and which would be consistent with the draft for the uniform bills of lading statute drawn for the Commissioners on the Uniform State Laws. Such a Federal law was enacted and known as the (Atlee) Pomerene act of 1916.

Another of Williston's contributions was the *Restatement of the Law of Contracts* (1932) prepared under the auspices of the American Law Institute. This was the first of a series of restatements of various branches of the law. In the *Restatement of Contracts* common law concepts were restated in a concise, exact and accurate manner. The significance of this work can be evaluated by considering the many judicial opinions, lawyers' briefs and scholarly articles which have been predicated upon it. The Carnegie Corporation granted $1,000,000 to support this work, which was begun in 1921. It was carried on by a committee of distinguished American lawyers, who gave years of effort to it under Williston, who was reporter, or head of the committee.

The monumental *The Law of Contracts* appeared in 1920 after nearly ten years of steady work. Williston is the outstanding exponent of the objective theory of the analysis of the contract as distinct from the subjective theory; that is, it is not the unexpressed mental assent which constitutes a contract, but the manifestation of assent by the parties.

He also stated explicitly the rights of the third party beneficiary, thereby popularizing the concept that a third person not actually a party to the contract but for whose benefit a contract has been entered into, should have the right to enforce that contract, which was made in his behalf, in a court of law.

Lord Wright of Durley has written of the treatise on contracts: ". . . this is a great work . . . not only in learning but in breadth of open-mindedness of view. I am inclined to agree with what Williston says more than once, that American law is at present in many respects more liberal and progressive than English law. . . . Williston has played a great part in making it so" (*Legal Essays and Addresses,* 1939).

"Law is a science but it is a pragmatic science," Williston has written. "It can rarely deal with the absolute. Questions of how far and how much constantly intrude, and the questions of degree thus introduced require for their solution determination of doubtful facts and comparative valuing of interests, which have no mathematical equivalent."

Among his many books are *Selected Cases and Statutes on the Law of Bankruptcy* (Harvard Law Review Publishing Association, 1901-1902), *Some Modern Tendencies in the Law* (Baker, Voorhis, 1929), *Negotiable Instruments* (American Institute of Banking, 1931), and *A Selection of Cases on the Law of Contracts* (Little, 1949).

On October 25, 1929 Williston became the first recipient of the American Bar Association's gold medal for "conspicuous service to American jurisprudence" for his "monumental work in restating the law of contracts." At the diamond jubilee meeting of the American Bar Association in August 1953, members who had studied under Williston paid tribute in a declaration which read in part: "You are one of the Olympians of the School and have contributed more than anyone that our generation knows to its creation as a great fountain of learning. . . . Your success as a teacher has been proverbial and your sympathy with us your students has been returned in our universal love for you" (*American Bar Association Journal,* November 1953).

Mary Fairlie Wellman and Samuel Williston were married on September 12, 1889. Mrs. Williston died in 1929. They had two children: Dorothea (Mrs. Murray F. Hall) and Margaret Fairlie (Mrs Chester B. McLaughlin, Jr.). Professor Williston now lives in what was, at one time, a school which his father owned and directed. Honorary LL.D. degrees have been conferred upon him by Harvard (1910), Amherst College (1923), Yale University (1926), Williams College (1938), and Boston College (1949). He is a fellow of the American Academy of Arts and Sciences.

References

Directory of American Scholars (1951)
Harvard Legal Essays (1934)
World Biography (1948)

WILLS, ROYAL BARRY Aug. 21, 1895-
Architect
Address: b. 3 Joy St., Boston, Mass.; h. 5 Wood Lane, Winchester, Mass.

Of some 2,000 houses of varied types and sizes designed by Royal Barry Wills and built in many parts of the United States and in Canada and the tropics, those for which the Boston architect is best known are low-cost homes in Early American tradition. Because of his special skill in combining architectural forms indigenous to northeastern United States, particularly New England, with the mechanical conveniences that meet the needs of contemporary living, Wills has been called "America's foremost exponent of Colonial-brought-up-to-date." He has specialized in space-flexibility for the small house of functional design and he is the winner of many architectural awards.

The small-homes designer is also a popular author of books and magazine articles offering practical information on financial and aesthetic matters to homeowners and builders, including *Houses for Homemakers* (Watts, 1945) which has sold over half a million copies.

America's homeowners are moving back into the kitchen, Wills told W. Clifford Harvey, real estate editor of the *Christian Science Monitor*. The modern family requirement is for a combination kitchen-dining-living room. Early New Englanders lived in the kitchen from necessity, since it was the only room that could be well heated. Today, the family lives and eats in the kitchen from choice. In Wills-designed kitchens, meal-getting activities are simplified, and disguised by halfway partitions, gleaming rows of copper pots and pans, and screens. Refrigerators and ranges are as decorative as television cabinets and ovens are built into the walls (*Christian Science Monitor,* February 19, 1954).

A native New Englander of English descent, Royal Barry Wills was born in Melrose, Massachusetts on August 21, 1895, the son of George Augustin Wills, a businessman, and Mabel Grace (Barry) Wills. For his early education he attended Melrose public schools and upon completing his high school course in 1914, entered Massachusetts Institute of Technology to study architectural engineering. He was a member of the institute's Architectural Society and Lambda Chi Alpha fraternity.

When Wills was graduated from M.I.T. in 1918 with a B.S. degree in architecture, he was "a popular though modest young man, whose excellent sense of humor had brought him renown through many an admirable cartoon in the institute's publications" ("The Architect and the House" by Leon Keach in *Pencil Points,* February 1937). Enlisting in the U.S. Naval Reserve, Wills took a training course for construction officers in 1918 at the Boston Navy Yard and in the same year received from M.I.T. a certificate in naval architecture.

At the end of World War I the young architect went to Philadelphia to work from January until July 1919 as a ship draftsman in the design department of William Cramp and Sons Shipbuilding Company. Returning to Boston, he was employed for the next six years as a designing engineer for the Turner Construction Company.

Commenting on the complexities of a profession in architecture, Wills said in his book *Houses Have Funny Bones* (1951), "An architect should be all things to his client. . . . Fortunately, in my formative years, I worked as a bellhop, surveyor, carpenter's helper, chipper and caulker, ship designer, mason's helper, cartoonist and necktie salesman." The bellhop experience taught him diplomacy, he said, and the salesman experience how to "make friends and influence people."

Not long after Wills entered independent practice in Boston in 1925, he won the first of his many awards when he was presented in 1929 with the first regional prize in the National Better Homes Competition. He was called to the White House in Washington in 1932 to receive from President Herbert Hoover a Gold Medal for the best small house of that year. Other medals from the Better Homes in American Competition followed in 1934 and 1935. He also won awards in the Jordan-Marsh Company Small House Competition (1935) and the Modernize Main Street Competition (1935) and various competitions of *House Beautiful, Pencil Points* and *Ladies' Home Journal.*

Further recognition came to Wills in 1938 when he was chosen as one of the eight leading architects in the United States to design a house for *Life* magazine. The house assigned to him was of the traditional type in the $10,000 class (Frank Lloyd Wright was asked to design the modern type). In 1939 a Wills-designed house was selected for construction at the Golden Gate Exposition in San Francisco. He accepted a commission from the United States Government in 1942 to design a 300-unit housing development for defense workers in Springfield, Massachusetts known as Lucy Mallary Village.

In 1943 *Architectural Forum* chose him to design a rural development. The Massachusetts State Association of Architects conferred on Wills its Honors Award in 1949.

Among Wills's designs are some that derive from Regency and English Cotswold styles, French cottages and farms, lodges and Western ranch houses. He has also produced a considerably large number of homes of the modern type, frequently in association with Hugh Stubbins, Jr. However, he gained prominence chiefly for designs of small residences in Early American tradition.

He takes much of his inspiration from Cape Cod cottages. Colonial farmhouses, block houses with overhanging second stories, and houses with salt-box roofs and gambrel roofs. In character with these larger forms is his use of cornices, doors and doorways, fire-places and chimneys, wallpaper, corner cupboards, stairways, small windowpanes, hardware and other details based on Colonial precedent.

As pointed out in *Life* (August 26, 1946), since Wills is the "leading United States designer of small traditional houses, [he] has become a focal point for the distaste of the country's more vociferous, but less popular modern architects." In his article "Confessions of a Cape Codder" (*Architectural Record,* April 1949), dealing with the relationship between an architect and his clients' needs and tastes, Wills summed up his attitude toward the traditional-modern controversy. "When I started to practice," he recalled, "the professional world seemed to be at peace within itself . . . and not until the early Thirties was its serenity disturbed by brawling between the Five Orders and the Pipe Columnists. My immediate impulse was to give the new thought a whirl, to check its virtues against the stridency of its protagonists. So we did a fair number of houses in the contemporary manner and still get a big kick doing them on occasion, but we never became rabid enough to wage an unholy war against the inherent desires of our clients."

In combining the traditional with the modern Wills believes that a home can have the beauty, graciousness and dignity of Early American architectural forms as well as all the mechanical equipment and conveniences of modern domestic architecture. "It can also enjoy some of the advantages of picture windows which are placed at the rear where the family can look out without having the entire neighborhood looking in" (*Christian Science Monitor,* May 22, 1953). He stresses the importance of a homelike atmosphere and maintains, as *Life* explains, that "good residential architecture should be primarily emotional and, like good art, be part of the people and understood by them."

One of the country's most widely read architectural authors, Wills has written six books about home building and design. *Houses for Good Living* (1940) and *Better Homes for Budgeteers* (1941), both published by Architectural Book Publishing Company, are now in their fourth printing. They contain designs and plans of houses representative of his work, with practical advice on building, budgeting and ways to save money. Half of the more than seventy houses pictured in *Better Homes for Budgeteers* are for families with modest incomes. *This Business of Architecture* (Reinhold, 1941) was written with the collaboration of Leon Keach on the subject of professional practice.

To aid the many prospective homeowners who had awaited the end of World War II to build their houses, Wills wrote *Houses for Homemakers* (published by F. Watts, 1945). "Most important of its many good points," commented the *Architectural Forum* book reviewer (December 1945), "is the interesting treatment of such inherently dull subject matter as deeds and title searching."

While not agreeing with all the architect's ideas about combining the traditional and the modern, the reviewer noted that Wills had tried to strike a balance between the two types and that almost half the houses pictured in the book were of modern design. "But these examples themselves," he added, "reveal that Wills's technique is more successful within the restrictions

Fabian Bachrach

ROYAL BARRY WILLS

of Colonial than in the freer contemporary idiom."

Planning Your Home Wisely (F. Watts, 1946) is another book of practical value to the home builder. The humorous *Houses Have Funny Bones* (Bond Wheelwright Company, 1951), with illustrations by the author, deals with the relationship between the architect and his clients. *Living on the Level* (Houghton Mifflin, 1955) discusses one-story dwellings and their many advantages.

The architect has contributed articles to many nationally circulated magazines in the United States as well as to architectural periodicals in Canada, England, South Africa, and Germany. Wills is further known to the American public through his guest appearances on a number of radio and television programs.

In keeping with his interest in Colonial architecture, Wills belongs to the historical societies of Narragansett, Old Newbury and Cohasset, Massachusetts and to the Early American Industries Association and the Society for the Preservation of New England Antiquities. He is affiliated also with the Marblehead Arts Association, the American Institute of Architects, the Massachusetts State Association of Architects and the Boston Society of Architects (vice-president, 1952-53).

The architect is a member of the New England Council Committee, Planning Board of the City of Melrose, and past chairman (1926-27, 1932-33) of the Melrose Board of Appeal. For the past few years he has awarded an annual scholarship to young students at the Boston Architectural Center. He retains his association with the Massachusetts Institute of Technology as a member of the alumni council and executive committee of the Alumni Association and as class agent of the class of 1918. His clubs are the Bear Hill Golf Club and the

WILLS, ROYAL BARRY—*Continued*
Cohasset Golf Club, and the City and University clubs of Boston.

Married on June 19, 1920 to Marguerite Waggett, Wills has two sons, Charles Barry, who has a contracting business, and Richard, who is associated with his father in his office in Boston. Wills is an Episcopalian and a Democrat. He is five feet nine inches tall and weighs 187 pounds; he has brown hair and hazel eyes. Tennis, reading, cartooning, attending auctions and collecting antiques are his favorite recreations. He spends his holidays at his summer home "Deep Run" in Cohasset or at his camp in East Wakefield, New Hampshire.

References

Life 21:67+ Ag 26 '46
Pencil P 18:65+ F '37

National Cyclopædia of American Biography Current Vol H (1952)
Who Knows—and What (1949)
Who's Who in America, 1954-55
Who's Who in New England (1949)
Wills, R. B. Houses Have Funny Bones (1951)
World Biography (1954)

H. Sato, Tokyo

DONALD V. WILSON

WILSON, DONALD V(ON STEIN) Sept. 20, 1909- Social service organization official
Address: b. c/o International Society for the Welfare of Cripples, 17 E. 52d St., New York 22; h. 445 W. 240th St., New York 63

When Donald V. Wilson was appointed secretary-general of the International Society for the Welfare of Cripples in December, 1949, he brought to this post twenty years of experience as a social worker in Ohio and Illinois, as a public welfare official in Louisiana, and as a welfare officer with the United States Army on General Douglas MacArthur's staff in Tokyo.

World congresses of the International Society for the Welfare of Cripples are held every three years; the latest convened in September 1954 at The Hague at which 800 experts from twenty-six countries pooled their knowledge and experience on the problems of physical disability.

Born in Kansas City, Missouri, on September 20, 1909, Donald Von Stein Wilson is the son of Robert Hayes and Jessie (Von Stein) Wilson. After graduation in 1931 from Muskingum College, in New Concord, Ohio, with an A.B. degree in political science, young Wilson studied in Cleveland at Western Reserve University's School of Law where he received the LL.B. degree in 1934. From the School of Social Service Administration at the University of Chicago, he obtained the M.A. degree in 1937.

He had, however, already begun his social work career in 1931 as a boys' club worker at Hiram House, a social service settlement in Cleveland, Ohio. From 1932 to 1934 he was a case worker for Cuyahoga County (Ohio) Relief Administration. Wilson first became associated with welfare work for the disabled in 1935, as a case worker in Cleveland, Ohio, for the Association for the Crippled and Disabled.

For five years, from 1937 to 1942, Wilson was a lecturer in the Graduate School of Social Welfare, Louisiana State University, at Baton Rouge. During the same period he was a representative of the Louisiana Department of Public Welfare, serving also as principal social analyst for the department. Out of this experience Mr. Wilson wrote a comprehensive study: *Public Social Services in Louisiana,* which was issued in 1943 as a booklet by the Louisiana Conference on Social Welfare. This study contains a chapter on Vocational Rehabilitation, in which Wilson wrote: "The person with a physical handicap presents many problems which cannot be solved without coordination of the various services available to him."

It was this theme of coordination, both national and international, which Wilson was later to stress in an article written after he became secretary-general of the Society for the Welfare of Cripples, and published in *Social Service* by The National Council of Social Service, London. In this article, entitled "Action on the World Level", he says: "It is the function of international health and welfare programs to facilitate the sharing among all peoples of the best knowledge and techniques that have been evolved."

From 1942 to 1946 Wilson served with the United States Army, advancing to the rank of lieutenant. He was a welfare officer on the Tochigi military government team, Japan; chief of the public welfare branch, military government section, Eighth Army, Yokohama, Japan; and, from 1947 to 1948, social welfare officer in the public health and welfare section of General Douglas MacArthur's staff in Tokyo. Out of this experience Wilson wrote an article entitled "Social Work in the Japanese Occupation", published in the *Social Work Journal* (April, 1950).

Returning to the United States in 1949, Wilson accepted the position of dean of the School of Applied Social Sciences at Western Reserve University from which post he was called, in the same year, to his present position as secretary-general of the International Society for the Welfare of Cripples. This Society is a federation of national, non-governmental organizations devoted to the service of disabled persons and to the removal of the causes of disability.

Established in Elyria, Ohio, in 1922 as the International Society for Crippled Children, it now has twenty-two affiliated national societies, councils or associations in as many countries. The founder, Edgar F. Allen, and many of the original officers were members of Rotary International which had been active in establishing services for crippled children. The society was reorganized in 1939, its present name was adopted, and, in 1949, offices were established in New York City under the direction of Donald Wilson.

The society has been granted consultative status by the Economic and Social Council of the United Nations and by the executive board of the United Nations International Children's Emergency Fund and it also has official relations with the World Health Organization.

In 1953 Wilson served as chairman of a conference called by the United Nations and its specialized agencies to plan improved services to the handicapped on a world-wide scale. The conference was attended by representatives of twenty-six international voluntary agencies.

Writing of this conference in the New York *Times*, Dr. Howard A. Rusk, director of the Institute of Physical Medicine and Rehabilitation, New York University-Bellevue Medical Center, said: "The governmental and voluntary agencies represented at the conference have reason to be greatly encouraged by the development of rehabilitation services throughout the world. Worthy as this objective is in itself, international activities in rehabilitation mean far more than the return of countless millions of hopeless, helpless people throughout the world to lives of dignity and productivity.

"With dynamic leadership from the United Nations, it can mean another step toward the international understanding that is essential to world peace, the greater political goal of the United Nations."

On December 21, 1939, Wilson married Marie Walker Reese, a social worker. They have two daughters, Donna Lynn and Fay Elizabeth. Wilson is a member of the American Association of Social Workers. He is six feet tall, weighs 160 pounds, has blue eyes and brown hair. In 1952 he was elected a member of the United States Committee of the International Conference of Social Work.

References

N Y Times p42 D 15 '49
Social Work J Ap '50
Who's Who in America, 1952-53
Who's Who in the United Nations (1951)

WILSON, H(ALSEY) W(ILLIAM) May 12, 1868—Mar. 1, 1954 Founder and chairman of the board of the The H. W. Wilson Co., New York, publishers of bibliographic works and library reference books; was educated at Beloit College and University of Minnesota; began his career in bookshop on University of Minnesota campus, 1889; married Justina Leavitt, 1895; conceived idea of publishing a cumulative monthly list of books which would include in one alphabet author's name, title of book and general subject heading; launched *Cumulative Book Index*, 1898; hired Marion E. Potter as editor; issued *Readers' Guide to Periodical Literature*, 1901; began publication of *Book Review Digest* (1905); until 1913 published in Minneapolis, then moved to White Plains, N.Y., and in 1917 to five-story building in the Bronx, New York City; added eight-story building in 1929 and six-story building in 1938; increased staff to over 425; increased recurrent publications to more than twenty; was the recipient (June 1948) of Distinguished Achievement Award, University of Minn.; awarded honorary degree of Doctor of Letters (1939) by Brown University; life member of American Library Association; Lippincott Award for Outstanding Achievement in Librarianship (1950); author of *The Bookman's Reading and Tools;* compiled *Toaster's Handbooks;* instituted debate handbooks and *Reference Shelf;* inaugurated "service basis" method of charge to libraries; system of interfiling linotype slugs in publishing indexes. See *Current Biography* (May) 1948; Lawler, John L., *The H. W. Wilson Company: Half a Century of Bibliographical Publishing* (Univ. of Minn. Press 1950).

From an oil painting by Raymond P. R. Neilson, 1952
H. W. WILSON

Obituary

N Y Times p25 Mr 2 '54

WILSON, LOUISE MAXWELL *See* Baker, L. (WLB) Yrbk 54

WINCHESTER, ALICE July 26, 1907- Editor; author

Address: b. c/o Antiques Magazine, 601 5th Ave., New York 17; h. 212 E. 48th St., New York 17

Through her books and her work as editor-in-chief of the magazine, *Antiques,* Alice Winchester has helped to secure a wider recognition of heirlooms as part of American culture and history. She has emphasized that antiques are both history and art, and appreciation of them leads to a broader understanding of this country's past. Her book, *How to Know American Antiques,* published in a hard-cover edition by Dodd, Mead & Company in 1951, has gone through three printings and has also been issued in a Mentor paper-back edition by the New American Library.

Among her other books are *Living With Antiques* (R. M. McBride, 1941) and *American Antiques in Words and Pictures* (1943). She also edited *The Antiques Book* (published by A. A. Wynn, 1950) which was a selection of the Seven Arts Book Society. She is a frequent lecturer at historical societies, museums and collectors' clubs and is an active participant in the National Council for Historic Sites and Buildings, of which she is a charter member. Her annual forums on antiques and decoration held at Williamsburg, Virginia, under the joint sponsorship of *Antiques* magazine and Colonial Williamsburg, Inc., have brought her national distinction. In 1950 she was named a Fellow of the Rochester, New York, Museum of Arts and Sciences.

Alice Winchester was born in Chicago, Illinois on July 26, 1907 to Benjamin Severance Winchester and Pearl Adair Gunn Winchester. On her paternal side, her ancestors included many ministers and teachers in New England. Her father is a Congregational minister, now retired. Her mother was born while the family were moving west from Kentucky. Many ministers and engineers are in her maternal ancestry. She has three sisters and one brother.

Reared in New England, she attended Roger Ludlow High School in Fairfield, Connecticut, graduating in 1925, having founded and edited the school paper. She attended Smith College, Northampton, Massachusetts, where she obtained tuition scholarships, studied in France at the Sorbonne during her junior year, and was graduated with a Bachelor of Arts degree in 1929. She earned extra money by baby-sitting and waiting on tables during her college years. She was a member of the Glee Club, won an Old French prize, and earned a Phi Beta Kappa key.

She is occasionally surprised to find herself editor of the magazine *Antiques,* because after graduation from Smith College she considered herself something of a modernist. However, she had been exposed to a good deal of antique and historical influence during her early childhood in Concord, Massachusetts, which she calls "the cradle of democracy."

After college she spent a few months working as a clerk in a Wall Street office, a short time with the Rockefeller Foundation, and then studied stenography. In 1930 she became secretary to Homer Eaton Keyes, editor of *The Magazine Antiques.* At that time, Miss Winchester remembers, antiques were to her just beautiful old pieces, most of them surrounded with fascinating legends, but "her knowledge of the field was negligible" (*Smith Alumnae Quarterly,* February, 1942). She began to find the subject exciting, and to develop a critical approach both to antiques and to editing and publishing problems.

Following the death of Homer Keyes in 1938 she was made editor, and her job became not only the supervision of all material published, but also travelling over the country visiting museums and private collections, tracking down rare antiquarian items, and giving lectures and radio talks. Since the magazine was founded in 1922 it has become a leader in its field and is widely consulted by antiquarians and connoisseurs.

In 1942, according to *Time, Antiques* had only 8,043 readers, but in 1950 after "the wartime shortage of household furnishings caused a boom in the second-hand market," *Antiques* "boomed with it, now has 20,921 readers."

For beginners in antique collecting, Miss Winchester advises that they just go around looking at as many good antiques as they can. Williamsburg, Virginia, is a fertile field for this, she declares, as well as more formal museums and also Colonial houses in New England and in the South. "Start reading," she urges, "and don't let yourself be baffled. You will find that gradually these things will pattern themselves. Instead of studying each field separately, you will discover a certain relationship in design within a period among glass, ceramics, furniture, silver and architecture" (Richmond, Virginia *Times Dispatch,* February 4, 1951).

Asked the inevitable questions "how old is antique?" or "how can one tell what is regarded as an antique?" Miss Winchester replies: "In 1930 the United States Government ruled that objects had to be at least a hundred years old to be classed as antiques, and so admitted duty free to this country. Since then, antiques have often been defined as objects made before 1830."

She emphasizes that Americans enjoy living with antiques "from the functional pine chests of the Pilgrims to the last carved rose of the Victorians," partly because we find them "satisfying artistically, and partly because they are a link with the past." She has stated that people often count among their antiques things made by machine as well as those wrought by hand. Most of the machine-made objects are later than 1830, but that date does serve generally as a dividing line between the age of craftsmanship and the machine age. It had begun in 1800, with gradual industrialization of old-time crafts.

Miss Winchester points out many prevalent fallacies about antiques. "One of the most common beliefs is that early American objects and furniture are crude compared to those made in Europe during the same time. That is really a fallacy," she states. "Fine things were made here during the early Colonial days. . . . A lot of Chippendale was made in Philadelphia, and the Philadelphia highboy is a high point in craftsmanship" (Worcester, Massachusetts *Telegram,* April 19, 1951). Eighteenth century English cabinet makers, she said, influenced those in the American colonies. "We come naturally by our affinity for English antiques."

In discussing other fallacies about antiques, Miss Winchester commented: "Age alone does not make antiques important. They must have artistic merit as well as age." She referred to Currier and Ives prints—now so popular—as "neither old nor particularly valuable. The ones that are the most valuable are historically interesting. The prints were produced as recently as 1907."

Pointing out in her book, *How To Know American Antiques,* that "legends grow on antiques the way moss grows on trees," Miss Winchester wrote: "As a family heirloom is passed from one generation to the next, its history takes on added flourishes. A spinning wheel made in 1820 becomes the spinning wheel brought over on the *Mayflower.* A bed of 1840 becomes the bed George Washington slept in. But while the personal associations of our heirlooms add to their interest, we do not need to rely on traditions to place their date and source." She stated that not every old piece has a maker's mark or label, but every one has certain characteristics that help to identify it in a certain period.

Prior to the founding of *The Magazine Antiques* in 1922, collecting antiques was chiefly a hobby for a few wealthy Americans who transported treasures from Europe. Today, although the majority of rare finds are in museums, the desire to own and appreciate antiques has spread to people in moderate circumstances. Miss Winchester has discovered that university professors, lumber dealers, doctors, insurance agents, librarians, salesmen all find in antiques a common interest "as the understanding of America's past grows and faith in her future endures."

One of Miss Winchester's favorite theories is that modern and antique things are compatible. "It is wonderful, of course," she said, "if one wants to make a conscientious restoration of an old house to its original period; but it is quite possible to mix fifteenth century Italian, ninth century Chinese and twentieth century American, and if they are things that express the same kind of taste, they ought to be harmonious and be in some ways more interesting than a strictly homogeneous period décor."

She is still something of a modernist—and her favorites in the modern field are the big public buildings "with their eminently fitting design." She thinks, however, that a lot of modern designers "don't take the proper advantages of traditional designs, which have had many variations and can go right on being adapted" (Richmond, Virginia *Times Dispatch,* February 4, 1951).

The editor has an encouraging word for despairing husbands who are frequently admonished: "Don't sit on that; it's an antique!" She explains: "Good antiques don't collapse; that's one of the things that make them valuable; they are well made, they've lasted sometimes 200 years and they're good for a couple hundred more. If an antique is in poor condition, it should be either properly restored, or used for kindling."

ALICE WINCHESTER

Her first work to be issued in a "pocketbook edition," *How To Know American Antiques* (1951), is designed to interest the novice collector. It covers the whole field including furniture, china, glass, silver, pewter, tinware, iron, brass, copper, lighting, coverlets and rugs, prints, pictures, and fireplace equipment. "A good many people of moderate means are turning to the nineteenth century for their antiques," Miss Winchester said. "There are a lot of interesting Victorian things and they have a certain antique charm."

Miss Winchester stresses the point that many things that people cherish because they are old and because they have family associations would have no great value to anyone else. "In many cases," she says, "the satisfaction of owning family pieces cannot be compensated for by the dollars and cents they would bring if offered for sale. Really, the value of an antique is what it is worth to you." "The best way to enjoy antiques is to live with them, as part of the home," she told a radio audience on *Women in the News.* "To avoid being cheated when buying antiques, compare, shop around, and read books and study examples in the museums."

Miss Winchester wrote an article, "How to Behave at an Auction" in *House and Garden,* July, 1944, in which she gave this advice: "The blithe belief that buying at auction means, perforce, getting a bargain is a fallacious theory of the unwary. An object sold at auction goes to the highest bidder and the price depends entirely on the amount of competition. If no one

WINCHESTER, ALICE—*Continued*

happens to want the item you want, you get it for a low price. If your competitor wants it to complete a set, or for a sentimental reason, or has been commissioned to get it regardless of cost, prices soar out of ordinary range . . . as a general rule, if bidding on a piece is low and slow, it is because the piece is not worth any more."

She believes that the ability to recognize an authentic antique requires the critical knowledge gained only by years of handling and study. Connoisseurs of antiques have developed a sixth sense which is described as the "feel" for an object, not an intangible but "the sum of critical judgment gained from absolute familiarity with the objects produced in various periods of history."

She is the author, with Jean Lipman, of *Primitive Painters in America* (Dodd, Mead, 1950), and with Joseph Downs of *The Henry Francis du Pont Winterthur Museum* (The Magazine *Antiques,* 1951). With her staff she edited *The Antiques Book* which contains thirty-five articles by experts in eleven fields of major antique interest (ceramic; furniture; glass; silver; pewter; architecture; prints; folk art; textiles; firearms and toys) and illustrated with 348 photographs. This was a selection of the Seven Arts Book Society in 1950.

The New York *Times* reviewer wrote of *The Antiques Book*: "People who are not already collectors are warned to beware of it, for the interest it excites is insidious. The fellow who gets started learning about antiques . . . is presently reading about the people who made the things and the life that went on around the makers. . . . Collectors will find the book handy for reference, each in his own specialty, and improving reading in broader but related fields."

In recognition of "her constant efforts in preserving and in making known the value of objects of the past, the Rochester Museum of Arts and Sciences named her a Fellow in the field of culture history in 1950. She has also lectured at the Henry Ford Museum at Dearborn, Michigan; at Old Sturbridge Village, Massachusetts; at Cooperstown, New York Seminars on American Culture; at the National Gallery, Washington, D.C. and other museums.

Described in the *Independent Woman* magazine as "slim, light-haired, blue-eyed with a Grecian profile and a buoyant laugh," Alice Winchester is five feet five inches tall, weighs 125 pounds, and says that her eyes are "green." She is an independent voter, and her religion is Protestant. One of her hobbies is "roughing it in the Hudson Bay region and Saskatchewan where you can't find an antique in a thousand miles." Another hobby is French cooking. Her New York apartment is furnished in "mixed" periods. Her prized antiques are two Ming paintings which she bought at an auction in New York.

References

Ind Woman p282 S '41
Richmond (Va.) Times Dispatch F 4 '51
Who's Who in America, 1952-53

WISE, JAMES DECAMP Oct. 7, 1898-
Business executive; lawyer

Address: b. c/o Bigelow-Sanford Carpet Company, 140 Madison Ave., New York 16; h. 172 E. 93d St., New York 28

A leader of new developments in the rug industry, James DeCamp Wise, president of the Bigelow-Sanford Carpet Company, has instituted a long range program of modernization of the 129-year-old company. A corporation lawyer, he was elected to the presidency in 1944 after having served as general counsel and a director since 1932. Under his management new styles and types of carpets have been introduced, and a far-reaching organization of men and methods has transformed Bigelow-Sanford from a semi-handicraft to a mass production business.

Wise pioneered in introducing synthetic fibers into carpets with the result that wool is playing a constantly diminishing role in the industry. He stated on June 22, 1953 at a wholesale home furnishings conference in Chicago that "40 per cent of the industry's woven yardage now contains man-made fibres, while another 15 to 20 per cent consisted of cotton. This means that only about 40 per cent of the industry's production is now in the form of the traditional wool rug or carpeting."

James DeCamp Wise, son of William Henry and Florence (Line) Wise, was born in Greencastle, Indiana, October 7, 1898. His family moved to Los Angeles while he was still very young, and there he attended school. He studied at Stanford University from 1916 to 1919, then came to New York to complete his B.A. degree, with election to Phi Beta Kappa, at Columbia College in 1921. After graduation he entered Columbia Law School, was an editor of Columbia *Law Review* in 1924, and in 1925 he received his LL.B degree and was admitted to the New York bar.

From 1925 to 1933 Wise was a member of the law offices of Cotton & Franklin, working in the fields of finance, corporate reorganization, labor law, and general industrial counseling. He was financial counsel to the firms of Dillon Read and White Weld, among others. He appeared many times before the New York State and the National Labor Relations Boards, representing such clients as the New York City Omnibus Corporation and the Fifth Avenue Coach Company. Some of the companies he represented as general counsel were the National Broadcasting Company, the Radio Corporation of America, and W.R. Grace and Company.

Wise became a partner in Cotton & Franklin and in its successor, Cahill, Gordon, Zachry & Reindel where he was a senior partner at the time of his resignation in 1945. In 1940 Wise went to Washington as a special consultant to the Reconstruction Finance Corporation. In December of the same year, and until February 1941, he served as special assistant to the then Under Secretary of the Navy, James Forrestal. His duties involved the handling of procurement problems connected with the Navy's expansion program. In recognition of this service Wise received the Distinguished Civilian Service Award in 1947, the Navy's highest civilian award.

While a member of the law firm he began his association with Bigelow-Sanford in 1932, becoming the company's general counsel. In 1939 he was elected to the board of directors of the company, and in the following year he was elected to the executive committee. When, in December 1944, on the death of John A. Sweetser, president of Bigelow-Sanford, Wise was invited to take over the office, he was thoroughly familiar with the corporate structure of the firm, but he had, according to *Business Week,* "few preconceived notions of how to run a carpet company."

Converting its factories for defense production during World War II, Bigelow-Sanford turned out 7,500,000 blankets for the armed forces. It also produced 19,000,000 square yards of cotton duck for military use; made parts for torpedoes, periscopes and airplane landing gear; machine tools; gun mounts; and radar and electronic equipment. Since converting back to civilian production, the company has established a defense contracts division, set up blanket and cotton looms to handle sudden military orders. Its staff of over 100 engineers and technicians is prepared to take on machine tool production in the event of a national emergency.

A Market Research Company survey for the Carpet Institute in 1943 had revealed that the industry was "afraid of anything new" and was operating in much the same way for the past century. Under Wise's administration, the changes at Bigelow-Sanford have been rapid and widespread. *Business Week* reported in 1949 that "Bigelow-Sanford today is doing practically nothing it did when Market Research made its survey." The New York *Herald Tribune* describes the result as "a completely revamped organization which has attained top rank in the industry."

The first step in Wise's program of modernization and reorganization was the bringing of new men into top management posts. Since 1945, he writes in his annual report for 1952, "the Company has been engaged in a program of employee development and selective training for management positions." Bigelow sponsors a school of craftsmanship (a four-year course in carpet making), an institute of management, conducted in cooperation with Cornell University and the University of Connecticut, and an annual one-year course for management trainees. In 1948 he established a school of carpet installation in Thompsonville, Connecticut and in 1949 a school in New York City to teach on-the-floor cleaning of carpets and developed a compound, Karpet-Kare, for this purpose.

Significant changes in production systems have also been made. Production was reduced from more than 900 colors and patterns to approximately 200, thus simplifying both manufacturing and distribution. In 1946 a products research and development department was created to aid in the development of new fabrics and designs. Wise has encouraged the development of synthetic fibers, largely because of the rise in wool prices and the uncer-

Herman Leonard

JAMES DECAMP WISE

tainty of supplies. "We are certain that it will be a more stable industry with synthetics than it will be with wool as the source of supply," he announced in September 1950 when Bigelow-Sanford introduced its first line of synthetic wool blend carpets.

Three years later he reported: "In 1952 over half of all soft-surface floorcoverings sold in the United States contained surface fibers other than wool. The industry is no longer fully dependent upon a single surface fiber."

Another change instituted under Wise's administration was a revision of the company's sales and distribution policies. Before World War II some 10,000 dealers handled Bigelow products. When a survey revealed that only 17 per cent of the dealers were handling 80 per cent of the company's business, the number of dealers was cut to 4,500.

On the occasion of Bigelow-Sanford's 125th anniversary in 1950 it was announced that "Bigelow-Sanford today is doing business on a new basis, a more efficient basis . . . and expanding the market for floor coverings. . . . For the first time in the history of any carpet company, Bigelow-Sanford's gross sales in 1950 topped $100,000,000."

In marketing and promoting the company's products, Wise has encountered regional problems: for example, people in different parts of the United States show preference for different colors and patterns. Since 1949 most of the company's twenty-eight show rooms have been renovated and "glamorized," and new designs are offered to convince housewives that prewar carpets are outdated.

Bigelow-Sanford shut down for one week in May 1953 its Axminister carpet mill in Amsterdam, New York because of "overproduction and a normal seasonal decline in orders from carpet retailers". Wise explained that the market for woven carpet weakened after a

WISE, JAMES DECAMP—*Continued*

strong first quarter in 1953 and that "present selling prices were unsatisfactory in relation to costs" (New York *Times*, February 12, 1954.) However, the company reported a net profit of $3,471,000 for 1953 in contrast to a $1,252,000 loss suffered in 1952. Net sales were $73,179,000 as compared with the 1952 volume of $67,273,000.

Active in many outside activities as well as in his company's operations, Wise has given much time to his alma mater, Columbia University. As president of the Columbia University Associates, he has been particularly interested in encouraging a free flow of ideas between businessmen and the university, pointing out to management students at Columbia that they are "just a subway ride from big business."

He was elected in 1951 to the newly-created post of vice-president for the general management division of the American Management Association. His other memberships and offices include membership in the board of trustees of the Carpet Institute, director of the Boston Manufacturer's Mutual Fire Insurance Company, trustee of Consolidated Edison Company, trustee and vice-chairman of the National Industrial Conference Board, and director and treasurer of the United Neighborhood Houses of New York.

He was married to the former Katherine Ulrich on June 19, 1930, and they have two children, Henry Ulrich and Joanna. Wise and his family divide their time between a Manhattan apartment and a farm in New Jersey where the executive likes to relax on weekends.

References

Bsns W p6 Je 25 '49
N Y Herald Tribune p43 D 6 '51
Who's Who in America, 1952-53 (1953)
Who's Who in Commerce and Industry

WOOLLEY, SIR (CHARLES) LEONARD Apr. 17, 1880- Archaeologist

Address: h. Sedgehill Manor, Wilts., nr. Shaftesbury, Dorset, England

One of the most exciting moments in Sir Leonard Woolley's career as an archaeologist was when he stood in the ruins of a temple near Ur of the Chaldees and one of his workmen handed him a clay tablet inscribed with the names of the kings of the First Dynasty of Ur, hitherto rejected by historians as a mythical kingdom. This was one episode in a half-century of discoveries in which Sir Leonard has been "digging up the past," as he calls it, and rescuing whole eras from oblivion. He is recognized among scholars as one of England's leading archaeologists.

To the general reader Woolley's name is familiar from his popular "Penguin" book, *Digging Up the Past* (1930; reprinted 1952), his "King Penguin" *Ur: The First Phases* (1946), and *Ur of the Chaldees* (latest edition, Crowell, 1954). He is the author of more than twenty-five books. He was engaged in field work from 1906 to 1950, interrupted by distinguished service in both World Wars and by occasional summers at the University of Pennsylvania and the British Museum. He was knighted in 1935. He was archaeological adviser (1943-1945) to the British War Office, and organized the protection of historical monuments and art treasures in war areas.

Charles Leonard Woolley (he does not use his first name) was born in London, April 17, 1880, son of the Reverend George Herbert Woolley and his wife, Sarah. He spent two years at the Hackney Grammar School, London, and then attended St. John's, Leatherhead, Surrey, a public school especially devoted to the education of the sons of clergymen of the Church of England. In 1901 he entered New College, Oxford, where he read in the classics and theology.

Woolley became an archaeologist almost by compulsion—the compulsion of a masterful mind. The mind was that of William Archibald Spooner, an Anglican clergyman and dean (1876-1889) and warden (1903-1924) of New College, Oxford. He had occasional lapses of speech, whereby he transposed sounds in two or more words (as a "blushing crow," for a "crushing blow"); this led to coinage of the word "spoonerism." Woolley relates how, in 1904, he was summoned to Dr. Spooner's office. Asked whether it was true that he had given up the idea of following his father into the Church, he replied that that was so, and was then asked what he proposed to do. "Well," Woolley answered, "I want to be a schoolmaster." Spooner said, "Oh yes, a schoolmaster, really. Well, Mr. Woolley, *I* have decided that you shall be an archaeologist." Woolley relates that he was not quite sure what an archaeologist was, but, "There was no gainsaying Warden Spooner, so I became one, and I have never regretted it."

In 1905, therefore, the young graduate was installed as an assistant-keeper at the Ashmolean Museum, Oxford, a post he occupied for two years. In 1906 he was first employed on field work, in charge of Roman excavations in Northumberland. With a mixture of flair and beginner's luck, he was highly successful, and has to his credit the discovery of the famous Corbridge Lion, a unique fountain, Roman granaries, pottery, and a terra-cotta relief nicknamed "the Roman Harry Lauder," bare-kneed and tunic-clad, and bearing an uncanny resemblance to the Scotch comedian.

His "luck" held, and in 1907 he was invited to join the Eckley B. Coxe Expedition to Nubia, sponsored by the University of Pennsylvania Museum, Philadelphia, Pennsylvania. In Nubia he directed operations which excavated the first cemetery ever dug belonging to the Meroitic civilization of the Lower Nile.

"I am convinced," Woolley wrote, "that nobody ought to undertake field work in the Nile Valley unless he has at least a fair knowledge of Egyptian, and can decipher . . . the hieroglyphic inscriptions which he may find. I never had that knowledge. . . . I could not read the hieroglyphics, nor was there anyone to help me, and my work suffered in consequence." His linguistic competence is nevertheless considerable. Besides Greek, Latin, Italian, French and German, Woolley has a knowledge of sundry dialects of spoken Arabic, indispensable for the direction of workers and management of "diggings" in the Near and Middle East.

From 1907 to 1911 Woolley worked for the Eckley B. Coxe expedition in Nubia and spent the summers in Philadelphia. In 1911 he again went to Nubia, this time for the University of Oxford. In 1912, under the aegis of the British Museum, he obtained his first independent command of an archaeological expedition. This was at the village of Jerablus, in Turkey, alongside the famous ruins of Carchemish, the ancient capital of the southern Hittites. His colleague here was T. E. Lawrence (soon to become famous as "Lawrence of Arabia," who led the revolt in the desert and wrote The *Seven Pillars of Wisdom.*

In *Dead Towns and Living Men,* Woolley noted Lawrence's "marked ascendancy over the Arab workmen, partly by his genuine interest in and sympathy with them, partly because his impish humour was of a sort that they could relish." The expedition uncovered temples and sculptures, impressive dado with relief carvings, and the statue of the god Atarluhas on his lion throne. "Very magnificent must Carchemish have been," writes Woolley, "when its sculptures were gay with colour, when the sunlight glistened on its enamel walls, and its sombre brick was overlaid with panels of cedar and plates of bronze; . . . but even now, when it lies deserted and in heaps, it has perhaps in the melancholy of its ruin found a subtler charm to offset the glory of its prime."

In 1914 Woolley did some work in Sinai for the Palestine Exploration Fund. While he was home for the summer intermission the war broke out, and he joined the 61st Howitzer Brigade of the Royal Artillery, but before the year was out was ordered to Egypt for intelligence work with Stewart Newcombe, Aubrey Herbert, T. E. Lawrence, and George (later Lord) Lloyd. At first he was in Cairo, and then, ranking as captain, supervised an independent branch at Port Said. Captured by the Turks in 1916, he was imprisoned successively at Adana, Ankara, Kastamuni and Kedos, and, in his own words "treatment varied from tolerable or even good to very bad, according to the character of the Turkish officer commanding." He was home for Christmas 1918, having been honored by the French Croix de Guerre and a mention in dispatches by the British Army. In 1919 he was sent out to Syria to organize a monuments service, but was soon transferred, and became political officer (in the rank of major) in northern Syria, until the British handed that region back to the French.

There followed twenty more years of almost uninterrupted field work in Turkey, Iraq, and Syria (he generally spent the summers in London, based at the British Museum, but not directly employed by that institution). In 1919 he was at Carchemish again; between 1921 and 1922 at Tel el Amarna, for the Egypt Exploration Society; and then, also in 1922, began the great work at Ur of the Chaldees, which is considered to be Woolley's major contribution to archaeology. This was a joint expedition financed by the British Museum and by the Museum of the University of Pennsylvania. It resulted in the book *Ur of the Chaldees* (1929) and the imposing series *Ur Excavations* (five volumes, 1927-1929).

British Inf. Services
SIR LEONARD WOOLLEY

Ur was a city of southern Mesopotamia, with a busy and active history stretching back some 4,000 years to the beginning of human records. Although other scholars had preceded Woolley, it was he who effectively uncovered the evidences of a non-Semitic civilization (in a region of Semites), originating in the Persian highlands. He brought to light many manifestations of a culture to which scholars have applied the name Sumerian. These people had an elaborate code of laws, a well-established religion with a hierarchy of gods, a well-equipped army, a high standard of domestic comfort, and high ability in both arts and handicrafts. Riven by successive wars, neglected and built up again by successive conquerors, Ur finally fell into ruin about 300 years before the Christian era, and since then has been an uninhabited desert. Woolley's dug-up treasures were distributed between the Iraq Museum, the British Museum, and the Museum of the University of Pennsylvania.

Members of the Ur expedition lived during the winters in Expedition House, a bungalow built of bricks of the time of Nebuchadnezzar. Every summer it got covered with sand, and every autumn Woolley, and his wife, and his staff had to excavate it. Housekeeping was complicated, he recalls. Water was carried in kerosene tins on the backs of donkeys from the Euphrates, ten miles away. Tough mutton and chickens were purchased from the Arabs, who lent the expedition a cow every season in

WOOLLEY, SIR LEONARD—*Continued*

return for her keep. Season by season the expedition made new discoveries, including the Ziggurat, the tower on which the moon-god's temple stood; golden head-dresses and helmets and jewels and ornaments. Woolley found geological proof of the Flood (as recorded in the Bible)—an eleven-foot layer of flood silt, several strata down, with ruins of other buildings underneath, which could only have been caused, he believes, by an immense upheaval.

The archaeologist found thousands of "documents"—inscribed clay tablets. Since the clay was often the consistency of cream cheese he developed his own method of preserving it: the tablets were put into kerosene tins which were filled with sand and placed in a kiln until the clay hardened; then the earth fell off and left the tablets firm and the inscriptions clearly decipherable.

When the work at Ur came to an end in 1934, Woolley looked around for another site to excavate. He found it by a process of intuitive reasoning. Somewhere, he thought, there must have been a community which made its living along the Euphrates by supplying the people of Mesopotamia with essential hardwood timber. He selected two likely mounds and discovered near Antioch, Syria, the royal city of Alalakh and its seaport al Mina, in the forgotten kingdom of Atchana, proving definite links with the Minoan civilization. He found a temple of Mithras older than those the Romans built in Europe, and he dug up silver coins bearing the owl of Athens. From 1937 to 1939, and between 1946 and 1949 he was at Atchana, and at Hatay, Turkey, in expeditions fostered privately but financed by the British Museum and other museums. He himself regards his findings here as of equal importance with his work at Ur. He recorded the results of his excavations of the two mounds at Atchana and al Mina in his book *A Forgotten Kingdom* (Penguin, 1953).

On the outbreak of World War II, September 3, 1939, Woolley was instantly summoned to the War Office, for work in the information and propaganda branch of Military Intelligence. While there (in 1942) he delivered the Huxley Memorial Lecture under the auspices of the Royal Anthropological Institute. In 1943 he became archaeological adviser to the War Office. He made visits of inspection to North Africa and Italy, but his work was essentially at Whitehall itself, collecting information, appointing officers in the field, drafting orders, drawing up regulations, and generally briefing the Secretary of State. The protection of ancient monuments was made a matter of Army responsibility and military discipline, and all rules and regulations were issued by the supreme Commander-in-Chief. After the war the Dutch Government commented that the British War Office had done more to protect works of art than any other agency in Europe. While engaged on these tasks Woolley held the ranks of major (General Staff), public relations directorate (1939-43) and lieutenant-colonel (General Staff), and archaeological adviser to the Civil Affairs Directorate (1943-46).

He has been given the honorary degrees of D.Litt. by Trinity College, Dublin and of LL.D. by the University of St. Andrew's, Scotland. He is also an honorary associate of the Royal Institute of British Architects and a fellow of the Society of Antiquaries. He was knighted in 1935. He married Katharine Elizabeth Keeling in 1927, widow of Lieutenant-Colonel Francis Keeling. She was an archaeologist and a gifted sculptor. She died in 1945.

Sir Leonard gave up active excavation in 1950 and retired to a country place at Shaftesbury, Dorset. He does not, however, regard himself as completely retired, for he is still working on his official report of the results obtained at Ur and at Hatay. But he has time for two absorbing outside interests. One is fishing, and the other the collection of pictures, in which he has a catholic taste, with some preference for the old Italians.

References

Who's Who, 1954
Woolley, L. Dead Towns and Living Men (1954); Digging Up The Past (1930); Spadework in Archaeology (1953)

WORSHAM, LEW(IS ELMER, JR.) Oct. 5, 1917- Professional golfer

Address: b. c/o Oakmont Country Club, Oakmont, Pa.; Coral Ridge Country Club, Fort Lauderdale, Fla.

"The most spectacular shot in golf" is the usual description of the over 100-yard eagle 2 which clinched the $25,000 first prize of the 1953 Tam O'Shanter "world's championship" tournament for Lew Worsham of Oakmont, Pennsylvania. The golfer came out of obscurity to win the national open title in 1947, but then dropped out of public notice for several years until he became the leading money winner in 1952 golf tournaments.

Born October 5, 1917 in Level Run, Virginia, Lewis Elmer Worsham, Jr. is one of the five children (four boys and a girl) of Lewis Elmer and Irene Lena Worsham. He was reared in Washington, D.C., where his father is a carpenter. When he was still young, he began caddying at the Kenwood Country Club to earn expense money. He had no interest in golf as a game, at first, but after a year or so of caddying during week-ends and school vacations, he began to play on Mondays the day when business was slack and the caddies were allowed to use the course. After six years, he entered the Hearst-sponsored Tri-Civic caddies' tournament in Chicago in 1935 and finished second. Worsham's dream was to play well enough to compete in regular tournaments, but it seemed only a dream to him.

After attending the Hampton (Virginia) High School, young Worsham went to work as assistant professional to Bob Barnett at the Chevy Chase Country Club in Maryland where he served the three-year apprenticeship required before admission to the Professional

Golfers Association. During this period, he learned to make and repair golf clubs and to run the golf shop. At that time, according to Lawrence Robinson of the New York *World-Telegram,* the assistant "figured he was the worst golfer extant and wanted to remake his game because of his big hook," but Barnett advised him to keep hitting the ball the way he had been hitting it.

When his apprenticeship was completed in 1939, twenty-one-year-old Lew Worsham was engaged as a "pro" at the famous Burning Tree Club in Bethesda, Maryland. Notables who took lessons from him included Robert Hannegan, James T. Forrestal, Steve Early and senators Robert Taft and Arthur Capper. Worsham has told a *Current Biography* interviewer that a major source of income for a "pro," in addition to teaching and the golf shop, is bag storage—there may be as many as 600 sets of clubs stored at the shop, at $10 to $15 apiece per year. While he was at the Burning Tree Club, he competed in and won the Mid-State Open championship in 1941 and 1942, and the Middle Atlantic PGA tournament in the latter year.

Worsham entered the Navy in 1943 and was sent to physical instructors' school. Stationed at the Bainbridge, Maryland officers' club, and later at Norfolk and Bannockburn, he conducted golf tournaments for servicemen. "While in the Navy," Worsham told *Current Biography,* "I met Jimmy Demaret and we became good friends and he gave me the idea that I could play well enough to make money playing in tournaments." While in the Navy, Lew Worsham, Jimmy Demaret and Rut Coffey competed in George S. May's 1944 "world's championship" Tam O'Shanter tournament. With one round to go, Worsham was apparently headed for prize money, when he, Demaret and Coffey each received a letter from Navy headquarters stating that their participation in civilian competitive sports was in violation of regulations. Worsham was nominated for the "hard luck player" prize of $1,000, but received $100 from May instead.

Back in civilian life in 1946, Lew Worsham returned to the Burning Tree Club and competed in a number of tournaments. He reached a tie in the Philadelphia *Inquirer* tournament and in the Jacksonville open that year, but lost in both play-offs. (Winning tournaments is not essential, although desirable, for the professional player; cash prizes are so arranged that any golfer among the first ten winners can make a "reasonable living," in Worsham's phrase.)

The Washington "pro" had never won a major tournament until November 1946, when he nosed out his friend Demaret by one stroke in the $12,000 Druid Hills open in Atlanta, Georgia. Worsham's 279 strokes for the seventy-two holes was 9 under par. Worsham was wondering if he should give up the security of his club job for the possible rewards of a tournament player, when luck saved him from having to make that decision. A temporary position opened for him as "pro" at the Congressional Country Club in Rockville, Maryland.

LEW WORSHAM

"I could play in most any tournament I wanted," Worsham said, "and was paid a salary to teach when I wasn't playing in tournaments." After a time, however, he resigned and became "pro" at the Oakmont Country Club, near Pittsburgh, Pennsylvania.

Carding consistent 70s and 71s, the golfer reached a play-off with Sammy Snead in the United States Golf Association open at the St. Louis Country Club in June 1947. Snead led all the way to the last hole, but with his last putt Worsham won the most respected title in golf by 69 to 70—2 under par, to Snead's 1. His prize was $2000, plus a $500 bonus for the extra day's work. Another $2500 came to "the Chin," as Worsham's fellow "pros" call him, that September when he won the Denver open golf tournament with a seventy-two-hole total of 276 strokes, 4 ahead of the field. This was his last important victory for several years.

In January 1951 he set a new competitive record of 63 for the Phoenix (Arizona) Country Club course, went over par on three holes, but scored 5 birdies on the first nine holes the next day, and sank an eight-foot putt on the final hole to win the Phoenix open tournament with 272, 1 stroke ahead of Lawson Little. That December he scored a double victory at the annual La Gorce "pro" tournament at Miami Beach—his 5-under-par 66 earned him a $500 prize.

Competing for the "world championship" in the 1952 Tam O'Shanter, the golfer led the field for the first sixty-six holes, then lost his lead on the last holes with a "stretch of bogies" which gave him a final 280. His winnings were less than $1000 and the Washington *Post* sports writer, John Gonella, referred to "the belief held by many that Lew would never again win a major event after his nerve-wracking experience. . . ."

In the race for the 1953 first prize of $25,000, Worsham again started brilliantly and scored

WORSHAM, LEW—*Continued*

a 7-under-par 65 on the first round, despite taking thirty-one putts. On the next day's round he arrived at the twelfth hole 12 under par, then "nervously came apart," missed a six-foot putt, and ended with a 72. His third-round 73 gave him a total of 210, or fifth place—Al Besselink, Dave Douglas, Doug Ford, and Chandler Harper were tied for first with 209 each.

By the last hole of the final round, Worsham was running second to Harper. Harper's last putt, a birdie, brought his seventy-two-hole total to 279, and he was already being congratulated when Worsham selected a sand wedge and shot over 100 yards into the hole for an eagle 2 that made his total 278. The golfer had hoped to make it in three strokes, which would force a playoff, but the shouts of the crowd near the hole told him he had shot an eagle and won the $25,000 as well as an enormous silver cup. "Never have I seen anything so dramatic as Worsham's finish," said Dutch Harrison. "It was the luckiest shot I ever had in my life," exclaimed Worsham. "I'm sorry I had to do it to my friend Harper."

Seen by millions on television, Worsham's "$25,000 swing" became a household word. In his mild-mannered way, the golfer objects to the statement that he won with one stroke. "I had to hit 277 pretty good shots to ever get into position to make that one shot," he told a *Current Biography* writer. As a result of his victory, which made him the year's top money-winning "pro," Worsham was signed by George S. May for thirty-five exhibition matches with a guarantee of earning $35,000. He prefers exhibitions to tournaments—"in an exhibition you always win."

The $1800 which the golfer garnered for second place in the National Celebrities Tournament brought his prize earnings up to $33,807 by September 7, 1953.

Worsham has earned $62,000 in 1953 and 1954 from exhibitions and endorsements, making him the top money-winning pro, according to the Professional Golf Association. On July 4, 1954 he was appointed professional at the Coral Ridge Country Club, Fort Lauderdale, Florida. He retains his post at the Oakmont, Pennsylvania Country Club. He won the $1800 top prize on March 24, 1954 for carding a four-under-par 68 in the pro-amateur tournament at the Seminole Golf Club, Palm Beach, Florida.

Lew Worsham has blue eyes and brown hair, is five feet, eleven inches tall, and he weighs 185 pounds. He was married to Margaret Virginia Shoemaker on June 3, 1939 and has a daughter, Margaret Lynda, and a son, Richard Lewis. The soft-spoken Virginian lists his church affiliation as Baptist, and has no political affiliation. His spare time is spent in hunting quail, pheasant and grouse, and in "any kind of fishing."

References

N Y Herald Tribune p21 Je 16 '47
N Y Times p14 Je 16 '47
N Y World-Telegram p20 Je 16 '47 por

WRONG, (HUMPHREY) HUME Sept. 10, 1894-Jan. 24, 1954 Canadian Under Secretary of State for External Affairs; assistant professor of history at University of Toronto (1921-1927); first secretary, counselor and, later, chargé d'affaires of Canadian Legation in Washington (1927-1937); appointed permanent delegate to League of Nations (1937); senior counselor of the Legation in Washington (1941-1942); represented Canada at first meeting of the U.N. General Assembly in London; as Ambassador Extraordinary and Plenipotentiary to U.S. (1946-1953) supported North Atlantic pact, aid to Europe, U.S.-Canadian economic-military integration; became Under Secretary of State for External Affairs in June 1953. See *Current Biography*, (Oct.) 1950.

Obituary

N Y Times p19 Ja 25 '54

YEAGER, CHARLES E. Feb. 13, 1923- United States Air Force officer; test pilot

Address: c/o Edwards Air Force Base, Muroc Calif.; 12th Air Force base headquarters, Ramstein, Germany

The recipient of two unique aviation records, Major Charles E. Yeager is the first man to have penetrated the sound barrier and the first to fly at a speed of more than 1,600 miles an hour, which he achieved in December 1953. Until October 1954, when he was assigned to the Iron Curtain air frontier in Germany, at United States 12th Air Force headquarters, he was the assistant chief of the flight test operations laboratory at Edwards Air Force Base in the Mojave Desert in California. During World War II Yeager served overseas as a flight officer, flying sixty-four missions with the Eighth Air Force Fighter Command in Europe. He was an Air Force test pilot when selected to fly the rocket research plane X-1 on October 14, 1947, the day he first broke the sound barrier. As one of the outstanding pioneers of the supersonic era, Yeager has shared in the award of the Collier Trophy.

His 1954 awards include the General William Mitchell Memorial Trophy (shared with General Curtis E. LeMay) presented by the American Legion, and the Harmon Air Trophy Award for outstanding achievements in aeronautics.

Charles E. Yeager was born in Myra, West Virginia on February 13, 1923. When he was six months old, his family moved to Hamlin, West Virginia. As a boy he was interested in sports, gardening and playing the trombone. He was graduated from Hamlin High School in 1941 and considered working for his father, A. Hal Yeager, a contract gas well driller. However, because of the possibility of war, Yeager enlisted in the Air Force in September 1941. He was commissioned a flight officer in March 1943 and was assigned to the 363d Fighter Squadron, 357th Fighter Group, at Tonapah, Nevada.

The squadron was sent to England the following November. Yeager made eight successful missions and destroyed two German planes.

On the ninth mission, March 5, 1944, he was shot down by Nazi planes near Regensburg and wounded in the leg. He made his way out of Germany and was picked up by the French underground. Disguised as a French peasant, Yeager was passed along into Spain by way of the Pyrenees. He was imprisoned by the Spanish police, but sawed his way out of jail. After forty-five days in Spain he was picked up by the Royal Air Force and soon was reunited with his squadron in England.

Air Force policy at that time did not permit a flier assisted by the underground to fly in the same theater again. In case of capture, the Germans might force him to reveal underground secrets. Yeager was determined to fly in Europe again and with other "evadees" virtually camped near General Dwight D. Eisenhower's headquarters, hoping to persuade him to authorize their return to combat.

The policy was changed when the cross-channel invasion began. In July 1944 Yeager was made a second lieutenant in the Air Reserve. During the remainder of the war he flew fifty-five more combat missions in P-51 Mustangs and destroyed eleven more enemy aircraft. He had flown a total of 270 combat hours. The flier was awarded the Silver Star with one oak leaf cluster, the Distinguished Flying Cross with two clusters, Bronze Star Medal, Air Medal with six clusters, and Purple Heart.

At Perrin Field, Texas, where he was next assigned, Yeager took the pilot instructors' course and in May 1946 became a basic flying instructor. Two months later he was assigned to the fighter flight test branch at Wright-Patterson Air Force Base in Ohio. He received his regular Air Force commission in February 1947.

From the many test pilots at the Wright-Patterson Base who volunteered to fly the X-1 research plane, Yeager was selected because of merit and size. Only a small man could comfortably fit in the cockpit of the X-1. Wesley Price (*Saturday Evening Post,* July 1, 1950) has written that the X-1 had been constructed to answer two questions: Could a straight-wing plane fly faster than sound? Could a man control its flight in battering shock waves? It was rumored that the X-1 would fail and neither Yeager nor Major Jackie L. Ridley, his engineering officer, were overconfident when they went to the California desert.

The tests were to be made at Muroc, about sixty-five miles from Los Angeles, in a secret zone which includes Rogers Dry Lake, a solid bed of clay that has been called the best landing field in the world. On arrival, Yeager and Ridley studied the technical background of their project. Yeager made glide and powered trial flights and became enthusiastic about the X-1. When they returned to Wright-Patterson Base to report, it was agreed that Yeager could hit the sonic barrier.

Yeager's own story of October 14, 1947, when he became the first man to cross the sonic barrier, appeared in *This Week* (August 22, 1948). The X-1 was ferried by a B-29 to 7,000 feet, at which point Yeager climbed down a ladder and sealed himself inside the cockpit of

U.S. Air Force

MAJOR CHARLES E. YEAGER

the X-1. Then, at the 20,000-foot mark, he made a fast recheck of the approximately fifty instruments and at 26,000 feet, the B-29 dipped its nose for the 1,000-foot dive that would precede the drop. Seconds were counted off, ending with the signal word, "drop".

Yeager dropped. His first reaction was of a "fiery sun that seemed about six feet away" and blinded him as "the plane bucked and fell." As he oriented himself, "the plane came to life and lunged forward into space." The B-29 was far behind as he shot up "into the sky at a forty-five degree angle." The sky deepened to purple, stars came out, but the sun still glowed. He leveled off and watched the Mach needle on his instrument panel creep past .9 which indicates 90 per cent of the speed of sound. "The X-1 was caught up in the full rush of its power." Finally the Mach needle went past 1.0, and he was flying ahead of sound. Sound travels about 763 miles per hour at sea level and approximately 662 miles per hour at 40,000 feet. Yeager recalls, "I was so high and so remote, and the airplane was so very quiet that I might almost have been motionless." Soon his fuel was about gone and he leveled off. Then without power, he started the down glide.

"It took seven and a half minutes to come down. I glided at 300 and 400 miles per hour, rolling and doing wing overs for the fun of it. . . . I saw a heavily-timbered mountain and thought it looked good for hunting, thought maybe it had a hidden lake where the fishing would be good. That's where I want to end up. Hunting and fishing. Lake Tahoe area. I'll give myself four or five more years of this kind of flying. Then I'll drive an old truck like the C-47, and when the 20/13 vision goes I'll get a desk. . . ." Yeager slowed his plane gradually to 160 miles per hour and came to a safe landing.

(Continued next page)

YEAGER, CHARLES E.—*Continued*

The news was not officially released until June 10, 1948, when Secretary of the Air Force W. Stuart Symington announced that Yeager had exceeded the speed of sound in a plane designed to reach a speed of more than 1,000 m.p.h. Aviation experts commented on the possibility of supersonic speeds, perhaps up to 1,700 or 2,000 miles per hour, which would be of incalculable value in war or peace.

The late Staff General Hoyt S. Vandenberg, Air Force Chief of Staff, presented Yeager with the Mackay Trophy for the outstanding military aviation performance of the year on June 15, 1948. On the forty-fifth anniversary of the Wright brothers first flight, December 17, 1948, President Harry S. Truman presented the Collier Trophy to Captain Charles E. Yeager who shared the award with Lawrence D. Bell, producer of the X-1, and John Stack, government scientist specializing in supersonic problems.

In the ensuing years Yeager continued to make test flights. After a civilian test pilot for the National Advisory Committee for Aeronautics had flown a Navy Skyrocket at 1,327 miles per hour on November 20, 1953, Yeager set out to fly faster. He established a new record of 1,650 miles per hour on December 12, 1953. He had regained his title as the world's fastest man in the Air Force's X-1A rocket plane.

Newsweek (February 22, 1954) reported that after the X-1A had been released from the bomb bay of the B-29 on that trip, Yeager leveled off at 70,000 feet and as he glanced back, saw "the wings buffeting and shock waves on them." He had reached a speed of 1,650 miles per hour when the plane "went out of control" and "dropped some 50,000 feet" (nearly ten miles), before he regained control. This was his fourth flight in the X-1A, which was built by Bell Aircraft Corporation. The X-1A is fueled by liquid oxygen and a special alcohol-water mixture.

As an Air Force major, Yeager earns $782.18 a month. He might earn as high as $30,000 a year as a civilian pilot and has had offers, but the jobs would be routine and he feels the Air Force offers other compensations. He has been sent to France to fly late model jets. In the fall of 1953, he went to the Far East and flew the MIG-15 that had been surrendered by a North Korean pilot. In January 1954 Yeager was among the "Wings-for-the-Americas" pilots who made a good-will tour of Latin American nations demonstrating United States jet air power.

On August 9, 1954 the Air Research and Development Command announced that Major Yeager was to be assigned in October to the 12th Air Force headquarters in Germany to "bring his test-pilot experience into the front line of the cold war to help develop increased combat capability in tactical units of the command." The force has more than 400 F-86 Sabre jets, and is the main air arm of the United States in Europe.

Chuck Yeager was married in 1945 to Glennis Faye Dickhouse for whom he had named all his P-51's while flying in Europe. He later christened the X-1 "Glamorous Glennis." The flier has four children, Donald, Michael, Sharon Christine, and Susan. The major has been described as "half scientist and half adventurer, a daredevil who must operate with mathematical precision" and who flies "like part of the plane." He is of fighter-pilot size and has brown hair and blue eyes. For vacationing, Yeager enjoys camping with his family.

Film rights to the life story of Major Yeager have been acquired by Sam X. Abarbanel. The film will include the story of the Bell X-1 plane and of the Air Research and Development Command.

References

N Y World-Telegram p5 D 16 '53 por
Newsweek 43:31+ F 22 '54 por
Sat Eve Post 223:26+ Jl 1 '50 por
Scholastic 59:4 Ja '52 por
This Week p6+ Ag 22 '48 por
Time 53:64+ Ap 18 '49 por

YOUNG, MILTON R(UBEN) Dec. 6, 1897- United States Senator from North Dakota; farmer

Address: b. Senate Office Bldg., Washington 25, D.C.; h. La Moure, N.D.

North Dakota's junior Senator, Milton R. Young, is a grain farmer and landowner who is a long-standing member of the U.S. Senate agriculture committee and of the influential Senate Republican Policy Committee. Shortly before the inauguration of Dwight D. Eisenhower, Young was one of four high-ranking Senators who conferred with the President-elect on Cabinet appointments, legislative plans and the establishment of a working relationship between Congress and the White House. Before Young's appointment and subsequent election to the Seventy-ninth Congress in 1945, he had served for twelve years in the North Dakota state legislature.

During the past two years he has become identified with a farm bloc opposing the Eisenhower Administration's policy of lower farm subsidies. He headed a sizable Senate group in an unsuccessful effort to prevent passage in 1954 of a bill providing flexible, rather than rigid, price supports for farm commodities.

Milton Ruben Young was born in Berlin, North Dakota on December 6, 1897 to John Young, a farmer and real estate dealer, and Rachel (Zimmerman) Young. He grew up in a rural community and attended the La Moure county public schools. Following his high school graduation in 1915, he studied at the state's North Dakota Agricultural College in Fargo and later at Graceland College in Lamoni, Iowa.

All through his political career Young has taken an active part in the operation of his large grain farm, located near Berlin in the southeastern part of the state. He was a member in this district of the school, township and county Agricultural Adjustment Administration boards.

He entered politics in 1932, with his election to the lower house of the North Dakota state legislature. Two years later he won a seat in the state Senate, where he served until his resignation on March 14, 1945. At various times in the Senate he held the chairmanship of committees on corporations, state affairs, ways and means, and appropriations. He was made president pro tempore of the Senate in 1941 and majority floor leader in 1943.

During the Presidential election contest of 1940 Young was division campaign manager of the Republican National Committee for Willkie Farm Voters and Republican state campaign manager. He again managed the state campaign in 1944, at which time his reorganization of the North Dakota Republican party resulted in the election of a Republican Governor. Among the defeated candidates of the party was Gerald P. Nye, an isolationist, who lost his seat in the United States Senate to John Moses, a Democrat and an outspoken internationalist.

When Senator Moses died a few months later, Young was appointed by Governor Fred G. Aandahl on March 12, 1945 to fill the vacancy in the Senate. Known as an advocate of an international police agreement for maintenance of world peace, Young reportedly gave assurance to the North Dakota Governor that he would support the foreign policies of President Franklin D. Roosevelt's Administration.

The appointment of Young was endorsed by North Dakota voters at a special election on June 25, 1946 when he was chosen to serve out Moses' unexpired term. For the second time, on July 25, 1946 he took his oath of office as a member of Congress. He was re-elected to a full six-year Senatorial term on November 7, 1950, receiving more than a two-to-one majority of the total votes cast.

Since his freshman year in Congress the North Dakota Republican has been a member of the Senate's Committee on Agriculture and Forestry. He served for a time on committees for immigration, manufactures and the District of Columbia, before receiving his present assignment to the Committee on Appropriations. Young also has a place on the eleven-member Senate Republican Committee, which directs legislative strategy in the upper chamber. In the Eighty-third Congress he has been secretary of the Senate Republican Conference, the party organization of all Republican Senators.

A leader of the farm bloc that championed high price supports for agricultural products, Young co-sponsored the Young-Russell Amendment to the 1949 farm bill, calling for continuation of rigid wartime price supports. This amendment passed the Senate in October by the margin of the tie-breaking vote of Vice-President Alben W. Barkley, but the bill was returned to the committee on the motion of Senator Clinton P. Anderson.

Under the Republican Administration, beginning January 1953, the Senator from North Dakota continued his fight against establishment of a flexible price support system and in October 1953 proposed a three-point plan to "halt our farm depression overnight." He recommended extending high price supports for three more years and adding certain non-basic crops to the list for which support at 90 per cent of parity was mandatory. (Parity is a formula for determining a fair price for crops in relation to the cost of the goods a farmer must buy.) Young's program also called for an increase in exports of farm products and a tightening on import curbs of unneeded foreign agricultural commodities.

Wide World

MILTON R. YOUNG

Part of Senator Young's criticism of the Administration's farm policies was directed at Secretary of Agriculture Ezra T. Benson. At first reluctant to confirm the nomination of Benson, Young in January 1953 decided not to oppose the new Secretary when he was assured that Benson had a "completely open mind" on the question of extending high farm price supports. Before the end of the year, however, Young reported that there was widespread discontent among the farmers because of "uncertainty over Secretary Benson's policies" (New York *Times*, October 18, 1953).

In the agriculture committee and on the floor of the Senate, Young argued against the Administration's 1954 farm bill providing for a flexible price support system and offered a motion for a one-year extension of the rigid 90 per cent support system. His efforts to prevent a reduction of the farm subsidy formula were defeated when the Senate in August 1954 voted to approve the Administration's bill.

Senator Young was a member of the survey commission formed by President Harry S. Truman in January 1952 to study ways of developing the Missouri River basin, which comprises one-sixth of the area of the United States. Dissenting in February 1953 from the majority which recommended a five-man Fed-

YOUNG, MILTON R.—*Continued*

eral commission to supervise the over-all development program, he headed a group favoring a Federal-state compact arrangement. With two other members of the survey commission he noted in a minority report that "the ultimate power would reside wholly in the Federal government, and the decisions of the proposed commission would be for the people rather than by the people" (New York *Times*, February 21, 1953).

The Senator's record on other domestic issues shows him in favor of the Equal Rights Amendment (July 1946) and the Taft-Hartley bill (May 1947), against a proposal to repeal Federal taxes on oleomargarine (March 1948) and a measure to forbid segregation in public housing (April 1949). He voted "nay" to cuts in reclamation funds and soil conservation (1951) and to a $46,000,000 reduction in the T.V.A. appropriation (June 1952).

Voting on legislative measures in foreign affairs, Young favored the Bretton Woods Agreement bill (July 1945), the United Nations Charter (July 1945), the Greek-Turkish aid bill (April 1947) and the European recovery bill (March 1948). In September 1947 he predicted that Congress would approve the Marshall Plan to aid economic restoration of Europe. The Senator, who had just returned from a conference in Geneva of the U.N. Food and Agriculture Organization, said that he would support any program "if the facts are clearly known and demonstrated, and if it is a long-range effort made after the European countries have made every effort to help themselves" (New York *Times*, September 8, 1947). He voted "yea" to a 10 per cent cut in Marshall plan authorization in April 1949.

On other bills in the field of international activity Young opposed the North Atlantic Security Pact (July 1949) and allocation of $45,000,000 for the Point IV program (May 1950). During 1951, 1952 and 1953 he voted for substantial reductions in foreign economic aid.

After making a tour of Europe to study problems of defense as a member of the appropriations committee, Senator Young recommended in December 1951 that the United States spend more money on its own defense. "We ought to build an air force at least three times as strong as that of any potential enemy," he told newsmen (New York *Herald Tribune*, December 17, 1951). When the Republican Administration proposed a cut in air force appropriations in May 1953, he protested that such a reduction would leave the air power of the United States inferior to Russia's. "We can't match the Russians in the number of men they can put into armies," he said, "but we can certainly do it in the air and should" (New York *Times*, May 24, 1953).

Among the legislative measures sponsored by the junior Senator from North Dakota was a resolution to have the Secretary of the Interior make a study leading to the possible restoration of Ford's Theatre as it was when President Lincoln was assassinated. Young began his campaign to restore the theatre in 1946 after discovering that the playhouse had been stripped of its original furnishings and equipment. His resolution, sponsored in the House of Representatives by George A. Dondero, was approved by Congress in May 1954.

During the Eighty-third Congress he opposed profits tax relief for small business (July 1953); favored the St. Lawrence Seaway authorization (January 1954), the Bricker Treaty Control Amendment (February 1954) and a bill allowing for 140,000 public housing units (June 1954). He was one of six Republicans who voted with the majority of Democrats in June 1954 to approve the proposal to add $35,000,000 to the Rural Electrification's loan authority.

Senator Young married Malinda V. Benson, daughter of a La Moure farmer, on July 7, 1919. They have three children: William M., Duane C., and John M. The legislator is a member of the Masonic Order and the Elks and belongs to the Reorganized Church of Jesus Christ of the Latter-Day Saints.

References

N Y Times p 1+ Mr 10 '45
Biographical Directory of the American Congress, 1774-1949 (1950)
Congressional Directory (1954)
Who's Who in America, 1954-55
Who's Who in United States Politics (1950)

ZAHEDI, FAZLOLLAH 1897- Premier of Iran

Address: Teheran, Iran

General Fazlollah Zahedi, the "strong man" of Iran, was appointed Premier of that country by Shah Mohammed Riza Pahlevi in August 1953, and took a leading role in the uprising that forced the former Premier Mohammed Mossadegh out of power at that time. To Zahedi, who had been a soldier-adventurer all his life, this revolt was only one of many similar blood-and-thunder episodes in his career. He had fought different Persian tribesmen, had been kidnapped and jailed in exile by the British, and had served as a military governor, as Teheran police chief, and as Senator and Minister of the Interior.

On October 21, 1954 Zahedi's regime received a vote of confidence when the Majiis (the lower house of Parliament of Iran) ratified the international oil agreement with eight major foreign oil firms to operate the Iranian oil industry and to split half of the profits with the Iranian Government.

Fazlollah Zahedi was born in 1897 to a moderately wealthy landowning family. He was educated at the Teheran Military Academy and studied the French, Arabic, Turkish and English languages in addition to the Persian.

At the age of twenty-three, Zahedi joined the Cossack Brigade and as a company commander led his command successfully against insurgents of Tangabun and Gilan who were led by Khuchik Khan and supported by the Bolsheviks. In 1922 he was promoted to the rank of Brigadier General.

That year Zahedi was captured by Kurdish outlaws and escaped. In 1923 he subdued the forces of Ismail Simitku, a noted Kurdish outlaw and received the Order of Zolfaghar (Sword of Ali) from the Shah. He was made commanding officer of the Fars Brigade and of the southern ports, and directed a military campaign against the tribal leader Sheikh Kazal, Lord of Khuzistan province.

Appointed in 1926 by Riza Shah—the present Shah's father—to be military governor of Khuzistan, the province in which Abadan, the hub of the nation's oil industry is located, Zahedi was later made military governor of Gorgon, in order to subdue Turkoman tribesmen and to assert government authority there.

In 1929 he was recalled to Teheran as commanding officer of the Gendarmerie. Then followed (1932-34) a term as Chief of Police of Teheran, and a term (1935-41) as Inspector-General of the Army.

In 1942 came an incident that halted Zahedi's progress upward. Early in World War II, when the British and Russians jointly occupied Iran and forced the abdication of the former Shah, Zahedi was commander of the Isfahan military district in the south. The British believed he was plotting with the Nazis, and sent Colonel Fitzroy Maclean to handle the matter. Colonel Maclean kidnapped Zahedi and shipped him to Palestine where he remained in custody until the war ended. This operation was described in Maclean's book, *Escape to Adventure* (American edition, Little, Brown, 1950).

Home again as hostilities ceased, Zahedi was promoted to Major General and in 1946 was made divisional commander of Fars Province. In 1947 he again became Inspector-General; he was retired from the Army in May 1949 and became adjutant to the Shah. In November 1949 he was made Chief of Police of Teheran once again, and in February 1950 was appointed a Senator by the Shah.

General Zahedi's elevation to Premier was foreshadowed by affairs in the spring of 1951 when the seventy-year-old Mossadegh urged the Iranian people to "break the chains" of foreign interests in Iran. His wishes were obeyed, and the Anglo-Iranian Oil Company's wells and giant Abadan refinery—said to be worth $750,000,000—were seized and nationalized. This meant the end of Iran's royalties of $4,200,000 a month.

Nevertheless, Dr. Mossadegh maintained his position for more than two years. As negotiations failed between the Anglo-Iranian company and the Mossadegh government, and as Iran was able to sell very little oil on world markets, the country's financial position grew rapidly worse. By August 1953 the Iranian treasury was empty, the government was deep in debt, 40,000 or more workers were idle at Abadan, and their $1,800,000 monthly payroll unpaid.

Meanwhile, Zahedi had acted as Minister of the Interior in Mossadegh's first Cabinet in 1951 and had aided with the oil nationalization program. He soon left this post, returned to the Senate, and worked with independents hostile to Mossadegh. The General found trouble awaiting him. On October 13, 1952, the Mossadegh government announced that it had broken up a foreign-aided plot instigated by Zahedi and others. As a Senator, Zahedi was immune from arrest, but a guard was placed around his home. In October 1952 the Senate was voted out of existence. On April 30, 1953 Zahedi was arrested in connection with the murder of Brigadier General Mahmud Afshartous, Chief of Police of Teheran. Zahedi escaped and took refuge with the Bakhtiari tribe which was generally favorable to the Shah.

Wide World

FAZLOLLAH ZAHEDI

In mid-August 1953, events rushed to a climax. On August 13 the Shah appointed Zahedi as Premier and he accepted the appointment on August 15. Rioting followed: mobs tore down statues of the Shah and of Zahedi, and both the thirty-three-year-old monarch and the Premier were forced to flee—Zahedi into hiding and Riza Pahlevi to Rome.

The tide turned, however, on August 19, when thousands of demonstrators in Teheran jammed the streets shouting the cry "Long live the Shah!" Aided by Army units, they captured Mossadegh's stronghold and smashed the headquarters of the Tudeh (Communist party) and of the pro-Mossadegh Pan-Iranian party. Late that afternoon, after a day of chaos, Zahedi assumed the direction of the government and was soon rewarded with the military rank of General.

Zahedi's first radio message to the people, according to Neal Stanford in the *Christian Science Monitor* (August 24, 1953) was: "I will raise the workers' wages, give free medicine to the poor. I shall give you a detailed program later." A cable was promptly sent to the Shah: "Shahinshah (King of Kings) of Iran, Rome: now that the people have been able to capture the capital, we are eagerly awaiting your return." The revolt had succeeded, Mossadegh was arrested and was put on trial for violation of the Shah's orders and

ZAHEDI, FAZLOLLAH—*Continued*

of the Iranian Constitution. (He was sentenced on December 21, 1953 to three years' imprisonment in solitary confinement.)

Since taking over the premiership, General Zahedi has been extremely active. He led an intensive fight against the leaders of the outlawed Tudeh (Communist party) and has jailed many. On one day, according to newspaper reports, about a thousand portraits of Stalin and hundreds of bales of anti-government, pro-Communist leaflets were seized. His security forces quashed a Communist effort to burn four hangars full of new fighter planes at a Teheran airbase. The Premier sent Army troops into the southern city of Shiraz, where 10,000 Ghashgha tribesmen were calling for the release of Dr. Mossadegh.

Finding imports reduced by a half, a budget deficit of $210,000,000, and a loss of about as much in oil revenue, Zahedi promptly tackled the problem of finances. He made a personal plea to President Eisenhower: "Iran needs immediate financial aid to enable it to emerge from a state of economic and financial chaos."

On September 3 the United States government announced that it had agreed to continue technical assistance to Iran at the annual level of $23,400,000. On September 5 President Eisenhower promised a $45,000,000 grant from the United States for emergency assistance. Iran also receives about $30,000,000 in U.S. military assistance. A supplementary trade agreement was signed with the Soviet Union which doubled the volume of barter trade between the two nations to a total of $84,000,000. The Soviets will supply steel rails, nickel, copper, brass, sugar, electrical cables in exchange for Iranian rice, carpets, opium, oil seeds, gum and cotton.

Zahedi, during his first days as Premier promised to encourage the mechanization of agriculture, and the formation of peasant cooperatives. He has stated that "some kind of land reform is necessary in Iran. A way must be found to give landlords fair compensation for their land, and the peasants must be trained to assume the responsibilities of land ownership and to take the initiative that goes with it." A program to improve living conditions for the lower-income groups was initiated with the decision to build 200 new clinics, 7,000 workers' houses in Teheran, and new schools throughout the country. The completion of irrigation, hydroelectric and railroad-building projects was planned.

Telling the Iranian people that the oil industry owed over $87,000,000 and needed 600 experts and about $30,000,000 in aid, Zahedi hinted that negotiation with Great Britain would be necessary in the near future if proposed reforms for Iran were to be carried out. In August he ended Mossadegh's policy of selling Iranian oil at half price on the world market. By October 11, the government announced its willingness to reach a settlement with the British over the nationalization of the Anglo-Iranian Oil Company, and to resume diplomatic relations with Great Britain which had been broken off on October 22, 1952.

Great Britain and Iran decided to exchange diplomatic representatives on December 5, 1953 and six days later Zahedi stated that he was confident that the oil dispute would be settled soon "with justice and reason and with safeguards for the national prestige of Iran."

As Zahedi had predicted, a settlement of the oil dispute was announced in October 1954. Iran signed a marketing and production contract with oil companies from four foreign countries. (See Herbert Hoover, Jr.'s biography in this Yearbook for details of the international oil agreement.)

Zahedi brings to the Premiership "abundant physical and moral courage," wrote Robert C. Doty in the New York *Times*. He continued: "[Zahedi] has the energy to work eighteen hours a day. He is forceful, even autocratic. . . . He is tall—six feet, two inches—and erect, deliberate in movement and austerely handsome, but with an over-all appearance of grayness that makes him appear older than his fifty-six years." *Time* calls him "an ambitious nationalist . . . [he has] straight, graying hair; he stands tall and straight despite severe arthritis." General Zahedi is president of the Retired Officers' Association. His hobbies include deer hunting, horse racing and poker.

General Zahedi has been married twice. By his first wife he had two sons, one of whom was killed in an air crash. The other, Ardeshir, attended the Utah State Agricultural College in the United States, worked for the United States "Point Four" administration in Iran, and is now his father's private secretary and the "civilian adjutant" to the Shah. Zahedi's home community is Resht, where he is an owner of extensive properties. He also owns a summer home in Shemiran.

References

N Y Herald Tribune p2 Ag 20 '53
N Y Times p2 Ag 20 '53; II p6E S 20 '53
Nation 177:192+ S 5 '53
Newsweek 42:38+ S 7 '53
Reporter 9:19+ N 10 '53
Sat Night 68:11 S 5 '53
Time 62:15 Ag 31 '53
U S News 35:61+ S 11 '53
International Who's Who, 1953

ZANUCK, DARRYL F(RANCIS) (zăn'ŭk) Sept. 5, 1902- Motion picture producer

Address: b. c/o Twentieth Century-Fox Film Corp., Beverly Hills, Calif.; h. 546 Ocean Front, Santa Monica, Calif.

NOTE: This biography supersedes the article which appeared in *Current Biography* in 1941.

One of Hollywood's most colorful and controversial producers for the past twenty-seven years, Darryl F. Zanuck has had many box office successes including *Grapes of Wrath, Gentleman's Agreement* and *Snows of Kilimanjaro*. He is credited with starting numerous actors such as Tyrone Power, James Cagney, Henry Fonda and Edward G. Robinson on the road to stardom. "As a trail blazer," *Time* commented, "Zanuck has no Hollywood equal." On

July 1, 1953 he was unanimously voted the annual Screen Producers Guild Milestone award for his "historic contributions to the American motion picture."

With the announcement that Twentieth Century-Fox would convert its entire production to a new three-dimensional process called CinemaScope, beginning February 16, 1953, Darryl F. Zanuck, vice-president in charge of production, predicted that movies were about to enter an era comparable to the transition made from silent to talking films.

The first film to be made in the new CinemaScope process, *The Robe,* opened at the Roxy theatre in New York on September 17, 1953, with Zanuck predicting that the motion picture industry would rise or fall on the success of this picture. However, some critics agreed with Bennett Cerf that "the case for those who envision CinemaScope as the salvation of the movie industry remains decidedly unproven" (*Saturday Review,* November 14, 1953). Nevertheless, according to Zanuck, *The Robe* is proving a big money-maker: receipts from the company's theatres showing the film in nine key cities are running four times above the weekly average business of those theatres. The weekly average gross at the Roxy in New York had been $65,000 for other pictures, but the giant screen newcomer increased that average to $150,000.

Darryl Francis Zanuck was born on September 5, 1902 in Wahoo, Nebraska, the son of Frank and Louise (Torpin) Zanuck. His father, of Swiss descent, was owner and operator of the Grand Hotel in that city. Taken to Los Angeles by his mother, who hoped to regain her health in that climate, young Darryl was sent to the Page Military Academy but he played hooky frequently, and broke into motion pictures at the age of eight, working as an extra on the old Essanay lot in Glendale, in the costume of an Indian maiden for a dollar a day. Promptly shipped back to Nebraska when his activities were discovered, Zanuck attended school until the eighth grade.

He enlisted in the Sixth Nebraska Infantry, persuaded the recruiting officers that he was eighteen (he was fourteen at the time), and was sent to the Mexican border. He served in France as a private in the 163rd Division of the A.E.F. He was used primarily as a messenger or runner, because of his small size, and saw action for nearly a year at the frontlines. He learned to box and fought in twenty-six camp shows as a bantam-weight.

Some of his letters were printed in the A.E.F. newspaper *Stars and Stripes,* and this determined Zanuck's career. Mustered out in 1920, he settled in New York and began to write stories. After a year of hard work he finally sold a story to *Physical Culture* magazine. He set out for Hollywood where he obtained odd jobs which included selling shirts and newspaper subscriptions, catching rivets in shipyards and working as a longshoreman at the San Pedro waterfront. Zanuck also organized the Darryl Poster Service, an outdoor advertising company, and it was the income from this enterprise that enabled him to return to his writing. His first sale was five hundred dollars for an original story sold to the Fox Film Company.

DARRYL F. ZANUCK

It was the selling of hair tonic which indirectly led to Zanuck's first important job in Hollywood. As a salesman for *Yuccatone,* he wrote a one hundred page testimonial for the tonic, and succeeded in persuading the maker, A. F. Foster, to publish a book entitled *Habit and Other Short Stories.*

Habit consisted of one short story, two scenarios, and the testimonial by Zanuck who sold all the contents of the book, and movies were made from the story and the two scenarios. Warner Brothers hired Darryl Zanuck as a writer for the dog star Rin Tin Tin in 1924, at a salary of one hundred and fifty dollars a week. Zanuck worked so hard that he got nineteen screen credits in one year.

He learned to cut and edit films, and in 1927 Warners promoted him to executive producer at a reputed salary of $5,000 a week. It was Zanuck who was responsible for the first use of sound dialogue in a full-length talking picture in 1928, *The Jazz Singer,* starring Al Jolson.

The young producer then began his innovations in earnest and soon made a reputation for plucking sensational drama out of the day's news. Having been made chief executive in charge of all Warner Brothers productions in 1931, Zanuck inaugurated the trend towards realistic gang warfare pictures, producing *Little Caesar, Doorway to Hell* and *Public Enemy.* In addition to these films, which were very successful, Zanuck produced the first of the "working girl" pictures, *Office Wife,* followed by another in the same genre, *Illicit.*

In 1933 Zanuck suddenly severed his relations with Warners, giving as his reason

ZANUCK, DARRYL F.—*Continued*

that Warners had extended a pay decrease of fifty per cent two weeks beyond the time Zanuck had promised his employees that the cut would be restored. On twenty-four hours' notice, Zanuck tore up his contract.

He joined with Joseph M. Schenck, then president of United Artists, in setting up Twentieth Century Pictures. Zanuck, who became vice-president, made their first picture, *The Bowery,* which starred Wallace Beery, Jackie Cooper and George Raft. This was followed by *The House of Rothschild* which starred George Arliss, and was widely credited with having started the biographical type of film. In May 1935, eighteen months after establishing the new company, Zanuck had made eighteen films, of which seventeen were successful.

When Schenck agreed to merge with the Fox Films Company to form a new combine called Twentieth Century-Fox, Zanuck, at the age of thirty-three assumed charge of all production at their Movietone City plant. At the end of the first year of operation, Twentieth Century-Fox showed a profit of $3,500,000 the first year and $16,000,000 the next two years.

Schenck was chairman of the corporation, while Zanuck was named a vice-president at a salary of $260,000 per year, a position and stipend he has continued to hold. It is said that the original contract between Zanuck and Schenck was drawn up on one sheet of paper, without legal advice. In 1949 Zanuck signed a ten-year contract at the $260,000 figure, with an option to advise for another ten years, at $150,000.

In 1941, Zanuck was commissioned a lieutenant-colonel in the United States Signal Corps, to make training films and combat documentary pictures for the War Department. Advanced to colonel in 1942, he accompanied the Allied Command in the invasion of Africa, of which he made a photographic record.

Upon leaving the service in 1943, Zanuck returned to his post in the Twentieth Century-Fox studios, where he continued his unorthodox moviemaking ways. Although he lost money with *The Ox-Bow Incident* in 1943 and $2,000,000 in 1944 on *Wilson* (which had for its theme the need to guard against postwar isolationism), Zanuck more than made up for these with a list of successful and well-remembered films.

Among these were *The Grapes of Wrath,* which won the New York Film Critics award in 1940; *Winged Victory,* made for the Air Force in 1944; *The Razor's Edge,* in 1946 starring Tyrone Power, and *Gentleman's Agreement,* which dealt with anti-semitism.

The latter film drew this comment from Alton Cook, of the New York *World-Telegram* on November 11, 1947: "*Gentleman's Agreement* is a rousing, memorable experience, a climax to a lifetime of moviegoing. Not a single calm person will emerge from the Mayfair these next few months that the picture remains there." The film set a new opening-day mark at the 1700-seat Mayfair by grossing $12,549.

Other distinguished pictures which Zanuck has produced are *Pinky,* starring Ethel Waters and Jeanne Crain; *Twelve O'Clock High,* an Air Force picture starring Gregory Peck, and *Snows of Kilimanjaro,* an outstanding box-office success of the 1952 season, which dramatized a story by Ernest Hemingway.

He pioneered by using authentic locations in foreign countries (such as in his films *Prince of Foxes, The Big Lift,* and *Snows of Kilimanjaro*) and "melting Hollywood's frozen funds abroad." Since the war, Zanuck's company has "consistently led the field in the quality of its films, by the verdict of both the box office and the critics" (*Time,* June 12, 1950).

He usually holds two long story conferences each day. According to Niven Busch's portrait of him in *Life* (April 14, 1941), Zanuck was "never a good writer himself. He was and still is, a great idea man. At his best his conference ideas are brilliant, rapid and powerful; he is capable of contributing characterizations and structural changes which add immensely to a picture's success." His revisions of Irving Berlin's *Alexander's Ragtime Band* resulted "in this picture making more money than anything else he has produced."

When Twentieth Century-Fox announced that it would convert its entire output of films to a process called CinemaScope, once again it was apparent that Zanuck had blazed another trail. CinemaScope is a process by which images are photographed with a special wide-angle lens attached to a regular camera. This results in a distortion, but when the films are put onto a projector, the projector being equipped with a special compensating lens, this lens corrects the distortion and gives the filmed images additional size and depth when they are projected onto a concave screen two and a half times larger than the regular screen which has been heretofore used. Zanuck speaks enthusiastically of the new "3-D" process. "It never fails to impress me, every time, that suddenly I'm right up there with the people on the screen. They're not off in the distance somewhere but up close! Everything on that screen seems to be really happening."

Although the total of sixteen pictures scheduled by Twentieth Century-Fox for 1954 is 50 per cent under the studio's average annual output before it adopted the CinemaScope process, Zanuck stated that his employment requirement would be practically the same as when he was making thirty-two pictures. "The pictures we make from now on will be twice as big and twice as costly," he explained. Commenting on the extraordinary earnings of *The Robe* and *How to Marry a Millionaire* (the second CinemaScope picture introduced), he said, "I knew I was right from the very start in going into CinemaScope. Now the public has shown me just how right I was."

Twentieth Century-Fox's production of *The Egyptian* cost $5,000,000, and although it received praise for its opulence, the critics generally agreed that "the pomp of the Pharaohs does not live again in this . . . pageant of Egypt's great age" (New York *Herald Tribune,* August 25, 1954). On the other hand,

Three Coins in the Fountain, also made in CinemaScope, received the critics' acclaim for its magnificent scenes of Rome and for its "glorious sightseeing adventure." Otis L. Guernsey, Jr. wrote in the New York *Herald Tribune,* May 21, 1954: "CinemaScope is still in its tryout stage as far as its esthetics are concerned, and one of its happiest experiments is *Three Coins in the Fountain. . . .*"

On July 16, 1954 Zanuck announced plans to make twenty-four CinemaScope pictures in the next twelve months at a cost of more than $55,000,000. Among these are *The Greatest Story Ever Told,* the life of Christ written by the late Fulton Oursler.

Zanuck helped to establish a department at Twentieth Century-Fox for making CinemaScope nonfiction short subjects which will be shown along with the CinemaScope full-length films.

Zanuck was the first producer to receive the coveted Irving G. Thalberg Memorial Trophy, awarded in 1937. He has also received the Legion of Merit for his services during World War II. He is the author of the book *Tunis Expedition* (Random House, 1943), which is an account of his experiences in the African landings. The five feet six inch tall producer weighs 142 pounds, has medium blonde hair and blue eyes. In addition to being fond of big game hunting he enjoys skiing and polo. Zanuck married Virginia Fox, a former actress, on January 14, 1924. They have three children, Darrylin, Susan and Richard.

References

Christian Sci Mon p4 Ap 21 '53
Life 10:99+ Ap 14 '41
N Y Herald Tribune p9 Ja 28 '50
N Y Times p17 F 2 '53
N Y World-Telegram p12 N 11 '47
Time 55:64+ Je 12 '50
Variety 188:7 S 24 '52

International Who's Who, 1953
Motion Picture and Television Almanac, 1953-54
Who's Who, 1953
Who's Who in America, 1952-53
World Biography (1948)

ZIFF, WILLIAM B(ERNARD) Aug. 1, 1898—Dec. 20, 1953 Publisher; author; began career as a commercial artist; attended Chicago Art Institute; aviator World War I; founded W. B. Ziff advertising agency (1920); established Ziff-Davis Publishing Company (1935); founder of *Aeronautics* Magazine; advocated strong air arm in modern warfare; publisher of aviation, photography, radio and science fiction magazines; author of best-selling books: *The Rape of Palestine* (1938); *The Coming Battle of Germany* (1942); *The Gentlemen Talk of Peace* (1944); *Two Worlds* (1946), and *He, the Maker* (a long poem) (1949). See *Current Biography,* (Oct.) 1946.

Obituary

N Y Times p31 D 21 '53

BIOGRAPHICAL REFERENCES

Consulted by the research staff of CURRENT BIOGRAPHY.

American Catholic Who's Who, 1954-55
American Medical Directory, 1950
American Men in Government (1949)
American Men of Science (1949)
American Women, 1939-40
America's Young Men, 1938-39
ASCAP Biographical Dictionary of Composers, Authors, and Publishers (1952)
Author's and Writer's Who's Who (1948-49)

Baker, T. ed. Biographical Dictionary of Musicians (1940)
Baseball Register (1954)
Biographical Directory of the American Congress, 1774-1949 (1950)
Blue Book of American Aviation, 1942
British Film Annual, 1949
Burke's Landed Gentry (1952)
Burke's Peerage, Baronetage, and Knightage (1953)
Business Executives of America (1950)

Canadian Who's Who, 1949-51
Catholic Who's Who, 1952
Chemical Who's Who, 1951
Chi è? (1948)
Chujoy, A. ed. Dance Encyclopedia (1949)
Congressional Directory (1954)

Dictionnaire Biographique des Artistes Contemporains, 1910-30
Dictionnaire Biographique Français Contemporain (1954)
Dictionnaire de Biographie Française (1933-)
Dictionnaire National des Contemporains (1936)
Directory of American Scholars (1951)
Directory of Medical Specialists (1951)
Directory of Medical Women, 1949
Directory of the American Political Science Association, 1953

Ewen, D. ed. Composers of Today (1936); Living Musicians (1940); Men and Women Who Make Music (1949); European Composers Today (1954)

Grove, G. Dictionary of Music and Musicians (1940)

Hindustan Year-Book & Who's Who, 1954
Hoehn, M. A. ed. Catholic Authors (1952)
Hvem er Hvem? 1950

Indian and Pakistan Year Book and Who's Who, 1948
International Press Who's Who; New Zealand, 1938
International Who's Who, 1954
International Who's Who in World Medicine, 1947
International World Who's Who (1949)
International Year Book and Statesmen's Who's Who, 1954
Italian-American Who's Who (1946)

Japan Who's Who, 1950-51

Kelly's Handbook to the Titled, Landed and Official Classes, 1951
Kraks Blaa Bog (1950)
Kunitz, S. J., and Haycraft, H. eds. Junior Book of Authors (1951); Twentieth Century Authors (1942)
Kürschners Deutscher Gelehrten Kalender, 1954

Leaders in Education (1948)

Martindale-Hubbell Law Directory, 1952
Motion Picture and Television Almanac, 1953-54
Musicians' International Directory and Biographical Record (1949-50)

Nalanda Year-Book and Who's Who in India and Pakistan, 1951-53
National Cyclopædia of American Biography Current Volumes A-H (1926-52)
Near and Middle East Who's Who, 1945-46
New Century Cyclopedia of Names (1954)

Österreicher der Gegenwart (1951)

Prominent Personalities in American Methodism (1945)

Quem é Alguém (1947)

Religious Leaders of America, 1941-42

Salter, J. T. ed. Public Men in and Out of Office (1946)
Slavonic Encyclopaedia (1949)
South African Who's Who, 1952

Thompson, O. ed. International Cyclopedia of Music and Musicians (1949)
Turkin, H. and Thompson, S. C. Official Encyclopedia of Baseball (1951)

Universal Jewish Encyclopedia (1948)

Vem är Det, 1949
Vem och Vad, 1948

Warfel, H. R. American Novelists of Today (1951)
Webster's Biographical Dictionary (1951)
Wer ist Wer? (1951)
Who is Who in Music (1951)
Who Knows—and What (1954)
Who's Important in Medicine, 1945
Who's Who, 1954
Who's Who in Alaska, 1947
Who's Who in America, 1954-55
Who's Who in American Art (1953)
Who's Who in American Education, 1951-52
Who's Who in American Jewry, 1938-39
Who's Who in Art (1952)
Who's Who in Australia, 1950
Who's Who in Aviation, 1942-43
Who's Who in Canada, 1949-50
Who's Who in Central and East-Europe, 1935-36
Who's Who in Chicago and Illinois (1950)

Who's Who in Colored America, 1950
Who's Who in Commerce and Industry (1953)
Who's Who in Egypt and the Near East, 1953
Who's Who in Engineering, 1948
Who's Who in France (Paris), 1953-54
Who's Who in Government (1932-33)
Who's Who (in) Israel, 1952
Who's Who in Japan, 1940-41
Who's Who in Labor (1946)
Who's Who in Latin America Pts 1-7 (1946-51)
Who's Who in Law, 1937
Who's Who in Library Service (1943)
Who's Who in Modern China (1954)
Who's Who in New England (1949)
Who's Who in New York, 1952
Who's Who in New Zealand (1951)
Who's Who in Philosophy (1952)
Who's Who in Railroading, 1946
Who's Who in Switzerland, 1950-51
Who's Who in the East (1953)
Who's Who in the Midwest (1954)
Who's Who in the Nation's Capital, 1938-39
Who's Who in the South and Southwest (1954)
Who's Who in the Theatre (1952)
Who's Who in the United Nations (1951)
Who's Who in the West (1954)
Who's Who in United States Politics (1952)
Who's Who of the Allied Governments, 1943
Wie is Dat? (1948)
Wier, A. E. ed. Macmillan Encyclopedia of Music and Musicians (1938)
Winchester's Screen Encyclopedia (1948)
Women of Achievement (1940)
World Biography (1954)
World Diplomatic Directory, 1951

Yearbook of the United Nations, 1953
Yost, E. American Women of Science (1943)

PERIODICALS AND NEWSPAPERS CONSULTED

including abbreviations used

NOTE: Most, but not all, of the publications below are listed in Wilson Company periodical indexes found in most libraries. For addresses, subscription price, etc., consult your librarian.

A. L. A. Bul—American Library Association Bulletin
Adult Ed—Adult Education
Formerly Adult Education Journal
Adv Age—Advertising Age
Adv Agency—Advertising Agency
Formerly Advertising Agency & Advertising & Selling
Am Artist—American Artist
Am Assn Univ Women J—Journal of the American Association of University Women
Am Collector—American Collector (discontinued)
Am Federationist—American Federationist
Am Hist R—American Historical Review
Am Home—American Home
Am Mag—American Magazine
Am Mercury—American Mercury
Am Phot—American Photography. See Photography
Am Pol Sci R—American Political Science Review
Am Scand R—American Scandinavian Review
Am Scholar—American Scholar
Am Sociol R—American Sociological Review
America—America
Américas—Américas
Ann Am Acad—Annals of the American Academy of Political and Social Science
Apollo—Apollo Magazine
Arch Forum—Architectural Forum, the Magazine of Building
Arch Rec—Architectural Record
Art Bul—College Art Association of America. Art Bulletin
Art Digest—Art Digest
Art N—Art News
Arts & Arch—Arts & Architecture
Asian R—Asian Review
Atlan—Atlantic Monthly
Automotive Ind—Automotive Industries
Aviation W—Aviation Week

Banking—Banking
Bet Hom & Gard—Better Homes & Gardens
Book-of-the-Month Club N—Book-of-the-Month Club News
Books Abroad—Books Abroad
Bronx Home News—See N Y Post
Bsns W—Business Week
Bul Bibliog—Bulletin of Bibliography and Dramatic Index
Bul Pan Am Union. See Américas

Can Forum—Canadian Forum
Can Hist R—Canadian Historical Review
Cath Lib World—Catholic Library World
Cath N—Catholic News
Cath Sch J—Catholic School Journal
Chem & Eng N—Chemical and Engineering News
Christian Cent—Christian Century
Christian Sci Mon—Christian Science Monitor
Christian Sci Mon Mag—Christian Science Monitor Weekly Magazine Section (discontinued)
Civil Eng—Civil Engineering, the Magazine of Engineered Construction
Col Engl—College English
Colliers—Collier's
Commonweal—Commonweal
Cong Digest—Congressional Digest
Connoisseur Mag—The Connoisseur Magazine
Contemp R—Contemporary Review
Coronet—Coronet
Cosmop—Cosmopolitan
Cue—Cue (Manhattan edition)
Cur Hist—Current History

Dance Mag—Dance Magazine
Design—Design
Dublin R—Dublin Review

Ed—Education
Ed & Pub—The Editor and Publisher
El Engl—Elementary English
Engl J—English Journal
Esquire—Esquire
Etude—Etude

Facts on File—Facts on File
Far East S—Far Eastern Survey
Finance—Finance
Flying—Flying
For Affairs—Foreign Affairs
For Policy Bul—Foreign Policy Bulletin
Forbes—Forbes
Fortnightly—Fortnightly
Fortune—Fortune

Gen Army—Generals of the Army and the Air Force
Good H—Good Housekeeping

Harper—Harper's Magazine
Harpers Bazaar—Harper's Bazaar
Holiday—Holiday
Horn Bk—Horn Book
House & Gard—House and Garden
House B—House Beautiful

Illus London N—Illustrated London News
Ind Woman—Independent Woman
Inland Ptr—Inland Printer
Inter-American—Inter-American

J Am Med Assn—Journal of the American Medical Association
J Home Econ—Journal of Home Economics
J Negro Hist—Journal of Negro History

PERIODICALS AND NEWSPAPERS CONSULTED

Knickerbocker—"The Knickerbocker"—The Netherlands Magazine

Ladies Home J—Ladies' Home Journal
Library J—Library Journal
Life—Life
Look—Look

MacLeans Mag—Maclean's Magazine
Mag Art—Magazine of Art (discontinued)
Mag of Wall St—Magazine of Wall Street and Business Analyst
Mlle—Mademoiselle
Mo Labor R—Monthly Labor Review
Motion Pict—Motion Picture and Television Magazine
Mus Am—Musical America
Mus Courier—Musical Courier
Mus Mod Art—Museum of Modern Art Bulletin
Mus Q—Musical Quarterly
Musician—Musician

N Y Herald Tribune—New York Herald Tribune
N Y Herald Tribune Book R—New York Herald Tribune Book Review
N Y Post—New York Post
Bronx Home News consolidated with N Y Post February 16, 1948.
N Y State Ed—New York State Education
N Y Sun—New York Sun. See N Y World-Telegram and Sun
N Y Times—New York Times
N Y Times Book R—New York Times Book Review
N Y Times Index—New York Times Index
N Y Times Mag—New York Times Magazine
N Y World-Telegram—New York World-Telegram and Sun
Nat & New Engl R—National and New English Review
Nat Ed Assn J—Journal of the National Education Association
Nat Geog Mag—National Geographic Magazine
Nation—The Nation
Nations Bsns—Nation's Business
Natur Hist—Natural History
Nature—Nature
Nature Mag—Nature Magazine
New Engl Q—New England Quarterly
New Repub—New Republic
New Statesm—New Statesman and Nation
New Yorker—New Yorker
Newsweek—Newsweek
19th Cent—Nineteenth Century & After

Opera N—Opera News

Parents Mag—Parents' Magazine
Pathfinder—See The Town Journal, Pathfinder
Phot—Photography
Photoplay—Photoplay
Poetry—Poetry
Pol Sci Q—Political Science Quarterly
Pop Mech—Popular Mechanics Magazine
Pop Sci—Popular Science Monthly
Progres Ed—Progressive Education
Pub W—Publishers' Weekly

Q R—Quarterly Review
Queen's Q—Queen's Quarterly

Read Digest—Reader's Digest
Ref Shelf—Reference Shelf
Reporter—The Reporter
Rotarian—Rotarian

Sales Management—Sales Management
Sat Eve Post—Saturday Evening Post
Sat Night—Saturday Night
Sat R—Saturday Review
Sch & Soc—School and Society
Sch R—School Review
Scholastic—Senior Scholastic
Sci Am—Scientific American
Sci Mo—Scientific Monthly
Sci N L—Science News Letter
Science—Science
Sign—The Sign
So Atlan Q—South Atlantic Quarterly
Spec—Spectator
Sport—Sport
Sport Illus—Sports Illustrated
Sporting N—Sporting News
Studio—The Studio
Sunset Mag—Sunset Magazine
Survey—Survey (discontinued)

Theatre Arts—Theatre Arts
This Week—This Week Magazine
Time—Time
Town and Country—Town and Country
Town J—The Town Journal, Pathfinder
Name changed from Pathfinder April 1953.
Travel—Travel

U N Bul—United Nations Bulletin. See United Nations Review
U N R—United Nations Review
U N World—United Nations World (discontinued)
U S Bur Labor. See Monthly Labor Review
U S Bur Labor Bul—United States Bureau of Labor Statistics. Bulletins.
U S News—United States News & World Report
U S Office Educ Bul—United States Office of Education. Bulletins.

Va Q R—Virginia Quarterly Review
Variety—Variety
Vital Speeches—Vital Speeches
Vogue—Vogue

Washington (D.C.) Post—Washington Post and Times Herald
Wilson Lib Bul—Wilson Library Bulletin
Womans Home C—Woman's Home Companion
Writer—Writer

Yale R—Yale Review

NECROLOGY

This is a list of biographees' obituaries which are in this Yearbook, including those of late 1953. Deaths which occurred in late 1954 are recorded in the early 1955 issues of CURRENT BIOGRAPHY.

Armstrong, Edwin Howard (biog 1940)

Bacon, Leonard (biog 1941)
Bax, Sir Arnold (Edward Trevor) (biog 1943)
Beals, Ralph A(lbert) (biog 1947)
Benavente (y Martínez), Jacinto (biog 1953)
Beria, Lavrenti P(avlovitch) (biog 1942)
Blandy, W(illiam) H(enry) P(urnell) (biog 1942)
Blunt, Katharine (biog 1946)
Braniff, T(homas) E(lmer) (biog 1952)
Brooke-Popham, Sir Robert (Moore) (biog 1941)
Butler, Hugh (Alfred) (biog 1950)

Camrose, William Ewert Berry, 1st Viscount (biog 1941)
Carpenter, J(ulius) Henry, Rev. Dr. (biog 1943)
Christopher, George T. (biog 1947)
Chute, Charles Lionel (biog 1949)
Clark, Bennett Champ (biog 1941)
Compton, Karl T(aylor) (biog 1941)
Coolidge, Elizabeth Sprague (biog 1941)
Creel, George (Edward) (biog 1944)

Davenport, Russell W(heeler) (biog 1944)
Denham, R(obert) N(ewton) (biog 1947)
Dickson, Marguerite (Stockman) (biog WLB 1952)
Du Pont, Pierre Samuel (biog 1940)

Echols, Oliver P(atton) (biog 1947)
Edman, Irwin (biog 1953)

Fairchild, David (Grandison) (biog 1953)
Farrington, Joseph R(ider) (biog 1948)
Forbes, B(ertie) C(harles) (biog 1950)
Fraser, James Earle (biog 1951)

Gasperi, Alcide de (biog 1946)
Greenstreet, Sydney (Hughes) (biog 1943)
Greenwood, Arthur (biog 1940)
Griswold, Dwight P(almer) (biog 1947)

Hays, Will H(arrison) (biog 1943)
Head, Walter W(illiam) (biog 1945)
Higgins, Daniel Paul (biog 1950)
Hoey, Clyde R(oark) (biog 1949)
Hollenbeck, Don (biog 1951)
Hooton, Earnest Albert (biog 1940)
Hormel, Jay C(atherwood) (biog 1946)
Hovde, Bryn(jolf) J(acob) (biog 1946)
Hunt, Lester C(allaway) (biog 1951)
Hutcheson, William L(evi) (biog 1943)

Ibn Saud, King of Saudi Arabia (biog 1943)
Ives, Charles E(dward) (biog 1947)

Jackson, Robert H(oughwout) (biog 1950)
Jouhaux, Léon (biog 1948)

Kapell, William (biog 1948)
Kiam, Omar (biog 1945)
Kurusu, Saburo (biog 1942)

Lasser, J(acob) K(ay) (biog 1946)
Locke, Alain (Le Roy) (biog 1944)

McCarran, Patrick A(nthony) (biog 1947)
McCormick, Anne O'Hare (biog 1940)
McCoy, Frank R(oss) (biog 1945)
MacGregor, Ellen (biog WLB 1954)
Marcantonio, Vito (biog 1949)
Marsh, Reginald (biog 1941)
Martland, Harrison Stanford (biog 1940)
Maverick, Maury (biog 1944)
Maybank, Burnet R(hett) (biog 1949)

Millikan, Robert A(ndrews) (biog 1952)
Moody, (Arthur Edson) Blair (biog 1951)

Norwich, Alfred Duff Cooper, 1st Viscount (biog 1940)

Pascal, Gabriel (biog 1942)
Plesman, Albert (biog 1953)
Procopé, Hjalmar Johan (biog 1940)

Rau, Sir Benegal Narsing (biog 1951)
Rawlings, Marjorie Kinnan (biog 1942)
Rice, Grantland (biog 1941)
Rohde, Ruth Bryan Owen (biog 1944)
Rothery, Agnes (Edwards) (biog WLB 1946)

Samuel, Bernard (biog 1949)
Saracoglu, Sükrü (biog 1942)
Schorr, Friedrich (biog 1942)
Shafer, Paul W(erntz) (biog 1952)
Shay, Frank (biog WLB 1952)
Shellabarger, Samuel (biog 1945)
Simon, John Allsebrook Simon, 1st Viscount (biog 1940)
Slye, Maud (biog 1940)
Sperry, Willard L(earoyd) (biog 1952)
Stark, Louis (biog 1945)
Stine, Charles Milton Altland (biog 1940)
Straus, Oskar (biog 1944)
Street, James (Howell) (biog WLB 1946)

Terrell, Mary Church (biog 1942)

Vandenberg, Hoyt S(anford) (biog 1945)
Vargas, Getúlio Dornelles (biog 1951)

Waller, Fred(eric) (biog 1953)
Wilson, H(alsey) W(illiam) (biog 1948)
Wrong, (Humphrey) Hume (biog 1950)

Ziff, William B(ernard) (biog 1946)

CLASSIFICATION BY PROFESSION—1954

Agriculture

Blundell, Michael
Brunsdale, (Clarence) Norman
Cardon, P(hilip) V(incent)
Pacheco e Chaves, Joao
Thornton, Dan(iel I. J.)
Young, Milton R(uben)

Archaeology

El Mallakh, Kamal
Woolley, Sir (Charles) Leonard

Architecture

Butts, Alfred M(osher)
Ditchy, Clair W(illiam)
Hamlin, Talbot (Faulkner)
Wills, Royal Barry

Art

Aaltonen, Wäinö (Waldemar)
Arp, Jean
Blanch, Arnold (Alder)
Borne, Mortimer
Chamberlain, Samuel
Cox, Allyn
El Mallakh, Kamal
Eyüboglu, Bedri Rahmi
Farnsworth, Jerry
Fingesten, Peter
Goodman, Bertram
Krohg, Per (Lasson)
Lee, Doris (Emrick)
Marini, Marino
Moore, Henry (Spencer)
Romano, Umberto
Sawyer, Helen (Alton)
Shahn, Ben(jamin)

Aviation

Beau, Lucas Victor
Hobbs, Leonard S(inclair)
LeMay, Curtis E(merson)
Lindbergh, Charles A(ugustus, Jr.)
McGregor, G(ordon) R(oy)
Pierson, Warren Lee
Starr, Chauncey
Yeager, Charles E.

Business

Backstrand, C(lifford) J(ulius)
Binns, Joseph Patterson
Borden, Neil H(opper)
Bunker, Ellsworth
Burns, H(endry) S(tuart) M(ackenzie)
Connell, Arthur J(oseph)
Cowen, Joshua Lionel
Cross, Burton M(elvin)
Dodge, Cleveland E(arl)
Ebbott, Percy J(ohn)
Gregg, Hugh
Hillary, Sir Edmund (Percival)
Hobbs, Leonard S(inclair)
Hopkins, John Jay
Howell, Charles R(obert)
McClellan, Harold C(hadick)
McGregor, G(ordon) R(oy)
Nyborg, Victor H(ugo)
O'Malley, Walter F(rancis)
Pierson, Warren Lee
Richards, Wayne E.
Serratosa Cibils, Joaquin
Thomas, Charles S(parks)
Viscardi, Henry, Jr.
White, Francis W(ilford)
Wise, James DeCamp

Dance

Adams, Diana
Atwood, Donna
Azuma IV, Tokuho
Balanchine, George
Caron, Leslie
Charisse, Cyd
Holm, Hanya
Slavenska, Mia

Diplomacy

Ardalan, Ali Gholi
Bunker, Ellsworth
Conroy, Pat(rick Dominic)
Dean, Arthur H(obson)
Dixon, Sir Pierson (John)
Donovan, William J(oseph)
González, César
Hoover, Herbert (Clark), Jr.
Lodge, Henry Cabot, Jr.
MacArthur, Douglas, 2d
Mendès-France, Pierre
Molotov, Viacheslav M(ikhailovich)
Wan (Waithayakon), Prince
Wilgress, (Leolyn) Dana
Willis, Frances E(lizabeth)

Education

Albion, Robert Greenhalgh
Arciniegas, Germán
Aron, Raymond (Claude Ferdinand)
Ascoli, Max
Bloch, Felix
Bond, Horace Mann
Borden, Neil H(opper)
Brownell, Samuel Miller
Burns, Edward McN(all)
Charlesworth, James C(lyde)
Durgin, C(alvin) T(hornton)
Early, William Ashby
Farnsworth, Jerry
Fingesten, Peter
Fisher, Harry L(inn)
Gipson, Lawrence Henry
Hayes, Samuel P(erkins)
Hayes, Samuel P(erkins), Jr.
Hutchins, Robert Maynard
Ingalls, (Mildred Dodge) Jeremy (WLB)
Jamali, Moh(amme)d Fadhel
Keck, Lucile L(iebermann)
Kinsey, Alfred C(harles)
Krohg, Per (Lasson)
La Gorce, John Oliver
Libby, W(illard) F(rank)
Newell, Homer E(dward), Jr.
Parkes, Henry Bamford
Picken, Mary Brooks
Poole, Lynn
Purcell, Edward M(ills)
Sawyer, Helen (Alton)
Swings, Pol(idore F.F.)
Taylor, John W(ilkinson)
Terrell, Daniel V(oiers)
Underhill, Ruth M(urray)
Williston, Samuel

Engineering

Hobbs, Leonard S(inclair)
Hoover, Herbert (Clark), Jr.
Sillcox, Lewis K(etcham)
Terrell, Daniel V(oiers)
Vogel, Herbert D(avis)

Fashion

Balenciaga, (Cristóbal)
Balmain, Pierre (Alexandre)
Chanel, Gabrielle (Bonheur)
McCardell, Claire
Picken, Mary Brooks
Victor, Sally (Josephs)

Finance

Anderson, Samuel W(agner)
Andrews, T(homas) Coleman
Bush, Prescott S(heldon)
Ebbott, Percy J(ohn)
Emmons, Glenn L(eonidas)
Frear, J(oseph) Allen, Jr.
Martínez Trueba, Andrés
Pierson, Warren Lee

Reese, Everett D.
Schneider, Alma K(ittredge)
Tuomioja, Sakari (Severi)
Wente, Carl F(redrick)

Government—Foreign

Ardalan, Ali Gholi
Bennett, W(illiam) J(ohn)
Blundell, Michael
Conroy, Pat(rick Dominic)
Coty, René (Jules Gustave)
Dixon, Sir Pierson (John)
Edelman, Maurice
Ely, Paul (Henri)
Fowler, R(obert) M(acLaren)
Franco (y Bahamonde), Francisco)
el-Glaoui, Thami el-Mezouari, Pasha of Marrakech
González, César
Grantham, Sir Alexander (William George Herder)
Haile Selassie I, Emperor of Ethiopia
Jamali, Moh(amme)d Fadhel
Khrushchev, Nikita S(ergeyevich)
Laniel, Joseph
MacDonald, Malcolm (John)
Martínez Trueba, Andrés
Menderes, Adnan
Mendès-France, Pierre
Mohammed, Ghulam
Molotov, Viacheslav M(ikhailovich)
Nasser, Gamal Abdel
Norodom Sihanouk, King of Cambodia
Odría (Amoretti), Manuel A(polinario)
Pacheco e Chaves, Joao
Pérez Jiménez, Marcos
Raab, Julius
Rubattel, Rodolphe
Saud, King of Saudi Arabia
Schreiber, (Karl Rudolf) Walther
Sisavang Vong, King of Laos
Tuomioja, Sakari (Severi)
Wakehurst, John de Vere Loder, 2d Baron
Wan (Waithayakon), Prince
Wilgress, (Leolyn) Dana
Zahedi, Fazlollah

Government—United States

Anderson, Samuel W(agner)
Andrews, T(homas) Coleman
Aronson, J(ohn) Hugo
Austin, Margretta (Stroup)
Bailey, Consuelo Northrop
Bingham, Jonathan B(rewster)
Bolton, Frances P(ayne Bingham)
Brossard, Edgar B(ernard)
Brownell, Herbert, Jr.
Brownell, Samuel Miller
Brunsdale, (Clarence) Norman
Burke, Thomas A(loysius)
Bush, Prescott S(heldon)
Butler, John Marshall
Cherry, Francis A(dams)
Coblentz, W(illiam) W(eber)
Cole, Albert M(cDonald)
Cole, W(illiam) Sterling
Crosby, Robert (Berkey)
Cross, Burton M(elvin)
Curtis, Carl T(homas)
Donovan, William J(oseph)
Emmons, Glenn L(eonidas)
Frear, J(oseph) Allen, Jr.
Gregg, Hugh
Hennings, Thomas C(arey), Jr.
Hoover, Herbert (Clark), Jr.
Howell, Charles R(obert)
Kee, Elizabeth (Frazier)
Kennon, Robert F(loyd)
Kuchel, Thomas H(enry)
Libby, W(illard) F(rank)
Lodge, Henry Cabot, Jr.
MacArthur, Douglas, 2d
Malcolm, George A(rthur)
Mechem, Edwin L(eard)
Mitchell, James P(aul)
Morse, Wayne (Lyman)
Moses, Robert
Potter, Charles E(dward)
Rodino, Peter W(allace), Jr.
Schneider, Alma K(ittredge)
Smathers, George A(rmistead)
Sullivan, Leonor (Alice) K(retzer)
Thomas, Charles S(parks)
Thornton, Dan(iel I. J.)
Vogel, Herbert D(avis)
Wagner, Robert F(erdinand, Jr.)
Warren, Earl
Wilkins, J(esse) Ernest
Willis, Frances E(lizabeth)
Young, Milton R(uben)

Industry

Abrams, Benjamin
Backstrand, C(lifford) J(ulius)
Fowler, R(obert) M(acLaren)
Hopkins, John Jay
White, Francis W(ilford)

International Relations

Ardalan, Ali Gholi
Austin, Margretta (Stroup)
Candau, Marcolino G(omes)
Cardon, P(hilip) V(incent)
Coulter, John B(reitling)
Dean, Arthur H(obson)
Dixon, Sir Pierson (John)
Hull, John E(dwin)
Lodge, Henry Cabot, Jr.
Mayo, Charles W(illiam)
Mendès-France, Pierre
Molotov, Viacheslav M(ikhailovich)
Taylor, John W(ilkinson)
Thimayya, K(odendera) S(ubayya)
Wan (Waithayakon), Prince
Wilgress, (Leolyn) Dana
Wilkins, J(esse) Ernest
Willis, Frances E(lizabeth)

Journalism

Aron, Raymond (Claude Ferdinand)
Blackwell, Betsy Talbot
Block, Herbert L(awrence)
Bruns, Franklin R(ichard), Jr.
Carraway, Gertrude S(prague)
Cousins, (Sue) Margaret
Frederick, Pauline
Herbert, Elizabeth Sweeney
Kuekes, Edward D(aniel)
McBride, Mary Margaret
Merz, Charles
Peltz, Mary Ellis (Opdycke)
Pulitzer, Joseph, 2d
Reid, Whitelaw
Rubattel, Rodolphe
Singer, Kurt D(eutsch)
Smith, (Oliver) Harrison
Vanderbilt, Amy
Van Horne, Harriet
Winchester, Alice

Labor

Conroy, Pat(rick Dominic)
Freitag, Walter
Meany, George
Mitchell, James P(aul)
Wilkins, J(esse) Ernest

Law

Bailey, Consuelo Northrop
Bingham, Jonathan B(rewster)
Bok, William Curtis
Brownell, Herbert, Jr.
Burke, Thomas A(loysius)
Butler, John Marshall
Cherry, Francis A(dams)
Cole, Albert M(cDonald)
Dean, Arthur H(obson)
Donovan, William J(oseph)
Fowler, R(obert) M(acLaren)
Hall, William Edwin
Hennings, Thomas C(arey), Jr.
Hopkins, John Jay
Hutchins, Robert Maynard
Jameson, William J(ames)
Jenkins, Ray H(oward)
Kennon, Robert F(loyd)
Kuchel, Thomas H(enry)
Mahady, Henry J(oseph)
Malcolm, George A(rthur)
Marshall, Thurgood
Mechem, Edwin L(eard)
Morse, Wayne (Lyman)

Library Service

Literature

Medicine

Military

Motion Pictures

Music

Naval

Nonfiction

Organizations

Achelis, Elisabeth
Borden, Neil H(opper)
Cameron, Charles S(herwood)
Carraway, Gertrude S(prague)
Ditchy, Clair W(illiam)
Early, William Ashby
Fisher, Harry L(inn)
Fitz Gerald, Leslie M(aurice)
Fowler, R(obert) M(acLaren)
Hitchcock, Charles B(aker)
Jameson, William J(ames)
Keck, Lucile L(iebermann)
Lacy, Dan (Mabry)
McClellan, Harold C(hadick)
McGregor, G(ordon) R(oy)
Mahady, Henry J(oseph)
Mumford, L(awrence) Quincy
Pierson, Warren Lee
Rau, Dhanvanthi (Handoo) Rama
Reese, Everett D.
Richards, Wayne E.
Serratosa Cibils, Joaquin
Sillcox, Lewis K(etcham)
Terrell, Daniel V(oiers)

Philosophy

Tillich, Paul J(ohannes), Rev. Dr.

Politics—Foreign

Blundell, Michael
Coty, René (Jules Gustave)
Edelman, Maurice
Franco (y Bahamonde), Francisco
Jamali, Moh(amme)d Fadhel
Khrushchev, Nikita S(ergeyevich)
Laniel, Joseph
Martínez Trueba, Andrés
Menderes, Adnan
Mendès-France, Pierre
Mohammed, Ghulam
Molotov, Viacheslav M(ikhailovich)
Nasser, Gamal Abdel
Odría (Amoretti), Manuel A(polinario)
Pérez Jiménez, Marcos
Raab, Julius
Rubattel, Rodolphe
Schreiber, (Karl Rudolf) Walther
Tuomioja, Sakari (Severi)
Zahedi, Fazlollah

Politics—United States

Aronson, J(ohn) Hugo
Bailey, Consuelo Northrop
Bolton, Frances P(ayne Bingham)
Brownell, Herbert, Jr.
Brunsdale, (Clarence) Norman
Burke, Thomas A(loysius)
Bush, Prescott S(heldon)
Butler, John Marshall
Cherry, Francis A(dams)
Cole, Albert M(cDonald)
Cole, W(illiam) Sterling
Crosby, Robert (Berkey)
Cross, Burton M(elvin)
Curtis, Carl T(homas)
Frear, J(oseph) Allen, Jr.
Gregg, Hugh
Hennings, Thomas C(arey), Jr.
Howell, Charles R(obert)
Kee, Elizabeth (Frazier)
Kennon, Robert F(loyd)
Kuchel, Thomas H(enry)
Lodge, Henry Cabot, Jr.
Mechem, Edwin L(eard)
Morse, Wayne (Lyman)
Potter, Charles E(dward)
Rodino, Peter W(allace), Jr.
Schneider, Alma K(ittredge)
Smathers, George A(rmistead)
Sullivan, Leonor (Alice) K(retzer)
Thornton, Dan(iel I. J.)
Wagner, Robert F(erdinand, Jr.)
Warren, Earl
Young, Milton R(uben)

Publishing

Ascoli, Max
Astor, John Jacob
Ballantine, Ian (Keith)
Barnhart, Clarence L(ewis)
Beecroft, John (William Richard)
Briney, Nancy (Wells)
Canfield, Cass
Cowles, John
Farrar, John (Chipman)
Foyle, Gilbert (Samuel)
Foyle, William Alfred
Haycraft, Howard
Kirkus, Virginia
Lacy, Dan (Mabry)
La Gorce, John Oliver
Lane, Sir Allen (Lane Williams)
Macy, George
Pulitzer, Joseph, 2d
Reid, Whitelaw
Rinehart, Stanley M(arshall), Jr.
Shimkin, Leon
Smith, (Oliver) Harrison
Winchester, Alice

Radio

Abrams, Benjamin
Albert, Eddie
Barlow, Howard
Cantor, Eddie
Conley, Eugene (Thomas)
Cox, Wally
Day, Doris
Fisher, Eddie
Frederick, Pauline
Liberace, (Wladziu Valentino)
McBride, Mary Margaret
McCormick, Myron
Moore, Garry
Toscanini, Arturo

Religion

Donegan, Horace W(illiam) B(aden), Rt. Rev.
Feltin, Maurice, Cardinal
Tillich, Paul J(ohannes), Rev. Dr.

Science

Bloch, Felix
Bolt, Richard H(enry)
Borst, Lyle B(enjamin)
Bullard, Sir Edward (Crisp)
Burnet, Sir (Frank) Macfarlane
Cameron, Charles S(herwood)
Coblentz, W(illiam) W(eber)
Fisher, Harry L(inn)
Goudsmit, Samuel A(braham)
Kinsey, Alfred C(harles)
Krebs, H(ans) A(dolf)
Libby, W(illard) F(rank)
Lindbergh, Charles A(ugustus, Jr.)
Lipmann, Fritz (Albert)
Newell, Homer E(dward), Jr.
Poole, Lynn
Purcell, Edward M(ills)
Rostand, Jean
Salk, Jonas E(dward)
Starr, Chauncey
Staudinger, Hermann
Sveda, Michael
Swings, Pol(idore F.F.)
Teller, Edward

Social Science

Albion, Robert Greenhalgh
Arciniegas, Germán
Ascoli, Max
Brossard, Edgar B(ernard)
Burns, Edward McN(all)
Charlesworth, James C(lyde)
Gipson, Lawrence Henry
Hayes, Samuel P(erkins)
Hayes, Samuel P(erkins), Jr.
Hitchcock, Charles B(aker)
Parkes, Henry Bamford
Underhill, Ruth M(urray)

Social Service

Sports

Technology

Television

Theatre

Other Classifications

BIOGRAPHIES OF WOMEN—1954

Achelis, Elisabeth
Adams, Diana
Adams, Edith
Arnow, Harriette (Louisa) Simpson (WLB)
Atwood, Donna
Austin, Margretta (Stroup)
Azuma IV, Tokuho

Bachauer, Gina
Bailey, Consuelo Northrop
Baird, Cora
Baker, Louise (WLB)
Best, Edna
Bialk, Elisa (WLB)
Blackwell, Betsy Talbot
Bolton, Frances P(ayne Bingham)
Breckinridge, Aida de Acosta
Briney, Nancy (Wells)
Burnett, Hallie Southgate (WLB)

Caron, Leslie
Carraway, Gertrude S(prague)
Castagnetta, Grace
Caulfield, Joan
Cavanah, Frances (Elizabeth) (WLB)
Chanel, Gabrielle (Bonheur)
Charisse, Cyd
Claire, Ina
Collier, Constance
Cousins, (Sue) Margaret

Day, Doris
Disney, Doris Miles (WLB)

Frederick, Pauline

Galard Terraube, Geneviève de
Greenwood, Joan

Hepburn, Audrey
Herbert, Elizabeth Sweeney
Holm, Hanya
Howe, Helen (WLB)

Ingalls, (Mildred Dodge) Jeremy (WLB)

Jaynes, Clare (WLB) (pseud. of Mayer, Jane, and Spiegel, Clara)
Jordan, Sara M(urray)

Keck, Lucile L(iebermann)
Kee, Elizabeth (Frazier)
Kirkus, Virginia

Lambert, Janet (Snyder) (WLB)
Lee, Doris (Emrick)

McBride, Mary Margaret
McCardell, Claire
MacGregor, Ellen (WLB)
Moore, Ruth (WLB)

Peltz, Mary Ellis (Opdycke)
Peters, Roberta
Picken, Mary Brooks

Raedler, Dorothy (Florence)
Rau, Dhanvanthi (Handoo) Rama
Russell, Anna

Sawyer, Helen (Alton)
Schneider, Alma K(ittredge)
Shippen, Katherine B(inney) (WLB)
Simon, Edith (WLB)
Slavenska, Mia
Sullivan, Leonor (Alice) K(retzer)
Sumner, (Bertha) Cid Ricketts (WLB)

Underhill, Ruth M(urray)

Vanderbilt, Amy
Van Horne, Harriet
Victor, Sally (Josephs)

Wilde, Louise K(athleen)
Willis, Frances E(lizabeth)
Winchester, Alice

MAJOR AWARD WINNERS

(whose biographies are included in this Yearbook)

ACADEMY OF MOTION PICTURE ARTS AND SCIENCES AWARD ("OSCARS")

Hepburn, Audrey
Holden, William

ROBERT J. COLLIER TROPHY (AVIATION)

Hobbs, Leonard S.
Yeager, Charles E.

NOBEL PRIZE

Bloch, Felix (physics)
Krebs, H. A. (physiology and medicine)
Lipmann, Fritz (physiology and medicine)
Purcell, Edward M. (physics)
Staudinger, Hermann (chemistry)

PULITZER PRIZE

Block, Herbert (newspaper cartoon)
Catton, Bruce (history)
Kuekes, Edward D. (newspaper cartoon)
Lindbergh, Charles A. (biography)

CUMULATED INDEX—1951-1954

This is a four-year cumulation of all names which have appeared in CURRENT BIOGRAPHY from 1951 through 1954. The dates after names indicate monthly issues and/or Yearbooks in which biographies and obituaries are contained.

For the index to 1940-1950 biographies, see CURRENT BIOGRAPHY 1950 Yearbook; that eleven-year cumulated index is also available separately. Inquire of the publisher for price.